ETHICS AND LAW FOR THE HEALTH PROFESSIONS

Third Edition

Ian Kerridge

Michael Lowe

Cameron Stewart

THE FEDERATION PRESS
2009

Published in Sydney by

The Federation Press
PO Box 45, Annandale, NSW, 2038.
71 John St, Leichhardt, NSW, 2040.
Ph (02) 9552 2200. Fax (02) 9552 1681.
E-mail: info@federationpress.com.au
Website: http://www.federationpress.com.au

First edition   1998 Social Science Press
Second edition   2005 The Federation Press
Third edition   2009 The Federation Press

National Library of Australia cataloguing-in-publication
    Kerridge, Ian H.
    Ethics and law for the health professions / Ian Kerridge, Michael Lowe,
        Cameron Stewart

    3rd ed.
    Includes index.
    ISBN 978 1 86287 730 6 (pbk)

    Medical ethics – Australia.
    Medical laws and legislation – Australia.

174.2

Typeset by Federation Press Pty Ltd, Leichhardt, NSW
    Printed by Ligare Pty Ltd, Riverwood, NSW.

Preface

Ethics and Law for the Health Professions is intended as an introductory and scholarly text in bioethics and law. The previous editions of this book have been used widely for training doctors, nurses and other health professionals throughout Australia and were also used in many undergraduate and postgraduate law courses. The present edition thoroughly revises and updates previous editions in line with new developments in medicine, ethics and the law.

In writing this book we have followed three major objectives. First, the book is structured to enable its use as a primary teaching resource in bioethics and health law. In doing this, we have attempted to cover topics in a logical, sequential order. Each chapter introduces new concepts and builds on those introduced previously.

Second, we have attempted to draw a clear line between ethical principles and the principles of law. We have found that many textbooks of ethics use legal examples for ethical discussion, and use ethical and legal concepts interchangeably. To a degree, this borrowing of concepts between the two disciplines is understandable. However, ethics and law are not the same and confusion between the two is widespread within the health-care environment. To prevent such confusion we have structured most chapters so that discussions of the ethical and legal implications of issues are considered separately.

Third, we have attempted to make this book usable by all members of the health-care professions and by lawyers involved in health care. We have structured the book upon the assumption that the ethical problems encountered by health professionals are common to all the health professions. We believe that each profession brings a different perspective to the same set of problems rather than there being separate ethics for each profession. We understand that this is somewhat controversial, particularly with regard to nursing, and have therefore included a separate chapter about nursing ethics in order to discuss this point. Cases that introduce each chapter have been drawn from our own experiences and from the ethics literature. These cases are intended to provide a focus for discussion and reflection on the issues in each chapter that are relevant to all professional groups

Since the previous edition, the major change in this book is that Cameron Stewart has taken on the authorship of the legal sections of the book, after John McPhee's untimely death from metastatic melanoma. John approached his final illness with courage and insight; and his analytical and intelligent observation of the health system, which continued until a few days before his death, continues to inform many aspects of this book. As we (including John) observed his final journey we saw many examples of both good practice and bad practice, ethical care and poor or ill-informed care, situations where the legal framework contributed strength to practitioner's expertise, and where practitioners were legally at risk. It reinforced to all of us that there is a great need for practitioners to reflect carefully on their values and on the care they provide and their contribution to the health-care system. John – we miss you and we hope that you would be happy with this edition which we dedicate to you.

The major change to the content of the current edition can probably best be described as a move away from 'exceptionalism'. Exceptionalism is the idea that certain groups, diseases or concepts are so different from similar things that they must be looked at entirely separately. So, in the second edition, we talked about HIV as an exceptional illness, and now we discuss it in the broader concept of infectious diseases. Animal experimentation is now discussed as part of a broader chapter about the effects that the health system has on the environment and the natural world, and Aboriginal health is discussed in the context of broader theories of development and disadvantage.

The entire text has been extensively revised and updated to take account of changes in law, biomedical science, health-care delivery and bioethics. We have also added entirely new chapters on chronic illness, children, international health and resource allocation, and a new chapter on the environment. There are many new sections added to existing chapters on issues such as disability, nano-technology, evidence-based medicine and community involvement in health care. We have substantially increased the amount of legal case analysis from Australia and added considerable comparative analysis, particularly from the United Kingdom, United States, Ireland, New Zealand and Canada. Where possible, references have been made to legislation from all the Australian jurisdictions. We were conscious of the fact that lawyers and health-care professionals from all over Australia should be able to refer to the legal issues that directly affect them. The legal content is current to 30 January 2009.

We have also tried to clarify our own positions on some of the more contro-versial subjects. This is not done as an attempt to persuade the reader, but to enable the reader to more critically evaluate what we have written.

We would like to thank our friends at The Federation Press for all their hard work in getting this edition out, particularly Chris Holt and Kathryn Fitzhenry. In writing this edition we set new world records for broken promises and we thank Chris and Kathryn for their understanding. Ian would also like to thank Gabriel, Niamh, Aisling and Isobel for their tolerance and joy and his colleagues at the Centre for Values, Ethics and the Law in Medicine for their advice, particularly Stacy Carter, Rob Irvine, Chris Jordens and Miles Little. He would also like to acknowledge his debt to his father, Professor Gordon Kerridge, who never had the opportunity to read this edition but whose values and critical insights inform every part of it. Michael would like to thank Chris Watson, Max and Joske for their comments and their sense of fun. Cameron thanks Nerida Stewart for her advice and his former colleagues at Macquarie University, particularly Peter Radan, Denise Meyerson, Bryan Horrigan, George Tomossy and Ingrid Day. He would also like to thank Rosalind Croucher, Sheila McLean, Loane Skene and Roger Magnusson for their professional help and support. Cameron's children (Max, Hannah, Beth and Angus) were no help at all, but that is as it should be.

Finally we note that technological change and the passage of time mean that our ethics must also change. One day it may be possible that brain-dead people will recover, that foetuses miscarried at 12 weeks' gestation may survive outside the womb, or that parts of our brain may be transplanted to others. Each new change will bring new possibilities and new challenges. We look forward to ongoing developments in ethics and law.

Ian Kerridge
Michael Lowe
Cameron Stewart
February 2009

List of Chapters

For detailed table of contents, see over

Contents

About the Authors

Ian Kerridge trained in medicine at the University of Newcastle, philosophy at the Universities of Sydney, Newcastle and Cambridge, and haematopoietic stem cell transplantation at the Royal Free Hospital, London. He is Director and Associate Professor in Bioethics at the Centre for Values, Ethics and the Law in Medicine at the University of Sydney and Staff Haematologist/Bone Marrow Transplant physician at Westmead Hospital, Sydney. Ian is Chair of the Australian Bone Marrow Donor Registry Ethics Committee, a member of the NSW Health Department's Clinical Ethics Advisory Panel and a member of the Editorial Boards of the *Journal of Medical Ethics*, the *Journal of Bioethical Inquiry* and the *Asian Bioethics Review*. In 2005 Ian was a member of the Legislation Review Committee (Lockhart Committee) which reviewed the *Prohibition of Human Cloning Act 2002* and the *Research Involving Human Embryos Act 2002*. His current research interests in ethics include the philosophy of medicine, stem cells, synthetic biology, end-of-life care, the experience of illness and survival following cancer and bone marrow transplantation, public health ethics, donor issues in transplantation, publication ethics and the pharmaceutical industry.

Michael Lowe worked as a registered nurse until graduating in medicine in 1989. He became interested in ethics as a junior doctor at Royal Darwin Hospital, and from 1999 to 2002 he worked at the Fiji School of Medicine. In 2003 he moved to Royal Darwin Hospital and the Northern Territory Clinical School where he is now the Clinical Dean. His current interests include clinical ethics, medical education, chronic disease, and Indigenous health.

Cameron Stewart did his law and economics degrees at Macquarie University and worked as a legal research officer and judge's associate in the Supreme Court of New South Wales, before becoming a commercial litigator in a large Sydney law firm. He studied for a masters of law at Sydney University and went on to complete his doctorate there which is concerned with law and end-of-life decision-making. He began teaching law at University of Western Sydney (1998-1999) and then later at Macquarie University (1999-2008), where he acted as Dean of Law in 2008. He is now Associate Professor in the Centre for Health Governance, Law and Ethics at Sydney Law School and Honorary Associate Professor in the Centre for Values Ethics and the Law in Medicine in the Faculty of Medicine, University of Sydney. His main interests are in dying and the law, guardianship law, human tissue regulation, property law and equity.

Introduction

Students of the health professions spend many years learning the specific details of how to care for ill patients. They learn that patients with leukaemia can be treated with bone-marrow transplants, that unconscious patients can be kept alive with artificial methods of feeding and hydration, that human ova can be inseminated in test-tubes, and that premature babies can be sustained with humidicribs, ventilators and medications. But the limits of medicine are being continually stretched by new discoveries and health professionals must continuously update their knowledge to keep abreast of these developments.

Thoughtful observers of medicine have always pondered whether all of this activity is necessarily a good thing. Should the fact that we *can* do something, necessarily imply that we *should* do it? We can do bone-marrow transplants – but should we? We can keep unconscious people alive – but should we? We can resuscitate premature babies – but should we?

People who work in the health professions are sometimes very uncomfortable when these questions are asked, and rightly so. It is rare that this kind of question can be answered by reference to journals, to experiments or to learned opinion. These questions require an entirely different and unfamiliar form of reasoning that has been explored in the field known as 'ethics'. Lawyers in the health fields also spend many years studying the rules of law, practice and procedure, but often without asking the bigger questions about the role of law in health care.

In large health-care institutions, people of many different persuasions and beliefs work and come to decisions together. But they may not always come to the same conclusions when they think about ethical issues, indeed it has been said that ethics is the 'disciplined reflection on ambiguity' (Jonsen 1990). To some people, this is a great weakness of ethics because it seems to imply that ethical issues are usually insoluble and that there may be nothing to decide between differences of opinion regarding any issue. Yet, this ambiguity also reflects a fact of human life that is more profound. Human affairs are, by their nature, complex and unpredictable, and solutions to one problem may create new problems and new questions. Nowhere is this more obvious than in the health care and the biomedical sciences. We find ways to reduce childhood mortality, but then find we are confronted with the problems of over-population. We cure a patient from life-threatening disease but may then find them litigating for an unsightly scar or unwanted blood transfusion. We may discover a new and effective therapy for an illness but then find that it kills more people than it cures. Ethics, by explicitly acknowledging this ambiguity, allows us to appreciate the complexity of health-care practice, and gives us tools to analyse the situation when the unexpected occurs.

Over the past 40 years there has been a remarkable increase in interest in ethics and bioethics. One can read about issues in bioethics almost every day in the mainstream newspapers, and they are widely discussed both among those who are involved with health care and also among those who are not. Although people will often disagree about ethical responses to new dilemmas, it is important that they continue to communicate and learn from each others' views.

Ethics and Law for the Health Professions aims to provide an accessible, scholarly and clinically relevant introduction to ethics and health law for health professionals, lawyers, teachers and students of the health care and regulation. By studying ethics and health law in a more formal way, we hope that health professionals, lawyers and students will recognise that questions of ethics and law are unavoidable in health care, and that considered reflection of these topics may provide new insights, and new ways of reasoning, may reveal new and interesting ideas, and may provide the impetus to join the on-going public and professional debate in these fascinating areas.

Reference

Jonsen, AR (1990) *The new medicine and the old ethics.* Cambridge, Massachusetts, Harvard University Press.

CHAPTER 1

WHAT IS ETHICS?

What ethics is

Ethics is the study of what we *ought* to do. The terms 'ethics' and 'morality' are often used interchangeably. The word 'ethics' comes from the Greek words *ethickos* – meaning a habit, pattern of behaviour or prevailing attitude, and *ethos* – meaning disposition or character. The classical Greek philosophers defined ethics by the questions 'How should I live?', or 'What should a good person do?'

The word 'morality' is derived from the Latin *morales* – meaning customs, conventions or social norms. Ethics and morality have come to have very similar meanings – but morality is perhaps more concerned with widely shared public or communal norms about right and wrong actions, whereas ethics has come to refer to a more subjective individual or organisational understanding of right and wrong.

Ethics, or moral philosophy, is one branch of philosophy. Other major branches are epistemology, the study of knowledge; logic, the study of thinking and reasoning; metaphysics or ontology, the study of entities or the nature of things; aesthetics, the study of the nature and expression of beauty; and political philosophy.

The field of ethics can be broken down into various divisions. One major division is into meta-ethics, normative ethics and practical ethics. Meta-ethics is concerned with the meaning of terms such as 'right', 'good', 'virtue' and 'justice'. One of the goals of meta-ethics is to examine the general characteristics of an ethical system. Normative ethics attempts to develop moral frameworks (principles, rules, theories and guidelines) to guide our actions and evaluate our behaviour.

Practical ethics refers to the implications that questions arising from ethics have in specific contexts. 'Bioethics' may be understood as one type of practical ethics, as it refers to ethics applied to anything in the biological sciences. 'Medical ethics', 'Nursing ethics', 'Psychological ethics' and 'Environmental ethics' are all parts of bioethics. 'Clinical ethics' refers specifically to the ethical aspects of the clinical encounter between patients and health professionals.

Some general statements have been applied to systems of ethics. First, ethics is broadly concerned with *human flourishing and well-being* and the construction and maintenance of a peaceful society in which all may benefit. Second, ethics is *prescriptive* – that is it refers more to what we *should* do than what we actually do. Third, ethics is a *systematic approach* that uses reason to define what ought or ought not be done, either as action or as process. Fourth, and perhaps most controversially, ethics embodies ideas that are *universalisable* – so ethics is relevant to all individuals; and if we develop moral concepts, principles and action-guides, they should apply equitably to all persons. Finally, it is often stated that ethics is of *overriding importance* – that is, ethics is of greater significance than the law, politics or self-interest (although in practice ethics is often overridden by considerations of law, politics or self-interest).

Some of these points are open to dispute. Nietzsche, for example, argued strongly that ethics should not be privileged above other forms of human endeavour, such as sport or creativity, and many argue forcefully from a sociological, postmodern or feminist perspective that ethics should be particular, rather than universalisable.

What ethics is not

Some authors have approached the task of defining ethics by turning the question upside down and considering in some detail what ethics is not (Singer 1979; Gillon 1980). In many ways this is easier than approaching the topic directly.

Ethics is not ... Professional codes of ethics

Since ancient times, doctors' actions have been guided by oaths that defined medical practice and listed responsible and irresponsible medical acts. The Hippocratic Oath (Box 1.1) was the first and most famous of these, although similar statements of medical ethics exist in other cultures (Etziony 1973).

The Hippocratic Oath is named after Hippocrates, who was born on the Greek island of Cos in about 460 BC. Little is known about Hippocrates other than that he belonged to a guild of doctors called the Ascelepiadae, travelled widely, and was in great demand as a doctor throughout his life. The books that are known as the Hippocratic Corpus were written at different times and reflect most of the major schools of ancient Greek philosophy. The Hippocratic Oath – the most influential core of Hippocratic ethics – was probably written by members of a philosophical sect called the Pythagoreans in the late fourth century BC. The Hippocratic Oath was passed on from teacher to pupil together with other detailed statements and instructions on the principles of patient care.

At the time of its drafting the oath served professional self-interest, binding a group of professionals into a cohesive and effective social force and enabling them to dominate the medical market-place of Ancient Athens. The Oath provides an important insight into the foundations of Western medicine and philosophy as it reflects the socio-cultural context of Ancient Greece and the ideas and values explored in the writings of Socrates, in the Greek tragedies and in the Homerian epics. But it is in relation to the ethics of the medical profession that the Oath has had the most significant influence. For the Oath reveals how physicians of that time understood illness, their patients, their medical obligations and the limits of their capacity. Minor modifications of the Hippocratic ethic have occurred over the millennia since it was formulated, but it has remained central to the ethics of many physicians until the present day. In recent years oaths like the Hippocratic Oath have become fashionable again after a period of decline, and an increasing number of medical schools require their graduates to swear them before graduating. Several groups have also proposed updates to the Hippocratic Oath. Other professional groups have also developed oaths. Oaths are probably best seen as texts that perform a social role in the professions – binding members of the profession together and providing technical codes of practice against which the profession can measure itself and be judged (Miles 2004).

Box 1.1: The Hippocratic Oath

I swear by Apollo Physician, and Ascelepius, and Hygieia and Panaceia and all the gods and goddesses, making them my witnesses, that I will fulfil according to my ability and judgment, this oath and this covenant:

To hold him who taught me this art equal to my own parents and to live my life in partnership with him, and if he is in need of money to give him a share of mine, and to regard his offspring as equal to my brothers in male lineage and to teach them this art – if they desire to learn it – without fee and covenant; to give a share of precepts and oral instruction and all the other learning to my sons and to the sons of him who has instructed me and to pupils who have signed the covenant and have taken an oath according to the medical law, but to no-one else.

I will apply dietetic measure for the benefit of the sick according to my ability and judgment; I will keep them from harm and injustice.

I will neither give a deadly drug to anyone if asked for it, nor will I make a suggestion to this effect. Similarly I will not give to a woman an abortive remedy. In purity and holiness I will guard my life and my art.

I will not use the knife, not even on sufferers from stone, but will withdraw in favour of such men as are engaged in this work.

Whatever houses I visit, I will come for the benefit of the sick, remaining free of all intentional mischief and in particular of sexual relations with both female and male persons, be they free or slaves.

What I may see or hear in the course of treatment or even outside the treatment in regard to the life of men, which on no account one must spread abroad, I will keep to myself holding such things shameful to be spoken about.

If I fulfil this oath and do not violate it, may it be granted to me to enjoy life and art, being honoured with fame among all men for all time to come; if I transgress it and swear falsely, may the opposite of all this be my lot.

(Reich 1982)

Apart from oaths, most health professions require their members to comply with an ethical code or code of conduct. Compliance with such codes is mandatory and breaches can result in a professional being disciplined by registration authorities (see Chapter 7).

Yet oaths, vows and codes of ethics seem somehow to miss the point of ethical behaviour. Ethics must start with an internal conviction of how to behave, and should not be defined by behaviour that simply conforms to rules set down by an outside body. While codes of ethics do serve important functions, they can often over-simplify ethical and clinical richness and complexity, overstate their authority, strip ethics of its context, evidence and process, and confuse ethics with law.

Ethics is not ... Professional etiquette

Etiquette has developed within the health professions to regulate the professional contacts of members with each other. Professional etiquette consists primarily of pragmatic standards or rules of behaviour such as when and how to seek second opinions, and how one may advertise one's services. Professional etiquette is often dismissed somewhat scornfully as being concerned chiefly with decorum, reputation, and traditional standards of courtesy.

Professional etiquette does not provide a moral basis for behaviour towards individual patients, indeed by encouraging the professions to close ranks around those who misbehave, it may even go against ethical behaviour. Yet there is also another side to professional etiquette. If market conditions alone are allowed to prevail, practitioners may be driven to cut their fees, increase the number of patients they see and reduce the time and attention they give to each. This may result in substandard care. Codes of professional etiquette traditionally provided a framework for practice that limited the extent of competition between practitioners. Professional etiquette, although it is open to abuse, can therefore be seen as a form of 'institutional ethics' that provides an environment in which some of the threats to ethical practice are removed (Friedson 1999).

Ethics is not ... Hospital policy or medical authority

Institutional policies and the opinions of higher authorities are often thought to legitimise professional opinions and resolve ethical conflict. However, authority and seniority do not in themselves guarantee justifiable behaviour or provide a basis for determining morality. Hospital policy usually reflects the interests of the administrative or political structure of the hospital and may be more concerned with defensive institutional policy than with the ethical status of decisions that affect clinical practice.

Ethics is not ... Religion

Ethics and morality have always been strongly associated with religion. Religion is generally regarded as a major source of moral guidance and has provided the basis for much of the development of moral, clinical and legal attitudes toward health care. While religious traditions are concerned with values and 'right' moral behaviour, they differ in important ways with regard to their key moral concepts, cosmologies, processes of ethical reasoning and the degree of guidance they offer in the face of ethical challenges raised by modern biomedicine. Some may give explicit rulings about whether an action is permissible or not; some may offer general guidance about the moral significance of specific actions, such as withdrawal of life-sustaining treatment; and others may offer no specific guidance, but provide a means of framing the issues by extrapolating from its traditional stories or its history of debates (Ankeny, Clifford et al 2005).

The major monotheistic traditions – Christianity, Judaism and Islam – often present moral norms as divine command, or as a 'natural law' – a moral order established by God. In contrast, the Indian religions – Hinduism, Buddhism and Jainism – emphasise an interdependent world with *karma* (a cosmic moral order that states that an individual's present is determined by past conduct and their future by present decisions) as the major determinant of moral life.

But just as there are differences between religious traditions, there is also enormous heterogeneity of interpretations, beliefs and practices within each religious tradition. Likewise, people who identify themselves with a particular religious tradition will differ in the importance they attach to their beliefs and the extent to which they influence the choices they make and the way in which they live (Curlin, Roach et al 2005).

Perhaps most importantly, however, is the fact that while religious people of many faiths share certain principles – the desire to avoid harm to others, the desire to look after the needy and the desire to avoid acts like murder, theft and immoral sexual relations – those without any religious conviction also share these principles and the virtues that form the basis of religious morality, such as love and compassion. Indeed those with religious and secular views are likely to find considerable common ground within a public discourse inclusive of basic values such as human dignity, non-violence, compassion, selflessness and respect for life.

In multicultural societies – where people of many different religions live side by side – one cannot refer to a single religion and expect it to be an authoritative source that will be agreed upon by all. Ancient religious sources do not provide direct answers to questions about the morality of platelet transfusion, or the morning-after pill, or whether ventilators can be removed from brain-dead people. Each of these developments requires religious leaders, ethicists, individual patients and practitioners to reason their way from what they have previously believed to be right towards new methods for dealing with the changed circumstances (Charlesworth 1993).

Ethics is not ... Law

When confronted by difficult ethical issues, health-care professionals frequently invoke the law as a means of resolving conflict. This is extremely misleading as law and ethics concern themselves with similar issues but are quite distinct. The relationship between morality and the law is complex. In contrast to morality, law incorporates central notions of social order, political and social consensus, governmental politics, punishment and legal sanction. Both ethics and the law do, however, share many features. Both are normative, in that they aim to provide answers to the question of how a person *should* act. Both are historically determined human creations. Both reflect the profound influence of religion, science, human experience and custom. Ethics and law also both emphasise reasoning, justification via argument and critical reflection.

The law also shares a respect for autonomy and independent moral judgment. Laws frequently use terms such as 'reasonable', 'sufficient' and 'disproportionate' – allowing for their interpretation in specific contexts and for the use of judicial discretion. Indeed, the law is replete with examples where courts have acknowledged moral complexity – particularly in cases involving treatment or non-treatment at the beginning and end of life.

In some cases, such as the laws relating to consent that emerged after World War II, legal argument has had a great influence upon ethical thinking; but the law should not be seen as the primary basis for ethical thought, rather it is the other way around – morality can be a fundamental influence on the law. For example, we believe that killing is morally wrong and formulate a law prohibiting murder, but we do not believe that killing is morally wrong simply because there is a law against it. We enact laws to safeguard what we believe to be morally or socially important.

There have been many instances where laws offer little guidance about ethical issues. For example, laws in some Australian States relating to cardio-pulmonary resuscitation (CPR) are very unclear and do not explicitly recognise patients' right to refuse CPR, although most ethics commentators believe that patients clearly do have this right. There have also been many cases – such as laws enacted in Nazi Germany, Stalinist Russia and Apartheid South Africa – in which laws were enacted by states which most people consider to be evil. To that extent, it is argued by some legal theorists, called *positivists*, that there is no *necessary* connection between law and morals: a law can still be legal even if is immoral (see Chapter 4). Others dispute this claim and say that law must have a minimum moral content for it to be able to exert normative force. These theorists are generally referred to as *natural lawyers* (see Chapter 4).

The main difference between law and ethics lies in the ability of law to close normative debate. Unlike ethics, where reasonable people may continue to take opposing views and continually justify them using their own ethics, law requires that debates be finalised and answers be given. Once parliament or the judges have created a binding legal norm there is no capacity for further legal debate. The legal norm therefore has become *normatively closed* in a way that ethical norms can never be. Legal systems are capable of providing final and binding resolutions; ethical systems are not.

Law should therefore be considered as part of the process of ethical reasoning. It is essential that health professionals first formulate an explicit ethical decision and then review the legal framework in which they need to work. In rare situations an ethical decision may require one to work outside the law.

Ethics is not ... Gut-feeling

Although 'gut-feelings' or intuition are rarely used to justify clinical decisions, it is not unusual for ethical behaviour to be justified because it 'feels right'. Contemporary bioethics has probably overemphasised rationality at the expense of emotion, intuition, virtues and care; but it is still generally agree that one cannot rely purely upon 'gut-feeling'. 'Gut-feelings' and intuitions do have a role in ethical decision-making, but it is important that they be balanced by a reasoned approach that insists on some degree of consistency and objectivity.

Ethics is not ... Public opinion or consensus

The use of consensus as a basis for determining morally correct action has come to prominence as the focus of decision-making in the health-care setting has shifted from the individual physician to the health-care team. However, consensus is not necessarily the most optimal process of collective deliberation. The purported consensus of health teams or committees may reflect institutional demands, power imbalances between health professionals, fear of litigation or desire for 'safety in numbers', rather than a true process of democratic decision-making (Caws 1991). In the end, the process of consensus may have little to do with determining morality and may be primarily a question of interpersonal relationships (Moreno 1988).

Sources such as opinion polls and referenda are often used to support moral actions, even though public opinion may be easily swayed by charismatic personalities or appeals to attractive and fashionable notions. Whilst group decision-making and collective activity provide strength, groups remain collections of individuals each of whom may have a different moral perspective and the capacity (or responsibility) to systematically engage an ethical issue. Group decision-making may therefore best be seen as a way of incorporating debate, argument, moral compromise and agreement into a process of decision-making – rather than as a way of reaching a simple moral consensus.

So, what *is* ethics?

Having discussed what ethics is not, we will now try and offer a description of what we believe ethics is. To do this we will return to our opening statement: ethics is the study of what we ought to do. Or if we restate this in the way of the Ancient Greeks, ethics asks each of us 'How should I live?'

This book is called *Ethics and Law for the Health Professions*. It is therefore about what members of the health professions – doctors, nurses, and other health professionals – ought to do. But this is not only the business of health professionals, everyone in society is concerned about this, and there are many different views about what should be done.

If we look at the question 'How should I live?', it is apparent that part of the answer must address how I should live in relation to others. This leads to an important insight: that ethics demands acknowledgement and respect for others and that ethics has a social dimension. It also brings up the question of who or what is important in determining how I should live or what I should do. For example, does one need to think of the interests of a foetus or an animal in ethical deliberations?

One of the key features of ethical questions is that people care about them. Some questions – such as the importance of consent and confidentiality – are questions that people in Western societies largely agree about We explore these bioethical 'issues' early in the book. Other ethical questions – such as the role of abortion or euthanasia – are unlikely to ever elicit widespread agreement. According to Caplan, bioethics 'continues to be a cultural flashpoint where disagreements run deep, the stakes continue to be high, and the voices and sources of authority diverse' (Caplan 2008). We will discuss the more controversial bioethical 'dilemmas' later in this book.

If we think of all possible ethical questions together, they become like a maze, or a poorly defined area of interlocking subjects, approaches and perspectives. This intellectual domain isn't owned by any particular discipline, indeed it would not be ethical if only doctors could comment on medical ethics, only nurses on nursing ethics. Bioethics is accessible to any number of different disciplines or perspectives and can be approached through the many different methods of inquiry familiar to each discipline. Thus, philosophy can explore the ethical domain using logic, bioethics using ethical principles or normative theory, linguistics by discourse analysis, law by legal reasoning, economics by cost-benefit analysis, nursing by reference to an ethics of care or phenomenological approaches, clinical medicine by randomised controlled clinical trials, sociology by stakeholder analysis, and so forth. In each case the discipline defines the boundaries of the region it either wishes or is compelled to explore, identifies the questions that need to be asked, and provides insights that may often be taken beyond the discipline itself.

But no discipline, method, or theory can completely describe the complexity and richness of the ethical space or ever entirely resolve the uncertainties, ambiguities and conflicts that are a feature of human experience and of ethics (Komesaroff 1995). This means that ethics must ultimately be about discourse, communication, social relationships and politics. Thus, while the ethical space ideally requires mutual respect, process, argument, transparency and shared critical reflection, it must also admit to the possibility of self-interest, incommensurability and intractable conflict (Frank 2004).

References

Ankeny, RA, R Clifford et al (2005) 'Religious perspectives on withdrawal of treatment from patients with multiple organ failure'. *Med J Aust* **183**(11-12): 616-21.

Caplan, A (2008) 'Putting bioethics in a suit and tie'. *Lancet* **371**: 107-8.

Caws, P (1991) 'Committees and consensus: How many heads are better than one?' *J Med Philos* **16**: 375-91.

Charlesworth, M (1993) *Bioethics in a liberal society*. Cambridge, Cambridge University Press.

Curlin, FA, CJ Roach et al (2005) 'How are religion and spirituality related to health? A study of physicians' perspectives'. *South Med J* **98**(8): 761-6.

Etziony, M (1973) *The Physician's Creed*. Springfield, Ill, Charles C Thomas.

Frank, A (2004) 'Ethics as process and practice'. *Int Med Jn* **34**: 355-7.

Friedson, E (1999) Professionalism and institutional ethics. *The American Medical Ethics Revolution*. R Baker, A Caplan, L Emanuel and S Latham. Baltimore, John Hopkins University Press.

Gillon, R (1980) *Philosophical Medical Ethics*. Oxford, Humana Press.

Komesaroff, P (1995) From bioethics to microethics. Ethical debate and modern medicine. *Troubled bodies: critical perspectives on postmodernism, medical ethics and the body*. P Komesaroff. Melbourne, Melbourne University Press.

Miles, S (2004) *The Hippocratic Oath and the ethics of medicine*. Oxford, Oxford University Press.

Moreno, J (1988) 'Ethics by committee: The moral authority of consensus'. *J Med Philos* **13**: 411-32.

Reich, WT, Ed (1982) *Encyclopedia of bioethics*. New York, Free Press.

Singer, P (1979) *Practical Ethics*. Cambridge, Cambridge University Press.

CHAPTER 2

Ethical Theories and Concepts

Introduction to ethical theory

We think about ethical issues in ways that reflect our own experiences, attitudes, and culture. Our actions and decisions may therefore embody implicit theories of ethics. Moral philosophers have attempted to explore these underlying concepts in order to deepen our understanding of the decisions we make and to facilitate ethical behaviour in our day-to-day lives. In this chapter we briefly examine some of the major ethical theories that have contributed to the development of philosophical and biomedical ethics. For a deeper understanding of moral philosophy we would encourage the reader to see the texts listed in the references.

Deontology

One of the major schools of moral philosophy is known as deontology. Deontology (from the Greek *deon* meaning 'binding duty') is also known as *intrinsicalism* because it embodies the notion that things or actions are right or wrong in and of themselves. For example, a deontological theory might maintain that there is something *intrinsically* wrong with acts of infanticide, rape or genocide that is independent of outcome or consequences. Many religions are based on deontological theories.

The central theoretical focus of deontological theories is on doing one's duty, which may be expressed by certain universal statements or action-guides. These central rules find expression in laws – such as 'Do not kill'; principles – such as respect for human life; institutions – such as the legal system; and 'relational laws' – such as respect for one's parents.

In order to determine what action is required in a particular circumstance, the deontological approach to moral reasoning involves the application of the appropriate universal statement to the specific situation. An example of such reasoning would be: killing is wrong; giving potassium chloride to this patient is killing; therefore this action is wrong.

This approach clearly separates the assessment of the action from the assessment of the outcome or consequences. According to deontologists, if fundamental moral principles are violated then the action is ethically wrong, even if it has good consequences. An extreme deontologist may go so far as to say that consequences are irrelevant to moral evaluation and that an act is right only if it conforms to a principle of duty; and wrong if it violates such a principle. The majority of deontologists are more moderate than this and hold that consequences are relevant to determining what is morally right or wrong, but that they are not the only things that are relevant and are certainly not of primary importance.

Some philosophers make a distinction between Act Deontologism and Rule Deontologism. Act Deontologism argues that we must decide separately in each particular situation what is right or wrong without appealing to any rules. It rejects the idea that a general rule may ever supersede a particular judgment as to what action should be taken because it claims that each situation is unique. Many philosophers believe that Act Deontologism is essentially untenable, as they believe that whenever a person acts morally they will always come to implicitly make and use a set of general rules even if they do not acknowledge them explicitly (Frankena 1973).

Rule Deontologism suggests that standards of right and wrong consist of one or more rules that are valid independently of their consequences. There are many versions of Rule Deontologism, and each differs from each other with regard to the rules they advocate, the importance they ascribe to different rules, the flexibility they allow in making exceptions to rules, and the methods they use to justify rules.

Four major types of justifications of moral rules have been presented: *Theological* arguments justify rules by appeal to divine revelation, suggesting that the proper moral rules are those that God wills us to follow. Although attractive to many, the great problem with these arguments is that there is so much conflict about the existence of God and about what actually *is* God's will.

Societal approaches argue that the correct moral rules are those believed in by most members of society. Unfortunately, this is also inadequate as consensus is not necessarily a guide to correct moral behaviour and may indeed justify what we would normally regard as morally repugnant actions. It is also true that in many difficult situations one cannot easily identify a consensus view (Brody 1983).

Intuitionist approach suggests that morality is actually an intrinsic feature of the world and that the proper moral rules or actions are those that possess the intrinsic property of 'rightness', a property that we can all perceive through our special faculty of moral intuition. Unfortunately, by appealing to direct apprehension of right moral rules or actions, the intuitionist approach bypasses the normal reasoning process and thus is not susceptible to either proof or disproof.

The most influential proponent of rule-based morality was Immanuel Kant (1724-1804). Kant sought to establish the ultimate basis for valid moral rules in a fourth approach – that of *pure reason*. Kant's metaphysics of morals, which is outlined in three main works, *Groundwork for the Metaphysics of Morals*, *Critique of Practical Reason* and *Metaphysics of Morals*, is based on the idea that using pure reason one can deduct *a priori* (something formulated by reason alone – without the need for empirical observation), universal and binding rules or laws which may guide one's decisions and actions and enable one to live a good life.

Further, he argued that people (moral agents) act or choose according to these laws, or are 'duty-bound', because they have 'good will'. In other words their (moral) actions result from practical consideration of moral laws and not out of habit, nor following consideration of consequences (ie, moral people do the right thing for the right reasons).

Kant's work is famously difficult to understand. In *Groundwork* he explains how rules that describe right actions should be 'univeralisable' – ie they should be able to be applied to everyone, in agreement with what he calls the 'categorical imperatives'. Kant provides (at least) three different formulations of the 'categorical imperative':

- 'act only according to that maxim whereby you can at the same time will that it should become a universal law';
- 'act in such a way that you treat humanity, whether in your own person or in the person of another, always at the same time as an end and never simply as a means'; and
- 'act as if the maxim of your action were to become through your will a universal law of nature'.

In summary, therefore, Kant suggests: first, that the ideal moral life consists of submission to a certain will or command that could be expressed in universal moral imperatives that are absolute and binding; second, that people themselves have an absolute, inalienable, irreducible and unconditional value that derives from the fact that they are rational beings who are self-legislating and have personal dignity; and, third, that this dignity is violated whenever a person is treated merely as a means to an end.

The value of deontological theory is that it reminds us of the importance of rationality in moral judgment and of moral standards independent of consequences. It has tremendous appeal for those who seek certainties in life and for institutions (such as the church or government) that have a need to bind together groups of people under some identifiable moral code.

However, deontological theory has also been criticised because its rules and principles are controversial, vague or difficult to define. For instance, even if it is accepted that is wrong to kill, it is still not clear whether this means that killing is always wrong in every circumstance. This gives rise to the major objection to deontological theory – the problem of conflicting morals. If all rules or prohibitions are equal, what should be done when two or more moral rules come into conflict? If they are not equal, then this implies that rules can sometimes be overruled or that there is a hierarchy of rules of different importance.

Some philosophers such as Ross speak of *prima facie* and *actual* duties (Ross 1939). A *prima facie* duty is binding, but it may to yield to some stronger duty, whereas an *actual* duty is one that may not yield to another demand. Fidelity to a promise, for example, may be a *prima facie* duty that would have to yield to an *actual* duty such as the obligation to save life.

Unfortunately, it has proven impossible for those who support intrinsicalism to provide an exception-free and conflict-free hierarchy of rules.

Consequentialist theories: utilitarianism

The difficulties found with rule-based morality may have led many contemporary philosophers towards *consequentialist* theories instead. The basic tenet of consequentialism is that the rightness or wrongness of an action is based solely on the consequences of performing it; the right act is defined as that which leads to the best consequences. The nature of the action or the motives and intention of the agent are largely irrelevant. For a consequentialist, actions are neither intrinsically right nor wrong; rather, the moral value of any action is dependent upon the consequences of that action.

There are many variants of consequentialist theory but they share a common rational process of moral reasoning. To decide if an action is moral or not, a consequentialist will attempt to consider all the feasible alternative actions in a given situation, and calculate all the possible consequences for the parties involved. They will then choose the action that will result in the best outcome.

The most prominent consequentialist theory is *Utilitarianism*. Utilitarianism is the normative moral theory that states that the single fundamental principle of ethics should be the 'principle of utility' – that the morally right action is the action that produces the best possible outcome as determined from a perspective that gives equal weighting to the interests of each party. For utilitarians, the central principle of utility is absolute, and all moral rules, actions or behaviours must be justified solely on the basis of an analysis of their consequences. Thus, killing, abortion or even infanticide may each be justifiable in certain circumstances.

The classical utilitarians, Jeremy Bentham (1748-1832) and John Stuart Mill (1806-73), conceived utility entirely in terms of happiness or pleasure, as they maintained that pleasure alone is intrinsically good, and pain (or the absence of pleasure) is intrinsically evil. But there is no satisfactory reason why pleasure should be the only standard for judging consequences as there are many other conditions (eg, truth, justice, knowledge) that also seem to be good in themselves. 'Ideal' utilitarians, such as GE Moore, contend that values other than happiness have intrinsic worth and consider that friendship, knowledge, health, autonomy and understanding may be considered intrinsically valuable (Moore 1903).

Another approach to utilitarianism is based on maximising individual preferences or desires. A number of prominent contemporary utilitarians, such as Richard Hare and Peter Singer, favour this view as they contend that whilst it may be impossible to adequately measure 'pain' or 'pleasure', it is possible to measure preferences (Hare 1964; Singer 1979). However, this approach fails to confront the issue of valid but morally unacceptable preferences (eg, those who actually enjoy killing or inflicting pain).

Controversy has also arisen over whether the principle of utility pertains to *acts* in specific contexts or, instead, to *rules* that determine the rightness or wrongness of actions. According to *Act utilitarianism*, individuals should act in each situation using rules only as rules of thumb and each action should be judged independently to bring about the greatest balance of good over evil. This approach has been supported by philosophers such as GE Moore and JJC Smart

(Moore 1903). Joseph Fletcher has enunciated another form of act utilitarianism called *Situationalism* (or *agapism* from the Greek 'love') in which each action or situation is judged purely on its own merits, in order to produce the most 'loving' result (Fletcher 1996). Unfortunately, it is extremely difficult to adequately define, measure or compare 'loving' outcomes, and hence situationalism is open to the same criticisms as other forms of utilitarianism.

Rule utilitarianism has been proposed as a defence against the objection that utilitarianism leads to morally indefensible conclusions. Like deontology, rule utilitarianism emphasises the centrality of rules in morality but, unlike deontology, it states that these rules should be formulated by reference to the principle of utility. Thus, the morality of actions is determined by reference to a system of moral rules formulated by society or individuals that are based on their ability to produce the best possible consequences. Rules are selected, revised and replaced on the basis of the principle of utility, which remains the ultimate standard. Importantly, the rules recognised as valid need not be rules that most people accept and act on (conventional morality); rather, valid rules are those everyone should act on because this would lead to the best results (Reich 1982).

Criticisms of consequentialist theories fall into several main groups. One group involves questions about the validity of the claim that consequentialism provides us with a simple, rational process of moral reasoning. Such criticisms consider consequentialism as fundamentally flawed because of methodological difficulties in assigning values to outcomes.

These methodological difficulties are basically threefold. The first methodological weakness is that the concept of utility or happiness is so unclear as to make it practically unworkable. Indeed, despite the efforts of Bentham, Singer, Hare and others, we still await a clear, practical definition of utility. Empirical research suggests that it is difficult, if not impossible, to quantify variables such as 'happiness' or 'quality of life' and to compare all the possible outcomes of an action. Making comparisons between quantitative and qualitative outcomes themselves or assessing such outcomes for individuals and between individuals seems difficult if not impossible.

The second weakness is that it is often unclear as to who are the parties involved in any moral action and what moral significance each of their interests should have. For example, when considering the morality or consequences of abortion, should you consider equally all those who may have an interest, that is, the mother, foetus, father, society and future generations, or should you not consider any one of these parties?

The third methodological weakness of consequentialism is that one cannot decide, on the basis of consequences alone, what moral action to follow. It is often difficult to predict or to determine outcomes in advance, and yet, if consequentialism is to be successful, then we need to know how to estimate, evaluate, compare and rank consequences in order to determine which consequences are more important and which preferences ought to be given priority. Unfortunately, we have no clear way of doing any of these things.

Thus, it appears that consequentialism is susceptible to many of the same criticisms as deontological theories because it is no easier to rank consequences than it is to rank moral rules. In practice, ethical theory must confront and deal with values and consequences that are not quantifiable in empirical terms and there are immense difficulties with measurement even in those areas where utilitarianism is popular such as health resource allocation (Williams 1972).

Another criticism of consequentialism is that it does not account for certain aspects of ordinary moral thinking such as the importance of individual rights in deciding moral issues. Ordinarily, we believe that others may not infringe upon an individual's rights such as the right to life or property, even when some social gain could be realised from such infringements. Consequentialism is unable to do justice to this aspect of morality because it fails to make provision for individual rights (Williams 1973).

The most strident argument against consequentialism is that it clashes with a broad range of considered beliefs and can lead to morally unacceptable conclusions. Utilitarianism may permit actions that are incommensurable with common morality, such as killing or torture, if these actions result in the best net balance of good over evil.

A final argument advanced against consequentialism is that no consequentialist theory can account for basic convictions about justice and injustice. For example, it may be unjust to allow policies that discriminate against people on the basis of race, sex, creed or socio-economic status even if they are indicated by a consequentialist analysis of a particular situation. The emphasis in consequentialist thought is upon net satisfaction rather than considerations of justice or equality and hence consequentialist theories can sanction unjust rules and allow the interests of the majority to override those of the minority.

Consequentialists have adopted several arguments that attempt to meet these criticisms. Hard-line utilitarians suggest that if consequentialism does not accord with traditional morality this is because common morality is the result of incorrect moral reflection which should be rejected in favour of consequentialism. More commonly, consequentialists accept that there are significant difficulties with absolute utilitarianism, but argue that the natural solution is to expand consequentialist principles to make them more reconcilable with existing moral beliefs, rather than to abandon consequentialism altogether.

Another way to answer criticism of consequentialism has been to develop 'rule-utilitarianism' whereby the rightness of a particular action lies in its conformity with a proper moral rule. Such moral rules are in turn based upon the value of their consequences. Rule-utilitarianism has thus been viewed by some critics as an attempt to occupy the philosophical 'middle ground' and thus obtain the benefits of both consequentialism and non-consequentialism. The claim is that a 'two-tier' model of rights, whereby consequentially justified rules take precedence over situational calculations, brings us closer to our everyday moral intuitions. Whilst this may be true, critics suggest that any attempt to reach a theoretical compromise in which the principle of utility remains the central aspect of morality is, by its very nature, philosophical unsound. As Bernard Williams notes in *Morality*:

> Whatever the general utility of having a certain rule, if one has actually reached the point of seeing that the utility of breaking it on a certain occasion

is greater than that of following it, then surely it would be pure irrationality not to break it. (Williams 1972)

The value of consequentialism is that it reminds us that the consequences of our actions have moral significance and must be taken into account in the evaluation of actions and situations (Sen 1987). This is apparent in the health sector where utilitarian criteria are frequently employed in areas such as the allocation of scarce health resources and the selection of recipients for donor organs. Consequentialism at least attempts to develop a rational process of moral reasoning that enables the resolution of moral conflict, although in the end it probably does not succeed. Finally, consequentialism attributes moral worth to specific situations or contexts in a manner that has immediate intuitive and clinical appeal, even for those who profess the central importance of rules.

Virtue theory

In recent years a number of philosophers have challenged both deontological and utilitarian philosophy and the emphasis in bioethics on rights, moral rules, ethical principles and rigid schemas of moral reasoning (MacIntyre 1984). They suggest that bioethics would be much better served by returning to the philosophy of Aristotle and his concept of moral virtue.

Virtue ethics contains the notion that the rightness or wrongness of an action is derived from the underlying motive of the person making that action. An analysis based upon virtue ethics would inquire into the attributes of persons we consider 'virtuous' rather than accepting that persons who follow certain moral rules or ethical obligations are necessarily virtuous (Frankena 1982). 'Virtue' here refers to competence in the pursuit of moral excellence and character traits that are morally valuable such as honesty, gentleness, integrity and discernment. Thus, the model of the moral person is one who is disposed by character to have the right motives and desires. By understanding moral behaviours as action that proceeds from virtue, one obviates the need for thinking of morality as 'rule following'. Bernadette Tobin has argued the case for virtue theory by claiming that '[h]uman affairs are deep and complicated and it is often very hard to know how one should act. In the end, one heeds wisdom rather than principles' (Tobin 1992). (For a further discussion of virtue, see Foot (Foot 1978), Pence (Pence 1980), MacIntyre (MacIntyre 1984).)

The concept of moral virtue derives from ancient philosophical traditions. To Plato, virtue was an intellectual trait synonymous with excellence in living a good life and it could be attained and maintained by practice. To Aristotle, and later Aquinas, virtue was expressed as a disposition to act in the right way and was the result of a balance between intellect, feeling and action. In the *Nichomachean Ethics,* Aristotle developed his own philosophy of virtue ethics, which he considered to be the study of how to live well as an individual and to promote human flourishing within society (Ross 1964). Aristotle used the term *ethika arête* to mean 'matters having to do with character'; the right character being modelled on a person of virtue or excellence. Aristotle considered happiness, or *eudaemonia,* to be the highest form of goodness, and argued that this was gained through excellence of function, which, in man's case, was the capacity to reason. This, in turn, was manifest through a life-long practice of making virtuous choices and acting in virtuous ways. For Aristotle, this involved choosing, and acting between two extremes of vice. (This is known as the rule of the 'Golden Mean'.) Thus, for example, the virtuous person would choose and act in ways that were magnificent (the virtue that lies between excess and deficiency) and courageous (the virtue that lies between rashness and cowardice). Each such choice was voluntary and rational and was both made possible by, and contributed to, the development of *phronesis* (practical wisdom). In other words, virtue was not regarded as an innate capacity but was felt to be a disposition cultivated by proper training, experience and critical reflection.

In recent times, virtue ethics has been further developed by a number of contemporary philosophers, including Alaisdair MacIntyre, Hannah Arendt, Martha Nussbaum and Ed Pellegrino. Some, like Pellegrino, have focused on the role of virtues in professional practice, whereas others, such as Martha Nussbaum, have addressed the role of particular virtues, such as compassion, in moral life (Pellegrino 1995; Nussbaum 1996). Andre Comte-Sponville, for example, has described 18 human virtues which provide a basis for considering 'what we should do, who we should be, and how we should live'. He list these as; politeness, fidelity, prudence, temperance, courage, justice, generosity, compassion, mercy, gratitude, humility, simplicity, tolerance, purity, gentleness, good faith, humour and love (Comte-Sponville 2003).

Unfortunately, although virtues do have a special place in practical ethics, it is not at all clear that virtues are a sufficient basis for determining the moral basis of behaviour or that virtue theory should take precedence over moral philosophies that emphasise rights, principles or ethical obligations. Virtue ethics broadly defines each of the concepts of moral goodness and virtuousness in terms of the other. The virtuous person is defined as a person who does good things, and good things are those acts a virtuous person does. As noted by Pellegrino:

> Virtue ethics does not tell us how to resolve specific moral dilemmas. It de-emphasises principles, rules, duties and concrete prescriptions. It only says that the virtuous person will be disposed to act in accord with the virtue appropriate to the situation. This lack of specificity leads to a distressing circularity in reasoning. The right and good is that which the virtuous person would do and the virtuous person is one who would do the right and good. (Pellegrino 1989)

This argument is not only circular, but it also clearly ignores the importance of rights, moral obligations and the significance of one's *actions*. Virtue theory, therefore, appears to be too simplistic and imprecise to adequately explain or justify the rightness or wrongness of actions. This problem is amplified by the difficulty that many virtue theorists have had in defining the 'essential' moral virtues, in providing a standard by which the relative merits of specific virtues can be judged and in determining whether these are a matter of nature, custom, convention or learning.

Obligations and rules, such as the right to life or the right to free speech, serve to protect the interests of individuals independent of the virtues of others; and it is surely not enough to claim that if a person has a virtuous character their actions are morally acceptable. Professional virtue must be concerned about the rightness or wrongness of acts, as well as the goodness or badness of the agent or his or her intent; and in medicine as in other areas of life it is not uncommon for people to act wrongly out of the best of intentions or as a consequence of emphasising one virtue to excess. To use an extreme example, the experiments of Nazi doctors could be seen as 'virtuous' expressions of patriotism, communalism or loyalty. By emphasising the importance of professional virtues and the moral significance of 'practical wisdom', virtue ethics runs the risk of basing ethics on the beliefs and judgments of health professionals and giving moral sanction to unacceptable paternalism.

While virtue ethics appears to be deficient in several ways, the upsurge of interest in contemporary virtue ethics reminds us that when considering ethical issues in health care, these issues cannot be separated from either the moral characteristics of the individuals involved or the process of moral reasoning that forms the basis of their decisions. Quite clearly, virtue, intent and practical wisdom may each determine, personalise and complement the moral judgments that health-care professionals may make in the process of caring for patients. Character traits such as honesty, integrity and fortitude enable health professionals to establish a therapeutic relationship with patients and provide effective health care. At the very least, virtue ethics helps us to recognise the subtle, emotional and intensely personal nature of ethical decisions in health care, the importance of professional virtue and beneficence, and the inadequacy of attempts to reduce ethics to mathematical calibration of consequences, hierarchies of rules, or the inflexible application of principles.

Values

'Value' refers to a thing's worth or importance. The terms 'values' and 'virtues' are often used interchangeably in ethics, whereas in fact there are substantial differences between the two. Their place in moral philosophy, bioethics and professional practice is quite distinct.

Philosophers have traditionally distinguished between different forms of value. *Intrinsic* value is taken as basic and all the other forms of value are defined in terms of it. Thus, something has *instrumental* value if it is a means to obtaining something that is intrinsically valuable; something has *inherent* value only if the experience or contemplation of it is intrinsically valuable; something has *contributory* value if it contributes to the value of some whole of which it is a part; and something has *relational* value if it is valuable by virtue of its bearing some relationship to something else that has intrinsic value.

The branch of philosophy that is concerned with the nature of value, and with what kinds of things have value, is called *value theory* (or *axiology*). Value theory is concerned with all forms of value including the aesthetic value of beauty and the moral values of right, wrong, obligation, responsibility, virtue and vice. Understood more narrowly, value theory is concerned with what is intrinsically valuable or desirable for its own sake (Audi 1999).

The central question of value theory ('what are those things that have intrinsic value?') may be used as a basis for any construction of a 'moral' society. This question has been answered in a number of different ways. The first is *hedonism* – the idea that pleasure, happiness or the satisfaction of preferences is the ultimate good. Hedonism has been defended by philosophers such as Epicurius, Voltaire, Bentham, Sidgwick and, with qualification, by JS Mill (Singer 1994).

Other philosophers have held that what is intrinsically valuable are experiences that exhibit 'satisfactoriness', where pleasure is but one form of satisfaction. Contemporary philosophers, including Moore, Ross, Bretano, Scheler and Little, tend to subscribe to different forms of value pluralism, whereby a range of things have intrinsic value (Moore 1903; Little 2004). These may include: consciousness, human flourishing, knowledge and insight, moral virtue, friendship and community, self-expression or creative freedom, a just distribution of goods, aesthetic experience and ontological security (where ontology refers to the nature or essence of existence).

John Finnis, in his book *Natural Law and Natural Rights*, lists seven things that are good in and of themselves, and are required for human well-being. These are: life itself, knowledge, play, aesthetic experience, sociability (friendship or community), practical reasonableness (the complex alignment of freedom, reason, integrity and authenticity that allows the genuine realisation of one's own preferences, hopes and self-determination), and 'religion' (which he describes as a recognition of, and concern about, an order of things 'beyond' each and every man) (Finnis 1980). He argues that all other forms of good are simply means for pursuing one of these basic goods, whereas none of those things on his list can be reduced to being a component of the others, or are instrumental in the pursuit of the others. While Finniss's choice of values is open to interpretation and debate, the notion that they are, either individually or in combination, those things that are required for a 'good' life, is extremely attractive.

Social contract theory (Contractarianism)

Social contract theories provide a very different approach to defining moral behaviour in that they are irreducibly political. In other words, contractarians assume that moral rules exist to provide social order, ensure a just society and to improve the lives of individuals – individuals who are both rational and self-interested. One of the earliest, and most famous, contractarians was the English philosopher, Thomas Hobbes (1588-1697). Hobbes famously argued that man's 'natural state' was 'solitary, poor, nasty, brutish and short', and that because people were rational they could see, first, that a society governed by moral and legal rules provided safety and escape from this natural state and, second, that a social contract enable creation of such a society (Pence 2000).

The most prominent recent social contract theories have been those advanced by Robert Nozick and John Rawls. Nozick, a libertarian philosopher, argues that the primary role of ethics is not to create a just society in which all prosper, but to create a society in which individuals can freely advance their own interests and government plays a limited role. In contrast, Rawls argues that it is possible to construct a morally defensible social contract that advances social justice and privileges equality.

John Rawls (1921-2002) has had a major impact on contemporary discussion of ethics, justice and health care, in large measure because philosophers and social theorists since Rawls have had to respond to the ideas that Rawls developed in his seminal work, *A Theory of Justice* (1971), and situate her or himself in relation to Rawls (Rawls 1971).

A Theory of Justice was in large part written as a critical response to utilitarianism – which dominated political thought in the post-World War II period. Rawls maintained that utilitarianism advocated the subordination or compromise of individual liberties if this worked to the benefit of the general good and that this was wrong.

In place of utilitarianism, Rawls built upon the work of John Locke in developing a form of social contract theory that described the principles of justice that people would be governed by and that would apply to the basic structures of society. Rawls called his formulation of the principles of justice – 'justice as fairness'. Rawls argues that the 'basic structure' of society – its political constitution, economy and property rules – is determined by principles that everyone would accept from a 'fair position'. This 'fair position' is one where everyone is impartially situated as equals by a hypothetical 'veil of ignorance'. This veil requires that people set aside their particular differences, eg, talents, wealth, social position, religious and philosophical views and conceptions of value. Rawls argues that from this position everyone would reject utilitarianism, perfectionism and intuitionism and that instead they would accept justice as fairness. This concept of justice consists of two principles. The first principle, known as the principle of liberty, says that certain liberties are basic and must be provided to all, including liberty of conscience, freedom of association, equal political liberties, freedom and integrity of the person, and the liberties that maintain the rule of law. These liberties are 'basic' because they are required for a person to exercise their 'moral powers'. (These moral powers – the capacity to be rational and the capacity to have a sense of justice and act on it – are essential aspects of the moral person as they enable each person to be a free, cooperative and responsible social citizen.) The second principle, known as the difference principle, regulates permissible differences in rights, power and privileges. It defines the limits of inequalities in wealth, income and power that may exist in a just society by asserting that social positions must be open to equal competition and inequalities are only permissible if they maximally benefit the least advantaged. Rawls's theory and principles therefore describe a liberal egalitarian society (or a form of liberal socialism) where wealth and income are distributed on moral grounds.

Rawls's theory, principles of justice and hypothetical veil of ignorance have all been subject to extensive criticism on the grounds that they make invalid assumptions about what people would choose, are naïve and unrealistic with regards to the possibility that people would set aside power and status, and discriminate against women and those who are dependent on others to care for them and to advocate for them. These are important criticisms, both because they point out possible flaws in Rawls's work and because they continue a crucial dialogue about global justice and equity and the links between ethics and socio-political organisation.

Arguments against rationality

A number of alternative moral theories dismiss the central role of reason in ethics and argue instead that it is emotion, attitude and intuition that are determinative in the formulation of moral truth.

David Hume (1711-76) and Charles Stevenson (1908-79) contend that moral statements are nothing more than expressions of feelings or attitudes and are not reliant on reason (McNaughton 1988). This is known as *Emotivism*. Another school of thought, *Intuitionism*, also rejects the importance of rational justi-fication and argues instead that moral truths are self-evident and known simply by intuition (Goldberg 1983). Both schools of thought believe that actions or decisions may be intrinsically good or bad but that such judgments have only *prima facie* standing, that is, they may be overridden by stronger moral demands. Other philosophers, such as the atheistic Friedrich Nietzsche (1844-1900) and the existentialists Blaire Pascal, Søren Kierkegaard, Martin Heidegger (1889-1976), and Jean-Paul Sartre (1905-80) have also attacked rationalistic Western philo-sophical ethics and defended a more emotional and individualistic approach to life and behaviour.

Emotivism, intuitionism and existentialism remind us that reason is clearly not the only determinant of moral actions and that intuition, attitude, desire, will or 'gut-feeling' may each contribute to our decisions. However, each of these theories fails to provide a coherent means for understanding or resolving ethical issues in health care, and they fail to understand the importance of some degree of rationality in ethics (Swanton 1987).

Casuistry

The term ' casuistry' refers to case-based moral reasoning. Casuistry rejects the need for universal ethical principles and claims instead that ethical decision-making results from a detailed understanding of particular situations and from interpretation of general moral rules in light of individual cases. Casuistry is based on clinical experience, practical wisdom and medical tradition (Jonsen and Toulmin 1988).

Casuistry has its earliest origins in the deliberations in the Greek Sophists. It was further developed in Aristotelian ethics, which maintained that morality incorporated practical judgments about what ought to be done in specific circum-stances.

For modern day casuists, moral authority and ethical norms develop from a consensus based upon the consideration of specific cases, rather than the consideration of underlying principles. The lessons learnt from such cases may then be generalised by analogy to other cases. This technique of 'paradigm analogue' – of placing each case in context rather than considering it in isolation – is a cornerstone of casuistical analysis as it facilitates the development of moral maxims, the elucidation of exceptions or qualifications to general principles and the resolution of each case by an experienced and prudent person (Arras 1991).

Casuistry emphasises the importance of clinical context in making ethical judgments. Casuistry can be very attractive to clinicians, but it is deficient in a number of ways. First, moral truths may not be clinically self-evident. The ethical aspects of individual cases may be interpreted in different ways by different persons, just as different clinicians may interpret the significance of clinical data differently. Health-care professionals may interpret cases and make moral judgments in a manner that reflects their own biases, value systems or ignorance and this is not a satisfactory basis for moral judgments. Second, because casuistry relies heavily upon health-care professionals' moral judgments it may simply reinforce strong paternalism as a means of decision-making. This idea, that casuistry lacks a substantive ethical basis and has no central conception of human welfare, flourishing or 'the good', and so is open to simplistic representations of ethical concerns and 'lazy thinking', represents one of the most persistent criticisms of casuistry (Gert 1998). Defences of casuistry's ethical substance generally tend to argue that it is based on 'common morality' – ie, those values and norms that are intuitively and informally (and often unconsciously) shared by all people. While this defence may provide popular appeal – it generally fails to rescue casuistry from criticisms that it lacks rigour or coherence. Third, the relationship between clinical cases and theory is unclear and there is a risk that overemphasis on the facts of a case may lead to overly subjective assessments of the ethical aspects of particular cases. Finally, while case analysis might be necessary for moral reasoning it might not be sufficient. It is probably more appropriate for ethical decision-making to consider both moral principles and the specific detail of cases or contexts.

Feminist moral philosophy and the ethics of care

Contemporary feminist philosophers have challenged the rationality, practicality and inherent (masculinist) sexism of much of Western moral philosophy. They contend that male-dominant Western traditions have failed to provide a coherent or universal moral philosophy that incorporates the needs of women and the substantial philosophical contributions women have made regarding the relative importance of *care* (as opposed to rationality), *interpersonal relationships* (as opposed to autonomy) and *communitarianism* (as opposed to individual rights). Modern bioethics has been challenged both by gender-attentive research, which has emphasised sexual oppression and discrimination against women in health care (American Medical Association Council on Ethical and Judicial Affairs 1991; Shaw 1994; Davidson 2001); and by the emergence of feminist moral theory (Gilligan 1982; Held 2002; Walker 2006).

It is often difficult to define feminism, in large measure because it is not a homogenous entity but can take many forms – radical feminism, liberal feminism, Marxist feminism, lesbian feminism and so on. In broad terms, however, feminism can be defined as a social movement of and for women, a project aimed at the emancipation of humanity and at sexual equality, and a method of analysis, ie, in terms of how one approaches issues and what one takes to be important political, philosophical, ethical and social questions (Fricker and Hornsby 2000). Feminist ethics, similarly, includes a range of different approaches – all of which owe some debt to the work of the feminist psychologist, Carol Gilligan. In her landmark text, *A Different Voice*, Gilligan disputed Lawrence Kohlberg's claims about moral development and asserted that women 'speak' in a different voice and that this voice had been excluded from serious thinking about morality. In fact, women speak in a number of voices, as there is no single feminist ethics and there is often significant disagreement between feminist theorists with regards to such issues as AIDS, surrogacy, pornography and sexual harassment (Garner 1995; Wolf 1996; Lumby 1997).

Despite differences in approaches, feminist ethics tends to reformulate those aspects of contemporary ethics that devalue women's experiences, highlight the differences between women and men, and provide strategies for dealing with ethical issues in a manner that counters the subordination of women (Jaggar 1998). Most feminist moral theories also share a number of other characteristics including:

(a) rejection of the overemphasis on individual rights, autonomy and rationality in bioethics (Parsons 1986);

(b) criticism of the dualistic thinking (or traditional dichotomies) that has structured Western philosophy and ethics and supported the subordination of women, eg, reason-emotion, mind-body, objective-subjective, public-private, general-particular, fact-value, male-female, autonomous-dependent etc;

(c) denial of the requirement for value-neutral philosophies or abstract ethical principles (Harding 1991);

(d) rejection of the adversarial nature of moral conflict as a means for resolving ethical issues in clinical practice;

(e) stressing the significance of values such as empathy, interdependence and caring, and the importance of the shared responsibility all members of society have to each other; and

(f) emphasis on the importance of context and the relevance of politics and power to understanding ethics and health care.

The development of feminist bioethics has been described as a succession of 'waves' (Charlesworth 1993). The 'first wave' feminists shared an optimistic view of technology as a value-neutral means for women to liberate themselves from the biological tyranny of pregnancy, childbirth and mothering (Firestone 1971). In the 1970s and 1980s the 'second wave' feminists adopted a more critical and pessimistic attitude to technology whereby it was viewed as a means for the continued oppression of women (Overall 1983). 'Third wave' feminists embody a diverse range of perspectives that reflect the growth, vitality and philosophical maturity of feminism. These thinkers may accept that technology is not value-neutral but argue that technology can be used by women, for women, to end oppression (Warren 1988; Purdy 1989). While the description of the 'waves' of feminism has historical importance and 'places' feminist ethics in terms of biotechnology, it is of limited relevance to contemporary thought as feminist bioethics is now a large, rich, mature and extraordinarily diverse field.

In recent times, what has become known as an *ethics of care* (sometimes called 'feminine ethics') has been developed from within nursing ethics and contemporary feminist philosophy, and has had a major impact on the concepts of health care and professional roles. The 'ethics of care' derives largely from the work of developmental psychologist Carol Gilligan and her thesis that the primary moral orientation of girls and women is an ethic of 'care' and that this may be contrasted with the 'justice' orientation of men and boys that has domi-nated health care and bioethics (Gilligan 1982). Supporters of the 'ethics of care' reject the philosophical emphasis on universal moral rules, impartiality, indi-vidual rights, law, objectivity and autonomy; and instead emphasise the impor-tance of personal responsibility, love, trust and caring (Baier 1986). They contend that dominance of a 'justice orientation' within bioethics and the priority given to autonomy has obscured the significance of the special commitment health professionals have to care for their patients.

This argument has been enthusiastically endorsed by many nurse ethicists and educators but has had less of an impact in clinical ethics; and has been criticised by some feminist philosophers as reinforcing the subordination of women by its emphasis on caring (Sherwin 1992). Critics of an ethics of care point out that women's competency at caring for others has developed within sexist societies and that emphasis on caring as an exclusively feminine virtue may serve simply to reinforce the sexual status quo. Those who reject an ethics of care generally suggest that care and justice are not mutually exclusive and that an emphasis on care without consideration of autonomy, justice and a language of rights is of limited value at the social and institutional level (van den Broek 1997).

Feminist ethics and the 'ethics of care' have helped refocus attention on the importance of caring, relationships, emotion, tolerance and humanity. Gender-attentive research has explored the relevance of issues such as power, authority and discrimination to bioethical analysis, to remind us that ethical issues only make sense when considered in light of the specific contexts. Feminist ethics have served both to reveal the diverse nature of the oppression of women and also to make explicit the importance of political change to eliminate oppression and imbalances of power.

Human rights, liberalism and communitarianism

Concepts of human rights are often invoked in discussions about health care. The question of human rights has played a large part in modern ethics, but there continues to be disagreement as to whether rights are a fundamental part of human existence, or are something that may or may not be granted by the state.

The concept of rights dates from the English Bill of Rights in 1689, and was incorporated into the American Declaration of Independence of 1776. The civil and political rights enshrined in such documents are known as first generation rights. They are based upon the rights of individuals to be free from the arbitrary interference by the state. Some of the rights defined in the amendments to the American Constitution include the rights to freedom of religion, freedom of expression, assembly, freedom from unreasonable search and seizure, and the right to due process in law.

Second generation rights are economic, social and cultural rights that were included in later Constitutions such as those of the Soviet Union, Mexico and Germany. These include the right to education and health care.

Third generation rights have been asserted by developing states in the post-colonial era in the 20th century. These states wish to see the creation of international order that will guarantee rights such as the right to development, to disaster relief, to peace and to a good environment.

When international treaties were set up to guarantee human rights, countries disagreed as to which of these rights should be obligatory. In particular, the United States of America and the United Kingdom did not believe that second and third generation rights could be implemented or enforced. This problem was resolved by drafting a number of separate treaties that recognise different obligations to different human rights. These treaties include the International Covenant on Civil and Political Rights and the International Covenant on Economic, Social and Cultural Rights among others (Davidson 1997).

While the idea of universal human rights can be traced back to Aristotle and to philosophical doctrines of natural law (particularly the works of Locke and Kant), contemporary ideas regarding human rights emerged out of the horrors of World War II and the Holocaust. They manifest a desire of the international community to establish both a collective expression of human conscience and a mechanism for mediating disputes between nations and defusing international crises. The principal international statement of human rights is the Universal Declaration of Human Rights (UDHR), which was approved by the United Nations on 10 December 1948. The UDHR comprises 30 articles – the first 21 are civil and political rights, covering such things as rights to non-discrimination, political participation, privacy, while articles 21 to 30 are more aspirational (and controversial) and proclaim the rights of people to the services of a welfare state, including rights to social security, education and an adequate standard of living (United Nations 1948). The UDHR has been the subject of extensive criticism from utilitarian, indigenous, socialist, anthropological and communitarian perspectives on the grounds that it is largely empty rhetoric (to paraphrase Bentham – 'nonsense on stilts'), imprescribable, culturally imperialist, tied to the economic principles of capitalism, egocentric, derived from a false understanding of individuals as free, autonomous and altruistic, and dominated by Western norms (Pollis and Schwab 2006; Editorial 2008). Despite such criticism and despite the continued global presence of war, injustice, poverty and genocide, the UDHR has profoundly influenced the way we think about politics, social order and the meaning and value of rights in moral discourse.

Rights can be defined as justifiable claims that individuals or groups can make upon society or upon other individuals. They may be expressed as *positive* rights or *negative* rights. A positive right is a right to be provided with a particular good or service by others whereas a negative right constrains others from interfering with an individual's exercise of that right. Thus, the right of liberty is a negative right because it merely suggests that no-one should hold one against once wishes. The right to education is a positive right as it means that someone must teach. Beauchamp describes the difference between positive and negative rights very simply:

> A positive right is a right to well-being, that is, a right to receive goods or services. A negative right is a right to liberty, that is, a right not to be interfered with. Presumably, all that must be done to honour negative rights is to leave people alone, but the same is not true with respect to positive rights. To honour positive rights, someone must provide something. Because of the correlativity between rights and obligations, everything true of positive rights is true of positive obligations, and everything true of negative rights is true of negative obligations. If a person has a positive right to food, medical care, and insurance, then others have a positive obligation to provide them. If a person has a negative right against interference, then another person has an obligation to abstain from interfering. (Beauchamp 1991)

It is clear from Beauchamp's description that the concept of 'rights' also entails definite but often ill-defined notions of associated obligations. For example, if one person possesses a right to life, this imposes an obligation upon others not to deprive that person of life. The extent of this obligation is defined by the specific context and by consideration of the wishes, beliefs and values of each party. Thus, a right to life does not necessarily prevent an individual being killed in war, or by another in self-defence, or an individual contracting with another to assist them to die.

The language of rights has been critical to the development of ethics and has played a vital role in protecting individuals from the excesses of the state. The question of what role rights should play in defining law, morality and political organisation remains controversial.

The notions that rights should provide the basis for an understanding of morality, and that the primary function of moral codes is to protect the interests and liberties of individuals, form the cornerstone of liberal theories of ethics. *Liberalism* and the language of rights have assumed a central role in ethics and law. The belief that individual liberty or autonomy has moral primacy and that this should be respected and protected by the state forms the core of the liberal ethics of philosophers such as Mill, Feinberg, Dworkin and Charlesworth.

Philosophical liberalism has been repudiated by a number of philosophers on the basis that it overemphasises the significance of autonomy and fails to appreciate the role of the community and social relationships in shaping moral rules. Indeed, critics of liberalism frequently view the decay of 'community values' and the reduction in the political commitment to social welfare in many industrialised nations as the logical end-point of the emphasis on philosophical and political liberalism in Western democracies (Sandel 1982).

A broad competing school of thought – *communitarianism* – is frequently advanced as the sociopolitical and philosophical alternative to liberalism. Communitarian theories emphasise communal values, cooperative virtues and social relationships and contend that social and moral rules are grounded not in individual rights but in community standards of 'common good'. Individuals within the community, be that the political state, the health-care institution or the family, are therefore expected to conform to and promote this 'common good'.

Communitarianism can be classified as either 'extreme' or 'moderate' (Beauchamp and Childress 1994). Extreme communitarians such as Michael Sandel, Alasdair MacIntyre and Charles Taylor are generally hostile to individual rights and contend that individuals are defined by, and embody, communal values that are best expressed through participation in community (MacIntyre 1984). Moderate communitarians emphasise the importance of community and communally derived moral rules but accept that communities may also embody autonomy and respect for individual rights as central moral principles.

Emphasis on community and notions of the common good can be found in many areas of debate in health ethics – most notably in relation to resource allocation, reproductive technology and organ procurement policies.

The distinction between community and liberty need not be as absolute as it has been laid out in the discussion above. Individuals are simultaneously members of many different communities including families, hospitals, nations and the global community. From each of these communities is inherited a range of different and not always compatible social roles and communal obligations. The communities are themselves shaped by the values, perspectives and actions of their members (Little, Jordens et al 2003). In fact, respect for rights and individual liberty allows individuals to prosper in communities, promotes social cohesion and enables peaceful coexistence between individuals with divergent cultural, moral, religious or political beliefs (Galston 1991).

The Capabilities approach

In recent years, increasing sensitivity to global inequity as a 'moral problem', rather than simply an economic one, has prompted intense scholarly activity in both the developing and the developed world. Collaboration between the Indian economist, philosopher and Nobel prize-winner, Amartya Sen, and the American philosopher, classicist and public intellectual, Martha Nussbaum, led to the elaboration of an important and influential approach to morality, poverty, hunger and development known as the Capabilities approach. This approach grounds Sen's idea that in relation to equity and development what matters is positive freedoms (the ability to be or do something) and the capacity of people to function, with Nussbaum's (Aristotelian) account of human good (Sen, Nussbaum et al 1993; Nussbaum 2006a; Nussbaum 2006b).

The Capabilities approach argues that one must begin by establishing what it is to live well, and that once this is defined one can then ask how social and political institutions are addressing this and making it possible for citizens to 'live well'. Nussbaum and Sen propose a model of what is required to live, and live well, which they term the *thick vague theory of the good*. The first level of this theory includes those capabilities required for human life, such as the capacity to feel pleasure and pain, cognitive ability, affiliation with other human beings, and so forth, whereas the second level includes the functional capabilities that are necessary for *good* human life and should be the concern of legislation and public policy. These functional capabilities include:

- being able to live to the end of complete human life; not dying pre-maturely, or before one's life is so reduced as to be not worth living;
- being able to have good health; be adequately nourished; have adequate shelter; have opportunities for sexual satisfaction; to move from place to place;
- being able to avoid unnecessary and non-beneficial pain; have pleasurable experiences;
- being able to use the five senses, to imagine, think and reason;
- being able to have attachments to things and persons outside ourselves; to love others, grieve their absence, love, grieve, feel longing;
- being able to form a conception of the good; engage in critical reflection about the planning of one's own life;
- being able to live for and with others, recognise and show concern for other human beings, engage in various forms of familial and social inter-action;
- being able to live concern for and relation to animals, plants and the world of nature;
- being able to laugh, to play, to enjoy recreational activities;
- being able to live one's life and nobody else's, live one's own life in one's very own surroundings and context.

The Capabilities approach provides an important break with liberalism, social contract theory and human rights theory – although it shares certain aspects of each of them. Although it has been criticised for being too vague and too idealistic and to have contributed to deeper misperceptions of the disabled, at the very least the Capabilities approach provides an alternative perspective on justice, happiness and global responsibilities.

Continental philosophy

'Continental philosophy' is the name given to a large number of philosophies to emerge from the continent of Europe over the past two centuries since the work of Immanuel Kant at the end of the 18th century. It is a term that is used most often by non-European thinkers and is generally aligned against the 'analytical', or mainstream philosophy that has dominated the Anglo-American philosophi-cal tradition. The term generates an enormous amount of confusion because it does not include an agreed set of philosophers in its canon, includes modern and postmodern philosophers, and does not refer to a single philosophical method, style, concern, tradition, or even territorial domain, as much of what goes under the label of continental philosophy is now produced in North America, the United Kingdom and Australasia (Solomon and Sherman 2003).

The history of continental philosophy is complex and dynamic, generating, consolidating and rejecting a number of philosophical movements and figures. The early period of continental philosophy was dominated by the 'modern' philosophers, GFW Hegel, Søren Kierkegaard, Karl Marx, Franz Bretano and the pre-postmodern philosopher, Friedrich Nietzsche. While these thinkers differed in major ways, each offered radical critiques of reason, identity, politics, social organisation, culture, the human experience and ethics. Nietzsche, for example, provided an extensive critique of the 'self', free will and rationality, rejected Christian morality as base and decadent and affirmed life, passion, power, (self) discipline and sexuality (Audi 1999).

The turn of the 20th century saw the ascendancy of the phenomenono-logists, notably Edmund Husserl, his student, Martin Heidegger, and, much later, Maurice Merleau-Ponty and Hans-Geor Gadamer, and the existentialism of Jean-Paul Sartre. The 1930s and 1940s gave rise to two very different currents in Continental, and particularly German philosophy. On the one hand, a group of philosophers flirted with Nazism, before developing a radically conservative agenda known as logical positivism, which was to have its greatest impact on North American analytical philosophy. Another group (the Frankfurt School) embarked on a social criticism of the rise of totalitarianism and the construction of modern European society. These philosophers, including Theodor Adorno and Herbert Marcuse, were critical of many of the tenets of the Enlightenment, particularly the existence of truth and the construction of unifying 'meta-narratives'. In the latter part of the 20th century a number of diverse and openly hostile philosophical movements emerged which either emphasised discourse and communicative action but remained sympathetic to the Enlightenment (Jurgen Habermas), critiqued the construction of philosophy and culture from postmodern sociological, linguistic or political perspectives (Jacques Derrida, Roland Barthes, Claude Levi-Strauss and Michel Foucault), anchored ethics in relationships (Emmanuel Levinas, Zygmunt Bauman), or rejected the edifice of modern philosophy and society on gender grounds, most notably the French feminists (Solomon 2003).

These philosophies would seem to have little in common, apart from the fact that they arose in Europe. And, indeed, the attributes most often credited to continental philosophy, such as scepticism of grand narratives and totalising theories, and attention to language, text and narrative belong, for the most part, to other philosophical movements, including postmodernism, phenomenology and post-structuralism. If there are any characteristics that set continental philosophy apart they are its historical and cultural particularity; its disunity and diversity; its capacity for radical critique; its suspicion about morality itself; its acceptance of interdisciplinary concerns, sources and methods; its emphasis on human flourishing; and its location within real human experience (Schroeder 2000).

A number of continental philosophers have had a particularly important influence on the structure, content and method of contemporary bioethics.

Levinas, Bauman and Derrida are important because they each remind us that ethics is ultimately concerned with relationships and moral sensitivity. Levinas, for example, argued that ethics is principally about responsibility and our responsiveness to the 'other' that we encounter in 'face-to-face' relationships (Levinas 1974). Derrida, most famous for devising the philosophical method of 'deconstruction', where a text is examined to reveal its underlying assumptions and rules, also drew upon Levinas's formulation of the 'other', arguing that the most important feature of ethics is 'hospitality', by which he meant openness to the 'other' (the 'arrivant') and acceptance of the possibility of our own transformation as a consequence of our interaction with others.

The other thinker to have had a major influence on contemporary bioethics is the French philosopher, humanist, historian and sociologist, Michel Foucault (1926-84). Foucault is best known for his critical studies of social institutions, most notably psychiatry, medicine, the human sciences, and the prison system, and for his work on the history of human sexuality. His work on power, and the relationships between power, knowledge and discourse, has enriched a number of fields of inquiry including bioethics; and many of the terms and concepts coined by Foucault, such as biopower, biopolitics, disciplinary institutions governmentality, state racism, technologies of the self and medical gaze, have become a part of both academic and lay discourse (Foucault 1997). Foucault's ethics can be (loosely) categorised as a form of secular humanism as he rejects the idea that religion or moral codes are a sufficient basis for ethics. Instead, Foucault argues that ethics involves freeing ourselves from the forms of identity imposed on us by the state and by society and examining how we decide what kind of person to be and how we become that kind of person (Foucault 1984). While Foucault has been extensively criticised for the coherence, historical accuracy, logic and internal consistency of his work, there is no doubt that his work has made a major contribution to the emergence of critical bioethics.

Postmodernism

Continental philosophy is often confused with postmodernism, whereas in fact, while postmodern approaches are a feature of contemporary continental philosophy, as we have described above, continental philosophy has a much broader history and method.

While the term 'postmodernism' has entered into popular culture, there is very little agreement about what it actually means, and what impact it has had on a range of subjects, including art, literature, history, architecture, media and ethics. For some, postmodernism represents the final escape from modern European metaphysics and philosophy, for some it represents the attempt by left-wing intellectuals to destroy Western civilisation, and for others it describes a diverse family of thinkers who have contributed very little to contemporary thought. All three descriptions of postmodernism are unsatisfactory (Cahoone 1996).

A more accurate description of postmodernism refers to either the philosophical movement that developed in France in the 1960s, more precisely called 'poststructuralism', or to the general reaction against modern rationalism, utopianism and 'foundationalism' (the attempt to establish the foundations of knowledge, morality and judgment). It is not possible to understand either of these descriptions of postmodernism without first understanding something about modernism and the rejection of the 'modern'.

The term 'modern', derived from the Latin modo, means 'of today', or what is current. 'Modernity' has a more precise meaning, referring to the 'modern' civilisation that developed in Europe and North America following the Enlightenment. The characteristics of this civilisation, the markers of modernity, were capitalism (the free market), liberal democracy, secularism, rationalism, humanism, science, industry and technology.

In the late 19th century and early part of the 20th century, modernism came under sustained attack from a series of philosophers, including Kierkegaard, Nietzsche and Heidegger, who each critiqued the basic assumptions of modern philosophy and spawned provocative 'postmodern' modes of discourse, writing and criticism. In their wake, a series of intellectual movements emerged that tended to emphasise the authentic 'self', most notably, phenomenology, Marxism, psychoanalysis and existentialism. Subsequent theoretical movements, particularly structuralism, which was developed by Ferdinand de Saussure and championed by Claude Levi-Strauss, rejected the focus on the self and argued instead that the emphasis should be on cultural symbols and structures, including language, ritual and kinship, on the ground that it is culture that creates the self.

The new 'poststructuralist' philosophers of the 1960s, the most significant of whom were Jacques Derrida, Gilles Deleuze, Michel Foucault and Jean-Francois Lyotard, accepted the rejection of the 'self' and of authenticity, but went much further, criticising the rational inquiry into truth, the certainty of meaning, the legitimacy of Western civilisation and the institutional claims of beneficence.

While it is difficult to characterise the common features of postmodernism, some generalisations can be made. First, postmodern philosophy questions the central tenets of modernity (the period in the history of the Western World since the Enlightenment) – that knowledge is possible and that truth is discoverable through human reason and the scientific method. Second, postmodern approaches are characterised by rejection of a single subject, system of knowledge, value system or process in ethics (Lyotard 1986; Jameson 1990). Postmodern ethics, *in turn*, rejects the ideologies of scientific medicine and ethics, and attempts to address issues of ethics through a diverse group of new perspectives, new languages and new paradigms grounded in and formed by their social and clinical context.

One critic of postmodern thinking is the physicist, Alan Sokal, who caused controversy in 1996 when a paper he had written as a 'parody' on postmodernism was taken seriously and published by the journal *Social Text* (Sokal and Bricmont 1999). Sokal's major objection to postmodernism is that postmodern thinking is intellectually sloppy, and that it invalidly applies social and political critiques to the natural sciences. He says:

> [T]he idea is that there are no objective truths either in the social sciences but even in the natural sciences; that's what is most shocking – somehow that the

validity of any statement is relative to the individual making it or relative to the social groups or culture to which that individual belongs ... [V]ery few people would say it in so many words, so explicitly and so precisely. But they say vague things that come down to that, if taken seriously ... We need to develop an analysis of society which would be more convincing to our fellow citizens than the analyses they would read in Newsweek and the New York Times. And to do that we need good arguments. We can't afford sloppy thinking. (Mukerjee 1998)

Sokal's criticisms of postmodernism serve to remind us that the inter-actions between facts and values can be confusing and are susceptible to being misconstrued. Many aspects of medicine, such as the biochemical effects of medication or the biological effects of micro-organisms, are not dependent on one's moral perspective, and one should hesitate before rejecting theory, prin-ciples, universal knowledge and empirical observation in all spheres of life.

Nevertheless, postmodernism and ethical pragmatism have each made major contributions to contemporary bioethics. Radical critique, deconstruction, sociological analysis and empirical study have each deepened the appreciation of the social, cultural, and moral context in which health care occurs, enriched the study of language and power, and reminded us about the interaction between facts and individual values.

Discourse ethics

In recent years 'process' or communicative models of ethics have been advo-cated as providing more appropriate bases for moral deliberation in the health professions. One of the most influential is known as Discourse Ethics.

Discourse ethics owes much to the work of the German philosopher and social theorist, Jurgen Habermas. In *The Theory of Communicative Action*, Habermas developed a comprehensive social theory based upon communicative rationality and discourse – the second-order communication that takes place both in everyday interaction and in institutionalised practices such as law and science (Habermas 1984). His theory of rationality is linguistic, or discursive, and argues for a universal or 'formal' system of speech whereby effective discourse occurs between individuals or groups who are prepared to respect each other, to accept some notion of practical reason, and to recognise a series of rules or norms of communication. These rules include the setting aside of power and self-interest, and the assumption of possibility of sincere, truth-governed speech. He then applies this theory to ethics and suggests that universal moral norms can be justified only by intersubjective discourse (the discourse principle). That is, a norm (for example, do not kill except in self-defence) is justified if, and only if, it can meet with the reasoned agreement of all those affected.

Habermas's theory has been extensively critiqued, most notably by Michel Foucault and Jacques Derrida, on the grounds that his theory provides process without substance, does not provide any criteria for deciding what constitutes the 'best' argument in any situation, and fails to take account of power differ-ences between discussants, the impossibility of engagement without self-interest, and the subjective nature of language itself. These would seem to be valid criticisms as discourse ethics provides an incomplete model of normative ethics and does not appear to provide an adequate framework for the moral interaction between individuals, particularly those who are poor, powerless or voiceless, and major commercial institutions, or for macroeconomic concerns in health care, such as resource allocation, patent laws or issues relating to global human rights.

Nevertheless, Habermas's suggestion that discourse is a deeply public activity, that it may be structured in such a way that it has moral value, and that it provides the means by which we construct ourselves, the meaning that we assign to our own and other people's lives, and the basis for moral action or social consensus, have been enormously influential in contemporary ethics. Indeed, discourse ethics has provided a reminder that ethics is fundamentally a social and communicative notion, and that resolution of moral conflict is only likely to result from genuine, mutually respectful and transparent discussion. Regardless of whether or not one accepts Habermas's theory, these claims appear intuitively correct, at least in the setting of the clinical dyad.

Narrative ethics

Ethics has traditionally sought rational and universalisable explanations of moral truth, or the 'good life', with little reference to the subjective experience of that life. In recent years, however, there has been a retreat from the ideals of objectivity, rationality and universality in ethics (the beliefs that drove the so-called 'Enlightenment project') (Lyotard 1986). In its place we have seen a flourishing of interest in narrative, storytelling, anecdote and autobiography as ways of structuring and interpreting the experiences of patients, carers and health-care professionals. Philosophically the emphasis on narrative has its origins in casuistry, continental philosophy, linguistics and phenomenology. Professionally, narrative ethics has been championed by nursing, but has recently achieved credibility within medicine and medical ethics.

The narrative is at the very heart of medicine. Not only is diagnosis encoded in the narratives patients tell of symptoms, but deep and therapeutically important understandings of the persons who bear symptoms are made possible in the course of hearing the narratives told of illness (Charon 2004). Many patients want to share their experiences and to find meaning within their predicaments, and this may be more important to them than a prescription or a diagnostic label. This can only be achieved through narrative, for we live in words and our experiences are all remembered, dreamt of, recounted and explained through words and narrative. Health professionals also tell stories, to teach, to share experiences and to understand generalities. They also recall their own experiences as a means for comprehending their patient's ordeals and their own lives with the sick, and to gain some understanding of the human condition (Verghese 2001).

However, while it would seem self-evidently true to say that the narrative is central to medicine, it is not at all clear what narrative ethics actually is, and what the relationship is between narrative and moral justification in bioethics (Arras 1991).

John Arras has suggested that there are at least three distinct formulations of narrative ethics. The first, and least controversial, is that narrative functions primarily to enrich moral theory and ethical principles. This assertion is based on the observation that narrative elements are embedded in all forms of moral reasoning (stories often have a moral and attention to the patient's narrative may reveal ethical concerns); that ethical principles and cases coexist in a 'reflective equilibrium'; and that a complete story, or history, is a prerequisite to responsible moral analysis (Arras 2002). As Bernard Williams has argued, in order to bring the moral individual into clearer focus we must attend to his or her particularity, desires, needs, character and full biography, and we can only do so by telling and retelling stories (Williams 1981). It is difficult to argue against this conception of narrative ethics.

The second formulation of narrative ethics contends that foundational historical stories and traditions form the basis of ethics. Thus, for example, stories from the Hippocratic corpus or from the Bible or the Talmud provide the basis for exhortation not to kill, or perform terminations of pregnancy. The problem with this way of thinking is that it is conservative, historically anchored, entrenches power, and describes both who we are, as well as who we are not. For example, foundational Christian stories may provide a very different moral justification for the Stolen Generation than an Aboriginal foundational story. Attempts to resolve conflicts among such competing stories, by reference to a series of abstract criteria, or by development of 'better' narratives, seem, ultimately, to be unsuccessful (MacIntyre 1988).

The final formulation of narrative ethics is the most radical, as it is a postmodern formulation of ethics which sees narrative as a substitute for the entire enterprise of moral justification. Postmodernism has been characterised by its retreat from theories and grand narratives and the emphasis it gives to the *petit recit*, or 'little narrative'. For many postmodern philosophers and sociologists, ethics is not definition of the 'good life' but about the construction of language and meaning through stories and a continuing conversation (Rorty 1989; Nussbaum 1990; Frank 1995). The difficulty with this conception of ethics is that it privileges the internal truth of narratives over judgments regarding those narratives, or the insights gained from those narratives. For example, while the Nazi physician, Dr Richard Brandt's narrative regarding human experimentation in Nazi Germany may have internal coherence, it would seem that ethics should also be to pass judgment as to the moral worth of his narrative and provide a statement regarding human dignity and the moral significance of consent in research. A further problem with attending only to the 'little narrative' is that this may blind us to larger social, cultural and institutional concerns and prevent any form of meaningful social critique (Arras 2002).

Guillemin and Gillam have proposed a different typology of the ways that narratives may be used in ethics. They suggest that there are four broad categories of narrative in ethics: the use of stories as an analytical or persuasive device; foundational stories used to determine and justify moral actions by placing them within a moral tradition, such as the stories of the Bible, Greek epics or Hippocrates; literary narratives used to develop moral sensitivity and reason; and personal experience or illness narratives (Guillemin and Gillam 2006).

Because narratives may be used in many different ways in ethics, Nelson has proposed that there are four questions that should be asked by anyone wanting to understand why (and how) a narrative is being used and/or wanting to use a narrative approach to ethics themselves.

> First, what is done with the story? This is the question about the *narrative act*. Second, with what kind of story is it done? This is a question about *genre*. Third, who does something with the story? This is a question about the *narrative agent*. And fourth, why is this done? This is a question about *moral purpose*. (Nelson 2001)

While there is considerable disagreement about the extent to which narratives offer any assistance in answering the question of how we should live (Clouser 1996), there is no doubt that narrative (and literature) provides the detail and richness that is crucial to ethical analysis and to any examination of human experience.

Empiricism and ethical pragmatism

In a paper entitled 'Shifting Paradigms in Bioethics and Health Law: The Rise of a New Pragmatism', Susan Wolf noted:

> [A] plethora of alternative methods has recently been put forth, a new empiricism has challenged the content of previously accepted principle, and burgeoning feminist and race-attentive work has rendered suspect any bioethical approach geared to the generic patient. (Wolf 1994)

This 'new' pragmatism has arisen because of frustration with types of ethical analysis that are remote from the world of genuine moral experience and the empirical realities of patients and disease. Pragmatism stresses the importance of empiricism – or reference to research and the 'real world' – in describing, explaining or clarifying the territory of moral behaviour (Musschenga 2005). It does not, however, suggest that data, surveys or referenda can or should resolve moral conflict or determine public policy. Bioethics must take account of clinical realities and the insights gained from empirical research; however, it is important to recognise that the principal task of bioethics is not to conform to medical tradition or accepted clinical practice. Rather, the task of ethics is to illustrate moral issues in clinical practice and describe how decisions should be made rather than how they have been made.

Empirical research has challenged firmly held convictions about the ethics of informed consent, no-CPR orders, decisions about withholding and withdrawing treatment, the use of advance directives and surrogate decision-making (Sugarman, Weinberger et al 1992; Orona, Koenig et al 1994; Rubin, Strull et al 1994). Of particular interest has been the finding that many patients do not wish to make decisions for themselves and that judgments made for incompetent patients by doctors or families may be no more likely to concur with the patient's wishes than if they were made by chance (Degner and Sloan 1992).

Pragmatism is also a reaction against the tendency for bioethics to emphasise autonomy and abstract reasoning but to ignore issues of race, gender and ethnicity. In this way ethical pragmatism shares with postmodernism an openness to the insights from a range of different approaches and methods.

Conclusion

The tension between different types of ethical theories has contributed enormously to the growth of moral philosophy, yet all theories have significant theoretical and methodological deficiencies that become particularly apparent in their application to practical bioethics. Moral philosophy is full of disagreement about how each of these normative theories should guide action or allow resolution of specific moral problems. What makes this debate more difficult is the fact that each philosophical theory is embedded in its own historical and theoretical settings and each embodies a view about how it applies to the resolution of moral problems. It is therefore difficult to judge the comparative merit of each theory because there are not clear 'theory-independent' criteria by which these may be judged.

This inconsistency within moral theory is an important aspect of intellectual life. Indeed, the inability to formulate a completely adequate normative moral theory may reflect more the complexity of ethics, particularly bioethics, than a significant philosophical impasse, and distinctions between theories may not be as significant for *practical ethics* as they would appear. Furthermore, many of the alternative moral philosophies need not be viewed as competing theories but as complementary. An individual may endorse a variety of different moral theories and employ them in different situations. Moreover, complicated moral issues may be distorted if we attempt to reduce them to coverage by a single moral theory. Recognising that the resolution of ethical problems may require the incorporation of a number of opposing ethical approaches may actually facilitate critical analysis and discourse (Habermas 1992).

Approaching bioethical issues by utilising a range of philosophical approaches to explore the 'moral space' does have some problems. We cannot be sure which approach should be used in a given situation, and we may be tempted to choose the approach that is most convenient to us. However, the advantages of using a range of approaches is that we will be forced to justify our decisions and defend them, since we must accept that they are always fallible and open to challenge.

References

American Medical Association Council on Ethical and Judicial Affairs (1991) 'Sexual misconduct and the practise of medicine'. *JAMA* **266**: 2741-5.
Arras, J (2002) Nice story, but so what?: Narrative and justification in ethics. *Stories and their limits: Narrative approaches to bioethics.* H Lindemann Nelson. New York, Routledge: 65-88.
Arras, JD (1991) 'Getting down to cases: The revival of casuistry in bioethics'. *J Med Philos* **16**: 29-51.
Audi, R (1999) *The Cambridge Dictionary of Philosophy* (2nd ed). Cambridge, Cambridge University Press.
Baier, A (1986) 'Trust and antitrust'. *Ethics* **96**: 248.

Beauchamp, TL (1991) *Philosophical ethics: An introduction to moral philosophy*. New York, McGraw Hill.

Beauchamp, TL and J Childress (1994) *Principles of biomedical ethics*. Oxford, Oxford University Press.

Brody, BA (1983) *Ethics and its applications*. Oxford, Clarendon Press.

Cahoone, L (1996) *From Modernism to Postmodernism: An Anthology*. Cambridge, MA, Blackwell.

Charlesworth, M (1993) *Bioethics in a liberal society*. Cambridge, Cambridge University Press.

Charon, R (2004) 'Narrative and medicine'. *N Engl J Med* **350**(9): 862-4.

Clouser, K (1996) 'Philosophy, Literature, and Ethics: Let the Engagement begin'. *Jnl Med Phil* **21**: 321-40.

Comte-Sponville, A (2003) *A short treatise on the great virtues: the uses of philosophy in everyday life*. London, Vintage.

Davidson, A (2001) Sex and the emergence of sexuality. *The Emergence of Sexuality: Historical Epistemology and the Formation of Concepts*. A Davidson. Cambridge MA, Harvard University Press.

Davidson, S (1997) *Human Rights*. Buckingham, Open University Press.

Degner, LF and JA Sloan (1992) 'Decision-making during serious illness: What role do physicians really want to play?' *J Clin Ethics* **45**: 941.

Editorial (2008) 'The right to health: from rhetoric to reality'. *Lancet* **372**(9655): 2001.

Finnis, J (1980) *Natural Law and Natural Rights*. Oxford, Clarendon Press.

Firestone, S (1971) *The dialectic of sex*. London, Jonathon Cape.

Fletcher, J (1996) *Situation Ethics*. Philadelphia, Westminster Press.

Foot, P (1978) *Virtues and Vices*. Oxford, Basil Blackwell.

Foucault, M (1984) The Use of Pleasure. *History of Sexuality (Vol 2)*. New York, Pantheon.

Foucault, M (1997) *Ethics: Subjectivity and truth – The Essential Works of Foucault 1954-1984*. Harmondsworth, Penguin.

Frank, A (1995) *The Wounded Storyteller*. Chicago, The University of Chicago Press.

Frankena, WK (1973) *Ethics*. New Jersey, Prentice Hall.

Frankena, WK (1982) Beneficence in an ethics of virtue. *Beneficence and health care*. EE Shelp. Dordrecht, Reidel.

Fricker, M and J Hornsby (2000) *The Cambridge Companion to Feminism in Philosophy*. Cambridge, Cambridge University Press.

Galston, WA (1991) *Liberal purposes*. Cambridge, Cambridge University Press.

Garner, H (1995) *The first stone*. Sydney, Picador.

Gert, B (1998) *Morality: Its nature and justification*. New York, Oxford University Press.

Gilligan, C (1982) *In a different voice: Psychological theory and women's development*. Cambridge MA, Harvard University Press.

Guillemin, M and L Gillam (2006) *Telling Moments: Everyday Ethics in Health Care*. Melbourne, IP Communications.

Habermas, J (1984) *The theory of communicative action*. Boston, Beacon Press.

Habermas, J (1992) *Moral consciousness and communicative action*. Cambridge, Polity Press.

Harding, S (1991) *Whose science? Whose knowledge? Thinking from women's lives*. Milton Keynes, Open University Press.

Hare, RM (1964) *The language of morals*. Oxford, Oxford University Press.

Held, V (2002) Reason, gender and moral theory. *Ethics: History, Theory and Contemporary Issues* (2nd ed). S Cahn and P Markie. New York, Oxford University Press: 667-92.

Jaggar, A (1998) 'Globalising feminist ethics'. *Hypatia* **13**(2): 7-32.

Jameson, F (1990) Postmodernism. *Feminism/postmodernism*. L Nicholson. London, Routledge: 85-6.

Jonsen, AR and S Toulmin (1988) *The abuse of casuistry: A history of moral reasoning*. Berkeley, University of California Press.

Levinas, E (1974) *Otherwise than Being, or Beyond Essence*. Pittsburgh, Duquesne University Press.

Little, J, C Jordens et al (2003) 'Discourse communities and the discourse of experience'. *Health* **7**: 73-86.

Little, JM (2004) *Community, security and human flourishing : an exploratory essay*. Sydney, University of Sydney, Centre for Values, Ethics and the Law in Medicine.

Lumby, C (1997) *Bad girls: the media, sex and feminism in the '90s*. Sydney, Allen and Unwin.

Lyotard, JF (1986) *The postmodern condition: A report on knowledge*. Manchester, Manchester University Press.

MacIntyre, A (1984) *After virtue: A study in moral theory*. Notre Dame, Ind, University of Nitre Dame Press.

MacIntyre, A (1988) *Whose justice? Whose rationality?* Notre Dame, Notre Dame Press.

McNaughton, D (1988) *Moral vision: an introduction to ethics*. Oxford, Basil Blackwell.

Moore, GE (1903) *Principia ethica*. Cambridge, Cambridge University Press.

Mukerjee, N (1998) 'Undressing the emperor'. *Scientific American*(March): 16-17.

Musschenga, A (2005) 'Empirical ethics, context-sensitivity, and contextualism'. *J Med Philos* **30**: 467-90.

Nelson, H (2001) *Narrative identities, Narrative Repair*. Ithaca, NY, Cornwell University Press.

Nussbaum, MC (1990) *Love's knowledge: Essays on Philosophy and Literature*. New York, Oxford University Press.

Nussbaum, MC (1996) 'Compassion: the basic social emotion'. *Social Philosophy and Policy* **13**: 27-58.

Nussbaum, MC (2006a) Capabilities and Disabilities. *Frontiers of Justice: Disability, Nationality, Species Membership. Tanner Lectures on Human Values* MC Nussbaum. Cambridge, MA, Harvard University Press: 185-222.

Nussbaum, MC (2006b) Human Functioning and Social Justice: A Defence of Aristotelian Essentialism. *Moral Issues in Global perspective I: Moral and Political Theory* (2nd ed). C Koggel. Peterborough, Boardview Press: 4-25.

Orona, CJ, BA Koenig et al (1994) 'Cultural aspects of non-disclosure'. *Camb Q Healthcare Ethics* **3**(3): 338-46.

Overall, C (1983) *Ethics and human reproduction*. London, Allen and Unwin.

Parsons, S (1986) 'Feminism and moral reasoning'. *Australasian J Philos* **Supplement**(64): 75-90.

Pellegrino, ED (1989) 'Character, virtue and self-interest in the ethics of the professions'. *J Contemp Health Law Policy*(5).

Pellegrino, ED (1995) 'Toward a virtue-based normative ethics for the health professions'. *Kennedy Inst Ethics J* **5**: 253-60.

Pence, G (2000) *Classic works in Medical Ethics*. Boston, McGraw Hill.

Pollis, A and P Schwab (2006) Human Rights: A Western Construct with Limited Applicability. *Moral Issues in Global perspective I: Moral and Political Theory* (2nd ed). C Koggel. Peterborough, Boardview Press: 60-71.

Purdy, LM (1989) 'Surrogate mothering: exploitation or empowerment'. *Bioethics* **2**.

Rawls, J (1971) *A theory of justice*. Cambridge, Mass, Harvard University Press.

Reich, WT (ed) (1982) *Encyclopedia of bioethics*. New York, Free Press.

Rorty, R.(1989) *Contingency, Irony and Solidarity*. Cambridge, Cambridge University Press.

Ross, WD (1964) *Aristotle*. New York, Barnes and Noble.

Rubin, SM., WM Strull et al (1994) 'Increasing the completion of the durable power of attorney for health care'. *JAMA* **271**(3): 209-12.

Schroeder, W (2000) Continental Ethics. *Ethical Theory*. H LaFollette. Malden, MA, Blackwell Publishing.

Sen, AK (1987) *On ethics and economics*. Oxford, UK; New York, NY, USA, B Blackwell.

Sen, AK, MC Nussbaum et al (1993) *The Quality of life*. Oxford; New York, Clarendon Press.

Shaw, LJ (1994) 'Gender differences in the non-invasive evaluation and management of patients with suspected coronary artery disease'. *Ann Intern Med* **120**: 559-566.

Sherwin, S (1992) *No longer patient: Feminist ethics and health care*. Philadelphia, Temple University Press.

Singer, P (1979) *Practical Ethics*. Cambridge, Cambridge University Press.

Singer, P (1994) *Rethinking life & death : the collapse of our traditional ethics*. Melbourne, Text Publishing.

Sokal, A and J Bricmont (1999) *Intellectual impostures: Postmodern philosophers' abuse of science*. London, Profile Books.

Solomon, M (2003) 'Donation after cardiac death: Non-heart beating organ donation deserves a green light and hospital oversight'. *Anesthesiology* **98**: 601-2.

Solomon, R and D Sherman (2003) *Continental Philosophy*. Oxford, Blackwell Publishing Ltd.

Sugarman, J, M Weinberger et al (1992) 'Factors associated with veteran's decisions about living wills'. *Arch Intern Med* **152**(2): 343-7.

Swanton, C (1987) 'The rationality of ethical intuitionism'. *Aust J Philos*. **65**(2): 172-86.

Tobin, B (1992) *Practical wisdom and health care: An account of the contribution of 'virtues ethics' to the practice of medicine and nursing*. ANZAAS Conference, Sept 1992, University of Technology, Brisbane.

United Nations. (1948) 'Universal Declaration of Human Rights'. <http://www.udhr.org/un/default.htm>.

van den Broek, K (1997) A critical look at the ethics of care. *Health care law and ethics*. L Shotton. Katoomba, NSW, Social Science Press.

Verghese, A (2001) 'The physician as storyteller'. *Ann Intern Med* **135**: 1012-17.

Walker, M (2006) What does the different voice say? Gilligan's women and moral philosophy. *Moral Issues in Global perspective I: Moral and Political Theory* (2nd ed). C Koggel. Peterborough, Boardview Press: 31-9.

Warren, MA (1988) 'IVF and women's interests'. *Bioethics* **2**.

Williams, B (1972) *Morality*. Cambridge, Cambridge University Press.

Williams, B (1973) A critique of utilitarianism. *Utilitarianism: For and against*. JJC Smart and B Williams. Cambridge, Cambridge University Press.

Williams, BAO (1981) *Moral luck : philosophical papers, 1973-1980*. Cambridge, UK; New York, Cambridge University Press.

Wolf, S (1994) 'Shifting paradigms in bioethics and health law: The rise of a new pragmatism'. *Am Jn of Law and Medicine* **XX**(4): 395-415.

Wolf, SM (1996) *Feminism & bioethics : beyond reproduction*. New York, Oxford University Press.

CHAPTER 3

RELATIVISM AND PLURALISM

Resistance to formal examination of ethics in health care comes from two main sources. On the one hand, many people are attracted to the health professions by religious ideals. Those with more fundamentalist religious ideals often dispute the idea that specific training in biomedical ethics has anything to offer that is not found in their own faiths. The other source of scepticism is based on the idea of relativism. Relativists believe that what is right and wrong varies from culture to culture and individual to individual. In many ways these ideas are opposite to each other, and disputes between those who believe in them go back at least as far as Plato. However, there is a logical basis for both types of objection and both deserve further attention.

In this section we will examine these ideas in more detail. We will begin by looking at the idea of neutrality and whether neutrality is possible or desirable for those with strong beliefs (including religious beliefs). We will then examine the question of relativism in greater detail. Finally, we will explain the approach to ethics that will be taken in this book, which, we hope, treads a careful path between these two schools of thought.

Neutrality

If a reader of this book comes from a strong religious position, it will become apparent fairly quickly that the authors of this book do not approach ethical issues in this way. In a fascinating literary analysis of bioethics entitled *The Fiction of Bioethics*, Tod Chambers has shown that even the apparently simple documentation of case-studies in the bioethics literature rapidly exposes the bias of authors (Chambers 1999). Cases in bioethics are inevitably written in such a way that they support the authors' philosophical positions, even if the authors pretend to be neutral.

For example, consider the following case (from the first edition of this book):

> CD is a 19 year-old woman who presents to her GP requesting an abortion. Although she has become pregnant to her steady boyfriend – a man whom she intends to have children with one day – she wishes to finish her university degree before doing this. Her GP believes that her interests would be best served by having an abortion and refers her to a clinic.

This case is expressed in the third person, as if an onlooker is watching what is going on. The onlooker appears to know the innermost thoughts of both the woman and her GP. There is very little background information to place the woman or her GP in the context of their lives or their relationship. In effect, the way that the case is written suggests (without even commencing the ethical discussion) that abortion is primarily a medical procedure that can be approached without deep involvement, from an abstracted position.

Reading such a case, in which the ethical position that is taken is implicit, can be very frustrating to those who come from different ethical positions. It is as if the rug has been pulled out from under them before they have begun the argument, and they may justifiably feel that the entire discussion is unfair. Yet we are all prisoners of our ideas, to at least some extent, and no matter how we attempt to disguise our biases, we cannot remove them altogether. In this book we have tried to be aware of this problem, but resolution of the problem does not rest entirely with the authors. When anyone reads about ethics, it is important that they are aware of the underlying biases that occur in the construction of the discussion and take these into account, since no authors can entirely remove their own beliefs from what they are writing.

If we are unable to hide our biases should we even attempt to be neutral? We believe that we should, and the reason for this arises mostly from political considerations. Western societies are based on a vision of individual citizens freely living their lives according to their own beliefs or values (a concept known as autonomy) with minimal interference by the state or others. This package of ideas is known as 'liberalism'.

According to Agich:

> [P]roponents of the liberal theory defend two further concepts, namely pluralism and toleration, as unavoidable corollaries of autonomy. Pluralism is the view that there are many viable concepts of the good life, many viable concepts of how one's life should be conducted. These concepts are neither different versions of a single homogenous good nor related in any discernable hierarchical pattern. Thus, difference is unavoidable and ineliminable. Because of difference, conflicts and disagreement unavoidably arise in the course of daily living. For this reason, toleration is an essential corollary of pluralism. Because we can expect that even reasonable persons will disagree about fundamental values and concepts of the good life, practical acceptance of the views of others – views that we might find wrongheaded, objectionable or even repulsive – is required. Since liberals accept that we may live with those who do not share our own ideals or else succumb to interminable conflict or resort to force to settle disagreement, toleration is the logical requirement.
>
> Given that diversity of viewpoints (pluralism) and disagreement among reasonable persons have become features of modern life and medical practice, political liberalism is the doctrine that the state should be neutral with respect to such disputes. An action or decision will count as neutral only if its justification does not appeal to some presumed intrinsic superiority of its own concept of the good life. (Agich 2003)

What Agich is saying is that because Western states are now based on a great diversity of ideas and ways of living, the only way that such societies can function is by maintaining a degree of tolerance. Most importantly, the state itself must be tolerant, which can occur only if it attempts to maintain a neutral position.

Citizens of liberal societies, including those who are employed by the state, will all have their own views, but in order for multicultural societies to work, citizens must be tolerant of the views of others. (Those who work for the state must especially attempt to hold a neutral position in respect of their public duties.) Australia, for example, claims to be a multicultural, liberal democracy and tolerates cultural, religious and political pluralism, provided that these beliefs and practices do not interfere with the beliefs and practices of other individuals or groups.

There is an ongoing debate about these issues, particularly in the USA. In one example, Justice Roy Moore, the Chief Justice of Alabama, was ordered by the Federal Court to remove a 2.6 ton granite block carved with the Ten Commandments from the Alabama State judicial building where he had placed it. The statue was removed because it was held to indicate a non-neutral (pro-Christian) position with regard to religion. This caused an outcry among more conservative commentators who saw the Ten Commandments as an important foundation of ethics rather than an example of prejudice.

Health workers form an important part of the apparatus of society, and are mostly employed either directly or indirectly by the government. In order to be part of a tolerant society, health workers are required to uphold a public position that is as neutral as possible with respect to the different ideas that are current in society. Of course, the nature of ethics is such that this is not always possible, and there may even be times where a health-care worker feels that his or her personal ethics are not compatible with a publicly held neutral position. Yet, for the most part, health-care workers must be aware of the spectrum of ethical beliefs in the community and be tolerant when beliefs that are found in the community are different to their privately held beliefs.

We believe that this is one of the main values of critical examination of ethics. Through it health professionals can explore a range of different views, become aware of where other people's views fit or conflict with their own, and come to a better understanding of how they might take a tolerant and reflective position that is suitable for their role in the health services.

Relativism

One of the more common views of ethics that is found among health workers is the idea that ethics is somehow irrelevant because there is no objective right and wrong. The view that right and wrong varies from person to person is known as relativism.

Relativism is sometimes divided into two different parts. 'Subjectivism' is the claim that the subjective views of individuals are the basis for right and wrong. 'Cultural relativism' is the claim that cultures set the standards for right and wrong (Levy 2002). These terms are not particularly clear, and different authors use the terms 'subjectivism' and 'relativism' interchangeably. We will use the term 'relativism' except when authors whom we quote use other terms.

Relativists often accuse those who are not relativists of being 'absolutists'. An absolutist believes that they know what is right and wrong, and that their standards should apply to everyone. Few people will overtly admit to being absolutists, but one imagines that there could be absolutists whose view are derived from such diverse philosophies as feminism, Marxism, Christianity, Islam, Hinduism, atheism and so forth. The relativism versus absolutism split in medical ethics is not one that is purely academic. Students and health professionals encounter these issues quite often.

For example, imagine that as a health worker you have just discovered that a patient (who happens to be from a large Greek family) has cancer. You decide that you should tell the patient about this, but are met at the door by the patient's son. He says, 'don't tell her that she has cancer, it will kill her'. What should you do? One absolutist position is that 'the patient has an absolute right to know'. If you took this position you would ignore the wishes of the son and tell the patient. A different, relativist, perspective would be that different cultures have different ethical systems concerning disclosure. If you were happy that the son was correctly representing his mother's culture, you would not tell the mother. (There are many other ways that this situation could be dealt with – some will be discussed in future chapters.)

Relativism is an extremely prevalent view of ethics. Allen Bloom, in his famous book *The Closing of the American Mind*, suggested:

> There is one thing a professor can be absolutely certain of: almost every student entering the university believes, or says he believes, that truth is relative. If this belief is put to the test, one can count on the students' reaction: they will be uncomprehending. That anyone should regard the proposition as not self-evident astonishes them, as though he were calling into question 2 + 2 = 4. These are things you don't think about. The students' backgrounds are as various as America can provide. Some are religious, some atheists; some are to the Left, some to the Right; some intend to be scientists, some humanists or professionals or businessmen; some are poor, some rich. They are unified only in their relativism and in their allegiance to equality. And the two are related in a moral intention. The relativity of truth is not a theoretical insight but a moral postulate, the condition of a free society, or so they see it.... The danger they have been taught to fear from absolutism is not error but intolerance. Relativism is necessary to openness; and this is the virtue, the only virtue, which all primary education for more than fifty years has dedicated itself to inculcating. Openness – and the relativism that makes it the only plausible stance in the face of various claims to truth and various ways of life and kinds of human beings – is the great insight of our times. The true believer is the real danger. The study of history and of culture teaches that all the world was mad in the past; men always thought they were right, and that led to wars, persecutions, slavery, xenophobia, racism, and chauvinism. The point is not to correct the mistakes and really be right; rather it is not to think you are right at all. (Bloom 1987)

Bloom maintains that young people in America (and the argument also applies to Australia) have been taught, from the moment that they first turn on 'Sesame Street', that tolerance is the only virtue that they should consider to be absolute. Most of us would agree that tolerance is something that we hold to be important. But there are many different philosophies that can lead us to a position of tolerance (ie human rights). Bloom feels that most modern education is ignorant of these alternative philosophies, so that most young people today see relativism as the only way to preserve tolerance for others' beliefs.

Relativism probably does lead to a degree of tolerance towards other individuals. It does this by suggesting that we should not make moral judgments about them. While this means that we should not disapprove or condemn other people, it also logically suggests that we should not respect or emulate them, as these positive views also involve moral judgments. Many relativists would be appalled by such a suggestion but it is a logical consequence of the idea of relativism.

Relativism has a number of other logical inconsistencies that diminish its relevance to daily life. To illustrate this argument we will consider the particular form of relativism known as cultural relativism. Cultural relativism is a theory based on the following argument:

1. Different cultures have different moral codes.
2. Therefore there is no objective 'truth' in morality. Right and wrong are only matters of opinion, and opinions vary from culture to culture. (Rachels 1978)

There are two types of problems with this argument. The first type is logical problems – statement 2 does not follow from statement 1. The existence of cultural difference says nothing about whether there are, or should be, shared ethical values or principles.

Also this argument is sometimes used to say that we have no right to judge or impose our views on other cultures. But, the statement, 'one has no right to judge or impose one's views upon other cultures', is itself a moral statement – so it is either right or wrong. According to cultural relativism, the rightness or wrongness of this statement varies from culture to culture, and it is quite possible that there are cultures where it is not correct. Therefore, according to cultural relativism, it would be right for these cultures to judge or impose their values upon other cultures, leading to a contradiction with the original statement. (Williams 1972; Levy 2002)

The second group of problems with moral relativism relate to the consequences of this belief. If we were to take moral relativism seriously we could not criticise any practices of other societies, and would be impregnable to criticism ourselves. Slavery, anti-Semitism, circumcision, cannibalism, human sacrifice, apartheid and consumerism would all be off limits to observers from outside each culture. Similarly, we would be unable to approve of other society's practices or moral norms. In fact we would have no reason to be challenged by the morality of other societies at all. It then follows that cultural relativism would allow only a limited or impoverished capacity for moral progress or social reform (Rachels 1978; Moody-Adams 1997).

Peter Singer says:

> It is sometimes said that to intervene in other countries to protect human
> rights is a form of cultural imperialism. By what right, those who take this

view ask, do we in the West impose on other peoples our view of the kind of society that they should have? Are we not repeating the errors of the Western missionaries who sailed out to Africa, or the South Sea Islands, and told the 'primitive' people they found there to cover their nakedness, to practice monogamy, and to have sex only when prone, with the man on top? Have we not learned from this experience that morality is relative to one's own society, and our morals are no better than theirs?

We should reject moral relativism. A much better case against cultural imperialism can be made from the standpoint of a view of ethics that allows for the possibility of moral argument beyond the boundaries of one's own culture. Then we can argue that distinctive cultures embody ways of living that have been developed over countless generations, that when they are destroyed the accumulated wisdom that they represent is lost, and that we are all enriched by being able to observe and appreciate a diversity of cultures. We can recognise that Western culture has no monopoly on Wisdom, has often learned from other cultures, and still has much to learn. We can urge sensitivity to values of other people, and understanding for what gives them self-respect and a sense of identity. (Singer 2002)

And while cultural relativism emphasises difference between cultures, there are of course many similarities across cultures. Societies can probably not exist without some acknowledgement of the need for personal safety, the value of child-rearing, the value of truth telling, and other ethical norms.

The importance of cultural relativism is that it warns us about the dangers of assuming that all our preferences are based in some absolute rational standard, and reminds us that we should keep an open mind (Rachels 1978).

Moral pluralism

An alternative position to either moral relativism or absolutism is moral pluralism. (The term pluralism here is used slightly differently to how it is used in the quote by Agich above. In that quote, pluralism applied to a variety of ways of living rather than to a variety of morals.)

Moral pluralism accepts that the world has many different value systems and that there are many different views about what constitutes a good life. Moral pluralists believe that different moral theories each capture part of truth of the moral life, but none of those theories has the entire answer. Because of this, it is important to discuss and critique moral systems, which also requires self-examination and a willingness to apply standards to one's self as well as to others.

Pluralism also recognises the value of having many different viewpoints. Acceptance of difference adds to the richness and depth of ethical debate. As Appiah says:

[E]very human civilisation has ways to reveal to us values we had not previously recognised or undermine our commitment to values we had settled on. Armed with these terms, fortified with a shared language of value, we can often guide one another, in the cosmopolitan spirit, to shared responses; and when we cannot agree, the understanding that our responses are shaped by some of the same vocabulary can make it easier to agree to disagree. (Appiah 2006)

Pluralism shares with relativism the idea that where values conflict there may be no way to say that one is better than the other – indeed, both may be good. But a pluralist does not think that, because values and perspectives are plural and conflicting, all values or perspectives are of equal worth or that there is *never* any way to judge whether one belief is better than the other. The difficulty this raises for pluralism is how to establish standards, or limits to tolerance, such that society can function effectively without intractable conflict or moral anarchy. Should female circumcision or revenge killings be tolerated on cultural grounds? There is considerable debate about how such decisions are made in pluralist societies, with most arguing that resolution is only possible through consensus, attention to social values and norms, and ultimately through respect for the security and flourishing of both the individual and the community (Rescher 1992; Little 2004).

A useful example of pluralism is given by Levy:

> [The pluralist] is much better placed to accord respect and recognition to other cultures than is a non-relativist who denies pluralism ... [the pluralist] can recognise the value of other cultures without feeling compelled to adopt those values. Imagine, for example, that she is the representative of a culture much like our own, which places a high value on individuality and auto-nomy. She is engaged in the process of assessing an alien culture; one in which autonomy and individuality are accorded little weight. Instead, this culture values community cohesion, harmony between its members and respect for tradition. Our autonomous judge might admire these qualities in the alien culture, thinking that they are the realization of values that are real. She might regret the lack of community in the life of her own society. Nevertheless, since she also thinks that autonomy is a real value, and that it is incompatible with a robust community, she will not feel compelled to adopt the lifestyle of the alien culture. (Levy 2002)

A pluralist may also note that many different value systems do agree on some points. Examples might include that one should not murder others or do things to them against their will. We may disagree about the sources of these moral positions (do they come from God, evolutionary biology, or just the need to get on with each other?), but unlike relativists, pluralists can accept some universalisable moral norms or values.

An example of these different types of reasoning can be found in the debate that occurred over a number of editions of *The Australian* in October 2002; after a Northern Territory Supreme Court judge sentenced Jackie Pascoe also known as Jamilmira, a 50-year-old tribal Aboriginal man, to only 24 hours in prison for having unlawful intercourse with his promised 15-year-old wife. The sentence was increased by the Northern Territory Court of Appeal to 12 months in prison to be suspended after serving one month. The High Court refused to hear a final appeal on the sentence (*Jamilmira v Hales* [2004] HCATrans 18). Nevertheless, the original sentence generated a heated debate about the role of cultural practice in defending criminal conduct.

Acting Justice John Gallop said the man was exercising his conjugal rights in traditional society and the girl 'knew what was expected of her'. Ever since the girl's birth, the defendant had been paying her parents with gifts – spears, food and more recently cash – so she would be handed to him upon her coming of age. When asked why he had sex with a 15-year-old, he told police: 'She is my promised wife. I have rights to touch her body'. Asked if he knew he had committed an offence, he said: 'Yes, I know. It's called carnal knowledge, but its Aboriginal custom – my culture' (Toohey 2002).

After details of the case were published a number of letters to the editor and articles commented upon it. Troy Williams, of Melbourne, suggested: 'We need to reconcile Aboriginal custom and our community's legal system. However objectionable Mr Pascoe's actions may be to us, it is apparently acceptable in his society, which shouldn't make it a crime'. This could be seen as an example of cultural relativism.

Dave Edwards, of Brisbane, wrote:

> Had this man been white he would be reviled as a paedophile and an exploiter of Aboriginal girls ... That a judicial officer would bow and scrape before Aboriginal custom at the expense of the rights and freedoms of an Australian citizen is both horrific and disappointing.

This comment is worded in an inflammatory style, and would be offensive to many Aboriginal people and their supporters. It is probably best characterised as an absolutist position as it is based on the idea that one should absolutely not 'bow and scrape before Aboriginal custom at the expense of the rights and freedoms of an Australian citizen'.

However, a similar conclusion is reached from a much more pro-Aboriginal position by Dawn Lawrie, a prominent citizen of Darwin:

> As a politician and then as the NT's first Anti-Discrimination Commissioner I have spent the best part of my adult life fighting for the rights of Aboriginal women and girls – it is sickening that in 2002 a young girl should be denied the protection offered to any other young girl just because she is Aboriginal.

This statement might also be regarded as absolutist – as it is based on the absolute belief that young girls should not be denied their rights for protection that are offered to every other Australian.

A fourth approach was taken by Kenneth Maddock of Sydney:

> Both the hopeful husband-to-be and the girl's parents must have known when entering into their contract in 1986 that the system was breaking down because of the rebelliousness of the rising generation. They should also have known that even in earlier times promises were not always kept, that a girl might be promised to more than one man (meaning that some promises had to be broken) and that girls would sometimes resist being handed over to men, especially men a lot older than themselves. Are diverse traditions to be treated as so many holy cows or should they be subject to rational and humane scrutiny even though this may anger some members of those groups? After all, it could be said that a woman living in a fundamentalist Muslim society will know what to expect if she commits adultery. She will be stoned to death.

This statement might be thought to be more pluralist in that it acknowledges the existence of the tradition, and appears somewhat sympathetic to it. The tradition is nonetheless rejected after making an analogy with the practice of stoning a woman to death in some Islamic states – a process that the author clearly finds unacceptable. (Note that some people might regard this comment as being as absolutist as the previous two – but just worded in a more obscure manner.)

Moral friends and moral strangers

An interesting example of a pluralist philosophy has been developed by Tristram Engelhardt in his book *The Foundations of Bioethics* (1996). Engelhardt is a Roman Catholic philosopher with strong views on subjects such as abortion, contraception and euthanasia. However, he also recognises that in a modern, multicultural society, these views are unlikely to hold great weight with secular thinkers or those of other religious persuasions. According to Engelhardt, all attempts to justify a content-full ethics (ie, one that attempts to set out which actions are right or wrong) will fail in the wider society, although it may be very successful within the community of believers.

Engelhardt argues that we can divide society into communities of 'moral friends', and a wider society of 'moral strangers'. Between moral friends it is possible to form a content-rich ethical consensus. For example, within a feminist group, it is likely that the issue of abortion will be approached in terms of a woman's right to control her body. Members of the group – ethical friends – will be able to debate this subject, learn from each other's views and reach consensus. The same is true of members of the Catholic Church, or perhaps of atheistic members of the Humanist Society. However, when one of these groups attempts to have an ethical discourse with a member of another group, they may find each other to be ethical strangers – and be totally unable to form a consensus or to respond adequately to each other's views.

According to Engelhardt:

> Because the division separating moral strangers is often obscured by (1) the political usefulness of ignoring or discounting differences, (2) the management of consensus and the projection of its existence through political processes, including bioethics committees, and (3) the existence of many individuals with muted commitments, many persons may doubt that moral strangers in fact frequently present themselves. Again to emphasise, moral strangeness does not require that the other be incomprehensibly other, only that the other be seen as other because of differences in moral and/or metaphysical commitments. Moral strangers can be the best of affective friends. Indeed they can even be spouses (for that matter, spouses can be mortal enemies). Still, to be moral strangers is to inhabit different moral worlds. An atheistic physician in the Netherlands may regard the refusal of physician-assisted suicide by a patient in terminal agony as alien to the moral commitments of the physician. So, too, the woman who on religious grounds refuses abortion after rape may be regarded not as a brave witness to exemplary moral convictions, but as a woman exploited by a false and patriarchal understanding of values. (Engelhardt 1996)

Engelhardt's work explores whether it is possible to develop a value-free, but content-filled, ethics that can be shared by moral strangers. A moral pluralist would suggest that this was not possible, and Engelhardt also concludes this.

However, he does suggest that there is a bare minimum of ethical thought that can be shared by moral strangers. He proposes two principles that can be shared in this way. The first he calls the 'principle of permission'. This states that one can only do something to another person if one has received their permission to do so. The second is what he calls the 'principle of beneficence', which states that the goal of moral action is the achievement of goods and the avoidance of harms. To Engelhardt, these principles do not provide the basis for a full morality – they provide only a minimalist framework that allows us to maintain a peaceful moral society in which more complete ethical structures can be sought.

Moral pluralism in the health-care setting

If we think about the health-care system using Engelhardt's terminology, it is questionable whether health-care professionals form a community of moral friends or a society of moral strangers. Members of the health-care team are clearly not complete moral strangers. Many difficult ethical decisions are reached within the health-care system with minimum conflict and disagreement. And although health-care professionals tend to use different philosophical structures to approach different problems, there are some areas of ethics in which they seem mostly to be in agreement. For example, within hospitals it is commonly understood that health resources do require rationing, although this point does not appear to be universally recognised in the community. Similarly, within the health-care community, the idea that a patient's medical condition has some bearing upon their entitlement to health-care (in particular the notion of 'futility') has also gathered wide support.

But health workers are not all moral friends either. Health professionals come from a plurality of religious, cultural and moral backgrounds. They do not share a complete, content-full morality that enables consensus always to be reached easily. At times consensus may be impossible to achieve.

Perhaps the best way to view the health-care community is as a group of 'moral acquaintances'. Like other acquaintances, they share certain habits, they try not to offend each other and, although they sometimes think that they are friends, they may be shocked to find the actual extent of their differences. The health-care institution provides a critical framework for moral agreement where otherwise people would disagree. It allows for moral pluralism but shapes it in a way that provides for effective social cooperation without recourse to illusory 'universal answers'.

As moral acquaintances, we probably share more of our ethical structure than moral strangers do (and indeed there is more to bioethics than the principle of permission and the principle of beneficence), but we do not share a complete, content-full morality. Moral disagreement is an inescapable facet of any society and it would be a mistake for any institution, committee or proponent of a single normative ethics to believe that moral difference can be eliminated.

In the rest of this book we will explore the way that ethical and legal problems thrown up by the health-care system have been approached. We will show how certain moral frameworks for dealing with these problems have been developed among the 'moral acquaintances' of the health-care system (starting with a principle-based approach to moral reasoning) and how the wider community has reacted to these. We will then look at a diverse series of ethical and legal issues in health care from the standpoint of moral pluralism.

Pluralism does not provide any simple answers to moral questions. There is no such thing as 'ethics made easy'. We must think and argue, challenge our own beliefs and those of others, compromise or refuse to compromise. Most importantly, as philosophers such as Jurgen Habermas have argued, we must listen and communicate effectively, and be genuinely open to the range of values, needs and perspectives that share the ethical space, because it is only by doing so that we can facilitate the flourishing of the entire community, establish a means for action and examine the validity of our own attitudes and beliefs (Habermas 1992).

References

Agich, G (2003) *Dependence and autonomy in old age*. Cambridge, Cambridge University Press.

Appiah, K (2006) *Cosmopolitanism; Ethics in a world of strangers*. London, Allen Lane.

Bloom, A (1987) *The closing of the American mind*, Simon and Schuster.

Chambers, T (1999) *The fiction of bioethics*. New York, Routledge.

Engelhardt, HT (1996) *The foundations of bioethics*. New York, Oxford University Press.

Habermas, J (1992) *Moral consciousness and communicative action*. Cambridge, Polity Press.

Levy, N (2002) *Moral relativism: A short introduction*. Oxford, Oneworld.

Little, J (2004) Community, security and human flourishing: An exploratory essay. *CVELIM Occasional Monograph Series. No 1*. Sydney.

Moody-Adams, M (1997) The empirical underdetermination of descriptive cultural relativism. *Fieldwork in familiar places*. M Moody-Adams. Cambridge, MA, Harvard University Press.

Rachels, J (1978) *Elements of moral philosophy*. New York, McGraw-Hill.

Rescher, N (1992) *Pluralism – Against the demand for consensus*. New Haven, Hale University Press.

Singer, P (2002) *One World – The ethics of globalisation.*, Text Publishing.

Toohey, P (2002). Black and White and Blurred. *The Weekend Australian*: 12 October 2002.

Williams, B (1972) *Morality*. Cambridge, Cambridge University Press.

CHAPTER 4

INTRODUCTION TO LAW

One of the questions often raised by health profession students when discussing moral issues is: 'What does the law say about this?' This question is often asked as if the answer to this question would resolve the moral issue. It must be said plainly that *the law is not the same as ethics*. The law may be influenced by moral considerations, but it is a separate form of normative reasoning that is not necessarily dependent on morals or ethics.

In the NSW case of *Woods v Lowns* (1996) Aust Torts Reports ¶81-376 at 63,166 Mahoney J (dissenting) said:

> [M]oral obligations are not legal obligations. The two must not be confused. A great deal of the time of the legislature is taken up in deciding whether moral obligations should become legal obligations, under what circumstances, and with what qualifications and exceptions. Law, as an instrument of social control, is a blunt instrument. It is often inappropriate to the qualifications and exceptions to which, if made law, a moral obligation should be subject. But the imposition of a legal obligation produces consequences which often make it inappropriate as a means of enforcing moral obligations. We are concerned with whether the moral obligations to which (as I assume) the doctor was subject should be a legal obligation.

In the criminal law area, Lord Atkin for the Judicial Committee of the Privy Council in *Proprietary Articles Trade Association v Attorney-General for Canada* [1931] AC 310 at 324 wrote:

> Criminal law connotes only the quality of such acts or omissions as are prohibited under appropriate penal provisions by authority of the state. The criminal quality of an act cannot be discerned by intuition; nor can it be discovered by reference to any standard but one: Is the act prohibited with penal consequences? Morality and criminality are far from co-extensive; nor is the sphere of criminality necessarily part of a more extensive field covered by morality – unless the moral code necessarily disapproves all acts prohibited by the State, in which case the argument moves in a circle. It appears to their Lordships to be of little value to seek to confine crimes to a category of acts which by their very nature belong to the domain of 'criminal jurisprudence'; for the domain of criminal jurisprudence can only be ascertained by examining what acts at any particular period are declared by the State to be crimes, and the only common nature they will be found to possess is that they are prohibited by the State ...

The relationship between law and ethics is therefore not necessarily dependent. But having said that there are many situations where the law and ethics come into contact. In developing areas of law (particularly health law), where there may not yet be a decided view, judges rely heavily on the views of professionals in those fields and their forms of ethics reasoning. As is discussed below and in further chapters, there are many legal tests (for example, in negligence, or assessment of futility of treatment) which are centred on the normative values of health professionals. So while the law is not the same as ethics, there are many situations where the law takes normative ethics and fashions it into law.

The rule of law and the separation of powers

One of the most basic principles in the Australian legal system is the recognition of *the rule of law*. Joseph Raz (1977) defined the rule of law as encompassing two features:

- that all people (including the government) should be ruled by the law and obey it; and
- that the law should be such that people should be able to be guided by it.

From these two features it is possible to list three basic principles that are central to the rule of law concept (Stewart 2004). The first is *certainty*, which requires that all law should be prospective, open, clear and stable so as to maximise the autonomy of individuals and groups in society. The second principle is that of *generality* which requires that, in addressing the control of the conduct of people from different classes, law must be impersonal and non-particularised. *Equality* is the final principle. It embodies the idea that all people should be equally subject to the law. Traditionally this has been seen to encompass a formal conception of equality, meaning that everyone is treated the same regardless of the differences between them. It requires that all have the same negative liberties (freedoms from interference). It also requires that these liberties should be protected in the same manner. However, the rule of law has also been said to encompass a wider notion of equality, such as equality of concern and respect. Viewed in this fashion legal equality requires that not only should like cases be treated alike but that different cases should be treated differently.

A system that values the rule of law can be distinguished from rule by dictator or absolute monarch. In these systems justice may depend upon the whim or beliefs of an individual. No individual in our system of government or justice system can hold absolute power. This is facilitated in the Australian system of government by the operation of the doctrine of the *separation of powers*. This doctrine was advocated by the French political philosopher Charles Montesquieu in the 18th century. Montesquieu argued that there were three governmental functions – the legislative, the executive and the judicial – and that there should therefore be three corresponding organs of government – the legislature, the executive and the judiciary (Srivastava, Deklin et al 1996). Montesquieu based his work *De l'esprit des lois* (1748) on his observations on the English system. His work was influential in the writing of the Constitution of the United States.

In the Australian system of government the separation of powers doctrine is recognised to varying degrees at both the State and Commonwealth levels:

- The legislature is the parliament that passes laws. All parliaments in Australia (except for Queensland) have *bicameral* legislatures, meaning that they have two houses each. Proposals for law (*bills*) must be passed by both houses to be made into law.
- The executive consists of the government ministers (who form a *Cabinet*) and the Queen's vice-regal representatives (the *Governor-General* for Australia and the *Governors* of the States). However, the Queen's representatives follow the advice of the government as a matter of convention so that, practically, the executive in each Australian polity is made up of the Cabinet in each parliament.
- The judiciary decide on the validity of the legislation and its application in individual cases.

There is no strict separation of powers in Australia. There is an imperfect separation between the legislature and the executive because executive government is made up of ministers of state who are also members of the legislature. Neither is there a strict constitutional separation of power between the State legislatures and State judiciaries in Australia. For example, State legislatures have the power to detain prisoners beyond their sentences, and have done so on occasion. In the federal sphere there is a strict separation between the judiciary and the legislature as this is provided for in Chapter III of the Australian Constitution.

What is law?

This is a difficult question which, like the question of what is ethics, has troubled philosophers for centuries. Putting it simply, there are two main ways to approach the question of how to define law:

Positivism defines laws as those norms that have been created by a person, or body who has been given the authority to make law. This approach to the definition of law is referred to as *positivism*, because it defines a norm as a law (rather than as some other kind of norm, like a moral principle or religious rule) purely because the norm was created or *posited* by someone with law-making power. Jeremy Bentham argued strongly for this definition of law, and his utilitarian approach was adopted by legal theorists like John Austin (1790-1859). Under Austin's theory, law is defined by its being a command coming from a sovereign, who threatens to punish the wrongdoer for failure to comply with the command. According to positivism there is no necessary connection between law and morality. Law is defined purely by its form, by whether it was handed down by someone with law-making power. An evil law, is still law (but that, of course, does not prevent the positivist from being highly critical of it).

One of the problems with the commend theory is that not all laws take the form of a command with a sanction. HLA Hart (1907-1992) argued that Austin's definition was limited. Hart said that laws consisted not only of rules with sanctions (which he referred to as *primary rules*) but also consisted of laws about how to do things in society (for example, become registered as an osteopath, make a will, form a company or sell a house). He also said that the legal system contained many rules about how to change rules (which he referred to as *secondary rules* like those contained in constitutions or company rules).

Hart argued that most people obey and follow law because they have adopted laws as a guide for their conduct, rather than through the fear of being punished. For example, ask yourself whether you have failed to murder anyone because of the fear of punishment or because you generally feel that murder is wrong. Hart described the general attitude of most people to the law as the *internal point of view*. He also said that ultimately people respect law because they have adopted a *rule of recognition* and that this rule of recognition is not really able to be explained by *positivism*, but rather it is a sociological fact.

The primary concern is that positivism fails to distinguish between good and evil laws, as it is based solely on the question of where laws come from rather than their content.

Natural law – natural lawyers argue that there is a necessary minimum content to law. Natural lawyers believe that if laws fail to comply with these minimum standards they lose their standing as laws even if they may have been handed down by a sovereign lawmaker. To that extent the minimum content suggests some correlation between law and morality. Strong natural law traditions can be found in Ancient Greek philosophy, Christianity and Islam. They can also be found in modern human rights instruments such as the *American Declaration of Independence* and the *International Covenant on Civil and Political Rights*.

Natural lawyers assume that humans have natural rights and that governments have to respect those rights in the form that their laws take. If they fail to do so then their commands do not have the force of law. Sometimes these arguments are based on theories of social contract, such as those put forth by John Locke (1632-1704), Hugo Grotius (1583-1645) and Samuel von Pufendorf (1632-1694), all of whom argued that humanity's innate powers of reason lead to the creation of social contracts where sovereignty was created but also limited in scope.

More modern theories of natural law do not necessarily adopt a social contract form. For example, John Finnis (1940-) has argued that life consists of the following intrinsic goods: life, knowledge, play, aesthetic experience, sociability, practical reasonableness and religion. According to Finnis, governments are obliged to respect the intrinsic goods in the way they rule and, to the extent that they deviate radically from them, there is no obligation to follow such laws.

Lon Fuller (1902-1978) also argued for a non-social contract form of natural law which he referred to as *procedural natural law*. For Fuller, law had to be defined by eight 'desiderata' that comprise a procedural morality of law. They are: that law is sufficiently general (there must be rules); law is publicly promulgated; prospective; clear and intelligible; law is free of contradictions; sufficiently constant to enable people to order their relations; not impossible to obey; and law must be administered in a way sufficiently congruent with the wording of its written rules so that people can abide by them (Fuller 1969).

These desiderata meant for Fuller that there was a minimum set of standards that law had to follow and that if the proposed law substantially failed to satisfy the standards it would lose its status as a law.

There are two main criticisms made of natural law theory. The first is that is it hard to apply. Using Finnis, for example, it is hard to disagree with his general proposition that laws should respect life, but what does that mean when one is faced with the question of whether to perform a late term abortion to save the mother's life?

The second criticism is aimed at Fuller. Fuller's desiderata avoid the first criticism by being specific, but, according to the famous criticism of Hart, by reducing them down he has made them purely rules of efficiency, rather than rules of morality and natural law. Hart argued that Fuller's desiderata were fully compatible with a Nazi-style regime. The Nazi state could still have passed many of their laws and complied with the desiderata (although it must be said that many of their laws *would have* offended the desiderata). As such Hart argued that Fuller had failed to show any connection between the law and morality. That is not to say that positivists do not believe people cannot be critical of laws and the legal system on morals grounds. It merely is saying that there is no requirement for a law to be moral for it to be understood as a law (Meyerson 2007).

For present purposes, it is impossible to conclude which theory is correct or more correct than the other. What can be said is that positivism is dominant amongst practitioners of law and judges in Australia. Australian courts have steadfastly refused to recognise fundamental natural laws, outside of those recognised in our constitutions (Stewart 2004).

Outside of the basic dualism of positivism and natural law, there are many schools of legal philosophy or *jurisprudence* which examine and critically analyse the Western legal tradition. They include:

Legal realism – this philosophy of law arose primarily in 20th century America. It main adherents included Chief Justice Oliver Wendell Holmes of the US Supreme Court, Judge Jerome Frank and Australian law Professor Julius Stone. Legal realism argues that law is indeterminate and that rules are incapable of being applied with reference to other social and political factors. Realists are sceptical about how predictably rules can be applied, and are also sceptical about how judges can manipulate findings of facts. Realists have argued that judges make their decisions based on a 'judicial hunch' and then retrospectively apply facts and rules to justify their conclusions. Legal realism gave rise in the 1970s to the Critical Legal Studies (CLS) movement, which aimed at 'trashing' legal concepts such as human rights. For the 'Crits', law is a form of legitimised domination that results from the conflict of political groups, the market and bureaucratic organisations. At every level of law, politics forms the basis of decision and, hence, law is politics all the way down.

Principles theory or *Law as integrity* – this is the theory of Ronald Dworkin that law is determinate and that legal problems always have a right answer. His philosophy states that laws are not just made up of rules but also of principles and those principles need to be determined by a judge working within the political morality of the community. Together, rules and principles allow the judge to come up with a correct answer to any legal problem. Dworkin's theory is based on the primacy of human rights. He believes that humans rights 'trump' other legal obligations.

Feminist jurisprudence – feminist movements have criticised the way the legal person is constructed in our legal system. They state that the rule-of-law principles presuppose a constructed individual or 'every-person' on which to focus protection from unwanted intrusion. The aim of feminist jurisprudence has been to show how this 'every-person' is male. The construction of the legal person relies on the notion of a separate, autonomous and rational being who approximates a man capable of employing rights aggressively and assertively and in ways that follow rules. By virtue of the underlying nature of the legal person, the experience of women is silenced and unknowable in law. The formal law cannot see the way women are tied to a private sphere in which they are disempowered. To the extent that the rule of law describes ways of protecting individuals from public powers, it ignores the manifest exercise of private power and private violence.

Where can law be found?

One of the features of the law in Australia is that the body of law and legal principles are not all to be found in one instrument. The two main sources of law in Australia are the common law and legislation. The common law consists of the principles developed by judges in cases that come before them. Legislation is the law passed by the parliament, or by some other bodies under delegation. The laws passed by parliaments are also often referred to as statutes.

Common law is based partly upon a vast body of case law developed by the English courts over many hundreds of years and then adopted into Australia. The direct influence of English law on Australian courts has significantly lessened since the passing of the *Australia Act* in 1986. Before that time, appeals from Australian courts could be taken to the Judicial Committee of the Privy Council, but this has now been abolished.

This does not mean that English law is irrelevant in Australia since Australia is a part of the common law 'family', which originated in England. English decisions will, where appropriate, continue to be cited before Australian courts. So, too, decisions from Canadian and New Zealand courts will be influential, but not binding, for Australian judges. For example, the English House of Lords judgment in *Gillick v West Norfolk and Wisbech Area Health Authority* [1986] AC 112 has been influential in the development of the law of the consent by children to medical procedures and has been cited with approval by the High Court of Australia in *Secretary, Department of Health and Community Services v JWB And SMB* (*Marion's* case) (1992) 175 CLR 218.

Australian law is not so greatly influenced by American case law. Sir Anthony Mason, formerly Chief Justice of the High Court of Australia, described his problems with American precedent in the following terms:

American case law is a trackless jungle in which only the most intrepid and discerning Australian lawyers should venture. It is possible to find American authority to support almost any conceivable proposition of law. Frequently one finds that there are competing and conflicting propositions, some commanding acceptance in particular jurisdictions, other commanding acceptance in other jurisdictions. It is essential, therefore, to use American authority with care and discrimination. Knowledge of the courts and judges who have been influential is important. (Mason 1988)

Thus, in the significant US Supreme Court decision of *Roe v Wade* 410 US 113 (1973), the court found a (US) constitutionally protected privacy right which provided a trimester-based approach to abortion decisions (Bennett 1997). Since the Australian Constitution does not provide for the protection of individual rights in the same way as the US Constitution, the decision in *Roe v Wade* has little or no precedential value in Australia.

The language of the law

A sometimes confusing feature of the law is that lawyers use language in different ways than common usage. Words used in a legal context have come to have different meanings than the words used in their everyday context. For example, where a health professional may talk about their 'duty of care' to a patient, a lawyer may use this expression in a more restricted sense – meaning the first step to be proven in a negligence action. Even among lawyers, expressions may be used in different ways depending upon the context – for example, the expression 'common law' may have at least three different meanings depending upon the context of its usage (see below). The best approach to studying law is to treat it like the study of a foreign language that is similar to, but not the same as, English. The language comes with its own history and culture and an understanding of these factors will help a student understand the way the law works.

Classification and types of law

The classification of laws is rather an arbitrary matter based on the purpose that is sought to be achieved by such classification. One method of classification, already discussed, is based on the sources of law: common law is the law that is derived from court judgments, whereas statute law is the law that is passed by parliaments.

Lawyers may also use the term 'common law' in a slightly different way to distinguish it from 'equity'. The doctrines of equity evolved through the office of the Lord Chancellor, whose role it was to grant relief from the hardships of an intractable common law in individual cases. Equity developed a number of remedies and forms of relief not available at common law. Eventually, decisions in equity became subject to the doctrine of precedent in the same manner as decisions at common law. In modern times these two systems have become intertwined and now all judges are able to try both common law and equity matters (although there still may be separate Divisions within the Supreme Courts). Lawyers may still refer to common law and equity as distinct areas when, for example, an 'equitable remedy' (such as an injunction) may be sought rather than the usual 'common law remedy' of damages.

The term 'common law' may also be used in a third way to distinguish English 'common law' from European or various other legal systems. In this context 'common law' is used to describe a *system* of law. Other legal systems have much less regard for precedent (see below) and have different systems for gathering evidence and reaching decisions.

Law may also be classified by subject matter into:

- contract law
- tort law
- criminal law
- administrative law
- constitutional law
- real property law
- personal property law
- commercial law
- company law
- taxation law, and so on.

Another of the major distinctions that can be made when classifying the law in this way is the distinction between the civil and criminal law. The criminal law proscribes behaviour that society deems to be unacceptable and worthy of punishment. The civil law can be referred to as all of the law that is not regarded as criminal. The most important difference between the trial of civil and criminal matters in the courts is the standard of proof required in each type of trial. In the criminal trial the Crown must prove the matter 'beyond reasonable doubt'. In civil matters the standard of proof is on the 'balance of probabilities'.

A further means of classifying law is as being 'substantive' or 'procedural'. 'Substantive' represents 'what the law is'. 'Procedural' law refers to how the law is implemented. For example, procedural law includes the law of evidence that determines what information may be heard before a court.

These different classifications of law are useful in legal communication and in legal writing and teaching. However, the circumstances that occur in real life may not fit easily into legal classifications. Real problems often (perhaps usually) cross the boundaries between the different classifications.

Common law

The common law (in this section) refers to the law that has developed over the centuries when judges have been asked to adjudicate over disputes. Common law arose when judges began to keep records of disputes and the reasons for their judgments. These early records developed into an elaborate system of law reporting which allowed detailed records to be kept of the facts of the case and the principles of law used to decide the case. When a new case came before a judge, the judge would refer to earlier reports to find cases that had similar features and use these cases as a guide to arrive at a decision. Over time, judges began to be bound by the principles developed in these earlier cases, and a somewhat rigid system developed whereby judges became *bound* by the rules established in the earlier cases. However, as not every case has identical facts or has the same issues raised, there is still some ability for judges to develop existing principles or, in some cases, develop new rules.

When Australia established a legal system, the common law of England became incorporated into Australian law. Upon Federation in 1901 (*Commonwealth of Australia Constitution Act 1900* (UK)) this common law became the common law of Australia. Unfortunately in a book such as this the way in which English law came to have effect in Australia cannot be discussed in detail. However, note should be taken of the High Court of Australia decision in *Mabo v Queensland (No 2)* (1992) 175 CLR 1, where the High Court recognised that some of the traditional property rights of the indigenous peoples of Australia may have survived into modern times. Importantly, the decision makes it clear that the laws of the Indigenous Australian peoples do not form part of the modern law of Australia.

The doctrine of precedent

One of the distinguishing features of the common law is that judges decide cases according to the *doctrine of precedent*. This rule, simply stated, provides that cases involving the same essential or material facts must be decided in the same way. This is called the doctrine of *stare decisis*. The orthodox interpretation of *stare decisis* is an obligation for judges to follow the *ratio decidendi* of past cases. The *ratio decidendi* (frequently simply referred to as the 'ratio') is the reasoning in a judgment on which the ultimate result (decision) of the case is based. Another way of stating this is that courts should follow the reasons for decisions given in previous cases. The doctrine of precedent, as applied in the common law system, is no more than a refined and formalised example of a decision-making process that seeks to avoid arbitrariness and to promote certainty and consistency. Although this is a simple enough rule to understand it is not necessarily clear which cases will be precedent for others.

Generally speaking, the key elements that must exist before a case will be a precedent for another will be:

- the material facts must be substantially the same; and
- the court whose previous decision is relied upon must be a higher court in the same legal hierarchy of courts as the court the present case is before.

It is the *ratio* that creates the binding law. It may be difficult to predict with certainty the form of the *ratio* that will be accepted by a later court. It is also possible that different judges will disagree about the correct interpretation of the *ratio* of a case.

Comments made by judges on legal principles that are not the deciding factor in the case are not binding – such comments are called *obiter dictum* (or if more than one such comment is made, *obiter dicta*). *Obiter dicta* expressed by eminent judges in superior courts are often very weighty, persuasive authorities for judges deciding later cases, but according to the doctrine of precedent they will never be binding.

Sometimes it may appear that a judge is bound by a precedent that might give a bad or unjust result in a later case. The judge may be able to distinguish the earlier decision in such a way that it can be argued that it is not binding in the current case. Given the flexibility of language and the complexities inherent in the concept of *ratio decidendi*, there are ways of arguing that a precedent should not be followed. Some of the most common arguments in achieving this aim are that:

- the statement of law in the earlier case is too wide and should be confined to its facts;
- the statement of law in the earlier case is *obiter dictum* rather than *ratio decidendi*;
- the precedent is distinguishable on its facts;
- the precedent was wrongly decided;
- the case was argued without reference to binding authority; and
- the precedent cannot apply to changed social conditions.

The doctrine of precedent is limited by the legal system a court is part of (also referred to as 'jurisdiction'). Thus a court in one legal system (for example, the NSW Supreme Court) generally must follow a decision of a higher court in the same legal system or hierarchy of courts (for example, the NSW Court of Appeal). Decisions of courts in one legal system may well be persuasive but are not technically binding on a court in another legal system (for example, the findings of the Victorian Supreme Court are not binding on the NSW District Court).

Law reporting

For a system of precedent to work successfully, a system of reporting the judgments of courts is necessary in order for lawyers and other to know what courts have decided. Not all judgments of courts can be reported in published series of law reports. Only the decisions from the superior courts are generally published, and even then only those decisions thought by the courts and the publishers to be of significance.

In Anglo-Australian law reporting a standard system of citation is generally used. The standard format is:

- The names of the parties to the action; the plaintiff (the person bringing the action) is listed first and then the defendant (the person defending the action). If the case is an appeal, the appellant (the person appealing to a higher court) and then the respondent (the person answering the appeal) are listed.
- The year of the decision. This will normally appear between round brackets, for example, '(2004)'. If the year is significant in identifying the

volume of the report then it will appear between square brackets (this is particularly so in UK reports), for example, '[2004]'.

- The volume number of the report (there will not be a volume number if the date is in square brackets unless there was more than one volume published in that year).
- The name of the series of the law report, usually as an abbreviation.
- The page number on which the report commences.

In the significant decision of the High Court in an appeal between Dr Christopher Rogers (the appellant) and Mrs Maree Lynette Whitaker (the respondent) the report is cited (referred to) as *Rogers v Whitaker* (1992) 175 CLR 479. The name of the case, *Rogers v Whitaker*, refers to the parties; the case was decided in 1992; it is reported in volume 175 of the Commonwealth Law Reports (CLR) and the report begins at page 479. We can also tell from the case name that the matter is a private law action and not a case from the criminal law, as criminal law cases have the Crown as a party (normally indicated by the words 'The Queen' or 'Regina', or even the initial 'R').

With the growing availability of reports of decisions on the Internet, new ways of referring to cases have been established. The Australian Institute of Judicial Administration has established a system of case citation that is independent of legal publishers and the print media. Most Australian courts now include paragraph numbers in their judgments so that citation of page numbers is no longer necessary to identify parts of the text of a judgment. The new 'medium neutral' citations are based on the following format: (the parties) [the year of the decision] (the court abbreviation) (the sequential number of the judgment). For example, the first decision of the High Court in 2004 appears as: *A Solicitor v Council of the Law Society of New South Wales* [2004] HCA 1. Where necessary, a specific location within the judgment can be identified with the additional reference to the applicable paragraph number. For example: *A Solicitor v Council of the Law Society of New South Wales* [2004] HCA 1 at [17].

Legislation

The Australian Constitution

The Australian Constitution was passed as part of a British Act of Parliament in 1900, and took effect on 1 January 1901. A British Act was necessary to form the Commonwealth of Australia because, before 1901, Australia was merely a collection of six self-governing British colonies and ultimate power over those colonies rested with the British Parliament. On the commencement of the British Act the Commonwealth of Australia came into being and the six colonies became the six States of Australia. The Constitution establishes a federal system of government. Under the Australian federal system powers are distributed amongst the Commonwealth and the six States. Chapters I, II, and III of the Constitution confer the legislative, executive, and judicial powers of the Commonwealth on three different bodies that are established by the Constitution –

the Parliament (Chapter I), the Commonwealth Executive (Chapter II), and the Federal Judicature (Chapter III).

The State and Commonwealth Parliaments have different powers to pass Acts. The powers of the parliaments are listed in their Constitutions. Federal law applies to all Australia, while a State law only applies to people and things in that State. State Parliaments have a general power to pass laws for the peace, welfare and good government of the State. Where there is a conflict between the law of a State and a federal Act the State law is invalid – to the extent of any inconsistency between the two laws (Australian Constitution, s 109).

Statutes

Statutes are passed by the Parliament of the Commonwealth or the States. Each parliament has two Houses (except for Queensland and the two Territories, which have only one House of Parliament). The Lower House of Parliament returns members who represent various seats or electoral divisions. The Upper House of Parliament is returned on a different basis and does not usually represent a specific electoral seat. The Upper and Lower Houses have different names in the States, Territories and the Commonwealth.

In order for a statute (an Act) to be validly enacted, it must be passed by both Houses of Parliament (or one only in Queensland and the Territories) and receive Royal Assent. An Act will come into force in accordance with its terms. In some cases, the Act will be effective from the date of assent, in other cases the Act will come into effect on a specific date, or a 'date to be proclaimed' by the Governor (State laws) or Governor-General (Commonwealth laws). An Act of Parliament will override the common law, should there be any conflict.

Although the parliament is the source of legislation, most Acts provide for a power to make regulations (also referred to as 'subordinate legislation') in order to implement the purposes of the main Act. This is because parliament does not usually include in the legislation the mass of detail required to make the Act effective. The legislation states the broad matters of policy and leaves the details to be included in regulations. The regulations are 'proclaimed' in the Government *Gazette* (a publication of each government in relation to administrative matters). The regulation takes effect, unless disallowed by parliament, on the date specified in the relevant proclamation. Regulations are very important to study for the reason that they can vary the impact of legislation in quite major ways. These regulations have the same force and effect as the Act itself and can override the common law.

Statutory interpretation

All modern statutes have a common form. The statute has a title and most have numbers that are useful in finding the particular Act in the published volumes of legislation. The main body of an Act is divided into numbered *sections*. These in turn may be divided into *subsections*, and then further into *paragraphs*. It is common today to arrange groups of sections in lengthy statutes in *Divisions* or *Parts*, which are usually provided with headings. A *table of contents* is often provided for lengthy Acts.

In individual cases, courts will generally not be asked to interpret whole Acts of Parliament but only that part of the law that is relevant to the particular case. The court then has to apply that law to the facts of the case to reach a result. Where the Act is uncertain or unclear as to its meaning the judge must first decide what is meant by the law before he or she can apply it.

The modern approach to statutory interpretation is to consider the text of the statute and, if necessary, adopt a 'purposive approach' to the meaning of the Act. In the High Court judgment in *CIC Insurance Ltd v Bankstown Football Club Ltd* [1997] HCA 2, the court said:

> [T]he modern approach to statutory interpretation (a) insists that the context be considered in the first instance, not merely at some later stage when ambiguity might be thought to arise, and (b) uses 'context' in its widest sense to include such things as the existing state of the law and the mischief which, by legitimate means such as those just mentioned, one may discern the statute was intended to remedy. Instances of general words in a statute being so constrained by their context are numerous. In particular, as McHugh JA pointed out in *Isherwood v Butler Pollnow Pty Ltd* (1986) 6 NSWLR 363 at 388, if the apparently plain words of a provision are read in the light of the mischief which the statute was designed to overcome and of the objects of the legislation, they may wear a very different appearance. Further, inconvenience or improbability of result may assist the court in preferring to the literal meaning an alternative construction which, by the steps identified above, is reasonably open and more closely conforms to the legislative intent. [Footnotes omitted]

The courts and tribunals

The Commonwealth of Australia, its six States, the Australian Capital Territory and the Northern Territory, all have their own systems of courts. In addition, there exist a number of courts exercising federal jurisdiction at a variety of levels. The High Court of Australia was created by Chapter III of the Constitution. Section 73 of the Constitution confers appellate jurisdiction on the High Court to hear appeals from decisions of:

- the High Court in its original jurisdiction;
- federal courts;
- courts exercising federal jurisdiction; and
- State Supreme Courts.

All other courts in Australia have been created by an Act of a Commonwealth, State or Territory Parliament.

State and Territory courts

The basic structure of the courts in each State is very similar, although there may be some variations in the names and functions of certain of the lower courts. The courts of law in the States and Territories form a hierarchy with the courts of summary jurisdiction at the base, then courts of intermediate jurisdiction as 'inferior courts', and the supreme courts as 'superior courts' at the apex. It is possible for a decision of a State Supreme Court to be appealed to the High

Court of Australia, but 'special leave' must be sought from the High Court and this will only be granted in a limited number of cases when an important issue of law has to be decided.

The courts of summary jurisdiction are referred to by different titles in the States and Territories. Generally they may be referred to as 'Magistrates' Courts' or 'Local Courts'. Since these courts are presided over by a magistrate we will refer to them as magistrates' courts. These courts are of vast importance in the administration of the law, for the magistrates' courts are responsible for most of the judicial decision-making. The civil and criminal jurisdictions of the magistrates' courts vary between the States and Territories and are limited by statute. Magistrates' courts deal with relatively minor criminal matters (traffic offences, smaller larceny cases, and lesser assault cases, for example) and exercise a restricted civil jurisdiction (up to $60,000 in New South Wales, or up to $72,000 if all parties agree to stay in the Local Court).

With the exception of Tasmania, Australian Capital Territory and the Northern Territory, the District (NSW, Qld, SA and WA) or County Courts (Victoria) are courts of intermediate jurisdiction; between the State Supreme Court and the Magistrates' Court. District or County Courts have both a civil and criminal jurisdiction. In the criminal area, these courts deal with more serious crimes. The courts have a limit in the civil jurisdiction on the award of damages ($750,000 in New South Wales). These courts also have an appellate jurisdiction in the case of appeals from magistrates.

The highest courts in the State structure are the various superior courts known as 'Supreme Courts'. These courts may have both an original jurisdiction (hearing cases for the first time) and an appellate jurisdiction (hearing cases on appeal from a single judge or from summary or intermediate courts). The State Supreme Courts exercise unlimited civil jurisdiction. They also exercise criminal jurisdiction in serious crimes (such as homicides and major drug cases). The State Supreme Courts also exercise a wide appellate jurisdiction (ie, they may hear appeals against judgments from other courts). In New South Wales, for example, the appellate civil jurisdiction is exercised by a separate Court of Appeal and, in criminal cases, is exercised by a separate Court of Criminal Appeal. The State Supreme Courts may also exercise jurisdiction under federal legislation where such jurisdiction is conferred.

Federal courts

The Federal Court of Australia was created by the *Federal Court of Australia Act 1976* (Cth) and began to exercise its jurisdiction on 1 February 1977. The Federal Court sits as required in each State, in the Australian Capital Territory and the Northern Territory. The court has such original jurisdiction as is invested in it by laws made by the Commonwealth Parliament, including, for example, in bankruptcy, corporations law, industrial relations, taxation and trade practices law. The Court also has appellate jurisdiction in relation to the decisions of single judges of the Court, decisions of the respective Supreme Courts of the Australian Territories, except the Northern Territory, and certain decisions of State Supreme Courts when exercising federal jurisdiction.

The *Family Law Act 1975* (Cth), which commenced operation on 5 January 1976, introduced a new law dealing with the dissolution and nullity of marriage, custody and welfare of the children, maintenance and the settlement of property between the parties to a marriage in Australia. The Act created the Family Court of Australia as a specialist court dealing only with matrimonial and associated proceedings. The Court's jurisdiction has been expanded significantly in recent years, including a wider federal jurisdiction in matters such as bankruptcy, administrative law and taxation appeals. The Family Court exercises original and appellate jurisdiction throughout mainland Australia except in Western Australia and the Northern Territory. In Western Australia, original jurisdiction under the Act is exercised by the Family Court of Western Australia (a State court which is funded by the Commonwealth Government). Since 1987, the judges of the Family Court of Western Australia have also held commissions as judges of the Family Court of Australia. In the Northern Territory, the Supreme Court of the Northern Territory and the Family Court of Australia exercise concurrent original jurisdiction under the Act.

The Industrial Relations Court of Australia was established in March 1994 to deal with a range of industrial relations matters. However, in 1997 the jurisdiction of the Industrial Relations Court was transferred to the Federal Court. The Industrial Relations Court will continue to exist formally until there are no judges remaining who hold office as judges of the Industrial Relations Court.

The Federal Magistrates Court was established in 1999 and is an independent federal court. The Federal Magistrates Court's jurisdiction includes matters such as family law, intellectual property, child support, administrative law, bankruptcy law and consumer protection law. Currently the Commonwealth government is considering merging the Federal Magistrates Court with the Federal Court and the Family Court.

Following the passing of 'cross-vesting' legislation, State courts may hear certain federal matters (or matters from other States or Territories) where it would be impractical or unjust to refer the matter to the correct court. Federal courts cannot, however, hear State matters (*Re Wakim; Ex parte McNally* (1999) 198 CLR 511).

Administrative and other tribunals

In addition to courts of law in Australia there also exist a substantial number of tribunals that are concerned with administrative matters in a wide variety of areas of activity. These tribunals differ markedly in both constitution and procedure. A general feature of tribunals is that the conduct of their sittings is usually more informal than courts and rules of evidence are less strictly interpreted. The extent to which the informality of procedure is practised in fact will frequently depend upon the actuality of how a tribunal operates rather than upon what the particular parliamentary enactment says on the subject. Tribunal membership is often constituted to include members with particular expertise in the area of deliberation, although it is often a legal practitioner who chairs the tribunal.

Coroner's Courts

Coroner's Courts exist in all States and both Territories. Legislation in the States and Territories varies somewhat in terms of when a Coroner is obliged to hold an inquest. In general, where there is reasonable cause for the Coroner to suspect that a person has died a violent or unnatural death or died in circumstances that are unclear, or in a prescribed facility, such as a prison or mental hospital, an inquest must be held. Provision is made in the legislation of the various jurisdictions for the appointment of Coroners and Deputy Coroners. The conditions of appointment and the powers of Coroners vary between the various States and Territories. Coronial inquiries are conducted in an inquisitorial rather than adversarial manner. The inquiry is not a trial but has a fact-finding goal. The coronial inquest is not bound by the rules of evidence and Coroners can conduct the inquiry in the manner that they think fit. Despite this, the conduct of most inquiries is along the adversarial model.

Trial process

In criminal matters a distinction is drawn between cases that are triable summarily and those that are triable on indictment. A magistrate sitting alone normally tries summary offences, which are the less serious and more common offences. Trials on indictment are usually those that involve the more serious crimes and are tried by judge and jury. In some cases, if the accused person so chooses, indictable offences may be tried summarily.

In most Australian jurisdictions civil proceedings are commenced by serving a writ of summons on the defendant, which will be accompanied by a statement of claim. (In New South Wales, the statement of claim is the initiating document.) The statement of claim states the material facts, the cause of action, and the judgment that it is desired to be obtained from the court. Once the statement of claim has been filed with the court and served on the defendants the parties will then begin to sort out what issues are actually in dispute through a process known as 'pleading'. The defendants will prepare a defence and may also initiate a counterclaim against the plaintiff. This process may be very complex. Once this process has been completed documents relevant to the case must be produced and inspected ('discovery') and a series of written questions and answers under oath (interrogatories) must be completed. At this stage, if there has been no settlement between the parties, then the case is set down for hearing. This whole process may be quite protracted.

Law reform

The law is in a constant process of change. The various parliaments at State and federal level pass large numbers of Acts each year (in 2003 the Commonwealth Parliament passed 150 Acts). The various appellate courts also hand down large numbers of judgments every year as well. This process allows the law to change with changes in society, although sometimes there is an unfortunate delay.

As well as these formal processes of changing law, there are a number of bodies that have an influential role in investigating changes that should be made in the law and then, where appropriate, recommending change. These bodies may be Law Reform Commissions, Royal Commissions and other influential groups in society such as trade unions and political parties. Law Reform Commissions are charged with specific responsibility for law reform, and both the State and federal bodies usually investigate questions referred to them by the Attorneys General. The Law Reform Commissions usually consult widely, often holding public meetings in which various points of view can be put forward. Issues relating to health care have been referred to various Law Reform Commissions for consideration. Notably, the Law Reform Commission of Victoria, New South Wales Reform Commission and the Australian Law Reform Commission in 1989 produced a joint report called 'Informed decisions about medical procedures'. One of the most widely implemented reports was the report on *Human tissue transplants* produced by the Australian Law Reform Commission in 1977. The draft Bill included with that report was substantially adopted by all jurisdictions.

The work of various Royal Commissions has also been influential in causing laws to be changed. Some of the more notable Royal Commissions include the Royal Commission into Aboriginal Deaths in Custody, which investigated the deaths of 99 Aboriginal and Torres Strait Islander people, who died between 1 January 1980 and 31 May 1989, and the New South Wales Royal Commission into Deep Sleep Therapy in 1990.

Human rights and the law

Law translates standards of human rights into reality. Creating a world that is respectful of law is a journey, a utopian journey, and we are still not absolutely sure how to get there. But just as democratic rights were the big idea at the beginning of the twentieth century so human rights are the big idea of the century we have recently entered. They have the potential of radically affecting the way in which we relate to each other as nations and as next-door neighbours. Human rights is where the law becomes poetry ... (Kennedy 2004)

Of increasing concern for all health-care professionals is the influence of human rights; both as law and rhetoric. The British Medical Association in *The medical profession and human rights: handbook for a changing agenda* lists four reasons why health workers need to be informed about human rights:

As citizens of the modern world they should know about this most "dynamic, complex and challenging modern movement".

Health policies, programs, practices and research may inadvertently violate human rights;

Violations of human rights have important adverse health effects on individuals and groups; and

Promoting human rights is now understood as an essential part of efforts to promote and protect public health. (British Medical Association 2001)

It is important that when considering the issue of human rights and the law we are aware of some of the background and sources of human rights law.

Categories of human rights

Three 'generations' of human rights can be identified. 'First generation' rights include political and civil rights and can be found in the revolutionary Constitutions of France and the United States. They were first enshrined at the global level by the 1948 *Universal Declaration of Human Rights* and included in the 1966 *International Covenant on Civil and Political Rights*. First generation rights include the right to life, liberty, security of person; freedom of movement; free from torture, cruel, inhumane or degrading treatment or punishment; or freedom from arbitrary arrest and detention. These rights are largely negative – to refrain from arbitrary use of power rather than in the sense of resource provision.

'Second generation' rights are economic, social and cultural rights. These rights are reflected in the *International Covenant on Economic, Social and Cultural Rights*. Second generation rights include the right to the highest attainable standards of health, to work, social security, adequate food, clothing, housing and education. They are mostly positive rights, representing things that the state is required to provide to the people under its jurisdiction.

'Third generation' rights are generally regarded as solidarity rights. They cover group and collective rights: the right to self-determination, to economic and social development, and to participate in the common heritage of mankind. These rights are not generally recognised by governments and human rights declarations.

Common law civil liberties

The common law has a long history of protecting what would now be considered to be human rights. Traditionally these rights have been called *civil liberties* and they fall into the first generation human right category. The framers of the Australian Constitution thought so highly of the common law protections that they decided not to follow the United States example and incorporate a Bill of Rights with the Constitution. Very few human rights are mentioned in that document. These are voting rights, rights to trial by jury for indictable federal offences, rights to freedom of religion, and rights of citizens not to be discriminated against because they are the resident of any Australian State. Apart from these rights, the framers believed that the common law would be sufficient protection of liberty.

Some of the common law rights that courts have recognised include:

- rights of protection from bodily interference;
- rights to protection of property;
- protections against self-incrimination;
- rights to natural justice, meaning a right to expect procedural fairness in government decision-making; and
- rights of access to the courts (for example, after being arrested).

These common law liberties may be infringed by legislation, but the legislation needs to be very clear about its intent, otherwise the courts will interpret the legislation narrowly.

Incorporating human rights into domestic law

Other common law nations took a different path to Australia and decided to recognise human rights in other ways in addition to the common law. One way this can be done is through recognising the rights by incorporating them into a Constitution. This offers the widest protection for citizens. Other law becomes subservient to the constitutional protections. This is the method used in the United States of America. A Bill of Rights incorporated into a Constitution can only be amended in the same manner as any other amendment to the Constitution.

Another method, such as that used in the *Canadian Charter of Rights and Freedoms* in the Constitution of Canada, allows a law or part of a law to apply temporarily 'notwithstanding' that it may be inconsistent with a right otherwise protected by the Constitution. This is known as an 'override power' or 'notwithstanding clause'.

Another mechanism for incorporating rights into law is through legislation which creates certain rights that must be taken in account by parliament and the courts when making decisions. This is similar to the way in which the *Human Rights Act 1998* in the United Kingdom incorporates the *European Convention on Human Rights* into United Kingdom Law. English courts are required to interpret existing laws so that they comply with the rights enumerated in the *European Convention*. If they believe that legislation infringes human rights they can issue a declaration of incompatibility, which does not change the legislation, but at least brings the incompatibility to the parliament's attention.

This type of human rights recognition has been introduced into the Australian Capital Territory and Victoria. The Australian Capital Territory's *Human Rights Act 2004* and the Victorian *Charter of Human Rights and Responsibilities Act 2006* recognise a number of basic human rights, and require government departments and public bodies to observe these rights when they create laws, set policies and provide services. Courts must interpret legislation in line with these rights and can declare that the legislation is incompatible with the human rights enumerated in the Acts. As in the UK, such a declaration has no legal effect on the legislation but triggers a report to the parliament. Similar approaches to human rights are currently being considered in Western Australia, Tasmania, the Northern Territory and the Commonwealth.

Finally, ordinary legislation may also incorporate human rights values in a form which does give direct rights but which may be amended or repealed by parliament. In Australia, the has been done at the Commonwealth and State levels primarily in relation to anti-discrimination laws; for example, a number of Acts have been enacted which prohibit discrimination on the grounds of race, sex, marital status, pregnancy, family responsibility, age and disability. Rights to privacy in sexual relationships between consenting adults have also been recognised in legislation (*Human Rights (Sexual Conduct) Act 1994* (Cth)). Privacy rights over personal information have been created. Additionally, the Commonwealth Government and most State and Territory governments have created special commissions with the function of promoting human rights and powers to investigate alleged breaches of human rights.

EXAMPLES OF CATEGORIES OF LAW RELEVANT TO HEALTH-CARE PROVIDERS

It is not possible in this book to give examples from all of the categories of law listed above. There are, however, three areas that need to be referred to because of their significance for the health-care provider. These three areas are: the law of contract, the law or torts and the criminal law.

The law of contract

The traditional way of regarding the doctor-patient relationship is that it is grounded in the law of contract (*Sidaway v Board of Governors of Bethlem Royal Hospital* [1985] AC 871 at 904). The High Court has also recognised this (either explicitly or impliedly) in *Breen v Williams* (1996) 186 CLR 71. The same principle probably applies where there is a relationship between a patient and an institution such as a hospital or nursing home whose services are provided by health-care providers who are employees of the institution with whom the patient has a contractual relationship.

It should be noted that, although there may be some contracts that the law requires to be reduced to writing (like those regarding land), by far the majority of contracts in the health area are not written down. This does not affect the validity of the agreement – in most cases where the courts have examined an alleged breach of contract between a health-care provider and a patient, the existence of the contract has not been disputed.

Before examining the nature of the health-care contract we need to examine some of the contractual principles. There are five basic requirements for a legally enforceable contract:

(a) *An intention to create legal relations* – there must be a voluntary assumption of a legal duty;

(b) *An agreement* – there must be an 'offer' and an 'acceptance';

(c) *Consideration* – the agreement must be supported by one party giving something in exchange for something else. (There are some contracts, those 'under seal' (known as *deeds*), which do not require consideration);

(d) *Legal capacity* – the capacity to understand the nature and effect of the agreement. Traditionally, for example, minors lacked legal capacity to enter into most forms of contract. Common law and statute have modified this principle.

(e) *Genuine consent* – the effectiveness of an agreement may be affected if it has been entered into under duress or as a result of fraud.

Intention to create legal relations

The law makes an assumption that there is no intention to create legal relations when family members make agreements. Conversely, the law presumes that there was an intention to create a contract if an agreement is made between strangers. These presumptions can be overturned depending on evidence relating to the nature of the agreement and the circumstances in which it was made. In the health-care context there will usually be a presumption that there is an intention to create legal relations because health services are being provided by health workers in a professional setting.

Agreement – offer and acceptance

A contract is formed after one party has made an offer and that offer has been accepted by another party. The contract is formed at the time when the offer is accepted. In the commercial context the timing of the formation of the contract may be very important.

There is a large body of case law that examines the question of which actions constitute an offer and which an acceptance. This is often not certain as the law recognises that there is a process of negotiation undertaken before the parties are ready to enter into the contract. The cases also examine the question of whether particular conduct is an offer of merely an 'invitation to treat'. For example, is an advertisement an offer or does it merely indicate that the advertiser is in business and ready to accept offers on goods or services included in the advertisement? This question may arise in the context of a health-care provider refusing to treat a patient.

Consideration

'Consideration' usually refers to the payment that is given by one party in exchange for the goods or service. In health care, this issue is made more difficult because services are sometimes paid for by a third party (like the government) or are given charitably.

Lack of capacity

At common law, infants and persons of 'unsound mind' lack the capacity to enter into contracts. A person who wishes to avoid the obligations under a contract because of a claim that they were of unsound mind when the agreement was made must be able to prove both the incapacity and that the other party knew of the incapacity. For example, a person who entered into a contract while intoxicated will be held to the contract unless they can show that the other party knew they were intoxicated at the time.

Terms of the contract

All contracts contain 'terms' that are the subject matter of the contract (that is, what the parties have promised to do). Most health-care contracts are not formal contracts that have been reduced entirely to writing. It is necessary, therefore, for courts to imply various terms into the contract in order for it to be made workable. An example of an implied term in the health-care contract is that the health-care professional will owe an obligation of confidence to the patient.

Termination of the contract

There are a number of ways that a contract may come to an end:

- *Performance* – when the parties have completed what they agreed to do the contract will come to an end.
- *Agreement* – the contract can be terminated by agreement between the parties.
- *Occurrence of a specified condition or event* – the contract may have provided for its termination upon the occurrence of a specified event or condition.
- *Frustration* – a contract may be terminated when it becomes impossible to complete because of some supervening event. For example, the ill health or death of one of the parties, where the participation of that person is a necessary part of the contract.
- *Breach* – when one of the parties to the contract, either expressly or impliedly refuses or fails to carry out their obligations under the contract.

Remedies for breach of contract

When one of the parties has breached their obligations under the terms of the contract the other party has a right to bring an action seeking a remedy. The main remedy is the award of *damages*, which are a monetary amount equivalent to the financial loss incurred as a result of the breach. The courts are also, on occasion, able to award discretionary remedies. These are only awarded when the payment of monetary damages is thought to be inappropriate. The main discretionary remedies are:

- *Specific performance* – which is a court order that the party in breach must perform their obligations under the contract.
- *Injunction* – this is an order by a court forbidding a person from doing something.

An example of the application of contract law: Breen v Williams

The facts in *Breen v Williams* (1996) 186 CLR 71 are as follows. In 1977 Ms Breen had a bilateral augmentation mammoplasty (that is, a breast enlargement). Thereafter she developed bilateral breast capsules. In 1978 she consulted Dr Williams, who was a plastic surgeon, but not the plastic surgeon who performed the implant. Dr Williams advised Ms Breen that the capsules should be compressed and he performed that operation. Ms Breen experienced severe pain and, after two further consultations with her, Dr Williams operated and performed a bilateral capsulotomy. Ms Breen had not consulted Dr Williams since that operation.

Ms Breen became interested in litigation in the United States by way of a class action against the manufacturer of the breast implants claiming that they were defective. Ms Breen sought to have access to the medical records kept by Dr Williams. Dr Williams would only do this if Ms Breen gave him an indemnification from any future legal action against him. Ms Breen did not wish to do this. Ms Breen sought an order from the New South Wales Supreme Court that Dr Williams allow her access to her medical records to examine them and obtain copies of the information contained in them. Ms Breen was unsuccessful before both the NSW Supreme Court and the Court of Appeal. A further appeal to the High Court was also unsuccessful.

Two of the issues that were canvassed in the court cases were the question of consideration in health-care contracts, and the question of what sort of terms could be implied into health-care contracts.

Regarding the first question, in the High Court judgment, Brennan CJ said that '[t]he consideration for the undertaking may be either a payment, or promise of payment, of reward or submission by the patient, or an undertaking by the patient to submit, to the treatment proposed' (at 78). However, with the greatest respect to the Chief Justice, the second option for establishing consideration, the submission by the patient to treatment, cannot be supported, as it would imply that the doctor receives a personal benefit by having the patient submit to treatment. If the patient were to refuse to submit to some aspect of the treatment, could the doctor say that the contract has been breached because of a failure by the patient to provide consideration?

In the same case Gummow J said that 'the medical practitioner [performed] services in consideration for fees payable by the patient'. While all members of the High Court recognised the existence of a contract, only Brennan CJ and Gummow J dealt with the issue of consideration. Gummow J also said '[t]hat established pattern now may require adjustment to accommodate wholly or partly state operated or financed health schemes, established by statute. The "bulk-billing" provisions of the *Health Insurance Act 1973* (Cth) ... provide an example of this' (at 123). In the case of bulk-billing it could be argued that the consideration given by the patient is the signed Medicare slip.

With regard to the second question, the issue of implied terms, Gaudron and McHugh JJ said:

> The doctor-patient relationship is contractual in origin. In general terms, "(a) doctor offers a patient diagnosis, advice and treatment", the objectives of which are "the prolongation of life, the restoration of the patient to full physical and mental health and the alleviation of pain". Given the informal nature of the relationship, however, a contract between a doctor and a patient rarely contains many express terms. Because that is so, the courts are obliged to formulate the rights and obligations of the parties to the contract. As Lord Wilberforce has put it, in cases where the parties to a contract have not attempted to spell out all the terms of their contract, the function of the court is "simply ... to establish what the contract is, the parties not having themselves fully stated the terms". The court does so by implying terms in the contract in accordance with established legal principles. (at 102)

One of the arguments that Ms Breen used was that there were various terms implied in her contract with Dr Williams that would give her a right to access her records. Brennan CJ wrote:

> The appellant argued for an implied term in the contract between the appellant and respondent that the respondent would act in the appellant's "best interests", even to the extent of testifying for her in litigation. The propounded "best interests" obligation was said to encompass an obligation to give a patient access to the doctor's records. The term implied in the ordinary contract does not go so far. It is limited by the subject matter to which the contract relates, namely, benefiting the health of the patient. (at 79-80)

The other members of the High Court came to similar conclusions. Thus it can be seen that a court will be cautious about implying too many obligations into the contract.

Similar issues were raised in *AAA v BBB* [2005] WASC 139. In this case a husband sued the medical practitioner who had been contracted by his wife to provide marriage counselling. In the course of providing that advice the doctor began a sexual relationship with the wife and the marriage fell apart. The husband sued the doctor in negligence for economic loss that he suffered as a result of the failed marriage. As part of this claim he argued that the doctor had an implied contractual duty to act in his patient's best interests and not commence an affair with her. Hasluck J dismissed this argument and said there was no such implied contractual duty nor was there an implied duty to consider the husband's interests.

The discussion of contract above has been, by necessity, brief and can only offer an overview of the law of contract as it affects the provision of health care. There a number of issues that have not been addressed such as contracts that are entered into under a mistake or misrepresentation; contracts formed under duress or undue influence; illegal contracts or contracts against public policy; and the statutory modification of contractual principles (such as under the *Trade Practices Act 1974* (Cth)).

Torts

Torts are civil wrongs. If one party does not act towards another party in accordance with proper societal standards, the law may provide a remedy. Examples of torts include negligence, defamation, nuisance and trespass (this list is not exhaustive). There is a significant overlap between many of the torts and the criminal law. This is because historically they developed out of the same legal rules as both areas deal with interferences to an individual's person or property. The difference between a crime and a tort is that the former is concerned with the protection of society and punishing of the wrongdoer while the latter involves some form of compensation for the harm done. Two torts – trespass to the person and negligence – are dealt with in some detail in Chapter 13 (trespass to the person) and Chapter 9 (negligence).

Criminal law

Broadly speaking, crime may be said to be conduct that the law proscribes. The law may declare that the conduct is an offence and a penalty may be prescribed. While parking offences and minor traffic violations may be technically described as crimes they are not generally regarded as criminal behaviour. Crimes are normally prosecuted by the state, although it is possible for an individual to commence criminal proceedings. An activity may be actionable as both a crime and a civil wrong.

One of the differences between criminal and civil law is the degree to which the fault must be shown. The criminal law requires proof *beyond reasonable doubt* whereas the civil standard is *on the balance of probabilities*. The burden of proving guilt is on the prosecution although, if a specific defence is relied upon by the accused, then it may be up to them to produce sufficient evidence to prove such defence. One of the fundamental principles of criminal law is that the accused *is innocent until proven guilty*. No person should be punished more than once for the same offence and they should not be placed in jeopardy of being tried twice.

In this section we do not attempt to discuss the criminal law in any comprehensive fashion. We merely attempt to illustrate the application of the criminal law by reference to some examples, namely fraud (as it relates to the *Health Insurance Act 1973* (Cth)) and manslaughter.

An example of criminal law: Medicare fraud

Dix et al note that 'the word *fraud* does not appear in the Health Insurance Act, but it is the expression commonly used to indicate offences under the Act which are seen to be of a fraudulent nature' (Dix, Errington et al 1996). It is an offence under s 128B of the Act to knowingly make a false statement in writing that was capable of being used in connection with a claim for payment under the *Health Insurance Act 1973*. The penalty for such an offence is a fine of up to $10,000 or imprisonment for five years, or both. There are a number of other similar offences under the Act.

One significant aspect of an offence under this provision is that it can have an effect on professional registration as well as the criminal penalty. In the South Australian case of *Medical Board of South Australia v Markey* (unreported, SADC, 19 December 1996), a medical practitioner had his registration cancelled after he had pleaded guilty in the Adelaide Magistrates Court to 10 counts alleging breaches of the *Health Insurance Act*. In a hearing considering disciplinary proceedings, the District Court said:

> It is difficult to envisage a circumstance where the behaviour of a medical practitioner which amounted to a deliberate and ongoing fraud upon the revenue could not attract the severest sanctions set out in the Act [*Health Insurance Act 1973* (Cth)]. This must be so to ensure that the public remains protected from others who may be so inclined to act, even where other tribunals, exercising other powers and protecting other interests, have considered the matter and imposed penalties. Thus, in our opinion, notwithstanding all that has been said in favour of the respondent, including his very long period

of practice and his professional and financial loss since the AAT delivered its decision in mid-1996, behaviour such as he has acknowledged is deserving of the severest condemnation. Pursuant to Section 58 of the Act [*Medical Practitioners Act 1983* (SA)] the order of the Tribunal is that the registration of the respondent as a medical practitioner on the general and specialist registers be cancelled.

An example of criminal law: Criminal negligence

Where a mistake causes the death of a patient, it is possible that the health-care provider could be prosecuted for criminal negligence. For this to happen there must have been not merely negligence, but gross negligence. The House of Lords considered this issue in a case concerning an anaesthetist – *R v Adomako* [1995] 1 AC 171.

The defendant was an anaesthetist who was charged with manslaughter after a patient who was undergoing surgery for a detached retina had a cardiac arrest and died due to anoxia because a connection in the anaesthetic equipment became disconnected. From the evidence there was an elapse of four and a half minutes between the disconnection of the endotracheal tube and the sounding of an alarm. Despite falls in the patient's heart rate and blood pressure, the anaesthetist thought that the alarm was caused by faulty equipment. At no stage before the cardiac arrest did the defendant check the integrity of the endotracheal tube connection. The jury found the defendant guilty on the charge of manslaughter. Experts stated that a competent anaesthetist should have noted the disconnection within 15 seconds – the conduct was said to be 'a gross dereliction of care' and 'abysmal'.

The House of Lords held that the question whether the degree of culpability was such that the anaesthetist should be liable to criminal sanctions was essentially a matter for the jury. Lord Mackay accepted that this was essentially a circular proposition: that criminal negligence is when a jury thinks the negligence was criminal. However, the House of Lords declined to offer a more precise definition. It did approve tests from earlier cases, which adopted the suggestion that gross negligence describes cases where the defendant has shown such disregard for the life and safety of others as to deserve punishment.

Adomako was applied in *R v Misra* [2004] EWCA Crim 2375, where two doctors appealed convictions for manslaughter after their patient died from toxic shock syndrome after routine knee surgery. Both doctors had been responsible for the post-operative care of the patient and had failed to realise that the patient was suffering from a post-operative infection. The doctors appealed on the basis that the law regarding negligent manslaughter was unclear and a breach of the *Human Rights Act 1998* (UK). The Court of Appeal disagreed and upheld the convictions. The court said:

> In our judgment the law is clear. The ingredients of the offence have been clearly defined, and the principles decided in the House of Lords in *Adomako*. They involve no uncertainty. The hypothetical citizen, seeking to know his position, would be advised that, assuming he owed a duty of care to the deceased which he had negligently broken, and that death resulted, he would

be liable to conviction for manslaughter if, on the available evidence, the jury was satisfied that his negligence was gross. A doctor would be told that grossly negligent treatment of a patient which exposed him or her to the risk of death, and caused it, would constitute manslaughter. (at [64])

Both *Misra* and *Adomako* were applied in *R v Pegios* [2008] NSWDC 104. In that case a dentist had been accused of manslaughter for the death of his patient under anaesthetic. It was alleged that the patient had been negligently over-dosed with sedatives. The dentist made an application to have the matter dismissed by the judge for lack of evidence, but the judge refused the application as the issue of whether there was gross negligence had to be decided by the jury.

These issues of negligent manslaughter will be examined as part of the upcoming trial of Jayant Patel, an Indian-born American surgeon, who was linked to the injury and death of several patients in the Queensland health system, particularly at Bundaberg Hospital. The Queensland Public Hospitals Commission of Inquiry recommended that that Queensland police investigate Dr Patel for several criminal offences, including negligent manslaughter (Davies 2005). At the time of writing Dr Patel has been charged with three counts of manslaughter (of 14 charges in total).

Recommended reading

In a work such as this, it has not been possible to examine all of the legal issues in relation to the topics we have covered in a great deal of detail. Further information will need to be investigated before forming a view about any particular issue. There have recently been a number of excellent publications available to assist health-care providers and students to find out more about the law as it relates to health care. Some of these works are listed below.

Books

Devereux, J (2006) *Australian Medical Law* (3rd ed). Sydney, Cavendish Publishing.
Skene, L (2008) *Law and Medical Practice: Rights, Duties, Claims and Defences* (3rd ed). Sydney, LexisNexis Butterworths.
Staunton, P and M Chiarella (2006) *Nursing and the Law* (6th ed). Sydney, Elsevier.
McIllwraith, J and B Madden (2006) *Health Care and the Law* (4th ed). Sydney, Law Book Co.

Looseleaf Service

Bate, PW, JC Dewdney and the CCH health and medical law editors *Australian Health & Medical Law Reporter* (Looseleaf Service). Sydney: CCH Australia (1988 – present).

Journals

Journal of Law and Medicine, published by LBC Information Services, Sydney
Australian Health Law Bulletin, published by Butterworths, Sydney

Online material

An excellent source of legal material, that has been consulted widely in preparing this book, can be found at the World Wide Web site of the Australasian Legal Information Institute (AustLII). AustLII is a joint facility of the Faculties of Law at the University of Technology, Sydney and the University of New South Wales. The aim of this organisation is to be a source of all Australian primary legal material. The URL of AustLII is <http://www.austlii.edu.au/>.

References

Austin, J (1971) *The province of jurisprudence determined and the uses of the study of jurisprudence*. London, Weidenfeld and Nicolson.

Bentham, J (1789) 'An Introduction to the principles of Morals and Legislation'. *A Fragment on Government and an Introduction to the Principles of Morals and Legislation*. W Harrison (1960), Oxford, Basil Blackwell.

British Medical Association (2001) *The medical profession and human rights: handbook for a changing agenda*. London, Zed Books.

Chiarella, M (2002) *The Legal and Professional Status of Nursing*. Sydney, Elsevier.

Davies, G (2005) *Queensland Public Hospitals Commission of Inquiry* <http://www.qphci.qld.gov.au/>.

Editorial (2004) 'How complicit are doctors in abuses of detainees?'. *Lancet* **364**: 1741.

Finnis, J (1980) *Natural Law and Natural Rights*. Oxford, Clarendon Press.

Fuller, L (1969) *The Morality of Law*. New Haven, Yale University Press.

Gilligan, C (1982) *In a different voice: psychological theory and women's development*. Cambridge, Mass, Harvard University press.

Grotius, H (1625, trans 1925) *De Jure Belli ac Pacis*. New York, Bobbs-Merrill.

Hart, HLA (1994) *The Concept of Law* (2nd ed). Clarendon Press, Oxford.

Kennedy, H (2004) *Just Law: The changing face of justice – and why it matters to us all*. London, Chatto & Windus.

MacKinnon, CA (1989) *Towards a Feminist Theory of the State*. London, Harvard University Press.

Mason, A (1988) 'The Use and Abuse of Precedent'. *Australian Bar Review* **4**(2): 93.

Meyerson, D (2007) *Understanding Jurisprudence*, Routledge-Cavendish, Oxford

Pufendorf, S (1994) *The political writings of Samuel Pufendorf*, edited by CL Carr, translated by MJ Seidler. New York, Oxford University Press.

Raz, J (1977) 'The Rule of Law and its Virtue'. *Law Quarterly Review* **93**: 195.

Srivastava, DK, T Deklin et al (1996) *Introduction to Australian Law*. Sydney, LBC Information Services.

Stewart, C (2004) 'The Rule of Law and the Tinkerbell Effect: Theoretical Considerations, Criticisms and Justifications for the Rule of Law'. *Macquarie Law Journal* **4**: 135.

CHAPTER 5

INTRODUCTION TO PRINCIPLE-BASED ETHICS

Principle-based ethics is an approach to ethics that specifies a number of rules or 'principles' to guide moral actions. Systems of principle-based ethics have been described by Beauchamp and Childress (Beauchamp and Childress 2009), Engelhardt (Engelhardt 1996), Veatch (Veatch 1981), Gillon (Gillon 1994) and Pellegrino and Thomasma (Pellegrino and Thomasma 1981) The most notable example is the 'four-principles' approach developed by Beauchamp and Childress (Beauchamp and Childress 2009).

Beauchamp and Childress derive their approach from three basic theses: that morality is concerned with right and wrong human conduct; that a universal, non-relative core exists within all morality that they call 'common morality'; and that appeals can be made to this common morality by suggesting either that people should behave in this way or do behave in this way. The four principles described by Beauchamp and Childress lie within the domain of 'common morality', that is, they are accepted as universal and non-relative. Because they are part of common morality, they are implicit in most theories of ethics, and they form a strong basis for ethical analysis and action (Beauchamp & Childress 2009).

Beauchamp and Childress describe a complex analytical framework including 'principles, 'rules', 'rights', 'virtues' and emotions. The principles provide the most comprehensive and general moral guidance. The rules are more specific, more restricted in scope, and provide clearer action guides.

Beauchamp and Childress recognise four basic moral principles that operate in health care – 'autonomy', 'beneficence', 'non-maleficence' and 'justice'. The principle of autonomy states that people should be allowed to be self-governing and make decisions for themselves. The principle of beneficence states that health workers (and others) should be actively altruistic. The principle of non-maleficence states that health workers (and others) should avoid doing harm. The principle of justice suggests that the goods that are available should be shared fairly. Each of these principles is derived both common morality and philosophical reflection.

Each principle is said to be 'prima facie', meaning that in all situations there needs to be consideration of their specific context (specification), and no principle takes automatic precedence over any other. Each principle needs to be balanced with other principles, as obligations that are derived from one principle may conflict with those derived from another. There is no predetermined hierarchy of the principles; each is essentially of equal importance and may be given different priority by different individuals in different situations. As balancing addresses the weight and strength of each principle it requires good arguments and consideration of outcomes. Ethical principles should therefore not be seen as a set of rules to be obeyed, or as a formula for deriving a single right answer, but as a framework for making justifiable clinical-ethical decisions.

It can be seen that principle-based ethics is pluralistic, as it can incorporate a range of moral stands, but at the same time it acknowledges the possibility of shared values. It cannot provide a single, reliable way to resolve all moral disagreement. Indeed, disagreement may arise over facts, scope, judgments about principles, specification and balancing of principles, and because there are genuine moral dilemmas there are times that disagreement may be unavoidable.

We believe that principle-based ethics provides an accessible means for exploring ethical issues in health care, particularly those issues that arise in clinical practice. While principle-based approaches to ethics offer an incomplete understanding of the ethical domain, and at times may not be the most appropriate means for exploring ethical concerns, they do provide sufficient structure and language that moral discourse can at least *begin*.

Principle-based ethics arose in part from the examination of medical practice in Western countries in the late 20th century, and is influenced by the culture of that time and place. One major impetus for the development of biomedical ethics at that time was the realisation that medical authority often usurped the rights of individual patients. In response to this realisation, both law and ethics placed primary emphasis on the rights of the individual and hence on the concept of individual autonomy. Indeed, one of the major criticisms of principle-based ethics is that it has placed too much emphasis on individual autonomy.

In his final editorial at the *Journal of Medical Ethics*, Gillon suggested that the primary emphasis of bioethics in the 21st century will shift from autonomy to justice (Gillon 2001). The reason for this is that it is increasingly apparent that the rising costs of health care for richer people in many societies appear to be restricting the health choices of poorer people. In addition, there is an increasing awareness that the health situation in the third world cannot be ignored in the West as was done previously. We will commence discussion of the four principles by looking in more detail at the concept of justice.

The principle of justice

'Justice' refers to standards and expectations which any society holds concerning relations between the members of that society; and the rights and services that are due to any member of that society. The word 'justice' suggests concepts such as fairness, rightness and equity

Modern ideas about justice began with the philosophical explorations of the ancient Greeks. Aristotle distinguished between a legal sense of justice (the concept used in courts of law and among the judiciary) and a more general sense of the concept.

Much of the fabric of democratic societies rests on the understanding that litigation should be a last resort to solving problems of justice. Some would even suggest that litigation is a very poor mechanism for ensuring justice. Some laws may be open to manipulation by power brokers and can even be used to flout and confound justice. Indeed, many societies possess unjust laws that do not guarantee fairness but perpetuate its opposite. To that degree, such laws fail to comply with the ethics of the rule of law. When such laws are unjust, it is just to fight them. Some lawyers (particularly the natural lawyers) would argue that such laws have no force or legitimacy. So far as the philosopher is concerned, this suggests that the general sense of justice might be superior to the positivistic legal sense of following legal rules, regardless of the moral quality of those rules.

In the 17th century, the British social philosopher John Locke (1632-1704) considered the hallmarks of the just society to be the establishment of a means to guarantee equality such that no individual would suffer from subordination or subjection (Benn and Peters 1975). He believed that humans were naturally free, equal and independent, and that everyone had natural rights to their life, health and the fruits of their own labour. Civil society grows out of this state of nature in a form of social contract, so that natural liberties can be further protected by government. To that extent government is only legitimate when it respects these pre-government, natural rights. Laws which offend them should be disobeyed. The American Declaration of Independence, in which it is declared that all people were created equal, was strongly influenced by this philosophy. In the domain of health-care ethics, justice as fairness is not usually taken to mean that every person must be offered identical service and treatment. It does, however, suggest that all persons – irrespective of wealth, power, status, religion or affiliation – should be offered fair access to services which accord with their health needs.

The philosopher David Hume believed that what constituted justice could only be examined by weighing up the competing claims of other people. Hume believed that this was necessary because of the obvious limitations of human and social life. He believed that every person could be accorded unlimited access to the goods of society only if all material things were plentiful. Because this is not the case, resources need to be distributed on the basis of need and not on the basis of wealth, power, ethnicity, religion, gender or social class (Gillon 1994). The implication of these ideas for health care is that, although we cannot hope to satisfy everybody's needs, the resources that are available should be apportioned on the basis of an impartial indicator such as 'need', rather than on the basis of favouritism or discrimination.

The most influential account of the concept of justice found in recent philosophical writings comes from John Rawls' book *A Theory of Justice*. Rawls begins his discussion of the concept of justice in the following way:

> Justice is the first virtue of social institutions, as truth is of systems of thought. A theory however elegant and economical must be rejected or revised if it is untrue; likewise laws and institutions no matter how efficient and well arranged must be reformed or abolished if they are unjust. Each person possesses an inviolability founded on justice that even the welfare of society as a whole cannot override. For this reason justice denies that the loss of

freedom for some is made right by a greater good shared by others. It does not allow that the sacrifices imposed on a few are outweighed by the larger sum of advantages enjoyed by many ... an injustice is tolerable only when it is necessary to avoid an even greater injustice. Being first virtues of human activities, truth and justice are uncompromising. (Rawls 1971)

Rawls' concept of justice is based (like Locke's theory and those of others like Thomas Hobbes and Jean Jacques Rousseau) on the idea of a 'social contract'. Rawls believed that the basic principles of a just and fair society could be discerned if people engaged in a thought experiment where they could imagine an *original position* where the state has not yet formed and where their identities and characteristics are not yet known. Rawls said that this *veil of ignorance* would prevent us from knowing who we will be in society. So, for instance, if we were to live in Ancient Rome we might like to be a Roman Emperor, but we would be much more likely to be a slave. It would be inadvisable, therefore, to decide to set up the society of Ancient Rome as an ideal society.

Rawls suggests that the most rational society that could be set up in this way would be based upon two principles. First, each person should have an equal right to the most extensive basic liberty compatible with a similar liberty for others (the *liberty principle*). Secondly, social and economic inequalities would only be allowed if they are both (a) reasonably expected to be to everyone's advantage including the worst off members of society, and (b) attached to positions and offices open to all (the *difference principle*). Rawls also referred to the notion of the *maximum principle* where unequal distribution of resources could still be just if it maximised the benefit to those who have the worst allocation of resources. Rawls does not appear to see a need for any publicly shared morality apart from these principles – each person should be free to pursue the goods that they choose, as long as they abide by these principles. This is one of the reasons that his ideas are so attractive in today's multicultural society.

An example of how these principles would be applied is as follows. If we consider the Australian health system, everyone is guaranteed a certain level of health care by the government. A follower of Rawls might see some value in adding an additional system of optional private health care, even if this would markedly improve the health of only a few people in society. This would be seen as just if the option of private care were open to all, and if the addition of private cover improved the lot of all people (perhaps by decreasing the waiting lists in the public system). It would be unjust if the costs of introducing such a system dragged money away from the public system, and hence resulted in some people being worse off.

Unfortunately, we do not live in a world that is entirely just. From a global perspective it is clear that basic ideas of justice are not applied to health care, and that a fair distribution of health resources do not occur worldwide. Within Australia, there are groups such as Indigenous Australians and the elderly who have great health needs that are not being met. Within the health professions there is an on-going debate about whether the role of health professionals should include working for greater social justice and worldwide equity, or whether their role is confined to distributing the resources that are already available (Gruen, Pearson et al 2004). These questions are thrown into greater prominence when health professionals are asked to comment on issues such as the health of refugees, the value of aid programs, or upon Aboriginal health. Many professional bodies now have policies about these topics and are prepared to advocate for justice on a more global scale.

The principle of respect for autonomy

The word 'autonomy' is derived from the Greek *autos* (self) and *nomos* (rule) and has been variously interpreted as self-determination, liberty, rights and 'free will'. There are many different theories and definitions of autonomy, but they generally all make some reference to individual liberty or independence, and the capacity for intentional or rational action (Dworkin 1988; Childress 1990). The most famous expression of the principle of respect for autonomy comes from John Stuart Mill: 'Over himself, over his own body and mind, the individual is sovereign' (Mill 1859).

Autonomy is a concept that has far broader application than in bioethics – it is the value that liberal democracies place on individuals controlling their own lives. In contemporary bioethics the principle of autonomy asserts that humans have a right to non-interference when making decisions about themselves. This perspective is often referred to as the principle of respect for persons because it promotes the view that the individual is the rightful determiner of his or her own life. It should be noted, however, that the principle of justice places some constraints upon the principle of autonomy – a person's autonomous actions should not restrict the autonomous actions of others beyond what is fair.

In Western medicine it is widely perceived that there is an imbalance in the power relationships between doctors (and other therapists) and patients. This imbalance has the potential to decrease the autonomy of individual patients, especially if therapists attempt to make decisions without the input of patients. The original response to these concerns was to insist upon the process of consent – whereby competent, informed patients could express their autonomy by either giving or refusing consent to the treatment suggested by their therapists.

The legal concept of informed consent has greatly influenced the ethical debate about autonomy. In order to give consent properly, the legal require-ments are that the person giving consent be fully informed, mentally competent and under no duress. In medical care, these are sometimes seen as sufficient requirements for individuals to make autonomous decisions; but there are many other factors that are required if autonomy is to be taken seriously. These include factors such as adequate time to make decisions, an environment that is not perceived as threatening or hostile, and the presence of adequate social support.

The concept of informed consent is widely supported, but it has also been suggested that a better approach to assuring patient autonomy would be an approach known as *shared decision-making*. In this model of decision-making the autonomy of the patient is seen as a more active principle than simply con-senting or not consenting to the doctor's suggestions. It is hoped that such a model would better reflect the complexity and individuality of the relationship between patients and their therapists (Brock 1991). Unfortunately, the concept of shared decision-making is very poorly defined (Moumjid, Gafni et al 2007), and in most situations it remains an aspiration rather than a reality (Holmes-Rovner, Valade et al 2000; Edwards, Wood et al 2005).

Part of the reason for this is that shared decision-making is difficult. Respect for patients' autonomy does not necessarily imply a value-neutral role for health workers; but it does require a delicate balancing of roles. Therapists need to set limits on the extent to which they interfere with patients' treatment choices, even if those choices may be seen as ultimately unhealthy. Also, different patients have very different attitudes towards the relationship that they wish to have with health-care professionals. Some patients require extremely detailed information about alternative approaches to their condition; others prefer to maintain a distance from their therapists, and others autonomously authorise health workers to make all treatment decisions for them. A model of shared decision-making should recognise such differences, and also recognise that health professionals are not simply value-neutral providers of facts, but are independent moral agents who have their own values and beliefs in relation to health and disease.

Deber and colleagues undertook an interesting study in which they divided the process of medical decision-making into two parts – 'problem solving' and 'decision-making' (Deber, Kraetschmer et al 1996). Patients' attitudes towards 'problem solving' were assessed by questions such as 'who should determine the diagnosis?', 'who should determine the treatment options?' and 'who should determine the risks and benefits of treatment?'. Patients overwhelmingly suggested that the doctor should be responsible for these aspects of care. The investigators also assessed 'decision-making', using questions such as 'who should determine what is done' and 'who should decide how acceptable risks and benefits are?' Patients mostly thought that decisions about these aspects of care should be shared. The authors noted that if patients are merely given a choice between 'autonomy', in which they are given a stack of textbooks and are told to figure it out themselves, and 'paternalism', in which they must abide by the decisions of a provider, it is not surprising that some will reject total autonomy. But the reality is more complex, and most patients prefer to delegate some aspects of medical decision-making to their health-care professionals but to be involved in other aspects.

Is it possible for autonomy to go too far? A number of recent articles have looked at the condition known as apotemnophilia – the desire to have a perfectly normal limb amputated. Recent publicity has meant that increasing numbers of people have requested this and a number of surgeons are willing to provide it (Elliott 2000). In another recent case, a man advertised that he wished to be murdered and cannibalised, and achieved his wish when he met someone with complementary desires (Dalrymple 2004). In the health sphere, there have been recent debates on whether women should be allowed to have elective caesarean sections simply because they request it, or be given the option of avoiding menstruation altogether by hormonal suppression.

The pre-eminent role of autonomy in contemporary bioethics has been criticised in the ethics literature. Some authors maintain that health-care decisions should depend less upon respecting autonomy and more on providing care and compassion (Thomasma 1984).

Alastair Campbell has argued that dependency, rather than autonomy, should be the most fundamental principle in health care and bioethics. He notes that illness inevitably involves a loss of freedom or the restriction of choice and argues that:

> What is required in the place of such an overstress on autonomy is a reaffirmation of the beneficent aspects of health care – those aspects which provide protection, nurture and support to those who need a restoration of their power to cope unaided. … Much of the time the ethical challenge is not to demand autonomous responses from ill people, but to find ways of moving them from an inappropriate and self-perpetuating dependency, to a restorative and releasing one. To do this we require more than simply the tools of rational analysis of possible choices of action. We need a relationship of mutual respect and trust between the providers and recipients of health care, based on a communal value which regards care for the weak and vulnerable as a fundamental ethical imperative. (Campbell 1994; Campbell and Lustig 1994)

Others, notably communitarian and feminist theorists, have rejected the primacy of autonomy – arguing that the focus on individualism and independence diminishes the importance of human relationships, community, caring and interdependence (Sandel 1982; MacIntyre 1984; Sherwin 1992; Mackenzie and Stoljar 1999). Rather than rejecting the notion of autonomy altogether, these writers argue instead that it is only the narrow libertarian construction of autonomy that is the problem and that, if conceptualised in a richer and more socially contextualised manner, autonomy remains central to the way we understand agency, freedom, vulnerability and oppression. This idea that autonomy is socially dependent is sometimes called 'relational autonomy'. Mackenzie and Stoljar define relational autonomy as follows:

> The term 'relational autonomy' … does not refer to a single unified conception of autonomy but is rather an umbrella term, designating a range of related perspectives. Those perspectives are premised on a shared conviction; the conviction that persons are socially embedded and those agents' identities are formed within the context of social relationships and shaped by a complex of intersecting social determinants, such as race, class, gender and ethnicity. Thus the focus of relational approaches is to analyse the implications of the intersubjective and social dimensions of selfhood and identity for conceptions of individual autonomy and moral and political agency. (Mackenzie and Stoljar 1999)

Similar arguments have been suggested by MacIntyre and Callaghan who argue that an individual's actions and beliefs are comprehensible only within their social, cultural or institutional context, and cannot be understood without consideration of these factors (Callaghan 1984; MacIntyre 1984). Indeed, for Sherwin, autonomy only has meaning if there are sufficient social and political support structures in place to provide individuals with sufficient freedom that they have meaningful choice (Sherwin 1992). The importance of relational views of autonomy are that they shift the focus from rationality, capacity and choice to social and political determinants of autonomy and agency, and the role played by social context, institutions and health-care providers in developing and maintaining autonomy (Dodds 2000).

Some non-Western philosophers see the emphasis on autonomy as being culturally biased – as their cultures do not place such value on the rights of the individual (Gbadegisin 1993; Qui 1993; Glick 1997). While these criticisms may have some validity, they should not lead one to reject autonomy altogether. Even in cross-cultural settings, most individuals value their own autonomy to some extent.

The final, and perhaps most significant, objection to the emphasis on autonomy is that in both health care and bioethics our primary concern should be not with autonomy, but *agency*. Whereas autonomy is concerned primarily with the capacity to choose, agency is concerned with the attributes and capacities that enable the expression of realistic choice and its enactment. Agency, therefore, can be expressed non-verbally and non-rationally through work, creativity, relationships and so forth, and requires physical, mental and relational capacities that may be determined by one's cultural learning, environment and personal experiences. Agency is essential for well-being, and illness inevitably causes disruption of agency – even where autonomy appears to be left intact (Ryff and Singer 2000). Thus, to fully and more richly appreciate the impact of illness on an individual, we should be concerned with how it has restricted their agency.

The principle of non-maleficence

The principle of non-maleficence can be summed up by the famous saying, *'primum non nocere'*, which means 'above all, do no harm'. The principle is also stated in the Hippocratic Oath where it says: 'I will use treatment to help the sick according to my ability and judgment, but I will never use it to injure or wrong them'. In philosophical terms, non-maleficence accords with Mill's harm principle and with contractarianism, which both suggest that the state and society should not attempt to shape all citizens' lives and that the first obligation we have is to leave one another alone so that we each may live as we choose.

Medical care can cause a wide range of harms, many of them difficult to predict. In addition to harms to the individual, medical care can also cause harms to relatives and other members of the community, the economy and the environment. (The so-called 'triple bottom line'.)

As with the other principles, the principle of non-maleficence may sometimes be overridden. In modern medicine people are often hurt, in particular people often undergo dangerous and painful procedures in the hope that this will lead to improvements in the long run. These situations can be seen as cases where autonomy and beneficence take precedence over non-maleficence.

The principle of beneficence

One of the principles expressed in the Hippocratic Oath was 'I will use treatment for the benefit of the sick, according to my ability and judgment'. This statement expressed what is now known as the principle of beneficence. Beneficence can be defined as active well-doing, altruism, or conduct aimed at the good and well-being of others. It is interesting to note that whereas the other three main principles of health-care ethics can be derived from considerations of justice, the same is not true of the principle of beneficence. Instead, doing good can either be thought of as a duty arising out of the role of the health professions or as arising out of other ethical concepts. Beneficence, therefore, can be seen as both a principle and a virtue.

The extent to which beneficence is a natural part of being human has been the subject of many debates in the history of ethics. The 'naturalists' have argued that doing good has proven more beneficial for everybody than doing harm, and so it is part of the natural processes that people should be beneficent towards each other. The 'hedonists' have argued that beneficence is just a covert form of self-seeking: the 'do-gooder' really wants praise, approval and an inner good feeling and cares little for the recipient of the goodness. The 'Jansenists' have argued that beneficence is totally at odds with corrupt human nature and therefore is impossible without direct divine intervention and help.

The principle of beneficence in health care should not be interpreted as doing something beyond the call of duty or from the goodness of one's heart. It was central to the Hippocratic ideals that physicians were not created for their own glory and honour but purely for the good of society: and that any honour, status or remuneration which they gained was said to only heighten the degree of obligation which physicians had to society. This ethos has carried over to the present day in a much diluted form, but it is commonly believed that the duty that health-care workers have to provide care is quite beyond any duty which non-medical or non-health professionals might have to do the same.

Health professions have responsibilities towards society in addition to the responsibilities that they owe the individual patient. Health workers are employed by society to provide medical care that is both appropriate and affordable. The practical expression of beneficence therefore requires judiciousness and genuine concern for the well-being of the total society. This must include the wise use of scarce resources, and some recognition of the financial limits to clinical medicine. In other words, beneficence towards individual patients, like the other major moral principles, presents an obligation that may be overridden by other considerations.

There is a very strong tradition within Western medicine that suggests that health-care workers should do *all* that is within their power to benefit patients. But the principle of beneficence requires that practitioners provide both appropriate treatment and an assurance that treatment will not produce more harms than good. Expensive technology that is used to treat patients may often appear to onlookers to be overly burdensome or not efficacious and in many instances it seems that the principle of beneficence may actually be contravened by the use of technology. For example, patients who are resuscitated following cardiac

87

arrest often die soon afterwards from complications of their illness or treatment; and infants placed in neonatal care nurseries may have severe malformations which require multiple surgical procedures. Nevertheless, technology is becoming increasingly refined, and treatments that are extremely costly are becoming increasingly feasible. In such a climate it is necessary to be very meticulous in defining the obligations that are owed to the principle of beneficence.

If a patient's autonomy is overridden due to a concern for beneficence, this is known as paternalism. Paternalism has been divided by some authors into two forms, based upon the competency of the patient, and the permanency and seriousness of the harm that may accrue. 'Weak' paternalism consists of beneficent action towards people who are clearly not in a position to make informed decisions themselves (Feinberg 1973). For example, decisions might be made in the perceived best interests of an intellectually disabled person who is unable to make autonomous decisions. By contrast, 'strong' paternalism is an approach based upon the supposition that it is sometimes ethical and proper for the health-care worker to effect beneficent actions even if the patient is competent and disagrees with the decision made. For example, there are several cases reported in which doctors have rendered women sterile in the belief that they should not bear further children, when the women themselves have wanted to continue child-bearing. Most modern ethicists accept the need for weak paternalism, but consider strong paternalism to be indefensible. (There has also been discussion of 'maternalism' – getting someone to do what you want by inducing a guilty conscience (Häyry 1991).)

Many bioethical issues involve a consideration of both non-maleficence and beneficence and, indeed, some philosophers suggest that they are different aspects of the same concept. However, it is usual to distinguish between them because 'doing good sometimes seems to conflict with not doing harm in relation to the same person (eg euthanasia) or to different persons (eg non-therapeutic research). And in cases of conflict, the duty of non-maleficence ... has priority' (Childress 1982).

A good example of the difference between the duties of beneficence and non-maleficence can be found in a debate about experiments in Africa aimed at developing new ways to prevent the spread of HIV from mothers to their babies. In 1994 it was shown that a complex and expensive regimen of drugs administered to pregnant women and their babies reduced maternal-foetal transmission of HIV from 25.5% to 8.3%. This regime had become commonplace in the Western world, but it was too expensive to use in the third world – indeed, to treat one woman cost 100-500 times the total health-care funds available per person per year in many countries (Halsey, Sommer et al 1997). A number of experiments were proposed to see whether there were cheaper ways to prevent maternal-foetal transmission of HIV. For the sake of these experiments it was proposed that women should be randomly allocated to receive either one of the new protocols or to receive no treatment, and that the outcome for the babies of these two groups of mothers should then be compared.

From an ethical point of view, it seems likely that no woman or baby would have suffered additional harm from entering such an experiment. Those who received the new treatment may have obtained some benefits, those who did not would have been no worse off than they would have been otherwise. So according to the principle of non-maleficence, there is nothing ethically wrong with such a trial. However, these experiments caused a great deal of controversy, because critics argued that the triallists had a duty to beneficence that outweighed their duty to non-maleficence. They suggested that it was unethical for half the study group to receive no treatment, when it was known that a treatment was available that would decrease the risk of HIV transmission. They argued therefore that the experiment should compare the new methods with the expensive previous regime that was only used in the West and was not available in Africa.

The example above demonstrates that beneficence is sometimes seen as an obligation that is added on top of non-maleficence, but is less binding. One cannot ethically push an innocent person off a bridge (non-maleficence), but one might have a lesser obligation to jump in to save them if they have fallen themselves (beneficence). In health care, the ethical issues of non-maleficence and beneficence are particularly apparent in decisions regarding the institution of dangerous therapy, or withdrawal of therapy that is no longer thought to be beneficial.

Conclusion

Principle-based ethics has been criticised by some because it does not provide a general theory of morality nor precisely specify what health-care workers should or should not do in every specific clinical context (Holmes 1990). Others have criticised the principle-based approach as being insufficient to account for complex systems, institutions, public health and government, too abstract, too rationalistic and too removed from the psychological milieu in which moral choices are made (Pellegrino 1994; Callahan 2003; Harris 2003). (We are in partial agreement with each of these criticisms.) In response to such criticism a number of philosophers have explored means for complementing, supplementing or systematising the four *prima facie* principles (Engelhardt and Rie 1988).

We believe that the great strengths of the principle-based approaches to ethics are that they are simple, provide a jumping-off point for those entering ethical debates and implicitly recognise that conflict and uncertainty are integral and unavoidable aspects of health care and of ethics. According to Beauchamp and Childress:

> Principles do not function as precise action guides that inform us in each circumstance how to act in the way more detailed rules do. Principles are general guides that leave considerable room for judgment in specific cases and that provide substantive guidance for the development of more detailed rules and policies. This limitation is no defect in principles; rather, it is a part of the moral life in which we are expected to take responsibility for the way we bring principles to bear in our judgments about particular cases. (Beauchamp and Childress 1994)

While it is true that principle-based ethics does not provide a moral hierarchy for explicit decision-making, it does provide a moral language and an analytical framework for bioethics that can be incorporated within many people's individual moral, religious, political and philosophical perspectives (ie it is pluralistic) (Gillon 1994).

Critics of principle-based ethics sometimes overlook the fact that principles are only broad action guides. The model of Beauchamp and Childress shows how we can use such broad guidelines through a process of specification and balancing to develop more action-oriented rules to specify what we should do, who should be involved and how we should go about it.

Within this book, we will provide a principle-based approach to ethical thinking, but at the same time attempt to recognise the many other perspectives and disciplines that crowd the 'ethical space'.

References

Beauchamp, T and J Childress (2009) *Principles of biomedical ethics* (6th ed). New York, Oxford University Press.

Beauchamp, TL and J Childress (1994) *Principles of biomedical ethics*. Oxford, Oxford University Press.

Benn, SA and R Peters (1975) *Social principles and the democratic state*. London, George Allen and Unwin.

Brock, DW (1991) 'Shared decision making'. *Kennedy Institute of Ethics Journal* **1**: 28-47.

Callaghan, D (1984) 'Autonomy: A moral good not a moral obsession'. *Hastings Cent Rep* **14**(5): 40-2.

Callahan, D (2003) 'Principlism and communitarianism'. *J Med Ethics* **29**(5): 287-91.

Campbell, A (1994) Dependency: the foundational value in medical ethics *Medicine and moral reasoning*. KW Fulford, GR Gillett and JM Soskice. Cambridge, Cambridge University Press: 184-92.

Campbell, CS and BA Lustig (1994) *Duties to others*. Dordrecht; Boston, Kluwer Academic Publishers.

Childress, J (1982) *Who should decide? Paternalism in health care*. New York, Oxford University Press.

Childress, J (1990) 'The place of autonomy in bioethics'. *Hastings Cent Rep* **20**(1): 12-17.

Dalrymple, T (2004) 'The case for cannibalism (Why not if everything is permissible for consenting adults?)', <www.freerepublic.com>.

Deber, RB, N Kraetschmer et al (1996) 'What role do patients wish to take in decision making?' *Arch Int Med* **56**: 1414-20.

Dodds, S (2000) Choice and control in feminist bioethics. *Relational Autonomy: Feminist perspectives on autonomy, agency and the social self*. C Mackenzie and N Stoljar. New York, Oxford University Press: 214.

Dworkin, G (1988) *The theory and practice of autonomy*. New York, Cambridge University Press.

Edwards, E, F Wood et al (2005) 'Shared decision making and risk communication in practice: A qualitative study of GPs' experiences'. *Br J Gen Practice* **55**(510): 6-13.

Elliott, A (2000) 'A new way to be mad'. *The Atlantic Monthly*.

Engelhardt, HT (1996) *The foundations of bioethics*. New York, Oxford University Press.

Engelhardt, HT and MA Rie (1988) 'Morality and the medical-industrial complex: A code of ethics for the mass marketing of health care'. *N Engl J Med* **319**: 1086-9.

Feinberg, J (1973) *Social Philosophy*. Englewood Cliffs, NJ, Prentice Hall.

Gbadegisin, S (1993) 'Bioethics and culture: An African perspective'. *Bioethics* **7**(257-62).

Gillon, R (1994) 'Medical ethics: Four principles plus attention to scope'. *BMJ* **309**: 184-8.

Gillon, R (2001) 'After 20 years, some reflections and farewell'. *J Med Ethics* **27**(2): 75-7.

Glick, SM (1997) 'Unlimited human autonomy – a cultural bias?' *N Engl J Med* **336**(13): 954-6.

Gruen, RL, SD Pearson et al (2004) 'Physician-Citizens – Public Roles and Professional Obligations'. *JAMA* **291**(1): 94-8.

Halsey, NA, A Sommer et al (1997) 'Ethics and international research'. *BMJ* **315**(7114): 965-6.

Harris, J (2003) 'In praise of unprincipled ethics'. *J Med Ethics* **29**(5): 303-6.

Häyry, H (1991) *The Limits of Medical Paternalism*. London, Routledge.

Holmes-Rovner, M, D Valade, et al (2000) 'Implementing shared decision-making in routine practice: barriers and opportunities'. *Health Expectations* **3**(3): 182-91.

MacIntyre, A (1984) *After virtue: A study in moral theory*. Notre Dame, Ind, University of Notre Dame Press.

Mackenzie, C and N Stoljar (1999) *Relational autonomy : feminist perspectives on autonomy, agency, and the social self*. New York, Oxford University Press.

Mill, J (1859) *On Liberty*.

Moumjid, N, A Gafni et al (2007) 'Shared decision making in the medical encounter: are we all talking about the same thing?' *Medical Decision Making* **27**: 539-46.

Pellegrino, ED (1994) 'The metamorphosis of medical ethics'. *Arch Pathol Lab Med* **118**: 1065-9.

Pellegrino, ED and DC Thomasma (1981) *For the patients' good: The restoration of beneficence in health care*. New York, Oxford University Press.

Qui, R (1993) 'What has bioethics to offer the developing countries?' *Bioethics* **7**: 108-25.

Rawls, J (1971) *A theory of justice*. Cambridge, Mass, Harvard University Press.

Ryff, C and B Singer (2000) 'Interpersonal flourishing: a positive health agenda for the new millennium'. *Personality and Social Psychology Review* **4**: 30-44.

Sandel, M (1982) *Liberalism and the limits of justice*. Cambridge, Cambridge University Press.

Sherwin, S (1992) *No longer patient: Feminist ethics and health care*. Philadelphia, Temple University Press.

Thomasma, DC (1984) 'Dependency and the care of the very old'. *J Am Geriatr Soc* **12**: 906-14.

Veatch, R (1981) *A theory of medical ethics*. New York, Basic Books.

CHAPTER 6

CLINICAL ETHICS AND ETHICAL DECISION-MAKING

Students of the health sciences often encounter great difficulty when they attempt to apply their knowledge of medical ethics to the specific demands of particular clinical problems (Hoffmaster 1989). Difficulties may arise either because health workers lack strategies to relate their ethical-knowledge-base to the ethical aspects of patients' problems, or because they lack a process for reasoning through ethical aspects of clinical cases. Failure to systematically address ethical issues in clinical contexts can create what seem to be intractable conflicts, yet open communication and a systematic approach to clinical ethical reasoning can often easily lead to resolution (Savulescu 1997).

Clinical ethics cannot realistically provide answers to all the moral questions that arise in health care. In any institution, different individuals will have different moral perspectives that reflect their own life experiences and belief systems. Moral pluralism is unavoidable in modern society, and a discourse that incorporates many ways of thinking (so-called 'wide reflective equilibrium') is often the most appropriate means for ethical decision-making (Habermas 1992).

It is an inevitable consequence of pluralism that there may be many right solutions to any single problem or issue. This in turn may lead to either acceptance of difference, or intractable conflict. The capacity to think broadly around a subject and discern the various possibilities has been termed the 'moral imagination' (Johnson 1993; Scott 1997). Unfortunately in many situations health professionals fail to recognise that there may be more than one solution to a problem.

Perhaps the real value of clinical ethics is to provide a process for ethical deliberation, rather than to define the outcomes of decision-making. Health professionals often confront difficult clinical decisions in which there appears to be no clear right or wrong answer, yet they are still able to move through a process that will arrive at a considered judgment. In other words, even though there may not be a right answer, there are ways of thinking that are better, more rigorous and inclusive, than others. It is no different when faced with difficult moral choices. Health-care professionals can learn to systematically analyse the ethical dimensions of their work to solve ethical problems, even where there may be a number of differing and sometimes conflicting moral perspectives that need to be taken into account.

Ethical thinking and problem-solving

Contemporary discussions of clinical ethical decision-making often present it as a type of problem-solving. However, ethical thinking must begin (and end) with the patient. In philosophical terms, this comes down to three main factors. First is recognising 'the other' – that is, the values, perspectives, experiences and narrative of another person (Hendley 2000). Second is the need to empathise with that person. Third is the need to have compassion for them (Nussbaum 2001).

With this in mind, a number of models for ethical decision-making have been developed. These models all present orderly approaches to identifying and evaluating ethical issues in health care. Each model of ethical reasoning has strengths and weaknesses and each works best in a particular context. Legal or judicial approaches to ethics work well in relation to international issues, such as global patents, or in relation to human rights; principle-based, relational, discursive or care-based approaches to ethical reasoning all work best in relation to the clinical encounter; and critical decision-analysis or stakeholder analysis work best at the level of health policy or at the point where micro- and macroethics collide. In fact, no single approach to moral reasoning will consistently resolve all moral disagreements, reflecting the complex character of moral life and the need for compromise as an indispensable aspect of moral discourse. Despite their shortcomings, frameworks for clinical ethical analysis are valuable because they make internal reasoning processes visible, and encourage reflection and rigour.

One example of a model for ethical reasoning has been described by Jonsen, Siegler and Winslade in their text, *Clinical Ethics*. In it they outline a systematic process for identifying all morally relevant information required to make justifiable decisions in clinical practice. Their format asks the health professional to consider four types of information: medical indications, patient (or surrogate) preferences, quality of life and contextual features (Jonsen, Siegler et al 1992).

Other structures of moral reasoning emphasise moral virtues, professional values and human rights (Pellegrino and Thomasma 1993; Koehn 1994).

Many of these models have much in common – including reference to principles, communication, care, patient preferences (or autonomy), a problem-solving approach and an emphasis on ethical concepts or ideas, such as power, vulnerability and virtues, rather than a unifying theory. In Table 6.1 (*see over*) we have attempted to incorporate the features of these into a single model. We will demonstrate how such a model can be used to assist clinical ethical decision-making by referring to a case-study.

Table 6.1 A Model for Ethical Decision-Making

Clearly state the problem:

Consider the problem within its context and attempt to distinguish between ethical problems and other medical, social, cultural, linguistic and legal issues.

Explore the meaning of value-laden terms, eg futility, quality of life.

Get the facts:

Find out as much as you can about the problem through history, examination and relevant investigations.

Take the time to listen to the patient's narrative and understand their personal and cultural biography.

Are there necessary facts that you do not have? If so, search for them.

Consider the ethical principles:

Autonomy: what is the patient's approach to the problem?

Beneficence: what benefits can be obtained for the patient?

Non-maleficence: what are the risks and how can they be avoided?

Justice: how are the interests of different parties to be balanced?

Confidentiality/privacy: what information is private and does confidentiality need to be limited or breached?

Veracity: has the patient and their family been honestly informed and is there any reason why the patient cannot know the truth?

Consider how the problem would look from another perspective or using another theory

Who are the relevant stakeholders? What is their interest? What do they have to lose? How salient are their interests? How powerful are they? How legitimate are they? How urgent are they?

How would the problem look like from an alternative ethical position? For example, consequentialist, rights-based, virtue-based, feminist, communitarian, care-based

Identify ethical conflicts:

Explain why the conflicts occur and how they may be resolved.

Consider the law:

Identify relevant legal concepts and laws and how they might guide management.

Examine relationship between the clinical-ethical decision and the law.

Making the ethical decision: Clearly state the clinical ethical decision, justify it, enact it and evaluate it:

Identify ethically viable options;

> Make the decision and justify it, for example, by specifying how guiding principles were balanced or by clarifying what issues or processes were considered most significant, and why;
>
> Take responsibility for the decision;
>
> Communicate the decision and assist relevant stakeholders determine an action plan;
>
> Document the decision;
>
> Assist/mediate resolution of any conflict;
>
> Evaluate the decision.

Case study (An example of ethical reasoning):

JD was an 82-year-old man who lived in a nursing home and had had several strokes. He was aphasic (unable to speak) and, although he appeared to understand some of what was said to him, the extent of his understanding was never certain. He was paralysed down one side and spent much of his day in a large chair in front of the television at the nursing home. He had two children who visited him infrequently. During the winter time, JD often developed chest infections that usually responded to oral antibiotics. During one of these infections he appeared to be more unwell than usual and began spitting all his medications out, as well as spitting out all food and fluid. He became quite dehydrated, and was transferred to the local hospital. An IV infusion was commenced, but he kept pulling it out and seemed much more settled when it was removed.

The question arose as to whether he should be restrained in order to continue with the infusion, or should be allowed to die of dehydration, malnutrition and infection.

Step 1: Identifying the ethical problem

The first stage of the ethical decision-making process can be surprisingly difficult. Part of the reason for this is that there are a number of ethical questions that can be asked in relation to the care of any patient. In the case of JD, the main question appeared to be whether it was ethically reasonable to allow him to stop eating and drinking. The issue was complicated by the fact that JD was unable to communicate and he may or may not have been confused; indeed, he may not have been mentally competent to make the decision.

The degree of mental competence exhibited by JD has great ethical significance; but it is not in itself an ethical question. However, we cannot proceed further with solving his problem until we decide on this point. In the case of JD, one of the first clinical facts that will be required is whether he is mentally competent. We can find out whether he is mentally competent by a careful history and examination. In some cases, attention to these sorts of facts will solve the ethical problem. For instance, if we find that Mr D is mentally competent, and that he is able to communicate with us in some way, and that he regards any drip or method of feeding him as an unbearable assault upon his person – then the decision to forgo treatment will become straightforward. On the other hand, if we find that he is not competent to make decisions we must re-define the ethical issue; and our question becomes something like: 'Can we ethically refrain from providing food and fluid to a mentally incompetent individual who appears to have a poor quality of life but will need to be restrained by force to feed him?'

Step 2: What facts are available?

Moral disputes frequently have 'non-moral' elements (scientific or factual data) at their core. To address our refined moral question we will again need to find a number of facts from the patient, his carers, his relatives and from other sources. One of the questions that seems most relevant is whether he will be likely to suffer more from not feeding him or from restraining him and forcing food upon him.

By searching through the literature we can find some data that will help us with this problem; however, this issue is very difficult to research. Some of the data seems to disagree with other data and some of it appears to be actually opinions disguised as facts. The unfortunate reality is that we can probably never know what patients like this feel as they die, unless by chance we end up in this position ourselves, and in that case we will be unable to tell others.

On reviewing the literature we find there are clearly two extremes in this argument. On the one hand, a doctor who testified in a 1986 court case presented a very disturbing view of death from starvation.

> [The man's] mouth would dry out and become caked or coated with thick material. His lips would become parched and cracked. His tongue would swell and might crack. His eyes would recede back into their orbits and his cheeks would become hollow. The lining of his nose might crack and cause his nose to bleed. His skin would hang loose on his body and become dry and scaly. His urine would become highly concentrated, leading to burning of his bladder. The lining of his stomach would dry out and he would experience dry heaves and vomiting. His body temperature would become very high ... etc. (Aronheim and Gasner 1990)

This description was very influential in America, even being quoted almost word for word in the television show 'LA Law' (although the patient in question died peacefully without such complications). It also became accepted by many health professionals. For example, in a 1991 study of attitudes towards dehydration in the terminally ill, it was found that many nurses believe that dehydration causes a wide variety of unpleasant effects, including apathy, depression, dysphagia, headaches, nausea, vomiting etc (House 1992).

Equally gory scenarios are suggested by proponents of the other side of the debate:

> If people are fully hydrated just before they die, their bladders fill, causing either incontinence or distressing restlessness. Their salivary glands work overtime producing drooling and a death rattle on dying. The failing heart may become overloaded, redoubling the rattle and causing dyspnoea due to

waterlogged lungs. Equally important is the nuisance of needles and tubes that make a cuddle almost impossible. (Lamerton 1991)

A more moderate review of the literature on this subject found that dying patients did not suffer greatly from lack of food or fluids as long as their mouths were kept moist with small amounts of ice or water. The authors concluded:

> Our experience is that it is rarely necessary artificially to provide fluids to terminally ill patients whilst maintaining full palliative care; symptom control can be quite effectively achieved in less invasive ways. However occasions arise when a patient requests it, or empirically feels the better for it. Being able to find out what suits the individual patient best is the key to this question. Furthermore, where the decision is taken in conjunction with the relatives, the quality of emotional contact possible between patient, carer and relative will be greatly enhanced. (Chadfield-Mohr and Byatt 1997)

Attempting to discover the facts in this case provides many insights into this problem. Yet, as is often the case in clinical ethics, the results are ambiguous, and do not in themselves provide a solution. However, they do provide some added information that will be of use in making decisions – even if they only point out that the situation is not straightforward.

Clarification of the details of the case cannot be achieved solely by reference to the medical aspects of the case or through a review of the relevant literature. Often the details of a case will become apparent if time is taken to speak with all the major stakeholders and listen to their story. While it is most important to understand the patient's illness narrative and their personal and cultural biography, it is also important to listen to the beliefs and values of those caring for the patient and those affected by their decisions. Attention to the details of the case will also enable clarification of the meaning of any value-laden terms used by any of the relevant stakeholders, particularly terms such as 'futility' and 'quality of life', which are often at the centre of disputes regarding withdrawal of therapy.

Step 3. Consider the ethical principles

An important aspect of the decision-making process is that, when we consider individual cases, we should not think about ethical principles in a detached and academic fashion. Clinical ethics involves 'getting one's hands dirty' with the practical aspects of peoples' lives and deaths.

For example, we should not attempt to sit back objectively to consider how to respect this patient's autonomy. In practical terms, respect for autonomy means that we should negotiate with patients at every stage of the decision-making process. Patients have their own views about many aspects of their care – from the interpretation of physical symptoms and signs to the overall aims of treatment. Respect for autonomy suggests that we should become intimately involved with their understanding of the disease process.

In JD's case, we cannot negotiate fully with him as he is not mentally competent (see below). So, in order to respect his autonomy, we must fall back on other ways of dealing with him – such as involving his family or close friends, ascertaining whether he has ever left instructions about what to do in this circumstance (advance directives), talking to his general practitioner and keeping him as informed as possible even though we are unsure how well he understands.

Issues of beneficence and non-maleficence also require both intellectual and emotional involvement. Patient management and clinical decision-making can only be successful if they reflect the particular circumstances of the patient's situation. This requires the development of efficient and effective communication skills and the ability to work well in teams. These skills are not often thought of as ethical issues, but they are at the heart of good, ethical practice.

Although we wish to do our best to help him, we are still unsure as to whether he will be best served by being allowed to die or by being forced to live. Which option will entail the greater burdens? Which option will afford him and his family the most justice? If we allow him to stop eating or drinking, then we should also consider the possibilities of physician-assisted suicide or active voluntary euthanasia? There is no single answer to these questions, and a solution will only be obtained from collaboration within the health team and with others who are close to the patient.

Issues of justice most commonly arise in terms of resource allocation and the costs of a patient's care. In modern Australia, these issues are unlikely to take great prominence in cases like this, although if JD required long-term artificial feeding or further intervention then the costs involved may become more important. Many practitioners still believe that those who care for patients at the bedside should not concern themselves with these issues. We disagree with this viewpoint and believe that issues of resource allocation are relevant to the care of individual patients. This will be discussed further in the chapter dealing with resource allocation.

Step 4: Consider how the problem would look from another perspective or using another theory

When deliberating about ethical issues in clinical practice it is important to recognise that issues may be problematised and resolved differently by different people in light of their own values, beliefs, and needs. Different stakeholders in any situation may see different problems. For these reasons it is always important to clarify exactly who has an interest in any given situation (who is a stakeholder), what exactly is their interest and how salient are they, that is, how important are they to the resolution of this case. So, for example, while our attention should be directed to JD, we may also wish to consider his two children, the nursing home staff and JD's carers when making decisions about withdrawal of feeding. This may be particularly important where they disagree about the morality of ceasing feeds.

But the way that we approach a case is also dependent on the theoretical (normative ethics) approach that we take to thinking through the issues involved. We have suggested that many different approaches may be taken to any case (within the moral space). While one person will never have sufficient expertise or capacity to approach a case from all of these perspectives, it is important to at least respect other approaches, acknowledge the richness that may result from multiple perspectives on a single problem, and recognise how the perspective taken may lead to completely different resolutions. In this case a consequentialist analysis may be concerned primarily with JD's outcome and with issues surrounding cost-effectiveness, and so recommend against continuing feeding. A deontological position may be concerned primarily with the moral injunction against intentional actions aimed at ending a life and express serious reservation about cessation of nutrition and hydration. And a virtue-based position may be more concerned with the best interests of JD, with the genuine efforts to provide care for him and with the motives of his carers and with the nursing home staff. Each moral perspective will be valid in some way and will add to the depth and intensity of the discussions surrounding cessation of feeding.

Step 5. Identify ethical conflicts

In the case of JD, one of the major conflicts that occurs is between the principles of beneficence and non-maleficence. We wish to help this man, but we are unsure if our help will actually harm him. Let us imagine that in this case, the closest person to him is his ex-neighbour who comes and visits him. She tells us that he has always been terrified of becoming a 'vegetable' and would not like to see himself like this. Furthermore, his previous poor state of health is confirmed by the nursing home. Let us suppose that the other workers on the health-care team believe that they would be able to recognise if he became greatly uncomfortable, and they confirm that he is more comfortable without his IV feeding.

In this circumstance we may be justified to use our knowledge that patients can die comfortably without fluids to suggest that the burdens of IV therapy outweigh the benefits. But in other cases, we may resolve the conflict between beneficence and non-maleficence differently.

Some degree of conflict between ethical principles, rules or rights will always occur and in each instance will require specification (defining their meaning and scope) and balancing (providing reasons or justification) (Beauchamp and Childress 2009). How one balances the ethical principles, virtues or rights does not depend upon an *a priori* moral order but on the strength of argument, the clinical context and the moral perspective of the agent making the judgment.

Step 6. Consider the Law

Law creates a structural background to the ethical debate. There may be cases where an ethical answer conflicts with what is legal, but this is rare. Most often the legal principles run parallel with the ethical principles, or they support the kind of ethical decision-making that has been discussed above. The primary legal principle is that of self-determination – which is the legal equivalent of the principle of autonomy. The law assumes all adults are competent; but from the facts it appears that JD is unable to communicate and is now incompetent. The next legal issue to determine is whether JD had previously made a decision about what kinds of treatment he would consent to in this situation. This decision may have been made in the form of an advance directive or it may have been recorded as part of an advance care plan. In the absence of any such decision being made by JD, the health professionals could then seek advice from JD's relatives or close friends (in this case his ex-neighbour) about whether JD had expressed views in the past about treatment that he would have declined.

Assuming that JD had not made any such statement, it may be possible to get a substitute decision-maker to make a decision regarding the treatment. Each jurisdiction has different rules regarding this process and they are outlined in Chapter 13. If no substitute is available, the health-care team may seek the guidance of the guardianship authorities or the Supreme Court, as to the best approach to take.

Step 7. Making the clinical decision

Having gathered all relevant information in a sensitive and systematic manner, the task is to make carefully reasoned ethical judgments. These decisions should be communicated and documented, and efforts should be made to assist relevant stakeholders deal effectively with the decision or options and develop an action plan. Often there will not be a single correct decision and a number of ethically viable alternatives will be put to the patient or the health-care team. In these situations the development of a way forward may require negotiation, compromise, mediation and planned review.

As members of the health-care team deliberate, they will consider a range of actions reflecting a number of different moral perspectives ('wide reflective equilibrium'). Each of these perspectives – their strengths, inadequacies, justifications and consequences – must be considered within the context of the actual case. Let us suppose that in this case we decide that the patient should not be restrained, that he should continue to be offered food and fluid regularly but that this should not be forced upon him, and that if he appears uncomfortable then this should be treated with a Morphine infusion. This decision should be discussed with all concerned and documented clearly in the notes – specifying who was involved in making the decision and why the decision was made. The decision should be reviewed at regular intervals as determined by the clinical context. The decision may also be reviewed after the patient has died, either as part of an audit, or by the coroner or legal system. It is also important that individual practitioners evaluate their own moral decisions. In so doing, health professionals should consider what impact the decision had on all involved parties, how they felt about their own role and whether there are lessons to be learnt from the decision (le Coz and Tassy 2007).

Dealing with moral disagreements

Health-care decision-making involves teamwork, involving people from many different professional and non-professional backgrounds. It is inevitable that disagreements will arise at times. Engelhardt suggests that there are some forms of moral disagreement in which agreement cannot be reached. However, there are a number of techniques by which differences in moral outlook can be bridged (Engelhardt 1996). Beauchamp suggests the following techniques for dealing with disagreement: specification, adopting a code or policy, obtaining information, providing definitional clarity, using examples and counterexamples, and analysing arguments (Beauchamp 1996). In addition, many ethical disagreements are resolved by paying scrupulous attention to keeping communication lines open between concerned parties in the debate.

Specification

Most practical moral problems require us to make our general rules more specific. If two people disagree about whether a patient has the right to refuse a form of treatment, it is difficult to arrange compromises if they maintain their positions based upon very general moral arguments. In the case above a nurse, for example, might say that a person has a right to make decisions for themselves. A doctor might argue that doctors have a duty to do their best for patients, regardless of the patients' wishes. Such an argument looks insoluble. However, if they are both asked to specify exactly what they mean by these statements in relationship to a particular patient, it may turn out that their disagreement is much more minor. The nurse might support the position that people who are not mentally competent should not decide things for themselves, and the doctor might agree that people who are mentally competent can refuse doctors' treatments. In that case, the question might then be resolvable by testing a patient's mental competence.

Adopting a code or policy

In some cases, adopting a code or policy may allow disagreements to be resolved by referring to this policy. For example, in many poor countries, renal dialysis is too expensive to be offered to all people who need it. If there is no policy about this, this needs to be re-negotiated with every patient who has renal failure, and there is a risk that the wider resource issues will be ignored in fights over individual patients. By having a general policy about this, disagreements can be avoided in a way that is open and fair to all.

Obtaining information

In many cases moral arguments in health care can be resolved by obtaining better information. For example, clinicians may disagree about whether it is reasonable to release information over the telephone to members of the press about an important person's illness. Instead of arguing about this point on general grounds, it may be possible to ask the patient their wishes, and if they say that they are happy for certain types of information to be released, this would resolve the issue.

Providing definitional clarity

Controversies can sometimes be resolved by the realisation that, although different parties are using the same terms, they mean different things by these terms. For example, to some people the term 'informed consent' means the legal definition of the term, to others it may mean a more holistic view based upon mutual decision-making. An argument about whether a patient needs to give informed consent might be resolved by settling this question of definition.

Using examples and counterexamples

Resolution of moral controversies can sometimes be aided by creative use of examples and counterexamples. For example, if a research ethics committee is discussing whether to accept a proposal, it may come across differences of opinion about the degree of information needed to give to patients. By looking at examples of how things could go wrong with the research, and counterexamples of how patients could become over-concerned by different types of wording, the parties may be able to agree about the final wording of information sheets.

Analysing arguments

This is one of the most important tools in philosophy because arguments can often be disproved and discounted by exposing inconsistencies, gaps and fallacies in them. For example, a researcher might propose that because his research subjects are schizophrenic, they would be unable to give consent to research, and therefore consent need not be requested. However, this argument rests upon a faulty supposition – that all schizophrenics are mentally incompetent. Since this is not the case, the argument is flawed and has no validity.

Communication

Appropriate management of ethical issues in health care depends crucially upon effective communication between health professionals, patients, families, and between members of the health-care team. Communication is a complex process and many factors, including the physical environment, time constraints, education in communication skills and differences between the health professional and patient in sex, age, educational background, social status, ethnic background, or deeply held moral convictions, may influence the quality of communication. Failures of communication not only diminish the quality of and satisfaction with health care (Comstock, Hooper et al 1982) but increase the likelihood of litigation as a consequence of adverse events. Unfortunately, hospitals and health facilities frequently do not provide an optimal environment in which communication can easily occur. It is essential that health professionals learn to listen to patients, to respect their autonomy, to provide time for them and to acknowledge and respect cultural differences where they exist.

Stakeholder analysis

While principle-based approaches to ethical reasoning are helpful, particularly in the clinical context, other approaches are needed to think through the ethical issues that arise where ethical principles are in conflict and appear equally valid, or where macro-ethical issues, such as those surrounding health resource allocation or public health, impact upon the clinical encounter. A number of sociological and political models of analysis have been proposed for situations such as these. Perhaps the best known, and most useful, is *stakeholder analysis*.

References to stakeholders and the use of stakeholder analysis as a tool have become increasingly popular in the management, development and health policy fields during the past decade. This reflects an increasing recognition of the role and relevance of stakeholders (literally those who have a stake, or interest), such as individuals, groups and organisations, and the manner in which they may influence decision-making at the individual and policy level. While stakeholder analysis has most often been applied to health policy (Brugha and Varvasovsky 2000), it may also be valuable as an alternative model for examining complex clinical problems (Montgomery and Little 2001). The primary objective of stakeholder analysis is to map the power, interest and influence of relevant stakeholders around a decision, issue or policy. Montgomery and Little describe the steps involved in stakeholder analysis of bioethical concerns as follows:

1. Define the issue, event or enterprise in which the stakeholders have an interest.
2. Define the stakeholders
3. Characterise the salience (prominence or significance) of each stakeholder by analysing their power, legitimacy and urgency. (Montgomery and Little 2001)

Perhaps the major benefit of stakeholder analysis is that it provides a means for reflecting upon the values, needs and perspectives of all relevant stakeholders in health care when other normative frameworks are unhelpful because consequences are unclear, rules and principles appear in intractable conflict and/or virtues are difficult to identify or apply.

Mediation and conflict resolution

Where conflict arises between health care professionals and patients or between family members, mediation strategies may be used for resolution and to prevent escalation. Mediation here refers to the intervention into a dispute by an acceptable, impartial and neutral third party who has no authoritative decision-making power, to assist disputing parties in voluntarily making their own mutually acceptable settlement of issues in dispute. Mediation provides an opportunity for all narratives to be heard, moves parties from entrenched positions to options based upon common ground or consensus, and may neutralise power imbalances. In situations of bioethical conflict, mediation may enhance the autonomy of the patient, support the values of the patient and family, and lead to the development of an action plan consistent with institutional policy, individual values and law (Dubler and Liebeman 2004).

As with all strategies to resolve disagreement, mediation will not always solve disputes. It will have limited success where one of the parties holds rigid or fixed positions, where one of the parties is incapable of rational discourse or where either party is extremely emotionally distraught.

Conflict resolution and the courts

In cases where mediation cannot resolve disputes, it may be necessary to resort to legal intervention. Legal teams have the advantage of being able to bring another layer of mediation expertise, as well as having the capacity to advise parties about the realistic prospects for resolution through litigation.

Generally speaking, most intractable disputes concerning the provision of health care have to be resolved within the traditional court structure. The traditional structures are often criticised for the expense and delay in their proceedings, although it should be said that court hearing times have generally improved in the past decade. Emergency applications can also be made to the Supreme Courts at any time of the day or night, and there is now a growing body of health cases which have been heard and resolved very quickly (for example, *Messiha v South East Health* [2004] NSWSC 1061 and *Melo v Superintendent of Royal Darwin Hospital* [2007] NTSC 71).

Apart from the traditional courts there is a growing number of tribunal and quasi-tribunal venues for dispute resolution. Guardianship tribunals and boards have an ever increasing role in decisions regarding incompetent patients, and health-care complaints and disciplinary tribunals are also being increasingly involved with matters, especially since the tort law reforms have made it harder to bring actions in negligence.

Clinical ethics consultation

The ethical aspects of medicine and the biological sciences have attracted much public comment and criticism over the past half-century. In the research setting, this has led to the development of a comprehensive system of institutionally based ethics committees aimed at ensuring the protection of participants in research. In the clinic, the importance of ethical issues has also been widely recognised, although, except in the United States, formalised systems for addressing ethical problems or dilemmas have been less widely adopted. In the past, when ethical concerns have arisen in clinical practice, health professionals have sought the guidance of respected colleagues. While practical, this 'three wise men' approach can be criticised on several grounds: it is unrepresentative of non-clinical views, it is likely to reinforce the values of the clinician who seeks the consultation, it misconstrues questions of value as questions of technical expertise, and it assumes that medical expertise confers the capacity to make difficult moral decisions.

The practice of 'clinical ethics' – that is, the consideration of ethical issues arising directly in the context of patient care – has been a feature of hospital practice in the United States since the 1960s. The development of clinical ethics was given great impetus by the President's Commission for the Study of Ethical Problems in Medicine and Biomedical and Behavioural Research and by the Joint Commission for the Accreditation of Healthcare Organisations, which in 1992 recommended that all healthcare facilities develop processes to address ethical issues based upon a framework that recognises the interdependence of patient care and organisational ethical issues (Rosner 1985). These processes, or 'clinical ethics services', take various forms, such as structured committees to which appeal may be made, the provision of specialist 'ethics consultants' or 'patient advocates', or other mechanisms for receiving and responding to complaints and grievances. The tasks they undertake also vary, and include direct involvement in case consultations, retrospective case reviews, development of policies and clinical guidelines, and education of clinical staff.

Clinical ethics services are increasingly a feature of health care in the United Kingdom and Germany (Slowther and Hope 2000), but elsewhere in Europe, Asia, Australia and in other parts of the world there has been little coordination, training or professionalisation of clinical ethics and the vast majority of institutions do not have access to clinical ethics services. Instead, it has been assumed that ethical issues should be resolved by health professionals themselves or through discussions between practitioners. The idea that patient care can be improved by considering issues of value separately from those concerning the scientific or technical aspects of diagnosis and management has been widely resisted. There has been wariness about intrusions into the relationship between practitioners and patients which, quite appropriately, has been regarded as the central locus of clinical care. There have also been concerns regarding legal liability and concern about changes that are perceived to erode the independence of judgment of clinicians. In addition, it has been pointed out that outcome data regarding ethics consultations in the United States are sparse, and, with a few notable exceptions, there is limited evidence that they have contributed to better quality of care, increased transparency, enhanced communication, or more satisfactory resolutions of disputes (Slowther and Hope 2000; Hendrick 2001; McGee, Spanogle et al 2002; Schneiderman, Gilmer et al 2003). There are, however, few well constructed studies of clinical ethics services, with many studies being predicated on the belief that there is a single correct moral response to any clinical problem and consequently focusing more on the frequent absence of consensus between clinical ethicists than on detailed exploration of process (Fox and Arnold 1996).

Why have a clinical ethics service?

While it is undoubtedly the case that for the most part health professionals are adept at effectively and sensitively managing ethical issues in clinical care, multi-disciplinary clinical ethics services may on occasions provide valuable resources to support clinical practice. The increasing complexity of the technical possibilities confronting patients, carers and health services and the increasing social and moral heterogeneity of Australian society support an intensified, deliberate focus on ethical issues that may not always be possible within everyday clinical practice. In some cases, the divergence of moral viewpoints may be such that special skills are required to establish and maintain critical dialogues. In addition, there are settings to which the conventional doctor-patient relationship simply does not extend – for example, where issues arise in relation to relatives or friends of patients, or between doctors and other health care practitioners. Increasing pressures on doctors in public hospitals may in any event limit both the time available for detailed exploration of ethical issues and the opportunities for providing education in this area to medical, nursing and other health-care personnel. The American Medical Association position on the role of a Clinical Ethics Committee, which largely reflects the de facto position adopted in Australia, is that a Clinical Ethics Committee should be:

> educational and advisory in purpose. Generally, the function of the ethics committee should be to consider and assist in resolving unusual, complicated ethical problems involving issues that affect the care and treatment of patients within the health care institution. Recommendations of the ethics committee should impose no obligation for acceptance on the part of the institution, its governing board, medical staff, attending physicians, or other persons. However, it should be expected that the recommendations of a dedicated ethics committee will receive serious consideration by decision makers. (American Medical Association 2002)

The clinical situations in which the assistance of a clinical ethics service may be sought include all those where the goals or outcomes of care are interpreted differently by different individuals and where conflict arises due to explicit moral or philosophical disagreement, and are therefore extremely varied. For example, the need for a clinical ethics consultation may arise:

- where there is uncertainty about the appropriate level of treatment in a chronically or terminally ill patient;
- where one party holds firm religious or philosophical views about a certain course of action, such as blood transfusion or enteral feeds;
- where, as a result of differences in philosophical outlook, personality or other factors, communication between doctor and patient has become impaired;
- where there is disagreement between the members of the health-care team, or between the patient and one or more health professionals;
- where differences arise between the administration of a hospital and clinical staff regarding issues of clinical practice; or
- where issues arise outside the doctor-patient relationship – for example, involving relatives or friends of the patient, or where members of the health-care team themselves require support or advice. (DuVal, Sartorius et al 2001)

As several of these examples demonstrate, a dispute need not be required to provoke a consultation, but merely a perceived need to clarify issues of an ethical or a philosophical nature; indeed, one of the objectives of such services is to encourage anticipation of potential problems and to avoid them through prior reflection and clarification. Even when genuine consensus is not possible, ethics consultation may benefit clinicians and the hospital community by encouraging communication; by clarifying what is and is not 'accepted practice'; and by facilitating transparency, veracity and critical reflection on shared values and on points of difference between patients and health professionals. Indeed, ethics consultation may serve as much to highlight moral differences as to resolve them .

How might a clinical ethics service work?

At least in some settings, therefore, a clinical ethics service may offer the possibility of enhancing clinical practice by assisting clinicians and other health professionals, patients and their families and others in identifying, understanding and managing ethical issues. However, there is disagreement about many key aspects of such a service (La Puma and Toulmin 1989). There is disagreement about who should conduct ethics consultations, how a clinical ethicist/ethics service should liaise with clinicians, and about the role of a clinical ethics services in the clinical decision-making process (Agich 1990). Questions also remain about the authority, accountability, processes, membership and requisite expertise of clinical ethics services. Some believe that there is a role for 'experts' in philosophy or moral theory, while others explicitly reject this approach. Some argue that an ethics service needs to be assessed in relation to its substantive outcomes, while others argue that its key role is merely to precipitate processes of critical reflection (Fletcher and Siegler 1996).

Much debate has focused on the role that ethics consultation should play in decision-making, specifically, whether ethics consultation should be seen primarily as the provision of structured, expert ethical responses to substantive moral issues or whether it is fundamentally a matter of interpretation, communication, consensus building and conflict resolution . To some extent this is, however, a false dichotomy, as there is an interplay between theory and practice and between 'technical' expertise and moral discourse, and all are features of both everyday clinical practice and clinical ethics consultations. Within any clinical process there may be a need for clarification and sensitive discussion of the value-basis or moral context of the issues being faced, whether these relate to professional values, personal beliefs, individual moral frameworks or institutional policies, and it is precisely in this area that ethics consultations may offer assistance. Such consultations should help participants to identify ethical issues arising in clinical situations, and where conflicts arise, facilitate processes that allow them to negotiate mutually satisfactory resolutions through the evaluation of all reasonable options open to them. They may make available alternative perspectives from outside institutional boundaries or from outside the biomedical model. They cannot, however, provide legal advice, medical opinions, institutional advocacy or grievances procedures, or definitive, unequivocal moral 'answers'.

An ethics consultation may be conducted by a single individual or a small team of individuals with different experiences, values or perspectives, who talk with all the parties involved and, where appropriate, bring them together in direct communication. Such individuals may include clinicians, lawyers, ethicists, philosophers, psychologists, economists, consumer advocates, to name but a few possibilities.

What philosophical framework should clinical ethics consultation use?

Many theories have been advanced or updated to take account of clinical ethics and to describe the expertise required of ethics consultation. These include principle-based ethics, narrative ethics, casuistry, discourse ethics, virtue ethics, process ethics and situationism (Ashcroft, Lucassen et al 2005). Of these, the first four are perhaps the most valuable, because they propose a practical method for resolving or mediating bioethical disputes. Although no single theory can provide an all-encompassing explanation of clinical ethics or the process of ethical decision-making, each provides tools that may help resolve ethical conflicts in healthcare.

Principle-based ethics provides a framework for describing conflicting principles in clinical decision-making (autonomy, beneficence, non-maleficence and justice), and thereby a language for describing the ethics of medicine. Narrative ethics emphasises the central relevance of the patients, their carers, and the health professional's story in enriching the moral analysis of the case or as a source of moral 'truth'. Casuistry is an ancient form of reasoning that considers similarities and differences between emergent cases and previous 'paradigm cases'. Possible courses of action are then ranked according to their moral strength. Its advantage lies in its reference to experience, common morality and the clinical context ('moral truth resides in the details') (Arras 1991). Discourse ethics sees ethical disputes as a 'disruption of consensus'. According to this approach, the task of ethics consultation is one of rebuilding consensus, by taking as many different perspectives into account as possible and, through an iterative process of consultation, ensuring that all parties agree with the final recommendations. Discourse ethics rests on a belief in the moral power of communication and the validity of discourse and experience. In practice, it provides an effective means of mediating between widely divergent perspectives to generate agreement.

We believe that each of these moral frameworks may help working groups to examine and mediate ethical conflicts and generate conclusions that are rigorous, valid, inclusive and morally defensible. Regardless of the moral framework adopted, it would seem that many ethical 'conflicts' will be able to be worked through by listening to the patient and to others involved in the case, by attention to basic and widely held values, by commonsense and by adopting a position somewhat outside the hospital hierarchy. A good example of this is given by Caplan in his book, *If I were a rich man could I buy a pancreas?*

> Are philosophers and others engaged in what has come to be called 'applied ethics' in the 'real world' of medicine able to do anything useful there? In mulling over such questions, it may be useful for the reader to ponder ... [examples] ... which stand out in my own mind as the occasions upon which,

through my involvement in a medical center, I felt I was most effective with reference to matters of applied ethics.

The first incident occurred in the course of teaching in the hospital of a large urban medical center. The elective was entitled 'Ethics Rounds' and was team taught with a psychiatrist and an internist. The course consisted of visiting various patients selected by students, interviewing the patients, and discussing some of the moral issues that the students and teachers felt were raised by the cases.

Early on in the course, the students had selected a 90-year-old woman with a fractured arm for an interview. She had no relatives, and the students were worried about what might happen to her upon discharge from the hospital. I came to the class fully prepared to discourse on theories of distributive justice at a moment's notice, since I rather naively believed the students might benefit greatly from a disquisition on Mill, Rawls and Nozick in trying to figure out what to do with the old woman.

As soon as the medical instructors and students had gathered together, we hurriedly set off to find and interview the old woman. We all burst into her room just as she was in the process of defecating. To my surprise, no one was deterred by her behaviour, and both the psychiatrist and the internist proceeded immediately to interview the woman about her life plans, goals and personal aspirations. I remained uncharacteristically silent during this exchange, and it was only when the class returned to the confines of the psychiatry lounge to discuss the case that I proffered the opinion that it might have been better to wait until the woman had finished her excretory functions before interviewing her. This observation was greeted with consternation by both students and the other teachers. Of course I was correct, they conceded. Privacy was important to patients, as my comments showed, and physicians should not allow the press of their own busy schedules to override a patient's needs for a certain amount of privacy. My insight was acknowledged with a great degree of gravity, and my esteem among the members of the course was assured for the duration of that particular clinical rotation. (Caplan 1992)

Ethics consultations will not resolve all ethical tension or uncertainty in clinical practice. Nor will they vouchsafe outcomes that are beyond critical examination. Because ethics committees are guided by the values and biases of those who comprise them, they may reach different conclusions when confronted with the same or similar cases, and they may, at times, be unable to reach any form of consensus when conflicting viewpoints based upon long-held and deeply felt moral views are brought to bear.

Conclusion

Ethical conflicts often stand at the intersection of different perspectives, including moral, medical, legal, sociological and religious, and as such the knowledge or expertise required of ethics consultation could reasonably include a knowledge of bioethics or moral philosophy, expertise in health law, communication skills, the ability to identify ethical issues and value positions, the capacity to appreciate clinical and moral uncertainty, and skills in mediation or conflict resolution. Appreciating the broad range of skills and expertise required of clinical ethics has two important implications: first, that the expertise of ethics consultation may lie either in depth of knowledge or in the ability to integrate knowledge from different disciplines and to facilitate reconciliation of different ethical perspectives (Yoder 1998; Moreno 1991); and, secondly, that ethics consultation is ultimately an interdisciplinary endeavour to which no single discipline can lay a definitive claim (Cassaret, Dashal et al 1998).

In the short term clinical ethics services are unlikely to be a feature of the Australian hospital system. In time, however, it is likely that they will play an increasingly important role as there is growing recognition of the need to increase the quality of care (in its broadest sense) to patients, reduce litigation, facilitate the fair distribution of limited community resources and, increasingly, ensure public confidence in medical institutions – all tasks that are broader than the functions of clinical governance or risk management services (Campbell 2001). Although there is currently limited evidence of their impact, clinical ethics services may, in principle, contribute to all these processes and there is likely to be a place for them in supporting and enriching the clinical process. If clinical ethics services are to be established and accepted, however, then it is essential that they are supportive of clinical decision-making and not remove ultimate responsibility or authority from the health-care team. If they are to have an impact then the processes adopted by such services must also be rigorous, transparent, inclusive and carefully articulated. Only then will explicit consideration of issues of value become an important part of the clinical landscape. Ethics consultation is not easy, and setting up an ethics consultation service should not be undertaken lightly. Such a service may have many benefits, but, if implemented poorly and without the support of the hospital community, is likely to be underutilised, ineffective or destructive. If, however, it is powerful, inclusive, plural and independent enough to provide a critical voice, then it may ultimately contribute to ethical practice and become a valuable hospital resource. In the foreseeable future, however, efforts to facilitate reflective, more ethically sensitive, practice should concentrate not on clinical ethics services but on encouraging all health professionals to see that dealing effectively with ethical issues raised by clinical practice is an integral part of patient care.

References

Agich, GJ (1990) 'Clinical ethics: A role theoretic look'. *Soc Sci Med* **30**(4): 389-99.

American Medical Association (2002) Ethics Committees in Health Care Institutions. *Policy Recommendations E-9.11.*

Aronheim, JC and MR Gasner (1990) 'The sloganism of starvation'. *Lancet* **335**: 218-19.

Arras, JD (1991) 'Getting down to cases: The revival of casuistry in bioethics'. *J Med Philos* **16**: 29-51.

Ashcroft, R, A Lucassen et al (2005) *Case Analysis in Clinical Ethics*. Cambridge, Cambridge University Press.

Beauchamp, T (1996) Moral Foundations. *Ethics and epidemiology*. S Coughlin and T Beauchamp. New York, Oxford University Press.

Beauchamp, T and J Childress (2009) *Principles of biomedical ethics* (6th ed). New York, Oxford University Press.

Brugha, R and Z Varvasovsky (2000) 'Stakeholder analysis: a review'. *Health Policy and Planning* **15**(3): 239-46.

Campbell, AV (2001) 'Clinical governance – watchword or buzzword?' *J Med Ethics* **27 Suppl 1**: i54-6.

Caplan, A (1992) *If I were a rich man could I buy a pancreas?* Bloomington and Indianapolis, Indiana University press.

Cassaret, D, F Dashal et al (1998) 'Experts in ethics? The authority of the clinical ethicist'. *Hastings Cent Rep* **28**(6): 6-11.

Chadfield-Mohr, S and C Byatt (1997) 'Dehydration in the terminally ill – iatrogenic insult or natural process?' *Postgrad Med J* **73**: 476-80.

Comstock, L, E Hooper et al (1982) 'Physician behaviours that correlate with patient satisfaction'. *J Med Educ* **57**: 105-12.

Dubler, N and C Liebeman (2004) *Bioethics mediation: a guide to shaping the shared solutions.* New York, United Hospital Fund of New York.

DuVal, G, L Sartorius et al (2001) 'What triggers requests for ethics consultations?' *J Med Ethics* **27 Suppl 1**: i24-9.

Engelhardt, HT (1996) *The foundations of bioethics.* New York, Oxford University Press.

Fletcher, J and M Siegler (1996) 'What are the goals of ethics consultation. A consensus statement'. *J Clin Ethics* **7**(2): 122-6.

Fox, E and R Arnold (1996) 'Evaluating outcomes in ethics consultation research'. *J Clin Ethics* **7**: 127-38.

Habermas, J (1992) *Moral consciousness and communicative action.* Cambridge, Polity Press.

Hendley, S (2000) *From communicative action to the face of the other: Levinas and Habermas on language, obligation and community.* Lexington, Lexington Books.

Hendrick, J (2001) 'Legal aspects of clinical ethics committees'. *J Med Ethics* **27**: 50-5.

Hoffmaster, B (1989) Philosophical ethics and practical ethics: Never the twain shall meet. *Clinical Ethics Theory and Practice.* B Hoffmaster, B Freedman and G Fraser. New Jersey, Humana Press.

House, N (1992) 'The hydration question: hydration or dehydration of terminally ill patients'. *Prof Nurse* **1**: 462-6.

Johnson, M (1993) *Moral imagination: implications of cognitive science.* Chicago, University of Chicago Press.

Jonsen, A, M Siegler et al (1992) *Clinical ethics: A practical approach to ethical decisions in clinical medicine.* New York, MacMillan.

Koehn, D (1994) *The Ground of Professional Ethics.* London, Routledge.

La Puma, J and S Toulmin (1989) 'Ethics consultants and ethics committees'. *Arch Intern Med* **149**(5): 1109-12.

Lamerton, R (1991) 'Dehydration in dying patients'. *Lancet* **337**: 255-70.

le Coz, P and S Tassy (2007) 'The philosophical moment of the medical decision: revisiting emotions felt to improve ethics of future decisions'. *J Med Ethics* **33**: 470-2.

McGee, G, JP Spanogle et al (2002) 'Successes and failures of hospital ethics committees: a national survey of ethics committee chairs'. *Camb Q Healthc Ethics* **11**(1): 87-93.

Montgomery, K and J Little (2001) 'Ethical thinking and stakeholders'. *MJA* **174**: 405-6.

Nussbaum, M (2001) *Upheavals of thought: the intelligence of emotions.* Cambridge, Cambridge University Press.

Pellegrino, E and D Thomasma (1993) *The virtues in medical practice.* Oxford, Oxford University Press.

Rosner, F (1985) 'Hospital medical ethics committees: a review of their development'. *JAMA* **253**: 2693.

Savulescu, J (1997) 'Liberal rationalism and medical decision-making'. *Bioethics* **11**(2): 115-29.

Schneiderman, L, T Gilmer et al (2003) 'Effects of ethics consultations on nonbeneficial life-sustaining treatments in the Intensive Care setting: A randomised controlled trial'. *JAMA* **290**: 1166-72.

Scott, P (1997) 'Imagination in practice'. *J Med Ethics* **23**(1): 45-50.

Slowther, AM and T Hope (2000) 'Clinical ethics committees'. *BMJ* **321**(7262): 649-50.

CHAPTER 7

PROFESSIONALISM

Case

A 1991 review of fraud in the relations between American doctors and the government insurer Medicaid reported several extraordinary examples. In Illinois, for instance, a psychiatrist was found to have billed Medicaid for 4800 hours in the year, or almost 24 hours every workday. Other physicians have been caught billing for services on persons who were dead at the time the alleged service was performed. A physician billed Medicaid for $3000 for a time when he was in Africa on Safari. A psychiatrist charged Medicaid for sexual liaisons with a patient, claiming that he had submitted the bills for professional services so that his wife, who handled his books, would not become suspicious of the dalliance. Another physician billed Medicaid for abortions on women who were not pregnant, including one who had a hysterectomy. In 48 separate instances, he billed Medicaid for performing two abortions within a month on the same patient. ...

Perhaps the most marked [impression in the interviews conducted] was the almost ubiquitous unwillingness of the members of the sample to indicate greed as the root cause of their difficulties. None of the physicians took full personal blame for his or her violation of a legitimate law or rule ... At the most, the physicians that we interviewed might acknowledge that they had been a little careless, but this was said to have been because they were fundamentally trusting people, more interested in the welfare of others than their own salvation, and that this character flaw had stood them in ill stead ... The physicians typically saw themselves as sacrificial lambs hung out to dry because of incompetent or backstabbing employees, stupid laws, bureaucratic nonsense, and a host of similar reasons. (Jesilow, Geis et al 1991)

What are the health professions?

The term 'health professions', refers to medicine, nursing, physiotherapy, clinical psychology, social work, occupational therapy, pharmacy, dietetics and a variety of less common occupations such as prosthetists and podiatrists. In their book *Social Work Processes*, Compton and Galaway describe the birth of the professions as follows:

A profession develops when society identifies a complex problem of social importance that appears to demand knowledge and skill for its solution that are greater than those possessed by the average member of society. The solution of the problem is seen as requiring specialised knowledge and skill involving nonroutine decision making and tasks that cannot be standardised. The knowledge and skill demanded are usually such that persons desiring to practice in the name of the profession must invest considerable time in their development and must demonstrate a satisfactory level of competence. (Compton and Galaway 1995)

A different view has been given by Friedson:

It is difficult to find very much agreement on a definition of the word 'profession' ... virtually all self-conscious occupational groups apply it to themselves at one time or another either to flatter themselves or to try to persuade others of their importance. Occupations to which the word has been applied are thus so varied as to have nothing in common save a hunger for prestige. (Friedson 1970)

Unfortunately, Friedson's view seems closest to the historical truth. The oldest professional medical body in the English-speaking world was the College of Physicians – now known as the Royal College of Physicians – founded by Henry VIII in 1518. The charter that created this body allowed members to control medical practice within seven miles of the city of London and exclude 'lesser breeds without the law'. Unfortunately, those who were eligible for membership of this society appeared uniquely incapable of practising medicine. Members were required to be graduates of Oxford and Cambridge, and were required only to pass a 20-minute examination conducted in Latin that was designed to show familiarity with the ancient masters of medicine. Graduates were not required to have ever touched or seen patients; indeed, it was only in 1815 that the Apothecaries Act finally required candidates to have 'walked the wards' of recognised hospitals before sitting their exams (Cartwright 1997).

Competition with the physicians was provided by two fiercely oppositional groups – the barber-surgeons and the apothecaries; as well as by a large selection of midwives, 'wise-women', grocer-apothecaries, quacks and semi-quacks. Both barber-surgeons and apothecaries taught through apprenticeship rather than through universities. Each of the three main groups claimed the right to practise all forms of medicine, and each accused the others of trespassing upon their specialties. In 1794 Thomas Perceval, a liberal-minded physician, circulated a pamphlet that was eventually published under the name of *Medical Ethics*, in which he outlined a code of behaviour to be observed by the various professions so that they could get along together; but the sparring between the three main professional groups continued until well into the 20th century.

Eventually, the medical profession became associated with high entrance standards, a demanding course of study, effective licensing, a high average standard of living, social prestige, a strong national organisation and a favourable public image – characteristics that continue to be part of the modern medical profession. In the early 20th century, professional organisations were also set up to regulate and represent nurses, midwives and many (but not all) of the other health professions. However, there are on-going discrepancies between the privileges and community respect accorded to the medical profession and those accorded to other health professionals, a situation that provides a continuing stimulus to debates about the value of the health professions and the meaning of professionalism.

In the 1970s and 80s extensive critiques of medicine, medical professionalism and professional self-regulation emerged (Friedson 1970). By the 1980s and 1990s, the term 'medical professionalism' had developed unpleasant connotations of elitism and exclusivity. In response, the medical profession sort to reassert the importance of medical self-regulation and rehabilitate the idea of professionalism.

In 2002, the Medical Professionalism Project (a cooperative project of the American Board of Internal Medicine, the American College of Physicians, and the European Federation of Internal Medicine) published their 'Charter on Medical Professionalism', reigniting debate within the medical profession about this subject (Medical Professionalism Project 2002). The Charter was based on three principles: the primacy of patient welfare, patient autonomy and social justice, and a number of professional responsibilities including commitment to professional competence, patient confidentiality and the just distribution of finite resources.

In the 15 months after the charter was published, it was cited by several hundred US and international newspapers in related stories; more than 70 radio, television and online interviews were conducted with project members; over 65,000 reprints were requested from around the world; and, websites related to the charter logged more than 70,000 related visits (Blank, Kimball et al 2003). Clearly the concept of professionalism continues to hold people's attention!

What is professionalism?

The word 'professionalism' has more than one meaning. Dictionaries define a profession as a 'calling' or vocation, carrying the connotation that health professionals are engaged in occupations that have a 'higher aim'. This aim is generally said to be the welfare of others – be they patients, clients or the community at large. An example of this sort of thinking can be found in the following quote:

> By a profession we mean a group of men pursuing a common calling as a learned art and as a public service – nonetheless a public service because it may incidentally be a means of livelihood. Gaining a livelihood is not a professional consideration. The spirit of a profession, the spirit of public service, curbs the urges of that incident. An organised profession does not seek to advance the money-making feature of professional activity. It seeks rather to make as effective as possible its primary character of a public service ... What a member of a profession invents or discovers as to the art of his profession is not his property. It is at the service of the public. (Scarlet 1991)

We will refer to this view of professionalism as the 'higher aim' view of professionalism.

A second connotation of the word 'professionalism' refers to a certain coldness and detachment in relations between the health professions and the clients they serve. We will refer to this as the 'professional detachment' view of professionalism. It is well illustrated by the following quote from William Osler from his famous speech entitled 'Aequanimitas':

In the first place, in the physician or surgeon no quality takes rank with im-perturbability ... Imperturbability means coolness and presence of mind under all circumstances, calmness in storm, clearness of judgement in moments of grave peril, immobility, impassiveness, or, to use an old and expressive word, phlegm. It is the quality which is most appreciated by the laity though often misunderstood by them; and the physician who has the misfortune to be without it, who betrays indecision and worry, and who shows that he is flustered and flurried in ordinary emergencies, loses rapidly the confidence of his patients ... Cultivate, then gentlemen, such a judicious measure of obtuseness as will enable you to meet the exigencies of practice with firmness and courage, without, at the same time, hardening 'the human heart by which we live'. (Osler 1932)

A third meaning of the word 'professionalism' refers to the idea that professions differ from other occupations through the right to control their own work. Professionals expect to be able to make judgments and take actions independently of the judgments of those outside the profession; considering themselves truly accountable only to their personal standards and to their peers. Professions are regulated by bodies composed of their own members who define entrance standards, standards of professional practice and punishments for members who transgress their rules (Compton and Galaway 1995). We will refer to this approach as the 'professional autonomy' view of professionalism.

A final, and in many ways the most satisfactory, connotation of the word refers to a general standard of all-round proficiency and accountability. The word 'professional' is used this way in common speech. For example, if we hire tradespeople to repair our house, we will consider them to have done a 'professional' job if they not only do the job well, but are also efficient, clean up after themselves, and make sure that they fit with our individual requirements. Furthermore, if they do not meet these standards, we would expect them to be held accountable to us, to their peers and to legal scrutiny. We will refer to this broad, all-round view of proficiency and accountability as the 'professional competence' view of professionalism.

Criticisms of professionalism

One major difficulty with the concept of professionalism is that the many different understandings of the word conflict with each other. One example of such a conflict can be found in a 1994 review that looked at donations from the American Medical Political Action Committee (AMPAC). AMPAC donated money to congressmen who supported the professional interests of doctors (such as payment and working conditions). Unfortunately, the congressmen who supported the conservative political agenda of AMPAC also tended to sup-port the tobacco industry. It became apparent that, by supporting professional objectives, doctors were also undermining public health! (Sharfstein and Sharfstein 1994)

A second type of conflict that occurs within the concept of professionalism is between the 'detached view' and the 'higher aim view of professionalism'. This can best be seen in the nursing agenda of 'professionalisation'. For much of this century, nursing has aspired to the status of profession, largely in an attempt to gain public respect and prestige (Porter 1992). However, at the same time as nurses have been attempting to attain professional status, another major movement within nursing has emphasised the central role of caring in patient-nurse relationships – an idea that is in direct opposition to the 'professional distance' view of professionalism. This point is well illustrated by an essay by Celia Davies entitled 'Cloaked in a tattered illusion', in which she characterises professionalism as an expression of the stereotypically masculine self. She describes a professional's actions as:

> [He] makes a momentary appearance, quizzes those who have more con-tinuous association with 'his patient', gives an opinion, proposes or confirms a course of action and moves on. His demeanour is cool, calm and collected; his decisions appear to arise rationally from his evaluation of the evidence as marshalled before him. The work is organised according to his convenience. (Davies 1995a)

If this is professionalism, Davies believes that nurses should have none of it. Instead, she suggests that nurses should adopt a new type of professionalism based upon 'reflective practice' rather than individual knowledge, interde-pendent decision process rather than unilateral decision processes, collective responsibility rather than individual accountability, and engagement with patients rather than detachment.

But she acknowledges that there are many problems with this model. 'Engagement' may lead to over-involvement and burnout, so she suggests instead that what is needed is a 'meaningful distance' between nurses and patients that would avoid both over- and under-involvement. But in making this suggestion, she seems to echo William Osler, and almost comes back to the 'professional distance' view again (Davies 1995b).

The other main difficulty with professionalism is that it inevitably focuses attention on the practitioner rather than the patient. Statements of profes-sionalism, such as the Charter, claim to put the patient foremost, but a sceptical reading suggests that their aim is more political. By reasserting the values of the profession, they restate the authority of the profession and defend the profession against external critique. Statements of professionalism are by their nature inward looking, and so they may be poorly responsive to needs arising from outside the profession.

Statements such as the charter are in many ways similar to oaths or codes of ethics. Ultimately, they take the form of lists of principles, values and respon-sibilities that do not account for the complexity of medicine. Like many codes of ethics, one could argue that the professionalism movement has reaffirmed the moral and socio-political power of biomedicine, stripped moral discourse of its history, contextual richness and complexity, and made a group of attitudes, values and behaviours come to be seen as immutable under the label of professionalism (Dudzinski 2004). And like codes of ethics, it is questionable that the professionalism movement has had any real impact on standards of care, professional integrity or public trust (Wear and Kuczewski 2004).

Strikes and industrial action

The internal tensions within the meaning of the word 'professionalism' are well illustrated by the controversies that arise from industrial action within the health-care system. On the one hand, industrial action may be viewed as the antithesis of professionalism – as a breach of trust between health professionals and patients and an abrogation of professional responsibility towards the welfare of the community (Tschudin 1986). Striking may be seen as rejection of accepted standards of altruism and self-sacrifice, a violation of patients' own rights to health care and an unjustified use of patients as a means to achieving political ends. On the other hand, strike action may also be seen as a democratic right that is open to all members of society and as a valid expression of professional autonomy.

To be effective, strikes need to have an impact upon employers and policy-makers, which inevitably harms or inconveniences patients. This creates a conflict between the 'higher aims' view of the profession, which must reject any possibility of harm to patients, and the 'professional autonomy' view that allows professionals to have a duty to themselves as well as to patients.

Health workers who engage in industrial action require a balance between self-interest and the public interest. And for industrial action to be successful, it generally requires wide agreement amongst those involved that the action is justifiable. This in turn requires a degree of consensus regarding the rationale for the strike, the risk to patients, the exhaustion of other means of settling disputes and the likelihood of success.

Within the health professions, there is great moral disagreement over what constitutes reasonable justification and reasonable mechanisms for industrial action (Chadwick and Thompson 2000). While many health professionals might support striking if a substandard health system created an obligation to act, and if strikes were unlikely to cause harm to patients, few professionals feel that striking is justifiable if it is driven purely by self-interest or if the risk of harm to patients is high (Kravitz and Linn 1992). However, this seems likely to depend upon both the standards of care available and the current working conditions for health-care professionals.

Human rights abuses

An increased focus on the political aspects of health care has also drawn attention to situations in which health professionals are complicit in abuses. All of the health professions commit themselves to powerful ethical ideals, such as justice, and to 'higher' duties to provide care to the community. When they engage in actions which directly transgress these ethical principles or professional roles we are forced to confront the 'bare edges' of ethics and human rights, and consider whether ethics can exist at all in oppressive environments where all fundamental human rights are systematically removed. We may also be forced to acknowledge that health professionals are no more or less moral than other people and may, be complicit in 'evil' acts (Zion 2004).

In June 2007, an attack on Glasgow airport was thwarted when the devices that had been prepared failed to explode. This followed unsuccessful bombings in London the previous day. What caught the public attention most was the fact that seven of the eight arrested were physicians, the eighth was a medical technician, and all eight worked for the National Health Service. The chair of the International Doctors' association called the involvement of doctors 'beyond belief'. But this is not the first time that doctors have been suspected of partici-pating in political violence. Presumably, these people acted, at least in part, with the goal of improving society. Wessley makes the point that idealism and a desire to improve society are desirable characteristics of the health professions. But, if untempered by respect for life and empathy, they may lead to such undesirable extremes (Wessley 2007).

Doctors have also done evil in the interests of the state. Chilean doctors have served as torturers, Russian doctors have incarcerated political dissidents in psychiatric hospitals, Egyptian doctors have performed unnecessary and invasive examinations on homosexual men, South African doctors have falsified medical reports on black South Africans who were tortured or killed, and American doctors and nurses have been complicit in Afghanistan, Guantanamo Bay and Iraq (notably Abu Ghraib prison) (de Gruchy and Fish 2004; Lifton 2004; Gawande 2006). Doctors developed many of the methods used and both doctors and nurses participated in the atrocities in Nazi Germany (Gallagher 1990; Schmidt 2007). Even where they have not directly participated in abuses, health professionals have sustained unjust institutions or regimes by virtue of their medical authority, by attempting to continue with their healing role despite the evidence of abuse around them, or because they had become socialised to the political environment and, over time, had had their own integrity compromised.

Naomi Klein demonstrated that the torture techniques used by the United States in places such as Guantanamo Bay were developed by the Canadian psychiatrist Dr Ewen Cameron while working at McGill University and funded by the CIA. His use of sensory deprivation and intense electroshock therapy was aimed at breaking down psychiatric patients' personalities. This formed the basis of the program MKUltra – which later was used for writing the interro-gation manuals for the CIA (Klein 2007). Cameron treated patients in sound-proof rooms, with piped-in white noise, with lights turned off and the patients wearing dark goggles and 'rubber eardrums' as well as cardboard tubing on the arms and legs to stop them touching any part of themselves. Some patients were kept like this for 35 days. As Klein puts it:

> The unidentified woman in the basement of the Allan Memorial Institute, straining to hear the engine of an airplane through a haze of darkness, drugs and electroshock, was not a patient in the care of a doctor; she was for all intents and purposes, a prisoner undergoing torture. (Klein 2007)

According to the *Tokyo Declaration* of the World Medical Associations, a physician should not 'countenance, condone or participate in the practice of torture or other forms of cruel, inhuman or degrading procedures, whatever the offence of which the victim of such procedures is suspected, accused or guilty, and whatever the victim's beliefs or motives, and in all situations including armed conflict and civil strife' (Singh 2003). So how do health professional become involved in such situations?

Many of the cases of human rights abuse describe situations arising from 'dual loyalties'. These have been defined as clinical role conflicts between professional duties to a patient and obligations, express or implied, real or perceived, to the interests of a third party such as an employer, an insurer or the state (Dual Loyalties and Human Rights in Health Professional Practice: Proposed Guidelines and Institutional Mechanisms 2002). Dual loyalties are common in clinical medicine, as health professionals frequently have obligations to other parties besides their patients, and are an integral feature of much of public health care. They become particularly problematic when they compromise the interests of the patient, and/or the moral integrity of the health professional, or when they lead to a violation of human rights. This type of outcome is particularly likely to occur in repressive political regimes or in closed institutions like prisons and some health-care institutions.

Conclusion

As we have seen, it may be difficult to define standards of competency and ethical behaviour that can be applied universally – even within professional groups. It may also be very difficult for practitioners to recognise when their behaviour no longer meets the appropriate standards of competence for the profession. Professionals cannot necessarily rely on either patient satisfaction, family views, views of colleagues or views of administrators to clarify this issue although these views will provide some guidance. And although professional bodies do specify some broad limits to professional behaviour, it is not necessarily the case that even these will be acceptable to all practitioners or their patients. As Tristam Engelhardt points out:

> When a patient confronts a physician (or a nurse or other health professional) the physician is encountered within the complex context of a profession with diverse goals, only some of which are directed to the treatment and care of that patient. If the patient wants what the profession does not usually give or wants treatments that depart from the standards of the profession, the physician must bear the judgement of the profession in mind. Any negotiation with a particular patient will involve the physician in a possible negotiation with the profession. (Engelhardt 1996)

This is particularly the case if the patient requests something that is controversial or illegal – such as euthanasia.

Engelhardt goes on to say that:

> Circumstances are, however, complex, for there is not one unambiguous sense of the health care professions or the medical professions ... Thus, as patients negotiate with health professionals about their treatment and care, they will need to determine the professional commitments of those with whom they are about to enter into the agreement for care and treatment. A woman of liberal moral persuasions will need to know, for example, whether the gynaecologist with whom she is considering developing a professional relationship holds views against sterilisation and abortion. So, too, it will be prudent for

119

someone diagnosed with disseminated cancer to know the physician's views regarding the use of narcotics and other drugs in the control of pain ... So, too, the physician will need to understand the patient's expectations from care. (Engelhardt 1996)

This implies that professionals and patients cannot rely entirely on professional groups to set standards of ethical behaviour for them to abide by. An equally important part of professionalism is that many of these standards must come from within the individual or from the patient-therapist relationship.

We believe that the modern emphasis on professionalism has gone too far. Professionalism centres on the practitioner, and discussions about professionalism seem sometimes to even ignore the existence of the patient. It is important for all health professionals to bear in mind that patient autonomy, patients' rights, and patients' needs and desires are the key to what medicine is about – not the autonomy, rights and interests of the profession.

LEGAL ASPECTS OF PROFESSIONALISM: PROFESSIONAL REGISTRATION AND ACCOUNTABILITY

Registration boards

Legislation provides for the creation of boards that are responsible for regulating the members of many health professions, including allied and complementary health professionals. These professions include medical practitioners, nurses and midwives, chiropractors, dentists, dental technicians, optometrists, osteopaths, pharmacists, physiotherapists, podiatrists and psychologists. In Victoria, practitioners of Chinese medicine are also registered. The boards set standards for registration, maintain registers of qualified persons and maintain discipline within the professions. The composition of the boards vary between the professions, but they often consist of a number of professionals nominated by relevant professional associations, a professional nominated by a university (or universities), a legal professional, a nominee from the minister of the relevant department and frequently a layperson.

It should be noted, however, that not all health professions are regulated in this way and some rely only on membership of professional associations or licensing by other regulatory bodies. For example, radiographers in New South Wales are not subject to registration in the same way as medical practitioners, nurses or midwives. However, radiographers in New South Wales must hold a licence, issued by the Environment Protection Authority, in order to use radioactive substances and certain radiation apparatus. Some health professionals also need to be members of specified organisations before payments for their services can be received from government agencies.

On 26 March 2008 the Council of Australian Governments (COAG) agreed to create a single national registration and accreditation system for nine health professions: medical practitioners; nurses and midwives; pharmacists; physiotherapists; psychologists; osteopaths; chiropractors; optometrists; and dentists (including dental hygienists, dental prosthetists and dental therapists). This

National Registration and Accreditation Scheme for the Health Professions commences on 1 July 2010 and, it is hoped, will standardise the regulation of these professions (see <http://www.nhwt.gov.au/natreg.asp>). It appears that while registration and accreditation will be unified disciplinary matters will still be run by each jurisdiction.

Functions of the boards

The functions of the boards also vary depending on jurisdiction and profession. Generally, however, boards set the standard of education and experience necessary for registration and may grant exemptions from meeting the minimum qualifications in certain circumstances. Most applicants for registration are also required to be of good character (sometimes described as being a 'fit and proper person') to fulfil the practice of the profession. Some boards have additional powers to carry out research, advise governments, consult with employers, establish codes of practice and to disseminate information to the profession (Wallace 2001).

Boards also exercise a supervisory function to ensure that the conduct of registered practitioners continues to meet the standards required by the profession. If standards are not met the board may decide on disciplinary measures to be taken, including removal from the register of authorised practitioners.

Registration

Once a person has met the appropriate educational, experience and general character requirements of the board then their name may be entered onto the register on payment of an appropriate fee. Where boards refuse registration, most legislation provides for an appeal process, usually to a court or tribunal (Edginton 1995).

The legislation varies in its approach to unregistered practitioners. All legislation prohibits an unregistered person from representing themselves as registered professionals. This is to prevent health consumers from being misled into believing that the person has received a form of state endorsement that is designed to ensure the competence and good character of the practitioner. The legislation may also prohibit an unregistered practitioner from charging for their services (or enforcing a debt) in relation to the professional field being regulated. For example the *Medical Act 1894* (WA) provides (s 21) that:

> Every medical practitioner registered under this Act may, whilst so registered, sue in any Court of law of competent jurisdiction for the recovery of his fees or other remuneration for professional services, whether medical or surgical; and no person other than such registered medical practitioner shall be entitled to sue or counterclaim for set-off or recover any charge or remuneration for any medical or surgical advice, attendance, service, or operation, or for any medicine which he shall have both prescribed and supplied.

Other legislation may go so far as to prohibit an unregistered person from practising the profession. For example, the *Optometry Practice Act 2007* (SA) provides (s 35):

(1) A person must not hold himself or herself out as a registered optometry student or an optometrist, or permit another person to do so, unless registered on the appropriate register.

Maximum penalty: $50 000 or imprisonment for 6 months.

Mutual recognition

Modern professionals are mobile and often wish to change the location of their practice from one State or Territory to another. To be forced to undergo a new process of registration may be difficult and time-consuming, particularly if there are different registration requirements in the new location. Following the Special Premier's Conference in 1991 all jurisdictions have passed legislation that allows a practitioner in one jurisdiction to apply for equivalent registration in another jurisdiction (Dix, Errington et al 1996). Another advantage of the mutual recognition scheme is that if a registered person were disciplined in one jurisdiction then any condition, suspension or cancellation would be applied in all jurisdictions.

Discipline

Most boards have a role in the investigation and disciplining of the persons on their register. With the development of health care complaint organisations (see following) the tasks sometimes overlap but often, such as in New South Wales, the complaints body undertakes an investigative and prosecutorial role while the board is responsible for adjudicatory aspects.

In the early development of the professional boards, they were mostly concerned about 'quackery, false qualifications and improper advertising' while in more recent times they are more concerned with complaints concerning 'poor treatment, inadequate communication, drug and alcohol abuse, sexual misconduct and physical or mental impairment' (Dix, Errington et al 1996). Complaints that may be referred to boards can include professional misconduct, physical or mental incapacity, alcohol or drug addiction or conviction of a serious offence. For example, the New South Wales *Nurses and Midwives Act 1991* provides (s 44(1)):

> A complaint may be made that a nurse or midwife:
> (a) has been convicted of or made the subject of a criminal finding for an offence (either in or outside New South Wales) and the circumstances of the offence render the nurse or midwife unfit in the public interest to practise nursing or midwifery, or
> (b) suffers from an impairment, or
> (c) has been guilty of unsatisfactory professional conduct, or
> (d) has been guilty of professional misconduct, or
> (e) does not have sufficient physical or mental capacity to practise nursing or midwifery, or
> (f) is not of good character.

As the legislation varies so widely between the various health professions and the different jurisdictions it is not possible in this book to cover them all comprehensively. It is sufficient to note that the central criteria relate to the professional conduct required of a professional person. The conduct of a registered health professional that may be subject to disciplinary action (and for the worst examples, deregistration) has been described in the various pieces of legislation to include expressions such as 'unsatisfactory professional conduct', 'professional misconduct', 'misconduct in a professional respect', 'unprofessional conduct', 'unethical conduct' or 'infamous or improper conduct'. An example of conduct that is considered to amount to unsatisfactory professional conduct can be found in s 36 of the *Medical Practice Act 1992* (NSW). It involves:

- Any conduct that demonstrates a lack of adequate knowledge, skill, judgment or care, by the practitioner in the practice of medicine.
- Any contravention by the practitioner (whether by act or omission) of a provision of this Act or the regulations.
- Any contravention by the practitioner (whether by act or omission) of a condition to which his or her registration is subject.
- Any conduct that results in the practitioner being convicted of or being made the subject of a criminal finding for certain specified offences.
- Accepting from a health service provider (or from another person on behalf of the health service provider) a benefit as inducement, consideration or reward for:
  (i)   referring another person to the health service provider, or
  (ii) recommending another person use any health service provided by the health service provider or consult with the health service provider in relation to a health matter.
- Accepting from a person who supplies a health product (or from another person on behalf of the supplier) a benefit as inducement, consideration or reward for recommending that another person use the health product.
- Offering or giving any person a benefit as inducement, consideration or reward for the person:
  (i)   referring another person to the registered medical practitioner, or
  (ii) recommending to another person that the person use any health service provided by the practitioner or consult the practitioner in relation to a health matter.
- Referring a person to, or recommending that a person use or consult:
  (i)   another health service provider, or
  (ii) a health service, or
  (iii) a health product,
  when the practitioner has a pecuniary interest in giving that referral or recommendation, unless the practitioner discloses the nature of that interest to the person before or at the time of giving the referral or recommendation.
- Engaging in overservicing.

- Permitting an assistant employed by the practitioner (in connection with the practitioner's professional practice) who is not a registered medical practitioner to attend, treat or perform operations on patients in respect of matters requiring professional discretion or skill.
- By the practitioner's presence, countenance, advice, assistance or co-operation, knowingly enable a person who is not a registered medical practitioner (whether or not that person is described as an assistant) to:
    (i) perform any act of operative surgery (as distinct from manipulative surgery) on a patient in respect of any matter requiring professional discretion or skill, or
    (ii) issue or procure the issue of any certificate, notification, report or other like document, or to engage in professional practice, as if the person were a registered medical practitioner.
- Refusing or failing, without reasonable cause, to attend (within a reasonable time after being requested to do so) on a person for the purpose of rendering professional services in the capacity of a registered medical practitioner in any case where the practitioner has reasonable cause to believe that the person is in need of urgent attention by a registered medical practitioner, unless the practitioner has taken all reasonable steps to ensure that another registered medical practitioner attends instead within a reasonable time.
- Any other improper or unethical conduct relating to the practice or purported practice of medicine.

As you can see the list is quite extensive! Section 37 of the Act defines 'professional misconduct' as 'unsatisfactory professional conduct of a sufficiently serious nature to justify suspension of the practitioner from practising medicine or the removal of the practitioner's name from the Register'. The registration legislation may also authorise the registration board to create codes of ethics or codes of conduct, the breach of which could amount to unsatisfactory conduct.

A common approach taken when addressing issues of professional conduct is that the protection of the public is paramount. The primary aim of disciplinary proceedings is not to punish the health professional but to protect the public from harm. Often an adverse finding against a health professional will not involve removal from the register. It is far more likely that an adverse finding will result in supervision, further education, a reprimand, or suspension from practice for a period of time or a fine.

For example, in a New South Wales Court of Appeal judgment (*Health Care Complaints Commission v Litchfield* (1997) 41 NSWLR 630) the court had to consider the appropriate penalty where the Medical Tribunal had found that a medical practitioner had engaged in inappropriate sexual conduct with three female patients. The Medical Tribunal had suspended the medical practitioner from practice for nine months and ordered him to submit to psychiatric assessment to be referred to the Medical Board. The Health Care Complaints Commission appealed, seeking an order that the doctor's name be removed from the register.

The doctor in this case had been tried and acquitted on criminal charges arising from the incidents with the three female patients. However, in general, the Medical Tribunal uses a lesser standard of proof than that required in criminal trials in reviewing the facts of a case. In this case, the Court of Appeal found that the decision of the Tribunal with respect to penalty was not appropriate and ordered that the order of the Tribunal be set aside and the medical practitioner's name be removed from the Register. The court emphasised that the purpose of the Tribunal hearing was purely protective (of patients), and that no element of punishment was involved.

The court said:

> Female patients entrust themselves to doctors, male and female, for medical examination and treatment which may require intimate physical contact which they would not otherwise accept from the doctor. The standards of the profession oblige doctors to use the opportunities afforded them for such contact for proper therapeutic purposes and not otherwise. This is the standard that the public in general and female patients in particular expect from their doctors, and which right thinking members of the profession observe, and expect their colleagues to observe. (at 638)

Impaired practitioners

Some of the health profession legislation or registration boards provide for circumstances where the health professional may be 'impaired'. A practitioner is generally considered to be impaired if he or she suffers from any physical or mental condition which detrimentally affects, or is likely to detrimentally affect, his or her capacity to practise their profession. A uniform definition is used in NSW in s 10 of the *Physiotherapists Act 2001*, the *Chiropractors Act 2001*, the *Optometrists Act 2002*, the *Pharmacy Practice Act 2006*, the *Podiatrists Act 2003*, the *Osteopaths Act 2001* and the *Dental Practice Act 2001*. It states:

> (1) For the purposes of this Act, a person suffers from an impairment if the person suffers from any physical or mental impairment, disability, condition or disorder that detrimentally affects or is likely to detrimentally affect the person's physical or mental capacity to practise physiotherapy [chiropractic, dentistry etc ...].

> (2) For the purposes of this Act, a person who habitually abuses alcohol or is addicted to a deleterious drug is taken to suffer from an impairment.

It is important to recognise that a health professional may be unwell or disabled without being impaired. Impairment is specifically related to risk to the public.

Self-reporting of impairment is sometimes mandatory for the impaired professional and the failure to self-report may be unsatisfactory conduct. For example in NSW, the *Code of Professional Practice* of the Psychologists Registration Board states:

> 4 iv. Psychologists should withdraw from practice (and seek professional help where appropriate for their impairment) when a physical or psychological condition (for example, as a result of alcohol, drugs, illness or personal stress)

seriously impairs their abilities or professional judgement. In cases of less serious impairment, Psychologists should consult with colleagues about the extent they should withdraw from or adjust their practice. (NSW Psychologists Registration Board 2004)

In Victoria, the law provides for registered health professionals to self-report impairment, but it does not make it mandatory. Under s 38 of the *Health Professions Registration Act 2005*, Chinese medicine practitioners, chiropractors, dentists, doctors, medical radiation practitioners, nurses, optometrists, osteopaths, pharmacists and physiotherapists can report themselves to their responsible boards when they believe that:

(a)   his or her ability to practise as a health practitioner is affected because —
   (i)   of his or her physical or mental health; or
   (ii)   he or she has an incapacity; or
   (iii)   he or she is an alcoholic or drug-dependent person; or
(b)   he or she has engaged in unprofessional conduct or professional misconduct; or
(c)   his or her professional performance is unsatisfactory...

Health professionals involved in the treatment of other health professionals may also need to report their colleagues to registration authorities. In Victoria s 36 of the *Health Professions Registration Act 2005* makes it a requirement for registered medical practitioners to report the ill-health of allied health professionals or students when the professionals/students are suffering from an illness or condition which:

(i)   has seriously impaired or may seriously impair that person's ability to practise as a registered health practitioner or that student's ability to undertake clinical training; and
(ii)   may result in the public being put at risk ... (s 36(b))

In NSW if a treating health professional finds that a registered doctor has mental incapacity they must report that to the Medical Board under both s 70 of the *Medical Practice Act 1992* and cl 11 of the *Medical Practice Regulation 2003*. In South Australia under s 49 of the *Medical Practice Act 2004*, health professionals, hospital administrators, and teachers of medical students must report on health professionals and medical students they suspect of being medically unfit to provide medical treatment. In Tasmania, a registered medical practitioner who signs an order under the *Mental Health Act 1996* or a medical recommendation under the *Alcohol and Drug Dependency Act 1968,* in relation to registered a medical practitioner, must give the Medical Council notice of that fact: *Medical Practitioners Registration Act 1996*, s 75. Generally, health professionals who report a colleague or student with an impairment are given protection from any civil liability, if the report is made in good faith.

After reporting, the registration authority can take disciplinary action, or may also refer to the allied health professional to an impairment panel, which has powers to investigate the professional's impairment, supervise the professional and/or make orders as to their work. Impairment panels are common in the regulation of psychologists, physiotherapists, dentists, pharmacists, chiropractors and osteopaths. There is now a greater emphasis on treatment and rehabilitation of the impaired practitioner, negotiated where possible on an individual and confidential basis. Formal disciplinary powers are usually kept in reserve. The registration boards often establish impairment programs overseen by an impairment committee or panel. The objective of such programs is to protect the public, although there is a strong secondary objective to maintain the health professional in safe practice whenever possible.

Reporting colleagues for unethical, incompetent or criminal behaviour

Outside of impairment, health professionals may also report their colleagues to regulating authorities for unethical behaviour, incompetent practices and criminal acts. Normally the reporting of such conduct is covered by professional codes so that the failure to report would be dealt with as a form of unsatisfactory conduct or professional misconduct. In some jurisdictions, the right to report colleagues is enshrined in legislation. For example, in the ACT s 78 of the *Health Professions Act 2004* empowers registered health professionals to report other health professionals for contravening standards, and gives the reporting health professional civil and criminal protection by deeming such a report not to be a breach of confidence, professional etiquette, professional ethics or professional conduct. No civil or criminal liability is incurred through the making of a report.

In NSW such reporting has become mandatory for registered medical practitioners. Amendments to the *Medical Practice Act 1992* (NSW) by the *Medical Practice Amendment Act 2008* create a new category of conduct defined as 'reportable misconduct' which must be reported to the NSW Medical Board when a registered medical practitioner believes, or ought reasonably to believe, that such misconduct has occurred. 'Reportable misconduct' is defined to include:

- a medical practitioner practising when under the influence of drugs or alcohol;
- a medical practitioner practising medicine in a manner that constitutes a flagrant departure from accepted standards of professional practice or competence and risks harm to some other person; and
- a medical practitioner being involved in sexual misconduct. (s 71A)

Under the amendments if a medical practitioner fails to report their colleague for such conduct, the medical practitioner will have committed either unsatisfactory professional conduct or professional misconduct.

The changes were in response to the investigation into the practice of Dr Graham Reeves, dubbed by the media as the 'Butcher of Bega'. Reeves is alleged to have been involved in improper practices in obstetrics and gynaecology. It has also been alleged that Reeves's colleagues were in a position to know about these practices and could have perhaps prevented them. However, it has also been reported that the registration authorities and his employers did know about Dr Reeves's past conduct and restrictions that had been placed on his practice by registration authorities. At the time of writing the matter is being investigated but it is possible that this case may not have actually been a failure to track and report behaviour but rather a failure by authorities to act on the information they already had in their possession (Australian Broadcasting Corporation 2008).

The existence of a sexual relationship between a patient and a colleague should also be reported, according to most codes of professional practice. For example, in Queensland a uniform policy applies to nurses, doctors, radiation technologists, dental technicians, prosthetists, pharmacists, physiotherapists, speech pathologists, psychologist, podiatrists, chiropractors and optometrists. The *Statement on Sexual Relationships Between Health Practitioners and their Patients 2005* contains the following:

> 5.1 A health practitioner who becomes aware that another practitioner has behaved improperly and unprofessionally by engaging in sexually exploitative or abusive behaviour toward a patient or former patient should take appropriate action including reporting to the relevant Board or the Health Rights Commissioner and/or encouraging the patient to report the matter.

> 5.2 When informed by a patient that another health practitioner may have been involved in sexually exploitative or abusive behaviour, health practitioners have an obligation to:

>> 5.2.1 inform the patient of their rights;

>> 5.2.2 endeavour to answer any questions the patient raises about the issue of sexual exploitation or abuse by health practitioners;

>> 5.2.3 ask whether the patient wishes to make a report to the Health Rights Commissioner or appropriate Board;

>> 5.2.4 refer them to an independent third party who may provide support and assistance in writing their report;

>> 5.2.5 keep accurate and detailed records of the patient's disclosure of the other health practitioner's behaviour.

> 5.3 If the patient does not want their name revealed, but still wants the matter reported, the health practitioner should report to the appropriate Board, disclosing the details provided by the patient, and the reasons for anonymity.

> 5.4 If the patient does not want to report, the health practitioner needs to make a judgement based on the specifics of the case weighed against the patient's choice. While there is no obligation for the health practitioner to take the matter further, evidence of, for instance, ongoing abuse, exploitation or criminal activity would be grounds to disregard the patient's wishes.

Health-care complaints

While regulatory boards do address complaints about quality of care and the standards of individual practitioners, it seems desirable for other mechanisms to exist that can assist in resolving complaints at the point of service.

All jurisdictions in Australia have provided mechanisms to allow for the establishment of independent complaints organisations to receive, assess, investigate, review, refer and conciliate health consumer complaints (see Table 8.1). The independent complaints commissions provide an important avenue for resolving many patient concerns regarding the quality of care or about specific health professionals without the need for litigation.

Table 8.1   Health Care Complaints

Jurisdiction	Legislation
NSW	Health Care Complaints Act 1993
Qld	Health Quality and Complaints Commission Act 2006
SA	Health and Community Services Complaints Act 2004
Tas	Health Complaints Act 1995
Vic	Health Services (Conciliation and Review) Act 1987
WA	Health Services (Conciliation and Review) Act 1995
ACT	Human Rights Commission Act 2005
NT	Health and Community Services Complaints Act 1998

Health service complaints legislation varies between States and Territories in its coverage of the different health professions. In each of the jurisdictions a 'health service' may include: medical, hospital and nursing services; dental services; psychiatric services; pharmaceutical services; ambulance services; community health services; health education services; relevant welfare services; services provided by dieticians, masseurs, naturopaths, acupuncturists, audiologists, audiometrists, optical dispensers and services provided in other alternative health care fields. Different jurisdictions may also cover services such as: radiography, psychiatric services, chiropractors, osteopaths, optometrists, physiotherapists, psychologists, occupational therapists, speech therapists, chiropodists, traditional Chinese medicine and podiatrists (reference should be made to the appropriate legislation to confirm coverage).

Complaints may be made by any user of the health services or by their representatives (in some States, like New South Wales, any person may make a complaint). There are some minor differences between jurisdictions with respect to additional persons and circumstances where others may make a complaint. Generally, the complainant must be identified but there are various provisions that may allow the complainant's name to be kept confidential. There is a general requirement that complaints must be in writing, although there may be circumstances where an oral complaint is sufficient.

In all jurisdictions the legislation allows for a complaint to be investigated, and provision is made to allow conciliation of health complaints by persons appointed as conciliators. The conciliation process is confidential and nothing revealed during the process can be used before a court or tribunal. Conciliators make reports on the outcome of the conciliation process; and if there has been no agreement between the parties the conciliator can make a recommendation that the complaint should be investigated or that the complaint should be referred to a relevant registration board. The complaint between the parties can be resolved at any time and, where the matter has been resolved, the Commission must be notified of the outcome and so cease dealing with the complaint. The various complaints commissions and registration boards usually cooperate when any complaint is received.

References

Australian Broadcasting Corporation (2008) Govt seeks charges against banned Bega doctor. <http://www.abc.net.au/news/stories/2008/07/31/2320414.htm>.

Blank, L, H Kimball et al (2003) 'Medical Professionalism in the New Millennium: A Physician Charter 15 Months Later'. *Ann Intern Med* **138**(10): 839-41.

Cartwright, F (1997) *A social history of medicine.* London, Longman.

Chadwick, R and A Thompson (2000) 'Professional Ethics and Labor Disputes: Medicine and Nursing in the United Kingdom'. *Cambridge Quarterly of Healthcare Ethics* **9**(483-497).

Compton, B and B Galaway (1995) *Social Work Processes.* Belmont, California, Wadsworth Publishing Company.

Davies, C (1995a) 'Cloaked in a tattered illusion'. *Nursing Times* **92**(45): 45-6.

Davies, C (1995b) 'A new vision of professionalism'. *Nursing Times* **92**(46): 54-6.

de Gruchy, J and J Fish (2004) 'Doctor's involvement in human rights abuses of men who have sex with men in Egypt'. *Lancet* **363**: 1903.

Dix, A, M Errington et al (1996) *Law for the medical profession.* Butterworth Heinemann Australia.

Dudzinski, DM (2004) 'Integrity in the relationship between medical ethics and professionalism'. *Am J Bioeth* **4**(2): 26-7.

Edginton, J (1995) *Law for the Nursing Profession and allied health care professionals.* Sydney, CCH Australia Ltd.

Engelhardt, HT (1996) *The foundations of bioethics.* New York, Oxford University Press.

Friedson, E (1970) *Profession of Medicine.* New York, Dodd, Mead.

Friedson, E (1970) *Professional dominance.* New York, Atheron.

Gallagher, H (1990) *By trust betrayed. Patients, physicians and the license to kill in the Third Reich.* New York, Henry Holt and Company.

Gawande, A (2006) 'When law and ethics collide--why physicians participate in executions'. *N Engl J Med* **354**(12): 1221-9.

Jesilow, P, G Geis et al (1991) 'Fraud by physicians against Medicaid'. *JAMA* **266**: 318-22.

Klein, N (2007) *The shock doctrine.* London, Allen Lane.

Kravitz, R and L Linn (1992) 'Conditions that justify strikes as perceived by housestaff at a public hospital'. *Acad Med* **67**(5): 342-4.

Lifton, R (2004) 'Doctors and torture'. *N Engl J Med* **351**(5): 415-16.

Medical Professionalism Project (2002) 'Medical professionalism in the new millennium: a physician charter'. *Ann Intern Med* **136**: 243-6.

Osler, W (1932) *Aequanimitas.* McGraw Hill.

Porter, S (1992) 'The poverty of professionalization: a critical analysis of strategies for occupational advancement of nursing'. *J Adv Nurs* **17**(6): 720-6.

Scarlet, E (1991) What is a profession? *On Doctoring.* R Reynolds and J Stone. New York, Simon and Schuster.

Schmidt, U (2007) *Karl Brandt: the Nazi doctor: Medicine and power in the Third Reich.* London, Hambeldon and London.

Sharfstein, J and S Sharfstein (1994) 'Campaign contributions from the American Medical Political Action Committee to members of Congress – for or against the public health'. *N Engl J Med* **330**(32-7).

Singh, J (2003) 'American physicians and dual loyalty obligations in the "war on terrorism".' *BMC Med Ethics* **4**: 1-10.

Tschudin, V (1986) *Ethics in nursing; the caring relationship.* London, Heinemann.

Wallace, M (2001) *Health care and the law.* Sydney, Lawbook Co.

Wear, D and M Kuczewski (2004) 'The professionalism movement: can we pause?' *Am Jn Bioethics* **4**(2): 1-10.

Wessley, S (2007) 'When doctors become terrorists'. *N Engl J Med* **357**: 635-7.

Zion, D (2004) 'Caring for detained asylum seekers, human rights and bioethics'. *Aust NZ J Public Health* **28**(6): 6-8.

CHAPTER 8

STANDARDS OF CARE, ERROR AND NEGLIGENCE

Case 1

An occupational therapist was called upon to assess the home skills of an 89-year-old man with multiple problems. The client was very insistent that he wished to return home and, despite reservations about his ability to cope, the occupational therapist felt that his wishes should override other considerations. She therefore recommended that he be discharged. Three days later he was admitted again, seriously unwell after falling and breaking his hip and spending the night lying on the floor before he was found.

The client's family, who flew from interstate when he was readmitted, were extremely unhappy that he had been 'allowed to go home' after the first admission. They lodged a complaint with the hospital and the Department of Health and stated that they were considering legal action. The occupational therapist was asked to explain her actions to the hospital administration and to write an apology for what had occurred to the client's family. However, despite the patient suffering an adverse effect, the family being upset, the medical administration blaming her, and despite her having to write an apology, she still felt that she had behaved appropriately.

Case 2

In June 1998, the Professional Conduct Committee of the General Medical Council of the United Kingdom (the body which regulates British doctors) concluded the longest-running case it has considered this century. Three medical practitioners were accused of serious professional misconduct relating to 29 deaths (and four survivors with brain damage) in 53 paediatric cardiac operations undertaken at the Bristol Royal Infirmary between 1988 and 1995. All three denied the charges but, after 65 days of evidence over eight months (costing 2.2 million pounds), all were found guilty ... The central allegations were that the Chief Executive and the Medical Director of the Trust allowed to be carried out, and the two paediatric cardiac surgeons carried out, operations on children knowing that the mortality rates for these operations, in the hands of these surgeons, were high. Furthermore, the surgeons were accused of not communicating to the parents the correct risk of death for these operations in their hands ... (Bolsin 1998)

Perhaps the only common ground that is held by all professions is that professionalism involves a commitment to proficiency. Professional proficiency may be sought through long training periods and difficult entry requirements, through periodic review and through the oversight of disciplinary bodies. But, most importantly, professionals are expected to internalise the standards of the profession that guide their day-to-day work.

Adverse events

When patients are treated in the health system they may suffer negative consequences of that treatment. Part of this is inevitable – most forms of treatment have some risk and when patients consent to treatment it is accepted by all that there is some risk of a poor outcome.

Adverse events are generally defined as injuries or setbacks to a person's interests (Davies, Hebert et al 2003). Some adverse events are preventable, many are not. Of those that are preventable, some are due to error on the part of the practitioners. An error has been defined as a failure to complete a planned action as it was intended, or when an incorrect plan is used in an attempt to achieve a given aim (Leape 1994). Some errors are due to an understandable lapse in human judgement, others may be defined as negligent (Hebert, Levin et al 2001). Adverse events due to wilful violation of health practice and procedures (such as refusal to abide by infection control guidelines) are not errors at all, and cannot be tolerated (Goldmann 2006).

There are high levels of adverse events experienced by people being treated within the health-care system. Several studies have demonstrated that the number of adverse events that occur is much larger than was previously thought.

The Harvard Medical Practice Study of 1984 reviewed medical records from 30,000 hospital discharges and 3500 malpractice claims in New York. They showed that adverse events occurred in 3.7% of hospitalisations, and they attributed 27.6% of these to medical negligence (Brennan, Leape et al 1991).

The Quality in Australian Health Care Study, using a similar methodology, found that 16.6% of admissions were associated with adverse events, 51% of which were considered preventable (Wilson, Runciman et al 1995). 13.7% of patients who suffered adverse events ended up with some degree of permanent disability and 4.9% of identified cases died. The authors extrapolated their results to all acute hospitals in Australia and suggested that, in 1992, 18,000 patients would have died as a result of their health-care and 50,000 patients would have suffered permanent disability.

In a more recent study, 6.8% of patients admitted to Victorian hospitals in 2003-04 suffered adverse events. These patients stayed an estimated 10 days longer in hospital, had seven times the risk of in-hospital death, and cost 15.7% of the total hospital expenditure ($460 million) (Ehsani, Jackson et al 2006). This is consistent with studies from the UK, Denmark, France, New Zealand, Canada and Spain which show similar rates of adverse events (3-16% of hospitalised patients) and preventability (20-50% of such events) (Hebert, Levin et al 2008). All of these studies have limitations, but together they clearly suggest that adverse events and errors are significant issues in health care.

Responding to adverse events

The Harvard study looked specifically at whether the legal system dealt with these adverse events appropriately. First, they found that there were 7.6 times as many negligent injuries as there were legal claims. And when they attempted to match the legal claims with the cases that had been identified as negligent, they found that only 2% of negligent injuries resulted in claims and only 17% of claims appeared to involve a negligent injury (Localio, Lawthers et al 1991). A similar mismatch between legal claims and adverse events has been noted in other American studies (Studdart, Mello et al 2004).

Many health professionals greatly fear such a haphazard legal response to errors, and feel that they must be very careful to protect themselves. Some argue that this results in the practice of so-called 'defensive medicine', in which unnecessary investigation and treatment is carried out for the sole purpose of decreasing medico-legal risk. Several studies have looked at the costs of defensive medicine in the American setting by comparing States in which there is a cap on the amount for which a doctor can be sued for negligence compared to those in which there is no cap (Kessler, Summerton et al 2006). States with caps reduced hospital expenditures by 5-9%, and had an increased overall retention of doctors compared to uncapped States.

If we extrapolate these results to Australia, then it seems possible that the Australian legal response to negligence may be the cause of similar problems, and may lead to an increase in defensive medicine (Nash, Tennant et al 2004).

The main problem with defensive medicine is that it is both illogical and counterproductive. First, on any assessment of risk, the likelihood of being sued in Australia for professional negligence is low, especially when one compares the rates of preventable and serious adverse injuries with the number of claims made. Secondly, defensive medicine also has the potential to increase the risk of being sued as it necessarily exposes the patient to further inventions, which consequently further exposes the patient to medical injury. To that degree, health professionals need to be cognisant that the best approach to minimising the risk of being sued is to ignore the legal risk altogether and focus on providing the best care that is possible in the patient's circumstances. This approach is even more appropriate in recent times given the changes in the test for standards of care that are discussed below.

Openness

The professions have responded to the problem of adverse events through increasing emphasis on quality assurance and patient safety. One of the key insights of the 'quality' movement has been that there has been a culture of secrecy in the health professions (in response to the threat of medico-legal litigation) that has made it very difficult to deal with problems when they occur. This recognition has led to a call for increasing openness about mistakes and adverse events, so that they can be examined properly and prevented.

From an ethics point of view, disclosure is desirable:

1. to prevent further harm to patients;
2. to facilitate public trust;
3. it is consistent the moral obligation of the patient:therapist relationship;
4. it is consistent with social trends towards transparency;
5. it manifests for patients as people;
6. it enables patients to seek restitution where appropriate;
7. it enables efforts to improve patient safety. (Bok 1979)

In the past, many people who have experienced adverse events have had this hidden from them. This sort of lying is obviously unethical. It has also been found that people who have been damaged by medical error are more likely to commence legal proceedings if they feel that they have been lied to. An example of this was given to the NSW Government Standing Committee into Complaint Handling within NSW Health.

An 18-month-old child was given an accidental overdose of an anti-convulsant by an inexperienced team in an emergency department. The child arrested and died despite 30 minutes attempted resuscitation, from which the parents were excluded. The hospital management expressly prohibited staff from approaching the parents. This is a brief extract from the statement by the child's mother. She is talking about the Coroner's Court 10 months later:

> We later found out that the doctor wanted to be the one to tell us. He wanted to tell us then and there but the hospital protocol did not allow it. I had to wait 10 months to hear, "I'm sorry."

> The nurse that was involved in the procedure ... we had to wait 10 months to meet her, and she was banned from approaching us. And we were actually at the Coroner's Court. I am standing in the line to the ladies toilet. I am in a public toilet and the lady's standing behind me, I happened to recognise her, and I said, "You are one of the nurses from the hospital, aren't you?" She said, "I am the nurse." She breaks down and cries and I break down and cry. And this is all happening in the public toilet, the last place this should happen. It is one of the most emotional meetings I have ever had, and all she ever wanted to say to me was, "I'm sorry" and all she could keep saying was, "I'm sorry, I'm so sorry." We ended up embracing and it was something we needed to do. I needed to hear that "I'm sorry" and she needed to say it. And it is happening in the public toilet. It is something the hospital should have organized. (NSW Parliament. Legislative Council. General Purpose Standing Committee Number 2 2004)

Another reason for the increasing emphasis on quality assurance and patient safety is that there has been increasing recognition that most adverse events and medical errors are due to multiple issues, not just the actions of individual practitioners. In a 1994 article, Leape stated that '[p]hysicians and nurses need to accept the notion that human error is an inevitable accompaniment of the human condition, even amongst conscientious professionals with high standards. Errors must be accepted as evidence of system flaws not character flaws' (Leape 1994).

For example, a patient may die suddenly from a pulmonary embolus. Although this may not be recognised as an adverse effect of therapy, it may have occurred because the junior doctor forgot to chart prophylactic heparin or because the hospital has a routine of not using any prophylactic measures for thrombo-embolism, or because orders were charted but were somehow mis-filed, or any combination of these. Systems errors may also result from management by staff who are unfamiliar with the patient, and tiredness and overwork (Wu, Folkman et al 1991; Peterson, Brennan et al 1994).

Health workers, and the health-care system, must learn to anticipate and prevent errors, and respond to errors that do occur in order to prevent them from recurring. This focus on identifying and correcting errors requires openness of reporting, and has become part of the basis for quality assurance activities that are now carried out in most health institutions.

Patients who have suffered from adverse events

At an institutional level, the balance between a 'blame-free' systems approach to medical error and a more traditional legalistic approach continues to be nego-tiated. From an ethical perspective, however, patients who have been harmed by medical care need to experience good communication including a clear explanation of what went wrong, how the error occurred, and what steps have been taken to prevent it happening again, accompanied by an apology from the person responsible.

According to Allsopp:

> The patient is entitled to a prompt, sympathetic and, above all, truthful account of what has occurred. This should be given either by the practitioner concerned or, if appropriate, by a senior colleague such as the consultant in charge. It is plain that for a patient to hear of such an event from a third party such as a porter or receptionist is the worst of all possible options. It is very important that a sincere and honest apology is made. Any patient who has had the misfortune to suffer through an error of whatever nature should receive a proper expression of regret. To apologise that such an incident should have occurred is, after all, only common courtesy and should not be confused with a formal admission of legal liability. (Allsopp 1986)

It should be noted however, that while such an approach may decrease the practitioner's risk of being sued by disgruntled patients (although the evidence for this is largely anecdotal), it will not eradicate the risk entirely and may increase the likelihood of success in any such case.

It is emotionally very difficult to be involved in adverse events and the subsequent legal and institutional responses to these. Health workers should actively seek help to debrief and be counselled after such events. Many people deal with such stresses by talking to colleagues, friends and family in an effort to 'share the stress around'. In situations in which there are legal ramifications this might not always be possible, and here professional advice should always be sought. Many hospitals have provision for staff counselling and care in the event of going to court and many professional bodies now also provide such support.

Health professionals tend to judge themselves harshly if they make mistakes that impact upon patients, and often ignore the fact that many mistakes are multi-factorial and involve systems errors. A more constructive approach to errors is to attempt to separate one's own role in the error from problems within the system that can be rectified. At times all that can be gained from such situations is the knowledge and conviction to avoid making such an error again – an insight that should be disseminated to one's colleagues and addressed both within the health-care institution and the profession as a whole.

There are now guidelines for reporting, disclosure and management of adverse events in most health institutions (Runciman, Merry et al 2007). Disclosure should take place at an appropriate time – such as when the patients is stable enough to absorb information, at an appropriate place – preferably a quiet, calm environment where the patient has support. There should be a clear explanation of what has occurred, acknowledgement of error, an explanation of the steps taken to respond to this error and, where appropriate, an apology should be offered (Hebert, Levin et al 2008). It should be noted that there is a greater duty to disclose major errors than to disclose minor errors where there is no apparent harm (Bogardis, Holmboe et al 1999).

Government and public responses to adverse events

Government bodies have enthusiastically promoted the quality assurance and patient safety agenda. In Australia, hospitals have been urged to set up quality assurance procedures, and limited legal liability has been given to committees within the health system so practitioners can talk about mistakes in an open fashion. Government-mandated professional regulatory bodies have begun offering counselling to members who are thought to be impaired, or else have imposed conditions of registration such as restricting the hours of work or withdrawing the right to prescribe opiates, instead of always taking a heavy-handed approach to these issues.

All of this has represented an attempt to move to a 'no-blame' culture rather than a culture that blames individuals for mistakes and hence discourages them from speaking about and dealing with their mistakes.

Unfortunately, neither the public nor the legal system has wholly supported these changes. The media and legal proceedings continue to emphasise 'blame' and, indeed, at times it appears that many members of the public would like to see a culture of blame continue.

A good example of these issues came when in November 2002, when four nurses who had been employed by Camden and Campbelltown hospitals made allegations of substandard care to the NSW Minister of Health. This eventually resulted in an investigation by the NSW Health Complaints Commission and subsequently a commission of inquiry into Campbelltown and Camden Hospitals. The Health Care Complaints Commissioner dealt with these complaints as systems errors rather than as complaints against particular practitioners. This was criticised severely by the subsequent Commission of Inquiry. The Commissioner stated:

The very notion that a public regulator such as the HCCC could prepare a report which substantiates ... allegations of inadequate care etc on the part of identifiable doctors, without regarding those allegations as a complaint *against* that doctor is offensive to a sense of fairness.

In his interim report, the Commissioner also noted:

In the next phase of this Inquiry, opportunities will be provided for those who espouse the view that the medical and nursing disciplinary system is excessively concerned with blame and thereby sacrifices systemic improvement, to explain and defend it. For my part, as a preliminary to the next phase, I should say that this Inquiry to date discredits the notion that individual accountability through professional discipline is inconsistent with systemic improvement of clinical care and institutional administration. The health system requires individual professionals to do their work well. Improvement of the system cannot possibly require removal of the possibility of disciplinary sanction for those who fall badly below proper standards of conduct. (Walker 2004)

Whistleblowing

A whistleblower is an employee, former employee or member of an organisation, especially a business or government agency, who reports misconduct to people or entities that have the power and presumed willingness to take corrective action (Wikipedia accessed 12/6/2008). In the health system, whistleblowers have exposed a number of breaches of practice in Australia (Kennedy and Walker 2007), the UK and elsewhere (Bolsin 1998; Paul 2000; Walker 2004).

Many whistleblowers in Australia and elsewhere have been nurses. Wilmot has analysed nurse whistleblowing from the view that nurse's duties to patients must take preference to their duties to employers. She says:

Although both duties are based on an implicit or an explicit promise, the promise to a person (the patient) must take precedence over the promise to an organization. It can even be argued that duty to the employer may in fact justify whistleblowing by nurses in some circumstances. However, the consequences of whistleblowing are forced upon nurses in a different way by the fact that the danger of reprisals acts as a deterrent to whistleblowers, however justified their actions may be (Wilmot 2000).

According to Faunce, 'without exception, public inquiries initiated by healthcare whistle blowers have validated their central allegations' (Faunce and Bolsin 2004). While this may generally be true, there is no guarantee that whistleblowers have not got things wrong, so all allegations by whistleblowers must be fully investigated.

Organisations commonly react to whistleblowers by marginalising them, criticising them, blaming them and sometimes dismissing them. For example, Dr Stephen Bolsin, after blowing the whistle on high death rates in a British cardiac surgical unit, said 'I was seen as the problem, rather than the death rates being the problem' (Editorial 1998). It is therefore an act that must be considered carefully. Whistleblowers must be absolutely clear of the factual details, must reflect carefully about other mechanisms for complaint before going outside the system and must be prepared for possible adverse reactions. Whistleblowing is a courageous response to injustice, but it should be a last option rather than a first option.

It is essential that governments and institutions have mechanisms in place to protect whistleblowers, and some legislation is now available to do this (Northern Territory Department of Justice (Policy Division) 2004).

LEGAL ASPECTS: STANDARDS OF CARE AND NEGLIGENCE

In this chapter we are concerned with the tort of negligence and its role in influencing the standards of care expected of health professionals.   In the New South Wales Court of Appeal judgment in *Cekan v Haines* (1990) 21 NSWLR 296 at 299-300, Kirby P (as he then was) said of the tort of negligence:

> [T]he law of negligence has a dual aspect. It exists both to compensate a person who has suffered a wrong and also to state the standards of the community in respect of wrongs. There is no doubt that those standards change over time. Economic and social change, community expectations and knowledge in relevant people affect those changing standards. The advent of insurance has also, doubtless, had a consequence upon the development of common law principle, although rarely acknowledged.

The above quote indicates that negligence has two functions: a *compensation* function (to return an injured party to his or her pre-tort position) and an *educational/deterrence* function (to set standards of behaviour and to deter sub-standard conduct). But tort law also has a third function as well: that of *retribution*, to punish the wrongdoer (or *tortfeasor*). The retribution function is very much based on the concepts of fault which underpin negligence claims.

There are four basic elements that need to be established before negligence can be proven:

- that a defendant owed a duty of care to the plaintiff;
- that the appropriate standard of care has been breached;
- that as a result of the breach damage has been caused to the plaintiff and the damage was not 'too remote'; and
- there are no defences which wholly or partially excuse the defendant's negligent behaviour.

Each of these elements is examined in turn, but before they are examined it is important to reflect on the recent history of tort law. In the past eight years there have been substantial changes to tort law because of a perception that there was an unsustainable increase in the amount of tort claims being made and an unsustainable increase in the amount of damages being awarded for injuries. Groups of health professionals, including the Australian Medical Association, argued that Australia was in the grip of a 'litigation crisis'. These concerns reached high levels when a prominent provider of medical indemnity insurance, United Medical Protection, went into voluntary liquidation.

On 30 May 2002, a Ministerial Meeting on Public Liability, comprising Ministers from the Commonwealth, States and Territory governments, jointly agreed to appoint a Panel of four persons to examine and review the law of negligence including its interaction with the *Trade Practices Act 1974* (Cth). The Panel was chaired by Justice David Ipp and a final report ('the Ipp Report') was submitted to the Minister for Revenue and Assistant Treasurer on 30 September 2002. The recommendations of the Committee ('the Ipp reforms') have been implemented to varying degrees by each State and Territory. Those changes are canvassed below but it can be said that most of the legislative reforms merely codified existing common law positions or made modest changes to substantive elements of tort law. The real changes made were in the area of damages calculation and assessment. A number of severe limits have now been placed on the assessment of damages, including caps (which are discussed below).

Table: Ipp Reform legislation

Jurisdiction	Legislation
New South Wales	*Civil Liability Act 2002*
Queensland	*Civil Liability Act 2003*
South Australia	*Civil Liability Act 1936*
Tasmania	*Civil Liability Act 2002*
Victoria	*Wrongs Act 1958* (Vic)
Western Australia	*Civil Liability Act 2002*
Australian Capital Territory	*Civil Law (Wrongs) Act 2002*
Northern Territory	*Personal Injuries (Liabilities and Damages) Act 2003*

Interestingly, the Ipp committee was not asked to examine whether there was, in fact, a litigation crisis taking place – they were instructed to proceed on the basis that there was one. There is conflicting evidence as to whether there was a noticeable increase in the amount of litigation in Australia in the past 10-15 years. The Legal Process Reform Group of the Australian Health Ministers' Advisory Council stated:

> 3.25 It seems likely that there has been an increase in claims numbers over the past 10-15 years – possibly doubling over that period in some jurisdictions. However, this is not simply explained by a theory of more litigious patients. Over that same period, the number of Medicare services provided has increased by 66% and the number of hospital admissions has increased by 76% so a significant proportion of that increase will have arisen from greater exposure to risk. (Legal Process Reform Group 2002)

Contrastingly, Professor Ted Wright's study of litigation patterns during the period concluded that there was little evidence that there had been a substantial increase in the number of claims made or in payouts from courts over the period. In some jurisdictions claim numbers were trending downwards before the introduction of the Ipp changes (Wright 2006).

While the cause of this insurance crisis is still debated it is true that the insurance industry was undergoing pressure from other quarters. It was certainly the case that for some medical specialty areas, such as obstetrics, neuro-surgery and orthopaedic surgery, indemnity premiums had reached very high levels. The issue is therefore how to balance the need to provide affordable insurance with the need to provide fair compensation for those who have been injured. Unfortunately, as stated by the Legal Reform Process Group:

> Many changes which are suggested as so-called tort reforms are simply benefit reductions, which if not well-considered will have the affect of increasing the harm and disadvantage suffered by those people who are most in need of assistance. Cost containment is an appropriate aim for reform. However the means of doing so needs to be considered and the basis for changes justified by the evidence.

It is arguable that the current reforms are simply a response to the Australian insurance industry's need for greater profitability, rather than any great leap forward for tort law reform. The past few years represent a real lost opportunity to rethink and reform the laws regarding preventable injuries. Critically, the Ipp 'reforms' do nothing directly to address issues of how to reduce accidents and adverse events. If the numbers of severe adverse events continue at currently estimated levels, the Ipp reform will do little to reduce the number of claims in the longer term. Professor Loane Skene has estimated that claim numbers may soon start to rise again and that the initial fall in claim numbers was just a temporary lull brought on by the rush of lawyers lodging claims in time to avoid the onset of the reforms (Skene 2008). If, in a few years time, claim numbers have climbed it will be worth asking the question of why our legislatures so severely curtailed the rights of injured people to compensation, for so little, if any, public benefit.

Did the defendant owe a duty of care?

Reasonable foreseeability, proximity, and incrementalism

In most cases it is accepted by the parties that a health professional owes a duty of care to a patient. However, there may be some cases (see below) where this will be in doubt and so we need to be aware of how a duty of care is established in law. The modern test for establishing the existence of a duty of care may be found in the 1932 House of Lords decision in *Donoghue v Stevenson* [1932] AC 562 at 580:

> [I]n English law there must be, and is, some general conception of relations giving rise to a duty of care, of which the particular cases found in the books are but instances. The liability for negligence, whether you style it such or treat it as in other systems as species of 'culpa' is no doubt based upon a general public sentiment of moral wrongdoing for which the offender must pay. But acts or omissions which any moral code would censure cannot in a practical world be treated so as to give a right to every person injured by them to demand relief. In this way rules of law arise which limit the range of complaints and the extent of their remedy. The rule that you are to love your

neighbour becomes in law, you must not injure your neighbour; and the lawyer's question, 'who is my neighbour?' receives a restricted reply. You must take reasonable care to avoid acts or omissions which you can reasonably foresee would be likely to injure your neighbour. Who, then, in law is my neighbour? The answer seems to be – persons who are so closely and directly affected by my act that I ought reasonably to have them in contemplation as being so affected when I am directing my mind to the acts or omissions which are called in question.

The above guiding principles are now firmly embedded in the law of negligence of most common law countries. This is often referred to as the 'neighbour principle' or 'reasonable foreseeability test'. The neighbour principle has been expanded as the courts have recognised changed social attitudes and technology.

In recent years the High Court of Australia has been attempting to develop principles that can be used in determining with greater certainty when a duty of care will be owed in new or changed circumstances. The aim has been to find a methodology or approach to cases where liability is in dispute. Adopting a methodology encourages consistency and the avoidance of legal error (Kirby J in *Graham Barclay Oysters Pty Ltd v Ryan* (2002) 211 CLR 540). This aim has proved to be elusive. During the 1980s and mid-1990s the court developed the notion of 'proximity' as a touchstone when identifying a duty of care. In the High Court decision in *Council of the Shire of Sutherland v Heyman* (1985) 157 CLR 424, Deane J identified three types of proximity that act as limits on the notion of foreseeability in establishing duty of care. The three types are:

- physical proximity;
- circumstantial proximity;
- causal proximity.

While some other members of the court adopted Deane J's proximity test, not all of the court agreed, most notably Brennan CJ. The approach adopted by Brennan CJ was to recognise an incremental development in the identification of new categories of the duty of care ('incrementalism').

In a 1997 decision of the High Court, *Hill v Van Erp* (1997) 188 CLR 159, four members of the High Court (Dawson, Toohey, McHugh and Gummow JJ) recognised the limitations in the usefulness of the notion of proximity in determining individual claims to the existence of a duty of care enforceable at law. This led Kirby J in *Pyrenees Shire Council v Day* (1989) 192 CLR 330 at 414 to say:

> When to these voices is added the consistent criticism of "proximity" expressed for a decade by Brennan CJ, it is tolerably clear that proximity's reign in this Court, at least as a universal identifier of the existence of a duty of care at common law, has come to an end.

Since these cases the approach taken by the High Court in *Sullivan v Moody* (2001) 207 CLR 562 is a single test of 'reasonableness in the circumstances according to community standards' (Derrington 2004). In examining community standards the courts are to look at issues such as the probability of the harm occurring and its significance, the costs of avoiding the harm and the social utility of the activity that gave rise to the injury.

The incrementalist approach to duties of care has now been enshrined in legislation in all jurisdictions barring the Northern Territory, as part of the Ipp reforms. For example, s 43 of the *Civil Law (Wrongs) Act 2002* (ACT) states:

43 Precautions against risk – general principles

(1) A person is not negligent in failing to take precautions against a risk of harm unless –

   (a)   the risk was foreseeable (that is, it is a risk of which the person knew or ought to have known); and

   (b)   the risk was not insignificant; and

   (c)   in the circumstances, a reasonable person in the person's position would have taken those precautions.

(2) In deciding whether a reasonable person would have taken precautions against a risk of harm, the court must consider the following (among other relevant things):

   (a)   the probability that the harm would happen if precautions were not taken;

   (b)   the likely seriousness of the harm;

   (c)   the burden of taking precautions to avoid the risk of harm;

   (d)   the social utility of the activity creating the risk of harm.

Equivalent provisions can be found in the *Civil Liability Act 2002* (NSW), s 5B; *Civil Liability Act 2003* (Qld), s 9; *Civil Liability Act 1936* (SA), s 32; *Civil Liability Act 2002* (Tas), s 11; *Wrongs Act 1958* (Vic), s 48; *Civil Liability Act 2002* (WA), s 5B.

Where then does this leave the duty of care for health-care providers? The relationship between doctor and patient, and hospital and patient, has been long recognised in the law of negligence. The same principles apply to other health-care providers. In *Cassidy v Ministry of Health* [1951] 2 KB 343 at 359-60, Denning LJ dealt with the duties of hospital authorities and said:

> In my opinion, authorities who run a hospital, be they local authorities, government boards, or any other corporation, are in law under the self-same duty as the humblest doctor. Whenever they accept a patient for treatment, they must use reasonable care and skill to cure him of his ailment. The hospital authorities cannot, of course, do it by themselves. They have no ears to listen through the stethoscope, and no hands to hold the knife. They must do it by the staff which they employ, and, if their staff are negligent in giving the treatment, they are just as liable for that negligence as is anyone else who employs others to do his duties for him. Is there any possible difference in law, I ask, can there be, between hospital authorities who accept a patient for treatment and railway or shipping authorities who accept a passenger for carriage? Not one whatever. Once they undertake the task, they come under a duty to use care in the doing of it, and that is so whether they do it for reward or not.

But when does the relationship begin? Treatment need not necessarily have commenced for a duty to be imposed. In *Albrighton v Royal Prince Alfred Hospital* [1980] 2 NSWLR 542, a patient with kypho-scoliosis and spina bifida was said to have been owed a duty of care by a neurologist, even though the neurologist had not yet physically seen the patient at the time of her injury. The patient had a large hairy naevus on her lower back. She was admitted to hospital for corrective surgery of her spine and for traction. The naevus raised the chance that the spinal tissue had connected with surrounding tissue and this increased the chance that traction would cause paraplegia. A neurologist had been asked to see the patient regarding the traction but had not done so. The doctor did not see the patient but wrote that he would see her after traction. After the traction was applied she became paralysed. A duty was said to be owed by the neurologist as he had been asked to examine the patient and, though he had not actually done so, he had nevertheless indicated that he would treat her.

Similarly, in *Wang v Central Sydney Area Health Service* [2000] NSWSC 1339, a person who had attended at emergency for a head injury was owed a duty even though he had left the hospital before being seen by a doctor. A duty was owed by the triage nurse to explain properly why he should stay and be seen, given the treacherous nature of head injuries.

Duties of care outside of therapeutic relationships

It is possible for health professionals to owe a duty of care to people outside of the therapeutic relationship. Health professionals have been found to owe duties of care to people who are not their patients in the following circumstances:

A duty to attend an emergency

In *Lowns v Woods* (1996) Aust Torts Reports ¶81-376 a doctor was found to have been negligent when he failed to attend an emergency. In January 1987 Patrick Woods, then aged 10 years old, was holidaying with his family on the NSW Central Coast. Patrick suffered a major and prolonged epileptic fit that left him permanently and totally disabled. When he was found fitting by his family, his elder sister Joanna ran to the nearby home and surgery of a general practitioner, Dr Peter Lowns, informed him of the situation and asked that he come to the home unit where the family was holidaying. Joanna Woods said that the doctor refused to attend Patrick. Dr Lowns denied that he was ever asked to attend the boy but the trial judge, Badgery-Parker J, preferred the evidence of Joanna on this issue rather than that of Dr Lowns. The judge accepted 'on a clear balance of probabilities' that Patrick's sister had told Dr Lowns her brother was having a fit but that he refused to leave his surgery to treat him.

The case is significant as the New South Wales Supreme Court recognised that:

> In general the common law does not impose a duty to assist a person in peril even where it is foreseeable that the consequence of a failure to assist will be the injury or death of the person imperilled. Something other than the foreseeability of harm is required before the law imposes a duty to intervene. It has been held in other common law jurisdictions that a doctor is under no duty to attend upon a person who is sick, even in an emergency, if that person is one with whom the doctor is not and never has been in a professional relationship of doctor and patient. (Badgery-Parker J, in the trial judgment)

Dr Lowns appealed to the Court of Appeal. On appeal, Kirby P and Cole JA upheld (on this aspect of the case) the decision of Badgery-Parker J. Kirby P said that 'in the special circumstances, the relationship of proximity between

Patrick Woods and Dr Lowns was established, notwithstanding their lack of previous professional association' (at 63,155). Cole JA also upheld the decision of the trial judge, identifying that there was physical, circumstantial *and* causal proximity, as identified by Deane J in *Council of the Shire of Sutherland v Heyman* (1985) 157 CLR 424. Mahoney JA dissented in the decision on this point.

Following recent High Court of Australia decisions on establishing a duty of care it is interesting to speculate whether another court would follow the decision in *Lowns v Woods*. It may be relevant that Dr Lowns himself acknowledged that within the ordinary standards of a local medical practitioner in his position, had he received the emergency call from Joanna Woods, he would have been obliged to respond and would in fact have responded. It also seemed to be significant to Kirby P that a medical practitioner who does not assist a 'person ... in need of urgent attention' may have committed professional misconduct under the terms of the *Medical Practitioners Act 1938* (NSW), s 27(2) (the legislation in force at that time – the current equivalent is the *Medical Practice Act 1992* (NSW), s 36(l)). Kirby P argued that this section represented the community expectation for the behaviour of medical practitioners in this situation.

English authority, however, would suggest that there is no common law duty to rescue. Lord Goff of Chieveley put it in *In re F (Mental Patient: Sterilisation)* [1990] 2 AC 1 at 77:

> The "doctor in the house" who volunteers to assist a lady in the audience who, overcome by the drama or by the heat in the theatre, has fainted away, is impelled to act by no greater duty than that imposed by his own Hippocratic oath.

As well, Stuart-Smith LJ said in *Capital & Counties plc v Hampshire County Council* [1997] QB 1004 at 1035:

> [A] doctor who happened to witness a road accident will very likely go to the assistance of anyone injured, but he is not under any legal obligation to do so (save in certain limited circumstances which are not relevant) and the relationship of doctor and patient does not arise. If he volunteers his assistance, his only duty as a matter of law is not to make the victim's condition worse.

These opinions need to be treated with care as they are not binding upon Australian courts and can also be distinguished in circumstances such as Dr Lowns. Dr Lowns was not a passer-by or member of an audience. He was at work, practising as a medical practitioner ('on duty') at the time.

Importantly, the Ipp reforms in some jurisdictions completely excuse health professionals who attend an emergency from any breach of the duty of care. This is discussed below.

A duty of care owed by staff without health-care qualifications

There have also been cases where a duty of care existed even though there was no health professional/patient relationship at the time. The New South Wales Court of Appeal in *Alexander v Heise* [2001] NSWCA 422 recognised that a medical receptionist owed a duty of care to a patient and considered the need for the prioritisation of patients and the necessity for a receptionist to exercise proper judgment in making appointments for potentially seriously ill patients. In the particular case the court found that there was no breach of her duty of care.

A duty of care to sexual partners of patients to avoid exposing them to infection

In *BT v Oei* [1999] NSWSC 1082, a doctor was found to have owed a duty of care to the sexual partner of his patient, and was subsequent found to be responsible for the sexual partner's HIV infection. The doctor had negligently failed to diagnose that the patient had HIV. The evidence suggested that had the HIV been diagnosed the patient would have taken precautions against infecting his sexual partner. The court found that it was reasonably foreseeable that the patient, if HIV positive, would transmit the virus to a sexual partner. A duty of care was therefore imposed on the doctor. The duty was an indirect one, to offer an HIV test to the patient. Because such a test had not been offered the patient was left undiagnosed and had infected his partner. It was also a key finding that had the patient known of his HIV infection he would have informed his sexual partner and they would have taken precautions against transmission. This and other cases are discussed in Chapter 28.

A duty to the sexual partners of patients when providing contraceptive treatments

Health professionals also owe a duty to sexual partners when they provide contraceptive treatments. Australian courts have long recognised claims for wrongful conception, where the patient sues for the economic loss of having to raise a child born after a failed sterilisation. In such cases it is also possible for the partners of the patient to sue for consequent losses upon the rearing of the child. For example, in both *Cattanach v Melchior* (2003) 215 CLR 1 and *McDonald v Sydney South Western Area Health Service* [2005] NSWSC 924, claims were successfully brought by fathers of children born after failed tubal ligations. Duties of care were owed to the fathers as their loss was clearly foreseeable and there was no conflict between the doctors' duties to the women seeking treatment and their partners. These cases of conception torts are discussed in more detail in Chapters 18 and 19.

A duty of care owed to third parties injured by mentally ill patients

It is also arguable that health professionals owe duties of care to third parties who might be injured by mentally ill patients when they are negligently treated. The most cited example of this is the Californian case of *Tarasoff v University of California* 551 P 2d 334 (1976). In this case, a psychologist was found to be negligent for failing to warn a woman that his patient intended to kill her. After the murder was committed, the woman's parent successfully sued the psychologist and the University for failing to directly warn the victim.

Tarasoff has been considered many times in the United States and in the overwhelming majority of cases it has been accepted as good law. Some States have sought to limit the *Tarasoff* duty through legislation. For example, the Californian Civil Code § 43.92 states that a physician's duty to warn of a patient's threatened violent behaviour arises only 'where the patient has communicated to the psychotherapist a serious threat of physical violence against a reasonably identifiable victim or victims'. More recently in *Munstermann ex rel Rowe v Alegent Health-Immanuel Medical Center* 716 NW 2d 73 (Neb 2006). the Supreme Court of Nebraska stated:

> [A] psychiatrist is liable for failing to warn of and protect from a patient's threatened violent behavior, or failing to predict and warn of and protect from a patient's violent behavior, when the patient has communicated to the psychiatrist a serious threat of physical violence against himself, herself, or a reasonably identifiable victim or victims. The duty to warn of or to take reasonable precautions to provide protection from violent behavior shall arise only under those limited circumstances, and shall be discharged by the psychiatrist if reasonable efforts are made to communicate the threat to the victim or victims and to a law enforcement agency.

There are no directly relevant cases in Australia. In *Hunter Area Health Service v Presland* (2005) 63 NSWLR 22, a mentally ill patient was discharged and subsequently killed his brother's fiancé. The patient sued the health service successfully at trial for the damage he suffered after realising that he had killed the victim. On appeal, the NSW Court of Appeal dismissed the claim saying that it was against public policy to find the area health service liable for non-physical injuries caused by the unlawful acts of a patient (the patient was not criminally liable due to mental illness, but the killing was unlawful nonetheless). The facts of *Presland* are rather unique and it is arguable that if a third party were injured by a negligently released psychiatric patient a duty would be imposed (Madden and McIllwraith 2008).

A duty of care owed to the unborn

Health professionals owe duties of care to unborn children to avoid causing them harm during foetal development. In *X and Y v Pal* (1991) 23 NSWLR 26, a specialist obstetrician and gynaecologist was negligent for not testing his pregnant patient for syphilis. The duty of care was also extended to the unborn child, and the doctor was also liable for the child's congenital syphilis. Mahoney JA said:

> In my opinion there is no difficulty in this regard from the fact merely that the act or default occurred before the plaintiff was born. If A is negligent in building a building and five years later it falls down, A is liable not only to those who were born when the building was built but also to those who have been born since the building was built. ... Liability in negligence does not depend upon the defendant being able, when the act or default occurred, to identify the person ultimately injured. It is sufficient, at the least, that he can identify a class of persons apt to be injured and that the plaintiff is, in the event, of that class. (at 30)

The duty to the unborn does not extend to claims for wrongful life, where a child argues that the doctor was negligent due to the doctor's failure to abort the child: *Harriton v Stephens* (2006) 226 CLR 52. This is discussed in Chapter 19.

Duties not owed to third parties

The above examples of duties owed to third parties by health professionals are special circumstances where the courts have expanded duty concepts. But the courts are generally reluctant to do so. Health professionals were not found to owe a duty to the parents of children suspected of having been sexually abused when making a report of the suspected abuse: *Sullivan v Moody* (2001) 207 CLR 562. In such cases, a duty is not owed to the parents as the health professionals have the protection of the children as their primary duty. The High Court stated:

> The statutory scheme that formed the background to the activities of the present respondents was, relevantly, a scheme for the protection of children. It required the respondents to treat the interests of the children as paramount. Their professional or statutory responsibilities involved investigating and reporting upon, allegations that the children had suffered, and were under threat of, serious harm. It would be inconsistent with the proper and effective discharge of those responsibilities that they should be subjected to a legal duty, breach of which would sound in damages, to take care to protect persons who were suspected of being the sources of that harm. (at [62])

Nor was a doctor found to owe a due of care to his patient's husband in *AAA v BBB* [2005] WASC 139. A husband claimed that the doctor had negligently inflicted economic injuries after the doctor commenced a sexual relationship with the wife during the course of providing marriage counselling. The judge denied the existence of a duty owed by the doctor to the husband and said that the duty was owed only to the wife. The doctor's role was not to advise the wife to stay in the marriage but rather to provide the wife with counselling and that could very well have entailed advising her to leave the relationship.

Breach of the standard of care: did the defendant's conduct fall below the standard of care?

The second step, after finding that a duty of care is owed, is to establish the relevant standard of care and to decide whether there has been a breach of that standard. The criteria for identifying the standard of care and breach has been stated by Mason J in *Wyong Shire Council v Shirt* (1980) 146 CLR 40 at 47:

> In deciding whether there has been a breach of the duty of care the tribunal of fact must first ask itself whether a reasonable man in the defendant's position would have foreseen that his conduct involved a risk of injury to the plaintiff or to a class of persons including the plaintiff. If the answer be in the affirmative, it is then for the tribunal of fact to determine what a reasonable man would do by way of response to the risk. The perception of the reasonable man's response calls for a consideration of the magnitude of the risk and the degree of the probability of its occurrence, along with the expense, difficulty and inconvenience of taking alleviating action and any other conflicting responsibilities which the defendant may have.

In summary it can be said that the criteria are what risks would a *reasonable person* be able to *foresee* and then having identified those risks what would the reasonable person do in response to those risks. A reasonable person is said to consider the *magnitude* of the risk and the *probability* of that risk occurring balanced against the expense of preventing the risk and any conflicting responsibilities.

Those who undertake work or activities requiring special skill must not only exercise reasonable care but also measure up to the standard of proficiency that can be expected from 'the ordinary skilled person exercising and professing to have that special skill': *Rogers v Whitaker* (1992) 175 CLR 479 at 483. In *Rogers v Whitaker* the majority of the High Court said:

> The law imposes on a medical practitioner a duty to exercise reasonable care and skill in the provision of professional advice and treatment. That duty is a "single comprehensive duty covering all the ways in which a doctor is called upon to exercise his skill and judgment"; it extends to the examination, diagnosis and treatment of the patient and the provision of information in an appropriate case. (at 483, footnotes omitted)

The standard of care required when providing information to patients is examined in Chapter 14.

The courts rely heavily on the advice of health professionals about what the standard should be, although it may not always be conclusive. For example, in *Marko v Falk* [2008] NSWCA 293, the NSW Court of Appeal refused to find that a surgeon had fallen below the requisite standard of care when he inadvertently perforated a patient's duodenum when removing a polyp. The perforation was not discovered until too late and the patient suffered sepsis. The evidence at trial suggested that the perforation could happen without negligence and that the surgeon had followed common practice in performing the procedure. The Court of Appeal refused to ignore the evidence of the experts that the procedure was carried out appropriately.

The Bolam principle

The *Bolam* principle states that a doctor is not negligent if he or she acts in accordance with what is accepted as proper by a responsible body of his or her peers. This principle is derived from a jury instruction given by McNair J in the English case of *Bolam v Friern Hospital Management Committee* [1957] 1 WLR 582 at 587, in which he said:

> A doctor is not guilty of negligence if he has acted in accordance with a practice accepted as proper by a responsible body of medical men skilled in that particular art.

The *Bolam* principle deviates from the ordinary test for standards of care in the way that it closes off the judge's (or jury's) inquiry into what a reasonable doctor would have done, and leaves that issue to be determined solely by a responsible body of the medical profession. Once it has been established that a responsible body of medical opinion would have acted in the way that the defendant acted, it is not open to the judge to disagree with that body of opinion and require a higher standard of care. At common law, the principle only applies to the medical profession (although as discussed below statutory modifications have now expanded its coverage).

In British law the *Bolam* principle has been extremely influential, particularly after it was adopted in *Sidaway v Governors of Bethlem Royal Hospital* [1985] AC 871. Lord Scarman made this quite clear:

> The *Bolam* principle may be formulated as a rule that a doctor is not negligent if he acts in accordance with a practice accepted at the time as proper by a responsible body of medical opinion even though other doctors adopt a different practice. In short, the law imposes the duty of care: but the standard of care is a matter of medical judgment. (at 881)

Australian courts have tended to be uncomfortable with the *Bolam* principle and preferred to opt for standards of care that are defined by the courts, rather than the profession itself. In 1983 the Chief Justice of the South Australian Supreme Court (*F v R* (1983) 33 SASR 189 at 194) said:

> The ultimate question, however, is not whether the defendant's conduct accords with the practices of his profession or some part of it, but whether it conforms to the standard of reasonable care demanded by the law. That is a question for the court and the duty of deciding it cannot be delegated to any profession or group in the community.

The High Court of Australia considered the issue in *Rogers v Whitaker* (1992) 175 CLR 479. The High Court said (Mason CJ, Brennan, Dawson, Toohey and McHugh JJ):

> In Australia, it has been accepted that the standard of care to be observed by a person with some special skill or competence is that of the ordinary skilled person exercising and professing to have that special skill. But, that standard is not determined solely or even primarily by reference to the practice followed or supported by a responsible body of opinion in the relevant profession or trade. Even in the sphere of diagnosis and treatment, the heartland of the skilled medical practitioner, the *Bolam* principle has not always been applied. Further, and more importantly, particularly in the field of non-disclosure of risk and the provision of advice and information, the *Bolam* principle has been discarded and, instead, the courts have adopted the principle that, while evidence of acceptable medical practice is a useful guide for the courts, it is for the courts to adjudicate on what is the appropriate standard of care after giving weight to "the paramount consideration that a person is entitled to make his own decisions about his life". (at 484)

This principle – that it is up to the courts to adjudicate on what is an appropriate standard of care rather than being up to the professions – was developed in cases like *Rogers v Whitaker* that involved questions about how much advice and information should be given to patients. The use of the principle in cases concerning diagnosis and treatment rather than the provision of advice and information has been more difficult, for the very practical reason that judges are reliant on medical experts as to what the standard of care should be.

Developing the Bolam principle in the United Kingdom

In *Bolitho v City and Hackney Health Authority* [1998] AC 232, the House of Lords examined the meaning attributed to the *Bolam* case in establishing the appropriate standard of care for medical practitioners.

The plaintiff in this case, Patrick, was a two-year-old deceased boy (the action was continued by his mother as administrator of his estate) who was admitted to St Bartholomew's Hospital suffering from croup. On the morning after admission he was examined by a consultant who was not concerned about his condition. At around 12.40 pm the senior paediatric registrar, Dr Horn, was paged after Patrick's condition began to deteriorate. Dr Horn indicated that she would attend as soon as possible. In the event, neither she nor the senior house officer in paediatrics, Dr Rodger, attended Patrick. Patrick's condition began to improve. At around 2 pm a second episode occurred. The nurse in charge, Sister Sallabank, again contacted Dr Horn, who was on afternoon clinic. Dr Horn advised that she had asked Dr Rodger to come in her place. While Sister Sallabank was talking to Dr Horn it was reported that Patrick's condition had improved. Dr Rodger did not attend Patrick after the second episode, her evidence being that her pager was not working because of flat batteries. At around 2.30 pm Patrick collapsed and suffered a cardio-respiratory arrest. It took nine to 10 minutes before the restoration of respiratory and cardiac functions. Patrick suffered severe brain damage and subsequently died.

The trial judge, Hutchinson J, accepted the claim by the plaintiff that Dr Horn was in breach of her duty of care by not attending, or arranging for a suitable deputy to attend, Patrick after receiving the telephone calls. However, although this was a breach of duty of care, it had not been established that the injury had been caused by the breach. Dr Horn gave evidence, accepted by the judge, that even if she had attended Patrick she would not have intubated him (which it was agreed would have prevented the cardiac arrest). It then had to be shown that if Dr Horn had not intubated Patrick in these circumstances there would have been a breach of the appropriate standard of care. Distinguished medical experts for both sides gave evidence (five for the plaintiff, three for the defendant). The judge found that the evidence from the most impressive experts from both sides represented 'a responsible body of professional opinion espoused by distinguished and truthful experts'. The judge held that, if Dr Horn had attended and not intubated, she would have met a proper level of skill and competence. He therefore found that the admitted breach of the appropriate standard of care had not caused the damage suffered by the plaintiff, as this damage would have occurred even if she had attended.

On appeal, the House of Lords, commenting on the application of *Bolam*, noted that a doctor would not be found negligent if 'he has acted in accordance with a practice accepted as proper by a responsible body of medical men skilled in that particular art' ([1998] AC 232 at 239). Therefore, the onus according to *Bolam* appears to be more upon proving that the medical witnesses are 'a responsible body of medical men' rather than upon examining what they have said. Lord Browne-Wilkinson (for the House) noted that:

> In the *Bolam* case itself, McNair J stated [1957] 1 WLR 583, 587, that the defendant had to have acted in accordance with the practice accepted as proper by a "responsible body of medical men". Later, at p 588, he referred to a "standard of practice recognised as proper by a competent reasonable body of opinion." Again, in the passage which I have cited from *Maynard's* case

[*Maynard v West Midlands Regional Health Authority* [1984] 1 WLR 634], Lord Scarman refers to a "respectable" body of professional opinion. (at 241)

However, he went on to add:

> The use of these adjectives – responsible, reasonable and respectable – all show that the court has to be satisfied that the exponents of the body of opinion relied upon can demonstrate that such opinion has a logical basis. In particular in cases involving, as they so often do, the weighing of risks against benefits, the judge before accepting a body of opinion as being responsible, reasonable or respectable, will need to be satisfied that, in forming their views, the experts have directed their minds to the question of comparative risks and benefits and have reached a defensible conclusion on the matter. (at 241)

So, in the past the epithets 'responsible, reasonable and respectable' have been applied to the exponents of the opinion (that is, the medical witnesses) and not to the opinion itself. The court had to make a judgment about the exponents, it did not have to consider what was being said by that group. The judgment of Lord Browne-Wilkinson goes further and says that a court must examine the logical basis of an opinion put forward by its exponents, in particular the way in which consideration has been taken of comparative risks and benefits. Lord Browne-Wilkinson expressed caution that it would be only in rare instances that a court would find it necessary to substitute its own judgment for that of the experts.

The Ipp reforms and the modified Bolam test

The Ipp reforms have introduced a modified *Bolam* test into most Australian jurisdictions (see the table *over page*). In these jurisdictions the provisions apply to 'professionals' – persons practising a profession – and are not limited to the medical profession. The term 'profession' is not defined within the legislation and it would be up to a court to decide whether, in the circumstances of a particular case, a person was practising as a professional or not. A health professional does not incur liability if it can be established that he or she acted in a manner that was widely accepted in Australia by peer professional opinion as competent professional practice. The fact that there are differing peer professional opinions concerning the practice does not prevent any of those opinions being relied on. Nor does the peer professional have to be universally accepted. The only exception is where the peer professional opinion being relied on was *irrational* (in NSW, Qld, SA, Tas), *unreasonable* (in Vic) or was *so unreasonable that no reasonable health professional would have adopted it* (in WA). All of these jurisdictions specifically state that this rule does not apply to the giving of a warning, advice or other information and some re-state the *Rogers v Whitaker* test. This is discussed further in Chapter 14.

When examining the NSW provisions in *Dobler v Halverson* [2007] NSWCA 335, the NSW Court of Appeal stated that the wording of the section indicated that it was meant to act as a defence to negligence, so that the obligation of proving compliance with rational, widely accepted, competent professional practice would lie with the health professional. In this particular claim the 18-year-old patient suffered a heart attack and hypoxic brain injury. Before the cardiac arrest the patient had seen his doctor on a number of occasions after fainting and

Jurisdiction	Legislation
NSW	*Civil Liability Act 2002*, s 5O
Qld	*Civil Liability Act 2003*, s 22
SA	*Civil Liability Act 1936*, s 41
Tas	*Civil Liability Act 2002*, s 22
Vic	*Wrongs Act 1958*, s 59
WA	*Civil Liability Act 2002*, s 5PB

having migraines. The doctor had noted a heart murmur but had not ordered an electroencephalogram (EEG). Had one been ordered, it would have uncovered that the patient had a prolonged QT interval and treatment could have been initiated to prevent cardiac arrest. There was conflicting expert evidence of whether it was competent professional practice not to order an EEG. The trial judge found that the failure to order the test was not supported by widely held competent professional practice, and hence there was negligence. The Court of Appeal upheld the finding of negligence. Giles JA examined how the section was intended to work:

> Section 5O was amongst the tort law reforms consequent on the *Review of Law of Negligence Final Report, September 2002* ("the *Review*"). It was intended to introduce a modified *Bolam* principle. Its importance does not lie so much in questions of onus of proof as in who determines the standard of care. Commonly, as in the present case, there will be expert evidence called by the plaintiff to the effect that the defendant's conduct fell short of acceptable professional practice and expert evidence called by the defendant that it did not; the expert evidence may or may not recognise that the opposing professional practice is one which has some currency. Apart from s 5O the Court would determine the standard of care, guided by the evidence of acceptable professional practice. It would not be obliged to hold against the plaintiff if the defendant's conduct accorded with professional practice regarded as acceptable by some although not by others. Section 5O has the effect that, if the defendant's conduct accorded with professional practice regarded as acceptable by some (more fully, if he "acted in a manner that … was widely accepted … by peer professional opinion as competent professional practice"), then subject to rationality that professional practice sets the standard of care.
>
> In this sense, s 5O provides a defence. The plaintiff will usually call his expert evidence to the effect that the defendant's conduct fell short of acceptable professional practice, and will invite the court to determine the standard of care in accordance with that evidence. He will not be concerned to identify and negate a different professional practice favourable to the defendant, and s 5O does not require that he do so. The defendant has the interest in calling expert evidence to establish that he acted according to professional practice widely accepted by peer professional opinion, which if accepted will (subject to rationality) mean that he escapes liability. (at [59]-[60])

Giles JA also stated that:

> For s 5O, the question is not necessarily one of preferring A's evidence of acceptable professional practice to the evidence of B. If B's evidence supports

the manner in which the defendant acted, the question is whether there is established a professional practice widely accepted by (rational) peer professional opinion. If A and B both gave their evidence as evidence of whether the manner in which the defendant acted accorded with professional practice widely accepted by (rational) peer professional opinion, the question will be one of preferring A's evidence to that of B, but otherwise it will be one of acceptance of B's evidence, its weight and what it establishes. The conceptual distinction must be made, although in the acceptance of B's evidence and its weight regard to the evidence of A is likely to remain relevant. (at 103])

Compare the finding in *Dobler* with that of *Walker v Sydney West Area Health Service* [2007] NSWSC 526. Walker was a 19-year-old mental health patient who injured himself during a suicide attempt. The plaintiff argued that he was negligently treated because he should have been medicated and detained by the defendant health service. The court found that, while there was some disagreement between the health professionals about what would have been the best treatment options for the plaintiff, the doctors had not failed to act in a manner that was widely accepted as competent professional practice by refusing to medicate the patient and by releasing him.

Causation: did the breach of the duty of care cause the injury?

Common sense causation

The High Court has stated that causation in tort law is based on common sense: *March v E & MH Stramare Pty Ltd* (1991) 171 CLR 506; *Travel Compensation Fund v Tambree* (2005) 224 CLR 627. The common sense inquiry requires the court to examine two issues: factual causation and the scope of liability. Factual causation exists when the it can be said that the injury would not have occurred 'but for' the breach of duty, meaning that the negligence was a necessary condition of the injury occurring. The scope of liability test requires the court to examine whether it is appropriate for the injury to be considered as having been caused by the breach. It is therefore a normative decision as to whether the judge should find the party responsible for the harm. The approach in the Ipp reform legislation confirms this two-pronged investigation (apart from in the Northern Territory): *Ruddock v Taylor* (2003) 58 NSWLR 269; *O'Gorman v Sydney South West Area Health Service* [2008] NSWSC 1127. The legislation is set out below in the following table:

Jurisdiction	Legislation
New South Wales	*Civil Liability Act 2002*, s 5D
Queensland	*Civil Liability Act 2003*, s 11
South Australia	*Civil Liability Act 1936*, s 34
Tasmania	*Civil Liability Act 2002*, s 13
Victoria	*Wrongs Act 1958* (Vic), s 51
Western Australia	*Civil Liability Act 2002*, s 5C
Australian Capital Territory	*Civil Law (Wrongs) Act 2002*, s 45

No action can be brought in negligence unless some damage has resulted from the breach of the standard of care. No matter how careless a health-care provider has been, an action will not be successful unless damage can be proven to have resulted from the breach of duty.

In *Barnett v Chelsea and Kensington Hospital Management Committee* [1968] 1 All ER 1068, three night watchmen attended the defendant hospital, clearly appearing ill, and they informed a nurse that they had been vomiting. The nurse telephoned the casualty officer, who did not see the men, but said that they should go home and see their own doctors. They left, and about five hours later one of the men died from arsenic poisoning. The court found that the casualty officer had been in breach of his standard of care by failing to have seen and examined the deceased. However, the medical evidence indicated that even if the deceased had received prompt medical attention it would not have been possible to diagnose the condition and administer an antidote in time to save him. Thus, the breach did not cause the death.

In *South Eastern Sydney Area Health Service v King* [2006] NSWCA, a 13-year-old patient was being treated with a radical and experimental treatment. The treatment protocol had been amended because of risk of neurological damage but one of the team doctors had failed to pass on the change to the treating specialist. The 13 year old became a quadriplegic. In holding the health service negligent the court upheld the finding that, had the treating specialist been made aware of the protocol amendment, he would have change the doses and the quadriplegia would have been avoided.

Loss of a chance of a better outcome as an tortious injury

There is a growing body of cases where patients have successfully argued that negligence reduced their chances of a better outcome, rather than directly causing their injury. In *Gavalas v Singh* [2001] VSCA 23 (a case where the patient argued that he had lost the chance of an earlier, complete removal of a tumour), Smith AJA stated:

> It is difficult to see any reason in principle why a plaintiff should not be compensated in appropriate circumstances for a lost opportunity if it flows from the alleged negligence. It has been said:
>
>> "The law of negligence may be seen as directed to several purposes, but purposes of compensating the injured and promoting reasonable co-nduct are prominent among them." [*Chappel v Hart* (1998) 195 CLR 232 at 285]
>
> In appropriate cases, an entitlement to compensation for the lost opportunity of a more favourable outcome addresses those purposes. Bearing such policy in mind, there is a strong case for saying that lost opportunity should be recognised by the law as a head of damage and compensated because it enables a plaintiff to obtain compensation in circumstances where negligence has deprived that plaintiff of a real chance or opportunity while at the same time avoiding the potentially unreasonable result of excessive compensation or no compensation despite the negligence of the defendant. (at [38])

In *Rufo v Hoskings* (2004) 61 NSWLR 678, the plaintiff claimed a loss of chance due to negligent treatment of her systemic lupus erythematosus. The plaintiff was treated with corticosteroids, which led to osteoporosis and eventual microfractures in her spine. The plaintiff believed that the there was a failure to use the correct steroids and 'steroid sparers' in her treatment regime. It was argued that this represented a less successful treatment regime and that she lost the chance of a better outcome. The trial judge agreed with these claims and found that the loss of chance at a better outcome was an injury.

The plaintiff was successful on appeal to the NSW Court of Appeal. Santow JA stated:

> [T]he present claim can be framed in terms of losing the benefit ... of a superior treatment regime with better chance of circumventing the risks of bone microfractures, while still curing the Lupus ... [T]hat better chance was less than even, but still material. There could be no question but that the better chance was a thing of value, even if its quantification posed considerable difficulty. (at [42])

Hodgson JA stated that:

> That chance must be inherent in the circumstances, not merely an artefact of the way evidence is presented in the case. Thus, if it appears to be a plain fact as to whether treatment would or would not have been successful, and the element of uncertainty arises merely from different expert views, then the plaintiff will not be compensated for the chance that one expert might be correct. On the other hand, if it appears that the very best medical science can do is to say that the treatment had a quantifiable chance of success, then in my opinion that can be treated as a valuable chance for the loss of which a plaintiff can be compensated. As with other questions concerning causation, a common sense approach should be taken to the question of whether a valuable chance has been lost, or whether the situation is rather one where one or other alternative would definitely have occurred, and the only uncertainty is due to imperfections in the evidence. (at [10])

The plaintiff was compensated by an amount for her total damages discounted by the percentage chance of success that she had lost.

After *Rufo* a number of issues still remain. The primary one is the way that these claims open up the capacity for claims to be made 'in a dual manner' (Tibballs 2007). The plaintiff can frame their injury under the classic negligence claim where the breach was a material cause of the loss (based on the balance of probabilities), and, the plaintiff can also claim that the breach led to a loss of a better outcome (which may have been less than a 50% possibility). Arguably, if the plaintiff fails to prove causation on the balance of probabilities test, he or she may get a second bite of the cherry through loss of chance. This happened in *Tabet v Mansour* [2007] NSWSC 36, where the plaintiff failed to prove that the defendants' negligence in failing to order a CT scan was causative of harm generated by the patient's medullablastoma. Nevertheless, Studdert J found that the failure to order the CT scan did reduce the patient's chance of a better outcome by 40% and assessed damages on that basis.

Another issue is concerned with what to do when the breach creates a small risk which then eventuates, leading to damage. Should this be viewed on common sense causation grounds as a material contribution or should the defendant only be liable instead for the creation of risk? In *O'Gorman v Sydney South West Area Health Service* [2008] NSWSC 1127, the plaintiff had undergone biannual screening for breast cancer. There were noticeable changes in a breast mass between 2004 and 2006 yet the patient was not recalled for an ultrasound or biopsy. The mass was later found to be malignant. The cancer had also metastasised in the patient's lungs and brain. It was agreed between the parties that the delay in diagnosis increased the chance of the cancer metastasising by 10%. The health service argued that the injury should be treated as one of a loss of chance to prevent the cancer's spread and as such damages should only be provided on a percentage basis of the actual loss. The plaintiff argued that while the risk was increased by only 10% the risk actually eventuated, so that the delay was a material cause of the metastatic tumours, leaving the defendant responsible for all the loss. Hoeben J, after applying s 5D of the *Civil Liability Act 2002* (NSW), found for the plaintiff as '[t]he events which occurred, ie the development of tumours in the plaintiff's lungs and brain, occurred within the very area of risk which had been increased by the delay in diagnosis' (at [150]).

Damages

Damages are primarily calculated on a compensatory basis. The aim is to place the injured party back to their pre-tort position: *Butler v Egg and Egg Pulp Marketing Board* (1966) 114 CLR 185. At common law damages could also be awarded to punish the tortfeasor for a 'contumelious' disregard for the plaintiff's rights, meaning a malicious and insulting injury. Such damages are referred to as *exemplary* damages. *Aggravated damages* also exist for injuries to the plaintiff's dignity and feelings, but such damages can only be awarded in causes of action, like defamation, which exist to protect dignity. The Ipp reforms have removed exemplary and aggravated damages for negligence in New South Wales, Queensland and the Northern Territory: *Civil Liability Act 2002* (NSW), s 21; *Civil Liability Act 2003* (Qld), s 52; *Personal Injuries (Liabilities and Damages) Act 2003* (NT), s 19.

Compensatory damages are further divided into special damages and general damages. Special damages are those losses which are already quantified, such as medical expenses already incurred or wages already lost. General damages relate to those losses which are not capable of precise accounting and include matters such as economic losses of future medical expenses, future lost earning capacity, as well as non-economic losses for pain and suffering, loss of amenity, loss of life expectancy and disfigurement.

Many jurisdictions have introduced caps and thresholds on the recovery of economic and non-economic loss. Barring South Australia and Tasmania, all Australian jurisdictions have capped loss of earnings at three times average weekly earnings: *Civil Liability Act 2002* (NSW), s 12; *Civil Liability Act 2003* (Qld), s 54; *Wrongs Act 1958* (Vic), s 28F; *Civil Liability Act 2002* (WA), s 11; *Civil Law (Wrongs) Act 2002* (ACT), s 38; *Personal Injuries (Liabilities and Damages) Act 2003* (NT), s 20.

Caps have also been imposed on non-economic losses in all jurisdictions (except for Tasmania, Western Australia and the ACT): *Civil Liability Act 2002* (NSW), s 16 ($350,000); *Civil Liability Act 2003* (Qld), s 62 ($250,000); *Civil Liability Act 1935* (SA), s 52 ($241,500); *Wrongs Act 1958* (Vic), s 28G ($371,380); *Personal Injuries (Liabilities and Damages) Act 2003* (NT), s 27 ($350,000).

In addition to the cap New South Wales, Queensland, South Australia, Western Australia and the Northern Territory also apply a threshold so that, if the injury is not a comparatively serious one, no damages for non-economic loss are awarded regardless of how much has been suffered. Above the threshold, a sliding scale is then applied to reduce damages. For example in New South Wales, under s 16 damages are not awarded for non-economic loss if the injury is less than 15% of a 'most extreme case'. If the loss equates with or is greater than 15%, a sliding scale is applied, where at 15% of a most extreme cases, 1% of the actual loss is awarded, and so on until when the injury is at least 33% of a most extreme cases 100% of the loss is awarded.

In Queensland s 61 of the *Civil Liability Act 2003* requires the court to allocate an injury scale between 0 and 100. Once scored, a fixed monetary amount is made payable to the score.

In Victoria, s 28L of the *Wrongs Act 1958* requires that the injury be significant for the plaintiff to recover. Non-economic losses have to be assessed by a medical panel. The decision of the medical panel can be appealed but on limited grounds. For example, in *Dixon v Hacker* [2007] VSC 342, the plaintiff was suing for post-traumatic stress disorder after botched breast implantation surgery. The panel found that the injury of the plaintiff was significant as it was a moderately severe post-traumatic stress disorder. The doctor appealed but failed on appeal as there was no evidence that the wrong decision had been made.

In South Australia a scale system is applied of a 60-point scale for 'a most gravest kind' of economic loss and there is a threshold of injury where the injured person must have been significantly impaired for at least seven days with medical expenses totalling at least $2750.

Finally in Western Australia the threshold sits at $12,000. Two sets of restrictive formulae are applied to damages until the damages reach $48,500.

Vicarious liability and non-delegable duties of care

An employer is liable for the negligent acts of his or her employee, provided the act is committed in the course of employment. This is known as 'vicarious liability'. This does not absolve the employee of liability, and patients could choose to sue an individual, although this is rarely the case. Where health professionals act as independent contractors (and not as employees) then they will not be able to rely upon the vicarious liability of an employer. In these cases it is important that the health professional arrange for the coverage of an appropriate professional indemnity insurance policy.

What acts are considered to be in the course of employment? Is the employer also liable for criminal acts done by the employee? In *Deatons Pty Ltd v*

Flew (1949) 79 CLR 370, a barmaid threw a beer glass at a patron and he lost an eye. The High Court found that the employer was not responsible as the act was not authorised, nor was it connected to any authorised act so that it could be considered as a 'mode of performing that act'. Rather it was a personal act which was not connected to employment.

Outside, and sometimes in addition to, vicarious liability, there are situations where the courts have found that defendants owe a duty of care, even when they have delegated the responsibility for performing functions to others. This duty of care is known as a *non-delegable duty of care*. The courts have found that there are special relationships where defendants are held to still owe a duty of care, even though another person has been contracted to do the work. These duties are imposed in cases of special vulnerability and dependence. For example, hospitals have been found to owe a non-delegable duty of care to their patients, and in such cases they cannot escape liability for negligence, even if that negligence was the caused by non-employees, such as visiting medical officers: *Samios v Repatriation Commission* [1960] WAR 219.

Non-delegable duties impose a duty to take reasonable care to prevent harm. As such, non-delegable duties of care only cover negligent acts and cannot be used to impose liability for intentional and criminal acts. In *New South Wales v Lepore* (2003) 212 CLR 511, the High Court considered three separate cases of students suing schools for being sexually assaulted by teachers. In each case the student argued that the school owed a non-delegable duty of care to prevent the sexual assaults. The majority of the High Court disagreed. Gleeson CJ (in the majority) used the following example of why non-delegable duties of care should not be used to cover intentional criminal acts:

> If a member of a hospital's staff with homicidal propensities were to attack and injure a patient, in circumstances where there was no fault on the part of the hospital authorities, or any other person for whose acts or omissions the hospital was vicariously responsible, the common law should not determine the question of the hospital's liability to the patient on the footing that the staff member had neglected to take reasonable care of the patient. It should face up to the fact that the staff member had criminally assaulted the patient, and address the problem of the circumstances in which an employer may be vicariously liable for the criminal acts of an employee. Intentional wrong-doing, especially intentional criminality, introduces a factor of legal relevance beyond a mere failure to take care. Homicide, rape, and theft are all acts that are inconsistent with care of person or property, but to characterise them as failure to take care, for the purpose of assigning tortious responsibility to a third party, would be to evade an issue. (at [31])

Interestingly, while the High Court refused to find a breach of the non-delegable duty of care owed to students, it did find that the schools were vicariously liable for the teachers' conduct. This was primarily due to the fact that:

> [T]he teacher-student relationship is invested with a high degree of power and intimacy, the use of that power and intimacy to commit sexual abuse may provide a sufficient connection between the sexual assault and the employment to make it just to treat such contact as occurring in the course of employment. (per Gleeson CJ at [74]).

A case which illustrates non-delegable duties of care in a hospital setting is *Sherry v Australasian Conference Association (t/a Sydney Adventist Hospital)* [2006] NSWSC 75. The patient was treated with minimally invasive direct coronary arterial bypass (MIDCAB). After surgery the patient had chest pains caused by a haemothorax (blood collecting in his pleural cavity). X-rays were ordered, a chest drain was later attempted but the patient died of cardiac arrest before the drain could be inserted. Allegations were made that the treatment provided by the staff of the hospital (nursing and physiotherapy) and by specialists (some of whom were on contract) was negligent. One of the specialists had been retained by the patient (Dr Marshman). Another had been appointed by the hospital as a 'CMO' or 'career medical officer' (Dr Walsh). An issue arose as to whether the hospital owed a non-delegable duty of care concerning the treatment provided by Dr Walsh. On this issue Simpson J stated:

> Whether the relationship with Dr Walsh and SAH was that of an employee and employer, or independent contractor and principal, does not seem to me to matter in the context of this determination. It was SAH who engaged Dr Walsh; it was SAH who paid Dr Walsh; it was SAH who rostered Dr Walsh on duty; while, obviously, Dr Walsh had a great deal of independence in respect to the treatment he administered to individual patients, he was subject to the direction of SAH in certain important respects: for example, in being responsible for CMO duties in the whole of SAH; in being required to allocate first priority to the ICU; and in being required to be available, if called upon, for the Accident and Emergency Department. Dr Walsh was, properly speaking, one of many agents of SAH (along with nursing staff, physiotherapists, and, no doubt, cleaning staff, nurses' aides, pharmacists, laboratory technicians, radiographers and probably many others) to enable SAH to provide the services it had contracted and undertaken to provide.
>
> Also relevant is the arrangement between SAH and Mr Sherry. That was that Mr Sherry would be admitted to SAH; SAH would provide him with all necessary medical services (other than those of the surgeon, with whom a separate arrangement was made by Mr Sherry); Mr Sherry had no input into the identity of the CMO who would be undertaking his care while he remained an inpatient; Mr Sherry had no input into the extent to which Dr Walsh would be available for his care.
>
> Accordingly, I am satisfied that the non-delegable duty owed by SAH to Mr Sherry incorporated liability for any negligent acts or omissions of Dr Walsh. (at [550]-[552])

Outside of the hospital contexts, non-delegable duties of care have been found to be owed by birth control clinics (*KT v PLG & Ardlog Pty Ltd* [2006] NSWSC 919), medical centres (*Rooty Hill Medical Centre v Gunther* [2002] NSWCA 60) and pathology services (*Chambers v Macquarie Pathology Services Pty Ltd* (unreported, NSWDC, 9 February 2001) (Madden and McIllwraith 2008).

New South Wales and Victoria now require the test for determining breach of non-delegable duties of care to be the same test as that of vicarious liability: *Civil Liability Act 2002* (NSW), s 5Q; *Wrongs Act 1958* (Vic), s 61.

Defences

Apart from the modified *Bolam* test introduced by the Ipp reforms, discussed above, there are two main defences available to a defendant once negligence has been established. The defences are – *contributory negligence* and *voluntary assumption of risk*. In health care there are no recorded Australian cases where courts have accepted a defence of voluntary assumption of risk. The reason for this may be that this is a complete defence. This means that if the court should find that the plaintiff had voluntarily agreed to accept the negligence of the defendant, then the plaintiff can recover no damages at all.

Contributory negligence, as a defence, has also been rare in Australian health litigation. In a recent New South Wales case of *Kalokerinos v Burnett* (unreported, NSWCA, 30 January 1996) the patient consulted her doctor in 1991 because she had experienced prolonged vaginal bleeding. The doctor referred her to a specialist in Tamworth. The patient alleged that she returned to the doctor later that day and told him that she was unable to travel to Tamworth and wanted a referral to a specialist at a town closer to home and that the doctor failed to make any alternative arrangements. The doctor denied this version of events. The patient was subsequently diagnosed with gynaecological cancer. It was agreed at the trial that had the cancer been diagnosed earlier it could have been treated by a hysterectomy. Early detection would have avoided radical radiation treatment which led to serious side-effects.

It was conceded by the doctor at the trial that a failure to refer the patient to a specialist in the other town, when the doctor was aware that she could not make arrangements to travel to Tamworth, would constitute negligence. The trial judge accepted the patient's version of events and found the doctor liable in negligence. The Court of Appeal found that the evidence did not disclose any real impediment to the patient seeking further medical advice. It therefore found that the patient's own negligence had contributed to the delay in diagnosis. The patient's damages were reduced by 20% to reflect the finding of contributory negligence.

More recently in *Young v Central Aboriginal Congress Inc* [2008] NTSC 47, the defendant medical clinic was found to be negligent in failing to follow-up the deceased patient and make sure he attended for further medical tests in relation to suspected heart disease. There was further negligence when the file of another patient with the same name was mistakenly used in a consultation. Nevertheless, the judge found the patient had contributed to his death by failing to attend a fasting cholesterol test, failing to attend the clinic for further consultations and failing to tell any of the doctors about the advice he had been given by the doctor at the clinic about possible heart disease. Damages were reduced by 50%.

No liability for attending an emergency: 'Good Samaritan' legislation

A further defence is now available under the Ipp legislation for 'good samaritans' who attend an emergency. There are no recorded cases of health professionals being sued in Australia for voluntarily attending an emergency and providing substandard care. However, it was noted in the Ipp Report that:

The Panel understands that health-care professionals have long expressed a sense of anxiety about the possibility of legal liability for negligence arising from the giving of assistance in emergency situations. However, the Panel is not aware, from its researches or from submissions received by it, of any Australian case in which a good Samaritan (a person who gives assistance in an emergency) has been sued by a person claiming that the actions of the good Samaritan were negligent. Nor are we aware of any insurance-related difficulties in this area. (Ipp, Cane et al 2002)

As a response, all jurisdictions, except for Tasmania, have created protections for people who attend an emergency, in good faith and without expectation of payment or other reward (see table below). Such people have complete immunity from civil liability as long as they are not under the influence of drugs or alcohol voluntarily taken. Nor can rescuers seek protection if they caused the emergency.

Jurisdiction	Legislation
NSW	*Civil Liability Act 2002*, ss 56, 57
Qld	*Law Reform Act 1995*, s 16 *Civil Liability Act 2003*, s 26
SA	*Civil Liability Act 1936*, s 74
Vic	*Wrongs Act 1958*, s 31B
WA	*Civil Liability Act 2002*, Pt 1D
ACT	*Civil Law (Wrongs) Act 2002*, s 5
NT	*Personal Injuries (Liabilities and Damages) Act 2005*, s 8

Alternatives to negligence?

There is no doubt that there is a great deal of dissatisfaction with the application of the tort of negligence amongst health-care professionals. The threat of litigation has been said to be the number one source of stress for general practitioners (Schattner and Coman 1998). In response to the concerns about litigation and the effect on health professionals the most frequently cited suggestion is to abandon the adversarial negligence system and move to a 'no-fault' system such as the existing workers' compensation or motor traffic accident schemes. Fenn et al have written that 'patient compensation schemes are a means by which two objectives can be pursued: the cost of the harm can be transferred from the patient (the "compensation" objective); and the clinician can be given an incentive to take appropriate care to avoid making mistakes which may harm other patients (the "deterrence" objective)' (Fenn, Gray et al 2004).

In common law jurisdictions, the tort of negligence is the main means of compensating those persons injured as a result of the negligence of a health professional. The tort of negligence has, however, been criticised for:

- significant delay and cost in hearing proceedings;
- failing to provide compensation for a substantial majority of persons injured because they cannot establish fault to the standard of proof required by a court;

- leading to defensive medicine;
- inconsistency in the provision of compensation; and
- excessive indemnity premiums for health professionals. (Accident Compensation Corporation 2003)

Only a very few countries have implemented no-fault schemes for medical injury. Notably these schemes are in Scandinavian countries and New Zealand.

Scandinavian schemes

Sweden, Norway, Denmark, Iceland and Finland all have similar patient-insurance schemes. These schemes are based on 1972 Swedish legislation that fixes the amount of compensation payable for any tort case. The coverage offered by these schemes is focused around providing compensation for 'avoidable' injuries, although the definition varies between the countries. Originally coverage applied to public services but has been extended (except in Norway and Denmark) to private providers. In Sweden, the Patient Insurance Scheme has been in operation since 1975 and specifically covers patients injured by medical treatment. The scheme covers treatment injuries, diagnostic failures, accident injuries, infection injuries and any injury suffered during the course of diagnosis. There is also a Pharmaceutical Insurance Scheme, funded by contributions from the pharmaceutical industry, which covers injuries caused by a drug.

The Scandinavian schemes vary between the coverage rules for claims and the schemes' prevention and disciplinary roles. The medical disciplinary systems are kept entirely separate from the insurance schemes. This affirms the principle in these countries that the patient insurance schemes are principally for compensation, rather than discipline and complaints resolution. This is said to enhance a 'blame free' culture with respect to mistakes. A basic principle in these schemes is that it is not necessary to prove negligence but it is necessary to prove causation between the treatment (or the drug) and the injury suffered.

New Zealand

The *Accident Compensation Act 1974* created the Accident Compensation Corporation (ACC) and introduced the concept of 'medical misadventure' into New Zealand law. It was intended to be a no-fault scheme to the extent that a claimant did not have to establish negligence on the part of another in order to receive compensation. The cost of the scheme is funded partly by New Zealanders in paid employment and partly by the government for those not in employment. Health professionals in New Zealand are therefore protected from civil claims for damages that arise from their own negligence. Claims for exemplary damages are, however, still available.

Because of the rising costs of the scheme during the 1980s it was reformed in 1992 by limiting the coverage and benefits that were available to claimants. Since 1992 lump sum payments for pain and suffering and loss of enjoyment of life were no longer available. A 'disability allowance' was paid in lieu of a lump sum. One of the significant changes made by the 1992 reforms was to introduce the finding of fault back into the 'no-fault' scheme. Before 1992 the term 'medical misadventure' was not defined in the Act. The interpretation of the expression was left to the ACC, the Accident Compensation Appeal Authority and the courts. The 1992 *Accident Rehabilitation, Compensation and Insurance Act* defined medical misadventure as a 'personal injury resulting from medical error or medical mishap'. Medical error was defined as 'the failure of a registered health professional to observe a standard of care and skill reasonably to be expected in the circumstances'. This meant that the scheme required a process of fault-finding before patients were entitled to compensation.

Despite the reforms in 1992 the scheme was under further pressure because of the continuing growth in expenditure. Additional reforms came into effect on 1 July 1999. The effect of the 1999 amendment was to remove the ACC as the monopoly insurer for workplace injuries and to challenge the dominance of general practitioners as the gatekeepers to other health-care services. However, these changes were reversed by 1 July 2000 after which the ACC became the sole provider for accident insurance for both work and non-work injury.

More recently, the *Injury Prevention, Rehabilitation and Compensation Act 2001* was introduced. The Act was the result of a long-running *Review of ACC Medical Misadventure* undertaken by the ACC and the Department of Labour (Coates and Smith 2004). The Review found that the requirements to establish fault focused too much on the actions of individual health professionals and led to the creation of an overly 'blaming' culture. The Act replaced the definition of 'medical misadventure' with the concept of 'treatment injury'. A 'treatment injury' is an injury caused by treatment provided by health professionals which was not an ordinary consequence or necessary part of the treatment (s 32). A treatment injury does not arise from underlying health conditions, resource allocation decisions or the patient's own refusal to give consent (s 32(2)). The fact that the treatment did not achieve a desired result does not, of itself, constitute treatment injury (s 32(3)). Infections that travel from patients to family members may also be considered a 'treatment injury' (s 32(7)).

Advantages and disadvantages of schemes

Many health professionals see the advantage of a scheme that removes the risk of being sued for negligence. This means not only the avoidance of the cost, inconvenience and stress associated with litigation but also the effect on reputation that concerns many professionals. There is still, however, the possibility of disciplinary actions as well as the possibility of criminal actions. In New Zealand there were a number of manslaughter actions against New Zealand medical practitioners, although the expansive definition of manslaughter has now been narrowed in the case of health-care professionals. Medical practitioners, who pay around $NZ1200 per year in medical indemnity insurance costs, also report widespread concern that 'New Zealand is a hostile and litigious environment for medical practice' (Tapper, Malcolm et al 2004).

An economic analysis of the value of introducing a NZ type no-fault scheme suggests that in the UK, which has a conservative approach to negligence claims, introduction of a no-fault scheme would result in a many-fold increase in compensation costs. Introducing the scheme in the USA may be cost effective (Kessler, Summerton et al 2006). The Australian system is likely to be somewhere between these two extremes.

References

Accident Compensation Corporation (2003) *ACC Background Paper: Comparison of International Schemes that compensate for medical injury.* Wellington, Accident Compensation Corporation.

Allsopp, KM (1986) *J Med Def Union* **2**(2): 2.

Bogardis, S, E Holmboe et al (1999) 'Perils, pitfalls and possibilities in talking about medical risk'. *JAMA* **281**: 1037-41.

Bok, S (1979) *Lying, moral choice in private and public life.* New York, Vintage Books.

Bolsin, S (1998) 'Professional misconduct: the Bristol case'. *Med J Aust* **169**(7): 369-72.

Brennan, TA, L Leape et al (1991) 'Incidence of adverse events and negligence in hospitalised patients: results of the Harvard Medical Practice Study II'. *N Engl J Med* **324**: 377-84.

Coates, J and K Smith (2004) 'Reform of the ACC Medical Misadventure'. *New Zealand Medical Journal* **117**: 1.

Davies, J, P Hebert et al (2003) *The Canadian Patient Safety Dictionary.* Ottawa, Royal College of Physicians and Surgeons of Canada.

Derrington, D (2004) 'Theory of negligence advanced in the High Court of Australia'. *ALJ* **78**: 595.

Editorial (1998) 'First lessons from the "Bristol case".' *Lancet* **351**: 1669.

Ehsani, J, T Jackson et al (2006) 'The incidence and cost of adverse events in Victorian hospitals 2003-04'. *Med J Aust* **184**(11): 551-5.

Faunce, T and S Bolsin (2004) 'Three Australian whistleblowing sagas: lessons for internal and external regulation'. *Med J Aust* **181**(1): 44-7.

Fenn, P, A Gray et al (2004) 'The Economics of Clinical Negligence Reform in England'. *The Economic Journal* **114**: F272-F292.

Goldmann, D (2006) 'System failure versus personal accountability: the case for clean hands'. *N Engl J Med* **355**: 121-3.

Hebert, P, A Levin et al (2001) 'Disclosure of medical error'. *CMAJ* **164**: 509-13.

Hebert, P, A Levin et al (2008) Disclosure of medical error. *The Cambridge Textbook of Bioethics.* P Singer and A Viens. Cambridge, Cambridge University Press: 257-65.

Ipp, D, P Cane et al (2002) *Review of the Law of Negligence: Final Report.* Canberra, Commonwealth of Australia.

Kennedy, V and D Walker (2007) *Dancing With Dr Death: The Inside Story of Doctor Jayant Patel and the Bundaberg Base Hospital.* Sydney, New Holland.

Kessler, D, N Summerton et al (2006) 'Effects of the medical liability system in Australia, the UK, and the USA'. *Lancet* **368**(9531): 240-7.

Leape, L (1994) 'Error in medicine'. *JAMA* **272**: 1851-7.

Legal Process Reform Group of Australian Ministers' Advisory Panel (2002), *Responding to the Medical Indemnity Crisis: An Integrated Reform Package.*

Localio, A, A Lawthers et al (1991) 'Relation between malpractice claims and adverse events due to negligence: results of the Harvard Medical Practice Study III'. *N Engl J Med* **325**: 245-51.

Madden, B and J McIllwraith (2008) *Australian Medical Liability.* Sydney, Lexis Nexis Butterworths.

Nash, L, C Tennant et al (2004) 'The psychological impact of complaints and negligence suits on doctors'. *Australasian Psychiatry* **12**(3): 278-81.

Northern Territory Department of Justice (Policy Division) (2004) *Whistleblowers Protection Legislation: Discussion Paper.* Darwin.

NSW Parliament. Legislative Council. General Purpose Standing Committee Number 2 (2004) *Complaints handling within NSW Health*: [report] / General Purpose Standing Committee No 2. Sydney.

Paul, C (2000) 'Internal and external morality of medicine: lessons from New Zealand'. *BMJ* **320**: 499-503.

Peterson, L, A Brennan et al (1994) 'Does housestaff discontinuity of care increase the risk for preventable adverse events?' *Ann Intern Med* **121**: 866-72.

Runciman, B, A Merry et al (2007) *Safety and ethics in healthcare*. Melbourne, Ashgate Publishing.

Schattner, P and G Coman (1998) 'The stress of metropolitan general practice'. *Med J Aust* **169**: 133-7.

Skene, L (2008) *Law and Medical Practice: Rights, Duties, Claims and Defences* (3rd ed). Sydney, LexisNexis Butterworths.

Staunton, P and M Chiarella (2003) *Nursing and the Law*. Sydney, Churchill Livingstone.

Studdart, D, M Mello et al (2004) 'Medical malpractice'. *N Engl J Med* **350**(3): 283-91.

Tapper, R, L Malcolm et al (2004) 'Surgeons' experiences of complaints to the Health and Disability Commissioner'. *New Zealand Medical Journal* **117**: 975.

Tibballs, J (2007) 'Loss of chance: a new development in medical negligence law' *Med J Aust* 187(4): 233-5.

Walker, B (2004) *Interim report of the Special Commission of Inquiry into Campbelltown and Camden Hospitals*. Sydney, NSW Government.

Wilmot, S (2000) 'Nurses and whistleblowing: the ethical issues'. *Jn Advanced Nursing* **32**(5): 1051-7.

Wilson, R, W Runciman et al (1995) 'The Quality in Australian Health Care Study'. *Med J Aust* **163**: 458-71.

Wu, A, S Folkman et al (1991) 'Do house officers learn from their mistakes?' *JAMA* **265**: 1089-94.

Wright, EW (2006) 'National Trends in Personal Injury Litigation: Before and After "Ipp?"' *Torts Law Journal* **14**: 233.

CHAPTER 9

THE STUDENT IN THE HEALTH-CARE ENVIRONMENT

Case 1

JS, a fourth year medical student, was asked to prepare a long case to present to the Professor of Medicine. The Professor suggested that he examine Mr AB, an 85-year-old man with alcoholic liver disease and hepatocellular carcinoma. When Mr B was asked for permission he replied: 'You can if you have to but I'd rather not, I've just seen three medical students and I'm a bit sore'.

JS asked the registrar for another patient to examine but was told that he ought to be a bit more persistent. 'You'll never get anywhere if you don't push these guys a bit'.

Case 2

A patient was admitted to have one of her kidneys removed because it was no longer functioning. At the start of the procedure, a medical student who was watching the operation told the surgeon that she thought he was taking out the wrong kidney. The surgeons dismissed her comments, telling her she had got it all wrong. No one else in the operating theatre voiced concerns. The surgeons removed the wrong kidney, the patient died and the doctors were charged with manslaughter. (Dwyer 2002)

The aim of training in the health professions is to develop students into competent practitioners. Students enter the health professions with varying backgrounds, ideas, and moral orientation (Bore, Munro et al 2005). Many students are very idealistic, and it is not surprising that some of this idealism wears off, or is even replaced with cynicism (Feudtner, Christakis et al 1994). On the other hand, students' ethics may also develop positively, influenced by the role models they find around them and the patients and situations that they find themselves encountering. Indeed disciplinary action is much more commonly taken in the student years than later in careers (Paice, Heard et al 2002; Papadakis, Teherani et al 2005).

Students often find their introduction to working in the health professions to be extremely challenging. They may often be placed in situations where real ethical dilemmas are ignored or denied by those in higher positions. If managed badly, this lack of recognition may lead to a process of 'ethical erosion' in which the student's ethical standards and compassion are gradually eroded by the hospital environment.

Feudtner and colleagues describe five main areas in which conflicts between the various roles of medical students result in ethical dilemmas –and similar considerations probably apply to the other health professions (Feudtner, Christakis et al 1994). These include: the witnessing of unethical acts committed by other team members, trying to be a good team player, being evaluated for grades, knowing a patient more personally than the rest of the team, and being subtly coerced to put oneself at risk of personal injury.

Learning 'on' patients, learning from patients

The literature suggests that medical education frequently fails to accord respect to patients and often involves them in undergraduate and postgraduate education without first obtaining meaningful consent. Studies have demonstrated that patients are infrequently informed that students would be involved in their care, that supervisors often misrepresent student's status, and that student's attention to explaining their own status to patients deteriorates over time (Cohen, McCullough et al 1987; Beatty and Lewis 1995; Silver-Isenstadt and Ubel 1999). Students themselves are also often concerned about the need to learn and practise on patients when others could provide services in a more expert manner. The manner in which students deal with these issues shapes their future development as professionals.

Medical, nursing and allied health students and junior hospital staff often find it difficult to balance the conflicting demands created by being both a learner and a carer (Jagsi and Soleymani Lehmann 2004). For example, students may hurt patients in the process of learning examination or technical procedures when both they and their patients are aware that such procedures do not benefit patients directly and could be performed more expertly in other hands (Coldicott, Pope et al 2003). This dilemma continues throughout professional life; in fact, whenever a surgeon performs a new procedure or a physician uses a new drug, the patient acts partly as a tool for learning.

We are all patients at some stage in our lives, and would probably all prefer to be operated on by a surgeon with the greatest experience or be given an intramuscular injection by the nurse who is least likely to cause adverse effects. However, if patients always demanded such standards of care, then new doctors and nurses would never be able to learn the practical aspects of patient care. Who then should be responsible for providing the teaching material for inexperienced health professionals?

In countries such as the United States, it may be argued that patients in public hospitals receive a better standard of health care than they could otherwise afford and should pay for this health care by allowing themselves to be used for learning purposes. Indeed, there is some evidence to suggest that the burdens of medical education are not distributed fairly. In one US study, medical students saw a disproportionately high number of non-white patients and patients with Medicaid (public insurance for the indigent) (Frank, Stange et al 1997). Such disparities exist because disempowered patients are not able to withhold consent or are never actually asked to consent to participate in student education. In fact it is likely that few patients would be aware of such justifications as this 'deal' is mostly kept hidden.

A more ethically satisfying approach to the issue is provided by patients, who commonly state: 'Well you've got to learn sometime don't you!' This form of selflessness, or altruistic commitment to community, appears to be the primary motivation for participation in education and provides a compelling argument for respecting patients by obtaining consent for participation in teaching (Magrane, Gannon et al 1996).

All patients, whether they are rich or poor, expect to receive expert medical care and many understand that expert care can only be provided by a health professional who has practical experience and clinical wisdom because they have learnt with and from patients. The right to expert medical care is therefore dependent on a duty that is owed by patients towards health professional training.

The extent of this duty is not clear. For example, several authors have examined how medical students learn vaginal examination. They have demonstrated that medical schools in the UK and the USA have markedly different approaches to teaching this skill. In one study, 70% of students in the USA learnt vaginal examination with non-patient volunteers, 23% with conscious patients and only 2% with unconscious patients. By contrast, in the UK, only 1% of students learned with volunteers, 41% used conscious patients and 46% used unconscious patients (Cohen, Wakeford et al 1988). Whenever these figures have become publicly known, they have tended to provoke public outrage.

Many women have reservations about students performing vaginal examinations and most wish to be informed about the status of the examining practitioner. In a study of an inner-city population in Birmingham, 54% of women objected to having an internal examination by a medical student, and 84% felt that no more than two medical students should be present at a consultation. All patients believed that permission should be sought for a vaginal examination under anaesthetic and all believed that a maximum of one student should be present in a consultation if a vaginal examination is to be performed (Bibby, Boyd et al 1988).

We no longer believe that patients have a 'duty' towards the training of medical, nursing, allied health and paramedical students, although patients may choose to participate in education out of altruism (Lowe, Kerridge et al 2008). Advances in technology and simulation mean that many of the skills that in the past needed to be learnt with real patients can now be learnt in simulated settings first. We also believe that, wherever possible, skills should be practised with well patients (often paid for their time) rather than sick patients. Skills such as vaginal and rectal exam are commonly learnt this way now.

Students who are approaching patients to learn from them should inform them truthfully of their status and the reason that they wish to see them, and students must be supervised adequately for any potentially distressing or hazardous procedure. If patients refuse to see students this should be accepted gracefully and without attempts at coercion.

Witnessing unethical acts

In addition to their other roles in the hospital system, students act as interested observers, part way between the layman and the full professional. It is disturbing that in some studies, 65% of students felt that they had witnessed unethical behaviour by a member of the health-care team to which they were attached and 80% believed that they had acted unethically or wilfully misled patients themselves. Fifty-four per cent of the students in this study who had witnessed unethical behaviour felt that they were in some way an accomplice to one or more of these actions (Feudtner, Christakis et al 1994). Similarly, in another survey of Canadian medical students, half reported pressure to act unethically, 60% had observed unethical conduct in a clinical teacher and many felt intimidated by their teacher and so unable to object or act differently (Hicks, Lin et al 2001).

Students do not enter the health professions as ethically neutral beings, developing all their skills and beliefs as they proceed; rather, they tend to approach it with their own set of values and beliefs and with a shared commitment to caring for patients. The process of learning about medicine, both in the academic and the clinical environments directs and perhaps limits this diffuse sense of moral concern. 'What students learn is to clarify and define their obligations and responsibilities to patients and others' (Dwyer 1994). This process is analogous to other forms of learning in health care – one begins with imprecise ideas and gradually modifies them in the face of experience.

For many students, the exposure to the hospital environment results in an erosion of their ethical values rather than a strengthening of them. For example, one student stated: 'Slowly I'm seeing my classmates become "destroyed" and it scares me. I've become so cynical that it's just not right!!' (Feudtner, Christakis et al 1994).

Much of the negative impact that hospitals have may relate to the long hours, poor working conditions and inadequate supervision and support that is offered in them, and it may be the case that the adoption of ethically dubious practices is useful for survival in this environment. Some medical students report that, although they recognise that their ethical principles are being eroded, they are not displeased by this. According to Feudtner, it is 'as though they have accepted that becoming a doctor requires a transformation of character' (Feudtner, Christakis et al 1994).

Students often react with a policy of silence when they observe or take part in ethically suspect actions. This has some rewards – it prevents ridicule, being graded poorly or being seen as a poor team player. However, it is not enough to observe unethical behaviour now and to vow to act if similar situations arise in the future. The skills involved in responding to unethical behaviour need to be practised and developed if they are to be available when needed. Keeping quiet becomes a habit, and it represents a failure in teaching, learning and caring (Dwyer 1994; Bloch 2003).

The duty to speak out

People like to conform to expectations. In 1963, a series of experiments designed by Stanley Milgram investigated the reactions of people placed in an environment that encouraged unethical actions (Sutherland 1994). Experimental subjects where asked to give electrical shocks to others as part of an experiment. Unbeknown to them, those who received the shocks were actually paid volunteers or 'stooges' who pretended to be in pain. Milgram advised the subjects to give shocks of increasing severity, even using equipment that was labelled: 'Danger: severe shock'; to the point where the victims screamed in agony or no longer appeared responsive, perhaps even dead. When the subjects protested about giving such severe shocks, they were told only 'you have no other choice, you must go on' or 'the experiment requires that you continue'. Over 60% of experimental subjects were persuaded to give shocks that they believed were severely dangerous or life threatening.

Milgram's experiments were conducted in an attempt to understand why ordinary German citizens, including many health professionals, complied with the orders that led to the atrocities in Nazi Germany. Before the Holocaust more than 200,000 German citizens were killed by German doctors, nurses and other individuals in an attempt to wipe out retarded, ill and 'defective' individuals throughout Germany (Gallagher 1990). This is not an isolated incident, doctors in the Soviet Union have incarcerated and tortured dissidents, doctors in America have castrated patients who were thought to have 'poor genetic material' and doctors throughout the world have participated in torture and killing. We do not maintain that the ethical standards in the Western world at present conform to those of the Nazis, but we do believe that everyone has some obligation to refuse to participate in unethical actions and speak out against unethical acts.

Unfortunately, it is difficult for junior staff and students to know exactly when they should speak out in matters of ethics or medical law. Junior medical, nursing, allied health staff or students are under no obligation to follow commands that are illegal such as torture or deliberate harm; indeed, there is a legal obligation to speak out against such actions. In addition, a strong ethical and legal case can be made for refusing to participate in actions that they believe to be morally wrong. An example of this is that one need not participate in abortions if one has a conscientious objection.

Unfortunately, the majority of conflicts of this type do not fall into either category but are characterised by legal and ethical uncertainty. Dwyer, in a 1994 Hastings Center Report, provides some interesting insights into this problem (Dwyer 1994). He believes that in trying to decide whether to speak up in a particular case, students should consider the potential harm to patients, their specific role in the situation, the nature and certainty of their judgments, the probable effectiveness of speaking up and the likely cost to themselves if they do speak up.

The major factor to be considered is the possibility of harm to patients. If patients have been harmed by unethical actions it may be necessary to speak out even if one is only peripherally involved. But students may often be unsure of their judgments, either because they feel that they do not have enough experience to judge the appropriateness of an action, or because they doubt the value of their own ethical judgments. Students need to find an appropriate threshold for certainty in expressing their concerns, taking into account the other factors mentioned by Dwyer.

It is also reasonable to consider the likely efficacy of speaking up and the possibilities for harm to one's self if one does speak up. Students may not have an obligation to speak out if it will be ineffective or cause harm to themselves that is out of proportion to the benefit to the patient. The relative importance of each of these factors is difficult to judge but it is our experience (and that of Dwyer's) that speaking out can make a difference and need not always involve great personal sacrifice. It is difficult to gather the courage to speak out but one should not be disheartened. Attempting to speak out in even small ways offers at least some potential for further moral growth.

Professional bodies, such as the American College of Physicians, state that 'it is unethical for a physician not to report fraud, professional misconduct, incompetence or abandonment of a patient by another physician' (American College of Physicians 1992). They also state, however, that 'it is unethical for a physician to disparage the professional competence, knowledge, qualifications, or services of another physician to a patient or a third party or to state or imply that a patient has been poorly managed or mistreated by a colleague, without substantial evidence'. Statements of the second sort are generally seen more as statements of 'professional etiquette' rather than ethics, and may at times even contradict community standards of ethical behaviour. Certainly, it is better to keep complaints and 'speaking out' within the usual channels where possible, but if this is not possible then it may be necessary to go outside them.

Cases of ethical conflict may be extremely difficult to recognise and one may only see on later reflection that one has participated in or acquiesced to unethical actions. There are several approaches to such situations.

First, one should develop a plan of action for future management of similar situations if they arise. Most people are taken aback when they first encounter situations in which they feel that something wrong has occurred.

Second, it is often possible to discuss these issues among one's peers, and develop a forum where such problems can be discussed in future (although it is particularly important for all concerned that this be done with the highest standards of confidentiality). James Dwyer states:

> It will not be easy to transform fearful silence into concerned conversation, but that is what needs to be done. There is a need for people to question and report the obviously bad. And in cases that are less obvious, there is a need for people to initiate discussions about what is good. … When students (and residents) fail to express their concerns … everyone stands to lose. (Dwyer 1994)

Third, there are a number of ways in which one can use the role of a student to bring up issues and institute change. One way for students to do this is to use their position as junior person in the team to pretend ignorance and ask questions as if they were learning-issues. For example, if a patient undergoes an HIV test without permission, the student might start asking about where they can find out the hospital policy on this or why, in this case, did the doctor decide to use a different approach to the hospital policy. They might also ask if it is all right to use this case for their ethics write-up, so could the doctor explain why he or she did this? (Kushner and Thomasma 2001). Or, to use a more mundane example, if a student were to note that a senior colleague had failed to start a patient who had experienced a myocardial infarct on aspirin, which is proven to be effective as secondary prophylaxis, they may ask a series of questions aimed at encouraging the doctor to commence appropriate therapy. These questions could become increasingly direct according to the response of the senior clinician. So, for example, the student may start by asking 'is there any treatment shown to reduce the chance of subsequent heart attacks?', then 'is aspirin of any benefit in this setting?', then 'aspirin is effective in cases like this, isn't it?', then 'shouldn't this patient be on aspirin?', then perhaps 'why aren't we starting this patient on aspirin?'. Such an approach is known as Graded Assertiveness, and is often used by medical students when dealing with teachers and by non-medical health professionals when dealing with doctors (Runciman, Merry et al 2007).

Where possible, students should always try to work within the system, by talking about the issue with the person who they feel is behaving unethically. This has to be done in a non-confrontational way. If it is impossible to talk to the person concerned, then students can move up the hierarchy. Indeed, there are numerous hierarchies within hospitals and, if it is not possible to address issues within one of these, it might be possible within another. For example, if placement with a particular physician exposes students to unethical behaviour, it may be possible for this to be discussed within the university and students be placed elsewhere in future.

It is usually less threatening if the student consults first with their supervisor, rather than moving up the hospital hierarchy, but in many cases these will be the same person. In general, it is best not to skip levels in the hierarchy (ie do not go directly to the head of the hospital) as this will introduce other complications. If no satisfaction is found at one level, the next level of the hierarchy should be approached.

Occasionally health professionals in hospitals feel that they need to speak out publicly about injustices that they perceive. Doing so is always fraught as it exposes situations, issues and people to public critique, and so should only be entertained where there is clear evidence of harm, where the individual concerned is very certain of their moral assessment, and after all other avenues have been exhausted. Historically, the approach of any organisation that finds this occurring has been to persecute and sack the 'whistle blower'. Reassuringly, there are policies now being developed to protect such people.

Unprofessional students

In 2005, Papadakis and colleagues published a study in which they looked back to the medical school records of 235 doctors who had been disciplined by medical boards in the United States and compared this to doctors who had not been disciplined. They found that doctors who were disciplined were three times as likely to have been noted to have unprofessional conduct in medical school as those who were not disciplined. The forms of unprofessional behaviour that were most likely to be associated with later disciplinary action were severe irresponsibility and severely diminished capacity for self-improvement (Papadakis, Teherani et al 2005).

In one way this study suggests that lack of professionalism may be a life-long phenomenon – little influenced by training or education. If this is the case, the answer is surely to exclude unprofessional students as early as possible. Perhaps some students are even unable to develop appropriate ethical frameworks (eg if they have certain personality disorders), and should be excluded from medical courses (Lowe, Kerridge et al 2001). The fact that one of the strongest predictors was 'severely diminished capacity for self-improvement' suggests that better education is unlikely to fix this problem.

On the other hand, the authors also note that unprofessional behaviour in medical school is much more common than disciplinary action once the student has graduated. Up to 20% of the control group – who were not subject to disciplinary action – had some evidence of unprofessional behaviour in their student years, although this tended to be mild. This suggests that doctors may be able to become more professional with training, education and experience.

Conclusion

Students of the health professions are both learners and participants within the health-care system. They are frequently exposed to situations in which they confront ethical dilemmas. These need to be addressed honestly as they are an integral feature of health care and health-care education. It has been stated that '[t]he ideal relationships between colleagues, within the medical profession and between health care professionals generally is one of both mutual support and mutual and honest criticism' (Campbell, Gillett et al 1992).

We have already discussed Milgram's experiments about the power of authority and conformity, but it is also worth noting that a few of his subjects refused to shock patients further. In one case the experimenter attempted to bully the subject by stating 'you have no other choice'. The subject replied: 'I do have a choice. Why don't I have a choice? I came here of my own free will' (Schwartz 1987). The same is true of students, health professionals and patients.

LEGAL ISSUES OF STUDENTS IN THE HEALTH-CARE SETTING

Health profession students must accept that they have both an ethical and legal responsibility to persons they may be involved with during their training. These obligations may extend to patients they are seeing, the relatives and friends of those patients, staff of the institution they may be in and other students. Even though students may be under supervision they still have a personal responsibility for their actions, although this responsibility will be judged against the standard expected of a student with their level of training.

A student's duty and standard of care

There is no doubt that a student health professional owes the patient they may be examining or interacting with a duty of care. The student will be expected to exercise a reasonable standard of care, whether the interaction is a purely learning exercise for the student or where the student may be providing some therapeutic benefit for the patient.

The standard is the same as that exercised by an ordinary person exercising that special skill. This was discussed in *Wilsher v Essex Area Health Authority* [1986] 3 All ER 801 (reversed on other grounds at [1988] AC 1074). Glidewell LJ stated that 'the law requires the trainee or learner to be judged by the same standard as his more experienced colleagues. If it did not, inexperience would frequently be urged as a defence to an action in professional negligence' (at 831). That requires a trainee nurse, for example, to satisfy the skills of a registered nurse, but not higher level skills such as that of a nurse practitioner or nurse unit manager. Specialists have a higher duty of care as represented by their added qualifications, skill and experience.

The result of this is that students should be under supervision at all times. The supervision of students and junior practitioners is an important role under-taken by health professionals. The level of supervision will vary depending on the experience of the student and the level of their learning. At first students will only act under close supervision, where a supervisor is physically present and actively works with the student as they carry out a procedure. As the student progresses and gains more experience the supervisor may decide that it is appropriate that the student can carry out a procedure without the supervisor being physically present. Even in this situation, however, a supervisor should always be available (or have made other suitable arrangements) for consultation or assistance should the student need help.

A student who undertakes a task, knowing it is beyond their level of learning or ability, will be judged against the standard of care expected from a suitably qualified practitioner: *Collins v Hertfordshire County Council* [1947] KB 598 (HC). It is important that the student health professional is aware of his or her own limitations and seeks assistance and further instruction where appro-priate. Students cannot be forced to provide services which are beyond their skill base. In *Luck v Blamey & Assoc* [2000] VSC 77, a woman sought a court order to force her surgeon to provide her with a treatment for her scleroderma. The surgeon refused to provide the treatment because he believed that it should be provided by a dermatologist. The court refused to order the surgeon to provide the treatment.

If students do go beyond their skill base without supervision the hospital may be found to have breached its duty of care to the patient. In *Brus v Australian Capital Territory* [2007] ACTSC 83, a hospital was found liable for injuries sustained by a patient, when she was operated on by a registrar who was not yet qualified to perform the operation in question. Connolly J stated:

> I do not accept that there is a general duty of care on a public hospital to in effect provide public patients with a choice of doctor, or to appraise a patient as to the academic standing of a registrar. However, there is a duty on a

hospital to ensure that it provides patients with suitably qualified staff. The rigorous College training program, it seems to me, ensures that, at each stage of their training, a registrar in good standing is suitably qualified to perform the range of procedures commensurate with their level of training. In this case, a registrar known to the hospital to have major deficiencies in surgical techniques for a level 2 Registrar was held out to Dr Heaton as a level 3 Registrar, and he allowed her to perform a procedure that he would not have permitted a level 2 Registrar to perform. (at [62])

Consent

It is important that patients consent to being seen or attended to by a student health professional. The fact that a hospital may have signs or information in patient handbooks indicating that it is a 'teaching' or 'training' hospital does not mean that patients are impliedly consenting to student participation in their health care. There may be some circumstances where it is not possible to gain consent from the patient for a student to be involved in their care or to observe treatment being given. This will be the case in emergency departments and intensive care units in hospitals. These units should have protocols in place to cover student involvement.

Care should be taken that the student is introduced as a student and not by another description that may be considered to be misleading. For example, a medical student should not be introduced as 'Dr' or as a 'doctor in training'. If the patient is misled about the status of a student it is not clear whether any consent may be invalidated (see the discussion in Chapter 13), but it may be a possibility.

Consent is a necessary part of all health care. Consent is repeatedly gained from patients during their treatment. As discussed further in Chapter 14 consent should be viewed as a *process* rather than an *event*. For example, the taking of the patient's blood pressure would require the consent of the patient (or where the patient is not competent this may be given by the person responsible or under provisions of guardianship legislation). It is also the case that a more formal consent is sought for investigations or procedures that may be the reason that a patient is admitted to a hospital. It is the responsibility of the treating doctor to obtain this 'informed consent' from the patient and to advise the patient of any material risks inherent in the procedure (*Rogers v Whitaker* (1992) 175 CLR 479).

Sometimes a doctor may delegate the task of explaining the risks to patients to other hospital staff. Doctors who delegate the task of providing information to patients bear the liability if others do not properly advise the patient. Students must be careful that they do not themselves undertake the task of providing information to patients. A situation may arise where a patient suggests to a student health professional that the patient did not really understand what they had been told by the doctor (or other health professional) and could the student please explain it to them. In this case it is important that the student does not independently undertake to provide the information to the patient. If they were to do so their standard of care would be judged against that of an appropriately qualified health professional. The best response may be to notify their supervisor or treating doctor so that the patient can be appropriately informed by the health professional.

All students have to undertake tasks for the first time. The first, or first few times, should always be under direct supervision. How much subsequent supervision is required will depend on the nature of the task to be performed and the risks that may be associated with the task. Should the patient be informed that the student (or trainee health professional) has limited experience in performing the procedure? In *Rogers v Whitaker* the High Court said that patients should be informed about 'material risks'. Material risks were said to be those risks to which a reasonable person in the patient's position would attach some significance or those risks that this particular patient has given some indication they may attach significance. Although *Rogers v Whitaker* was concerned about *risks* it could be inferred from the judgment that patients should be provided with *material information* about the procedure. Would material information include the fact that the student was inexperienced in the procedure?

The 1998 High Court decision in *Chappel v Hart* (1998) 195 CLR 232 provides some support for the proposition that such disclosure is required. In this case the patient, Mrs Hart, was not warned of a particular risk of a procedure that she underwent. Mrs Hart asserted that if she had been warned of the particular risk associated with the procedure (although the risk came about through a rare concurrence of events) she would not have agreed to go ahead at that time and would have sought the most experienced surgeon in the field to perform the procedure. Gaudron J said, in passing, that:

> If the foreseeable risk to Mrs Hart was the loss of an opportunity to undergo surgery at the hands of a more experienced surgeon, the duty would have been a duty to inform her that there were more experienced surgeons practising in the field. (at 239)

Ultimately, the Court's decision did not determine this issue. However, it does provide some support for the proposition that there may be a duty to warn a patient when the doctor is junior or inexperienced in relation to particular procedures. It would be advisable that, where the patient may be clearly nervous about the outcome or requests information about the health-care team, they be advised about the level of experience of the team and the type of supervision that will be exercised.

Confidentiality

In the same way that health professionals owe a duty of confidence to their patients so too do student health professionals. All confidences revealed to a student should remain confidential. There may be some circumstances where a patient may reveal to the student information that they have not told the health professionals responsible for their care. This can create a dilemma for a student, particularly if the patient explicitly states that they do not want the health-care team to be told. The best path is to avoid such a situation in the first place! The nature of the discussion the student will be having with the patient needs to be established with the patient before information is collected. This may include the fact that the student may be discussing the conversation with their supervisor as part of the training process.

Whilst there is a general recognition that it is necessary to gain the patient's consent before being seen by a student the same does not seem to apply, in practice, to students' gaining access to confidential information about patients. This may happen directly by students reviewing a patient's medical record (without consent), often before they gain consent to approach the patient or indirectly through attending departmental meetings where patient cases are discussed. This would seem to indicate a difference in the approach to the 'physical autonomy' of the patient and their 'informational autonomy' (Case 2003).

It may be that it is not practicable to seek a patient's consent in all cases, particularly where students participate in health-care teams where it may be quite appropriate that the health professionals be informed about aspects of the patient's care. Principle 2.2(f) in Sch 1 to the *Health Records Act 2001* (Vic) recognises that information can be provided for training purposes as long as a reasonable attempt is made to de-identify the records. In NSW the Statutory Guidelines to the *Health Records and Information Privacy Act 2002* include 'Statutory Guidelines on Training'. The Guidelines provide that a breach of the Act will not occur where students gain access to health records with the permission of their supervisor and where the students have agreed, in writing, not to reveal further the confidential information that they access. Neither the *Privacy Act 1988* (Cth) nor the *Health Records (Privacy and Access) Act 1997* (ACT) deal explicitly with the use of information for training purposes but they do allow information to be used without consent for 'management, funding, or quality' purposes. It might be arguable that training is both part of management and quality assurance, and for teaching hospitals may also have funding implications. All these privacy schemes allow for the information to be used where the patient consents or is aware that the information would be used in that way. The use of patient information in teaching hospitals may therefore be covered by patient consent or by making the patient aware that students will have access to the information for education and training.

Boundary violations

Maintaining clear professional boundaries is an important part of patient care. This applies as much to health profession students as it does to health professionals. While the provision of health care has become less formal it is still important that inappropriate relations are not developed with patients. A distinction has been drawn between boundary crossing (departures from usual practice that are not exploitive and can sometimes be helpful to the patient) and boundary violations (boundary crossing that is harmful to the patient) (Galletly 2004).

Hospitals and universities have a responsibility to ensure that health profession students understand issues relating to boundary violations and the student's responsibility not to cross the line inappropriately. Health profession supervisors have a responsibility to prevent breaches and to take appropriate action where breaches do occur. An example of a boundary violation can be found in *Southern Area Health Service v Brown* [2003] NSWCA 369.

The female patient in this case had a long history of psychiatric disturbance and had been treated over a long period of time at the defendant hospital. The patient became acquainted with a (male) first-year student nurse who was on placement at the hospital where she was being treated. The student was assigned to take the patient outside when she wanted to have a cigarette. According to the hospital manager the student nurse was under close supervision and was not involved in the medical treatment of the patient. However, the court described the supervision thus:

> [The student] was not closely supervised in the sense of being under the constant and vigilant eye of a member of staff at every moment of the shift. Since part of his duties included mundane activities, such as accompanying [the patient] outside, he had the opportunity, in the course of his rostered shift as a trainee, to engage in conversation with her. These were not described by [the patient] in terms which suggested any overt impropriety about their nature or the topics dealt with. (at [25])

After the patient was discharged from the hospital the student nurse had further contact with the patient, and members of the hospital's Mental Health Service were aware of this contact. In the early hours of the morning, after accepting an invitation to accompany her home, the student nurse sexually assaulted the patient.

The trial judge, affirmed by the New South Wales Court of Appeal, found that the members of staff of the hospital had a duty to warn the student that the relationship with the patient ought not to be fostered and found that 'there was nothing to suggest that, had [he] been rebuffed and/or warned off by the [hospital's] staff, he would have forced the issue' (at [61]). Thus, when they found out that the student intended to contact the patient privately it was the duty of the hospital staff, and in particular his supervisors, to warn him against such contact.

There is a limit to the duty owed by hospitals to prevent their staff having relationships with their patients. In *Mills v Central Sydney Area Health Service* [2002] NSWSC 728, a psychiatric nurse commenced a sexual relationship with a patient during his treatment, and that sexual relationship continued after the treatment ceased. Not long after the start of the relationship the patient was murdered by the nurse. The family of the patient argued that the health service had provided negligent treatment by allowing the nurse to enter into a sexual relationship with the patient and had that not happened the patient would not have been killed. Master Harrison dismissed this argument. He found that the nurse's later actions were not foreseeable and hence there was no duty. Moreover, the Master found that even if there was a duty to prevent such conduct there was no causation as the murder took place six weeks after the patient had left the care of the hospital. The health service had no duty to prevent sexual relationships occurring outside of hospital grounds and outside the nurse's working hours.

Impaired students

Impairment is discussed in Chapter 5. Students with health problems, such as mental illness and drug addiction, should seek help for their impairments. In some jurisdictions, reporting of such conditions is required. For example, in South Australia s 49 of the *Medical Practice Act 2004*, requires health professionals, hospital administrators and teachers of medical students to report medical students to the authorities if they suspect students of being unfit to provide medical treatment.

References

American College of Physicians (1992) 'Ethics Manual. (Third Edition)'. *Ann Intern Med* **117**: 947-960.

Beatty, M and J Lewis (1995) 'When students introduce themselves as doctors to patients'. *Acad Med* **70**: 175-6.

Bibby, J, N Boyd et al (1988) 'Consent for vaginal examination by students on anaesthetised patients'. *Lancet* (Nov 12): 1150.

Bloch, S (2003) 'Medical students and clinical ethics'. *Med J Aust* **178**(4): 167-9.

Bore, M, D Munro et al (2005) 'Selection of medical students according to their moral orientation'. *Medical Education* **39**(3): 266-75.

Campbell, A, G Gillett et al (1992) *Practical Medical Ethics*. Auckland, Oxford University Press.

Case, P (2003) 'Confidence matters: The rise and fall of informational autonomy in medical law'. *Medical Law Review* **11**: 208-36.

Cohen, D, L McCullough et al (1987) 'Informed consent policies governing medical students interaction with patients'. *J Med Educ* **62**: 789-98.

Cohen, D, R Wakeford et al (1988) 'Teaching vaginal examination'. *Lancet* (Dec 10): 1375.

Coldicott, Y, C Pope et al (2003) 'The ethics of intimate examination – teaching tomorrows doctors'. *BMJ* **326**: 97-101.

Dwyer, C (2002) 'Doctors go on trial for manslaughter after removing wrong kidney'. *BMJ* **324**: 1476.

Dwyer, J (1994) 'Primum non tacere. An ethics of speaking up'. *Hastings Cent Rep* **Jan-Feb**: 13-18.

Feudtner, C, D Christakis et al (1994) 'Do clinical clerks suffer ethical erosion? Students' perceptions of their ethical environment and personal development'. *Acad Med* **69**: 660-79.

Frank, S, K Stange et al (1997) 'Direct observation of community-based ambulatory encounters involving medical students'. *JAMA* **278**: 712-16.

Gallagher, H (1990) *By trust betrayed. Patients, physicians and the license to kill in the Third Reich*. New York, Henry Holt and Company.

Galletly, C (2004) 'Crossing professional boundaries in medicine: the slippery slope to patient sexual exploitation'. *Med J Aust* **181**(7): 380-3.

Hicks, LK, Y Lin et al (2001) 'Understanding the clinical dilemmas that shape medical students' ethical development: questionnaire survey and focus group study'. *BMJ* **322**(7288): 709-10.

Jagsi, R and L Soleymani Lehmann (2004) 'The ethics of medical education'. *BMJ* **329**: 332-4.

Kushner, T and D Thomasma (2001) *Ward ethics: Dilemmas for medical students and doctors in training*. Cambridge, Cambridge University Press.

Lowe, M, I Kerridge et al (2001) 'Is it possible to assess the "ethics" of medical school applicants?'. *J Med Ethics* **27**(6): 404-8.

Lowe, M, I Kerridge et al (2008) 'Do patients have an obligation to participate in student teaching?'. *Med Education* **42**(3): 237-41.

McIllwraith, J and B Madden (2006) *Health Care and the Law*. Sydney, Thomson Lawbook Co.

Magrane, D, J Gannon et al (1996) 'Student doctors and women in labour: attitudes and expectations'. *Obstet Gynaecol*. **88**: 298-302.

Paice, E, S Heard et al (2002) 'How important are role models in making good doctors?'. *BMJ* **325**(7366): 707-10.

Papadakis, M, A Teherani et al (2005) 'Disciplinary Action by Medical Boards and Prior Behavior in Medical School'. *N Engl J Med* **353**(25): 2673-83.

Runciman, B, A Merry et al (2007) *Safety and ethics in healthcare*. Melbourne, Ashgate Publishing.

Schwartz, S (1987) *Pavlov 's Heirs*. Sydney, Angus and Robertson.

Silver-Isenstadt, A and P Ubel (1999) 'Erosion in medical students attitudes about telling patients they are students'. *J Gen Intern Med* **14**: 481-7.

Sutherland, S (1994) *Irrationality. The enemy within*. London, Penguin Books.

CHAPTER 10

NURSING

Case 1

Mrs C was an elderly Polish woman who was admitted to hospital with chest pain. Her son could not be contacted at the time of her admission because he had gone on holidays. When he returned one week later he stated that his mother had only recently begun living with him, which had caused him considerable stress. Her admission to hospital had provided him an opportunity to get away for a much needed holiday.

Mrs C was adamant that she wished to live with her son and the staff persuaded her son to take her home. Two months later, the community nurses were asked to assist with the care of Mrs C at home. When they looked closely at the home situation, it became clear that Mrs C had severe urinary incontinence – which was worse than had been apparent in hospital – and she required a full-time carer to look after her. Her discharge from hospital had caused a family crisis as her daughter-in-law did not wish to care for her and had left the small flat that they lived in. The son had taken long-service leave to care for his mother, but did not know what he would do once his leave ran out.

The community nurse felt that she faced a dilemma in this situation. Although she felt that her first concern should be the best interests of the old lady, who wished to stay at home, she could not see how she could do this but still take into account the conflicting needs of the other family members who were experiencing such disruption.

Case 2

A researcher investigated the care of dying patients by sitting in their rooms and noting down any care that was given. The following case – that of a 41-year-old woman who was dying from hepatic carcinoma – is one of several similar case histories reported.

> *'At 5.25 pm a supper tray was placed before her, and she was lifted to the side of the bed and placed unsupported with her legs dangling over the side. Being unable to support herself she fell back.*

> *At 5.42 pm a cup of tea was placed on the tray. She struggled to reach the tea but was unable to do so. 'Did you have a drink?' asked a nurse. There was no response and '120ml tea' was recorded on the fluid balance chart.*

At 5.50 pm the patient tried to reach a drink on her locker without success. At 6.05 pm she rolled over, drew in her legs, and tried to cover herself with a sheet.

At 6.10 pm the tray was removed with the food untouched; no contact was made with the patient. At 6.50 pm a member of the staff placed a glass of water on the locker, there was again no contact.

Visitors attended the patient between 7.00 and 8.00pm.

At 8.15 pm a nurse approached and asked the patient if she would like tea or coffee. 'I've got juice.' she replied. She tried to raise herself to reach the drink on her locker, but it was beyond her reach. She struggled but eventually lay back exhausted. She continued this struggle for half an hour, moaning as the nurses passed, and then called out at 9.20 pm to a nurse.

'What's wrong?' asked the nurse. The patient indicated that she wanted her juice. The nurse handed the patient her juice and then left (nine-second contact). The patient attempted to drink, but could not keep her head up to do so. She could neither drink the juice, nor lay the juice down on the locker, which was beyond her reach. She looked once more in the direction of the observer. Observations were discontinued, and the patient was helped to drink.'
(Mills, Davies et al 1994)

Case 3

JS is a nurse who works in a hospital in which there is a policy that all patients should have CPR if they have a cardiac arrest, unless there is a written order to the contrary. One evening, she realised that Mr D, a man with metastatic carcinoma whom she knew very well, was slipping into unconsciousness and appeared to be dying. She knew that he was a man with who had suffered greatly from his disease and he had frequently said that he just wanted to 'slip away'.

She reviewed his notes and found that a CPR order had not been written. She paged the medical officer on duty to discuss the situation, but before she received a reply, was called to Mr D's room because he had stopped breathing. She decided not to commence CPR. The following day, when the events of the night had been discussed, she was asked to account for her actions by the hospital administration and was threatened with disciplinary action.

What is different about nursing?

The birth of modern nursing is often dated to the work of Florence Nightingale in the military hospitals of the Crimean War. Early nurses in the Nightingale tradition stressed a model of nursing that was based on the rank system of the British Army – with the officer class represented by the doctors, and the lesser ranks represented by nurses. In this environment, loyalty to the doctor was emphasised as one of the chief moral requirements of nurses. Such loyalty was supposed to inspire patient confidence in the doctor, which in turn was thought to aid the patient's recovery. For the most part nurses accepted this as a solemn obligation (Winslow 1984).

However, this attitude also led to deep moral difficulties for nurses when they felt that the moral authority of doctors was not justifiable, such as when doctors were incompetent or out of touch with their patients. It also led to situations in which doctors who made mistakes were able to blame nurses, and hence maintain their own reputations. One of the most notorious cases of this sort occurred in Manila in 1929 when a nurse called Lorenza Somera was found guilty of manslaughter after following a doctor's mistaken order to give an injection of cocaine. The doctor in the case was acquitted. This led to a world-wide protest campaign, and eventually Somera was pardoned. This campaign represented the beginnings of a realisation among nurses that their ethical standards could no longer be delegated to the doctors who provided their medical orders.

In the 1960s and 1970s, the growth of technology in medicine caused changes in the way that the public perceived the role of medicine; it was no longer seen as entirely beneficent, and aspects of medical care came to thought of as cold, cruel and impersonal. Although the public standing of doctors slipped, nurses continued to enjoy enormous community standing, in part because they were seen by the public and by themselves as a humanising influence that could blunt some of the excesses of medicine. Over the subsequent decades, Australian nurse-training moved out of the hospitals and into universities, new career structures developed and nursing adopted a model of practice based upon a new type of professionalism – one that emphasised nursing as a separate discipline from medicine.

One aspect of health care that was explored by nurses was the way in which the impersonal, logical, sterile ways of the modern hospital seemed to be mirrored in the impartial, intellectual logic of modern biomedical ethics. Nursing ethicists realised that this impartiality was not necessarily a feature of good nursing or medical care, where the ultimate value of encounters often seems to rest in the individual human contact between patients and their carers rather than in the intellectualism of diagnosis and treatment. Hence nursing ethics arose as a separate area within bioethics, primarily because nurses could not identify with the medical profession and indeed sometimes felt that they were acting in opposition to it.

Nursing theory

As nursing moved away from the Nightingale model, nurses needed to develop new models to explain to themselves and others exactly what they did. If not the doctors' handmaiden, what precisely is a nurse? This question has led to the ongoing development of a large number of theories of nursing, and questions of nursing theory have become central to much of the academic discipline of nursing. Nursing theorists have embraced feminism, sociological theories and cultural theory as sources of inspiration for theories of nursing practice and nursing ethics (Alligood and Mariner-Tomey 2002).

Some academic nurses believe that there is even a moral requirement for nurses to derive their work from overarching theories (Grace 2002). However, this is not universally agreed either within nursing (Speedy and Kermode 1996) or without. If we look at the more general question as to whether professions need to be based on agreed 'grand theories', authors such as Sunstein (writing about the law) believe that it is preferable to look for low-level agreements ('minimally-theorised agreements') rather than basing practice on deep, all-encompassing theories (Sunstein 1994). The 'evidence-based medicine' movement in clinical medicine has also been anti-theory, believing that the benefits of health care should be found in its results, and discounting the role of theory unless it has concrete outcomes. (Yet, in another way, the 'evidence-based' movements in medicine and nursing are also theories of what medicine and nursing should be about, and many of the same reservations apply to them – see Chapter 27.) There are real doubts whether any particular theory can capture the richness and variety of professions such as nursing and medicine, which are by their nature complex and diverse, and whose boundaries are defined by both the professions themselves and also by changing needs of the wider society.

Some nursing theory, such as Virgina Henderson's pioneering work, has arisen out of careful and deep examination of nursing practice. Many other nursing theories have arisen entirely out of theoretical constructs rather than from an empirical basis (Schmieding 2002). As a result, some nursing theory is difficult to apply in practice or is difficult to comprehend, and some of it is clearly meaningless. (For example, see Erikson's belief that theories of holistic nursing can be derived from quantum physics and string theory (Erikson 2007).) This is, of course, also true of many other bodies of theory including philosophy, sociology, linguistics and cultural studies. There is a tendency for some nursing theory to be written in terms that are very difficult to understand and full of jargon. Academic writing needs to communicate complex ideas, but the best of academic writing in both nursing and other areas should try to be both clear and commonsense.

Nursing ethics

One of the defining features of nursing ethics has been the emphasis given to the experience of illness and the patient's narrative. In part this focus has arisen as part of nursing's rejection of the emphasis of medicine on the scientific, technological, general and abstract features of disease and health care. This type of writing is known as 'phenomenology'. The case quoted above in Case 2 is a phenomenological account.

Phenomenology is a way of thinking first developed by European philosophers. Its primary concern is with the nature and meaning of human experience *as it is lived* (Merleau-Ponty 1962). Phenomenological accounts of illness often provide intensely personal, subjective and complex accounts of experience (Frank 1995; Madjar and Walton 1999). The insights gained through such accounts of illness are invaluable for enriching any discussion of ethics and health care.

While the methods of nursing ethics may differ from medical ethics, the subjects of nursing ethics are also somewhat different. Nursing ethicists have been largely concerned with five main moral concepts: advocacy, accountability, power, interdisciplinary collaboration and caring (Fry 1995). Three of these areas – the ethics of care, advocacy and collaborative models of health-care delivery – are probably the most discussed topics in nursing ethics. In the rest of this chapter we concentrate mainly on these areas.

The ethics of care

In the 1960s and 1970s, the moral psychologist Leonard Kohlberg developed an influential theory of moral development based on the work of developmental psychologists such as Jean Piaget. Kohlberg came to the conclusion that moral development occurred in six defined stages, leading from a state of moral immaturity towards higher levels of moral development. The higher stages (stages five and six) involved individuals acting objectively, rationally and impartially, following universal ethical principles of a higher morality based on concepts of justice.

Kohlberg's work was strongly criticised by his former colleague Carol Gilligan. One of Gilligan's main criticisms was that Kohlberg had studied a purely male sample and that when he applied his findings to women he tended to find them to be morally undeveloped and 'immature'. In a famous paper that looked at women who were making decisions about abortions, Gilligan found that many women did not regard morality in terms of justice and competing rights but instead saw it in terms of the need to nurture and maintain human relationships involving emotional responses to the concrete details of particular situations. (Note that this does not imply that a care orientation is exclusively female.) Gilligan therefore claimed that women had a 'care focus' in moral reasoning that had been ignored or underplayed by Kohlberg (Gilligan 1982).

Gilligan's ideas about an ethics of care strongly influenced the views of many nurse-ethicists; who saw them as providing a viable alternative to the dominance of principle-based ethics. It was even suggested that while principle-based ethics with its emphasis on universality and justice might be appropriate for doctors, a more personal, caring ethics might be more appropriate for nurses (Davis 1985).

'Caring' is a concept that is difficult to define. The primary characteristics of the ethics of care have been summarised as:

- a primary concern with avoidance of harm, and a general preference for values of nurturance over those of justice and equality;
- a focus on relatedness and relationships in contrast to individualistic conceptions of rights and contractual social interaction, including a rejection of ideas of impartiality in favour of recognition that an agent's location in specific relationships may have moral implications;
- a preference for concrete, as opposed to abstract, deliberation, rejection of the use of abstract and universal principles in favour of attention to the specific contextual details and the nuances of particular situations;

- an emphasis on empathetic awareness of the needs and perceptions of others. (Crossthwaite 1994)

There are a number of reasons why an ethics of care might be attractive to the nursing profession. First, nursing is a predominantly female profession. In Australia about 90% of registered nurses and 95% of enrolled nurses are women. Interestingly, while medicine continues to be dominated by men, it is not as gender-specific as nursing. The proportion of doctors who are female has increased from 11% in 1961 to 38% of general practitioners and 31% of specialists in 2006 (Australian Institute of Health and Welfare 2008).

A second reason why the 'ethics of care' might be more attractive to nurses is that nursing procedures are less likely to be invasive, mutilating or painful than medical procedures, and are more likely to be supportive and nurturing.

Thirdly, the traditions of nursing have always placed great emphasis on the caring aspects of the profession, a tradition that carries over today.

Finally, by virtue of their prolonged contact with patients and the physical and emotional closeness that they may achieve with patients, the profession of nursing may be particularly suited to the development of an 'ethics of care'.

There is also some empirical evidence that nurses tend to focus on issues of caring more than doctors. For example, one study involved recording conversations about issues of relevance to ethics among staff in a British psycho-geriatric ward. The recordings were then classified by the ethical principles that best described them. Forty seven different interactions were recorded in which doctors discussed issues relating to beneficence. Forty four of these conversations were based on utilitarian concepts such as attempts to impartially distribute benefits and burdens. Only three conversations involved relationship-based or virtue-based considerations of beneficence. By contrast, 16 of a total of 56 of the nurses' conversations discussed issues of relationships or virtue (Robertson 1996). The author concluded that there were some real differences between the ethical viewpoints of doctors and nurses, although these were a matter of degree rather than being absolute. He also noted that both attitudes had their strengths and weaknesses. Whereas doctors maintained more distance from patients, and could therefore be seen as somewhat aloof or arrogant, they also expressed less frustration with difficult cases. Similarly, while nurses' emphasis on virtues such as 'caring' could often foster patient's well-being and allow staff to respond to their social needs, it also risked allowing decisions to be coloured by frustration, tension and negative feelings towards difficult patients. (The idea that nurses and doctors use different approaches to ethics is not born out by all studies. In mixed doctor/nurse discussion groups in Denmark, nurses and doctors were found to use very similar styles of ethical reasoning. However, 'physicians use more of the discussion time than nurses, they use a more assertive style of argumentation, and the solutions chosen are usually first put forward by physicians' (Holm, Gjersøe et al 1996).)

Although care-based ethics arises in part from a rejection of principle-based ethics, the closest concept to caring that can be found in principle-based ethics is the principle of beneficence – the duty to do what is best for patients. This comparison suggests that caring might have some of the same flaws as beneficence – in particular that it might lead to paternalism. Some evidence for this can be found in studies that show that patients and nurses have very different views of the roles of nurses. For example, some studies have shown that patients tend to emphasise the instrumental activities of nursing (such as responding quickly to calls and knowing how to give shots), whereas nurses tend to emphasise the emotional aspects of nursing (Gooding, Sloan et al 1993, Webb 1996). While this is not the case in all studies (eg, see Sivamalai 2008), it does suggest that in caring for patients by emphasising emotional needs, nurses may not necessarily be following the wishes of patients but pursuing their own values, beliefs or professional needs instead. This should 'provide staff with a cautionary note not to assume that intended caring is always seen as such by the patient' (von Essen and Sjödén 1991).

Some critics of the ethics of care have also claimed that by stereotyping nursing as an exclusively 'caring' profession, and hence following traditional stereotypes of female behaviour, nurses have backed themselves into a position of irresponsibility, powerlessness and ineffectiveness (Nelson 1992). Indeed, according to more extreme views, caring may even represent a vice: as it may foster dependency, inefficiency, emotional attachment and burnout (Curzer 1993).

A good example of some of these concepts came in a discussion of 'therapeutic reciprocity' in a recent edition of the *American Journal of Nursing*. Joan Vivaldelli, a clinical ICU nurse, wrote about caring for the daughter of a woman who was dying of cancer. Joan's own mother had died when she was a similar age to the daughter, so she was able to help the daughter in part by sharing her own experiences (Vivaldelli 2007).

The (male) ethics commentator on this paper valued this example of caring, but warned against both the dangers of partiality and of subjectivity when one is involved in this way. He stated:

> [E]mpathy tends to occur between like people and with likeable people. Nurses, like all people, are prone to having special feelings for others who are like them or who are endearing … the real ethical problem is not how to refine relations with patients whom nurses see as similar, but rather how to connect with patients whom they see as different … A more potent danger occurs when a nurse's need to see similarities interferes with her or his ability to have a therapeutic nurse-patient relationship, such as if the nurse distorts understanding of a patient and the patient's problems in an effort to see the patients as more like herself or himself. (Olsen 2007)

It seems then that caring is an important characteristic of both nurses and other health-care professionals. However, the concept of caring is difficult to define, and it may be open to misunderstanding and even abuse (Tarlier 2004). Hence, although caring is an important moral virtue and a significant moral concept, it should not be considered in isolation, but should be complemented and expanded by other moral concepts.

Fry and Johnstone have described a useful model of nursing ethics that integrates caring with other aspects of ethics (Fry and Johnstone 2008). This model suggests that a theory of nursing ethics:

1. should have a focus on human well-being as its central moral good;
2. should emphasise caring as a moral obligation;
3. should emphasise the importance of moral character in the nurse-patient relationship; and
4. should set aside the notion that principles and rules should have a *primary* role to play in moral justification, but should allow the use of moral principles in justification of nursing decisions.

Approaches like this that integrate care into a broader framework are a promising direction forward in nursing ethics.

Advocacy

In recent years the patient-rights movement has encouraged patients to seek information from their carers and to take an active role in decision-making. Books such as *99 questions you should ask your doctor and why* suggest that patients should ask doctors questions such as 'why do I have to wait so long when I am on time for my appointment?', 'do you accept gifts from pharmaceutical companies?', 'will you honour my living will?' and even 'do you know my name?' (Keckley 1994).

However, many patients are unable to ask for information, to understand it or to act upon it. Patients may be too unwell or too powerless to participate in decisions, and at times the whole health-care system seems to conspire against patients taking a more active role in their treatment. Rather than standing by and allowing patients to be disempowered, many nurse ethicists have come to the conclusion that nurses are ideally placed to act as patient advocates.

Advocacy is a term that is taken from the legal system where it is used to refer to someone who pleads the cause of another. Early theorists who examined the concept of advocacy in nursing used this model to argue that the role of the nurse was to help patients to stand up for their rights, and to act as surrogates in helping powerless patients to obtain what they were entitled to. In many ways, the role of the nurse in advocacy follows from Virginia Henderson's original definition of nursing:

> The unique function of the nurse is to assist the individual, sick or well, in the performance of those activities contributing to health or its recovery (or to peaceful death) that he would perform unaided if he had the necessary strength, will or knowledge. And to do this in such a way as to help him gain independence as rapidly a possible. (Henderson 1966)

The concept of advocacy has three basic assumptions: that health-care professionals are proactive as opposed to being passive and subordinate, that they speak up and act on behalf of the patient, and that some kind of difficulty, challenge or opposition must exist without which advocacy would be unnecessary.

Practising nurses tend to define advocacy in fairly simple terms. For example, '[a]n advocate is someone who stands up for the patient and kind of watches out for the patient; intervenes with physicians and looks out for patients' personal wants and desires' or '[i]t means protecting and defending a patient's best interests as defined by the patient or their family' (Sellin 1995).

Nurse ethicists like Gadow and Curtin have attempted to go further than this and evolve a concept of advocacy as a complete philosophical basis for nursing. Gadow, in an influential article titled 'Existential advocacy: philosophical foundation of nursing', argued that the major role of nurses was 'that individuals be assisted by nursing to authentically exercise their freedom of self-determination' (Gadow 1983). By this, Gadow appears to be suggesting an autonomy-based model of advocacy, in which nurses must steer a careful line between paternalistic manipulation of patients on the one hand, and acting as purely instrumental agents of medical care on the other.

A different view of advocacy was proposed by Leah Curtin in her 1986 essay 'The nurse as advocate: a philosophical foundation for nursing' (Curtin 1986). Curtin argues for what she calls 'human advocacy' – which is derived from the common humanity, common needs and common human rights that patients and nurses share. Curtin believes that the moral end of nursing is the promotion of the health and welfare of the patient, something which is usually valued by both patients and nurses. She goes further to state that human advocacy – nurse and patient working together for this aim – is *as natural as living and dying*.

More recent nursing ethicists have emphasised the difficulties that nurses experience when attempting to act as advocates and some of the philosophical problems that arise from concepts of nurse advocacy. According to Winslow, the rise of advocacy as a concept has even generated a whole new genre of literature – the 'nurse-as-advocate short story' (Winslow 1984). Such stories generally take the form of nurses becoming aware of an injustice in the health system, pointing it out to the appropriate authorities, then suffering the consequences such as job loss or legal proceedings. Such stories highlight the fact that advocacy is in many ways an ethic of conflict, and to many people it is not something that comes easily or naturally.

There is some empirical evidence both in favour and against the role of nurse-advocacy. Studies of women during labour consistently show that the presence of a support person reduced the use of pain medication, reduced the rates of caesarean delivery, decreased perineal trauma, reduced the baby's chance of having a low APGAR score, and reduced the chance that the mother would have a bad experience of childbirth (Enkin, Keirse et al 1995). These changes were found whether the support person was a partner or was a trained health worker with no prior social bond with the labouring woman.

By contrast, the SUPPORT trial was a large study of the formalised use of nurse advocacy in intensive care units in the United States. This trial was unable to find any beneficial effects from the use of nurse advocates in this setting (The SUPPORT Principal Investigators 1995).

An unresolved issue with the concept of advocacy is the question as to how far advocacy should be taken outside the context of the nurse-patient relationship. Some authors have suggested that advocacy may involve a social responsibility, in which nurses have an obligation to protest against public aspects of medical care such as unscrupulous actions by pharmaceutical companies and substandard services such as polluted air and water. However, views of advocacy that are based upon assuring patient autonomy also seem to argue against viewing medicine from a social perspective. For example, in the case of Mrs C cited at the beginning of this chapter, if the nurse's aim was to act as a patient advocate, then she should do her best to allow the lady to stay with her son. But there seems to be something very unjust about this as it ignores the needs of the son. In a similar way, if a nurse is to act as the advocate for a patient who requests expensive but futile treatment, the concept of advocacy does not allow her to consider how that money could be better spent, or whether other community members have a greater right to those resources.

Another issue concerns the question of whether nurses are the ideal group or the only group who should act as the patient's advocate. Nurse theorists tend to see nurses as ideal patient advocates because of the sustained and personal contact that nurses have with patients. But there are many other professionals who may have similar contact, such as the family general practitioner or the rehabilitation physiotherapist. And, given the current shift away from in-patient care and towards out-patient or community-based care, nurses' involvement with many individuals in hospital seems likely to become even more curtailed.

A final difficulty with the notion of nurse-advocacy lies with its focus. Nurse advocacy must be directed at something, and frequently it is directed at doctors. This book will provide plenty of evidence that doctors may make unjustifiable or unethical decisions, but issues surrounding the need for patient advocacy are broader than this. The entire organisation of health care, the use of medical technology, the ways we have of teaching about health and the reactions of the public towards health issues, all have the potential to generate serious and fundamental ethical questions. All health professionals have the potential to stand outside and criticise the health-care system, but all are part of the system as well. Many patients do require advocates, but they may require nurse advocates to speak out against medical practices, medical advocates to speak out against nurses, or any other health-care professionals to help preserve their rights against the health-care system as a whole.

A good example of advocacy, in the spirit of writers such as Curtin, can be found in an article by Rader and colleagues about bathing older people with dementia. The authors noted that the daily bathing of elderly people with dementia is often a frightening experience for patients and a period of confrontation for staff. One of the authors even had herself bathed on a shower chair in a nursing home to experience what it was like, and found it uncomfortable and threatening. They then developed new protocols for bathing elderly people in a non-threatening way, tried these out and are now advocating a completely different approach to bathing such patients. This will involve breaking down many customs and rituals in aged care, and will require advocacy at many levels if it is to come about (Rader, Barrick et al 2006). This sort of advocacy is not the public, political advocacy that is often thought to be essential. Nonetheless, this type of advocacy can be seen to go to the heart of quality care.

Collaborative models of health-care delivery: The ethics of interprofessionalism

Changes in the health sector over the past two decades have led to calls for interprofessional models of care to replace traditional models of health-care delivery that were based around the sole medical practitioner (Irvine, Kerridge et al 2002). Interprofessional models of care, which emphasise multidisciplinary teams, collaboration, and sharing of responsibility for patient care, have grown to be regarded as the optimal approach to patient care and one of the best means for empowering nurses in hospitals and in the community (World Health Organization 1988).

Unfortunately, despite the theoretical benefits of interdisciplinary care, success in achieving it has often proved elusive. A review of the empirical literature on multidisciplinary teamwork in health-care settings suggests that the relationships between service providers remain variable and complicated (Loxley 1997). And even where health professionals recognise their interdependence and are enthusiastic supporters of multidisciplinary teams there has only been limited success in terms of health outcomes such as length of stay, improved coordination and integration of services, or the number of consultations between health professionals (Zwarenstein 2007). Indeed, while the concept of mutual respect between health professionals and functional multidisciplinary teams seems self-evidently valuable, much of the available evidence suggests that relationships between health professionals, and particularly between doctors and nurses, continue to be characterised by conflict and mutual suspicion rather than by cooperation. Part of this arises from disparities between the way that a particular profession views itself and how it is viewed by other professional groups (Bernhofen and Opie 1997; Cott 1997), a factor which may be difficult to change.

It is, of course, not surprising that so little has changed, as simply instructing professions to collaborate is insufficient to bring about effective teams able to deliver improved services. A variety of structural, political, cultural and legal barriers exist that inhibit interprofessional collaboration including differences in the professions' power, size, gender composition. This includes differences in educational attainment, status and income; the continued authority of the medical profession to direct and coordinate health-care delivery; the dominance of 'teams' by doctors; differences in work schedules and processes; the particularity of knowledge and values; linguistic differences due to professions developing their own 'talk'; and professional protectiveness. Significant advances in the development of multidisciplinary teams or in the empowerment of nursing are unlikely to occur without attention being given to the existing patterns of professional communication and the impact of culture and organisation settings in determining the function of health-care teams (Boaden and Leavis 2000). And this must occur, as the fact that no single profession can provide for all the health and welfare needs of patients and their families creates a moral obligation for all health professionals to collaborate and to share responsibility for providing appropriate care. Draper, writing in relation to midwifery, defines some of these issues very acutely.

The frustration of professional autonomy occurs when a professional is not permitted to exercise appropriate judgement while working as that professional. One of the difficulties facing midwifery is how the boundaries of the profession are defined and who should define them ... This is not just a problem for midwifery ... As a profession, midwifery ought to define its own boundaries and professional responsibilities but this is often something that has to be negotiated with other professions who also have a professional interest (for instance, obstetrics and paediatrics) and as a result some of the professional boundaries have become blurred. This means that at these boundaries professional autonomy is also unclear. (Draper 2004)

The difficulties with role definition across the health-care team means that the professional relations between doctors and nurses continue to be a key issue in nursing ethics (although it is hardly discussed in medical ethics.) Authors like de Raeve have explored the legitimacy or illegitimacy of medical authority over nursing work. Her conclusion is that acting in accordance with legitimate medical authority enhances rather than compromises the nurse's professional integrity. Difficulties, however, may lie in disentangling legitimate from illegitimate attempts to control nursing work (de Raeve 2002).

Draper states that 'where a midwife's professional judgement is overridden in a way that is casual and disrespectful there is cause for legitimate complaint ... There is less cause for complaint when legal responsibility is not equally shared, unless the midwife has the greater responsibility' (Draper 2004). She goes on to add:

[Any professional] asserting what they see to be their rights using the concept of [professional] autonomy must be mindful of the fact that autonomy is a double-edged sword. To be autonomous is certainly to be able to exercise choice, but it is also to be held responsible – accountable – for the choices that have been made. It is unfair to be held accountable for situations over which one has no control, but it is also for this reason that it would be unfair for one professional to insist on making a decision, and then to expect or allow another professional to take responsibility if things go wrong as a result. (Draper 2004)

Conclusion: Is there a need for a separate ethics of nursing?

Since the 1960s, nurses have attempted to gain recognition for nursing's status as a separate profession. One influential approach to this goal was through the identification of six sociological criteria that could be used to determine its progress towards professionalism. These consisted of a long and disciplined educational process, discretionary authority and judgment, an active and cohesive professional organisation, acknowledged social worth, a strong level of commitment, and a unique body of knowledge and skill (Bishop 1996). The attainment and recognition of the goal of professionalism represents an ongoing subtext to modern nursing. In the field of bioethics, this quest for professionalism has been represented by assertions that nursing ethics provides a separate body of knowledge that is distinct from the rest of contemporary bioethics.

The care of patients in hospitals is increasingly moving away from the commanding role of the sole medical practitioner towards the notion of multidisciplinary teams working in cooperation with patients. The formation of such teams, however, does not guarantee optimal management or automatically resolve the ethical issues that arise in inter-professional decision-making. There is, for example, some evidence that doctors tend to dominate discussion time and use more assertive styles of argument than nurses, and that the solutions chosen by multi-disciplinary groups tend to be those that are first put forward by doctors (Holm, Gjersøe et al 1996). A theory of ethics that is confrontational – such as advocacy – may be required to prevent such domination, but team members must also be familiar with less confrontational approaches if they are to work together.

Skills in caring and curing are required by all members of health-care teams. It would be wrong to implacably separate these roles by gender or profession. However, nursing's traditional, and renewed, emphasis on care, its largely female work-force and its history of ethical inquiry into areas such as advocacy and care may make such areas particularly attractive for nursing study.

Nursing offers many different insights into the ethical foundations of health care and contributes to a more sophisticated model of bioethics. However, nursing ethics does not appear to provide a completely separate body of know-ledge or method from the rest of bioethics, even though there may be professional imperatives within nursing to declare it as such. (In the same way, we do not believe that there is a separate medical ethics, physiotherapy ethics, social work ethics and so forth.) Concepts of nursing ethics such as care and advocacy should be incorporated into the ethics of all health professions, and these ideas should be balanced within nursing by other ethical frameworks and concepts such as those discussed elsewhere in this book.

NURSES AND THE LAW

The law applies to nurses in the same way in which it applies to any other health-care professional, other than nurse-specific registration legislation in each jurisdiction.

Megan-Jane Johnstone, in her book *Nursing and the Injustices of the Law*, has critically examined the relationship between law, the legal system and nurses (Johnstone 1994). Johnstone concludes that nurses must examine the way in which the law has unjustly treated nurses and nursing practice. She outlines the role that the law has played in obstructing the professional development of nursing and supporting the continued 'subordination to the (male dominated) medical profession' (Johnstone 1994: xiii). Johnstone cites many individual examples, from many varied jurisdictions, of decisions that have worked against the interests of a nurse or nursing in general. However, it seems likely that these instances do not represent a systematic attempt by the law to subordinate nurses; rather that the law merely reflects the wider social and professional context of nursing.

More recently, Mary Chiarella, in *The Legal and Professional Status of Nursing*, has used the perspective of 'outsider scholarship' to examine the con-flicting images of the nurse in the law (Chiarella 2002). Chiarella describes this approach in this way:

It is a useful technique for oppressed and/or minority groups. It propounds a counter approach to the positivist school of thought that the findings of authoritative institutions, such as courts, constitute the authentic truth, which accordingly suggests that all other parties' accounts become devalued in formal decision making processes. (Chiarella 2002)

Chiarella analyses case law from a number of jurisdictions and identifies both social change and the manner in which recurrent images of nurses are portrayed within the case law. From the analysis she has identified five images – 'a ministering angel', 'a domestic worker', 'the doctor's handmaiden', 'the subordinate professional' and 'the autonomous professional'. Chiarella concludes her book by arguing that 'there is no coherent body of law which addressed the status and responsibilities of the registered nurse in Australia'. This is so, she says, because the role of the nurse in health care is neither recognised nor legitimised and that nurses operate 'inside (or outside)' a legal framework which insufficiently recognises their work and their presence.

Despite these critiques of nursing and its relationship with the law, we do agree with Johnstone's conclusion that nurses need to understand the law as it currently affects nurses and to engage in critical debate and reform of the law. This needs to be done, not only in the narrow professional concerns, but also in the wider social context.

Nurse Heathcote

Mary Chiarella's book begins and ends with a discussion of the case of Sophia Heathcote (*Re Nurses Registration Act 1953* and *In re Heathcote and Nurses Registration Board and Walton* (unreported, NSWDC, 12 April 1991). As well, Megan-Jane Johnstone's text and the major textbooks on nurses and law (Edginton 1995; Wallace 1995; Wallace 2001; Staunton and Chiarella 2003) make mention of this case. The case exemplifies many of the issues around the role of nursing and the law, and some of the injustices that can arise in particular cases.

The NSW Nurses Registration Board found Sophia Heathcote, a registered nurse, guilty of professional misconduct and had her name removed from the register. She then appealed to the District Court which overturned the decision of the Board and her name was restored to the register. The events that led to this result were as follows.

Nurse Heathcote and a nursing assistant were on duty at Wilcannia hospital. The nearest 'supervising' doctor (the Flying Doctor Service) was 200 kms away. A young Aboriginal man was brought by his relatives to the hospital as he was suffering from alcohol withdrawal. He wandered away on a couple of occasions and the police were called as Nurse Heathcote was concerned about his safety. At about 2.30 am the police returned with the young man. Nurse Heathcote telephoned the 'on-call' doctor. The doctor agreed that it was in the patient's best interests to go to the police station as there were no facilities at the hospital to secure an uncontrollable patient. She was also advised to check the patient's blood sugar levels. The patient was then taken to the police station. The young man was found dead in his cell due to hanging.

At a coronial inquiry the coroner said that Nurse Heathcote's actions should be referred to the Nurses Registration Board which found her guilty of professional misconduct and deregistered her for a period of one year. The alleged instances of misconduct were:

- failure to elicit further information from the relations;
- failure to assess the patient properly;
- the judgment as to the management of the patient;
- failure to adequately inform the doctor of the patient's condition; and
- placing the patient back into the care of the police. (Staunton and Whyburn 1997; Staunton and Chiarella 2003)

The District Court dismissed all of the allegations against Nurse Heathcote. The court emphasised that Nurse Heathcote was placed in a situation where she had to contend with a wandering patient in difficult circumstances. She had done all that was required of her.

Johnstone sees this as an example of a nurse being used as a 'scapegoat' for the negligent or unprofessional actions of others (Johnstone 1994). However, this case can also be used as an example of an injustice against a nurse that was corrected upon judicial review.

Regulation of nurses and midwives

Nurses and midwives are registered and regulated at the State and Territory level. The following table sets out the legislation and bodies which govern the regulation of nurses and midwives.

	Legislation	Registration and Disciplinary Body
NSW	Nurses and Midwives Act 1991	Nurses and Midwives Board (http://www.nmb.nsw.gov.au/)
Qld	Nursing Act 1992	Queensland Nursing Council (http://www.qnc.qld.gov.au/home/index.aspx)
SA	Nurses Act 1999	Nurses Board of South Australia (http://www.nursesboard.sa.gov.au)
Tas	Nursing Act 1995	Nursing Board of Tasmania (http://www.nursingboardtas.org.au/)
Vic	Nurses Act 1993	Nurses Board of Victoria (http://www.nbv.org.au/)
WA	Nurses Act 1992	Nurses Board of Western Australia (http://www.nbwa.org.au/)
ACT	Health Professionals Act 2004	Nursing and Midwifery Board (http://www.actnmb.act.gov.au/)
NT	Health Practitioners Act 2004	Health Professions Licensing Authority (http://www.health.nt.gov.au/Health_Professions_Licensing_Authority_HPLA/index.aspx) Nursing and Midwifery Board (http://www.health.nt.gov.au/Health_Professions_Licensing_Authority_HPLA/Health_Registration_Boards/Nursing_and_Midwifery_Board/index.aspx)

At the time of writing, the Council of Australian Governments has agreed to create a single registration and accreditation scheme for nurses and midwives as part of the National Registration and Accreditation Scheme and work is being done to put that scheme into place.

Nurses and hospitals

A nurse who is employed by a hospital, or other institution, may make the employer liable for her or his acts under the principle of 'vicarious liability'. This principle is based on the fact that an employer is responsible for the acts of its employees. In the early part of this century a number of English cases found that hospitals were not responsible for the actions of their employees (including nurses) (*Hall and Wife v Lees* [1904] 2 KB 602 and *Hillyer v St Bartholomew's Hospital* [1909] 2 KB 820). The courts were reluctant to find against the hospital as they were charitable institutions and large awards of damages made against them could affect their viability. Responsibility for the acts of nurses was often instead placed on the surgeons who were performing procedures in the operating theatre.

The approach of the courts subsequently changed to allow recovery of damages from hospital authorities for the acts of their employees. In *Gold v Essex County Council* [1942] 2 KB 293, the Court of Appeal held a hospital liable for the negligent conduct of an employee radiographer. In discussion the issues and earlier cases Goddard LJ commented:

> I cannot understand on what principle a hospital authority is to be exempt from liability if a nurse carelessly administers a dose of poison to a patient instead of medicine, and yet is liable if a cook mixes some deleterious substance in the patient's food. (at 312-13)

In a later case, *Cassidy v Ministry of Health* [1951] 2 KB 343 at 361-2, Denning LJ said:

> [T]here can be no doubt that the nurses remain the servants [traditionally the employer and employee relationship was referred to as a master-servant relationship, this expression is now seldom used] of the hospital authorities, even when they are under the directions of the surgeon in the operating theatre. The reason is because the nurses are employed by the hospital authorities, paid by them, and liable to be dismissed by them; and the consulting surgeon has not that 'entire and absolute control' over them which is necessary to make them his servants, even temporarily.

An important principle that may be gained from Denning LJ's judgment is that in a negligence action a nurse will be independently accountable for her or his acts. Chula Dahanayake has commented that '[n]ursing negligence therefore has become indefensible in terms of a hospital pleading a "master of the ship" slogan in operating theatre conditions' (Dahanayake 1991). These principles have also been recognised by Australian courts (see *Samios v Repatriation Commission* [1960] WALR 219; *Albrighton v Royal Alfred Hospital* [1980] 2 NSWLR 542).

The scope of the nursing function is increasing and the profession has been put under maximum pressure in meeting the challenge of the expanding role of the nurse in the health-care team (Dahanayake 1991). This means that nursing practice will increasingly come to be examined by the courts, particularly with greater recognition of nursing professionalism.

An example of the way in which a court has approached nursing responsibility can be found in a Queensland Court of Appeal decision in *Langley and Warren v Glandore Pty Ltd* [1997] QCA 342. A patient underwent an abdominal hysterectomy in a private hospital in 1990. The operation was carried out by Dr Langley with the assistance of Dr Warren and two nurses. After the operation was finished an absorbent pack ('sponge') was left inside the patient's abdomen. It was only after the patient developed painful symptoms that the presence of the sponge was discovered and removed about 10 months after the original operation.

The patient sued the two doctors and the hospital, as employer of the two nurses, for negligence. The trial was heard by a judge and jury (the use of a jury in a negligence action is very uncommon in Australia). The jury found that Dr Langley was entirely responsible for leaving the sponge in the patient's abdomen and Dr Warren was responsible for a separate claim that he had not properly advised the patient before the operation. The jury found that the hospital was not in breach of its duty to the patient. The doctors appealed to the Court of Appeal on the basis that the verdict of the jury was perverse and that there was no basis on which a reasonable jury could not have found the hospital in breach of its duty of care to the patient.

The evidence before the court was that the nurses had an obligation to count and check the surgical sponges being used in the operation. There was a well-established standard, the 'ACORN' standard, for the 'counting of sponges, swabs, instruments and needles'. The Court of Appeal found that on the balance of probabilities there had been some breakdown in the checking of the sponges that led to one of them being left in the patient's abdomen. The surgeon had fulfilled his duty by physically checking to see if any sponges remained (it was accepted that missing a sponge in this way was not necessarily a breach of the standard of care, that is why there is a rigorous process of counting and checking by the nurses) and checking with the nurses that the count of sponges removed from the patient was accurate. The Court of Appeal set aside the jury's verdict and found against the hospital which was vicariously liable for the negligence of the nurses. In his judgment Williams J referred to the argument that the surgeon was responsible for the actions of all those in the operating theatre. He said that the analogy with the surgeon as 'captain of the ship' was 'not helpful'.

Another example of how nursing standards of care are judged comes from *Warner v Queensland* [2006] NSWSC 593 where a patient argued that he had been negligently assigned to the wrong triage category by a triage nurse and that, as a result, he had left the emergency department and self-harmed. Hislop J examined triage practice and listened to evidence from experts in both medical and nursing fields before finding that the nurse had followed appropriate standards in her triaging of the patient and, in doing so, had fulfilled her duty of care.

Part of the nurse's standard of care is also to call for specialist help when it is required. In *Ballard v Cox* [2006] NSWSC 252 a nurse was found negligent for not repeatedly calling for the aid of an obstetrician to attend a delivery. The nurse had called once and the obstetrician had failed to attend but when the condition of the woman and child deteriorated the nurse failed to call again for the obstetrician to attend. The child suffered brain damage from asphyxia. The judge found both the nurse and the doctor responsible and apportioned the damages 60% to the doctor and 40% to the hospital (which was vicariously liable for the nurse's negligence).

Nurse practitioners

All Australian jurisdictions now either recognise a classification of nurse – the nurse practitioner – or have projects underway to evaluate and implement such a classification of nurse. The Australian Nursing and Midwifery Council defines a nurse practitioner as follows:

> A nurse practitioner is a registered nurse educated and authorised to function autonomously and collaboratively in an advanced and extended clinical role. The nurse practitioner role includes assessment and management of clients using nursing knowledge and skills and may include but is not limited to the direct referral of patients to other health care professionals, prescribing medications and ordering diagnostic investigations. The nurse practitioner role is grounded in the nursing profession's values, knowledge, theories and practise and provides innovative and flexible health care delivery that complements other health care providers. The scope of practice of the nurse practitioner is determined by the context in which the nurse practitioner is authorised to practise (Australian Nursing and Midwifery Council 2006)

Generally speaking nurse practitioners are licensed to do all regular nursing tasks but may also assess and manage patients, initiate diagnostic tests, prescribe and supply medications, and refer patients to other health professionals. In New South Wales nurse practitioners are registered under s 19A of the *Nurses and Midwives Act 1991*. In Queensland nurse practitioners are endorsed by the Queensland Nursing Council under s 77 of the *Nursing Act 1992* and in accordance with the *Professional Standards Statement for Nurse Practitioner Practice*. The Tasmanian Nurses Board has power to registered restricted practice areas under s 31 of the *Nursing Act 1995* and nurse practitioners are recognised as such under regs 4-6 of the *Nursing Regulations 2005*. Section 20 of the *Health Professions Registration Act 2005* allows the Nurses Board of Victoria to endorse nurse practitioners and the practitioners must select a practice category under s 13(ba) of the *Drugs, Poisons and Controlled Substances Act 1981*. In the ACT s 195 of the *Health Act 1993* allows for regulation to create nurse practitioner positions. In the Northern Territory nurse practitioner positions are determined by the Health Professions Licensing Authority under s 32 of the *Health Practitioners Act 2004* and in accordance with the *Nurse Practitioner Authorisation Process Policy 2008*.

Workers' compensation

An examination of recent case law where nurses have been involved in litigation reveals that nurses are frequently involved in workplace-related accidents, particularly back injuries, for which they seek compensation. An employee who is injured at work may be compensated for losses suffered. Compensation is statutory in nature and is known as workers' compensation. From the early part of the 20th century, all of the States and the Commonwealth have had schemes of workers' compensation which have been based on the English workers' compensation legislation of 1906.

In recent years there has been a great deal of pressure placed on these schemes by a perceived blowout in the cost of the system and a consequent increase in insurance premiums for employers. Many States and Territories repealed their legislation and introduced new schemes which placed greater emphasis on rehabilitation and the administrative efficiency of the schemes (*Safety, Rehabilitation and Compensation Act 1988* (Cth); *Workers Compensation Act 1987* (NSW), *Workplace Injury Management and Workers Compensation Act 1998* (NSW); *Workplace Health and Safety Act 1995* (Qld), *Workers' Compensation and Rehabilitation Act 2003* (Qld); *Workers Rehabilitation and Compensation Act 1986* (SA); *Workplace Health and Safety Act 1995* (Tas); *Accident Compensation Act 1985* (Vic); *Workers Compensation and Rehabilitation Act 1981* (WA), *Workers Compensation (Common Law Proceedings) Act 2004* (WA); *Workers Compensation Act 1951* (ACT); *Workers Rehabilitation and Compensation Act 1986* (NT), *Workplace Health and Safety Act 2007* (NT)). Although all schemes have differences there are also a number of common features.

There are a number of entitlements that may be available to an injured worker, for example, social security benefits from the Commonwealth, sick leave, and civil actions for negligence, as well as the various workers' compensation schemes. An employee may only keep one type of benefit. Many of the workers' compensation schemes limit actions that may be taken under the common law. For example, in New South Wales there are only limited common law rights that are subject to various thresholds.

A worker is entitled to compensation even if she or he was negligent. If the worker's injury was caused by the worker's own serious and wilful misconduct then the worker may not be able to be compensated. However, this requirement is generally interpreted very narrowly.

References

Alligood, M and A Mariner-Tomey (2002) Significance of theory for nursing as a discipline and profession. *Nursing theorists and their work* (5th ed). M Alligood and A Mariner-Tomey. St Louis, Mosby.

Australian Institute of Health and Welfare (2008) *Australia's Health 2008*. Canberra, AIHW.

Bernhofen, D and A Opie (1997) 'Thinking teams thinking clients: issues of discourse and representation in the work of health care teams'. *Sociology of Health and Illness* 19(3): 259-80.

Bishop, A (1996) Nursing as a profession. *Encyclopedia of Bioethics*. W Reich: 1827-31.

Boaden, N and J Leavis (2000) 'Putting teamwork in context'. *Medical Education* **34**(11): 921-7.

Chiarella, M (2002) *The Legal and Professional Status of Nursing*. Sydney, Elsevier.

Cott, C (1997) 'We decide, you carry it out: a social network analysis of multi-disciplinary long-term care teams'. *Social Science and Medicine* **45**(9): 1411-21.

Crossthwaite, J (1994) 'Feminism and medical ethics'. *Monash Biomedical Review* **13**(3): 13-19.

Curtin, L (1986) The nurse as advocate: a philosophical foundation for nursing. *Ethical issues in nursing*. P Chinn. Rockville, Maryland, Apen Systems. **11-20**.

Curzer, H (1993) 'Is care a virtue for health care professionals?' *J Med Philos* **18**: 51-69.

Dahanayake, C (1991) 'The Nurse and the Law (Part 1)'. *Med Law* **10**: 249-67.

Davis, D (1985) 'Nursing: an ethic of caring'. *Hum Med* **2**: 19-25.

de Raeve, L (2002) 'Medical authority and nursing integrity'. *J Med Ethics* **28**(6): 353-7.

Draper, H (2004) Introduction. *Ethics and Midwifery* (2nd ed). L Frith and H Draper. London, Elsevier.

Edginton, J (1995) *Law for the Nursing Profession and allied health care professionals*. Sydney, CCH Australia Ltd.

Enkin, M, M Keirse et al (1995) *A guide to effective care in pregnancy and childbirth*. Oxford, Oxford University Press.

Erikson, H (2007) 'Philosophy and theory of Holism'. *Nursing Clinics of North America* **42**(2): 149.

Frank, A (1995) *The Wounded Storyteller: Body, Illness and Ethics*. Chicago and London, University of Chicago Press.

Fry, S (1995) Nursing ethics. *Encyclopedia of Bioethics*. W Reich. New York, MacMillan: 1822-26.

Fry, ST and M-J Johnstone (2008) *Ethics in Nursing Practice*. Oxford, Blackwell Publishing.

Gadow, S (1983) Existential advocacy: philosophical foundation of nursing. *Ethical problems in the nurse-patient relationship*. CP Murphy, H Hunter. Boston, Allyn and Bacon: 40-58.

Gilligan, C (1982) *In a different voice: Psychological theory and women's development*. Cambridge MA, Harvard University Press.

Gooding, B, M Sloan et al (1993) 'Important nurse caring behaviours: perception of oncology patients and nurses'. *Can J Nurs Res* **25**(3): 65-76.

Grace, P (2002) Philosophies, Models and theories: Moral obligations. *Nursing Theory: Utilization and application* (2nd ed). M Alligood and A Mariner-Tomey. St Louis, Mosby.

Henderson, V (1966) *The nature of nursing: A definition and its implication for practice, research and education*. New York, MacMillan.

Holm, S, P Gjersøe et al (1996) 'Ethical reasoning in mixed nurse-physician groups'. *J Med Ethics* **22**: 168-73.

Irvine, R, I Kerridge et al (2002) 'Interprofessionalism and ethics: consensus or clash of cultures?'. *J Interprofessional Care* **16**(3): 199-210.

Johnstone, M (1994) *Nursing and the Injustices of the Law*. Sydney, Harcourt Brace & Company.

Keckley, P (1994) *99 questions you should ask your doctor and why*. Tennessee, Rutledge Hill Press.

Loxley, A (1997) *Collaboration in health and welfare: working with difference*. London, Jessica Kingsley.

Madjar, I and J Walton (1999) *Nursing and the experience of illness: Phenomenology in Practice*. Sydney, Allen and Unwin.

Merleau-Ponty, M (1962) *Phenomenology of Perception*. New York, Routledge.

Mills, M, H Davies et al (1994) 'Care of dying patients in hospital'. *BMJ* **309**: 583-6.

Nelson, H (1992) 'Against caring'. *J Clin Ethics* **3**: 8-15.

Olsen, D (2007) 'Ethical caution for nurses'. *American Journal of Nursing* **107**(7): 75.

Rader, J, A Barrick, et al (2006) 'The bathing of older adults with dementia'. *American Journal of Nursing* **106**(4): 40-8.

Robertson, D (1996) 'Ethical theory, ethnography and differences between doctors and nurses in approaches to patient care'. *J Medical Ethics* **22**: 292-9.

Schmieding, N (2002) Orlando's nursing process theory in nursing practice. *Nursing theory: Utilisation and application* (2nd ed). M Alligood and A Mariner-Tomey. St Louis, Mosby.

Sellin, S (1995) 'Out on a limb: a qualitative study of patient advocacy in institutional nursing'. *Nurs Ethics* **2**(1): 19-29.

Sivamalai, S (2008) 'Desired attributes of new graduate nurses as identified by the rural community'. *Rural and Remote Health* **8**: 938 (Online).

Speedy, S and S Kermode (1996) Nursing theory: whose interests are being served? *Nursing theory in Australia*. J Greenwood. Sydney, HarperEducational Publishers.

Staunton, P and M Chiarella (2003) *Nursing and the Law*. Sydney, Churchill Livingstone.

Staunton, P and B Whyburn (1997) *Nursing and the Law*. Sydney, Harcourt, Brace and Company.

Sunstein, C (1994) *Political Conflict and Legal Agreement*. The Tanner Lectures on Human Values, Harvard University, Boston. 29 November–1 December 1994.

Tarlier, D (2004) 'Beyond caring: the moral and ethical bases of responsive nurse–patient relationships'. *Nursing Philosophy* **5**: 230-41.

The SUPPORT Principal Investigators (1995) 'A controlled trial to improve care of seriously ill hospitalised patients'. *JAMA* **274**(20): 1591-8.

Vivaldelli, J (2007) 'Therapeutic reciprocity'. *AJN* **107**(7): 74-76.

von Essen, L and P Sjödén (1991) 'Patient and staff perceptions of caring: review and replication'. *J Adv Nurs* **16**: 1364-74.

Wallace, M (2001) *Health care and the law*. Sydney, Lawbook Co.

Webb, C (1996) 'Caring, curing and coping: towards an integrated model'. *J Adv Nurs* **23**: 960-8.

Winslow, G (1984) 'From loyalty to advocacy: a new metaphor for nursing'. *Hastings Cent Rep*(June): 32-9.

World Health Organization (1988) Learning together to work for health. Report of a WHO study on multiprofessional education of health personnel: the team approach. *WHO Technical Report Series*. WH Organization: 1-72.

Zwarenstein, M (2007) 'Interventions to promote collaboration between nurses and doctors'. *Cochrane Database of Systematic Reviews*. **4**.

CHAPTER 11

TRUTH-TELLING (VERACITY)

Case 1

JD is a 38-year-old woman who has had recurrent episodes of abdominal pain since sustaining a penetrating abdominal injury in a car accident four years ago. The underlying cause of these episodes has never been clear. They are generally treated by admitting her to hospital and giving her fourth hourly injections of Morphine.

During her most recent admission, her consultant thought that it might be possible to differentiate whether her pain was due to physical or psychological factors by giving her injections of tranquillisers instead of painkillers. Accordingly, he prescribed six-hourly injections of Chlorpromazine instead of Morphine but continued to tell her that he was prescribing Morphine. Events came to a head when the patient requested a further injection after four hours and, when this was refused, began to suspect that she was being tricked in some way. The nurse looking after JD felt that she had been placed in a particularly difficult position as she had been asked to lie to the patient and to provide inadequate pain relief.

Case 2

In traditional Navaho culture, it is held that thought and language have the power to shape reality and to control events. Discussing the potential complications of diabetes with a newly diagnosed Navaho patient may, in the view of the traditional patient, result in the occurrence of such complications. Restated, in the Navaho view, language does not merely describe reality, language shapes reality.

... a middle-aged Navaho woman, who is a nurse, speaking about how the risks of bypass surgery were explained to her father said the following: 'The surgeon told him that he may not wake up, that this is the risk of every surgery. For the surgeon it was very routine, but the way that my Dad received it, it was almost a death sentence, and he never consented to the surgery.' (Carrese and Rhodes 1995)

The rule of veracity may be defined as the duty that one has to tell the truth. In general, we expect a moral person to be as honest, straightforward and truthful as possible. In health care, the rule of veracity is strongly associated with the principle of autonomy, since for patients to make autonomous decisions they must be in possession of the facts.

From an ethics perspective, there are three main reasons for truth-telling:

1. It is a manifestation of respect for people as persons.
2. It may improve outcomes by enabling people to make fully informed decisions about their care.
3. It is central to maintenance of a trusting health professional: patient relationship.

However, veracity may at times conflict with other principles such as beneficence and non-maleficence and there are a number of reasons why health-care professionals may not always be honest with patients. Reasons (not all of them ethically justifiable) why therapists may not tell the truth to patients include: the belief that patients may not want to know the truth or may not be able to understand it, the belief that truth-telling would be inappropriate in the context of the patient's personal values or culture, the inability of some therapists to admit the truth where it involves a sense of their own failure, and lack of skill in communicating the truth. Another reason is that they may believe that the condition of the patient is so fragile that full disclosure of all information may harm the patient, causing them to suffer, give up or even commit suicide. Non-disclosure on this basis is called 'benevolent deception' or 'therapeutic privilege'.

Issues of veracity arise when informing patients about diagnoses and possible treatments. They also occur when it is necessary to inform patients about adverse effects of care, medical mistakes, or lapses of professional competence. Different approaches to this will depend on whether veracity is interpreted narrowly as a prohibition of lying or, more broadly, as an obligation to full and honest disclosure. Professional loyalties and the fear of litigation also affect individual's interpretations of the obligation to truth-telling.

Despite these reservations about truth-telling, the literature about it is clear – the vast majority of patients wish to be told the truth about all aspects of their care (Hebert, Hoffmaster et al 1997).

Therapeutic privilege

It has been suggested that at times it is necessary to lie to patients to avoid harming them. Many health-care workers are concerned that the release of distressing information may cause severe mental anguish and even physical illness for some patients. For example, it is often questioned whether patients should be told the truth if members of their family have been killed in a car accident and they themselves are unstable. It is feared that this information might cause such patients to give up hope or die. It has been suggested that in these circumstances health workers may be exempted from the normal duty of ensuring veracity. This concept is known as 'therapeutic privilege'.

Therapeutic privilege is based on consequentialism, and the idea that the bad effects of truth-telling might outweigh the good effects. Whilst there is some evidence that severe emotional stress may cause harm to some patients, empirical evidence suggests that truth-telling is often beneficial. Many patients want to be informed, and most deal with 'bad news' well. What evidence exists also tends to suggest that information disclosure may actually increase patients' abilities to cope, their pain control and their satisfaction and compliance with care, and that informing patients truthfully about a life-threatening disease does not result in a greater incidence of anxiety, despair, sadness, depression, insomnia or fear (Ell, Nishimoto et al 1989; Centeno-Cortes and Nunez-Olarte 1994).

Although it is difficult to predict how much individual patients wish to know, non-disclosure may threaten the relationship between health-care professionals and patients, and threaten health-care professionals' own moral integrity. A web of elaborate deception is often woven around patients as a consequence of requests for non-disclosure. This is particularly difficult to sustain in the context of institutional care where many different people are involved in the care of each patient. But not all members of the team will agree with the policy of lying to the patient, and the situation is usually untenable. Before long the patient will usually find out the truth and therapeutic relationships will be invariably damaged.

The placebo effect

Placebos (from the Latin 'I will please') are inert substances such as sugar pills that are given to patients because they have been led to believe that such substances will help them. Surprisingly, placebos often do help and 35% of the physically ill and 40% or more of the mentally ill respond to some extent to placebos. It is likely that the placebo effect is incorporated into most forms of medical therapy and that some of the benefits that patients experience from all therapy is due to their expectation that they will receive such benefit. Placebos are also used in trials of experimental medication – a topic that will be explored in more detail in the chapter on research ethics.

According to Laurence and Bennett:

> The deliberate use of drugs as placebos is a confession of failure by the doctor. Failures however are sometimes inevitable and an absolute condemnation of the use of placebos on all occasions would be unrealistic ...

They go on to remark that:

> [T]hose who have qualms of conscience about prescribing pharmacologically useless medicines tend to use semi-placebos, such as vitamins, in the vague hope that these may do some good. This is wrong, for thereby the prescriber deceives himself as well as the patient. If deception there must be ... let it be wholehearted, unflinching, and efficient. A placebo medicine should be red, yellow or brown; for blue or green are colours popularly associated with poisons or with external applications. The taste should be bitter but not unpleasant. Capsules should be coloured and either very small ... or impressively large; they should not look like everyday tablets such as aspirin. (Laurence and Bennett 1987)

Such concepts have obvious ethical implications as they represent a form of paternalism, in which patients are deceived 'for their own good'. Patients who find out about such deception tend to feel betrayed and let down by their physicians.

Moerman and colleagues have suggested that the term 'the placebo effect' should be replaced by 'the meaning response' (Moerman and Jonas 2002). They refer to research that shows that the effects of treatment of duodenal ulcer with either active agents or with placebos varies enormously across different cultures. Cultures with a low rate of placebo response to anti-ulcer treatment also had a low rate of response to active treatment. Cultures with a high rate of response to placebo also had a high rate of response to active treatment (Moerman 2000). Moerman has also demonstrated that different cultures have varying placebo responses to different medical conditions.

This research suggests that much of the response that is seen to medical interventions may be due to the meaning that patients see as being inherent in the treatment, rather than being due to the treatment itself. If this effect is exploited, such as by strongly suggesting to patients that the treatment will work, its effects can be maximised (Thomas 1987).

This creates a conundrum for health practitioners. To meet the legal and ethical criteria for informed consent, it is necessary to inform patients of the risks and possible side-effects and give a realistic appraisal of likely treatment benefits. But the effects of treatment would be likely much greater if this was not done, and the patient was instead encouraged and reassured. The healing rituals of alternative medicine, which do not necessarily involve warnings and doubts, may be more efficacious as placebos than those in Western medicine.

The emphasis on autonomy in modern medical ethics provides little justification for the use of the placebo effect in its purest form. But the placebo effect should not be relinquished altogether. Patients are likely to respond better to any medication when therapists express optimism and confidence in the outcome. A degree of professional optimism is likely to be a large part of the 'art' of being a therapist, but this must be constrained within the bounds of truth, even if this limits treatment effectiveness.

Breaking bad news

In the past, concealing the truth from patients was often justified on paternalistic grounds. This is no longer the case. The most important issues now are not whether to tell the truth, but how to tell it, when to tell it, who should tell it and what should be told.

Therapists often dislike breaking bad news to patients because it is distressing to both the patient and themselves. But it is important that health-care workers should be trained adequately to learn how to break bad news effectively in order to lessen its impact. There has been a large amount of research to show that it is easier to break bad news when one has been trained to do so, and if one follows certain rules (see Table 10.1 *over page*). In some situations, such as when standing in a busy hospital corridor, it may not be appropriate to break bad news, and in these circumstances it should be postponed until conditions are more suitable. Few would consider the postponement of bad news for these reasons to be unethical.

Table 10.1. Breaking Bad News

1.	The news should be delivered in a comfortable, private, quiet location.
2.	The time should be convenient, there should be sufficient time allocated, and interruptions should be minimised.
3.	Bad news should be given in person; the therapist should be face to face, making eye contact and with no physical barriers between them and the patient.
4.	The patient's support network should be identified, and may be present during the interaction if desired by the patient.
5.	A 'warning shot' should be given – such as 'I'm afraid that I've got some bad news to tell you'.
6.	If possible, the therapist should convey some message of hope.
7.	The therapist should acknowledge and explore the patient's reaction and allow for emotional expressions.
8.	The therapist should summarise the discussion (perhaps in written or taped form) and allow for questions.
9.	The therapist should deliver bad news with empathy and respect.
10.	The language must be kept simple, without euphemisms or technical jargon.
11.	News should be given at the patient's pace, allowing them to dictate what they are told.

(Ptacek and Eberhardt 1996)

Veracity implies much more than simply the passing on of facts. It is possible to avoid lying to a patient and yet be untruthful by concealing facts, creating false impressions, or obscuring the truth in euphemisms or medical terminology (Bok 1979). However the requirement for honesty does not imply brutal or destructive communication of data, without compassion, tact or sensitivity (Anon 2000). As Jonsen has noted, while the truth may be brutal, the telling of it should not be (Jonsen, Siegler et al 1992).

Cultural factors

The way that patients exercise their autonomy may be shaped by age, level of education, gender, clinical context, religious beliefs and culture. In pluralistic societies, health-care professionals and patients may not share assumptions about appropriate disclosure of information. In many cultures it is seen as important to know that one is dying in advance, so that one can prepare for this eventuality both materially and spiritually. However, in other cultures it is traditional that patients are not told about some diagnoses, and that respon-sibility for health-care decision-making is delegated to other family members. For example, in Japan the diagnosis of stomach cancer is very common, but patients are frequently told that they have stomach ulcers instead. Families in these cultures often go to great lengths to prevent patients being given information and many believe that the diagnosis should only be told to patients if their family consents (Akayabashi, Kai et al 1999).

To many Western health workers, the idea of concealing crucial information from patients is repugnant, and indeed one cannot legally treat a patient without informing them of the risks and benefits of a procedure – which cannot be done if they are ignorant of their diagnosis. Similarly, it may be difficult to discuss options for cardiopulmonary resuscitation if patients are unaware that their condition may be life-threatening. But perhaps these concerns reflect a degree of cultural insensitivity, and we should be hiding diagnoses from people from cultures where disclosure is thought inappropriate.

Considerable uncertainty surrounds the issue of whether patients have the right not to hear information. Some have affirmed that the patient's 'right not to know' is a valid autonomous choice, and have suggested that forcing information on patients constitutes unjustifiable paternalism (Gillon 1990; Pellegrino 1992). Others have argued that in some circumstances patients have an obligation to hear the truth and be involved in decision-making. For example, if a patient has a sexually transmitted disease and would rather not know, it is argued that health workers may be able to justifiably inform them in the hope that they will modify their sexual practices.

In practical terms, it has been suggested that one approach to the problem of dealing with patients from cultures who may have different cultural norms regarding the exercise of autonomy is to ask them in advance whether they wish to know test results, or whether such results should first be communicated to their family. This has been termed 'offering truth' (Freedman 1993). While this approach seems intuitively appealing, we are unsure how this would work in practice, especially where a diagnosis comes as a surprise.

For the most part, we believe that patients should be given the opportunity to hear the truth, although this need not be necessarily be done by baldly stating the facts. Our experience is that if the doctor remains in a committed relationship with the patient and respects their values and beliefs, over time concerns about truth-telling tend to diminish. This is also consistent with the literature (Chiu, Hu et al 2000).

In her book *Pacific Journey*, New Zealand artist Valerie Hunton described one of the experiences that her husband Rex had noted while working as a physician in the Marshall Islands. He had diagnosed a Marshallese man as having advanced cancer of the lung and had carefully and sensitively explained the illness to him.

> The man responded in a stoical manner that is typical of people of the Pacific. They shook hands and on leaving the bedside, Rex felt their relationship was good and he had handled the situation well. The next morning however he was confronted in the corridor of the hospital by four close relatives who demanded to know why they had not been informed of this serious illness instead of the patient. Rex explained to them that this was the man's own personal information to do with whatever he wished. The relatives did not agree – they were adamant that he should never have been told by anyone.

When Rex asked whether their relative would ever learn the truth they said 'Yes! We would have taken him home and loved and cared for him so much that he would have known that he was dying.' (Hunton 2001)

This type of experience is common to those working with people from non-Western cultures (Ellerby, McKenzie et al 2000). It is also fairly common in the West, where families often wish to protect elderly people from the shock of some diagnoses. However, even in this circumstance, individual autonomy continues to be important, as people's wishes need to be taken into account and their need for information has to be addressed. Western health workers sometimes assume that the best way to tell someone their diagnosis is to state it bluntly, yet it is possible that many people in Western cultures would also prefer the oblique approach of the Marshallese. The issue of individual autonomy should not be ignored, but it must be approached in a culturally appropriate manner just as any ethical decision must be taken in the light of individual differences. Insensitivity to the cultural norms of a patient may result in the provision of information to someone who is not ready or willing to hear it and thus be a source of considerable distress (Gold 2004).

Munchausen's syndrome

It is sometimes asked whether patients also have a duty to tell the truth to health-care workers. It seems reasonable that patients should have the same social duty to tell the truth to their therapists as they do to any other person, but their duty is unlikely to extend further than this. There are a few instances in which it is not in a patient's interests to tell the truth (such as patients who have been refused care when they have acknowledged that they have AIDS). For the most part it is in the patient's interests to be as truthful as possible with their therapists, as this is more likely to lead to correct treatment and management of their medical condition.

In a condition known as Munchausen's syndrome, patients actively seek to mislead doctors in an effort to obtain medical care. Some such patients go through extensive diagnostic work-ups for diarrhoea, without disclosing that they are taking large quantities of laxatives; other patients put blood in their urine to get operated upon or inject themselves with faeces to be admitted to hospitals. If they are confronted with the evidence about what they have been doing, such patients often become very offended, discharging themselves from hospital and continuing their behaviour at a different geographical location.

This may represent an instance in which it is best not to tell the truth to patients, but instead to continue in a supportive relationship until they are able to admit their behaviour or recover from the psychological issues that cause them to behave in this way. By maintaining a relationship with these patients it may be possible to prevent excessive surgery that they would otherwise experience and to help them develop some insight into their behaviour.

In a related condition, Munchausen's disease by proxy, adults injure or kill children in order to obtain contact with hospitals. Some units now videotape mothers suspected of this behaviour without their knowledge and justify their actions by stating that their duty of beneficence to the child overrides their need to be truthful to the mother. However, many also believe that the condition, as well as other forms of child abuse, have been over-diagnosed, and that some of these people have been falsely accused (Chadwick, Krous et al 2006).

Recently, governments have also given increasing attention to the phenomenon of 'doctor shopping'. The Health Insurance Commission (HIC) defines doctor shoppers as people who have 30 or more Medicare consultations a year or see more than 15 different general practitioners to obtain more Pharmaceutical Benefits Scheme (PBS) prescriptions than appear to be clinically necessary. In 1995-96, there were 13,240 Australians who met this definition (Kamien 2004). Doctor shoppers for the most part are searching for access to drugs, and their approach frequently includes lying about symptoms and other drug use.

Health professionals who encounter patients who lie may be tempted to take a simplistic approach – of either believing everything they say, or refusing to deal with them. Yet those who lie to doctors are at high risk and health professionals need to engage with these people if tragedies are to be avoided (Martyres and Clode 2004).

Speaking out

Health professionals often find it difficult to tell the truth in matters where mistakes have been made, or where they have observed unprofessional or unethical conduct. Veracity may be ignored in situations such as medical malpractice, drug abuse by health workers and violation of professional boundaries such as sexual relationships between therapists and patients. When such situations are uncovered, it is frequently found that colleagues have known about them for a long time but have not spoken because of misplaced professional loyalties or because of fear of litigation. But disclosure in such situations may be morally required to enable investigation and management of problems, preservation of trust in institutions and professions, and to allow patients to seek help. It has been stated: 'The ideal relationships between colleagues, within the medical profession and between health care professionals generally is one of both mutual support and mutual and honest criticism' (Campbell, Gillett et al 1992).

People who work in hospitals are both participants and observers of the health-care process. In some studies, 65% of students felt that they had witnessed unethical behaviour by a member of the health-care team to which they were attached and 80% believed that they had acted unethically or wilfully misled patients themselves. 54% of the students who had witnessed unethical behaviour felt that they were in some way an accomplice to one or more of these actions (Feudtner, Christakis et al 1994).

Health-care workers often react with a policy of silence when they observe or take part in ethically suspect actions. This has some rewards – it prevents ridicule, being graded poorly or being seen as a poor team player; however, it is not enough to observe unethical behaviour now and to vow to act if similar situations arise in the future. The skills involved in responding to unethical behaviour need to be practised and developed if they are to be available when needed. Keeping quiet becomes a habit, and it represents a failure in teaching, learning and caring.

When there have been mistakes made in medical practices, patients usually accept apologies and explanations. Where there is continuing deceit, this merely undermines the therapeutic relationship and may make the risk of litigation even greater.

Conclusion

If we accept that health workers have an obligation to be truthful, there are still a number of issues that need to be clarified such as how to give information, who should be giving and receiving information, when to give information and what information to give.

A proper understanding of veracity recognises the inequality in the therapist/patient relationship and the fact that each brings different needs and values to the therapeutic relationship. Patients require truth but also need care, understanding and support when facing illness or death.

LEGAL ASPECTS OF TRUTH-TELLING AND VERACITY

There is no general obligation not to tell lies in the law. However, specific obligations to tell the truth may arise, for example, in the criminal law of fraud, the tort of deceit, and breaches of legislation such as the *Trade Practices Act 1974* (Cth), *Fair Trading Act* (all jurisdictions) or the various *Oaths Acts*.

Therapeutic privilege and withholding information

The High Court of Australia has recognised 'therapeutic privilege' as being a principle of common law. In the 1992 judgment in *Rogers v Whitaker* (1992) 175 CLR 479, the majority of the court recognised that, contrary to the basic principle of giving information to patients, there are some circumstances where the medical practitioner will be excused from providing information that the patient would want to know. Unfortunately, while recognising the existence of the principle of therapeutic privilege the court did not define it or explain the limits of the principle. There may be a question as to whether the term 'therapeutic privilege' is a fundamental principle of law, or whether it is just a line of argument that can be used in the defence to an otherwise actionable act.

Health professionals are required to provide patients with an appropriate standard of care, including providing patients with information about the likelihood of any material risks that they might suffer. The High Court said, when describing the method of establishing the standard of care in 'information and advice' cases, that:

> [A] risk is material if, in the circumstances of a particular case, a reasonable person in the patient's position, if warned of the risk, would be likely to attach significance to it or if the medical practitioner is or should reasonably be

aware that the particular patient, if warned of the risk, would be likely to attach significance to it. *This duty is subject to the therapeutic privilege.* ((1992) 175 CLR 479 at 490, emphasis added)

The court adopted the following meaning of the expression:

However, at the same time, his Lordship [Lord Templeman in *Sidaway* [1985] AC 871] gave quite substantial scope to a doctor to decide that providing all available information to a patient would be inconsistent with the doctor's obligation to have regard to the patient's best interests. This is the doctor's so-called therapeutic privilege, an opportunity afforded to the doctor to prove that he or she reasonably believed that disclosure of a risk would prove damaging to a patient. (at 486)

Gaudron J, delivering a concurring, but separate opinion, specifically restricted the application of the principle:

Again leaving aside cases involving a medical emergency or a situation where the circumstances of the individual require special consideration, I see no basis for treating the doctor's duty to warn of risks (whether involved in the treatment or procedures proposed or otherwise attending the patient's condition or circumstances) as different in nature or degree from any other duty to warn of real and foreseeable risks. And as at present advised, I see no basis for any exception or "therapeutic privilege" which is not based in medical emergency or in considerations of the patient's ability to receive, understand or properly evaluate the significance of the information that would ordinarily be required with respect to his or her condition or the treatment proposed. (at 494)

It is perhaps unfortunate that the High Court used the expression 'therapeutic privilege'. The principle is not actually a privilege or an 'entitlement', rather it is an obligation not to do harm – including doing harm by divulging information. This obligation is related to the general principle in negligence included in the standard of care.

Examples of the application of the principle are limited. The closest example of its application can be seen from the South Australian case of *Battersby v Tottman* (1985) 37 SASR 524. There are a number of unfortunate aspects of this case, but it can be used as an illustration of the application of the principle of therapeutic privilege.

Mrs Battersby suffered from a deep-seated psychosis with symptoms of depression and hallucinations and feelings of homicide and suicide. The only means of controlling her depression and preventing her from attempting suicide was to prescribe large doses of Melleril. One of the side-effects from large doses of Melleril is that it can affect the patient's eyesight (pigmentary retinopathy). Mrs Battersby was not informed of this side-effect. After using Melleril for a prolonged period Mrs Battersby's eyesight was affected to the extent that she became blind.

Mrs Battersby sued the doctor and hospital in negligence for not properly informing her about the risks associated with taking the drug. The court found that the doctor had not been in breach of the standard of care that he owed to Mrs Battersby as, if he had explained the side-effect, she may have stopped taking the drug and may have committed suicide. The risk of telling her was greater than the risk of the side-effect. That is, to tell her of the side-effect of damage to her eyesight may have caused her harm and thus excused what may have otherwise been a breach of the standard of care.

A final note on therapeutic privilege – the concept of therapeutic privilege, in modern times, was stated by Robinson J in the United States case of *Canterbury v Spence* 464 F 2d 772 (1972). But it should be noted that while Robinson J recognised the concept he also said that therapeutic privilege must 'be carefully circumscribed … for otherwise it might devour the rule [of informed consent] itself' (at 789). He continued 'the privilege does not accept the paternalistic notion that the physician may remain silent simply because divulgence might prompt the patient to forego therapy the physician feels the patient needs' (at 789).

Breaking bad news

The way in which bad news is conveyed to patients or their family forms part of the standard of care necessary to fulfil the duty of care owed to the person. Health-care professionals, as part of their training or continuing education, should hone their skills in communicating bad news and a failure to do so could form the basis of a complaint (whether disciplinary or within the legal system). The difficult case of *Hunter Area Health Service v Marchlewski* (2000) 51 NSWLR 268 could be used as an illustration of this point.

Maria Marchlewski was born at the defendant hospital. During her delivery there were avoidable complications that (by the time of the subsequent trial) were conceded by the hospital to be a breach of their duty of care. Maria was born 'clinically dead', suffering brain damage caused by cerebral hypoxia, which was caused by asphyxia during the delivery. She was resuscitated and placed on a ventilator. What occurred thereafter was the subject of some dispute between the parties; the trial judge made certain findings that, by the time the matter was heard by the NSW Court of Appeal, were not challenged. Based on the damage to Maria's brain, kidney and lungs the hospital formed a firm opinion that her prognosis was very poor. The opinion of the doctors was that the prognosis for the child was so bad that the likelihood of a 'normal or near normal outcome was zero'. Senior hospital staff attempted to explain their diagnosis and prognosis to the parents. This task was unusually difficult because of a number of reasons – each parent had a limited understanding of English (the first language of the mother was Thai, that of the father was Polish), there were cultural and religious differences that needed to be accommodated and, significantly, the parents were 'distraught and angry about the unexpected outcome of a perfectly normal pregnancy and their perception that the medical people had been at fault'.

Although Maria was eventually weaned off ventilator support her condition was still poor and a decision was made that she should not be re-ventilated in the event of a deterioration in her condition. The trial judge found (and this was not challenged on appeal) that the 'decision was made without consultation with, or the consent of' the parents. Almost one month after her birth Maria had a respiratory arrest, did not respond to any resuscitation and she died. The parents were very angry about this outcome and the father demanded a full inquiry. When asked if he wanted an autopsy he said that he wanted a full examination of the baby to see why she had died.

The parents sued the hospital claiming that they had suffered 'nervous shock' as a result of the circumstances surrounding the death of their daughter. By the time that the case came to trial in the NSW Supreme Court, before Dowd J (*Marchlewski v Hunter Area Health Service* [1998] NSWSC 771), the hospital had admitted to a breach of their duty of care to the parents and that this had caused them damage. The question to be decided by the court was the extent of the damage suffered by the parents. The mother was awarded $346,400 and the father $691,023 which included an amount for aggravated damages.

Part of the claim made by the parents was that the staff had initiated a coronial inquest and arranged for an autopsy to be performed without any explanation of the nature of an autopsy. They said that if they had been told what was involved they would have objected on religious and cultural grounds. On this issue Dowd J said that:

> [I]n the circumstances of the exacerbated sensibilities of [the parents], and in the knowledge of her religious beliefs, some degree of care should be taken to ensure that the consent or instruction to have a coroners inquiry was based on proper knowledge of what was involved, particularly as to the way an autopsy is carried out. Multicultural Australians include people from diverse religious nations and cultures. Sensitivity should be shown to different burial rituals. There is no evidence before the Court that in fact there was a proper explanation of what was involved.

The hospital appealed the decision and was successful on the issue of aggravated damages. The Court of Appeal set the awards for aggravated damages aside.

Cultural factors

> So many family members say, 'If the test result is bad, we want you to tell us first and let us decide whether to tell our father or our mother.' But the providers say, 'I have responsibilities here – and liabilities. I have to tell,' said Gheisar, whose work in multicultural Seattle puts her in contact with families from the Asian Pacific Islands, Southeast Asia, East Africa, and recently, Bosnia and Iraq, among many other locales. (Kreier 1999)

The principle of autonomy is one of the central values of our legal system. In the High Court case of *Perre v Apand Pty Ltd* (1999) 198 CLR 180 at 223-4, McHugh J wrote:

> One of the central tenets of the common law is that a person is legally responsible for his or her choices. It is a corollary of that responsibility that a person is entitled to make those choices for him or her self without unjustifiable interference from others. In other words, the common law regards individuals as autonomous beings entitled to make, but responsible for, their own choices.

The legal doctrines of duress, undue influence and criminal liability are premised on that view of the common law. In any organised society, however, individuals cannot have complete autonomy, for the good government of a society is impossible unless the sovereign power in that society has power in various circumstances to coerce the citizen. Nevertheless, the common law has generally sought to interfere with the autonomy of individuals only to the extent necessary for the maintenance of society.

An important aspect of the respect for the autonomy of the individual is their right, within constraints mentioned by McHugh J, is to determine how they exercise their autonomy.

Some health professionals, in a naive understanding of the notion of consent, insist that patients *must* make decisions for themselves and *must* be given all possible information about their condition. This is not so. One of the important features of the decision in *Rogers v Whitaker* (1992) 175 CLR 479 is that the provision of information is patient centred. The focus is on the needs of the patient and the context of their care. Issues such as cultural beliefs and values will be important to many patients in the decisions around their health care. The provision of information is also a process where the needs of the patient may change over time and constantly need to be reassessed.

The common law is flexible enough to account for differences in the relations between various parties and, as stated by Gaudron J in *Rogers v Whitaker*, 'a patient may have special needs and concerns which, if known to the doctor, will indicate that special or additional information is required' (at 493). One of these special needs may be the need to have their cultural beliefs respected and honoured.

Waiver of rights and autonomy

The common law recognises the concept of 'waiver', where an autonomous person may waive their right or rights, including the right they may have to receive specific information. Waiver is an imprecise term which covers a variety of legal concepts (*Commonwealth v Verwayen* (1990) 170 CLR 394). Caution must always be exercised to identify the extent of any waiver. Healy (1999) has identified the elements of a valid waiver and writes that the patient must know that:

- the doctor has a duty to disclose further information;
- the patient has the right to make an informed decision;
- the patient can decline to opt for the recommended treatment; and
- the doctor must obtain consent before proceeding.

It is clear that when the issue of waiver arises there is an obligation on the doctor to explore the issues with the patient to determine whether, and how, the waiver is to be exercised. What will be important is the manner in which the doctor expresses themselves to the patient and the way in which the issues are raised. Healy points out that a purported waiver 'should not be used as an outlet to facilitate significantly less communication and understanding between doctor and patient' (Healy 1999).

Beauchamp and Childress note that 'physicians should ask their patients if they wish to receive information and make decisions or if they prefer that their families handle such matters' and that 'this recommendation accepts [autonomy's] central condition that the choice is rightly the patients' (Beauchamp and Childress 2001). However, they also warn that 'a general practice of allowing waivers is dangerous [as] it would be easy to violate autonomy and fail to discharge our responsibilities by inflexible rules that either permit or prohibit waivers in institutional settings' (Beauchamp and Childress 2009).

Given that Australia is said to be a 'multicultural' society it would seem to represent a reasonable standard of care that health professionals make themselves aware of the needs of different cultures. One important issue, however, when discussing culture and the information to be provided to the patient is that we do not stereotype. Whilst a person may come from a particular racial, ethnic, religious or cultural group, the individual may have views that may be different and this difference must be accommodated.

Truth-telling and certificates

Health professionals, particularly medical practitioners, will be asked to issue certificates, reports or other documents stating the existence of specified facts. These certificates may be requested by employers, insurers and for court proceedings. It is essential that any certificate or report is not false or misleading in any particular.

Issuing a false certificate may be in breach of professional registration legislation or may be a crime if the purpose is knowingly to assist in perpetrating a fraud. Such actions may also constitute unsatisfactory professional conduct or professional misconduct for the purposes of professional registration and discipline.

Any health professional preparing a certificate should, at a minimum, consider the following:

- any certificate should be based on known facts;
- should be addressed to the party requiring the certificate (eg, the employer or insurer);
- the date when any examination took place;
- the patient's confidentiality should be respected and only information that is necessary for the purpose of the certificate should be included – for sickness certificates, issued by medical practitioners, the diagnosis should not be included without the patient's consent; and
- under no circumstances should a certificate be backdated.

Many professional registration boards have guidelines or policies on medical certificates.

Reporting colleagues and whistleblowing

Health professionals' obligation to report unethical, incompetent and criminal conduct has already been discussed in Chapter 7. Health professionals sometimes have knowledge about the conduct of others within their professional workplace that is not otherwise known. When a professional discloses information that evidences some objectionable misconduct, not otherwise known or visible, this is commonly known as 'whistleblowing'. Whistleblowers generally do so out of a sense of public duty arising from high personal ethical standards.

There are a number of notable examples of whistleblowing, such as the inquiry into the deaths of children undergoing paediatric cardiac surgery at the Bristol Royal Infirmary in the UK, the Campbelltown and Camden Hospital investigation in NSW, the Canberra Hospital inquiry into neurological services and the Inquiry into Gynaecological and Obstetric Services at King Edward Memorial Hospital in Perth (Faunce and Bolsin 2004). These examples show that blowing the whistle can come at high personal cost as whistleblowers, particularly those in junior positions, may be vulnerable to action being taken against them by way of reprisal (Faunce and Bolsin 2004).

Specific whistleblower legislation has been enacted in all Australian States and the Australian Capital Territory (*Protected Disclosures Act 1994* (NSW), *Whistleblowers Protection Act 1994* (Qld), *Whistleblowers Protection Act 1993* (SA), *Public Interest Disclosures Act 2002* (Tas), *Whistleblowers Protection Act 2001* (Vic), *Public Interest Disclosure Act 2003* (WA) and *Public Interest Disclosure Act 1994* (ACT)). The Northern Territory Law Reform Committee has made recommendations about the adoption of such legislation and recommended (with qualifications) following the Victorian and Tasmanian models (Northern Territory Law Reform Committee 2002).

The basic objectives of whistleblower legislation are to:

- protect the whistleblower who, in good faith, makes a disclosure in the public interest from detrimental action;
- ensure that the person to whom the disclosure is made takes appropriate action; and
- facilitate the making of disclosures.

Apart from Victoria and Tasmania, each jurisdiction has adopted different approaches to the encouragement of disclosures, the protection of whistleblowers and the obligations of agencies on receiving disclosures. The Northern Territory Department of Justice (Policy Division) has produced a discussion paper on proposed legislation for the Northern Territory (Northern Territory Department of Justice (Policy Division) 2004). In this discussion paper they have produced an attachment that contains a detailed comparison of aspects of the legislation from the various jurisdictions.

Importantly, the whistleblower legislation applies to disclosures within the public sector. The legislation does not apply to the private sector.

Admitting mistakes

The common law has long recognised that medical professionals have a duty to inform their patients of any error which has made their conditions worse. This was described in *Naylor v Preston Area Health Authority* [1987] 2 All ER 353 as a 'duty of candour' which rests on health professionals, and while the decision was concerned with doctors it could equally be applied across the range of allied health professionals. This duty requires that the patient be informed of errors, especially in circumstances where a preventable injury will be made worse if further treatment is not provided. The duty is primarily sourced in the law of negligence but arguably it may also arise from an equitable fiduciary duty to act in the patient's best interests (Faunce and Bolsin 2005).

In *Wighton v Arnott* [2005] NSWSC 637, a patient had three operations to remove a lump in her shoulder. During the third operation the surgeon severed her accessory nerve but he neglected to inform her that this had happened. Because the patient was not informed she went several months without appropriate treatment and lost the opportunity to repair the severed nerve. She suffered from problems such as a wasted arm and frozen shoulder. The patient alleged that the failure to inform her of the severing of her nerve was a breach of duty. Studdert J said:

> I accept that repair of a severed accessory nerve was outside the scope of the defendant's speciality and the exercise of due care on his part did not require of him that he endeavour to repair the severed nerve himself either on the day it was severed or subsequently. What the exercise of due care required of the defendant was that he take reasonable steps to determine whether it was the accessory nerve which had been severed and that he alert the plaintiff as to what had occurred. (at [38])

Apologies

One of the reasons patients decide to sue health professionals for negligence is that they believe that the practitioner 'doesn't care'. This may result from the lack of an explanation, an apology or an expression of regret following an unexpected result of treatment. One of the reasons put forward by health professionals for not providing an apology or an expression of regret is that this may be seen as an admission of liability and open themselves to the prospect of a legal action.

The Ipp reforms (see Chapter 8) did not include recommendations on the issue of apologies. Nevertheless, all jurisdictions now have legislation which prevents an apology or an expression of regret from being considered an admission of liability.

Jurisdiction	Legislation
NSW	*Civil Liability Act 2002*, s 69
Qld	*Civil Liability Act 2003*, s 72
SA	*Civil Liability Act 1936*, s 75
Tas	*Civil Liability Act 2002*, s 7
Vic	*Wrongs Act 1958*, ss 14J-14K
WA	*Civil Liability Act 2002*, s 5AH
ACT	*Civil Law (Wrongs) Act 2002*, s 14
NT	*Personal Injuries (Liabilities and Damages) Act 2003*, s 13

References

Akayabashi, A, I Kai et al (1999) 'Truth telling in the case of a pessimistic diagnosis in Japan'. *Lancet* **354**(1263).

Anon (2000) 'Delivering bad news'. *BMJ* **321**: 1233.

Beauchamp, T and J Childress (2001) *Principles of biomedical ethics* (5th ed). New York, Oxford University Press.

Beauchamp, T and J Childress (2009) *Principles of biomedical ethics* (6th ed). New York, Oxford University Press.

Bok, S (1979) *Lying, moral choice in private and public life*. New York, Vintage Books.

Campbell, A, G Gillett et al (1992) *Practical Medical Ethics*. Auckland, Oxford University Press.

Carrese, J and L Rhodes (1995) 'Western bioethics on the Navajo reservation – benefit or harm?' *JAMA* **274**(10): 826-9.

Centeno-Cortes, C and J Nunez-Olarte (1994) 'Questioning diagnosis disclosure in terminal cancer patients: a prospective study evaluating patients' responses'. *Palliat Med* **8**: 39044.

Chadwick, D, H Krous et al (2006) 'Meadow, Southall, and the General Medical Council of the United Kingdom'. *Paediatrics* **117**: 2247-51.

Chiu, T, W Hu et al (2000) 'Ethical dilemmas in palliative care: a study in Taiwan'. *J Med Ethics* **26**: 353-7.

Ell, K, R Nishimoto et al (1989) 'A longitudinal analysis of psychological adaptation among survivors of cancer'. *Cancer* **63**(2): 406-13.

Ellerby, J, J McKenzie et al (2000) 'Bioethics for clinicians: 18 Aboriginal cultures'. *CMAJ* **163**(7): 845-50.

Feudtner, C, D Christakis et al (1994) 'Do clinical clerks suffer ethical erosion? Students' perceptions of their ethical environment and personal development'. *Acad Med* **69**: 660-79.

Freedman, B (1993) 'Offering truth: One ethical approach to the uninformed cancer patient'. *Arch Intern Med* **153**: 572-6.

Gillon, R (1990) 'Deceit, principles and philosophical medical ethics'. *J Med Ethics* **16**(2): 59-69.

Gold, M (2004) 'Is honesty always the best policy? Ethical aspects of truth telling'. *Int Med Jn* **34**: 578-80.

Hebert, P, B Hoffmaster et al (1997) 'Truth telling'. *CMAJ* **156**: 225-8.

Hunton, V (2001) *Pacific Journey: A celebration* Auckland, Resource books.

Jonsen, A, M Siegler et al (1992) *Clinical ethics: A practical approach to ethical decisions in clinical medicine*. New York, MacMillan.

Kamien, M (2004) '"Doctor shoppers": at risk by any other name'. *Med J Aust* **180**(5): 204-5.

Laurence, D and P Bennett (1987) *Clinical pharmacology*. New York, Churchill Livingstone.

Martyres, R and D Clode (2004) 'Seeking drugs or seeking help? Escalating "doctor shopping" by young heroin users before fatal overdose'. *Med J Aust* **180**: 211-14.

Moerman, D (2000) 'Cultural variations in the placebo effect: ulcers, anxiety, and blood pressure'. *Med Anthrop Q* **14**: 51-72.

Moerman, D and W Jonas (2002) 'Deconstructing the placebo effect and finding the meaning response'. *Ann Intern Med* **136**(6): 471-6.

Pellegrino, E (1992) 'Is truth-telling to the patient a cultural artefact?' *JAMA* **268**(13): 1734-9.

Ptacek, J and T Eberhardt (1996) 'Breaking bad news: a review of the literature'. *JAMA* **276**(6): 496-502.

Thomas, K (1987) 'General practice consultations: is there any point in being positive?' *BMJ (Clin Res Ed)* **57**: 253-61.

CHAPTER 12

CONFIDENTIALITY AND RECORD-KEEPING

Case study 1

VZ is a 32-year-old social worker, who was admitted to a psychiatric hospital during a manic episode. During his illness, he was loud, aggressive and at times sexually disinhibited. When he recovered from his illness he was extremely ashamed of his previous behaviour. He was terrified that information about his illness would be common knowledge at the nearby hospital where he worked as he felt that this would result in the loss of his temporary job.

Case study 2

BC is a 78-year-old woman who was admitted to hospital with acute pulmonary oedema and dementia. The following day her son rang to find out how she was going. 'We can't release that information over the phone', he was told. 'But I'm her son!' he said. 'But I don't know that, do I', was the reply, 'and in any case, the hospital policy is that we cannot release that information over the phone.'

The word confidentiality derives from the Latin roots *con* – meaning completeness – and *fidere* – meaning to trust; hence to confide is to trust wholly or to impart knowledge with reliance upon secrecy.

Privacy is a related concept that is often used interchangeably with confidentiality but is actually quite distinct. Privacy refers to one's ownership of one's body or information about one's self, whereas confidentiality refers specifically to restrictions upon private information revealed in confidence where there is an explicit or implicit assumption that the information shared will not be disclosed to others.

The provision of care always involves some invasion of privacy. Patients give health workers permission to discuss their most intimate secrets, to view their naked bodies and to perform painful and embarrassing procedures upon them. Patients allow access to this private information because they are actively seeking help and trust that their best interests will be maintained. However, patients generally expect that this information will not be disclosed to others. When such information is disclosed, then a breach of confidentiality may have occurred.

It should be noted that the importance of confidentiality is both socially and culturally determined. Confidentiality is greatly emphasised in Anglo-Celtic societies such as USA or Australia which emphasise individualism, autonomy, rights and individual liberty. Confidentiality may be less important in cultures with less individualistic and more community-oriented traditions and where the role of families in decision-making is more privileged (Perez-Carceles, Pereniguez et al 2005). However in these situations, patients may still be very concerned if information spreads beyond the group for whom it is allowed.

In Western societies, respect for confidentiality is underpinned by the common law, professional codes of practice and legislation. Injunctions to maintain confidentiality have been laid down in a number of professional codes including the Hippocratic Oath, the World Medical Association's Declaration of Geneva (1948), the International Council of Nursing Code of Ethics (1973), and the Australian Association of Occupational Therapists Code of Ethics.

Confidentiality in the health-care setting includes all the information relating to the practitioner's professional relationship with the patient. This may include the information that a patient shares with a health professional as well as the results of physical examination findings, tests and procedures, the information that patients may convey non-verbally, such as their emotional state, and the fact that they have been a patient at all (Hamblin 1992). Ethically and legally, the rule of confidentiality obliges all health-care workers to not only refrain from disclosing information obtained from patients to others, but also to take every reasonable precaution to ensure that any records of such information remain confidential. This obligation remains in force even after the death of the patient. Because of the links between rights, duties and obligations, the rule can be expressed either as a person's right to have health information treated confidentially, or as a health-care worker's duty or obligation to ensure that such information is not disclosed to others without the person's permission.

It is difficult to maintain confidentiality in a health-care system that is increasingly team-oriented, fragmented and complex. Patients come into contact with large numbers of health professionals and many others who are indirectly involved in their care. Recent trends in information technology have resulted in an increasing ability to document various aspects of patient care, coupled with increasing opportunities to breach confidentiality. This has occurred during a period of rapidly increasing litigation, much of it concerned with either breaches of confidentiality or lack of documentation. There is a fundamental conflict between the need to maintain the confidentiality of the doctor-patient relationship, and the need to document its details for future reference. Considerations such as these have led some critics such as Mark Siegler to suggest that professional exhortations to maintain confidentiality are meaningless and that confidentiality in medicine is now a 'decrepit concept' as it no longer exists (Siegler 1982).

Four types of philosophical arguments have been used to support the concept of confidentiality. The first is a principle-based argument derived from respect for autonomy. This argument claims that maintaining confidentiality is a crucial part of respecting a patient's autonomy – for if an individual is to be self-determining, he or she must be able to maintain their sense of personal integrity and control what personal information others have about them (Bok 1982).

The second argument is a virtue-based argument which maintains that trust and fidelity to an implicit or explicit promise to maintain confidentiality is a fundamental part of the health worker–patient relationship.

The third argument is that the moral right to protection of secrets and the corresponding duty to maintain confidentiality is fundamental to all human relationships. This 'relational' or communitarian basis for confidentiality is that most often referred to in feminist and 'care' ethics.

The final argument is a consequentialist one that maintains that the assurance of patient confidentiality is necessary for achieving the medical goals of effective diagnosis and treatment (Oakley 1997). According to this argument, patients will only agree to fully disclose their personal histories and submit to examinations and investigations where they are certain that the results of these will not be disclosed or become public knowledge. In this way, maintaining confidentiality produces a direct medical benefit and prevents harm occurring to patients and the public.

These arguments provide a sound basis for respecting confidentiality, yet they do not support an absolute obligation to maintain confidentiality. There may be circumstances in which confidentiality may be overridden, and at times the disclosure of confidential information may be morally permissible or even obligatory. The question then becomes, what are the limits of confidentiality and under what circumstances may breaches of obligation be justifiable?

We believe that confidentiality can be best thought of as two related concepts: the implied confidentiality that is found within the health professional–patient relationship, and a more explicit form of confidentiality that can be negotiated between health workers and patients. It is useful to make a distinction between the *scope* or *limits* of confidentiality, which may be discussed and negotiated in advance of the consultation, and *breaches* of confidentiality, when a confidential relationship is broken on the grounds of a more pressing obligation.

Limits of confidentiality

There are many aspects of the patient–professional relationship that are excluded from complete confidentiality by statute, law or convention. For example, in the field of occupational health, doctors frequently are asked by employers to assess patients' fitness to work. The American College of Occupational and Environmental Medicine has published a position paper on this topic that recognises that employers may be entitled to information about an individual's medical work fitness as long as this is made explicitly clear before the consultation begins. They do not recognise any entitlement by employers to individual diagnoses or specific detail except in compliance with laws or regulations (American College of Occupational and Environmental Health 1995). Likewise, doctors who fill out sickness certificates may comment upon individual capacity to work but should usually avoid comment about actual diagnoses.

There are other limits to confidentiality that have been established in law. Many countries have laws that require mandatory reporting of blood alcohol levels for those involved in car accidents, gun-shot wounds or domestic violence, and in cases of infectious disease. Such limits to confidentiality are legislated as a means to address the larger issues of the common good. It may also be possible for health professionals and students to negotiate other exceptions to the rule of confidentiality. For example, a medical student could negotiate with a patient at the beginning of a consultation so that all information that is obtained in the consultation is shared with the hospital team. Similarly, one could refuse to accept information from patient's relatives which is offered under the condition that the patient is not to be told.

Breaches of confidentiality

There are some rare occasions in which it may be necessary to breach confidentiality, without the patient's permission and acting against the patient's trust. It is widely accepted in ethics and law that the rule of confidentiality may be breached if the patient voluntarily consents, or without the consent of the patient if a higher obligation is threatened (most commonly to protect the patient from harm, or to protect other parties from harm). An example of the latter would be when confidentiality is breached to protect the 'public good' in cases of child abuse, infectious disease or potential violence.

The duty to maintain confidentiality takes on an added significance in psychiatry and psychotherapy. Patients disclose the most intimate details of their lives to psychotherapists, at a time when they are vulnerable and explicitly asking for help. They do so on the understanding that they are secure within the therapeutic relationship. At times, however, the patient may disclose an intention to injure or kill another.

The moral obligations to maintain or breach confidentiality in such situations have been widely debated since the *Tarasoff* case (which was discussed in Chapter 8). In that case a patient, Prosenjit Poddor, confided to his psychologist, Dr Lawrence Moore, that he intended to kill his ex-girlfriend Tatiana Tarasoff. Dr Moore informed the University of California police but did not warn Tatiana. Poddor subsequently murdered Tarasoff, leading her parents to sue Dr Moore for negligence. The court subsequently found Dr Moore and the University of California liable for negligence for failure to follow a legal duty to breach confidentiality – a decision broadened in a re-hearing of the case in 1976 (*Tarasoff v Regents of the University of California* 551 P 2d 334 (1976)).

The moral and legal justification for breaching confidentiality in this case was that there was a foreseeable harm to an identifiable third party that was serious and probable. However, the simplicity of this justification is misleading and does not recognise the enormous complexity in cases such as these in which one must attempt to balance the *prima facie* obligation to preserve confidences on the one hand with obligations to preserve justice and non-maleficence on the other. It is also extremely difficult for therapists to assess the sincerity of a lethal threat when expressions of harm to one's self or others may not be predictive of action but may be a symptom of the mental illness or a 'cry for help'.

There is some empirical evidence that patients under psychiatric care may be harmed by breaches of confidentiality. One study found that 95% of patients would resent others having unauthorised access to their medical records 67% would be angry if information was disclosed to their relatives without their approval and 17% would consider this adequate reason to terminate the therapeutic relationship (Schmidt 1983).

The therapist is therefore required to perform a risk assessment. They must decide whether it is better to err on the side of caution and breach confidentiality or whether it is more important to reaffirm the moral basis for confidentiality and recognise the potential harms that may arise from breaching confidences.

Problems with confidentiality

In the hospital environment, the principle of confidentiality is widely espoused but is frequently breached in practice. Beauchamp and Childress discuss Mark Siegler's critique of the 'decrepit concept of confidentiality' as follows:

> Siegler presents the case of a patient who became concerned about the number of people in the hospital who appeared to have access to his record and threatened to leave prematurely unless the hospital would guarantee confidentiality. Upon inquiry, Siegler discovered that many more people than he had suspected had legitimate needs and responsibilities to examine the patient's chart. When he informed the patient of the number, approximately seventy-five, he assured the patient that "These people were all involved in providing or supporting his health care services." The patient retorted, "I always believed that medical confidentiality was part of a doctor's code of ethics. Perhaps you should tell me just what you people mean by confidentiality?" (Beauchamp and Childress 2009)

In many ways the hospital environment appears to be organised in a manner that is counter to any principle of confidentiality. Records are freely accessible, patient's histories are presented at open meetings and health workers can often be heard talking about patients in lifts (Vigod, Bell et al 2003), in corridors (Olsen and Sabin 2003), in nearby pubs and coffee shops and over the dinner table at home. While such discussions are difficult to avoid and may even be necessary for optimal care, it is imperative that greater care is taken so that individuals cannot be identified, even by the most indirect means. According to one poll, 83% of patients were satisfied with the way physicians handled confidential information, but there is widespread ignorance of what actually occurs. In a study by Weiss most patients did not expect cases to be discussed in medical journals, at parties or with the physician's spouse, although 50% of house staff and medical officers do discuss cases with their spouses, and 70% discuss cases at parties (Weiss 1982). Patients have a variety of different views about what information should be kept confidential (Sankar, Mora et al 2003; Jenkins, Merz et al 2005). Concerns about confidentiality, particularly in the setting of sexual health, may affect patients' willingness to present to services (Carlisle, Shickle et al 2006).

Police, the press and legal representatives frequently attempt to gain information about patients in hospitals when it is unethical or illegal for health workers to provide it. If such information is disclosed, it is important to note that it is the health worker who has breached confidentiality, not the person who requested the information.

Record-keeping

Accurate and comprehensive medical records are an essential part of medical care – functioning as a store of clinical data and as a means of communication between health professionals. They are used in research, audit, planning, administration and litigation.

Medical records have, in the past, been considered as aids to help doctors remember patient details, and were therefore owned by the practitioner or the institution that created them. In recent years, changing perspectives regarding the rights of patients and the health worker–patient relationship have altered our understanding of the medical record. Some people now view records from an autonomy perspective – as a data source collated by the health team that is held in trust for the benefit of the patient; or as a shared record of a collaborative relationship that is kept by the institution yet is accessible by the patient.

Due to an increased recognition of autonomy and recent developments in law, patients in most English-speaking countries are now allowed access to their medical records. In fact, patients have always been able to obtain a degree of access to their medical records through the process of legal discovery. Such access may assist patients who wish to make a complaint or to take legal action about their medical care. What has changed is that this can now be done more informally.

There are many positive aspects of this trend towards greater accountability and increased patient access to medical records. It has been argued that a right to access one's own records may allow patients to create comprehensive dossiers of their medical history and hence allow better continuity of care; and that free access to careful and well-kept records is likely to enhance trust in the health-care system (Gilhooly and McGhee 1991). Certainly, improved communication between doctors and patients in other areas has been shown to decrease litigation, a process that may be further advanced by patients having access to their medical records. Indeed, most studies that have examined patients' reaction to having access to their medical records have found that they find the experience beneficial and may become more involved in therapeutic decision-making (Roth, Wolford et al 1980).

Electronic records

The growth of electronic record-keeping is inevitable. By 2000 over half of the hospitals in the US were in the process of implementing electronic patient record (EPR) systems, and the industry was spending $15 billion per year on information technology (IT), an amount that was expanding by 20% per year (Anderson 2000).

Anderson says:

> The collection, storage and communication of a large variety of personal patient data, however, present a major dilemma. How can we provide the data required by the new forms of health care delivery and at the same time protect the personal privacy of patients? Recent debates concerning medical privacy legislation, software regulation, and telemedicine suggest that this

dilemma will not be easily resolved. The problem is systemic and arises out of the routine use and flow of information throughout the health industry. Health care information is primarily transferred among authorized users. Not only is the information used for patient care and financial reimbursement, secondary users of the information include medical, nursing, and allied health education, research, social services, public health, regulation, litigation, and commercial purposes such as the development of new medical technology and marketing. The main threats to privacy and confidentiality arise from within the institutions that provide patient care as well as institutions that have access to patient data for secondary purposes. (Anderson 1990)

There are two main types of electronic records used in health care: electronic medical records – which have been developed primarily to support the operation of health-care services; and personal health records – which have been developed to enable patients to manage their own health-care management and illnesses (Young, Chaney et al 2007).

There is as yet no conclusive evidence of the value of electronic records for patient care (van der Kam, Mooman et al 2000; Clamp and Keen 2007), but electronic records are of particular use for administrative tasks such as compiling health statistics, the development of performance statistics and analysing health trends. However, IT is strongly associated in the public mind with threats to confidentiality, and there is a real risk of such breaches (Bomba, Cooper et al 1995).

A good example of some of the issues that arise with electronic health records in Australia is the development of HealthConnect. HealthConnect is a partnership between the Commonwealth, State and Territory governments that aims to coordinate e-health systems in different parts of the health sector. HealthConnect was introduced to respond to the diversity of existing health records: the aim is that every time a person goes to a different health-care provider or moves interstate, their important health information will be readily available (with their consent). The hope is that better access to more complete information for health-care providers will lead to better decision-making, improved delivery of health care and better consumer safety.

The strategy has had to take particular care with the privacy of personal health information, including reviewing existing legislation to comply with the changes to e-health technology. Consumers are able to authorise the creation of, and subsequent access by health-care providers to, their electronic health records and electronic health plans. They also have the ability to remove authorisation for providers they no longer wish to have access to their health records.

It is claimed that the benefits of the strategy will be:

- in an emergency situation patients' lives could be saved as health professionals can access health information more readily;
- errors in clinical decisions and medication management will be reduced as health providers can keep in touch electronically, no matter where they are located;
- referrals, test results and other important information will be transferred more accurately, quickly and securely between doctors and any other

member of the health-care team – this will prevent health risks caused by unnecessary duplicate procedures or tests and reduce costs;

- convenience and time saving will be inherent as patients will not have to chase health records created by different providers;

- wherever patients go in the health system their electronically stored health data can be transferred quickly and accurately to another provider with their consent. (<http://www.health.gov.au/internet/hconnect/publishing.nsf/Content/faqs-1lp#4>)

The advantages of systems such as HealthConnect is that they allow complete, automatic and integrated entry of clinical and pathological data, rapid access to the system, users at multiple sites, and the transferring of patient information from site to site. Unfortunately, these same factors mean that information is likely to become less secure – being potentially accessible to anyone with computer skills (Wyatt 1994).

According to Hodge and colleagues:

> Principal among the legal challenges presented by the computerization of health data information is how to protect individual privacy interests in personally identifiable health information. Health data about individuals are among the most sensitive types of personal information. Protecting the confidentiality of personally identifiable health data is critical. Insufficient protections can lead to unauthorized use and disclosures of data … Computerized databases of personally identifiable information may be accessed, changed, viewed, copied, used, disclosed, or deleted more easily and by more people (authorized and unauthorized) than paper-based records. With little more than basic information about a person, detailed medical profiles of individuals can be quickly assembled by private or commercial actors through online networks, Internet chat boards, and retrieval services. (Hodge, Gostin et al 1999)

Health institutions have responded to the threat to confidentiality posed by electronic systems through a number of security measures. These include allowing patients to be treated under a pseudonym, allowing patients to opt out of electronic databases, creating separate systems for sensitive data such as HIV and mental health information, and creating access and dissemination protocols that incorporate passwords, coded data, keystroke auditing and record monitoring. It is possible that some of these measures will in turn limit the effectiveness of electronic records. For example, a patient who shops among multiple doctors for narcotics is unlikely to consent to their records being shared. It also remains to be seen whether such measures will prevent violations of patient confidentiality.

Conclusion

Confidentiality and record-keeping are areas in which many of the traditional ethical and legal arguments are being rapidly eroded by technological change. Patients expect greater confidentiality in hospitals than they presently receive and, to meet this expectation, health workers need to be clear about their duties regarding confidentiality and record-keeping. There are limits to confidentiality, in both legal and ethical senses, and health-care workers should be open and truthful in discussing these with patients. There are also rare occasions in which patient confidentiality must be breached in the public good. However, there are good reasons to maintain a policy of confidentiality, and it should only be breached for matters of the utmost importance.

LEGAL ASPECTS OF CONFIDENTIALITY, RECORD-KEEPING AND PRIVACY

The obligation of confidence

The law recognises the significant need to protect the secrets disclosed by a patient to a health-care provider during the course of their professional relationship. The secret acquired is that of the patient, not of the health-care provider. Health information that has been anonymised (ie, has had all identifying characteristics removed from the record) is not generally considered to be confidential as the information cannot be related to the individual person concerned (*R v Source Informatics Ltd* [2000] 1 All ER 786).

Confidences between health-care providers and patients may be legally protected (and thus able to be enforced) in three ways:

- contract;
- equity;
- specific statutory provisions.

Contract and confidence

Many obligations of confidence arise between parties who are in a contractual relationship. Contractual confidences can arise in two main ways: through an express term of the contract or, impliedly, when such a term is assumed to be in the contract but not expressly stated. If an obligation of confidence is expressly referred to in the contract then the extent of the obligation is determined by that condition: *Deta Nominees Pty Ltd v Viscount Plastic Products Pty Ltd* [1979] VR 167 at 190, per Fullagar J.

In health-care contexts express terms about confidentiality can be found in contracts between employers and employees. Express covenants are often used restrictively in employment contexts to prevent use of confidential information after the termination of employment. While there were earlier doubts, it now appears that an express clause can extend contractual obligations of confidence beyond what would be imposed by other laws like equity: *Wright v Gasweld Pty Ltd* (1991) 22 NSWLR 317.

Obligations of confidence can also be implied into contracts: *Deta Nominees Pty Ltd v Viscount Plastic Products Pty Ltd* [1979] VR 167. When the contractual duty of confidence is implied it mirrors the equitable duty of confidence (discussed below). The obligation can survive the termination of the working relationship. In *Mid-City Skin Cancer and Laser Centre v Zahedi-Anarak* [2006] NSWSC 844, a doctor was found to have breached an implied term of confidence when he took a number of patient files with him after he ceased working for a corporate medical centre. He then used the files to compile of list of patients whom he then contacted about providing further treatments. Similarly, in *Ashcoast Pty Ltd v Whillans* [2000] 2 Qd R 1, the Queensland Court of Appeal held that a medical practitioner had breached an implied obligation owed to the operator of a medical centre by copying patient names and addresses and then contacting them after leaving the centre.

But what of contracts between patients and health-care professionals? Most contracts between health-care providers and patients are informal (ie, not in writing), and the terms of contracts are therefore not usually explicitly agreed upon: *Breen v Williams* (1996) 186 CLR 71. Because of this courts will imply a term in the contract to require the health-care provider to protect any confidences that may have been divulged: *Parry-Jones v Law Society* [1969] 1 Ch 1. There will be instances, however, when it may be more difficult (if not impossible) to identify a contract between health-care providers and patients. This may be because there is no 'consideration' between the parties which is usually necessary to support a contract. (Although, if broad concepts of consideration mentioned in *Breen v Williams* (1996) 186 CLR 71 were followed the requirements may be present). (Herdy 1996)

Equity and confidence

Equity imposes an obligation of confidence in certain conditions. In *Coco v AN Clark (Engineers) Ltd* [1969] RPC 41 at 47, Megarry J set out the three elements of the equitable action for breach of confidence:

> In my judgment, three elements are normally required if, apart from contract, a case of breach of confidence is to succeed. First, the information itself must … 'have the necessary quality of confidence about it.' Secondly, that information must have been imparted in circumstances importing an obligation of confidence. Thirdly, there must be an unauthorised use of that information to the detriment of the party communicating it.

Information concerning a person's medical history has the 'necessary quality of confidence', especially when the disclosure of the patient's medical condition would subject the patient to ridicule or embarrassment. For example, in *X v Y* [1988] 2 All ER 648 newspapers were prevented from publishing information that two GPs working for a health service were HIV positive. Another example is that of supermodel Naomi Campbell, who was able to claim damages for breach of confidence when a newspaper published details of her group therapy for narcotics addiction and photographs of her attendance at meetings: *Campbell v MGN Ltd* [2004] UKHL 22.

Anonymised medical records are no longer confidential and there is no breach if the information is published: *R v Dept of Health; Ex parte Source Informatics Ltd* [2000] 1 All ER 786. The court will judge whether information has been sufficiently anonymised: *Local Authority v Health Authority (disclosure: restriction on publication)* [2004] 1 All ER 480.

Where a breach of confidence is anticipated an injunction may be sought which, if granted, can prevent the confidential information from being used or disclosed. For example, in *IVF Australia Pty Ltd v Palantrou Pty Ltd* [2005] NSWSC 810 a limited injunction was granted against doctors who had set up a rival IVF clinic after using patient information taken from their former clinic's database.

Injunctions may be difficult to request from the court if the information has already entered the public domain because such information loses the 'necessary quality of confidence'. However, if information has been made public only briefly then it still may remain confidential and an injunction may be ordered. This occurred in *Australian Football League v Age Company Ltd* [2006] VSC 308, where the names of three AFL players who had tested positive to drugs were published on an internet discussion forum. An electronic newspaper article had also named the players to a limited group of subscribers for about five hours. A further publication of one of the player's names had occurred when a phone caller named the player on the 'Fox Footy' television program. Regardless, Kellam J found that the information had still not yet fully entered the public domain and therefore remained confidential. A permanent injunction was ordered on the release of the player's identities.

Once the information has been published in the public domain a claimant may not seek an injunction but may have access to other remedies like equitable compensation for any damages that they have suffered.

Statutory provisions

A number of pieces of legislation provide for the protection of confidences. For example, in NSW, legislation such as the *Health Administration Act 1982*; *Human Tissue Act 1983* and the *Public Health Act 1991* all provide that some information must not be disclosed. The legislation usually provides for a penalty to be imposed if information is inappropriately disclosed.

Professional codes of conduct

Most health profession codes of conduct include a requirement to protect the confidences entrusted to the health-care provider. Although the breach of a professional code of conduct does not create an enforceable right for the patient a professional standards board or tribunal could find that a breach of confidence (without an appropriate defence) may amount to unsatisfactory professional conduct or professional misconduct.

An example of this can be found in *Health Care Complaints Commission (HCCC) v Guilfoyle* [2007] NSWPST 1, where a psychologist was found to have been guilty of unsatisfactory professional conduct. The psychologist had (amongst other things) breached the confidentiality of two clients (who were married to each other) by sending out an invoice with a notation on it that both clients used cannabis heavily.

Does the obligation of confidence continue after the death of the patient?

Despite many professional codes of ethics requiring that confidences are to be kept following the death of the patient the legal position on this matter is uncertain. Some legal commentators have suggested that analogies can be drawn with the law of defamation where actions are not sustainable after the death of the deceased person (Kennedy and Grubb 2000). Others have argued that the interest in the context of breach of confidence is different in its nature and that such an obligation could continue after death (Savulescu and Skene 2000).

Privacy legislation (see below) may cover the circumstances around the disclosure of health information of deceased persons for 30 years (Victoria and NSW) or indefinitely (Australian Capital Territory) of a deceased person.

Medical records

Medical records are defined by statute in some jurisdictions (*Medical Practitioners Registration Act 2001* (Qld), s 259; *Health Records (Privacy and Access) Act 1997* (ACT)). The most comprehensive definition of 'health information' is given by the *Health Records and Information Privacy Act 2002* (NSW), which is:

(a) personal information that is information or an opinion about:
>   (i)   the physical or mental health or a disability (at any time) of an individual, or
>   (ii) an individual's express wishes about the future provision of health services to him or her, or
>   (iii) a health service provided, or to be provided, to an individual, or
(b) other personal information collected to provide, or in providing, a health service, or
(c) other personal information about an individual collected in connection with the donation, or intended donation, of an individual's body parts, organs or body substances, or
(d) other personal information that is genetic information about an individual arising from a health service provided to the individual in a form that is or could be predictive of the health (at any time) of the individual or of any sibling, relative or descendant of the individual,

but does not include health information, or a class of health information or health information contained in a class of documents, that is prescribed as exempt health information for the purposes of this Act generally or for the purposes of specified provisions of this Act. (s 6)

Medical records are the contemporaneous record of events. The records are used by health-care providers to assist them in the care of patients. If records are not kept adequately then it could be argued that there has been a breach of the appropriate standard of care and, should damage result, there may be a successful action in negligence. A number of criteria have been identified as being necessary for good record-keeping. Records must be clear, concise, unbiased, free of abbreviations (other than those accepted by the wider body practising in the area of recording), legible, objective and accurate (Field 1997).

Medical records are of significant medico-legal importance. Courts rely upon accurate records in order to ascertain what may have happened in the disputed events. It is a regrettable fact that civil legal actions may take many years before they come the courts. In turn, legal proceedings may have only commenced many years after the events (this is particularly so in cases involving children). Courts recognise that health-care providers may have no independent recollection of events and so may use their records to refresh their memory.

If notes have not been made, or the notes are inadequate, then courts may draw an adverse inference from this fact. For example, in a NSW Supreme Court case *(Strelec v Nelson,* unreported, NSWSC, 13 December 1996, Smart J) a specialist obstetrician was found to have acted negligently during the delivery of a child. The court was influenced in reaching this conclusion because the doctor had not kept a record of events that occurred during labour. Smart J at one point in the judgment said:

> He [Dr Nelson] rejected that he had made an error of judgment. He acknowledged that his failure to make any note of what he had done and what had happened was a serious departure from proper practice. It was his usual practice to record what happened at a delivery. He denied that he had failed to make notes because he did not know why the delivery had gone wrong or to prevent anyone from reviewing what he had done and discovering a mistake. Dr Nelson was acutely embarrassed by what had happened. He was hoping that the baby would recover. He had no satisfactory explanation for what had happened. He probably asked himself whether he should have pursued a different course, eg a caesarean section, which would have avoided the damage to the baby and had an uneasy feeling in that regard. He was worried that he had made a mistake. It was a subject that he found disturbing. It was a combination of such reasons that led him not to make notes.

The failure to keep appropriate medical records may also lead to a finding of unsatisfactory professional conduct or professional misconduct: *Lindsay v Health Care Complaints Commission* [2004] NSWCA 222. This occurred in *HCCC v Moore* [2008] NSWPST 2, where a psychologist was de-registered for failing to take an adequate clinical history (including the patient's history of child sexual assault) and failing to develop an appropriate treatment plan. This shortcoming was part of a wider pattern of inappropriate behaviour. The psychologist employed a number of inappropriate treatment methods such as 'prismology', the use of crystals, allegedly inserting herself into the patient's dreams, giving the patient liquid remedies (referred to as 'Rescue Remedy', and 'Sexuality Remedy') and giving the patient pink personal items to 'de-masculinise' her. There were a number of gifts made by the psychologist to the patient and the psychologist gave the patient her personal address and that of her father's. Bizarrely the psychologist gave the patient a ring so that the patient would give the ring to the Van Halen brothers (of the 1980s rock group 'Van Halen'). She also had engaged in a sexual relationship with the patient.

Ownership of medical records

In the past, some patients who wished to have access to their records had been denied access by their medical practitioner (usually on legal advice). However, limited rights of access to medical records have been allowed by statute (eg,

Freedom of Information Act 1982 (Cth); *Freedom of Information Act 1989* (NSW)). These statutes allow access to records kept by public institutions (ie public hospitals) upon payment of an appropriate fee. Access may also be gained to records kept by non-government organisations where these organisations are regulated by statute (eg, *Private Hospitals Regulation 1996* (NSW); *Day Procedures Centres Regulation 1996* (NSW)).

The issues of ownership of, and access to, medical records were discussed further in the High Court decision in *Breen v Williams* (1996) 186 CLR 71. In 1977 Ms Breen had a bilateral augmentation mammoplasty (breast enlargement). Thereafter she developed bilateral breast capsules – a painful condition in which fibrous tissue builds up around breast implants. In 1978 she consulted Dr Williams, who was a plastic surgeon, but not the plastic surgeon who performed the implant. Dr Williams advised Ms Breen that the capsules should be compressed and he performed that operation. Ms Breen experienced severe pain and, after two further consultations with her, Dr Williams operated and performed a bilateral capsulotomy. Ms Breen has not consulted Dr Williams since that operation.

Ms Breen became interested in litigation in the United States by way of a class action against the manufacturer of the breast implants claiming that they were defective. Ms Breen sought to have access to the medical records kept by Dr Williams. Dr Williams would only do this if Ms Breen gave him an indemnification from any future legal action against him. Ms Breen did not wish to do this. Ms Breen sought an order that Dr Williams allow her access to her medical records to examine them and obtain copies of the information contained in them. Ms Breen was unsuccessful before both the NSW Supreme Court and the Court of Appeal. A further appeal to the High Court was also unsuccessful.

Following the High Court decision in *Breen v Williams* there can be no doubt that the originator of a medical record is the owner of that record. This is the case whether it is a hospital, nursing home, general practitioner, specialist or independent practitioner. The only exception would be parts of the medical record such as X-rays or pathology reports which have been prepared by other professionals and paid for separately by the patient (see the discussion of Dawson and Toohey JJ in *Breen*). In *Mid-City Skin Cancer and Laser Centre v Zahedi-Anarak* [2006] NSWSC 844, it was said that pathology reports belong to patients and, when they are sent by pathologists to the treating doctor, the doctor takes possession of them on behalf of the patient (in law this is referred to as a *bailment*).

In *Breen v Williams* the High Court decided that there was no general legal right that would allow patients to access their records in the absence of legislation. As a consequence of this decision a number of jurisdictions (including the Commonwealth) have passed 'privacy' legislation to allow patients access to information recorded about them and, where appropriate, have any errors in the record corrected (this is discussed below).

Disputes about the ownership of medical records can also arise between health professionals and their former employers. In *Health Services for Men Pty Ltd v D'Souza* (2000) 48 NSWLR 448 there was a dispute between doctors and the corporate owner of their former practice over who had ownership of the medical records of the practice. The doctors had been asked to use an 'examination sheet' which was basically a standard form used by the doctors to make notes during patient consultation. The NSW Court of Appeal found that the sheet belonged to the corporate owner of the practice and not the doctors. This was a clinic where services were not provided to patients by individual doctors and patients would see whoever was rostered on and available at the time. Large expenditure on advertising for the clinics suggested that patients were patients of the clinic and not of individual doctors. Patients would be invited to the clinic after ringing an information line. All of this evidenced a common intention that ownership of the medical records would commence, and remain, with those who were in control of the whole organisation, and not the individual doctors.

Privacy

'Privacy' is a term that carries different meanings, depending upon the context of its use. Sometimes privacy is equated with liberty or autonomy; at other times with seclusion or solitude. Privacy legislation is primarily concerned with enhancing the protection of information held about a person and allowing that person access to ensure that any information that is held about them is accurate and appropriate for the purpose for which it was collected. Thus privacy legislation has a wider coverage than the obligation of confidence, which deals primarily with issues of the disclosure of information.

There is no general protection of privacy under Australian law and for many years, following the High Court decision in *Victoria Park Racing and Recreation Grounds Co Ltd v Taylor* (1937) 58 CLR 479, it was believed that there was no tort remedy available for breaches of privacy. However, the High Court, in *Australian Broadcasting Corporation v Lenah Game Meats Pty Ltd* (2001) 208 CLR 199, left open the possibility that the equitable doctrine of breach of confidence may be used to fashion a new right of privacy.

This approach has been taken by the House of Lords on numerous occasions. In *Campbell v MGN Limited* [2004] UKHL 22, the House upheld a claim for damages for invasion of privacy. The plaintiff (Ms Campbell) was a well-known fashion model and the defendant was a newspaper that published articles about Ms Campbell, revealing that she was a drug addict who was receiving treatment for her addiction. The newspaper also published photographs of her outside a branch of Narcotics Anonymous. Although Ms Campbell had publicly stated that she did not use illegal drugs (and thus her addiction would be a matter of legitimate public comment) the House of Lords held that the publication of details of her treatment and the photographs constituted a breach of her right to privacy in her private life. This right was based on the equitable doctrine of breach of confidence which was discussed above, but the House of Lords extended its meaning so that it could be said that the UK had laws which protected privacy.

Commonwealth legislation

The *Privacy Act 1988*, as originally enacted, applied principally to Commonwealth and Australian Capital Territory government agencies. The Act contains 11 Information Privacy Principles (IPPs) that cover the collection, storage, security, access and use of personal information. The Act was amended at the end of 2001 to expand coverage to include private sector businesses, including health service providers in private practice. The Act does not affect State and Territory authorities such as public hospitals.

The amended Act introduced 10 National Privacy Principles (NPPs) which legally bind non-government organisations in the way they must collect and handle personal information. The NPPs cover areas such as the collection, use, disclosure, data quality and security, openness, access and correction, identifiers, anonymity, transborder data flows and sensitive information.

Both the IPPs and NPPs control the use and disclosure of health information. Both differentiate between the primary purpose for use and disclosure (which is the dominant reason for the patient consenting to the provision of information) and secondary purposes (which are not the dominant reason for the provision of the information). Use or disclosure of information is permitted if the use or disclosure is related to the primary purpose of collection. Use or disclosure for a secondary purpose is also permitted but only when it directly relates to the primary purpose. For example, the use of personal information to send an invoice for treatment may not have been consented to directly by the patient, but it is sufficiently related to the primary purpose of treatment for the information to be used in that way (Stewart, Kerridge et al 2008).

The IPPs and NPPs have given patients the right to access their health information (IPP 6; NPP 6) which overcomes the problem of *Breen*. However, the right to access is limited and access can be refused if the provision of the record would pose a serious risk to the life or physical, mental or psychological health of the patient or another person. It can also be refused if the provision breaches some other obligation of confidence, for example, legal professional privilege. It can also be refused when the provision of the record would have an unreasonable impact on the privacy of other individuals: *Re F and Osbourne Park Hospital* [2008] WAICmr 44. An example of this is *R (Mrs) v Ballarat Health Services* [2007] VCAT 2397, (which occurred under similar Victorian legislation) where VCAT refused to allow a patient access to entries in her medical records created during her time as an involuntary patient in a mental hospital. The entries related to phone conversations made with other persons. The Tribunal found that the entries were personal and confidentially given, and that there was no justifiable interest in allowing access.

The IPPs and NPPs also give patients the power to correct health records when they contain errors and to demand that the information be properly stored and securely transferred. Issues of secure transfer occurred in *S v Health Service Provider* [2008] PrivCmrA 19, where the Privacy Commissioner found that it was a breach of NPP 4.1 for a health service provider to send a patient's X-rays via the regular post.

Patients also have a right to seek the destruction of records when they are no longer needed (NPP 4.2). However, in *P v Private Health service Provider* [2008] PrivCmrA 16, the Privacy Commissioner found that a patient could not demand the destruction of health records if the records had to be preserved under other laws such as the *Medical Practice Regulation 2003* (NSW) which requires that records be kept for seven years.

The *Privacy Act* allows organisations an option of adopting a 'privacy code', which must be approved by the Federal Privacy Commissioner. An approved privacy code effectively replaces some or all of the NPPs.

Because a strict interpretation of the NPPs may have some undesirable outcomes, the Federal Privacy Commissioner can authorise particular practices by issuing a 'Public Interest Determination'. One of the first issues to arise in this context was the taking of a patient's family history. The collection of health information about a family member is the collection of information from a third party and the NPPs would require that the third party would have to be informed of this and their consent would have to be obtained. The medical profession argued that the taking of a family history was a fundamental part of diagnosis and treatment of a patient and to require that a third party be informed that information about them had been recorded and to gain their consent for such collection would be impractical. The Privacy Commissioner issued Public Interest Determinations 9 and 9A, which make it clear that doctors taking a family history will not be in breach of the NPPs.

New South Wales

The *Privacy and Personal Information Act 1998* covers public sector organisations while the *Health Records and Information Privacy Act 2002* (HRIPA) covers health information held in both the public and private sectors.

The *Health Records and Information Privacy Act* creates 15 'Health Privacy Principles' (HPPs) outlining how health information must be collected, stored, used and disclosed. The Act also allows for the creation of 'Statutory Guidelines' that can vary the application of the HPPs. Four statutory guidelines have been prepared:

- use or disclosure of health information for the management of health services;
- use or disclosure of health information for training purposes;
- use or disclosure of health information for research purposes; and
- notification when collecting health information about a person from someone else.

The HRIPA also sets out how complaints regarding the handling of health information can be dealt with.

Victoria

The *Health Records Act 2001* is broadly similar to the Commonwealth *Privacy Act* with 11 Health Privacy Principles which cover much the same ground as the NPPs but in greater detail and with a health focus. The *Health Records Act* provides protection for a health-care provider against liability for defamation or breach of confidence where a patient is given access to their health information under the terms of the Act.

Australian Capital Territory

The *Health Records (Privacy and Access) Act 1997* has removed health records from the jurisdiction of the Federal Privacy Commissioner and placed it in the hands of the ACT Human Rights Commissioner. The Act contains Privacy Principles based on the Commonwealth IPPs and gives people access to their own health records in both the public and private sectors.

Defences to breaches of confidentiality and privacy

Neither the obligation to maintain confidence nor the statutory rights of privacy are absolute. There are a number of exceptions and defences, including the following:

Express or implied consent of the patient

As discussed above, use and disclosure of confidential information is limited by the patient's consent, whether it be express or implied. This is also recognised in all the statutory regimes: *Privacy Act 1988* (Cth) IPP 10, NPP 2(b); *Health Records and Information Privacy Act 2002* (NSW), HPP 10(1)(e); *Health Records Act 2001* (Vic), HPP 2.2(b); *Health Records (Privacy and Access) Act 1997* (ACT), PP 9(a).

Overriding duty to the public

Both equity and the privacy regimes recognise that in some circumstances the obligation to protect a patient's confidence may be overridden by the need to protect others or the public generally: *Privacy Act 1988* (Cth) NPP 2.1(e); *Health Records and Information Privacy Act 2002* (NSW), HPP 10(1)(c); *Health Records Act 2001* (Vic), HPP 2.2(h); *Health Records (Privacy and Access) Act 1997* (ACT), PP 9.1(b).

A balancing exercise must be undertaken in order to determine whether the interests of the public outweigh the interests of the individual. An example of the application of this principle can be found in the English case of *W v Egdell* [1990] 1 All ER 835.

A paranoid schizophrenic patient, detained indefinitely in a secure hospital for the killing of five people years earlier, requested a consultant psychiatrist to prepare a report which the detainee intended to rely on for the purposes of obtaining a discharge from detention. The report was unfavourable and the detainee withdrew his application which was to have been heard before a mental health review tribunal. However, the psychiatrist released copies of the report without the detainee's permission to the authorities. An action was brought against the psychiatrist for breach of confidentiality. The court held that the psychiatrist's duty to the patient was overridden by the duty to the public, in that the public interest required the practitioner to place his report and opinions before the appropriate authorities because of the potential danger to the public.

As mentioned previously, in the US case of *Tarasoff v Regents of the University of California* 551 P 2d 334 (1976), it was found that there may be circumstances where there is an obligation to breach a confidence in order to protect a known person. This case must be relied on with caution as the application of this principle has not been considered by Australian courts. It should also be noted that even in the US the principle has not been followed, or distinguished, in about the same proportion of cases as it has been followed.

In the context of a hearing concerning professional misconduct the Psychologists Registration Board of Victoria in *Re Noble* [2002] PRBD (Vic) 6 gave some consideration to this issue and stated:

> The panel accepts that there are some extreme circumstances such as those articulated in the Canadian Supreme Court decision of *Smith v Jones* (1999) 132 CCC (3d) 225 where a psychologist should disclose information learned in the course of a confidential relationship in order to protect persons at risk. However, the criteria set out by the majority of the court in that decision make it clear how high the bar is raised against breach of confidentiality:
>> 'First, is there a clear risk to an identifiable person or group of persons?
>> Second, is there a risk of serious bodily harm or death?
>> Third, is the danger imminent?'

The requirement of an 'imminent threat' in the privacy legislation is an imprecise term that indicates that the risk may soon result in harm. The Federal Privacy Commissioner has indicated that this would mean days or weeks, depending on the risk: Office of the Federal Privacy Commissioner (2001). Interestingly, in the ACT the requirement is not limited to 'imminent' threats. The disclosure must be necessary 'to prevent or lessen a significant risk to the life or physical, mental or emotional health of the consumer or another person' (PP 9.1(b)).

Mandatory disclosure under compulsion of law

There are many instances where the law allows or even requires the disclosure of confidential information.

The common law can require that in judicial or quasi-judicial proceedings communications between health-care professionals and patients may have to be divulged. There is no general doctor-patient privilege (ie, the confidentiality of communications between doctors and patients does not carry into the courtroom). Even though there is no general privilege, courts have a discretion to prevent the disclosure of information where the court considers this necessary (*Hunter v Mann* [1974] 2 WLR 742 at 746). Some jurisdictions (*Evidence Act 2001* (Tas), s 127A; *Evidence Act 1958* (Vic), s 28 (but see *Evidence Act 2008* (Vic), Part 3.10); and *Evidence Act* (NT), s 12(2)) allow doctor-patient privilege in civil proceedings only: *Elliot v Tippett* [2008] VSC 175. The New South Wales and Victorian *Evidence Acts* contain provisions to allow a limited privilege for communications between counsellors and victims of sexual assault in order to prevent notes being made available to the defendant.

Some of these issues were discussed in *Royal Women's Hospital v Medical Practitioners Board of Victoria* (2006) 15 VR 22. In that case the hospital refused to supply health records to the Medical Practitioners Board of Victoria. The Board sought the records as part of an investigation sparked by Senator Julian McGauran, into a late-term abortion that had been performed in the hospital.

The abortion had been performed as the child had been diagnosed with dwarfism and the pregnant woman had threatened self-harm should an abortion not be performed. The Senator alleged that the child had been misdiagnosed and made a complaint to the Medical Board.

The main thrust of the hospital's argument was that there was a public interest immunity which protected it from the Board's power of investigation. Public interest immunity is normally claimed by government officials and members of the executive to keep sensitive governmental information secret. The Victorian Court of Appeal found that the hospital had no right to claim such an immunity and that the Board's powers of investigation could not be resisted. The doctors were later cleared of misconduct by the Board (Stewart 2007).

Questions arise in civil proceedings between patients and their doctors whether patient have waived their rights of confidentiality over their medical records. Health professionals often seek access to the medical records to defend themselves against claims of negligence. Sometimes the breaching of confidence in these circumstances is classed as protecting the public interest in the administration of justice. In *Campbell v Tameside Metropolitan Borough Council* [1982] QB 1065, a teacher brought an action in negligence against an education authority after she was badly beaten by a student. In pursuance of her claim she sought access to the authority's psychological assessment records to prove that the authority had been aware of the student's mental instability. The Court of Appeal found that the public interest in allowing the teacher to properly litigate her claim was of enough weight to override the authority's duty of confidence to the student.

However, this approach has not always found favour in Australia. In *Richards v Kadian* [2005] NSWCA 328, the NSW Court of Appeal refused to follow this line of thought. The child plaintiff had brought proceedings against his doctor, alleging that the doctor had been negligent in failing to diagnose a congenital heart condition. In preparing a defence to the claim, the doctor sought to interview the child's treating specialists. Access had been granted to the specialists' records but the plaintiff refused to give the specialist permission to be interviewed. It was argued by the defendant doctor that the obligations of confidence had been waived by the plaintiff when the action had commenced. The court found that, in order for the obligations of confidence to have been waived, there had to be an identifiable public interest which went beyond the effects on the private rights of the parties. As no other public interests were affected by the confidentiality apart from those of the parties, the court refused to find that the obligations of confidence had been waived.

Providing information to relatives

Generally speaking it is a breach of both the equitable duty and privacy statutes to give relatives health information without the consent of the patient. Obviously an exception exists for disclosure to the person's substitute decision-maker, if the patient is incompetent: *Privacy Act 1988* (Cth) NPP 2.4; *Health Records and Information Privacy Act 2002* (NSW), ss 7-8; *Health Records Act 2001* (Vic), HPP 2.2(d); *Health Records (Privacy and Access) Act 1997* (ACT), PP 10.4.

There is also an exception for disclosure in the Federal NPP 2.4, for disclosure to the person responsible for the care of the patient, if the disclosure is made for compassionate reasons and is not contrary to any wish expressed by the patient. Similar provisions can be found in the other jurisdictions. In the ACT, disclosure to relatives without the consent of the patient or substitute decision-maker is permissible if it is made for compassionate reasons, there are reasonable grounds for believing that the disclosure would have been expected by the patient and the disclosure is not contrary to the patient's express wishes: *Health Records (Privacy and Access) Act 1997* (ACT), PP 6.3.

In NSW and Victoria it is an added requirement that the disclosure not be made to a relative under the age of 18 years, unless the health professional reasonably believes that the child has sufficient maturity to receive the information: *Health Records and Information Privacy Act 2002* (NSW), HPP 11(1)(g); *Health Records Act 2001* (Vic), HPP 2.4 but see also *Health Services Act 1988* (Vic), s 141(3)(c)(ii).

An exception also exists in the *Privacy Act 1988* (Cth) for the disclosure of genetic information to a relative, when the genetic information has been obtained in the course of providing a health service to a patient. The genetic information can be disclosed to the 'genetic relative' of the patient if the disclosure is necessary to lessen or prevent a serious threat to the life, health or safety (whether or not the threat is imminent) of the relative. This is discussed further in Chapter 17.

Providing information to other health professionals

All members of a treatment team are entitled to view patient information, either because consent has been given expressly or impliedly or because the use is related to the primary purpose for which it was collected. Express permission is given for such use in the *Health Records (Privacy and Access) Act 1997* (ACT), PP 6.1, 9.1-9.3, 10.2. The *Health Services Act 2001* (Vic) also allows for disclosure when necessary for patient care or further treatment and support functions (Skene 2008).

Quality assurance, management and training

Privacy legislation also allows for medical records to be used without consent for use in quality assurance and training: *Health Records and Information Privacy Act 2002* (NSW), HPP 10(d)-(e), 11(1)(d)-(e); *Health Administration Act 1982* (NSW), s 20J; *Health Records Act 2001* (Vic), HPP 2(f); *Health Services Act 1988* (Vic), s 139(5); *Health Records (Privacy and Access) Act 1997* (ACT), PP 9.1(e) and 10.2(f).

Medical research

Privacy legislation does allow for access for research purposes without consent if approval is given for such access by an ethics committee, properly constituted under the *National Health and Medical Research Council Act 1992* (Cth). The committees can only give approval if seeking the consent of patients is impractical, and where the public benefit in allowing the research outweighs the public benefit in the maintenance of privacy. Each jurisdiction has requirements on the type of information that must be provided to an ethics committee in its assessment. The *Privacy Act 1988* (Cth) does this through ss 95-95A, in NSW via HPP 10(f), in Victoria the disclosure is governed by HPP 2(g) and in ACT through PP 10.3. Both NSW and Victoria also have statutory guidelines for controlling the disclosure for research (see above).

Mandatory reporting

There are many reporting requirements that authorise and sometimes mandate reporting of health information without consent. For example, public health legislation may require notification of cases of infectious diseases to health authorities (see Chapter 28) or for mental health problems in people who own firearms: *Firearms Act 1996* (NSW), s 79; *Weapons Act 1990* (Qld), s 151; *Firearms Regulations 1993* (SA), r 44; *Firearms Act 1996* (Tas); *Firearms Act 1996* (Vic), s 183; *Firearms Act 1973* (WA), s 23B; *Firearms Act 1996* (ACT), s 115. Driving authorities may also have to be notified when a health professional believes that a driver is impaired: *Road Transport (Driver Licensing) Regulation 1999* (NSW), cl 31; *Transport Operations (Road Use Management) Act 1995* (Qld), s 142; *Motor Vehicles Act 1959* (SA), s 148; *Vehicle and Traffic Act 1999* (Tas), s 63; *Road Safety Act 1986* (Vic), s 27; *Road Transport (Driver Licensing) Regulation 2000* (ACT), s 78; *Motor Vehicles Act 1999* (NT), s 11.

Most jurisdictions require the notification of suspected child abuse: *Children and Young Persons (Care and Protection) Act 1998* (NSW); *Public Health Act 2005* (Qld); *Children's Protection Act 1993* (SA); *Children, Young Persons and Their Families Act 1997* (Tas); *Children and Young Persons Act 1989* (Vic); *Children and Young People Act 1999* (ACT); *Care and Protection of Children Act 2007* (NT). In Tasmania, the *Family Violence Act 2004* requires health professionals to report suspected family violence, although at the time of writing this section (s 38) had not yet commenced.

The impairment of health-care professionals is also reportable in some jurisdictions (this is discussed in Chapter 7).

Finally, there is a general common law requirement to report a crime. The crime of misprision of felony applies to a failure to report serious criminal activity. A person commits the offence if he or she fails to disclose his or her knowledge of a crime to those responsible for the administration of justice. Doctor/patient confidentiality may provide a reasonable excuse for non-disclosure for the purpose of misprision of felony (Stewart, Kerridge et al 2008).

In NSW, s 316 of the *Crimes Act 1900* (NSW) also obliges a person to notify police when they possess information that will be of 'material assistance' in securing the conviction of an offender. The punishment for failing to report is two years' imprisonment. The regulations state that a prosecution for an offence under this law is not to be commenced against a medical practitioner, psychologist, nurse, social worker or researcher without the approval of the Attorney General.

Equity excuses a breach of confidence when the confidential information related to a crime or other kinds of misconduct: *Gartside v Outram* (1856) 26 LJ Ch 113. The statutory privacy regimes allow the disclosure of information when there is suspected unlawful activity: *Privacy Act 1988* (Cth) NPP 2.1(f) and (h); *Health Records and Information Privacy Act 2002* (NSW), HPP 10(1)(h), 11(1)(i); *Health Records Act 2001* (Vic), HPP 2.2(i).

References

American College of Occupational and Environmental Health (1995) 'Position on the confidentiality of medical information in the workplace'. *J Occup Environ Health* **37**(5): 594-6.

Anderson, E (1990) 'Is women's labour a commodity?' *Philosophy and Public Affairs* **19**(1): 71-92.

Anderson, J (2000) 'Security of the distributed electronic patient record: a case-based approach to identifying policy issues'. *International Journal of Medical Informatics* **60**(2): 111-18.

Beauchamp, T and J Childress (2009) *Principles of biomedical ethics* (6th ed). New York, Oxford University Press.

Bok, S (1982) *Secrets: on the ethics of concealment and revelation*. New York, Pantheon Books.

Bomba, B, J Cooper et al (1995) 'Working towards a national health information system in Australia'. *Medinfo* **8 Pt 2**: 1633.

Carlisle, J, D Shickle et al (2006) 'Concerns over confidentiality may deter adolescents from consulting their doctors. A qualitative exploration'. *J Med Ethics* **32**: 133-7.

Clamp, S and J Keen (2007) 'Electronic health records: is the evidence base any use?' *Med Inform Internet med.* **32**(1): 5-10.

Field, S (1997) Documentation in Health Care. *Health Care Law and Ethics*. L Shotton. Katoomba, Social Science Press.

Gilhooly, M and S McGhee (1991) 'Medical records: practicalities and principles of patient possession'. *J Med Ethics* **17**: 138-43.

Hamblin, J (1992) 'Confidentiality, public interest and the health professional's duty of care'. *Australian Health Review* **15**: 422-34.

Herdy, WM (1996) 'Must the doctor tell?'. *J Law Med* **270**: 270.

Hodge, J, L Gostin et al (1999) 'Privacy, Quality, and Liability'. *JAMA* **282**: 1466-71.

Jenkins, G, J Merz et al (2005) 'The qualitative study of women's views on medical confidentiality'. *J Med Ethics* **31**: 499-504.

Oakley, J (1997) The morality of breaching confidentiality to protect others. *Health Care Law and Ethics*. L Shelton. Katoomba, Social Science Press.

Olsen, J and B Sabin (2003) 'Emergency department patient perceptions of privacy and confidentiality'. *J Emerg Med* **25**: 329-33.

Perez-Carceles, M, J Pereniguez et al (2005) 'Balancing confidentiality and the information provided to families of patients in primary care'. *J Med Ethics* **31**: 531-5.

Roth, L, J Wolford et al (1980) 'Patient access to records: tonic or toxin'. *Am J Psychiatry* **137**: 592-6.

Sankar, P, S Mora et al (2003) 'Patient perspectives on medical confidentiality: a review of he literature'. *J Gen Intern Med* **18**: 659-69.

Schmidt, B (1983) 'Confidentiality in psychiatry. A study of the patient's view'. *Hosp Comm Psych* **34**: 353-5.

Siegler, M (1982) 'Confidentiality in medicine – a decrepit concept'. *N Engl J Med* **307**: 1518-21.

Stewart, C, I Kerridge et al (2008) *The Australian medico-legal handbook*. Sydney, Churchill Livingstone Elsevier.

van der Kam, W, P Mooman et al (2000) 'Effects of electronic communication in general practice'. *Jn Medical Informatics* **60**(1): 59-70.

Vigod, S, C Bell et al (2003) 'Privacy of patients' information in hospital lifts: observational study'. *BMJ* **327**: 1024-5.

Weiss, B (1982) 'Confidentiality expectations of patients, physicians and medical students'. *JAMA* **247**: 2695-7.

Wyatt, J (1994) 'Clinical data systems Pt 1. Data and medical records'. *Lancet* **334**: 1543-7.

Young, A, E Chaney et al (2007) 'Information technology to support improved care for chronic illness'. *J Gen Intern Med* **22**(Suppl 3): 425-30.

CHAPTER 13

IMPAIRMENTS OF DECISION-MAKING CAPACITY

Case 1

JG is a 67-year-old man who lives in a boarding house. He spends his days wandering through the city streets, picking up rubbish. He has no close family, and since arguing with the boarding-house proprietor has had no other friends. He was admitted to hospital when the boarding-house proprietor noted that he was looking increasingly unwell and had not left his room for several days.

In hospital he was found to be in complete heart block and required the insertion of a pacemaker in order to maintain enough cardiac output to be able to walk. In discussions with him about this, his replies did not appear to make sense, as he mostly seemed to talk about the 'Japanese coming to get him'. It was felt that he was unable to make decisions for himself, so his case was referred to the Guardianship Tribunal.

Case 2

EF is a 24-year-old man who was born with complicated congenital deformities and has spent his life being cared for by his mother. He spends his day either lying in a bed or being wheeled around in a modified wheel chair. He smiles at times although his mother has never heard him speak. He has had recurrent admissions with urinary infections that are thought to be due to kidney stones and is known to have a large staghorn calculus in one kidney. On one of these admissions it was suggested that nephrectomy (removal of a kidney) should be performed to prevent further recurrences. His mother was concerned that this would cause him more pain and suffering and decided not to go ahead with this, but rather to accept the fact that he was likely to need repeated admissions

Case 3

GH is a 32-year-old man with known HIV. He was brought by his partner to the out-patient clinic, febrile and delirious with a one-week history of cough. His oxygen saturation was 52%. According to his partner, Mr H had noticed his memory declining for several months and often forgot to take his medications. His partner stated that he did not believe that Mr H would benefit from ventilation and produced a document signed by Mr H that assigned all decision-making responsibilities to his partner.

A central tenet of modern bioethics is the concept of autonomy – the idea that individuals have the right to make decisions about their own medical care. However not all people are able to make decisions about themselves – some, in particular, do not have the mental abilities to do so.

There are two different terminologies used for describing this situation: impaired 'competence', and impaired 'decision-making capacity'. Some authors make a distinction between these two terms, referring to 'competency' as a legal decision made by judge that a patient is able to make medical decisions for themselves; and 'decision-making capacity' as a physician's determination based on clinical examination that a patient is able to make medical decisions for themselves (Arnold 2006). In the clinical setting, these terms are often used interchangeably. In this book we mostly use the term 'competence' or 'mental competence', apart from where it is confusing due to other meanings of the word (such as professional 'competence').

Mental competence can be seen as a continuum, with some patients unable to make any decision for themselves; with others who are fully autonomous; and with many who fall somewhere between these extremes. One of the difficulties with the concept of competence is that there are no objective, universally defined, standards for assessing patients' competence. Various criteria for assessing competence have been suggested including: rationality of choice (Stanley, Stanley et al 1988; Marson, Cody et al 1995), reasonableness of choice, evidence of choice (Marson, Ingram et al 1995), or patients' understanding (Fitten, Lusky et al 1990) or appreciation of their situation (Hoffman and Srinivasan 1992).

Authors such as Pellegrino (Pellegrino and Thomasma 1981) have identified a number of capacities that they believe make up the concept of competence (such as the capacity to receive, comprehend, retain and recall relevant information, the capacity to integrate the information received and relate it to one's self/own situation, the capacity to evaluate benefits and risks in terms of personal values, etc). Yet this approach is also open to question as there are no agreed standards for how capacities are to be assessed or integrated into the overall assessment of competence (Sugarman, McCrory et al 1998).

There is also uncertainty about how to approach decision-making once a patient is found to be incompetent. In general, decisions need to be made by a surrogate such as a family member, who must attempt either to consider the patient's best interests, consider what the patient would wish to do in the circumstance ('substituted judgment'), or refer to an 'advance directive'. There are problems associated with all of these approaches, and each may be inappropriate if it is poorly understood or poorly applied.

Cognitive testing

It is generally assumed that people are competent to make decisions about their own health care unless proven otherwise. It is therefore important that health professionals are alert to the factors that may impair cognitive capacity. Unfortunately, while only 5% of those aged over 68 have significant cognitive impairment, mild to moderate cognitive impairment goes undiagnosed in about 60% of patients in inpatient and primary care settings and even up to 50% of family members of cognitively impaired relatives may fail to recognise their impairments (Boustani, Callahan et al 2005; Watson, Lewis et al 2005).

Cognitive testing plays an important role in assessing competence and establishing whether a person has impaired decisional capacity. Cognitive testing looks at whether a person has adequate intellectual functions to be oriented to time, place and person; to recognise objects, to speak, to remember things, etc. Cognitive tests can only look at a small subset of normal mental functions, but they give some idea about a person's overall level of intellectual ability.

One way of screening for impairments of cognitive function is to ask patients to state the exact day and date. Although about 25% of unimpaired persons (including the authors) will be unable to answer such a question, very few cognitively impaired patients will be able to answer this question correctly (Sapira 1990). If a person answers this correctly, they are probably cognitively intact.

The next stage of cognitive testing consists of the use of a more formal test such as the Mini-Mental State Examination (MMSE) (Folstein, Folstein et al 1975). This is a well-validated questionnaire that is extensively used, especially for the elderly. MMSEs may yield false-negative results in some forms of cognitive impairment such as frontal lobe or non-dominant lobe damage and can also be influenced by age, and verbal ability. Low educational levels (finishing school before the age of nine) increase the likelihood that normal patients will be misclassified as impaired. High education levels lead to an increased chance that an impaired patient will be misclassified as normal (Tomaugh and McIntyre 1992). The MMSE is also, to some extent, culture-specific and alternative tests are available for some cultures. For example, Aboriginal people in Northern Australia may be assessed with the Kimberley Indigenous Competence Assessment tool (see <http://www.healthykimberley.com.au/chronicdisease.html>).

When assessing cognitive function it is important to take into account factors that may influence patients' mental abilities, such as their mood, the presence of significant co-morbidity and the environment in which they are being tested. Patients may not be capable of rationality if they are tired, anxious, stressed or under the effects of medication. Elderly patients may be better assessed in their own homes than in the intimidating environment of a hospital (Finucaine, Myser et al 1993).

The most immediate action after an assessment that a patient is cognitively impaired is to diagnose the cause of the disorder. Between 10% and 40% of patients in acute medical or surgical wards will have an organic brain syndrome, often due to medications or infection. If reversible factors can be identified, then it may be possible to return a patient to a normal cognitive state.

Integrating cognitive testing into a competence assessment

It is often emphasised that cognitive function is only one of the capacities required to make competent decisions and there may frequently be a disparity between cognitive capacity and competency. For example, psychotic patients may be cognitively intact but may lack decision-making capacity, and some cognitively impaired patients, such as those with Alzheimer's disease, may be able to make less complicated decisions (Rosin and van Dijk 2005; Kitamura and Takahashi 2007; Moye and Marson 2007).

In general, assessment of competence should not be based solely on cognitive assessments, although a partial exception to this rule occurs with elderly patients. Cognitive deficits are common in the elderly due to the onset of dementia or the presence of delirium. These are also common causes of diminished decision-making capacity in the elderly. It may therefore be possible to use cognitive testing as a more reliable indication of competence in the elderly than in younger people, where cognition and decision-making capacity may not be so tightly linked. (Molloy, Silberfeld et al 1996).

A large number of measures are available that attempt to assess competence, or decisional capacity, rather than simply cognitive function (Dunn, Nowrangi et al 2006). While some of these instruments have established psychometric validity and reliability, all have limitations and it is often unclear how the thresholds they use to establish competence or the domains they use to measure competence should be applied in different contexts and with different decisions. Of the available instruments, the MacArthur Competence Assessment Tools for Treatment and Clinical Research are the most comprehensive and have been the most widely validated (Appelbaum and Grisso 1997; Appelbaum, Grisso et al 1999). While these instruments may provide aids to capacity assessment, none is capable of integrating assessment of a wide range of factors that affect competency; all make questionable assumptions about the importance, definition and measurement of the different components of competence, including 'reasoning' and 'understanding'; few account for 'executive function' (the capacity to actually carry out a decision or enact a preference) or the patient's values or narrative; none replicates the complexity and richness of clinical decisions; and none is a substitute for clinical judgment or for carefully constructed discussions with the patient and those around them (Breden and Vollmann 2004; Lai and Karlawish 2007; Moye and Marson 2007).

Rationality

Health professionals tend to place great emphasis on rationality, but competent patients need only to be sufficiently rational to understand and reflect on their conditions in accordance with their own belief systems.

The term 'rational' is difficult to define. It may be applied to persons, actions or beliefs. A rational person may therefore be someone who is a reasonable, sensible or logical thinker. In economics, a rational action is one that maximises self-interest and an irrational action is that one that harms an agent or leaves them worse off. Beliefs may be rational if they are comprehensible to us or if we understand them. These senses of the word may also disagree so, for example, a person who sacrifices him or herself for a cause may be acting for a comprehensible belief but not in a self-interested way, and a person may in general be a reasonable person but may on occasion act in an incomprehensible manner (Elliott 1996).

When we are considering whether an act is rational we should ask whether the person is 'reasonable' or 'sensible' according to broadly held social or cultural norms, whether the act is in the person's best interest and whether their beliefs are in some way comprehensible. We should then attempt to form a judgment out of these three factors.

Another approach to rationality describes three types of rationality: substantive, formal and procedural rationality (Junermann 1986). According to this approach, decisions are substantively rational if they are realistic, formally rational if they are in agreement with the values and beliefs of the individual making the decision, and procedurally rational if they are based on a careful and neutral assessment of all relevant information.

This classification of rationality demonstrates many of the problems associated with applying standards of rationality to judgments of competence. First, the question as to what constitutes the 'real' world is frequently central to disputes regarding competence and often incorporates the values and perspectives of the observer. Secondly, decisions may have internal consistency or coherence and yet still be open to question, as what may appear rational to one person may seem irrational to another. Thirdly, decisions are rarely, if ever, based only on information, but are a much more complex phenomenon. A broad range of factors influence the decisions or judgments that people make about their own care and about those they care for, including information, beliefs, emotions (Nussbaum 2001), fears, the weight of prior experience, a sense of responsibility to others, and a desire to avoid regretting the outcomes that may result from our actions (Gilovich and Medvec 1995). Fourthly, decisions are frequently so complex, particularly in contemporary health care, that even if individuals were able to only consider information relevant to a decision, they would not have the time or cognitive capacity to consider all relevant information. Finally, when people are required to make decisions about health care, or indeed any major decision, they generally do not (and can not) act completely rationally by weighing up all relevant data, but often construct simple models (or heuristics) that take account of the data that they believe to be most important and the biases, process or values that they hold dear (Tversky and Kahneman 1974).

No clear consensus exists as to how free and rational a decision must be or how much irrationality must be displayed before a patient or a decision should be considered incompetent. Under the stress of illness, decisions made by competent patients may vary markedly in their degree of apparent rationality.

How should standards of competence vary with different decisions?

It is frequently stated that the degree of competence required varies with the decision in question. Yet it is not clear exactly how different decisions affect acceptable standards of competence. There are two main schools of thought about this: (a) that the degree of competence required depends on the severity of the consequences of the decision, and (b) that the degree of competence required varies only with the complexity of the decision.

Some forms of decision-making have easily defined parameters, and the corresponding capacities required by patients may also be easily defined. For example, in the case of a patient who needs their leg amputated for gangrene,

247

there are really only two outcomes that need to be considered – death from sepsis or survival with an amputation. If a patient is capable of deciding between these choices, they are competent to make the decision.

There are some more complex types of decision whose parameters have been formally defined in law. For example, in filling out a will the capacities required include having enough long-term memory to remember the claims of various heirs, enough comprehension and judgment to understand what a will is; and enough immediate memory or registration to apply to the task of making the will (Peisah and Brodaty 1994). Each of these capacities can be specifically tested, and it may therefore be possible to get a good idea as to whether a person is capable of making a will through specific tests of individual cognitive functions.

However, there are also some situations in which the exact capacities re-quired to make decisions are not so clearly defined. An example might be a com-plex choice between a number of different forms of therapy. A logical approach to assessing competence in decisions like this might be to carefully work through the decision with the patient, assessing his or her rationality at each point. Yet working through a decision like this may place a patient in an unfair situation as it leads to a type of circular reasoning. If a patient's decision forms the basis of the examiner's assessment of their competence, then the examiner might disallow decisions that he or she disagrees with. Indeed, according to Finucaine, 'it is remarkable how often a question of competence arises because a patient's wishes conflict with those of his or her doctor' (Finucaine, Myser et al 1993).

Furthermore, while some decisions may be easy to work through, other decisions lead inevitably to a range of further decisions. For example, decisions about accommodation may lead to further decisions about food, cleanliness, mobility, safety, finances and acceptance of services. These may, in turn, require many more capacities than can be easily recognised. In these situations, rather than working through each of these decisions, the assessment of patients' general capacities (through cognitive or neuro-psychological testing) might be parti-cularly useful.

A different model of competence was proposed by Alexander (Alexander 1988; Lowe et al 2000; Hurst 2004). Alexander suggests that there are a number of different properties that define competent behaviour. First, there is the capacity to recognise that a purposeful decision-making response is required; secondly, there is the capacity to activate the cognitive mechanisms necessary to process the decision; and, thirdly, there is the capacity required for implementation of the decision's resolution. Alexander's model differs from Beauchamp and Childress' and Pellegrino's model in that their attentions appear to occupy only the second of his three properties. Alexander's view is that each of his properties of compe-tence can be understood in terms of specific neurological capacities. Patients may lose specific capacities that make them incompetent for some decisions yet not for others, although the decisions may have equal risks or equal complexity.

Such considerations suggest that the degrees of competence required for individual decisions vary in both quantity and quality. Patients require different levels of competence depending on the complexity of the decision and (perhaps) on the severity of its consequences. But they also require different types of com-petence for different types of decision.

Clinical assessment of competence

How can we put all of these factors together? It seems that, in general, the assessment of competence requires consideration of three different domains. *Qualitative factors* are those that vary with the type of the decision – people need different types of competence to deal with different types of decisions. *Quantitative factors* depend on the complexity of the decision – more complicated decisions require greater competence. The *degree of certainty* that is required about a person's competence depends on the severity of the consequences of the decision – a patient's decision that has very severe consequences should only be accepted if one is relatively certain about their degree of competence!

In the table below (Table 11.1) we provide a model for managing situations where questions about a patient's decisional competence arise in clinical care that looks at each of these factors in a systematic way (Lowe, Kerridge et al 2000; Barilan and Weintraub 2001; Hurst 2004).

Table 11.1: A model for managing decisional competence in health care

1.   Assess the problem:

How complex is it?

What are its consequences?

What qualitative aspects require consideration?

2.   Assess the patient's decision

If it appears rational, accept it.

If the decision does not appear rational, or if it is unclear and the consequences are great:

   (a) Identify (where possible) the cognitive factors involved in the decision using tests of capacity, such as the MMSE, and decisional competence, such as the MacCAT-T, where appropriate.

   (b) Identify the patient's broader cognitive state, paying particular attention to the factors in (a).

3.   If the patient's broader cognitive state, and the cognitive factors required for the decision are adequate, accept the decision. If they are not adequate:

   (a) 'Defuse' the decision if possible by changing the complexity or consequences of the decision.

   (b) Otherwise attempt to persuade the patient of an alternative course of action/decision or consider overriding the patient's decision to protect his or her best interests and/or advance his or her established preferences for care.

Who should decide for patients with impaired capacity?

Once it is clear that a person has impaired decision-making capacity, we may then be faced with the question as to how best to make decisions for them. One of the first questions is *who* should make decisions for them?

In emergency situations (where treatment is immediately necessary to save a person's life or prevent serious deterioration of their condition) it may not be possible, or appropriate, to establish a patient's wishes or even to identify the relevant surrogate decision-maker. In these situations patients may be treated without their explicit consent according to an assessment of their medical best interests. Such treatment should, where possible, be the least restrictive of the patient's future choices. This type of 'emergency provision' for decision-making should also cease when the patient regains capacity or where an appropriate surrogate decision-maker is identified, regardless of the clinical circumstances.

In general, family members, acting in concert with the health-care team, are the usual, and the preferred, people who should be making decisions for incompetent patients. There are a number of reasons why family members are best suited for this role – including that family members are often the people most affected by decisions about the patient, that family members are often the people preferred by patients to make decisions, and that family members may best be able to predict what patients would wish to do (and hence preserve some measure of their autonomy) (Arnold and Kellum 2003).

Family decision-making in Western societies often occurs by consensus. In other societies, the oldest son, or another relative may have a formal position as the decision-maker. 'Family' must also be interpreted loosely in some situations, a gay or lesbian partner or close friend may sometimes be better considered family than the biological or legal relatives. According to the NHMRC:

> [T]he term 'family' should be understood broadly to include those closest in knowledge, care and affection to the person in PCU or MRS. This may include the immediate biological family, the family of acquisition (related by marriage/contract), as well as the family of choice and friends (not related biologically or by marriage or contract). For Aboriginal and Torres Strait Islander peoples, it may also include traditional kinship groups and structures. (National Health and Medical Research Council 2007)

Some of the most difficult situations in health care occur when families cannot agree, or where families disagree with other close friends or partners.

When family decision-making becomes too complex, or if there are legal connotations to the decision-making (such as managing the person's money), a formal representative of the person may be appointed. There are three ways in which someone may become a person's legal representative':

(a) the representative was appointed by the person before he or she became incapable of making decisions about his or her medical treatment;

(b) the representative is appointed by a court or tribunal after the person has become incapable of making such decisions; or

(c) the representative has legal authority conferred automatically by statute, for example, as the person's spouse, carer, other next of kin or close friend. (National Health and Medical Research Council 2007) (For further discussion see section below.)

Once it is clear who should make the decisions, we must then consider how to make the decision This question is often approached by looking at three 'standards' for decision-making for patients with impaired capacity – 'best interests', 'substituted judgments' and 'advance directives'.

Best interests

The 'best interests' standard of decision-making for incompetent patients requires surrogate decision-makers to make the decision that provides the maximum anticipated benefit to patients. Best-interests judgments are consequentialist assessments that are based primarily on the principles of beneficence and non-maleficence. They involves assessment of the benefits and burdens of each therapeutic alternative including consideration of pain, disability and quality of life. A best-interests standard of decision-making is patient-centred, excludes consideration of the interests of others and focuses on the patients' current needs (Griffith 1991). On the basis of best-interests standards, surrogate decision-makers may decide whether treatment is clearly beneficial – and is therefore morally required; futile – and may be withheld or withdrawn; or offers uncertain benefits – and is thus dependent on the judgment of the surrogate decision-maker (President's Commission for the Study of Ethical Problems in Medicine and Biomedical and Behavioural Research 1983).

Best-interests judgments have been widely used in health care, particularly in decisions for never-competent patients (eg, children) and for previously competent adult patients whose prior preferences cannot be ascertained. However, there are several problems that are associated with best-interests judgments. Best-interests decisions often involve quality-of-life assessments, yet judgments about quality of life depend greatly on the values of the person making the assessment and the factors included in the assessment. This may lead to conflicts when there are differing views about what constitutes a person's best interests. For example, the parents of a Jehovah's Witness child might refuse their child a blood transfusion based on their religious views of the child's best interests, whereas medical views of the child's best interests may be dominated by the fact that the transfusion is life-saving.

Despite these problems, health professionals are morally required to make best-interests judgments in many situations, particularly in the care of children and neonates.

'Substituted judgments'

A different standard of decision-making based on 'substituted judgments' has been proposed as a way to overcome some of the problems with the 'best interests' standard. Substituted judgments are decisions in which proxy decision-makers, who are often partners or close family members, attempt to reach the same decision that the patient would reach if he or she were competent. It is based on the premise that decisions about treatment belong to the incompetent patient by virtue of respect for autonomy.

Substituted judgments cannot be made for patients who have never been competent as no basis exists for a judgment of autonomous choice if a patient has never experienced autonomy. The standard should only be used for previously competent patients where a belief exists that a decision can be made as the patient would have made it. Substituted judgments are most valid where the patient has clearly expressed their wishes before becoming incompetent. In the absence of clearly stated preferences, substituted judgment may sometimes be inferred from the surrogate's understanding of the patient's actions, value system and beliefs. The most important aspect of substituted decision-making is therefore that the surrogate must truly know the patient.

Unfortunately, a large number of studies have found that patients infrequently discuss treatment issues with their surrogates (High 1988), that surrogates (including family members) frequently disagree (30-50%) with patients (Hare, Pratt et al 1992) and that there is a substantial lack of accuracy in surrogate determinations of patient preferences for care under diverse clinical circumstances (Ouslander, Tymchuk and Rahbar 1989; Zweibel and Cassel 1989; Tomlinson, Howe et al 1990). A recent systematic review of surrogate decision-making established that patient-designated and next-of-kin surrogates incorrectly predict patient's end-of-life preferences in one third of cases and that the two most widely endorsed methods for improving surrogate accuracy, patient designation of surrogates and prior discussion of patient preferences, do not improve surrogate accuracy (Shalowitz, Garrett-Mayer et al 2006). These results underscore the fact that the mere identification of a surrogate does not guarantee either their awareness of the patient's wishes, or improved decision-making. Designated decision-makers may be unavailable when needed, may be incompetent to make decisions for the patient, may selectively choose patient's values that accord with their own, may experience conflicts of interest and may not truly understand the patients' perspective. Furthermore, it is unclear whether a surrogate decision-maker can ever legitimately infer a patient's wishes from their previously stated values or their behaviour and whether surrogate decision-makers offer any advantage over population-based treatment indicators (which predict which treatments a given patient may prefer based on studies of the choices of similar patients in similar situations) (Varma and Wendler 2007).

While the practice of surrogate decision-making is clearly sub-optimal, research suggests that surrogates generally do try to do the right thing for their loved one, and are often concerned with protecting their dignity, are often more accurate than physicians at predicting patients' preferences for treatment and provide a more holistic picture of their loved one than simply than that of a patient, and that patients continue to trust partners and family members to make decisions for them in the belief that the family's decisions are most likely to reflect their own wishes and values (Chambers-Evans and Carnevale 2005; Shalowitz, Garrett-Mayer et al 2006). However, where a previously competent patient has left no reliable indication of their wishes and where there is no one available who adequately knows the patient, surrogate decision-makers should not attempt to make substituted judgments but should make decisions in the patient's best interests.

Advance directives

Advance directives for health care have been proposed as another means by which the autonomy of incompetent individuals can be respected and by which they can maintain control over their medical care when they can no longer participate in the consent process. Advance directives have received widespread public and professional endorsement in the hope that they will promote patient autonomy, enable more humane and ethical use of medical technology, diminish the individual responsibility that surrogates may bear for decision-making and perhaps provide a more ethical approach to reducing health-care costs than rationing (Davidson, Hackler et al 1989; Martin, Emanuel et al 2000; Prendergast 2001). As a consequence, advance directives have received considerable political and legislative support, and the United States, most European countries and most Australian States now have provision for advance directives and for advance care planning (Fassier, Lautrette et al 2005; Parker, Stewart et al 2007). Indeed, much debate about advance directives now centres upon how advance directives should be used rather than whether they should be used. However, empirical research suggests that the apparent simplicity of advance directives is deceptive and that, although promising, there are major problems with their validity, reliability, durability, accessibility, portability, popularity and efficacy (Emanuel and Emanuel 1990; Brock 1991; Fletcher and Spencer 1995).

Advance directives may be oral or written, explicit or implicit. Most attention has focused on two specific types of advance directives – Living Wills and Durable Powers of Attorney for Health Care. A Living Will is a written document in which a competent person sets out health-care preferences before incapacity occurs. A Durable Power of Attorney for Health Care authorises individuals to appoint another person to act as their agent to make all health-care decisions after they become incapacitated. Both forms of advance directive can be combined in a single document.

Living Wills are often limited by linguistic vagueness, using ambiguous terms such as 'heroic measures' or 'resuscitation' that provide little guidance for clinical management (Teno, Licks et al 1997). For these reasons it is generally recommended that patients should designate a surrogate for decision-making, in combination with their Living Will.

Advance directives allow the projection of an individual's wishes to a period of anticipated incapacity and thus assume that patient choices will remain stable over time. However, patients often change their mind over time and decisions made about hypothetical situations that differ from those made when faced with actual health problems. (Patrick, Danis et al 1988; Kellogg, Crain et al 1992; Potter, Stewart et al 1994). Those who interpret a patient's advance directive may therefore be required to make judgments about how well informed patients were and their degree of rationality at the time that the directive was made, and whether their preferences would be different now that they had experience of the specific medical condition that previously was simply a theoretical abstraction.

Ryan has argued that directives made by healthy individuals who opt for withdrawal of active treatment in a situation where the inability to consent is potentially reversible should be prohibited on the basis that individuals are likely to underestimate their desire for medical intervention should they become ill (Ryan 1996). Other commentators such as Dworkin have argued that advance directives should always be respected on the grounds that, should a person become incompetent, they cannot be said to have changed the values or views that lend genuine meaning to their life; rather they are simply no longer competent to express them (Dworkin 1993).

Discussing advance planning and documenting an advance directive has limited utility if such information is unavailable when decisions must be made. Data drawn from the USA have found that advance directives are frequently not available at hospital admission – particularly where the admission is non-elective (Morrison, Olson et al 1995). Furthermore, even where a directive is completed appropriately and is available on admission, it may often be over-looked or disregarded because of a judgment by those caring for the patient that the directive refuses justified treatment or requests unjustified treatment. This may sometimes represent unjustifiable medical paternalism, but it may also be consistent with evidence that suggests that patients may not want their directive followed to the letter but would rather their directive be interpreted in the clinical context (Collins, Parks et al 2006).

Despite the public and professional enthusiasm for advance directives, advance care planning remains the exception rather than rule. Studies from the USA have found that less than 10% of the general population have advance directives. There are a number of reasons for the low rate of completion of advance directives. Many patients do not wish to prepare advance directives – believing either that they do not require advance planning or that health professionals or their families should be responsible for their end-of-life decisions. Others may have little knowledge of advance directives, or have had little opportunity to discuss advance planning, or believe that it is the physician's responsibility to initiate such discussions (Collins, Parks et al 2006).

Physicians rarely initiate discussions regarding life-sustaining treatment and advance planning. The exact reasons for this are also unclear but may be because physicians are uncertain about the benefits or legality of advance directives, may not fully understand what an advance directive is or how to enact one, may lack the time to discuss such issues with patients, or may believe that advance directives are required only by those who are elderly or terminally ill. Most studies suggest that patients prefer that discussions be initiated earlier in the course of a terminal disease rather than later, whereas practitioners prefer discussions to commence later. Finally, both patients and physicians may find the issues surrounding death, dying and advance planning difficult to confront. Patients may feel that signing such a document is the psychological equivalent of 'giving up' or that the directive will result in their receiving less treatment than they need or desire. Physicians may also believe that such discussions will cause psychological harm to their patients, despite the fact that the evidence for this is largely anecdotal (Schade and Muslin 1989).

While there are many persuasive theoretical arguments to support the use of advance directives, a series of large studies have failed to demonstrate that advance directives positively influence end-of-life decision-making or have any impact on the pattern of care. The most comprehensive study about the utility of advance directives has been the Study to Understand Prognoses and Preferences for Outcomes and Risks of Treatment (SUPPORT) trial. This study was undertaken in two phases. Phase One was a prospective observational study of 4301 patients admitted to Intensive Care Units in the United States. Of these patients, 618 reported having an advance directive, but this was mentioned in the hospital notes in only 36 cases (5.8%) and was filed in the notes in only two cases. Furthermore, the presence of an advance directive appeared to have no effect on decision-making concerning resuscitation (Teno, Lynne et al 1994). In Phase Two of the study, the investigators tried to improve communication and decision-making in the management of a further 4804 patients by providing doctors with brief written reports about their patients' likely prognosis, providing information about patients' preferences for treatment including advance directives, and by initiating and maintaining communication between patients, families and doctors, using specially trained nurse-facilitators. The outcome of the trial was that advance planning appeared to have no impact on the care of seriously ill patients. Specifically, advance directives had no clinically important effect on decision-making, the use of hospital resources, pain management, patient satisfaction, physician practice, the application of CPR, or the use of do-not-resuscitate (DNR) orders – even among those who had a living will or chose to forego resuscitation (The SUPPORT Principal Investigators 1995). The authors concluded from these results that either advance directives are simply not effective in improving decision-making, or that advance directives are effective in altering decision-making but only in a small subset of the population or if implemented in a different manner to that of the SUPPORT trial. In the decade since the SUPPORT trial a large number of studies have been conducted into the use and impact of advance directives. For the most part these studies replicate the findings of SUPPORT – advance care directives are still rarely available and, even when they are available, do little to direct medical decision-making (Collins, Parks et al 2006).

In Australia, a number of States have pursued advance directives and/or advance care planning processes and policies, often in concert with end-of-life or chronic disease programs or as part of reviews of consent practices or guardianship legislation. The Austin hospital, in Melbourne, implemented a program originally from the USA called the 'Respecting Patient Choices' program. This has since been rolled out to many other hospitals within Australia with Commonwealth support. In this program, nursing and allied health staff are trained to assist patients understand and complete advance care planning documents. In the Austin hospital, before the program was introduced less than 10% of all in-patients (excluding palliative care) had ever completed an advance care plan and only 55% of these forms were currently active. Furthermore, only 14.3% of patients had completed an enduring power of attorney. After the intervention, 47% of patients had been given the opportunity to complete an advance care plan, and 70% of the introduced patients went on to include expressions of treatment that they would and would not want in the future, in their medical record. Of patients who subsequently died, 95% had their expression of treatment choices respected and their end-of-life wishes followed (Lee, Heland et al 2003). (However, it should be recognised that not all of these patients would have been incompetent.)

Advance care planning

A recent review article on advance directives, provocatively entitled 'Enough: the failure of the Living Will', concluded that any sensible examination of the literature would lead to the conclusion that policies promoting advance directives should be abandoned (Fegerlin and Schneider 2004). While we agree that there is limited value in simply making advance directives available (or in mandating their use), recent international and Australian experience suggests that there may be some modest benefit in advance care planning processes and that what is important is not the individual instrument used, or the form of the particular directive, but rather the process of communication around health care (Ditto, Danks et al 2001; Jordens, Little et al 2005; Collins, Parks et al 2006; Emanuel 2008).

Advance care planning becomes especially important if we lose mental capacity before we die. Not everyone will have strong preferences about what happens if that is the case, but where a patient has a condition that may affect the length or quality of their life, has a condition that will inevitably impair their capacity as it progresses, such as dementia, or is facing a situation where loss or impairment of capacity is at least a possibility, then it makes sense to encourage them to consider their goals, hopes, fears and preferences for future care, and reflect on what they may want for themselves in the event that they cannot make their own decisions, and then discuss their feelings, values, concerns and choices with their relatives and health care team. (General Medical Council 2008) For even if one remains competent in the final stages of life, or questions never emerge in relation to the appropriateness of medical care, advance discussion and planning may still have some benefits.

Advance directives may be a component of advance care planning, and should be considered in light of the patient's own preferences for documentation, the clinical context, the scope of the proposed directive and the predictability of various anticipated outcomes. For example, a patient with end-stage cardiac failure who has few relatives and knows that the likely mode of their own death will be cardiorespiratory arrest may choose to document their wishes regarding CPR, but little else, in an advance directive. Where a decision is made to incorporate an advance directive within an advance care planning process, a review of the literature suggests that it should:

1. be completed by a competent patient (perhaps after formal assessment of competence to complete an advance directive) with documentation of competence included in the directive;
2. be made on the basis of informed consent;
3. be activated only when the patient is incompetent;

4. be able to be revoked at any time – orally or in writing;

5. be carefully drafted and validated;

6. employ both medical terminology and terminology that is understood by lay-persons;

7. be simple and concise;

8. allow for disease-specific statements, eg, preferences for ventilation in chronic airways limitation;

9. include treatment-specific statements, eg, preferences for CPR ventilation, intensive care, artificial nutrition and hydration, and palliative care (perhaps by reference to clinical scenarios);

10. include a personal statement of the individual's 'life values' that the health-care team or surrogate should consider when making decisions in their best interest – including an indication of what the individual considers an unacceptable quality of life, their goals for care, their fears about disability and their hopes for what the end of their life may look like;

11. provide guidance for both continuation and refusal of treatment;

12. allow for nomination of a proxy decision-maker (including directions for contact);

13. allow for periodic review and documentation, and include validation of each revision;

14. be co-signed by the patient, physician and nominated proxy;

15. be retained by the patient, the nominated proxy, the patient's primary physician and the patient's legal adviser. A copy should also be retained in the treating hospital's case records. The patient should also carry a card on their person indicating that an advance directive has been completed;

16. discussed with patient's physician, nominated proxy and chosen relatives;

17. be offered in a clinical, non-administrative setting;

18. be incorporated into a process of advance care planning involving a series of consultations/discussions between the patient and their physician;

19. be incorporated into an education program directed at health providers (ie, physicians nurses, social work etc) and at consumers (ie, patient advocacy groups).

Advance care planning resembles the process of obtaining informed consent, in that it is an iterative process that enables education and the expression of preferences. And in the same way that consent forms only document the outcome of a process, advance directives only document the outcome of the advance care planning process.

Where this process of decision-making is not informed, or is communicated inadequately, or is referred to a surrogate with no understanding of the patient's values and preferences, then any form of advance planning will inevitably fail. As Greg Sachs has noted:

Advance directives, like new medications or devices, are only tools. Patients only benefit from the use of such tools once they and their physicians have learned how to use them appropriately and effectively. Advance directives are most likely to benefit patients when adequate thought and communication go into preparing the directive. I believe most of the efforts of the clinical ethics community should be directed towards teaching patients, families, and physicians how to have meaningful, ongoing, advance directive discussion. (Sachs 1993)

The results of empirical research suggest that the impact of advance directives on patient care may be more limited than was expected. This may be because the conceptual framework underpinning advance care planning does not reflect the needs and experiences of patients; because some of the problems associated with advance directives are simply intractable; because advance care planning prioritises autonomy and so may be inconsistent with non-Anglo-American cultures; because advance care planning may function not to enable decisions to be made in the event of incapacity but simply to allow patients prepare for death; and because decision-making at the end of life involves much more than simply an expression of individual preference (Martin, Emanuel et al 2000; Jordens, Little et al 2005). *Values histories*, where a health-care professional assesses the patient's beliefs regarding health care and then attempts to identify the patient's preferred approach to a variety of situations (Leland 2001), and *combined directives*, which merge components of instructional advance directives, the health-care proxy and the values history in an attempt to obtain a more complete understanding of a patient's wishes (Kirschner 2005), offer promise but neither has been adequately assessed in large scale studies. It remains to be seen if legislation and policies institutionalising advance care planning will be any more effective.

LEGAL ASPECTS OF COMPETENCE, ADVANCE DIRECTIVES AND SUBSTITUTE DECISION-MAKING

Competence is the capacity to understand the nature and consequences of medical procedures to be undertaken. At common law there is a general presumption that an adult person is competent to make decisions about their medical care. There may be many reasons why a person may not be capable of making decisions for themselves – dementia, intellectual disability, brain damage due to trauma, alcohol and drugs. The test for competence is 'functional', that is, based on the ability of the person rather than other criteria such as the rationality of the decision or the status of the patient (eg, 'a person who refuses blood products is incompetent' or 'all people with Down's Syndrome are incompetent') (Stewart and Biegler 2004).

The only status-based criterion used in the determination of competence is age. Adult patients (over the age of 18 years) are presumed to have competence to consent. People under the age of 18 are presumed to be incompetent. In both situations the presumption can be rebutted. In New South Wales and South Australia, the presumption of competence has been lowered to 14 and 16 respectively: *Minors (Property and Contracts) Act 1970* (NSW), s 49; *Consent to*

Medical Treatment and Palliative Care Act 1995 (SA), s 6. Issues concerning children and competence are discussed in Chapter 20.

Disproving the competence of adults

At common law the presumption of competence for adults is rebuttable: *Re T (Adult: Refusal of Treatment)* [1993] Fam 95. In Queensland the *Powers of Attorney Act 1998* provides that '[a]n adult is presumed to have capacity for a matter' (Sch 1, s 1). Evidence may be produced to indicate that the person lacks capacity.

The competence of a person may be an issue in many legal situations. For example, in Chapter 5 it was mentioned that the competence of a party to an agreement may be relevant to its enforceability under the law of contract. Also, competence may be an issue when a person makes a will. The High Court of Australia, in *Gibbons v Wright* (1954) 91 CLR 423, addressed the general approach to establishing competence in the following way:

> The law does not prescribe any fixed standard of sanity as requisite for the validity of all transactions. It requires, in relation to each particular matter or piece of business transacted, that each party shall have such soundness of mind as to be capable of understanding the general nature of what he is doing by his participation ... The principle ... appears to us to be that the mental capacity required by the law in respect of any instrument is relative to the particular transaction which is being effected by means of the instrument, and may be described as the capacity to understand the nature of that transaction when it is explained ... Ordinarily the nature of the transaction means in this connection the broad operation, the 'general purport' of the instrument; but in some cases it may mean the effect of a wider transaction which the instrument is a means of carrying out. (at 437-8)

Most of the case law in this area involves an assertion that a patient is not competent to refuse medical treatment. It seems that there are very few situations where there will be an action before courts or tribunals concerning capacity when the patient agrees with the recommendations of the medical team!

Competence may also be variable within the same person. Fluctuating mental states may mean that the patient is competent to make decisions at some times, but not at others. Competence can also vary over time.

The common law test for competence to consent to medical treatment

Common law decisions have examined situations where patients have refused medical treatment where the medical team feel that it is in the best interests of the patient that it should be done (see Chapter 15). The general test is that the patient should understand the broad nature and purpose of the proposed treatment. Lord Donaldson in *Re T (Adult: Refusal of Treatment)* [1993] Fam 95 at 112-13 has written:

> The right to decide one's own fate presupposes a capacity to do so. Every adult is presumed to have that capacity, but it is a presumption which can be rebutted. This is not a question of the degree of intelligence or education of the adult concerned. However a small minority of the population lack the

necessary mental capacity due to mental illness or retarded development: see, for example, *In Re F (Mental Patient: Sterilisation)* [1990] 2 AC 1. This is a permanent or at least a long-term state. Others who would normally have that capacity may be deprived of it or have it reduced by reason of temporary factors, such as unconsciousness or confusion or other effects of shock, severe fatigue, pain or drugs being used in their treatment.

In the English case of *Re C (Adult: Refusal of Medical Treatment)* [1994] 1 All ER 819, the patient, C, suffered from paranoid schizophrenia and lived in a psychiatric facility (Broadmoor). His doctors thought that he needed to have his leg amputated, as it had become gangrenous, and that he might die if the operation was not performed. He refused to consent to the procedure and sought a declaration from the court that the amputation could not proceed without his consent. The court held that C's general incapacity due to schizophrenia was irrelevant to his decision to refuse treatment. It had not been proven to the court that C did not understand the choice he was being asked to make, and consequently he was competent to withhold his consent. An order was made forbidding the amputation without C's written consent.

The court held that in order to ascertain whether the patient understood the nature, purpose and effects of a proposed treatment, the capacity to adopt three stages of decision making should be examined:

- the comprehension and retention of the information about the treatment;
- believing that information; and
- weighing up that information in the balance so as to arrive at a choice.

Comprehension of information

One of the difficult questions for this part of the test is to discern the level of information that the patient has to be able to comprehend. As discussed in Chapter 14, there are two standards of information provision that are relevant to consent:

(a) *the battery standard*, which requires that a patient be given general information about the broad nature and purpose of the proposed treatment to avoid a claim of battery; and

(b) *the negligence standard*, which is the duty in negligence that requires the health professional to disclose risks that are material to the individual patient, or risks that a reasonable person would be likely to attach significance to (this is sometimes referred to as 'duty of informed consent').

Which standard does a patient have to comprehend to be considered competent? On one view, 'a patient need not be informed of (nor understand) the risks of the procedure, in order to be competent to consent to treatment' (Devereux 1999). According to this view, the law of consent is concerned solely with battery. Patients should not be classed as incompetent merely because a material risk has not been communicated to them. One the other hand it might be suggested that if a patient is incapable of understanding material risks then they should be deemed incompetent to make the decision. American commentators Grisso and

Appelbaum (1998) have recommended that the patient should understand the nature of the illness and proposed treatment, as well as the risks and benefits of that treatment, of alternative treatments and of no treatment at all.

The view of UK Professor Andrew Grubb is that the law of competence should take a middle course between these two standards:

> The patient must be able to understand more than the 'broad nature and purpose' of the procedure. He must also be able to understand the likely (or possible) effects or consequences of undergoing (or not) the procedure in question. (Grubb 1998)

Because of the difficulties of being able to delineate exactly what a middle course would be, Stewart and Biegler (2004) have argued that the negligence standard be adopted as the one health professionals ought to apply in assessing competence. Stewart and Biegler state:

> This means from a practical perspective that doctors should try to inform the patient of the material risks of having or refusing treatment. If the patient understands those risks then the patient can satisfy this step of the functional competence test. If the patient cannot understand a material risk then they have not satisfied this step and they are incompetent. If, however, the doctor fails to inform the patient of material risk but the broad nature and effects of the treatment have been communicated and these are understood, the failure to inform the patient of the material risk ought not to render the patient incompetent. Instead, liability for negligent advice might arise.

Believing information

The requirement that the patient believe the treatment information is normally a factor in cases where the person exhibits some delusion regarding the nature of their illness, and cannot accept the medical reality regarding its cause or treatment. For example, in *Tennessee v Northern* 563 SW 2d 197 (1978), the patient thought her toes were merely dirty and not gangrenous, and in *NHS Trust v T* [2004] EWHC 1279 (Fam), the patient believed that her blood had been infected with evil and that any transfusion of fresh blood would turn evil as soon as it entered her body. Neither patient was competent because neither could believe the reality regarding their conditions and treatments.

Weighing the factors and making a choice

In *Re T (Adult: Refusal of Treatment)* [1993] Fam 95 at 116, Butler-Sloss LJ said that '[a] decision to refuse medical treatment by a patient capable of making the decision does not have to be sensible, rational or well- considered'.

On the issue of the rationality of decisions made by patients, Lord Donaldson also said in the same case that:

> [T]he patient's right of choice exists whether the reasons for making that choice are rational, irrational, unknown or even non-existent. That his choice is contrary to what is to be expected of the vast majority of adults is only relevant if there are other reasons for doubting his capacity to decide. The nature of his choice or the terms in which it is expressed may then tip the balance. (at 113)

As Stewart and Biegler emphasise, 'it is the making of the decision which needs to be 'rational' and not the outcome' (Stewart and Biegler 2004).

Communication of the decision

An inability to communicate means that the person will be found incompetent even though their mental processes may be unaffected. For example, in *Auckland Area Health Board v Attorney-General* [1993] 1 NZLR 235, a patient with Guillain-Barré syndrome (a condition which impairs communication through progressive paralysis but does not impair cognition) was presumed to be incompetent by the court seemingly because of his inability to communicate.

Degrees of capacity

Again, in *Re T (Adult: Refusal Of Treatment)* [1993] Fam 95 at 113, Lord Donaldson also says that '[w]hat matters is that the doctors should consider whether at that time [the patient] had a capacity which was commensurate with the gravity of the decision which he purported to make. The more serious the decision, the greater the capacity required'.

But Stewart and Biegler (2004) write:

> This statement is confusing because if a person has the capacity to make a decision, they have that capacity. It is a 'yes' or 'no' proposition. But the better way to understand Lord Donaldson is to interpret this statement as requiring greater scrutiny of capacity in cases where the decision is about life-threatening conditions, before the patient is accepted as competent or not.

Whilst we agree with Stewart and Biegler and also Malcolm Parker that 'the more serious the risk, the greater the *level of evidence* of capacity that should be sought' (Parker 2004), it is clear that the assessment of capacity is dependent on the type and complexity of the decision to be made. For example, an adult with Down's syndrome may be competent to consent to having a small wound stitched but not competent to give consent to radical surgery.

Later judgments have appeared to adopt an evidence approach advocated by Stewart, Biegler and Parker. In *Fitzpatrick v K* [2008] IEHC 104 (facts discussed below), Laffoy J of the High Court of Ireland stated:

> Counsel for Miss K took issue with the proposition enunciated by Lord Donaldson ... that the patient's capacity should be commensurate with the gravity of the decision which he purports to make, suggesting instead that the level of capacity required should be measured against the nature of the decision, that is to say, its complexity, rather than its consequences. It was also submitted that the proposition may have the effect of reversing the burden of proof of capacity. In my view, Lord Donaldson, who clearly recognised the presumption in favour of capacity, was saying no more than that, where the patient's choice is of death over life, the question for the doctor is whether the patient has the capacity at the time to make a decision of that gravity. The principle enjoins the doctor to view the issue by reference to the gravity of the outcome ... Clear and convincing proof is required.

Abuse of competence assessment?

Autonomy is undoubtedly a central value recognised by the law. However, the weight that is given to the principle of autonomy may produce results that are so counter-intuitive that decision makers (including courts) may stretch notions of incapacity to achieve the results that they want (McCall Smith 1997). But as Justice Michael Kirby has pointed out, 'woe betide the professional who forgets that the law hovers over such decisions' (Kirby 2003). Two English cases may illustrate this point.

In *St George's Healthcare NHS Trust v S; R v Collins, ex parte S* [1998] 3 All ER 673, veterinary nurse, S, was 36 weeks pregnant and was suffering pre-eclampsia which was severe enough to require a hospitalisation and induction of labour. Even though she understood the life threatening risks to herself and the baby, she refused to be hospitalised as she believed that pregnancy was a natural process that should proceed without any medical intervention. She was detained by the health professionals under the provisions of the *Mental Health Act 1983* on the basis of a previous diagnosis of 'moderate depression' but the real reason was found to be a concern for the foetus and S's physical health. Ms S was transferred to St George's Hospital and an *ex parte* application was made to the court resulting in a court order authorising treatment without her consent. A caesarean section was performed and she safely delivered a baby girl. At no time did S receive treatment for any mental disorder.

S appealed to the Court of Appeal, which found that the treatment she had received was unlawful. There was never a question of S's competence. The Court of Appeal affirmed the principles stated in *Re MB (An Adult: Medical Treatment)* [1997] 2 FCR 541 (see further discussion in Chapter 14).

In *Re B (Adult: Refusal of Treatment)* [2002] 2 All ER 449, Ms B, following an illness, became a tetraplegic and suffered complete paralysis from the neck down, although she was able to move her head and speak. She gave formal instructions to the hospital verbally, in an advance directive and through her solicitors, that she wanted her artificial ventilation to be removed, even though she realised that if this were to happen she would almost certainly die.

Two psychiatrists interviewed Ms B and, after an initial disagreement, formed the view that she was not competent to refuse the continued ventilation, even though her consent was thought sufficient for all other forms of treatment that she was undergoing. Ms B applied to the High Court for a declaration that she was competent to refuse ventilation and that it would be unlawful for the hospital to continue treatment against her will.

The case was heard by Dame Elizabeth Butler-Sloss P. A further psychiatric assessment was arranged. Her Ladyship found that Ms B was competent to refuse the ventilation and warned against a 'benevolent paternalism which does not embrace recognition of the personal autonomy of the severely disabled patient'. She also said that:

> The doctors must not allow their emotional reaction to or strong disagreement with the decision of the patient to cloud their judgment in answering the primary question whether the patient has the mental capacity to make the decision. (at 474).

These cases can be contrasted with *bona fides* cases where the competence of the patient is at issue. For example, difficulties arise when competence assessment has to occur in an emergency. In *Fitzpatrick v K* [2008] IEHC 104, an African woman in Ireland haemorrhaged after giving birth. After emergency treatment had commenced the staff were told by the patient that she was a Jehovah's Witness and that she refused blood, even though on admission she had claimed to be a Roman Catholic. On one occasion during the episode she suggested that she should be given Coke, tomatoes, eggs and milk as an alternative to blood products. The treating obstetrician (the 'Master') doubted the patient's capacity to make a decision and approached the court for a determination on competence and for an order authorising treatment in the interim. These orders were made. The woman later appealed the decision. The court found that, while the patient may have been competent to refuse treatment, at the time there was sufficient uncertainty with regards to the patient's ability to retain and understand information to justify the court order. Laffoy J stated that:

> The duty of the clinician caring for a patient in the circumstances which prevailed in relation to Ms K … is to advise the patient of, and afford him or her the opportunity to receive, appropriate medical treatment. If, as a competent adult, the patient refuses to accept the treatment and no issue arises as to the capacity of the patient to make that decision, the clinician's duty to provide such treatment is discharged. However, if an issue arises as to the capacity of the patient to refuse treatment, the duty of the clinician to advise on and provide the appropriate treatment remains. As a matter of law and common sense, the duty of care which the clinician owes the patient in those circumstances is no different from what it would be if there was no refusal or if the patient was unconscious. What is required of the clinician is to take the steps to have the capacity issue be resolved, with the assistance of the court if necessary.
>
> It follows that the assessment of the patient's capacity to refuse treatment falls to be determined by reference to the clinician's responsibility to give to the patient the relevant information in relation to the appropriate treatment and the risks attendant on the patient refusing the treatment. The *C case* test requires an objective assessment as to whether the patient assimilates, understands and weighs that information in the balance

In some Australian jurisdictions a statutory defence has been created for doctors when they incorrectly conclude that a person has the capacity to consent to treatment. For example, s 69(3) of the *Guardianship and Management of Property Act 1991* (ACT) states:

> Where a person, who is not competent to do so, purports to consent to the performance of a medical procedure or the provision of other treatment for the person by a doctor, no action or proceeding, civil or criminal, lies against the doctor by reason only of the performance of that procedure or the provision of that treatment without the person's consent if:
> (a) the doctor did not know, or could not reasonably be expected to know, that the person was not competent to give the consent required; and
> (b) the doctor otherwise acted in good faith in performing that procedure or providing that treatment.

However, this section does not cover the situation where a physician wrongfully concludes that a patient is incompetent and treats in the patient's best interests. Grubb (1998) has argued that in such circumstances a defence of reasonable mistake should apply, but mistake is not a defence to a claim in battery: *O'Donohue v Wille* [1999] NSWSC 661. Stewart and Biegler have argued that an uncertainty defence should be created to protect health professionals from claims of battery, when they mistakenly and in good faith override a competent patient's objection and provide emergency treatment, on the basis that the person is incompetent (Stewart and Biegler 2004).

Statutory definitions of competence

The *Powers of Attorney Act 1998* (Qld) and the *Guardianship and Administration Act 2000* (Qld) define the test for capacity in very similar ways to that in *Re C (Adult: Refusal of Medical Treatment)* [1994] 1 All ER 819. In Sch 3 to the 1998 Act and Sch 4 to the 2000 Act 'capacity' is defined as:

(a)   understanding the nature and effect of decision about the matter; and
(b)   freely and voluntarily making decisions about the matter; and
(c)   communicating the decisions in some way.

Similar definitions can also be found in New South Wales, Tasmania and Victoria: *Guardianship Act 1987* (NSW), s 33(2); *Guardianship and Administration Act 1995* (Tas), s 36(2); *Guardianship and Administration Act 1986* (Vic), s 36(2).

In relation to advance health directives the *Powers of Attorney Act 1998* (Qld) provides:

42. (1) A principal may make an advance health directive, to the extent it does not give power to an attorney, only if the principal understands the following matters:
(a)   the nature and the likely effects of each direction in the advance health directive;
(b)   a direction operates only while the principal has impaired capacity for the matter covered by the direction;
(c)   the principal may revoke a direction at any time the principal has capacity for the matter covered by the direction;
(d)   at any time the principal is not capable of revoking a direction, the principal is unable to effectively oversee the implementation of the direction.

In relation to powers of attorney, including those concerning health care, the *Powers of Attorney Act 2006* (ACT), s 9, stated that a person has impaired decision-making capacity if they cannot understand the nature or effect of their decisions.

The Queensland capacity definition was tested in *Re PVM* [2000] QGAAT 1, where a 39-year-old Aboriginal man with traumatic brain and spinal cord damage was not found to be incompetent to refuse ventilation support. It was tested again in *Re Bridges* [2001] Qd R 574, where a mentally ill patient was found to be incompetent to refuse dialysis, after she had ceased taking her anti-psychotic medication. The court authorised treatment for both dialysis and medication until such time as the medication took effect and the patient had regained competence, after which she could then make a decision regarding her treatment.

Advance directives

Advance directives and the common law

One way a patient can deal with incompetence is to plan ahead and give direction about what he or she would like for future care. 'Advance directives' are decisions made by patients about what medical treatments they would like in the future, if at some point they cannot make decisions for themselves (Stewart 2006). When thought of in these broad terms, advance directives can be seen as an existing part of everyday medical practice, particularly surgical procedures, where patients consent to treatments many days, even weeks, before they are sedated for their operation. Most academic and legal discussion of advance directives focuses particularly on those decisions about withholding or withdrawing treatments at the end of life (see Chapters 14 and 15). These directives (sometimes referred to as 'living wills') usually record decisions about refusing life-sustaining treatments, but they can also contain the patient's preferences and desires about a whole range of treatment matters.

There are three questions that need to be answered before an advance directive becomes binding:

1. Was the decision-maker competent when they made the directive?

The test for competence was discussed above. In *NHS Trust v T* [2004] EWHC 1279 (Fam) (see facts above) the woman was found incompetent to make an advance directive to refuse blood, because of her delusion that her blood was evil and that any transfused blood would be infected by the evil blood. Contrastingly, in *In re W* [2002] EWHC 90 (Fam), a prisoner with a severe psychiatric disorder was not found incompetent, when he made an advance directive refusing treatment for a self-inflicted wound. The prisoner wounded himself in the shin and repeatedly inserted objects and rubbed faeces into the wound. He had also shoved two tap fittings up his anus, all to protest his prison conditions. His advance directive refusing all treatment was upheld. Butler–Sloss P found that there was no evidence of a lack of competence on the prisoner's part (in fact the deliberate nature of the injuries suggested he was fully competent – but see Chapter 14 for other cases on prisoners refusing treatment).

2. Was the advance directive intended to apply in the circumstances that have arisen?

This question is normally answered by an interpretive analysis of the patient's language in their decision and the meaning of particular words and phrases employed. Courts will ordinarily err on the side of preserving life if remote, general, spontaneous or casual comments were made: *Matter of Jobes*, 529 A 2d 434 at 443 (NJ, 1987). Contrastingly, evidence of clear and serious decision-making which consists of written evidence or eye-witness accounts is usually strong enough to support the applicability of an advance directive: *Matter of Peter* 529 A 2d 419 (NJ, 1987).

Circumstances sometimes change and the directive may no longer apply. This happened in *HE v A Hospital NHS Trust* [2003] EWHC 1017 (Fam), where a 24-year-old female Jehovah's Witness had signed an advance directive, but had, two years later, promised to convert to Islam after becoming engaged to a Muslim. She had been raised as a Muslim but had become a Jehovah's Witness after her parents separated and her mother joined the faith. An application was brought by her father after the woman became seriously ill following an operation. A blood transfusion was deemed necessary by medical staff but the woman's mother was adamant that the directive be followed. Mumby J found the woman's promise to convert back to Islam an 'essential and compelling aspect' for finding that the advance directive was no longer intended to apply.

3.   Was the decision-maker unduly influenced?

Decisions to refuse treatment must be free from the undue influence of others (see Chapter 14). In *Re T (An Adult) (Consent to Medical Treatment)* its was found that an advance directive had been made by a patient (who was not a Jehovah's witness) to refuse blood, but that the patient had made the decision because of the undue influence of the patient's mother (who was a Jehovah's Witness). The court found that the woman's mother had exerted undue pressure on the woman to make her refuse the treatment prior to her becoming incapacitated. The woman's decision was therefore invalid and treatment could be provided by the doctors according to the patient's best interests. The court stated that, when examining undue influence, one must inquire as to both the strength of will of the patient and the relationship of the patient with the persuader.

Legislation on advance directives

All jurisdictions apart from New South Wales and Tasmania have legislative mechanisms for creating advance directives. All these schemes preserve a patient's right to make advance directives at common law (except for South Australia and Queensland) (Stewart, Kerridge and Parker 2008).

	Legislation
Qld	*Powers of Attorney Act 1998*
SA	*Consent to Medical Treatment and Palliative Care Act 1995*
Vic	*Medical Treatment Act 1988*
WA	*Guardianship and Administration Act 1990* (NB: at time of writing provisions under Part 9B were not yet in effect)
ACT	*Medical Treatment (Health Directions) Act 2006*
NT	*Natural Death Act 1988*

The legislative right to make an advance directive is limited in each jurisdiction to people over the age of 18. Directives to refuse treatment can relate to refusal of treatment generally, or of a particular kind of treatment. In Queensland, the patient can also consent to future health care and require the withdrawal of life-sustaining treatment, as well as authorise the use of force: *Powers of Attorney Act 1998* (Qld), s 35.

Each jurisdiction places limitations on what can be refused. In Victoria and the ACT a patient can be prevented from refusing palliative care: *Medical Treatment Act 1988* (Vic), s 4(2); *Medical Treatment Act 1994* (ACT), s 5(2).

In Victoria the patient can only refuse treatment that is related to a 'current condition': s 5(1)(a). Unfortunately the meaning of 'current condition' is not defined, but presumably it relates to treatment for a medical condition which is being suffered by the patient at the time the advance directive is completed. This means that these statutory directives are not available to people who would refuse treatment for conditions which they have not yet suffered, eg, strokes, or physical injuries which sustain blood loss.

In the Northern Territory, the direction can be made at any time but only becomes effective when the patient is suffering from a 'terminal illness', which is defined as an illness, injury or degeneration leading to an imminent death and from which there is no reasonable prospect of temporary or permanent recovery: s 3.

South Australia has similar restrictions. The direction only becomes operative when the patient is in a terminal phase of a terminal illness, and is no longer competent: s 7(1).

In Queensland (under s 36) the directive generally becomes effective on incapacity but a direction to withhold life-sustaining treatment will not operate unless:

(a) the principal is terminally ill and is not expected to live more than a year, or is in a persistent vegetative state, or is permanently unconscious, or has a severe illness with no reasonable prospect of being able to live without the continued application of life-sustaining measures; and

(b) if the direction concerns artificial hydration or nutrition) the life sustaining measure would be inconsistent with good medical practice; and

(c) the patient has no reasonable prospect of regaining capacity for health matters.

In Western Australia, a treatment decision in an advance directive will not operate if circumstances have arisen that the patient had not anticipated and would cause a reasonable person to change their mind about the treatment decision: s 110S(3)-(4).

Problems with advance care directives

The discussion in the first part of the chapter set out the problems of institutional resistance to advance directives that is evidenced in studies like the SUPPORT trial. Such resistance can also come from the legal profession. In *Qumsieh v*

Guardianship and Administration Board (1998) 14 VAR 46, a Jehovah's Witness from Victoria had made a common law advance directive before giving birth in which she outlined her objection to blood products. She also had the hospital make notes of her objections. She haemorrhaged after giving birth and lapsed into unconsciousness. The hospital convinced her husband to ignore her wishes and both parties approached the Guardianship Board (now merged with the Victorian Civil and Administration Tribunal) to have the husband appointed guardian for the purpose of giving consent to the transfusion. The Board was not told of the woman's advance directive and nor was the woman represented. After recovering, the woman sought judicial review of the decision to appoint a guardian. The trial judge dismissed the application and did not give reasons. She appealed that decision to the Victorian Court of Appeal. Again, the woman's claims were dismissed. It was said that the issue was moot and that the Court should not encourage further disagreement between the woman and her husband. Stewart (1999) has argued that the case represents a series of failures of the legal system to deal seriously with the obvious issues of Mrs Qumsieh's rights to refuse treatment and her rights to procedural fairness.

Another serious limitation relates to the legal response to the breach of an advance directive. The legal system's ordinary response to medical treatment without consent is the tort of battery (see Chapter 14). In *Malette v Schulman* (1990) 67 DLR (4th) 321 a doctor was held liable in battery when he ignored a Jehovah's Witness's advance directive to refuse blood products. At trial and on appeal, the plaintiff was awarded $20,000. The court stated the sum was appropriate given the patient's mental and emotional suffering. This suggests that even in the absence of substantial physical harm a patient wrongly given life-sustaining treatment should be able to claim damages beyond the nominal, because non-consensual touching is considered to be a very serious infringement even where it causes no physical harm.

However, not all courts have been happy to give damages for breaching an advance directive, even in those cases where the patient appears to have suffered a consequential physical injury. In *Anderson v St Francis – St George Hospital* 671 NE 2d 225 (1996), a patient was wrongfully resuscitated in violation of a 'do not resuscitate' order. The day after being resuscitated he had a stroke and remained partially paralysed and needing nursing home care until his death two years later. The court found that life was not a compensable injury as the court could not weigh the relative benefits of being versus non-being. Furthermore, it was said that there are some mistakes and technical assaults for which there should be no monetary compensation (similar approaches have been taken to 'wrongful life' claims which are discussed in Chapter 19). The court also refused to find that the continuation of the patient's life was the cause of his stroke. The mere fact that patient continued to live did not mean that further injuries sustained by the patient (those being, the stroke and attendant care costs) were caused by his life.

Stewart (2006) has argued that:

> *Anderson's case* exhibits a particularly narrow view of harm and causation, and it reflects a policy bias in favour of the sanctity of life ethic ... By stating

that the life of the patient was not a recognisable harm, the judgment has the effect of filing down the teeth of the tort of battery, by leaving no option for enforcing the patient's own choice about how he valued his own life. The judgment ignores the fact that Mr Anderson did view his continued life as a harm and that, in all other aspects, the legal system recognized his right to make that choice.

In some jurisdictions statutory penalties apply for breaching advance directives, such as the statutory offence of medical trespass in Victoria: *Medical Treatment Act 1988* (Vic), s 6. But, given no one has ever been prosecuted under the section, it is difficult to assess its effectiveness. The general lack of civil and criminal responses to breaches of advance directives evidences a real danger that the right to make an advance directive will become a right without a remedy (Stewart 2006).

Substitute decision-makers

Generally speaking, there are four different types of substitute decision-maker in Australia. They are:

- the Supreme Courts of each State and Territory;
- the guardianship authorities (tribunals or boards) in each jurisdiction, and the guardians they appoint;
- health attorneys, enduring guardians and medical agents appointed by the patient; and
- relatives and friends under 'person responsible' legislation.

Doctors also have power to provide treatment without consent when such treatment is necessary. This is discussed in Chapter 14. Each substitute decision-maker will now be examined.

The Supreme Courts' parens patriae jurisdiction

The Supreme Courts of the States and Territories have the power to consent to treatments on behalf of incompetent adults and children under their inherent jurisdiction. The inherent jurisdiction arises out of the two concepts of the Royal Prerogative and the *parens patriae* jurisdiction. The Royal Prerogative relates to the 'powers and privileges of the sovereign' and the *parens patriae* concept is the notion of the sovereign as the 'father of the people' (Powell 2004).

The prerogative is ancient and its limits have never been exhaustively defined. The jurisdiction was originally exercised after a finding that the person was an *idiot* (sometimes *natural fool*) or a *lunatic* where those deemed to be idiots were born with a disability and those who were classed as lunatics had developed their disability later in life. On occasion the terminology of idiot and lunatic has been retained, albeit modernised: *MS v ES* [1983] 3 NSWLR 199; *RH v CAH* [1984] 1 NSWLR 694. However, in recent times, courts have not relied on the distinctions and instead have found the *parens patriae* jurisdiction applicable in cases where the proposed patient is incompetent.

The best interests test

Judges exercising the jurisdiction must make a decision in the patient's 'best interests'. The best interests test is difficult to define. Some judges have simply refused to attempt any general mapping out. In *Re T (A Minor) (Wardship: Medical Treatment)* [1991] Fam 33 at 52 Balcombe LJ stated that any attempt to lay down a test would be unhelpful. Similarly, in *Re T (A Minor) (Wardship: Medical Treatment)* [1997] 1 WLR 242 at 254, Waite LJ stated that any generalisations about the test were out of place as each case turned on its own facts and circumstances.

In *Airedale NHS Trust v Bland* [1993] AC 789, the majority of the House of Lords found that the best interests test should be determined by the medical profession in accordance with what a responsible body of medical opinion believed would be in the patient's best interests. This was an adaptation of the *Bolam* test of medical negligence (see Chapter 8). The problem with this formulation is the way that the equation of medical assessment with best interests ignores the subjective personal and social dimensions of a person's best interests. Not all English judges were comfortable with this result and the Court of Appeal in later judgments stated firmly on a number of occasions that the best interests test is wider than medical interests: *In re MB (Medical Treatment)* [1997] 2 FLR 426; *Re A (children) (conjoined twins)* [2000] 4 All ER 961 at 994 (Ward LJ). In *Re A (Male Sterilisation)* [2000] 1 FLR 426 at 555, Butler-Sloss LJ stated that 'best interests encompasses medical, emotional and all other welfare issues'. In *Re S (Adult Patient's Best Interests)* [2000] 2 FLR 389 at 400-1, the *Bolam* test was said to be irrelevant to the best interests test, once a decision had been made about the acceptable alternatives for treatment. In light of this change in attitude, judges in England now approach the question of bests interests by drawing up a list of the advantages and disadvantages of the proposed course of treatment: *NHS Trust v Ms D* [2005] EWHC 2439 (Fam); *An NHS Trust v MB* [2006] EWHC 507 (Fam).

Judges in Australia have done more to provide guidance of the content of the test. In *Re Marion (No 2)* (1992) 17 Fam LR 336 (a case involving the sterilisation of a minor), Nicholson CJ created a checklist of factors to consider in assessing best interests. Those factors include:

(1) The particular condition of the patient which requires the procedure or treatment;

(2) The nature of the procedure or treatment proposed;

(3) The reasons for which it is proposed that the procedure or treatment be carried out;

(4) The alternative courses of treatment that are available in relation to that condition;

(5) The desirability of and effect of authorising the procedure or treatment proposed rather than the available alternatives;

(6) The physical effects on the patient and the psychological and social implications for the patient of:
   (a) authorising the proposed procedure or treatment
   (b) not authorising the proposed procedure or treatment

(7)   The nature and degree of any risk to the patient of:
    (a)   authorising the proposed procedure or treatment
    (b)   not authorising the proposed procedure or treatment
(8)   The views (if any) expressed by the carers of the patient:
    (a)   the guardian(s) of the patient;
    (b)   the relatives of the patient;
    (c)   a person who is responsible for the daily care and control of the patient;
    (d)   the patient;
to the proposed procedure or treatment and to any alternative procedure or treatment.

Guardianship authorities and guardians

Each jurisdiction has a guardianship authority which has power under legislation to consent to treatment on behalf of an incompetent patient. These authorities also have the power to appoint guardians, or remove and replace them. The guardianship authorities are not courts and are not subject to the rules of evidence. They are normally multi-disciplinary, meaning that the tribunal members will come from different professions.

Jurisdiction	Guardianship authority	Legislation
NSW	Guardianship Tribunal	Guardianship Act 1987
Qld	Guardianship and Administration Tribunal	Guardianship and Administration Act 2000
SA	Guardianship Board	Guardianship and Administration Act 1993
Tas	Guardianship and Administration Board	Guardianship and Administration Act 1995
Vic	Guardianship & Administration List, Victorian Civil and Administrative Tribunal	Guardianship and Administration Act 1986
WA	State Administrative Tribunal	Guardianship and Administration Act 1990, s 51
ACT	Guardianship and Management of Property Tribunal	Guardianship and Management of Property Act 1991
NT	Guardianship Panel and the Local Court	Adult Guardianship Act 1988

Each guardianship authority, and the guardians they appoint, must make treatment decisions according to a number of key principles set out in each piece of legislation. Generally speaking, they are bound to make decisions in the patient's best interests, or which promote and maintain the patient's health and well-being. They are also subject to whatever is known about what the patient would have wanted in the circumstances, and they must make the decision in a way that is the least restrictive of the person's rights: *Guardianship Act 1987* (NSW), s 4; *Guardianship and Administration Act 2000* (Qld), Sch 1, s 12;

Guardianship and Administration Act 1993 (SA), s 5; *Guardianship and Adminis-tration Act 1995* (Tas), ss 6, 43(2); *Guardianship and Administration Act 1986* (Vic), ss 4, 38; *Guardianship and Administration Act 1990* (WA), ss 4(2)(a), 51; *Guardian-ship and Management of Property Act 1991* (ACT), s 4; *Adult Guardianship Act 1988* (NT), s 4.

Health attorneys, enduring guardians and medical agents

Unlike guardians appointed by the courts or guardianship authorities, health attorneys, enduring guardians and medical agents are appointed by the patient, before their incapacity. An attorney's primary duty is to follow the instructions in the power (Stewart, Kerridge and Parker 2008). General powers are granted to consent to medical treatment but, in addition to these, specific instructions can be stipulated by the patient.

Jurisdiction	Legislation
NSW	*Guardianship Act 1987*, Part 2 (enduring guardian)
Qld	*Powers of Attorney Act 1998*, Part 3 (health attorney)
SA	*Consent to Medical Treatment and Palliative Care Act 1995*, Part 2, Division 3 (medical agent) *Guardianship and Administration Act 1993*, Part 3 (enduring guardian)
Tas	*Guardianship and Administration Act 1995*, Part 5 (enduring guardian)
Vic	*Guardianship and Administration Act 1986*, Division 5A (enduring guardian) *Medical Treatment Act 1988*, Part 2 (medical agent)
WA	*Guardianship and Administration Act 1990* (enduring guardian)
ACT	*Powers of Attorney Act 2006* (enduring attorney)

Interestingly, South Australia and Victoria have two separate types of health attorneys, who must make their decisions in quite different ways. In both jurisdictions, enduring guardians must make a decision that generally accords with the best interests of the patient (the exact wording differs in each juris-diction), whereas medical agents must make a substituted judgment.

Persons responsible

At common law the relatives of incompetent patients have no power to consent to their medical treatment (Skegg 1984). To that extent treatment would be provided to such patients by doctors under the doctrine of necessity (Stewart, Kerridge and Parker 2008).

All States (but not the ACT or Northern Territory) have passed legislation granting rights to relatives and close friends to consent to treatment. In New South Wales, Queensland, Victoria, Tasmania and Western Australia a person responsible for consent can be chosen from a list of candidates: *Guardianship Act 1987* (NSW), Part 5; *Powers of Attorney Act 1998* (Qld), Chapter 4; *Guardianship and Administration Act 1995* (Tas), Part 6; *Guardianship and Administration Act 1986* (Vic), Part 4A; *Guardianship and Administration Act 1990* (WA), s 119.

In general the order for appointment of persons responsible works as follows:

1.   a court or tribunal appointed guardian;
2.   an enduring attorney or enduring guardian;
3.   the spouse of the person in a close and continuing relationship with the person (including de facto relationships and homosexual partners in New South Wales, Queensland and Tasmania);
4.   the unpaid primary carer (people receiving a carer's pension are not considered to be paid and whoever cared for the patient before they were admitted to institutional care may still be regarded as their carer);
5.   a close friend or relative of the person. A person is considered a close friend or relative when they have maintained a close personal relationship through frequent personal contact and have a personal interest in the patient's welfare. (Stewart, Kerridge and Parker 2008)

In Victoria, a further hierarchy is given for non-spousal relatives, namely the eldest of any of the following who are over 18 years (*Guardianship and Administration Act 1986* (Vic), s 3):

(a) son or daughter;
(b) father or mother;
(c) brother or sister;
(d) grandfather or grandmother;
(e) grandson or granddaughter;
(f) uncle or aunt; or
(g) nephew or niece.

Finally, in Queensland, a further personal responsible is the Adult Guardian who may be asked to consent as 'statutory health attorney' if no close friends or relatives are available.

In South Australia, the *Guardianship and Administration Act 1993* (SA), s 59, grants powers of consent to the nearest relative, in the absence of a guardian. A relative is defined to be:

(a) a spouse;
(b) a parent;
(c) a person (not being a guardian appointed under this Act) who acts in *loco parentis* in relation to the person;
(d) a brother or sister of or over 18 years of age;
(e) a son or daughter of or over 18 years of age.

Limits on consent: special and prescribed medical treatments

Guardianship legislation in all jurisdictions has definitions of special or prescribed medical treatments which can only be consented to by the Supreme Court or the guardianship authority. These treatments are normally concerned with reproduction (abortions, sterilisations or contraceptives), psychiatric treatments (like electro-convulsive therapy and psychosurgery), donation of tissue to third parties, or experimental medical treatments. The tests for whether the authority should consent range from requirements that the treatment be in the patient's best interests, to the requirement that the treatment be necessary to save the patient's life or prevent serious damage to the patient's health.

Jurisdiction	Legislation
NSW	*Guardianship Act 1987* (NSW), ss 33, 45, 45A *Guardianship Regulation 2005*, cll 8- 9.
Qld	*Guardianship and Administration Act 2000* (Qld), ss 68-74
SA	*Guardianship and Administration Act 1993* (SA), s 61
Tas	*Guardianship and Administration Act 1995* (Tas), s 45
Vic	*Guardianship and Administration Act 1986* (Vic), ss 3, 42B-42G
WA	*Guardianship and Administration Act 1990* (WA), ss 57, 67
ACT	*Guardianship and Management of Property Act 1991* (ACT), Dictionary, s 70 *Powers of Attorney Act 2006* (ACT), s 73
NT	*Adult Guardianship Act 1988* (NT), s 21

Because the *parens patriae* jurisdiction is wider than the statutory jurisdiction of the guardianship authorities, claims are more likely to be brought before the Supreme Court. This occurred in *Northern Sydney and Central Coast Area Health Service v CT by his Tutor ET* [2005] NSWSC 551, where the Supreme Court approved the donation of bone marrow by an intellectually disabled adult (CT) to his brother NT, who was suffering from non-Hodgkin's lymphoma. Consent could not be given by CT's other relatives of the Guardianship Tribunal because their powers to consent were limited to treatments which promoted and maintained CT's health and well-being. Donating bone marrow served no therapeutic purpose for CT and as such did not promote the physical welfare of CT. The court approved of the treatment as it was in CT's best interests to be able to help his brother (see Chapter 25 for more regarding donation of human tissue by incompetent adults).

References

Alexander, M (1988) 'Clinical determination of mental competence. A theory and retrospective study'. *Arch Neurol* **45**: 23-6.

Appelbaum, PS and T Grisso (1997) 'Capacities of hospitalized, medically ill patients to consent to treatment'. *Psychosomatics* **38**(2): 119-25.

Appelbaum, PS, T Grisso et al (1999) 'Competence of depressed patients for consent to research'. *Am J Psychiatry* **156**(9): 1380-4.

Arnold, R (2006) 'Fast Fact and Concept #55: Decision Making Capacity. 2nd ed', 2008, <http://www.eperc.mcw.edu/fastFact/ff_55.htm>.

Arnold, R and J Kellum (2003) 'Moral justifications for surrogate decision-making in the intensive care unit: Implications and limitations'. *Crit Care Med* **31**(5): S347-S353.

Barilan, YM and M Weintraub (2001) 'Persuasion as respect for persons: an alternative view of autonomy and of the limits of discourse'. *J Med Philos* **26**(1): 13-33.

Bennett, B (1997) *Law and Medicine*. Sydney, LBC Information Services.

Boustani, M, CM Callahan et al (2005) 'Implementing a screening and diagnosis program for dementia in primary care'. *J Gen Intern Med* **20**(7): 572-7.

Breden, TM and J Vollmann (2004) 'The cognitive based approach of capacity assessment in psychiatry: a philosophical critique of the MacCAT-T'. *Health Care Anal* **12**(4): 273-83; discussion 265-72.

Brock, D (1991) 'Trumping advance directives'. *Hastings Cent Rep* **Sept-Oct**: 55-6.

Chambers-Evans, J and FA Carnevale (2005) 'Dawning of awareness: the experience of surrogate decision making at the end of life'. *J Clin Ethics* **16**(1): 28-45.

Collins, LG, SM Parks et al (2006) 'The state of advance care planning: one decade after SUPPORT'. *Am J Hosp Palliat Care* **23**(5): 378-84.

Davidson, K, C Hackler et al (1989) 'Physicians' attitudes on advance directives'. *JAMA* **262**(2415-9).

Devereux, J (1999) Competency to Consent to treatment: An Introduction. *Controversies in Health Law*. I Freckelton, K Petersen. Sydney, Federation Press.

Ditto, P, J Danks et al (2001) 'Advance directives as acts of communication'. *Arch Intern Med* **161**: 421-30.

Dunn, LB, MA Nowrangi et al (2006) 'Assessing decisional capacity for clinical research or treatment: a review of instruments'. *Am J Psychiatry* **163**(8): 1323-34.

Dworkin, R (1993) *Life's Dominion : an argument about abortion and euthanasia*. London, Harper Collins.

Elliott, C (1996) *The rules of insanity*. Albany, New York Press.

Emanuel, E and L Emanuel (1990) 'Living wills: Past, present and future'. *J Clin Ethics* **1**: 9-19.

Emanuel, EJ (2008) *The Oxford textbook of clinical research ethics*. Oxford; New York, Oxford University Press.

Fassier, T, A Lautrette et al (2005) 'Care at the end of life in critically ill patients: the European perspective'. *Curr Opin Crit Care* **11**(6): 616-23.

Finucaine, P, C Myser et al (1993) 'Is she fit to sign doctor? Practical ethical issues in assessing the competence of elderly patients'. *Med J Aust* **159**: 400-3.

Fitten, L, R Lusky et al (1990) 'Assessing treatment decision-making capacity in elderly nursing-home residents'. *J Am Geriatr Soc* **38**: 1097-104.

Fletcher, J and E Spencer (1995) 'Incompetent patient on the slippery slope'. *Lancet* **345**(271).

Folstein, M, S Folstein et al (1975) 'Mini-mental state: a practical method for grading the cognitive state of patients for the clinician'. *J Psychiatr Res* **12**: 189-98.

Gilovich, T and V Medvec (1995) 'The experience of regret – what, when and why'. *Psych Rev* **102**(379-95).

Griffith, D (1991) 'The Best Interests Standard: a comparison of the State's parens patriae authority and judicial oversight in best interest determination for children and incompetent patients'. *Issues in Law and Medicine* **7**(3): 287.

Grisso, T and P Appelbaum (1998) *Assessing Competence to Consent to Treatment: A Guide for Physicians and other Health Professionals*. New York, Oxford University Press.

Hare, J, C Pratt et al (1992) 'Agreement between patients and their self-selected surrogates on difficult medical decisions'. *Arch Intern Med* **15**(2): 1049-54.

High, D (1988) 'All in the family: Extended autonomy and expectations in surrogate health care decision-making'. *Gerontologist* **28**: 46-52.

Hoffman, B and J Srinivasan (1992) 'A study of competence to consent to treatment in a psychiatric hospital'. *Can J Psychiatry* **37**: 179-82.

Hurst, SA (2004) 'When patients refuse assessment of decision-making capacity: how should clinicians respond?' *Arch Intern Med* **164**(16): 1757-60.

Jordens, C, M Little et al (2005) 'From advance directives to advance care planning: current legal status, ethical rationales and a new research agenda'. *Intern Med J* **35**(9): 563-6.

Junermann, H (1986) The two camps on rationality. *Judgement and decision making: an interdisciplinary reader*. H Arkes and K Hammond. Cambridge, Cambridge University Press: 627-41.

Kellogg, F, M Crain et al (1992) 'Life-sustaining interventions in frail elderly persons. Talking about choices'. *Arch Intern Med* **152**: 2317-20.

Kirby, M (2003) 'Book Review: Who can decide? The six step assessment process'. *Elder Law Review* **2**: 1.

Kirschner, KL (2005) 'When written advance directives are not enough'. *Clin Geriatr Med* **21**(1): 193-209, x.

Kitamura, T and N Takahashi (2007) 'Ethical and conceptual aspects of capacity assessments in psychiatry'. *Curr Opin Psychiatry* **20**(6): 578-81.

Lai, JM and J Karlawish (2007) 'Assessing the capacity to make everyday decisions: a guide for clinicians and an agenda for future research'. *Am J Geriatr Psychiatry* **15**(2): 101-11.

Lee, M, M Heland et al (2003) 'Respecting Patient Choices: advance care planning to improve patient care at Austin Health'. *Health Issues* **77**: 23-26.

Leland, J (2001) 'Advance directives and establishing the goals of care'. *Prim Care* **28**(2): 349-63.

Lowe, M, I Kerridge et al (2000) 'A question of competence'. *Age and Ageing* **29**(2): 179-82.

Marson, D, M Cody et al (1995) 'Neuropsychologic predictors of competency in Alzheimer's disease using a rational reasons legal standard'. *Arch Neurol* **52**: 955-9.

Marson, D, K Ingram et al (1995) 'Assessing the competency of patients with Alzheimer's disease under different legal standards: A prototype instrument'. *Arch Neurol* **52**: 949-54.

Martin, DK, LL Emanuel et al (2000) 'Planning for the end of life'. *Lancet* **356**(9242): 1672-6.

McCall Smith, A (1997) 'Beyond Autonomy'. *Journal of Contemporary Health Law and Policy* **14**: 23.

Molloy, D, M Silberfeld et al (1996) 'Measuring capacity to complete an advance directive. Journal of the American Geriatrics Society'. *J Am Geriatr Soc* **44**(6): 660-4.

Morrison, R, E Olson et al (1995) 'The inaccessibility of advance directives on transfer from ambulatory to acute care settings'. *JAMA* **275**(6): 478-82.

Moye, J and DC Marson (2007) 'Assessment of decision-making capacity in older adults: an emerging area of practice and research'. *J Gerontol B Psychol Sci Soc Sci* **62**(1): P3-P11.

National Health and Medical Research Council (2007) *Ethical Guidelines for the Care of People in Post-Coma Unresponsiveness (Vegetative State) or a Minimally Responsive State – DRAFT*. Canberra, National Health and Medical Research Council.

Nussbaum, M (2001) *Upheavals of thought: the intelligence of emotions*. Cambridge, Cambridge University Press.

Ouslander, J, A Tymchuk and B Rahbar (1989) 'Health care decisions among elderly long-term residents and their potential proxies'. *Ann Intern Med* **149**: 1367-72.

Parker, M (2004) 'Judging capacity: Paternalism and the risk-related standard'. *Journal of Law and Medicine* **11**(4): 482-91.

Parker, M, C Stewart et al (2007) 'Two steps forward, one step back: advance care planning, Australian regulatory frameworks and the Australian Medical Association'. *Intern Med J* **37**(9): 637-43.

Patrick, D, M Danis et al (1988) 'Quality of life following intensive care'. *J Gen Int Med*(3): 218-23.

Peisah, C and H Brodaty (1994) 'Dementia and the will-making process: the role of the medical practitioner'. *Med J Aust* **161**: 381-4.

Pellegrino, ED and DC Thomasma (1981) *For the patients' good: The restoration of beneficence in health care*. New York, Oxford University Press.

Potter, J, D Stewart et al (1994) 'Living wills: would sick people change their mind?' *Postgrad Med J* **70**: 818-20.

Powell, P (2004) *The Origins and Development of the Protective Jurisdiction of the Supreme Court of New South Wales*. Sydney, Francis Forbes Society.

Prendergast, T (2001) 'Advance care planning: pitfalls, progress, promise'. *Crit Care Med* **29**(2 [Suppl]): N24-9.

President's Commission for the Study of Ethical Problems in Medicine and Biomedical and Behavioural Research (1983). *Decisions to forgo life-sustaining treatment: a report on the ethical, medical and legal issues in treatment decisions*: 197-229.

Rosin, AJ and Y van Dijk (2005) 'Subtle ethical dilemmas in geriatric management and clinical research'. *J Med Ethics* **31**(6): 355-9.

Ryan, C (1996) 'Betting you life: an argument against certain advance directives'. *J Med Ethics* **22**: 95-9.

Sachs, G (1993) Improving advance directives: More dialogue not more laws'. *J Clin Ethics* **4**(2): 171-3.

Sapira, J (1990) *The art and science of bedside diagnosis*, Williams and Wilkin.

Schade, S and H Muslin (1989) 'Do not resuscitate decisions: discussions with patients'. *J Med Ethics* **15**: 186-90.

Shalowitz, DI, E Garrett-Mayer et al (2006) 'The accuracy of surrogate decision makers: a systematic review'. *Arch Intern Med* **166**(5): 493-7.

Skegg, P (1984) *Law, Ethics and Medicine*. Oxford, Clarendon Press.

Stanley, B, M Stanley et al (1988) 'Functional competence of elderly patients at risk'. *Gerontologist* **28**: 53-8.

Stewart, C (1999) 'Advance Directives, the Right to Die and the Common Law: Recent Problems with Blood Transfusions'. *Melbourne University Law Review* **23**: 161

Stewart, C (2006) Advance directives: Disputes and dilemmas. *Disputes and Dilemmas in Health Law*. I Freckelton and K Petersen. Sydney, Federation Press.

Stewart, C and P Biegler (2004) 'A primer on the law of competence to refuse medical treatment'. *Australian Law Journal* **78**(5): 325-42.

Sugarman, J, D McCrory et al (1998) 'Getting meaningful informed consent from older adults: A structured literature review of empirical research'. *J Am Geriatr Soc* **46**: 517-29.

Teno, J, S Licks et al (1997) 'Do advance directives provide instructions that direct care?' *J Am Geriatr Soc* **45**: 508-12.

Teno, J, J Lynne et al (1994) 'Do formal advance directives affect resuscitation decisions and the use of resources for seriously ill patients?' *J Clin Ethics* **5**(1): 23-30.

The Support Principal Investigators (1995) 'A controlled trial to improve care of seriously ill hospitalised patients'. *JAMA* **274**(20): 1591-8.

Tomaugh, T and N McIntyre (1992) 'The Mini-mental State examination: A comprehensive review'. *J Am Geriatr Soc* **40**: 922-35.

Tomlinson, T, K Howe et al (1990) 'An empirical study of proxy consent for elderly persons'. *Gerontologist* **30**: 54-64.

Tversky, A and D Kahneman (1974) 'Judgement under uncertainty: heuristics and biases'. *Science* **185**: 1124-31.

Varma, S and D Wendler (2007) 'Medical decision making for patients without surrogates'. *Arch Intern Med* **167**(16): 1711-5.

Watson, LC, CL Lewis et al (2005) 'Asking family about memory loss. Is it helpful?' *J Gen Intern Med* **20**(1): 28-32.

Zweibel, N and C Cassel (1989) 'Treatment choices at the end of life: A comparison of decisions by older patients and their physician selected proxies'. *Gerontologist* **29**: 615-21.

CHAPTER 14

CONSENT

Case 1

AB is a 39-year-old sheet-metal worker who was admitted to hospital for a laparoscopic cholecystectomy. The surgical resident medical officer, Dr D, was asked to 'consent' him as part of his pre-operative work-up. She had never seen a laparoscopic cholecystectomy performed but had a good understanding of the anatomy of the biliary tree and was able to answer most of Mr B's questions and obtain his signature on the consent form.

Unfortunately, due to the patient's obesity, laparoscopic cholecystectomy was unsuccessful and an open procedure was performed. Following surgery he required a day in the intensive care unit before returning to the wards. Dr D was embarrassed that the operation, post-operative course and scars remaining after the procedure bore so little resemblance to what she had described to the patient. She was also concerned that she would be legally liable if Mr S took legal action.

Case 2

A 31-year-old male was admitted to hospital with acute myeloblastic leukaemia. The patient stated on admission that he was a Jehovah's Witness and would not accept any blood products, although he was aware that the usual treatment of acute leukaemia involves the need for a large quantity of blood products. No blood products were used during the course of his therapy and blood tests were restricted to not more than twice per week.

The patient's blood count fell markedly during therapy until results were at the absolute limit at which he could be expected to remain alive. During the course of this therapy the patient developed severe air hunger and confusion, both of which were relieved by the administration of 50% oxygen. On day 25 his blood count began to show signs of recovery and he was discharged on day 31.

It is now accepted that individuals have the right to make decisions about their own health care. Consent is the most visible way in which the health-care system manifests respect for patient autonomy, ensuring that competent patients are able to make autonomous decisions and that non-competent patients are protected from harm. Consent can be defined as the 'autonomous authorisation of a medical intervention … by individual patients' (Beauchamp and Faden 2004).

Although there is broad recognition of the importance of consent, the concept is not particularly clear. Understanding of its practical application in clinical practice is imperfect, particularly in patients with serious illness, and there are many conflicting views of its nature and procedures (Little and Leeder 1996; Cassel, Leon et al 2001). In this book we use the term 'consent', rather than 'informed consent', as this is more consistent with Australian law – however, we believe that neither term is entirely satisfactory for describing the complex interactions between health-care professionals and patients at the time of decision-making.

Consent is primarily concerned with the elements, substance and process of communication between health professionals and patients – as defined by law, clinical practice and moral theory (Faden and Beauchamp 1986). A number of different models of consent have been described, each of which incorporates assumptions about the process of decision-making, and none of these models entirely captures the complexity of the consent process (Lidz, Appelbaum et al 1988; Brody 1989; Wear 1998; Katz 2002). Taken together they suggest that consent is best thought of as a process that occurs as part of the relationship between patient and therapist, involving shared and considered reflection on the goals of treatment and on both the patient's and therapist's values and beliefs.

For consent to be legally or ethically valid the person consenting must have the capacity to give consent (he or she must be *competent* and have the capacity to *understand* information relevant to the decision), consent must be *freely and voluntarily* given, the consent must be *specified* (for a specific purpose) and the consent must be based on adequate *disclosure* of material information by the clinician. While consent should be regarded as an ongoing part of all health-care relationships, it becomes a particular concern whenever the management of a patient's medical problems involves invasive procedures or material risks.

We have already discussed the assessment of competence and the processes by which decisions can be made for non-competent patients in Chapter 13. In this chapter we will expand on other aspects of consent.

Table 14.1: The elements of consent

Elements which *enable* a valid consent:

1. Competence
2. Voluntariness

Elements which *inform*:

3. Disclosure of Information
4. Understanding of Information

Elements which *enact* consent

5. Decision (including specificity)
6. Authorisation (of the chosen treatment plan)

Voluntariness

If an action is voluntary it means that one is able to exercise choice, sufficiently free from undue manipulation or coercion; where manipulation can be defined as the deliberate distortion or omission of information in an attempt to induce a patient to make a certain decision, and coercion can be defined as the use of implicit or explicit threats to ensure that a treatment is accepted (Etchells, Sharpe et al 1996; Kuczewski and McCruden 2001).

A number of 'internal' and 'external' factors may impact on a patient's health-care decisions. Pain, anxiety, depression, physical impairment, weakness or debility, immobility, isolation or threats to personal identity may all influence the decisions a person makes about their own health care. While it may be possible to reduce the impact of these factors on decision-making, ultimately such internal influences may be an unavoidable feature of health care.

Illness may leave patients prone to influences from partners, family members, clinicians and others, so great care must be taken to ensure that patients do not become the objects of deceit, force or manipulation. There is a variety of ways in which a sick person maybe coerced, ranging from strong forms of coercion such as threats and violence to milder forms such as persuasion or emotion-laden appeals. At times it may be necessary for health workers to intervene to prevent patients being coerced by family members or authority figures such as lawyers or the police.

A range of strategies can also be used to reduce the possibility of coercion or manipulation, such as providing sufficient information to enable the patient to make an informed decision; presenting this information in an unbiased manner; encouraging the patient to ask questions, and offering the patient opportunities both to have a private consultation without others being present; or providing the opportunity to have a family member or support person present in all consultations.

Health-care workers generally have a duty to refrain from influencing patients if such influence would cause their decisions to be substantially non-voluntary. In the rare situations where the use of force or coercion is justifiable, such as where a patient is at immediate risk of harming herself or himself, health-care workers should use the least restrictive technique possible. Finally, and perhaps most obviously, health workers should not be involved with procedures that are by their very nature coercive, such as torture or executions.

Disclosure

The moral justification for open disclosure in health care derives from respect for patients' freedom to make autonomous choices and from recognition of its importance in the development and maintenance of a trusting and effective health professional-patient relationship (Parascandola, Hawkins et al 2002). The opportunity for voluntary decision-making is only present where there has been adequate disclosure by the health professional. A patient with a problem for which there is more than one management option cannot give consent if information regarding some of the options has not been disclosed. Therapists may therefore directly affect patients' freedom of choice through their control of the type and amount of information they provide.

Most patients wish to be given sufficient information to enable them to make health decisions consistent with their values and goals (Jenkins, Fallow-filed et al 2001; Miyata, Takahashi et al 2005). Information facilitates decision-making, family communication and involvement in care; assists patients to cope with illness and with therapy; and provides them with a sense of control and a way to manage uncertainty (Clarke, Hall et al 2004; Kirk, Kirk et al 2004; Thorne, Hislop et al 2006).

Many patients expect health professionals involved in their care to identify their particular health problems, develop a list of treatment options, formulate a management plan and make a recommendation, but also expect that they themselves will ultimately make decisions about their own health care and about whether to accept or refuse a recommended treatment plan/option. However, different patients will have different preferences for involvement in decision-making (Ford, Schofield et al 2003; Hagerty, Butow et al 2004). Some may wish to retain all authority while others, particularly those who are elderly, ill or vulnerable, may often choose to follow their physician's or nurse's recommendations for treatment and/or cede decision-making responsibility to them (Pinquart and Duberstein 2004; Levinson, Kao et al 2005). Preferences for participation in decision-making may also vary according to a patient's experience of health care, the relationship they have established with their carer and their cultural background. But health professionals cannot and should not make assumptions regarding a patient's preferences for participation in decision-making on the basis of the community that they belong to, and preferences for participation in decision-making should not be assumed to be a stable 'personal trait' as they may change with time, illness experience and proximity to death or disability.

Among the most important information that is required to be disclosed is the potential benefit and the degree of risk attached to the therapy or intervention that is of most significance. In clinical practice risk can be understood as both the probability of a particular event (the product of the magnitude of the potential harm one is exposed to multiplied by the probability of that harm occurring), and the harms that are associated with those events. On some occasions attempts to quantify risks like this give reasonable guidance as to what should be disclosed. For example, where potential harm is very great, and the probability of its happening is very high, then that risk should be disclosed. Likewise, where the potential harm is minor but there is a very high probability of it happening, for example a rash with antibiotics, then that risk should also be disclosed. Alternatively, where the potential harm is insignificant and there is an extremely small risk of it occurring, then that risk need not always be disclosed (Bogardis, Holmboe et al 1999). Whether such risks *should* be disclosed may arise in the context of discussion between the health professional and the patient, and clarification of the patients' goals and fears. Risk communication is therefore both qualitative and quantitative and descriptive and normative and is as much concerned with values and beliefs as it is with information transfer (Edwards and Elwyn 2001).

A number of strategies have been advanced to improve risk communication, including the use of risk comparisons (comparing a medical risk with a non-medical risk, such as the risk of being attacked by a shark), the presentation of risk in both descriptive and numerical terms and as absolute and relative risks, and the use of visual and pictorial formats (Edwards and Elwyn 2001; Paling 2003).

Unfortunately, patient management often involves decisions where the risks are poorly understood, difficult to predict or involve death and serious disability. In such situations the degree of information required, and the risk assessment itself, is value-laden and not easily delineated by legislation or decision analysis. While information disclosure needs to be tailored to each situation and to each patient's needs and preferences, guidelines for information disclosure such as those provided by the National Health and Medical Research Council (Table 14.2) provide a systematic approach to information disclosure.

Table 14.2: Requirements for information transfer in clinical practice

1. Diagnosis (including degree of uncertainty about this)
2. Prognosis (including degree of uncertainty about this)
3. Options for investigations/treatments
4. Burdens and benefits of investigations/treatments
5. Whether intervention conventional/experimental
6. Who will perform intervention
7. Consequences of choosing or not choosing treatment
8. Significant expected short-term and long-term outcomes
9. Time involved
10. Cost involved

Information given may be modified by:
1. Seriousness of patient's condition
2. Nature of the intervention
3. Degree of possible harm
4. Likelihood or risk
5. Patients' needs, attitude, understanding, etc

While such guidelines provide some direction, there remains considerable confusion as to what information should be disclosed in any given situation and whether patients actually want large amounts of information, particularly when they are seriously ill. Perhaps more importantly, models such as that provided by the NHMRC assume that all health information is amenable to reason and to good communication skills. While this may be true of technical information, it is genuinely unclear whether it is ever possible to communicate the types of experiences that characterise serious illness, such as pain, fear, debilitating lethargy, loss of identity and sense of isolation (Little, Jordens et al 2008). These types of concerns have led some to argue that information disclosure requirements laid out in professional guidelines and in legal judgments are far removed from the practicalities of medicine and from the real experiences of patients – who may be more interested in understanding the rationale behind their health carer's recommendations than in the details of the care plan (Henman, Butow et al 2002; Leydon, Leydon et al 2002).

Regardless of the informational content provided, it is important that information be communicated sensitively and effectively and in a manner that is consistent with the patient's personal values and cultural beliefs (Kagawa-Singer and Blackhall 2001). Consent is not a simple event or action, but a highly complex process and it is essential that health professionals have the necessary communication skills to provide clarity, direction, compassion and reassurance (Edwards and Elwyn 2001).

Specificity

Consent should be specific to an intervention or treatment; it cannot be generalised to other treatments (except where related to the primary treatment and/or where necessary to save the patient's life or prevent serious injury). Unfortunately, it is often extremely difficult to adequately delineate many medical therapies, particularly where these are complex, ongoing or characterised by diagnostic, therapeutic or prognostic uncertainty. For example, does consent to a chemotherapy regimen extend to the use of intravenous fluids, anti-gout drugs and antimicrobial prophylaxis or does consent to diabetic care extend to alterations in insulin regimens, adjustments to monitoring protocols or additions of oral hypoglycaemic agents? Alternatively, should a patient be asked to consent to a complex therapeutic entity such as transplantation, which may involve multiple specific interventions, have no single end-point and be associated with considerable, but unpredictable, risks? While these issues have received scant attention in the ethics literature, within the law there has been considerable debate regarding the scope of consent and the probity of 'blanket' consent clauses (*Brushett v Cowan* (1990) 3 CCLT (2d) 195 (Nfld CA) at 199; *Davis and Barking, Havering and Brentwood Health Authority* (1993) 4 Med LR 85).

Understanding and acceptance of information

The main difficulty with consent is that it is not always easy to find out what a patient wishes to know, or to determine whether they have been adequately informed. The crucial issue here is not whether patients have been provided with information but whether they appreciate and understand that information.

There are many barriers to understanding between patients and members of the health-care team, including time constraints, differences in terminology and knowledge, and the fact that it is difficult to imagine one's self in another's position. When information is given to patients there are several ways in which it is possible to check their understanding. Important information should be reinforced, repeated and checked for understanding, and diagrams are a useful aid in helping patients remember and relate information. The presentation of information to the patient in clinical practice must be informative and be couched in language that is simple and free of jargon. Patients must be given adequate time to make decisions and should be encouraged to consider other options or seek alternative opinions if they require. In cases where English is a second language the use of an interpreter is usually appropriate.

Decision aids are sometimes used to assist patients to understand the risks, benefits, outcomes and probabilities of outcomes associated with specific interventions, clarify their own values and express their preferences for treatment (O'Connor, Legare et al 2003; Trevena and Barratt 2003). While decision aids are time consuming and not appropriate for all patients, there is some evidence that they are effective in increasing knowledge, encouraging realistic expectations of treatment, reducing conflict and clarifying patients preferences for treatment (O'Connor, Llewellyn-Thomas et al 2004). There is no evidence that they influence health outcomes or increase the moral congruence of health-care decisions (Kennedy 2003; O'Connor, Legare et al 2003).

Critiques of consent

It is clear that the construction and attainability of each of the elements of consent is open to question. While this creates a challenge for clinicians and policy makers, it does not really threaten the very notion of consent. In contrast, in recent years a number of other critiques have challenged the philosophical basis of consent and the descriptive adequacy of the concept of consent.

Consent requirements in health care are perhaps the most visible representation of the socio-cultural emphasis given to respect for autonomy. The pre-eminent role of autonomy in bioethics and health law has, however, come under sustained attack. It has been suggested, for example, that health-care decisions should depend less on respecting autonomy and more on providing care and compassion; because the focus on autonomy and individualism diminishes the importance of human relationships, caring and interdependence, and fails to acknowledge how vulnerable people may become in the setting of serious illness. It has also been noted that the choices that a person makes are only comprehensible within their social, cultural and institutional context; and the emphasis on autonomy is largely a cultural construction, as non-Western cultures tend not to place such value on the rights of individuals. Neither of these criticisms requires that the commitment to consent be abandoned – rather, they suggest that consent in medicine needs to be critically examined within its social, cultural and relational context.

The idea that consent is simply an exercise in rational choice based around logical consideration of the burdens and benefits associated with an intervention has also been criticised on the grounds that health-care decisions are rarely amenable to the simple logic of consequentialism and that they are frequently intuitive or based on over-riding concerns, such as fear of death, or the anticipated regret that may follow a decision to not 'try everything' (Landman 1993; Reynolds and Nelson 2007; Little, Jordens et al 2008). Critics of consent as 'rational choice' assert that consent can never be completely rational when one's life is at stake and when outcomes are uncertain, and that consent is ultimately imprecise, discursive, contextual, culturally determined and value laden (Kopelman 2004).

A number of different models of consent have been described in the bioethics literature. Wear fashions consent as an 'event', a tool for medical management, Brody describes consent in terms of transparent decision-making, Lidz describes consent as a process that respects the active participation of the patient in decision-making, and Katz describes consent as a conversation between the patient and physician where each relate to the other as equals and each shares their values, beliefs and vulnerabilities (Lidz, Appelbaum et al 1988; Brody 1989; Wear 1998; Katz, Fitzgerald et al 2002). Each of these models has some strengths and, taken together with the critiques of consent described above, it is arguable that consent should be conceptualised as a staged, dynamic process, an ongoing 'conversation of consent' that takes place within a context shaped by the skills, values, expectations, needs and experiences of the patient and the health professional (Nelson and Nelson 1999). If viewed in this way, disclosure of information, particularly about material risks, remains important, but other concepts are also emphasised, such as vulnerability, trust, regret and responsibility, as are other moral values, such as professional commitments to care and presence (an implicit contract to provide ongoing explanation, reassurance and support during a patient's course of treatment). These concepts and values are fundamental to the health professional–patient relationship and are a pre-requisite for effective communication; and any construction of consent that fails to account for them cannot adequately capture its complexity or contextual specificity.

Trust

The values of honesty, integrity, benevolence, respect, compassion and courage, among others, have all been advanced as traits that are central to professional morality and to the therapeutic relationship.

The concept that has been most closely examined in relation to the status and survival of the professions is trust (O'Neill 2002). The psychologist, Carl Rogers, has argued that trust is one of the prerequisites of the therapeutic relationship; the sociologist, Anthony Giddens, has described how social change has led first to the investiture of trust in the expert professions, and then inevitably to erosion of that trust; and the Australian medical ethicist, Wendy Rogers (2002), has argued that doctors have a moral duty to trust their patients (Rogers 1957; Giddens 1990; Rogers 2002). What then is trust? And why is it regarded as so fundamental a concept to the health professions?

The word trust has many meanings, but in relation to health care it tends to have connotations of faith, commitment, a general expression of respect, belief and confidence. As Baier has noted: 'We count on all sorts of people for all sorts of vital things, without any contracts, explicit or implicit, with them or with any third coordinating party' (Baier 1995).

Trust is particularly important in medicine because of medicine's complexity, because of the degree of expertise required to provide appropriate care and because of the risk, ambiguity and uncertainty inherent in medicine. Those who are ill and require care do not have the knowledge or expertise necessary to cure their ills and they can never know everything relevant to their care or develop the skills needed to care for themselves. They must trust that those caring for them have these skills, use their knowledge wisely, respect them and have their best interests at heart. Trust, therefore, is an expression of vulnerability, as it results from need and is manifest in the discretionary powers provided to those entrusted with someone's care. Trust is fundamental to the health professional–patient relationship, for it provides the security necessary for an individual to consult a health professional, share their biography, describe their deepest fears or secrets and allow their body to be exposed and examined.

But trust is fragile, and can be misplaced or destroyed. Abuse of power, boundary violations, incompetence, deception, manifest conflict of interest, experience of harm and lack of care and respect all can damage trust (Gilson 2003). And relationships between health professionals and patients cannot survive a loss of trust. Therapeutic relationships where trust has been lost are characterised by adversarial communication, inadequate information transfer, unilateral decision-making, anger, poor compliance, secrecy and increased litigation.

The health professions are sometimes mistrusted (particularly the medical profession). O'Neill has argued that much of this mistrust is misplaced. The question of how to re-gain public trust goes beyond what is required to make the professions trustworthy, because institutions may be trustworthy but still be mistrusted. However, making the professions more trusted and more trustworthy must continue to be among the greatest priorities of the professions (O'Neill 2002).

Shared decision-making: The ethical ideal?

Historically, both legal and institutional standards of consent have focused on disclosure of information by the doctor to the patient, rather than the two-way communication that has been referred to by some authors as 'shared decision-making' (Brock 1991). Narrow interpretations of consent that involve a one-way flow of information from therapist to patient lead to an unsatisfactory, simplistic model of information transfer – of health workers talking 'at' rather than 'with' patients. This has led to considerable misunderstanding of consent in the clinical context. Consent is commonly regarded as an action such as 'consenting a patient'. Seen in this light, the aim of consent is to prevent litigation and to adhere to institutional guidelines rather than to improve communication with patients. Such an interpretation often leads to a perfunctory approach to consent.

Consent is better thought of as a two-way process of shared and informed decision-making. Although several definitions of shared decision-making (SDM) exist (Charles, Whelan et al 2003), there is no consensus regarding the concept in the literature (Moumjid, Gafni et al 2007). Differences in definitions of shared decision-making relate to the role of the patient and health professional in the decision-making process, the sequencing of the involvement of each, and what is shared between them. Some definitions see SDM as the process by which health professionals provide information to patients so that they can make decisions according to their own values (Eddy 1990), whereas others view SDM as an interactive process in which patients and physicians participate in all phases of the decision making process and together negotiate a treatment plan (Charles, Gafni et al 1999). The definition provided by Coulter describes SDM as follows:

> In SDM, the intention is that patients and health professionals share both the process of decision-making and ownership of the decision made. Shared information about values and likely treatment outcomes is an essential prerequisite, but the process also depends on a commitment from both parties to engage in the decision-making process. The clinician has to be prepared to acknowledge the legitimacy of the patient's preferences and the patient has to accept shared responsibility for the treatment decision. (Coulter 1999)

All models of SDM maintain as their central focus the autonomy and interests of the patient but avoid a simplistic health professional–patient division of labour and the separation between 'facts' and information on the one hand ('the professional's role'), and preferences, choices or beliefs on the other ('the patient's role') (Veatch 1972). All recognise that health professionals are not simply value-neutral providers of facts regarding diagnosis, prognosis and treatment alternatives but are independent moral agents with well-defined professional roles. When health professionals talk with patients, present information to them, give advice or encourage compliance, they cannot help but express their own values and beliefs in relation to health, disease and their role as an advocate for the patients' health (Brock 1991).

Decision-making is unavoidably *shared* because each participant brings their own beliefs, values, perspectives and knowledge to the therapeutic relationship. For example, one patient may request extremely detailed information about alternative therapies whereas another may prefer to maintain a 'distance', making decisions in isolation. Other patients may autonomously authorise therapists to make decisions about medical treatment for them.

Clinical ethical practice demands much more of the health professional than a superficial recognition of patient self-determination. Although consent may be superficially seen as an action – an authorisation of a specific intervention, in a deeper sense it is an integral and continuing part of the process of shared decision-making. When seen in this light, the development of legal standards of disclosure, and better institutional guidelines for consent, may be less important than ensuring that professional education includes the teaching of efficient interactional skills and related values to all health-care professionals.

Jehovah's Witnesses and blood transfusions

The Jehovah's Witnesses are a Christian sect founded in the 1870s by Charles Russell in Pittsburgh, Pennsylvania, which now claims membership of 4.5 million people world-wide (Watt 1994). The philosophy of the Jehovah's Witnesses is that the transfusion of blood products is prohibited by the Old Testament.

The refusal of blood transfusion dates back to a 1945 church decision that is based on Biblical passages prohibiting the eating of blood (Anon 1945). Verses that are used to support this objection include Genesis 9:3,4: 'Only flesh with its soul – its blood – you must not eat'; Leviticus 17:13,14: '[You must] pour its blood out and cover it with dust'; and Acts 15:19-21: 'Abstain from … fornication and from what is strangled and from blood'. Modern Jehovah's Witnesses are aware of a large body of medical literature about the hazards of blood transfusion and of ways to avoid its use, and they feel that their stand is somewhat vindicated by recent epidemics of blood-borne viral illnesses such as Hepatitis C and HIV.

Jehovah's Witnesses accept that the application of biblical verse to some aspects of modern medical care is not always clear. They therefore divide blood products into two main groups: products that they will not accept such as whole blood, red cells, plasma, platelets of white cells; and products that must be decided by each individual's conscience such as immunoglobulins, coagulation factor preparations, albumin, vaccines, sera and organ transplants. Jehovah's Witnesses will not accept pre- and intra-operative storage of blood for later autologous transfusions but allow individuals to decide personally about haemodilution, haemodialysis, plasmapheresis, heart-lung bypass and blood salvaging techniques, providing that there is continuous extra-corporeal circulation and the blood does not stand still. Non-blood plasma expanders are generally accepted.

In essence, the philosophy of Jehovah's Witnesses is that blood has been designed and created by God, and should therefore be used as God intended it to be. The consequences of violating the prohibition against transfusions are considerable for Jehovah's Witnesses as this is regarded as a sin and may result in excommunication from the church and forfeiting the opportunity to attain eternal life.

Conflict between Jehovah's Witnesses and health workers occurs when health workers believe that the patient's best interests are served by giving them a blood transfusion but the patient refuses consent on religious grounds. There is now a clear legal recognition of the fact that patients have the right to refuse any form of treatment, although many health workers find this difficult to accept. Conflict between patients and doctors about this matter has been dealt with by three different techniques – coercion, deception or through attempts at mutual respect for both patient and physician autonomy (Macklin 1988).

An example where coercion has been thought to be a reasonable option can be found in the treatment of the children of Jehovah's Witness parents. Courts will generally support the transfusion of these children on the basis that parental autonomy is not unlimited and children should not be martyrs to the parent's beliefs (Frackiewicz, Lee et al 1991)(Quintero 1993). In the event that a child of a Jehovah's Witness parent requires blood transfusion, where all non-blood alternatives have failed, a court order should be obtained and the child transfused against the parent's wishes. Coercion is a tactic that cannot be used in other circumstances – indeed to do so would be to invite legal consequences.

An example of doctors who advocate the use of deception can be found in the results of a 1991 survey of 242 members of the European Society of Intensive Care Medicine who were asked about attitudes towards the use of blood transfusions in a hypothetical case involving an exsanguinating Jehovah's Witness patient. Twenty-six per cent (26%) of doctors stated that they would transfuse patients in these circumstances but would never inform the patient of this (Vincent 1991).

A model of shared decision-making suggests that in most cases neither coercion nor deception can be justified since they undermine the basis of the patient-therapist relationship. Much of the philosophy of Jehovah's Witnesses is left to individual interpretation and personal discretion, so, early, open and continuing communication is of vital importance. Witnesses should be informed adequately about the consequences of refusing blood products but their right to refuse treatment must be respected, even if this results in their death. Most Jehovah's Witnesses carry 'medical directive' cards that explicitly refuse blood transfusion under any circumstances and these are given due weight by the law.

Early consultation with liaison groups will allow complications to be anticipated and therapy to proceed without confrontations or undue delay. The governing body of Jehovah's Witnesses has published an informative and practical guide to the medical management of Jehovah's Witnesses and has set up Hospital Liaison Committees in many major cities. These committees help Witnesses find cooperative doctors and surgeons prepared to provide bloodless surgery and are available to support patients and their families in difficult situations and provide liaison for consultation with medical personnel.

The treatment of Jehovah's Witnesses demonstrates that patients and therapists often have very different beliefs about health care. If the process of obtaining consent is treated merely as unilateral information-giving, it is unlikely that these differences will be recognised or resolved. By using a shared process of decision-making, management can be tailored to individual patients in most cases. When consent is approached in this way, both sides can learn from the experience.

LEGAL ASPECTS OF CONSENT

In many areas of health law, consent is necessary in order to avoid legal liability. Consent generally works as a defence to a claim of wrongdoing. For example, although medical information is usually considered to be confidential, confidential information may be revealed to others if the patient consents to the confidence being broken (see Chapter 12).

It is particularly important to gain consent where it is necessary for the health provider to touch patients or carry out procedures with them. This is a crucial area in law, because both the criminal law and the tort law provide redress for those who have suffered an unwanted interference.

Consent becomes very significant when there is an unwanted interference with another person's body, so practitioners need to be very conscious of the legal environment affecting this area in order to avoid liability. Traditionally this area is treated in the criminal law of assault and in the tort law of trespass, which covers assault, battery and false imprisonment.

Criminal assault

Under the criminal codes and legislation of each Australian jurisdiction the term 'assault' is used to include the actual application of force as well as the threat or attempt to do so (Howard 1982). The criminal law (under the common law or statute) will punish a common assault. An assault has been defined as:

> A person who strikes, touches, or moves, or otherwise applies force of any kind to, the person of another, either directly or indirectly, without his [sic] consent, or with his [sic] consent if the consent is obtained by fraud, or who by any bodily act or gesture attempts or threatens to apply force of any kind to the person of another without his [sic] consent, under such circumstances that the person making the attempt or threat has actually or apparently a present ability to effect his [sic] purpose, is said to assault that other person, and the act is called an assault. (Howard 1982)

Section 61 of the *Crimes Act 1900* (NSW) provides that '[w]hosoever assaults any person, although not occasioning actual bodily harm, shall be liable to imprisonment for two years'. Consent is a defence to this provision. In the NSW Court of Appeal judgment in *Fitzgerald v Kennard* (1995) 38 NSWLR 184 at 201, Cole JA said:

> [T]he normal issue will be ... whether the victim consented to the physical contact. In such a case no question arises regarding whether the victim was put in fear of physical violence by acts of the accused which might be categorised as angry, revengeful, rude, insolent or hostile. The physical contact, absent consent, establishes the assault. Where the physical contact was intended, the element of **mens rea** in such an assault is established. (*'Mens rea' refers to the requisite mental element of a crime. For a crime to take place, there must be both a 'guilty action' and a 'guilty mind' – the 'mens rea'.*)

Trespass to the person

The tort of trespass to the person includes three types of actions – assault, battery and false imprisonment. An assault is a threat made to a person that they will be touched without consent. Battery occurs when the person is touched. False imprisonment covers situations where a person is unlawfully prevented from leaving a place against their will. In the health context this may include refusing or preventing a person from leaving premises or placing physical, chemical or mental restraints on a person (Madden and McIllwraith 2008).

An example of a successful civil action in battery and false imprisonment can be found in *Hart v Herron* (1984) Aust Torts Reports ¶80-201. In this case Mr Hart was admitted to Chelmsford Private Hospital. While he was there, Dr Herron (a psychiatrist) and the hospital, without his consent, treated him by what became known as Deep Sleep Therapy. This treatment involved narcosis and electro-convulsive therapy (ECT). Mr Hart was awarded compensatory and aggravated damages against the defendant doctor for false imprisonment, assault and negligence, and against the defendant hospital for false imprisonment.

In claims of trespass there is no requirement in law for there to be any harm to the patient (it is 'actionable *per se*'). In fact, even if the treatment has saved the person's life an action in battery may be successful if there was no effective consent (see *Malette v Shulman* (1990) 67 DLR (4th) 321, discussed below).

The slightest touching of another person's body constitutes a battery if it occurs without consent, or if it falls outside the generally acceptable range of physical conduct which is part of everyday life (like being jostled on a crowded train): *Collins v Wilcock* [1984] 1 WLR 1171. A battery may occur even if the patient does not know that it has happened. The patient may be unconscious, anaesthetised, asleep or comatose (McIllwraith and Madden 2006). For example, if students were to perform a pelvic examination on an anaesthetised patient who has not consented (Coney 1988), the patient could sue for battery, even if they were not aware of the examination at the time and no harm has come to them. Even more significantly, an examination in these circumstances could also amount to a sexual assault (rape) for the purposes of the criminal law (Johnstone 1989).

In older cases it was also said that some element of ill-will or 'hostility' was required on the part of the defendant: *Wilson v Pringle* [1987] QB 237. However, more recent UK and Australian case law indicates that 'hostility' is not a requirement: *Re F (Mental patient: sterilisation)* [1990] 2 AC 1 at 73 per Lord Goff; *Rixon v Star City Pty Ltd* (2001) 53 NSWLR 98. In *Boughey v R* (1986) 161 CLR 10 at [24], Mason, Wilson and Deane JJ stated:

> There is strong authority for the proposition that the application of force to another, 'be it never so small', will constitute common law battery if it is 'actually done to the Person of a Man, in an angry, or revengeful, or rude, or insolent Manner, as by Spitting in his Face, or any Way touching him in Anger, or violently justling him out of the Way' (Hawkins, A *Treatise of the Pleas of the Crown*, (1716) ch LXII, sect 2, p 134). It has never, however, been the common law that actual hostility or hostile intent towards the person against whom force is intentionally applied is a necessary general ingredient of an unlawful battery

Emergencies and necessity

The law recognises that there may be circumstances where consent cannot be gained (eg, where the patient is unconscious or otherwise lacks the capacity to consent), and yet where not offering treatment may cause great harm to the patient (eg, the death of the patient). It might be argued that consent of the patient may be implied in these circumstances but a better view is that there is a common law defence of 'necessity' available to both criminal charges and to claims in tort.

There are three steps in establishing necessity as a common law defence. First, the criminal or tortious act must have been done in order to avoid a threat which is an 'irreparable evil upon the accused or upon others whom he was bound to protect': *R v Loughnan* [1981] VR 443 at 448. Secondly, the accused must have had no reasonable alternative to breaking the law: *Perka v R* [1984] 2 SCR 232; *R v Latimer* (2001) 193 DLR (4th) 577 at 592. Finally, the acts done to avoid the imminent peril must not be disproportionate to the peril to be avoided.

Questions can be raised about whether the threat needs to be imminent. In criminal law, it was said in *Morgentaler v R* [1976] 1 SCR 616 that the accused must show that he or she honestly believed on reasonable grounds that it was an urgent situation of imminent peril before the defence can be raised. Some doubt was cast on this requirement in *Re A (children) (conjoined twins)* [2000] 4 All ER 961 at 1051 by Brooke LJ who stated that the principle is one of 'necessity not emergency'. Similarly, in the earlier case of *Re F* [1989] 2 AC 1 Lord Goff rejected urgency as an element of necessity in cases of non-consensual medical treatment. However, in *R v Loughnan* Young CJ and King J stated that '[i]f there is an interval of time between the threat and its expected execution it will be rarely if ever that a defence of necessity will succeed' (at 448). More recently in *Bayley v Police* [2007] SASC 411, it was said that '[t]he event justifying the conduct must be imminent and operational. If the threat abates there can be no emergency, nor can an action in response be said to be reasonable or proportionate' (at [53]). Tort law appears to be more settled and clearly requires the imminent threat of grave harm: *London Borough of Southwark v Williams* [1971] Ch 734.

Legislation also recognises that consent (whether by the patient or their substituted decision-maker) is not necessary in emergency situations. For example, s 37(1) of the *Guardianship Act 1987* (NSW) provides:

> Medical or dental treatment may be carried out on a patient to whom this Part applies without consent given in accordance with this Part if the medical practitioner or dentist carrying out or supervising the treatment considers the treatment is necessary, as a matter of urgency:
>
> (a) to save the patient's life; or
> (b) to prevent serious damage to the patient's health; or
> (c) except in the case of special treatment – to prevent the patient from suffering or continuing to suffer significant pain or distress.

Also, s 13(1) of the *Consent to Medical Treatment and Palliative Care Act 1995* (SA) provides:

> Subject to subsection (3), a medical practitioner may lawfully administer medical treatment to a person (the 'patient') if –
>
> (a) the patient is incapable of consenting; and
> (b) the medical practitioner who administers the treatment is of the opinion that the treatment is necessary to meet an imminent risk to life or health and that opinion is supported by the written opinion of another medical practitioner who has personally examined the patient; and
> (c) the patient (if of or over 16 years of age) has not, to the best of the medical practitioner's knowledge, refused to consent to the treatment.

See also *Children and Young Persons (Care and Protection) Act 1998* (NSW), s 174; *Guardianship and Administration Act 2000* (Qld), ss 63, 64; *Guardianship and Administration Act 1995* (Tas) ss 40, 41; *Guardianship and Administration Act 1986* (Vic), s 42A; *Guardianship and Administration Act 1990* (WA), s 119; *Emergency Medical Operations Act 1992* (NT), s 3.

New South Wales, Queensland, Tasmania and Victoria also allow for non-consensual treatment to be provided in non-emergencies if there are no substitute decision-makers available; the treatment is necessary and will most successfully promote the patient's health and well-being; and the patient does not object to the carrying out of the treatment. See *Guardianship Act 1987* (NSW), s 37; *Guardianship and Administration Act 2000* (Qld), s 64; *Guardianship and Administration Act 1995* (Tas), s 41; *Guardianship and Administration Act 1986* (Vic), s 42K.

It should be emphasised that the doctrine of necessity only applies where the patient is not able to consent and there has not been any specific instructions given by the patient before their inability to consent (see Chapter 13 for treatment decisions for incompetent patients).

The limits of consent

Consent is not a universal defence to all civil claims and criminal charges and there are limits to the range of behaviours a person can consent to. The most obvious example of this is that a person cannot consent to being murdered. Nor is consent a defence to assisted suicide: *Crimes Act 1900* (NSW), s 31C; *Criminal Code* (Qld), s 311; *Criminal Law Consolidation Act 1935* (SA), s 13A(5); *Criminal Code* (Tas), s 163; *Crimes Act 1958* (Vic), s 6(2); *Crimes Act 1900* (ACT), s 17; *Criminal Code* (NT), s 168.

Consent also fails as a defence to assaults occasioned via consensual homosexual sado-masochism which leads to actual bodily harm. Actual bodily harm is defined to be injuries which are calculated to interfere with the health and comfort of a victim as long as they are more than merely transient and trifling injuries. In *R v Brown* [1994] 1 AC 212, the House of Lords upheld the conviction of a group of men who had engaged in rather painful acts of consensual sado-masochism. Consent was not seen as a valid defence to these assaults, as the activity was seen as dangerous, possibly leading to the spread of disease or to attracting young people into such activities. Following *Brown* there are many examples of convictions for such behaviour. For example, in both *R v Stein* [2007] VSCA 300 and *R v McIntosh* [1999] VSC 358, defendants were convicted for manslaughter after their sexual partners died during consensual sado-masochism. In *R v Emmett* [1999] EWCA Crim 1710 a man (who later became the victim's husband) was convicted for assault for consensually asphyxiating his wife with a plastic bag and a ligature during sex, as well as burning her breasts with lighter fluid.

Nevertheless, people are legally empowered to consent to a wide range of behaviours that exposes them to serious risk of harm (even death). Classic examples of such conduct includes hard contact sports, like boxing and rugby union, body modification through tattooing and piercing, and religious body modification like male circumcision. What is it that distinguishes these accepted forms of bodily interference from the consensual sado-masochism in *Brown*? The answer would appear to be that the public interest justifies the use of consent as a defence in these examples, but goes against them in cases like *Brown*.

Of course, public interest tests are not certain and leave the judge with a high degree of flexibility. This is illustrated by *R v Wilson* [1997] QB 47, where a man had been convicted for assault for consensually branding his initials into his wife's backside with a hot knife. His appeal was upheld as it was said that there was a public interest in allowing married couples to engage in such private activities. Many view the contrast between the results in *Brown* and *Wilson* as evidence of legalised homophobia, rather than of solid legal principle.

How do these principles effect medical treatment? Clearly medical treatment is in the public interest when it goes towards saving lives or reducing the burden of disease and disability. Lord Mustill in *Brown* went so far as to say that medical treatment was in a special category:

> Many of the acts done by surgeons would be very serious crimes if done by anyone else, and yet the surgeons incur no liability. Actual consent, or the substitute for consent deemed by the law to exist where an emergency creates a need for action, is an essential element in this immunity; but it cannot be a direct explanation for it, since much of the bodily invasion involved in surgery lies well above any point at which consent could even arguably be regarded as furnishing a defence. Why is this so? The answer must in my opinion be that proper medical treatment, for which actual or deemed consent is a prerequisite, is in a category of its own. ([1994] 1 AC 212 at 266)

But what of medical treatments that are not aimed at the treatment of disease and disability, such as extreme cosmetic surgery and body modification? It might be argued that such procedures are not in the public interest and cannot be supported by a defence of consent. It might be said that such interventions are the equivalent of *maiming*, an older crime where a person could be convicted of hurting him or herself so to avoid serving in the armed forces (see *Brown* at 221). In *Bravery v Bravery* [1954] 3 All ER 59, Lord Denning took this view of male sterilisation. He said:

> Take a case where a sterilisation operation is done so as to enable a man to have the pleasure of sexual intercourse without shouldering the responsibilities attached to it. The operation is plainly injurious to the public interest. It is degrading to the man himself. It is injurious to his wife and any other woman whom he may marry, to say nothing of the way it opens to licentiousness, and unlike other contraceptives, it allows no room for a change of mind on either side. It is illegal, even though the man consents to it … (at 68)

Lord Denning's views are clearly incorrect for modern times (and may well have been at the time he voiced them!). But the idea that non-therapeutic surgical interventions should be banned occasionally returns to popularity. For example, the media have in recent times reported widespread concern over teenagers having cosmetic surgery. The Queensland government reacted to this concern by passing the *Health Legislation (Restriction on Use of Cosmetic Surgery for Children and Another Measure) Amendment Act 2008*. The Act makes it an offence to treat children with cosmetic surgery unless there are reasonable grounds for believing that the treatment is in the child's best interests. More about the best interests test in children's medical treatment is said in Chapter 20, but it should be noted here that such a legislative requirement adds nothing to the protection of children as the law already required that such interventions be in the child's best interests. It would appear that the sole purpose of the legislative change was to placate public feeling.

Elements of a valid consent

Consent must be voluntary

Any consent gained from a patient must be free and voluntary. All health-care providers must ensure that they do not pressure the patient into making a decision they think is the preferred course of action, but which the patient does not want (Dix, Errington et al 1996). The English case of *Re T (Adult: Refusal of Treatment)* [1993] Fam 95 is an example of a patient's wishes being overcome by another. A 20-year-old, pregnant (34 weeks) woman, Ms T, was involved in a motor traffic accident and admitted to hospital. Ms T had been brought up as a Jehovah's Witness, although she was never a member of the sect. During the day following her admission her condition deteriorated. In the afternoon, when only her mother (who was herself a Jehovah's witness) had been with her, Ms T stated spontaneously to a nurse that she did not want a blood transfusion. In the evening she went into labour and needed a caesarean section. Ms T agreed to the caesarean section but signed a form signifying that she did not want a blood transfusion. The following morning her child was delivered stillborn. Her condition deteriorated to such an extent that, had she not signed the form, she would have been given a blood transfusion.

Her father and boyfriend (who were not Jehovah's Witnesses) applied to the court for a declaration that it would not be unlawful in Ms T's circumstances to give her a blood transfusion. The judge made an interlocutory order and a transfusion was given forthwith. This decision was then appealed to the Court of Appeal which held that:

> [T]here is abundant evidence which would have justified this court in substi-tuting findings that Miss T was not in a physical or mental condition which enabled her to reach a decision binding on the medical authorities and that even if, contrary to that view, she would otherwise have been in a position to reach such a decision, the influence of her mother was such as to vitiate the decision which she expressed. (Lord Donaldson MR at 111)

Consent cannot be general

Authority is limited to the specific procedure for which consent has been given. That is, consent to one specific procedure does not grant a right to perform any other procedure that may be thought to be convenient. If another procedure is performed without consent then there will be a battery. Some consent forms attempt to provide for situations where additional procedures can be performed. The validity of a very general authorisation included in a consent form to per-form any additional procedures thought necessary must be doubted. Any additional procedure will be limited to those that could be reasonably antici-pated prior to the procedure being performed, and should have been mentioned when information was being provided about the procedure. Of course, should an emergency arise during a procedure and it is necessary, as a matter of urgency, to perform an additional procedure it can be done without consent under the doctrine of necessity.

General understanding of the nature of the act

The law is concerned about the quality of the patient's understanding of what is about to be done and is interested in the 'nature of the act'.

There have been a series of criminal cases where courts have found that there has been no understanding of the nature of the act performed, including:

- a girl who agreed to sexual intercourse with a singing teacher wrongly believing it to be a procedure to improve her singing voice (*R v Williams* [1923] 1 KB 340);
- a girl who had sexual intercourse with a doctor, wrongly believing it was a medical procedure (*R v Case* (1850) 4 Cox CC 220);
- a girl who agreed to have sexual intercourse with a man wrongly believing him to be a doctor and it to be treatment (*R v Harms* (1944) 2 DLR 61 (Sask CA));
- a woman who agreed to sexual intercourse with the defendant in the belief (wrongly) that he was medically qualified and that he was treating her (*R v Flattery* (1877) 2 QBD 410 (CCCR));
- a woman who agreed to an intimate examination by the defendant believing (wrongly) that he was a doctor and she was receiving treatment (*R v Maurantonio* (1967) 65 DLR (2d) 674 (Ont CA);
- a woman who consented to her breasts being fondled by a man who deceived her into thinking he was conducting a medical examination (*R v Linekar* [1995] 2 HKC 599);
- two prostitutes who agreed to provide discounted and free sexual services to a person masquerading as a policeman: *Michael v Western Australia* [2008] WASCA 66.

Cases where it was found that there had been a general understanding of the nature of the act include:

- a woman who agreed to a vaginal examination by a doctor in the presence of his friend whom she wrongly believed to be a medical student (*R v Bolduc and Bird* (1967) 63 DLR 82 (Can Sup Ct));
- a woman who agreed to sexual intercourse with a man whom she wrongly believed to be her husband (*R v Papadimitropoulos* (1957) 98 CLR 249 – in this case the 'wedding' ceremony they had gone through was not a valid marriage ceremony).

In the first group the patient mistakenly believed that the act was therapeutic in nature when it was, in fact, not (Grubb 1988).

The Full Court of the Victorian Supreme Court, in *R v Mobilio* [1991] 1 VR 339, acquitted a person on appeal against a conviction for three counts of sexual assault. The defendant was a radiographer employed to undertake ultrasound examinations. In 1989 a number of women were referred for ultrasound examination to the defendant. During the examination he manipulated the ultrasound transducer in such a way that it penetrated the women's vaginas. The women apparently consented to the penetration on the understanding that it was an accepted part of the ultrasound examination. It was found that penetration was done for the sexual gratification of Mr Mobilio and that there was no medical justification for what he did. He was convicted of a number of counts of sexual assault. The Full Court examined the question of whether the women had actually consented in law to what took place. It found that each of the women had consented to being penetrated and that it mattered not that their consent was obtained on the understanding that the penetration was medically justified. The court said that 'no mistake as to the man's purpose deprives her consent of reality'.

The decision received significant academic criticism (Grubb 1988; Morgan 1991). The law in Victoria (and other jurisdictions) was amended following this decision. The *Crimes Act* 1958 (Vic) now provides:

> **36. Meaning of consent**
> For the purposes of Subdivisions (8A) to (8D) 'consent' means free agreement. Circumstances in which a person does not freely agree to an act include the following – ...
> > (g) the person mistakenly believes that the act is for medical or hygienic purposes.

The Queensland criminal provisions in this area (ss 348-349 of the *Criminal Code*) were tested in *R v BAS* [2005] QCA 97. In this case the accused had committed multiple acts of indecent dealing, sexual assault and rape by pretending to offer natural and alternative therapies which included touching of breasts by hand and by machines, blowing air onto breasts, and touching the genitals of the victims with his hands and machines. The prosecution had argued that the accused had performed these acts for sexual gratification and not for therapeutic purposes and that consent had been obtained by fraud. Section 348 requires that the consent not be obtained by 'false and fraudulent representations about the nature or purpose of the act'. The Court of Appeal upheld the finding of the jury that the accused had dishonestly represented his purpose for seeking consent to acts he performed.

Identity

Generally, consent for one person to perform a procedure is not consent for any other person to perform the procedure. Again, consent forms often try to cover the situation where another person, other than a nominated person, is to perform a procedure. Care must be taken that the nature of the substitute performance is explained to the patient. Usually it will be implied that in a surgical procedure the surgeon will not be performing all aspects of the operation but if assistants are to be used this should be explained to the patient (Dix, Errington et al 1996).

The English courts have held that the 'identity' of the person cannot be stretched to cover qualifications or attributes. In *R v Richardson* (1998) 43 BMLR 21, the appellant was a registered dental practitioner until suspended by the General Dental Council. Despite the fact of her de-registration she continued to practise as a dentist. She was charged with six counts of assault occasioning actual bodily harm. The basis of this charge was that any consent that had been gained from her patients was vitiated because of her fraudulent conduct. On the basis of a direction from the trial judge she pleaded guilty on all counts. The Court of Appeal allowed an appeal and all charges were quashed. The fact of the dentist's de-registration did not affect the validity of the consent given to undergo the dental procedure. The patients agreed to therapeutic dental work and that is precisely what they got.

In another English case, *R v Tabassum* [2000] 2 Cr App R 328, a medical representative (who had no medical training) was found guilty of indecent assault where a woman consented to the touching of her breasts in the mistaken belief that the appellant was medically qualified. There was no sexual motive – the appellant's interest was to prepare a database software package to sell to doctors.

Withdrawing consent

Consent may be withdrawn at any time. As medical treatment can be framed in terms of a contractual relationship (see Chapter 4) any decision by the patient to change their mind and withdraw from the procedure may involve contractual remedies. In most contracts, both parties to the contract are under some obligation. No court, however, would order that, having entered into the contract, the patient is obliged to continue. Any remedy for breach of contract would be in damages rather than specific performance (ie, an order from a court to complete all unfulfilled obligations). Hence no patient should be made to feel that since they have signed a consent form or verbally agreed to undergo a procedure they cannot change their mind. If an indication of a change of mind was given by the patient and was met by any form of duress (forcefully encouraging or threatening statements) it may vitiate the consent.

Refusal of consent

In *Schloendorf v Society of New York Hospital* 195 NE 92 (1914) at 93 Cardozo J made the classic statement:

> Every human being of adult years and sound mind has a right to determine what shall be done with his own body; and a surgeon who performs an operation without his patient's consent commits an assault, for which he is liable in damages.

While it is an American case it correctly summarises a fundamental legal principle that all common law jurisdictions share. Competent adults have the right to refuse treatment even if that means they will die as a result. In *Smith v Auckland Hospital* [1965] NZLR 191 at 219, TA Greeson J stated that '[a]n individual patient must, in my view, always retain the right to decline investigation or treatment however unreasonable or foolish this may appear in the eyes of his medical advisers'. Similarly, in *Re T* [1993] Fam 95 at 102 (discussed above) Lord Donaldson MR said:

> This right of choice is not limited to decisions which others might regard as sensible. It exists notwithstanding that the reasons for making the choice are rational, irrational, unknown or even non-existent ...

In the same case Butler-Sloss LJ stated: 'A decision to refuse medical treatment by a patient capable of making the decision does not have to be sensible, rational or well considered' (at 116). Straughton LJ agreed:

> An adult whose mental capacity is unimpaired has the right to decide for herself whether she will or will not receive medical or surgical treatment, even in circumstances where she is likely or even certain to die in the absence of treatment. (at 120)

As *Re T* illustrates, the clearest example of a refusal of consent is where a blood transfusion is refused for religious reasons. Blood transfusion is a relevantly simple treatment in critical care situations but it is one that some have a religious objection to. The Canadian decision in *Malette v Shulman* (1990) 67 DLR (4th) 321 held that a medical practitioner could not give a blood transfusion to an unconscious patient after he had become aware that the patient carried a card which identified her as a Jehovah's Witness and instructed that she was not to be treated with any blood products. The Ontario Court of Appeal held that to administer a blood transfusion, contrary to the instructions on the card, was a battery – even though the card was not witnessed or dated. This is the clearest case where a court has recognised an advance declaration of a refusal of particular treatment. The instruction regarding treatment is very specific and limited to particular treatment, the reasons for the request from this class of person are also well known. *Malette's case* is an example of advance directives which are discussed in more detail in Chapter 1.

Limits to the right to refuse treatment

As with any right, there are limits to the right to refuse treatment. Most obviously relevant is the competence of the patient. Decisions to refuse treatment often occur in cases where the patient's capacity to make such decision may be impaired and medical practitioners have to be careful to properly assess any claims of incapacity on the part of the patient. For example, in both *Re B (Adult: Refusal of Medical Treatment)* [2002] EWHC 429, and *Re PVM* [2000] QGAAT 1, ventilator-dependent patients who refused further life-sustaining treatment were found to be competent to make such a decision (see Chapter 13).

Other limitations also exist. Some patients in public health settings and mental health environments lose their rights to refuse treatment, even when they are competent (see Chapters 21 and 27). Prisoners may be treated against their will, if their refusal will have a detrimental effect on the maintenance of security and discipline: *R v Ashworth Hospital; Ex parte Brady* [2000] Lloyds Rep Med 355. Price reported that Australian immigration detention detainees were being forcibly treated, but argued that that was illegal under international humanitarian law (Price 2003).

Much often turns on the reason for the prisoner's refusal. Hunger strikes are not uncommon, particularly with political prisoners. Early British cases involving suffragettes found that there was a duty to force feed: *Leigh v Gladstone* (1909) 26 TLR 139. However, later cases have found that there is no common law duty to force feed prisoners: *Schneidas v Corrective Services Commission* (unreported, NSWSC, 8 April 1983); *Secretary of State for the Home Department v Robb* [1995] 1 All ER 677. Nevertheless, in some jurisdictions, corrective services have the power to treat prisoners against their will. For example, in NSW the Chief Executive Officer of Justice Health can forcibly treat prisoners if he or she is of the opinion, having taken into account the cultural background and religious views of the inmate, that the treatment is necessary to save the inmate's life or to prevent serious damage to the inmate's health: *Crimes (Administration of Sentences) Act 1999* (NSW), s 73.

These exceptions to the right to refuse treatment are primarily based on the protection of third parties or the public. Perhaps the most difficult situations are those involving pregnant women refusing treatment, because here the interests of the woman and the unborn child conflict in ways that are more difficult to untangle. There have been a number of American and English cases where women have refused to undergo a caesarean section (sometimes for religious reasons) or other types of treatment late in pregnancy and courts have been asked to override the woman's decision.

In *Re AC* 573 A 2d 1235 (1990) the District Court of Appeals of Columbia had to decide whether it should confirm the order of an inferior court to authorise the caesarean section of a pregnant woman (in week 26 of her term) who was close to death with cancer. The woman had refused the procedure, although there was a question mark over her capacity. As the inferior court had authorised the caesarean, it had gone ahead with the result that the baby died after two hours and the mother died two days later. It was argued that the lower court had erred in weighing the public interest in the life of the foetus higher than the refusal of the mother.

The Court of Appeals found against the procedure on the grounds that the patient's wishes, once they are ascertained, must be followed in 'virtually all cases' (at 1249) unless there are 'truly extraordinary or compelling reasons to override them' (at 1247). The court was concerned that any other finding would undermine the relationships between pregnant women and their physicians. Furthermore, the hasty and pressured nature of these types of proceedings meant that there had to be a stronger emphasis on the security of the rights of self-determination.

In *In re Baby Boy Doe* 632 NE 2d 326 (1994) the Appellate Court of Illinois went further and found that the pregnant woman's rights of privacy, bodily integrity and religious liberty remained undiminished during pregnancy. The woman was said to retain the same right to refuse invasive treatment, even of lifesaving and other beneficial nature, that she could exercise when she was not pregnant. The potential impact on the foetus was not relevant. However, the court did question the possibility that less invasive procedures, such as blood transfusions, may be treated differently in future cases.

The question of blood transfusions was answered in *Re Fetus Brown* 689 NE 2d 397 (1997). The Appellate Court of Illinois was asked to determine the legality of a court-ordered blood transfusion for a Jehovah's Witness who was 35 weeks pregnant. The woman was competent and had the support of her husband. A lower court had appointed a guardian for the foetus and ordered that blood transfusions take place. Transfusions took place and the mother had to be forcibly restrained during the transfusions. The child was born healthy and the mother sought to have the lower court's decision overturned. The court found that, upon examination, a forced blood transfusion was not relatively non-invasive and risk free and that no state interest existed in protecting the foetus which could justify overriding her refusal. The decision of the lower court was reversed.

The UK courts have trod a similarly difficult path. In *Re S (Adult: Refusal of Treatment)* [1993] Fam 123, Sir Stephen Brown P was asked to authorise a caesarean section on a 30-year-old woman who was refusing to undergo the procedure on religious grounds. Both the life of the woman and the unborn child were at risk if the procedure was not performed. The application was brought on urgently before the judge (it came to the notice of court officials at 1.30pm, the hearing commenced in chambers just before 2.00pm and the decision was announced at 2.18pm). The court, relying on a misinterpretation of *Re AC* 573 A 2d 1253 (1990), made a declaration that the procedure could be performed.

In March 1997 the English Court of Appeal upheld a judgment of Hollis J that a woman was suffering from a mental impairment when she refused an anaesthetic necessary for her caesarean section (*Re MB* [1997] 8 Med LR 217). Her mental impairment was caused by her fear of needles, which made her temporarily incompetent. The court *held that medical treatment could be undertaken in an emergency even if, through lack of capacity, no consent had been competently given, provided the treatment was a necessity and did no more than was reasonably required in the best interests of the patient.*

The court recognised that all of the recent decisions in caesarean section cases arose in circumstances of urgency or extreme urgency. To assist further decision-makers the court set out the basic principles that should be considered:

(1) Every person was presumed to have the capacity to consent to or to re-fuse medical treatment unless and until that presumption was rebutted.

(2) A competent woman who had the capacity to decide might, for religious or other reasons whether rational or irrational or for no reason at all, choose not to have medical intervention even though the consequence might be the death or serious handicap of the child she bore or her own death. In that event the court did not have jurisdiction to declare medical intervention lawful and the question of her own best interests, objectively considered, did not arise.

(3) Irrationality connoted a decision which was so outrageous in its defiance of logic or of accepted moral standards that no sensible person who had applied his mind to the question to be decided could have arrived at it. Although it might be thought that irrationality sat uneasily with competence to decide; panic, indecisiveness and irrationality in themselves did not as such amount to incompetence, but might be symptoms or evidence of incompetence. The graver the consequences of

the decision the commensurately greater the level of competence was required to take the decision.

(4) A person lacked capacity if some impairment or disturbance of mental functioning rendered the person unable to make a decision whether to consent to or refuse treatment.

(5) Temporary factors such as confusion, shock, fatigue, pain or drugs might completely erode capacity but only if such factors were operating to such a degree that the ability to decide was absent.

(6) Another such influence might be panic induced by fear. Again careful scrutiny of the evidence was necessary because fear of an operation might be a rational reason for refusal to undergo it. Fear might also, however, paralyse the will and thus destroy the capacity to make a decision.

A year later these principles were tested in *St George's Healthcare NHS Trust v S* [1998] 3 All ER 673. This case concerned a woman who refused a caesarean section offered to her for pre-eclampsia. After refusing treatment she was declared mentally ill by staff and detained under mental health legislation. The hospital then sought a court order authorising treatment. The trial judge was not presented with any formal evidence and was misled by the hospital as to the patient's condition. Moreover, no evidence was led as to the patient's competence. Neither the patient nor her solicitors had been informed of the hearing. After performing the operation they released her. On review, the Court of Appeal found that the unborn child's need for medical attention could not override the patient's express and competent refusal. Even where the interference with the woman's body is minor and the refusal of treatment unreasonable, the court will not sanction treatment because the principle of autonomy would be extinguished.

The duty to provide information to patients when seeking their consent

As long as the patient has a general understanding of the treatment proposed, then there will not be an assault or battery if consent has been gained. However, a separate duty is also owed to give the patient information so that the patient can make the decision about whether or not to consent to treatment. This separate duty is a professional one and the failure to comply with it is treated under the law of negligence. If the patient has been given inadequate information then an action in negligence may be successful (as long as the other requirements of the tort have been met: see Chapter 8).

The duty to provide information is sometimes referred to (particularly by North American authors) as the duty to seek informed consent. As noted above, the High Court in *Rogers v Whitaker* (1992) 175 CLR 479 did not find the term 'informed consent' useful in the discussion of what information was necessary to be given to a person when asking them to consent to a procedure. The majority of the court (Mason CJ, Brennan, Dawson, Toohey and McHugh JJ) said:

> In this context, nothing is to be gained by reiterating the expressions used in American authorities, such as 'the patient's right of self- determination' or even the oft-used and somewhat amorphous phrase 'informed consent'. The right of self-determination is an expression which is, perhaps, suitable to cases where the issue is whether a person has agreed to the general surgical procedure or treatment, but is of little assistance in the balancing process that is involved in the determination of whether there has been a breach of the duty of disclosure. Likewise, the phrase 'informed consent' is apt to mislead as it suggests a test of the validity of a patient's consent. Moreover, consent is relevant to actions framed in trespass, not in negligence. (at 490)

In *Rogers v Whitaker* the question to be decided by the court was whether an ophthalmic surgeon should have warned his patient (who had sight in only one eye) of the one in 14,000 chance of a complication, sympathetic ophthalmia and subsequent risk of blindness, arising from a proposed procedure to her damaged eye. The High Court affirmed the decisions of the NSW Supreme Court and Court of Appeal that the doctor should have warned his patient of this remote risk.

The test stated by the court for establishing what information is to be given to the patient is as follows:

> The law should recognize that a doctor has a duty to warn a patient of a material risk inherent in the proposed treatment; a risk is material if, in the circumstances of the particular case, a reasonable person in the patient's position, if warned of the risk, would be likely to attach significance to it or if the medical practitioner is or should reasonably be aware that the particular patient, if warned of the risk, would be likely to attach significance to it. This duty is subject to the therapeutic privilege. (at 490)

The notion of 'therapeutic privilege' is discussed further in Chapter 11.

Although the judgment was specifically focused on risk, it is clear that the High Court intended the principle to cover information beyond simply risks associated with the procedure. Additional factors need to be considered when providing information to patients including:

- the nature of the matter to be disclosed;
- the nature of the treatment;
- the desire of the patient for information;
- the temperament and health of the patient; and
- the general surrounding circumstances. (*F v R* (1983) 33 SASR 189)

In summary *Rogers v Whitaker* can be interpreted as requiring that the provision of information to patients needs to be 'patient focused'. What information may the patient require – not what information does the profession think a patient needs.

Once the court has found that appropriate information had not been provided to the patient then it must be established that the breach caused the harm that is the subject of litigation. In *Rogers v Whitaker* the plaintiff had argued that if she had known of the possibility of going blind she would not have consented to the procedure. This aspect of the case was accepted by the trial judge and was not challenged before the High Court.

Since 1992 the High Court has considered two additional cases on the provision of information – *Chappel v Hart* (1998) 195 CLR 232 and *Rosenberg v Percival* (2001) 205 CLR 434.

In *Chappel v Hart*, an ear, nose and throat specialist performed a procedure on Mrs Hart during which her oesophagus was perforated. The perforation of the oesophagus was a known complication of this surgery and could occur without fault on the part of the surgeon. A chain of events was set off by the perforation. Bacteria escaped from the oesophagus causing an infection that in turn damaged the laryngeal nerve that led to paralysis of Mrs Hart's right vocal cord. This left her with a weak and husky voice.

It was found at trial that Mrs Hart had made a comment in passing to Dr Chappel that she didn't 'want to wind up like Neville Wran' (the trial judge noted that 'this remark was taken to be an allusion to a contemporaneous problem which, following an operation, the then Premier of New South Wales had experienced with his voice which had been partly restored by a teflon injection to his vocal cords'). The court found that the doctor had not warned her of the risk of damage to her vocal cord and that not doing so was in breach of the standard of care owed to the patient. This was not challenged when the case went to the High Court.

Mrs Hart claimed, which was accepted by the court, that if she had known of the risk to her voice she would not have gone ahead with the procedure at that time and would have sought out the most experienced surgeon available to perform the procedure. Dr Chappel argued that Mrs Hart would have had to undergo the procedure at some stage and that his failure to warn did not cause the loss sustained.

The High Court dismissed Dr Chappel's appeal by a 3:2 majority. The five judges each delivered a separate judgment. All five judges accepted that the test for causation in negligence is a question of 'commonsense' but seemed to differ in the understanding in this particular case! It could be argued that the difference of opinion between the majority and minority opinions was a matter of interpretation of certain evidence that was presented before the trial court.

Chappel v Hart is a difficult case. Because of the nature of the case, the way it was argued before the court and because of the factual findings made by the trial court, it is a difficult precedent to apply. It would seem that the reason the appellant was granted special leave to appeal to the High Court was because it was seen as an opportunity to consider the issue of 'loss of chance', although this was not the way the issue was finally argued before the court.

In *Rosenberg v Percival* a dental surgeon failed to warn his patient (a nurse with a doctorate in philosophy) appropriately about risks associated with a sagittal split osteotomy. Following the procedure the patient suffered severe temporomandibular joint complications. In that case (as in *Rogers v Whitaker*) the patient asserted that if she had been appropriately warned about the risks associated with the procedure she would not have undergone it at that time. Each of the High Court judges who decided this case (on appeal from the Full Court of the Western Australian Supreme Court) delivered a separate judgment, but all affirmed the principle stated in *Rogers v Whitaker*.

The High Court unanimously decided that even if she had been warned of the risk associated with the procedure she would still have gone ahead. The High Court noted that findings on causation do not depend solely on the patient's credibility (noting that their evidence may be affected by the patient's knowledge of the outcome of the procedure) but should also take into account the seriousness of the need for treatment, their willingness to undergo risks, professional background, whether the patient asks any questions about risk and what type of warning would have been given to the patient.

The decision in *Rogers v Whitaker* was subject to significant criticism (Mendelson 2001) in Australia and suggestions that there would be a substantial increase in litigation as a result. In *Rosenberg v Percival*, Kirby J examined many of these arguments but was not convinced that the decision in *Rogers v Whitaker* was incorrectly decided.

Since 1992 there have, indeed, been a significant number of cases where the issue of inadequate information being provided by medical practitioners has been raised. In 2000 Rachael Mulheron examined many of the 'provision of information' cases that had been heard by Australian courts since the *Rogers v Whitaker* decision had been handed down (Mulheron 2000). From this analysis she identified 12 tests to identify whether a medical risk is 'material'.

It is important to remember when examining the cases that there is a need to focus on the principles behind the decision and not the specific facts of individual cases. For example, the fact that the risk of sympathetic ophthalmia was one in 14,000 in *Rogers v Whitaker* does not mean that all risks up to this number have to be disclosed to patients. Whether the risk is 'material' depends on a number of different factors. In *Rosenberg v Percival* the Chief Justice warned that:

> Recent judgments in this Court have drawn attention to the danger of a failure, after the event, to take account of the context, before or at the time of the event, in which a contingency was to be evaluated. This danger may be of particular significance where the alleged breach of duty of care is a failure to warn about the possible risks associated with a course of action, where there were, at the time, strong reasons in favour of pursuing the course of action. ((2001) 205 CLR 434 at 441-2)

As Mulheron points out:

> The goal in this difficult area of medico-legal litigation is to strike a balance between encouraging disclosure and imposing a duty on doctors that they can meet in practice. (Mulheron 2000)

Tort reform and the provision of information

The Ipp Reforms

The recent recommendations in the Ipp Report (discussed in Chapter 8) and legislative change in most Australian jurisdictions do not seem to alter the common law standards for the provision of information to patients.

The Ipp Report made some specific recommendations (specific to medical practitioners) with respect to the provision of information:

Duties to inform

Recommendation 5

In the Proposed Act the professional's duties to inform should be legislatively stated in certain respects, but only in relation to medical practitioners.

Recommendation 6

The medical practitioner's duties to inform should be expressed as duties to take reasonable care.

Recommendation 7

The legislative statement referred to in Recommendation 5 should embody the following principles:

(a) There are two types of duties to inform, a proactive duty and a reactive duty.

(b) The proactive duty to inform requires the medical practitioner to take reasonable care to give the patient such information as the reasonable person in the patient's position would, in the circumstances, want to be given before making a decision whether or not to undergo treatment.

(c) The information referred to in paragraph (b) should be determined by reference to the time at which the relevant decision was made by the patient and not a later time.

(d) A medical practitioner does not breach the proactive duty to inform by reason only of a failure to give the patient information about a risk or other matter that would, in the circumstances, have been obvious to a reasonable person in the position of the patient, unless giving the information is required by statute.

(e) Obvious risks include risks that are patent or matters of common knowledge; and a risk may be obvious even though it is of low probability.

(f) The reactive duty to inform requires the medical practitioner to take reasonable care to give the patient such information as the medical practitioner knows or ought to know the patient wants to be given before making the decision whether or not to undergo the treatment.

The standard of care when providing information

All the jurisdictions barring ACT and the Northern Territory responded by excluding the duty to warn from the standard of care provisions, which effectively preserves the common law (Madden and McIllwraith 2008). The provisions in New South Wales, Queensland, South Australia, Tasmania, Victoria and Western Australia relate to advice given by all professions whereas the provisions in South Australia and Western Australia just cover advice given regarding health-care services.

Jurisdiction	Legislation
New South Wales	*Civil Liability Act 2002*, s 5P
Queensland	*Civil Liability Act 2003*, s 22
South Australia	*Civil Liability Act 1936*, s 41
Tasmania	*Civil Liability Act 2002*, s 22
Victoria	*Wrongs Act 1958*, s 60
Western Australia	*Civil Liability Act 2002*, s 5PB

There were also specific enactments concerning health advice made in Queensland, Tasmania and Victoria. The *Civil Liability Act 2003* (Qld), s 21, and the *Civil Liability Act 2002* (Tas), s 21, state that a doctor does not breach a duty to warn of a risk unless the doctor fails to provide:

(a) information that a reasonable person in the patient's position would, in the circumstances, require to enable the person to make a reasonably informed decision about whether to undergo the treatment or follow the advice;

(b) information that the doctor knows or ought reasonably to know the patient wants to be given before making the decision about whether to undergo the treatment or follow the advice.

The *Wrongs Act 1958* (Vic), s 50, says:

A person (the defendant) who owes a duty of care to another person (the plaintiff) to give a warning or other information to the plaintiff in respect of a risk or other matter, satisfies that duty of care if the defendant takes reasonable care in giving that warning or other information.

Obvious risks

The *Civil Liability Act 2002* (Tas), s 17(2)(c), states that a medical practitioner is not under a duty to warn of obvious risks. The other jurisdictions have removed a general duty to warn of obvious risks but this does not apply to professionals providing services. However, in these jurisdictions it is presumed that a plaintiff is aware of such risks but that presumption may be rebutted.

Evidence of what the patient would have done had they known of the risk

As can be seen in cases like Rosenberg, courts have developed a natural scepticism when dealing with evidence from injured patients about what they would have done had they known of the risk that eventuated into their injury. For example, in *Richards v Rahilly* [2005] NSWSC 352 at [256]-[257] (a case involving the treatment of a child), Hoeben J stated:

Reliance was also placed upon the evidence of Mr Richards when he was recalled after the conclusion of the evidence ... The evidence of Mr Richards was that had treatment options been explained to him, he would have chosen Vigabatrin.

The evidence of Mr Richards to which I have referred, is of little value. He understood how important that answer was to Rhiannon's case. Although his evidence on this question may well have been truthful, it suffers from the problem identified by McHugh J in *Chappel v Hart* [1998] HCA 55; (1998) 195 CLR 232 at 246 (note 64) and restated in *Rosenberg v Percival* (p 443, para 25). The reliability of such evidence needs to be assessed by reference to other evidence.

Even though it was probably unnecessary, some legislative changes were made to the way that evidence can be led as to what the patient would have done had they been made aware of a material risk. These changes exclude evidence being given by the injured person about what they would have done, except where that evidence works against their claim.

Jurisdiction	Legislation
New South Wales	*Civil Liability Act 2002*, s 5D
Queensland	*Civil Liability Act 2003*, s 11
Tasmania	*Civil Liability Act 2002*, s 13
Victoria	*Wrongs Act 1958* (Vic), s 60
Western Australia	*Civil Liability Act 2002*, s 5C

'Consent forms'

Consent does not need to be in writing to be enforceable. In fact, most consent will be verbal or implied. The more serious the intervention, the more formal should be the consent. For example, if major surgery is anticipated the consent will be evidenced in writing (the consent form) and it may be deemed appropriate to give the patient information in a written form (information sheet). It may also be appropriate to give the patient time to reflect upon the decision.

In principle, a valid consent does not have to be in writing but it should be noted that in some circumstances legislation will require the consent to be evidenced in writing (eg, *Human Tissue Act 1983* (NSW), s 23(3)(b)).

Health-care providers often confuse the purpose of consent forms. Sometimes the signing of a consent form is seen as the gaining of consent. This is incorrect – although the signing of a consent form may happen at some stage during the consent process. The consent form is a piece of documentary evidence. It is useful if there should be some doubt about whether the patient has agreed to go ahead with a procedure but it is not, in itself, determinative of the issue. Consent forms may be useful to escape liability in battery, but their usefulness in a negligence action is limited.

For interventions where the consequences are less or not serious, consent may be verbal or implied. For example, a request to take the temperature of a patient does not need to be evidenced in writing and, in fact, may not even be verbalised. The nature of the consent process is usually the subject of an appropriate professional judgment, although institutions may have their own policies concerning the process to be undertaken when gaining consent.

References

Anon (1945) 'Immovable for the right to worship'. *Watchtower* **66**: 195-6.

Baier, A (1995) *Trust and antitrust. Moral prejudices: Essays on ethics.* Cambridge, MA, Harvard University Press.

Beauchamp, T and R Faden (2004) Informed consent: II. Meaning and elements of informed consent. *Encyclopedia of Bioethics* (3rd ed). S Post. New York, MacMillan Reference USA.

Bogardis, S, E Holmboe et al (1999) 'Perils, pitfalls and possibilities in talking about medical risk'. *JAMA* **281**: 1037-41.

Brock, DW (1991) 'Shared decision making'. *Kennedy Institute of Ethics Journal* **1**: 28-47.

Brody, H (1989) *Transparency: Informed Consent in Primary Care.* Mountain View, Mayfield Publishing Company.

Cassel, E, A Leon et al (2001) 'Preliminary evidence of impaired thinking in sick patients'. *Ann Intern Med* **134**(12): 1120-3.

Charles, C, A Gafni et al (1999) 'Decision-making in the physician-patient encounter: revisiting the shared treatment decision-making model'. *Soc Sci Med* **49**(5): 651-61.

Charles, CA, T Whelan et al (2003) 'Shared treatment decision making: what does it mean to physicians?' *J Clin Oncol* **21**(5): 932-6.

Clarke, G, R Hall et al (2004) 'Physician-patient relations: no more models'. *AM J Bioethics* **4**: W16-19.

Coney, S (1988) *The Unfortunate Experiment.* Auckland; Melbourne, Penguin Books.

Coulter, A (1999) Shared decision-making: a summary and future issues. *Breast Cancer: Sharing the decision.* A Maslin and T Powles. Oxford, Oxford University Press.

Dix, A, M Errington et al (1996) *Law for the medical profession.* Sydney, Butterworth Heinemann Australia.

Eddy, DM (1990) 'Clinical decision making: from theory to practice. Anatomy of a decision'. *JAMA* **263**(3): 441-3.

Edwards, A and G Elwyn (2001) 'Understanding risk and lessons for clinical risk communication about treatment preferences'. *Qual Health Care* **10**(Suppl 1): i9-i13.

Etchells, E, G Sharpe et al (1996) 'Voluntariness'. *CMAJ* **155**: 1083-6.

Faden, R and T Beauchamp (1986) *A history and theory of informed consent.* New York, Oxford University Press.

Ford, S, T Schofield et al (2003) 'What are the ingredients for a successful evidence-based patient choice consultation? A qualitative study'. *Soc Sci Med* **56**: 589-602.

Frackiewicz, E, R Lee et al (1991) 'Use of a blood substitute in a patient who refuses to accept a transfusion'. *Am J Hosp Pharm* **48**: 2176.

Giddens, A (1990) *The consequences of modernity.* Cambridge, Polity Press.

Gilson, L (2003) 'Trust and the development of health care as a social institution'. *Social Science and Medicine* **56**: 1453-68.

Grubb, A (1988) 'United Kingdom – R v Richardson'. *Med Law Rev* **6**: 247.

Hagerty, R, P Butow et al (2004) 'Cancer patients preferences for communication of prognosis in the metastatic setting'. *J Clin Oncol* **22**: 1721-30.

Henman, M, P Butow et al (2002) 'Lay constructions of decision-making: perceptions of women with cancer'. *Psych-Oncology* **11**: 295-306.

Howard, C (1982) *Criminal Law.* Sydney, Law Book Company.

Jenkins, V, L Fallowfiled et al (2001). 'Information needs of patients with cancer: results from a large study in UK cancer centres'. *Br J Cancer* **84**: 48-51.

Johnstone, M (1989) *Bioethics: A Nursing Perspective.* Sydney, WB Saunders.

Kagawa-Singer, M and L Blackhall (2001). 'Negotiating cross-cultural issues at the end of life'. *JAMA* **286**: 2993-3002.

Katz, J (2002). *The Silent World of Doctor and Patient.* Baltimore, John Hopkins University Press.

Katz, MG, L Fitzgerald et al (2002) 'Issues and concerns of couples presenting for pre-implantation genetic diagnosis (PGD)'. *Prenat Diagn* **22**(12): 1117-22.

Kennedy, AD (2003) 'On what basis should the effectiveness of decision aids be judged?' *Health Expect* **6**(3): 255-68.

Kirk, P, I Kirk et al (2004) 'What do patients receiving palliative care for cancer and their families want to be told? A Canadian and Australian qualitative study'. *BMJ* **328**: 1343.

Kopelman, LM (2004) 'Minimal risk as an international ethical standard in research'. *J Med Philos* **29**(3): 351-78.

Kuczewski, M and P McCruden (2001) 'Informed consent: does it take a village? The problem of culture and truth-telling'. *Camb Q Health Ethics* **10**: 34-46.

Landman, J (1993) *Regret – The persistence of the possible.* New York, Oxford University Press.

Levinson, W, A Kao et al (2005) 'Not all patients want to participate in decision-making. A national survey of public preferences'. *J Gen Intern Med* **20**: 531-5.

Leydon, G, G Leydon et al (2002) 'Cancer patient's information needs and information seeking behaviour: in-depth interview study'. *BMJ* **320**: 909-13.

Lidz, C, P Appelbaum et al (1988) 'Two models of implementing informed consent'. *Arch Intern Med* **148**: 1385-9.

Little, J and S Leeder (1996) 'Logic, hermeneutics and informed consent'. *Eur J Surg* **162**: 3-10.

Little, M, C Jordens et al (2008) 'Informed consent and medical ordeal: a qualitative study'. *Intern Med J* **38**: 1-5.

Macklin, R (1988) 'The inner workings of an ethics committee: Latest battle over Jehovah's Witnesses'. *Hastings Cent Rep* **Feb/Mar**: 15-20.

Madden, B and J McIllwraith (2008) *Australian Medical Liability.* Sydney, Lexis Nexis Butterworths.

Miyata, H, M Takahashi et al (2005) 'Disclosure preferences regarding cancer diagnosis and prognosis: to tell or not to tell?' *J Med Ethics* **31**: 311-15.

Morgan, J (1991) 'Rape in medical treatment: The patient as victim'. *MULR* **18**: 403.

Moumjid, N, A Gafni et al (2007) 'Shared decision making in the medical encounter: are we all talking about the same thing?' *Med Decis Making* **27**(5): 539-46.

Mulheron, R (2000) 'Twelve tests to identify whether a medical risk is "material"'. *National Law Review*: 1.

Nelson, J and H Nelson (1999) Meaning and medicine: a reader in the philosophy of health care. *Reflecyive bioethics.* H Nelson and H Nelson. New York, Routledge.

O'Connor, AM, F Legare et al (2003) 'Risk communication in practice: the contribution of decision aids'. *BMJ* **327**(7417): 736-40.

O'Connor, AM, HA Llewellyn-Thomas et al (2004) 'Modifying unwarranted variations in health care: shared decision making using patient decision aids'. *Health Aff (Millwood)* **Suppl Web Exclusives**: VAR63-72.

O'Neill, O (2002) *Autonomy and trust in bioethics.* Cambridge, Cambridge University Press.

Paling, J (2003) 'Strategies to help patients understand risks'. *BMJ* **327**(7417): 745-8.

Parascandola, M, J Hawkins et al (2002) 'Patient autonomy and the challenge of clinical uncertainty'. *Kennedy Inst Ethics J* **12**: 245-64.

Pinquart, M and P Duberstein (2004) 'Information needs and decision-making processes in older cancer patients'. *Crit Rev Oncol Haematol* **51**: 69-80.

Price, P (2003) 'Who has jurisdiction over the mind? An individual rights approach to forced medication in Australia'. *Aust Jn Human Rights* **10**: 219.

Quintero, C (1993) 'Blood administration in paediatric Jehovah's Witnesses'. *Pediatr Nurs* **19**: 46.

Reynolds, WW and RM Nelson (2007) 'Risk perception and decision processes underlying informed consent to research participation'. *Soc Sci Med* **65**(10): 2105-15.

Rogers, C (1957) 'The necessary and sufficient conditions of therapeutic personality change'. *J Consult Psych* **21**(2): 95-103.

Rogers, W (2002) 'Is there a moral duty for doctors to trust their patients?' *J Med Ethics* **28**: 77-80.

Thorne, S, G Hislop et al (2006) 'Hope and probability: patient perspectives of the meaning of numerical information in cancer communication'. *Qual Health Res* **16**: 318-36.

Trevena, L and A Barratt (2003) 'Integrated decision making: definitions for a new discipline'. *Patient Educ Couns* **50**(3): 265-8.

Veatch, R (1972) 'Models for ethical medicine in a revolutionary age'. *Hastings Cent Rep* **2**: 5-7.

Vincent, J (1991) 'Transfusion in the exsanguinating Jehovah's Witness patient – the attitude of intensive-care doctors'. *Eur J Anaesthesiol* **8**(4): 297-300.

Watt, J (1994) 'Alternative management procedures should be used'. *BMJ* **308**: 1424.

Wear, S (1998) *Informed Consent. Patient Autonomy and Clinical Beneficence within Health Care*. Washington DC, Georgetown University Press.

Wear, S (1998) *Informed Consent. Patient autonomy and clinician beneficence within health care* (2nd ed). Washington DC, Georgetown University Press.

CHAPTER 15

TREATMENT AND NON-TREATMENT ISSUES: THE LIMITS OF MEDICAL CARE

Case 1

BL is a 12-year-old boy who was born with complicated congenital abnormalities, including cyanotic heart disease and mental retardation. For the past two years he has had increasing breathlessness on exercise, until now he is breathless on any activity at all. His cognitive state is such that he recognises his family, but is unable to speak and needs most activities of daily living to be done for him. The only way to treat his present condition is through a heart-lung transplant. His parents are unsure of whether he should have this, and his cardiologist does not believe that it would be justifiable, however other family members believe that it should be offered on the grounds that it is the only procedure that has any chance of saving his life.

Case 2

Amyotrophic lateral sclerosis (ALS) is a severe condition of the spinal cord that causes progressive weakness and eventual total paralysis so that people cannot even breathe by themselves. It is sometimes argued that therapy (including the provision of ventilators) to patients with ALS is futile because of the disease's progressive nature. The Honourable Justice Sam Filer – a ventilator-dependent American with ALS – spoke at a 1991 conference using a voice synthesiser to describe his thoughts about the condition: "Throughout the ALS process, I have learned many things. I have learned that ALS does not necessarily mean a death sentence, that I am not living with a life-threatening disease, but rather with a life-enhancing condition." (Bach and Barnett 1995)

Sanctity of life

Respect for the sanctity of life is often thought of as a major basis for the ethics of medical care. In fact there are many problems with this concept, and few ethicists now accept the rule of sanctity of life without a number of qualifications. In its most basic form, the rule of sanctity of life states that it is morally prohibited to intentionally kill a person, to intentionally let a person die or to base decisions relating to the prolongation or shortening of human life on considerations of the kind or quality of a person's life (Kuhse 1987). Such a version of the rule of sanctity of life is rarely advocated, as there are many situations in which this degree of respect for human life seems inappropriate or impossible to maintain. (For example, many Christian churches allow killing in self-defence or in the course of war – although this would be prohibited by the rule of sanctity of human life.)

An example of the use of a strict form of the rule of sanctity of life is found in the Reagan administration's 'Baby Doe regulations'. These regulations arose out of a 1982 case in which a baby with Downs' syndrome died after life-saving surgery for a tracheo-oesophageal fistula was intentionally omitted. The case caused outrage among sections of the American community, and caused the Reagan administration to notify all providers of health care that received federal funds that they must not discriminate against the handicapped. Furthermore:

> American hospitals received new guidelines, telling them that in each delivery ward, maternity ward, paediatric ward and intensive care nursery, they must display a poster indicating that 'DISCRIMINATORY FAILURE TO FEED AND CARE FOR HANDICAPPED INFANTS IN THIS FACILITY IS PROHIBITED BY FEDERAL LAW'. This poster then said that any person knowing of such discriminatory denial of food or customary medical care should immediately contact a 'Handicapped Infant Hotline', for which a toll-free twenty-four hour contact number was given. (Singer 1995)

Squads of lawyers, doctors and government officials were set up to investigate any calls (and there were 1633 of these in 1983) and doctors began resuscitating many children whom they would not otherwise have treated – including some with severe deformities that were incompatible with life. After several appeals, the final version of the law was struck down by the Supreme Court in 1986 on the grounds that it ignored the accepted role of parental consent in the medical care of infants. The court also found that conditions such as multiple handicaps and extreme prematurity might legitimately be used as grounds for non-treatment (Singer 1995).

A more common interpretation of the rule of sanctity of life allows some exceptions. For example, in some cases it may be thought permissible to refrain from preventing death in conditions which are treatable but where the outcomes are thought to be excessively burdensome. Such exceptions depend on us drawing a moral distinction between causing death and refraining from preventing death. Whether such a distinction is reasonable will be discussed further in the section on passive and active euthanasia.

The doctrine of ordinary and extraordinary means

Another approach to the issue of how much it is necessary to strive to keep patients alive is provided by the 'Doctrine of Ordinary and Extraordinary Means'. This Roman Catholic doctrine arose from the dilemmas that faced patients in the days when surgery was carried out without anaesthetics, and with very limited chance of success. If a patient needed an amputation, the question arose as to whether refusing this unpleasant and often unsuccessful procedure was morally equivalent to refusing food or water or even to committing suicide. The dilemma was resolved by dividing treatments into two categories – ordinary means of treatment – which patients were morally obliged to accept, and health professionals obliged to offer, and extraordinary means of treatment – which were thought to be morally optional.

'Ordinary means' were defined as forms of therapy that offer a reasonable hope for benefit and can be obtained without excessive expense, pain or other inconvenience. 'Extraordinary means' were those forms of treatment that involve excessive expense, pain or inconvenience and do not offer a reasonable hope of benefit. In the modern world the distinction between ordinary and extraordinary means is often ambiguous as the exact forms of therapy that are 'ordinary' or 'extraordinary' vary over time: few would now consider an amputation to be an 'extraordinary' means of therapy. It has been argued that this ambiguity allows a certain freedom of interpretation that might enable the doctrine to remain relevant as a modern ethical tool.

An alternative view, given by Beauchamp and Childress, is that it would be better if these terms were abandoned.

> [M]oral discourse would improve if the terms were replaced by terms such as 'optional' and 'obligatory'. 'Ordinary' would then be reconstructed to mean morally obligatory, mandatory, required, or imperative, while 'extraordinary' would be reconstructed to mean morally optional, elective, or expendable. (Beauchamp and Childress 1994)

Gillon, in a defence of the doctrine of ordinary and extraordinary means, inadvertently identifies the weakness of both the ordinary/extraordinary and optional/obligatory distinction.

> Only after the assessment of whether the burden of treatment would be too great for, or disproportionate to, the likely benefit in the particular circumstances, can the treatment be labelled ordinary if it is morally obligatory or extraordinary if it is morally optional. Furthermore, even if it is morally optional, there remains a decision to be made by the patient or his proxies whether to carry it out. (Gillon 1986)

In other words the issues of critical moral importance do not relate to the means or therapy in question, but appear to relate to the patients or surrogate's wishes and an assessment of the burdens and benefits of treatment.

The benefits may include improvements in life expectancy, physical functioning, physical appearance, diminished pain and improved overall quality of life. Burdens may include the riskiness of a therapy; the pain, discomfort, or distress it may cause; any negative impacts that the treatment may have on patients' lives; the psychological effects of treatments; and the costs of treatment. Although burdens–benefits analysis is enormously appealing, its promise of mathematical simplicity is misleading and it places considerable emphasis on the competency of the patient, their degree of rationality and their intent, that is, whether they are depressed or suicidal. If patients should be able to refuse treatment that is excessively burdensome, or (more controversially) health professionals not be obliged to offer excessively burdensome therapies, then health professionals are ethically required to identify clearly the expected burdens and benefits of treatment and the patient's preferences, and have valid consent as their goal.

Futility

There are some instances in which the burdens of a therapy seem to be out of all proportion to any possible benefits. Such therapy is sometimes described as 'futile'. The debate about the definition of futile medical treatment dates back to the time of Plato who stated that to attempt futile treatment is to display an ignorance that is allied to madness. The Hippocratic Corpus encouraged physicians to recognise the limits of medicine and to refuse to treat those who are overmastered by their diseases, realising that in such cases medicine is powerless. There has been a revitalisation of the debate about futility because it has been suggested that both suffering and expense may be diminished by the avoidance of futile medical care. Supporters of the concept of futility argue that patients should not be entitled to care that is judged to be futile, nor should the therapist be under any obligation to offer it (Lantos 1994). Unfortunately it has proven very difficult to provide a definition of futility that is both philosophically coherent and clinically useful.

One way of judging whether care is futile or not is through the use of quantitative measures. Schneiderman has proposed that if a treatment has not been successful in the last 100 cases, then commonsense dictates that such a treatment should be regarded as futile (Schneiderman, Jecker et al 1990). Unfortunately, there are many inherent difficulties with this definition – in many situations it is not possible to gather sufficient data to make accurate predictions of outcome, and even where data does exist to predict the outlook for certain disease groups it may be difficult to apply to individual patients. A number of studies have also demonstrated the limitations of physicians' clinical estimation of both prognosis and diagnosis (Poses, Bekes et al 1989). Expressions of probability also have different meanings for different people – some might consider treatment futile only where the success rate was 0%, whereas others may invoke futility for treatments with success rates as high as 10% (Nakao and Axelrod 1983). Indeed, physiological or biological outcomes are not the sole measure of the worth of an intervention and therapy that is thought to be futile from a medical perspective may still be valued for its emotional, psychological or symbolic importance. For example, continuing intravenous fluids for a patient who is unconscious following a major intracerebral haemorrhage may be of great symbolic importance to a family who believes such treatment to be essential. Data of this sort makes clear that all quantitative 'thresholds for futility' (below which an intervention may be judged futile) are relative to the desired outcome or goal, epistemologically arbitrary and subject to conflicting interpretations (Kite and Wilkinson 2002; Shevell 2002).

An alternative approach to questions of futility was developed by philosophers such as Plato, who emphasised that any treatment which left patients with a useless life was inappropriate. He stated that medicine was not intended for such patients, and they should not be treated even if they were richer than Midas. Unlike quantitative definitions, such qualitative definitions define a futile treatment as one which does not achieve its desired goals. (It is therefore sometimes described as 'normative futility'.) In this way, futile therapy has been defined variously as therapy that is useless or ineffective, that cannot achieve the patient's wishes or goals, that does not offer a reasonable chance of survival, that fails to achieve a physiological effect or that fails to offer a minimal quality of life or medical benefit.

But there are also considerable difficulties with qualitative definitions of futility. Qualitative assessments of outcome are intrinsically subjective and value laden and hence they may be contaminated by bias and discrimination. In fact, qualitative estimations of futility may be entirely dependent on who is making the judgment. According to Youngner, a decision that treatment is futile or that certain goals are not worth pursuing reflects a conflict of values that runs the risk of 'giving opinions disguised as data' (Youngner 1988). As Gillon has noted – futility judgments are fraught with ambiguity and both clinical and moral complexity.

> It involves assessment of outcomes of interventions in terms of value-free descriptions (for example whether or not restoration of heartbeat is possible); in terms of probabilities (how likely or probable are the outcomes); and in terms of values (how valuable or otherwise, and according to whose values – patient's or their surrogate's, doctors' and other health professionals', managers', or society's values?) (Gillon 1997)

Thus, while it may be possible to make decisions on the basis of 'normative futility' where patients and their health carers are in agreement as to goals of treatment and the extent to which those goals are attainable and worth pursuing, normative futility does not provide a means for resolving conflict. Given the difficulties in defining futility and establishing any type of consensus regarding thresholds for futility, in recent years increasing numbers of clinicians, ethicists and legislators have accepted that disagreement is inevitable where questions of futility arise and argued in favour of a *procedural* approach to resolving futility questions (Halevy and Brody 1996). According to this approach, disputes over whether a therapy is futile are resolved not through a policy that attempts to define futility but through a predefined and fair process that addresses specific cases (Zucker and Zucker 1997).

In 1999, the Council on Ethical and Judicial Affairs (CEJA) of the American Medical Association concluded that 'objectivity is unattainable' when defining futility and that the best approach is to implement a fair process (Council on Ethical and Judicial Affairs 1999). The CEJA defined a fair process as one that included extensive deliberation and consultation in an attempt to reach a resolution, followed by efforts to transfer care to a physician willing to comply with the patient's wishes or withdrawal or withholding of treatment where no other physician or facility is prepared to accept care and administer the treatment in question.

Since that time a number of US States, notably Texas and California, have enacted legislation that validates an extrajudicial, procedural approach to resolving disputes over futility. The Texas Advance Directives Act requires:

- review of the physician's decision to withhold or withdraw life-sustaining treatment on the basis of futility by an 'ethics or medical committee';

317

- that the patient or surrogate be given the right to attend the committee meeting and obtain a written explanation of the committee's findings;
- that transfer to another physician or facility should be sought if the physician, patient or surrogate disagrees with the committee's findings (and that the patient is liable for any costs incurred in the transfer if it is requested by the patient or surrogate);
- that the physician may withhold or withdraw life-sustaining treatment if a transfer cannot be arranged within 10 days;
- that the patient or surrogate have the right to go to court to extend the period of time to arrange for a transfer. (Tex Health and Safety Code S166.046)

Procedural approaches to resolving futility disputes have been examined in a number of empirical studies. All offer preliminary evidence that such approaches may assist in resolving conflict and keep disputes between patients and health professionals out of the courtroom (Cassaret and Siegler 1999; Cantor, Braddock et al 2003; Fine and Mato 2003).

Another approach is provided by Lofmark and Nilstun, who set a series of questions derived from a review of empirical studies of futility that may assist clinicians to make explicit the conditions and consequences of futility assessments in any given situation (Lofmark and Nilstun 2002). The questions include:

Identify the conditions of futility
- Who has the final authority to decide about whether and why an intervention is futile?
- What measure (intervention) is at stake?
- What goal is to be reached?
- What is the probability of reaching that goal?

Identify the moral consequences of a judgment that something is futile
- May, ought or should health-care professionals forgo the intervention?
- Can/should this be done with or without communication with the involved or affected?
- Who will be responsible for the decision to forgo the intervention?

Given the problems associated with the term 'futility' and the ethical and medical uncertainty surrounding futility judgments, it is our belief that questions regarding futility should not be seen as offering a value-free point of clinical closure but as providing an opportunity to re-examine the goals of medical care and to deepen communication between health professionals, patients and carers.

Quality of life

The concept of futility depends on weighing the burdens and benefits of medical care. While it is possible to measure burdens and benefits solely in terms of mortality and economic cost, this approach misses a great deal of the flavour of clinical interactions and ignores many outcomes that are among the main objectives of medical care and are the outcomes most valued by patients. The most fundamental aim of many health interventions is to restore, maintain or improve quality of life, but the term 'quality of life' is extremely difficult to define and is surrounded by considerable controversy.

When researchers attempt to measure quality of life they can do so either by asking patients with specific medical conditions to rate their own quality of life or by asking others to rate the quality of life of such patients. There are some theoretical reasons to use the latter approach and it is often much easier to do (Russel, Gold et al 1996). But such determinations may not be accurate. Even severely disabled, long-term ventilator-dependent individuals with poliomyelitis, muscular dystrophy and spinal cord injury may have very positive views of their lives and life satisfaction that may be at odds with those not affected (Bach and Barnett 1995).

Onlookers commonly underestimate the quality of life of disabled people, suggesting that using outsiders to estimate quality of life is likely to be unreliable and biased (Bodenhamer, Achterberg-Lawlis et al 1983). Estimations of a patient's projected quality of life may reflect cultural, racial, ageist, sexist or social bias and may also obscure the realisation that aspects of a person's life circumstances may improve with recognition and remediation rather than being dismissed as poor 'quality of life'. For example, in 1989 Larry McAfee, a Georgian man with quadriplegia, wished to receive legal assistance to end his life because his quadriplegia and the need for ventilation had confined him to a poor quality existence in a nursing home. He made his decision after discovering that his father had become terminally ill. The Supreme Court of Georgia upheld his right to be sedated while someone turned off his ventilator. Disability-rights advocates did not regard this case as a 'right-to-die' issue, rather they saw it as a consequence of the failure of society to make resources available to improve his life. The case of Larry MacAfee became 'a battle-cry in the disability-rights community for more adequate funding for personal-assistance services' (DeJong and Banja 1995). A simplistic view of Larry McAfee's quality of life obscured the underlying reasons for his poor level of existence. Interestingly, McAfee never had the ventilator turned off and he died in the nursing home in 1995 of pneumonia.

Health-care professionals need also to be aware that differences in social, cultural and economic background can lead to divergent views of quality of life that may impact on the clinical management of individual patients or on resource-allocation decisions. Health workers are overwhelmingly middle-class, introducing biases in assessing patients from disadvantaged backgrounds. Inadequate housing or education may result in poor hygiene, inability to obtain employment and difficult social conditions, which may all contribute to judgments that a person has a poor quality of life. Empirical research suggests that health professionals generally do make quality of life judgments about their patients/clients – often rating their quality of life lower than patients themselves do (Starr, Perlman et al 1986). There is also evidence that health professionals tend to emphasise the importance of cognitive function to quality of life, whereas non-health professionals are more likely to emphasise the importance of social relationships. Such studies illustrate the complex and subjective nature of quality of life assessments and are a reminder of the dangers of allowing descriptive judgments to become prescriptive, that is, determining what should or should not be done.

Because quality of life assessments are so closely tied to one's values, perspectives and goals, if the value-laden nature of quality of life assessments is not made explicit then they may conceal a lack of understanding of a patient's values, beliefs and needs, and may conceal bias, discrimination, and social worth criteria in 'medical' judgments. This type of error is common in health care and may underpin decisions not to transplant patients who drink to excess and not to investigate or treat elderly patients (Nantais and Kuczewski 2004).

When we consider quality of life measurements, it is apparent that they are made up of many separate measures of different qualities of life such as pain, disability, physical function, happiness, life satisfaction or intellectual function. It is not actually possible to find a single or global scale that will allow these disparate entities to become commensurable (Hirskyj 2007). Many of us have been advised, when making difficult decisions, to make a list of the various things in favour or against the decision and to weigh them against each other. While such advice can be useful, in that it urges us to consider all the different aspects of a decision, it is not usually possible to come to a conclusion in this way. The same problem is encountered in burdens and benefits analysis.

There is great interest in quantifying concepts of futility and quality of life, but this is often not appropriate. From a philosophical perspective, measurements of quality of life seem to frequently fall into a logical fallacy known as reification – the application of numerical scales to concepts that are not able to be measured in this way. The Nobel prize-winning physicist Richard Feynman provides a story that illustrates this problem:

> Nobody was permitted to see the Emperor of China, and the question was, 'What was the length of the Emperor of China's nose?' To find out you go all over the country asking people what they think the length of the Emperor of China's nose is and you average it. And that would be very 'accurate' because you averaged so many people. But it's no way to find anything out; when you have a very wide range of people who contribute without looking carefully at it, you don't improve your knowledge by averaging. (Feynman 1986)

In many ways, the notion of quality of life resembles the length of the king's nose – we know that it exists, we can ask questionnaires about it and arrive at some public consensus, but we can never be certain that this consensus in any way captures the proper meaning of it.

Conclusion

The rule of sanctity of life continues to be an important basis for medical care. However, it has always been recognised that there are times when patients' wishes or the consideration of their best interests will lead to the conclusion that an absolute commitment to sanctity of life is not appropriate. The limitations of medical care in such cases may be considered using concepts such as 'futility' or 'quality of life' and 'burdens and benefits' although these concepts have their own problems, and should not be viewed simplistically.

Despite the recognition that quality of life is an important determinant of health care, considerable psychological, philosophical, definitional and methodological difficulties complicate the use of such assessments in patient management. There is a considerable evidence to suggest that physicians *do* take quality of life considerations into account when making management decisions but that they base such evaluations on criteria that differ from those of their patients (Starr, Perlman et al 1986).

Quality of life judgments are complex, multifactorial and highly subjective. It may be more reliable to measure only individual factors that make up quality of life such as pain, nausea or functional ability rather than quality of life in general. It may also be more justifiable, given the subjective nature of quality of life judgments, to use quality of life data on a *within-patient* basis (ie, to assess the adequacy of treatment), rather than as a basis for comparison with other patients or groups.

Medical and nursing professionals consistently rate the quality of life of their patients lower than patients do themselves and they base such judgments on medical or disease criteria rather than 'non-medical' criteria, such as happiness, relationships and financial security, that their patients consider more important. The most difficult issue is therefore not whether to take account of factors that affect quality of life, but whether this is being done appropriately. Where patients are competent, their *own* assessment of quality of life will be a major factor in guiding clinical management. Where they are incompetent, enormous care should be taken by others such as partners, families and health-care professionals, who seek to make such judgments.

Like many topics in ethics, these issues remain ambiguous. In many cases, answers to the question of whether life is overly burdensome, or whether quality-of-life is excessively affected by a form of therapy will be best approached by open communication between staff, patients and their families. Much of the ambiguity and conflict associated with determinations of qualitative futility can be reduced by ensuring the patient, their carers and/or their surrogate are both informed and involved interactively in the decision-making process throughout the health-care period. Such an approach not only takes account of the perspectives of the patient and the health team, but is most likely to assist in clarifying the goals of treatment and the relevant values and beliefs that relate to clinical management. In the rare case where it is impossible to reach consensus about the value of therapy – such as where patients or their families insist on medical care that is expensive but thought to be futile by therapists – recourse to more formal committee-based approaches or to legal mechanisms may be necessary. For examples of how these situations may be managed, see Halevy and Brody (Halevy and Brody 1996).

The ethical issues surrounding quality of life and the limitation of treatment will not be resolved simply by refusal to use the terms themselves. Further discussion on what constitutes futility will necessarily involve a consideration of whose values are considered in decision-making and a re-examination of medicine's existing values and their current extension and expression as health-care goals in a time of rapidly expanding technology.

LEGAL APPROACHES TO END-OF-LIFE DECISION-MAKING

This part of the chapter examines the legal aspects of end-of-life decision-making, including the key legal concepts, the legal requirements for how decisions are made, and the distinctions made in criminal law between permissible withholding and withdrawal of treatment and homicide. Chapters 13 and 14 have already examined the rights of patients to refuse treatment and make advance directives. This chapter concentrates on end-of-life decisions for patients who are incompetent.

The sanctity of life

The sanctity of life ethic is a foundational principle of the common law (Stewart 2005). Rehnquist CJ of the United States Supreme Court has recognised that the state has an interest in preserving life which is 'symbolic and aspirational as well as practical': *Washington v Glucksberg* 521 US 702 at 729 (1997). In the United Kingdom, Lord Donaldson said that '[s]ociety's interest is in upholding the concept that all human life is sacred and that it should be preserved if at all possible': *Re T (An Adult) (Consent to Medical Treatment)* [1992] 2 Fam 458 at 470. Similarly, in *Airedale NHS Trust v Bland* [1993] AC 789, the House of Lords considered the situation where the doctors and family of a patient in a persistent vegetative state wished to withdraw treatment. They asked the courts to rule on the legality of this course of action. The members of the House of Lords discussed the application of the principle of the sanctity of life in the following ways:

> **Lord Keith**: [T]he principle of the sanctity of life, which it is the concern of the state, and the judiciary as one of the arms of the state, to maintain … is not an absolute one. It does not compel a medical practitioner on pain of criminal sanctions to treat a patient, who will die if he does not, contrary to the express wishes of the patient. It does not authorise forcible feeding of prisoners on hunger strike. It does not compel the temporary keeping alive of patients who are terminally ill where to do so would merely prolong their suffering. On the other hand it forbids the taking of active measures to cut short the life of a terminally ill patient. (at 859)

> **Lord Goff**: [T]he fundamental principle is the principle of the sanctity of human life – a principle long recognised not only in our own society but also in most, if not all, civilised societies throughout the modern world, as is indeed evidenced by its recognition both in article 2 of the European Convention for the Protection of Human Rights and Fundamental Freedoms (1953) (Cmd 8969), and in article 6 of the International Covenant on Civil and Political Rights 1966. But this principle, fundamental though it is, is not absolute. Indeed there are circumstances in which it is lawful to take another man's life, for example by a lawful act of self-defence, or (in the days when capital punishment was acceptable in our society) by lawful execution. We are not however concerned with cases such as these. We are concerned with circumstances in which it may be lawful to withhold from a patient medical treatment or care by means of which his life may be prolonged. But here too there is no absolute rule that the patient's life must be prolonged by such treatment or care, if available, regardless of the circumstances. (at 863-4)

Lord Mustill: The interest of the state in preserving the lives of its citizens is very strong, but it is not absolute. There are contrary interests, and sometimes these prevail; as witness the over-mastering effect of the patient's refusal of treatment, even where this makes death inevitable. (at 894)

In New Zealand (*Auckland Area Health Board v Attorney General* [1993] 1 NZLR 235), an application was made by doctors of the intensive care unit of Auckland Hospital and by the Auckland Area Health Board for a declaration from the High Court (in New Zealand this is an intermediate court) clarifying whether, in law, they would be guilty of culpable homicide under ss 151(1) or 164 of the *Crimes Act 1961* (NZ), were they to withdraw the ventilatory-support system which maintained the breathing and heartbeat of a patient with an extreme case of Guillain-Barré syndrome. The judge, Thomas J, reflected on the sanctity of life principle:

> Life, and the concept of life, represents a deep-rooted value immanent in our society. Its preservation is a fundamental humanitarian precept providing an ideal which not only is of inherent merit in commanding respect for the worth and dignity of the individual but also exemplifies all the finer virtues which are the mark of a civilised order. Consequently, the protection of life is, and will remain, a primary function of the criminal law. It was said by Blackstone to be the first regard of the English law ... and I entertain no doubt that it receives no less regard today. Indeed, our New Zealand Bill of Rights Act 1990 recognises the individual's right to life and emphasises the role of the law in preserving life. Section 8 of the New Zealand Bill of Rights Act 1990 provides:
>
>> '8. Right not to be deprived of life – No one shall be deprived of life except on such grounds as are established by law and are consistent with the principles of fundamental justice.'
>
> This is not to say, of course, that the sanctity of life represents an absolute value. Few, if any, values can be stated in absolute terms. The qualification in s 8 itself confirms that to be the case. (at 244-5)

In these two cases the courts balanced the obligation to preserve life with doing what was in the best interests of the patient. In both cases, following withdrawal of treatment, the patient was allowed to die.

The Supreme Courts, *parens patriae* and end-of-life decisions

In Australia, each Supreme Court has a *parens patriae* jurisdiction which allows it to make treatment decisions for incompetent adults and children in their best interests (see Chapter 13). This jurisdiction has been used on numerous occasions to review decisions about treatment being withheld and withdrawn.

The first case to consider the application of *parens patriae* to end-of-life decisions in Australia was *Northridge v Central Sydney Area Health Service* (2000) 50 NSWLR 549, where the patient, Thompson, had overdosed on heroin and was admitted to the hospital. He had suffered a significant brain injury from having stopped breathing. It was decided by the medical team treating Thompson that a 'not for resuscitation' order be place on his chart and that he be given no antibiotics after a few days of treatment, as it was believed that Thompson was in a vegetative state. It was claimed that such treatment was futile (see the discussion below). However, Thompson's sister sought a court order overturning the decision, on the basis that there had been a misdiagnosis and that Thompson was recovering. O'Keefe J agreed with Northridge and ordered that all decisions to withdraw treatment be reviewed by him under the *parens patriae* jurisdiction. He was critical of the hastiness of the diagnosis, the fact that the hospital's own policies regarding not for resuscitation orders had not been followed and with the inadequacy of communication between the hospital staff and Thompson's family. His Honour stated:

> There is undoubted jurisdiction in the Supreme Court of New South Wales to act to protect the right of an unconscious person to receive ordinary reasonable and appropriate (as opposed to extra-ordinary, excessively burdensome, intrusive or futile) medical treatment, sustenance and support. In this day and age ordinary reasonable and appropriate treatment, for a person of the age and condition of Mr Thompson, would extend to the administration of antibiotics and appropriate feeding. The court also has jurisdiction to prevent the withdrawal of such treatment, support and sustenance where the withdrawal may put in jeopardy the life, good health or welfare of such unconscious individual. What constitutes appropriate medical treatment in a given case is a medical matter in the first instance. However, where there is doubt or serious dispute in this regard the court has the power to act to protect the life and welfare of the unconscious person. (at [24])

The courts will not overturn a medical decision when there has been a good faith attempt to seek alternative opinions and those opinions are in agreement about the treatment options. In *Messiha (by his tutor) v South East Health* [2004] NSWSC 1061, the family of a patient sought a court order for the continuation of life-sustaining treatments. The patient had had a cardiac arrest and suffered severe brain damage as a result. He had a history of heart disease and severe lung disease. There was unanimous medical opinion that the best interests of the patient would be served by the managed withdrawal of treatment. However, the patient's family disputed this and believed that treatment was not futile if it continued to support the patient's life. Howie J decided that the managed withdrawal of treatment was in the patient's best interests. He was swayed by the unanimous medical opinion as to the patient's prognosis, and believed that the treatment was burdensome and futile.

Similarly, *In the application of Herrington; re King* [2007] VSC 151, continued treatment was found to be futile for a patient with hypoxic brain damage and who had multiple serious health problems, including kidney failure. She was described as being in a vegetative state. The court found that withholding treatment was in her best interests given the unanimous medical opinion that treatment was futile.

Finally, in *Melo v Superintendent of Royal Darwin Hospital* [2007] NTSC 71, the Supreme Court of the Northern Territory refused to order the continuation of ventilation for a brain-damaged man. Paulo Melo had been severely injured in a motor vehicle accident, with compromised blood flow to his brain and severe spinal damage. He had a Glasgow Coma Scale rating of 3 (the lowest) indicating extremely low brain function. The hospital treatment team had determined that continued ventilatory support was futile. The patient's family disagreed and stated that they believed his eye movements to be meaningful. The treatment team countered by saying that the movement was involuntary and probably caused by spasms from the spinal injury. Further opinions were sought from the Royal Adelaide Spinal Unit, the Royal Adelaide Intensive Care Unit, a visiting neurologist and a visiting neurosurgeon. These all concurred with the decision to cease ventilation. A further opinion was sought by the family but that doctor had not yet seen the patient at the time of the trial.

The judge expressed a real concern with extending the ventilation given all the evidence was against it. He refused to order the continuation of the ventilation on the ground that there was unanimous medical opinion that it was not in the patient's best interests.

Other substitute decision-makers' powers at the end-of-life

The range of available substitute decision-makers for incompetent adults was discussed in Chapter 13. These substitute decision-makers have limited powers to consent to medical treatment as set out in relevant legislation and questions can be asked as to whether their powers cover refusing treatment or consent to its withdrawal. Each jurisdiction will now be examined.

Australian Capital Territory

The ACT expressly gives power to enduring attorneys to refuse treatment for their principals. In the ACT under the *Powers of Attorney Act 2006*, s 46, enduring attorneys may refuse treatment for a principal if:

(a) the attorney has consulted a doctor about –
  (i)   the nature of the principal's illness; and
  (ii) any alternative forms of treatment available to the principal; and
  (iii) the consequences to the principal of remaining untreated; and
(b) the attorney believes, on reasonable grounds, that the principal would ask for the medical treatment to be withheld or withdrawn if the principal –
  (i)   could make a rational judgment; and
  (ii) were to give serious consideration to the principal's own health and wellbeing.

Section 86 requires the attorney to have regard to the patient's right to receive relief from pain, suffering and discomfort to the maximum extent that is reasonable in the circumstances. Moreover, the patient has a right to the reasonable provision of food and water. In providing relief from pain, suffering and discomfort to the patient, the health professional must give adequate consideration to the principal's account of the principal's level of pain, suffering and discomfort.

The power of guardians to refuse treatment is less clear. The *Guardianship and Management of Property Act 1991*, s 7(3)(f), gives power to guardians to consent to treatment (which arguably must include the power to refuse treatment: see discussion below). Importantly, guardians must comply with any advance directive given by the patient before incapacity, but the appointment of an enduring attorney will revoke any previous advance medical directive given by the patient: *Medical Treatment (Health Directions) Act 2006*, ss 18, 19.

Apart from guardians and enduring attorneys, there are no other substitute decision-makers recognised in the ACT (see Chapter 13).

New South Wales

In New South Wales, all substitute decision-makers, including the Guardianship Tribunal, guardians, enduring guardians and persons responsible must make decisions which promote and maintain the health and well-being of the patient: *Guardianship Act 1987*, ss 32, 40, 45. It has been argued that this phrase cannot include decisions to withhold-or withdraw treatment. In *WK v Public Guardian (No 2)* [2006] NSWADT 121, the NSW Administrative Decisions Tribunal (NSWADT) found that a guardian could not make a decision to withdraw treatment, as death was not promoting or maintaining health and well-being. The patient in question was a 73-year-old man with end-stage kidney disease, advanced heart disease, dementia and bowel cancer, who was receiving haemodialysis. A decision was made by his treating physician, the patient's sister-in-law and other relatives and friends to stop the dialysis and give palliative care. However, a friend of the patient, WK, objected to the decision to withdraw treatment and the decision was referred to the Guardianship Tribunal. The Tribunal appointed the Public Guardian as guardian. The Public Guardian, amongst other things, consented to the withdrawal of treatment, a not for resuscitation order and palliative care.

WK appealed the decision of the Public Guardian to the NSWADT. The Deputy President of NSWADT issued a stay on the decision to withdraw treatment and ordered that further evidence be presented: *WK v Public Guardian* [2006] NSWADT 93. On the return of the application the NSWADT decided that the decision to withdraw dialysis and to refuse 'aggressive' treatment was beyond the power of the Public Guardian.

There are obvious failings in such an interpretation (Stewart 2006). It ignores the fact that, when a patient is dying, treatment withdrawal and palliative care can substantially enhance a patient's welfare and, in that sense, promote their health and well-being. The interpretation also means that disabled patients who are not competent to refuse treatment will be left with aggressive treatment as the only option and will effectively be battered to death. This simply cannot be the correct interpretation of the Act and since *WK (No 2)* competing interpretations have surfaced.

In *Re AG* [2007] NSWGT 1, the Guardianship Tribunal reviewed the findings in the *WK* matter, and gave a decision which substantially diverted from the findings of the NSWADT. The patient was a 56-year-old woman with mild intellectual disability, who was born in Malta but raised in Australia. Both her parents were dead and she lived alone in her own home, receiving support services on a daily basis from a specialist care provider. AG had been diagnosed with a renal tumour with lymphadenopathy. There was also the possibility that she had secondary brain tumours and her prognosis was consequently very poor. Miss AG had a history of refusing medical treatment, including fear of needles. She also refused to acknowledge the existence of the kidney tumour, although she had accepted that she had cancer. The Public Guardian had previously been appointed to manage AG's care but was now faced with a decision concerning a palliative care plan which included decisions to forego CPR and dialysis. The Public Guardian approached the Guardianship Tribunal for directions on the care plan, given that the WK (No 2) decision seemed to conclude that it was not possible for the Public Guardian to consent to such a plan.

The Tribunal decided that, generally, consent could be given or refused for medical treatment under the *Guardianship Act*, which included palliative care. Palliative care could include treatment limitations, such as the non-provision of treatment, on the proviso that the palliative care promoted and maintained the patient's health and well-being. The Tribunal stated that the weight of authority supported the notion that treatment limitation can promote and maintain a person's health and well-being, if it prevents futile treatment and if it allows the person to die with comfort and dignity.

The Tribunal also found that guardians with health-care functions could be given the power to be involved in advance care planning. The Tribunal also recognised that advance care planning could also be engaged in without the necessity of appointing a guardian with a health-care function.

In conclusion, the Tribunal felt that it was necessary for a specific order to be made to give the Public Guardian the power to consent to the proposed palliative care plan, and that could only be done after further medical investigations, mentioned above, were completed.

After *Re AG* the NSWADT was given another chance to re-interpret the power of substitute decision-makers under Part 5 of the *Guardianship Act* in *FI v Public Guardian* [2008] NSWADT 263. The applicant, FI, was the mother of DFI, a 24-year-old patient who had been severely brain damaged in a car accident. FI claimed that DFI was in a vegetative state, although this was disputed by her medical carers. The Public Guardian had been appointed as DFI's guardian and had been given powers to make end-of-life decisions. FI requested the Public Guardian to exercise those powers to refuse treatment for DFI. The Public Guardian refused to do so on the basis that such a decision was beyond power, given the findings in *WK (No 2)*. O'Connor J re-examined *WK* and whether decisions to withdraw treatment could promote and maintain health and well-being. O'Connor J found that:

> In my view, the Guardianship Act does not seek to fetter a guardian in a way that is inconsistent with the ordinary law. A plenary order bestows on the guardian 'all the functions of a guardian of that person that a guardian has at law or in equity' (s 21(1)(b)). Accordingly, in my view, a specified function in a limited guardianship order should be interpreted in accordance with what is permitted by law or in equity in relation to the kind of conduct the subject of the specified function. The only difference between the rights enjoyed under the law as between an autonomous individual with capacity, and a guardian responsible for a person without capacity, is that the guardian must always act according to best interests considerations whereas the autonomous individual, in the exercise of free will, may make decisions which, objectively, appear to be against his or her best interests ...

It would, in my view, be a strange outcome if the order-making powers of the Guardianship Tribunal were to be read down, as compared to the powers available to the Supreme Court in the protective jurisdiction, so as to prevent guardians as substitute decision makers to be involved in the making of care decisions that have elements that involve the cessation of medical treatment. The Supreme Court's inherent protective jurisdiction and the Guardianship Tribunal's statutory jurisdiction are both seeking to serve the same end. (at [47], [49])

The effect of the decision is to make it clear that guardians do have the power to refuse treatment, as long as the decision is made in the patient's best interests. It remains to be seen whether other persons responsible also have this power. Logically, all the substitute decision-makers in Part 5 of the Act should be subject to the same restrictions and able to exercise the same powers. However, O'Connor J appears to have been very careful to concentrate the wording of the decision on guardianship alone.

Northern Territory

The Northern Territory only recognises guardians as substitute decision-makers and does not have enduring attorney or person responsible legislation. A guardian is given all the powers and duties which the guardian would have if he or she were a parent and the represented person was his or her infant child: *Adult Guardianship Act*, s 17. It might be argued that this would include a decision to refuse treatment, along the same reasons as those advocated by O'Connor J in *FI* (see under New South Wales, above).

Queensland

In Queensland, the *Guardianship and Administration Act 2000*, ss 66-66A, give express power to substitute decision-makers (including guardians, health attorneys and statutory health attorneys) to refuse life-sustaining treatments. This includes guardians, health attorneys and statutory health attorneys. However, a consent given by these decision-makers to the withholding or withdrawal of treatment cannot operate unless the patient's health provider considers the commencement or continuation of the treatment to be inconsistent with 'good medical practice' (s 66A). This wording raises quite a high bar to the removal of treatment as practitioners may feel that withdrawal is in the patient's best interests but may not be inclined to say that its continuation is inconsistent with good medical practice. Nevertheless, the phrase has been interpreted as not to require unanimous opinion regarding withdrawal. In *Re HG* [2006] QGAAT 26, a patient with Wernicke's encephalopathy and Korsakoff's psychosis, had a brain stem stroke which left him in a 'locked-in state'. The Queensland Guardianship and Administration Tribunal (GAAT) was asked to determine whether artificial feeding and hydration (ANH) should be continued. Even though there were differing opinions about whether ANH should be ceased the QGAAT found that on the balance of medical evidence it would be inconsistent with good medical practice to continue ANH.

In *Re TM* [2002] QGAAT 1, the GAAT had to consider a dispute between the brother and sister of a 62-year-old patient with Alzheimer's disease, and the patient's children as to whether the patient be given a PEG tube for ANH. The brother and sister of the patient were in favour of the insertion of the tube but the children were not. For the purposes of the Act it was determined that the children were the statutory health attorneys and not the brother and sister. The children had cared for the mother and made previous health decisions for her, so were the more appropriate choice.

A number of applications to withdraw treatment have been approved in Queensland. For example, in *Re MC* [2003] QGAAT 13, permission was sought to withdraw artificial feeding from an 80-year-old woman in a persistent vegetative state. The QGAAT found that the treatment was of no benefit to her and should be ceased. In *Re RWG* [2000] QGAAT 2, the wife of a 73-year-old male with an acquired brain injury made an application for a no-CPR order and for the power to refuse antibiotics. The QGAAT agreed to the no-CPR order but would not consent to the refusal of antibiotics given the patient was not suffering from an infection at the time of hearing and, as such, it would be premature to examine the issue. In *Re SAJ* [2007] QGAAT 62, the QGAAT approved of the withdrawal of ANH from an 86 year old who had suffered numerous strokes on the ground that continued treatment was inconsistent with good medical practice.

South Australia

The *Guardianship and Administration Act 1993, s* 31, is very similar to the Northern Territory legislation. It grants a guardian all the powers of a guardian at law and in equity, again suggesting a power to refuse treatment.

However, no express mention is made of a power being given to persons responsible to refuse consent. Arguably, if a person is given the power to consent one could say that it includes a power to refuse consent, but this is conjectural.

Tasmania

In Tasmania, the *Guardianship and Administration Act 1995, s* 25(2)(e), states that guardians (including enduring guardians) can consent to any health care that is in the best interests of the represented person and to refuse or withdraw consent to any such treatment. However, the powers of persons responsible are less clear. Under s 43, persons responsible can consent to treatment in the patient's best interests. Arguably this includes the power to refuse treatment when it is no longer in the patient's best interests (based on arguments raised above).

Victoria

In Victoria, the *Guardianship and Administration Act 1986, s* 42H, allows guardians and enduring guardians to refuse consent to treatment when it is not in the patient's best interests. Under the *Medical Treatment Act 1988*, both medical agents and guardians may use a refusal of treatment certificate. Section 5B(2) of the *Medical Treatment Act* states that a guardian can only make a refusal of treatment certificate (under s 5B) when:

(a) the medical treatment would cause unreasonable distress to the patient; or

(b) there are reasonable grounds for believing that the patient, if competent, and after giving serious consideration to his or her health and well-being, would consider that the medical treatment is unwarranted.

Refusal of treatment certificates cannot be used to refuse palliative care, which is defined to include the reasonable provision of food and water. This issue was examined in *BWV* [2003] VSC 173, in which the Supreme Court found that artificial nutrition and hydration (ANH) was not the reasonable provision of food and water, but rather medical treatment which could be refused under the *Medical Treatment Act* by an appointed guardian or medical agent.

Since *BWV* there have been are a number of cases now recorded where guardians have exercised their power to refuse treatment under the *Medical Treatment Act*. In *RCS* [2004] VCAT 1880, the wife and brother of a patient with severe brain damage were appointed as limited guardians for the purpose of refusing medical treatment, namely antibiotics. In *Korp* [2005] VCAT 779, the Public Advocate was appointed to make decisions for a woman who had been injured in an attempted murder and had fallen into a permanent vegetative state. The Public Advocate sought an order that would authorise him to issue a refusal of treatment certificate refusing ANH. It was argued by her husband (who at the time had been charged with her attempted murder) that the patient was a devout Catholic who would not have refused ANH. Morris J decided that the appointment of the Public Guardian was in her best interests. The fact the patient was Catholic did not necessarily mean that she would have wanted ANH to be continued. It was said that the hypothetical question posed by s 5B(2)(b) of the *Medical Treatment Act* is not one 'that is automatically answered in a particular way because a person holds a particular religious faith': at [36].

Persons responsible arguably also have the power to refuse treatment in Victoria as their powers to consent are based on the best interests test. Section 42L of the *Medical Treatment Act* expressly mentions a person responsible refusing consent to treatment. The section allows a medical practitioner to provide treatment over the objections of the person responsible, when the practitioner believes on reasonable grounds that the proposed treatment is in the best interests of the patient. The practitioner must send a written notice to the person responsible informing them of their decision and the avenue for appeal of the decision to the Victorian Civil and Administrative Tribunal.

Western Australia

In Western Australia the *Guardianship and Administration Act 1990*, s 119, states that a number of alternative decision-makers can consent to medical treatment. Consent to medical treatment has been considered by the WA Guardianship Board (which has now been subsumed within the State Administrative Tribunal) to include decisions to withhold and withdraw life-sustaining treatments. The section was considered in *BTO* [2004] WAGAB 2. The Guardianship Board did authorise the withdrawal of treatment. While s 119 only mentioned consent to treatment, the Board found that the concept of consent to treatment not only included the giving of consent but also the decision to withhold or withdraw life-sustaining measures. The *Guardianship and Administration Act 1990* was amended in 2008 by the West Australian government to recognise advance directives and enduring guardianship (amongst other things). Many of these amendments are not yet in force. One of these new sections, s 110ZJ, clearly states that guardians, enduring guardians and persons responsible have the power to refuse treatment.

Problems with the law in end-of-life decisions

The best interests test lacks clarity

One of the primary problems with the use of the best interests test is that it fails to offer a solid set of recognisable signs for people to follow. One of the most critical opponents of the best interests approach was Brennan J (as he was then) in *Secretary, Department of Health and Community Services v JWB and SMB (Marion's case)* (1992) 175 CLR 218 at 270-1 where he spoke out against the use of the test in sterilisation cases.

> The … best interests approach offers no hierarchy of values which might guide the exercise of a discretionary power to authorize sterilization, much less any general legal principle which might direct the difficult decisions to be made in this area by parents, guardians, the medical profession and the courts … [I]n the absence of legal rules or a hierarchy of values, the best interests approach depends upon the value system of the decision-maker. Absent any rule or guideline, that approach simply creates an unexaminable discretion in the repository of the power.

His Honour's criticism points out one of the major flaws of the majority decision in *Marion's case*. By allowing the bests interests test to apply to circumstances which, on the whole, are not subject to broadly accepted community standards, the majority did not achieve any certainty or surety in the law. This problem is also experienced in decisions about withholding treatment. The reluctance of appeal judges, particularly in earlier decisions from the United Kingdom, to develop guidelines about the content of best interests has created the tendency for 'best interests' to become a label which justifies the judge's conclusions. Some work has since been done on the best interests test (see Chapter 13) and the more recent cases from the United Kingdom now approach the question of best interests by drawing up a list of the advantages and disadvantages of the proposed course of treatment, which is an improvement on earlier efforts: *NHS Trust v Ms D* [2005] EWHC 2439 (Fam); *An NHS Trust v MB* [2006] EWHC 507 (Fam).

Futility

Medical treatment that is futile need not be attempted as, by definition, futile treatment is not in the patient's best interests. Generally, the law leaves the question of what treatment is considered futile up to the medical profession. Although, as we have seen above, the courts may be asked to review the decision-making process used in deciding the question of futility, if there has been some misdiagnosis or possibility that the decision had been unfairly made.

In *Airedale NHS Trust v Bland* [1993] AC 789 at 869, Lord Goff considered futile treatment:

> I cannot see that medical treatment is appropriate or requisite simply to pro-long a patient's life, when such treatment has no therapeutic purpose of any kind, as where it is futile because the patient is unconscious and there is no prospect of any improvement in his condition ... [I]n the end, in a case such as the present it is the futility of the treatment which justifies its termination. I do not consider that, in circumstances such as these, a doctor is required to initiate or to continue life-prolonging treatment or care in the best interests of his patient. It follows that no such duty rests upon the respondents, or upon Dr Howe, in the case of Anthony Bland, whose condition is in reality no more than a living death, and for whom such treatment or care would, in medical terms, be futile.

In a New Zealand case (*Shortland v Northland Health Ltd* [1998] 1 NZLR 433), the court had to consider whether a patient could demand treatment that the treating medical team thought was futile. The patient, Mr Rau Williams, a 63-year-old man, suffered from diabetes and was admitted to Whangarei Hospital with a non-functioning kidney which was fatal unless treated by dialysis until transplant. Over an extended period Mr Williams' suitability for acceptance onto a dialysis treatment program was assessed, the assessment process including interim dialysis. Mr Williams was not accepted onto the renal replacement program and the interim dialysis treatment was to be discontinued on 17 September 1997. The reasons given for not being accepted onto the program were that Mr Williams suffered from moderate dementia and could not understand or provide the high level of cooperation required for his treatment.

The Court of Appeal considered a set of guidelines used by the hospital in reaching its conclusions. The guidelines had been drawn up on 26 July 1996 and were called the 'Guidelines for Entry into the Northern Region's End Stage Renal Failure Programme'. These guidelines were developed to 'assist providers to ensure comparable services across the region, determine when it is appro-priate to offer life-prolonging therapy and decide priorities for therapy on the basis of greatest probable benefit'. The court noted evidence from one of the expert medical witnesses that the physicians 'assess the patient's best interests using the guidelines as a framework'.

On an issue arguing that the hospital was not supplying the 'necessaries of life' to Mr Williams as required by New Zealand law, the court said:

> The extent of the duty to supply the "necessaries of life" has to be assessed in the particular context. In this case that context is the clinical assessment process already described. We need do no more than recall some critical elements of that process. NH, through its staff and other persons involved, carefully assessed Mr Williams' situation over a ten-week period. As well, they had knowledge of his condition and his ability to take advantage of, and benefit from, dialysis from his hospitalisation in the previous year. That

assessment was informed by five or six meetings of an interdisciplinary team, including family members. Among other things that assessment included the opinion, in terms of the guidelines, that MR Williams would not have the ability to cooperate with active therapy. The conclusion reached at the end of that process was that Mr Williams should not be placed on a dialysis treatment programme. ([1998] 1 NZLR 433 at 445)

This case (and the others discussed above such as *Northridge, Messiha* and *Melo*) illustrates the importance of following a proper decision-making process when reaching decisions about the futility of any treatments. Once a fair determination has been made, it is highly unlikely that treatment will be ordered by the courts, against the wishes of doctors. In *Messiha*, Howie J stated:

[I]t seems to me that it would be an unusual case where the Court would act against what is unanimously held by medical experts as an appropriate treatment regime for the patient in order to preserve the life of a terminally ill patient in a deep coma where there is no real prospect of recovery to any significant degree. This is not to make any value judgment of the life of the patient in his present situation or to disregard the wishes of the family and the beliefs that they genuinely hold for his recovery. But it is simply an acceptance of the fact that the treatment of the patient, where, as here, the Court is satisfied that decision as to the appropriate treatment is being made in the welfare and interest of the patient, is principally a matter for the expertise of professional medical practitioners ... ([2004] NSWSC 1061 at [25])

It is safe to conclude that once a fair process has been adopted, it will not be possible for patients or their substitute decision-makers to demand treatment. Nor is it possible to demand treatment via an advance directive. In *R (On the application of Burke) v General Medical Council* [2005] EWCA Civ 1003, a patient with spino-cerebellar ataxia, a condition which would eventually require him to receive artificial nutrition and hydration (ANH), sought to review the General Medical Council's policy, *Withholding and Withdrawing Life-prolonging Treatments: Good Practice in Decision-making*. The patient believed the policy breached his human rights because it did not recognise his right to make an advance directive *requesting* ANH to be provided when he was no longer competent (see below for more on advance directives). Instead the policy focused solely on the right of patients to *refuse* treatments and, in the absence of advance directives, the right of doctors to *withdraw* treatments. The patient argued that the policy allowed a doctor to withdraw ANH from him when he became incompetent, even though he wished for it to be continued.

The Court of Appeal of England and Wales did not agree with the patient. It found that the patient could not demand ANH be provided to him via an advance directive. The advance directive could give consent to treatment but only treatment that the health professionals were offering at the time. The court stated that at common law the doctor's duty was to provide a range of treatment options. If the patient sought another treatment which the doctor believed was not clinically indicated, the health professional was not under a legal duty to provide it.

The key issue is whether the determination of futility has been made fairly. The *Northridge* case (discussed above) shows that if a determination is made outside of clinical guidelines and hospital policies, and triggers a breakdown in communication with the patient's relatives, the courts are more likely to intervene. O'Keefe J stated:

> I have no disagreement with that proposition in general provided that the questions of which treatment is futile and why it is so have been adequately and expressly addressed. There are usually considered to be two components of medical futility. Firstly, a procedure may be considered futile because it is most unlikely to achieve its goal, that is, to be successful. Secondly, it may be that the specific goal of the therapy is judged to be futile. However, not infrequently, the context in which the term futility is introduced admits of no interpretation other than that the patient's life itself is regarded as futile.
>
> In Mr Thompson's case it would be difficult to maintain that suitable antibiotics treatment ... would be futile in treating his chest infection. Secondly, it would be difficult to maintain that treatment of a chest infection in a comatose patient 9 days after admission whose prognosis remains quite unclear, was a futile goal. ((2000) 50 NSWLR 549 at [99])

Assessment of quality of life

Criticisms are often levelled at courts when they approve of treatment withdrawal on the basis that they have included quality of life assessment in their determination of whether the patient's life should be prolonged with medical intervention. Such claims attack the judges for supposedly discriminating against the disabled and breaching the sanctity of life principle. Courts will often try to say that their determinations are based on an assessment of what the treatment will provide rather than on the patient's own worth as a person. For example, the Victorian Civil and Administrative Tribunal has warned that expressions like 'quality of life' are dangerous and are avoided by the Tribunal. They note that their view is that 'as a central proposition ... the question is never whether the patient's life is worthwhile but whether the treatment is worthwhile' (*BWV* [2003] VCAT 121 at [21]).

However, when one reviews the history of court and tribunal determinations it is clear that the patient's quality of life is a factor in determining whether treatment should be continued. Examples of this come from cases, mainly concerning disabled newborns and infants, where the courts have found that the life of the patient is so demonstrably awful and full of pain and suffering that further life-prolonging treatment cannot be justified. This is often referred to as *intolerability*.

The first case to consider this issue in detail was *Re B (A Minor) (Wardship: Medical Treatment)* [1981] 1 WLR 1421. In *Re B* the court had to determine whether an operation should be authorised for an infant with Down's Syndrome who had an intestinal blockage. The parents of the child believed that the baby should not be treated and doctors were reluctant to carry out the operation. The Court of Appeal ordered that the operation be performed on the basis that the life of the child was not so 'demonstrably awful' that in effect the child must be condemned to die. It would only be in the best interests of the child to withhold treatment if the child was suffering 'severe proved damage where the future is so certain and where the life of the child is so bound to be full of pain and suffering' (at 1424).

The Court of Appeal returned to the question of quality of life in *Re J (A Minor) (Wardship: Medical Treatment)* [1990] 3 All ER 930. This case concerned an infant who had been born premature and had suffered severe and permanent brain damage, epilepsy, severe spastic quadriplegia, blindness and deafness. It was likely that he would never speak or develop any limited intellectual abilities. He was not expected to survive to late adolescence although he might have lived on for some years. It was likely that he was able to feel pain. He had twice been ventilated in circumstances where his breathing had stopped.

The Court of Appeal decided that further resuscitation and ventilation be withheld. Lord Donaldson MR said that while there were strong presumptions in favour of life, the value of life was not absolute (at 938). Lord Donaldson saw the decision to withhold treatment as being made in a balancing process where the best interests of the child were to be determined by a number of factors, which include, but was not limited to, the value of life (at 938.) The court had to consider the child's current level of pain and suffering and its quality of life. Furthermore, account should be taken of the pain and suffering caused by further treatment.

Both Lord Donaldson MR and Balcombe LJ rejected any mechanical application of the phrases and terms 'demonstrably so awful' or 'intolerable' to the question of best interests (at 938 and 942 respectively). Instead, after considering the factors of pain and suffering, Lord Donaldson found that it was not in the best interests of the child to treat when 'treatment which will cause [the child] increased suffering and produce no commensurate benefit, giving full weight to the child's, and mankind's, desire to survive' (at 938).

Taylor LJ was more willing to use the *Re B* terminology, and as a result his formulation of the best interests test appears to be more strict. He said:

> I am of the view that there must be extreme cases in which the court is entitled to say: 'The life which this treatment would prolong would be so cruel as to be intolerable.' If, for example, a child was so damaged as to have negligible use of its facilities and the only way of preserving its life was by the continuous administration of painful treatment such that the child either would be in continuous agony or would have to be sedated continuously as to have no conscious life at all, I cannot think counsel's absolute test should apply to require the treatment to be given. In those circumstances, without there being any question of deliberately ending life or shortening it, I consider the court is entitled in the best interests of the child to say that deliberate steps should not be taken artificially to prolong its miserable life span. (at 944-5)

The intolerability criteria has also been used for adults. In *South Buckinghamshire NHS Trust v R (a patient)* [1996] 7 Med LR 401, a group of carers sought judicial review of a decision to place a do-not-resuscitate notice (DNR) on the patient's chart. Sir Stephen Brown P found that the 'best interests of the patient' could be determined by judging the quality of the patient's life to see if it was 'so afflicted as to be intolerable'. It was decided that the decision to withhold treatment was lawful and within power, given the patient's condition.

On occasion the patient is described as being in a 'living death'. In *Re C (A baby)* [1996] 2 FLR 43, Sir Stephen Brown P approved of the withdrawal of ventilatory support from a child suffering a 'living death' caused by cerebral blindness brought on by a premature birth and meningitis. Similarly, the adult patients in *Auckland Health Board v Attorney-General* [1993] 1 NZLR 235 and *Airedale NHS Trust v Bland* [1993] AC 789 were described as being the 'living dead' before it was found that their treatments should be withdrawn.

One of the most controversial and well publicised cases on intolerability is *Wyatt v Portsmouth* [2005] EWCA Civ 118. Charlotte Wyatt became a media cause célèbre, after a decision had been made by hospital authorities not to ventilate her should she get an infection at some point in the future. She had been born at 26 weeks and suffered chronic lung disease and kidney problems. She was also profoundly brain damaged and could not see, hear or make voluntary movements or respond to stimulus. Her parents demanded that all treatments be provided to her. At trial Hedley J had twice decided in favour of the hospital's decision: *Portsmouth NHS Trust v Wyatt* [2004] EWHC 2247 (Fam) and *Wyatt v Portsmouth NHS Trust* [2005] EWHC 693 (Fam). In the first trial Charlotte was 100% oxygen dependant for survival and required continuous deep sedation. Hedley J found her condition to be intolerable, and authorised her doctors to withhold ventilation if she became ill with an infection. At the second trial, her condition had improved but Hedley J still thought that it was in her best interests to withhold ventilation should she get an infection.

Hedley J had made his decision by reference to the intolerability of treatment. The Court of Appeal, when upholding Hedley J's decision, was cautious of the use of intolerability as a 'gloss' or touchstone and said that the appropriate test was not intolerability but best interests. Intolerability may be a relevant issue but only as a factor in determining best interests. Interestingly, Charlotte is, on last report, still alive but in foster care (<www.savecharlotte.com>).

The problem with the intolerability criteria is the risk that it becomes a conclusion rather than a test to be used in assessing the facts of the patient's best interests. Butler-Sloss P raised this issue in *Re L (Medical Treatment: Benefit)* [2004] EWHC 2713 (Fam), when she ordered that ventilation not be offered to a child with Edwards syndrome (trisonomy 18), a fatal and incurable genetic condition, who had suffered numerous arrests and had multiple heart defects, chronic respiratory failure, reflux, epilepsy and hypertonia. According to Butler-Sloss P the court's focus should be on the child's best interests and not intolerability.

Similarly, Holman J in *An NHS Trust v MB* [2006] EWHC 507 (Fam) at [17] said:

> I avoid reference to the concept of 'intolerability'. It seems to me that it all depends on what one means by 'intolerable' and that use of that word really expresses a conclusion rather than provides a test. If it is correct to say, or once it has been concluded, that life is literally 'intolerable', then it is hard to see in what circumstances it should be artificially prolonged. If, conversely, it is 'tolerable' then it is hard to see in what circumstances it should be permitted, avoidably, to end.

This case concerned whether ventilation should be withdrawn from a child with spinal muscular atrophy, who was completely paralysed apart from some possible thumb and eyebrow movement. The judge did not find that withdrawal of ventilation was in the child's best interests as he was presumed not to be brain damaged, had close family relationships and gained some pleasure from watching television. However, permission was given for the withholding of resuscitation should the child arrest.

An NHS Trust v MB was followed soon after in *Re K (A minor)* [2006] EWHC 1007 (Fam), where treatment was withdrawn from a child with an incredibly severe case of congenital myotonica dystrophy, a neuromuscular disorder causing chronic muscle weakness and associated with learning difficulties. The child could not tolerate milk and suffered chronic vomiting. To avoid this she was being fed intravenously by a central venous line (a catheter passed into a large vein near the heart) but such feeding would not sustain her long term. Other types of feeding had been tried but were unsuccessful. She was also being given ventilatory support. The child's condition was terminal and there was no evidence that she took any enjoyment for outside stimulus. She had arrested several times and required intensive care for blood infections. Both parents, the child's guardian and the health professionals agreed that it was not in her best interests to be given life- support when she next suffered an arrest. They also wanted to cease the artificial feeding. The judge agreed and distinguished the case from *MB* on best interests grounds. Mark Potter J stated:

> On the evidence before me there is no realistic sense in which one can assign to her the simple pleasure of being alive or having other than a life dominated by regular pain, distress and discomfort and unrelieved by the pleasures of eating. Her muscular function is already severely diminished and any pleasure which might otherwise develop through increased activity and stimulation of the senses is denied to her. She has no prospect of relief from this pitiful existence before an end which is regarded as virtually certain by the age of one year and likely to be appreciably less. If her line is not removed she will continue to suffer pain and distress from the invasive treatment which she already experiences and the prospect is of the likely necessity for removal of her line in the near future which will merely add to her distress. If she were to have the necessary further surgical operation to replace the line, she would require mechanical ventilation which is also invasive and painful. There would be no improvement in her condition or improvement in her expectation of life. In these circumstances, I have no doubt that it would not only be a mercy, but it is in her best interests, to cease to provide [the feeding] while she is still clinically stable, so that she may die in peace and over a comparatively short space of time, relieved by the palliative treatment contemplated, which will cause her neither pain nor discomfort and will enable her to live out her short life in relative peace in the close care of her parents who love her. (at [57])

While these more recent decisions have moved away from intolerability and back to best interests, they do not resolve the issue of how a patient's quality of life should be considered (if at all) in end-of-life decisions. Professor John Keown has argued extensively that quality of life assessment breaches the sanctity of life principle (Keown 1997; Keown 1998; Keown and Gormally 1999). While the doctrine of the sanctity of life, allows decision-makers to consider whether particular treatments may be worthwhile, Keown says that it forbids any consideration of whether a patient's life is worthwhile.

The problem with these arguments is that the distinction between considering the worth of treatment, as opposed to the worth of the patient's life, is only semantic. When one asks the question about whether a treatment is worthwhile, one is inevitably led to an examination of what the treatment is going to achieve for the patient. If the treatment is merely prolonging a life of pain and suffering or one of completely insensate existence, the treatment is futile. The worth of the treatment can only be assessed in such cases by considering the effect of it on the patient's quality of life. If the patient's quality of life is diminished by the treatment or unaffected by it, then the treatment is not in the patient's best interests. Keown's sanctity of life principle, and the quality of life approach that he dismisses, are really one and the same.

Criminal law and the withholding and withdrawal of treatment

How is it that the withholding and withdrawal of treatment is not a crime? In the common law homicide occurs when a person intentionally causes the death of a person. Homicide, in that sense, has a mental element (sometimes called *malice aforethought* or *mens rea*), and a causation element (the *actus reus*). In the common law, omissions to act will not be found to be a cause of death, unless the accused was under a duty to act in the circumstances.

The orthodox explanation for why withholding withdrawing treatment is legal is given by two cases. The first is the California case of *Barber v Superior Court of the State of California* 195 Cal Rptr 484 (1983), where two doctors, who had discontinued the life support of a patient in a vegetative state, were found not guilty of murder and conspiracy to murder. The court found that the removal of artificial nutrition and hydration was an omission to continue futile treatment. As the treatments were futile, the physicians had breached no duty in omitting to continue them and could not be found to have caused the death of the patient.

This approach was repeated in the English case of *Airedale NHS Trust v Bland* [1993] AC 789, which again involved the withdrawal of artificial feeding and hydration. As the court did in *Barber,* the House of Lords focused on the question of the doctors' duty to continue treatment they believed was futile. The House of Lords found that doctors were not bound to provide treatment that has no beneficial effect. As was discussed in Chapter 13, the question of 'benefit' was said to be determined by the *Bolam* test, meaning that if a responsible body of medical opinion believed that there was no benefit then the treatment was futile.

There are major problems with the explanations of legality given in *Barber* and *Bland,* which are examined below.

The intention to kill

It is clear from *Barber* and *Bland* that a health professional who withdraws or withholds life-sustaining treatment intends to kill. In *Barber* the court found that doctors acted intentionally and with the knowledge that their patient would die.

In *Bland* Lord Browne-Wilkinson found that the doctors satisfied *mens rea* as the whole purpose of stopping artificial feeding was to bring about Anthony Bland's death.

Why? This is because *mens rea* is satisfied, not only in those situations where a person desires the death of another, but also when the accused knows or believes that death is a probable consequence of his or her actions: *R v Crabbe* (1985) 156 CLR 464. In that sense, the term *malice aforethought* is somewhat misleading as it does not require spite, ill will or premeditation: *Royall v R* (1990) 172 CLR 378 at 416.

Importantly, throughout the common law world, the motive of the defendant is irrelevant to the question of culpability, once an intention to kill has been established. It does not matter that the killing is inspired by compassionate motives. It was said in *Bland* by Lord Mustill that:

> The fact that the doctor's motives are kindly will for some, although not for all, transform the moral quality of his act, but this makes no difference in law. It is intent to kill or cause grievous bodily harm which constitutes the *mens rea* of murder, and the reason why the intent was formed makes no difference at all. ([1993] AC 789 at 892)

Causation in homicide

The reasoning in both *Bland* and *Barber* therefore rests on the acts and omissions distinction and, consequently, on the characterisation of the withholding and withdrawal of treatment, as an omission in circumstances where there was no duty to act. An 'act' can be defined as a 'willed body movement': *Ryan v R* (1967) 121 CLR 205. An omission be contrast is the failure to act. A failure to act does not cause death unless it can be shown the accused was obligated to act by some overriding duty.

Clearly, the withholding of treatment (such as through a no-CPR order, or a decision not to commence antibiotics or ventilation) is an omission because no active involvement is required. What is more difficult are situations where ongoing treatment is terminated (such as ANH or artificial ventilation). These are much more difficult to understand as omissions as they necessarily involve people acting, by turning off machines or removing tubes. For example, when ventilation is ceased, the patient is usually also sedated so that they will not struggle when asphyxiating (this occurred in cases like *PVM* and *B* which were discussed in Chapter 14).

Even though these decisions by health professionals clearly involve them acting, the common law treats them as omissions. In *Bland* Lord Goff stated:

> I agree that the doctor's conduct in discontinuing life support can properly be categorised as an omission. It is true that it may be difficult to describe what the doctor actually does as an omission, for example where he takes a positive step to bring the life support to an end. But the discontinuation of life support is, for the present purposes, no different from not initiating life support in the first place. In each case, the doctor is simply allowing his patient to die in the sense that he is desisting from taking a step which might, in certain circumstances, prevent his patient from dying as a result of his pre-existing con-

dition; and as a matter of general principle an omission such as this will not be unlawful unless it constitutes a breach of duty to the patient. I also agree that the doctor's conduct is differentiated from that of, for example, an interloper, who maliciously switches off a life support machine because, although the interloper may perform exactly the same act as the doctor who discontinues life support, his doing so constitutes an interference with the life supporting treatment then being administered by the doctor. Accordingly whereas the doctor, in discontinuing life support , is simply allowing his patient to die of his pre-existing condition, the interloper is actively intervening to stop the doctor from prolonging the patient's life and such conduct cannot possibly be categorised as an omission. ([1993] AC 789 at 866)

This argument is logically untenable. This is because the question of whether an accused owed a legal duty to act in particular circumstances is irrelevant to the characterisation of a causal event as an act or omission. *Either a causal event is an act or it is an omission.* It is only after a causal event has been characterised as an omission that the question arises as to whether a duty is owed by an accused to act. The criminal law does not characterise acts and omissions by reference to whether a duty to act exists between an accused and a victim. It looks first at the causal event itself and only later for legal duties once a finding of an omission has been made.

What Lord Goff is really trying to argue is that the law should allow some people to turn off ventilators (competent patients and doctors) and not others (meddlers), in special situations. This is an imminently sensible proposition but it cannot be achieved by reversing the logic of the criminal law's approach to omissions. Nor can it be achieved by turning logic on its head by finding that voluntary or willed movements (pressing buttons, pulling plugs, flipping switches etc) are omissions.

Ultimately the acts and omissions distinction is a poor tool for discriminating between acceptable and unacceptable forms of conduct. Not all judges have been happy with its use and many have pointed to the inherent defects of this approach. In *Bland*, Lord Mustill expressed 'acute unease' at the proposed use of the distinction and found it to be 'illogical', but felt constrained by authority to adopt it. In New Zealand in the *Auckland Area Hospital Board case* [1993] 1 NZLR 235, Thomas J found that the distinction could not be used to clarify the issue of the cause of a patient's death. In the United States the use of distinction was ridiculed by Scalia J in *Cruzan* 497 US 261 at 296 (1990) and the distinction was rejected by the court in *Matter of Conroy* 486 A 2d 1209 (1985).

Characterising conduct as active or passive is often an elusive notion, even outside the context of medical decision-making ... The distinction is particularly nebulous, however, in the context of whether to withhold or withdraw life-sustaining treatment. In a case like that of Claire Conroy, for example, would a physician who discontinued naso-gastric feeding be actively causing her death by removing her primary source of nutrients; or would he merely be omitting to continue the artificial form of treatment, thus passively allowing her medical condition, which includes her inability to swallow, to take its natural course? ... The ambiguity in the distinction is further heightened when one performs an act within an overall plan of non-intervention, such as when a doctor writes an order not to resuscitate a patient.

Statutory defences

If one accepts these criticisms the only two available options are either to pass legislation which clarifies the rights of health professionals and protects them form liability; or for judges to abandon the acts and omission distinction, recognise that death has been caused by withdrawal, but that the withdrawal was justified (essentially creating a defence to homicide).

The first option has been adopted in some Australian jurisdictions (particularly in relation to possible liability arising from advance directives). The ACT protects health professionals from liability for withdrawing life-sustaining treatment in accordance with an advance directive, when they act honestly: *Medical Treatment (Health Directions) Act 2006*, s 16. In the Northern Territory, the non-application of medical treatment in compliance with an advance directive is not considered a cause of death: *Natural Death Act 1988*, s 6. In Queensland, the *Powers of Attorney Act 1999*, *s* 101, says that any person acting in accordance with an advance health directive, or a decision of an attorney for a health matter, is not liable for an act or omission to any greater extent than if the act or omission happened with the patient's consent. Section 80 of the *Guardianship and Administration Act 2000* (Qld) repeats this protection.

South Australia's *Consent to Medical Treatment and Palliative Care Act 1995*, s 16, protects health professionals from civil and criminal liability for an act or omission done or made:

(a) with the consent of the patient or the patient's representative or without consent but in accordance with an authority conferred by this Act or any other Act; and

(b) in good faith and without negligence; and

(c) in accordance with proper professional standards of medical practice; and

(d) in order to preserve or improve the quality of life.

Under 17(2) medical practitioners caring for patients in the terminal phase of a terminal illness are said to have no duty to use, or continue using, life-sustaining measures if the effect of doing so would be merely to prolong life in a moribund state without any real prospect of recovery, or in a persistent vegetative state.

In Western Australia, s 11ZL of the *Guardianship and Administration Act 1990* (which at the time of writing has not yet been enacted) provides protection to health professionals from criminal liability when they withdraw treatment under an advance directive or in accordance with the instructions of the substitute decision-maker, even if it hastens the patient's death.

A common law defence?

For those jurisdictions without statutory protection, the issue of a common law defence is an important one. The benefit of a defence is that there is no need to rest on the shaky and ineffectual acts and omissions distinction. A defence would require the person to justify their actions.

The most suitable defence for this purpose is necessity. Necessity was discussed in Chapter 14. The three elements of the defence of necessity were set out in Chapter 14. First, the criminal act must have been done in order to avoid an irreparable evil. Secondly, the accused must have had no reasonable alternative to breaking the law. Thirdly, the acts done to avoid the imminent peril must not be disproportionate to the peril to be avoided.

In the context of withdrawing treatment from incompetents it could successfully be argued that any positive action taken to withdraw treatment was a necessitous one. The defence would arise when a doctor or health-care professional actively removes treatment from the patient when that treatment is no longer in the patient's best interests. The first step of the test of necessity is met as any positive act on the part of a health-care professional to withdraw treatment is done to avoid the evil of continued unlawful bodily interference. Continued treatment is unlawful as treatments should be withdrawn when they are no longer in the patient's interests. The second step is also met as there is no reasonable alternative for a health professional. Either the unlawful treatment continues or it does not. There is no alternative but to act positively to remove treatment. As for the third requirement of proportionality, it would seem that those acts that are directly related to the removal of treatment (withdrawing tubes or turning off ventilation machines, for example) will be proportionate acts that are necessary to discontinue the unauthorised touching of the patient. Other incidental acts such as the continued provision of palliative care, which allows the withdrawal of treatment to be more effective, will also be justified.

The third requirement of proportionality also allows the prohibition against more active forms of involuntary euthanasia to be maintained. Lethal injections would not be a proportionate response to the need to withdraw treatment as there are many less drastic options which make the withdrawal of treatment possible (sedation, removal of feeding tubes, cessation of artificial nutrition and hydration, ceasing ventilatory support etc). Hence, the defence of necessity would work to provide a more sensible and workable distinction between legal forms of withdrawal of treatment and active voluntary euthanasia than the current use of acts and omissions. There is no need to pretend that some acts are omissions. Instead the courts could accept these acts as acts, but distinguish them from active voluntary euthanasia by reference to necessity.

The only major problem to this approach is that necessity has not traditionally been available as a defence to murder. The main authority for limiting the defence is *R v Dudley and Stephens* (1884) 14 QBD 273, a case where the defence was not availed to sailors who were cast adrift after a shipwreck and cannibalised a cabin boy to save their lives. There were two reasons for this:

1. No one should have the power of deciding who should live and who should die.
2. To allow people to choose who should live and who should die would totally divorce law and morality.

However, *Dudley and Stephens* was distinguished by the Court of Appeal of England and Wales in *Re A (children) (conjoined twins)* [2000] 4 All ER 961. In this case two of the three judges recognised that necessity could justify the killing of a conjoined twin by separating it from the other, in circumstances where neither child would survive without being separated. The judges distinguished the case from *Dudley and Stephens* by arguing that there was no element of choice, as the child would have died anyway, and, secondly, there was no clear divorce of law from morality in allowing one child to live when both would die without the operation. A similar approach was also taken in *Queensland v Nolan* [2001] QSC 174, where Chesterman J found that doctors could separate conjoined twins in circumstances where the separation would kill one of the twins.

The Supreme Court of Canada has also questioned whether *Dudley and Stephens* prevents necessity from being raised as a defence to murder: *R v Latimer* (2001) 193 DLR (4th) 577 at 596. In the United States, there is some division on the issue of the availability of necessity as a defence to homicide, but the Model Penal Code does not exclude the possibility of its use: Model Penal Code s 3.02. To that extent it may be arguable that necessity could form the basic of a defence to the withdrawal of treatment.

References

Bach, J and V Barnett (1995) 'Ethical considerations in the management of individuals with severe neuromuscular disorders'. *Am J Phys Med Rehab* **74**(1): S34-S40.

Beauchamp, TL and J Childress (1994) *Principles of biomedical ethics*. Oxford, Oxford University Press.

Bodenhamer, E, J Achterberg-Lawlis et al (1983) 'Staff and patient perceptions of the psychosocial concerns of spinal-cord injured persons'. *Am J Phys Med Rehab* **62**: 183-93.

Cantor, M, C Braddock et al (2003) 'Do-not-resuscitate orders and medical futility'. *Arch Intern Med* **163**: 2689-94.

Cassaret, D and M Siegler (1999) 'Unilateral do-not-attempt resuscitation orders and ethics consultation: a case series'. *Crit Care Med* **27**: 1116-20.

Council on Ethical and Judicial Affairs (1999) 'American Medical Association. Medical futility in end-of-life care'. *JAMA* **281**: 937-41.

DeJong, G and J Banja (1995) Health care and physical disability. *Encyclopedia of Bioethics*. WT Reich. New York, MacMillan.

Feynman, R (1986) *Surely you're joking Mr Feynman*. London, Unwin.

Fine, R and T Mato (2003) 'Resolution of futility by due process: Early experience with the Texas Advance Directives Act'. *Ann Intern Med* **138**(9): 743-6.

Gillon, R (1986) 'Ordinary and extraordinary means'. *BMJ* **29**: 259-61.

Gillon, R (1997) 'Futility – too ambiguous and pejorative a term?' *J Med Ethics* **23**: 339-40.

Halevy, A and B Brody (1996) 'A multi-institutional collaborative policy on medical futility'. *JAMA* **276**(7): 571-4.

Hirskyj, P (2007) 'QALY: an ethical issue that dare not speak its name'. *Nurs Ethics* **14**(1): 72-82.

Keown, J (1997) 'Restoring Moral and Intellectual Shape to the Law After *Bland*' *Law Quarterly Review* **113**: 481.

Keown, J (1998) 'The Legal Revolution: From "Sanctity of Life" to "Quality of Life" and "Autonomy" ' *Journal of Contemporary Health Law and Policy* **14**: 253

Keown, J and L Gormally (1999) 'Human Dignity, Autonomy and Mentally Incapacitated Patients: A Critique of *Who Decides?*' *Web Journal of Current Legal Issues* **4**.

Kite, S and S Wilkinson (2002) 'Beyond futility: to what extent is the concept of futility useful in clinical decision-making about CPR?' *Lancet Oncol* **3**(10): 638-42.

Kuhse, H (1987) *The sanctity-of-life doctrine in medicine*. Oxford, Clarendon Press.

Lantos, J (1994) 'Futility assessments and the doctor-patient relationship'. *J Am Geriatr Soc* **42**(8): 868-70.

Lofmark, R and T Nilstun (2002) 'Conditions and consequences of medical futility – from a literature review to a clinical model'. *J Med Ethics* **28**(2): 115-19.

Meisel, A (1997) 'Rights and Risks to Vulnerable Communities: Physician-Assisted Suicide: A Common Law Roadmap for State Courts'. *Fordham Urban Law Journal* **23**: 817.

Nakao, M and S Axelrod (1983) 'Numbers are better than words; verbal specifications of frequency have no place in medicine'. *Am J Med* **74**: 1061-5.

Nantais, D and M Kuczewski (2004) 'Quality of life: the contested rhetoric of resource allocation and end-of-life decision making'. *J Med Philos* **29**(6): 651-64.

Poses, R, C Bekes et al (1989) 'The answer to "What are my chances Doctor?" depends on whom is asked: prognostic disagreement and inaccuracy for critically ill patients'. *Crit Care Med* **17**: 827-33.

Russel, L, M Gold et al (1996) 'The role of cost-effectiveness analysis in health and medicine'. *JAMA* **276**: 1172-77.

Schneiderman, L, N Jecker et al (1990) 'Medical futility: its meaning and ethical implications'. *Ann Intern Med* **112**: 949-54.

Shevell, MI (2002) 'Reflections on futility'. *Semin Pediatr Neurol* **9**(1): 41-5.

Singer, P (1995) *Rethinking life and death*. Melbourne, Text Publishing.

Starr, T, R Perlman et al (1986) 'Quality of life and resuscitation decisions in elderly patients'. *J Gen Int Med* **1**: 373.

Stewart, C (2005) The Sanctity of Life in Law: Comparisons between Jewish, Catholic, Islamic and Common Law Approaches. R Atherton, D Meyerson and P Radan. *Law and Religion: God the State and the Common Law*. London, Routledge.

Stewart, C (2006) 'Problems with substitute decision-making in NSW' *Journal of Bioethical Inquiry* **3**: 128.

Youngner, S (1988) 'Who defines futility?' *JAMA*(269): 209.

Zucker, MB. and HD Zucker (1997) *Medical futility : and the evaluation of life-sustaining interventions*. New York, Cambridge University Press.

CHAPTER 16

CPR AND NO-CPR ORDERS

Case study

Mr TH was a 69-year-old man with end-stage Amyotrophic Lateral Sclerosis (ALS or Motor Neurone Disease). He was admitted to hospital with a chest infection – his fourth admission in the last year. He was very depressed and could no longer cope at home. In the middle of one night the nurse was called to see him because he was very agitated. She realised that he was confused because of lack of oxygen, but before she could get him some oxygen he collapsed and suffered a cardiac arrest. She called for the cardiorespiratory arrest team, who resuscitated him briefly before his heart stopped again. As they were about to try again, his daughter rushed into the room and insisted that they should stop, as he did not wish to be resuscitated. The arrest team decided to leave him alone with his family.

When closed-chest massage was first developed in 1960, it was applied to victims of myocardial infarction, electrical shock, drownings and other acute events (Kouwenhaven, Jude et al 1960). CPR was very successful for these patients and between 12% and 50% survived to discharge from hospital. Since the 1960s, however, CPR has also come to be applied as a 'standing order' to other patients, and it is now frequently used for those who experience a cardiac arrest that is secondary to underlying chronic or debilitating diseases.

Survival after cardiac arrest depends critically on the setting in which it is used. Overall, about 30% of people who suffer cardiac arrest in Australian hospitals survive to discharge (Weerasinghe, MacIntyre et al 2002) In patients with severe acute illness, such as sepsis or pneumonia, or chronic debilitating disease, including cancer, renal failure, cardiac failure and cerebrovascular disease, survival following CPR may be as low as 4% (Murphy 1988; Weil and Fries 2005). Outcomes from out-of-hospital cardiac arrest depend on the presence of trained bystanders and appropriate equipment (Weston, Wilson et al 1997). In a Western Australian study, there was a survival rate of 6.8% for witnessed arrests, and 33% if that bystander was an equipped paramedic (Finn, Jacobs et al 2001). In patients with asystolic cardiac arrest (ie, those in whom the heart was not beating when the paramedics arrived), survival rate may be less than 1% (Meyer, Bernard et al 2001).

CPR is also not a totally benign procedure. It may entail considerable burdens to the patient, including fractured ribs, multiple venepunctures and prolonged stays in intensive care units, however, the side-effects of CPR also vary depending on the setting. Fractured ribs and injuries are relatively common when elderly people are resuscitated by inexperienced people. In a different setting – children given CPR in a tertiary hospital – injuries were rare (Ryan, Young et al 2003).

Of those who survive CPR, many die in the days following the resuscitation. In one study of survivors of cardiac arrest, 61.5% died before discharge, mostly due to neurological injuries (Laver, Farrow et al 2004). The prevalence of brain injury following CPR varies from 10-83% (Berek, Lechleitner et al 1995; Rogove, Safar et al 1995; Sandroni, Nolan et al 2007) and the worst possible scenario, survival in a state of post-coma unresponsiveness, is estimated to occur in about 2.7% of patients (Krischer, Fine et al 1987).

Medical Emergency Teams (METs)

Ideally, cardiac arrests would be prevented rather than treated when they occur. In recent years, many Australian hospitals have embraced the concept of Medical Emergency Teams (METs) in the hope that the rapid provision of skilled medical responses to early changes in patients' vital signs would prevent further deterioration and ultimately reduce the incidence of intensive care unit (ICU) admission, cardiac arrest or death (Lee, Bishop et al 1995) While there is some evidence that METs may provide a benefit, recent Australian studies have provided intriguing, and perhaps surprising, insights into means for improving outcomes for critically ill hospitalised patients.

The Medical Early Response Intervention and Therapy (MERIT) study investigators, in collaboration with the Australian and New Zealand Intensive Care Society's Clinical Trials Group, conducted the first large multi-centre randomised controlled trial of MET versus standard (usual) care. This study, which was conducted in 23 hospitals and involved 36,000 patients, reported a reduction in composite endpoints (cardiac arrest, unexpected death or ICU admission) in both the intervention and control hospitals with no differences between those hospitals with MET systems and those without (Hillman, Chen et al 2005). At the same time, however, MET hospitals reported increased numbers of calls to hospital emergency teams and increased early designation of resuscitation status. Similarly, an audit of experience with a MET system at a Victorian teaching hospital found that cardiac arrest rates fell before and after the introduction of an education process and a MET system, and continued to fall despite there being no change in the MET system over a 10-year period (Buist, Harrison et al 2007). This suggests that the most significant aspect of a MET system may not be the MET at all, but the associated education of staff regarding resuscitation, the attention to assessment and documentation of vital signs, the designation of resuscitation status and the documentation of directives regarding CPR or the omission of CPR (Cooper and Buist 2008).

'No-CPR' policies

For the majority of acutely ill patients, cardiac arrest is an uncommon occurrence and should it occur (and where the wishes of the patient are unknown) there is an ethical presumption grounded in the principles of non-maleficence and beneficence in favour of attempting to preserve life. But for other patients, those with serious, chronic and terminal conditions, cardiorespiratory arrest is an anticipated consequence of their illness and CPR may be much less beneficial and more burdensome than in other acute situations. While it may be difficult to predict when cardiac arrest may occur, situations like those described make the likelihood of cardiac arrest so high that decisions can be made in advance as to whether CPR should be attempted.

Growing appreciation of the medical, legal and ethical implications of resuscitation has led to the development of formal 'Do-Not-Resuscitate' policies. According to the principle of autonomy, a competent patient has the right to refuse medical treatment even if it would be lifesaving. Patients who are thought to be at risk of cardiac arrest should therefore be fully informed of their condition and prognosis, and should be offered the choice to refuse CPR (Florin 1993).

Despite general agreement about these principles, there is still considerable apprehension among clinicians about the involvement of patients in this process. Many doctors do not routinely discuss CPR, arguing that patients would rather not know that they are dying or prefer not to discuss it with others (Schade and Muslin 1989). This may also reflect doctors' uncertainty regarding the most appropriate time to initiate discussions regarding prognosis or their fears that patients will be upset, even though most research suggests that patients are rarely upset by discussions regarding CPR.

A second reason why doctors may avoid discussion with patients about CPR is that they may believe that the clinical factors involved in critical care are too complex for patients to understand and deal with. For this reason, sick patients are often bypassed in favour of using their family as decision-makers. However, most research suggests that neither physicians nor family members are good at predicting patient preferences about resuscitation, suggesting that patients should be involved in these decisions where possible (Uhlmann, Pearlman et al 1988). Decisions about CPR depend critically on its likely burdens and benefits, as they are evaluated by the individual patient. If patients are mentally competent, then decisions should be reached as a shared process involving the patient and the clinical staff, with involvement of family and other staff members as desired by the patient. If patients are not competent then their wishes need to be inferred, either with the assistance of advance directives, or through surrogate decision-maker's – usually family members who are close to the patient.

A third reason why doctors may avoid discussing CPR with patients is that they may be concerned that patients will insist on resuscitation when the doctor believes that it is inappropriate or unavailable. This is particularly difficult as ICU departments develop increasingly stringent admission policies, leading to the real possibility that a person may be resuscitated at their request, be intubated and managed with complex medication regimes, and then refused admission to ICU. In order to have appropriate discussions with patients, doctors need to be aware of what they can offer and whether there are any limits on this, and they should take care not to offer treatment options that are unavailable.

Like all therapies, the application of CPR is sometimes inappropriate or not clinically indicated. In many cases, particularly in the care of the elderly and those who are terminally ill, doctors may not discuss the institution of a No-CPR order with patients when they believe that it is not clinically indicated or is 'futile' (Marik and Zaloga 2001; Ditillo 2002; Cherniack 2003). It is generally held that therapists are under no legal or ethical obligation to offer therapy that is futile. However, the determination that CPR is 'futile' or 'inappropriate' is not wholly objective and is influenced by physician's (and patient's) values and assumptions about the value of different outcomes (Wachter, Luce et al 1989). If CPR is thought to be futile then this opinion should be justified and the reasons for it should be recorded in the notes (Waisel and Truog 1995). A general consensus that is emerging about futile care is that it should be discussed with patients where possible, and that disagreement about what constitutes futile therapy should be resolved through procedural means (Cantor, Braddock et al 2003) – as discussed in Chapter 15.

The literature demonstrates that patients and their families and, to a lesser extent, health professionals have an over-optimistic view of patients' chances of surviving. This suggests that discussions about CPR are likely to be predicated on unrealistic expectations of benefit, that disputes about the goals of care and about whether treatment is futile are commonplace and that patients and their families may assume that CPR is beneficial and should be offered/applied (Wagg, Kinirons et al 1995; Kerridge, Pearson et al 1998; Jones, Brewer et al 2000; Heyland, Frank et al 2006). Nevertheless, there may come a time when it is clear either that there is an extremely low chance of survival or that the burdens of CPR far outweigh its benefits. Indeed, extensive medical literature supports selective use of CPR, rather than as a response to death occurring as a consequence of advanced age or illness. It may be reasonable, therefore, not to offer CPR in some cases. Some institutional bodies have attempted to define those instances where CPR is indicated and where it is not. Hilberman et al use a principle-based approach to CPR and suggest that on current evidence:

CPR is indicated: 1. For witnessed arrests; 2. For a cardiac rhythm of ventricular fibrillation or tachycardia; 3. During operations and procedures; and, 4. as part of well-justified experimental protocols.

CPR is not indicated: 1. If the patient does not want CPR; 2. If the arrest is unwitnessed, unless some sign of life persists; 3. If CPR is not started within six minutes of the arrest, or has continued more than thirty minutes (except hypothermia); 4. For patients in a Persistent Vegetative State, in coma, or with severe heart of lung failure, advanced cancer, or other end-state illness.

CPR is relatively contraindicated: 1. If it is known that the patient had significant physical deterioration prior to the cardiac arrest; 2. For persons who have severe dementia, and possibly for those with moderate dementia; 3. For patients with cancer (who rarely survive CPR according to the medical literature). However, some patients have minimal cancer and deserve CPR; 4. For victims of the AIDS epidemic for whom cardiac arrest is a late complication. Exciting advances in treatment, recently reported, seem most likely to delay the occurrence of cardiac arrest but not after subsequent outcome.

It is intended that indications will be revised as new knowledge emerges. In any scenario we expect that providers will need to make individual judgments. (Hilberman, Kutner et al 1997)

If CPR is not to be offered, then it should not be presented to patients as if they have a choice about the matter. This does not mean that it cannot be discussed; indeed, discussing such issues with patients may be an important part of terminal care as it enables elucidation of the patient's goals, clarification of the medical prognosis and definition of agreed treatment options. Where there is persistent disagreement about the application of CPR, or any other therapy, there are a number of strategies for resolving disagreement, including time and further discussions about the goals of care and the likelihood that CPR would contribute to attaining those goals; an offer of a second opinion; clinical ethics consultation; facilitation/mediation through a third party acceptable to the health team and the patient/family; institution of a time-limited treatment trial; and, if all else fails, consideration of transfer of the patient to another care team or facility or referral to legal processes, such as Guardianship Tribunals (NSW Dept of Health 2005).

Surveys of 'No-CPR' decisions have highlighted many problems with the formulation, documentation and communication of 'No-CPR' orders (Sidhu, Dunkley et al 2007). Decisions about the institution or omission of CPR need to be documented clearly and formally in the patient's notes. Such decisions may change as the patient's illness and attitudes change and they should be reviewed regularly. Decisions about CPR should be kept separate from decisions about care such as the use of antibiotics, oxygen or intravenous fluids. The fact that a patient does not want CPR does not necessarily imply that other methods of treatment should be withdrawn as well. Indeed, the literature suggests that the presence of a 'No-CPR' order reduces physicians' willingness to continue or institute a range of therapies not related to CPR (Beach and Morrison 2002). Such misunderstandings are the source of considerable anger and interprofessional conflict and as such the exact scope of any 'No-CPR' order should be made explicit in the notes.

We favour the use of the term 'No-CPR' rather than 'Not For Resuscitation' (NFR) or 'Do Not Resuscitate' (DNR) as this term refers only to CPR and it avoids confusion about the meaning of the word resuscitation.

Nursing staff should be involved at all stages of the decision-making process (NSW Dept of Health 2005). This is desirable, not only because nurses are the ones first called upon to act in the event of a cardiac arrest, but also because they have their own ethical concerns and important insights into individual patients. Where the patient agrees, close family members should also be involved. The decision to record a 'No-CPR' order on a patient's chart represents a crucial moment in the care of the critically ill patient and should usually be reached only after reflective and sympathetic discussion with the patient or, if the patient is not mentally competent, with their surrogate and appropriate members of the health-care team.

Table 16.1: Guidelines for a 'No-CPR' Order

1. A 'No-CPR' order should be recorded as a formal order in the patient's notes in a clear and unambiguous manner.

2. A 'No-CPR' order should include a brief assessment of the patient's competence/decision-making capacity.

3. A 'No-CPR' order should incorporate a brief description of discussions with the patient, person responsible and family (where appropriate), and
   (a) a statement of the patient's wishes (when the patient is competent), or
   (b) the wishes of the family/surrogate (when the patient is not competent).

4. Where a decision has been made not to involve a patient or surrogate in decisions regarding resuscitation status, an explanation should be provided in the progress notes as to the rationale underlying this decision.

5. A 'No-CPR' order should always involve appropriate members of the health team (eg nurses, allied health professionals and the medical staff) in decision-making, although the implementation of the 'No-CPR' order remains the responsibility of the senior attending medical officer.

6. Any 'No-CPR' order should include a statement of the medical condition justifying it.

7. Any 'No-CPR' order should include a statement of the scope of the order specifying the management plan subsequent to the 'No-CPR' order.

8. Any 'No-CPR' order should be subject to review on a regular basis and can be rescinded at any time. Any review should be implemented and documented in the patient's progress notes as above.

LEGAL ASPECTS OF CARDIOPULMONARY RESUSCITATION

Patients and substitute decision-makers refusing CPR

The right of competent adults to refuse life-sustaining treatments like CPR was discussed in detail in Chapter 14, whereas the right of substitute decision-makers to refuse CPR on behalf of incompetent patients was discussed in Chapter 15.

The only two Australian jurisdictions which specifically refer to CPR in legislation are Queensland and South Australia. In both the *Powers of Attorney Act 1998* (Qld), and the *Guardianship and Administration Act 2000* (Qld), s 5A of Sch 2 defines 'life-sustaining measures' to include CPR, meaning that it is amongst the types of treatment that can be refused by patients via an advance directive, and by guardians, health attorneys and statutory health attorneys. 'Life sustaining measures' is similarly defined by s 4 of the *Consent to Medical Treatment and Palliative Care Act 1995* (SA) to include cardiopulmonary resuscitation (which is relevant to the discussion below).

CPR has been refused by substitute decision-makers in a number of Australian cases. For example, in Queensland the Guardianship and Administration Tribunal (QGAAT) approved the withholding of CPR for a 73-year-old man with an acquired brain injury. The patient had been hospitalised with septicaemia and his wife made an application to withhold antibiotics and CPR: *Re RWG* [2000] QGAAT 49. Two of the three children of the patient supported the application, but the son resisted it as he believed withholding CPR would be inhumane. The Tribunal found that CPR was invasive and could cause pain to conscious patients. On that basis CPR was not found to be in the patient's best interests. It was not in accordance with good medical practice for it to be offered to the patient as the treatment came with significant risks of brain damage, pain and distress.

In New South Wales, CPR was not permitted to be refused in *WK v Public Guardian (No 2)* [2006] NSWADT 121 but, following the later decision in *FI v Public Guardian* [2008] NSWADT 263, it appears that substitute decision-makers in New South Wales do have the power to refuse life-sustaining treatment (including CPR).

Generally speaking, a decision about a No-CPR order should be reached with the patient or substitute decision-maker after having been given appropriate information about the consequences of having or not having the resuscitation, including all material risks and potential outcomes. To perform CPR after a clear indication of refusal had been given could amount to a battery. The patient or substitute can, of course, change their mind at any time after refusing treatment.

The fact of a No-CPR decision having been reached with the patient or substitute decision-maker must be appropriately documented so that other health-care providers are aware of the decision of the patient and respect that decision. This requirement is consistent with meeting an appropriate standard of care.

Patients and substitute decision-makers demanding CPR

If CPR is futile there is no duty to provide it. This follows from *R (On the application of Burke) v General Medical Council* [2005] EWCA Civ 1003, where a patient failed to argue that artificial nutrition and hydration (ANH) should be provided to him after he became incompetent, when health-care providers thought it was futile. *Burke* suggests that if an appropriate determination has been made regarding CPR being futile, a patient (or substitute decision-maker) cannot demand CPR.

Of course, this all hinges on the determination of futility being appropriately made. In *Northridge v Central Sydney Area Health Service* [2000] NSWSC 1241 (also discussed in Chapter 13), a patient, Thompson, had been admitted to the Royal Prince Alfred Hospital in an unconscious condition following a heroin overdose. Thompson was resuscitated and admitted into the intensive care unit.

It was found that Thompson had suffered a cardiac arrest and significant brain damage, and would not recover. He was transferred from the intensive care unit to a ward. At some stage in his admission a Not for Resuscitation (NFR) order was placed on Thompson's medical record. The effect of this order was 'to negate treatment inconsistent with its implementation'. Thompson's family objected to the treatment that was being provided to him and his sister, North-ridge, made an application to the New South Wales Supreme Court to have treatment reinstated. The matter came before O'Keefe J who made an interim order that included the suspension of the NFR order until a hearing could be held.

The evidence presented to the court was principally by way of affidavit. Part of evidence from the hospital was that the NFR order had been made following discussion with members of Mr Thompson's family – but the family disputed this. Before the final hearing of the case Mr Thompson's condition began to improve and he was eventually transferred to a rehabilitation facility. In the judgment that O'Keefe J finally handed down (on 29 December 2000, more than nine months from the initial application), his Honour noted:

> On 20 March 2000 Mr Thompson ... experienced a respiratory arrest. Had the NFR then been in force no steps would have been taken to ventilate him and thus restore his breathing. Because of the intervention by the court the NFR had been lifted. This resulted in his being ventilated, his breathing being restored and his recovery. (at [77])

In his judgment O'Keefe J said that the evidence revealed a lack of communication, a premature diagnosis and an inadequate adherence to the hospital's own policies in relation to consultation with relatives.

Is consent needed to make a No-CPR order?

There is some American authority which suggests that the patient or the patient's substitute needs to give consent to the making of a No-CPR order under the doctrine of informed consent. On that basis, some courts have found that the failure to get the patient's consent to a No-CPR order is a form of actionable negligence. In *Payne v Marion General Hospital* 549 NE 2d 1043 (1990, Ind App) the patient, a 65-year-old alcoholic, was extremely ill with multiple health issues including malnutrition, uremia, hypertensive cardiovascular disease, chronic obstructive lung disease, non-union of a fracture, and congenital levoscoliosis of the spine. A DNR order had been entered onto his chart with the consent of his sister but the evidence suggested that the patient was competent. A claim was made by his estate in negligence, a claim which the appeals court refused to dismiss, finding that the right of informed consent supported such an action.

Similarly, in *Belcher v Charleston Area Medical Center* 422 SE 2d 827 (1992), a hospital was sued for not gaining the consent of a 17-year-old boy with muscular dystrophy who was admitted to the hospital after a choking episode. The patient died after hospital staff followed a DNR order on the patient's chart. The parent (who themselves had not objected to the DNR order) brought the action on the basis that their son had been inadequately consulted before the DNR order was entered. The court refused to dismiss the action and remanded the case for a determination on whether the patient was a 'mature minor' whose consent was necessary before the issuance of the DNR order. The court found that, if the patient's competence were proven, damages could be sought.

In *Wendland v Sparks* 574 NW 2d 327 (1998), the Supreme Court of Iowa found that a claim for wrongful issuing of a No-CPR order could be treated like a case of loss of chance (see Chapter 8). The facts of this case were that a No-CPR order had been made without either the patient or her husband's consent where her chance of survival was less than 50%. A trial judge had dismissed the action but the Supreme Court reversed that decision and found that the loss of chance argument should be examined at trial.

Other American cases had found that a patient has no claim if the CPR is futile. In *Gilgunn v Massachusetts General Hospital* (unreported, 21 April 1995, Mass Super No 92-4820-H), the family of an elderly woman unsuccessfully sued the hospital that had entered a DNR order without the informed consent of the patient. The hospital had previously removed a DNR order at the request of the patient's family but had later reinstated it because the hospital's clinical ethics committee had found that CPR was futile. The jury found that, although the patient would have chosen to be resuscitated, no damages could be awarded because, inter alia, the CPR would have been futile.

Many of these decisions hinge on the relevant US State and federal legislation which mandates consent and can be distinguished from Australian conditions. For example, in *In re Baby K* 16 F 3d 590 at 596 (4th Cir, 1994), a court found that an anencephalic infant (a child born without an upper brain) had to be provided with life-sustaining treatment, because such treatment was mandated by the provisions of the *Emergency Medical Treatment and Active Labor Act*, 42 USC SS 139dd (1988 & Supp V 1993). The Act provides that if a provider is receiving federal funding for emergency health services it must provide treatment to all patients or transfer them to another provider. In the later case of *Bryan v Rectors & Visitors of the University of Virginia* 95 F 3d 349 (1996), it was found that the Act did not mandate CPR for a patient who had already been hospitalised for nearly two weeks. It imposed a duty on the hospital to admit the patient but not to provide emergency treatment for the rest of her stay.

Australia has no equivalent to the *Emergency Medical Treatment and Active Labor Act*. The only statute that might require consent for the withdrawal of treatment is the *Consent to Medical Treatment and Palliative Care Act 1995* (SA). Section 17(2) states:

> A medical practitioner responsible for the treatment or care of a patient in the terminal phase of a terminal illness, or a person participating in the treatment or care of the patient under the medical practitioner's supervision, is, in *the absence of an express direction by the patient or the patient's representative to the contrary*, under no duty to use, or to continue to use, life sustaining measures in treating the patient if the effect of doing so would be merely to prolong life in a moribund state without any real prospect of recovery or in a persistent vegetative state. (emphasis added)

The wording in emphasis seems to assume that the patient or substitute decision-maker needs to give their consent to the withdrawal of life-sustaining measures (which, as discussed above, include CPR). Professor Loane Skene (2004) has argued that Parliament would not have intended for that to mean consent was necessary for the withholding of futile treatment, but as she admits there is no guarantee that a court would interpret it that way.

A tort of wrongful resuscitation?

In Chapter 13 there was a discussion the case of *Anderson v St Francis – St George Hospital* 671 NE 2d 225 (1996). The patient had commenced a claim for being resuscitated, despite having consented to a 'do not resuscitate' order being placed on his chart. The day following the resuscitation he had a stroke and remained partially paralysed until his death two years after his resuscitation. The claim was continued by his estate. The claim was framed on both negligence and battery grounds and stated to be a claim for the 'wrongful administration of life-prolonging treatment' or 'wrongful living'.

As was discussed in Chapter 13, the court refused to recognise that Mr Anderson had suffered a harm that was compensable in law. His life was not a form of damage, nor were his medical treatment and economic damages considered to have been caused by his resuscitation. The cases have similarly failed to recognise an action for wrongful CPR. In *Allore v Flower Hospital* 699 NE 2d 560 (1997), the patient had asked not to be resuscitated in an advance directive but someone had mistakenly entered orders to resuscitate on his chart. The patient experienced breathing difficulties, was intubated and eventually placed on mechanical ventilation. On discovering the living will, the treatment was immediately discontinued and the patient died. His estate sued for the emotional distress and costs of unwanted medical treatment. The claims were dismissed summarily by the trial judge and the plaintiff appealed.

The Court of Appeals of Ohio found that any question of liability was limited to the damages for the alleged battery and no amounts could be awarded for distress, or the medical costs, as these were caused by the continuation of life and not by the battery itself.

The approach of these cases is very similar to the wrongful life cases which are discussed in Chapters 18 and 19. The cases use the sanctity of life principle as a reason for not awarding damages, but they ignore the fact that the sanctity of life includes a respect for the person's wishes. If there is a right to refuse treatment like CPR (and there should be) it needs to be protected and enforced by the legal system. Obviously, in emergencies it will be difficult to know whether CPR should be provided. But in institutional settings where there has been a clear choice made by the patient to refuse CPR, any non-consented administration of CPR should be appropriately dealt with under the existing tort law principles.

References

Beach, M and R Morrison (2002) 'The effect of do-not-resuscitate orders on physician decision-making'. *J Am Geratr Soc* **50**(12): 2057-61.

Berek, K, P Lechleitner et al (1995) 'Early determination of neurological outcome after prehospital cardiopulmonary resuscitation'. *Stroke* **26**: 543-9.

Buist, M, J Harrison et al (2007) 'Six year audit of cardiac arrests and medical emergency team calls in an Australian outer metropolitan teaching hospital'. *BMJ* **335**(7631): 1210-2.

Cantor, M, C Braddock et al (2003) 'D0-not-resuscitate orders and medical futility'. *Arch Intern Med* **163**: 2689-2694.

Cherniack, E (2003) 'Increasing use of DNR orders in the elderly worldwide: whose choice is it?' *J Med Ethics* **29**(6): 372-3.

Cooper, DJ and MD Buist (2008) 'Vitalness of vital signs, and medical emergency teams'. *Med J Aust* **188**(11): 630-1.

Ditillo, B (2002) 'Should there be a choice for cardiopulmonary resuscitation when death is expected? Revisiting an old idea whose time is yet to come'. *J Palliat Med* **5**(1): 107-16.

Finn, J, I Jacobs et al (2001) 'Outcomes of out-of-hospital cardiac arrest patients in Perth, Western Australia, 1996-1999'. *Resuscitation* **51**(3): 247-55.

Florin, D (1993) ' "Do not resuscitate" orders: The need for a policy'. *JR Coll Physicians London* **27**: 135-8.

Heyland, DK, C Frank et al (2006) 'Understanding cardiopulmonary resuscitation decision making: perspectives of seriously ill hospitalized patients and family members'. *Chest* **130**(2): 419-28.

Hilberman, M, J Kutner et al (1997) 'Marginally effective medical care: ethical analysis of issues in cardiopulmonary resuscitation (CPR)'. *J Med Ethics* **23**(4): 361.

Hillman, K, J Chen et al (2005) 'Introduction of the medical emergency team (MET) system: a cluster-randomised controlled trial'. *Lancet* **365**(9477): 2091-7.

Jones, GK, KL Brewer et al (2000) 'Public expectations of survival following cardiopulmonary resuscitation'. *Acad Emerg Med* **7**(1): 48-53.

Kerridge, I, S Pearson et al (1998) 'Decision-making in CPR – attitudes of hospital patients and healthcare professionals'. *Med J Aust* **169**(3): 128-31.

Kouwenhaven, W, J Jude et al (1960) 'Closed-Chest Cardiac Massage'. *JAMA* **173**: 1064-7.

Krischer, J, E Fine et al (1987) 'Complications of cardiac resuscitation'. *Chest* **92**(2): 287-91.

Laver, S, C Farrow et al (2004) 'Mode of death after admission to an intensive care unit following cardiac arrest'. *Intensive Care medicine* (Sep 9 (epub)).

Lee, A, G Bishop et al (1995) 'The Medical Emergency Team'. *Anaesth Intensive Care* **23**(2): 183-6.

Marik, P and G Zaloga (2001) 'CPR in terminally ill patients?' *Resuscitation* **49**(1): 99-103.

Meyer, A, S Bernard et al (2001) 'Asystolic cardiac arrest in Melbourne, Australia'. *Emerg Med (Fremantle)* **13**(2): 186-9.

Murphy, D (1988) 'Do-not-resuscitate orders. Time for reappraisal in long-term-care institutions', *JAMA* **260**(14): 2098-101.

NSW Dept of Health (2005) Guidelines for end-of-life care and decision-making. Sydney, NSW Dept of Health.

Rogove, H, P Safar et al (1995) 'Old age does not negate good cerebral outcome after cardiopulmonary resuscitation: analyses from the brain resuscitation clinical trials'. *Crit Care Med* **23**: 18-25.

Ryan, M, S Young et al (2003) 'Do resuscitation attempts in children who die, cause injury?' *Emerg Med J* **20**(1): 10-12.

Sandroni, C, J Nolan et al (2007) 'In-hospital cardiac arrest: incidence, prognosis and possible measures to improve survival'. *Intensive Care Med* **33**(2): 237-45.

Schade, S and H Muslin (1989) 'Do not resuscitate decisions: discussions with patients'. *J Med Ethics* **15**: 186-90.

Sidhu, N, M Dunkley et al (2007) '"Not-for-resuscitation" orders in Australian public hospitals: policies, standardised order forms and patient information leaflets'. *Med J Aust* **188**(2): 72-75.

Uhlmann, R, R Pearlman et al (1988) '"Physicians and spouses" predictions of elderly patients resuscitation preferences'. *J Geront* **43**: M115-M121.

Wachter, E, J Luce et al (1989) 'Decisions about resuscitation: Inequities among patients with different diseases but similar prognoses'. *Ann Intern Med* **111**: 525-32.

Wagg, A, M Kinirons et al (1995) 'Cardiopulmonary resuscitation; doctors and nurses expect too much'. *JR Coll Physicians London* **29**(1): 20-4.

Waisel, D and R Truog (1995) 'The cardiopulmonary resuscitation – not indicated order: futility revisited'. *Ann Intern Med* **122**(4): 304-8.

Weerasinghe, D, C MacIntyre et al (2002) 'The epidemiology of cardiac arrests in a Sydney hospital'. *Resuscitation* **53**(1): 53-62.

Weil, MH and M Fries (2005) 'In-hospital cardiac arrest'. *Crit Care Med* **33**(12): 2825-30.

Weston, CF, RJ Wilson et al (1997) 'Predicting survival from out-of-hospital cardiac arrest: a multivariate analysis'. *Resuscitation* **34**(1): 27-34.

CHAPTER 17

GENETICS AND BIOTECHNOLOGY

Case 1

DM is a 24-year-old woman whose mother, aunt and grandmother have died of breast cancer. She is extremely worried about breast cancer and is considering having prophylactic bilateral mastectomies. She requests a genetic test to assess her risk of breast cancer as she has read that these tests can identify one in two women who will get breast cancer.

Case 2

The local genetics unit is offering free screening for cystic fibrosis for pregnant women. CW, a 29-year-old pregnant woman, presents for screening. She states that, although she would not have an abortion if the child was found to have cystic fibrosis, she would like to know anyway as this would allow her to commence therapy early if she has a child with the disease.

Many of the recent advances in medicine and the biosciences have been made not at the bedside but in the laboratory and the factory. Advances in biotechnology have already provided considerable insights into normal biological function and the mechanisms of disease. Although (with a few exceptions) they have yet to make a major contribution to clinical care, they are widely believed to represent the future of medicine. It may be many years before these sciences are fully incorporated into clinical practice, yet it is important that health professionals are aware of how the biosciences may challenge human identity and transform ideas of health and disease, but may also entrench existing inequities. It is also particularly important that health workers are aware of the issues involved in the clinical application of genetics and in genetic research as they are likely to be increasingly exposed to them in their working environment and may be asked about their meaning and relevance by patients, families and other health professionals.

Genetic screening and diagnosis

Until recently, genetics was concerned largely with 'pure' or 'single gene' disorders. The scope of genetic testing has now increased well beyond this. Clinical genetics now incorporates many different practices: including the analysis of an individual's genes for the purpose of identifying specific chromosomal alterations associated with disease (eg, Cystic Fibrosis); the investigation of susceptibility to common diseases such as heart disease, diabetes and cancer; pharmacogenomics (the study of genetic predisposition to respond to a certain drug or to develop adverse effects from it) and the study of genetic variance across populations (Roses 2004).

Genetic testing produces an enormous amount of knowledge which may be used for diagnosis, for medical or anthropological study, for forensic or paternity testing and for predicting whether an individual will develop a genetic disease at some time in the future ('predictive' testing or 'screening'). Predictive testing has the potential for extraordinary health benefits as it may one day provide individuals with enough foreknowledge to make life, health, reproductive or behavioural choices that will avoid or ameliorate disease and disability (particularly if effective gene-therapy ever becomes available). On the other hand, predictive testing also opens the possibility of discrimination and stigmatisation and may force individuals to confront their future and make health and lifestyle choices that they would rather avoid (Harper and Clarke 1990; Richards 2006).

The first presymptomatic screening tests that were widely used were non-genetic tests for the detection of phenylketonuria, hypothyroidism, sickle cell anaemia and cystic fibrosis at birth. More recently, evolving knowledge in genetics has created the possibility of screening for the presymptomatic detection of 'late-onset' disorders such as breast cancer, Huntington's disease, diabetes, heart disease and dementia. The potential impact of these tests may be considerable – allowing 'risk profiles' to be established for individuals and populations which would form the basis of a range of therapeutic and preventative health interventions (Trent, Williamson et al 2003). However, enthusiasm for genetic testing should be tempered by biological and political realism (Parker 1995). A good example of some of the problems that have arisen from the introduction of genetic screening can be found in recent advances in the genetics of breast cancer.

Many cancers result from mutations or deletions from one of two types of genes – tumour suppressor genes that need to be inactivated, and oncogenes that need to be activated to promote tumour growth (Eeles, Ponder et al 1996). Following the discovery of the BRCA1 and BRCA2 genes for susceptibility to breast and ovarian cancer in 1994, presymptomatic testing rapidly became available – particularly in the private sector where it was performed as a profit-making venture. A United States company – Myriad Genetics Inc (Myriad) – held patents over methods and materials used to detect the BRCA1 and BRCA2 genes. In Europe and Canada, Myriad proposed licence conditions that would require testing laboratories to send DNA samples to its laboratories in the United States for sequencing, resulting in costs of testing about three times those charged by local laboratories. These problems were not so great in Australia, but concerns remained about whether other companies would proceed with the same approach that had been proposed by Myriad (Australian Law Reform Commission 2004). These fears were realised in 2008 when Genetic Technologies Ltd (which in 2002 had acquired from Myriad the right to use their patents to conduct diagnostic testing of the BRCA1 and BRCA2 genes) announced that it would enforce these patents, meaning that they would exclusively perform BRCA 1 and BRCA2 testing (at 'market cost') and that these tests would no longer be available within public hospitals (Robotham, Metherell et al 2008).

The story was complicated further when it was realised that the risk of breast and ovarian cancer among carriers of mutant breast cancer susceptibility genes had been grossly overestimated. It was reported that the odds of finding a BRCA1 mutation in women with a family history or breast cancer was found to be only 7 in 100 and not 1 in 2 as was originally proposed (Couch, De Shano et al 1997). The result of this was that 9 out of 10 tests for the BRCA1 were negative, and while the test is now used much more judiciously and appropriately in the investigation of women with a family history of breast and/or ovarian cancer, it has failed to live up to the claims that were made about the impact it would have on the investigation and management of either individual patients or 'at risk' populations.

Issues raised by this episode are relevant to the entire range of proposals for presymptomatic testing. It is clear that market forces, commercialisation and overenthusiastic predictions may drive the development of genetic testing before the true significance of genetic markers are established, before all the relevant genes have been identified (including so-called 'modifier' genes), before simple cost-effective mutation testing has been developed and certainly before the 'opportunity cost' of the program has been acknowledged (Levitt 1995; Schrag, Kunz et al 1997). Furthermore, most common diseases are likely to result from a complex interplay of multiple genes, environmental influences and spontaneous genetic mutations, and are unlikely to be amenable to a single genetic test. Health professionals will need to be very wary of applying the genetic information in wrong ways or too soon (Healy 1997; Roses 2004).

Another problem with genetic screening is that most of the conditions that can now be tested for cannot be treated very effectively. Examples include pre-senilin mutations for early-onset dementia, Huntington's disease and other rare neurological conditions.

Huntington's disease occurs in 50% of the offspring of affected people but only develops symptoms in middle age. Thereafter, there is a progressive decline manifested by the development of dementia and movement disorders. Before gene tests for Huntington's disease were developed, it was thought that uncertainty about whether a person had the disease was more stressful for those at risk than knowing that they had it. This suggested that most people at risk of getting Huntington's disease would have wanted to find out for sure. In fact, only a minority of people at risk of Huntington's disease request the gene test (eg, in Canada, the figure is about 18% (Creighton, Almqvist et al 2003)), and many at-risk people decide against the test once they receive full information of its implications. This suggests that, in the absence of effective treatment, genetic knowledge may be less useful than has been made out, and may, at times, be harmful. Indeed, the literature is replete with descriptions of cases where patients, families and communities were unclear of the rationale for testing and unable to understand, or cope with, the implications of positive or negative test results (Duncan 2004).

Because of the complexity of genetic testing, the subjective nature of risk assessment, and the implications that may result from erroneous (often deterministic) beliefs regarding genetic 'disease', it is critical that all those undergoing genetic testing receive both pre-test counselling and post-test support (Lloyd, Reyna et al 2001; Otlowski and Williamson 2003). This will often require referral to clinical genetics services.

Prenatal diagnosis

Prenatal diagnosis has been developed over the past 20 years to assist couples to have an unaffected child where there is a risk of genetic abnormality. Diagnosis can be by visualisation (ultrasound), amniocentesis, foetal blood sampling or chorionic villus sampling. This technology has been applied both to individuals making reproductive choices and as public health measures to decrease the prevalence of genetic diseases such as sickle-cell anaemia.

In the past, the value of prenatal diagnosis relied primarily on the capacity to eliminate foetuses with genetic abnormalities by abortion. This was the source of many of the ethical concerns raised by prenatal diagnosis. However, the introduction of preimplantation genetic diagnosis (PGD) in the early 1990s has made possible a degree of separation between prenatal diagnosis and the issue of abortion (Botkin 1998). In PGD, embryos created in vitro (by IVF) are analysed for well-defined genetic defects, and only those free of those defects are inserted into the uterus. PGD is generally used in individuals at high risk of having a child with genetic disease who have concurrent infertility, recurrent miscarriages, religious objections to termination of pregnancy, or who have repeatedly opted to terminate their pregnancies on the basis of prenatal tests (Sermon 2002). PGD has been applied to approximately 35 different monogenic diseases including: autosomal recessive diseases (cystic fibrosis, sickle cell anaemia, thalassaemia), autosomal dominant diseases (myotonic dystrophy, Huntington's disease, Marfan's Syndrome), X-linked diseases (Duchenne muscular dystrophy, Fragile X syndrome), and a number of chromosomal structural abnormalities (Sermon, Van Steirteghem et al 2004).

The utility of prenatal diagnosis for genetic diseases varies depending on the penetrance of the gene, age of onset, severity of symptoms and availability of effective treatment. Physicians and patients often elect for prenatal diagnosis for diseases that manifest in childhood, are untreatable and have a high degree of lethality. While many such indications are now an accepted part of clinical practice, more controversial applications of prenatal diagnosis and PGD include sex selection for 'non-medical' purposes, selection of embryos according to their suitability to act as a sibling donor, diagnosis of late-onset diseases and cancer susceptibility syndromes, and even for the positive selection of genetic disorders according to parental preference. (This has been called 'designer disability' by one author (Savulescu 2000).)

Opponents of prenatal diagnosis and PGD argue that it will lead to a devaluing of disabled individuals – particularly where the prevailing sociopolitical context may support the belief that the healthy should survive and the 'less than healthy' should never be born (Boss 1994; Mattei 1996). Many are also concerned that advances in prenatal diagnosis and PGD may allow the desire to avoid the birth of an 'abnormal' baby to be subtly replaced by demands for children who conform with their parents' desires. While it is important to avoid conflating judgments about disability with judgments about disabled *people*, there can be no doubt that we do make judgments about quality of life and about human flourishing and that our values and biases are manifest in the diseases for which we develop tests and therapies and for which we offer prenatal diagnosis. This, in turn, raises the question of how to define normality and abnormality, genetic order and disorder; and how we can maintain social justice so that not only the wealthy have access to prenatal diagnosis (Dawson and Singer 1990).

Sex selection

One area of great controversy is the practice of PGD for the determination of foetal sex. This is usually requested for social reasons, including 'family balancing' (the practice of seeking to have a child of one gender to 'balance' the presence of children of the opposite gender within the family). In the past this practice has generally been condemned, but in recent years there has been increasing recognition that such services are available within the private sector, and there has been less certainty that sex selection for family balancing is necessarily morally wrong (Human Genetics Society of Australasia 1997; Ray, Munnich et al 2002). Opponents of sex selection argue that that it represents a misuse of limited medical resources and of IVF and PGD, that it is unjust as it will only be accessible to the rich, and that it disrupts the rough equality of the 'sexual mix', devalues the equality of the sexes and may diminish the status of women in society (Warren 1985). Those in favour of sex selection respond to these objections by noting that sex selection is a reasonable extension of pro-creative autonomy and that sex selection in vitro is preferable to sex selection following prenatal diagnosis or after birth as the latter are associated with abortion and infanticide. Supporters of sex selection argue that gender discrimi-nation and gender stereotyping are best tackled through sociopolitical and legal change rather than through restriction of reproductive choice; that sex distri-bution is unlikely to be skewed as so few people will utilise PGD to choose their child's sex; and that where sex selection is utilised to achieve family balancing, issues of gender discrimination and skewed gender balance do not arise (Malpani, Malpani et al 2002; Pennings 2002).

Preimplantation genetic diagnosis for stem-cell donation

While PGD is most often used to screen for the absence of disease in order to prevent the transmission of a heritable disorder, in recent years PGD has also been used to select an embryo, according to its HLA type, so that the child born can be a stem-cell donor for a sick sibling (a so-called 'saviour sibling'). The first such case was described by Verlinsky and colleagues and concerned the use of PGD to ensure the birth of a baby boy with a suitable tissue type to act as a donor of umbilical cord blood cells to cure his sister of the fatal condition of

Fanconi's anaemia (Verlinsky, Rechitsky et al 2001). The main ethical arguments made against this practice, which has been specifically approved in the United Kingdom, are that it treats the child as a 'treatment' (so breaching the Kantian imperative that a person should never be used as a 'means' to another end), and that the child will feel diminished when they learn that they were conceived purely for the purpose of saving a sibling. Neither of these arguments is, however, either philosophically or empirically compelling. First, such cases do not breach the Kantian imperative as this refers to the treatment of a person *solely* as a means, and in such cases these children are also conceived to be loved and cherished as a valued family member and an individual in their own right. Secondly, there is no reason why children conceived in this manner should not feel more valued, having contributed in such an important way to the well-being of a sibling (Pennings, Schots et al 2002). And perhaps, most importantly, it is important to recognise that families are more than simply a collection of individuals, each with their own interests, but are complex and dynamic entities in which each member has freedom, 'relational autonomy' and mutual obligations. Since most parents would not hesitate to volunteer an existing child as a donor to save the life of a sick sibling, so it would seem reasonable to conceive a child to make the same 'gift' (Robertson 2003).

Consent and confidentiality

Genetic information is not only relevant to the individual but also to his or her family and community. However, information about a patient's genome is usually thought of as private information and, like all private information, access to it is controlled by the individual themselves. Conflicts may arise where others such as family members, employers, insurance companies and health professionals make a claim on that information.

Particular difficulties arise within families where one individual refuses genetic testing or refuses to divulge private genetic information, where this information may be of benefit to other family members. The Australian Law Reform Commission has suggested that:

> Privacy laws should be harmonised and tailored to address the particular challenges of human genetic information. Among other things, this will require extending privacy protection to genetic samples as well as genetic information. However, the familial dimension of genetic information also requires acknowledgment—for example, doctors should be authorised to disclose personal genetic information to a genetic relative in circumstances where disclosure is necessary to lessen or prevent a serious threat to an individual's life, health, or safety. (Australian Law Reform Commission 2003)

There have been many instances where people have refused family members access to information that may have been useful for their health. While it is sometimes difficult to understand why this should happen, causes may include such issues as fear, guilt or uncertainty over paternity. As a general rule a patient's genetic confidentiality should always be respected except where he or she consents to the information being disclosed to others to whom it is relevant. The moral obligations imposed by family relationships seem to justify honest disclosure and sensitive counselling but not 'strong' coercion, or involuntary disclosure (Clarke 1994).

One of the areas of genetic testing that has attracted most media and government attention has been the risk of discrimination in health or life insurance and employment on the basis of genetic testing. Insurance companies clearly have a claim on individuals' genetic information based on their fear of 'adverse selection' and a requirement to maintain commercial competitiveness (Harper 1993). This right to access to any genetic information that may be relevant to determining a person's insurability is frequently seen to conflict with an individual's right to genetic privacy and the desire of health professionals to maintain their patients' confidences. The argument put by the insurance industry is that the use of genetic information does not represent a major departure from current practice and that the results of genetic tests should be treated in the same manner as results of any other medical test. Insurance companies already adjust premiums on the basis of current co-morbidity (eg, HIV/AIDS or heart disease), or current risk factors (eg, smoking or other 'high-risk' behaviours such as parachuting), and taking genetic information into consideration would not seem any different.

However, many health professionals believe that genetic information is different to other forms of health information. Genetic mutations are not reversible and frequently not treatable, and the results of genetic testing will generally provide a 'risk estimate' of disease occurring at come time in the future rather than a precise indication that disease will occur or of its severity. Some individuals may have evidence of a genetic marker or a genetic predisposition and yet never develop overt disease whereas others may develop disease without any evidence of genetic susceptibility. At the current time these concerns have not been adequately resolved and will no doubt continue to trouble insurers, government, genetics services and community representatives as the availability of genetic technology increase. The continuing uncertainty, in turn, is also likely to reduce uptake of genetic testing and feed the fears that many in the community feel about confidentiality and potential misuse of information (Friedrich 2002). Some progress is being made. In 2002 the Investment Financial Services Association (IFSA), the peak body of the life insurance industry in Australia, announced that people who tested positive for haemochromatosis and agreed to take measures to prevent organ failure (regular blood donation) would not be refused life insurance or have their premiums loaded because of their genetic status (Delatycki, Allen et al 2002).

Genetic counselling

Clinical genetics services generally do not provide medical therapy. Clients/patients are generally healthy and the 'therapy' provided usually consists of providing information, pre-test and post-test counselling and follow-up. Although there is some dispute as to what 'genetic counselling' is, or what its aims should be, a useful definition is '[a]n educational process that seeks to assist affected and/or at-risk individuals to understand the nature of the genetic disorder, its transmission and the options open to them in management and family planning' (Kelly 1986). In other words, the focus of genetic counselling is the client's autonomy and the process of decision-making – rather than the prevention of disease or genetic abnormality.

The issue of how, and how much, counsellors should guide their client's/ patient's decision, that is, how 'directive' they should be, has generated considerable disquiet in clinical genetics. It is often claimed that counselling should ideally be 'non-directive' (Zare, Sorenson et al 1984; Wertz and Sorenson 1986); indeed, the 'Code of Ethical Principles for Genetics Professionals' produced by the Council of Regional Networks Committee on Ethics (1996) states that counsellors should 'provide counselling that is non-directive, supportive, and responsive to the individual's requests, and should respect the choices of patients and families' (Baumiller, Comley et al 1996).

On closer examination the directive/non-directive controversy would appear to arise from a misunderstanding of the ethical and legal requirements of consent. Valid consent does not require that clients are simply provided with a smorgasbord of choices and then abandoned to their own autonomy but nor does it accept a counselling process where the health professional manifestly coerces or manipulates the clients' choices. If one accepts that even the provision of information will influence a patient's/client's decisions, then counselling is unavoidably directive (Clarke 1991). The ideal process of counselling would therefore seem to be one that assists patients/clients to make informed decisions that best reflect their own values and beliefs. In other words the question is not so much whether counselling should be directive but whether it is inappropriately directive. This would require that counsellors acknowledge that facts are not value-neutral and that they have the capacity to influence decision-making.

Direct-to-consumer genetic testing (DTC-GT)

While many of the fears of genetic advances have proven unfounded, the increasing availability of 'direct-to-consumer' genetic testing seems more likely to challenge professional and regulatory attempts to control the 'genetic revolution' (Caulfield 2000). Private laboratories in the United States, Europe, Asia and Australia are now advertising their services directly to the consumer via the internet, meaning they are accessible to people in different countries regardless of that country's regulatory approach to DTC-GT. Iceland's deCODE Genetics offers a personalised genetic diagnostic services called 'deCODEme', California's 23andMe provides a service under the slogan: 'Genetics just got personal. Don't worry. We're here to help'; and many other companies provide a range of similar services to consumers around the world (Davies 2009). The explosion of such services suggests that people may be interested in what knowledge of their genetics may tell them about their ancestry, their biology, and what they can do to reduce their health risks and change their 'destiny'.

The emergence of the consumer genetics industry has caused concern among mainstream genetic services about the validity and legality of delivering genetic information directly to consumers. Many worry about the likelihood that the value of these tests will be overstated by companies or misunderstood by consumers without expert assistance and counselling (Chapman 2008). Since people may rely on these tests to make critical decisions about their health, lifestyle and family planning, we must take seriously the manner in which they are marketed, the way that results are presented and explained, and the availability, or otherwise, of personal support and counselling (Hogarth, Javitt et al 2008).

This degree of patient autonomy has not been seen before in the biomedical sciences, and serious attempts to engage with these new 'freedoms' will be required. The medical profession may dismiss these advances as consumerism and attempt to better control the market through national legislation, but this is unlikely to be an adequate response either to the attractions or the risks of DTC genetic tests (Otlowski 2003).

Gene therapy

Conventional approaches to treating genetic disorders include dietary restriction (phenylketonuria), hormone replacement (congenital adrenal hyperplasia), enzyme or protein replacement (haemophilia), drug therapy (familial hypercholesterolaemia), behaviour modification and organ transplantation (adult polycystic kidney disease). Unfortunately, many genetic disorders are characterised by progressive disability or chronic ill health for which there is no effective treatment.

Recent advances in molecular biology have raised the prospect of gene therapy for many genetic and non-genetic disorders. A wide number of disorders are possible candidates for gene therapy, including genetic diseases such as cystic fibrosis, muscular dystrophy, thalassaemia and sickle-cell disease, and non-genetic diseases such as cancer, HIV/AIDS, cardiovascular disease and rheumatoid arthritis. When addressing ethical issues arising from gene therapy, distinctions have been made in terms of the target of gene therapy – which can be either somatic (non-reproductive) cells or germ line (reproductive) cells – and the goal of genetic therapy – which can be either cure or prevention of disease, or enhancement of human capabilities (Anderson 1992).

Somatic cell gene therapy

In somatic cell gene therapy foreign genes are inserted into a target cell line (for cells other than germ cells) to correct a genetic defect. The first somatic gene therapy trials were approved in 1990 in the United States to treat adenosine deaminase deficiency. In Australia the first trial of gene therapy was approved in 1995. Although there have been considerable technical difficulties associated with the insertion, expression and regulation of new genes in somatic cells, a number of conditions including severe combined immune deficiency (SCID), thalassaemia, adrenoleukodystrophy, cystic fibrosis and muscular dystrophy have now been successfully treated using somatic gene therapy. Nevertheless, the promise of gene therapy remains largely unfulfilled, and some of the dangers that were thought to be largely theoretical, particularly the risk of inducing cancer, have been found to be a real risk in certain patient populations. The development of acute leukaemia in five children with SCID enrolled in gene therapy trials in France and the UK has, more than any other single event, caused a re-evaluation of both the risks and benefits of somatic gene therapy and the consent processes of gene therapy trials, particularly as it has become clear that these cases of leukaemia were directly related to insertional mutagenesis associated with the retroviral vectors used in the study (Hacein-Bey-Abina, Von Kalle et al 2003; Board of the European Society of Gene and Cell Therapy 2008; Caplan 2008; Wilson 2008).

Perhaps the most controversial aspect of somatic gene therapy is its potential application as a means for enhancing human characteristics, such as intelligence or sporting prowess. Advocates of genetic enhancement, such as the Australian bioethicist, Julian Savulescu, argue that genetic enhancement is a reasonable expression of liberty, is directly concerned with human flourishing, may serve to redress the unfair natural distribution of talent, and is compatible with environmental manipulations to achieve the same ends. Those who object to genetic enhancement argue, in response, that it is 'playing God' (always a weak argument in medicine, where the entire therapeutic enterprise is directed against allowing 'nature' to occur), that it is an inappropriate use of scarce medical resources, that it would give some individuals (the wealthy) an unfair competitive advantage, that it will entrench privilege and increase injustice, and that it will engender a culture where certain personal characteristics are excessively valued, where other characteristics are disvalued and where difference is not tolerated (Hope, Savulescu et al 2003). At the current time, arguments regarding genetic modification are largely theoretical as the choice of genetic characteristics occurs primarily through prenatal diagnosis and PGD. Given the current limitations of gene therapy, this situation is unlikely to change in the foreseeable future.

Germ-line gene therapy

Germ-line therapy refers to the insertion of a normal gene into the germ-line (sperm, ova and early embryos) to replace a defective or lethal gene so that all offspring will have the inserted gene rather than the abnormal gene. The major difference with somatic cell therapy is that germ-line therapy produces changes that can be transmitted through subsequent generations. The scientific rationale for germ-line therapy is that it allows treatment of genetic disorders that are not amenable to gene repair after birth and dispenses with the need for repeating somatic cell gene therapy in subsequent generations by eliminating the defective gene from the population.

Germ-line therapy raises profound ethical concerns and at the current time is not permitted by existing guidelines, including those of the NHMRC in Australia (Danks 1994). A number of deontological and consequentialist objections can be made to germ-line therapy. Many philosophers have categorically rejected germ-line therapy on the grounds that it offends against human dignity, autonomy and an individual's right to their own genetic identity, and reshapes the genetic make-up of future generations without their consent (Lappé 1991; Wachter and Lo 1993). Although initially appealing – the problem with these forms of arguments is that they give considerable moral weight to future generations, that is, those not currently autonomous, and fail to acknowledge that future generations may make the same decisions about germ-line therapy as are made by present generations based on similar consideration of autonomy and beneficence.

More consequentialist arguments contend that too little is currently known about the process of germ-line therapy, the stability of inserted genetic material, or the long-term consequences to individuals or to the species, to allow it to proceed. Indeed, animal experiments have found that germ-line therapy is associated with high risks, as gene expression may occur in inappropriate tissues and normal embryological development may be disrupted. This is a powerful argument against clinical trials in humans but does not exclude the possibility of advances in molecular biology and biotechnology or the potential benefits of continuing germ-line experimentation in animals (Zimmerman 1991).

The major objection to germ-line therapy is that it is essentially super-fluous. Germ-line therapy involves obtaining sperm, ova or embryos via IVF and then inserting the necessary gene before implantation. Given that the same clinical outcome may be achieved by preimplantation diagnosis and selective implantation (ie, simply not implanting defective embryos) or by prenatal diagnosis and selective termination – without the risks of mutation and genetic instability – there would appear to be little current need for germ-line therapy (Harris 1997).

While caution seems clinically and ethically appropriate, it is not incon-ceivable that germ-line therapy may become safer and more valuable in the future. Somatic cell gene therapy already holds enormous promise for the treat-ment of genetic disorders, cancers and even HIV/AIDS. It is likely that the potential applications of gene therapy will rapidly increase – making essential the consideration of ethical issues and the development of a regulatory process flexible enough to adapt to rapid change.

Eugenics: the abuses and limits of genetic enquiry

Many of the issues that arise in the context of clinical genetics and genetic research do so because of the beliefs that people have about genes, particularly the belief that genetic alleles have direct and powerful influences on human traits (genetic determinism) and the belief that human capabilities, health and illness can be largely understood as a function of human genetics (often called genetic reductionism or genetic essentialism). These beliefs, which may be view-ed as both an empirical belief and an ideology, are highly problematic because they confuse basic concepts such as aetiology and pathogenesis, cause and pre-disposition or risk, congenital and acquired genetic differences, and genotype and phenotype. Ethically, they are problematic because they have provided the scientific rationale for the treatment of individuals and populations on the basis of their genes.

Ethical concerns about the study and manipulation of the human genome are not new and many of the fears raised by genetic advances reflect a historical awareness of 'eugenics' (Garver 1994). Eugenics is a movement that attempts to improve the species by minimising the transmission of 'unfit' or 'unworthy' genes (negative eugenics) and/or maximising the transmission of desirable genes (positive eugenics). Mandatory sterilisation, involuntary euthanasia, infanticide and the societal acceptance of high infant and maternal mortality rates have all been used in different social and historical contexts to further negative eugenics against the 'unfit' – variously defined as criminals, the poor, homosexuals, the mentally and physically disabled, immigrants, Jews and Gypsies.

Many countries have had eugenic policies. In the early 20th century, the United States enacted compulsory sterilisation laws and restrictive immigration laws. Sixty thousand people were involuntarily sterilised under such legislation including the insane, criminals, mentally retarded, alcoholics, epileptics and prostitutes and some normal people (Kevles 1985). This was used to address concerns that the supposed Anglo-Saxon genetic superiority in the United States was being diminished by uncontrolled reproduction of the 'socially undesirable' and by immigration from southern and Eastern Europe (particularly of Jews).

International scientific and political debate about eugenics also formed the basis of 'race hygiene' policies developed in late 19th century Germany and subsequently adopted by Hitler's Nazi Party to suit a new set of ideological objectives. The Nazis accepted the genetic principles of inherited characteristics, and reinforced these with the language of microbiology and public health – aiming to cleanse the body, and the body politic, of contamination or disease (Weindling 1989). Scientists, lawyers and medical practitioners helped define and administer eugenic policies that included the compulsory sterilisation, and killing, of those with genetic disorders, physical and mental disability and psychiatric illness, and later, undesirable ethnic groups such as Jews, Russians, Gypsies and Poles (Muller-Hill 1988).

Although Nazism and the Holocaust provide the clearest example of eugenic policy, broadly eugenic principles continue to determine social policy and legislation. Singapore offers incentives to educated people to encourage them to produce more children (Dawson and Singer 1990) and China enacted the 'Law of the People's Republic of China in Maternal and Infant Health Care' in June 1995. The passage of this law, which provided for pre-marital checks, pre-natal diagnosis and compulsory sterilisation as a means for decreasing the prevalence of abnormal births, or births of 'inferior quality', was greeted with widespread but not uniform political and scientific condemnation (Editorial 1995).

While eugenic concerns are often quickly dismissed by those working in molecular and clinical genetics, they must be considered seriously as they reflect the ambiguous distinction between genetic 'normality' and 'abnormality', and the tension between individual autonomy and human dignity on the one hand, with the protection and beneficent promotion of the public good on the other.

The completion of the Human Genome Project has provided the entire human DNA sequence. Over the coming decades researchers will seek to determine the functions of the 35,000 or so genes in the human genome (Trent, Williamson et al 2003). This will generate an enormous amount of new knowledge and will inevitably present both promise and problems. Genetic differences will continue to be identified – permitting the identification of adverse genetic mutations, the development of predictive and presymptomatic genetic tests, the expansion of gene therapy, and increasing possibilities for prenatal diagnosis and selective termination (Morris, Tyler et al 1988). The question that medical science and society will be forced to ask of itself (for this question will never become irrelevant) is whether it retains eugenic principles, practices and policies and has simply redefined the 'unfit' in purely genetic terms. As Dr James Watson, the discoverer of the genetic code, noted in 1990:

> Genetic injustice arises through throws of the genetic dice that operate when our sperm and egg are formed. This genetic variability between humans reflects the fact that the gene distribution process is not perfect and that new genetic mutations are constantly arising. There is no way to stop this process. Moreover, the variation has been the basis of our evolution ... The question now faces us ... as to how we are going to deal with these differences between individuals. In the past, at the time of the eugenics movement ... and during the reign of racist thoughts in Nazi Germany, there was very little genetic knowledge. Most decisions were made without solid genetic evidence ... Now we have to face the fact that we soon will have real facts and how are we going to respond to them? (Watson 1990)

There is nothing intrinsically immoral with investigating the human genome and 'interfering with nature'. The limits of genetics would appear not to be determined by appeals to biological integrity but by the sociopolitical context in which genetic research and clinical practice occurs. Even efforts to explore the genetic basis of race, behaviour, intelligence or sexual orientation would not seem intrinsically unethical – despite the moral outrage that such research, including the Human Genetic Diversity Project, provokes. Problems with research of this type include that it may break the link between medicine and disease and, by defining normal human diversity as disease, may thereby compromise human dignity. It is also the case that the social context of research may sometimes be characterised by discrimination, bigotry, inequality and the potential for misuse and misinterpretation of genetic data. If this is so, then the failure to acknowledge this would seem unethical. History is replete with instances where medical science, and genetics in particular, have been used inappropriately to influence employment, reproductive freedom and social policy (Lewontin 1993).

Health professionals may therefore decide that a research project or health intervention is not, in itself, unethical, but that it should not be proceeded with in the prevailing social, scientific or political context. (Consider, for example, organ commerce or reproductive surrogacy.) This requires that health professionals consider not only the scientific merit of any proposal, but also the specific ethical issues that it raises and their social and political consequences.

Regenerative medicine

'Regenerative medicine' is the repair, replacement or regeneration of cells, tissues or organs to restore impaired function. The term 'regenerative medicine' is often used to refer to stem-cell research, but it may involve a much greater range of technologies including molecular genetics, proteomics, gene therapy, tissue engineering, immunology and stem-cell transplantation (Mironov et al 2004). Techniques of regenerative medicine, such as the use of stem cells, have been the focus of extraordinary public attention over the past decade – attracting attention both for their promise and for the ethical issues raised by their practice. Like gene therapy research, regenerative medicine has so far delivered very little, with only a small number of products such as tissue-engineered skin substitute so far developed.

Empirical studies suggest strong public support for stem-cell research, regenerative medicine and somatic cell nuclear transfer (therapeutic cloning) with approximately two thirds of those surveyed in the US, Europe and Australia supporting this research (Perry 2000).

Regenerative medicine raises a number of ethical concerns including:

- those relating to the moral status of the embryo and whether embryos can be used in the process of conducting stem-cell research;
- those associated with translating research into clinical practice;
- those surrounding consent to participation in clinical trials – there is a real question whether consent is genuinely possible given the coercive influence of the clinical context (severe irreversible illness and therapies available only through clinical trials), the complexity of the therapies being studied or tested, and the uncertainty of clinical outcomes (risks and benefits) in both the short and long term (Lo et al 2005; Kimmelman 2005);
- those associated with transplantation including those relating to tissue, cellular and organ procurement, risk assessment, safety concerns, xeno-transplantation issues (where hybrid or chimeric tissues are generated), compensation of donors and cross-cultural concerns; and
- those raised by the therapies that may be used to improve/enhance normal function as well as replace or repair it, including the impact of such therapies on human identity and concepts of health, illness and normalcy. (Wolpe 2002)

Human cloning (somatic cell nuclear transfer)

In 1997 the Roslin Institute in Scotland reported the birth of a viable lamb (Dolly) 'cloned' from an adult somatic cell. (While Dolly was regarded as the first cloned animal, in fact Soviet scientists had probably cloned a mouse in 1986 and researchers at the Roslin Institute had themselves cloned two highland sheep, Megan and Morag, from early embryonic cells in 1996.) Dolly was produced with funding from PRL Therapeutics and the UK Ministry of Agriculture, Fisheries and Food, for two purposes. First, it was envisaged that cloning could help create elite stocks of farm animals. Secondly, cloning offered an attractive advance for biotechnology companies seeking to produce medicinal products from transgenically modified animals.

A *clone* is an exact replica or group of genetically identical cells descended from a single common ancestor. In biology, cloning refers to the process of creating a genetic duplicate of an individual cell or organism through asexual reproduction, by stimulating a single cell. (Strictly speaking, Dolly was not an identical clone as part of one's genetic material comes from the mitochondria in the cytoplasm of the cell and, in Dolly's case, only the nuclear DNA was transferred.) A distinction is often made between different types of cloning, reproductive cloning (where the aim is to produce a liveborn offspring), and therapeutic cloning (where the aim is to produce tissues or organs for transplantation or biological products, such as proteins or cytokines).

Cloning non-human animals

Researchers have now successfully cloned frogs, carp, mice, sheep, rhesus monkeys, gaurs, cattle, cats, dogs, donkeys and horses. The potential benefits of cloning transgenic animals are clear. Cloning allows the rapid, precise and replicable production of animals modified to produce proteins (such as growth hormone), drugs for treating cancer and other diseases, and even organs that have sufficient similarity to human tissue that they will not be rejected. Cloning may also benefit the agriculture industry (providing a means for generating herds of 'elite' animals) and the environment (allowing genetic protection of endangered species). Much progress has already been made in this area. Transgenic goats, sheep and cows are already providing products for human use, such as blood clotting proteins for use by haemophiliacs, and pigs have been 'humanised' to reduce the risks of adverse immunological complications following transplantation.

Human reproductive cloning

It is likely that the first definite human clone was produced in 2008 by a research team led by Dr Samuel Wood using DNA from an adult skin cell and a human oocyte (French et al 2008). While the benefits of human cloning are less clear than those for animals there are still some theoretical benefits, including the treatment of people with presently untreatable infertility – such as men with total germ-cell failure; the avoidance of heritable genetic disease without the use of donor gametes; the production of children in order to provide transplantable tissue to a sibling, and the 'replacement' of lost children or great individuals (Lane 2006; Winston 1997).

The prospect of human (reproductive) cloning following the Roslin experiment sparked immediate moral outrage and calls for a ban on human cloning from bodies and individuals as diverse as the Vatican, the US Biotechnology Industry Organisation, the Council of Europe's Bioethics Convention, and most national governments. In the United States, President Clinton, citing 'serious ethical questions', referred the issue to the National Bioethics Advisory Commission, which concluded in June 1997 that at this time it was 'morally unacceptable for anyone in the public or private sector, whether in a research or clinical setting, to attempt to create a child using somatic cell nuclear transfer cloning' (Bloom 1997). Little has changed since that time and the international community tends to agree that human cloning for reproductive reasons should not be attempted. Currently even those countries that allow human therapeutic cloning prohibit human reproductive cloning and major international bodies, including the WHO and UNESCO, have all denounced reproductive cloning.

The arguments advanced against reproductive cloning are well known. The major secular argument against reproductive cloning is that it remains an unproven and technically problematic process and that non-human animal studies and the limited experience with human cloning raise real concerns about risk assessment and patient safety (Wakayama 2004).

Other consequentialist objections have been raised against reproductive cloning including that it will separate reproduction from human relationships; alter social relationships and change forever what it means to be a parent; cause clones psychological harm because they will already know their destiny – as it is the same as their DNA donor (this is sometimes referred to as the 'foreknowledge trap'); and that it will ultimately diminish genetic variability, making the species more susceptible to disease.

The issue of diminished genetic variability, while valid in agriculture and animal husbandry, would seem to have little force as an objection to human cloning. The effect of the variation on the human gene pool of 'natural' twins is incalculably small and there would be no reason to believe that the impact of human cloning would be any greater. The benefits of sexual reproduction – genetic diversity and hybrid vigour – in addition to its important social function – would limit any adverse genetic outcome of cloning.

It is also often claimed that cloning is inherently evil – an 'unnatural' and morally unjustifiable intrusion into human life. Such 'contrary to nature' arguments are difficult to sustain, however, as human beings have long manipulated the environment and animals to their ends, and have manipulated 'nature' wherever possible to diminish the mortality and morbidity of human disease.

A variant of this argument is that cloning represents unacceptable use of individuals as means for another's ends and so offends against 'human dignity' or 'human autonomy'. Although appealing, there are a number of problems with this argument. First, it is not clear how cloning differs from other instances where human products or organs are used as means for another's ends and do not appear to compromise human dignity. People donate blood or organs, provide spare IVF embryos for donation or research, and conceive children to be allogeneic bone marrow donors for dying siblings (Harris 1997). Secondly, there are instances where cloning would not appear to offend against dignity – for example, cloning a child to be a 'biological' child for a lesbian couple. Thirdly, cloning does not produce identical copies of the same individual person – it only produces identical copies of the same genotype. Human clones would not be strictly 'identical' as they would be born a generation apart, experience different environmental influences and generate different spontaneous genetic mutations. Each clone, like an identical twin, would be a distinct individual with their own dignity and own autonomy. Finally, given that society does not currently tolerate abuses of 'natural' twins, such as using them solely as organ banks for each other, it is unlikely to tolerate abuses of cloning.

Many of the arguments against human reproductive cloning are based simply on revulsion, rather than considered analysis, and many are based on mistaken beliefs of genetic determinism, ie, that there is a direct and complete association between genotype and phenotype and that health, personality and identity are based entirely in the genome (Kass 1997). Assertions of the immorality of human cloning are generally not compelling, and focusing on futuristic or hypothetical scenarios is no substitute for a balanced analysis of the issues involved. However, given the present low survival rates of clones, the propensity for epigenetic errors in somatic cell nuclear transfer embryos and the high risks of miscarriage and malformation, and the current uncertainties surrounding cellular aging, considerable caution will need to be exercised in human cloning until such time as a clearer assessment of the potential burdens and benefits of cloning is possible (Allegrucci, Denning et al 2004).

Human therapeutic cloning

In contrast to reproductive cloning, therapeutic cloning offers great promise across a range of fields of inquiry. Therapeutic cloning may help the exploration of genetic and degenerative disease, cancer biology, aging and reproduction, as well as opening possibilities in pharmocogenetics and large scale drug screening. Therapeutic cloning may also allow the development of cloned organs, tissues, proteins and molecules for use in therapy and transplantation – providing biological therapies to patients with organ failure, skin grafts for burns victims, bone marrow for patients undergoing chemotherapy, and solid organs for transplantation (Winston 1997; Lane 2006). Therapeutic cloning of tissue or organs may provide a means of treating those degenerative disorders for which there is currently limited therapies available, may ameliorate the discrepancy between the supply and demand of donor organs, and may allow production of tissues perfectly matched for the recipient, so avoiding the problems resulting from donor incompatibility and immunosuppressive medications.

Stem cells

Stem cells are defined by their capacity to self-renew, proliferate and differentiate to form one or more cell types. One type of categorisation divides stem cells into those isolated from the embryo, those found in umbilical cord blood, and those found in adult somatic tissue. Stem cells can then be further categorised according to the number of differentiated cell types they can produce.

- *Totipotent* stem cells are able to form all fully-differentiated cells in the body and placenta. The embryo, zygote and the immediate descendents of the first two cell divisions are the only cells considered to be totipotent.
- *Pluripotent* stem cells can differentiate into almost all cells that arise from the three germ layers (neuroectoderm, endoderm and mesoderm), but are unable to give rise to the placenta and supporting structures. The embryonic stem cells that form the inner cell mass of the blastocyst at around five days after fertilisation are considered pluripotent. At the current time the major source of embryonic stem cells is from human embryos that have been discarded during fertility treatments.

- *Multipotent* stem cells are capable of producing a small range of differentiated cell lineages appropriate to their location and are found in a wide range of adult tissues. Haematopoietic stem cells, which contribute to the generation of 200 billion red cells, 10 billion white cells and 400 billion platelets each day, are the best known and most widely utilised form of multipotent stem cell, but stem cells have also been identified in the brain, spinal cord, liver, pancreas, skin, intestine, kidney, mammary gland, bone, heart and skeletal muscle.

Traditionally, differentiation was considered to be a unidirectional process of sequential, irreversible commitment steps through a hierarchy of stem cells, which progressively restrict the range of cellular choices available. The notion of lineage commitment, and thus the use of the term multipotent, has been questioned by recent research which has found that the eventual fate of stem cells may be determined by the local environment. Thus, for example, haematopoietic stem cells, under the right conditions, may home to other organs and differentiate into non-blood cells, including cardiac skeletal muscle, pancreatic tissue, liver or brain. This is known as *transdifferentiation* or *plasticity* (Mathur and Martin 2004). The concept of plasticity has opened up the possibility of using haematopoitetic stem cells (which are easily and safely collected both from patients and normal donors) or indeed any other type of adult stem cell, for reparative therapy for a range of adult degenerative diseases, including ischaemic heart disease, neurodegenerative disorders and diabetes.

Rodent studies have demonstrated that focal implantation or intravenous delivery of bone marrow-derived stem cells improves function in models of cerebral ischaemia, Parkinson's disease, multiple sclerosis, amyotrophic lateral sclerosis, diabetes mellitus, Huntington's disease and trauma (Rice and Scolding 2004). Early clinical studies involving human volunteers suggests that administration of autologous bone marrow and peripheral blood stem cells may improve cardiac function following acute myocardial infarction (heart attack). However, the clinical significance of these findings and the mechanism by which stem cells improve organ function remain unclear.

In recent years there have been a number of important scientific developments in stem-cell research that illustrate the speed at which science can move, the time it takes to move from the 'bench to the bedside' in biomedical research, and the way that scientific and biotechnological advances can resolve some ethical issues and create others. Of note:

- In 2006 and 2007 researchers demonstrated that somatic cells can be directly reprogrammed into pluripotent embryonic stem cell-like cells in mice and primates, after transfection with key stem-cell specific genes (Byrne et al 2007; Takahashi and Yamanaka 2006).
- In June 2007 scientists from Roslin Cells reported that they had been able to create a stem-cell line from a human egg without introducing genetic material from another donor.
- In 2007 teams of researchers from Japan and the United States reported success in 'reprogramming' human skin cells into 'induced pluripotent

stem cells' (iPS cells), without needing to create human oocytes or embryos (Takahashi et al 2007; Yu et al 2007). While this process is inefficient and safety data is outstanding it provides the possibility that SC research may be able to proceed without the need for human (or animal) oocytes and without the need to create and/or destroy human embryos.

- In 2008 scientists at Harvard and Columbia universities reported that they had been able to create 'personalised' iPS cells from a patient with Amyotrophic Lateral Sclerosis and differentiate these into motor neurons that could be used for research and, theoretically, as a cellular therapy (Dimos et al 2008). Research in animals suggests that embryonic stem-cell therapies may have some therapeutic utility (improving symptoms of parkinsonism in mice) but as yet there is no data on the utility of embryonic stem-cell therapy in humans (Tabar et al 2008).

- In January 2008, the Human Fertilisation and Embryology Authority (HFEA) in the United Kingdom granted two licences for researchers to create hybrid embryos using bovine (cow) oocytes (eggs) and human DNA. (The first hybrid embryo was successfully created by researchers from Newcastle University in April 2008.)

While these developments may reduce the necessity for destructive research involving human embryos and for a supply of human oocytes for research purposes, as with all technological solutions to moral problems they do not address some fundamental moral issues, such as the capacity to create human life, including from a single individual, and they create others, such as the capacity of iPS cells to be developed into human gametes, ie, sperm and oocytes. Importantly, while it seems likely that induced pluripotent stem cells could reduce the necessity for embryonic stem cells for research and therapies, it is unlikely that developments in iPS research will make embryonic stem-cell research redundant, as human embryonic stem cells appear more adaptable ('plastic') than stem cells derived from body cells and also appear to have greater proliferative potential, and research on embryos and embryonic stem cells is still needed in order to better understand normal reproduction and normal and abnormal cellular biology.

In time, embryonic stem-cell research may lead to novel therapies for genetic, malignant or degenerative disorders, provide new insights into the pathophysiology of many conditions and be used to test drug therapies. But at this stage nothing is being used in humans from human embryonic stem cells, and many scientific obstacles remain before clinical applications are feasible. It may turn out that it is not embryonic stem cells themselves that prove to be most valuable, but therapeutic components and molecules produced by them, and the knowledge that they provide regarding normal and abnormal development.

Political, legislative and regulatory responses to stem-cell research

Stem-cell research has proven to be extremely controversial, and different countries have adopted different responses to it, depending on a series of complex local imperatives. For example, Pope John Paul II advised George W Bush that the work was the same as infanticide, because obtaining the cells involves destroying early stage human embryos. US Catholic bishops subsequently advised the President that the work was 'illegal, immoral and unnecessary'. In response, the US government adopted a policy that restricts federal government funding to research done on cell lines created before the enactment of relevant legislation and prevents the use of federal funding for research aimed at extracting stem cells from new embryos (there is no such restriction on private funding of stem-cell research) (Perrone 2001). The general idea behind this strategy was that it prevented the government from being implicated in the destruction of embryos. As US President George W Bush stated at the time, this strategy 'allows us to explore the promise and potential of stem-cell research without crossing a fundamental moral line, by providing taxpayer funding that would sanction or encourage further destruction of human embryos that have at least the potential for life' (White House 2001). The President's response to this issue was broadly criticised by the scientific community, since while federal funding through agencies like the National Institutes of Health was limited to cell lines on the 'Bush list', no such restrictions applied to private sources of funds. (The Obama administration may have different positions on issues such as human cloning. Barack Obama has previously voted against a bill outlawing human cloning in the Illinois State Senate, but later said he had done this by mistake because he had 'pressed the wrong button' (Wallstein 2008). In the 2008 election, Obama campaigned on a pledge to reverse Bush's policy on embryonic stem-cell research, though at the time of writing he had not as yet done so (Hewett 2009).)

In Europe some countries, including the UK, Belgium and Sweden, have more permissive legislation governing stem-cell research, while others, including Italy and Germany, have highly restrictive legislation (Knowles 2004). The UK, in particular, has adopted a very proactive stance in relation to stem-cell research, with stem-cell research attracting substantial government support and research funds from the Medical Research Council. In the UK, the creation and use of embryos up to 14 days old are controlled by the government's Human Fertilisation and Embryology Authority (HFEA) with legislation governing transfer of nuclei explicitly allowing for research for therapeutic purposes on cells derived from human embryos.

In Australia, stem-cell research was debated in Federal Parliament in 2002. Professor Alan Trounson, Australia's leading researcher in this area, applied for permission to create new lines of stem cells from excess IVF embryos. He showed parliamentarians a video of a paraplegic mouse walking after a procedure that he said was injection of embryonic stem cells. (Later this turned out to have been due to injection of a different sort of stem cell which had not come from embryos, and he was criticised heavily over this.) Subsequent to this debate, in November 2002, the House of Representatives passed the *Prohibition of Human Cloning Act 2002* (Cth) and the *Research Involving Human Embryos Act 2002* (Cth) that would ban both reproductive and therapeutic cloning, but would enable the use of excess frozen embryos produced by in vitro fertilisation technology for the production of embryonic stem cells. The use of fresh IVF embryos was also permitted, provided that these embryos had been created primarily for the purpose of assisted reproduction rather than research.

In 2005 a Legislative Review Committee (subsequently known as the Lockhart Committee after the late Chair of the Committee, Justice John Lockhart AO QC) was appointed to review the legislation. The Committee was required to consider the scope and operation of Commonwealth, State and Territory legislation regulating ART; developments in ART, medical and scientific research and the potential therapeutic applications of this research; community standards; the establishment of a National Stem Cell Bank; and implications for Australian science economic activity. The Lockhart Committee conducted a consultation process over the next six months during which it received over 1000 written submissions, held face-to-face meetings with relevant stakeholders, conducted site visits to major laboratory facilities, and held public and private hearings in all capital cities. (Ian Kerridge was a member of this committee and has been an advocate of stem-cell research.)

The Committee ultimately made 54 recommendations in a report tabled in both Houses of Parliament in December 2005. Many of these were uncontroversial, such as the recommendation to retain national legislation on human cloning and embryo research and to maintain prohibitions on reproductive cloning, implantation of an embryo into a woman (other than a gamete fusion – egg and sperm embryo), development of an embryo for more than 14 days, germline gene therapy, creation of sperm and egg embryos for research, creation of human-animal hybrids or chimeras (with limited exceptions) and sale of human sperm, eggs and embryos. However, the Committee also argued that embryo research should also be permitted under licence on the fertilisation of eggs and on 'impaired' embryos. And most importantly, and controversially, the Committee also recommended that creation of embryos by somatic cell nuclear transfer (SCNT) was justifiable, under licence, in order to conduct research aimed at developing stem cells 'matched' to the 'donor' and to construct disease models for research (Australian Government 2005).

Although the federal cabinet initially rejected the Committee's recommendations, after lobbying by a number of Coalition backbenchers the Prime Minister allowed a conscience vote in Parliament. In October and November 2006, a private member's Bill (the Patterson Bill) based around the majority of the recommendations of the Lockhart Committee was passed by the Senate (34 votes in favour to 32 votes against) and by the House of Representatives (82 votes in favour to 62 votes against). As the Commonwealth Parliament has no specific power to pass legislation on human cloning and embryos, in April 2007 the Council of Australian Governments resolved that they would introduce relevant legislation to ensure a nationally consistent scheme. To date New South Wales, Victoria, Tasmania and Queensland have enacted complementary legislation, while similar legislation was defeated in Western Australia (Skene et al 2008).

Australian legislation is consistent with guidelines produced by the International Society for Stem Cell Research (ISSCR) for human embryonic stem-cell research which prohibit human reproductive cloning, the development of embryos beyond 14 days etc (Daley 2007) and, for the most part, with guidelines/codes of ethics produced by international collaborations, notably the 'Hinxton' group (<www.hinxtongroup.org/au_pscdg.html>), regarding data sharing, open access to stem-cell lines stored in international repositories, such as the UK Stem Cell Bank, and for collaboration between scientists working in different legislative environments without fear of legal prosecution (Lott 2007).

Ethics of stem-cell research

Stem-cell research raises fundamental concerns regarding the moral status of the embryo and the ethics of using human blastocysts for research and therapy, as the embryo is destroyed during the process of collecting embryonic stem cells. However, stem-cell research is only really morally regarded as killing if one assumes that the embryo has full moral status at conception. There are many other views of the moral status of the embryo, including that moral status occurs at day 14, at six weeks, with the development of consciousness, when viable or at birth, and all of these would allow embryonic stem-cell research.

There are a number of reasons why the assertion that the blastocyst is a fully human person, deserving of protection, is problematic. First, until the blastocyst implants into the uterus (usually at 7-8 days post conception) it cannot develop into a person. Secondly, even after implantation, up until about 14 days' gestation, monozygotic twinning may occur, meaning that there would be two persons rather than just one. Third, even after implantation, spontaneous abortions can occur. Indeed, following normal conception approximately 60% of embryos spontaneously abort and, following IVF, approximately 75% of blastocysts are lost. Fourth, even after implantation a blastocyst may develop not into a person, but into a tumour called a hydatidiform mole. And we do not treat this tumour as a person. Fifth, if we accept that full moral status is achieved at conception, then the lawful destruction of frozen embryos would appear to be unjustifiable killing. Finally, if embryos have full moral status, it is unclear why we do not regard the 75-110,000 terminations of pregnancy each year in Australia as murder.

It is important to recognise that while recent changes to Australian law enable the destruction of embryos for research and the creation of SCNT embryos, the human embryo retains a special status in law. Scientists must obtain a licence to do any embryo research, must use the minimum number necessary to complete their research and must treat and dispose of embryos with 'respect' (although it is unclear exactly what this means). (Indeed it is noteworthy that very few ART embryos have been declared to be excess to ART requirements. At March 2007 only 329 excess embryos had been used in licensed research in Australia. The NHMRC Embryo Research Licensing Committee had issued nine licences authorising the use of up to 1915 excess ART embryos. Four of the nine licences were for the use of up to 550 excess embryos for derivation of ES cells (<http://www.nhmrc.gov.au/research/embryos/stemcells/index.htm#8>).)

This position would seem consistent with the contested social and moral status given to the embryo and foetus in secular liberal democracies like Australia. For while we recognise the importance of respect for human life, we also permit (or require) the disposal of excess embryos created by ART after women have completed their family, we allow destructive research on donated human embryos, we tolerate 'early' abortions but institute processes for critical assessment of late-term abortions, and culturally we treat early pregnancy loss (miscarriage) as a personal tragedy but as qualitatively different to the death of a child or adult.

Disagreements regarding the moral status of the embryo are unlikely to be resolved and neither adult stem cells nor iPS cells provide an ethically unproblematic 'replacement' for embryonic stem cells in research or therapy. But the moral status of the embryo is by no means the only ethical issue raised by stem-cell research and even if it were possible to derive stem cells from somatic cells without creating (or destroying) an embryo, and then to use those stem cells to derive specific cells or biological products that may be used as a therapy, then there would still remain ethical issues relating to translational research and bioproduct development in this area (Sugarman 2008).

Embryonic stem-cell research is still in its infancy and it is not yet clear what the risks of stem-cell therapies are likely to be. Research using adult stem cells in cardiac disease has already been associated with accelerated coronary stent stenosis in some patients, and embryonic stem cells carry the risk of teratoma formation if transplanted into patients. While these risks do not, in themselves, demand a cessation of clinical research in humans, they at least urge caution and careful oversight (Schuldiner, Itskovitz-Eldor et al 2003).

Stem-cell therapies are also likely to be expensive, at least initially, and so will probably benefit only the wealthy, or will be 'purchased' by the state at great cost. This will raise important questions of justice (Bok, Schill et al 2004).

A related concern focuses on equity and justice issues arising from the need for human oocytes in order to create embryos for research purposes. As it is illegal to import, buy or sell human oocytes in Australia, embryonic stem-cell research is currently reliant on altruistic donation of oocytes from women undergoing IVF who have completed their family or from altruistic donors motivated, perhaps, by compassion for those who have degenerative conditions. (Australian oocyte donors may receive compensation for 'reasonable expenses' associated with donation.) This is in contrast to both the situation in the United States (where women can sell their eggs to infertile couples but payment for oocyte donations for research is prohibited) and the United Kingdom (where it is also illegal to offer payments to oocyte donors, but fertility clinics can offer discounts for women who donate their oocytes for research). Interestingly, the ISSCR has attempted to balance conflicting interests and ethical principles by distinguishing between egg *donors* (who donate eggs while undergoing fertility treatment and should not receive payment), and egg *providers* (women who provide eggs outside of ART for the purposes of research and who may be paid) (Baylis and McLeod 2007). In general there is a real reluctance to establish policies that allow for payment for oocytes on the grounds that they simply reinforce existing gender inequities, commodify the (female) body, and create the environment in which women who lack other resources will be exploited, and women who have embryos in cryopreservation or are simply of reproductive age may feel coerced or compelled to 'donate' (Steinbrook 2006).

While animals provide an alternative source of oocytes, the creation of hybrid embryos for research or for quality control in ART remains illegal in Australia after the recommendation from the Lockhart Committee to allow their creation was rejected. This stands in stark contrast to the United Kingdom, where the creation of hybrid embryos has been permitted by legislation, leading to the creation of the first such embryos in 2008. A number of objections have been advanced against the creation of hybrid embryos, including that it offends against human dignity, that it offends against the dignity and welfare of non-human animals and treats them simply as commodities, that it creates the possibility of new types of disease, that it creates invalid models for research into human disease, that it is 'against nature' and that it is simply viscerally offensive (Karpowicz et al 2004). While it is likely that this issue will be revisited in the 2009-10 review of the Acts, it seems unlikely that there will be any change to the existing legislation.

Finally, the whole experience of embryonic stem-cell research raises questions regarding the manner in which the science has been 'sold' to the public by an enthusiastic media and research community at a time when there are few tangible clinical benefits to report and when many of the concepts, including the biological equivalence of different stem cells and the concept of in vivo plasticity, are contested (Nisbet 2004). The experience of Professor Trounson is part of a pattern, whereby researchers and some patient groups have expressed very high expectations of stem-cell research, which have not yet been met by the clinical applications of the work. The American actor Christopher Reeve, who was made quadriplegic in 1995 after a fall from a horse, was one of the most vocal supporters of stem-cell research in the United States. He declared that he would walk before the age of 50 through the benefits of this research, but died at 52 without achieving his aim. Researchers in this area report that there continues to be great pressure applied to them to start performing procedures using stem cells in spinal cord injury, despite the fact that the benefits and risks are currently unknown (Rosenveld and Gillett 2004). This seems to indicate that unrealistic expectations about this technology are currently being generated, which may be unethical if it raises the hopes of patients inappropriately. While publicity surrounding stem cells has had the effect of mobilising enormous visible public support for stem-cell research, it runs the risk of further eroding public trust in science and scientists, particularly if public expectations are not met, if research participants experience unexpected adverse effects or if commercial imperatives distort the research agenda or limit access to stem cell-derived therapies.

Gene patenting

Patenting laws, public policy and the commercial development of biotechnology companies have followed genetic research. In the late 1970s the US Supreme Court declared that genetically engineered 'oil-eating' microbes were patentable, and in 1988 Harvard University was given a patent for a transgenic mouse. Following this decision, further patents were applied for other transgenic animals, human DNA sequences, recombinant genes and gene products (Healy 1992). The issue that attracted most international attention occurred when the National Institutes of Health (NIH) in the United States took the step of publishing and simultaneously applying for a patent to protect more than 2000 partial gene sequences discovered in its laboratories – even though knowledge of the biological function of the genes was limited or absent. Although the application was rejected amid a general international consensus that patenting gene sequences of unknown function was unacceptable, efforts to broker international patent treaties have largely failed and the issue of patenting genes continues to generate controversy (Chalmers, Otlowski et al 1995).

Patents are generally issued to anyone who invents or discovers a new process, technique or material, providing the commercial exclusivity that encourages industry to invest in research and development. The arguments in favour of gene patenting are generally that, because research is important and expensive (and only the private sector has the resources to fund research), those who invest in research should be 'rewarded' for their efforts and their innovation and should be provided with sufficient time to recoup their investment.

A number of deontological and consequentialist objections can be made against gene patenting. First, it has been claimed that, in the absence of legalised slavery, human life or the human body cannot be owned and that patenting DNA, particularly where it remains in the human body, offends the dignity of human beings and the biological integrity of our 'universal heritage'. Interestingly, this argument – the human genome is not amenable to patent – has not been of major concern to many of the scientific community who have objected less to the patenting of genes *per se* than their premature patenting, that is, before their biological function and commercial potential are adequately defined.

A second argument raised against gene patenting is that patenting implies ownership and proprietorship – concepts counter to the whole ethos of scientific research, collaboration and collegiality. The concern is that new knowledge, new methods, and/or new therapies will not be immediately shared for fear of jeopardising the granting of potential intellectual and commercial property rights. In other words, patenting is inevitably against the professional, academic and public interest (Loughlan 1995). Those who defend patenting argue in response to this objection that the patent system requires full public disclosure and does not necessarily inhibit an invention or product's availability, but only enforces payment for that availability.

This response leads to a third major objection to gene patenting. Given that genetic research and development is inevitably monopolised by a limited number of biotechnology companies or institutions, the vast majority of which are located in industrialised nations, patenting will allow monopolisation of the genome. The riches of our universal biological heritage will therefore be exploited by the wealthy to develop tests, techniques, drugs or products that can then be sold at high cost – burdening medical institutions with huge fees and royalty payments and placing them out of the reach of individuals or societies (Coghlan 1993). While such concerns appear alarmist, recent events suggest that they might also be realistic. The Human Genome Project, for example, was completed earlier than anticipated both because of technological improvements in gene sequencing and the involvement of the private sector (Celera). At the same time, however, the involvement of the private sector arguably led to greater secrecy, less data sharing and less accuracy. Similarly, in the past few years, evidence has emerged of enforcement of intellectual property rights over human DNA adversely affecting medical care of patients in Australia, including genetic testing for diagnosis of children with seizure disorders due to Dravet's syndrome and BRCA1 and BRCA2 testing for women with breast and ovarian cancer (Robotham 2008). These are serious developments and are likely to become more of a feature of the health-care environment as health-care delivery merges with biotechnology.

Biobanks

While genetics, cellular biology and other biosciences have provided important insights into the development of disease in individuals, increasing awareness of the need to study associations between genetics, health status and disease (primarily for public health and scientific benefit rather than for the benefit of the individual) has led to the establishment of large numbers of population 'biobanks' to facilitate this research (Catchpoole, deFazio et al 2007). (The terms 'tissue bank', 'biobank' or 'biospecimen bank' all refer to the collection of human biological samples, including tissue samples, cell cultures, blood and blood products, genetic material, eg DNA, RNA etc and pathologically altered human tissue, and associated information about the donor.)

Biobanks differ in a number of respects including the type of sample/tissue collected; whether the samples are from an archive or prospectively collected; the degree of identifiability of the samples; the amount of clinical data linked to each sample; whether there is linkage with other data sources; the domain in which the samples were collected, eg clinical, research, pathological; the management/ownership of the samples, eg research institute, private/commercial; and the access of the biobank to 'external' researchers. Biobanks also may or may not be part of a consortium where a number of biobanks collaborate under an overarching governance structure, and/or a biospecimen network (or data linkage networks) which links data from different databases or biobanks and may provide a forum for sharing information, transferring knowledge or standardising governance or research processes. In Australia the Australasian Biospecimens Network (ABN) is the largest stakeholder and data linkage network – enabling researchers to search for samples and data according to cancer site/type, histopathology and sample type (Catchpoole, deFazio et al 2007).

Biobanking raises a number of concerns – many of which arise in other contexts, such as in research, regenerative medicine, genetics and public health, and many of which have gained greater prominence in the wake of high profile scandals surrounding the retention of human organs without consent in the United Kingdom (Alder Hey) and Australia (Glebe Morgue) (Barnes, Matthews et al 2005). These include issues related to ownership of human tissue (Skene 2007); the commercialisation of human tissue (Brown and Then 2007); privacy and confidentiality; and social justice concerns including the exploitation of indigenous and other vulnerable populations, benefit-sharing and access to biobanks for researchers from the developing world and those researching problems relevant to the developing world (Schuklenk and Kleinsmidt 2006).

Arguably, however, the major ethical issue that arises with regard to biobanking is that of consent (Gillett 2007). While biobanking is generally not associated with physical risks (as specimens are often collected in the context of medical care or surgery for a pre-existing condition), consent remains important because specimens may be used for purposes inconsistent with the values and preferences of the donor, because the results of research using these specimens may have clinical implications for the donor or their family, and because information arising from biobanks may be sought by third parties and/or may lead to discrimination or stigmatisation of individuals or groups. Questions therefore arise as to who can consent, what type of consent should be sought (narrow, project specific or broad and open-ended), what information should be provided to the donor, whether counselling is necessary, and whether it is necessary to re-contact the donor, either for consent to have their sample used in research projects or to provide information gained through research on their tissue.

The major practical challenge to obtaining consent to biobanking research relates to the fact that it may not be possible to inform the 'donor' about the details, risks and benefits of research as these may often not be known at the time of specimen donation. This has prompted extensive debate regarding the most appropriate approach to consent in biobanking research and the means by which a balance can be struck between the interests of the individual (and their family) and the interests of the community. In recent years concerns about the perceived constraints imposed by respect for individual or group autonomy on biobanking research have led to a critical re-examination of autonomy and consent processes in biobanks and population genetic studies (Knoppers and Chadwick 2005; Kaiser 2006; Gillett 2007). This has precipitated a move away from individualised (project-specific) consent to 'broad' or 'open-ended' consent and, associated with this, an emphasis on governance processes, and mechanisms for ensuring trust, benefit-sharing, communitarian values and altruism (Lipworth, Ankeny et al 2006).

Biobanking research has challenged not just our notion of how research should be done and what constitutes 'valuable' knowledge, but the philosophical assumptions that have underpinned research since Nuremberg. While this debate can appear, at times, simply to be a mechanism for reinforcing the moral and political power of science, medicine and industry, it is vital that biobanking be used as a means for thinking again about the values that underpin public health and about what it is we want, as a society, from science and medicine.

Nanotechnology and nanomedicine

Few developments in the biosciences and biotechnology have attracted as much attention as nanotechnology – in part because nanotechnology makes the familiar appear strange, in part because it is powerful and yet invisible and in part because it merges biology and engineering in ways that go far beyond simple prosthetics.

Nanotechnology refers to the science/technology of engineering devices whose structure is on the scale of single atoms or molecules. (A nanometre is one billionth of a metre or 1/80,000 the width of human hair or about the combined diameter of 10 hydrogen atoms.)

The appeal of nanotechnology is that the properties of matter at this scale differ from larger levels and so may make possible the development of new products with different properties or capacities. Many nano products already exist, including materials in cosmetics, sunscreens, fabrics, automotive paints and food (eg, to make milk whiter and ice-cream smoother). Nanoparticles also offer remarkable promise in environmental care – removing industrial contaminants from soil, oil from the sea and excess carbon from the air.

It is, however, the potential applications of nanotechnology in health care that have attracted the greatest attention. As most animal cells are 10-20,000 nanometres in diameter, this means that nanoscale devices (having at least one dimension less than 100 nanometres) can enter cells and the organelles inside them to interact with DNA and proteins. This may make possible the detection and treatment of disease faster and more efficiently than is currently the case. In cancer medicine, for example, nanotechnologies may make it possible to detect the molecular changes caused by cancer long before physical examination or medical imaging is effective, and may make it possible to deliver therapeutic agents to cancer cells without harming healthy, neighbouring cells. (The ultimate goal is to develop nanoparticles that will circulate through the body, detect cancer-associated molecular changes, assist with imaging, release a therapeutic agent, and then monitor the effectiveness of the intervention (Zu, Wenchi et al 2007).)

Unsurprisingly, while nanotechnology has generated great excitement, it also raises a number of ethical issues, many of which have emerged in the context of other biosciences, such as genetics, synthetic biology, regenerative medicine and genetics. These include ethical concerns relating to:

- patient safety, risk assessment and risk communication;
- environmental risks;
- conflicts of interest and the technological and commercial imperatives driving the development and introduction of nanotechnology;
- justice and access to nanoproducts;
- consent (including labelling);
- community involvement in the development of public policy; and
- respect for the 'human condition' raised by the enhancement of human nature and human capabilities. (Sparrow 2007)

Given that current state of knowledge about the application of nanotechnologies in health care, it is perhaps the ethical issues associated with risk assessment, risk management and risk communication that create the most pressing challenges (Resnik and Tinkle 2007). While animal studies and ex-vivo laboratory studies provide data regarding the interaction of nanoproducts in biological systems, they do not resolve all the uncertainty surrounding exposure to nanomedical products and, both in relation to the application of nanotechnology in environmental practices and in health care, questions inevitably remain regarding what can go wrong, how likely it is that things may go wrong, what the consequences may be (and for whom) and whether these risks are acceptable.

While some of the risks of nanotechnology sound far-fetched, such as the oft quoted scenario in which self-replicating nanomachines able to break down biological waste material run amok, replicating exponentially and turning terrestrial life into 'grey goo', other risks appear much more realistic, and much more understandable. Indeed, analogous human pathologies and data from nanoparticle exposures in animal studies suggest that nanomedicines may damage the lungs, cause cellular damage from the production of 'free radicals' and cross the blood-brain barrier and cause neurological injury (Zu, Wenchi et al 2007).

In the face of uncertainty regarding the likelihood and impact of risks associated with nanoproducts, some have suggested that the 'Precautionary Principle' should be applied to nanotechnology (Phoenix and Treder 2006). In its *strict* form the Precautionary Principle requires inaction where action might pose a risk, whereas its *active* form requires that the burden of proof for establishing the safety of any new technology lies with its proponents and that appropriate efforts be made to mitigate risk by investigating and choosing less risky alternatives where they are available and by taking responsibility for potential risks through monitoring and through transparent and democratic decision-making (Phoenix and Treder 2006). The Precautionary Principle cannot resolve questions of uncertainty and may require too great a guarantee of safety; yet it is a useful guide for thinking through some of the underlying issues that underpin the introduction of any new technology or science.

The synthetic life sciences

Few areas of science offer as much promise or pose as much threat as the synthetic life sciences, including synthetic genomics (the creation of novel or existing genes, chromosomes or genomes through the assembly of DNA molecules) and synthetic biology (the design, redesign and construction of new or existing biological systems or entities) (European Commission 2005). These technologies appear to offer enormous potential, particularly for the development of pharmaceuticals, the repair of defective genes, fuel production and environmental detoxification, and the success of researchers in synthesising the poliovirus, influenza virus and *Mycoplasma genitalium* bacteria suggests that rapid progress is being made in this field (Cello, Paul et al 2002; Tumpey, Basler et al 2005; Ro, Paradise et al 2006; Gibson, Benders et al 2008).

Yet the capacity to synthesise organisms and engineer their virulence, resistance and infectivity raises profound biosecurity and biosafety concerns. Some of these concerns are those of 'dual-use' technologies, ie technologies that may be used to benefit individuals or population but may also be used malevolently, which in this case could be as biological weapons (Miller and Selgelid 2007). Others concern the potential contamination of the 'genome pool' by genetic exchange between synthetic and wild-type organisms and the unintended consequences of the release of synthetic organisms into the environment (Bhutkar 2005).

While the safety and security issues raised by the synthetic life sciences have dominated the public and professional discourse, as with all biotechnologies, synthetic sciences also raise profound justice concerns, as they are likely to benefit the wealthy and the industrialised west, rather than the poor and the developing world.

The coming years are likely to reveal whether the synthetic sciences provide real benefit, as opposed to commercial gain and scientific curiosity, and whether the ethical debate surrounding the synthetic sciences is being fuelled not by a realistic assessment of its risks and benefits but by cultural constructions of risk and fear of the 'other'. At this time it is more important than ever that democratic processes are established that construct these debates in moral terms as well as in scientific terms, for it is the entire population that they gain benefit or be harmed.

GENETICS AND THE LAW

It has been said that the relationship between law and medicine is '[l]aw, marching with medicine but in the rear and limping a little' (Windeyer J in *Mount Isa Mines Ltd v Pusey* (1970) 125 CLR 383 at 395). In issues related to genetics, however, the law may be seen as reacting to developments as they are announced or speculated upon, not when a problem has arisen which then needs resolution (which is often the way that the law develops). It is interesting to note the reaction in many jurisdictions to the announcement of the cloning of 'Dolly'. Legislation that banned or regulated the cloning of humans was quickly enacted, despite the fact that these possibilities for humans were still a long way into the future.

Genetic testing and counselling

Two issues that arise in this area are the processes that must be established before and after genetic testing is conducted. This is particularly the case with regard to the provision of appropriate counselling and the confidentiality of information, including among members of the same family. Counselling, both before and after testing, is necessary in order for the health-care providers to meet the standard of care owed to the patient/ client. The common law, following the High Court decision in *Rogers v Whitaker* (1992) 175 CLR 479, requires information concerning 'material risks' to be given to patients. 'Material risks' are those to which a reasonable person in the patient's position, if warned of the risk and in the circumstances of the particular case, would be likely to attach significance.

The role of genetic counselling is to convey correct information to the patient/client, replacing vague or incorrect ideas. Due to the predictive nature of genetic information, counsellors may identify people at risk and help them to make difficult decisions about care or reproduction. Counsellors must consider the psychological impact that being at a genetic risk will have on the individual and the implications for other family members. The importance of genetic counselling is emphasised in the Australian Law Reform Commission and Australian Health Ethics Committee report *Essentially Yours: The protection of human genetic information in Australia* (discussed below). Because of the profound medical and psychological implications of genetic test information for individuals it is necessary to provide them with appropriate information about a genetic test and, in some cases, assistance in decision-making. Chapter 23 of the Report dealt with genetic counselling and medical education (Australian Law Reform Commission, National Health and Medical Research Council et al 2003). One of the recommendations in the report is that:

> **Recommendation 23-3.** The Human Genetics Commission of Australia (HGCA) should develop genetic testing and counselling practice guidelines, in consultation with the Human Genetics Society of Australia, state clinical genetics services, and other interested organisations. These guidelines should identify genetic tests, or categories of genetic tests, that require special treatment in relation to procedures for ordering testing and ensuring access to genetic counselling.

Genetic testing, privacy and discrimination

Genetic testing has implications for discrimination law, particularly in areas of insurance and employment. A team of Australian researchers banded together to form the Genetic Discrimination Project to study the prevalence of genetic discrimination in Australia (<www.gdproject.org>). A number of reports have issued from the project. One study examined the perceptions of clients of clinical genetics services regarding alleged discrimination associated with having genetic information (Taylor, Treloar et al 2008). A survey of several hundred such adults found that 10% of respondents reported some form of discrimination in life insurance (42%), employment (5%), family (22%), social (11%) and health (20%) areas.

In September 1996 the Federal Privacy Commissioner issued an information paper on the privacy implications of genetic testing (Privacy Commissioner 1996). The information paper noted that 'the prevailing medical ethics place considerable emphasis on doctor-patient confidentiality and there is little evidence of widespread mishandling of personal genetic information'. The information paper did note, however, that the existing protections in most clinical settings place less emphasis on the rights of the person tested than the information-privacy principles would suggest. The Privacy Commissioner noted that much genetic information is handled within regulatory frameworks that apply to a wide range of information.

The information paper examined seven areas in which genetic testing is performed:

- testing adults for genetic characteristics in a clinical setting;
- testing children in a clinical setting;
- testing or the use of testing information for medical research purposes;
- testing suspects in criminal cases;
- testing alleged parents in family law cases;
- assessing applicants for insurance cover; and
- testing prospective or existing employees.

The information paper outlined the issues in the areas and identified approaches that had been adopted in jurisdictions outside Australia. The paper finally recommended that:

> The wide range of social contexts across which genetic testing may be carried out and the lack of a coherent approach to privacy issues between and within contexts reinforces the arguments … for the wide application of a set of general policy principles. Application to specific industries or sectors could be set out in codes of practice developed in consultation with stakeholders and approved by a neutral authority, the Commissioner or some comparable officeholder. (Privacy Commissioner 1996)

A Committee of international governmental experts convened in July 1997 for the finalisation of a draft declaration on the human genome and examination of the revised preliminary draft prepared by the International Bioethics Committee of UNESCO. At the end of their deliberations on 25 July 1997, the committee of governmental experts, where more than 80 States were represented, adopted by consensus the Draft of a Universal Declaration on the Human Genome and Human Rights. At its 29th session, on 11 November 1997, the General Conference of UNESCO adopted, unanimously and by acclamation, the Universal Declaration on the Human Genome and Human Rights.

The Universal Declaration on the Human Genome and Human Rights includes the following articles that are intended to protect the rights of individuals from abuse:

Article 6
No one shall be subjected to discrimination based on genetic characteristics that is intended to infringe or has the effect of infringing human rights, fundamental freedoms and human dignity.

Article 7
Genetic data associated with an identifiable person and stored or processed for the purposes of research or any other purpose must be held confidential in the conditions set by law.

Article 8
Every individual shall have the right, according to international and national law, to just reparation for any damage sustained as a direct and determining result of an intervention affecting his or her genome.

Article 9
In order to protect human rights and fundamental freedoms, limitations to the principles of consent and confidentiality may only be prescribed by law,

for compelling reasons within the bounds of public international law and the international law of human rights.

As a result of concerns about the use (and abuse) of genetic information a major, two-year, public inquiry was conducted by the Australian Law Reform Commission (ALRC) and the Australian Health Ethics Committee (AHEC) of the National Health and Medical Research Council (NHMRC). The final report, 1200 pages, containing 144 recommendations for reform, was released in May 2003 (Australian Law Reform Commission, National Health and Medical Research Council et al 2003). Some of the issues considered in the report include:

- the ethical oversight of genetic research;
- the use of DNA collections by law enforcement authorities;
- the regulation of genetic testing in the workplace;
- the collection and use of genetic information by the insurance industry;
- genetic testing by immigration authorities;
- DNA parentage testing;
- the use of genetic testing as an element in the construction of kinship and identity; and
- the use of genetic testing to identify potential sporting champions.

The inquiry concluded that an omnibus genetic regulation legislation was not appropriate at present but existing law should be 'fine tuned' to cover the challenges of developments in genetics. One of the central recommendations is the establishment of a standing Human Genetics Commission of Australia (HGCA). The role of this organisation would be to provide independent, high-level, technical advice to governments, industry and the community, and to act as a 'consultative mechanism for the development of policy statements and national guidelines in this area' (Weisbrot and Breen 2003).

The Genetic Discrimination Project has examined the prevalence of genetic discrimination in the insurance area (Otlowski, Barlow-Stewart et al 2007). The study looked at insurance applications from 288 individuals who had disclosed a genetic test result in their applications for death cover, trauma/crisis, income protection/disability and total and permanent disablement on life insurance. The study found that conditions being disclosed were haemochromatosis (71%), Huntington disease (12%) and breast/ovarian cancer (6%). Importantly, the study found that in 49% of applications, the genetic test result was described as being the only influence in making a decision about whether to provide insurance and on what terms. The researchers have argued that in most cases the insurance underwriting was reasonable, but further education was needed so that insurance underwriters could avoid improperly accounting for the risk of genetic predisposition to disease.

The ALRC/AHEC report did not recommend that insurers should be banned from using genetic test information. Rather, it urged that insurers should be obliged to justify their use of genetic information and should provide clear reasons for any unfavourable decisions. It also argued that genetic testing by employers should not be allowed except where it may be necessary to protect health and safety.

While the Australian government has been slow to implement legislation, in May 2008 the United States implemented a new federal law, the *Genetic Information Nondiscrimination Act 2008*. The Act forbids discrimination in group premiums for health insurance, the mandatory use of genetic testing by health plans, and the use of genetic information for underwriting health plans.

Genetic information and the *Privacy Act 1988* (Cth)

Family histories

The law regarding confidentiality and privacy is discussed in Chapter 12. In 2001 the Commonwealth *Privacy Act 1988* was amended to apply to all health service providers in the private sector. The amendments included 10 National Privacy Principles (NPPs) that allow individuals to exercise rights and choices about how their personal and health information is handled. Before the amendments came into effect it was realised that the collection of the social, family and medical history of a patient may infringe some of the NPPs. This was because the collection of such information results in the collection of information about a third party. If this were the case then the collection of personal or health information about the third party without their consent would amount to a breach of the NPPs. Also, the NPPs would require that, where information about a third party was collected, that person must then be notified of the fact that information had been collected about them. This would extend to the collection of genetic information.

An application was made by ACHA Health for a 'Public Interest Determination' to clarify this issue. A Public Issue Determination (PID) enables the Federal Privacy Commissioner to reduce the privacy protections of the NPPs provided the public interest in the potential breach substantially outweighs the public interest in adhering to the NPP. In response to ACHA's application and following a wide community consultation process, the Commissioner issued Public Interest Determinations (PIDs) 9 and 9A. In summary, the PIDs allow a health service provider to collect information about a third party without the consent of that third party when:

- the collection of the third party's information into the patient's social, family or medical history is necessary to provide a health service directly to the patient; and
- the third party's information is relevant to the family, social or medical history of that patient.

In reaching the decision the Privacy Commissioner found that the definition of 'health information' under the *Privacy Act* clearly includes genetic information, 'including the predictive characteristics of genetic information'.

Duty to warn family members about a genetic risk

Do health professionals owe a duty to the relatives of a patient when they discover genetic information regarding heath risks that might affect the relatives' health? Professor Loane Skene has argued that genetic information is familial in nature and, as such, health professionals should be free to disclose information to other family members when it is relevant to their health (Skene 1998; Skene 2001). Others, like Dean Bell and Professor Belinda Bennett have countered that genetic information is not different from other health information, and that there may be overall negative effects on the treatment of such conditions if patients believe that they will not have their confidentiality maintained (Bell and Bennett 2001). Bell and Bennett recognise that privacy and confidentiality principles allow for disclosure to prevent or lessen a serious and imminent threat to life and health, but they argue that, overall, genetic information is more predictive than determinative and that patients have a right *not to know* which may be affected by non-consensual disclosure.

The ALRC and the AHEC made recommendations regarding disclosure of genetic information in their report, *Essentially Yours*. These recommendations led to amendments to the *Privacy Act 1988* (Cth) in 2006. National Privacy Principle 2.1 allows for disclosure by an organisation if the disclosure is to a genetic relative and the organisation reasonably believes that the use or disclosure is necessary to lessen or prevent a serious threat to the life, health or safety (whether or not the threat is imminent). Disclosure must occur in line with guidelines produced under s 95AA. At the time of writing the NHMRC has released draft guidelines for consultation.

Issues remain, even after the introduction of NPP 2.1. First, the NPP only relates to the private sector and does not cover those working in State public hospitals or Commonwealth agencies (Otlowski, Barlow-Stewart et al 2007). Secondly, the disclosure can only be to a genetic relative, which prevents disclosure to the reproductive partners of those with genetic conditions. This is a significant limitation given that withholding information of genetic conditions could seriously impact on the reproductive choices partners make. The arguments for allowing disclosure to genetic relatives apply equally to reproductive partners as, while they may not suffer from the condition themselves, they are directly affected by the transmission of genetic conditions to their children.

Finally NPP 2.1 only gives the health professional the power to disclose but it says nothing about whether there is a duty to disclose. They are no Australian cases on the failure to disclose genetic information, but, as Chapter 8 illustrates, there are numerous examples of health professionals owing duties to people outside of the therapeutic relationship. In the United States there has been some recognition of a duty to warn relatives of genetic risks. In *Pate v Threlkel* 661 So 2d 278 (1995), the Supreme Court of Florida found a duty could be owed to children of a patient with medullary thyroid carcinoma. A daughter of a patient sued the treating doctor for not warning the patient that his children could inherit the condition. The Supreme Court overturned a decision of a lower court which dismissed the matter for want of a duty of care. The risk of harm to the daughter was said to be reasonably foreseeable. However, the court found that the duty would be satisfied by the doctor warning the patient, rather than by directly contacting the genetic relatives.

A more expansive approach was taken in *Safer v Pack* 677 A 2d 1188 (1996), where the plaintiff argued that a doctor had a duty to warn the children of a patient he had treated for colon cancer and multiple polyposis. The Superior Court of New Jersey upheld the claim of duty, finding that the doctor's duty was similar to the duty owed by psychiatrists to potential victims of mentally ill patients (discussed in Chapter 8). While they recognised that there may be cases of a conflict between the privacy rights of the patient and the rights of the genetic relative, the court found that such a conflict did not exist in the present case.

As is always the case, American cases are not authority in Australia, but the arguments accepted in them are easily transmitted into the Australian context, and it could be argued that Australia courts would look at these duty concepts in a similar way.

Stem cells, cloning and research on human embryos

Spurred on by the developments in stem-cell research and community concerns about scientific developments in relation to human reproduction, the Council of Australian Governments (COAG) reached an agreement in April 2002 that the Commonwealth, States and Territories would introduce nationally consistent legislation, principally to regulate stem-cell research, but also covering other practices associated with reproductive technology. This legislation was enacted in all jurisdictions except Western Australia and the Northern Territory, although the Western Australian *Human Reproductive Technology Act 1991* already covered the same field of prohibited practices. The Acts were structured in such a way that for research involving human embryos the Commonwealth legislation was applied as if it were the law of the State. The State and Australian Capital Territory Acts facilitate the application of the Commonwealth regulatory regime. The legislation prohibiting human cloning and other practices mirrored the Commonwealth legislation and imposed penalties to be applied locally by the States.

A review of the initial legislation was undertaken in 2005 by the Legislation Review Committee, which became known as the Lockhart Review (named after Justice Lockhart, the Chair). The Review made a number of suggested reforms, primarily aimed at rolling back the prohibition on therapeutic cloning, while retaining the prohibition on reproductive cloning. The legislative changes recommended by that Review were introduced into the Commonwealth Parliament in 2006. They essentially create a set of completely prohibited practices and then create a secondary set of practices which are prohibited unless they are authorised by a licence.

Other jurisdictions soon followed suit with the exception of South Australia and Western Australia. In South Australia the *Statutes Amendment (Prohibition of Human Cloning for Reproduction and Regulation of Research Involving Human Embryos) Bill* was introduced towards the end of 2008 and is waiting clearance from the upper house. In Western Australia the Lockhart reforms were rejected by the parliament in May 2008, although there has been some discussion of reintroducing the Bill. This leaves South Australia and Western Australia in the pre-Lockhart position, where all cloning is illegal.

Table 17.1 Human Cloning and Research on Human Embryo Legislation

Jurisdiction	Legislation
Commonwealth	*Research Involving Human Embryos Act 2002* *Prohibition of Human Cloning for Reproduction Act 2002*
New South Wales	*Human Cloning for Reproduction and Other Prohibited Practices Act 2003* *Research Involving Human Embryos (New South Wales) Act 2003*
Queensland	*Research Involving Human Embryos and Prohibition of Human Cloning Act 2003*
South Australia	*Prohibition of Human Cloning Act 2003* *Research Involving Human Embryos Act 2003*
Tasmania	*Human Cloning for Reproduction and Other Prohibited Practices Act 2003* *Human Embryonic Research Regulation Act 2003*
Victoria	*Infertility Treatment Act 1995* *Assisted Reproductive Treatment Act 2008* (not in force at time of writing)
Western Australia	*Human Reproductive Technology Act 1991*
Australian Capital Territory	*Human Cloning and Embryo Research Act 2004*
Northern Territory	Nil

The following are examples of the completely prohibited practices created by the Lockhart reform legislation:

- placing a human embryo clone in a human body or the body of an animal;
- importing or exporting a human embryo clone;
- creating a human embryo for a purpose other than achieving pregnancy in a woman;
- creating or developing a human embryo by fertilisation that contains genetic material provided by more than two persons;
- developing a human embryo outside the body of a woman for more than 14 days;
- making heritable alterations to the genome;
- collecting a viable human embryo from the body of a woman;
- creating a chimeric embryo made from a human embryo where a cell or part of a cell from an animal has been introduced;
- developing a hybrid embryo made from the combination of animal and human gametes;
- intentionally placing a human embryo in an animal;
- intentionally placing a human embryo in a human in a place apart from a woman's uterus;

- intentionally placing an animal embryo in a human;
- importing, exporting or placing a prohibited embryo (of the kind described above);
- commercial trading in human eggs, human sperm or human embryos (excluding reasonable expenses).

Practices that are offences but which may be licensed include:

- creating a human embryo other than by fertilisation, or developing such an embryo;
- creating or developing a human embryo containing genetic material provided by more than two persons;
- using precursor cells from a human embryo or a human foetus to create a human embryo, or developing such an embryo; and
- creating a hybrid embryo.

The maximum penalty relating to human cloning offences is 15 years' imprisonment.

Research involving human embryos

Research using early stage excess ART (assisted reproductive technology) embryos, which would otherwise be discarded, will be allowed to continue within a rigorous regulatory framework. The Commonwealth *Research Involving Human Embryos Act 2002* is treated as an Act of the States. This means that the NHMRC's Licensing Committee established under the Commonwealth Act has powers and functions under State law and is the only body issuing licences for the use of excess ART embryos.

It is an offence to use an 'excess ART embryo' unless:

- the use is authorised by a licence issued by the NHMRC Licensing Committee; or
- the use is specifically exempt.

An 'excess ART embryo' is a human embryo created *in vitro* for the purpose of attempting to achieve pregnancy in a particular woman, that has been determined, in writing, by that woman (and her spouse, if any) as being excess to their needs. The exempt uses of excess ART embryos are:

- storage and removal from storage;
- transport;
- observation, including photography or video recording;
- allowing to succumb;
- diagnostic investigations by an ART clinic where the embryo is biologically unfit for implantation, in order to directly benefit the woman for whom the embryo was created; and
- use in the ART treatment of a woman other than the woman for whom the embryo was created (donation to another couple).

Sex selection

Sex selection (which is discussed in the first part of the chapter) is currently banned in Victoria, unless the child must be of a particular sex to avoid the risk of transmission of a genetic abnormality or a disease: *Infertility Treatment Act 1995* (Vic), s 50. The ban is reproduced in the *Assisted Reproductive Treatment Act 2008* (Vic), s 28.

Other jurisdictions have not used legislation to ban sex selection but IVF practitioners, who are bound by the NHMRC's *Ethical guidelines on the use of assisted reproductive technology in clinical practice and research 2007*, must have regard to [11.1] which states:

> Sex selection is an ethically controversial issue. The Australian Health Ethics Committee believes that admission to life should not be conditional upon a child being a particular sex. Therefore, pending further community discussion, sex selection (by whatever means) must not be undertaken except to reduce the risk of transmission of a serious genetic condition.

Gene therapy and tissue regulation

In Australia genetic therapy is regarded as being experimental, and reference may therefore be made to the National Health and Medical Research Council's (NHMRC) Statement on Human Experimentation (National Health and Medical Research Council 1999). Supplementary Note 7 to the Statement on Human Experimentation – *Somatic Cell Gene Therapy and Other Forms of Experimental Introduction of DNA and RNA into Human Subjects (1992)* – has been replaced from 1 January 2000 by *Guidelines for Ethical Review of Research Proposals for Human Somatic Cell Gene Therapy and Related Therapies*. Gene therapy is still a relatively new technique and between 1995 and 2003 approximately 10 trials of gene therapy and related therapies had been approved (Therapeutic Goods Administration 2003).

In 1994 the NHMRC's Research Committee formed a subcommittee – Gene and Related Therapies Research Advisory Panel (GTRAP) – to provide advice to the NHMRC and Human Research Ethics Committees (HRECs) on matters pertaining to human gene therapy trials and to assist researchers in the establishment of best practice standards. GTRAP also maintains a register of patients who have undergone gene therapy so that, should gene therapy be associated with long-term side effects, patients and their families could be followed up or contacted at some future time.

In summary the system for review and approval for gene therapy trials is as follows:

- proposals are submitted to the institution's HREC. When the HREC has completed its assessment the proposal is forwarded to GTRAP;
- GTRAP assesses the proposal and provides a recommendation back to the HREC;
- gene therapy proposals follow the Therapeutic Goods Administration's (TGA) Clinical Trial Exemption (CTX) Scheme, unless GTRAP considers the Clinical Trial Notification (CTN) scheme is suitable;

- any proposal that may pose an environmental risk must be considered by an Institutional Biosafety Committee for consideration and go to the Office of the Gene Technology Regulator; for example, where the therapy involves a live viable genetically modified organism (GMO) (Therapeutic Goods Administration 2003). For general purposes a person who has undergone somatic cell gene therapy is specifically excluded from the definition of a GMO for the purposes of the *Gene Technology Act 2000* (Cth);
- once approval from all relevant bodies has been received the clinical trial may proceed, subject to any conditions that may have been imposed.

In 2002 a meeting of the Australian Health Ministers' Conference agreed that the TGA introduce a national regulatory framework for human cellular and tissue therapies. The ministers also agreed that the legislation should also accommodate therapeutic goods manufactured from viable human or animal tissue (Therapeutic Goods Administration 2003). The three areas that were proposed to be regulated under this scheme were:

- human tissue and cells and cellular and tissue-based therapies;
- gene and related therapies; and
- xenotransplantation (use of animal tissues and cells).

In the Lockhart amendments to the *Research Involving Human Embryos Act 2002* (Cth), a new section, s 47C, was introduced which required the Health Minister to prepare a report on the feasibility of a national legislative scheme or regulatory approach for effective governance of non-blood human tissue based therapies. On 17 November 2006, the Australian Health Ministers Conference signed a *National Framework for Human Cellular, Tissue and Emerging Biological Therapies*. The framework excludes solid organs and reproductive materials from its regulation.

A report was also prepared by the Commonwealth Department of Health and Ageing on solid organs and reproductive tissues (Commonwealth Department of Health and Ageing 2008). The report recommends that:

- a legislative approach for governance of manipulated non-blood human tissue based therapies should be developed as part of the therapeutic goods regulatory reform program;
- the development of appropriate standards and regulatory arrangements for solid organs should be referred to the new statutory national organ donation and transplantation authority; and
- a national legislative or regulatory approach for effective governance of un-manipulated reproductive tissues was not necessary. (at 2)

The NHMRC is examining whether or not animal-to-human transplantation research should proceed in Australia and, if so, under what regulatory framework. There were two rounds of public consultations in 2002 and 2004 and draft guidelines and a discussion paper were released. The NHMRC said that there should be a five-year moratorium on any research into animal-to-human whole organ transplants in Australia primarily because:

- the risks of transmission of animal viruses had not been adequately resolved; and
- xenotransplantation was at such an early stage that it was unlikely to confer any benefit on research participants (National Health and Medical Research Council 2005).

Patenting genes

A patent is a monopoly granted by a government for a limited period in return for the development and disclosure by an inventor of a new invention. The patent takes the form of an exclusive right to prevent other people from using the invention. Thus an Australian patent can prevent the manufacture of a patented article in Australia, the sale of that article within Australia, the export of that article from Australia, and the importation of that article into Australia following its manufacture abroad by anyone other than the patentee.

Section 18(2) of the *Patents Act 1990* (Cth) provides that '[h]uman beings, and the biological processes for their generation, are not patentable inventions'. This provision has been interpreted by the Australian Patent Office to mean that DNA and genes in the human body are not patentable. However, once a DNA or gene sequence has been separated from the human body and manufactured synthetically, it would be patentable (Nicol 1996).

In mid-2004 the Australian Law Reform Commission (ALRC) completed an 18-month inquiry into gene patents. The ALRC produced a 700-page report, *Genes and Ingenuity: Gene Patents and Human Health*, which was tabled in the Commonwealth Parliament on 31 August 2004 (Australian Law Reform Commission 2004). The terms of reference of the inquiry directed the ALRC to consider the impact of current patenting laws and practices related to genes and genetic and related technologies on:

- research and its subsequent application and commercialisation;
- the Australian biotechnology sector; and
- the cost-effective provision of health care in Australia.

One of the key concerns for the inquiry was the question of whether there should be a statutory exemption for research or experimentation on patented inventions. The report noted that the *Patents Act* does not expressly exempt the experimental or research use of patented inventions for liability from infringement. They said that generally patent holders did not seek to enforce their rights against researchers. However, during the inquiry Genetic Technologies Limited 'revealed that it was asking some research institutions to take out a licence for research using its patented method for the use of non-coding DNA' (Australian Law Reform Commission 2004). The Report includes 50 recommendations for reform to customise the current system to accommodate emerging scientific breakthroughs. Some of these recommendations include:

- improving patent law and practice concerning the patenting of genetic materials and technologies;
- improving patent law and practice concerning the exploitation of gene patents;

- ensuring privately funded research, where commercialised, results in appropriate public benefit;
- encouraging universities and other research organisations to raise the awareness of researchers about patenting issues and the commercialisation of research; and
- establishing mechanisms for monitoring the implications of gene patents for research and health care so that governments have the ability to intervene where gene patents are considered to have an adverse impact.

Many of the submissions to the inquiry argued that it was wrong for patents to be granted on genetic sequences at all because they occurred naturally and were not an invention. However, as the practice had been widespread for a number of years in Australia and overseas, it was no longer practicable to recommend that gene sequences should not be patentable.

At the time of writing the Community Affairs Committee of the Australian Senate has commenced an inquiry into gene patents. The terms of reference are:

> The impact of the granting of patents in Australia over human and microbial genes and non-coding sequences, proteins, and their derivatives, including those materials in an isolated form, with particular reference to:
> (a) the impact which the granting of patent monopolies over such materials has had, is having, and may have had on:
>   (i) the provision and costs of healthcare,
>   (ii) the provision of training and accreditation for healthcare professionals,
>   (iii) the progress in medical research, and
>   (iv) the health and wellbeing of the Australian people;
> (b) identifying measures that would ameliorate any adverse impacts arising from the granting of patents over such materials, including whether the *Patents Act 1990* should be amended, in light of the any matters identified by the inquiry; and
> (c) whether the *Patents Act 1990* should be amended so as to expressly prohibit the grant of patent monopolies over such materials.

Genetics and negligence

The advent of widespread use of genetic screening raises the issue of what should be the law's response to negligent genetic screening on the unborn. Primarily, the types of claims must take two forms: *wrongful birth* claims (where the parents sue because a child has been born that should have been aborted) and *wrongful life* claims (where the child sues for not being aborted). Both types of claims are discussed in detail in Chapter 19, but it is worth noting here that only wrongful birth claims have been recognised in Australia, and that in some jurisdictions the damages available for wrongful birth have been limited to the special expenses relating to the treatment of the child's disability.

An example of a wrongful birth claim caused by negligent genetic screening is *Farraj v King's Healthcare NHS Trust* [2006] EWHC 1228 (QB). The plaintiffs argued that their child had been negligently screened for beta thalassaemia major (BTM). Both parents carried the BTM genetic trait and had sought out genetic screening when they fell pregnant with their third child. They argued that, had the test been performed properly, it would have revealed the genetic presence of BTM and they would have terminated the pregnancy. The parents sued both the hospital which had received the sample for genetic testing, and the private company which conducted culturing on the specimen to increase its volume for the test (CSL). CSL argued, on an interlocutory application, that it did not owe any duty to the parents as it had no relationship with them and the duty of the hospital was non-delegable.

Swift J disagreed and found that a duty was owed. Her Honour said:

> If negligence occurs in a hospital laboratory, the relevant hospital trust is liable to a person who suffers damage as a result of that negligence. It is difficult to see why a private laboratory should be in a different position. CSL was a commercial operation which was paid for its services. (at [77])

An example of a wrongful life claim based on negligent genetic screening is *Waller v James* [2006] HCA 16. The child had been born through IVF but the embryo had not been screened for a genetic condition which the father carried. The condition, AT3 deficiency, is a clotting disorder, and when the child was born he suffered severe brain damage. The child sued on the basis that the genetic screening had been negligent. Had it been done properly, the child would not have been selected for implantation and would not have been born. As discussed in Chapter 19, the High Court refused to recognise the claim, citing, amongst other things, the difficulty in calculating the difference between the pre-tort position of the child (namely, not being born) with the post-tort position of the child (living with a disability).

References

Allegrucci, CC Denning et al (2004) 'Stem-cell consequences of embryo epigenetic defects'. *Lancet* **364**(9429): 206-8.

Anderson, WF (1992) 'Human gene therapy'. *Science* **256**(5058): 808-13.

Australian Government (2005) *Legislation Review: Prohibition of Human Cloning Act 2002 and the Research Involving Human Embryos Act 2002* Reports. Canberra, December 2005.

Australian Law Reform Commission (2003) *Essentially Yours: The Protection of Human Genetic Information in Australia*. Sydney, Australian Law Reform Commission.

Australian Law Reform Commission (2004) *Genes and Ingenuity: Gene Patenting and Human Health*. Sydney, Australian Law Reform Commission.

Barnes, L, FE Matthews et al (2005) 'Brain donation for research: consent and re-consent post Alder Hey'. *Bull Med Ethics*(211): 17-21.

Baumiller, R, S Comley et al (1996) 'Code of Ethical Principles for Genetics Professionals'. *Am Jn of Medical Genetics* **65**: 177-8.

Baylis, F and C McLeod (2007) 'The stem cell debate continues: the buying and selling of eggs for research'. *J Med Ethics* 33: 726-31.

Bell, D and B Bennett (2001) 'Genetic secrets and the family'. *Med Law Rev* 9(2): 130-61.

Bhutkar, A (2005) 'Synthetic biology. Navigating the challenges ahead'. *J Biolaw and Bus* 8: 19-29.

Bloom, F (1997) 'Breakthroughs 1997'. *Science* **278**: 2029.

Board of the European Society of Gene and Cell Therapy, E. C. o. t. C. N. o. E. a. E. o. t. C. I. P. (2008) 'Case of leukaemia associated with X-linked Severe Combined Immuno-deficiency Gene Therapy Trial in London'. *Human Gene Therapy* **19**: 3-4.

Bok, H, K Schill et al (2004) 'Justice, ethnicity and stem cell banks'. *Lancet* **364**: 118-21.

Boss, J (1994) 'First trimester prenatal diagnosis: earlier is not necessarily better'. *J Med Ethics* **20**(3): 146-51.

Botkin, J (1998) 'Ethical issues and practical problems in preimplantation genetic diagnosis'. *Journal of Law, Medicine and Ethics* **26**(1): 17-28.

Brown, S and SN Then (2007) 'Commercialisation of regenerative human tissue: regulation and reform in Australia and England, Wales and Northern Ireland'. *J Law Med* **14**(3): 339-59.

Byrne, JA, DA Pedersen, LL Clepper et al (2007) 'Producing primate embryonic stem cells by somatic cell nuclear transfer'. *Nature* **450**(7169): 497-502.

Caplan, AL (2008) 'If it's broken, shouldn't it be fixed? Informed consent and initial clinical trials of gene therapy'. *Hum Gene Ther* **19**(1): 5-6.

Catchpoole, D, A deFazio et al (2007) 'The importance of biorepository networks: the Australian Biospecimen Network – Oncology'. *Australian Journal of Medical Science* **28**(1): 16-20.

Caulfield, T (2000) 'Underwhelmed: hyperbole, regulatory policy, and the genetic revolution'. *McGill Law J* **45**(2): 437-60.

Cello, J, AV Paul et al (2002) 'Chemical synthesis of poliovirus cDNA: generation of infectious virus in the absence of natural template'. *Science* **297**(5583): 1016-18.

Chalmers, D, M Otlowski et al (1995) 'Current research: project on the legal and ethical aspects of genetic research in Australia'. *J Law Med* **3**: 30-5.

Chapman, A (2008) 'DTC marketing of genetic tests: the perfect storm'. *Am J Bioeth* **8**(6): 10-2.

Clarke, A (1991) 'Is non-directive genetic counselling possible?' *Lancet* **338**: 998-1001.

Clarke, A (1994) 'Genetic screening: a response to Nuffield'. *Bull Med Ethics* **940**: 12-21.

Coghlan, A (1993) 'Vital research caught in patent crossfire'. *New Scientist*: 4.

Commonwealth Department of Health and Ageing (2008) *Report to the Parliament of Australia as Prescribed by Section 47C of the Research Involving Human Embryos Act 2002*. Canberra.

Couch, F, M De Shano et al (1997) 'BRCA1 mutations in women attending clinics that evaluate the risk of breast cancer'. *N Engl J Med* **336**: 1409-15.

Creighton, S, E Almqvist et al (2003) 'Predictive, pre-natal and diagnostic genetic testing for Huntington's disease: the experience in Canada from 1987 to 2000'. *Clin Genetics* **63**(6): 462-75.

Daley, G, RL Ahrlund, JM Auerbach et al (2007) 'Ethics. The ISSCR Guidelines for Human Embryonic Stem Cell Research'. *Science* **315**(5812): 603-4.

Danks, D (1994) 'Germ-Line gene therapy: No place in treatment of genetic disease'. *Human Gene Therapy* **5**(2): 151-2.

Davies, K (2009) 'Spit and SNP – The pros and cons of personal genomics'. *Australian Life Scientist* **6**(1): 8-14

Dawson, K and P Singer (1990) 'The Human Genome Project: for better or for worse?' *Med J Aust* **152**: 484-9.

Delatycki, M, K Allen et al (2002) 'Insurance agreement to facilitate genetic testing [letter]'. *Lancet* **359**: 1433.

Dimos, JT, KT Rodolfa, KK Niakan et al (2008) 'Induced Pluripotent Stem Cells Generated from Patients with ALS Can Be Differentiated into Motor Neurons'. *Science* **321**(5893): 1218-21.

Duncan, RE (2004) 'Predictive genetic testing in young people: when is it appropriate?' *J Paediatr Child Health* **40**(11): 593-5.

Editorial (1995) 'Western eyes on China's eugenics laws'. *Lancet Infect Dis* **346**: 131.

Editorial (1997) 'Human cloning requires a moratorium, not a ban'. *Nature* **386**: 2.

Eeles, R, B Ponder et al (eds) (1996) *Genetic predisposition to cancer*. London, Chapman and Hall.

European Commission (2005) *Synbiology: An analysis of synthetic biology research in Europe and North America*. Brussels, Belgium, The European Commission.

French, AJ, CA Adams, LS Anderson, JR Kitchen, MR Hughes and SH Wood (2008) 'Development of human cloned blastocysts following somatic cell nuclear transfer with adult fibroblasts'. *Stem Cells* **26**: 485-93.

Friedrich, M (2002) 'Preserving privacy, preventing discrimination becomes the province of genetic experts'. *JAMA* **288**: 815-16.

Garver, K (1994) 'The Human Genome Project and Eugenic concerns'. *Am J Hum Genet* **E54**(1): 148-55.

Gibson, DG, GA Benders et al (2008) 'Complete chemical synthesis, assembly, and cloning of a Mycoplasma genitalium genome'. *Science* **319**(5867): 1215-20.

Gillett, G (2007) 'The use of human tissue'. *J Bioethical Inquiry* **4**(2): 119-27.

Hacein-Bey-Abina, S, C Von Kalle et al (2003) 'LMO2-associated clonal T-cell proliferation in two patients after gene therapy for SCID-X1'. *Science* **302**: 415-19.

Harper, P (1993) 'Insurance and genetic testing'. *Lancet* **341**: 224-7.

Harper, P and A Clarke (1990) 'Should we test children for "adult" genetic disease?' *Lancet* **335**: 1205-6.

Harris, J (1997) 'Goodbye Dolly? The ethics of human cloning'. *J Med Ethics* **23**: 353-60.

Healy, B (1992) 'On Gene Patenting'. *N Engl J Med* **327**(9): 664-8.

Healy, B (1997) 'BRCA genes – Bookmaking, fortune-telling and medical care'. *N Engl J Med* **336**(20): 1449-51.

Hewett, H (2009) A defeat for pro-lifers, but the debate isn't over. *Los Angeles Times*. 28 January. <http://www.latimes.com/news/opinion/la-oew-hewitt-estrich28-2009 jan28,0,7714991.story>.

Hogarth, S, GH Javitt et al (2008) 'The current landscape for direct-to-consumer genetic testing: legal, ethical and policy issues'. *Annu Rev Genomics Hum Genetics* **9**: 161-82.

Hope, RA, J Savulescu et al (2003) *Medical ethics and law: the core curriculum*. Edinburgh, Churchill Livingstone.

Human Genetics Society of Australasia (1997) 'Prenatal Diagnosis Policy'. *Fellowship Affairs* **Nov**: 23-4.

Kaiser, J (2006) 'Patient privacy. Rule to protect records may doom long-term heart study'. *Science* **311**(5767): 1547-8.

Karpowicz, P, CB Cohen and D van der Kooy (2004) 'It is ethical to transplant human stem cells into nonhuman embryos'. *Nature Medicine* **10**(4): 331-5.

Kass, LR (1997) The wisdom of repugnance. *New Republic*. 1997.06.02: 17-26.

Kelly, T (1986) *Clinical Genetics and Genetic Counselling*. Chicago, Year Book.

Kevles, D (1985) *In the Name of Eugenics*. New York, Knopf.

Kimmelman, J (2005) 'Recent developments in gene therapy: risks and ethics'. *BMJ* **330**: 79-82.

Knoppers, BM and R Chadwick (2005) 'Human genetic research: emerging trends in ethics'. *Nat Rev Genet* **6**(1): 75-9.

Knowles, L (2004) 'A regulatory patchwork: human ES cell research oversight'. *Nat Biotechnol* **22**: 157-63.

Lappé, M (1991) 'Ethical issues in manipulating the human germ-line'. *J Med Philos* **16**: 628.

Levitt, M (1995) 'Ethics of genetic screening: a new report on genetic screening in the Netherlands'. *Euroscan* **3**: 1-5.

Lewontin, R (1993) *The Doctrine of DNA: Biology as Ideology*. Hammondsworth, Penguin Books.

Lipworth, W, R Ankeny et al (2006) 'Consent in crisis: the need to reconceptualize consent to tissue banking research'. *Intern Med J* **36**(2): 124-8.

Lloyd, FJ, VF Reyna et al (2001) 'Accuracy and ambiguity in counseling patients about genetic risk'. *Arch Intern Med* **161**(20): 2411-13.

Lott, JP and J Savulescu (2007) 'Towards a global human embryonic stem cell bank'. *Am J Bioethics* **7**(8): 37-44.

Loughlan, P (1995) 'The patenting of medical treatment'. *Med J Aust* **162**: 376-80.

Malpani, A, A Malpani et al (2002) 'The use of preimplantation genetic diagnosis in sex selection for family balancing in India'. *Reprod Biomed Ownline* **4**(1): 16-20.

Mathur, A and J Martin (2004) 'Stem cells and repair of the heart'. *Lancet* **364**: 183-92.

Mattei, J (1996) 'Prenatal diagnosis'. *World Health* **Sept-Oct**(5).

Miller, S and MJ Selgelid (2007) 'Ethical and philosophical consideration of the dual-use dilemma in the biological sciences'. *Sci Eng Ethics* **13**(4): 523-80.

Moronov, V, RP Visconti and RR Markwald (2004) 'What is regenerative medicine? Emergence of applied stem cell and developmental biology'. *Expert Opin Biol Ther* **4**: 773-81.

Morris, M, A Tyler et al (1988) 'Adoption and genetic prediction for Huntington's disease. *Lancet* **8619**(2): 1069-70.

Muller-Hill, B (1988) *Murderous Science*. Oxford, Oxford University Press.

National Health and Medical Research Council (2005) *Animal–to-human transplantation (Xenotransplantation): Final report and advice to the National Health and Medical Research Council*, September 2004. Canberra, National Health and Medical Research Council.

Nicol, D (1996) 'Should human genes be patentable inventions under Australian patent law?' *J Law Med* **3**: 231-48.

Nisbet, M (2004) 'The Polls-Trends: Public Opinion about stem cell research and human cloning'. *Public Opinion Quarterly* **68**(1): 131-9.

Otlowski, M (2003) 'Genetic discrimination: meeting the challenges of an emerging issue'. *UNSWLJ* **26**(3): 764-9.

Otlowski, M, K Barlow-Stewart et al (2007) 'Investigating genetic discrimination in the Australian life insurance sector: the use of genetic test results in underwriting, 1999-2003'. *J Law Med* **14**(3): 367-96.

Otlowski, MF and R Williamson (2003) 'Ethical and legal issues and the "new genetics".' *Med J Aust* **178**(11): 582-5.

Parker, L (1995) 'Breast cancer genetic screening and critical bioethics gaze'. *J Med Philos* **20**: 313-17.

Pennings, G (2002) 'Personal desires of patients and social obligations of geneticists: applying preimplantation genetic diagnosis for non-medical sex selection'. *Prenat Diagn* **22**(12): 1123-9.

Pennings, G, R Schots et al (2002) 'Ethical considerations on preimplantation genetic diagnosis for HLA typing to match a future child as a donor of haematopoietic stem cells to a sibling'. *Hum Reprod* **17**(3): 534-8.

Perrone, J (2001) Stem Cells. *Guardian Unlimited*, 10 August.

Perry, D (2000) 'Patient's voices: the powerful sound in the stem cell debate'. *Science* **287**: 1423.

Lo, B, P Zettler, MI Cedars et al (2005) 'A new era in the ethics of human embryonic stem cell research'. *Stem Cells* **23**: 1454-9.

Phoenix, C and M Treder (2006) 'Applying the Precautionary Principle to nano-technology', <http://www.crnano.org/precautionary.htm>.

Privacy Commissioner (1996) *Information Paper Number Five: The Privacy Implications of Genetic Testing*. Canberra, Human Rights and Equal Opportunity Commission.

Ray, PF, A Munnich et al (2002) 'The place of "social sexing" in medicine and science'. *Hum Reprod* **17**(1): 248-9.

Resnik, DB and SS Tinkle (2007) 'Ethics in nanomedicine'. *Nanomed* **2**(3): 345-50.

Rice, C and N Scolding (2004) 'Adult stem cells – reprogramming neurological repair?' *Lancet* **364**: 193-9.

Richards, FH (2006) 'Maturity of judgement in decision making for predictive testing for nontreatable adult-onset neurogenetic conditions: a case against predictive testing of minors'. *Clin Genet* **70**(5): 396-401.

Ro, DK, EM Paradise et al (2006) 'Production of the antimalarial drug precursor artemisinic acid in engineered yeast'. *Nature* **440**(7086): 940-3.

Robertson, J (2003) 'Extending preimplantation genetic diagnosis: the ethical debate – ethical issues in new uses of preimplantation genetic diagnosis'. *Hum Reproduction* **18**: 465-71.

Robotham, J (2008) Sick babies denied treatment in DNA row. *Sydney Morning Herald*: 1, 4.

Robotham, J, M Metherell et al (2008) Labs ordered to stop breast cancer tests. *Sydney Morning Herald*.

Rosenveld, J and G Gillett (2004) 'Ethics, stem cells and spinal cord repair'. *Med J Aust* **180**(12): 637-9.

Roses, AD (2004) 'Pharmacogenetics and drug development: the path to safer and more effective drugs'. *Nat Rev Genet* **5**(9): 645-56.

Savulescu, J (2000) 'Education and debate: deaf lesbians, "designer disability", and the future of medicine', *BMJ* **325**: 771-3.

Schrag, D, K Kunz et al (1997) 'Decision analysis-effects of prophylactic mastectomy and oophorectomy on life expectancy among women with BRCA1 or BRCA2 gene mutations'. *N Engl J Med* **336**: 1465-71.

Schuklenk, U and A Kleinsmidt (2006) 'North-South benefit sharing arrangements in bioprospecting and genetic research: a critical and ethical analysis'. *Developing World Bioethics* **6**(3): 122-34.

Schuldiner, M, J Itskovitz-Eldor et al (2003) 'Selective ablation of human embryonic stem cells expressing a "suicide" gene'. *Stem Cells* **21**: 257-65.

Sermon, K (2002) 'Current concepts in preimplantation genetic diagnosis (PGD): a molecular biologist's view'. *Hum Reprod Update* **8**(1): 11-20.

Sermon, K, A Van Steirteghem et al (2004) 'Preimplantation genetic diagnosis'. *Lancet* **363**(9421): 1633-41.

Skene, L (1998) 'Patients' rights or family responsibilities? Two approaches to genetic testing'. *Med Law Rev* **6**(1): 1-41.

Skene, L (2001) 'Genetic secrets and the family: a response to Bell and Bennett'. *Med Law Rev* **9**(2): 162-9.

Skene, L (2007) 'Legal rights in human bodies, body parts and tissue'. *J Bioethical Inquiry* **4**(2): 129-33.

Skene, L, I Kerridge, B Marshall, P McCombe and P Schofield (2008) 'The Lockhart Committee: Developing policy through commitment to moral values, community and democratic processes'. *J Law Med* **16**(1): 132-8.

Sparrow, R (2007) 'Revolutionary and familiar, inevitable and precarious: Rhetorical contradictions in enthusiasm for nanotechnology'. *Nanoethics* **1**(1): 57-68.

Steinbrook, R (2006) 'Egg donation and human embryonic stem cell research'. *N Engl J Med* **354**(4): 324-6.

Sugarman, J (2008) 'Human stem cell ethics: beyond the embryo'. *Cell Stem Cell* **2**(6): 529-33.

Tabar, V, M Tomishima, G Panagiotakos et al (2008) 'Therapeutic cloning in individual parkinsonian mice'. *Nat Med* **14**(4): 379-81.

Takahashi, K and S Yamanaka (2006) 'Induction of pluripotent stem cells from mouse embryonic and adult fibroblast cultures by defined factors'. *Cell* **126**: 663-76.

Taylor, S, S Treloar et al (2008) 'Investigating genetic discrimination in Australia: a large-scale survey of clinical genetics clients'. *Clin Genet*.

Therapeutic Goods Administration (2003) *Discussion paper: The regulation of human tissues and emerging biological therapies*. Canberra, Therapeutic Goods Administration.

Trent, R, R Williamson et al (2003) 'The "new genetics" and clinical practice'. *Med J Aust* **178**(8): 406-9.

Tumpey, TM, CF Basler et al (2005) 'Characterization of the reconstructed 1918 Spanish influenza pandemic virus'. *Science* **310**(5745): 77-80.

Verlinsky, Y, S Rechitsky et al (2001) 'Preimplantation diagnosis for Fanconi anemia combined with HLA matching'. *JAMA* **2001**(285): 3130-3.

Wachter, R and B Lo (1993) 'Advance directives for patients with human immuno-deficiency virus infection'. *Critical Care Clinics* **9**(1): 125-36.

Wakayama, T (2004) 'On the road to therapeutic cloning'. *Nat Biotechnol* **22**(4): 399-400.

Wallsten, P (2008) Obama said oops on 6 state Senate votes. *Los Angeles Times* 24 January <http://www.latimes.com/news/politics/la-na-obamavotes24jan24,0,713086. story>

Warren, M (1985) *Gendercide: the implications of sex selection.* Totowa, NJ, Rowman and Allenheld.

Watson, J (1990) Fundacion BBV *Human Genome Project, Ethics.* Madrid.

Weindling, P (1989) *Health, race and German politics between national unification and Nazism. 1870-1945.* Cambridge, Cambridge University Press.

Weisbrot, D and KJ Breen (2003) 'The protection of human genetic information'. *Med J Aust* **179**: 127-8.

Wertz, D and J Sorenson (1986) 'Client reactions to genetic counselling: self-reports of influence'. *Clin Genetics* **30**: 494-502.

White House, T (2001) 'Remarks by the President on stem cell research'.

Wilson, JM (2008) 'Adverse events in gene transfer trials and an agenda for the new year'. *Hum Gene Ther* **19**(1): 1-2.

Winston, R (1997) *The Future of Genetic Manipulation.* London, Phoenix.

Wolpe, PR (2002) 'Treatment, enhancement and the ethics of neurotherapeutics'. *Brain Cogn* **50**: 387-95.

Yu J, MA Vodyanik, K Smuga-Otto et al (2007) 'Induced Pluripotent Stem Cell Lines Derived from Human Somatic Cells'. *Science* **318**(5858): 1917-20.

Zare, N, J Sorenson et al (1984) 'Sex of provider as a variable in effective genetic counselling'. *Soc Sci Med* **19**: 671-5.

Zimmerman, B (1991) 'Human germ-line therapy: The case for its development and use'. *J Med Philos* **16**(2): 593-612.

Zu, L, W Wenchi et al (2007) 'New technology and clinical applications of nanomedicine'. *Medical Clinics of North America* **91**: 845-62.

CHAPTER 18

SEXUALITY AND REPRODUCTION

Case 1

ST is a 51-year-old woman. She is single, and until recently she was an executive in a large corporation. At the age of 49 she began to experience symptoms of menopause and realised that she strongly wished to have a baby. She attempted to have a child, first, by the use of intra-uterine insemination using donor sperm and, when this did not work, by searching for an egg donor. A donor was found who agreed, for a fee, to undergo a course of ovarian stimulation followed by oocyte (egg) harvesting. These oocytes were fertilised in-vitro with sperm from a donor and implanted in ST's womb. The child was born by caesarean section because her doctor did not think that ST's body could stand the rigours of labour.

ST was very pleased with the results. "I didn't know," she said, "that I could ever love anyone this much." (Belkin 1997)

Case 2

JL and BS are a lesbian couple who have been in a relationship for four years and who share a house. They wish to have a child, and have been referred to an infertility clinic for donor insemination using a sperm donor known to them.

Sexuality, intimacy and illness

Sexuality suffuses every aspect of our lives. Illness and the effects of medical treatment can have dramatic impacts on sexuality, relationships and identity. Loss of sexual identity and erosion of sexual intimacy can leave patients and their partners feeling anxious, depressed, inadequate and isolated. Conversely, the preservation of sexuality and intimacy may enhance people's ability to cope and maintain their quality of life.

The maintenance of sexuality and intimacy in the context of illness presents a major challenge for many patients and their partners. How people react to changes in their sexuality brought on by illness is strongly influenced by the willingness of health professionals to discuss issues regarding sexuality with their patients, including clarifying any misperceptions they may have and providing them with education, counselling or psycho-social interventions (Hordern and Street 2007). The ability of a couple to renegotiate sexuality and intimacy in the context of illness is also, unsurprisingly, influenced by their pre-existing sexual relationship, the quality of communication in their relationship, the dynamics of the care-giving relationship, and the way that they construct what sexual practices are possible or 'normal', and what are 'taboo' (Hordern and Street 2007).

The experience of patients and couples dealing with illnesses that affect sexual function is also shaped by broader cultural constructions of sexuality. This has important implications in many cultures for both gay and lesbian and heterosexual couples, because heterosexual couples may regard inability to have intercourse as catastrophic and may fail to see alternative sexual practices as 'real sex', while gay and lesbian couples may feel that their experiences and needs are excluded from even the possibility of discourse within the health-care system (Butler 1990).

Philosophy and sexuality

The philosophy of sex concerns itself with questions of sexuality and sexual identity, the meaning of gender, and the ethics of sexual practices and relationships. Historically, religious traditions have been the most powerful influence on cultural constructions of sexuality and the regulation of sexual practices (Blackford 2006). Christian ethics, for example, has an enormous literature devoted to demonstrating that homosexuality is, by light of 'natural reason' or by Christian revelation, a 'disordered' condition (Yarhouse 2004) (although there is also a large Christian literature that is accepting of homosexuality).

Different moral philosophers have had very different approaches to questions regarding the status and morality of sexuality. Plato wrote extensively on the benefits of homosexual love. Immanuel Kant regarded sexual desire as a threat to virtue and moral values. Other philosophers have tended to appeal to principles of liberty, consent and non-interference, and have regarded sexuality as a matter of individual choice. More recently, the philosophy of sexuality has been informed by feminist philosophers, Marxists, continental philosophers and disability theorists who have provided radical critiques of the social construction of sexual identity and sexual roles (Soble 2002). These philosophers have emphasised the role of power imbalances in sexuality, the pervasive impact of male dominance, the role of 'interdependence' in relationships, the oppression of women and non-heterosexual identity, and the political and commercial basis of sexuality including the 'commodification' of the body. ('Commodification' is the process by which something which is of great intrinsic worth but no commercial value is turned into a commodity that can be bought or sold. In these debates it refers to the way commercial opportunities can arise from exploiting the body in various ways.)

Health care is ultimately concerned with bodies and their meaning – patients permit health professionals access to their bodies, share intimate and personal stories, and open their lives, experiences and social relationships to medical scrutiny. Much of recent philosophical thought about human bodies has had little influence in health care, but it has transformed the way that philosophers think about sexuality, identity and bodies because it has demonstrated that bodies are socially embedded and inscribed by history, language, culture and experience (Merleau-Ponty 1964; Foucault 1990).

For example, where medicine has been concerned with sexuality it has tended to ignore many aspects of intimacy and relationships, and has concerned itself more with static conceptions of sexual health and normality, which may be expressed by identifying sexual 'pathology' or 'deviance', and with therapeutic interventions to treat such 'dysfunctions' (Komesaroff 2008). This is ethically problematic because it offers an impoverished view of human experience as the construction of human sexuality in scientific and medical terms and its classification into normal or abnormal is not value-free.

Some authors such as Schuklenk and Ristow have argued that these divisions are frequently based on heterosexual assumptions about 'normalcy' and 'deviancy' and are often predicated on the idea that deviance from this heterosexual norm should be 'understood', diagnosed and, if possible, cured or avoided (Schuklenk and Ristow 1996). This argument has been taken further by some to suggest that medical research into the origins of homosexuality might be unethical, or at least unjustifiable, because it is based on a heterosexual norm, has no significant utility and simply promotes heterosexist stereotyping and discrimination. Similar criticisms may be advanced against other approaches to sexuality such as the push by the pharmaceutical industry to have sildafenil registered for treatment of female sexual dysfunction and the ethics of behavioural genetics and genetic screening for sexual orientation (Fishman 2004).

Assisted reproductive technology (ART)

Reproduction and sexuality are closely tied together. In recent years, many new techniques for assisted reproduction have become available. These techniques have changed the links between reproduction and sexuality, and ethics has often struggled to catch up with them.

Becoming a parent and rearing a child are central features of many people's social identity. Childlessness can have a devastating impact on individuals and couples who wish to attain this identity but are unable to. In the past adoption was the only answer to this problem, but the growth of ART has opened up many new possibilities (Shanner and Nisker 2001).

Developments in ART, and the availability of donated reproductive tissues (such as sperm, eggs and embryos), have made childbirth possible for many women who otherwise would have found this impossible. The combination of ART and established genetic technologies has also enabled people with certain genetic conditions to have children in the knowledge that their children will not inherit their condition or, less commonly, to ensure that they will. At the same time it has raised a range of controversies about such fundamental concepts as identity, parenthood, the family and the moral status of the embryo and foetus. The ethical debate that has surrounded the introduction of these new technologies has also led to the development of clinical guidelines and legislation to regulate clinical practice, control research and clarify family relationships.

ART has changed our world. Among the authors' acquaintances are sperm and oocyte donors, children born from donor insemination and IVF, children who, as embryos, were frozen for two years before being implanted, children of lesbian parents born with donated sperm, children of homosexual male parents born using surrogacy arrangements, adopted children, and children conceived through sexual intercourse between their mother and father. ART has also made possible post-mortem insemination, postmenopausal pregnancy, virgin births and embryos being conceived at one time being born to different people at different times.

Sperm and oocyte donation

Sperm donation may be required when a woman's male partner has sperm of low quality or number or carries a hereditable disease, or when the woman is single or in a lesbian relationship. Oocyte donation may be required for women who wish to become pregnant but lack 'ovarian reserve' due to advanced age, ovarian disease or previous cancer therapy (Nisker, Baylis et al 2006).

Many of the world's cultures have taken great interest in sperm. Indian Brahmin men try to conserve their sperm and not squander it. In Chinese Taoism, men are encouraged to orgasm without ejaculation, in order to conserve the precious substance. Aristotle believed that sperm was 'the most refined of substances' (Mischewski 2001). And in the Bible, Onan spilled his seed upon the ground and was slain for this detestable act.

Sperm were first seen under the microscope by van Leeuwenhoek in 1677. In 1784, Spallanzani first artificially inseminated a dog (Foote 2002). In 1790, the renowned Scottish surgeon, Dr John Hunter, reported that he had successfully inseminated the wife of a linen draper, using her husband's sperm. In 1884, a letter to an American medical journal reported a case of artificial insemination from 25 years earlier (using the doctor as sperm donor).

In 1954, the first comprehensive account of donor insemination was published in the *British Medical Journal*. In that same year the Supreme Court of Cook County ruled that, regardless of a husband's consent, Donor Insemination (DI) was 'contrary to public policy and good morals, and considered adultery on the mother's part'. This perspective was maintained as late as 1963, when a court in the United States held that a DI child was illegitimate because the sperm donor was not married to the child's mother (Fader 1993). As late as 1977, a child born from donor sperm in the UK was regarded as illegitimate – and the parents then needed to apply for adoption (Kirkman 2005).

The first Australian doctor to report that he had used donor sperm was AM Hill in 1970. Over 22 years, he gave donor sperm to 16 patients – and 11 became pregnant. The first successful human pregnancy with frozen spermatozoa was reported in 1953. The first public announcement of a successful birth from frozen sperm was made in 1963 and the first commercial sperm bank opened in the early 1970s (Fader 1993).

There is now an international trade in sperm and oocytes – often obtained through the internet. Sperm from US banks costs between US$135 and US$410 per dose. Insemination at a Danish clinic costs around AU$900 per treatment.

Because of variations between countries in laws regarding the identification of sperm donors, and insemination of lesbian and single women, UK women commonly fly to Denmark for US sperm inseminations. Women may also pay up to US$20,000 to obtain donor oocytes, with prices proportional to the perceived 'attractiveness' of the donor's social and biological characteristics. The commercialisation and commodification of gametes has been extensively critiqued on the grounds that it offends against respect for human integrity and dignity, may compromise the health professional-patient relationship and, most importantly, because it endangers vulnerable oocyte 'donors', many of whom may be poor or socially disadvantaged women who sell their eggs in order to support themselves, their family or their own ART expenses and, arguably, may be unable to provide free and informed consent (although oocyte donors in the United States are frequently young, middle-class, often professional women) (Steinbock 2004; Sauer and Kavic 2006). For these reasons, while gamete donors may be offered 'reasonable' compensation, the purchase or sale of gametes is prohibited in Australia, New Zealand, Canada and most Western European countries.

Interestingly, while issues relating to vulnerability, consent and coercion have received large amounts of attention in the context of oocyte commerce, they have received much less attention in the context of oocyte donation within families or between friends. This is illogical as it is very difficult, if not impossible, to sufficiently reduce the coercive influence of pre-existing relationships (particularly within families) where one party has a serious need and/or has made a request for assistance from a sibling or friend. What evidence there is suggests that it is extremely difficult to refuse a family member's request for an oocyte or, indeed, for any regenerative or non-regenerative tissue, such as blood, bone marrow, a kidney or a liver segment (Ber 2000).

Sperm and oocyte donation continue to raise difficult ethical concerns. In recent years some of the issues that have arisen include the rights of children to know their sperm or oocyte donor, the rights of single and lesbian women to have children through sperm or oocyte donation, the rights of donors to be involved with their offsprings' care, the adequacy of consent processes in gamete donation, and the risks posed to both donors and recipients by commodifying gametes. These issues came up even more forcefully when the next stage of reproductive technology – IVF – was developed.

In-vitro fertilisation

The theoretical possibility of IVF was first considered in the 1930s but it was not until 1969 that human extracorporeal fertilisation was achieved in the laboratory (Edwards, Steptoe et al 1980). In 1978 it became a clinical reality when the world's first child – Louise Brown – was born following *in vitro* fertilisation (IVF), permanently altering the scientific and popular understanding of human reproduction.

IVF requires oocytes to be retrieved from a woman's ovaries and fertilised in the laboratory with donor sperm. The oocytes are aspirated from follicles in the woman's ovaries laparoscopically or transvaginally after the ovaries have been 'primed' with hormones that stimulate the development of egg-bearing follicles. Although it is relatively safe, there are some risks associated with this including the potentially fatal 'ovarian hyperstimulation syndrome'. The retrieved oocytes are then placed in culture with the donor sperm and examined for fertilisation after 20-24 hours. Of the 10 to 12 oocytes collected from a single cycle of ovarian stimulation about 80% are expected to fertilise. After a further 24 hours (during which the embryos have undergone further cell division to the four-cell stage) they are suitable for transfer to the woman's uterus.

In IVF, each attempt at implantation of an embryo is known as a 'cycle'. Pregnancy rates for IVF exceed 25% per cycle for women/couples whose infertility is caused by sperm problems, endometriosis or Fallopian tube pathology or is unexplained. Pregnancy rates are higher with transfer of cryopreserved embryos. Over 60% of couples entering ART programs become pregnant after four cycles and over 75% after nine cycles (Kovacs 1993; Mishell 2001). Recognition that the rate of pregnancy rises with the number of embryos simultaneously transferred to the uterus originally led to the practice of multiple embryo transfer. Unfortunately, the transfer of two or more embryos to the uterus increases the risk of multiple pregnancy (ie, twins, triplets etc) thereby increasing the risks for mother and foetuses. Cryopreservation (the freezing of preimplantation embryos for later use) has provided the means by which these risks can be reduced, by harvesting and fertilising a number of eggs, but freezing some embryos for later use if necessary. Following the demonstration that the rate of implantation and pregnancy from frozen and thawed embryos was essentially the same as 'fresh' embryos, cryopreservation of embryos has become a standard, safe and cost-effective process. For these reasons most fertility clinics now routinely transfer only one to two embryos.

In Australia in 2005, there were 51,017 treatment cycles reported to the Australian and New Zealand Assisted Reproduction Database (ANZARD). Single-embryo transfers (SET) cycles accounted for 48.3% of embryos transfer cycles in 2005, and babies born to women who had a single-embryo transfer had better outcomes compared to babies born to women who had a double-embryo transfer (DET). In 2005, the perinatal mortality rate was 14.7 deaths per 1000 ART births, a 23.8% decrease from 2004. The perinatal mortality rate was the lowest among singletons born following SET (7.3 deaths per 1000 births): <http://www.npsu.unsw.edu.au/NPSUweb.nsf/page/art11>.

While IVF is a relatively safe procedure, it does carry significant mortality and morbidity, and is associated with risks to the mother, child and family unit. The main risks to the mother are those associated with ovarian hyperstimulation syndrome, thromboembolism, pelvic surgery, obstetric complications, and the emotional and psychological consequences of IVF and infertility. While children born after ART are generally healthy and are developmentally similar to those born following spontaneous conception, lower birth weight, lower gestational age and multiple pregnancy are associated with a higher risk of intrauterine and perinatal complications. Most reviews also demonstrate a higher risk of congenital malformations and rare epigenetic defects. Further long-term follow-up of children born after ART is required to properly assess long-term outcomes.

Responses to assisted reproductive technology

Reproductive technologies and their impact on women have been the focus of considerable attention from feminist ethicists. Broadly speaking, feminist responses to ART have been either non-interventionist or pro-interventionist. Non-interventionists have tended to see reproductive technologies as manifestations of the oppression of women, and have speculated that ART reinforces the notion that women are socially valuable only if fertile (Mies 1987).

Pro-interventionists generally have welcomed reproductive technologies that sever biological reproduction from the social identity of women and afford the promise of freedom from 'biological tyranny'. 'Second wave' feminists regard reproductive technologies as having an inherent socio-political force that could provide a means for surrendering control of women's reproductive capacity to men, to science and to 'technopatriarchs' (Overall 1983). More recent feminist writings have emphasised the social and political aspects of reproductive technologies and the importance of consent.

Assisted reproductive technology has come under attack from social anthropologists, ecologists and philosophers on the grounds that in an over-populated world where millions of people die each year from preventable disease there is something very incongruous about using state funds and medical expertise to create more children. Although these objections seem reasonable enough, they can be equally applied to many other technological advances, indeed to any intervention that prolongs life, improves a person's reproductive ability or uses health funds. Other criticisms that have been levelled at ART include: whether separation of conception from sexuality is unnatural or immoral (a commonly expressed theological objection to ART), whether ART commodifies or commercialises reproduction and women's bodies, and whether the attention given to ART is indicative of a more fundamental social concern, that childlessness does not have the same status as childbearing or childrearing.

Access to assisted reproductive technology

The popularity of IVF and the fact that most IVF children are healthy and develop normally have raised the reproductive expectations of women and engendered the belief that ART should be universally available. While ART receives substantial public funding in Australia, in other countries, such as Canada, ART receives no public funding, while in many Western European countries restrictions are placed on the number of cycles, pregnancies or children for which public funding is available. In other words, access to ART is often limited to economically advantaged women/couples.

Fertility services often use a series of eligibility criteria reflective of the perceived effectiveness, benefits and risks of IVF to determine access to ART including the cause of infertility, the age of the potential mother and the presence of physical, intellectual or psychiatric disease in the mother. ART clinics may also deny access on the basis of other 'non-medical' criteria, including race, ethnicity, income, the marital status of the mother, the sexual preference/orientation of the potential mother, physical or cognitive disability and the perceived ability of the woman or couple to parent (Gurmankin, Caplan et al 2005; Peterson 2005; Vandervort 2006). The idea that not everyone is an appropriate parent is commonly expressed, when looking at how other people behave in supermarkets, restaurants, or late at night on city streets. Generally we cannot do anything about other people's parenthood – people have children whether we wish them to or not. However, when women seek access to ART, it is possible for health providers or other authorities to begin to have a say. Reproductive technology practitioners are often requested to provide services to people who they may not believe would make ideal parents – but should they have any say in this matter?

There are a number of problems with health professionals taking on the role of gatekeepers to control access to ART. First, it is not always clear why access should be restricted. Is it because of resource considerations, because of 'community values' and social policy (Keeping 1997), because of legislation or institutional guidelines, or on the basis of doctors' own ethical or religious beliefs? The issue is not so much whether there should be any restrictions – as judgments that some therapy is futile or medically contraindicated are inevitable; but that access to reproductive technology should not be discriminatory or based on medically or morally irrelevant considerations (Pearn 1997). Examples that the authors are aware of in which reproductive technology has been requested include where parents have criminal histories, where they already have large families but are now subfertile, where they have previously been sterilised but now have a new partner, where one or other partner is seriously or terminally ill, where one or other partner is extremely old, where previous children have been taken into care, where the request comes from a single woman, where the request comes from lesbian parents, where the request is for a surrogate parent for an infertile heterosexual couple, or where the request is from a surrogate parent for a homosexual male couple. There are many other possibilities.

Before the development of IVF, female fertility was largely limited by age and ended by menopause. Following the advent of IVF there has been the gradual realisation that this need no longer be the case. At first IVF was only made available to women in their 20s and early 30s – those thought to have the greatest chance of successful pregnancy. In the early 1990s ART was offered to those in their late 30s and early 40s, and since that time the use of donor eggs has become available to women approaching or even past their menopause (Antinori, Versaci et al 1993; Sauer and Kavic 2006).

The issue achieved major media prominence in early 1997 when Arceli Keh, a 63-year-old Californian woman, gave birth to an IVF child – an event both hailed as a symbol of the triumph of medicine over nature and decried as an immoral misuse of medical technology. While such cases seem biologically unusual, it is not at all clear why older women should not have access to ART. Age is clearly a strong biological determinant of fertility, but there is no evidence that age affects the capacity for motherhood, nor are there any age restrictions placed on men becoming fathers in their 50s, 60s and 70s. What IVF has demonstrated is that the dividing line that distinguishes those who are 'old enough' to have a baby from those who are 'too old' is actually a moving boundary determined in part by cultural and social factors.

Lesbians and motherhood

The sexuality of lesbian women is the subject of much prurient curiosity. Conception, pregnancy and child-rearing, touching as they do upon many aspects of sexuality, have become the victim of much misplaced moralising with regard to lesbian mothers.

Many ART clinics in Australia exclude lesbian women from ART services. This has generally been justified by reference to perceived social and cultural norms, by concerns for the welfare of children raised in 'fatherless' families (Jansen 1997) and by distinguishing between the treatment of 'medical' and 'non-medical' infertility. These arguments are now impossible to sustain. Freedom of sexual preference is now clearly accepted at law and regarded as an issue of personal choice rather than public policy. Where the welfare of potential children is at issue, as it must be, there seems no basis for excluding lesbian women from access to ART as there are no impediments to lesbian parents successfully raising children in a loving and nurturing environment (Leiblum, Palmer et al 1995; Tasker and Golombok 1995).

The other argument against lesbian women having access to ART is based on disagreements about the definition of the word 'infertility'. Infertility has been defined as the failure to conceive after 'trying' for one year. For many reproductive physicians this definition implicitly assumes that infertility can only be demonstrated by heterosexual couples. The lifestyle choices of single people or same-sex couples may make conception biologically impossible, and therefore they may not fit the 'trying' part of the definition of infertility. This assumption allows distinctions to be made between 'medical' infertility and 'social' or 'non-medical' infertility (Jansen 1995). The argument that is made is that those with medical infertility have a justifiable claim on resources whereas those who are 'suffering from childlessness' (ie, older women, single women and lesbian women) cannot claim a right to ART services. Critics of the distinction between medical and social infertility suggest that it is morally irrelevant and discriminatory, and does not take account of changing social concepts of motherhood, fatherhood and family structure or of advances in medical technology (Dowd 1997). They suggest that, just as an understanding of death has been changed by advances in ventilation and resuscitation, so our understanding of infertility should be responsive to medical science.

One case that has received widespread media attention, as much for the fact that it involved a lesbian couple as for the other issues concerned, occurred in 2002. Two deaf women, Sharon Duchesneau and Candy McCullogh, were both mental health professionals with graduate degrees from Gallaudet University – the world's only liberal arts university for the deaf. When they wished to have a baby, they wished to choose an embryo that had a genetic cause of deafness, and they chose their donor accordingly. This would presumably enable their child to participate more fully in the community of which they were part (Skattebol 2005). The story – reported in the *British Medical Journal* under the heading 'Deaf lesbians, "designer disability" and the future of medicine', caused widespread and sensational public debate (Savulescu 2000).

It is difficult to think logically about such a case, and the sensationalism that inevitably accompanies it makes it even harder. There is after all no one who has been harmed by this. As Collett points out:

> [T]he lesbian couple who have had a deaf baby have not deliberately made a child with 'normal' hearing deaf. The particular child born to them would always have been deaf and only by having a completely different child would they have had a hearing baby. This child would either have been born deaf or not born at all and therefore what critics of their behaviour are effectively saying is that a deaf child would have been better off if he/she had not been born at all. (Collett 2002)

And what has lesbianism got to do with it after all? Why does this take pride of place, even in bioethics discussions in eminent journals. It is as if we do not have the language to discuss such difficult dilemmas and fall back on our stereotypes to fill the void

In an Australian case, *Re Patrick* (2002) 28 Fam LR 579, a dispute occurred between a lesbian couple and their sperm donor over the donor's role in the raising of two-year-old Patrick. The couple had placed an ad looking for a sperm donor, that was answered by one of their acquaintances. The donor's evidence was that he had made it clear that he desired involvement in the child for 1-2 days per week.

After 30 attempts at conception the mother became pregnant and, in time, had Patrick. At the time of the birth, the couple went into hiding as a way of resisting the donor's request to be present at the birth. After learning of the birth from a friend, he then filed an application with the Family Court for joint responsibility for Patrick. After further breakdown of the relationship, the affair was eventually resolved in a hearing before Justice Guest, in which he gave visitation rights to Patrick's donor that were similar to that of an estranged parent in a divorce case. He did find, however, that the donor was not Patrick's legal parent as the status of being a parent is determined by State laws which do not recognise sperm donors as fathers. Several months after the conclusion of the case, Patrick's mother killed both herself and Patrick (Kelly 2005). In this tragic case Patrick's best interests were clearly not served, but there will be disagreement as to where his interests were lost. Was it from the technology that allows donor insemination, or the personalities involved, or the nature of the agreements that can be made about parenthood, or due to the court's attempt at reconstructing the 'family' in a way at odds with the mother and her partner's wishes? Throughout, one gets a distinct feeling that society has changed faster than we are able to respond, and that the legal models and other ways we have for dealing with these new possibilities are not yet up to the task.

Related issues were discussed *H v J* (2006) 36 Fam LR 316, where a child had been conceived by a lesbian couple after using donated sperm from a friend. The difference in this case was that the relationship between the two mothers had broken down and the biological mother had denied her former partner access to the child. The non-biological mother sought an order for access on the basis that she was a parent or, in the alternative, that she was someone who was significant to the child's care, welfare and development and who should have access. The Federal Magistrate found that the non-biological mother could not be considered as the parent as the provisions in the *Family Law Act 1975* (Cth), s 60H, specifically dealt with children being born to heterosexual couples and not homosexual couples via artificial conception. Nevertheless, the woman was found to be a person significant to the child's care, welfare and development. Orders were made to adduce further evidence about the relationship between the woman and the child. In 2008, the Act was amended to include long-term homosexual relationships within its definition of de facto relationships. The effect of this change is to bring homosexual de facto partners within the definition of 'parent' under s 60H, so that partners who are not the biological parent will be considered as parents for the purpose of the Act, regardless of whether they are heterosexual or homosexual.

Gestational agreements and surrogacy

Gestational agreements are often used in ART. Agreements between participants in conception, pregnancy and child-rearing may occur where a gestational 'carrier' is impregnated with the sperm of the partner of a woman who is unable to gestate her own embryo/foetus, or where a woman gestates a pregnancy arising from donor oocytes, donor sperm or both. The term 'surrogate mother' (literally meaning substitute or replacement mother) is sometimes used to describe situations where a woman, for commercial or altruistic reasons, conceives, gestates and delivers a baby on behalf of another woman who is unable or unwilling to sustain a pregnancy but becomes the 'real' (legal and social) mother of the baby.

Surrogacy can take a number of forms. 'Genetic' or 'partial' surrogacy refers to situations where the surrogate mother's egg is fertilised by the sperm of the commissioning father, or an anonymous donor, either through IVF or intercourse. 'Gestatory' or 'full' surrogacy refers to situations where an embryo obtained from IVF is transferred into the surrogate's uterus so that she gestates the embryo/foetus but has no genetic link with the child.

The practice of surrogate motherhood has attracted enormous amounts of criticism – much of it ill-informed, inconsistently applied or poorly argued. These criticisms have been of two fundamental types – deontological arguments that contend that surrogacy is intrinsically immoral, and consequentialist arguments that suggest the consequences (to the mothers, children and to social concept of family) of allowing surrogacy are so deleterious that it should be prohibited by law (Charlesworth 1993).

> Opponents of surrogacy claim that it offends against certain basic moral principles such as the dignity and autonomy of the mother and the child: and that it involves one person (the infertile woman) using another person (the surrogate mother) as a means to her ends. This objection has been used by theologians, feminists, lawyers and philosophers, and the argument has involved analogies comparing surrogate motherhood with slavery or prostitution. (Warnock 1985)

While there are certain similarities between prostitution and surrogacy – in both cases physical services are traded, material compensation is provided and a deep personal bond is not required to complete the transaction – these characteristics define most commercial transactions, such as employing a builder or cleaner, and do not seem sufficient reason to claim that the employee (or surrogate) is being exploited or being used immorally as a thing or instrument (Prokopijevic 1990). Exploitation occurs where the individual does not freely and voluntarily consent, or is coerced directly or indirectly through poverty or powerlessness (Charlesworth 1993). But one can accept services offered altruistically or pay another for their services without exploiting them.

A number of feminist critics of surrogacy suggest that it is impossible for a woman to make an autonomous choice to act as a surrogate mother both because surrogacy itself is so exploitative that it cannot ever be freely chosen (just as one cannot freely choose to be a slave) and because free choice is not possible in the current sociopolitical context where women are already oppressed (Dodds and Jones 1989). While it may be true that the subtle forms of social, political and economic coercion are inevitable aspects of surrogacy, it is more difficult to sustain the claim that autonomous choice in these matters is impossible. Women frequently make autonomous choices regarding a range of complex and emotionally fraught reproductive issues such as *in vitro* fertilisation, abortion and prenatal screening. Such choices are clearly possible and are even seen as a woman's right. It is not logically consistent to allow these decisions but to regard decisions about surrogacy as morally impossible.

A woman's reproductive labour does seem to be different from other forms of labour. Reproductive labour is not only a physical process but an emotional, social and psychological process, the product of which is not something but *someone*. Critics of surrogate motherhood suggest that it is the need to separate the psychosocial aspects of pregnancy from the physical gestation that make it ethically untenable (Anderson 1990).

Other arguments against surrogacy have concentrated on the deleterious consequences of such practices for the surrogate mother, the commissioning parents, the child and for society. Such arguments generally use well-publicised cases such as Baby M or Baby Cotton to demonstrate that surrogate motherhood will inevitably lead to the exploitation of women and to enormous psychological harm to any child born of such arrangements. The potential for the exploitation of women in surrogacy arrangements is given even greater emphasis by philosophers who worry that commercialising the process will divide society into two groups; the poor who bear children and the wealthy who pay others to do it for them (Singer 1985). Although plausible, the difficulty for these arguments is that there is very little empirical data to support them and it is not always clear how the harms to children or parents, resulting from surrogacy arrangements, differ from the harms of other social or reproductive processes such as IVF, adoption, marriage or divorce (Reame and Parker 1990).

Because surrogacy arrangements always involve more than two people, all of whom can legitimately claim to be the child's parent, potential conflicts of moral claims or 'rights' are an inherent aspect of surrogate motherhood. The danger always exists, therefore, that surrogacy arrangements may harm the child's well-being, diminish the commissioning parents' expectation that the pregnancy is theirs or 'dehumanise' or 'alienate' the mother's labour. These potential harms do not, however, seem sufficient justification for a legislative prohibition of surrogacy. Even if one denies liberal claims that choices regarding surrogacy are purely matters of personal morality rather than public policy, it does not follow that if surrogacy is morally questionable that it should be prohibited. The state may instead choose to regulate surrogacy arrangements – just as it does for adoption or IVF. Legislation may even be put in place that restricts surrogacy to non-commercial or altruistic arrangements, guarantees time for surrogate mothers to make informed choices regarding 'their' baby's well-being after birth, demands exclusion of women psychologically unprepared for surrogacy, and prevents couples from refusing to accept the baby if it is born with a defect.

This response – that surrogacy should be allowed under strict control with uniform national legislation – was the recommendation (subsequently rejected by federal and State health ministers) of the National Bioethics Consultative Committee's 1988 inquiry into surrogacy (National Bioethics Consultative Committee 1990).

More recently, the International Federation of Gynaecology and Obstetrics (FIGO) Committee for the Ethical Aspects of Human Reproduction and Women's Health also recommended against prohibition, proposing instead a series of conditions that would need to be met were surrogacy arrangements for ART to be pursued. These included: that only full surrogacy was acceptable, that all efforts should be made to avoid multiple pregnancy, that the autonomy of the surrogate mother should be respected at all times, that surrogacy arrangements should not be commercial and should only be pursued for 'medical' reasons, that the commissioning couple and surrogate mother should receive separate counselling before any agreement, that all parties should seek independent legal advice, that there should be prior agreement about the disposition of all unused embryos and that surrogacy arrangements should be practised under medical supervision and be approved by the ethics committee of the relevant fertility service (International Federation on Gynaecology and Obstetrics (FIGO) 2008). Although restrictive, guidelines such as these would appear to be one way to limit some of the most obvious problems of surrogate motherhood. It may be, however, that the moral issues arising from surrogacy arrangements are so problematic and so inseparable from the process itself that it should be restricted to all but the most extreme cases.

'Choosing children': ART and genetic determination

The combination of ART and preimplantation genetic diagnosis (PGD) of IVF embryos has long been used to avoid transmission of specific genetic conditions – indeed this possibility has been regarded as one of the most valuable applications of ART. While this application of ART has been readily incorporated into the management of many patients with genetic conditions and has been adopted by many couples wishing to have children but not pass on a genetic condition to their children, it may be ethically problematic because it rests on normative judgments about disability and 'normalcy' and because it is arguably eugenic (Shakespeare 1999).

The use of ART and PGD for other, less widely accepted, purposes, includes the selection of embryos with a specific histocompatibility in order to produce a 'saviour sibling' for a sibling requiring a bone marrow transplant (Pennings, Schots et al 2002), the (largely theoretical) selection of embryos with particular 'positive' characteristics, such as intelligence or eye colour (Robertson 2003), and the selection of embryos with particular disease states, such as congenital deafness and Duchene's muscular dystrophy, in order that they might share the identity, experience, culture and community as their parents. These uses of ART also raise significant ethical questions regarding the proper use of medical technology, the limits of parental autonomy, the use of children as 'commodities', and the persistence of inequity, social stigma and discrimination (Nunes 2006).

Using frozen embryos: research, donation and destruction

Cryopreservation of embryos has greatly diminished the risks of IVF but created a large bank of frozen embryos that are surplus to the reproductive requirements of their biological parents.

In Australia in 2001, 46,835 embryos were frozen and 31,194 were thawed. This resulted in a net increase in the numbers of frozen embryos in storage. Of the thawed embryos, 18,777 were used for IVF. At 31 December 2001, 38 IVF units reported holding a total of 81,627 frozen embryos in storage (Healy 2004). Embryos are now stored for a maximum of 5-10 years. It is difficult to know what to do with them at the end of this time – whether they should be destroyed, donated to other women or kept for research. This has been the subject of great controversy. In Britain in 1995, fertility clinics destroyed over 3000 embryos on one day when legislation prevented them from being kept any longer.

Many couples who have embryos in storage opt for discarding those that are surplus to their needs. Some groups have suggested that these embryos are being destroyed as part of a laboratory-based genocide program, analogous to the free availability of abortion. A more biological-based viewpoint is that these eggs are simply not being allowed to progress to the four-cell stage of development – the biological equivalent of failure of implantation following a normal conception.

Difficult moral problems occur when there is uncertainty and conflict about the 'ownership' of embryos. For example, occasions may arise when a couple who have IVF embryos in storage separate or divorce, and one partner wishes to have the embryos destroyed but the other wishes to have them remain for future use. In such cases it is unclear what the rights and responsibilities of each parent are and who should make decisions regarding the embryos' fate.

For many couples, the thought of discarding surplus embryos seems a waste of an extremely precious gift. The possibility of donating their embryos to other infertile couples appears to many as a caring, communitarian response to the shared burden of infertility. The number of couples who could benefit from embryo-donation is substantial and includes women who are unable to produce eggs of their own because of menopause, surgery or chemotherapy. Older women in particular would be likely to benefit from embryo donation as they have a lower rate of success with other forms of ART and have high miscarriage rates when they do conceive. However, despite the potential for embryo donation programs, little work has been done to establish a framework in which donation can occur.

The other possible use for 'spare' embryos is in medical research. There is great potential for such research and includes the further investigation of infertility, genetic diseases, pre-natal diagnosis, gene therapy, embryology, carcinoma and transplantation. Ethical issues raised by embryo research centre upon the moral status of the embryo – whether it can be regarded as a human, a potential human, a person, or even as genetically distinct tissue (Warnock 1985).

Many of these issues are argued by analogy to the abortion debate. But in contrast to foetuses that are being aborted, embryos do not have the potential for development unless they are transferred to a woman's uterus. In all other ways, the pre-implantation embryo is identical to the embryo *in-vivo*. Both are undeniably members of the species *homo sapiens*, but neither possesses properties such as sentience, cognition and the ability to form social relationships that are required by philosophers who value 'personhood' over 'humanness'. Pre-embryos can also be divided up to make a number of new people (such as occurs when identical twins are formed) (Eberl 2000). On the basis of these considerations, some have argued that IVF embryos have no right to life and may be used for research purposes, whereas others argue that IVF embryos have a sufficient basis for absolute protection.

The most common position, and that advocated by groups such as the Warnock committee in Britain and the Waller committee in Australia, has been that the IVF embryo has a special status due to its properties of humanness and potentiality, but that stringently controlled research may be acceptable. Strict guidelines establish the limits of such research – research should be scientifically valid, should be passed by an institutional ethics committee, should not involve cloning or genetic manipulation, should only be performed on embryos in their early stage of development, and should only use embryos that are superfluous to the reproductive needs of parents.

ART and the changing notion of parenthood

ART creates situations where the biological and social components of fatherhood can be separated and where motherhood can be divided into genetic, gestational and social motherhood. This can create multiple 'parents' with conflicting rights, stakes and obligations. While the majority of women and couples who undergo ART find that they are able to satisfactorily resolve any such conflicts, at times complex questions regarding parental roles, ownership, privacy and confidentiality and the moral status of the embryo can arise. For example, sperm and egg donors' 'right' to anonymity and privacy may conflict with a biological child's 'right' to know their genetic history. These types of questions are extraordinarily difficult to resolve as they embody conflicts between deeply held values – the value accorded to the child and family, and the values attached to liberty, autonomy and privacy. For these reasons culture and community values are likely to play a large role in determining the shape of ART services.

REPRODUCTION AND THE LAW

This part of the chapter examines legal issues surrounding reproduction, including sterilisation, wrongful conception, artificial reproductive technology, artificial insemination, surrogacy and posthumous conception. Issues concerning genetics and abortion are discussed in Chapters 17 and 19, respectively.

Consensual sterilisation and wrongful conception

In Chapter 14 there was a discussion of the limits of consent where Lord Denning's opposition to male sterilisation was quoted from *Bravery v Bravery* [1954] 3 All ER 59. His Lordship believed that a man could not consent to being sterilised because it would have allowed the man to 'have the pleasure of sexual intercourse without shouldering the responsibilities attached to it' and as such the sterilisation procedure was 'plainly injurious to the public interest'. Even the most conservative opponent of birth control would find such comments questionable in modern times and it is clear that competent adults may consent to be sterilised.

Issues then arise as to what the law's response should be to negligently performed sterilisations, which are sometimes referred to as cases of *wrongful conception*. On the one hand, if a person had sought advice from a medical professional and paid for treatment, they should have the right to recover their loss when that service has been negligent. On the other hand, there may be serious policy arguments against allowing a person to get damages for the birth of a child.

The House of Lords considered these issues in *McFarlane v Tayside Health Board* [1999] 4 All ER 961, where the parents of a child sued the health authorities for a negligently performed vasectomy and post-vasectomy testing regime. The House found that the woman could claim for her expenses related to the pregnancy (medical expenses, lost income, pain and suffering) but that the couple could not recover the costs of raising the healthy child. One of the reasons for not allowing damages was that it was not fair, just and reasonable for the parents to receive damages for child-rearing without taking into account the benefits of having a child. As those benefits could not be calculated they could not be offset against the damages. On that basis, allowing the parents to claim would be allowing them to receive more money than they deserved, so it was then better not to provide for any amount in damages.

Another argument raised by the House was that such a claim offended principles of distributive justice. Lord Steyn found that it was morally unacceptable to allow such a claim having regard to the Aristotelian principle of distributive justice which focused on the just distribution of burdens and losses among members of a society. He said:

> It is possible to view the case simply from the perspective of corrective justice. It requires somebody who has harmed another without justification to indemnify the other. On this approach the parents' claim for the cost of bringing up Catherine must succeed. But one may also approach the case from the vantage point of distributive justice. It requires a focus on the just distribution of

burdens and losses among members of a society. If the matter is approached in this way, it may become relevant to ask of the commuters on the Underground the following question: Should the parents of an unwanted but healthy child be able to sue the doctor or hospital for compensation equivalent to the cost of bringing up the child for the years of his or her minority, ie until about 18 years? My Lords, I have not consulted my fellow travellers on the London Underground but I am firmly of the view that an overwhelming number of ordinary men and women would answer the question with an emphatic "No". And the reason for such a response would be an inarticulate premise as to what is morally acceptable and what is not. [The general public] will have in mind that many couples cannot have children and others have the sorrow and burden of looking after a disabled child. The realisation that compensation for financial loss in respect of the upbringing of a child would necessarily have to discriminate between rich and poor would surely appear unseemly to them. It would also worry them that parents may be put in a position of arguing in court that the unwanted child, which they accepted and care for, is more trouble than it is worth. Instinctively, the traveller on the Underground would consider that the law of tort has no business to provide legal remedies consequent up upon the birth of a healthy child, which all of us regard as a valuable and good thing. (at 977)

The decision in *MacFarlane* left open the question of whether damages could be awarded for child-rearing expenses when the child is disabled. In *Parkinson v St James & Seacroft University Hospital NHS Trust* [2001] EWCA Civ 530, damages were awarded for a child born after a negligently performed sterilisation, where the child was born with Autistic Spectrum Disorder. The Court of Appeal found that, according to principles of distributive justice, ordinary people would consider that it would be fair for the law to make an award for the extra expenses associated with the child's disability. The court noted that the disability would need to be 'significant' and stated that 'significant disabilities' could include physical and mental disabilities. The court also found that any disability arising from genetic causes or foreseeable events during pregnancy would suffice to found a claim.

Two years later, the House of Lords refused to allow damages to a disabled woman who had fallen pregnant with a healthy child after a negligently performed sterilisation. The woman argued that the principles of corrective justice would support her claim given it was analogous to the situation in *Parkinson*. A majority of the House refused to depart from *MacFarlane*. They felt that the policy considerations were unchanged and that rearing expenses could not be recovered. However, the majority were persuaded that a conventional fixed sum should be awarded to parents in these cases given their rights had been affected. The sum was set at £15,000.

Australian courts have also struggled with these issues and have come to a different conclusion. In *Cattanach v Melchior* [2003] HCA 38, a husband and wife claimed damages for the costs of raising a healthy child, born after a negligently performed sterilisation. Only one of the woman's tubes was clipped because the doctor mistakenly believed that the other had been removed at an earlier time. The doctor did not inform the parents of the risk of pregnancy. Nor did he offer them tests to ensure that the procedure had been successful. If such tests had been taken they would have revealed the woman's continued fertility. The majority of the High Court found that the claim was an application of the ordinary principles of negligence. The claim was for the economic costs of raising the child, not for harm caused by the child's life. The majority did not accept the policy argument against recognising the claim. For example, McHugh and Gummow JJ stated:

> To suggest that the birth of a child is always a blessing, and that the benefits to be derived there from always outweigh the burdens, denies the first category of damages awarded in this case; it also denies the widespread use of contraception by persons such as the Melchiors to avoid just such an event. The perceived disruption to familial relationships by, for example, the Melchiors' third child later becoming aware of this litigation, is at best speculative. In the absence of any clear and accepted understanding of such matters, the common law should not justify preclusion of recovery on speculation as to possible psychological harm to children. (at [79])

The majority found it was unnecessary to offset the benefits of having a child as the economic costs of raising the child were unrelated to those benefits. McHugh J and Gummow JJ stated:

> The benefits received from the birth of a child are not legally relevant to the head of damage that compensates for the cost of maintaining the child. A different case would be presented if the mother claimed damages for 'loss of enjoyment of life' as the result of raising the child. If such a head of damage were allowable, it would be correct to set off against the claim all the benefits derived from having the child. But the head of damages that is relevant in the present case is the financial damage that the parents will suffer as the result of their legal responsibility to raise the child. The benefits to be enjoyed as a result of having the child are not related to that head of damage. The coal miner, forced to retire because of injury, does not get less damages for loss of earning capacity because he is now free to sit in the sun each day reading his favourite newspaper. Likewise, the award of damages to the parents for their future financial expenditure is not to be reduced by the enjoyment that they will or may obtain from the birth of the child. (at [90])

After the decision was handed down New South Wales, Queensland and South Australia all passed legislation to overturn the effects of the decision: *Civil Liability Act 2002* (NSW), s 71; *Civil Liability Act 2003* (Qld), ss 49A, 49B; *Civil Liability Act 1936* (SA), s 67. The changes effectively prevent damages being awarded for the costs of raising a healthy child. Damages remain recoverable for the special costs of raising a child with a disability, effectively adopting the decision in *MacFarlane* (without the conventional sum accepted in *Rees*).

MacFarlane and *Melchior* both make it clear that a duty is owed to the mother, but the duty of care also extends from the mother to her sexual partner. In *McDonald v Sydney South West Area Health Service* [2005] NSWSC 924, the NSW Supreme Court found that a father was owed a duty of care. The duty of care that was owed to the father was to ensure that his partner was properly treated so that she or the plaintiff did not suffer the financial burden of raising an additional child. The plaintiff tried and failed to raise an informed consent argument as the judge found that the information given to the couple was acceptable

Causation can also be difficult to prove, even where the defendant may have breached the duty of care. In *Moore v Queensland* [2005] QSC 48, the plaintiff was unable to prove that the placement of a Filshie clip in a ampullary section of a fallopian tube rather than on the isthmic section (where it would normally go) had caused the pregnancy. The evidence was supportive of the tube having fully occluded the tube, even though it was in a non-conventional position.

Note that the sterilisation of incompetent adults is discussed in Chapter 13, while the sterilisation of children is discussed in Chapter 20.

Regulation of artificial reproductive technology

There has been much debate in the community in the past 20 years about whether there is any need for legislation in relation to the provision of ART. Following the birth of Louise Brown there were a large number of law reform commission reports and committees of inquiry into whether this area should be regulated by legislation (Bennett 1997). Despite these many inquiries only four States have passed legislation regulating ART (although legislation has not yet been brought into force in New South Wales and Victoria).

Table: Australian ART legislation

Jurisdiction	Legislation
NSW	*Assisted Reproductive Technology Act 2007* (not yet in force)
SA	*Reproductive Technology (Clinical Practices) Act 1988*
Vic	*Infertility Treatment Act 1995* *Assisted Reproductive Treatment Act 2008* (not yet in force)
WA	*Human Reproductive Technology Act 1991*

Other jurisdictions have left the area largely unregulated, although there may be legislation on issues such as the status of children who were conceived using ART or the status of surrogacy arrangements.

In the jurisdictions with no specific legislation there would seem to be a view that, as ART has been developed primarily as a treatment for infertility, it should be regulated in the same manner as other medical treatments. Undoubtedly, the law already has some influence in the way artificial reproductive technology treatments are provided. However, because of the relatively recent development of these technologies, the common law has had little opportunity to develop in this area. There is, therefore, a great deal of uncertainty as to how the law may respond to disputes that arise in relation to ART.

Some people have suggested that ART is qualitatively different from other medical treatments. They argue that ART alleviates infertility by allowing for the birth of another person and thus the interests of a third person are affected by the treatment. They also suggest that in some cases the technology is not used as an alternative form of conception and not for the treatment of infertility.

In the unregulated jurisdictions medical practitioners who practise assisted reproductive technologies have certain guidelines that they should follow, although there is no legal sanction involved in the event of a breach of these Guidelines. The National Health and Medical Research Council (NHMRC) has issued the *Ethical Guidelines on the Use of Assisted Reproductive Technology in Clinical Practice and Research* 2007. In the event that the medical practitioner or clinic is accredited with the Fertility Society of Australia's Reproductive Technology Accreditation Committee, the practitioner must follow that body's Code of Practice in order to retain accreditation (NSW Department of Health 1997).

Jurisdictions with legislative schemes are now examined.

New South Wales

New South Wales passed the *Assisted Reproductive Technology Act 2007* in December 2007 but it has not yet commenced. The Act has the stated objects in s 3:

(a) to prevent the commercialisation of human reproduction, and
(b) to protect the interests of the following persons:
    (i) a person born as a result of ART treatment,
    (ii) a person providing a gamete for use in ART treatment or for research in connection with ART treatment,
    (iii) a woman undergoing ART treatment.

The Act governs treatments, storage of gametes and embryos for use in treatment, and the procurement of gametes from donors. ART is defined to include treatment to procure pregnancy in a woman by means other than sexual intercourse, and includes artificial insemination, in-vitro fertilisation, gamete intrafallopian transfer. ART services have to be undertaken by a registered medical practitioner and ART providers need to be registered. In providing ART services, providers need to make counselling services available to the women seeking treatment.

Another feature of the Act is the creation of a register of donors which can be accessed by adult offspring to learn information about the gamete donor, including the donor's identity: *Assisted Reproductive Technology Act 2007* (NSW), Part 3. Adult children can also learn information about other children born from the donor's gametes, but they can only be given identifying information if the other offspring consents to being identified: s 37. The non-biological parents can also access part of the register to gain non-identifying information about the donor and the donor's offspring: s 38. Identifying information can be accessed by parents but only when it is needed to 'save the life of the child or to prevent serious damage to the child's physical or psychological health and the information cannot reasonably be obtained by the parent in any other way': s 38(1)(c). Finally, the donor can access non-identifying information about their offspring, but can only be given information about the offspring's identity when the adult offspring consents: s 39. The Director-General has power to seek consent from a person on the register if another person makes a request for information: s 40.

Another interesting feature of the Act is that is allows donors to place conditions on their donation. Under s 17 a gamete provider can give a written notice which sets out the provider's wishes in relation to how the gamete (and embryos created from it) should be used and whether the gamete or embryo may be stored, exported or supplied to another ART provider. The consent can be waived or revoked by the donor up until the gamete has been used to create an embryo or has been placed into the body of a woman.

As noted by Stewart (2008), this effectively allows the donor to place restrictions on who may use the gamete, including the possibility of restrictions based on race, colour, sexual identity/preference and religion (as well as a myriad of other conceivable discriminators). Lesbian groups were particularly concerned that it may lead to their being excluded from having access to sperm.

The section is intended to encourage more donation. There have been fears that the disclosure provisions discussed above will discourage donors from providing gametes, so to counter point those risks donors have been given more choice about who may use their gametes. The problem with this reasoning is that discriminatory conditions may offend federal laws such as the *Racial Discrimination Act 1975* (Cth) and the *Sex Discrimination Act 1984* (Cth). Federal laws override State laws if they are found to be inconsistent. While private gifts are not usually subject to these laws, service providers are, and it may be that donors may express limitations which the providers are not permitted to carry out.

South Australia

The South Australian *Reproductive Technology (Clinical Practices) Act 1988* establishes the South Australian Council on Reproductive Technology whose major task is to formulate and implement a Code of Ethical Practice to govern the use of artificial fertilisation procedures and research involving experimentation with human reproductive material. In addition the Council has the following functions:

- to carry out research into the social consequences of reproductive technology;
- to promote research into the causes of human infertility;
- to advise the minister on any questions arising out of, or in relation to, reproductive technology;
- to promote (by the dissemination of information and in other ways) informed public debate on the ethical and social issues that arise from reproductive technology; and
- to collaborate with other bodies carrying out similar functions in Australia.

In carrying out these functions the Council must consider, as a fundamental principle in the formulation of the code of ethical practice, that the welfare of any child to be born as a result of an artificial fertilisation procedure is to be of paramount importance. Medical practitioners and health-care facilities are only permitted to carry out artificial fertilisation procedures if the doctor or the institution is the holder of a licence. Licences are not issued unless the Commission is satisfied that the applicant has adequate staff and facilities. A licence will only be granted where it is necessary to fulfil a genuine and substantial social need.

Victoria

The *Assisted Reproductive Treatment Act 2008* replaces the *Infertility Treatment Act 1995*, but, at the time of writing, its provisions had not yet come into force. The guiding principles of the *Infertility Treatment Act* include (in descending order of importance):

- the welfare and interests of any person born or to be born as a result of a treatment procedure are paramount;
- human life should be preserved and protected;
- the interests of the family should be considered;
- infertile couples should be assisted in fulfilling their desire to have children.

The Act provides both for the licensing of centres and the approval of doctors who carry out assisted reproductive procedures. The responsibility for licensing rests with the *Infertility Treatment Authority*, which is a body set up by the Act. The Authority is responsible for administering the licensing and approval systems for those organisations or individuals wishing to conduct reproductive technology and/or research programs. There is a right of appeal from a decision of the Authority to the Victorian Civil and Administrative Tribunal (VCAT).

A public or private hospital may apply to the Authority for a licence for all or any of the following activities:

- the carrying out of treatment procedures or treatment procedures of a particular kind;
- the forming of an embryo outside the body of a woman;
- the storage of gametes, zygotes or embryos and the undertaking of approved research.

A medical practitioner may only carry out a fertilisation procedure (ie, any ART not including donor insemination) if they are approved to carry out that kind of procedure. The place where the procedure is to be carried out must be licensed.

The 2008 Act aims to regulate the use of ART, to regulate access to information about ART, and to promote research into the incidence, causes and prevention of infertility. The Act also controls surrogacy (see below) and establishes the Victorian Assisted Reproductive Treatment Authority (as a replacement for the Infertility Treatment Authority).

The guiding principles of the Act are set out in s 5. They are:

(a) the welfare and interests of persons born or to be born as a result of treatment procedures are paramount;

(b) at no time should the use of treatment procedures be for the purpose of exploiting, in trade or otherwise—
  (i) the reproductive capabilities of men and women; or
  (ii) children born as a result of treatment procedures;

(c) children born as the result of the use of donated gametes have a right to information about their genetic parents;

(d) the health and wellbeing of persons undergoing treatment procedures must be protected at all times;

(e) persons seeking to undergo treatment procedures must not be discriminated against on the basis of their sexual orientation, marital status, race or religion.

Western Australia

The *Human Reproductive Technology Act 1991* (WA) established the Western Australian Reproductive Technology Council. The major functions of the Council are to advise the Minister and the Commissioner of Health in relation to reproductive technology and licensing matters. The Council gives advice on the issuing of licences. Before issuing the licence, the Commissioner must be satisfied as to the qualifications of the 'person responsible' for the licence. Another function of the Council is to consult widely in the compilation of a code of practice to apply to reproductive technology. The code may provide for such matters as:

- ovarian stimulation undertaken by a licensee;

- artificial fertilisation procedures likely to lead to multiple pregnancies;

- the treatment of any gametes intended for use in an artificial fertilisation procedure, including their genetic modification;

- the circumstances in which, the periods and purposes for which, and the methods by which, an embryo may be kept and maintained outside a human body, or any gametes, egg in the process of fertilisation or embryo may be stored;

- the donation, use, supply, export from the State, posthumous use, or other dealing in or disposal of, gametes, eggs in the process of fertilisation or embryos by licensees;

- the privacy of patients, and the conduct of authorised officers, during the carrying out of any inspection or investigation; and

- the giving or withdrawal of recognition to Institutional Ethics Committees by the Council for the purposes of the Act.

Access

Until recently, the Victorian, South Australian and Western Australian Acts required that a woman who undergoes a treatment procedure must be married and infertile. Marriage was not defined to include a de facto relationship, and therefore only legally married couples could have access to these technologies.

These provisions were first challenged in South Australia in *Pearce v South Australian Health Commission* (1996) 66 SASR 486. The plaintiff, a woman separated from her husband, was denied IVF treatment because she did not meet the marriage criteria set out in the Act. The court held that the provisions in the South Australian Act which prevented the application of procedures except for the benefit of married women were in direct conflict with the *Sex Discrimination Act 1984* (Cth) which prohibits discrimination in the provision of goods and services on the grounds of marital status. Hence, the provisions of the South Australian Act were held to be invalid in so far as they conflicted with the *Sex Discrimination Act*, because of the operation of s 109 of the Commonwealth Constitution.

The second case concerned the Victorian *Infertility Treatment Act* (which will be repealed with the commencement of the *Assisted Reproductive Treatment Act 2008*). In *MW v Royal Women's Hospital* [1997] HREOCA 6, the Human Rights and Equal Opportunity Commission held that denial of ART to three women in heterosexual de facto relationships was contrary to the *Sex Discrimination Act*, despite the fact that the Victorian legislation (at the time) allowed only married women to have access to the technology.

Following the decision in *MW v Royal Women's Hospital* the Victorian Act was amended to extend access to de facto couples. Lesbian couples and single women were still unable to access IVF services in Victoria and so had to travel interstate to access IVF. In 2000, Dr John McBain decided to challenge the con-stitutional validity of the Victorian restrictions. Dr McBain commenced proceedings in the Federal Court seeking a declaration that s 8 of the *Infertility Treatment Act 1995* (Vic) was inconsistent with the Commonwealth *Sex Discrimi-nation Act* (under s 109 of the Constitution a State law that is incompatible with a federal law is invalid to the extent of the inconsistency). Sundberg J held that there was an incompatibility between the two Acts and the Victorian Act was invalid to the extent of the inconsistency (*McBain v Victoria* (2000) 99 FCR 116). The Catholic Bishops and Episcopal Conference (who had been given the right to appear as *amici curiae*) appealed to the High Court of Australia. The Women's Electoral Lobby, the Human Rights and Equal Opportunity Commission and the Australian Family Association were granted leave to intervene. The Attorney-General for the Commonwealth also intervened. Dr McBain was not a party to the appeal. The High Court in a 7-0 result dismissed the application on proced-ural grounds and did not have to address whether there was an incompatibility between the two Acts (*Re McBain; Ex parte Australian Catholic Bishops Conference* (2002) 209 CLR 372). Following the High Court's decision it was reported that the Howard Government might amend the *Sex Discrimination Act* to allow States to pass laws stopping single women from receiving fertility treatment (Banham 2002). However, this was never attempted.

Since the *McBain* case, the attitudes of the States with regulation has changed towards access. Only the South Australian Act still retains a require-ment that the woman be married. In contrast the New South Wales Act does not regulate access at all.

The West Australian Act removed all references to marriage with the *Acts Amendment (Lesbian and Gay Law Reform) Act 2002*, but s 23 of the *Human Reproductive Technology Act 1991* (WA) still requires that the woman seeking treatment be unable to conceive because of medical reasons or needs ART to avoid passing on a genetic abnormality or disease. This would seem to exclude the use of ART for social infertility.

In Victoria, the provisions of the *Infertility Treatment Act* relating to access will be replaced with the *Assisted Reproductive Treatment Act 2008*, when the new Act is brought into force. As stated above, one of the new Act's aims is to eliminate discrimination on the grounds of sexual orientation, marital status, race or religion. Section 10 allows a woman to access treatment, if a doctor believes that she is unable to become pregnant without ART, or she is unlikely to carry a pregnancy without ART, or she is at risk of transmitting a genetic abnormality or disease with ART. Additionally, if a woman is refused access she can ask for the decision to be reviewed by a Patient Review Panel. The panel can decide in favour of treatment if the treatment complies with the guiding principles of the Act (see above), is for a therapeutic goal and is consistent with the best interests of a child who would be born as a result of the treatment (these provisions are particularly relevant to issues of saviour siblings: see below).

Negligence and ART

Cases of negligent ART raise similarly difficult issues as those raised in cases of *wrongful conception* (discussed above) and cases of *wrongful birth* and *wrongful life* (discussed in Chapter 19). As stated above, parents do have the right to sue for negligence in the provision of reproductive health services when those services lead to the birth of a child who is born with a disability.

In *G and M v Armellin* [2008] ACTSC 68, the parents had initially indicated on a form that they would like two embryos implanted but were advised that they could change their minds on the day of the procedure. On the day of the procedure the woman very clearly indicated that she wanted one embryo. However, the embryologist was not in the room at the time, and prepared two embryos in accordance with the written instructions. No conversation was had between the doctor and the embryologist and the embryologist inserted two embryos, in accordance with the form. The parents sued for the costs of the extra child as per *Cattanach v Melchior* [2003] HCA 38.

The Supreme Court found that the doctor had not breached his duty of care as there was nothing to alert the doctor that the patient's verbal instructions were inconsistent with the form she had submitted to the clinic. The woman was also found to have contributed to the mistaken transfer of two embryos by not making it clear to the doctor that she had changed her mind. Bennett J stated that had a breach of duty been found he would have reduced her damages by 35% given the contributory negligence.

The judge also dealt with issues of mitigation and causation, even though there was no need given the findings on breach of duty. It was argued by the doctor that the woman had increased her damages by not having an abortion of the extra child, or by adopting the child once born. The judge found that the failure to seek an abortion was not a failure to mitigate loss. Nor could it be argued that the woman should have adopted the child out. Such actions were considered to be unreasonable by the judge. They could not be expected of the plaintiff as forms of mitigation. Nor did these decisions break the chain of causation between the actions of the doctor and the damage.

Parents may also have rights in negligence and other torts if embryos made with their gametic material are used without their consent. A claim was brought in *NW v Invitro Laboratory Pty Ltd* [2005] WADC 20 by a man who argued that an embryo had been implanted into his ex-wife without his consent. He said that the implantation of the embryo after their divorce gave rise to claims in negligence, breach of a statutory duty and breach of fiduciary duty. The ex-wife and the fertility clinic sought to strike down the man's claim. The Registrar refused to strike out the claim completely finding that they had merit (except for a claim for emotional damages).

While the law recognises the rights of parents to bring action, children who have been born with disabilities due to negligent ART have not been permitted to seek damages for being born. Such claims fall into the category of *wrongful life*. Wrongful life is discussed in more detail in Chapter 20, but it is worth mentioning here the facts of *Waller v James* [2006] HCA 16. In this case the parents had used IVF to conceive a child, but the embryo had not been screened for a genetic condition which the father carried. The condition, AT3 deficiency, is a clotting disorder, and when the child was born he suffered severe brain damage. The child sued on the basis that the IVF process had been conducted negligently, as the parents had never been advised to screen out embryos with the genetic condition. The parents also brought a child for wrongful birth. A majority of the High Court refused to recognise a duty being owed to the child. Crennan J gave judgment for the majority. Her Honour found that a child cannot argue that it would have better off if it had not been born. These issues are discussed in more detail in Chapter 20.

Saviour siblings

'Saviour siblings' were discussed in the first part of the chapter. A saviour sibling is a child born using IVF, screened for genetic abnormalities and tested for histocompatibility, in order for the child's tissue (usually the umbilical cord blood) to be made available to treat an ill sibling. The obvious concern for those who oppose this use of technology is that the child is being created for 'spare parts', a most obvious attempt to use the Kantian dictum against not using another person solely as a means to an end.

The only reported legal case on saviour siblings is *Quintavalle v Human Fertilisation and Embryology Authority* [2003] EWCA Civ 667. In this case Mrs and Mr Hashmi were seeking approval from the Human Fertilisation and Embryology Authority to create a saviour sibling for their son Zain, who suffered from beta-thalassaemia major. A transplant of compatible stem cells from a sibling's umbilical cord or bone marrow would cure his condition. None of his four siblings was a good match, including Zain's younger brother who had been conceived naturally and in the hope of being a match. Mrs Hashmi had also aborted another pregnancy which showed the foetus to have beta-thalassaemia. The HFEA had agreed to issue a licence for the treatment as they saw that this treatment would be of benefit to the future child as it could be screened for beta-thalassaemia. An initial cycle of implantation was unsuccessful and then an interest group sought a review of the HFEA decision to grant the licence. It was argued that the decision of the HFEA was beyond power as under their legislation they could only approve treatments for the purpose of assisting women to carry children. The Court of Appeal found that it was open to HFEA to consider PGD as being of assistance to a woman to carry a child.

'Saviour siblings' have been born in Australia. In 2004, a Tasmanian couple used PGD with tissue typing to have a second child. The child was screened for Hyper-IgM syndrome, a family of genetic conditions that causes immuno-deficiencies due to a high level of immunoglobulin M antibodies. The child was also a matched tissue donor for the couple's existing child, who is affected by the same condition: Biotechnology Online <http://www.biotechnologyonline.gov. au/human/preimplant.html>.

Could a saviour sibling be born in the jurisdictions with legislation? Both the *Reproductive Technology (Clinical Practices) Act 1988* (SA), s 13, and *Human Reproductive Technology Act 1991* (WA), s 23, state that ART cannot be carried out unless it is to help a woman who cannot conceive due to medical reasons, or to help a couple or a woman who need to use ART to avoid passing on a genetic abnormality or disease. In cases like the Hashmis where the future child might get the same disease as the sick sibling, PGD could be employed to screen out the embryos with the genetic disease and, arguably, tissue matching could also occur. But with other diseases that could be treated with matched tissue from a donor there may be no chance of reoccurrence and the only reason for the ART is to check for histo-compatibility. This occurred in the British case of Whittaker where the parents were not granted a licence by the HFEA to create a sibling to treat their child with Diamond-Blackfan anaemia. This condition was not here-ditable and the procedure could not be seen as providing any benefit to the future child (Thomas 2004).

The *Assisted Reproductive Treatment Act 2008* (Vic) arguably has a wider ambit. Section 10, as discussed above, limits the types of situations in which treatment can be provided (much in the same way as the Western Australian legislation). However, there is still the option of then getting approval from the Patient Review Panel, on the grounds that PGD was for a therapeutic goal (treat-ing the sick sibling) and is *consistent* with the best interests of a child who would be born as a result of the treatment procedure. It could be said that the pro-cedure may not be directly *in* the future child's interest (as no therapeutic gain is achieved) but it certainly does not conflict with the child's interests, and in that sense could be said to be *consistent* with it.

The regulation of artificial insemination

Artificial insemination – the procedure of transferring sperm without also trans-ferring an ovum into the reproductive system of a woman (NSW Department of Health 1997) – has been used for many years as a means of promoting conception where the sexual act is not desired (Wallace 2001). When the practice of artificial insemination has been examined by law reform bodies it has generally been regarded as being different from other methods of assisted repro-duction. The New South Wales Law Reform Commission's artificial insemi-nation report in 1986 said:

> Neither the law nor the parliament should presume to regulate the private sexual behaviour of mature competent persons, that the principles of personal freedom and autonomy should apply so far as possible and that if a woman

chooses or a man and woman choose, to achieve pregnancy by AI that is no concern of the State. (NSWLRC 1986)

Meg Wallace has noted the following concerns that may arise in the unregulated jurisdictions:

- there may be no records concerning genetic origin;
- maintenance of medical history;
- control of the spread of disease;
- liability for negligent practice; and
- issues of consent. (Wallace 2001)

Artificial insemination, where donor sperm is introduced into the reproductive system of a woman, is legal at common law. There is legislation in New South Wales, South Australia, Victoria and Western Australia which affects its practice, but other jurisdictions have left the practice unregulated.

In New South Wales artificial insemination is included in the definition of ART and therefore can only be conducted by a registered provider under the supervision of a medical practitioner: *Assisted Reproductive Technology Act 2007*, s 4.

In South Australia artificial insemination services are not regulated if they are provided gratuitously, or provided by a medical practitioner who has submitted his or her name for registration to the minister and has made an undertaking to the minister to observe the code of ethical practice contained in the *Reproductive Technology (Code of Ethical Clinical Practice) Regulations 1995*: *Reproductive Technology (Clinical Practices) Act 1988*, s 13(7).

In Victoria, *Assisted Reproductive Treatment Act 2008*, ss 8-9, do not regulate women who are self-inseminating but, outside of that situation, all artificial insemination needs to be performed by a doctor, who must comply with the Act, including the provisions on checks, limits on treatment, counselling and consent.

In Western Australia, s 6 of the *Human Reproductive Technology Act 1991* requires a person carrying out artificial insemination to have a licence or to be an approved medical practitioner who has provided a written undertaking to agree to follow the code of practice of the Human Reproductive Technology Council.

An interesting case concerned with artificial insemination is *BM v DA* (2007) 39 Fam LR 168. The couple had been in a relationship that had broken down. After their breakup the woman told the man that she was pregnant and that she needed both a blood and semen sample for testing the baby for genetic abnormalities. A child was later born prematurely but at a much later date than would have been possible if she had been pregnant during the relevant time. The man alleged that the woman was not pregnant and had deceived him into providing sperm with which she later impregnated herself. It was later confirmed that the man was the genetic father of the child. The woman sought child maintenance orders from the man but the man argued that, as the child had been artificially inseminated, he was not the legal father. Henderson FM found for the man. As the parties were not married or in a de facto relationship no presumption arose that the man was the parent. Given the child was conceived through artificial insemination, the relevant State law applied to the effect that, as a sperm donor, he was not the legal father of the child.

Frozen embryos and disputes between 'parents'

The legislation in New South Wales, Victoria, South Australia and Western Australia provides that consent must be gained from the donors to store an embryo and it must not be removed from storage unless it is to be used for treatment or research. It does not appear that an appellate court has been asked to consider the issue of access to stored embryos, although in at least one family law case a frozen embryo has been the subject of dispute (see *In Marriage of A Husband and B Wife* (1990) FLC ¶92-126, although the fate of the embryo was not the subject of this report).

There have been a number of cases in the United States where the fate of frozen embryos has been in dispute. A case that was widely reported is *Davis v Davis* 842 SW 2d 588 (1992). The case arose as a divorce action, filed by Junior Davis against his then wife, Mary Sue Davis. The parties had been able to agree upon all the terms of the dissolution, with one unprecedented exception: 'who was to have custody of the seven frozen embryos stored in a Knoxville fertility clinic'. By the time the Tennessee Supreme Court heard the appeal both parties had remarried. Mary Sue Davis no longer wished to utilise the frozen embryos herself, but sought authority to donate them to a childless couple. Junior Davis was 'adamantly opposed' to such donation and preferred to see the embryos discarded. The court said that the essential dispute was 'not where or how or how long to store the pre-embryos, but whether the parties will become parents'. The court held that there were two rights of equal significance in the case, 'the right to procreate and the right to avoid procreation'. The court held that in most cases 'the party wishing to avoid procreation should prevail'.

In *Kass v Kass* 91 NY 2d 554 (1998), a dispute arose between a divorced man and woman over the use of five frozen embryos. The w6man wanted to use the embryos, as they were her only chance of parenthood. The ex-husband refused permission as he did not want to be a father with the woman. The court found against the woman and relied on the agreement signed by the parties with the IVF clinic which said that in the event of a dispute the embryos would not be implanted and could be used for research. Similarly, in *Roman v Roman* 193 SW 3d 40 (2006) and *Litowitz v Litowitz* 48 P 3d 261 (2002), similar contracts which stated that embryos would be discarded on divorce were also upheld.

Sometimes the contract is ambiguous on the issue of what to do on divorce. This happened in both *AZ v BZ* 725 NE 2d 1051 (2000) and *JB v MB* 783 A 2d 707 (2001), where the contracts were considered incomplete or ambiguous on the issue. Both courts refused on public policy grounds to force the unwilling party to be a parent. In *AZ*, the contract stated that on divorce the eggs would be given to the wife. There was a concern that the husband had signed a blank form and left it for his wife to fill, leaving doubt as to whether he had truly consented to the agreement.

Finally, in *In re Marriage of Witten* 672 NW 2d 768 (2003) the court refused to use the contract method and instead required 'contemporaneous mutual consent' which required the signed authorisation of both parties to any transfer, release, disposition or use of the embryos. If both parties could not agree then the status quo would be maintained, which would result in the embryos being stored indefinitely.

In the UK the issue arose in *Evans v Amicus Healthcare Ltd* [2004] 3 All ER 1025, where a woman, Evans, had six embryos created with her partner and frozen before being treated for ovarian tumours. The treatment rendered her infertile. Under the *Human Fertilisation and Embryology Act 1990* (UK) either one party was entitled to withdraw their consent for use of the embryos up to the point of implantation. The couple later separated and the man refused his consent to the eggs being used.

Evans argued that the man's initial consent could not be withdrawn and that her human rights would be violated if she were not permitted to use the embryos. She argued that the man's promises that he would always allow her to use the embryos were binding. The Court of Appeal disagreed. The Act clearly allowed consent to be withdrawn at any time until implantation. To the extent that any of her human rights had been effected this was objectively justifiable.

Two subsequent appeals to the European Court of Human Rights similarly failed (*Evans v United Kingdom* (2006) 43 EHRR 21; *Evans v United Kingdom* (2008) 46 EHRR 34), primarily because the *Human Fertilisation and Embryology Act 1990* (UK) was said to strike a fair balance between the competing rights of the parties.

The general approach from the US and UK decisions appears to be that, as long as one party does not agree to being a parent, then the frozen embryos cannot be implanted. A different approach was taken in *the* Canadian case of *Caufield v Wong* 2005 ABQB 290. In this case a former couple, who were then only friends, agreed to have IVF for the purpose of having children. Twins were born and four excess embryos were stored. A custody battle eventuated regarding the twins. Because of this battle, the man did not wish the further embryos to be implanted. The judge refused to make an order preventing the woman from using the sperm. He adopted property language to describe the control of the embryos:

> The gift was an unqualified gift given in order to conceive children. Mr Wong fully knew that Ms Caufield could use the fertilized embryos when and as she chose. That was implicit in his gift to her. The remaining fertilized embryos remain her property. They are chattels that can be used as she sees fit. Mr Wong is not in a position to control or direct their use in any fashion. They shall be returned to Ms Caufield. Conversely, as they are not Mr Wong's property and he has no legal interest in them, he is not responsible for paying for their storage. That responsibility lies with Ms Caufield who owns the embryos. (at [21])

The problem with this language is that property concepts are not an easy fit for human tissue disputes. Ordinarily the law forbids human tissue from being subject to property rights.

There are no recorded cases in Australia regarding disputes concerning frozen embryos. The only case which touched on these issues is *In Estate of K* (unreported, TASSC, 22 April 1996) where the court was asked to decide whether two embryos, the product of the ova of the widow and semen of the deceased, could be considered as children for the purposes of sharing in the deceased's estate and, if so, whether they were living at the date of death, or whether they become children of the deceased upon their being born alive. Slicer J found that '[t]here was no human in existence at the time of the death of the deceased' and so the frozen embryo could not inherit any property. However, Slicer J did hold that 'a child, being the product of his father's semen and mother's ovum, implanted in the mother's womb subsequent to the death of his father is, upon birth, entitled to a right of inheritance afforded by law'.

Surrogacy and the law

Most jurisdictions have made commercial surrogacy illegal: *Assisted Reproductive Technology Act 2007* (NSW), s 43; *Surrogacy Contracts Act 1993* (Tas); *Infertility Treatment Act 1995* (Vic), s 59; *Assisted Reproductive Treatment Act 2008* (Vic), s 44; *Parentage Act 2004* (ACT), s 41. Some jurisdictions make all surrogacy illegal whether it be commercial or gratuitous: *Surrogate Parenthood Act 1988* (Qld), ss 2-3; *Family Relationships Act 1975* (SA), s 10G. The ACT legislation forbids commercial agreements for surrogacy, but allows payment for costs associated with getting pregnant, having the baby and birth-related expenses. The new Victorian legislation allows the surrogate to be reimbursed for prescribed costs actually incurred: s 44. All the above legislation makes advertising surrogacy services illegal, and contracts for surrogacy are unenforceable.

The new Victorian regulatory model also requires that all surrogacy agreements be reviewed by a Patient Review Panel: s 39. Under s 40(1), the Panel can only approve agreements where they are satisfied that:

- (a) that a doctor has formed an opinion that—
    - (i) in the circumstances, the commissioning parent is unlikely to become pregnant, be able to carry a pregnancy or give birth; or
    - (ii) if the commissioning parent is a woman, the woman is likely to place her life or health, or that of the baby, at risk if she becomes pregnant, carries a pregnancy or gives birth;
- (ab) that the surrogate mother's oocyte will not be used in the conception of the child;
- (ac) that the surrogate mother has previously carried a pregnancy and given birth to a live child;
- (b) that the surrogate mother is at least 25 years of age;
- (c) that the commissioning parent, the surrogate mother and the surrogate mother's partner, if any, have received counselling and legal advice as required under section 43;
- (d) that the parties to the surrogacy arrangement are aware of and understand the personal and legal consequences of the arrangement;
- (e) that the parties to the surrogacy arrangement are prepared for the consequences if the arrangement does not proceed in accordance with the parties' intentions, including—
    - (i) the consequences if the commissioning parent decides not to accept the child once born; and
    - (ii) the consequences if the surrogate mother refuses to relinquish the child to the commissioning parent.
- (f) that the parties to the surrogacy arrangement are able to make informed decisions about proceeding with the arrangement.

Western Australia has passed the *Surrogacy Act 2008*, but its provisions have yet to take effect at the time of writing. When they do commercial surrogacy will be illegal but reasonable expenses related to pregnancy and birth, as well as expert advice, can be paid for: ss 6-8. The Act is very prescriptive about what is a reasonable expense and deals with medical expenses, wages foregone, psychological counselling and insurance. Surrogacy agreements are not binding except to the extent that they require the payment of reasonable expenses: s 7.

At the time of writing there is a great deal of activity in examining the legal regulation of surrogacy. Currently the Standing Committee of Attorneys General, the Australian Health Ministers' Conference, and the Community and Disability Services Ministers' Conference have created a Joint Working Group to examine a proposal for a national harmonised model of surrogacy (2009). The NSW Parliament is currently reviewing altruistic surrogacy laws and the Queensland Parliament has released a report on the decriminalisation of altruistic surrogacy (2008), which recommends (amongst other things) that it be decriminalised and that reasonable expenses be recoverable by birth mothers. The Tasmanian Legislative Council Select Committee (2008) has also issued a report on surrogacy which made a number of recommendations, including a 21-year-old limit for birth mothers, compulsory counselling, a requirement for the birth mother to have had their own child and that parenting issues be determined by the Family Court. The Social Development Committee of the South Australian Parliament has also reviewed surrogacy (2007) and made recommendations that altruistic gestational surrogacy be legalised as long as it is 'medical indicated', meaning necessary, because the intended parents have some medical problem. The report also recommends that any legislation comply with discrimination laws

In most jurisdictions the birth mother and her partner are presumed to be the parents. This necessitates a court order (either from the Family Court or State court) regarding parenting. In the ACT this is regulated through the *Parentage Act 2004* (ACT), Div 2.5, where the Supreme Court can make a declaration regarding parenting in line with a surrogacy agreement. In other jurisdictions the process is left to the courts, on the basis that the surrogacy agreement itself is not enforceable. In a case before the Full Court of the Family Court of Australia (*Re Evelyn* [1998] FamCA 55), the court had to consider a surrogacy arrangement. Mrs S from South Australia offered to carry a baby for her Queensland friends, Mr and Mrs Q. Mrs S, who had three children, was inseminated with Mr Q's sperm and gave birth to the child, Evelyn. The Qs, who had an adopted three-year-old son, took baby Evelyn back to Queensland six days after the birth.

Mrs S was unable to abide by the terms of the agreement and wanted the child returned to her. The trial judge, Jordan J, said that:

> It is apparent that this case is not about parenting capacity. The Court is dealing with four different personalities and quite different parenting styles. However, it is clear that each household has the capacity to provide a very high standard of care for Evelyn. Each of the adults love the child and they are each committed to her welfare for the future. Simply stated, all of the parties wish to have the pleasure of raising this young girl.

The judge gave custody of Evelyn to Mrs S, the birth mother, as this was in the best interests of the child, Evelyn. Jordan J did not recognise the agreement between the parties and ruled in the best interests of the child. He found that each family offered a high standard of care, but the S household, with three stepsiblings, would serve Evelyn's long-term interests best. The Full Court of the Family Court of Australia upheld this decision. The Full Court noted:

> Notwithstanding that the present case concerns a surrogacy situation, it remains clear, as a matter of principle, that there is no presumption in favour of a biological parent nor any presumption in favour of the biological mother where the child is female. In our view, his Honour correctly applied this approach in the present case. While it is true that he ultimately gave the biological mother a preferential position, he did so on the evidence before him in the particular circumstances of this case and after considering the various parenting capacities of the persons concerned, and the opinions of the expert witnesses on the subject.

Since *Evelyn's* case there have been a number of cases before the courts seeking to confirm the parenting arrangements for the child (eg, *PJ v DOCS* [1999] NSWSC 340, *Application of A and B* [2000] NSWSC 640, *Application of D and E* [2000] NSWSC 646 and *In the Matter of an Application Pursuant to the Birth, Deaths and Marriages Registration Act 1997* [2000] ACTSC 39). In some of the cases the courts are asked to exercise their power over adoptions to legalise the arrangement. This occurred in *Application of A and B* [2000] NSWSC 640 and *Application of D and E* [2000] NSWSC 646, where the birth mothers were the sisters of the intended mother and had been artificially inseminated with their brother-in-law's sperm. Bryson J made orders in favour of the adoptions by the intended parents although he expressed his strong sense of dissatisfaction with the use of adopted procedures to institutionalise surrogacy.

One of the more interesting cases is *Re Mark* (2004) 31 Fam LR 162, where two gay men requested that the Family Court declare that they were the parents of a child born through surrogacy (Mark). Mark was conceived in the United States by a surrogate who used a donor egg and the sperm of one of the men (Mr X). The conception had been arranged under a surrogacy agreement made in California. A US court had made an order to name the man and the surrogate mother as the child's parents on the birth certificate. Mark had been cared for by the men since birth.

The couple sought an order from the Family Court that they have joint responsibility for the long-term care, welfare and development of Mark, that he live with him, that they be jointly responsible for his day-to-day care, welfare and development. They also wanted the surrogate to have contact from time to time.

The application was granted. It was found that the word 'parent' used in the *Family Law Act 1975* (Cth) could be applied to Mr X and that, in any case, both men were concerned with the child's care, welfare and development, and had the rights to seek the application. It was in the child's best interests to make the order.

Posthumous conception

There have been a number of cases that have come before the courts where the spouse of a deceased man has sought possession of the deceased's sperm for the purpose of undergoing IVF. The cases are split into two kinds: emergency interlocutory applications to approve the removal of the sperm for storage, and hearings on whether the sperm can be used in an IVF procedure.

The courts have been split on whether they can make interim orders for removal. In *AB v Attorney General (Vic)* (unreported, VSC, 23 July 1998) the wife of a recently deceased man sought semen samples to be removed from his body. In an urgent hearing Gillard J granted the application, although he reserved for further consideration whether the sample could be used for IVF purposes in Victoria. Sometimes the approval is given under the court's power to make orders preserving the status quo before a full hearing: *Re Section 22 of the Human Tissue and Transplant ACT 1982 (WA); Ex parte M* [2008] WASC 276; *S v Minister for Health (WA)* [2008] WASC 262; *Fields v Attorney-General (Vic)* [2004] VSC 547.

But in other cases the courts have stated that they have no power to over the corpse to order the removal of sperm. In the UK, it has been said that there are no powers held by relatives to remove sperm from the deceased: *L v Human Fertilisation and Embryology Authority* [2008] EWHC 2149 (Fam). Similarly, in Queensland *In the matter of Gray* [2000] QSC 390, Chesterman J held that there was no common law power to interfere with a corpse and that to remove part of the body for whatever reason or motive is unlawful. Nor did the *parens* patriae power apply to the dead. Any change to the law would need to be made by parliament. His Honour also said that even if he did have power he would not make the order because:

- the deceased had not consented;
- the court could have no confidence that the applicant's desire was rational as she must have been suffering greatly from grief and shock; and
- the best interests of any child born would not be served by inevitable fatherlessness; the nature of the conception may cause the child embarrassment or more serious emotional problems as it grows up. More significant, because the court can never know in what circumstances the child may be born and brought up, it is impossible to know what is in its best interests.

With respect, the second and third arguments raised by Chesterman J are spurious and insulting to the woman applicant. The fact that the woman was able to engage and instruct legal counsel on an extremely difficult point of law, at a time when most people would be rendered incapable, suggests that this woman was completely rational and in control of herself. The best interests arguments are similarly weak. If it were true that being without a parent meant that you were better off not being born, then we would be happy to euthanise orphans and force pregnant women to have abortions when their partners died. Nor could it be seriously argued that the fact that a child might be teased is a reason for their not being born. Public policy reasoning should be employed by judges but only when it is based on sound reasoning, not discomfort with technology.

Unfortunately, *Gray* was followed in *Baker v Queensland* [2003] QSC 002 where the court held the facts were indistinguishable from those in *Gray*. However, in *In re Denman* [2004] 2 Qd R 595, Atkinson J refused to follow either case and found the court did have an inherent jurisdiction to order the retrieval of sperm. Her Honour stated that:

> As there is no express statutory prohibition on the removal of sperm from a deceased person in Queensland, it appears to me there is a serious question to be tried as to whether or not sperm can or should be removed from a deceased person and used for the purpose of posthumous reproduction.
>
> Both of the judges who decided the cases I have referred to in Queensland referred to what they regarded as strong public policy arguments against such a course. Those arguments are valid, but there are also valid public policy arguments in the other direction. ...
>
> As to the balance of convenience, in my view the balance of convenience clearly requires that the sperm be harvested so that its use can be determined.
>
> If it is not harvested then there is no relief that can be sought by the applicant.
>
> Whereas if it is harvested, then it can be determined by this Court or the Court of Appeal whether or not that sperm, once stored, ought be used.
>
> In my view, giving respect to the decisions in *Gray* and *Baker*, the Court has the inherent jurisdiction to allow behaviour which is not unlawful. (at 597-8)

Denman was followed in a brief judgment in *KJR v Attorney-General (Qld)* [2008] QSC 325.

In New South Wales in 2000 there was a slight variation, in that the man was not yet dead, although he would die very soon (*MAW v Western Area Health Service* (2000) 49 NSWLR 231). The man had suffered severe brain damage in an accident. His life was being maintained by mechanical means and his death was imminent. His wife made an application to the NSW Supreme Court to allow sperm to be removed before he died. O'Keefe J found that the jurisdiction of the Supreme Court did not extend to giving permission on behalf of a comatose and dying man for the removal of sperm as it could not be said to be for his welfare or protection. He echoed the comments made by Chesterman J regarding the emotional state of the woman and said it was likely that she might change her mind. O'Keeffe J also said that:

> Such a child would never have the prospect of knowing its father. Such a child would come to recognise that he or she was not sought to be procreated during the life of the father. Such a child would not have rights of succession under the law of New South Wales nor rights under the Compensation to Relatives Act arising out of the circumstances giving rise to the death of his or her father. Furthermore, should the circumstances of the child's conception come to be known there would be people in the community who would tend to regard the child as different – not a happy situation, especially for a child.
>
> In the circumstances of the present case I cannot conclude that such a child's best interests would be served by being brought into existence in the manner, at the time and in the circumstances contemplated as possible by the plaintiff. (at [43]-[44])

In Victoria, the situation on sperm removal has been complicated by the operation of the *Infertility Treatment Act 1995*. Section 43 prohibits the insemination of sperm to make a child from a person once they are deceased, unless they gave their consent. Nevertheless, approvals have been given on an inter-locutory basis. This has occurred in *AB v Attorney General (Vic)* (see above) and in *Fields v Attorney-General (Vic)* [2004] VSC 547, where an application was brought by the parents of the deceased. The deceased was aged 23 years and had died in a car accident. His wife was also involved in the accident and in inten-sive care. The couple had been attending a fertility treatment program at the Royal Women's Hospital. Coldrey J assumed that he could make a decision based on what had happened in *AB v Attorney General (Vic)* and left the question of whether the sperm could be issued 'for another day'. A similar approach was taken in *Y v Austin Health* [2005] VSC 427, where the deceased had died during the hearing from sepsis brought on by pneumococcal pneumonia. Habersberger J was critical of the comments made by Chesterman J and O'Keefe J regarding the emotional states of plaintiffs in these cases and said if such applications were not made then they would forever be denied the chance to make a decision.

The issue of whether the sperm could be used in Victoria was considered in *AB v Attorney-General* [2005] VSC 180, which concerned the sperm retrieved in *AB v Attorney General (Vic)*, discussed above. The judge found that s 43 of the *Infertility Treatment Act 1995* (Vic) prevented an order from being made to allow the sperm to be used in Victoria, without the consent of the deceased. The section had been amended by parliament but only to allow frozen embryos (made from a person who had subsequently died) to be implanted. The parliamentary change had occurred in response to the plight of Joanne Bandel-Caccamo, who became pregnant to her husband using IVF. Tragically, she miscarried the child after her husband died from cancer and she wanted to use the remaining embryos to become pregnant again. The Victorian parliament amended the law in 2001 to let this occur but they left the prohibition on the use of gametes from a deceased person. Given that s 43 clearly prohibited the use of the sperm, Hargrave J refused to make an order. However, he indicated that the woman could make an application to have the sperm taken to NSW. She later made an application to the ITA which refused to release the sperm. She had that decision reviewed by VCAT who agreed that the sperm could be taken to NSW for use: *YZ v Infertility Treatment Authority (General)* [2005] VCAT 2655.

As stated above, the *Infertility Treatment Act 1995* is being repealed by the *Assisted Reproductive Treatment Act 2008*. The new Act expressly deals with post-humous conception. Section 46 allows an ART provider to use the deceased's gametes and embryos made from the deceased gametes when the procedure is carried out on the deceased partner, or (if the deceased is a woman) a surrogate. However, the deceased must have given written consent, and the procedure must be approved of by the Patient Review Panel, which is required under s 47 to take into account the possible impact on the future child. Given these limi-tations it is unlikely that the majority of plaintiffs will benefit from the Act. In all the applications above, the deceased had not consented (or refused).

Arguably, a better approach would be to borrow from consent provisions used in relation to the post-mortem use of other human tissue (discussed in Chapter 25), namely that the tissue can be used when the deceased consented, or where the senior available next of kin consents.

In any event, even when there are schemes for written consent, problems remain. In *Mrs U v Centre for Reproductive Medicine* [2002] EWCA Civ 565, a woman argued that her husband had been unduly influenced into withdrawing his consent to the use of his sperm after death. The husband had agreed to it being made available but, after speaking with a senior nurse, changed his mind. The Court of Appeal could find no evidence of undue influence and alteration was upheld.

References

Anderson, E (1990) 'Is women's labour a commodity?' *Philosophy and Public Affairs* **19**(1): 71-92.

Antinori, S, C Versaci et al (1993) 'Oocyte donation in menopausal women'. *Human Reprod* **8**: 1487-90.

Belkin, L (1997) Sophia's choice. *Good Weekend Dec 6*: 68-73.

Bennett, B (1997) *Law and Medicine*. Sydney, LBC Information Services.

Ber, R (2000) 'Ethical issues in gestational surrogacy'. *Theor Med Bioeth* **21**(2): 153-69.

Blackford, R (2006) 'Sinning against nature: the theory of background conditions'. *J Med Ethics* **32**(11): 629-34.

Butler, J (1990) *Gender Trouble. Feminism and the subversion of identity*. New York, Routledge.

Charlesworth, M (1993) *Bioethics in a liberal society*. Cambridge, Cambridge University Press.

Collett, C (2002) 'Falling on deaf ears?', 15 May 2008, <http://www.bmj.com/cgi/eletters/325/7367/771.

Dodds, S and K Jones (1989) 'Surrogacy and autonomy'. *Bioethics* **3**: 13.

Dowd, H (1997) 'Should lesbians receive donor sperm? Debate goes beyond the law'. *Aust Med* **May 5**: 8-9.

Eberl, T (2000) 'The beginning of personhood: a Thomistic biological analysis'. *Bioethics* **14**(2): 134-57.

Edwards, R, P Steptoe et al (1980) 'Establishing full-term human pregnancies using cleaving embryos grown in vitro'. *Br J Obstet Gynaecol* **87**: 737-56.

Fader, S (1993) *Sperm banking: a reproductive resource*. California Cryobank Inc.

Fishman, JR (2004) 'Manufacturing desire: the commodification of female sexual dysfunction'. *Soc Stud Sci* **34**(2): 187-218.

Foote, R (2002) 'The history of artificial insemination: Selected notes and notables'. *J Anim Sci* **80**: 1-10.

Foucault, M (1990) *The history of sexuality Vols 1-3*. New York, Vintage.

Gurmankin, AD, AL Caplan et al (2005) 'Screening practices and beliefs of assisted reproductive technology programs'. *Fertil Steril* **83**(1): 61-7.

Healy, J (2004) *Issues in Society Vol 29: IVF and Surrogacy*. Thirroul, The Spinney Press.

Hordern, AJ and AF Street (2007) 'Communicating about patient sexuality and intimacy after cancer: mismatched expectations and unmet needs'. *Med J Aust* **186**(5): 224-7.

Hordern, AJ and AF Street (2007) 'Constructions of sexuality and intimacy after cancer: patient and health professional perspectives'. *Soc Sci Med* **64**(8): 1704-18.

International Federation on Gynaecology and Obstetrics (FIGO) (2008) 'FIGO Committee Report: Surrogacy'. *Int J Gynaecol Obstet* **102**(3): 312-13.

Jansen, R (1995) 'Older ovaries: ageing and reproduction'. *Med J Aust* **162**: 623-4.

Jansen, R (1997) 'Reproductive medicine and the social state of childlessness'. *Med J Aust* **167**: 321-3.

Joint Working Party, Standing Committee of Attorney's General, Australian Health Ministers' Conference, Community and Disability Services Ministers' Conference. (2009) *A Proposal for National Model to Harmonise Regulation of Surrogacy*.

Keeping, J (1997) 'Should lesbians receive donor sperm? Clinical, not personal, guidelines'. *Aust Med* **May 5**: 8-9.

Kelly, F (2005) In search of a father: Sperm donors, lesbian-headed families, and the *Re Patrick* case. *Sperm Wars*. H Jones and M Kirkman. Sydney, ABC Books.

Kirkman, M (2005) Going home and forgetting about it: donor insemination and the secrecy debate. *Sperm wars*. H Jones and M Kirkman. Sydney, ABC Books.

Komesaroff, PA (2008) *Experiments in Love and Death: Medicine, Postmodernism, Microethics and the Body*. Melbourne, Melbourne University Press.

Kovacs, G (1993) 'The likelihood of pregnancy with IVF and GIFT in Australia and New Zealand'. *Med J Aust* **158**: 805-7.

Leiblum, S, M Palmer et al (1995) 'Non-traditional mothers: single heterosexual/lesbian women and lesbian couples electing motherhood via donor insemination'. *J Psychosom Obstet Gynaecol* **16**(11-20).

Merleau-Ponty, M (1964) *Signs*. Evanston, North-Western University Press.

Mies, M (1987) Do we need all this? A call against genetic engineering and reproductive technology. *Made to order: the Myth of Reproductive and Genetic Progress*. P Spallone and D Steinberg. New York, Oxford University Press.

Mischewski, A (2001) Making your hair stand on end: the meaning of sperm. *Sperm Wars*. H Jones and M Kirkman. Sydney, ABC books.

Mishell, D (2001) Infertility. *Comprehensive Gynaecology*. M Stenchever, W Droegemuller, A Herbst and et al. St Louis, Mosby: 1169-215.

National Bioethics Consultative Committee (1990) *Discussion paper on surrogacy: 2 – Implementation*. Canberra, National Bioethics Consultative Committee.

Nisker, J, F Baylis et al (2006) 'Choice in fertility preservation in girls and adolescent women with cancer'. *Cancer* **107**(7 Suppl): 1686-9.

Nunes, R (2006) 'Deafness, genetics and dysgenics'. *Med Health Care Philos* **9**(1): 25-31.

Overall, C (1983) *Ethics and Human Reproduction. London: Allen and Unwin*. London, Allen and Unwin.

Queensland Parliament (2008) *Investigation into Altruistic Surrogacy* Committee Report

Pearn, J (1997) 'Gatekeeping and assisted reproductive technology'. *Med J Aust* **167**: 318-20.

Pennings, G, R Schots et al (2002) 'Ethical considerations on preimplantation genetic diagnosis for HLA typing to match a future child as a donor of haematopoietic stem cells to a sibling'. *Hum Reprod* **17**(3): 534-8.

Peterson, MM (2005) 'Assisted reproductive technologies and equity of access issues'. *J Med Ethics* **31**(5): 280-5.

Prokopijevic, M (1990) 'Surrogate motherhood'. *Journal of Applied Philosophy* **7**(2): 169-81.

Reame, N and P Parker (1990) 'Surrogate pregnancy: clinical features of forty-four cases'. *Am Jn Obstet Gynaecol* **162**: 1222.

Robertson, JA (2003) 'Extending preimplantation genetic diagnosis: the ethical debate. Ethical issues in new uses of preimplantation genetic diagnosis'. *Hum Reprod* **18**(3): 465-71.

Sauer, MV and SM Kavic (2006) 'Oocyte and embryo donation 2006: reviewing two decades of innovation and controversy'. *Reprod Biomed Online* **12**(2): 153-62.

Savulescu, J (2000) 'Education and debate: deaf lesbians, "designer disability", and the future of medicine'. *BMJ* **325**: 771-3.

Schuklenk, U and M Ristow (1996) 'The ethics of research into the cause(s) of homo-sexuality'. *J Homosex* **31**(3): 5-30.

Legislative Council Tasmanian Parliament (2008) Select Committee Report on Surrogacy.

Shakespeare, T (1999) 'Losing the plot? Medical and activist discourses of contemporary genetics and disability'. *Sociol Health Illness* **21**: 669-88.

Shanner, L and J Nisker (2001) 'Bioethics for clinicians: 26. Assisted reproductive tech-nologies'. *CMAJ* **164**(11): 1589-94.

Singer, P (1985) 'Technology and procreation: How far should we go?' *Technology Review* **Feb/ Mar**: 23-30.

Skattebol, J (2005) Difference, deafness and donor choice. *Sperm Wars*. H. Jones and M. Kirkman. Sydney, ABC Books.

Soble, AE (2002) *The Philosophy of Sex* (4th ed). Lanham Md, Rowman and Littlefield.

Social Development Committee, South Australian Parliament (2007) *Inquiry Into Gestational Surrogacy*.

Steinbock, B (2004) 'Payment for egg donation and surrogacy'. *Mt Sinai J Med* **71**(4): 255-65.

Stewart, C (2008) 'NSW Passes Assisted Reproductive Technology Act 2007' *Journal of Bioethical Inquiry* **5**: 9

Tasker, F and S Golombok (1995) 'Adults raised as children in lesbian families'. *Am J Orthopsychiatry* **65**: 203-15.

Thomas, C (2004) 'Pre-implantation Testing and the Protection of the "Saviour Sibling".' **5** *Deakin Law Review*. <http://www.austlii.edu.au/au/journals/DeakinLRev/2004/5.html>.

Vandervort, L (2006) 'Reproductive choice: screening policy and access to the means of reproduction'. *Hum Rights Q* **28**(2): 438-64.

Wallace, M (2001) *Health care and the law*. Sydney, Lawbook Co.

Warnock, M (1985) *A question of life: the Warnock report on human fertilisation and embryology*. Oxford, Basil Blackwell.

Yarhouse, M (2004) 'Homosexuality, ethics and identity synthesis'. *Christ Bioeth* **10**(2-3): 239-57.

CHAPTER 19

ABORTION

Case 1

CD is a 25-year-old woman who had been diagnosed with severe post-natal depression after her first child, and was still on anti-depressant tablets. The child had been born prematurely and continued to have some mild cerebral palsy due to the premature birth. CD now lived with her husband and the first child.

The present pregnancy was unplanned, and she had taken antibiotics, had a chest X-ray and had not taken any folic acid in early pregnancy. She stated that she believed that the combination of all of these things meant that she couldn't go through with this pregnancy. She stated that she would be unable to cope if anything went wrong with the next pregnancy, and felt that these factors meant that something could go wrong.

When she presented to her doctor, at 12 weeks' gestation, her doctor reassured her that the risk from these issues was minimal; however, the woman maintained that these were the reasons why she wished to have an abortion. She was referred for an abortion on the ground that the pregnancy was a potential harm to her psychological health.

Case 2

VL is a 20-year-old student nurse. She is strongly opposed to abortion for religious reasons. For her surgical experience she is assigned to work in the operating theatre of a local hospital. To her surprise, she finds that she is expected to assist with a series of terminations of pregnancies. She refuses to do so and asks to be transferred to a different theatre list.

The term 'abortion' refers to the termination of a pregnancy. In medical terminology it may be used to refer to either miscarriage or the artificial termination of pregnancies, but in everyday use it tends to be used only for artificial terminations. It is this sense of the word that we will be using in the rest of this chapter. Abortion is sometimes classified according to the time of pregnancy at which it occurs – the term 'first trimester' referring to the first three months of pregnancy, 'second trimester' to the second three months. 'Early abortion' occurs at less than 20 weeks' gestation, 'late abortion' occurs at greater than 20 weeks' gestation.

Abortion is common. In the world, there are about 210 million conceptions per year. Approximately one in five of these end in abortion (half of these abortions done illegally), and 16% end in unwanted or mistimed birth. Overall, about one third of pregnancies are unintended. Each year 66,500 maternal deaths are attributable to unsafe abortion (Brown 2007).

Abortion is also common within Australia, and is used by fertile women of all age groups. Women in their 20s account for most abortions that are performed. About one in five Australian teenage girls will become pregnant between the ages of 15 and 19, and about half will have an abortion (Adelson, Frommer et al 1990; Lancaster 1996). In total, an estimated 84,460 abortions were performed in Australia in 2003 (Chan and Sage 2005).

Abortion has touched most people's lives in some way – many have had abortions and most would know women who have had abortions. Given the frequency of abortion, and the undoubted need for a way to manage unplanned pregnancy, many people's position about abortion could probably best be termed 'pro-choice pragmatism' (Furedi 2002). But to many others, issues around abortion continue to be deeply problematic, either because abortion inevitably involves the death of the foetus, or because regulation of abortion represents a direct intrusion by mechanisms of the state into women's private decisions about their own bodies.

The Hippocratic Oath maintained that 'I will not give to a woman a pessary to cause abortion', but even at the time this was written there were different practices and attitudes to abortion, and since that time the complex issues surrounding abortion have always been the subject of controversy. Health professionals need to be aware of the issues involved in the abortion debate in order to develop their own viewpoints and understand those of others. In this chapter we will review some community attitudes towards abortion, and compare these with some philosophical and religious positions. In this we are particularly indebted to the book *Life's Dominion – an argument about abortion and euthanasia* by Ronald Dworkin (Dworkin 1993). Before doing so, however, it is important to consider how questions of *moral status* are relevant to the abortion debate and also to other areas of bioethics.

Moral status

Ethics is concerned primarily with how we should act or how we should live. Implicit in this understanding of ethics is the need to define the 'moral community', ie, those to whom we owe moral obligations and those we do not, and those who have moral rights or claims, and those who do not. All ethical theories make (often unstated) assumptions about who, or what, counts ethically, and about human nature. These assumptions, or arguments, are generally framed in terms of statements about what entities have moral status (and so deserving of the protection afforded by moral norms, principles, virtues, rules and rights). Most moral theories have excluded non-human animals from moral consideration. And in contemporary bioethics, debates about brain death, post-coma unresponsiveness, abortion, research involving non-human animals and stem-cell research turn on arguments about the moral status of embryos, foetuses, babies, the disabled, and those with permanent cognitive impairment or loss of consciousness.

There are a number of different theories of moral status. Different theories accord moral status on the basis of biological properties consistent with belonging to the species (Homo sapiens), cognition, sentience (consciousness and the capacity to feel pain and pleasure), moral agency (the capacity to make moral judgments about the rightness or wrongness of behaviour and act morally) and relationships that establish roles and obligations, such as the patient-physician relationship (Beauchamp and Childress 2009). Each of these theories provides an incomplete and contestable account of the complexities of moral communities. In the context of the abortion debate, the status that one attributes to embryos, foetuses and babies determines a large part of how one positions one's self in relation to the ethics of abortion (Warren 1973; Tooley 1983; Steinbock 1992).

The conservative position

The abortion debate is sometimes characterised as a polarisation between two basic rights – the foetus's right to life and a woman's right to terminate her own pregnancies. When seen in this way, our ability to resolve this conflict appears entirely hopeless. But while much of the academic and public debate about abortion is couched in these terms, few people actually hold such one-sided views.

The conservative position about abortion states that the foetus is a human being and thus possesses a right to life. And if one denies this right to life one is committing murder, which is by definition morally wrong. Conservatives vary about the consequences that they believe should follow from such reasoning, some believing that the force of the law should be used to prevent abortions, whereas others believe that other rights – such as the right to be free of government interference – should at times take precedence over considerations of foetal rights.

If one examines the conservative position in more detail it becomes apparent that, although many people accord the foetus with human rights, for many people these rights differ from those of other humans. Many moderate conservatives who hold that foetuses have basic human rights make exceptions in which abortion may at times be justified. For example, they may believe that abortion is morally permissible to end a pregnancy that began in rape, or where the foetus has either a potentially lethal or major physical malformation. But this is not totally consistent with a foetus having the same rights as any other individual, for why should a foetus be made to pay with its life for the wrong-doing of someone else or for having a disability or illness that in a child or adult would not constitute grounds for sanctioned killing? Another exception to the prohibition of abortion is sometimes made when the foetus is in some way a risk to the mother's life. This may be justified by recourse to the principle of double effect; but the principle of double effect could equally justify saving the foetus's life at the expense of the mother's – a state of affairs that is not generally advocated.

Such exceptions to the absolute censure upon abortion suggest that, even in the conservative view, the sacred life of the foetus is seen as slightly different from that of other humans.

The liberal position

The extreme liberal view is often expressed as 'a woman's right to choose' – meaning that a woman should have the right to abortion at any stage of pregnancy regardless of any consideration of the moral status of the foetus. However, a more common variant of a liberal position on abortion insists that abortion is always a grave moral decision and so is not justifiable for trivial or frivolous reasons. It is important to add that liberal perspectives also argue that abortions are rarely sought for 'frivolous reasons' (which the authors accept to be true) and that the pregnant woman is in the best position to make a determination on the adequacy of the reasons for her decision. Many people who hold liberal views believe that abortion may be morally permissible or even demanded in situations such as rape, incest or the presence of severe congenital disease. Likewise, many would consider that a woman's concern for her own interests might sometimes be considered to be an adequate justification for abortion if the consequences of childbirth would be permanent and grave for her or her family's life. Finally, many liberals would believe that the state has no business interfering even to prevent morally impermissible actions, because the question of whether an abortion is morally justifiable is ultimately up to the woman concerned (Dworkin 1993). The pro-abortion British gynaecologist Peter Huntingford has put it this way: 'The fetus has a right to life. But only the mother can protect that right' (Kenny 2002).

Seen in this way, the liberal position about abortion is not as far removed from the conservative view as might first be thought. Both view decisions about abortion as grave moral choices and both admit to certain situations in which abortion may be permissible. The major difference is one of emphasis, not of underlying principles.

Dworkin suggests that these differences are due to differences in one's views about the sources of the 'sacredness' of human life. He believes that the fundamental difference between the conservative and liberal views lies in their differing emphases placed on the natural or god-given investment in the development of human beings, as compared to the human investment in human development. The conservative position can be seen in this way to emphasise the intrinsic value of a life, which is not a value that changes across the life span but which may nevertheless be weighed and balanced against the value of other lives if necessary. The liberal position places more emphasis on the human investment in a life which must also be balanced against the human investment in the lives of the mother and her family (Dworkin 1993).

Late abortion

The idea that moral rights vary with development is common in both religious and non-religious arguments about abortion. Most of us accept a newborn baby as a person with the same rights to life as any other human. No one accepts an individual ovum and the spermatozoa that will fertilise it as an individual. Somewhere in between these points a 'person' develops.

Defining when this occurs leads to a type of problem known as a 'notch' problem. Notch problems occur when a tiny difference in one attribute results in a huge difference in how a person is treated. This term is used in economics, for example, where a one day difference in age can result in a person becoming eligible for a pension or other benefit where previously they were not. The development of a human being occurs as a continuum, not as a series of discrete events, so defining a particular point as the moment of most moral significance is likely to be problematic. This does not necessarily mean, however, that there is no moral difference between the two ends of the process – the ovum and the adult.

One cut-off point that has been proposed for deciding whether an abortion should be morally acceptable is that of 'Viability' – the capacity for the foetus to survive outside the uterus. This is attractive because it allows us to be consistent – we do all that we can to support the life of foetuses or infants that are viable, and we allow abortion of those who are not.

Unfortunately, viability has its own notch problem. The 'EPICURE' study looked at all births less than 26 weeks' gestation in England and Ireland in the final nine months of 1995. Eleven per cent of foetuses between 20 and 22 weeks' gestation were reported to show signs of life at birth. This rose to 39% at 23 weeks, and 67% at 25 weeks. Of those reported to show signs of life, 92% of those less than 23 weeks' gestation died in the delivery room whereas only 8% of those at 25 weeks' gestation did (Costeloe, Hennessy et al 2000). This study suggested that somewhere between 22 weeks' and 25 weeks' gestation, many infants become viable for life outside the womb in the neonatal intensive care setting. Whether a particular infant is viable or not depends on individual factors, not just the age of gestation. These figures will also change as technology improves. Indeed the mortality for these babies has roughly halved over the past 20 years (Riley, Roth et al 2008). The fact that it is not possible to draw a clear, generalisable and fixed dividing line between viable and non-viable foetuses is a valuable reminder that such points in biology and medicine are often somewhat arbitrary. But just because the lines between different states or categories are unclear does not mean that these categories do not exist or are not important. The fact that we cannot draw a clear and objective point at which day ends and night begins does not mean that day and night do not exist. In other words, we can recognise the arbitrary nature of claims about viability, use these distinctions because they have some utility, but also acknowledge that because they are normative they will always be open to different interpretations and contestation.

This uncertainty has led some authors to maintain that viability is irrelevant to the moral question of abortion. We (the authors) do not agree with this. If a foetus is considered viable, then (if the parents consider it appropriate), huge effort and expense are spent attempting to give it the best possible outcome. If, in the adjacent operating theatre, a foetus of the same characteristics is allowed to die, or is killed in the process of abortion, then this is simply inconsistent. We believe therefore that, while viability is dependent on technology and access to that technology, the time of viability retains clinical, social and moral significance, and provides one important place at which discourse and decision-making about abortion (or resuscitation) changes (Langerak 1979).

This significance has been emphasised by recent legal and ethical debate about late (>20 week) and 'partial birth' abortion. Some Australian States such as Victoria allow abortion in late pregnancy. In 2005, Victoria recorded 309 perinatal deaths (ie, deaths after 20 weeks' gestation) as a result of termination of pregnancies. Of these terminations, 129 were for congenital abnormalities, and 160 for psychosocial indications. This included the deaths of five foetuses greater than 27 weeks' gestation (four for psychosocial and one for congenital reasons) (Consultative Council on Obstetric and Paediatric Mortality and Morbidity 2007).

Late abortions can occur either through the medical induction of labour or through dilatation of the cervix followed by mechanical destruction of the foetus and evacuation of foetal parts. One form of late abortion known as either 'dilatation and extraction' or 'partial birth abortion' involves the foetus being partly delivered in the breech position and then the head being delivered after destruction of the intracranial contents. This form of abortion has been specifically made illegal in the United States after enormous and divisive political debate.

Destruction of the foetus may also be called 'foeticide'. A striking feature of the Victorian data for late abortions is that the majority (particularly of the psychosocial abortions) were classified as still birth rather than neonatal death. This implies that foeticide is part of most late abortions in Victoria.

Another striking feature of the Victorian data is that the majority of women having late abortions came from other Australian States or from overseas (Consultative Council on Obstetric and Paediatric Mortality and Morbidity 2007). Victoria has the only free-standing abortion clinic in Australia that undertakes late abortions, and other States 'effectively export these women for care' (de Crespiny and Savulescu 2008).

It is hard to know what to make of the medical literature on late abortion and foeticide. Some obstetricians involved in this area justify late abortion on the grounds that withdrawal of life-support in a neonatal ICU is little different from withdrawal of maternal support in the womb.

> There is an unreasonable contrast between obstetric and neonatal management after 20 weeks duration Paediatricians recommend that the parents of a normal infant born 24-26 weeks should decide whether or not their baby is treated, even if there is some chance of survival. Yet at the same gestation, late abortion is likely to be refused. Paediatricians will also discuss with the family the option of withdrawing intensive care in some cases where an older baby is severely affected with abnormalities but is still capable of surviving. It seems the fetus *inside* a woman's body has a higher moral status than a newborn infant of the same gestation *outside* a woman's body.
>
> The uterus is indeed the best intensive care unit; fetuses with the most terrible abnormalities usually do not die before birth. Denying abortion may only delay the inevitable and extend the suffering of the family. (de Crespiny and Savulescu 2008)

Yet this argument is not entirely convincing. Articles in favour of late-term abortion tend to play down the fact that most such abortions (in Victoria at least) are done for psychosocial reasons (Ellwood 2005). They also play down the active role that doctors and families have in the foetus's death, compared with the passive role that happens in intensive care units.

Those involved in late-term abortion believe that painless foeticide before late abortion can be justified as decreasing pain and suffering to the foetus that would occur through birth and death soon after (Dommergues, Cahen et al 2003). But the principle of double effect does not justify painless infanticide. Since the only difference between a late term foetus and a premature baby is that one is in the womb and one is outside it, the question arises as to whether this factor could justify any moral differences between the two.

We believe that there are some circumstances in which late abortion can be justified, and abortion must be readily available for such cases. The question then becomes how one can define and justify the circumstances in which late abortion should be available. In general terms there are four main alternatives: where continuation of the pregnancy would result in the death of the mother (and therefore the foetus) or a high probability of threat to her life; where the foetus has an abnormality that is inconsistent with life outside the uterus or has a severe abnormality; where late abortion is sought for 'good reasons'; or in any situation where a woman seeks a late abortion. Each of these conditions assumes that the foetus is attributed less moral status than either an adult or a newborn child and that birth has moral, as well as legal, symbolic, cultural and psycho-logical, significance. But each of these alternatives also raises other difficulties. If we accept late abortion in situations where there is a threat to the woman's life, the question then arises as to how serious must this threat be, what type of threat must it be (would it include psychological threat) and why would the possibility of maternal harm not also justify (or require) delivery, rather than abortion. If we accept late abortion for foetal malformation – how would we define a major malformation and why would such criteria not simply be a form of discrimination or eugenics (Savulescu 2001)? If we accept late abortion only in situations where there is adequate justification – what would we define as a 'good' or sufficient reason and what moral authority would allow us to restrict a woman's autonomy or judge her reasons (Woodrow 2003)? The final alternative, that late abortion should be available on request, offends against the idea that the foetus has (at least some) moral value.

For the most part, late abortion in situations where there is a genuine threat to the life and/or well-being of the mother, or in cases of serious foetal anoma-lies incompatible with life, appears to be more broadly accepted than other situations in which questions of late abortion arise (Epner, Jonas et al 1998; Gross 2002). Reassuringly, such situations are uncommon, as are other situations in which requests for late abortion arise. Given the moral importance of late abortion, and the different perspectives regarding justifications for late abortion, departments of obstetrics and gynaecology that perform late abortions have generally established clear processes and authority for decision-making (often called Termination Review Committees). These processes are not unproblematic and often make assumptions regarding the status and rights of the pregnant woman and foetus (Woodrow 2003). Regardless of the structures and processes adopted, it is important though that they be prompt and sensitive, as delaying such decisions only increases their moral difficulty (de Crespiny and Savulescu 2008).

Feminist perspectives

In an influential essay published in 1971, Judith Jarvis Thompson took quite a different approach to the abortion debate. In this essay she set out to examine whether abortions might still be morally admissible even if we accept full moral status for both mother and foetus. She used an argument that was based on a clever analogy (that some critics have found to be deeply objectionable!) (Jarvis Thompson 1971).

She asked the reader to imagine a situation in which they woke up one day after a deep sleep to find that they had been kidnapped by a group of music lovers who had grafted a famous violinist onto their back. This unlikely situation had occurred because the violinist was suffering from a rare disease that could only be alleviated by attachment to the reader's bloodstream and kidneys. If the violinist was unattached again, he would certainly die.

Thompson uses this fictional situation to argue that, while it would be commendable to remain grafted to the violinist, there is no real obligation to do so. No one could demand that you continue in this way, and any law which insisted on it would clearly be unjust. This is a situation in which, even though we must grant full moral rights to both parties, there is still no absolute obligation for the independent person to keep the dependent person alive. What Thompson attempts to show is that there is a great difference between the claim that a person has a right to life, and the claim that other people are obliged to do whatever is necessary to keep them alive, or be forced to so.

Thompson believes that this argument may be a reasonable analogy for pregnancy, particularly in cases in which a woman has been raped or otherwise forced to become pregnant against her will. But critics of this argument maintain that in the more common situations in which women request abortions, the degree of obligation that a woman might have might depend on her degree of responsibility for her pregnancy (Warren 1973).

Feminist critics of Thompson's argument believe that she ignores a particularly important aspect of the debate about abortion – the concept of interpersonal responsibility. In a famous study that was based on interviewing women who were considering abortions, Carol Gilligan found that women tended to see this decision as a conflict between responsibilities, and did not tend to focus upon questions such as the foetus's right to life (Gilligan 1982). Critics of Thompson believe that her arguments, and those of many others who speak on the subject, ignore the complex and often irreconcilable responsibilities that women have when they make this choice.

To many feminists, these interlocking relationships are characterised overwhelmingly by women's sexual subordination to men. Greater equality could ensure that pregnancy was a free and creative act, something that a woman had chosen for herself. But, at present, arguments based on the private decisions of women as autonomous, self-deciding individuals cannot be separated from the social milieu in which they occur. Women's decisions for abortion may therefore be necessitated by a great range of responsibilities – towards their families, their work and their communities, and these harsh realities may mitigate responsibilities that they owe to the foetus within them.

Some authors have suggested that abortion is best understood as a political issue rather than purely as an ethical issue. For example, Lewins argues that a large proportion of the women who have abortions would actually prefer to continue with their pregnancies if they had the economic or social means to do so (Lewins 1996). Abortion is viewed by these women, not necessarily as a good thing, but as the lesser of two undesirable outcomes. As such it is a practice that society need not regard as intrinsically good, but more as a way of avoiding worse practices such as 'backyard abortions' and unwanted children. Lewins further argues that we should avoid further attempts to change public thinking or to examine the ethical aspects of this issue, as this is unavoidably divisive. Instead, we should concentrate on the social context of abortion and the political processes that enable harm-minimisation for pregnant women.

Early pregnancy

Pregnancy begins with the fertilisation of the ovum with spermatozoa. After 24 hours the fertilised ovum begins to divide as it floats down the fallopian tube and into the uterus. At 5 days post-conception, the embryo begins implantation in the uterine wall, a process that is completed by 8-9 days. At 14 days, a 'primitive streak' begins to form in the cell mass – the beginning of the development of organs and tissues.

The early embryo has some characteristics that are not found in later stages of development. For example, up until the 8-cell stage, one or more cells can be removed from the developing embryo and a complete human being can still be produced (this may be done in IVF for pre-implantation diagnosis). Furthermore, until the 14-day period, the embryo may split into more than one individual – the process for development of identical twins (American College of Gynaecology 2006). When we hear that a fertilised ovum is a potential human, it is worth bearing in mind that it is actually potentially a number of humans!

There is something very strange about this. If a foetus is a person, but we can split it in two to make two different people, it is difficult to regard such a situation as being identical to what 'personhood' means at a later stage of development. There is debate about the moral significance of such physiological differences in early pregnancy, but the authors believe that these and many other aspects of foetal development do have moral significance. They also point to the possibility of other morally significant differences between early and late pregnancy.

One approach to this issue contends that what is significant about people in moral terms is not membership of the species Homo sapiens but the attainment of a cluster of mental characteristics or abilities such as rationality, sentience, self-awareness, social interaction and the capacity to communicate. Together, these characteristics are used to define 'personhood'. The argument then follows that since only persons have a right to life, and since early foetuses are not persons, they do not necessarily have a right to life.

Other characteristics that develop as the foetus matures have also been suggested as providing appropriate moral boundaries for allowing or disallowing abortion, including 'brain-life', 'quickening', viability, independence and birth (Himma 2003).

Christian views

In Western societies, the greatest opposition to abortion comes from the Christian, in particular the Roman Catholic, traditions. The Roman Catholic Church organises and orchestrates much of the opposition to abortion both at a political and a more informal level. As Dworkin notes:

> Roman Catholic clergy and laity are not alone in the pro-life movement, but the evidence requires the conclusion that it is they who have vitalised the movement, given it organisation and direction, and used ecclesiastical channels of communication in its support. (Dworkin 1993)

The Roman Catholic church has always opposed abortion, but the grounds for this opposition have changed considerably during the past two millennia. Early discussions about abortion explicitly rejected the concept that human life began at conception and focused instead on determination of the time at which the soul entered the human body, which was thought to be some time after conception. (Many of these proposals appear extremely anachronistic today as they were based upon fallacious understandings of human biology.) Abortion after the time of ensoulment was considered to be equivalent to murder.

Abortion was also opposed on the basis of a quite separate argument – that interference with the process of reproduction, even before the body was ensouled, was interfering with God's procreative function. In this way, prohibitions against abortion were included with other prohibitions including those against masturbation and contraception.

The rise of the liberal democracies led to increasing separation between the functions of the church and the state. Opposition to abortion on purely religious grounds could not be sustained in such an environment and, as more knowledge became available about the biology of foetal development, the Roman Catholic opposition to abortion shifted towards a more secular logic. This came through the assertion that human life began at the point of conception, and that abortion was therefore identified as a form of murder. A papal decree of 1869 marked the first official rejection of the view that a foetus could be ensouled at some time after conception and this position has continued to the present day (Dunstan 1984). (Unlike abortion, the issues of contraception and masturbation are not still seen as secular ethical concerns, and there is little discussion of these topics in most textbooks of biomedical ethics.)

The Roman Catholic opposition to abortion continues to this day. Pope John Paul II, in his Encyclical Letter, *Veritatis Splendor* (1993), stated that there are objects of the human act which are by their nature 'incapable of being ordered' to

God, in other words that there are acts which are intrinsically evil. According to this encyclical, intrinsic evils include: whatever violates the integrity of the human person; whatever is offensive to human dignity; and whatever is hostile to life itself, such as any kind of homicide, genocide, abortion, euthanasia and voluntary suicide. In this way, abortion is identified as being hostile to human life itself, and it is implied that human life begins at conception. However, this position does continue to acknowledge exceptions where the death of the foetus may be an inevitable (though not intended) consequence of therapy (eg, ectopic pregnancy or carcinoma of the uterus). These exceptions are justified philo-sophically by recourse to the principle of double effect.

The view of church leaders about abortion is not necessarily reflected in the views of all the ordinary members of the church. For example, in a 1992 Ameri-can poll, only 13% of American Catholics believed that abortion should never be permitted (Dworkin 1993).

Many Protestant Christians hold views similar to the Roman Catholic view, but this is by no means universal. Some Christian churches have quite liberal views about abortion. For example, the United Methodist church website states:

> Our belief in the sanctity of unborn human life makes us reluctant to approve abortion. But we are equally bound to respect the sacredness of the life and well-being of the mother, for whom devastating damage may result from an unacceptable pregnancy. In continuity with past Christian teaching, we recognize tragic conflicts of life with life that may justify abortion, and in such cases we support the legal option of abortion under proper medical pro-cedures. We cannot affirm abortion as an acceptable means of birth control, and we unconditionally reject it as a means of gender selection.
>
> We oppose the use of late-term abortion known as dilation and extraction (partial-birth abortion) and call for the end of this practice except when the physical life of the mother is in danger and no other medical procedure is available, or in the case of severe fetal anomalies incompatible with life. We call all Christians to a searching and prayerful inquiry into the sorts of conditions that may warrant abortion. We commit our Church to continue to provide nurturing ministries to those who terminate a pregnancy, to those in the midst of a crisis pregnancy, and to those who give birth. We particularly encourage the Church, the government, and social service agencies to support and facilitate the option of adoption.
>
> (<http://archives.umc.org/interior.asp?mid=1732>)

Non-Christian views of abortion

The variety of opinion that constitutes Christian views on abortion is also found in the non-Christian traditions. The basic propositions in Islamic law (*Shar'ia*) is that the foetus is like a drop of fluid (*nufta*) for 40 days, then like a leech or something that clings (*al-alaqah*) for another 40 days, and then like an unformed or chewed fleshy lump for another 40 days (*al-mughdah*), after which time Allah sends an angel to infuse the foetus with a soul. On this basis the four main Islamic schools of law – the Hanafite, Hanbalite, Malikite and Shafiite – agree that there can be no abortion after the end of the fourth month unless it can be established that to continue the pregnancy would endanger the life of the mother (Bowker

1986). In such cases the existing life of the mother is considered of greater value than the foetus's life, and abortion can be justified according to the principle of necessity. Alternatively, abortion might be warranted if the mother is still breast-feeding and the birth of another child would overtax the mother's capacity to breastfeed the existing child, putting it at serious risk. However, the four schools do not reach any consensus about abortion before that time. The Zaydis maintain that the unformed (ie unsouled) foetus is without human life, and hence abortion within the first four months is possible unconditionally. The Hanafites believe that abortion is possible at this time only with sufficient reason – such as if the mother is breastfeeding. The Malikites believe that the foetus at this stage, while not a human being, should not be interfered with in even the most exceptional circumstances. Similarly, the Shafi'i school states that a dead pregnant woman may be cut open to remove the foetus if there is a chance of it surviving.

The majority of Jewish scholars believe that the foetus lacks legal personality (it is not a person or *nefesh adam* and has no rights of inheritance). The foetus is considered to be part of the mother, until the head, or the greater part of the foetus, has emerged. Because of this, in Jewish law (*Halakah*), abortion is not murder but it is nevertheless considered to be morally wrong, unless it is necessary to preserve the health of the mother. The mother's duty to preserve her life outweighs her obligations to the foetus. If the foetus threatens the mother's life she is obliged to save herself by destroying it. In the *Mishnan Ohalot* 7:6, it is said that if a woman is having difficulty during childbirth, the foetus should be cut up and removed limb by limb. This was repeated by the great Jewish scholar and doctor, Maimonides, in the *Mishneh Torah*, with the justification that such a child is like a pursuer trying to kill the mother. Further evidence for this proposition can be found in the *Babylonian Talmud* (*Arakhin* 7a-b), where it is said that a pregnant prisoner who has been condemned to death should be executed without delay, to prevent the child from being born. Further, if there is a chance that the child will be born after the mother's death, the mother's belly should be struck to kill the child first. A mother would suffer if she saw the child born before execution and she would be disgraced if the child was expelled alive after her death. According to the passage, it is better to avoid causing suffering or disgrace to the mother than saving the life of the foetus.

Some have argued that abortion is therefore permissible in Jewish law for both physical and psychological threats to the pregnant woman. For example, the meaning of 'difficulty' in the passage from *Ohalot* has been taken by some as including psychological harms within its terms. Similarly, if the unborn child has a defect the child may be aborted, not because of an assessment of the child's future quality of life, but because the woman may suffer disgrace from giving birth.

Both Hindus and Buddhists emphasise non-violence against all living beings, whether they be human or not, and this prohibition may also apply to abortion. But, as we have seen within the other religions that we have discussed, there is a wide range of opinion in both religions that may support or reject abortions under different circumstances. In general it appears that most religious faiths do not accept abortion in the later stages of pregnancy unless there is great danger to the mother, and place varying restrictions on its use in the earlier stages of pregnancy.

There continues to be debate across many faiths and in the secular world about appropriate gestational limits for abortion. In early pregnancy we believe that abortion should be widely available, and the decision about whether to go through with this should be predominantly decided by the mother. The Australian obstetrician Caroline de Costa has written:

> What I have seen is this: the fetus becomes a person when the woman decides it does. With wanted pregnancy, even if unplanned, this may be very early on. With unwanted pregnancy, this often becomes a difficult and deeply personal decision for the woman but it is a decision *she* makes. And I believe that it is a decision that only the woman herself, with the help of whoever she chooses – partner, doctor, friends, family – should make. (De Costa 2007)

We do not believe that the same is true of late pregnancy when the foetus develops biological features that may have moral significance. In this we are in agreement with most of the religious views explored above.

The effects of abortion

The major outcome of abortion, as anti-abortion groups remind us, is the death and miscarriage of the foetus, but there are other effects as well. It is undoubtedly true that some women who have had an abortion regret it for the rest of their lives and feel blighted by this decision. It is equally true, however, that others may regard their abortion as an unpleasant but unavoidable choice and still others who may feel that, in the context of their life narrative, the fact that they had an abortion was of relatively little consequence.

There have been several studies that have looked at the effects of abortion on women who have had, or have been refused, an abortion, and on their families. The psychological sequelae of abortion for women are generally mild. After an estimated 3550 abortions in one area of England, only one woman was admitted to hospital with psychosis within three months of an abortion. In a study of 200 English women who underwent abortion, depression scores three months after abortion showed considerable improvement compared to pre-abortion scores, but 7% of women continued to feel guilt and nine of the women regretted the abortion 18 months after it occurred. In 1989, the American Surgeon General concluded that there was insufficient evidence to conclude that abortion was psychologically harmful to women and that the development of significant psychological problems from abortion was not a significant public health issue (Green 1992). Subsequent studies have, however, found a correlation between abortion and suicidality (Gissler, Hemminki et al 1996; Fergusson, Horwood et al 2006).

A study that reviewed the world literature on infanticide found that 83% of newborns and 11% of infants killed by their mothers were born of an unwanted pregnancy (Resnick 1970). A 1991 review of the psychological impact of abortion found that 40% of mothers who were refused abortion obtained abortions elsewhere, and that the effects on children for whom abortion was denied were long lasting and negative (Dagg 1991).

Other studies have looked at children whose parents had been refused access to an abortion. In a Swedish study, 68 children whose mothers were refused an abortion were compared with a similar group of controls with a 21-year follow-up. Nineteen per cent of the unwanted children had been placed with foster parents, 28% had attended a psychiatric clinic, 18% were registered with a child welfare board for complaints of delinquency and 8% had penal records. All these results were greatly in excess of the wanted children (Green 1992).

The effects of the widespread availability of abortion have probably influenced society more greatly than we are aware. The economist Stephen Levitt has argued that the most dramatic effect of legalised abortion has been its effect on crime. His justification for this is that unwanted children are more likely to commit crimes, so fewer unwanted children would result in fewer crimes. He uses American data to show how this may have occurred (Levitt and Dubner 2005).

In the late 1960s, some American States began allowing abortions under extreme circumstances. By 1970, five States made abortion legal and freely available, and in 1973 the *Roe v Wade* case legalised early abortion across the whole United States. In the year after *Roe v Wade*, 750,000 women had abortions, increasing to 1.6 million by 1980. In the early 1990s, at the time that those who had been aborted would have been reaching adolescence, crime rates in the United states began to fall markedly. This happened first in States in which abortion was legalised first, and only occurred in the age groups who would have been affected by this legislation. States with the highest abortion rates in the 1970s now have the lowest crime rates and vice-versa (Levitt and Dubner 2005).

Like so many aspects of the abortion debate, this argument has been controversial, and is seen by many as deeply objectionable. We (the authors) do not believe that this argument can be used to justify abortion. However, this theory does point out that the widespread availability of abortion may have changed society in many ways that we might not even recognise.

Health professionals' participation in abortion

Some professional codes of ethics include clauses that permit members of the health professions to refuse to participate in procedures when they have a conscientious objection to the procedure involved or some sort of moral objection to the disease concerned. These are known as 'conscience clauses'. An example of this can be found in the American Nurses Association 1976 Code for nurses where it states:

> The nurse's concern for human dignity and the provision of quality nursing care is not limited by human attitudes or beliefs. If personally opposed to the delivery of care in a particular case because of the nature of the health problem or the procedures to be used, the nurse is justified in refusing to participate. Such refusal should be known in advance and in time for other appropriate arrangements to be made for the client's nursing care. If the nurse must knowingly enter such a case under emergency circumstances or enters unknowingly, the obligation to provide the best possible care is observed. The nurse withdraws from this type of situation only when assured that alternative sources of nursing care are available to the client. If a client requests

information or counsel in an area that is legally sanctioned but contrary to the nurse's personal beliefs, the nurse may refuse to provide these services but must advise the client of sources where such service is available.

Many other health professions either allow or demand conscientious objection when a practitioner is morally opposed to abortion. According to Dickens:

> Physicians' conscientious objection to non-lifesaving interventions in pregnancy have long been accepted. Nurses' claims are less recognized, allowing non-participation in abortions but not refusal of patient preparation and aftercare. Objections of others in health-related activities, such as serving meals to abortion patients and typing abortion referral letters, have been disallowed. Pharmacists may claim refusal rights over fulfilling prescriptions for emergency (post-coital) contraceptives and drugs for medical (ie non-surgical) abortion. (Dickens 2001)

Such statements are often seen as providing health professionals with the right (or even the duty) to avoid participating in abortion services if they do not personally approve of them. These ideas are strongly supported by hospital staff. A recent US survey of labour and delivery-ward nurses in the United States found that 90% of respondents would agree to care for patients terminating pregnancy because of foetal demise, 77% would care for patients terminating pregnancy because of foetal abnormalities that were incompatible with life, and 37% would care for patients seeking termination for non-lethal foetal abnormalities. Few respondents suggested that they would care for a woman who sought termination for selective reduction, sex selection or 'personal reasons' (Marek 2004). However, this may lead to a contradiction if women believe that they have a right to abortion services, or if such a right is enshrined in law.

For example, in California there is a State-mandated legal obligation for counties to provide abortion services to those incarcerated in prisons and those who are mentally incompetent. Such positive rights of access to abortion services, whether they be legally sanctioned or otherwise, may lead to situations in which the rights of health-care providers to refuse abortion services might be compromised. An article in the *Journal of Medical Ethics* described a situation where this occurred, and a county was unable to provide the legally required abortion services because no doctor in the area would provide abortions (Meyers and Woods 1996). In this case the authors believed that the conscience clause that allowed health workers to refuse to treat women requiring abortions was fundamentally flawed for three reasons. First, it did not acknowledge a physician's fundamental obligation to provide services. Secondly, it trivialised the process of conscientious objection which became a simple procedure of opting out without requiring justification. Thirdly, it allowed mixed motives when doctors did not wish to perform abortions for other reasons such as insufficient financial rewards.

Meyers and Woods (1996) suggest that conscientious objection needs to be based on sincere religious or moral beliefs that are consistent with one's other beliefs or actions, and are a key component of one's overall belief framework. The authors also believe that there might be some situations in which practitioners should not be allowed conscientious objection and in which some alternative form of public-service commitment be acknowledged.

When a patient requests an abortion, health-care workers have an obligation to assist her to understand her decision and any other options she may have as fully as possible. As with other areas of medicine, we believe that the model of shared decision-making is the most appropriate way to deal with this situation. If health workers are morally opposed to abortion, but do not object to referring the patient to another for this service, then this should be discussed with the patient and they should be referred.

There are some health professionals who have such a strong conscientious objection to abortion that they will not even refer a patient to someone who will discuss the issue sympathetically. This course of action has a degree of logical consistency, but it totally denies patients any degree of autonomy in this decision. We believe that, if therapists feel this way, at the very least they must explain to the patient that their behaviour is due to their personal beliefs, that not all therapists feel this way and that the patient may be able to obtain a different opinion from another therapist. Health-care professionals should think very carefully about whether their right to conscientiously object in this manner is riding rough-shod over the rights of their patients, particularly where patients have few choices about which practitioners they visit.

Conclusion

There are several factors that have further complicated the debate about abortion. The first of these is the rise in terrorist and intimidation tactics against women who have abortions and doctors who perform them. This has occurred particularly in the United States where large numbers of abortion clinics have been burnt to the ground and women and clinic workers have been harassed, assaulted and murdered (Hern 1994; Gottlieb 1995). One example was that of Paul Hill, a former church minister, who murdered Dr John Britton and his escort outside a Penascola abortion clinic in July 1995 and was subsequently sentenced to die in the electric chair. (Recent political attention in the United States has been more concerned with revisiting legislative provision for termination of pregnancy and with explicitly protecting health providers who refuse to provide abortions, than in the broader social and liberal basis of termination of pregnancy (Tanne 2004).)

The other development is the emergence of reliable, non-surgical approaches to abortion such as the use of mifepristone (RU 486). Such agents have been shown to be safe, effective and to be preferred by many women (Hernshaw 1997). The promise of these new methods is that they may allow abortion to move from special clinics to the community, making abortion services more accessible, ensuring safety and privacy, and allowing increased integration of women's health services into primary health care. (De Costa 2007) There continues to be great opposition to these developments from some religious sources and from political conservatives, on the grounds that they will make abortion easier. (For example, Father Brian Lucas, a Catholic Church spokesman, states that 'RU486 is tantamount to chemical warfare on an unborn child' (*Sydney Morning Herald*, 19 May 1997).) The 2006 parliamentary debate about the availability of RU 486 in Australia, was one of the few moments where Liberal politicians in

Australia dared to vote against the then Liberal Prime Minister, John Howard. This again illustrates the fact that abortion cannot be viewed simply as either an ethical or medical issue in isolation from its social and political context.

LEGAL ASPECTS OF ABORTION

The legal status of the foetus

A foetus is not a legal person, but it is considered to be both human and alive, and hence worthy of protection in both the criminal and civil law: *St George's Healthcare NHS Trust v S* [1998] 3 All ER 673. The foetus has been said to be unique organism which is separate but connected to its mother: *Re A-G's Reference (No 3 of 1994)* [1998] AC 245. Foetuses do have some 'rights' but there are exercisable only when they are born alive. The born alive rule is as follows:

> [L]egally a person is not in being until he or she is fully born in a living state. A baby is fully and completely born when it is completely delivered from the body of its mother and it has a separate and independent existence in the sense that it does not derive its power of living from its mother. It is not material that the child may still be attached to its mother by the umbilical cord; that does not prevent it from having a separate existence. But it is required, before the child can be the victim of murder or of manslaughter or of infanticide, that the child should have an existence separate from and independent of its mother ... and is living by virtue of the functioning of its own organs. (*R v Hutty* [1953] VLR 338 at 339)

While still *in utero* a foetus does not have standing to bring an action against the mother to restrain her from acting in ways that might harm the foetus. For example, a woman cannot be stopped from having an abortion by a person representing the foetus: *Attorney-General (Qld) (ex rel Kerry) v T* (1983) 57 ALJR 285. Nor can the woman be injuncted from indulging in a lifestyle harmful to the foetus: *Re Winnipeg Child and Family Services (Northwest Area) v G* [1997] 3 SCR 925, (1989) 152 DLR (4th) 193 (gluesniffing); *Re F (In Utero)* [1988] Fam 122 (CA) (mother with poor mental state and nomadic lifestyle). Nor can an unborn child be made a ward of the court, even on the father's application to prevent its abortion: *Paton v British Pregnancy Advisory Service* [1979] QB 276.

Once born alive the rights of the foetus come into fruit. For example, foetuses are considered to be children of the marriage for testamentary purposes and can take up an inheritance if they were conceived and are born alive: *Elliot v Lord Joicey* [1935] AC 209. In *Re Elm* [2006] NSWSC 1137, order were made before the child's birth to take the child into care immediately upon birth for the purpose of administering treatment against HIV transmission.

Foetuses cannot be murdered but, if they are born alive and later die from pre-natal injuries, the assailant may be guilty of murder or manslaughter: *Re A-G's Reference (No 3 of 1994)* [1998] AC 245. In *R v King* (2003) 59 NSWLR 472, the father of an unborn child attacked the mother after she had refused to have an abortion. The father's intention was to cause a miscarriage. The child was not born alive. The court accepted that the foetus was part of the mother's body for the purpose of the law of assault occasioning grievous bodily harm, so that its death was an assault on the mother. In contrast, in *R v F* (1993) 40 NSWLR 245, a child was born prematurely and died after its mother was involved in a car accident caused by the defendant. The issue for the court was whether the child was a 'person' within the meaning of s 52A of the *Crimes Act 1900* (NSW), which deals with death caused by impact with a motor vehicle. Grove J stated:

> As observed by the learned trial judge the common law has long recognized that where an unborn child receives injuries, is born alive but dies of those antenatal injuries, the perpetrator may suffer criminal liability for homicide: *R v Senior* (1832) 1 Mood CC 346; 168 ER 1798; *R v West* (1848) 2 Cox CC 500. In New South Wales the definition of murder in s 18 of the *Crimes Act* refers to 'intent to kill or inflict grievous bodily harm on some person' and there is no reason to hold that the common law principle as to liability would not continue to apply. Legislation of provisions such as those penalizing procuration of miscarriage (Crimes Act, s 83) do not purport to nor operate so as to abrogate it. An offender may be convicted of the murder or manslaughter of a 'person' being an unborn infant at the time of the felonious act causing death and it can be noted that one arraigned for those crimes may by express provision (s 52A(5)) be convicted of an offence under s 52A. (at 247)

The foetus can also bring a civil action against a third party for injuries suffered *in utero*, but only after it has been born alive: *X and Y v Pal* (1991) 23 NSWLR 26; *Watt v Rama* [1972] VR 353.

Can a child sue its mother for pre-natal injury? This is a far more difficult proposition to the duty owed by third parties, as the mother has rights of her own, to have an abortion, to refuse treatment even when it causes the death of the foetus (see Chapter 14), or to engage in a lifestyle harmful to the foetus. The Supreme Court of Canada, in *Dobson (Litigation Guardian of) v Dobson* [1999] 2 SCR 753; 174 DLR (4th) 1, refused to find that a mother owed her unborn child a duty of care, on the grounds that it would severely curtail the rights of pregnant women. Nevertheless, in New South Wales, an action against the mother was allowed in *Lynch v Lynch* (1991) 25 NSWLR 411, on the basis that the claim was made against a mother with third party insurance which covered her against negligent driving. Similarly, in *Bowditch v McEwan* [2002] QCA 172, the Queensland Court of Appeal found that a duty could be owed by pregnant mothers in motor vehicle accidents. The reason given was that the woman's autonomy was not affected by the imposition of a duty in cases of motor vehicle negligence, and on that basis the case could be distinguished from cases concerning the lifestyle and social choices of the mother when pregnant. de Jersey CJ stated:

> It should be clearly expressed that this determination of the appeal says nothing in relation to the many complex social considerations raised in argument before us, and many of which moved the Supreme Court of Canada in dealing with the broader question it framed: such questions as whether a mother's smoking or consuming excessive amounts of alcohol during pregnancy, or engaging in other dangerous activity and the like, could give rise to a claim by an infant born exhibiting adverse consequent effects. (at [13])

Therefore the question remains as to whether in Australian law a pregnant woman owes a legal duty to her foetus regarding her social and lifestyle choices.

Arguably the best approach would be to say that the only duties owed exist when the woman's personal autonomy over her personal life is not affected by the duty.

Abortion law

The common law and abortion

In the early development of the common law (1200-1600), abortion was dealt with primarily by the Ecclesiastical Courts, although Keown has argued that abortion was a crime at common law during this period, at least beyond the point of 'quickening' (Keown 1988). 'Quickening' occurs when the pregnant woman can perceive the movement of the foetus in her womb, and this normally occurs between 16 and 18 weeks' (117 days to 126 days) gestation. In both Bracton and Fleta's treatises on the common law, abortion was said to be equivalent to homicide, after quickening (Keown 1988). However, in his *Institutes* Lord Coke wrote that abortion of a quickened child was not murder but rather a misprision or misdemeanour ((1641) 3 *Co Inst* 139). Matthew Hale found similarly in his *Pleas of the Crown* (1682) as did Blackstone, who stated that abortion after quickening 'is now no murder but a great misprision' (Blackstone, 1769: VI, 198).

In 1803 a number of changes were made to abortion regulation with the passage of *Lord Ellenborough's Act* (43 Geo III c 58). This Act made the offence of procuring a miscarriage of a quickened child punishable by death. It also made the abortion of a pre-quickened child a felony punishable by a variety of non-capital sentences including transportation and whipping. Further changes came in 1837 when the distinction between pre- and post-quickening abortions was removed: *Offences Against the Person Act 1837*. In 1861 further expansion came in the form of making it a crime for a woman to engage in self-abortion, as well as making it an offence to supply the means for an abortion: *Offences Against the Person Act 1861*, ss 58, 59. It also become unnecessary to prove the woman was actually pregnant, if an abortion was performed by a third party (Keown, 1988).

A defence to the 1861 Act was recognised in *R v Bourne* [1937] 3 All ER 617, which concerned an abortion performed on a rape victim. The judge stated in this case that:

> The law of this land has always held human life to be sacred, and the protection that the law gives to human life extends also to the unborn child in the womb. The unborn child in the womb must not be destroyed unless the destruction of that child is for the purpose of preserving the yet more precious life of the mother. (at 620)

As such an abortion could take place when it was necessary to prevent threats to the mother's physical and mental health.

Reforms in the United Kingdom and United States

In England the necessity defence was later recognised statutorily in the *Abortion Act 1967*, which put in place a scheme for therapeutic abortions to protect the mental and physical health of the mother. The Act also allows for abortion to take place when there is a substantial risk that the child would suffer from physical or mental abnormalities.

In the United States it was accepted in most jurisdictions that the common law only criminalised abortion after quickening. However, legislative criminalisation began in the 19th century and by the end of that century every State had criminalised the practice. The early part of that century saw criminalisation as part of a movement towards reducing death and injury caused by abortion. The early statutory enactments often repeated the common law rule that it was a crime to abort a quickened foetus.

By the middle of the 19th century, medical science had improved to the point where abortion had become relatively safe for women and its popularity, particularly among middle class Protestant woman, dramatically increased. As a response to pressure for the newly formed American Medical Association and from concerns that abortion was undermining racial and secular purity, quickening laws were replaced by laws prohibiting all abortion from conception. In 1973 the United States Supreme Court found that the right to access abortion was a fundamental right protected by privacy rights under the 14th Amendment in *Roe v Wade* 410 US 113 (1973). Since that decision abortion has been protected constitutionally although the Supreme Court has varied its approach as to acceptable State control over abortion practice: *Planned Parenthood v Casey* 505 US 833 (1992). Most recently the Supreme Court upheld a ban on late-term abortions via the method of intact dilation and extraction (which is often referred to as partial birth abortion): *Gonzales v Carhart* 550 US 124 (2007). The majority found that the procedure was only one of a number available at late term and, given there was no medical consensus that the method was necessary, Congress was free to ban the procedure. The court left open the possibility of latter challenges on an 'as applied' basis.

The current law in Australian jurisdictions

In Australia there is no legal right to an abortion on demand (indeed there are probably no treatments which can be *demanded* in Australia). Legislation differs greatly from jurisdiction to jurisdiction. The law on terminations of pregnancy has become fragmented, creating different rules between the different Australian jurisdictions. Because the laws are inconsistent between the jurisdictions and the fact the law in this area appears to be unclear and outdated there has been a call for the law on abortion in Australia to be made uniform (de Crespigny and Savulescu 2004) Each jurisdiction will be examined in turn.

New South Wales

The legislation in New South Wales prohibits the 'unlawful' administration of a drug or the use of any other means to deliberately cause a woman to miscarry. The *Crimes Act 1900* provides:

> **82.** Whosoever, being a woman with child, unlawfully administers to herself any drug or noxious thing, or unlawfully uses any instrument or other

means, with intent in any such case to procure her miscarriage, shall be liable to penal servitude for ten years.

83. Whosoever unlawfully administers to, or causes to be taken by, any woman, whether with child or not, any drug or noxious thing, or unlawfully uses any instrument or other means, with intent in any such case to procure her miscarriage, shall be liable to penal servitude for ten years.

Because the legislation mentions 'unlawfully' it implies that there may be circumstances where an abortion will be lawful. These circumstances usually fall within the defence known as 'necessity'. For this defence to be effective two conditions need to be met. First, the termination of pregnancy must be necessary and, second, the steps taken must be proportionate to the danger to be avoided. Two Australian decisions have considered this issue.

In a Victorian case (which dealt with the older legislation which was the same as that in New South Wales), *R v Davidson* [1969] VR 667 at 672, Menhennit J stated:

The Crown must establish either:

(a)   that the accused did not honestly believe on reasonable grounds that the act done by him was necessary to preserve the woman from a serious danger to her life or her physical or mental health (not being merely the normal dangers of pregnancy and childbirth) which the continuance of the pregnancy would entail; or

(b)   that the accused did not honestly believe on reasonable grounds that the act done by him was in the circumstances proportionate to the need to preserve the woman from a serious danger to her life or her physical or mental health (not being merely the normal dangers of pregnancy and childbirth) which the continuance of the pregnancy would entail.

The issue was also considered in New South Wales in the District Court decision of *R v Wald* (1971) 3 DCR (NSW) 25 at 29 where Levine J said:

[I]t would be for the jury to decide whether there existed in the case of each woman any economic, social or medical ground or reason which in their view could constitute reasonable grounds upon which an accused could honestly and reasonably believe there would result a serious danger to her physical or mental health.

The NSW Court of Appeal considered the defence in *CES v Superclinics (Australia) Pty Ltd* (1995) 38 NSWLR 47. CES (CES was a pseudonym given to the plaintiff in order to protect the identity of the plaintiff and her child) attended the 'Superclinics' clinic on 27 November 1986 and told the attending medical practitioner that she had missed her last period. She told the doctor that she was concerned about being pregnant. CES was told to return within a week if she had still not menstruated. She returned on 1 December 1986 and was attended by the same medical practitioner. She had still not menstruated. A blood test was taken in order to determine whether or not she was pregnant.

A report was received from the pathology service the next day. This report showed a negative result. CES was informed of the result a couple of days later when she telephoned the clinic. The test was a false negative result. She was pregnant at that time. CES attended the clinic again on 30 December 1986 as she had still not menstruated. (She had not had a period since 19 October 1986.) No blood test or any physical examination was carried out on this occasion.

On 6 January 1987 she again attended the clinic, but this time she saw a different medical practitioner. The contraceptive pill was prescribed at this visit as CES was to go on a holiday to Queensland with her boyfriend. On 23 January 1987, after returning from her holiday, she attended the clinic again and saw a third medical practitioner. She informed this doctor of her recent and relevant medical history and her desire to terminate the pregnancy if she were pregnant (CES claimed at the trial that she had informed all of her medical practitioners that if she were pregnant she would wish for the pregnancy to be terminated). A blood sample was taken and sent to a pathology service. The test was returned positive. When CES telephoned the clinic on 30 January she was informed that the test was negative!

On 24 March 1987 CES consulted another doctor (apparently not at the clinic) for a general check-up and a Pap smear test. CES showed external signs of being pregnant and was referred for an ultrasound pregnancy test. This showed her to be approximately 19 weeks' pregnant. She was informed that it was now too late for a termination.

On 30 August 1987 CES gave birth to a healthy child.

CES sued Superclinics for negligence. At trial Newman J found that there had been a breach of the appropriate standard of care owed to the plaintiff by the defendants. However, he found that damage was not proven as, at all times, CES would not have been able to have a lawful termination of her pregnancy.

CES appealed. The Court of Appeal overturned the judgment, reaffirming the formerly settled law under the *Wald* case. This ruling stands for the proposition that abortion is legal if, in the consulting physician's opinion, the woman's life or health would be detrimentally affected, taking into consideration her physical, mental or economic circumstances. Kirby P and Priestley JA held that the abortion, in this case, would not be unlawful and that CES therefore was entitled to claim for an amount of damages (which was to be determined by the lower court).

Meagher JA was very strong in his dissenting opinion:

> The position is perfectly clear: ss 82 and 83 of the Crimes Act make abortion illegal. There is an apparent and unstated exception in cases where an abortion is necessary to preserve the mother's health: *R v Wald* (1971) 3 NSWDCR 25. This apparent exception has no application on the present facts. Newman J found the plaintiff's health excellent at all times. Nor could a medical practitioner, however progressive, have had honest or reasonable grounds to think otherwise – so much is expressly found by his Honour. Moreover, in these circumstances the plaintiff could hardly have had honest or reasonable grounds for believing an abortion to be legal. But, I am also of the view that the plaintiff's action contravenes the general public policy of the law as well as the provisions of specific sections of the Crimes Act. ((1995) 38 NSWLR 47 at 85-6)

Superclinics appealed to the High Court. The case took a controversial turn when the High Court, on the casting vote of Brennan CJ, gave the Catholic Bishops leave to intervene as *amicus curiae* – a friend of the court. This status enables applicants to present a written submission on issues before the case, but not to appear and argue orally. The Women's Electoral Lobby also sought leave to intervene. Before the High Court could hear argument in the case the parties settled:

> It is understood the medical centre Superclinics and the woman involved have reached 'a meeting of minds' on a settlement, subject to the signing of precise terms, expected tomorrow. A lawyer for one of the parties said last night that 'the whole thing collapsed when everyone jumped on board'. The deal will be kept confidential. (Kingston 1996)

The most recent case from New South Wales on abortion is *R v Sood* [2006] NSWSC 1141. In this case the accused was a doctor who was asked to perform an abortion on a woman who was pregnant at 22 to 24 weeks' gestation. The patient had unsuccessfully sought an abortion from other practitioners before approaching Dr Sood. After quoting a fee of $1800 for the procedure, Dr Sood told the patient that heavy bleeding was the only complication of the procedure. There was no physical examination and nor was there a discussion about alternatives to abortion or about why the patient wanted the pregnancy terminated.

Dr Sood performed the procedure by inserting a prostaglandin tablet into the patient's vagina, gave the patient two more tablets with instructions to take them orally. She charged the patient $500 but the patient could only pay $400 at the time. Dr Sood also informed the patient to take the tablets and return the next day for the procedure and with the balance of the money. On returning home that evening, the patient went into labour. She eventually gave birth to the child in the toilet the following morning. There was conflicting evidence as to whether the child was born alive. Sood sought payment for the outstanding fees.

Sood was charged and convicted with the use of a drug to unlawfully procure a miscarriage. Sood was also charged but acquitted of the manslaughter of the child (presumably because of the problems of proving whether the child was born alive). On the issue of whether the abortion was lawful, Simpson J stated:

> Unlawfulness is thus established if the Crown proves, beyond reasonable doubt, one or more of the following:
> (i) that the accused person did not honestly and genuinely hold the requisite belief (ie that termination of pregnancy was necessary in order to protect the mother from serious danger to her life or health, whether physical or mental); or
> (ii) that, if and to the extent that, such a belief were held, it was not based upon reasonable grounds; or
> (iii) that a reasonable person in the position of the accused would have considered that the risk of termination was out of proportion to the risk to the mother of the continuation of the pregnancy. (at [17])

The problem with this formulation is that it is out of step with the formulation of the defence in *Davidson* and *Wald*. It makes the test of proportionality objective rather than subjective, by formulating the test as what a *reasonable person* would have considered regarding the balance of risks, rather than what the was thought by actual doctor.

Obviously Sood's conviction arose primarily because she completely failed to make proper inquiries regarding why the abortion was necessary. The judge stated that, had she made those inquiries, she may well have formed a reasonable belief about risk and proceeded to lawfully terminate the pregnancy.

Queensland

The *Criminal Code*, s 224, criminalises the termination of pregnancy in a similar way to the legislation in New South Wales. A defence is available under s 282 if the procedure is necessary for the preservation of the mother's life and is reasonable having 'regard to the patient's state at the time and to all circumstances of the case'. The Queensland District Court has interpreted this provision broadly along the lines of the ruling in Victoria by Menhennit J to include the preservation of the woman's physical and mental health: *R v Bayliss & Cullen* [1986] 9 Qld Lawyer Reports 8. In *Veivers v Connolly* [1995] 2 Qd R 326, s 282 of the *Criminal Code* was confirmed as a defence, and it was accepted that serious danger to mental health could crystallise *after* the birth of a severely damaged child.

South Australia

Sections 81 and 82 of the *Criminal Law Consolidation Act 1935* are in similar terms to the legislation in New South Wales. Section 82A, however, outlines when terminations may be lawfully performed. This section says that a medical practitioner may lawfully perform an abortion where it is immediately necessary to save the life of the woman or to prevent grave injury to her physical or mental health.

In cases where there is no emergency the legislation provides that a termination of pregnancy may be lawfully performed where the medical practitioner and another medical practitioner have both examined the woman and believe in good faith that:

- the continuation of the pregnancy poses a greater risk to the pregnant woman, either in terms of a risk to her life or to her physical or mental health, than the termination; or
- if the pregnancy continues there exists a substantial risk that the child 'would suffer from such physical or mental abnormalities as to be seriously handicapped'.

In contrast to New South Wales, the South Australian legislation recognises a termination for a foetal abnormality and not just on the basis of how this may affect the pregnant woman. However, a termination must not be carried out where the foetus is capable of being born alive (there is a statutory presumption of viability at 28 weeks' gestation) unless the termination is necessary to save the woman's life.

Tasmania

Following a complaint by a medical student that doctors were performing abortions illegally in Tasmania, doctors at Tasmania's public hospitals refused to perform abortions until the matter was cleared up. This led to amendment of the Tasmanian laws. While the *Criminal Code* still includes a prohibition on unlawfully procuring a miscarriage, the Code was amended in December 2001 to provide that an abortion is lawful if two doctors certify that the 'continuation of the pregnancy would involve greater risk of injury to the physical or mental health of the pregnant woman than if the pregnancy were terminated'. The woman must also give 'informed consent' unless it is impracticable for her to do so: s 164. At least one of the medical practitioners has to specialise in obstetrics or gynaecology. The requirement for informed consent requires the medical practitioner to counsel the woman about the medical risks of termination and of carrying a pregnancy to term, and the medical practitioner must refer her to counselling about other matters relating to termination and pregnancy.

Victoria

In the past the *Crimes Act 1958* (Vic), ss 65-66, contained similar provisions to those in New South Wales. However, in 2008 Victoria amended its laws to partially decriminalise abortion. Section 66 removed the crimes of abortion part from s 65, which now states that it is an offence for an unqualified person to perform an abortion. However, a woman who consents to, or assists in, the performance of an abortion on herself is not guilty of an offence. The *Abortion Law Reform Act 2008*, s 4, states that an abortion may be performed by a medical practitioner if the pregnancy is not more than 24 weeks' gestation. No other requirements are stated. Section 5 permits abortions after 24 weeks' gestation if the medical practitioner:

(a) reasonably believes that the abortion is appropriate in all the circumstances; and

(b) has consulted at least one other registered medical practitioner who also reasonably believes that the abortion is appropriate in all the circumstances.

Subsection (2) requires the medical practitioner to have regard to:

(a) all relevant medical circumstances; and

(b) the woman's current and future physical, psychological and social circumstances.

Medical practitioners may conscientiously object to performing the abortion, but there is a general duty to perform an abortion in an emergency where the abortion is necessary to preserve the life of the pregnant woman. This same restriction applies to nurses.

Western Australia

In early 1988, police seized a foetus from a household refrigerator where a Maori mother of three had intended to store it until she could return to New Zealand to bury it. Police were alerted by a primary school teacher concerned that the woman's son had told school friends of a 'baby' in the fridge.

On 10 February 1998 Dr Victor Chan and anaesthetist Dr Hoh Peng Lee were charged with offences under the *Criminal Code*. The doctors became the first medical practitioners in 30 years to be charged in a State where more than 9000 abortions were performed each year.

The prosecution of the two doctors caused a furore in Western Australia and debate throughout Australia. Doctors at Perth's two abortion clinics and the only public women's hospital, King Edward Memorial, refused to perform pregnancy terminations in all but the most dire of circumstances until the law was clarified (Le Grand 1988).

Amendments to the law were proposed. After a great deal of debate the West Australian Parliament repealed criminal sanctions against women for procuring an abortion and left a woman's informed consent as the minimum requirement for doctors to perform a lawful abortion. The charges against the doctors were dropped.

Abortion is illegal under s 199 of the Code unless it is performed by a medical practitioner in good faith and in accordance with s 334 of the *Health Act 1911*. If a doctor does not comply with the requirements of the Acts he or she may face a fine of $50,000. Any other person who performs an abortion is guilty of a crime and liable to imprisonment for five years. The *Health Act*, s 334, allows a medical practitioner to perform an abortion at up to 20 weeks' gestation as long as:

(a) the woman concerned has given informed consent; or

(b) the woman concerned will suffer serious personal, family or social consequences if the abortion is not performed; or

(c) serious danger to the physical or mental health of the woman concerned will result if the abortion is not performed; or

(d) the pregnancy of the woman concerned is causing serious danger to her physical or mental health.

'Informed consent' is defined to mean consent freely given by the woman over the age of 16 years where:

(a) a medical practitioner (apart from the treating doctor) has properly, appropriately and adequately provided her with counselling about the medical risk of termination of pregnancy and of carrying a pregnancy to term;

(b) a medical practitioner (apart from the treating doctor) has offered her the opportunity of referral to appropriate and adequate counselling about matters relating to termination of pregnancy and carrying a pregnancy to term; and

(c) a medical practitioner (apart from the treating doctor) has informed her that appropriate and adequate counselling will be available to her should she wish it upon termination of pregnancy or after carrying the pregnancy to term.

If informed consent cannot be practicably given the abortion may still be performed if:

(a) serious danger to the physical or mental health of the woman concerned will result if the abortion is not performed; or

(b) the pregnancy of the woman concerned is causing serious danger to her physical or mental health.

After 20 weeks' gestation an abortion cannot be performed unless:

(a) two medical practitioners who are members of a panel of at least six medical practitioners appointed by the Minister for the purposes of this section have agreed that the mother, or the unborn child, has a severe medical condition that, in the clinical judgment of those 2 medical practitioners, justifies the procedure; and

(b) the abortion is performed in a facility approved by the Minister.

Australian Capital Territory

The Australian Capital Territory is the only Australian jurisdiction to formally legalise abortion. The references to abortion in the *Crimes Act 1900* were deleted in 2002 by the *Crimes (Abolition of Abortion) Act 2002*. The *Health Act 1993*, Pt 5A, now provides that only a registered medical practitioner may carry out an abortion (s 81), which must be carried out in a medical facility (s 82). A health professional is not obliged to perform or assist in the performance of an abortion (s 84).

Northern Territory

In the Northern Territory, abortion is regulated via the *Criminal Code*, ss 208B, 208C, and the *Medical Services Act 1982*, s 11. Section 208B of the *Criminal Code* makes the administration, supply or use of a drug or instrument to procure an abortion illegal. The issue of whether the woman was actually pregnant is not material to the offence. An exception is created under the *Medical Services Act 1982*, s 11, which states that a medical practitioner may perform an abortion (when the pregnancy is 14 weeks or less gestation) if:

(a) the practitioner reasonably believes the woman to pregnant for not more than 14 weeks, after medically examining her; and

(b) two medical practitioners (one of whom must be a gynaecologist or obstetrician, unless it is not reasonably practicable) believe that:

   (i) the continuance of the pregnancy would involve greater risk to her life or greater risk of harm to her physical or mental health than if the pregnancy were terminated; *or*

   (ii) there is a substantial risk that, if the pregnancy were not terminated and the child were born, the child would be seriously handicapped because of physical or mental abnormalities; *and*

(c) the treatment is given in a hospital; and

(d) when giving the treatment, the practitioner reasonably believes she has been pregnant for not more than 14 weeks; and

(e) the appropriate person consents to the giving of the treatment.

If the pregnancy is less than 23 weeks' gestation an abortion is lawful if:

(a) the practitioner reasonably believes (after an examination) that the woman is pregnant for 23 weeks' gestation or less;

(b) the practitioner is of the opinion termination of the pregnancy is immediately necessary to prevent serious harm to her physical or mental health; and

(c) when giving the treatment, the practitioner reasonably believes she has been pregnant for not more than 23 weeks; and

(d) the appropriate person consents to the giving of the treatment

At any stage of the pregnancy, including beyond 23 weeks' gestation, it will be lawful to perform an abortion if:

(a) the treatment is given or carried out in good faith for the sole purpose of preserving the woman's life; and

(b) the appropriate person consents to the giving of the treatment.

The definition of 'appropriate person' is either the woman (if she is over 16 years and capable) or someone with lawful authority(which presumably must be a parent or guardian).

Child destruction

All Australian jurisdictions except New South Wales and Victoria have laws on 'child destruction' (see Table 19.1). The offence was created to cover the gap between offences relating to abortion and murder or manslaughter.

The elements of the offence are:

- the child must be capable of being born alive;
- the act or omission causing death must occur within the time-frame prescribed;
- the requisite mental element must be present; and
- the killing must be unlawful.

The timing of the conduct causing death may be critical in order to establish liability. In Victoria, South Australia and Tasmania the time frame is broad, once a child is capable of being born alive a termination of pregnancy could involve an offence of child destruction as well as procuring an abortion. In Queensland, Western Australia and the Northern Territory the conduct must occur 'when a woman is about to be delivered of a child' before an offence occurs. The provision in the ACT is very broad and relates to an act or omission 'occurring in relation to child birth'.

In practice, prosecutions for this offence are very rare.

In New South Wales the Honourable Mervyn Finlay QC was asked to review the law of manslaughter as a result of a highly publicised case where an unborn child died following a motor vehicle accident. The alleged offender was not charged because the foetus was not a person for the purposes of the law of manslaughter. His report was released in April 2003. He recommended that the law of manslaughter should not be altered but he did recommend a specific offence of killing an unborn child (preferring this term to 'child destruction' used in some jurisdictions) and also amendments to culpable driving offences. At the time of writing these recommendations had not been put into effect.

In Victoria the *Abortion Law Reform Act 2008* repealed the child destruction laws of Victoria (s 10 of the *Crimes Act 1958*).

Table 19.1 Child destruction laws

	Legislation
Qld	*Criminal Code*, s 313
SA	*Criminal Law Consolidation Act 1935*, s 82A
Tas	*Criminal Code*, s 290
Vic	*Crimes Act 1958* s 10
WA	*Criminal Code*, s 290
ACT	*Crimes Act 1900*, s 42
NT	*Criminal Code*, s 170

The role of fathers in abortion

As stated above, potential fathers do not have the right to prevent an abortion being performed. In *Attorney-General (Qld) (ex rel Kerr) v T* (1983) 46 ALR 275, a 26-year-old woman, Ms T, was unmarried and seven weeks' pregnant following an act of sexual intercourse with Mr Kerr. She wished to have the pregnancy terminated and informed Mr Kerr that this was her decision. Mr Kerr suggested that he live with and support her during the pregnancy and that the child, when born, should be adopted out. When she refused his request Mr Kerr approached the courts for an injunction to prevent her terminating the pregnancy.

Mr Kerr argued that the courts should act to prevent what he said would be an unlawful abortion. In the High Court of Australia Gibbs CJ (in a chambers decision) said that it would be unjustifiable to assume that Ms T would be convicted of an offence under the Queensland *Criminal Code*. Mr Kerr also argued that the foetus should be regarded as a person whose life can be pro-tected by the courts. Gibbs CJ agreed with the English judgment in *Paton v BPAS Trustees* [1979] 1 QB 276 that a foetus has no right of its own until it is born and has a separate existence from its mother. The application for an injunction to prevent the abortion was refused.

In a case in the Family Court of Australia, *In the Marriage of F* (1989) 13 Fam LR 189, a husband and wife separated when the wife was approximately 13 weeks' pregnant. She had indicated an intention to terminate both the preg-nancy and the marriage. The husband sought an injunction to prevent her from terminating the pregnancy. The court held that the foetus had no right at com-mon law which could be enforced on its behalf by the husband. The court also held that, on balance, the legitimate interest of the husband in having his intended offspring was subordinate to the legitimate interest of the wife in being free to decide a matter which affected her far more than it did the husband.

Abortion, negligence, wrongful birth and wrongful life

Injuries to women from negligent advice and treatment

Women are owed duties to be properly advised and treated during termination of pregnancy. The woman seeking a termination is owed a duty to be informed of material risks. For example, on *Hassan v Minister for Health (No 2)* [2008] WASCA 149 (also discussed in Chapter 31), the woman was admitted to hospital for an induced labour to remove her foetus, which had died *in utero*. The clinical method chosen was to artificially induce labour and then perform a uterine evacuation to remove the foetus and placenta. As part of this treatment, the patient was invited to participate in a clinical trial of prostaglandin, in the form of the drug Misoprostal. The drug induces labour and the trial was designed to test for suitable dosages of the drug in second trimester terminations. Unfortunately, the patient experienced complications with bleeding and, as the placenta was being removed, the patient had a massive haemorrhage which put her life in serious danger. A total hysterectomy was performed to stop the bleeding but the patient was left sterile.

The plaintiff alleged that the doctor had failed to warn her of the risk that she might have to have a hysterectomy by choosing to induce labour, and failed to inform her of alternative procedures such as dilatation and evacuation (D&E). Both the trial judge and the Court of Appeal agreed there was a duty of care but they did not find that there had been a breach of that duty which had caused the hysterectomy. The hysterectomy was found to have been an unavoidable complication, given the patient's obstetric history.

Another example comes from *KT v PLG* [2006] NSWSC 919. In this case a woman had sought a surgical termination of pregnancy but had experienced extensive pelvic damage and a torn uterus with her right fallopian tube and ovary having been completely ripped out. She was rendered infertile and suffered physical and psychological injuries. The cause of the injuries appeared to have been an incorrect assessment of duration of pregnancy, which had been believed to have been at 8-9 weeks but which, in fact, was at 16 weeks. The doctor and clinic were found to have been negligent in the failure to properly examine the plaintiff.

Wrongful birth claims

Negligent reproductive treatments and negligently performed sterilisations have been discussed in Chapters 17 and 18, respectively. Those chapters have already discussed claims for *wrongful conception* (were a child is born after a negligent sterilisation or contraception); *wrongful birth* (where the parents claim for the costs of caring for a child whom they could have aborted had they not been negligently advised); and *wrongful life* (claims by children who claim damage from having been born, in circumstances when there parents had been negligently advised about having an abortion). These terms are not terms of art and, on occasion, the terms *wrongful conception* and *wrongful birth* are used inter-changeably. In *Groom v Selby* [2001] EWCA Civ 1522 at [28], Hale LJ stated that '[t]he principles applicable in wrongful birth cases cannot sensibly be distin-guished from the principles applicable in wrongful conception cases'.

One of the earliest cases of wrongful birth is the Scottish case of *Scuriaga v Powell* (1979) 123 SJ 406, which was a contractual claim for failure to perform an abortion. The judge in that case awarded damages for pain and suffering, for loss of earnings and for diminution of marriage prospects.

After *Scuriaga* most cases have proceeded on a negligence basis. In some cases the negligence relates to the failure to diagnose pregnancy until such times as it is too late to have an abortion. This occurred in *CES v Superclinics (Australia) Pty Ltd* (1995) 38 NSWLR 47, which was discussed above.

In other cases the breach of duty relates to failure to diagnose an infection or disease in the pregnant woman. This occurred in *Veivers v Connolly* [1995] 2 Qd R 326, where the doctor failed to diagnose the pregnant woman as being infected with rubella. The child was born with congenital rubella embryopathy.

Sometimes the breach relates to the failure to diagnose an abnormality in the foetus itself: *Rand v East Dorset Health Authority* [2000] Lloyd's Rep Med 181; *Hardman v Amin* [2000] Lloyd's Rep Med 498; *Lee v Taunton & Somerset NHS Trust* [2001] 1 FLR 419. For example, in both *Lillywhite v University College London Hospitals NHS Trust* [2005] EWCA Civ 1466 and *P v Leeds Teaching Hospitals NHS Trust* [2004] EWHC 1392 (QB), the breach of duty related to the failure of the health professionals to observe quite significant abnormalities during ultrasound tests. In *Farraj v King's Healthcare NHS Trust* [2006] EWHC Civ 1228, the defen-dants had failed to properly test the foetus for beta thalassaemia major.

The issue of damages in wrongful birth claims is complicated by public policy considerations. These were discussed in Chapter 18 in the analysis of cases on wrongful conception. To summarise, it has been argued that damages should not issue for the birth of a healthy child because the benefit of having a healthy child is incalculable; unwilling parents could mitigate their losses by adopting the child out; and it is against public policy for children to be con-sidered an economic form of damage. The High Court has not considered these issues in relation to wrongful birth, but it has rejected them in cases of wrongful conception. Given that the legal elements of wrongful conception and birth are difficult to distinguish, it is hard to argue that damages are not recoverable in Australia for the costs of caring and raising children born through wrongful birth, whether they be disabled or not.

In some Australian jurisdictions, legislation has been introduced to curtail the effects of *Cattanach v Melchior* [2003] HCA 38, so that damages can only be claimed for the special costs of rearing a child with disability: *Civil Liability Act 2002* (NSW), s 71; *Civil Liability Act 2003* (Qld), ss 49A, 49B; *Civil Liability Act 1936* (SA), s 67. The changes prevent the parents being able to bring damages for the costs of raising a healthy child, even though the child was born via wrongful birth.

Wrongful life claims

As stated above, wrongful life claims are brought by children, who argue that health professionals breached a duty to advise their mother (and sometimes father) to have an abortion. A successful claim requires that the child prove that the mother would have had the abortion had she been so advised (Kapterian 2006). There are two practical reasons why plaintiffs bring wrongful life claims. First, a wrongful life claim allows damages to be brought for the pain and suffering of the child, which are not recoverable by parents in wrongful birth claims. Secondly, wrongful life claims can be brought by children when their parents have decided not to sue and where the parents' rights to sue may have disappeared due to limitations on the time for lodging tort claims.

Wrongful life claims have been rejected in the United Kingdom on public policy grounds. In *McKay v Essex Area Health Authority* [1982] QB 1166, a doctor had misinterpreted the result of a rubella blood test and the child had been born with disabilities. A majority of the Court of Appeal dismissed the claim of the child on a number of grounds including:

- the child's disabilities had not been caused by the doctor;
- doctors cannot be under a duty to terminate life;
- the claim was contrary to public policy as a violation of the sanctity of human life; and
- it would be impossible for the court to evaluate damages by comparing the value of non-existence and the value of existence in a disabled state.

The majority of the Australian High Court has also rejected wrongful life claims. In *Harriton v Stephens* [2006] HCA 15, the plaintiff had been born with significant disabilities due to congenital rubella embryopathy. Hayne J stated that the plaintiff had failed to show that she had suffered damage:

> It is because the appellant cannot ever have and could never have had a life free from the disabilities she has that the particular and individual comparison required by the law's conception of "damage" cannot be made. Because she has never had and can never have any life other than the life she has, with the disabilities she has, she cannot show that she has suffered damage, as that legal concept is now understood, as a result of a failure to give the advice she says her mother should have been given. (at [172])

Crennan J also thought the comparison between life and non-life was impossible (at [252]). Her honour felt that a life without pain was never a possibility for the plaintiff (at [270]). Moreover, she found that 'it is odious and repugnant to devalue the life of a disabled person by suggesting that such a person would have been better off not to have been born into a life with disabilities' (at [258]). She found the claim to be at odds with disability law and with the law's prohibition of the taking of life.

The High Court found similarly in *Waller v James* [2006] HCA 16, which was discussed in Chapter 18. The negligence in this case related to the failure of IVF technicians to advise the parents to screen for a genetic disorder carried by the father. The disorder (AT3 deficiency) was a clotting disorder which later caused brain damage in the child when it was born. The High Court refused to recognise the claim, primarily on the basis that there was no way to calculate the difference between the pre-tort position of the child (namely, not being born) with the post-tort position of the child (living with a disability).

Kirby J gave a forthright dissent in both cases. He found the label 'wrongful life' to misleading and said it should be avoided. The claim is not based on the plaintiff's life being wrongful but rather the claim is based on the suffering of the plaintiff being wrong. His Honour thought the argument that such claims entail a duty to kill were absurd. On the duty issue he stated in *Harriton*:

> The duty owed by health care providers to take reasonable care to avoid causing pre-natal injury to a foetus is sufficiently broad to impose a duty of care on the respondent in this case. In order to discharge that duty, the respondent did not need to engage in conduct that was significantly different from conduct that would ordinarily be involved in a medical practitioner's fulfilling the pre-natal injury category of duty. Furthermore, the damage involved immediate, discernible physical damage, which the duty relating to pre-natal injuries ordinarily encompasses. This is not a case involving pure economic loss or another type of loss which is distinguishable from physical damage that could take this case outside the ambit of the pre-natal injury duty of care. (at [71])

On the issue of whether the court could compare life with non-life his Honour said:

> The proposition that it is impossible to value non-existence is undermined by the fact that, for some time, the courts have been comparing existence with non-existence in other legal settings. Thus, courts have declared lawful the withdrawal of life-sustaining medical treatment from severely disabled newborns and adults and from the terminally ill. The English Court of Appeal authorised separation surgery on conjoined twins in order to preserve the life of one twin, although doing so would result in the death of the other. Such cases are distinguishable from the present. Unlike the case at hand, they are not concerned with assigning a monetary figure to the difference between existence and non-existence. However, one cannot escape the fact that they entail a judicial comparison between existence and non-existence ... (at [95])

The current situation is therefore that wrongful birth claims can be brought in Australia but wrongful life claims are excluded. Even if one accepts the public policy arguments raised in these cases, it still seems a rather curious thing that parents are able to recover damages in these cases, but the disabled child is not. Arguably, we have reached the untenable situation where the law is saying that it values and respects the economic costs of raising disabled children, but it affords no respect or value to the pain and suffering of the child. Under the current law the parents could very well take the money from a successful claim and spend it on themselves, without any recourse being made available to the child. This is patently ridiculous. It clearly shows the inadequacy of tort law and fault-based systems generally, and perhaps adds impetus to further consideration of no-fault based systems of compensation (see Chapter 8).

References

Adelson, P, M Frommer, et al (1990) 'Termination of pregnancy in New South Wales'. *Aust NZ J Publ Health* **20**: 64-8.

American College of Gynaecology (2006) 'Using preimplantation embryos for research. ACOG Committee opinion #347'. *Obstet Gynaecol* **108**: 1305-17.

Beauchamp, T and J Childress (2009) *Principles of biomedical ethics* (6th ed). New York, Oxford University Press.

Blackstone, W (1769) *Commentaries on the Laws of England* <http://www.lonang.com/exlibris/blackstone/>.

Bowker, J (1986) Religions and the status of the embryo. *Human embryo research: yes or no?* TC Foundation. London, Tavistock.

Brown, H (2007) 'Abortion around the world'. *BMJ* **335**: 1018-19.

Chan, A and L Sage (2005) 'Estimating Australia's abortion rates 1985–2003'. *Med J Aust* **182**(9): 447-52.

Consultative Council on Obstetric and Paediatric Mortality and Morbidity (2007) *Annual Report for the Year 2005, incorporating the 44th Survey of Perinatal Deaths in Victoria.* Melbourne.

Costeloe, K, E Hennessy et al (2000) 'The EPICure study: outcomes to discharge from hospital for infants born at the threshold of viability'. *Pediatrics* **106**(4): 659-71.

De Costa, C (2007) *RU-486. The abortion pill.* Salisbury, Boolarong Press.

De Crespigny, LJ and J Savulescu (2004) 'Abortion: time to clarify Australia's confusing laws'. *Med J Aust* **181**(4): 201-3.

De Crespiny, LJ and J Savulescu (2008) 'Pregnant women with fetal abnormalities: the forgotten people in the abortion debate'. *Med J Aust* **188**(2): 100-93.

Dommergues, M, F Cahen et al (2003) 'Feticide during second- and third-trimester termination of pregnancy: opinions of health care professionals'. *Fetal Diagn Ther* **18**(2): 91-7.

Dworkin, R (1993) *Life's Dominion: an argument about abortion and euthanasia.* London, Harper Collins.

Ellwood, D (2005) 'Late terminations of pregnancy – an obstetrician's perspective'. *Australian Health Review* **29**(2): 139-42.

Epner, JE, HS Jonas et al (1998) 'Late-term abortion'. *JAMA* **280**(8): 724-9.

Fergusson, DM, LJ Horwood et al (2006) 'Abortion in young women and subsequent mental health'. *J Child Psychol Psychiatry* **47**(1): 16-24.

Furedi, A (2002) Abortion is a fact of life. *Abortion: whose right?* C Fox. London, Hodder and Staughton.

Gissler, M, E Hemminki et al (1996) 'Suicides after pregnancy in Finland, 1987-94: register linkage study'. *BMJ* **313**(7070): 1431-4.

Gross, ML (2002) 'Abortion and neonaticide: ethics, practice, and policy in four nations'. *Bioethics* **16**(3): 202-30.

Kapterian, G (2006) 'Harriton, Waller And Australian negligence law: is there a place for wrongful life?' *J Law Med* **13**(3): 336-51.

Kenny, M (2002) Choices, rights and paradoxes in the abortion story. *Abortion: whose right?* C Fox. London, Hodder and Stoughton.

Keown, J (1988) *Abortion, doctors and the law.* New York, Cambridge University Press.

Kingston, M (1996) Settlement of landmark test case will confirm abortion legal in NSW. *The Australian.*

Lancaster, P (1996) 'The health of Australia's mothers and babies'. *Med J Aust* **164**: 198-9.

Langerak, EA (1979) 'Abortion: listening to the middle'. *Hastings Cent Rep* **9**(5): 24-8.

Le Grand, C (1988) Bill ends women's doubts on abortion. *The Australian.*

Levitt, S and S Dubner (2005) *Freakonomics.* New York, Harper Collins.

Riley, K, S Roth et al (2008) 'Survival and neurodevelopmental morbidity at 1 year of age following extremely preterm delivery over a 20-year period: a single centre cohort study'. *Acta Paediatrica* **97**(2): 159-65.

Savulescu, J (2001) 'Is current practice around late termination of pregnancy eugenic and discriminatory? Maternal interests and abortion'. *J Med Ethics* **27**(3): 165-71.

Steinbock, B (1992) *Life before birth : the moral and legal status of embryos and fetuses.* New York, Oxford University Press.

Tooley, M (1983) *Abortion and infanticide.* Oxford, New York, Clarendon Press; Oxford University Press.

Warren, M (1973) 'On the moral and legal status of abortion'. *The Monist* **57**(1): 43-61.

Woodrow, NL (2003) 'Termination review committees: are they necessary?' *Med J Aust* **179**(2): 92-4.

CHAPTER 20

CHILDREN

Case 1

Danika is a nine-year-old girl who is receiving chemotherapy for leukaemia. She is brought into the Emergency Department by her mother with a two-week history of breathlessness, lethargy and headache. She is found to be extremely anaemic, with a rapid heart rate and cold fingers and toes. The paediatric haemato-oncologist caring for Danika tells her mother that Danika needs a blood transfusion as a matter of some urgency. Danika's mother phones her husband who tells her that he would rather that Danika not have a blood transfusion as blood safety cannot be guaranteed and that it would be better if Danika simply rested and allowed her bone marrow to recover on its own.

Case 2

Gabriel is a four-year old boy. His 42-year-old grandmother was diagnosed with severe-early-onset dementia from a pre-senilin 2 mutation. This is a degenerative condition for which there is no cure. As part of the follow-up of the case, other family members were offered the option of genetic testing. Gabriel's 22-year-old mother asked whether she could have her son tested for the disorder as well.

Children have a special status in society. Their vulnerability, restricted auto-nomy, emotional significance and potentiality make them more 'valuable' than any other group in society. This provides the rationale for health spending on child care and forms the basis of debates regarding child abuse, children's rights and decision-making regarding the health care of children (United Nations 1989; British Medical Association 2001).

The care of children raises many complex issues due primarily to the fact that children are generally regarded as incapable of expressing autonomous informed preferences. In most societies parents are the natural surrogate decision-makers for children and have wide-ranging moral, social and legal res-ponsibilities for the determination of their children's best interests. This parental discretion is not, however, absolute. Children are also considered beings in their own right, with their own interests and needs. While society generally assumes that parents will make decisions that are in the best interests of their children, there are occasions where parents may be judged incapable of exercising that responsibility, or where it is believed that parental preferences conflict with the interest of their children. In such instances society generally assumes moral and legal responsibility for the child's welfare, and will act to protect them from harm (Royal Australian College of Physicians 2001).

Decision-making for children

Children have traditionally been excluded from decision-making about their own health care on the grounds that they were not competent. However, perspectives regarding the participation of children in decision-making have evolved and it is now generally recognised that children may have differing levels of capacity for decision-making and that decisional capacity is determined not so much by an arbitrary age criterion/cutoff, but by maturation. Decision-making for children differs from that for permanently incompetent adults because, unlike those who are permanently incompetent, children become increasingly mature and at some point express a desire to control their own life and own health-care decisions. Adulthood is often defined arbitrarily as a fixed age for all people. But the point at which children can make decisions varies, depending on both the person and the decision involved (Zawitowski and Frader 2003). There is some latitude in law to take this into account (see discussion of the *Gillick* case below).

Even when they are not competent, children's preferences should be taken into account (Santelli, Smith Rogers et al 2003). It is generally suggested that when doctors do not need to gain a child's consent, they should still attempt to gain the child's *assent* to courses of treatment proposed (Rossi, Reynolds et al 2003; Zawitowski and Frader 2003). Assent refers to an agreement with a decision or a course of action. The assent process should include: helping the child become aware of his or her illness in a developmentally appropriate fashion, telling the child what to expect with tests and treatments, assessing the child's understanding of the situation and factors influencing his or her response, and soliciting the child's willingness (or refusal) to accept the proposed care (American Academy of Pediatrics Committee on Bioethics 1995).

While combining assent and consent in making decisions for older children seems intuitively correct, the concept of assent is both theoretically and practically difficult. There are no clear standards for establishing with absolute certainty a child's decisional capacity and the relative importance of assent is often unclear, particularly where a child refuses to assent to a course of action that his or her parents have already agreed to (Miller, Drotor et al 2004).

This has led others to argue that what is required is not simply an assessment of a child's decisional capacity, but an assessment of what the child can understand, what the child wishes to know, the child's own preferences for participation in decision-making, the potential harms and benefits of involving the child in decision-making, and what the child needs to know in order to participate in decision-making and in their care plan (Kenny, Downie et al 2008). Thus, while there is no obligation to involve an infant in decision-making, a mature minor should be informed to the same standard as a competent adult and their decisions respected.

When a child cannot give consent, it is usually obtained from the parents. Parents of older children may be able to make decisions for children based on their knowledge of the child's preferences ('substituted judgment'), but decisions for younger children need to be made upon assessment of the child's best interests. To make decisions in this way, the parent must take into account the potential benefits of interventions and the real and potential burdens of treatment. Any health professionals involved in this process must ensure that the parent does this in a 'reasonable' manner. This is known as the 'rational parent' standard. According to Zawitowsky:

> A rational-parent standard requires the surrogate to demonstrate the ability to prioritize options for the child using the parent's or guardian's own coherent and consistent value system. A parental decision that may seem irrational to medical personnel may prove to be otherwise when examined more closely in the context of the parent's values. Goldworth proposed that surrogates would demonstrate a lack of rational decision making if evidenced ignorance of material facts that make it impossible for parents to be rational decision makers, neglected or abused the child, or did not show an awareness of the demands of family integrity. (Zawitowski and Frader 2003)

At certain times, the child's decision-makers may disagree about what is in the best interests of the child/patient, and a decision may be made to overturn parental authority. Such decisions are socially, psychologically and ethically difficult and should not be made without careful consideration. Instances where society, through the actions of health-care professionals, may act to protect the best interests of the child may include instances of child abuse or neglect; parental incompetence (eg, parental psychosis); parental beliefs that impose unjustifiable burdens on the child (eg, Christian Scientists who refuse medical care); or instances where parents insist that treatment must continue in the face of evidence that treatment is futile.

It must be recognised, however, that there are many instances where parents and health carers disagree in relation to a child's management and where the parents may believe that they know better what is in their child's best interests (eg, choosing not to continue chemotherapy for a terminal malignancy). This would suggest that an open process of shared and informed decision-making is optimal, both because it enables decisions to be made that are more clinically and ethically appropriate, and also because it may allow the burden of grief, guilt and responsibility to be shared so that a child's parents are neither saviour nor executioner.

Issues surrounding decision-making become particularly difficult during adolescence as this is when young people develop an independent identity and the capacity to make and enact choices. (Indeed the achievement of, and commitment to, a coherent identity is often regarded as the critical 'development task' of adolescence. Identity is best understood as psychological self-representation – the image of oneself as a unique, discrete entity with particular attributes that persist across space and time and that manifests in a variety of role in different social contexts. Identity, therefore, is constructed socially and culturally and during adolescence is (re)constructed through changing relationships with authority figures and peers and through rituals that demand self-transformation.) (Erikson 1968; Adams and Marshall 1996; Rose 1996; Gillies and Johnston 2004)

Adolescence is a time of enormous change and many of these changes impact upon decision-making capacity and participation. Physical and sexual maturation, cognitive and emotional development, shifts in familial, social and vocational roles, and acquisition of an independent conception of one's place in the world all contribute to, and derive from, major changes in moral, legal, political and economic rights and responsibilities (Harter 1999; Madan-Swain, Brown et al 2000).

Children's rights

The principle of beneficence has generally been regarded as the moral basis for parental and social judgments regarding the best interests of children. In recent years there has been increased interest in a human rights-based approach providing a more robust way to protect children's best interests.

While human rights has an ancient lineage that dates back to Plato, children's rights really only became a specific concern with the drafting of the United Nations Universal Declaration of the Rights of the Child in 1959. This document sought to explain the special application of human rights to children (those under 18), stating that 'mankind owes to the child the best it has to give' and that children must be protected so that they have an opportunity 'to develop physically, mentally, morally, spiritually and socially, ... in freedom and dignity'.

These rights were specified in the Convention on the Rights of the Child (CRC) in 1989, which described the need for care (the right to love and understanding and the right to basic health care), the need for protection (from abuse, discrimination and exploitation), the critical role that families play in providing love, support, care and protection, the importance of education and development opportunities for normal maturation and transition to adulthood, and the right of children to express their views and have them taken into account in decisions about their care (United Nations 1989). Many countries have incorporated the CRC's principles into legislation, and numerous professional bodies either refer to the CRC in their policy documents or adopt a children's rights approach to health service delivery.

A children's rights approach creates an obligation on health services to meet the range of developmental needs encapsulated by these rights; and on parents and health practitioners to solicit, acknowledge and incorporate the child's views and preferences into decisions regarding their health care. It is argued that doing so may not only meet a moral duty to respect the child's rights but may also have a range of other benefits – promoting intellectual, emotional and psychological development, increasing satisfaction with care, encouraging compliance with health are and ultimately cultivating responsibility and respect for others (Ross 1997; Kuther 2003).

Family-centred care

Families are generally recognised as having some rights to pursue their own goals and to prioritise and meet their members' needs according to their own value. Respect for families derives from philosophical and cultural values and, increasingly, from empirical data showing that the environment in which children are raised is a major determinant of later development of personal and social competence.

It has also been increasingly recognised that families may be harmed by the experience of health care. The separation of parents and children may have a detrimental impact on all parties (even where this decision is made by health or welfare authorities with the best of intentions), the values and beliefs of parents may often not be accorded respect, parents may be inappropriately judged against entrenched medical perceptions of the 'good' (generally compliant) parent, and families may be alienated from difficult medical decisions. This has led some to propose an alternative model of care – 'family-centred care' (American Academy of Pediatrics Committee on Bioethics 2003). This model of care still retains a clinical and moral focus on the child, but also recognises the family, recognising its strengths and limitations, acknowledging its uniqueness and explicitly including the family in a collaborative team charged with the child's care.

While this model of care is ethically sophisticated, it can raise substantial practical and philosophical difficulties when there is disagreement between the child and his and her parent(s), when there is disagreement between the parents themselves, and where there is disagreement between the parents and the health-care team. In these situations there is little option but for all concerned to (re)focus on the best interests of the child and for the health-care team to explicitly identify the child as the one to whom they have the primary moral responsibility. Regardless of whether this model provides for better outcomes or not, in the end it is an important reminder of the ambiguous and difficult role of parents and of the importance of family and community (Wertlieb 2003).

Transplantation

A good example of some of the complications that can arise comes when children are found to be suitable donors of organs for other family members. Children are usually seen as the 'donors of last resort' – only to be considered as donors when no other persons are available.

In 1957, Leonard Marsden, a 17-year-old, consented to donating a kidney to his identical brother. It might be thought that this was not in Leonard's best interests – since there is a 0.03% risk of death from kidney donation, and an increased risk of going on to renal failure one's self (Najarian, Chavers et al 1992). The US court that considered his case decided that if the transplant were not done and his brother died, Leonard would suffer an emotional disturbance that would adversely affect his health and well-being. The surgery would thus confer a 'medical benefit' on both brothers. This judgment is in fitting with what many people instinctively feel – that there may be some place for some children to act as organ donors in specific situations.

Genetic testing of children

A wide range of genetic tests are available for hereditary diseases. In childhood, genetic testing may be useful for diagnosis of conditions such as Trisomy 21 and cystic fibrosis. Genetic tests are also available for adult diseases that are often untreatable – such as Huntington's disease. Only a minority of at-risk adults who are offered these tests take them up. This suggests that these tests should not be performed on children, who would be unable to decide for themselves whether they prefer to live with the results of such tests or carry on in ignorance. According to the NHMRC and ALRC document *Essentially Yours*:

> The genetic testing of children, with the exception of DNA parentage testing and testing for law enforcement purposes, is not generally regulated by legislation. However, the World Health Organisation, the Nuffield Council on Bioethics, the American Society of Human Genetics and the HGSA have developed guidelines on the genetic testing of children. These guidelines proceed on the basis that predictive testing of minors should be restricted to situations in which the testing provides treatment options that are of direct benefit to the child. Testing for adult onset disease, for which there is no known treatment or preventive strategy, should not be carried out on children. Such testing should be deferred until adulthood, or until individuals are able to appreciate the implications of testing and make informed decisions for themselves. (Australian Law Reform Commission 2003)

Neonatal care

Even where the process of decision-making is optimised, making decisions for neonates/infants is made more difficult by diagnostic and prognostic uncertainty, the need to make judgments about the child's quality of life, and the potential burdens and benefits of treatment. The complex issues surrounding quality-of-life judgments are made more difficult when applied to neonates because one cannot accurately predict the child's future abilities, disabilities, function, quality of life, values, preferences, and even their prognosis. Because decisions rely on the best-interests assessment of others there is great potential for the introduction of social biases (such as the general disposition to devalue limited intelligence). This requires that those working with neonates and infants acknowledge their own biases and recognise that the attitudes, beliefs and values of those who make decisions for children will influence the decisions they make.

Nevertheless, judgments of burdens and net benefit as well as estimations of prognosis remain relevant to decision-making for neonates. There are many children whose condition demands careful consideration of issues of treatment or non-treatment. Such children may include those who have no capacity for consciousness or personal life (eg, anencephalic children) and those whose condition delivers such severe disability or suffering that the benefit of any therapy is far out-weighed by its burdens. In such instances 'reasonable' judgments of burdens, benefits, prospective quality of life, future health-care costs and clinical inefficacy may be a sound justification for withholding or withdrawing aggressive medical interventions.

Routine circumcision of newborn and infant males

The routine circumcision (surgical removal of the foreskin of the penis) of newborn and infant males illustrates many of the ethical complexities of decision-making for neonates, including the difficulties in establishing best interests, the limits to parental autonomy and the need to make decisions in the context of medical uncertainty.

Circumcision has an ancient lineage – having first been practised as an initiation rite for both girls and boys among tribal groups in east Africa and the Middle East. 'Therapeutic' circumcision of boys first arose in the United States and the United Kingdom in the late 19th century as a means for controlling masturbation and sexual impulsivity. Australia and New Zealand adopted circumcision from Britain and by the 1950s up to 85% of newborn boys were circumcised. Since then the rates in both countries have fallen to less than 5-10% (RACP 2008). In the United States approximately 65% of male infants are circumcised (Nelson, Dunn et al 2005; Cathcart, Nuttall et al 2006). Circumcision is uncommon in most other parts of the world. Circumcision of males is legal in Australia, the UK and the United States. In contrast, any routine operation on the genitalia of female infants or children is illegal in Australia (see below).

Following the rejection of masturbation as a disease and the gradual acceptance of sexual expression as a normal personal and social function, rates of circumcision have fallen over the past 40 years as it became evident that the major reasons that circumcision was performed was on the grounds of parental choice, perceived psychosocial benefit, identity with the father or increased acceptance within a group for cultural (most commonly) or religious reasons.

There is ongoing debate about the (medical) benefits of circumcision. Recent data suggests that circumcision may be associated with some benefits including a small reduction in the incidence of urinary tract infections (UTIs) in infancy (Singh-Grewal, Macdessi et al 2005), a reduced risk of HIV/AIDS, syphilis and chancroid in those from developing countries with a high prevalence of sexually transmitted infections (Siegfried, Muller et al 2005; Richters, Smith et al 2006; Weiss, Thomas et al 2006; Gray, Kigozi et al 2007), and, in those living in developed countries, a reduction in the lifetime risk of penile cancer in men and (less clearly) cervical cancer in female partners (Maden, Sherman et al 1993). The complications associated with circumcision are more clearly defined and are generally low (1-4%) and minor (Kaplan 1983; Cathcart, Nuttall et al 2006). Acute complications include bleeding (particularly in those with an inherited or acquired bleeding tendency), infection, urethral damage, pain and penile amputation. Longer term complications include secondary phimosis, meatal stenosis, poor cosmetic appearance, psychological trauma and reduced sexual sensation and sexual function (Kim and Pang 2007).

Our society accepts that parents have the right to make decisions on their child's behalf, without interference from the state, as long as they are informed and their decisions are consistent with the best interests of the child. There are a number of reasons why this framework does not simply resolve disputes regarding the 'ethics' of routine circumcision of male infants. First, the evidence regarding benefits (in particular) is contested and any comparative weighting of risks and benefits is likely to be determined in large measure by the values and interests of the parents. Second, it does not adequately account for cultural meaning and it is unclear how one can objectively judge parental weighting of medical risks against social or cultural benefits. Third, any other situation in which parents are asked to weigh up risks and benefits of an intervention are generally resolved by demanding simply that parents are adequately informed. Fourth, as with many other medical interventions, the benefits (with the exception of a decrease in UTI rates) accrue over time, and generally occur after the boy could be old enough to decide for himself) whereas the most significant risks are acute.

For all of these reasons, while professional bodies generally do not encourage non-therapeutic male circumcision, and the procedure receives no government support in most States, infant male circumcision is generally supported if performed with parental consent and by a competent medical practitioner with adequate analgesia (RACP 2008).

LEGAL ISSUES CONCERNING CHILDREN AND MEDICAL TREATMENT

Competence

Issues of competence were discussed in detail in Chapter 13. The age at which a person becomes an 'adult' in Australia is universally fixed by legislation as 18. People under the age of 18 are presumed to be incompetent, and health professionals must be satisfied that they have the capacity to consent to treatment. In the High Court of Australia decision in *Secretary, Department of Health and Community Services v JWB and SMB* (*Marion's case*) (1992) 175 CLR 218 at 290, Deane J noted that:

> The common law has long recognized that the transition from the complete legal disability of the newly-born baby to the full capacity of the mentally competent adult is, in many respects, a gradual one ... Well before a young person reaches the age of eighteen, she or he possesses legal capacity in a variety of different areas: the capacity to commit (and to be liable to be punished for) crimes requiring criminal intent; within limits, the capacity to make a contract and to be guilty of a tort; subject to any necessary authorization, the capacity to marry.

The test for competence in children comes from the House of Lords' decision in *Gillick v West Norfolk and Wisbech AHA* [1986] AC 112 (*Gillick*). In the *Gillick* case a mother sought to have the court rule that parents and guardians have a right to make decisions on behalf of children as to contraceptive advice or treatment. Young people had been receiving information about contraception through the family planning clinic without the prior knowledge and consent of their parents. Mrs Gillick, who had five daughters under the age of 16, sought an assurance from her local area health authority that her daughters would not be given advice and treatment on contraception without the plaintiff 's prior knowledge and consent while they were under 16.

One of the propositions endorsed by the majority in *Gillick* was that parental power to consent to medical treatment on behalf of a child diminishes gradually as the child's capacities and maturity grow and that this rate of development depends on the individual child. A minor is capable of giving consent when he or she 'achieves a sufficient understanding and intelligence to enable him or her to understand fully what is proposed' (at 189). This is sometimes referred to as being 'Gillick competent'. The House of Lords also held that the rights of a parent to control their child are for the child's benefit, and one recognised only so long as they are needed for the protection of the child. Absolute dominion over the child was held to be a thing of the past and parental rights dwindle proportionately with the child's maturity.

The principles established by the House of Lords in *Gillick's* case have subsequently been approved by the High Court of Australia in *Marion's case* (1992) 175 CLR 218 (discussed below).

Two Australian jurisdictions have reduced the age of the presumption of capacity. In New South Wales, s 49 of the *Minors (Property and Contracts) Act 1970* provides that the consent to medical or dental procedures by a child over the age of 14 years is to be treated the same as if an adult had consented. The section also provides that parents can consent to medical or dental treatment on a child under the age of 16 years. This effectively means that children of 14 years and older are presumed to be competent but parents may also consent to treatment for them until the age of 16, where the child is presumed to be emancipated from parental consent. Of course these are presumptions which may be rebutted and if the child is not competent the rights of the parents to consent to treatment remain in place until the child turns 18. After that time, parental powers disappear but consent can be provided to the treatment according to guardianship laws, which were discussed in Chapter 13.

Section 6 of the South Australian *Consent to Medical Treatment and Palliative Care Act 1995* provides that 'a person of or over 16 years of age may make decisions about his or her own medical treatment as validly and effectively as an adult'. Where a child consents to medical treatment, s 12 requires that the medical practitioner must be 'of the opinion that the child is capable of understanding the nature, consequences and risks of the treatment and that the treatment is in the best interest of the child's health and well-being; and that opinion is supported by the written opinion of at least one other medical practitioner who personally examines the child before the treatment is commenced'. Similar legislation has not been enacted in other jurisdictions.

Limits to parental power of consent

In *Marion's case* the High Court outlined limits to the types of treatments and interventions that parents can consent to on behalf of their children. Marion (which was not her real name) lived in the Northern Territory and had an intellectual disability. Her parents asked the Family Court of Australia either to give consent to carry out a hysterectomy and an oophorectomy, or to declare that it was lawful for them alone, as Marion's parents, to give the consent. In the Northern Territory there was no Territory legislation which dealt with the sterilisation of children and, therefore, the common law rules applied. The majority of the High Court, while adopting the 'Gillick' principle, held that the common law does not necessarily allow parents or guardians to give a valid and effective consent to *non-therapeutic* medical procedures where the treatment is not being provided for some malformation or disease. Only a court has that power and, in the Northern Territory, because there is no Territory legislation specifically dealing with this situation, the Family Court had jurisdiction to hear applications and, where appropriate, to authorise the performance of the surgery. The Family Court's jurisdiction is known as the welfare power, and is similar to the *parens patriae* power of Supreme Courts, which was discussed in Chapter 13.

The majority explained that it was considered necessary for an outside body (ie, one independent of the parents and the child) to authorise non-therapeutic treatments. Sterilisation (in common with some other medical procedures) requires invasive, irreversible and major surgery, and is to be considered appropriate only as a step of last resort. The majority distinguished it from other medical procedures, noting the significant risk of making the wrong decision, either as to a child's present or future capacity to consent or about what are the best interests of a child who cannot consent. A number of factors contribute to the significant risk of a wrong decision being made. These include:

- the complexity of the question of consent;
- the central role played by the medical profession both in decision-making and in the performance of the procedure (and the possibility of error);
- the clash of interests – decisions involve the possibly conflicting, though legitimate, interests of the child, the parents, carers and other family members;
- the gravity of the consequences of a wrong decision; and (perhaps most significantly), the fact that sterilisation interferes with a 'fundamental right to personal inviolability existing in the common law'. (at 253)

Because of these reasons the majority found that only the court should consent because parents might not make a decision in the child's best interests.

After *Marion's case* a number of other treatments have been classed as non-therapeutic, requiring the consent of the Family Court or State Supreme Courts.

Tissue donation

Donation of tissue by children is discussed in more detail in Chapter 25, but it is worth noting there is currently controversy over whether such donation can be consented to by parents without some third party review. In *GWW and CMW* (1997) FLC ¶92-748 the parents of a 10-year-old boy sought approval for a donation of the child's bone marrow to his aunt in treatment of her leukaemia. The child wished to make the donation. The Family Court found that the child was not competent and that it had the power to consent to the donation. The court said that such procedures should only be approved when they were in the child's best interests. In determining the child's best interests, regard should be had to the relationship between the child and the recipient, the value of a continued relationship with the recipient, and the risks and discomforts of donation. The court approved the donation because the balance was in favour of the donation being in the child's best interests.

The decision in *GWW* was questioned in *Re Inaya (Special Medical Procedure)* (2007) 38 Fam LR 546. Orders were sought from the Family Court to authorise the donation of bone marrow from a 13-month-old child to the child's seven-month-old cousin who suffered from infantile osteopetrosis. The child's condition was fatal and the bone marrow transplant was the only potential cure. The *Human Tissue Act 1982* (Vic) (the Victorian Act) prohibited the removal of tissue from the child. Section 15 of that Act only allowed donations to be made between siblings and a parent of the child. Cronin J found that donation of regenerative tissue was within parental power given that the Act already recognised the parent's right to consent to donations to siblings or the other parent. He found that bone marrow donation was not serious or irreversible, with minimal risks. Cronin J said:

> The High Court made it clear that most decisions relating to medical matters fell *within normal parental responsibility*. If that were not so, how could the piercing of the ears of a child or the ritual circumcision of a child be permitted without court order. (at [60], emphasis in original)

Because the power to consent was found to be within ordinary parental power and supported by the *Family Law Act 1975* (Cth), the Victorian prohibition on donation outside of immediate family members was struck down.

Gender reassignment

In *Re A (a child)* (1993) FLC ¶92-402, gender reassignment was found to be a special medical treatment requiring court approval. The child was a 14-year-old genetic female with an extreme masculinisation caused by abnormal adrenal gland activity. She had not received regular hormonal treatment in her earlier years and had become more male to the point where her treating doctors believed that she would be better off as a male rather than as a female. The court believed that the treatment was of a kind that required court authorisation as a safeguard.

Treatment for gender dysphoria

Similar approaches have been taken to treatments for gender identity dysphoria. In *Re Alex* [2004] FamCA 297, a 13-year-old genetic female wanted to undergo hormonal treatment for gender dysphoria. She had been raised as a male and identified herself as a male. The onset of puberty was disturbing her given she was starting to grow breasts. It was not clear to Nicholson CJ that the treatment was for a malfunction or disease. As such he believed it was appropriate for the treatment to fall into the class of treatments that the courts need to authorise. After reviewing the child best interests, the court ordered that treatment be commenced.

Similar issues arose in *Re Brodie (Special Medical Procedures: Jurisdiction)* [2007] FamCA 776, and *Re Brodie (Special Medical Procedure)* [2008] FamCA 334. The cases were concerned with a 12-year-old who wished to be treated with a gonadotrophin-releasing hormone analogue, so as to prevent her female development. The mother supported the treatment whereas the father did not. In the

first judgment Carter J thought the treatment may not be a special medical procedure as consent was only being sought for the first stage of the treatment
which was fully reversible. However, by the later decision, permission was
being sought for continued treatment (including testosterone) which would
cause permanent changes. On that basis Carter J was not satisfied that the treatment plan was a procedure for treating a bodily malfunction or disease (at [41]).
The treatment was found to be in the child's best interests and ordered to be
carried out.

Abortion

Issues relating to the legality of abortion were discussed in Chapter 19. In *K v
Minister for Youth and Community Services* [1982] 1 NSWLR 311, an abortion was
ordered for a child who was already a ward of court. More recently in
Queensland v B [2008] QSC 231, the Supreme Court of Queensland found that an
abortion for a 12-year-old girl needed the consent of the court, even when the
child and her parents agreed to the procedure. The judge found that the child
was not competent, and also found that the abortion was beyond parental
power. The child was found to be of less than average intelligence and maturity.
Both evidence from the parents and the health professionals was to the effect
that she had intellectual functioning close to that of a child half her age. On the
issue of parental power, Wilson J stated:

> For similar reasons [to those in *Marion's case*], B's parents should not be able
> to consent to the termination of her pregnancy. The Court in its role as *parens
> patriae* must act in the best interests of the child, B, whereas her parents may
> ultimately make a decision which favours other and possibly conflicting
> interests of the family as a whole (albeit one bifurcated by their own divorce).
> And, like the decision to sterilise, which was under consideration in *Marion's
> case*, the medical profession might be expected to play a central role in the
> decision to terminate the pregnancy as well as in the procedure itself. To
> terminate a pregnancy is to negate the possibility of the mother ultimately
> giving birth to a live baby. (at [17])

Circumcision

Female circumcision has been banned in most States of Australia or is presumed
to be illegal under ordinary criminal law principles: *Crimes Act 1900* (NSW), s 45;
Criminal Code (Qld), ss 323A-323B; *Criminal Law Consolidated Act 1935* (SA), s 33;
Crimes Act 1958 (Vic), ss 32-38A; *Crimes (Amendment) Act (No 3)* 1995 (ACT);
Criminal Code (NT), ss 186A-186D. In *Wadmal and Amrita (No 2)* [2008] FamCA
1062, orders were made by the Family Court to restrain a father or others from
performing female circumcision on his daughter.

Contrastingly, male circumcision is not banned, and (as the quote from
Cronin J above in *Re Inaya (Special Medical Procedure)* (2007) 38 Fam LR 546
suggests) is considered to be within parental power to consent to, even though it
is permanent, irreversible and often done for social or religious reasons.

United Kingdom courts have considered male circumcision disputes. In *Re J (Child)* [1999] EWCA Civ 3022, the dispute was between a Turkish-born Muslin father, and an English-born Anglican mother over whether their five-year-old son should be circumcised. Neither parent was particularly observant of their religion and the child had no contact with the Islamic community (apart from his father). The court found that the issue had to be determined by the court and that the father could not authorise the treatment on his own. Dame Elizabeth Butler-Sloss P stated:

> The issue of circumcision has not, to my knowledge, previously been considered by this court, but in my view it comes within that group. The decision to circumcise a child on ground other than medical necessity is a very important one; the operation is irreversible, and should only be carried out where the parents together approve of it or, in the absence of parental agreement, where a court decides that the operation is in the best interests of the child. This requirement for a determination by the court should also apply to a local authority with parental responsibility under a care order. (at [32])

The decision of the trial judge that the circumcision of the boy was not in his best interests was upheld. The child was not being raised as a Muslim and did not mix in Muslim circles. The bond between the father and the son would not be weakened without circumcision.

'Growth attenuation' and the 'Ashley treatment'

A great deal of interest was sparked by the American case of Ashley, a six-year-old-girl with static encephalopathy. She could not sit, walk or communicate. She was also unable to eat and was being fed by PEG tube. However, she did interact with her environment and with her family. Her parents were alarmed when she began to grow pubic hair and breast tissue due to an accelerated growth rate. The parents became concerned that Ashley would grow too big to be cared for at home and would have to be moved to an institution. They were also concerned about the risk of institutional sexual abuse. The family also had a history of fibrocystic breast disease and the parents were concerned that Ashley would suffer from this disease should she grow breasts and be strapped into a chair in an institutional setting.

The ethics committee of the Children's Hospital and Regional Medical Center in Seattle, Washington, approved of a treatment plan which included: high-dose oestrogen therapy (to close the growth centres in her bones), hysterectomy and the surgical removal of her breast buds. The ethics committee recommended that that court approval be gained before the treatment commenced. This was not done even though the law of Washington State required all sterilisations of incompetent patients to be court approved. The hospital later issued an apology where they admitted a mistake in understanding the requirements for court review.

Clearly any treatment like this would need to be approved in Australia. It obviously raises issues about the outer boundaries of what is in the best interests of the child. These extensive and irreversible procedures were being employed to avoid a perceived (but not actualised) risk. For that reason it would be unlikely that an Australian authority would authorise such a treatment regime. The case clearly illustrates the difficulties of conflict of interest when the treatment being provided is also of benefit to the parents

State legislation on special and prescribed treatments

Some jurisdictions have placed limits on parental power in statue. To the extent that these State-based laws conflict with the Family Court's power to consent in the child's best interests, they are void under the Constitution: *P v P* (1994) 181 CLR 583.

In New South Wales, treatment of children over 16 years is dealt with under the *Guardianship Act 1987* (see Chapter 13 for discussion of special treatments under that Act). Special treatments for children under 16 must be approved by the Guardianship Tribunal, except when they are necessary to save the child's life or to prevent serious damage to the child's psychological or physical health: *Children and Young Persons (Care and Protection) Act 1998*, s 175. 'Special medical treatments' include non-therapeutic sterilisations, vasectomy or tubal occlusions, contraception and treatment for menstrual regulation. Other special treatments have been added by regulation, namely, administration of addictive drugs for more than 10 days out of 30, experimental procedures not conforming to NHMRC guidelines, and the use of psychotropic drugs by a child in out-of-home care for the purpose of controlling his or her behaviour.

In Queensland, the *Guardianship and Administration Act 2000*, s 80C, deals with sterilisation procedures for children. The Guardianship and Administration Tribunal may consent to sterilisation if the procedure is in the child's 'best interests'. Section 80D states:

> (1) The sterilisation of a child with an impairment is in the child's best interests only if—
>   (a) one or more of the following applies—
>   (i) the sterilisation is medically necessary;
>   (ii) the child is, or is likely to be, sexually active and there is no method of contraception that could reasonably be expected to be successfully applied;
>   (iii) if the child is female—the child has problems with menstruation and cessation of menstruation by sterilisation is the only practicable way of overcoming the problems; and
>   (b) the child's impairment results in a substantial reduction of the child's capacity for communication, social interaction and learning; and
>   (c) the child's impairment is, or is likely to be, permanent and there is a reasonable likelihood, when the child turns 18, the child will have impaired capacity for consenting to sterilisation; and
>   (d) the sterilisation can not reasonably be postponed; and
>   (e) the sterilisation is otherwise in the child's best interests.

The section also states that sterilisation is not in the child's best interests if the sterilisation is for eugenic reasons or to remove the risk of pregnancy resulting from sexual abuse. The Act also sets down a procedure for seeking out the views of the child and the child's parents and carers as to what they think the child's best interests are.

Comments on special medical procedures since Marion's case

One of the problems with *Marion's case*, and the cases that have followed it, is that the therapeutic/non-therapeutic distinction has been difficult to maintain. The distinction was always problematic. Mason CJ, Dawson, Toohey and Gaudron JJ (who made up most of the majority in *Marion's case*) only used the distinction with some hesitancy. It was never employed in the UK: *In re B (A Minor) (Wardship: Sterilisation)* [1988] AC 199. In that decision, Lord Hailsham rightly saw it as 'meaningless' (at 204).

The cases above demonstrate that the therapeutic/non-therapeutic distinction has completely broken down. As cases of bone marrow donation and male circumcision show, not all non-therapeutic treatments have to be court or tribunal approved. If it were otherwise then a court order would be needed every time a 10-year-old girl had her ears pierced. The distinction fails to tell us why some treatments need court approval and others do not. Moreover, the use of the distinction is insulting to people with gender identity problems as they have been necessarily classified as needing 'non-therapeutic' treatment which sends a message that these illnesses are not real and devastating.

There are good reasons to require some treatments to be court-approved. But the therapeutic/non-therapeutic distinction does not help in explaining how the choice is made as to which ones should be reviewed. The better approach would be to jettison the distinction altogether and to work from an established list of treatments that require approval. New situations could be dealt with by a list factors for health professionals to consider, such as whether the treatment is reversible, whether it is painful, what the benefits of treatment, and the presence of conflicts of interest on the part of parents.

Another problem with *Marion's case* concerns whether it has been effective in stopping the number of non-approved sterilisations. The Human Rights and Equal Opportunity Commission (now known as the Australian Human Rights Commission) commissioned two reports which indicate that large numbers of sterilisations are performed each year without court approval (Brady, Britton & Grover 1997; Brady & Grover 2001). If these figures are correct, they either represent a massive campaign of civil disobedience on the part of the Australian medical profession, or its complete ignorance of the law. Either conclusion would be disturbing. There are some reasons to doubt the figures. Recent Medicare data shows the number of sterilisations of male and females under 20 years to be less than a handful for 2008, which is a dramatically lower figure compared to earlier years. However, these figures only represent claims on Medicare and it may be that there are sterilisations being performed privately which are not recorded.

If the figures are correct it must be said that *Marion's case* has failed to protect the rights of the disabled. Mandatory court-tribunal review is perhaps too expensive and cumbersome a mechanism to protect people with disabilities. Perhaps the better approach would be to incorporate clinical ethics committees with the power to make approvals in the institutional setting. Properly constituted and working under tight guidelines it may be that such committees would at least provide some mechanism for review of these decisions. The danger is that such committees would become rubber stamps which would not take proper accounts of the rights of those being sterilised.

Conflicts between parents and children

Situations will arise where there may be a conflict between the wishes of a child and those of the child's parent(s). In this case whose view will prevail? These conflicts may arise where a child refuses particular treatment while the parents wish it to be given. In the English case of *Re R (A Minor) (Wardship: Medical Treatment)* [1992] Fam 11, the question arose whether a judge has power to override a decision of a child to refuse medication and treatment irrespective of whether the child was competent to give her consent and whether the child had the requisite capacity to refuse such medication or treatment. The Court of Appeal of England and Wales held that the High Court had power to give authority for the medical treatment of a child who was competent to consent to treatment but who had refused consent and that, conversely, the court had an overriding power to refuse consent or forbid treatment even if the child consented.

In *Marion's case* McHugh J reaffirmed that 'the parent's authority is at an end when the child gains sufficient intellectual and emotional maturity to make an informed decision on the matter in question' and said that 'in so far as *Re R (A Minor) (Wardship: Consent to Treatment)* suggests the contrary, it is inconsistent with *Gillick* ((1992) 175 CLR 218 at 316-17). Although this comment is obiter dicta, it is likely that this is the situation that will prevail in Australia. In the New South Wales Supreme Court case of *K v Minister for Youth and Community Services* [1982] 1 NSWLR 311, the court held that a guardian could not refuse consent to a minor having an abortion when her doctor (among others) considered it necessary for her physical and mental well-being.

Conflicts between parents and health professionals

Conflicts often arise in clinical settings where the parents refuse emergency treatment for their child. Invariably the treatment involves the administration of blood products where the parents are Jehovah's Witnesses. Each jurisdiction has passed legislation (*see opposite*) which allows the treatment to be provided to save life or prevent serious injury.

In *Birkett v Director General of Family and Community Services* (unreported, NSWSC, Equity Division, 3 February 1994), the parents of a four-day-old child refused permission for a blood transfusion to be given to the child after the child developed gastro-intestinal tract bleeding. The parents were Jehovah's Witnesses and objected to the transfusion on religious grounds. Despite the objections of the parents the medical team gave blood transfusions to the child, relying on the authority of s 20A of the *Children (Care and Protection) Act 1987* (this Act has since been replaced by the *Children and Young Persons (Care and Protection) Act 1998*). Bryson J confirmed that the actions of the medical team were consistent with the authority under s 20A. It is useful to note that Bryson J said:

> In my view, when it falls to the Court to apply the words in subs 20A(1) relating to its being necessary as a matter of urgency to carry out treatment, the references to necessity and urgency require consideration, among other things, of the practicality of applying to a court for authorisation to carry out

Jurisdiction	Legislation	Requirements
NSW	*Guardianship Act 1987*, s 37	Emergency medical treatment generally allowed for children over 16 years to save life or prevent serious injury.
	Children and Young Persons (Care and Protection) Act 1998, s 174	Emergency medical treatment for people under 18 years, may be given to save life or prevent serious injury.
Qld	*Transplantation and Anatomy Act 1979*, s 20	Blood transfusions may be given (even over parental refusal) if necessary to preserve the life of the child. Two doctors must agree (or concurrence of medical superintendent of base hospital).
SA	*Consent to Treatment and Palliative Care Act 1995*, s 13	Emergency treatment may be given if an imminent risk to life or health and as long as two doctors agree in writing. A parental refusal may also be overridden if the treatment is in the child's best interests.
Tas	*Human Tissue Act 1985*, s 21	Blood may be administered (even over parental refusal) if two doctors agree that the child is in danger of dying and that the administration of a blood transfusion to the child is the best means of preventing the death of the child.
Vic	*Human Tissue Act 1982*, s 24	Blood may be administered (even over parental refusal) if two doctors agree that the child is in danger of dying.
WA	*Human Tissue and Transplant Act 1982*, s 21	Blood may be administered (even over parental refusal) if the child is in danger of dying.
ACT	*Transplantation and Anatomy Act 1978*, s 23	Emergency blood transfusions permitted if two doctors agree the transfusion is necessary.
NT	*Emergency Medical Operations Act 1973*, ss 2, 3	Emergency operations (including blood transfusions) when parental consent not available and two doctors agree

the treatment. The necessity and the urgency exist in relation to the practicalities of resorting to the court as the authority which can deal with the matter when there is no consent of parents.

This passage indicates that where there is no urgency for treatment, but it is desirable that it be given, and the parents refuse consent, then an application should be made to the Supreme Court for an order that the treatment be carried out. The Supreme Court can exercise its *parens patriae* power. The *parens patriae* power was explained by Bryson J in the following way:

The history of these powers of courts is explained by referring to powers exercised in past ages by the King as Parens Patriae, parent of the nation, and later delegated by kings to Courts, but they are more clearly understood as powers exercised on behalf of the community as a whole on the ground that the community has an interest in the welfare of children, and can take control of decisions relating to aspects of the welfare of children when it is appropriate to do so.

Parens patriae was employed in *Re Heather* [2003] NSWSC 532, where an 11-year-old child and her parents refused chemotherapy for the treatment of ovarian cancer. The parents wished to treat the cancer with a strict diet and 'oxygen therapy'. After reviewing the medical evidence the court ordered that the treatment be taken over by the doctors and that chemotherapy be administered, as this was in the child's best interests.

Similar issues arose in *Director-General, Department of Community Services; Re Jules* [2008] NSWSC 1193. The child was born with a high risk of contracting Hepatitis B from his mother, The parents had refused examination, vaccination and treatment with Vitamin K and had absconded with the child in defiance of an earlier court order. Brereton J felt that it was better to make the child a ward of court when making orders consenting to medical treatment. An interim order was made but later discharged as the parents later became compliant, apologising for their behaviour.

In *Re Paul* [2008] NSWSC 960, consent was given to administer blood to a one-year-old boy with an unresectable abdominal neuroblastoma where the parents of a child refused blood transfusions.

Children refusing treatment

One of the most difficult areas of law exists where a competent child refuses life-sustaining treatment. The position is the UK is that the child can be forcibly treated if the court believes the treatment to be in the child's best interests. As stated above, Lord Donaldson believed parental rights to consent to treatment remained effective and were held jointly and severally with minors until majority: *Re R (a minor) (wardship: treatment)* [1991] 3 WLR 593. This means that parents and courts cannot override a competent consent by a minor, but they may override a competent refusal. Lord Donaldson said in *Re W (a minor) (medical treatment)* [1992] 4 All ER 627 at 639-40:

> No minor of whatever age has power by refusing consent to treatment to override a consent to treatment by someone who has parental responsibility for the minor and *a fortiori* a consent by the court.

In Australia, courts have found that a competent child's refusal may be overridden. In *H and W* (1995) FLC ¶92-598 both Fogarty and Kay JJ cited Lord Donaldson's view with approval, finding that 'where a court is concerned with the welfare of a child, no question of "self-determination" by a mature child can arise' (at 81,947). In *DOCS v Y* [1999] NSWSC 644, a case concerning an incompetent child with anorexia nervosa, the judge accepted the court's power to override a child's competent refusal of treatment. In *Minister for Health v AS* [2004] WASC 286, the WA Supreme Court approved a non-consensual blood transfusion on a 15-year-old Jehovah's Witness. The child's *Gillick* competence was said to be a relevant, but not determinative, factor in the question of whether to treat the child. Finally, in *Royal Alexandra Hospital for Children v J* [2005] NSWSC 422 (later affirmed in [2005] NSWSC 465): J, a Jehovah's Witness over 16 years old, was given blood against his will during his treatment for acute lymphoblastic leukaemia.

References

Adams, GR and SK Marshall (1996) 'A developmental social psychology of identity: understanding the person-in-context'. *J Adolesc* **19**(5): 429-42.

American Academy of Pediatrics Committee on Bioethics (1995) 'Informed consent, parental permission, and assent in pediatric practice'. *Pediatrics* **95**: 314-17.

American Academy of Pediatrics Committee on Bioethics (2003) 'Family-centered care and the Pediatrician's role'. *Pediatrics* **112**(3 Pt 1): 691-7.

Australian Law Reform Commission (2003) *Essentially Yours: The Protection of Human Genetic Information in Australia.* Australian Law Reform Commission.

British Medical Association (2001) *Consent, rights and choices in health care for children.* London, BMJ books.

Brady, S, J Britton and S Grover (2001) *The Sterilisation of Girls and Young Women in Australia: issues and progress* (<www.hreoc.gov.au>).

Brady, S and S Grover (1997) *The Sterilisation of Girls and Young Women in Australia* (<www.hreoc.gov.au>).

Cathcart, P, M Nuttall et al (2006) 'Trends in paediatric circumcision and its complications in England between 1997 and 2003'. *Br J Surg* **93**(7): 885-90.

Erikson, E (1968) *Identity, youth and crisis.* New York, Norton.

Gillies, B and G Johnston (2004) 'Identity loss and maintenance: commonality of experience in cancer and dementia'. *Eur J Cancer Care (Engl)* **13**(5): 436-42.

Gray, RH, G Kigozi et al (2007) 'Male circumcision for HIV prevention in men in Rakai, Uganda: a randomised trial'. *Lancet* **369**(9562): 657-66.

Harter, S (1999) *The Construction of the Self.* New York, Guildford Press.

Kaplan, GW (1983) 'Complications of circumcision'. *Urol Clin North Am* **10**(3): 543-9.

Kenny, N, J Downie et al (2008) Respectful involvement of children in medical decision-making. *The Cambridge textbook of bioethics.* P Singe and A Viens. Cambridge, Cambridge University Press.

Kim, D and MG Pang (2007) 'The effect of male circumcision on sexuality'. *BJU Int* **99**(3): 619-22.

Kuther, T (2003) 'Medical decision-making and minors: issues of consent and assent'. *Adolescence* **38**(150): 343-58.

Madan-Swain, A, R Brown et al (2000) 'Identity in adolescent survivors of childhood cancer'. *J Pediatr Psychology* **25**.

Maden, C, KJ Sherman et al (1993) 'History of circumcision, medical conditions, and sexual activity and risk of penile cancer'. *J Natl Cancer Inst* **85**(1): 19-24.

Miller, V, D Drotor et al (2004) 'Children's competence for assent and consent: a review of empirical findings'. *Ethics Behav* **14**: 255-95.

Najarian, J, B Chavers et al (1992) 'Twenty years or more of follow-up of living kidney donors'. *Lancet* **340**: 807-10.

Nelson, CP, R Dunn et al (2005) 'The increasing incidence of newborn circumcision: data from the nationwide inpatient sample'. *J Urol* **173**(3): 978-81.

RACP (2008) *Routine Circumcision of Newborn and Infant Males.* Sydney, Royal Australasian College of Physicians, Paediatrics and Child Health Division.

Richters, J, AM Smith et al (2006) 'Circumcision in Australia: prevalence and effects on sexual health'. *Int J STD AIDS* **17**(8): 547-54.

Rose, N (1996) *Inventing our selves – psychology, power and personhood.* New York, Cambridge University Press.

Ross, L (1997) 'Health care decision making by children – is it in their best interests?' *Hastings Center Report* **27**(6): 41-6.

Rossi, W, W Reynolds et al (2003) 'Child assent and parental permission in pediatric research'. *Theor Med Bioethics* **24**: 131-40.

Royal Australian College of Physicians (2001) *Paediatric policy: ethics of research in children.* Melbourne, RACP.

Santelli, J, A Smith Rogers et al (2003) 'Guidelines for adolescent health research. A position paper for the Society for Adolescent Medicine'. *J Adolescent Medicine* **33**(5): 396-409.

Siegfried, N, M Muller et al (2005) 'HIV and male circumcision--a systematic review with assessment of the quality of studies'. *Lancet Infect Dis* **5**(3): 165-73.

Singh-Grewal, D, J Macdessi et al (2005) 'Circumcision for the prevention of urinary tract infection in boys: a systematic review of randomised trials and observational studies'. *Arch Dis Child* **90**(8): 853-8.

United Nations (1989) *Convention on the rights of the child.* Geneva, Office of the High Commissioner of human rights.

Weiss, HA, SL Thomas et al (2006) 'Male circumcision and risk of syphilis, chancroid, and genital herpes: a systematic review and meta-analysis'. *Sex Transm Infect* **82**(2): 101-9; discussion 110.

Wertlieb, D (2003) 'Converging trends in family research and pediatrics: recent findings for the American Academy of Pediatrics Task Force on the Family'. *Pediatrics* **111**(6 pt 2): 1572-82.

Zawitowski, C and J Frader (2003) 'Ethical problems in pediatric critical care: Consent'. *Crit Care med* **31**(5): S407-S410.

CHAPTER 21

PEOPLE WITH MENTAL ILLNESS

Case study

The following extract is from the 'Share a Secret' page of an Australian women's magazine, in which a woman describes her relationship with her psychiatrist:

> *I went to John for help with my low self esteem and habit of falling in love with the wrong man. And John was the kindly, attentive father figure who gave me his full attention. I soon realised full attention meant counter-transference – when therapist and patient get emotionally involved with each other … Finally John said the therapy was over. Then he asked me out. And a strange thing happened. He lost his power and charisma and the roles reversed. I became the therapist. As he poured out his parental and marital problems over a meal in a plush inner-city restaurant, he seemed to become small, like a little boy. I remember standing on the street with him thinking what a little man he was, not the strong virile person he had seemed to be before. We spent the night together but the attraction had gone. The next morning I felt uncomfortable and realized I had been hard and overly judgmental, so I phoned him and asked if we could give the relationship another try. But he wanted nothing more to do with me.*
>
> *I plunged into a deep depression, rejected by another uncaring man who only wanted me for a one-night stand. Over the next few weeks I became severely depressed, almost suicidal. I was saved from this state by my flatmate, who gave me affection and support. A good friend can be so much better than a paid therapist. A friend genuinely cares about you. Now, nearly ten years later, I'm much more in control of my life and my depression has gone. I look back at that experience with greater objectivity. John was a lonely man at a vulnerable time in his life – divorced, in his late forties, needing reassurance. He should not have become involved with me in a situation where I was paying him to help me to sort out my life.* (Anon 1992)

Power imbalances between therapists and patients are found throughout medicine, but they are particularly noticeable in psychiatry. Psychiatrists diagnose patients as having mental illness, institutionalise them against their wishes or free them from imprisonment, give them mind-altering substances and administer electro-convulsive therapy. These power imbalances are the cause of many of the ethical issues in psychiatry.

Ethical concerns that are associated with psychiatry include most of the topics discussed elsewhere in this book. Issues such as confidentiality and consent take on particular relevance in psychiatry because of the stigma associated with mental illness and the perceived unpleasantness of some psychiatric treatments such as ECT. In this chapter we limit the discussion of ethical problems in psychiatry to three particular topics – psychiatric diagnosis (including the diagnosis of depression), involuntary treatment (including suicide prevention), and problems that occur when the boundaries of the patient-therapist relationship are crossed. The issues are not unique to psychiatry; and even those therapists who are not involved in treating psychiatric patients will need to deal with them from time to time.

The ethical problems associated with psychiatry are sometimes discussed in textbooks under the heading 'Abuses of psychiatry'. When psychiatry is looked at in this way, its aims and methods are considered to be basically sound, and only 'rotten apples' such as the Chelmsford doctors or the psychiatrists from the old Soviet Union threaten to throw the movement into disrepute. It should be noted, however, that there is another view of psychiatry, espoused by groups such as the anti-psychiatry movement and the Church of Scientology, who maintain that psychiatry is in itself abuse and that the bad apples of psychiatry are in fact an expression of a deeper malaise.

Psychiatric diagnosis

The concept of disease is crucial to medicine because it explains and classifies human experience, determines the subject matter, goals, scope and outcome measures of medicine and performs important social functions – providing certainty and explanation, conferring legitimacy to symptoms and behaviours, connecting individuals with communities and marking a point at which a person may adopt a particular social role (the 'sick role'), and anticipate support from health and welfare systems and from their community(s).

Disease is one of a number of related concepts that include illness, disorder, malady, abnormality and dysfunction. Each may be understood (to some extent) as both a manifestation of biological variation and as an expression of the values and norms of the society in which they occur. Each may also have a different meaning according to the context and the perspective of the speaker. And each generally achieves its normative status, or moral weight, not as a consequence of an empirical discovery, but as the result of a particular cultural conception of health and disease (Tiles 1993; Aronowitz 2004; Clouser, Culver et al 2004).

Nowhere is this more apparent than in psychiatry.

The diagnosis of psychiatric illness may have a major effect on patients' lives. A diagnostic label explains aspects of a person's life that may have been puzzling or disturbing, provides an opportunity to assess the future development of illness, and suggests possible treatment modalities. Diagnosis also has a social function – the diagnosis of psychiatric illness validates people's symptoms, and has allowed people to avoid the military draft, to be eligible for therapeutic abortion and to escape punishment after certain crimes.

Diagnosis also has a darker side – the diagnosis of cancer provokes fear, the diagnosis of AIDS provokes discrimination, the diagnosis of some infectious diseases allows patients to be isolated and treated against their wishes, and the diagnosis of dementia may allow patients' houses and possessions to be sold without their permission. And, as experience in the former Soviet Union and, more recently, in China, has shown, psychiatric diagnosis may be a political act – suppressing political dissent through 'medical' control (Bloch and Reddaway 1983; Munro 2000; Lee 2001). The negative aspects of psychiatric diagnosis for individuals have been emphasised by the 'anti-psychiatry' movement, ethicists and the patient rights movement. These negative effects may include:

> not only the loss of personal freedom and the subjection to noxious psychiatric environments and treatments, but also the possibility of life-long labelling as well as a variety of legal and social disadvantages ranging from declarations of non-responsibility in family and financial affairs to, under the most extreme circumstance, the deprivation of life. (Reich 1981)

The effects of labelling patients with psychiatric diagnoses can be minimised by strict adherence to rules of confidentiality. But psychiatric diagnosis, and society's response to it, is pervasive – it colours the way that people are viewed and allows people to be treated in a manner that would otherwise not be acceptable. Psychiatric diagnosis allows us to dehumanise and exclude patients from normal human interactions, as illustrated in the following quote:

> Psychiatric hospitals may be unpleasant places; and some psychiatric techniques, such as the use of drugs, electric shock, restraints and confinement to seclusion rooms, may be experienced by patients as highly noxious. The psychiatrist knows that in hospitalising a patient he may be, in the service of treatment, also causing him a certain degree of harm. The awareness of possible harm is compounded if the patient is an involuntary one, if the most invasive or liberty-depriving techniques are used, and if the patient responds to these conditions and techniques with the insistence that he is not sick and with a plea that they should be altered and stopped and that he should be released. At such times the psychiatrist must harden his heart. And what enables him to do this, among other things, is the diagnosis. (Reich 1981)

Since the 18th century medicine has sought to base its theories and practices on evidence derived from scientific methods – seeking objectivity, rationality, and logic as means for separating facts from values. The extent to which psychiatric diagnosis, is 'natural' or 'real', ie exists as an objective physiological state or is 'socially constructed', has been a major preoccupation of psychiatrists and of philosophers of medicine over the past century (Burr 1995; Sadler 2005; Robertson and Walter 2007). For some, mental illness is no different from physical illness in the sense that it can be diagnosed according to set criteria and without value judgments or social bias (Kendell 1975). Others such as Boorse argue that disease can be defined in terms of interference with 'species normative function', and illness is where a disease state is judged to be undesirable (Boorse 1975; Boorse 1976). Wakefield defines mental disorders as 'harmful dysfunctions' of natural physiology where these dysfunctions are judged to be 'undesirable' (thus introducing the idea that mental illness incorporates biological realities, and social or moral values/judgments about behaviours) (Wakefield 1992a; Wakefield 1992b).

The general conclusion of many philosophers (including Georg Canguilhem and Michel Foucault) is that the use of medical science to define diseases such as mental illness as distinct entities can never be value-free (Canguilhem 1991). This idea, that the objects of our inquiry can never be known objectively, is picked up by the anti-psychiatrists, such as Tomas Szasz, who regarded mental disorders simply as a social construct created to marginalise or control those experiencing 'problems of living' (Szasz 1960).

The psychosocial model

Twentieth century psychiatry has been dominated by three main models of psychiatric diagnosis – the psychosocial model, the medical model and the bio-psychosocial model. The psychosocial model of psychiatry came to particular prominence after the experience of doctors treating soldiers with psychiatric illness caused by exposure to battlefield conditions in World War II.

> The assumptions of the psychosocial framework were 1) that the boundary between the mentally well and the mentally ill is fluid because normal people can become ill if exposed to severe-enough trauma, 2) that mental illness is conceived along a continuum of severity – from neurosis to borderline conditions to psychosis, 3) that an untoward mixture of noxious environment and psychic conflict causes mental illness, and 4) that the mechanisms by which mental illness emerges in the individual are psychologically mediated (known as the principle of psychogenesis). (Wilson 1993)

The emergence of the psychosocial model, and the implication that its techniques could be applied to normal as well as abnormal behaviour, allowed psychiatry and psychoanalysis to take on a major role in Western (particularly American) life. However, as competition for funding within medicine and criticism of the scientific basis for this model became more intense, psychiatrists were placed under increasing pressure to justify their actions. The psychosocial model came under increasing criticism on the grounds that its methods were private insights that were not publicly accountable and that, if mental illness had psychosocial roots, then it was not truly a medical issue but rather a social, political and legal one. Studies such as that by Ash also demonstrated that there was little more than random chance that two psychiatrists would agree on a diagnosis (Ash 1949).

The psychosocial model of psychiatry was particularly criticised by members of the 'antipsychiatry' movement who argued that many of the conditions that psychiatry was treating were actually just normal aspects of everyday life that should not be medicalised in this way.

This illustrates one of the main moral difficulties with psychiatric diagnosis – the question of whether diagnosis should be defined in 'normative' or 'descriptive' terms. A 'normative' judgment is a statement that a problem exists that needs fixing. For example, 'normative ethics' identifies moral problems and tells us how we ought to behave when faced with them. A descriptive diagnosis, on the other hand, merely describes something that is not usual (eg, the diagnosis of a twin pregnancy).

A good example of the difference between normative and descriptive diagnoses can be found in the different ways that homosexuality has been regarded. From a descriptive perspective, it seems clear that homosexuals behave in different ways than heterosexuals. However, in an early classification scheme for psychiatric illness (DSM-1), homosexuality was not viewed descriptively, but was seen normatively as an instance of sociopathic personality disturbance. The decision to stop viewing homosexuality in normative terms – as a disorder that needed correcting – was only taken after a nation-wide vote by the American Psychological Association in 1973. But it seems unlikely that homosexuality changed drastically in 1973 – what changed was the social environment in which the 'disease' existed. This illustrates the fact that while the identification of psychiatric diagnoses may be descriptive, the decision to see them in normative terms depends on social, political and personal factors. And, like homosexuality, syndromes such as repetitive strain injury, post-traumatic stress disorder and attention deficit disorder are all defined as illnesses partly in response to social and political factors.

The medical model and the biopsychosocial model

In response to criticisms of the psychosocial model, two new models of psychiatry were developed – the medical model and the biopsychosocial model. The medical model regarded psychiatric diseases essentially as varieties of medical illnesses. According to Engel:

> The medical model of an illness is a process that moves from the recognition and palliation of symptoms to the characterisation of a specific disease in which the aetiology and pathogenesis are known and the treatment is rational and specific. Thus [it] progresses from symptoms, to clusters of symptoms, to syndromes and finally to diseases with specific pathogenesis and pathology. (Engel 1977)

The medical model was supported by discoveries in anti-psychotic drug treatment and other medical advances that suggested that many psychiatric illnesses could be treated as medical conditions. However, this was not true of all psychiatric illnesses, and proponents of the biopsychosocial model pointed out that many of the criticisms of the subjectivity of psychiatric diagnosis could equally apply to physical diagnosis. They suggested that all disease, physical and psychiatric, would be better understood in terms of an interaction between biological, psychological and social perspectives, ie, by integrating the medical model and the psychosocial model.

A biopsychosocial model suggests that:

> The doctor's task is to account for the dysphoria and the dysfunction which lead individuals to seek medical help, adopt the sick role, and accept the status of patienthood. He must weigh the relative contributions of social and psychological as well as of biological factors implicated in the patient's dysphoria and dysfunction as well as his decision to accept or not accept patienthood and with it the responsibility to cooperate in his own health care. By evaluating all the factors contributing to both illness and patienthood, rather

than giving primacy to biological factors alone, a biopsychosocial model would make it possible to explain why some individuals experience as "illness" conditions which others merely regard as problems of living. (Engel 1977)

The Diagnostic and Statistical Manuals of the American Psychiatric Association (American Psychiatric Association 2000) are probably the foremost example of the biopsychosocial model. These schemes for classifying and diagnosing mental diseases originally started in 1918 as a statistical manual used for counting the numbers of patients in hospitals with mental disorders. After World War II, as psychiatry moved increasingly out of the hospitals into the community, new tools were needed to classify people with milder forms of illness, and the first Diagnostic and Statistical Manual (DSM-I) was published in 1952. This was followed by DSM-II in 1968, DSM-III in 1980, and DSM-IV in 2000 (Horwitz and Wakefield 2007).

DSM-IV, which lists 297 disorders, now forms the basis for many psychiatric diagnoses. It addresses the issues raised in the biopsychosocial model of psychiatric diagnosis, by describing patients using a 'multiaxial' system of diagnosis. Axis 1 describes the clinical psychiatric disorder that is the focus of clinical attention. Axis II consists of personality disorders or mental retardation. Axis III lists physical disorders or general medical conditions. Axis IV lists psychosocial and environmental problems that contribute to the development of the current disorder. Axis V is a global assessment of functioning.

The DSMs have been extensively criticised, both from within psychiatry, and from other disciplines and perspectives, most notably those from sociology, anthropology, law, gender studies, disability theory, continental and feminist philosophy, and narrative and care ethics. Some of these criticisms are that the DSMs are concerned more with the reliability than the validity of diagnostic constructs (Kirk and Kutchins 1992), are 'deeply value-laden and politically conservative' (Caplan 1995), embody Western ethnocentric interpretations of behaviour and may 'pathologise' non-Western people (Bhugara and Bhui 1999; Fabrega 2001), arose from a confluence of 'non-medical interests' including the pharmaceutical industry and the American Psychiatric Association (APA) (Schacht 1985; Lakoff 2005), and ultimately seek to medicalise all forms of human experience (Chodoff 2002).

Psychiatric syndromes and 'medicalisation'

The identification of 'Axis 1' psychiatric diagnoses is based on the identification of syndromes – a syndrome being a collection of symptoms and signs. Syndromes may be identified in physical medicine as well as in psychiatry – and the identification of a syndrome is not meant to imply that there is a single underlying disease process. For example, Parkinsonism is a syndrome characterised by immobility, rigidity and tremor. It may be caused by 'Parkinson's disease' – the degeneration of particular nuclei within the brain, or by various drugs, or by other neurological disorders.

Almost any set of behaviours can be described as a syndrome. The DSM contains lists of symptoms and signs that make up various Axis 1 syndromes.

So, for example, in DSM-IV, a 'major depressive episode' is defined as the presence of symptoms and signs such as:

- 'depressed mood most of the day, nearly every day, as indicated by either subjective report or observation made by others';
- 'markedly diminished interest or pleasure in all, or almost all, activities most of the day, nearly every day (as indicated by either subjective account or observation made by others)';
- 'significant weight loss when not dieting or weight gain (eg, a change of more than 5% of body weight in a month)';
- 'a decrease or increase in appetite nearly every day'; 'insomnia or hypersomnia nearly every day'.

The classification of psychiatric illnesses as a series of syndromes arose in part as a reaction to the huge number of contradictory theories about the causation of psychiatric illness. Rather than attempting to describe the underlying disease processes, theorists attempted to sidestep the value judgments that were inherent in various theories of disease causation by merely describing psychiatric syndromes. Yet because the biopsychosocial model incorporates the medical model, one of its major assumptions is that, at least in part, there is a biological basis for many of these syndromes.

This is not necessarily the case. Although there is some evidence that the brains of some of those with mental illness are affected by structural changes, studies generally point only to an association between mental illness and brain disease, not necessarily to causation. There is also evidence that drug therapy improves mental illness, but this is not necessarily evidence of underlying biological disease either. For example, while it may be possible to stop the sexual behaviour of a homosexual man by the use of drugs to reduce his libido, this does not imply that his homosexuality has a biological basis.

The idea that diseases such as alcoholism, schizophrenia or depression have a mostly biological causation is attractive to many and is the basis of some effective therapies – such as Alcoholics Anonymous. However such arguments are also used by some to excuse responsibility for their own or others' actions – particularly within the legal context. Thomas Szasz – one of the founders of the anti-psychiatry movement – points to the way in which behaviour such as shoplifting, fabricating signs of illness, and rubbing one's sexual organs against people, may now be diagnosed as syndromes, medicalised and treated as illnesses (Szasz 1979). But these behaviours can be understood in other ways as well – a person who fabricates illness may be thought of simply as a liar or cheat rather than a case of 'factitious disorder'. A person who steals may be thought of as a thief rather than a 'kleptomaniac' (Sadler 2002).

Antipsychiatrists like Szasz have been some of the greatest critics of the psychosocial model of mental illness, and the medical model was introduced partly as an answer to their criticisms. One of the main criticisms of the antipsychiatrists was that psychiatry acted outside the proper range of a medical specialty – that it did not confine itself to those who were unwell but began to 'take over' more and more of the range of normal human behaviour. Critics of the DSM approach are becoming increasingly concerned that the biopsychosocial model of mental illness is allowing psychiatrists to again claim an ever-expanding range of human behaviour as their domain (Wakefield and First 2003).

Depression

It has commonly been stated that Western countries are in the midst of an epidemic of depression. Diagnoses of depression have increased markedly in the past 20 years, antidepressant drugs have become among the best-selling medications in the world, scientific publications about depression have skyrocketed and there has been unprecedented public interest in depression from high-profile personalities discussing their own diagnoses and through the work of advocacy organisations such as the Black Dog Institute. However, while these changes may represent a gathering epidemic, it is possible that this may not be the case; that rather they merely represent a further encroachment of psychiatric diagnosis into everyday life.

This point has been strongly made by Horwitz and Wakefield in their book *The Loss of Sadness* (Horwitz and Wakefield 2007). They argue that the DSM-III and DSM-IV criteria for depression are inappropriately wide, and that they therefore capture many people who are 'sad' rather than depressed. They give examples of people with mood changes after relationship breakdowns, job losses or the diagnosis of illness in their children, who meet the criteria for major depression, but where they could also be seen to be reacting in a normal way to life's tragedies.

In some ways this is not a problem – people who are sad but who are diagnosed with depression might still derive benefits from counselling or drug treatment, and in countries like America may only be able to access services that they could not get without a diagnosis. The increasing rates of depression caused by misclassification also are good for advocacy groups, professional groups and drug companies, and may serve to destigmatise mental illnesses by making them seem more a part of everyday life.

However, there are also reasons why we should distinguish between normal sadness and depression. These include:

- that pathologisation of normal conditions may cause harm;
- that distinctions between depression and normal sadness should improve assessments of prognosis;
- that accurate diagnosis should point to better treatment, and that recognising the relations between normal sadness and social factors should identify appropriate social interventions;
- that more accurate epidemiological measures of depression would be possible, including a more accurate assessment of unmet needs; and
- that '[d]istinguishing nondisordered from dysfunctional loss responses avoids medicalizing our thinking about normal sadness and thus maintains the conceptual integrity of psychiatry'. (Horwitz and Wakefield 2007)

In the foreword to Horwitz and Wakefield's book, one of the originators of DSM-III – Robert L Spitzer – accepts Horwitz and Wakefield's criticisms of modern diagnosis of depression, and the need to change this in future editions of DSM. This will inevitably conflict with groups who benefit from having the widest definition possible.

Suicide

We intuitively feel that we should stop people from committing suicide. A lot of justifications have been proposed for this but (in the minds of the authors at least), no justifications adequately explain this intuition.

For example, Megan Jane Johnstone appears to see the major justification for preventing suicide as one of preventing harm to others:

> First, an act of suicide is never without moral consequences: not only does it have an impact on the significant moral interests of the person suiciding, but it can significantly affect the important moral interests of others. As experience tells us, suicide can shatter, injure and destroy the lives of other people; it can also cause substantial loss to society. (Johnstone 1994)

While this is undoubtedly true, it suggests that it is less important to prevent suicide in those with no close relatives and does not seem to capture the significant moral aspects of the act.

Heyd and Bloch present a different argument that seems to capture the issues more fully (Heyd and Bloch 1999). Their key insight is that suicide is irreversible, whereas prevention of suicide is not. If we allow a person to suicide, then they will never have the opportunity to change their mind, but, if we can delay their suicide, then many will do so. This also leads to some unexpected corollaries; including that the moral duty to prevent suicide in the terminally ill might not be as binding as for those who are well.

Heyd and Bloch also point to another moral issue – that where the aims of medical treatment in most conditions are agreed upon by doctor and patient, in suicide treatment and prevention there is a deep disagreement about the aim of treatment (Heyd and Bloch 1999). This brings up the question of the role of medicine, and reinforces that at times the principles of beneficence and non-maleficence may outweigh that of autonomy.

There are some situations in which suicide in the face of suffering is a rational event – such as the soldier killing himself to avoid inevitable torture. In medicine, the question of suicide and euthanasia in cases of severe pain is widely discussed (including elsewhere in this book) with there being quite a lot of support for the idea that this can be a rational choice at times. These questions are examined further in Chapter 26.

Treating patients against their will

Involuntary detention of psychiatric patients is generally justified on the grounds that it prevents patients harming themselves or others. This statement depends on our ability to predict whether patients actually will cause harm or not; but it is not possible to be entirely accurate about these predictions. If a very high threshold of suspicion is set, few people will be detained against their wishes but a larger number will be missed who will cause harm. If a very low threshold is set, increasing numbers of people will be involuntarily detained, but fewer will be able to cause harm. In fact, American figures from the early 1980s suggested that five or six people were detained unnecessarily for every suicide prevented (Group for the advancement of psychiatry 1984). The threshold for suspicion that is chosen will depend on economic, legal and political factors as well as clinical ones, as the economic costs of detaining too many harmless people, or the political costs of not detaining one very harmful person, may both be major. It is important to note, also, that there now been a number of legal cases in which patients have sued hospitals because they have been denied involuntary treatment at a time when it is clear that they would have benefited from it.

Patients are treated against their wishes when they are mentally incompetent and when their treatment is thought to be in their 'best interests' An important ethical consideration about these decisions is, if patients are to be treated against their will, it should be made certain that their best interests will be looked after. This has not always been the case. In 1991, two Royal Commissions presented their findings in relation to inquiries into the care of patients at Chelmsford Private Hospital and Townsville General Hospital's Ward 10A. In each case patients suffered harm from hospitalisation – by 'deep sleep therapy' at Chelmsford, and by inappropriate use of therapeutic communities and inappropriately excessive use of psychotropic drugs at Townsville (Lawrence 1991). Professional bodies were unable to institute appropriate action in either case and practices were not altered until media campaigns were instituted by patients' rights groups (Boettcher 1992).

When patients are admitted involuntarily to psychiatric hospitals, they come under the jurisdiction of bodies such as guardianship boards. However, decisions should still incorporate consideration of any previous expressions of their wishes (made when they were competent) and of their families' substituted judgments. When a patient is found to be mentally incompetent, this does not imply that they should play no further part in treatment decisions regarding their care. Patients should still be informed about all decisions and should be given the opportunity to participate in planning. Although in some cases their wishes will need to be overruled, this will not always be the case. For example, a patient may resist the use of a particular psychotropic drug, but be quite happy to be prescribed a drug with similar effects that they do not perceive to be causing the same side-effects. It must also be remembered that patients judged not competent to participate in decision-making regarding certain therapies, such as ECT, may not be generally incompetent, may still be able to participate in other treatment decisions and may regain the capacity to make all decisions at a later point.

Boundaries to the therapeutic relationship

The relationship between therapists and patients is marked by a commitment to strict confidentiality and by the presence of notable power imbalances. It is not surprising that in such an environment abuses of the therapeutic relationship sometimes occur. If a therapist has sex with a patient, borrows money or obtains financial advice from a patient, or even just becomes close personal friends with patients, the therapeutic relationship changes to satisfy non-therapeutic ends. Such changes are known as 'boundary violations'. (However, there are some therapeutic relationships which have different boundaries – such as sexual surrogates used in sex therapy. These roles continue to be very controversial.)

Sexual relationships between patients and doctors have been condemned since the formulation of the Hippocratic code which stated that doctors should 'abstain from every voluntary act of mischief and corruption and further from the seduction of females or males, of freemen or slaves' (Karasu 1981). These attitudes have continued to have a major influence on professional codes of ethics. Boundary violations have been examined in great detail in psychiatric and medical literature. They are comparatively neglected in nursing literature, perhaps because there is a perception that there is a lesser power imbalance between nurses and their patients. However, there is much anecdotal evidence of nurses having sex with, and even marrying, their patients – sometimes with disastrous results (Pennington, Gafner et al 1993).

Sexual feelings between therapists and patients are common. In a survey of Dutch doctors, 84% of male gynaecologists (but only 27% of female gynae-cologists) reported having felt sexually attracted to a patient (Wilbers, Veenstra et al 1992). In an American study, 95% of male psychologists and 76% of female psychologists reported experiencing sexual attraction to a patient on at least one occasion (Pope and Bouhoutsos 1986). But while sexual *feelings* are common, sexual *relationships* between doctors and patients are probably much less prevalent. The actual number of doctors who have sexual relations with patients is difficult to quantify, but up to 4% of Dutch gynaecologists and between 5 and 10% of psychiatrists admit having had sexual contact with patients (Ameri-can Medical Association Council on Ethical and Judicial Affairs 1991; Wilbers, Veenstra et al 1992).

Studies of patients who have initiated disciplinary action against physi-cians or who have been identified as having been sexually abused by doctors report that 85-90% of such patients experienced these sexual contacts as damag-ing. Although these studies are clearly influenced by selection bias, many patients who have been involved in patient-doctor sexual contact clearly exper-ience problems such as depression and anxiety, sexual problems, guilt, severe distrust of their own judgment and mistrust of both physicians and men in general (American Medical Association Council on Ethical and Judicial Affairs 1991).

Most of the research on sexual contact between therapists and patients comes from the psychiatric and psychological literature. This is partly because there is a special significance in the relationship between psychiatrist and their clients, but also because psychiatrists seem more willing to evaluate their own practices in this regard. Two central concepts in psychiatric literature are transference and counter-transference. Transference is a term that may be used loosely to describe the attitudes, feelings and thoughts that the patient has for the therapist and the ways in which these emotions have been influenced by previous authority figures such as the patient's parents. Transference is probably less important in relationships that are brief and procedure oriented (such as in ophthalmology) and more so in extended relationships that involve counselling or sexuality, such as gynaecology and general practice. Psychoanalysis uses transference to allow the patient to gain insight into difficult relationships that they have had with authority figures in the past, and to work through these difficulties in the context of the new relationship, eventually disengaging and continuing unsupported. The transference of past attitudes is something that heavily influences the feeling of the patient towards the therapist and may lead to feelings of an affectionate and sexual nature. These feelings may not terminate with the end of therapy and it is possible that they never actually resolve completely. There is a strong body of feeling that therapists should never have relationships with patients, particularly sexual relationships, during or after cessation of therapy as this would represent an unfair exploitation of transference.

The converse of transference is counter-transference – the feelings that the therapist has for the patient. In one study, 93% of psychiatrists who acknowledged having sexual contact with patients felt that the patient was in love with them and 65% felt that they were in love with the patient. In this study, one offender had contacted 12 patients following therapy and continued to maintain that his motivation in his most recent contact was 'love' (Epstein 1994).

Articles in the lay press often use strong emotional language expressing moral outrage at sexual relationships between therapists and patients. (For example, an article in the *Sun* in 1993 was titled: 'Randy Doc with holes in pants bedded Miss A thirteen times'.) Such relationships are often seen as exploitative, due to the great power differentials between therapists and patients. But, as Goodyear-Smith notes, there is probably the potential for exploitation in any relationship:

> [I]t is unrealistic to expect relationships to be always balanced with respect to power. There are also many ways a person can hold power in a relationship, and one member may hold power in one area, to be balanced by power held by the other in a different way. What is important is not necessarily who holds more power, but whether they use that power in an exploitative or manipulative way. (Goodyear-Smith 1993)

There is also some evidence that the power differential in the therapeutic relationship actually helps to decrease the risk of boundary violations. Gabbard, a highly experienced worker in this area, suggests that more problems occur in the area of 'supportive' psychotherapy rather than the more rigidly prescribed expressive or insight-based psychotherapy. This is important because supportive psychotherapy is commonly practised by untrained therapists and other health workers; indeed, it is the basis for much of the 'caring' relationship that is often advocated in health care. According to Gabbard:

> Many therapists relax their mental construct of the therapeutic frame and assume more of an attitude of 'anything goes' when they decide to shift from expressive to supportive tactics. Self-disclosure is often one of the first boundaries to go, and soon the therapist is engaged in an informal, friendly style of interaction that may be perilously close to extra-therapeutic relationships that

do not have treatment goals associated with them. When no immediate disaster is detected after crossing one boundary, the therapist may begin to feel that other boundary crossings will be just as safe. The therapist then develops a false sense of security that leads to a progressive slide down the slippery slope. (Gabbard 1997)

Articles that refer to sexual contact between nurses and patients tend to pay less attention to issues of power differentials between therapists and patients, but are more concerned with concepts such as the nurse's feelings of inadequacy and co-dependence. They suggest that many nurses who meet their own social and emotional needs by keeping care of others might be particularly prone to encourage boundary violations. Nurses might be prone to violate boundaries because of the pressures of single parenting, the need to meet social and emotional needs at work because of irregular hours, lack of awareness and education about boundary issues, and predispositions stemming from addictive or dysfunctional families of origin (Pennington, Gafner et al 1993).

In conclusion, sexual feelings for patients are common, but they should never be acted upon within the context of a professional relationship. If a sexual relationship with a patient is being considered then, as a minimum, therapists must terminate their professional relationship with patients and seek consultation with a colleague about the advisability of their actions. Such actions may still not protect therapists from disciplinary or legal action which may be undertaken even if the patient consents to the relationship. In one case in 1989, the plaintiff was awarded $1 million damages even though the psychologist concerned waited until therapy had ended before beginning a sexual relationship, had married the patient and had remained married for five years (Pope and Bouhoutsos 1986).

The therapeutic relationship between health-care workers and patients is of great moral significance. Patients go to the health-care system for care and the relief of suffering, whether this be psychological, physical or emotional. If, as a consequence of the therapist's poorly considered actions, the patient's suffering comes to outweigh any benefit from this contact, then the patient is entitled to redress.

Conclusion

Psychiatric ethics generally focuses on justice, rights and beneficence, with most concern directed at the rights of vulnerable patients to treatment, and to protection from excessive or unjustified coercion. Debate has also tended to focus on the competing rights of public safety and personal freedom (Bloch and Chodoff 1984). While the emphasis on human rights and justice in psychiatry has undoubtedly reduced the incidence of abuse of psychiatric patients, countered the assumption of incompetence and led to a global trend towards de-institutionalisation, it could be argued that too strong an emphasis on patient rights has also led to a failure to adequately address the stigmatisation of psychiatric illness and the construction of psychiatric diagnosis, and that too rapid a demand for clinical outcomes has led to patients with mental illness being discharged to a community unwilling and ill-prepared to care. Psychiatry raises substantial ethical, ontological and epistemological concerns, concerns that challenge not only our moral values, but also the very way that we construe health, illness and professional care.

MENTAL HEALTH LAW

All Australian jurisdictions have enacted mental health statutes.

Table 25.1 Mental Health Legislation

	Legislation
NSW	*Mental Health Act 2007*
Qld	*Mental Health Act 2000*
SA	*Mental Health Act 1993*
Tas	*Mental Health 1996*
Vic	*Mental Health Act 1986*
WA	*Mental Health Act 1996*
ACT	*Mental Health (Treatment and Care) Act 1994*
NT	*Mental Health and Related Services Act 1998*

Much of this legislation focuses on the involuntary patient and, in particular, on the administrative processes necessary to protect the legal rights of the patient; including issues of detention and treatment against their will. In recent years there has also been a focus on treatment within the community, and in some jurisdictions 'community treatment orders' have been developed.

Some of the issues addressed by the various Acts include:

- definitions of mental illness
- voluntary admission
- involuntary admission
- review, discharge, leave and treatment
- treatment (including ECT and psychosurgery)
- mental health review tribunals.

It is not possible here to cover in detail all of the mental health legislation, instead we will concentrate mainly on definitions of mental illness in law, voluntary and involuntary patients, and prohibited and special treatments.. '

Mental illness defined

Dix and Errington have commented that 'it has traditionally been an arduous task for legislators to define the terms "mentally ill person" and "mental illness"' (Dix, Errington et al 1996). In some jurisdictions there is no precise definition of mental illness, so definitions that are used tend to be somewhat circular. The more recent legislation attempts to define mental illness according to the symptoms displayed by the person.

Some of the difficulties with legal definitions of mental illness are illustrated by the case of Garry David. This Victorian case was an appeal from a decision of the Mental Health Review Board. David, a convicted murderer, carried out several acts of self-mutilation while in prison, had threatened prison officers and had made general threats against the public at large. He was certified under the *Mental Health Act 1986* so that he could be detained and treated, however he then appealed to the Mental Health Review Board who ruled that he was not mentally ill as he was suffering from a personality disorder and therefore could not be civilly committed. The government responded with an extreme measure, by passing the *Community Protection Act 1990* (Vic) 'to provide for the safety of members of the public and the care or treatment and management of Garry David'. Under this Act, an order for preventive detention (not exceeding 12 months) could be made by the Supreme Court if it was satisfied, on the balance of probabilities, that Garry David: '(a) is a serious risk to the safety of any member of the public; and (b) is likely to commit any act of personal violence to another person'. While a detention order was in force regular reports, on specific matters, to the responsible minister were required; and Garry David could be released only by a further order of the Supreme Court. In June 1993 Garry David died of peritonitis, a complication of his repeatedly slashing his abdomen and puncturing his intestines over the previous two years.

This case was an incredible response resulting from the difficulties associated with the meaning of 'mental illness'.

In the Federal Court decision of *Comcare v Mooi* (unreported, 20 June 1996), Drummond J observed:

> In the medico-legal context, the concept of mental illness is a notoriously difficult one to define or describe. Legislation providing for the committal to care of mentally ill persons generally avoids defining what is meant by the term ... Faced with the equally unhelpful English legislation, Lawton LJ, in *W v L* [1974] 1 QB 711 at 719, said that the statutory expression 'mental illness' consists of ordinary English words of no particular medical significance; in order to decide whether a person was mentally ill and thus liable to be kept in protective care under the English mental health legislation, his Lordship said that the right test was to ask whether an ordinary sensible person, aware of the patient's behaviour, would say that he was obviously mentally ill.

In most jurisdictions the legislation provides for certain behaviour that will not amount to mental illness. These provisions offer some degree of protection against the mental health legislation being used to suppress particular thoughts or activities. For example, the New South Wales Act provides in s 16:

> (1)   A person is not a mentally ill person or a mentally disordered person merely because of any one or more of the following:
> (a) the person expresses or refuses or fails to express or has expressed or refused or failed to express a particular political opinion or belief,
> (b) the person expresses or refuses or fails to express or has expressed or refused or failed to express a particular religious opinion or belief,

(c) the person expresses or refuses or fails to express or has expressed or refused or failed to express a particular philosophy,

(d) the person expresses or refuses or fails to express or has expressed or refused or failed to express a particular sexual preference or sexual orientation,

(e) the person engages in or refuses or fails to engage in, or has engaged in or refused or failed to engage in, a particular political activity,

(f) the person engages in or refuses or fails to engage in, or has engaged in or refused or failed to engage in, a particular religious activity,

(g) the person engages in or has engaged in a particular sexual activity or sexual promiscuity,

(h) the person engages in or has engaged in immoral conduct,

(i) the person engages in or has engaged in illegal conduct,

(j) the person has developmental disability of mind,

(k) the person takes or has taken alcohol or any other drug,

New South Wales

New South Wales passed a new *Mental Health Act* in 2007. The Act retained most of the key features of the older legislation but added, amongst other things, new objectives for care and treatment (s 68); added ambulance officers to the list of people who can take a person to a facility for assessment; created new community treatment orders which can be made without the need for inpatient admission; added new powers for travel, search and sedation; prohibited psychosurgery and limited the timing of orders for electro-convulsive therapy (ECT).

Section 4(1) states that:

> *mental illness* means a condition that seriously impairs, either temporarily or permanently, the mental functioning of a person and is characterised by the presence in the person of any one or more of the following symptoms:
> (a) delusions,
> (b) hallucinations,
> (c) serious disorder of thought form,
> (d) a severe disturbance of mood,
> (e) sustained or repeated irrational behaviour indicating the presence of any one or more of the symptoms referred to in paragraphs (a)–(d).

For the purpose of the Act, a 'mentally ill person' is not just a person who suffers from a mental illness, but must meet the criteria set out in s 14:

> A person is a mentally ill person if the person is suffering from mental illness and, owing to that illness, there are reasonable grounds for believing that care, treatment or control of the person is necessary:
> (a) for the person's own protection from serious harm, or
> (b) for the protection of others from serious harm.

The New South Wales Supreme Court, in *DAW v Medical Superintendent of Rozelle Hospital* (unreported, 14 February 1996), considered the meaning of former s 9 (now s 14). The plaintiff in this case, DAW, had been diagnosed as suffering from schizophrenia since her teenage years. She began using heroin at 22, had been on a methadone program since about 1980 and had been taking medication for psychosis for many years. On about 12 occasions, she had been admitted to hospital apparently because she had not maintained medication. Dr Large, a staff specialist psychiatrist, gave evidence that, on 11 January 1996, he became concerned about DAW's potential for suicide. DAW was transferred to Rozelle Hospital.

DAW's claim before the Supreme Court was that the Medical Superintendent of Rozelle Hospital had not proved on the balance of probabilities that DAW was a mentally ill person. DAW and her husband gave evidence before the court. DAW submitted to the judge that there was no suggestion in the notes that DAW had ever attempted suicide. The judge, Hodgson J, noted that DAW in giving her evidence in court 'presented as stable'. DAW's husband gave evidence that he had no concern that there was any danger of the plaintiff injuring herself or her new baby.

Despite this evidence Hodgson J said:

> However, against this, all the expert witnesses who have given evidence in this case, including Dr Clark who gave evidence for the plaintiff, were in agreement that the plaintiff was a mentally ill person within the definition of s 9. Case history notes from Royal Prince Alfred Hospital, of which the King George V Hospital is an adjunct, record that on 10th January 1996, the plaintiff said words to the effect that she was distressed by voices, and that those voices were swearing at her, threatening at her, and wanted her to kill people and kill herself; and that she said she did not have on-going intentions to kill herself, but she might one day. Dr Large gave evidence to the effect that on 11th January 1996, the plaintiff told him twice that she wished she was dead, and said she would not tell him any more for fear of being sent to a psychiatric hospital or him taking steps to prevent her from killing herself.
>
> I consider those notes taken on 10th January 1996, and Dr Large's evidence, to be reliable; and in my opinion, it is appropriate that statements such as those be taken seriously. In those circumstances, and having regard to the evidence of all the medical experts, in my opinion the defendant has shown, on the balance of probabilities, that the plaintiff is a mentally ill person. I might add that there is no contest that the other aspect of s 9 is satisfied, namely that the plaintiff is suffering from mental illness.

It appears from this case that medical evidence seems to be a considerable hurdle to overcome if a person wishes to prove that they are not a 'mentally ill person' for the purposes of the Act!

Queensland

In Queensland the definition of mental illness is a 'condition characterised by a significant disturbance of thought, mood, perception or memory'. Opinions, beliefs and sexual preferences are excluded as they are in New South Wales.

South Australia

The South Australian legislation defines mental illness as 'any illness or disorder of the mind'. There is no safeguard in the South Australian Act that protects certain behaviour that would protect unpopular or simply different points of view. A decision that a person has a mental illness must be made in accordance with internationally accepted medical standards.

Tasmania

Section 4(1) defines mental illness as a mental condition resulting in –

    (a) serious distortion of perception or thought; or

    (b) serious impairment or disturbance of the capacity for rational thought; or

    (c) serious mood disorder; or

    (d) involuntary behaviour or serious impairment of the capacity to control behaviour.

A diagnosis of mental illness may not be based solely on –

    (a) antisocial behaviour; or

    (b) intellectual or behavioural nonconformity; or

    (c) intellectual disability; or

    (d) intoxication by reason of alcohol or a drug. (s 4(2))

Victoria

Section 8(1A) defines mental illness to be a medical condition that is charac-terised by a significant disturbance of thought, mood, perception or memory. Serious temporary or permanent physiological, biochemical or psychological effects of drug or alcohol taking can be regarded as an indication that a person is mentally ill. Opinions, beliefs and sexual preferences are excluded as they are in New South Wales.

Western Australia

Section 4 defines mental illness to be a disturbance of thought, mood, volition, perception, orientation or memory that impairs judgment or behaviour to a significant extent. Opinions, sexual behaviour, immoral conduct, intellectual dis-ability, drug or alcohol dependence and anti-social behaviour are excluded from the definition.

Australian Capital Territory

In the Australian Capital Territory the terms 'mental dysfunction' and 'mental illness' have been defined as:

> *mental dysfunction* means a disturbance or defect, to a substantially disabling degree, of perceptual interpretation, comprehension, reasoning, learning, judgment, memory, motivation or emotion; ...

> *mental illness* means a condition that seriously impairs (either temporarily or permanently) the mental functioning of a person and is characterised by the presence in the person of any of the following symptoms:
>   (a) delusions;
>   (b) hallucinations;

(c)   serious disorder of thought form;

(d)   a severe disturbance of mood;

(e)   sustained or repeated irrational behaviour indicating the presence of the symptoms referred to in paragraph (a), (b), (c) or (d);

A court has also recently considered these provisions. The plaintiff in *Burnett v Mental Health Tribunal* [1997] ACTSC 94, Geraldine Burnett, had been a legal officer in the Public Service but retired in 1990 for what was described as 'psychiatric reasons'. She had been involved in a protracted series of disputes with neighbours. Police had attended from time to time and on occasion she had been taken into custody. The catalyst for her current admission to Canberra Hospital was an incident on 11 October 1997 in which she allegedly became aggressive towards a neighbour, physically assaulted him and caused damage to his property. Before her admission to the Psychiatry Unit of the Canberra Hospital on 11 October 1997 she had been admitted on five other occasions, all said to have been related to aggressive behaviour towards her neighbours.

Ms Burnett appeared before the Mental Health Tribunal, which ordered that she be detained in a mental health facility for a period of up to 28 days, and authorised the Director of Mental Health Services or his delegate to administer psychiatric treatment during that period. The Tribunal found that the appellant was suffering from a psychiatric illness.

Ms Burnett appealed the decision to the ACT Supreme Court. In reviewing the evidence that had been presented before the tribunal the judge, Crispin J said:

> Whilst there is much to suggest that the appellant's behaviour may have been irrational on a number of occasions, the paucity of evidence makes it difficult to determine whether it should be regarded as "sustained or repeated" as required by the definition. Having regard to the nature of this legislation and the potential consequences of a finding of psychiatric illness, I think that this phrase should be construed as requiring more than mere evidence that irrational behaviour occurred on more than one occasion. In my view, the word 'repeated', used as an alternative to 'sustained', refers to a pattern of irrational behaviour or at least to behaviour of that kind which occurs with some measure of frequency. On the basis of the evidence before me it is difficult to determine whether the irrational behaviour has been repeated in that sense. It is even more difficult to determine whether such behaviour was indicative of the presence of delusions or any of the other symptoms referred to in the definition.

Crispin J had 'regard to the intimation that the appellant intends to move to a new location and is willing to attend for counselling and since it is open to the respondent to bring a fresh application' and upheld the appeal.

Northern Territory

Mental illness is defined in s 6 as:

> A condition that seriously impairs, either temporarily or permanently, the mental functioning of a person in one or more of the areas of thought, mood, volition, perception, orientation or memory and is characterised –

(a) by the presence of at least one of the following symptoms:
  (i) delusions;
  (ii) hallucinations;
  (iii) serious disorders of the stream of thought;
  (iv) serious disorders of thought form;
  (v) serious disturbances of mood; or
(b) by sustained or repeated irrational behaviour that may be taken to indicate the presence of at least one of the symptoms referred to in paragraph (a).

The Act also specifies that any determination must be:

> in accordance with internationally accepted clinical standards and concordant with the current edition of the World Health Organisation, International Classification of Mental and Behavioural Disorders, Clinical Descriptions and Diagnostic Guidelines or the American Psychiatric Association Diagnostic and Statistical Manual of Mental Disorders. (s 6(2))

The Act also includes a category of 'mentally disturbed' person, meaning a person whose behaviour is so irrational as to justify the person being temporarily detained under the Act (s 4). Opinions, beliefs and sexual preferences are excluded as they are in New South Wales.

Voluntary treatments

All jurisdictions have schemes of voluntary treatment, but they are regulated in New South Wales, Northern Territory, South Australia and Tasmania. Generally speaking, the law allows people over the age of 14 to admit themselves to a mental health facility, or alternatively the parent or guardian of a person under 18 may seek to have them admitted. The patient's admission needs to be confirmed by a doctor. Medial practitioners may refuse admission but these decisions can be appealed. Voluntary patients are free to leave at any time, but in Tasmania their departure may be delayed for up to four hours for an assessment.

Involuntary treatment

Involuntary treatment regimes regulate the apprehension, detention, examination and treatment of people with mental illness without consent. These regimes are normally triggered by criteria related to the safety of the patient or the public. Most jurisdictions allow people to be apprehended and detained when they threaten suicide or present a serious danger to themselves of other. Examination must ordinarily happen within a quick time after being brought to a facility. After assessment it may be necessary to seek an order from a mental health authority. Stewart, Kerridge and Parker state that orders usually take two forms:

- psychiatric treatment orders, where the treatment is ordered to take place during a period when the person is detained;
- community care orders, where the person is allowed back into the community but ordered to comply with a treatment regime that might include taking medication, be engaged in counselling and seek regular visits to a mental health service. In some jurisdictions community care

orders can also order a person to live at a community care facility or be ordered not to engage in certain activities or meet with certain people. The breach of a community care order can trigger the right to apprehend the person and bring them back into the hospital setting for further assessment. (Stewart, Kerridge and Parker 2008)

Prohibited treatments, electro-convulsive therapy, restraint and seclusion

There are a number of psychiatric treatments which have been banned. Psycho-surgery has been banned in New South Wales and the Northern Territory: *Mental Health Act 2007* (NSW), s 83; *Mental Health and Related Services Act 1998* (NT), s 58. Sterilisations have also been banned as a treatment for mental illness in the Northern Territory: *Mental Health and Related Services Act 1998* (NT), s 60. The notorious deep sleep and insulin coma therapies employed at Chelmsford hospital have been banned in New South Wales, Queensland, Western Australia and the Northern Territory: *Mental Health Act 2007* (NSW), s 83; *Mental Health Act 2000* (Qld), s 162; *Mental Health Act 1996* (WA), s 99; *Mental Health and Related Services Act 1998* (NT), s 59.

In other jurisdictions psychosurgery is heavily regulated and normally must be approved by a board (Queensland, Victoria, Western Australia, ACT) or by two psychiatrists, with the patient's informed consent (South Australia): *Mental Health Act 2000* (Qld), s 161; *Mental Health Act 1986* (Vic), Part 5, Div 1; *Mental Health Act 1996* (WA), Part 5, Div 4; *Mental Health (Treatment and Care) Act 1994* (ACT), Part 7, Div 7.3.

Electro-convulsive therapy (ECT) is also heavily regulated. Ordinarily the law requires that the patient give informed consent or that the ECT be approved of by a mental health tribunal. Strict reporting guidelines are usually imposed and the number of treatments is limited, before further approval must be sought for more treatment: *Mental Health Act 2007* (NSW), Part 2, Div 3; *Mental Health Act 2000* (Qld), Part 7; *Mental Health Act 1986* (Vic), Part 5, Div 2; *Mental Health Act 1996* (WA), Part 5, Div 5; *Mental Health (Treatment and Care) Act 1994* (ACT), Part 7; *Mental Health and Related Services Act 1998* (NT), s 66.

Other difficult treatments include seclusion and restraint. Seclusion and restraint in elder care are discussed in Chapter 23. In the mental health setting orders can be sought in some jurisdictions to confine or restrain the patient, so as to prevent the patient from causing themselves harm: *Mental Health Act 2000* (Qld), Part 3, Divs 3-4; *Mental Health Act 1986* (Vic), Part 5, Div 3; *Mental Health Act 1996* (WA), Part 5, Divs 8-9; *Mental Health (Treatment and Care) Act 1994* (ACT), s 35; *Mental Health and Related Services Act 1998* (NT), s 61. Orders for res-traint and seclusion must be recorded, and ordinarily restricted to maximum times.

Non-psychiatric treatments

People with mental illness are often ill with other ailments and conditions. Most jurisdictions require the informed consent of a patient to non-psychiatric treatments, but they also provide for non-consensual treatment to be provided in an emergency if the treatment is necessary to prevent injury or save the patient's life and that patient is not capable of giving consent: *Mental Health Act 2007* (NSW), s 99; *Mental Health Act 1986* (Vic), Part 5, Div 4; *Mental Health Act 1996* (WA), s 110; *Mental Health and Related Services Act 1998* (NT), s 63.

Standards of care and the mental health patient

A New South Wales case decided by the Supreme Court in 2003 caused a great deal of controversy and raised issues of the standard of care owed to mentally ill or disordered persons (*Presland v Hunter Area Health Service* [2003] NSWSC 754). In 1995 Mr Presland suffered from delusional behaviour that culminated in a violent episode involving a friend and his friend's young child. Mr Presland suffered head injuries and was transported to a local hospital for treatment. His head wounds were treated at the hospital and an initial view was formed that he required psychiatric assessment. He was then taken to a psychiatric hospital for assessment and treatment. Mr Presland appears to have recognised that because of his delusional thoughts he needed assistance and agreed to be taken to the psychiatric hospital. Upon arrival he was assessed and admitted into a ward.

The next morning Mr Presland's brother brought some clothes to the hospital for him. There appears to have been some confusion about the purpose of Mr Presland's brother's purpose in coming to the hospital and it appears that the registrar on duty thought that Mr Presland wished to be discharged from the facility. During a brief interview the registrar seems to have formed the view that Mr Presland was currently not a mentally ill person for the purposes of the *Mental Health Act 1990* (NSW). He was released into the care of his brother. Shortly after his release he killed his brother's fiancé while in a psychotic state.

Mr Presland was tried for murder but found not guilty on the grounds of mental illness and was detained in a psychiatric unit at Long Bay Gaol. After he was released in December 1997 he sued the health service on the basis that it had breached its duty of care when the psychiatric registrar did not recognise that he was a mentally ill or mentally disordered person and should have been detained as an involuntary patient. He argued that if he had been detained his mental condition would have been treated and he would not have killed his brother's fiancé.

The trial judge was extremely critical of the assessment of Mr Presland undertaken at the hospital by the registrar. He described the assessment as 'seriously inadequate' and said that the registrar was 'merely going through the motions and, even then, only some of them'.

In discussing the role of the *Mental Health Act* and the responsibilities of the medical profession, the judge said that the 'best possible care and treatment' (required by the Act) was a medical question distinct from any policy considerations contained within the Act which are confined to how care and treatment are administered. Mr Presland was awarded approximately $300,000 in damages.

The decision was overturned by a majority of the Court of Appeal in *Hunter Area Health Service v Presland* [2005] NSWCA 33. Sheller JA was prepared to find that a duty was owed to Presland but also found that Mr Presland's acts were unlawful and that public policy was against damages being award to Mr Presland. Santow JA found that there was no duty on the part of the doctor to avoid damages for non-physical injuries. Moreover, the imposition of such a duty would go against the objectives of the *Mental Health Act 1990* by introducing a detrimentally defensive frame of mind, and by promoting a bias towards detention. Santow JA also said it would be unjust to make the defendants legally responsible for a non-physical injury traced back to unlawful but not criminal conduct. The fact that the plaintiff was insane did not make the act lawful. Spigelman CJ (in dissent) found that a duty was owed and that the death of the victim was precisely the kind of harm that the statute was designed to prevent.

The New South Wales government responded to *Presland* by amending the *Civil Liability Act 2002* to prevent the recovery of damages for the loss that results from a serious offence committed by a mentally ill person (s 54A). The *Mental Health Act* was also amended to exclude civil liability of police officers and health-care professionals for certain functions exercised under the Act (s 294).

Occupational health and safety and the mental health patient

The various mental health statutes include provisions that deal with the involuntary treatment of patients because they may pose a danger to themselves or others. The 'others' may also include members of staff who are responsible for the care and treatment of the mentally ill patient. Thus the treatment of a mentally ill person may involve the risk that staff may be injured during the treatment of such patients.

Employers also have a responsibility to ensure that employees have a safe workplace. Inevitably there will be a tension between obligations under mental health and occupational health and safety legislation. This tension can be illustrated by a 2002 decision of the New South Wales Industrial Relations Commission (*WorkCover Authority of New South Wales (Inspector Pompili) v Central Sydney Area Health Service* [2002] NSWIRComm 44).

This case involved a complaint that serious failures of a psychiatric hospital's management of patients resulted in a serious assault on staff by an ill patient, armed with broken glass, in an area that had no controlled point of entry. In considering the balance that must be arrived at between the care and treatment of patients and the safety of staff the Commission said:

> Given the evidence as to the conditions from which TR and other patients treated at Rozelle suffer, and the fact that the defendant and those whom it employs are dedicated to the care and treatment which such people require, it can readily be appreciated that staff might be slow to move to physically restrain a patient. That, indeed, would seem consistent with the policies in evidence. Empathy, care and even pity for such patients are, however, not a proper basis upon which employees may be permitted to place themselves into danger. There can be no doubt that in a situation where the choices facing the defendant are physical intervention in order to ensure that a patient is restrained from hurting others and a risk to the health, welfare or safety of

employees, if such steps are not taken, the absolute obligations imposed upon the defendant by s 15 of the Act, require that safety of employees be preferred.

No matter how dedicated to patient welfare a nurse or other employee might be, it is inconsistent with the requirements of the [Occupational Health and Safety] Act, that the defendant permit them to be the subject of physical assault, or indeed repeated physical assault, by patients who are not restrained from harming others. Employment on such a basis is not permitted by the Act.

The evidence which the defendant led was that it is only a small percentage of patients who give rise to risk of assault of staff and others to whom the defendant owes obligations under the Act. That fact does not, however, detract from the need for the defendant to ensure that its obligations are met, when such patients are admitted at Rozelle Hospital. (at [89]-[91])

References

American Medical Association Council on Ethical and Judicial Affairs (1991) 'Sexual misconduct and the practise of medicine'. *JAMA* **266**: 2741-5.

American Psychiatric Association (2000) *Diagnostic and Statistical Manual of Mental Disorders* (4th ed). Washington DC, American Psychiatric Association.

Anon (1992) *Woman's Day*, Sept: 34.

Aronowitz, R (2004) When Do Symptoms Become a Disease? *Health, Disease, and Illness: Concepts in Medicine*. A Caplan, J McCartney and D Sisti. Washington DC, Georgetown University Press: 65-72.

Ash, P (1949) 'The reliability of psychiatric diagnosis'. *J Abnorm Soc Psych* **44**: 272-6.

Bhugara, D and K Bhui (1999) 'Racism in psychiatry: paradigm lost – paradigm regained'. *Int Rev Psychiatry* **11**(2-3): 236-43.

Bloch, S and P Chodoff (1984) *Psychiatric ethics*. London, Oxford University Press.

Bloch, S and P Reddaway (1983) *Soviet Psychiatric Abuse*. London, Gollancz.

Boettcher, B (1992) 'Inquiries into psychiatry: Chelmsford and Townsville'. *Med J Aust* **156**: 222.

Boorse, C (1975) 'On the distinction between disease and illness'. *Philos Publ Affairs* **5**(1): 49-68.

Boorse, C (1976) 'What a theory of mental health should be'. *Jnl for the Theory of Social Behaviour* **6**: 61-84.

Burr, V (1995) *An Introduction to Social Construction*. London, Routledge.

Canguilhem, G (1991) *The Normal and the Pathological – Introduction to the Problem*. New York, Zone Books.

Caplan, A (1995) *They say you're crazy*. New York, Addison-Wesley.

Chodoff, P (2002) 'The medicalisation of the human condition'. *Psychiatr Serv* **53**(5): 627-8.

Clouser, K, C Culver et al (2004) Malady: A New Treatment of Disease. *Health, Disease, and Illness: Concepts in Medicine*. A Caplan, J McCartney and D Sisti. Washington, DC, Georgetown University Press: 90-103.

Dix, A, M Errington et al (1996) *Law for the medical profession*. Sydney, Butterworth Heinemann.

Engel, G (1977) 'The need for a new medical model: A challenge for biomedicine'. *Science* **196**(4268): 129-36.

Epstein, R (1994) *Keeping Boundaries. Maintaining safety and integrity in the psychotherapeutic process*. Washington DC, American Psychiatric Press Inc.

Fabrega, H (2001) 'Culture and history in psychiatric diagnosis and practice'. *Psych Clin Nth America* **24**(3): 391-405.

Fulford, K (1999) Analytic philosophy, brain science, and the concept of disorder. *Psychiatric ethics* (2nd ed). S Bloch, S Green and P Chodoff. New York, Oxford University Press: 161-91.

Gabbard, G (1997) 'Lessons to be learned from the study of sexual boundary violations'. *Aust NZ J Psychiatry* **31**: 321-7.

Goodyear-Smith, F (1993) 'Sexual issues in the doctor/patient relationship'. *NZ Med J* **106**: 227-9.

Group for the Advancement of Psychiatry (1984) *A casebook in psychiatric ethics*. New York, Brunner/Mazel.

Heyd, D and S Bloch (1999) The ethics of suicide. *Psychiatric ethics* (3rd ed). S Bloch, P Chodoff and SK Green. Oxford, Oxford University Press.

Horwitz, A and J Wakefield (2007) *The loss of sadness: How psychiatry transformed normal sorrow into depressive disorder*. Oxford, Oxford University Press.

Johnstone, M (1994) *Bioethics: A Nursing Perspective*. Sydney, Harcourt Brace.

Karasu, T (1981) Ethical aspects of psychotherapy. *Psychiatric ethics*. S Bloch and P Chodoff. Oxford, Oxford University Press.

Kendell, R (1975) 'The concept of disease and its implication for psychiatry'. *Br J Psychiatr* **127**: 305-15.

Kirk, S and H Kutchins (1992) *The Selling of the DSM: The Rhetoric of Science in Psychiatry*. New York, Aldine de Gruyer.

Lakoff, A (2005) *Pharmaceutical reason: Knowledge and Value in Global Psychiatry*. Cambridge, Cambridge University Press.

Lawrence, J (1991) 'Inquiries into psychiatry: Chelmsford and Townsville'. *Med J Aust* **155**: 652-4.

Lee, S (2001) 'Who is politicising psychiatry in China?' *BMJ*(179): 178-9.

Munro, R (2000) 'Judicial psychiatry in China and its political abuses'. *Columbia Jn Asian Law* **14**: 1-128.

Pennington, S, G Gafner et al (1993) 'Addressing ethical boundaries among nurses'. *Nurse Management* **24**(6): 36-9.

Pope, K and J Bouhoutsos (1986) *Sexual Intimacy between therapists and patients*. New York, Praeger.

Reich, W (1981) Psychiatric diagnosis as an ethical problem. *Psychiatric ethics*. S Bloch and P Chodoff. Oxford, Oxford University Press: 61-88.

Robertson, M and G Walter (2007) 'The Ethics of Psychiatric Diagnosis'. *Psych Annals* **37**(12): 793-7.

Sadler, J (2005) *Values and Psychiatric Diagnosis*. New York, Oxford University Press.

Sadler, JE (2002) *Descriptions and prescriptions: Values, mental disorders and the DSMs*. Baltimore, Johns Hopkins University Press.

Schacht, T (1985) 'DSM and the politics of truth'. *Ann Psychol* **40**(5): 513-21.

Stewart, C, I Kerridge and M Parker (2008) *The Australian Medico-Legal Handbook*. Sydney, Elsevier.

Szasz, TS (1960) 'The myth of mental illness'. *Am Psychol* **15**: 113-18.

Szasz, TS (1979) *The theology of medicine: the political-philosophical foundations of medical ethics*. Oxford; Melbourne, Oxford University Press.

Tiles, M (1993) 'The normal and the pathological: the concept of scientific medicine'. *Brit J Phil Sci* **44**: 729-43.

Wakefield, J (1992a) 'Disorder as harmful dysfunction: a conceptual critique of DSM-III-R's definition of mental disorder'. *Psychol Rev* **99**(2): 23-39.

Wakefield, J (1992b) 'The concept of mental disorder: on the boundary between biological facts and social values'. *Am Psychol* **47**: 373-88.

Wakefield, J and M First (2003) Clarifying the distinction between disorder and nodisorder. *Advancing DSM: Dilemmas in Psychiatric Diagnosis*. K Phillips, M First and H Pincus. Washington DC, American Psychiatric Association.

Wilbers, D, G Veenstra et al (1992) 'Sexual contact in the doctor-patient relationship in the Netherlands'. *BMJ* **304**: 1531-4.

Wilson, N (1993) 'DSM-III and the transformation of American Psychiatry: a history'. *Am J Psychiatry* **150**: 399-410.

CHAPTER 22

ETHICS AND CHRONIC DISEASE

Case 1

DE is an 8 year-old boy who has been identified at school as being overweight, and the school has offered extra fitness classes for him and a number of other children. He does not want to go as he feels these would make him be known in class as a 'fatty'. Should his parents encourage him to do these, in the interests of health, or reassure him and try to make him be proud of his body as it is?

Case 2

A Medicare item number for chronic disease plans has been introduced by the federal government to encourage GPs to develop treatment plans for patients with chronic disease. There are now a number of reports of patients for whom their usual GP develops such a plan, only to find that another GP has already done so. Sometimes the patient has been unaware of the other plan, which may have been done as part of a consultation for another problem, or as a single consult with a different GP. In many of these cases, the GP who has been funded to develop the plan is not the person who will provide the long-term care.

There is no clear, agreed definition of what exactly constitutes the set of conditions known as the chronic diseases (Australian Institute of Health and Welfare (AIHW) 2002). The first of the Australian chronic disease strategies – the NT Preventable Chronic Disease Strategy – identified Type II diabetes, Hypertension, Ischaemic Heart Disease (IHD), Chronic Kidney Disease (CKD) and Chronic Obstructive Airways Disease (COAD) as its main focuses – because these conditions were thought to have shared risk factors such as smoking, obesity and other lifestyle factors (Weeramanthri, Morton et al 1999). However, many of the new diseases that have been added to the list of 'chronic diseases' do not share these risk factors.

The Australian National Chronic Disease Strategy concentrated on diseases that can be approached using a common strategy based on prevention, screening, detection at an early stage, best practice management, and patient self-management. This approach is similar to what is recommended by leaders in the field such as Davis and Wagner (Davis, Wagner et al 2000). According to the Australian National Chronic Disease Strategy, chronic diseases:

- have complex and multiple causes;
- usually have a gradual onset, although they can have sudden onset and acute stages;
- occur across the life cycle, although they become more prevalent with older age;
- can compromise quality of life through physical limitations and disability;
- are long term and persistent, leading to a gradual deterioration of health;
- while usually not immediately life threatening, they are the most common and leading cause of premature mortality (National Health Priority Action Council (Australia) and Australia Dept of Health and Ageing 2006).

However, there are exceptions to most of these rules. For example, chronic obstructive airways disease is clearly due to smoking, ischaemic heart disease often presents abruptly and may be immediately life threatening, asthma is common in childhood but may go away later, etc. Some of the conditions included as chronic diseases may not even be best thought of as diseases. This is particularly true of conditions such as hypertension, obesity and Type 2 diabetes, whose major effects on mortality and morbidity are through predisposition to other diseases such as IHD.

Lumping all these disparate conditions together into one entity – chronic diseases – has led to the idea that their numbers are now growing to epidemic proportions, and that all chronic diseases may be treated in similar ways. But it is unclear whether they really should be lumped together. What makes these conditions similar enough that they can all be combined into one category?

Disease, illness and risk factors

One useful way of thinking about chronic disease is the distinction between disease, illness, and risk factor. The definition of these terms has been the subject of a long debate in the philosophy of medicine, but in this chapter we use the term 'disease' to refer to a problem that can be viewed from the biomedical model – such as an alteration in body structure or function. An 'illness' can be defined as the human experience of symptoms and suffering – how the disease is perceived, lived with and responded to by individuals and their families (Lubkin and Larsen 2002). A 'risk factor' can sometimes refer to demographic or other characteristics (such as age) that predispose to disease, and sometimes to a disease process (such as hypertension) that does not directly cause suffering but predisposes to other illnesses that do. Some chronic diseases have moved from being originally described as illnesses to now being regarded as risk factors. For example, hypertension was a cause of death in the past but is rarely a direct cause now – however it continues to be a risk factor for other diseases.

The one thing that we can say about the chronic diseases is that they last a long time. This means that people will react to their diseases differently at different stages of their lives, and at different times after the diagnosis of their disease. For example, a person newly diagnosed with diabetes will likely feel very different about it from someone who has had it for many years.

The sociologist Michael Bury has distinguished two main ways that people ascribe meaning to their chronic diseases. The first meaning lies in the likely consequences of the disease – how it may disrupt their life, everyday activities and lifespan. In the early stages of a chronic disease people often seek to minimise these consequences – seeking advice, reading literature, contacting support groups and so forth. They may begin this process tentatively, becoming more skilled and assertive in time. The second meaning of chronic illness can be seen in terms of its significance to the individual. The significance of conditions such as diabetes or hypertension varies across different sections of society, different socioeconomic layers, different ethnic groups and different individuals. Different conditions carry different stereotypes and imagery (Bury 1991).

The significance of symptoms, be they mild or severe, can be greatly altered by interactions with the health system. Today I feel perfectly healthy. But if I went to the doctor for a few tests, it could turn out that I have hypertension, hypercholesterolemia, impaired glucose tolerance and obesity, all without feeling any different to how I do currently, and without suffering any ill-effects for 10-20 years. Such diagnoses are likely to make me feel worse, not better. (This is quite different to acute diseases, where going to the doctor should make me feel better not worse.)

The significance of many common states of being has changed markedly as more and more aspects of life are defined as 'diseased'. For example, in the past someone might have been thought to be merely fat, whereas now they are part of an 'epidemic' of obesity. Where once someone might have been thought to be sad, they are now suffering from depression. Impaired glucose tolerance is now pre-diabetes. People who we once thought of as busy, we now think of as suffering from 'stress'.

The World Health Organization defined health as 'a state of complete physical, mental and social well-being and not merely the absence of disease or infirmity' (WHO 1946). People with chronic disease risk-factors may have good social and mental well-being, but cannot really be defined as healthy by this definition, yet they may feel perfectly well and suffer no ill-consequences of their diseases for many years. There is a clear ethical question as to whether we should label such people as diseased.

Three areas in which definitions of 'healthy' and 'diseased' have been particularly important are the debate around obesity and overweight, the concept of 'disability', and the way we regard people who have 'survived' life-threatening diseases such as cancer.

Obesity

In recent years the prevalence and mortality of many chronic diseases has fallen, but rates of obesity and Type II diabetes have risen. It is largely the increasing prevalence of these two conditions that has led to the idea that there is an 'epidemic' of chronic disease.

Obesity has been the subject of an acrimonious debate as to whether it should be classified as a disease or not (John-Sowah 2007), with the debate polarised between those who wish to normalise obesity and those who wish it to be medicalised. Part of the problem is that 'disease' can be either contrasted with health or with normality, either of which can in turn be defined as that which is normal or that which is ideal (Tiles 1993).

Obesity is 'normal' in many senses of the word: it is a normal physiological response to an environment of increased food and decreased exercise; obese and overweight people make up the majority of the Australian adult population (Australian Institute of Health and Welfare (AIHW) 2007); and the long-term effects of obesity on mortality appear to be confined to the small group of people with extreme obesity (Flegal, Graubard et al 2005). This suggests that obesity is only a disease when it is contrasted to the ideal. Obesity is not seen as ideal, both because of its physical effects and because of social reasons, whereas other groups such as athletes who also have increased morbidity and health service utilisation (Petridou, Kedikiglou et al 2003) are not seen as diseased because they are seen as ideal.

Obesity is, at least in part, a social construction. For while average weight has increased because of the increased availability of food (and particular types of food) and decreased exercise, the meanings and values attached to body size have also changed over time and vary between cultures. In the West, fat bodies used to be regarded as healthy, prosperous, attractive, sexually desirable and morally virtuous. In many other cultures fatness remains a signifier of social status in men and fertility and desirability in women. In more recent times, however, obesity has become an object of revulsion, shame and disgust, with overtones of moral weakness, greed, psychological maladjustment, impulsiveness, illness and disease (Maddox and Liederman 1969; Jutel 2005; Komesaroff 2008).

In response to the obesity 'epidemic' there has been an explosion of health interventions including pharmaceutical therapies, gastric banding surgery, weight loss programs, public restrictions on food advertising and marketing to children, imposition of food and exercise requirements in schools and public health campaigns encouraging people to exercise more and eat less. Many of these interventions are based on little, if any, evidence. And interventions to decrease obesity also run the risk of increasing morbidity, by increasing the stigmatisation of obesity (Parham 1999; Puhl and Brownell 2003). Indeed an emphasis on obesity in adolescence has already been suggested as one of the causes for an apparent increase in eating disorders such as anorexia and bulimia (Wallace 2007). The entire project of identifying obesity as a disease runs the great risk of losing track of the ultimate outcome – decreasing morbidity and mortality of conditions such as IHD and diabetes that are associated with obesity.

In fact, the mortality risks of obesity are decreasing. As improvements in risk-factor management spread through the population, morbidity and mortality attributable to obesity are likely to continue to fall even without interventions to decrease obesity *per se*. Indeed the extent of negative health consequences that occur from obesity is still unclear. This was demonstrated in a review of the three NHANES surveys from the 1970s to the 1990s showing that the most recent studies were unable to demonstrate any effect of obesity on mortality except at the highest levels of Body Mass Index (BMI). BMIs in the 'overweight' range were associated with better mortality than those in the 'normal' range. The authors commented:

> The impact of obesity on mortality may have decreased over time, perhaps because of improvements in public health and medical care. These findings are consistent with the increases in life expectancy in the United States and the declining mortality rates from ischemic heart disease. (Flegal, Graubard et al 2005)

Unfortunately, by grouping all chronic diseases together, much of the good news about falling mortality from chronic disease is lost in attention to the rising prevalence of obesity and diabetes. A good example of the way that these conditions are reported together occurred in a study that modelled the decrease in US deaths from coronary disease between 1980 and 2000. It concluded that major falls in death rates from cardiovascular disease in the US (by greater than 50%) were partially offset by increases in the body mass index and the prevalence of diabetes during that time (Ford, Ajani et al 2007). Yet an equally valid way of expressing the same information would be that the impact of increasing obesity and diabetes prevalence on cardiovascular death rates was more than made up for by a fall in other risk factors. This is not a message that is often heard!

There is no doubt that there is a lot of 'spin' involved in discussions of obesity and diabetes. Obesity is of key interest to three powerful industries – the food industry, the weight-loss industry and the health-care industry. Messages about obesity and diabetes may be distorted in either direction by any of these interests. For example, in 2004, the World Health Organization's proposed Global Strategy on Diet, Physical Activity and Health was watered down by United States representatives who complained of 'an unsubstantiated focus on "good" and "bad" foods, and a conclusion that specific foods are linked to non-communicable diseases and obesity'. In reply, a WHO official accused the US government of making the health of millions of young Americans 'a hostage to fortune' as a result of its links to business, particularly the sugar lobby (Dyer 2004).

The weight loss industry is also powerful. In 2004, 71 million Americans were reported to be actively dieting, 140,000 underwent bariatric surgery, and the USA collectively spent $46 billion on weight loss products (Gibbs 2005). Of course, most weight loss products are aimed at cosmetic effects rather than health. Major differences between the research community and the wider population about the actual health risks of obesity tend to get mixed up with messages about the aesthetics of obesity.

Disability

Many people with chronic disease are independent and apparently unaffected by their conditions, but there are also many who are disabled or dependent on others for care (House of Representatives Standing Committee on Family Community Housing and Youth 2008). There is a long debate about the philosophy of disability, which is important to understand if we are to understand chronic disease. Much of the thinking about disability seems to prefigure likely future debates about chronic disease.

The International Classification of Impairments, Disabilities and Handicaps (ICIDH) was developed by the World Health Organization in the 1980s to assist government agencies, NGOs and health-care professionals understand and respond to disability. The initial scheme had three major categories: impairment (defined as abnormality in the structure or function of the body due to disease or trauma), disability (defined as restriction in the ability considered normal for a human being), and handicap (defined as the social disadvantage associated with either impairment or disability). But the ICIDH was criticised by disability theorists as placing too much emphasis on disability as a decrease in ability rather than recognising that there are a range ways of being, none of them necessarily more valid then the others. (The ICIDH was subsequently revised with these criticisms in mind into a new classification known as the ICF.)

The disability rights movement arose in the 1970s, influenced by social and political activism in many fields including women's rights, civil rights, black civil rights, and the lesbian and gay movement. They asserted that disabled people were discriminated against because their bodies, behaviours, capacities and identities did not conform to dominant social standards and that social, intellectual and political change was required to end the systematic oppression of disabled people.

Disability theorists and philosophers of disability, including Eva Kittay, Michael Oliver, Magrit Shildrick and Ron Amundson, forced a re-examination of the way that disability is understood. While disability theorists differ in important ways, they generally argue that disability is largely a social and political phenomenon and that medicine, the social sciences and medical humanities, most particularly bioethics, have misunderstood disability.

British disability theorists argued that medicine has generally conceived of disability as a 'personal tragedy' and that this view has translated into medical policies and practices designed to repair, correct or prevent such individuals and social policies aimed at compensation (Oliver 1990). Oliver proposed an alternative 'social model of disability' based on definitions of disability advanced by the Union of Physically Impaired Against Segregation (UPIAS) which located the 'causes' of disability within society and social institutions. The UPIAS defined disability as:

> Disability is something imposed on top of our impairments by the way we are unnecessarily isolated and excluded from full participation in society. Disabled people are therefore an oppressed group in society. To understand this it is necessary to grasp the distinction between the physical impairment and the social situation, called 'disability', of people with such impairment. Thus, we define impairment as lacking part or all of a limb, organ or mechanism of the body; and disability as the disadvantage or restriction of activity caused by a contemporary social organization which takes no or little account of people who have physical impairments and thus excludes them from participation in the mainstream of social activities. Physical disability is therefore a particular form of social oppression. (UPIAS 1976)

The importance of this and similar social reconceptualisations of disability were that they severed the causal link between the bodies of disabled people (impairment) and their social situation (disability), instead defining disability as systematic oppressive and discriminatory social restrictions placed on disabled people through inaccessible buildings, public spaces and transport systems, exclusionary occupational arrangements, segregated education, 'disablist' health policies and practices, and personal prejudice (Oliver 1996).

In recent years philosophers of disability have argued that both medicine and bioethics (particularly utilitarian and libertarian perspectives) have failed to see the social problems associated with disability, have been ignorant of and insensitive to the subjective experiences of disabled people, and have misconstrued the extent to which disabled people are marginalised and discriminated against (Goering 2008; Ho 2008; Shildrick 2008). And, perhaps more controversially, they have maintained that both medicine and bioethics have perpetuated and legitimised the category of 'impairment' in the first place and put in place regulatory responses to control it (Tremain 2001).

These ideas have also been influential on the UN Convention on the Rights of Persons with Disabilities (entered into force 3 May 2008), which defines disability as an evolving concept resulting from the interaction between people with impairments and the environmental and attitudinal barriers that hinder their full and effective participation in society on an equal basis with others. It notes that 650 million people live with disability and about 2 billion people are directly affected by disability (one-third of the world's population).

Concern with the experience of people living with disability, both in the developing and the industrialised world, has prompted the US philosophers, Martha Nussbaum and Eva Kittay, to develop socio-political theories of disability based around human dignity, rights, care and justice (Kittay 1999; Kittay 2005; Nussbaum 2006). Nussbaum's 'capabilities approach' is based on the idea that a just society is one that ensures that each of its members has the capacities necessary for a 'good human life', such as life, food, drink, shelter, mobility, affiliation with others, infant development, practical reason, separateness and so forth.

In contrast, Eva Kittay provides a compelling critique of the adequacy of social contract and liberal theories for disability, through reflection on the experience of her daughter Sesha, who has severe mental retardation and cerebral palsy, cannot speak, walk unassisted or care for herself (Davidson 2007). While Kittay shares with Nussbaum an interest in social justice, she rejects the idea that human life, or good human life, requires the exercise of a predetermined set of human functions and argues instead that some people will be unable to fashion their own lives or exist independently, regardless of what resources are made available and whether or not social prejudices are banished. Kittay's point is that we should not assume that independence is the norm or aim of each individual, or stigmatise those who are dependent. Rather, we should accept that dependency is a fact of human existence and devote our attention to providing for the needs of long-term dependency and care, and providing people with incapacity or disability the space to develop their individuality, autonomy and independent agency (Fine 2005; Davidson 2007).

More recently, disability theorists such as Shakespeare and Hughes have argued that any distinction between disability and impairment 'has outlived its usefulness' and have started to move away from a model of disability as a *purely* social phenomenon (Shakespeare 2006; Hughes 2007).

According to Shakespeare:

> For example, people with intellectual impairments or dyslexia are disadvantaged by living in societies based on written information and expecting high levels of literacy and education. But this does not constitute oppression, any more than snow and ice or floods constitute oppression for people with mobility impairments. Not all barriers are discriminatory. Where people are penalised, through no fault of their own, because they are unable to read or get around, then societies which aspire to being inclusive and egalitarian have a duty to compensate such individuals. Failure to do so effectively undermines a society's claim to fairness and humanity. In other words, there are important additional steps to be made in the argument. (Shakespeare 2008)

This seems to lead us back from seeing disability purely as a social phenomenon, to one in which both biological and social factors need to be considered.

Cancer survivors: Chronic illness, chronic disease or health?

The ethical dimensions of the experience of chronic illness have been explored by authors such as Agich (Agich 1995). One area in which patients' experiences of chronic disease are becoming better known is the long-term experiences of cancer survivors. Increasing numbers of people are now surviving after being successfully treated for cancer. Worldwide, 54.5 million people have been diagnosed with cancer in the past five years and 45% of these people will be alive after five years (Cancer Research UK 2007).

There are a number of moral implications of this phenomenon. First, the fact that so many survive a cancer diagnosis suggests that the disease must not be treated as an acute event but, perhaps, as a diagnosis with long-term sequelae or, perhaps, a chronic disease (Aziz and Rowland 2003). Secondly, if we are to provide care for people with cancer and prepare them for survival beyond a cancer diagnosis, then we must understand what the experience of cancer, and surviving cancer, entails. Thirdly, cancer survivors are going to place a substantial burden on the health sector and this must be accounted for and planned for. As a society we are fortunate that we are now facing an 'epidemic' of cancer survivors, but we must plan accordingly.

Medical interest in the experience of survival after serious illness first developed in the 1960s with reference to life after myocardial infarction (Lew 1967). By the 1980s the concept of 'survivorship' appeared in cancer-related literature as health professionals and researchers became aware of the complex physical, psychosocial, spiritual and social impact of the experience of cancer (Shanfield 1980). While much of the early literature used quantitative measures and focused on biomedical survival, increasingly the literature dealing with life after a cancer diagnosis incorporated qualitative methods and narrative or biographical accounts of illness (Mullan 1985).

Survivorship is now regarded as a state or process that affects all those living after a diagnosis of cancer (Little, Sayers et al 2000; Deimling, Sterns et al 2005). This recognises that a diagnosis of cancer has an immense impact on people's lives and, while few have all the features of psychiatric illness (although some of the features of survivorship overlap with Post Traumatic Stress Disorder), most survivors are left with an enduring sense of their own vulnerability and mortality and most experience a sense of 'liminality' (from the Latin *limen* – describing a place between two living spaces) in that while their cancer may be in remission they can never return to 'normal' (Little, Sayers et al 2000; Carr 2004).

While different people and different cultures may experience cancer and its aftermath very differently, and words are generally incapable of truly capturing the experience of cancer survival, there are a number of elements that characterise survivorship (Little, Sayers et al 2000; Doyle 2008). These include:

- disruption of one's life, relationships and identity;
- a sense that one is always a cancer patient and that the routines of medical follow-up serve both to perpetuate anxiety and provide reassurance (Diamond 1998);
- distrust of one's own body;
- a sense of one's own mortality;
- a feeling of isolation from others and an inability to express or share with others the meaning of the cancer experience, as only those who have 'been there' can begin to understand;
- a sense of always having to live with the uncertainty or recurrence;
- a search for meaning (Frankl 1963);
- an inability to maintain or form relationships; and
- psychological outcomes that may be both positive (personal growth, appreciation of life, improved relationships etc) and negative (existential anxiety, fatigue, cognitive impairment, sexual dysfunction), may never be clearly identified and may not be easily remediable.

While research has now provided a comprehensive insight into the experience of cancer and its treatment, much less is known about the impact of individual and cultural differences on survivorship, or whether specific interventions, such as care plans, structured psychological follow-up, or 'exit interviews' may alter the consequences of a cancer diagnosis. What is clear, however, is that '[p]atient care does not end when treatment ends' (Institute of Medicine 2006).

Lifestyle choice and chronic disease

Chronic conditions such as obesity and diabetes are frequently said to be due to lifestyle choices. While to some extent this may be true, it may also open the door to great stigmatisation of people who suffer from these conditions.

Health professionals are familiar with people who continue to make bad lifestyle choices despite suffering from the bad consequences of these choices. Many people with COAD continue to smoke, many diabetics keep eating cakes, and many people with ischaemic heart disease continue to eat fatty foods and smoke. When we are faced with people like this, we may try to explain their behaviour in two main ways:

- Structural explanations are based on factors that are out of the control of the individual. Structural explanations may include that people smoke because they are addicted; drink as a response to the stressors in their lives; and make bad lifestyle choices because they are poor, ill-educated and oppressed. Structural explanations suggest that the answer to these problems is to change the underlying structure of people's lives – to educate people, improve their standards of living, legislate against addictive substances etc.

- Agency-based explanations explain people's behaviours in term of their choices as free agents. According to agency-based explanations, people choose their behaviours. Some of these choices are rational, some are irrational – but they are all the responsibility of the individual. Agency-based interventions depend upon trying to get individuals to change their choices. For example, Alcoholics Anonymous asks people to take responsibility for their actions and to stop blaming their personal choices on others. (Hays 1994)

When we think about patients with chronic disease, many of us move back and forth between these two models, and we may have difficulty in reconciling them. We talk about expert patients who know how to live with their disease, but we do not always accept that people who do not do what we say have their own expertise. We try to introduce laws to stop people smoking, drinking or eating too much, but we are also sometimes accused of trampling over people's individual choices.

If we explain people's behaviour in terms of free will, bad lifestyle choices seem to reflect poorly on the morality of individuals who make these decisions. When we see lifestyle choices as being due to structural reasons, we may no longer see people as being morally culpable but blame society instead. This makes structural explanations attractive for those of us who do not like making moral judgments about others, but agency-based explanations attractive to those of us who do.

Many people attempt to incorporate both models into their explanations of poor lifestyle choice. Some professionals see those who make bad lifestyle choices as being entirely at the whim of external forces such as poverty, poor education and oppression, but people who make healthy choices as doing so of their own free will. They may see their role as helping people escape their structural bonds, so that they will then be free to make healthy decisions. People who use this sort of explanatory model talk about 'teaching people to make decisions for themselves' or 'helping people to make the right lifestyle choices'. Unfortunately this approach sometimes seems hypocritical since it only allows for the possibility of free will when the patient is doing what the therapist wants.

A different way of understanding this is to remember that all of us have our virtues and vices. For example, some of us may recognise that we are particularly prone to lying around lazily and eating too much. It may also be clear to us that there are some situations in which our vices would be accentuated, and other situations in which they would be minimised. For example if we lived in a community in which we were unable to find a job, where junk food was plentiful, and where it was difficult to undergo recreational activities, then we would be likely to indulge our vices more. Other people have different vices and virtues, for example, the presence of cheap tobacco and alcohol will make those inclined that way to be more likely to drink and smoke, and difficulties obtaining contraceptives will make people less inclined to have safe sex.

As health professionals we can encourage health virtues and discourage health vices at both the individual and societal levels. At an individual level, we can help people to recognise when their behaviours lead them in unhealthy directions, and encourage them to resist going in these ways. At a society level we should be encouraging the development of communities that bring out our virtues and de-emphasise our vices. Making it a bit easier to make healthy choices, and a bit harder to follow our vices, will help us all.

As the epidemiologist S Leonard Syme says:

> No one would [question] that, as individuals, we are responsible for our health. In the final analysis, we are the only ones who can change our behaviour. We are the only ones who lift fork to mouth, who inhale smoke, who plant feet on sidewalk. And we are the only ones who can decide to do these things … [But] we don't live in a vacuum. Whether we like it or not, our thoughts, ideas, wishes and behaviours are influenced and conditioned by the people around us, by environments in which we find ourselves, and the customs, traditions, fads and fashions to which we are continuously exposed … Effective behaviour change therefore requires that we do our best as individuals, but also that we work together with one another to create more healthful and supportive social environments. (Syme 1997)

The epidemic of chronic disease

In 1967, the US Surgeon-General told a White House gathering that it was time to shift national attention from infectious diseases to chronic diseases (Garrett 1994). Since that time chronic disease has been described as an epidemic by WHO (WHO 2005), by academic publications (Horton 2005), and by economists and epidemiologists (Australian Institute of Health and Welfare (AIHW) 2002). Political leaders describe the situation as 'explosive' and 'a rising threat' (Australian Labor Party 2007).

Much of the current awareness about chronic disease has arisen from changes in the disease patterns in the developing world, where chronic disease prevalence has risen rapidly with increasing prosperity. For example, in India life-expectancy at birth has increased from 31 years in 1947 to 61 years in 2005 (Aiyar 2007) and the rise of the middle class means that people are now more likely to be eating better, doing less physically stressful labour and are less likely to suffer from severe infectious diseases. This is all good news, but the down side is that as people live longer they are more likely to suffer from diseases such as diabetes and heart disease. This is particularly the case in countries like India, where peoples' bodies are adapted to poor conditions, and where populations suffer more from chronic disease when conditions improve.

In China, life expectancy has also increased, from less than 50 years in 1950 to 72 years now. In 1973, communicable diseases were responsible for 27.8% of deaths, but only 5.2% in 2005. Chronic diseases have increased as a cause of death, from 41.7% of deaths in 1973 to 74.1% in 2005 (Yang, Kong et al 2008). The causes for the increase are twofold – one is that as more people survive, the diseases of old age become more common. The second is that the lifestyle changes that have resulted in greater lifespan have also resulted in a greater uptake of unhealthy behaviours – particularly smoking. People in China have seen an increase in age-adjusted mortality from diseases such as lung cancer, chronic obstructive airway disease, stroke and ischemic heart disease as well as an increase in life expectancy. The economic costs of this epidemic of chronic disease have been substantial (Yang, Kong et al 2008).

People in many other poor countries are also living longer, and developing chronic diseases more commonly. Funding the treatment of chronic diseases is becoming a great problem for many developing countries and the rising numbers of people requiring treatment for chronic diseases gives the impression that they are facing an 'epidemic' of chronic disease. But few people would recommend going back to previous disease patterns of high levels of communicable disease and reduced life-expectancy. This then is an odd epidemic, an epidemic that we would rather put up with than escape.

There is some justification for seeing chronic disease as an epidemic in countries such as China, but the idea has now also spread to Western countries. The idea that we are facing an 'epidemic' of chronic disease seems to have spread from poor countries to rich countries, and it is now commonly heard in countries like Australia, Great Britain and the USA. This is somewhat surprising because, unlike India and China, one of the most striking trends in health in the past 20 years in Western countries is a major fall in the age-adjusted mortality of most chronic diseases. While this is particularly true of ischaemic heart disease, mortality from other chronic illnesses that are associated with vascular disease (such as cerebrovascular diseases) has also fallen; as has the prevalence and mortality of chronic illnesses associated with smoking (such as asthma and COAD). There have also been general improvements in both life expectancy and levels of self-assessed health (Australian Institute of Health and Welfare (AIHW) 2007).

Although there have been falls in mortality from many chronic illnesses, there has also been an increase in the costs of preventing and treating these illnesses. Reasons for this include the increase in life expectancy, and the spread of chronic disease management and treatment into wider sections of the population (a good example is the increasing use of dialysis in older patients). Costs will continue to rise as more people survive serious illness and as people at lower risk thresholds and greater age take up more expensive preventative treatments. While these trends represent a real need for increased levels of support and funding, they do not represent an epidemic in the usual sense.

Managing chronic disease

Much recent discussion about the treatment of chronic illness emphasises patient self-management as a model of care. According to this model, 'optimal chronic care is achieved when a prepared, proactive practice team interacts with an informed, activated patient. The new patient-physician relationship for chronic disease features informed, activated patients in partnership with their physicians' (Bodenheimer, Lorig et al 2002).

There has been widespread support for the concept of patient self-management. The idea fits nicely into current ideas about patient autonomy, promises savings to government and has the support of many patient groups. (Indeed it has probably resulted in the development of many patient support groups.) But the effects of patient self-management are less clear – and so far this strategy has shown only modest benefits in certain sub-groups of patients with chronic disease.

It is also not entirely sure quite how patient self-management differs from usual good-quality care. There is a suspicion among some commentators that it represents just another way of enhancing medical dominance (Wilson, Kendall et al 2007). Trials that demonstrate the value of patient self-management have largely involved well-educated, middle class, volunteers – quite a different group from the people for whom such skills might be more valuable. There is also concern that the potential harms and costs to patients and their families of self-management have not been fully explored (Redman 2007).

Continuity of care

In the past, medicine often emphasised the importance of the single provider providing 'lifetime' care (Weiss and Blustein 1996). Today, single providers rarely provide ongoing care. The development of health-care teams and the increasing mobility of the workforce mean that there may be little continuity of practitioner or even treating team over the lifetime of a person with chronic disease. This has led to the development of a different model of care to replace the supposed virtues of single-provider care – a model known as 'continuity of care'.

The idea of continuity of care can be broken down into terms such as informational continuity, chronological continuity, interpersonal continuity, geographic continuity, interdisciplinary or team-based continuity, and family continuity (Saultz 2003). Most research has focused on interpersonal continuity – long-term relationships between doctors and patients. This has tended to show increased patient satisfaction, and improvement in some outcomes of care (such as rates of hospitalisation) when long-term relationships are maintained (Gill, Mainous et al 2000; Saultz and Lochner 2005).

In the Australian context, the term 'continuity of care' has come to refer largely to team-based continuity. This can be defined as the degree to which a series of discrete health-care events are experienced as coherent and connected and consistent with patients' or consumers' medical needs and personal context (RACGP 2007). According to Haggerty: 'For patients and their families, the experience of continuity is the perception that providers know what has happened before, that different providers agree on a management plan, and that a provider who knows them will care for them in the future' (Haggerty, Reid et al 2003).

Team-based continuity of care models focus on the way that patients (or consumers) interact with organisations or trans-organisational systems of care rather than with individuals. Many models of continuity of care stress the need for some continuity of provider but this need not necessarily be continuity of a particular doctor-patient relationship. Rather, providers may include practice nurses, case managers or other non- medical persons.

Trust in health care

Trust is a key factor in effective health care, particularly in chronic disease. Trust between patients and health-care providers ('interpersonal trust') is highly correlated with satisfaction with the physician and adherence to treatment (Safran, Taira et al 1998). Trust in health-care organisations such as those responsible for continuity of care (a type of 'impersonal trust') is also important. Mechanic and Schlesinger note that:

> The absence of trust creates substantial social costs as patients or purchasers seek information about physician performance and second or third opinions or otherwise grade themselves against adverse outcomes ... In short, a health care system without trust diverts a large share of the medical care dollar away from treatment to self-protection, regulatory enforcement, and physician compliance. (Mechanic and Schlesinger 1996)

Yet a legitimate question remains as to whether people can or should trust health-care organisations.

Philosophers such as Annette Baier and Tom Bailey stress that trust exposes our weaknesses. Bailey says:

> [W]hen we trust others, we are confidently relying on them to take care of something which we care about, but which they could harm or steal if they wished. When we trust, then, we make ourselves vulnerable. But we do so in the confidence that the trusted will not exploit this vulnerability, and generally in the confidence that the trusted will actively take care of what we make vulnerable. (Bailey 2002)

This point is also emphasised by analysts of trust in health care. Hall and colleagues have defined trust in health care as 'the optimistic acceptance of a vulnerable situation in which the truster believes the trustee will care for the trustee's interests' (Hall, Dugan et al 2001). This definition seems to suggest that the difference between trust in health care and trust in other situations is that, in health care, the 'patient' is already vulnerable so the trusting relationship arises, not from the trustee making themselves vulnerable, but from them optimistically accepting this.

This implies that trusting is forced upon people undergoing health care rather than being a choice. This can be exacerbated when continuity-of-care systems become so all-embracing that there is little actual choice remaining for patients. For example, all palliative care services in a city may be organised into a single service in the interests of continuity of care. But by decreasing choice, this can decrease the opportunity for patients to freely enter into trusting relationships.

According to Gilson:

> In relationships that result from lack of choice or occur in a context of inequality, such as that between health care provider and patient, a form of involuntary trust may appear to exist. However, as trust cannot be coerced into existence, the involuntary trust seen in these relationships is more correctly seen as a form of dependency. (Gilson 2003)

This suggests it is important for health-care organisations and systems that patients voluntarily and optimistically accept their care out of trust, rather than doing so grudgingly because of the lack of choice. But how can this occur?

Institutional trustworthiness

Part of what is required for patients to assign trust to a health-care provider is for the consumer to be able to evaluate the provider's trustworthiness. The philosopher Onora O'Neill has pointed out that trustworthiness is neither necessary nor sufficient for trust (one can both fail to trust the trustworthy and choose to trust the untrustworthy) but it is certainly a step in the right direction. The main difficulty lies in vouchsafing this quality (O'Neill 2002).

The trustworthiness of organisations and of the individuals within them are often linked in the minds of consumers. As Mechanic and Schlesinger note:

> Patients who trust their physicians may worry less about the trustworthiness of the hospitals or health maintenance organisations through which they get their services ... Similarly, trust in one's physicians and nurses can flow from confidence in the competence and commitment of the institutions with which they are affiliated. (Mechanic and Schlesinger 1996)

However, this cognitive link is probably illogical, and reflects a halo effect rather than something that can be depended on. Personally trustworthy individuals may be put under such pressure by an untrustworthy organisation that they do not act in the way expected of them. Alternatively, personally untrustworthy individuals may be so constrained by a trustworthy organisation that they must operate in a trustworthy manner.

Also it does not necessarily follow that because an organisation is composed entirely of trustworthy people then it is itself trustworthy. Organisations may be set up in such a way that they cannot be trusted – for example, so that junior people, who know the truth of the organisation's activities, cannot speak out; while those who speak for the organisation do not understand what is happening.

There is a large literature about trust, organisational ethics and health care (Gilson 2003), much of it focused on managed care in the USA (Mechanic and Schlesinger 1996). Much of this literature suggests that Hobbes's view of individuals should also apply to organisations – that we should trust them only if we are confident that they fear detection and punishment sufficiently to dissuade them from lying to us. A different view – that far-sighted organisations will see that it is in their interests to act truthfully – may be correct; but since it is known that organisations tend to work with short time horizons, and since there is clear evidence of organisations that prosper entirely through deception (such as public relations companies), this view seems tenuous.

What does this mean for continuity of care?

The view that organisational trustworthiness is possible, but only when enforced with big sticks, is one that is widely expressed. In response to this view, health organisations undergo strict accreditation, audit and quality control activities, and are regularly monitored and exposed by the press and a variety of investigatory bodies.

Monitoring and disciplinary institutions are supposed to promote consistent behaviour among trustees. As Gilson notes:

> Trust in strangers may, finally, be rooted in institutions that lower the risks you face in trusting them, and so allow delegated or fiduciary trust to develop … Such institutions enable us to trust the employees of organisations even when we have never had contact with them or share no relevant communal allegiance. As patients, they provide the basis for our judgement that health care providers will act in our best interests. (Gilson 2003)

Yet, as O'Neill has pointed out, the paradoxical results are that trust in health-care organisations appears to have fallen rather than being improved by such measures (O'Neill 2002).

Trusting a health-care system on the basis of one's interpersonal interactions with trustworthy people with in it can only be a rational response if those people have some degree of control of the organisation. If health professionals within an organisation or health-care system have full knowledge about the system, are empowered within the system and act under professional ethics, such individuals should be able to guarantee the integrity of the organisation. For example, if a doctor who is a member of a health-care organisation refers a patient for surgery for cancer, it is important that that patient is seen as quickly as possible and is treated as effectively as possible. At an individual level, professional ethics requires that health professionals do every reasonable thing within their power to ensure the well-being of their patient. On an organisational level, organisational ethics must require that professionals are empowered sufficiently to fulfil the requirements of their personal ethics. Health-care systems must therefore allow professionals to be fully aware of the fate of patients in the organisation, and to have enough power to fix problems if something has gone wrong.

In other words, even if health professionals are not the sole providers for patients, if they are sufficiently empowered then the trustworthiness of the organisation should be able to be vouchsafed by them. In this way, the trust that the patient holds in the organisation should be able to be maintained by the professional ethics of the health professionals who come in contact with the patient

Is chronic disease an ethical problem?

In this chapter we have reviewed some of the emerging ethical problems that arise from chronic diseases. This is a new area of ethics, and we have really only been able to sketch out some preliminary ideas. Some of the other problems that arise with chronic disease are shared with other subjects in this book – labelling is a problem in both psychiatry and chronic disease, and the question of rhetoric comes up repeatedly in public health and research. Other areas are thrown into particular focus by chronic disease – including the idea of patient self-management and the difficulties with providing continuity of care across a team of health-care professionals. In particular, many of the concepts in recent debates about disability seem to show promise in examining the ethical concerns in chronic disease, particularly for stigmatised conditions such as obesity and cancer survivorship. We expect that there will be increasing interest in looking at definitions of disability, normality and disease in relation to chronic diseases. Indeed, there seems little doubt that a rise in interest in the ethics of chronic disease will occur in parallel with the increasing attention being paid to chronic diseases themselves.

CHRONIC DISEASE AND THE LAW

Law and chronic disease prevention

The question whether law can have any role in preventing chronic disease is very much determined by how one conceptualises the problem of chronic disease. Martin has argued that if chronic diseases (like obesity) are considered to be a medical problem then responsibility for reducing obesity levels falls on the health professions (Martin 2008). In such an analysis the role of law is very limited, primarily to the professional regulation. However, if chronic disease is considered to be an economic or social problem, then law has a more direct role to play. Martin says:

> In particular law can:
> - impose enforceable duties on bodies which are in a position to improve the health environment
> - provide powers (such as powers of licensing, taxation, inspection) which give some leverage in ensuring that stakeholders recognise their responsibilities
> - provide tools such as judicial review and actions in tort to enable private bodies and individuals to protect health
> - provide protections against public health interventions which go too far and which impinge on the human rights of individuals
> - set norms to influence public opinion on what is and what is not acceptable health behaviour. (Martin 2008)

Magnusson and Colagiuri have argued that law can play an important role in chronic disease prevention. They list the following legal and regulatory mechanisms that can achieve better outcomes in the fight against chronic disease:

> - *health infrastructure and governance*: improving the quality and implementation of public health policies and programs through agencies that have a clear mandate to follow the evidence and to engage with stakeholders across all sectors;
> - shaping the *information environment* and creating 'information assets';
> - taxing, spending, making grants, subsidising and creating economic incentives;

- designing and altering the physical and built environment;
- *economic policies* addressing the socioeconomic gradient: confronting and addressing health inequalities; and
- *command and control regulation*: directly regulating persons, professionals, businesses and other organisations. (Magnusson and Colagiuri 2008)

The law faces difficulties with such attempts primarily because oftentimes such efforts are hampered by the food, tobacco and alcohol industries which do not support restrictive regulation and which argue that there products are legal, and that the problems caused by the products are the result of an individual's poor choices. However as Magnusson and Colagiuri point out, 'preaching self-control will not work if healthy choices are constantly being undermined by other more powerful influences' (Magnusson and Colagiuri 2008). The role of law is therefore to create supportive environments to counter these influences.

Targeting regulation at obesity

One of the biggest challenges for regulators is the question of what regulatory environment would be the best for tackling rising obesity levels. Some have argued that law can address the underlying environmental risk factors which naturally support better health choices, such as healthier food and better lifestyle (Magnusson 2008a). This shifts the focus from trying to change individual behaviour directly to creating an environment where healthy individual choices about food and exercise are more likely to be made.

Gary Sacks et al have stated that the first step is to examine current regulation to identify which existing laws and regulation:

- are obesogenic (ie create an environment that contributes to obesity) eg, land-use laws that allow for a large concentration of fast-food outlets selling energy-dense foods, and agricultural subsidies that result in an oversupply of sugar;
- serve as barriers to efforts to prevent obesity eg, public liability laws as a barrier to opening school grounds after hours, and food safety laws that encourage packaged and
- not fresh food in pre-schools; and
- serve as facilitators to obesity prevention eg, mandatory physical education in schools, car-free areas of cities. (Sacks, Swinburn et al 2008)

Once these laws have been identified, a restructured focus can re-organise the regulatory environment to make it more conducive to better living. Some of the areas where regulatory change could improve obesity rates include:

Workplace regulation

The change in working environments and the shift to more sedentary forms of employment in the past 50 years have had a major impact on the amount of physical exercise people do. Martin has stated:

> If the government is serious about obesity, then a change in the law on working hours to support a change in working culture, such that family time is recognised and valued, would be a starting point. (Martin 2008)

In the United States, where health insurance is paid for by employers, there is a direct correlation between work and private health. In Australia, other areas may prove fruitful. Magnusson suggests that governments could offer tax incentives to encourage the introduction of health and well-being programs in the workplace (Magnusson 2008b). As Australians spend increasing amounts of time at work, employment becomes more central to the fight against chronic disease. Magnusson points out that the workplace represents an opportunity to address issues of smoking cessation, weight control, regular physical activity, nutrition, health screening and diabetes management.

Breastfeeding

Martin has suggested that legislation can be used to both discourage formula feeding of infants and to encourage breastfeeding which, it is argued, can have positive effects on obesity (Martin 2008). Legislation can prevent milk products from being prescribed and advertising laws can prohibit the advertising of milk products for infants under six months. She also argues laws on maternity leave help to increase breastfeeding rates, as do laws which require breastfeeding spaces at work and laws which protect the right to breastfeed in public. In Australia, the State-based discrimination laws prohibit discrimination based on breastfeeding.

Food in schools

Laws can also dictate the type, quality and portion size of foods sold in schools. In the UK, where school lunches have always been provided by the government, there is an easy and direct line of regulation (Martin 2008). In Australia, where school canteens have been organised at the school level, there is not a history of direct regulation. Nevertheless, examples do exists, such as the NSW Government's *FreshTastes@School* strategy which limits the days soft drinks are available to two days per term and classifies food on a traffic light system.

Food labelling

Traditional food laws deal with poisonous materials and hygiene and have not traditionally been employed to tackle obesity. For that reason Martin believes that the traditional food laws are not useful in the control of obesity (Martin 2008). Magnusson and Colagiuri have suggested that labelling laws would useful, such as a traffic light labelling system to warn of foods high in saturated fat, sugar and salt (Magnusson and Colagiuri 2008).

Advertising

Advertising in traditional media has also been suggested as a possible regulatory market. Many have suggested that children's television advertising be tightly controlled. The Office for Communications in the UK has banned television advertisements for products with high levels of salt, sugar and fat during programs likely to appeal to children (Magnusson and Colagiuri 2008).

In Australia children's television advertising is regulated by the Australian Communications and Media Authority (ACMA). The ACMA enforces the Children's Television Standards (CTS), which place controls on advertising that is shown during children's television. The industry also self-regulates through the *Commercial Television Industry Code of Practice* (CTICP), a voluntary code set up through the industry group, Free TV Australia. The CTICP also has some regulatory impact on advertisements directed to children, including a requirement that food advertisements directed at children not promote unhealthy eating and drinking, an inactive lifestyle, or contain misleading nutritional information (Handsley, Mehta et al 2009). Unfortunately, according to Magnusson, the codes appear to be routinely ignored by food advertisers and are ambiguous (Magnusson 2008b).

In 2008, the *Protecting Children from Junk Food Advertising (Broadcasting Amendment) Bill 2008* was introduced into the Australian Senate. The Bill sought to proscribe junk food advertising during children's television viewing periods. The Bill also sought to make it a condition of financial assistance to schools that they do not display advertisements or sponsorship announcements that relate to food and beverage manufacturers, distributors or sellers. The Bill was referred to the Community Standards Committee of the Senate which recommended that the Bill not be passed. It was thought that the link between advertising and obesity had not been made out and that the development of new self-regulatory standards meant that legislation was premature.

Education programs and healthy food promotion

Australian governments have had a long history of being involved in education programs regarding nutrition and dietary guidelines (Pollard, Lewis et al 2008). Pollard et al have noted that regulatory efforts in this area do better when they are integrated across health departments, particularly when policy goals are shared between the three tiers of government (Pollard, Lewis et al 2008).

Taxation

Hodge et al argue that taxation laws are a useful tool to discourage unhealthy behaviours (Hodge, Garcia et al 2008). Taxation has been used to particular effect on alcohol and tobacco consumption, and some have argued that taxes could have a similarly depressing effect on the consumption of foods high in fat, sugar and salt. 'Fat taxes' have been introduced in a number of American jurisdictions, based on the idea that they will both reduce consumption and add to public coffers for other campaigns against obesity (Hodge, Garcia et al 2008; Magnusson 2008b). Magnusson suggests that other taxes could focus on advertising, either generally or at rates to reflect the health properties of advertised food and drinks.

Such taxes are not without criticism. Some studies have suggested that the taxes do not reduce consumption of low nutritional foods, or that they have unexpected outcomes that can distort healthy eating.

Environmental law

Swinburne argues that one of the major factors in rising obesity rates are environments which promote excessive energy intake and reduce physical exertion (Swinburn 2008). Environmental and planning law can play a role in making sure that appropriate public places are made available for the public to engage in physical exercise. Other aspects of environmental and planning law can be used to limit the amount of fast food restaurants in an area.

Civil Action

Hodge et al have described litigation against fast food chains in the US as a viable regulatory option (Hodge, Garcia et al 2008). Cases in the US have focused on claims for misleading and deceptive conduct, inadequately disclosed health risks, or misleading advertisements. In Florida, DeConna Ice Cream was sued after its ice cream contained three times as much fat as labelled. Similarly, Robert's American Gourmet Foods was sued when its products of rice snacks had unstated calories and fat content. Both suits settled for nuisance sums.

Perhaps the most famous, court case is *Pelman v McDonald's Corp* 452 F Supp 2d 320 (SDNY 2006). The plaintiffs were the parents of minors who sued McDonald's in negligence and for breach of state consumer laws. Eventually the negligence claim was dropped but the consumer law claim survived an interlocutory challenge and is still ongoing. The consumer claim was that McDonald's had created a false impression that their food was nutritionally beneficial and that McDonald's had not disclosed how their food processes rendered their foods less healthier than they claimed.

In response, the food industry aggressively pursued political protection and over 20 States passed legislation banning these claims (Smith 2006). Two attempts in the federal arena, the *Personal Responsibility in Food Consumption Act 2003* and *Commonsense Consumption Act 2005*, both failed.

Some are very critical of the use of litigation to pursue these claims and find tort law to be a poor choice of tool to improve public health. Frank has said:

> A closer look shows that the plaintiffs' successes have been thin gruel and that the obesity litigation to date has been much more successful in transferring wealth to attorneys than in advancing legitimate public policy concerns. (Frank 2006)

Global health and chronic disease

Global and international health law are discussed in Chapter 30, but it is worth mentioning here that international approaches may also be extremely important to the control of chronic disease. International law and global health law can be drivers for change by setting international standards backed up by state obligations. Magnusson lists the following as sources of change:

    (i)   international legal instruments creating legal obligations on signatories to implement certain policies;

    (ii) economic incentives; and

(iii) partnerships between global and national stakeholders for the advancement of shared policy objectives. (Magnusson 2007)

The need for international efforts is primarily a reflection of the fact that chronic
disease is often caused by products produced by large multinational corporations which operate across countries. Magnusson gives two examples of
international health law helping to curb chronic disease. The World Health
Organization (WHO) has pushed for countries to sign the Framework Convention on Tobacco Control (FCTC), a treaty which sees states agree to control
the sale and advertising of tobacco products. WHO has also adopted a Global
Strategy on Diet, Physical Activity and Health (GSDPAH) which, while not a
treaty, aims to provides countries with a policy framework to help states to
implement national policies to combat obesity. Governments who adopt the
strategy agree to implement policies on food labelling and marketing; on production of food, and promoting physical activity.

Magnusson comments:

> Ultimately, whether developed countries pass domestic laws in the areas
> identified above, or secure the health of their populations in other ways, is not
> the point. The point is that global standards provide a baseline for responsible
> transnational corporate behaviour. Appropriately implemented at country
> level, binding international standards on diet and nutrition will make the
> health of future generations less dependent upon corporate charity and
> voluntary commitments. It will also reduce the "regulatory gap" that might
> otherwise emerge between developed and developing countries, due to the
> vulnerability of the latter to pressure from large transnational corporations.
> (Magnusson 2007)

References

Agich, G (1995) Chronic illness and freedom. *Chronic Illness: From experience to policy.* A
    Toombs, D Barnar and R Carson. Indianapolis, Indiana University Press.
Aiyar, S (2007) Our greatest achievement: longer lives. *Times of India.*
Australian Institute of Health and Welfare (AIHW) (2002) *Chronic diseases and associated
    risk factors in Australia, 2001.* Canberra, AIHW.
Australian Institute of Health and Welfare (AIHW) (2007) *Australia's health 2006.*
    Canberra, AIHW.
Australian Labor Party (2007) Fresh ideas for health and the future economy: Rudd. *ALP
    Media Statement 28 June 2007,* Australian Labor Party.
Aziz, N and J Rowland (2003) 'Trends and advances in cancer survivorship research:
    challenges and opportunity'. *Seminars in radiation oncology* 13(3): 248-66.
Bailey, T (2002) 'On Trust and Philosophy'. <http://www.open2.net/trust/on_trust/
    on_trust1.htm>.
Bodenheimer, T, K Lorig et al (2002) 'Patient self-management of chronic disease in
    primary care'. *JAMA* 288(19): 2469-75.
Bury, M (1991) 'The sociology of chronic illness: a review of research and prospects'.
    Sociology of Health and Illness 13(451-468).
Cancer Research UK (2007) 'Cancer Worldwide'. <http://www.cancerresearch.uk.org>.
Carr, K (2004) *It's Not Like That Actually. A Memoir of Surviving cancer – And Beyond.*
    London, Vermillion.
Davidson, M (2007) 'Introduction'. *J Literary Disability* 1(2): i-iv.
Davis, R, R Wagner et al (2000) 'Advances in managing chronic disease'. *BMJ* 320: 525-6.

Deimling, G, S Sterns et al (2005) 'The health of older – adult, long-term cancer survivors'. *Cancer Nursing* **28**(6): 415-24.

Diamond, J (1998) *Because Cowards Get Cancer Too … ….* London, Vermillion.

Doyle, N (2008) 'Cancer survivorship: evolutionary concept analysis'. *J Adv Nursing* **62**(4): 499-509.

Dyer, O (2004) 'United States wins more time to lobby against WHO diet plan'. *BMJ* **328**: 254.

Fine, M (2005) 'Dependency work: A critical exploration of Kittay's perspective on care as a relational power'. *Health Sociology Rev* **14**(2): 153-6.

Flegal, K, B Graubard et al (2005) 'Excess Deaths Associated with Underweight, Overweight, and Obesity'. *JAMA* **293**: 1861-7.

Ford, E, U Ajani et al (2007) 'Explaining the decrease in US deaths from coronary disease'. *N Engl J Med* **356**: 2388-98.

Frank, T (2006) 'A Taxonomy of Obesity Litigation'. *Uni Ark Little Rock L Rev* **28**: 427.

Frankl, V (1963) *Man's Search for Meaning: An Introduction to Logotherapy.* New York, Pocket Books.

Garrett, L (1994) *The Coming Plague. Newly emerging diseases in a world out of balance.* New York, Penguin.

Gibbs, W (2005) 'Obesity: An overblown epidemic?' *Scientific American*(June): 48-55.

Gill, J, AI Mainous et al (2000) 'The Effect of Continuity of Care on Emergency Department Use'. *Arch Fam Med* **9**: 333-8.

Gilson, L (2003) 'Trust and the development of health care as a social institution'. *Social Science and Medicine* **56**: 1453-68.

Goering, S (2008) ' "You say you're happy but …": Contested quality of life judgments in bioethics and disability studies'. *J Bioethical Inquiry* **5**: 125-35.

Haggerty, J, R Reid et al (2003) 'Continuity of care: a multidisciplinary review'. *BMJ*(327): 1219-21.

Hall, M, E Dugan et al (2001) 'Trust in physicians and medical institutions: what is it, can it be measured and does it matter?' *Milbamk Quarterly* **79**(4): 613-39.

Handsley, E, J Mehta et al (2009) 'Regulatory axes on food advertising to children on television'. *Australia and New Zealand Health Policy* **6**: 1.

Hays, S (1994) 'Structure and agency and the sticky problem of culture. Sociological Theory'. *Sociological Theory* **12**(1): 57-72.

Ho, A (2008) 'The individualist model of autonomy and the challenge of disability'. *J Bioethical Inquiry* **5**: 193-207.

Hodge, J, A Garcia et al (2008) 'Legal themes concerning obesity regulation in the United States: Theory and practice'. *Australia and New Zealand Health Policy* **5**: 14.

Horton, R (2005) 'The neglected epidemic of chronic disease'. *Lancet* **366**(9496): 1514.

House of Representatives Standing Committee on Family Community Housing and Youth (2008) 'Better care for our Carers: New parliamentary inquiry announced', Media release. Canberra.

Hughes, B (2007) 'Being disabled: toward a critical social ontology for disability studies'. *Disability and Society* **22**(7): 673-84.

Institute of Medicine (2006) *Cancer Patient to Cancer Survivor: Lost in Transition.* Washington DC, National Academic Press.

John-Sowah, J (2007) 'Implications of Viewing Obesity as a Disease'. <http://www.ama-assn.org/ama/pub/category/15630.html>.

Jutel, A (2005) 'Weighing health: The moral burden of obesity'. *Social Semiotics* **15**(2): 113-25.

Kittay, E (1999) *Love's labor: Women, Equality and Dependency.* New York, Routledge.

Kittay, E (2005) 'Dependency, difference and the global ethic of long-term care'. *J Polit Philos* **13**(4): 443-69.

Komesaroff, PA (2008) *Experiments in Love and Death: Medicine, Postmodernism, Microethics and the Body.* Melbourne, Melbourne University Press.

Lew, E (1967) 'Survivorship after myocardial infarction'. *Am J Public Health* **57**: 119-27.

Little, M, E Sayers et al (2000) 'On surviving cancer'. *J Royal Soc Medicine* **93**(10): 501-3.

Lubkin, I and P Larsen (2002) What is chronicity? *Chronic illness: impact and interventions* (5th ed). I Lubkin and P Larsen. Sudbury, MA, Jones and Bartlett.

Maddox, GL and V Liederman (1969) 'Overweight as a social disability with medical implications'. *J Med Educ* **44**(3): 214-20.

Magnusson, R (2007) 'Non-communicable diseases and global health governance: enhancing global processes to improve health development'. *Globalisation and Health* **3**: 2.

Magnusson, RS (2008a) 'What's law got to do with it Part 1: A framework for obesity prevention'. *Aust New Zealand Health Policy* **5**: 10.

Magnusson, RS (2008b) 'What's law got to do with it Part 2: Legal strategies for healthier nutrition and obesity prevention'. *Aust New Zealand Health Policy* **5**: 11.

Magnusson, RS and R Colagiuri (2008) 'The law and chronic disease prevention: possibilities and politics'. *Med J Aust* **188**(2): 104-5.

Martin, R (2008) 'The role of law in the control of obesity in England: looking at the contribution of law to a healthy food culture'. *Aust New Zealand Health Policy* **5**: 21.

Mechanic, D and M Schlesinger (1996) 'The impact of managed care on patients' trust in medical care and their physicians'. *JAMA* **275**: 1693-7.

Mullan, F (1985) 'Seasons of survival: reflections of a physician with cancer'. *N Engl J Med* **313**(25): 270-3.

National Health Priority Action Council (Australia) and Australia Dept of Health and Ageing (2006) *National Chronic Disease Strategy and the Frameworks*. Canberra, ACT, Dept of Health and Ageing.

Nussbaum, MC (2006) Capabilities and Disabilities. *Frontiers of Justice: Disability, Nationality, Species Membership. Tanner Lectures on Human Values* MC Nussbaum. Cambridge, MA, Harvard University Press: 185-222.

O'Neill, O (2002) *Autonomy and trust in bioethics*. Cambridge, Cambridge University Press.

Oliver, M (1990) *The politics of disablement*. London, Macmillan Education.

Oliver, M (1996) *Understanding disability: from theory to practice*. London, Macmillan.

Parham, E (1999) Meanings of weight among dietitians and nutritionists. *Weighty issues: Fatness and thinness as social problems*. J Sobal and D Maurer. Hawthorne, NY, Aldine de Gruyter: 183-205.

Petridou, E, S Kedikiglou et al (2003) 'Sports injuries among adults in six European Union countries'. *Eur J Trauma* **29**: 278-83.

Pollard, CM, JM Lewis et al (2008) 'Selecting interventions to promote fruit and vegetable consumption: from policy to action, a planning framework case study in Western Australia'. *Aust New Zealand Health Policy* **5**: 27.

Puhl, R and K Brownell (2003) 'Psychosocial origins of obesity stigma: Toward changing a powerful and pervasive bias'. *Obesity Reviews* **4**: 213-27.

RACGP (2007) 'Royal Australian College of General Practitioners. RACGP standards for General Practices. Glossary'. <http://www.racgp.org.au/standards/glossary>.

Redman, B (2007) 'Responsibility for control; ethics of patient preparation for self-management of chronic disease'. *Bioethics* **21**(5): 243-50.

Sacks, G, BA Swinburn et al (2008) 'A systematic policy approach to changing the food system and physical activity environments to prevent obesity'. *Aust New Zealand Health Policy* **5**: 13.

Safran, D, D Taira et al (1998) 'Linking primary care performance to outcomes of care'. *J Fam Pract* **47**(3): 213-20.

Saultz, J (2003) 'Defining and measuring interpersonal continuity of care'. *Ann Fam Med* **1**: 134-43.

Saultz, J and J Lochner (2005) 'Interpersonal Continuity of Care and Care Outcomes: A Critical Review'. *Ann Fam Med* **3**: 159-66.

Shakespeare, T (2006) *Disability rights and wrongs*. London; New York, Routledge.

Shakespeare, T (2008) 'Debating disability'. *J Med Ethics* **34**(11-14).

Shanfield, S (1980) 'On surviving cancer: psychological considerations'. *Comprehensive Psychiatry* **21**(2): 128-34.

Shildrick, M (2008) 'Deciding on death: Conventions and contestations in the context of disability'. *J Bioethical Inquiry* **5**: 209-19.

Smith, J (2006) 'Setting the Stage for Public Health: The Role of Litigation in Controlling Obesity'. *Uni Ark Little Rock L Rev* **28**: 443.

Swinburn, BA (2008) 'Obesity prevention: the role of policies, laws and regulations'. *Aust New Zealand Health Policy* **5**: 12.

Syme, LS (1997) 'Explaining inequalities in coronary heart disease'. *Lancet* **350**: 231.

Tiles, M (1993) 'The normal and the pathological: the concept of scientific medicine'. *Brit J Phil Sci* **44**: 729-43.

Tremain, S (2001) 'On the government of disability'. *Social Theory and Practice* **27**(4): 617-36.

UPIAS (1976) *The fundamental principles of disability*. London, Union for the Physically Impaired Against Segregation.

Wallace, N (2007) Teens' fear of fat fuels eating disorders. *Sydney Morning Herald*.

Weeramanthri, T, S Morton et al (1999) *Northern Territory Preventable Chronic Disease Strategy – Overview and Framework*. Darwin, Territory Health Services.

Weiss, L and J Blustein (1996) 'Faithful patients: the effect of long-term physician-patient relationships on the costs and use of health care by older Americans'. *Am J Public Health.* **86**: 1742-7.

WHO (1946) *Preamble to the Constitution of the World Health Organization*. Geneva, WHO.

WHO (2005) 'Stop the global epidemic of chronic disease'. <http://www.who.int/media centre/news/releases/2005/pr47/en/index.html>.

Wilson, P, S Kendall et al (2007) 'The expert patients programme: a paradox of patient empowerment and medical dominance'. *Health and Social care in the Community* **15**(5): 426-38.

Yang, G, L Kong et al (2008) 'Health system reform in China 3. Emergence of chronic non-communicable diseases in China'. *Lancet* **372**: 1697-705.

CHAPTER 23

THE ELDERLY

Case

Mrs D is a 79-year-old woman who was admitted to hospital because of her decreasing ability to care for herself. Although Mrs D has never had much money, she has a son who is known to be very wealthy. During her stay in hospital it became apparent that Mrs D would be unable to go home but would have to move to a hostel specialising in aged care. She could either pay $60,000 to move in to a private hostel immediately or wait in hospital until a government-funded 'disadvantaged' position became available.

Mrs D had been living in considerable luxury in her son's home but was eligible for the 'disadvantaged' bed because she did not have any money of her own. In consultation with her son, she elected to wait in hospital until such a bed was available. Many of her carers felt uncomfortable with this decision because they believed both that she was taking up a bed that could be used for someone more deserving, and that her son should have a moral duty to pay for his mother's care

Case 2

Miss M is an 82-year-old retired clerical worker who has always lived alone and spent much of her day sitting in a chair, smoking. Local community groups help her with washing, cooking, shopping and cleaning. Her GP has seen her several times for 'neglect', being 'filthy', and having severe cellulitis of her legs. Miss M has always refused to move from her home.

Recently, her niece visited her from another state and was appalled by her aunt's situation. The niece arranged to take Miss M to an aged-care hostel near her home for a 'holiday'. The local geriatric service was then asked to provide an opinion about Miss M's suitability for permanent placement there. Miss M was adamant that she wished to return to her previous living arrangement.

The proportion of elderly people in Western societies is increasing. In Australia in 1991, 11% of the population was aged 65 and over (2.0 million). By 2021 this is projected to increase to 18% (4.2 million). Other characteristics of the older population are also changing. The proportion of people who are very old – aged 85 or over – has increased at an even more rapid rate, from 8% in 1991 to 11% in 2001. The proportion of elderly people from culturally and linguistically diverse backgrounds is also likely to increase, from 18% of the older population in 1996 to 23% of the older population in 2011 (Australian Institute of Health and Welfare 2002).

People who are older than 60 become unwell and die from three major groups of diseases, each producing a different sort of end of life:

> The first is cancer: most victims functioning reasonably well before entering a steep decline. Cancer deaths peak at 65-plus, and more and more sufferers recover. If they do, two other clouds appear on the horizon. One of these is chronic organ failure and the other is frailty, dementia and decline. Chronic problems with an organ – usually heart disease or emphysema – bring a gradual decline punctuated by severe episodes, such as heart attack or lung failure. Dementia or frailty can mean a long poor-quality end of life. As more cures are found for cancer, and sensible types give up smoking and bacon, more people will find that a slow decline is the meagre reward for their virtuous behaviour. (Anon 2008)

Because of these major changes, ethical issues regarding the care of elderly people are likely to gain increasing prominence over the next 20 years. Many of these issues are the same as for other recipients of health care (Mueller, Hook and Fleming 2004) but some issues are thrown into particular prominence in relation to the elderly.

The first of these issues arises because elderly people require more health services than younger people do. In America the elderly constitute 12% of the population but consume more than 30% of health-care resources (Moody 1998). Yet, despite the increased health resources spent upon the elderly, they may not return to a quality of life that is valued by younger, able-bodied people. The issue is further complicated by the fact that there is widespread discrimination against the elderly, and younger members of society undervalue many aspects of the lives of elderly people. Because of these problems, a common but often unspoken agenda is whether health resources should be rationed for the elderly so that they could be used elsewhere where they might 'do more good'.

Limiting care to the elderly

There are several reasons why we might wish to limit care to the elderly. First, there is some evidence that many of the interventions that are commonly used in younger people may be unnecessary or inappropriate for elderly people. For example, Kaw and Sekas examined changes in nutrition and survival for 46 demented nursing-home residents who were treated with percutaneous endoscopically-placed gastrostomy (PEG) tubes. (PEG tubes are tubes that are placed through the abdominal wall directly into the stomach to allow patients to be fed without them swallowing. In many places they are used in elderly people who can no longer swallow effectively because of dementia or strokes.) In this study, no patient's functional or nutritional status improved significantly after PEG placement (Kaw and Sekas 1994).

Secondly, there are interventions that, although they may be medically appropriate in some senses, may not be desired by elderly people. For example, elderly people sometimes refuse surgical procedures on the grounds that they are too old and have 'had a fair innings'; and many do not desire CPR or intensive care admission (Ubel and Goold 1997). The 'fair innings' argument, which has its roots in the Christian idea that our life-span is three score and 10 years (70 years), suggests that anyone who achieves or exceeds this life-span has had a 'fair innings' and anyone who has not has died 'tragically young'. This attitude is reflected in popular folklore and appears to be loosely shared by health professionals, and by the community (Williams 1997).

The philosopher Daniel Callaghan has developed this idea further by suggesting that some of the goals of medicine (such as prolonging life) may no longer be appropriate when applied to the care of the elderly. He says: '[T]here will be better ways in the future to spend our money than on indefinitely extending the life of the elderly. That is neither a wise social goal nor one that the aged themselves should want, however compellingly it will attract them' (Callaghan 1987). He goes on to suggest that society should define the 'natural life span' and that, once patients reach this age, it should no longer be obligatory to offer them life-extending technology. Instead the priority of health care should shift to the relief of suffering only. This idea has been the subject of great controversy and is not widely accepted.

In some ways these ideas are attractive as they imply that it might be possible to save money and to improve care of the elderly at the same time. But there is also some data to suggest that this is not the case. In many studies, elderly people appear to benefit as much or more from expensive, high-technology interventions, such as intensive care units and cardiac investigations, as younger people; and, even after careful explanation of the risks and benefits of invasive therapy, a substantial proportion of elderly people opt for CPR, mechanical ventilation and other aggressive interventions (Levinsky 1996). Even Callaghan's proposal of 'comfort measures' for those who are past their natural lifetime is likely to result in only small savings, as the quantity of highly expensive interventions that occur in this age group is already limited.

Another difficulty with age-based rationing is known as the 'notch problem'. Proposals such as Callaghan's require a cut-off point where patients lose their rights to full medical care and become entitled only to relief of suffering. It is very important that this barrier is set appropriately and that the point of cut-off should not be seen to be an arbitrary one. However, it is likely that for any age that is proposed as the cut-off point examples could be found of those who are older but are deserving of life-extending care, and of those who are younger but for whom such care should be denied. Wide individual variation exists in ageing and many people in later life function physiologically within the normal range for people much younger. Furthermore, any proposal for a cut-off age must in some way be arbitrary, as increasing it or decreasing it by a year or two is unlikely to make a substantial difference to the state of health of the people concerned. This leaves us in a paradoxical situation where the cut-off point cannot be arbitrary but cannot be anything but arbitrary. This identifies a major problem with Callaghan's argument. Not surprisingly, he has been particularly criticised for treating the elderly as a homogenous group that ignores the significance of sexual differences in life-span and individual variation in morbidity. Those who object to such age-based rationing suggest that the only solution, therefore, is to make each decision on the basis of a competent assessment of individual risk (Grimley-Evans 1997).

Callaghan proposes that we should limit the care provided to elderly patients because such expenditure does not offer them sufficient benefits. Many others have suggested that we should limit the care to the elderly because this expenditure does not offer maximum benefit to society. Indeed, this concept is inherent in cost effectiveness and cost-benefits analysis.

To illustrate why this may be so we will consider the example of an elderly patient who requires replacement of a heart valve. In a 1993 article, the case was presented of an 87-year-old lady who had rapidly developed increasing short-ness of breath (Thibault 1993). She was found to have severe aortic stenosis (a narrowing of the outflow valve of the heart), a common condition that usually leads to death within two years unless it is treated with open-heart surgery. She underwent surgery and, after a difficult post-operative course, was able to be discharged on the 32nd post-operative day.

The costs of operating on this woman were several times those of operating on a younger patient with a similar condition. After the operation, the older woman might have been expected to live about six years – a gain of only three to four years from what she would have if she was treated non-surgically. By comparison, the costs of operating on a younger person would be less and they might have many times this life expectancy. Furthermore, a younger patient may be able to go back to paid employment – something that is unlikely with an 87-year-old lady.

If we were to think about this case from the viewpoint of the patient, she is likely to be in favour of valve replacements for the elderly, as they offer her the likelihood that she would more than double her life-expectancy. However, if we were to perform a costs-benefits analysis – and think from the point-of-view of attempting to maximise the economic benefit to society – then it seems likely that we would always chose to operate on a younger patient instead. Similar reasoning would lead us to avoid treating the unemployed, the mentally ill, women and some minority racial groups who are likely to have less income in the longer term or may even place burdens on society. None of this would seem to be supportable in a democratic society.

Many of the difficulties that arise from using age as a basis for resource allocation can be placed in perspective by consideration of ageing and dying as fundamental parts of life. The elderly are deserving of value, care and respect by virtue of their social roles and interactions. Using age as a basis for decision-making and resource allocation without critical reflection or examination of the inappropriate or erroneous language, attitudes, beliefs and behaviours that may be associated with such judgments is nothing more than crude ageism, and should be avoided (Penson, Daniels and Lynch 2004). However, being valued does not constitute an unlimited claim for medical care and resource. Just as we value neonates, but are not required to expend unlimited resources on their care, the same is true of other sectors of the population.

Dementia

One of the characteristic features of ageing, and particularly of extreme ageing, is the increased prevalence of dementing illnesses. Dementia is uncommon before the age of 65, and after the age of 65 the likelihood of living with dementia doubles every 5 years, and it affects 24% of those aged 85 or over (Australian Institute of Health and Welfare 2007). In 2002, the estimated cost of caring for people with dementia in Australia was $3.2 billion (Access Economics 2003).

Dementia develops insidiously, and people who suffer from dementia eventually lose their capacity to make their own decisions. Without mental capacity, demented people are unable to maintain full autonomy. One of the key factors about the ethics of dealing with people with dementia is that this loss of capacity is irreversible.

Much of the discrimination against the elderly that is expressed in our society comes from our attitudes towards their loss of autonomy. (And the elderly also have multiple other reasons for their loss of autonomy.) George Agich, in an essay on autonomy in American culture, notes that autonomy is not only an important philosophical concept, but it is also a significant cultural ideal. The same can be said of Australia.

> Indeed, some authors have noted that the concept of individual freedom held by elderly Americans and their families rests on a sweeping faith and confidence of the individual in his own competence and mastery, which in turn, produces a definition of personal identity predicated on independence and self-reliance. This cultural ideal results in a variety of secondary defences against dependence: a denial of need, hostility towards helpers even in the face of disabilities and limitations that require assistance from others, contempt for the real or imagined weakness of others, and, in some cases, an inflated self-image. The cultural attitude that constitutes an aversion for dependence has been termed counterdependence. The attitude of counterdependence assumes that any form of dependence is tantamount to degrading submission. (Agich 2003)

Given these attitudes, it is not surprising that some of the major ethical and legal approaches to the problems of dementia concentrate on maintaining individual autonomy. They have included the use of substituted decision-makers and advance directives. Unfortunately, there are problems with both these approaches.

One of the main problems is that it has now been clearly demonstrated that decisions made by substitute decision-makers bear little correlation with what people actually wish (Ouslander and Tymchuk 1989; Zweibel and Cassel 1989; Tomlinson, Howe et al 1990; Hare, Pratt et al 1992). This means that the use of surrogate decision-makers probably does not maintain the autonomy of demented people.

There are also many problems with advance directives. Dementia deteriorates over many years. If a patient writes an advance directive, by the time it is required, he or she may be in a completely different physical and mental circumstance. Because of these factors, the idea that autonomy can be preserved into a dementing illness is probably untenable when it comes to making major treatment decisions such as consent for medical procedures and placement. Clinical experience suggests that most of these decisions are actually made by relatives and health professionals on the basis of their own views of the patients' best interests.

In a 1994 article, Athena McLean described a case that she had observed as an anthropologist working at a geriatric centre (McLean 1994). One night, two elderly demented people were disturbed during a sexual act. This led to a number of meetings between the nursing staff, the administration and the families of both patients, as onlookers were concerned that, because the woman was not mentally competent to give informed consent, the relationship was thus vulnerable to charges of sexual assault. The demented man's wife (who was not demented herself but was estranged from him) then authorised the staff to use any means necessary – physical or chemical – to control him. The staff began by attempting to use behaviour therapy but finally placed him on a regime of thioridazine, a major tranquilliser, and carbemazepine, an anticonvulsant, to reduce his 'agitated' behaviour. When these measures did not work, the woman was relocated to another floor. She became withdrawn and combative and also needed treatment with major tranquillisers.

This case illustrates how the wishes of patients before developing dementia cannot necessarily be assumed to represent their wishes once they are demented. There are many cases of demented patients who may have been horrified if they had known how they would change as their disease progressed, but who seem fairly contented in their new demented state. In ethics and law, a considerable emphasis is placed upon the presence of cognitive abilities as evidence of competence, yet people with poor cognitive abilities may continue to have a degree of emotional competence such as the ability to form lasting, satisfying emotional relationships.

We tend to presume that individuals have an 'authentic moral self' that is preserved over time and is best represented by a person's state before they become demented. If that is the case than departures from expected behaviours must be seen as tragic evidence of pathology. But if we accept a different concept of personhood that allows different aspects of people or even different personalities to be expressed over a lifetime, the changes that occur with dementia might even be seen as new possibilities.

What is frequently overlooked is that demented people can often make the smaller decisions of everyday life for themselves. In many ways this is a more important aspect of preservation of autonomy, as these decisions may be more important for the person concerned. In order for demented patients to be able to make such decisions for themselves, the environment of care for elderly demented people must be carefully designed and managed, so that autonomy can be preserved while safety is maintained.

For example, many elderly demented people wander around their environment. If that environment can be made safe, then the person can chose where they wander at liberty without problems occurring. And, if wandering is not viewed as problem, it can be regarded as an opportunity to support mobility and independence (Agich 2003). If on the other hand, the environment is not set up well, and patients are always being shepherded away from dangerous situations, then wandering will become a severe stressor for patients and staff, and patients will find their autonomy severely restricted.

Another example of this principle is that in the past, elderly people were frequently either sedated or restrained in chairs for fear that they would damage themselves when they got up. It has since been shown that with proper attention to the environment, the use of physical and chemical restraints can be markedly reduced or eliminated (Sloane, Mathew et al 1991; Levine, Marchello et al 1995; Hoffman, Powell-Cope et al 2003). (One intervention that has been particularly successful in reducing the use of restraints has been the passing of legislation in the United States that explicitly demands the reduction of psychotropic drugs and restraints. The Bill that accomplished this resulted in a substantial reduction (26.7%) in anti-psychotic medication use (Shorr et al 1994).)

Institutional care

Seven per cent of Australian women and 3% of Australian men aged 65 or over are residents in aged care homes at any time. However, the lifetime risk of becoming a resident of an aged care home is much higher than this. Forty-two per cent of women who are born today can expect to enter an aged care home for permanent care at least once over their lifetime. For men the figure is 24% (Mason, Liu et al 2001).

Mortality rates for demented patients in nursing homes are much higher than those of the general population, especially during the first months after admission (van Dijk et al 1992). The combination of dementia and loss of functional capacities is the most important factor in predicting mortality. Food intake has also been shown to be a strong predictor of survival in elderly patients (Frisoni, Franzoni et al 1995). However, invasive interventions aimed at increasing the life expectancies of demented patients, such as restraints, phar-macological treatments or PEG feeding, have not been shown to be effective in reducing the high rate of mortality found in these patients. By contrast, some of the less technological approaches, such as the use of pets, are well validated and suggest that a more humane approach to nursing home care may be desirable (Fritz, Farver et al 1995).

Many elderly people fear admission to aged care establishments. David Morgan has studied negotiation strategies that are used by elderly people to attempt to avoid this, in a study of an institution in the United States that included both apartment-style accommodation and a nursing home (Morgan 1982). He found that elderly people in this situation used five strategies:

(1) They attempted to disguise their health problems.
(2) They minimised the problems that could not be disguised.
(3) They denied that their problem required treatment or that the nursing home was the appropriate setting for their treatment.
(4) They sought alternatives to a move to the nursing home.
(5) They created conflict among the institution's staff.

Staff responded to these strategies by increasingly monitoring residents with surveillance for behaviours such as drooling, mild confusion or appearing poorly dressed at meals. Any of these suspicious activities were met with an increase in surveillance. The residents, in turn, stepped up their attempts to evade monitoring.

Morgan presented the following case study as an example. Medical staff warned one woman that her general instability made a fall probable if she continued independent living. However, she slipped on a scale and cut her leg. She attempted to hide this and care for herself, but the wound ulcerated and she became bed bound. At that stage it was noted that she was absent from the dining area, and she was transferred to the nursing home where she remained bedridden for two months.

Morgan's research shows quite profoundly how the care of elderly people in institutions can lead insidiously into situations of distrust and to poor health outcomes. Agich, who has also discussed Morgan's work, feels that it is an example of how a society that unrealistically prizes independence can lead to isolation, conflict and adversarial process (Agich 2003). On reading his account one is struck by how the role of care-giver can be eroded by the simultaneous role of gatekeeper. Monitoring patients to assess their need for nursing home can easily merge into general nosiness, and the dignity of both patients and staff can be compromised in the process.

Community care of patients with dementia

Patients with dementia may require many years of nursing care and impose a considerable burden on the health sector. The elderly therefore often become the focus of cost-control measures. It has been suggested that one solution to the economic burden of caring for patients with dementia is to encourage community-based systems of care.

Most patients markedly prefer community care to institutional care. Unfortunately, a number of studies have documented that community care may not be cheaper than institutional care and may place great stresses on carers. For example, one study that examined the relationship between dementia and abusive behaviour in a group of demented patients and their care-givers found that 12% of care-givers reported that they had directed physically abusive behaviour towards patients and 33% reported that patients had directed abuse toward them (Coyne, Reichman et al 1993). This illustrates the fundamental point that, when costs are being added up, it is important to consider non-economic costs and the different viewpoints of those who may have a stake in health care. By shifting the cost of care to the community, increased economic and other burdens are placed on those who do the caring. Within this context it is interesting to note that the majority of home care is provided by women – wives, daughters, other female relatives or neighbours.

Health policies based upon shifting the costs of care to family members break down when families require two incomes to survive, where they are separated by distance and where there has been family breakdown. Under such circumstances governments and health-care workers cannot be moralistic in asserting that people have a duty to care for their older relatives, because for many people this will be neither possible nor desirable.

Despite the problems with community care, there are many people for whom it is appropriate and works well. In fact, as Moody points out:

> Many care-givers remain in their role for a long time and never 'burn out'. There is a normalcy to family care-giving, especially between spouses, that makes it seem non-extraordinary to those who render care. Moreover, significant help for care-giver burden does exist. Social supports, especially the informal support of family and friends, can prove crucial to people under stress. (Moody 1998)

Conclusion

The interests of elderly people are not necessarily the same as the interests of their families, health professionals or health institutions. It is important that a balance is achieved between the needs of these parties and those of elderly people. Approaches to obtaining this balance have not been well delineated in medical or ethical literature but must include considerations of both the patient's autonomy and their best interests.

THE ELDERLY AND THE LAW

The law applies to the elderly in the same way in which it applies to other members of the community. There are a number of areas that have been dealt with in other chapters that may be of particular concern to the elderly. For example, the issues dealt with in Chapters 13, 14 and 15 (competence, surrogate decision-making and the limits of care) may be of concern because older people are more likely to encounter these issues. Such issues will not be re-examined in this chapter, rather we will consider legislation that places limits on discrimination against older people, and some of the rights of people who are in nursing homes or hostels.

Age discrimination

All jurisdictions have legislation that places limits on discrimination on the basis of the age of the person (*Anti-Discrimination Act 1977* (NSW), *Anti-Discrimination Act 1991* (Qld), *Equal Opportunity Act 1984* (SA), *Anti-Discrimination Act 1998* (Tas), *Equal Opportunity Act 1995* (Vic), *Equal Opportunity Act 1984* (WA), *Discrimination Act 1991* (ACT), *Anti-Discrimination Act 1993* (NT). All of these Acts, however, also include exceptions to their application. Each Act needs to be carefully examined in order to determine if a particular activity will be allowed or prohibited by the Act.

These issues were discussed in *Central Northern Adelaide Health Service v Atkinson* [2008] SASC 371. In this case the 77-year-old plaintiff complained that he was being denied access to health care on the grounds of his age. He had sought and been refused health care from a community health-care organisation, which provided services to patients who were Aboriginal or Torres Strait Islander or from a non-English speaking background or under 25 years of age (amongst other things). His complaint of discrimination on the basis of age and race were upheld by the Equal Opportunity Tribunal. The Tribunal directed that there should be a written apology. No compensation was ordered.

On appeal, the Supreme Court of South Australia found that the discrimination was lawful under the *Equal Opportunity Act 1984* (SA), s 85P. This section states that it is not unlawful to carry out a scheme or undertaking for the benefit of persons of a particular age or age group. The court found that, as the age-related criteria were based on the medical needs of young people in the area of drugs, education, employment, poverty, mental health and family and sexual relationships, it was protected under the section.

Federal legislation

The Commonwealth passed the *Age Discrimination Act 2004* which became law on 22 June 2004. This Act makes direct or indirect discrimination on the basis of a person's age unlawful. The areas covered by the Act include employment, education, access to premises, provision of goods, services and facilities, and the provision of accommodation.

The Act brings federal legislation into line with existing State legislation although, unlike State legislation, the Act uses a 'dominant reason' test which requires age as the main reason for the discrimination. For most State legislation it is usually enough if age is just one reason for the discrimination.

The provision of health services would be covered by s 28 of the Act which provides that 'it is unlawful for a person who, whether for payment or not, provides goods or services, or makes facilities available, to discriminate against another person on the ground of the other person's age ...'. It should be noted, however, that the Act provides for exemptions to these requirements for certain health-related purposes. Section 42 says that certain 'exempted health programs' are not subject to the general requirement against discrimination. Exempted health programs are defined as:

> a program, scheme or arrangement that:
> (a) relates to health goods or services or medical goods or services; and
> (b) to the extent that it applies to people of a particular age, is reasonably based on evidence of effectiveness, and on cost (if cost has been taken into account in relation to the program, scheme or arrangement).
> The evidence of effectiveness mentioned in paragraph (b) is evidence that is reasonably available from time to time about matters (such as safety, risks, benefits and health needs) that:
> (c) affect people of the age mentioned in that paragraph (if no comparable evidence is reasonably available from time to time in relation to people of a different age); or
> (d) affect people of the age mentioned in that paragraph in a different way to people of a different age (in all other cases).

An example of an exempted health program included in the Act (although not forming part of the Act itself) is 'a program for providing free influenza vaccines to older people, based on evidence showing that older people are at a greater risk of complications as a result of influenza than are people of different ages'.

Section 42 also includes an exemption for 'individual decisions':

> (3) This Part does not make it unlawful for a person to discriminate against another person, on the ground of the other person's age, by taking the other person's age into account in making a decision relating to health goods or services or medical goods or services, if:
>
> (a) taking the other person's age into account in making the decision is reasonably based on evidence, and professional knowledge, about the ability of persons of the other person's age to benefit from the goods or services; and
>
> (b) the decision is not in accordance with an exempted health program.

While the Bill was being examined by the Australian Senate Legal and Constitutional Committee, COTA National Seniors expressed some reservations about these exemptions, specifically the privileging of 'professional knowledge, about the ability of other persons of the same age to benefit from the goods or services'. COTA noted that:

> Health professionals are amongst occupational groups who accept negative stereotypes of age and base decisions on these false assumptions. In addition health professionals commonly acknowledge that they use 'old age' as a simplistic even though accurate synonym for the effects of chronic disease/disabling conditions on older people. (COTA National Seniors Partnership 2003)

The new Act has not yet been subject to any major judicial consideration in relation to health care. In *Thompson v Big Bert Pty Ltd t/as Charles Hotel* [2007] FCA 1978, a woman unsuccessfully claimed age discrimination in relation to her employment. She claimed that she had lost shiftwork at a pub due to her age and that she was being replaced by 'young glamours'. On the facts Buchanan J found that she had lost work because of her attitude and poor work relationship with other staff, not because of her age.

The High Court of Australia had to address similar age discrimination legislation (under the *Industrial Relations Act 1988* (Cth)) in *Qantas Airways Limited v Christie* [1998] HCA 18. On 21 November 1994, Mr John Christie, a Jumbo Jet B747 Captain with Qantas Airways Ltd ('Qantas'), reached the age of 60 whereupon his employment with Qantas came to an end. International rules would not allow Mr Christie to fly certain international air routes. Qantas would only be able to roster him on domestic air routes which, it was said, was very difficult to accommodate. Mr Christie brought proceedings in the Industrial Relations Court of Australia, asserting that his termination by Qantas was in breach of the federal termination protection laws, which prohibited termination of employment on the grounds of age. Although his claim did not succeed at first instance before Wilcox CJ, a majority of the Full Court of the Federal Court upheld Christie's claim and held that the termination was contrary to law. The primary question, which the High Court was asked to answer in this appeal, was under what circumstances may an employer dismiss an employee on the impermissible ground of age because the employee is unable to perform the 'inherent requirements' of the job. The High Court found that, as Mr Christie could not meet the 'inherent requirements' required by his position, the conditions of his employment that set the mandatory retirement age were effective. The High Court (by majority) allowed Qantas' appeal. The New Zealand Court of Appeal made an almost identical decision in *Air New Zealand Ltd v McAlister* [2008] 3 NZLR 794.

Even though similar cases do not seem to have been considered in the area of health care, it can be inferred that decisions on appropriate treatment should not be made strictly on the age of the patient but on their current health status (although age may be a relevant consideration to take into account). In *Qantas Airways Limited v Christie* [1998] HCA 18 at [1], Brennan CJ said:

> The experience of … courts … in applying anti-discrimination legislation must be built case by case. A firm jurisprudence will be developed over time; its development should not be confined by too early a definition of its principles.

It remains to be seen how the courts will approach the issue of rationing decisions that are based on criteria such as the age of the patient.

The rights of the elderly in institutions

Nursing homes are facilities regulated by State legislation that provide health-care services for the aged or for people with major disabilities. The Commonwealth, however, controls the administration of nursing homes through the provision of finance and subsidies in approved nursing homes.

In 1997 the Commonwealth enacted the *Aged Care Act 1997*. This Act concerns the licensing of approved providers, as well as the funding and allocation of places in aged care. Amongst other things, it sets out the responsibilities of approved providers for the quality of care they provide and the rights of those being cared for. The Act has not been without its critics, particularly in relation to entry contributions for intending residents of nursing homes and hostels for the first time.

The minister may make principles under s 96-1(1) of the Act for regulating the care to be provided. The current version of the *Quality of Care Principles 1997* sets out standards for accreditation, residential care, community care and flexible care. The minister has also made the *User Rights Principles 1997* which deal with the responsibilities of providers in relation to: any accommodation bond charged; fees; security and tenure; compliance with extra service agreements; and establishment of complaints resolution.

Failure to observe principles can result in loss of approval to provide services. In 2000 the Secretary to the Commonwealth Department of Health and Aged Care (as the Department was then known) revoked the licence under the *Aged Care Act* of a Melbourne nursing home – Riverside Nursing Home. This action followed sensational publicity about the standard of care provided to residents of the facility, including 'kerosene baths'. The licence of the nursing home was revoked after an investigation that identified evidence of a severe risk to the health and well-being of residents. An appeal by the nursing home against the decision was unsuccessful (*Riverside Nursing Care Pty Ltd v Bishop* [2000] FCA 1054).

A more recent example comes from *Re Saitta Pty Ltd and Secretary, Department of Health and Ageing* (2008) 105 ALD 55. In this case the Administrative Appeals Tribunal upheld the decision of the Department of Health and Ageing to revoke the applicant's approval as a provider of aged care services. The approval was revoked for allowing a disqualified person to be involved in management; for poor infection control (including poor food handling, poor wound management, poor waste management, soiled clothing not being washed properly and toilet brushes not being cleaned regularly); non-maintenance of buildings and furniture in a poor state; inadequate medication management (drugs were not properly secured; tablets were found on the floor, residents were given medication when lying down; medication was mixed with food; drugs charts were not kept properly).

Particular note was made of the fact that the dignity of the residents was not being afforded by their living conditions. The Tribunal stated:

> The Standards state that the aim is to accord dignity to residents. Keeping residents and the environment in which they live clean not only maintains that dignity but also promotes better health. Clothes which after washing still retain faecal matter are clearly undesirable and unacceptable from both a dignity and health point of view. The leaving of a faecally soiled kylie on the floor in a room occupied by two residents, without making an arrangement for the floor to be cleaned, while the carer attends a training session, is undignified for the resident. The lack of effective strategies to assist residents and greater monitoring and use of ameliorative strategies for those who are apt to void inappropriately all result in residents not being accorded proper dignity and constitute non compliance with Standard Pt 3 Item 3.6 (dignity). (at [118])

The fact that the buildings and furniture were not properly maintained also was said to affront the dignity of the residents. Rubbish bins were not regularly emptied and male residents often urinated in them. There was a strong smell of urine in the carpet. A resident was observed being restrained with a lap belt in a chair an hour after breakfast had finished. Food was hurriedly shovelled into the resident's mouths and they were left with food over their faces. The resident were found to be in a basically filthy condition and inadequately cared for. On the basis of these findings the Tribunal was satisfied that the decision to revoke the approval was necessary and appropriate.

Some States also provide some protection for the elderly who are in institutional care (Bates, Dewdney et al 1988-present). For example, the principles outlined in the *Health Services Act 1988* (Vic), s 10, require proprietors of 'residential care services' to ensure that:

    (a)   residents are entitled to high quality health care and personal care, to their choice of registered medical practitioner or other provider of health services and to an informed choice of appropriate treatment;

(b) residents should be provided with a sufficient level of nutrition, warmth, clothing and shelter in a home-like environment;

(c) services should be provided in a safe environment and the residents' right to choose to participate in activities involving a degree of risk should be recognised;

(d) residents should be treated with dignity and respect and are entitled to privacy;

(e) residents should be provided with and be encouraged to participate in activities appropriate to their interests and needs and to physical and social rehabilitation;

(f) residents are entitled to social independence including the right to choose and pursue friendships and relationships with members of either sex, to practise religion and cultural customs and to exercise rights as citizens;

(g) residents are entitled to the right to manage their own finances wherever possible;

(h) residents are entitled to freedom of choice to the extent that it does not unreasonably infringe the rights of others and the freedom to comment about the provision of health services.

More detailed standards are outlined in the *Health Services (Supported Residential Services) Regulations 2001* (Vic).

Restraints, seclusion and the use of reasonable force

There may be occasions where a patient, perhaps because of the effects of dementia, mental illness or disability, poses a threat to themselves or to others. Elderly patients may also become disorientated and hence prone to wandering away from their carers. They may also be abusive, violent and aggressive. In circumstances such as these the question needs to be considered as to whether these people, in these circumstances, can be restrained or secluded?

At law, it is a general principle that people should not be detained against their will unless there is some lawful reason for doing so (Edginton 1995). In the civil law the unlawful restraint or seclusion of a person may amount to the tort of 'false imprisonment' (see Chapter 14). If the restraint or seclusion is accompanied by physical force there may also be a 'battery'. For example, a competent patient cannot normally be detained against their will in a hospital, even if it is in their best interests to remain. Even the act of hiding the patient's street clothes in order to prevent them from leaving (without any other action) could amount to a false imprisonment. Drugs should also not be given if the purpose of administering the drug is to restrain the person rather than for their treatment.

There may be occasions when a patient may need to be restrained in order to protect:

- the patient from injury;
- other patients who may be at risk;
- themselves from unnecessary risk or harm. (Staunton and Chiarella 2003)

Staunton and Chiarella make a particularly important point when they write that it must be remembered that 'such restraint is for the protection [of the patient] and not the convenience of staff' (Staunton and Chiarella 2003). Any application of restraint must be done after consideration of all of the issues involved, consultation with staff who may be involved in the care of the person and, where possible, the relatives (or person responsible) of the person.

The power to authorise seclusion, restraint and reasonable force most probably emanates from the *parens patriae* jurisdiction over incompetent adults and children. In *Re PS (an adult)* [2007] EWHC 623 (Fam), it was said in the United Kingdom context that the court has an inherent jurisdiction (similar to *parens patriae*):

> to direct that the child or adult in question shall be placed at and remain in a specified institution such as, for example, a hospital, residential unit, care home or secure unit. It is equally clear that the court's powers extend to authorising that person's detention in such a place and the use of reasonable force (if necessary) to detain him and ensure that he remains there: see *Norfolk and Norwich Healthcare (NHS) Trust v W* [1996] 2 FLR 613 (adult), *A Metropolitan Borough Council v DB* [1997] 1 FLR 767 (child), *Re MB (Medical Treatment)* [1997] 2 FLR 426 at page 439 (adult) and *Re C (Detention: Medical Treatment)* [1997] 2 FLR 180 (child). (at [16])

Re PS (an adult) was concerned with an elderly incompetent woman who was in need of care but whose daughter was threatening to remove her from that care, in contravention of her best interests. Mumby J used the inherent power to order PS be detained. Mumby J made similar orders authorising 'reasonable and proportionate measures' in *Matter of GJ NJ and BJ* [2008] EWHC 1097 (Fam) and *Primary Care Trust v AH* [2008] EWHC 1403 (Fam), where caring relatives of disable adults were unable or refused to consent to assessment for medical treatment.

In Australia, there is some legislative recognition of the need for detention, restraint and reasonable force in aged care and disability services (such control measures in the mental health setting are discussed in Chapter 21). Section 32(c) of the *Guardianship and Administration Act 1993* (SA) states that 'the use of such force as may be reasonably necessary for ensuring the proper medical treatment, day-to-day care and wellbeing of the person'. The South Australian Office of Public Advocate has argued that it is best to get consent from a substitute decision-maker before applying restraint and that it must be recorded in the patient's records (Harley 2002).

In Queensland, s 75 of the *Guardianship and Administration Act 2000* contains similar wording. Detention under this section (although not in an aged care context) was raised in *Re JD* [2003] QGAAT 14. Ms JD was aged 23 years at the time of the application before the Tribunal. She was diagnosed as having a moderate level of mental retardation following a brain haemorrhage after an injury when she was three and a half years of age. It is said that Ms JD displayed immature and destructive behaviours, was quick to anger and prone to yell, hit and break things. As Ms JD lacked the capacity to make personal decisions for herself the Adult Guardian was appointed as her guardian. The issue before the

Tribunal was whether a guardianship order can be used to require the detention of Ms JD against her will.

The Guardianship and Administration Tribunal (GAAT) believed that s 75 provided sufficient authority for a guardian to authorise the use of minimum force necessary to carry out the health care that is authorised under the Act (where the health care is likely to cause no distress or temporary distress which is outweighed by the benefit to the adult of the proposed health care (s 67)).

However, it was drawn to the attention of the Tribunal that the Queensland Health Department (which was not a party to the proceedings) had received legal advice that the guardian did not, in fact, have such powers. The GAAT also noted similar concerns expressed in 2002 by a Victorian Law Reform Commission Discussion Paper on 'People with Intellectual Disabilities at Risk'. The GAAT was also aware of concerns that had been expressed in recent cases in the European Court of Human Rights in relation to the use of restraint and detention in relation to adults with impaired capacity.

In light of these concerns the GAAT recommended that the Adult Guardian should take the matter on appeal to the Supreme Court to determine the issue. The outcome of any application to the Supreme Court is not known.

The issue was reconsidered again in *Re WMC* [2005] QGAAT 26. The person under guardianship was a 45-year-old man who had been intellectually disabled since birth. He had been institutionalised since he was five years of age. He often behaved in ways that could harm others, including yelling, pounding walls and doors, punching and breaking windows. Seclusion was often used as a means of settling him down. The GAAT accepted that seclusion and restraint were permissible only if they promoted and maintained his health and wellbeing or were in his overall best interests.

A different outcome can be found in *Re MLI* [2006] QGAAT 31. The question in this case was whether it was appropriate to use restrictive measures to treat an 18-year-old, mildly intellectually disabled man which included continued seclusion. MLI had a history of explosive outbursts and violent behaviour including assaulting staff and lighting fires. The GAAT was concerned that MLI was being detained indefinitely. While the Tribunal was satisfied that a guardian's power to consent to health care could extend to consenting to restrictive practices, detention behind locked doors permanently could not be so authorised. An urgent review of MLI's conditions was ordered.

Finally, in *Re HAB* [2007] QGAAT 13, restraint with a sash was referred to without objection by the GAAT in relation to the appointment of the Adult Guardian as guardian over an 88-year-old woman with dementia. The woman had impaired mobility and had suffered serious falls caused by her attempts to stand and had previously broken her hip after a fall.

Conceivably as a response to these problems, changes were introduced in 2008. In Queensland, the use of restraints can be consented to by the adult using an advance directive: *Powers of Attorney Act 1998*, s 35(2)(c). Otherwise restrictive practices (including restraints and seclusion) are governed by Chapter 5B of the *Guardianship and Administration Act 2000* and by Part 10A of the *Disability Services Act 2006*. Seclusion may only be ordered when the adult lacks capacity, is a danger to others, a positive behaviour support plan had been created for them and when restraining or secluding the patient is the least restrictive option. If the restraints are chemical in nature the adult's doctor must be asked for their opinion. Restrictive practice orders must be reviewed and can be in place for no longer than 12 months. Guardians can also be appointed for restrictive practices to give consent on the adult's behalf.

In Victoria powers are given to the Victorian Civil and Administrative Tribunal (VCAT) under the *Guardianship and Administration Act 1986*, s 26, to make an order authorising the use of restraints to unsure that the represented person complies with the guardian's decisions.

Additional powers have been given to VCAT under the *Disability Act 2006*, s 186, to order those in disability services residential accommodation to be placed under a supervised treatment order. The order can authorise restrictive interventions including seclusion and restraint (both physical and chemical). VCAT may only make the order if it is satisfied that:

(a)   the person has previously exhibited a pattern of violent or dangerous behaviour causing serious harm to another person or exposing another person to a significant risk of serious harm;

(b)   there is a significant risk of serious harm to another person which cannot be substantially reduced by using less restrictive means;

(c)   the services to be provided to the person in accordance with the treatment plan will be of benefit to the person and substantially reduce the significant risk of serious harm to another person;

(d)   the person is unable or unwilling to consent to voluntarily complying with a treatment plan to substantially reduce the significant risk of serious harm to another person;

(e)   it is necessary to detain the person to ensure compliance with the treatment plan and prevent a significant risk of serious harm to another person. (s 191(6))

VCAT employed its powers in *MM (Guardianship)* [2008] VCAT 1282. The case concerned a 35-year-old intellectually disabled man who was assessed as being a serious risk of committing sexual violence against young boys and adolescents. He was ordered to remain detained for continued treatment. A similar order was made in *LM (Guardianship)* [2008] VCAT 2084 to detain a 25-year-old woman with a mild to borderline intellectual disability, borderline personality disorder, depression, anxiety and non-epileptic seizures. She had had four seizures on roads and walked into traffic twice. She had also made numerous violent threats and threats to self-harm. She had also begun to secret a knife.

In Western Australia, chemical restraint has been approved by the State Administrative Tribunal (SAT) for people under guardianship: *Re Application for Guardianship Order (BCB)* (2002) 28 SR (WA) 338; *SJ and MET* [2006] WASAT 210; *PN* [2008] WASAT 158. For example, in *ADP* [2005] WASAT 131, the SAT ordered that the Public Advocate be appointed the guardian of an elderly patient with a history of abusive behaviour who was being treated with olanzapine for his psychosis. The Public Advocate was, amongst other things, given the power to consent to chemical restraints. More recently in *JP* [2008] WASAT 3, JP was a 59-year-old man with severe residual physical, cognitive and behavioural deficiencies as a consequence of a brain trauma. He was treated with antipsychotic medication. The SAT rejected an attempt by the Public Advocate to classify the medication as treatment for the man's condition. Its purpose was not to treat but to restrain the patient. In that sense a guardian needed to be appointed to consent to restraint but only when it was in JP's best interests, rather than for the convenience of the staff.

Mandatory reporting of elder abuse

The *Aged Care Act 1997* (Cth) , s 63-1AA, makes it mandatory for both approved providers of aged care and staff to report suspected 'reportable assaults'. Section 63-1AA(9) defines these as 'unlawful sexual contact, unreasonable use of force, or assault …', that is inflicted on a person in aged care. The approved provider must report within 24 hours to both the police and to the Secretary of the Department. Staff must report as soon as is reasonably possible to either (or all of) the approved provider, key personnel, another person approved by the provider to receive such reports, a police officer or the Secretary.

References

Anon (2008) Things to look forward to *The Economist*.

Access Economics (2003) *The dementia epidemic: economic impact and positive solutions for Australia*. Canberra, Access Economics.

Agich, G (2003) *Dependence and autonomy in old age*. Cambridge, Cambridge University Press.

Australian Institute of Health and Welfare (2002) *Older Australia at a glance*. Canberra, AIHW.

Australian Institute of Health and Welfare (2007) *Dementia in Australia: National data analysis and development*. Canberra, AIHW.

Bates, IW, JC Dewdney et al (1988-present) *Australian Health & Medical Law Reporter* (Looseleaf Service). Sydney, CCH Australia.

Callaghan, D (1987) *Setting limits: Medical goals in an aging society*. New York, Simon and Schuster.

COTA National Seniors Partnership (2003) Submission to Australian Senate Legal and Constitutional Committee: Provisions of the Age Discrimination Bill 2003.

Coyne, A, W Reichman et al (1993) 'The relationship between dementia and elder abuse'. *Am J Psychiatry* **150**(4): 643-6.

Edginton, J (1995) *Law for the Nursing Profession and allied health care professionals*. Sydney, CCH Australia Ltd.

Frisoni, G, S Franzoni et al (1995) 'Food intake and mortality in the frail elderly'. *J Geront A Biol Sci Med* **50**(4): M203-10.

Fritz, C, T Farver et al (1995) 'Association with companion animals and the expression of noncognitive symptoms in Alzheimer's patients'. *J Nerv Ment Dis* **183**(7): 459-63.

Grimley-Evans, J (1997) 'Rationing health care by age. The case against'. *BMJ* **314**: 822-5.

Hare, J, C Pratt et al (1992) 'Agreement between patients and their self-selected surrogates on difficult medical decisions'. *Arch Intern Med* **15**(2): 1049-54.

Harley, J (2002) *Office of Public Advocate Restraint Position Paper* (<http://www.opa.sa.gov.au>).

Hoffman, S, G Powell-Cope et al (2003) 'BedSAFE. A bed safety project for frail older adults'. *J Gerontol Nurs* **2003**(29(11)): 34-42.

Kaw, M and G Sekas (1994) 'Long-term follow-up of consequences of percutaneous endoscopic gastrostomy (PEG) tubes in nursing home patients'. *Dig Dis Sci* **39**(4): 738-43.

Levine, J, V Marchello et al (1995) 'Progress towards a restraint-free environment in a large academic teaching facility'. *J Am Geriatr Soc* **43**: 914-18.

Levinsky, N (1996) 'The purpose of advance medical planning – autonomy for patients or limitation of care?'. *N Engl J Med* **335**(10): 741-3.

Mason, F, Z Liu et al (2001) The probability of using an aged care home over a lifetime (1990-00). *Working Paper no 36*. Canberra, Australian Institute of Health and Welfare.

McLean, A (1994) 'What kind of love is this?'. *The Sciences* **34**(5): 36-9.

Moody, H (1998) *Aging: concepts and controversies*. Thousand Oaks California, Pine Forge Press.

Morgan, D (1982) 'Failing health and the desire for independence: two conflicting aspects of health care in old age'. *Social Problems* **30**(October): 40-50.

Mueller PS, CC Hook and KC Fleming (2004) 'Ethical issues in geriatrics: a guide for clinicians'. *Mayo Clin Proc* **79**(4): 554-62.

Ouslander, J and A Tymchuk (1989) 'Health care decisions among elderly long-term residents and their potential proxies'. *Ann Intern Med* **149**: 1367-72.

Penson RT, KJ Daniels and TJ Lynch (2004) 'Too old to care?'. *Oncologist* **9**(3): 343-52.

Shorr, R, R Fought and W Ray (1994) 'Changes in anti-psychotic drug use in nursing homes during implementation of the OBRA-87 regulations'. *JAMA* **271**(5): 358-62.

Sloane, P, L Mathew et al (1991) 'Physical and pharmacologic restraint of nursing home patients with dementia. Impact of specialised units'. *JAMA* **265**(10): 1278-82.

Staunton, P and M Chiarella (2003) *Nursing and the Law*. Sydney, Churchill Livingstone.

Thibault, G (1993) 'Too old for what?'. *N Engl J Med* **328**: 946-50.

Tomlinson, T, K Howe et al (1990) 'An empirical study of proxy consent for elderly persons'. *Gerontologist* **30**: 54-64.

Ubel, P and S Goold (1997) 'Recognising bedside rationing: clear cases and tough calls'. *Ann Intern Med* **126**(1): 74-9.

van Dijk, P, H van der Sande, D Dippel and J Habbema (1992) 'The nature of excess mortality in nursing home patients with dementia'. *J Gerontol* **47**(2): M28-34.

Williams, A (1997) 'Rationing health care by age. The case for'. *BMJ* **314**: 820-2.

Zweibel, N and C Cassel (1989) 'Treatment choices at the end of life: A comparison of decisions by older patients and their physician selected proxies'. *Gerontologist* **29**: 615-21.

CHAPTER 24

POST-COMA UNRESPONSIVENESS AND BRAIN DEATH

Case 1

JS is a 48-year-old man who suffered a cardiac arrest after taking a deliberate overdose of anti-depressant tablets and alcohol. He was found soon after the episode but required ventilation for 3 days before being able to breathe by himself. After weaning from the ventilator he remained deeply comatose for several weeks. He then began to develop periods in which he seemed more awake, opened his eyes at times and occasionally groaned, though he did not ever appear to interact with his surroundings. He was fed by naso-gastric tube and then by gastrostomy feeds. He developed recurrent episodes in which he became very sweaty and had a high blood pressure and pulse, and developed severe contractures of his legs and multiple bed-sores. Because he did not have any close relatives he was discharged to a nursing home and died soon after.

Case 2

JT is a 28-year-old woman who was sexually and physically assaulted, sustaining severe head injuries. She was found soon after the incident and required immediate intubation and ventilation. A CT scan on admission to hospital showed severe cerebral oedema. She was diagnosed with brain death 24 hours after admission. After discussion with her parents, her heart, lungs, liver, corneas and kidneys were removed for donation to others.

Case 3

On 25 February 1990, Terri Schiavo, a previously healthy young American woman, collapsed in her home following a cardiorespiratory arrest. She was resuscitated by paramedics and then transferred to the Intensive Care Unit of Humana Northside Hospital in Florida, where she was intubated and ventilated due to the extensive brain injury she had suffered following her arrest (anoxic-ischaemic encephalopathy). The cause of her cardiac arrest was never determined but may have been due to electrolyte disturbances resulting from excessive dieting/bulimia. Schiavo remained comatose for two and a half months and one year after her arrest was diagnosed as being in a persistent vegetative state (PVS). During this time she received nutrition via a percutaneous endoscopic gastrostomy (PEG) feeding tube inserted through her abdominal wall. Despite extensive rehabilitation and experimental thalamic (neurosurgical) stimulation therapy Terri's condition remained unchanged.

In 1998 her husband and guardian, Michael Schiavo, petitioned the Pinellas County Circuit Court to remove her feeding tube to allow her to die. This request was opposed by Terri's parents, Robert and Mary Schindler. The court determined that in the absence of an advance directive the evidence suggested that Terri would not have wished to continue life-sustaining measures. This decision, and Michael's authority to act as his wife's guardian, was subsequently appealed 14 times over the next seven years on the grounds that the diagnosis was incorrect, that Terri would not have refused nutrition and hydration, that Michael was an unfit guardian and served to gain by Terri's death, that Terri was disabled but not terminally ill, and that Terri had not received the full range of effective treatments for PVS.

The case attracted extensive national and international media attention, involved the Vatican, State and Federal politicians and pro-life and disability rights groups, and the Florida and United States governments passed laws that, unsuccessfully, sought to prevent the removal of Schiavo's feeding tube.

On 18 March 2005, Terri Schiavo's feeding tube was disconnected. Schiavo died of dehydration at a Pinellas park hospice on 31 March 2005. Post-mortem demonstrated extensive brain damage consistent with a clinical diagnosis of PVS (Caplan, McCartney et al 2006; Racine, Amaram et al 2008).

A number of terms are used to describe people with severe neurological impairments.

- **Coma** is a state of presumed profound unconsciousness from which the person cannot be roused when examined.
- **Post-coma unresponsiveness (PCU)** is a state or condition in which a person has emerged from coma to the extent that he or she is observed to have sleep/wake cycles over a period of time but no purposeful responses to stimuli.
- **Minimally responsive state (MRS)** may occur when a person has emerged from coma or PCU. There is a minimal level of purposeful response, with discernible but often inconsistent evidence of consciousness. Cognitively mediated behaviour occurs often enough or for long enough to distinguish it from reflex behaviour. (National Health and Medical Research Council 2007)

Post-coma unresponsiveness

The term 'post-coma unresponsiveness' (PCU) was introduced by the NHMRC in 2004 to clarify inconsistency in the terminology used to describe this state (variously described as the permanent vegetative state, persistent vegetative state and continuing vegetative state in different countries and clinical contexts), and to avoid the potentially pejorative term 'vegetative state' that was used previously (National Health and Medical Research Council 2004).

Post-coma unresponsiveness refers to a clinical condition in which patients appear to be awake following a period of coma but do not appear to be aware of their surroundings. In the first few months of the condition the vast majority of patients in such states will die (generally as a consequence of hypostatic pneumonia) or will emerge from the unresponsive state. Some, however, remain unresponsive and may exist like this for many years – up to 37 years in one case (Kinney, Korein et al 1994). Some guidelines, including those produced by the Royal College of Physicians of London, suggest that this state may be classified as permanent if it persists for more than one year in trauma cases and six months in non-trauma cases (Royal College of Physicians of London 2003). Other bodies, such as the NHMRC, reject the terms permanent or persistent on the grounds that the condition of people in PCU may not be static but may change slowly over time, with patients emerging to a state of MRS or better (National Health and Medical Research Council 2004).

A number of bodies have provided guidelines for the diagnosis of post-coma unresponsiveness or 'vegetative state' – all are different and many have been criticised on the grounds that they lead to an unacceptably high rate of misdiagnosis (Royal College of Physicians of London 2003). In Australia, the NHMRC guidelines are the preferred framework for the diagnosis of PCU. These guidelines state that the term PCU may generally be applied to patients emerging from coma in an apparently wakeful unconscious state in which there is:

- a complete lack of responses that suggest a cognitive component;
- preservation of sleep-wake cycles and cardiorespiratory function; and
- partial or complete preservation of hypothalamic and brain stem autonomic functions. (National Health and Medical Research Council 2004)

The framework recognises that PCU may be difficult to distinguish from other conditions that follow severe brain injury and that accurate diagnosis of PCU and MRS may take weeks or months – and should not be considered for a minimum of four weeks after emergence from coma.

There is no data on how many people in Australia have PCU, or where they are cared for, or who is involved in their care (National Health and Medical Research Council 2004). In 1994 the US Multi-Society Task Force estimated that there were between 10,000–25,000 people with PCU in the United States, which would equate to 1000–2500 people with PCU in Australia (Multi-Society Task Force on PVS 1994a).

The question that most concerns relatives and health professionals caring for patients with PCU is whether recovery is possible. In general terms, there is a low probability of functional improvement for people in a state of PCU and MRS, and the likelihood of emergence or functional improvement becomes increasingly poor with the progression of time (National Health and Medical Research Council 2004). But it is very difficult to predict with any certainty whether recovery is possible and what the quality of that recovery may be (Jennet 2002). In one study quoted by the Multi-Society Task Force on PCU, of 169 adults diagnosed with a persistent vegetative state following a non-traumatic brain injury, only 11% recovered consciousness within three months and only two additional patients recovered consciousness within six months. After one year, 32% remained in PCU and 53% had died. Fifteen per cent of patients regained consciousness but only one patient of the 169 made a good recovery, the other survivors having moderate to severe disability (Multi-Society Task Force on PVS 1994b).

Some generalisations can be made that may assist families and health professionals make management decisions regarding such patients: older patients and those who remain unresponsive for a long period following hypoxic brain injury are less likely to regain responsiveness; approximately 50% of patients left vegetative after an acute brain insult will die within the first year; and no specific treatment has been shown to increase the chance of recovery (Institute of Medical Ethics Working Party on the Ethics of Prolonging Life and Assisted Death 1991). While brain stimulation therapy, such as that administered to Terri Schiavo, may occasionally improve the minimally conscious state, there is no definite evidence of benefit in PCU (Bernat 2006).

A 1994 consensus statement by the Multi-Society Task Force on PCU emphasised that:

> [E]xtensive clinical experience, the results of positron-emission tomographic (PET) studies, and neuro-pathological examination support the belief that patients in a persistent vegetative state are unaware and insensate and therefore lack the cerebral cortical capacity to be conscious of pain. (Multi-Society Task Force on PVS 1994b)

This consensus has recently been called into question by the results of some interesting new research (Lewis 2007).

The first challenge to our current understanding of persistent coma arises from research showing that a proportion of patients in a state of PCU may be aroused by administration of the sleeping pill Zolpidem. A number of patients have been described who become alert and conscious once given this drug but relapse back into their previous condition once it wears off (Class and Nel 2006).

The second challenge to the status quo has resulted from recent developments in neuroscience and neuroimaging, which have provided insights into the working brain, consciousness, cognition and emotions, including pain (Bernat 2006; Laureys and Boly 2007; Fins 2008; Rousseau, Confort-Gouny et al 2008). These have raised questions as to whether those in a PCU state have lost all aspects of consciousness, as there appears to be some evidence of consciousness in patients in PCU using advanced imaging techniques in some people with PCU. For example, Owen and colleagues used functional MRI (fMRI) to study a 23-year-old woman who met the international criteria for PCU. They asked the woman to perform two mental imagery tasks at specific points during the scan. One task involved imagining playing a game of tennis and the other involved imagining visiting all of the rooms of her house, starting from the front door. The authors reported that:

> [D]uring the periods that she was asked to imagine playing tennis, significant activity was observed in the supplementary motor area of her brain. In contrast, when she was asked to imagine walking through her home, significant activity was observed in the parahippocampal gyrus, the posterior parietal cortex, and the lateral premotor cortex. (Owen, Martin et al 2006)

These neural responses were indistinguishable from those observed in healthy volunteers performing the same imagery tasks in the scanner. The authors commented: 'The most parsimonious explanation therefore remains that this patient was consciously aware and purposefully following the instructions given to her, despite her diagnosis of vegetative state' (Owen, Coleman et al 2007). It is currently uncertain what proportion of patients with post-coma unresponsiveness that this might apply to.

The third challenge results from well-publicised and increasingly well-defined examples of patients who recovered from a PCU state, sometimes years after first sustaining a major brain injury (Fins, Schiff et al 2007).

People in PCU and MRS are extremely vulnerable because they are totally dependent on others and unable to advocate for their own interests. There is a fundamental moral obligation to promote the interests of these patients (through respect for their dignity and rights, and through respect for their previously expressed wishes and for the views of their surrogate decision-maker) and to protect them from harm, abuse, neglect or exploitation (National Health and Medical Research Council 2004). Unfortunately, it is often difficult to know exactly what is in the best interests of a patient in PCU, particularly where nothing is known about their wishes or where there is conflict between the surrogates, health-care staff or other interested parties (as occurred in the case of Terri Schiavo).

Much of the controversy about patients with post-coma unresponsiveness concerns whether it is necessary to continue to artificially feed and give fluids to patients after they have been diagnosed (Fine 2006). This is ethically contentious because many people see the withdrawal of food and fluid as being different from withdrawing other medical therapies. Dresser notes:

> As applied to terminally ill or vegetative patients, this belief generally rests on the symbolic and emotional significance of providing nourishment, together with a reluctance to cease sustenance before a patient's illness takes its 'natural course'. Yet withholding or withdrawing medication, full resuscitation efforts, or respirator care can have consequences identical to removing patients from nutritional support. (Dresser and Boisaubim 1985)

The new findings about PCU further complicate this debate. There is at least one legal case reported in which the question of functional MRI and Zolpidem treatment has arisen, and where the courts required a trial of Zolpidem (but not imaging with fMRI) before treatment was withdrawn (Lewis 2007).

Whether a patient is conscious or not is of some significance to these cases, but it might not be the solely significant factor. Decisions to withhold or withdraw treatment are generally based on considerations of patients' previously expressed preferences, and on weighing up the burdens and benefits of therapy. A patient who is conscious but wholly unable to move or communicate – except through the medium of fMRI – suffers significant burdens. The question for patients with post-coma unresponsiveness then centres around whether their best interests will be served by maintaining food and fluid.

Brain death

A diagnosis of death is necessary for many aspects of societal functioning. Death is a prerequisite for wills to be read, for a charge of murder or manslaughter to be laid, for burial or cremation, for grieving to occur and for procurement of vital organs for transplantation. The diagnosis of death has traditionally fallen to doctors, as has the definition of death.

Death has traditionally been described in terms of circulatory failure – when the heart no longer beats and the lungs no longer take breath. However, the development of technology that takes over the functions of breathing and circulatory support has meant that a totally new, iatrogenic state has been created in which ventilation and circulation could be maintained in a body whose brain has ceased to function. This state is known as 'brain death' or 'brainstem death'.

Brain death was first described in France in 1959 as 'coma dépasse' – literally a state beyond coma, and the term 'brain death' was defined formally in 1968 in the report of the Ad Hoc Committee of the Harvard Medical School (Ad Hoc Committee of the Harvard Medical School 1968). This report set out criteria for brain death that have since been adopted, with some modifications, in most countries. (Guidelines for the diagnosis of brain death differ in regards to the requirement for ancillary testing, including EEGs and study of cerebral blood flow, in large measure because none of the existing confirmatory studies have the necessary positive predictive value for the reliable diagnosis of death (Young, Shemie et al 2006).) In 1981, the Report of the Medical Consultants on the Diagnosis of Death to the US President's Commission recommended that the criteria for diagnosis of brain death should be seen as synonymous with the definition of death of the organism as a whole. Since the publication of that report, recognition that the essential physiological component of brain death is the death of the brainstem has led to the terms 'brain death' and 'brainstem death' being used interchangeably (Gillett 1986).

If one examines the history of the concept of brain death, it is clear that it is closely linked to developments in intensive care and, more significantly, in organ transplantation. By redefining death in terms of brain function, society's increasing need for organ transplants was put on a philosophical footing that would allow the expansion of transplant programs. Unfortunately, this led to great potential for a conflict of interests between the demand for organs, and the need for a scientifically valid definition of human death.

When the concept of brain death was first introduced, it was argued that death of the brainstem inevitably implied the imminent death of the whole body, even where ventilatory support was continued. This appeared to provide good justification for defining death in terms of brainstem criteria. This argument is no longer tenable as we now know that bodies with a dead brain may be kept alive for many months. Indeed, a brain dead pregnant woman had been maintained on a ventilator for months and later gave birth to healthy children, and brain dead children have been reported to survive for up to 14 years with ventilatory and nutritional support (Washida, Okamoto et al 1992; Powner and Bernstein 2003).

It has also been found that many individuals who fulfil all of the tests for absent brainstem function may have evidence of some cortical function and spinal reflex movements (Truog and Fackler 1992; Dosemeci, Cengiz et al 2004). Despite uncertainty regarding their status, what is certain is that patients with brain death will not recover, and will continue in that state until the artificial support they receive either fails or is withdrawn. In other words brainstem criteria define prognosis, although the timing of 'actual death' depends on provision or withdrawal of intensive care.

For those who believe in the sanctity of life, it would not be permissible to kill a human being in order to take their organs for transplantation. But if donors are already dead, this would be perfectly permissible. This is known as the 'dead donor rule'. By defining brain dead people as 'actually dead', proponents of organ transplantation were able to sidestep the fact that organ transplantation requires the death of the donor. According to Pearson:

> [Brainstem death] had to be equated with 'death' because, unlike almost every other situation in which useless support might be withdrawn, in this case, removal of the ventilator was immediately followed by cessation of circulation ... Most societies recognize that although we all have to die at some time, it is wrong for our life to be ended by another person. What we might reconcile as an act of omission, we could not accept as an act of commission. There was no other word that could supply acceptance. (Pearson 1995)

This solution has a logical neatness, but if we redefine death to allow organ transplantation, there is no reason why it could not be further redefined when the need for organ transplantation increases. In the 1990s authors such as Shann (Shann 1995) suggested precisely this, recommending that the definition of death be extended to patients with post-coma unresponsiveness. More recently, Donation after Cardiac Death (DCD) policies, which allow declaration of death for the purposes of organ procurement after 2-5 minutes of asystole (absent heart activity), have been introduced in a number of countries, including in Australia, in order to increase the number and quality of cadaveric organs available for transplantation. (This issue is discussed in more detail in Chapter 25.)

Alternative approaches to defining death fall into two general categories:

1. traditional cardiopulmonary definitions of death based on irreversible cessation of circulation (which, recently, and somewhat controversially, have been defined in terms of the period of asystole); and

2. 'higher brain' or ' neocortical' definitions of death which conclude that individuals who have permanently suffered the loss of consciousness (including those with persistent vegetative states) should be considered as dead.

Proponents of neocortical criteria for death emphasise the importance of sentience, cognition and 'personhood' in defining life. Personhood has been variously described as rationality, sociality, self-awareness, capacity for intentional behaviour, and the ability to conceive and carry out projects (Lizza 1993). But the absence of a clear definition, anatomic localisation or tool to measure personhood make it difficult to support as a definition of death – particularly as it is divergent from traditional cardiorespiratory definitions of death (Powner, Ackeman et al 1996).

Death is a medical, legal and cultural category that fulfils a number of purposes and there is considerable confusion and ambivalence in both lay and health-care populations regarding brain death and organ donation (Macdonald, Liben et al 2008). If death is redefined in a way that is not in keeping with public perceptions, there is a risk that the public will become disillusioned about the process of organ transplantation (Kellehear 2008). According to Shann:

> [P]aradoxically, some of the strongest opposition to change, or even discussion of the issues involved, comes from the transplant lobby – who fear that any suggestion of change will be misinterpreted as an attempt to snatch organs, and so undermine public confidence in the public system. (Shann 1995)

Within this context it is interesting to note that the two primary reasons the public gives for not signing donor cards are fear that doctors 'might do something to me before I'm really dead' and fear that 'doctors might hasten my death' (Annas 1988).

Many commentators have noted that brain-dead people do not resemble our usual concepts of the dead. Brain-dead patients are pink and warm, their hearts beat and they continue to breathe with the aid of a ventilator. It is not surprising that about 20% of families of brain-dead patients continue to have doubts about whether their relative was actually dead, even after brain death was explained to them, and a further 66% accept that the patient is dead but feel emotionally that they are still alive. This experience does not appear to be related to whether families agree or disagree with organ donation (Pearson 1995). It is also noteworthy that many health professionals recognise that some families may not be able to accept that brain death is synonymous with death and that some jurisdictions, including Japan, New York State and New Jersey, accept cultural and religious objections to brain death criteria for a declaration of death.

Doctors and nurses also have difficulty in coming to terms with the concept of brain death. A study by Tomlinson showed that many believe that brain-dead patients are 'irreversibly dying' or have unacceptable quality of life rather than being actually dead. Nurses and physicians often seem to talk to families as if patients were still alive, using statements such as: 'If kept on the respirator, the patient will die of sepsis' or 'at this point in time it doesn't look as if the patient is going to survive' (Tomlinson 1990). Media headlines such as 'Woman is Kept Alive to Save Unborn Baby' and 'Brain Dead Woman Dies After Baby Born' occurred in the newspaper *USA Today* when a woman called Susan Torres delivered a healthy baby in August 2005 months after being diagnosed as brain dead. This also suggests that many people may find it difficult to reconcile a dead person gestating a pregnancy.

Definitions of death based on brainstem criteria blur the borders between the question of what it is to be human and the separate issue of what it means to be alive. Proponents of brainstem death argue for a radically different definition of death for humans than that used to describe the death of non-human animals or plants. Of course, many living organisms do not have brainstems, and hence brainstem definitions violate any trans-species generalisability for the definition of death. Proponents of brainstem death argue that death is the moment beyond which integration of the organism is lost, when structural disintegration is inevitable and biological sub-systems cannot be maintained without artificial support. In this respect, they argue that clinical death should be equated with the destruction of the critical integrating system of that organism, represented in humans by the functions of the brainstem (Korein 1978). Death of the brainstem is therefore the necessary and sufficient component of death of the body as a whole (Pallis 1983). However, proponents of brainstem definitions of death do not adequately define what is meant by 'living as an integrated and co-ordinated organism', a concept that is central to their argument. And suggestions that the brain is the supreme regulator of the body are both biologically and philo-sophically simplistic. For example, regulation of haematopoesis, glucose meta-bolism, immunity and many other bodily functions exist independently of the brainstem (Whetstine 2007).

The brainstem is not the only structure in the human body that is required to maintain the integration of the organism. The heart, the liver, the kidneys and other organs are all required, and loss of the functions of any of these organs will result in eventual disintegration of the organism without artificial support. We do not define a patient as dead from the moment that their liver has failed, rather we regard them as dying. We do not regard a patient with acute renal failure requiring urgent dialysis as dead from the moment that their kidney fails; instead we regard them as dying, unless they receive long-term dialysis. Being 'liver-dead' or 'kidney-dead' or 'heart-dead' all imply that the organism is dying, but there will be variable times from the moment when the organ dies until the time when the organism dies. We suggest that similar reasoning should apply to those who are brainstem dead. This view is not common yet in Aust-ralia, but there is increasing support from it in world literature (Truog 2004; Truog 2007).

Conclusion

Changes to medical technology have allowed patients with post-coma unres-ponsiveness and brainstem death to live beyond the short period that they once would have survived. Society is then faced with a dilemma when it has to consider what to do with these people. Various ethical and legal structures have been set up to allow us to deal with these people – and it is now generally accepted that we may withdraw life-sustaining therapy and allow such people to die. In the case of brain-dead patients, we may also use their organs for trans-plantation.

At present, the concept that brain death and actual death are synonymous has widespread support in the ICU and transplant community, but these con-cepts are now coming under scrutiny (Truog 2007; Karakatsanis 2008). The authors believe that arguments regarding the existence of life must never be confused with concerns about the need for organs for organ transplantation, and the 'value' of life. Where such concerns arise they must be seen for what they are

– questions about the ethics of treatment withdrawal, euthanasia and organ transplantation, not questions about the definition of death (see also Chapter 25).

Brain death has always been linked with organ donation. The histories of the two concepts run in parallel, the groups of physicians involved in both areas overlap, and organ donation depends on the concept of brain death for its existence. The nature of this articulation between brain death and organ donation needs to be explored rather than ignored.

It is crucial to the survival of organ transplantation that this linkage is seen as a parallel development rather than the horse of organ donation pulling the cart of new definitions of death (Joffe 2007). (An example of how this can go wrong may be seen in the recent case in which two American hospitals allowed a man's organs to be removed before he was declared brain dead. This led to a charge of homicide against the doctors (Anon 2004).) Brainstem criteria allow organ donation but do not allow burial or cremation. This suggests that, although it is not acknowledged in much of the medical community, brainstem definitions of death are already separated from definitions of 'actual death'.

Brainstem criteria provide good evidence that a patient has irreversible loss of consciousness and will not survive without intensive support. However, they do not provide absolute evidence for loss of all functions of the brain and a proportion of the medical and lay population do not appear to accept brainstem definitions of death on an emotional level, and many do not accept such definitions intellectually either. We believe that these problems can be overcome by defining death by cardiorespiratory criteria, and by using the term 'brain dead' in exactly the same way in which we advise patients that a gangrenous foot is dead, or that part of their heart muscle is dead. This would allow the term to be used in the same way as doctors, nurses and patients already talk about brain death, and the way that the public appears to understand it. Patients with brain death could then be accepted as dying rather than as already dead. Patients who meet criteria for brainstem death may have treatment withdrawn on the basis that they have no hope of recovery, and they may also be considered to be potential donors for organ transplantation. But they should not be considered to be dead. Abandoning the 'dead donor rule' and introducing legislation to allow the removal of organs from patients who are dying *and* fulfil brain death criteria would allow transplantation to continue and may potentially be acceptable to the public (Evans 2007; Verheidje, Rady et al 2007). Although this approach is coherent, we accept that the current unsatisfactory situation is likely to continue, at least until advances in regenerative medicine, immunology and stem cell therapies make brain death untenable (Truog 2007). According to Powner :

> The confirmation of a lifeless condition is the central prerequisite to burial, while organ donation is but a step along the way. Defining lifelessness without a requirement for absent cardiopulmonary function may be a pause for convenience, but cannot yet suffice as the necessary prerequisite for society's current ritual recognising that death has been defined. (Powner, Ackeman et al 1996)

Guidelines of the Australasian Transplant Coordinators Association and the Australian and New Zealand Intensive Care Society (ANZICS 1998) emphasise the need for declaration of brain death to *precede* any discussion of organ donation, and they encourage formal testing for brain death even where there is no intention to make a request for organ donation. This point is not always appreciated; for example, the ethics commentator in a discussion of brain death in the *Medical Journal of Australia* suggested that making the diagnosis of brain death 'is not required unless transplantation is considered' (Kennedy, Moran et al 1996). Such continuing emphasis on the necessary link between brain death and organ donation is unfortunate, and endangers the credibility of brain death declaration as a legitimate clinical tool that is independent of the transplant program.

Finally, we would suggest that there is a danger in tying any definition of death to the availability of technology as developments in science are just as likely to challenge our current notions of death as developments in intensive care did in the 1960s, and as recent findings with post-coma unresponsiveness have. It is very likely that developments in cell biology, stem-cell research, cardiopulmonary resuscitation, critical care and transplantation will continue to inform and challenge our understandings of life and death. Recent research into human embryonic stem (ES) cells has, for the first time, made tissue repair a possibility. In vitro and animal studies have already demonstrated that ES cells may differentiate into nerve cells, including cells of the brain stem, and that such cells may be biochemically and electrophysiologically active and may reverse cognitive and motor deficits. While ES cells have no current application, in the long term, as more is learnt about neurobiological development, tissue repair and the replacement of brain function, the entire notion of irreversible loss of brain function and of organ-based definitions of death will be called into question (Hess and Borlongan 2008; Joannides and Chandran 2008; Modo 2008).

LEGAL ASPECTS OF PCU AND BRAIN DEATH

Chapter 15 examined the different regimes for the withholding and withdrawal of treatment in Australia. Many of the laws discussed in that chapter were concerned with patients with PCU. This chapter will highlight the particular difficulties faced in PCU and brain death cases.

PCU and the law

Australian courts have been slow to get involved in cases concerning the withdrawal of treatment from patients in a persistent vegetative state. As Professor Ian Freckelton has noted, Australia has not adopted the practice which has evolved in England of making 'applications to courts for declaratory orders' (Freckelton 1993). It was the long practice of lawyers in Australia to refer to the major decisions from the United States – *Cruzan v Director, Missouri Department of Health* 110 S Ct 2841 (1990) (*Cruzan*) – and United Kingdom – *Airedale NHS Trust v Bland* [1993] AC 789 (*Bland*) – when discussing these issues.

The Cruzan case

In 1983, Nancy Beth Cruzan was involved in an automobile accident, which left her in a 'persistent vegetative state'. She was sustained after several weeks by artificial feeding through an implanted gastronomy tube. After their daughter had been in a PCU for five years, the Cruzan family requested removal of her feeding tube. Hospital employees refused to honour the request without a court order. The Missouri Trial Court found that Nancy Cruzan had the fundamental right to ask for the removal of death-prolonging procedures. The Supreme Court of Missouri reversed the decision because it was sceptical that the right to refuse treatment was applicable in this case. The court decided that the state's policy to preserve life should govern because there was insufficient evidence to support the parents' claim of Nancy Cruzan's wishes.

The US Supreme Court agreed to hear the case to determine whether the US Constitution protected Nancy Cruzan's right to withdraw life-sustaining treatment and, thus, whether the hospital is required to stop treatment. The Nancy Cruzan case provides the current US legal framework for care of a patient in a PCU. Five US Supreme Court Justices wrote opinions on the case. In 1990, the five-to-four decision of the US Supreme Court affirmed the state's right to determine its requirements for 'clear and convincing evidence' and affirmed the right of the patient in a PCU to discontinue nutrition and hydration when sufficient evidence is available. The definition of 'clear and convincing evidence' set by each state could require oral or written evidence from another person affirming the patient's wishes regarding life-sustaining treatment.

In the opinion, the US Supreme Court stated that the 'principle that a competent person has a constitutionally protected liberty interest in refusing unwanted medical treatment may be inferred from our prior decisions. ... We assume that the United States Constitution would grant a competent person a constitutionally protected right to refuse lifesaving hydration and nutrition' (at 2851-2). The various opinions also mentioned that the decision of life or death is a deeply personal issue.

The concurring opinion by O'Connor J stated that the *Cruzan* decision 'does not preclude a future determination that the Constitution requires the States to implement the decisions of a patient's duly appointed surrogate'. Stevens J's dissent stated that 'the best interests of the individual, especially when buttressed by the interests of all related third parties must prevail over any general state policy that simply ignores those interested ... To deny the importance of these consequences is in effect to deny that Nancy Cruzan has interests at all and thereby to deny her personhood in the name of preserving the sanctity of her life' (at 2889-90).

Six months after the US Supreme Court decision, three new witnesses testified of Nancy's stated desire not to continue with life-sustaining medical treatment in these types of circumstances. The court case was subsequently dismissed, and the court granted permission for the feeding tube to be removed. The decision of the court emphasises the need for patients to have written advance directives.

The Bland case

The *Bland* case has been mentioned in a number of chapters in this book, as the House of Lords examined many important principles in order to reach its final conclusion. The House of Lords determined that it was lawful to withdraw medical treatment and support, including nutrition and hydration, from Mr Anthony Bland, a patient in a persistent vegetative state.

Mr Bland, then aged 17½, went to the Hillsborough Ground on 15 April 1989 to support the Liverpool Football Club. In the course of the disaster that occurred on that day, his lungs were crushed and punctured and the supply of oxygen to his brain was interrupted. As a result, he suffered catastrophic and irreversible damage to the higher centres of the brain. At no time before the disaster did Mr Bland give any indication of his wishes should he find himself in such a condition. His family agreed that the feeding tube should be removed and felt that this was what Mr Bland would have wanted. The Airedale NHS Trust applied for declarations that they might:

> lawfully discontinue all life-sustaining treatment and medical support measures designed to keep Mr Bland alive in his existing persistent vegetative state including the termination of ventilation, nutrition and hydration by artificial means; and
>
> ... lawfully discontinue and thereafter need not furnish medical treatment to Mr Bland except for the sole purpose of enabling Mr Bland to end his life and die peacefully with the greatest dignity and the least of pain suffering and distress.

Mr Bland's case was an extreme one, in which there was no significant disagreement amongst the expert witnesses. The House of Lords found that treatment could be withdrawn from Mr Bland as it was not in his best interests to continue the treatment. The court also found that cases such as this should be brought before a court for consideration before withdrawal of treatment. It was anticipated that this type of case would benefit from an independent investigation by the Official Solicitor as the patient's guardian (in litigation). In a subsequent case, *Frenchay NHS Trust v S* [1994] 1 FLR 485, it was suggested that the courts need not in fact be involved in every PCU case. The Official Solicitor has subsequently issued a Practice Note (*Practice Note (Vegetative State)* [1996] 2 FLR 375) giving guidance on seeking court consideration of PCU cases.

Following the decision in *Bland* there have been a number of cases decided by the English courts. In *Re G (Persistent Vegetative State)* [1995] 2 FCR 46, the court held that treatment could be withdrawn, even where the patient's mother (although not his wife) objected to the withdrawal. The views of the next-of-kin or of others close to the patient cannot act as a veto to an application, but they must be taken fully into account by the court. The applicant in the PCU cases may be either the next-of-kin or other individuals closely connected with the patient or the relevant district health authority/NHS trust (*Re S (Hospital Patient: Court's Jurisdiction)* [1996] Fam 1, CA).

In 1996 the Inner House of the Court of Sessions in Scotland, sitting as a court of five judges (*Law Hospital NHS Trust v Lord Advocate* 1996 SLT 848), held that the Court of Session had power, in the exercise of the Sovereign's authority as *parens patriae* (parent of the country), to authorise a medical practitioner to discontinue life-sustaining treatment that was being provided to a patient who was permanently unconscious and insensate. The patient in this case, X, had been in a persistent vegetative state for at least three years. There was no prospect of any improvement in her condition. She remained alive only because feeding and hydration were provided to her artificially and because of the nursing care that she continued to receive. Her consultant physician and three consultant neurologists considered her position to be hopeless and that there were no useful avenues of treatment to explore. Her next-of-kin had agreed that life-sustaining and medical treatment should be discontinued. The patient herself, however, was unable to give her consent.

The court held that whether or not such authority should be granted depended on whether or not it was in the best interests of the patient that his or her life be prolonged by the continuance of the treatment. This is the same test as is used in England.

In 2000 Dame Elizabeth Butler-Sloss, the President of the English High Court's Family Division, has to consider in two cases (*An NHS Trust v M; An NHS Trust v H* [2001] 2 FLR 367) whether the accession of the United Kingdom to the *European Convention for the Protection of Human Rights and Fundamental Freedoms 1950* had changed the existing law set out by the House of Lords in *Bland*. The President held that it did not and that the English law was compatible with Article 2 of the Convention. The following year another case (*NHS Trust A v H* [2001] 2 FLR 501) came before the President where a patient was said to be in a permanent vegetative state although she did not meet all of the criteria set out in the 1996 Royal College of Physicians' criteria for diagnosing PCU. Dame Elizabeth Butler-Sloss called for a thorough review of the criteria used to find whether a patient should be deemed to be in a PCU.

Australia

Cases in the parens patriae jurisdiction

There has been one Australian case where a court has had to consider the clinical diagnosis of PCU under the *parens patriae* jurisdiction. This is the New South Wales case of *Northridge v Central Sydney Area Health Service* [2000] NSWSC 1241. This is not a case, however, where a court was being asked to consider the lawfulness, or not, of a proposed course of treatment. In this case there was a dispute between the family of an incompetent patient and the health-care team responsible for his treatment. The case has been discussed in Chapter 15.

Mr Thompson, following an overdose of heroin, was admitted into the defendant hospital. Following treatment in the intensive care unit it was found that he had suffered significant brain damage. This diagnosis was reached within about four days of his admission. On the basis of this diagnosis the provision of antibiotics and food was stopped and a 'not for resuscitation' order was written. The family disagreed with this course of care and sought an order from the New South Wales Supreme Court to have his treatment reinstated. It appears that, during discussion between the doctors and members of Mr Thompson's family, the expression 'vegetative state' was used on several occasions and that it was said that he was in a 'chronic vegetative state'.

Following the intervention of the Supreme Court a number of experts examined Mr Thompson and they were critical of the diagnosis of 'chronic vegetative state'. They suggested that this expression was unusual, as the usual descriptions of the vegetative state are either 'persistent' or 'permanent'. In his judgment O'Keefe J stated:

> A number of areas of serious concern are thrown up by the present case. The first relates to the way in which and time at which the diagnosis of "chronic vegetative state" was arrived at. The very terminology used in the diagnosis is challenged by medical practitioners knowledgeable and skilled in relation to the care and treatment of patients who have suffered brain damage either as a result of head injury or some other cause. The terminology adopted in the United Kingdom is "permanent vegetative state". Whilst there is no formal nomenclature in Australia it is, from a laymen's point of view, not difficult to equate "chronic" with "permanent" when describing a vegetative state. However the two descriptions may not be synonymous. A second problem is that, assuming that the diagnoses of chronic vegetative state and permanent vegetative state are synonymous, there is no adopted or recognised standard in Australia in relation to the making of such a diagnosis. On different occasions during the course of the matter the defendant confirmed that there was no standard for the making of such a diagnosis and, a fortiori, no standard or guidelines in relation to the withdrawal of conventional medical treatment and artificial feeding from patients who are diagnosed as being in such a vegetative state. (at [107])

Following the intervention of the court, Mr Thompson's condition improved (to a limited extent) and he was transferred to a rehabilitation facility. In response to the decision in *Northridge*, the NHMRC formed a working party to investigate the clinical diagnosis of persistent vegetative state. In 2004 (endorsed by the NHMRC on 18 December 2003) an information paper was released 'Post-Coma Unresponsiveness (Vegetative State): A Clinical Framework for Diagnosis' which is intended to assist health professionals involved in the assessment and diagnosis of post-coma unresponsiveness. The information paper notes that 'the term *post-coma unresponsiveness* is intended to be synonymous with the more established term *vegetative state*' and that 'both terms avoid the use of a time-based qualifier such as persistent or permanent' (National Health and Medical Research Council 2004).

Cases under guardianship legislation

There are a number of cases in New South Wales, Queensland, Victoria and Western Australia which have established the principle that treatment can be withdrawn from a person with PCU by the various substitute decision-makers created under the different legislative regimes.

In New South Wales, the Administrative Decisions Tribunal decided in *FI v Public Guardian* [2008] NSWADT 263, that it was possible for guardians under the guardianship legislation to refuse treatment for a woman who was alleged to be in a vegetative state. The decision did not deal with the question of whether the treatment should be withdrawn but it did clarify that it was possible for such a decision to be made under the New South Wales legislation (see Chapter 15).

In Queensland, artificial feeding and hydration can only be refused by patients with an advance directive, or by substitute decision-maker when its use is inconsistent with good medical practice: *Powers of Attorney Act 1998* (Qld), s 36(2); *Guardianship and Administration Act 2000* (Qld), s 66A. The Queensland Guardianship and Administration Tribunal (QGAAT) considered these provisions in *Re MC* [2003] QGAAT 13, where permission was granted to withdraw artificial feeding from an 80-year-old woman in persistent vegetative state. The QGAAT found that the treatment was of no benefit to her and should be ceased. More recently in *Re SAJ* [2007] QGAAT 62, the QGAAT made a similar order refusing artificial feeding for an 83-year-old man who had become vegetative after severe stroke. The medical evidence suggested that even with artificial feeding and hydration he would be in a 'starvation state' his muscles would wither and there was a high probability of his developing deep vein thrombosis, aspiration pneumonia and urinary tract infections. He was also at risk of developing pressure sores which could become infected and painful. On balance the QGAAT thought that the treatment was not consistent with good medical practice.

Victoria has also dealt with cases of PCU. The cases normally arise under the *Medical Treatment Act 1988* where a guardian can be appointed with the power to issue a refusal of treatment certificate (see Chapter 15). In *Re BWV* [2003] VSC 173, the issue was discussed as to whether artificial feeding and hydration was 'treatment' which could be refused using a refusal of treatment certificate. The Act stated that palliative care could not be refused using a certificate and palliative care was defined to include the reasonable provision of food and water. The Supreme Court found that artificial feeding was medical treatment and not the reasonable provision of food and water, under the Victorian legislation. Given the feeding was medical treatment, it could be refused by the guardian under the *Medical Treatment Act 1988*.

In *Re Korp* [2005] VCAT 779, the patient had fallen into PCU after being assaulted by her husband's lover and left in a car boot for four days. The lover later plead guilty to the crime and the husband was charged with attempted murder. Mr Korp opposed any withdrawal of treatment on the grounds that his wife would not have refused treatment as she was a Catholic. Morris J felt that even if she were a devout Catholic that did not follow that Mrs Korp would have consented to the treatment. The Supreme Court examined the question of who should be Korp's guardian. Mrs Korp's adult daughter, although accepting appointment as an administrator to manage her mother's financial and legal affairs, declined to be appointed guardian because of the gravity of the decisions that potentially had to be made. Instead, the public advocate was appointed by VCAT as Mrs Korp's guardian. A decision was made to refuse treatment and she died on 5 August 2005.

Difficulties arose with another guardianship appointment in *EK (Guardianship)* [2005] VCAT 2520. The case concerned a 94-year-old woman with advanced dementia. The patient's niece felt the woman was in a vegetative state, but on examination only one of three doctors said that she was 'virtually' in a vegetative state, the other two denying it altogether. Because the niece had persisted with this view, VCAT appointed the public advocate as the patient's guardian, rather than the niece, to determine the appropriate course of treatment.

Is artificial feeding and hydration a form of medical treatment or basic care?

One the most controversial aspects of treatment withdrawal from people with PCU is the issue of whether artificial feeding and hydration (ANH) is medical treatment (which can be withheld if no longer in the patient's best interests) or basic care (which should always be provided to patients, as it is always in the patient's best interests). We have already discussed *Re BWV*, the Victorian case which found that under the *Medical Treatment Act 1988* (Vic), ANH is not considered to be the reasonable provision of food and water, and hence can be refused using a refusal of treatment certificate. In all other common law jurisdictions ANH has been classed as medical treatment and not as basic care. In the United States, decisions in *Barber v Superior Court of the State of California* 195 Cal Rptr 484 (1983) at 490; *In re Estate of Longeway* 549 NE 2d 292 (1989); *Re Gardiner* 534 A 2d 947 (1987); *Matter of Guardianship of LW* 482 NW 2d 60 (1992) at 66; *Matter of Conway* 486 A 2d 1209 (1985) all confirm that ANH is medical treatment. England (*Bland* [1993] 2 AC), Scotland (*Law Hospital NHS Trust v Lord Advocate* 1996 SLT 848), Canada (*Nancy B v Hotel-Dieu de Quebec* (1992) 86 DLR (4th) 385), and Ireland (*In the Matter of a Ward of Court* [1995] 2 IRLM 401) have all agreed with this approach.

Of course the fact that the medical profession sees hydration and nutrition as treatment does not mean that it is accepted as so by the wider community. For example, much of the controversy surrounding Terri Schiavo focused on the issue of whether she was going to be 'starved to death', even though the Florida statute permitted ANH to be withdrawn when there was clear and convincing evidence that the person would not have wanted it (Faunce and Stewart 2005).

Brain death

The common law has always deferred to the medical profession on the issue of when biological death occurs. In *Smeaton v Secretary of State for Health* [2002] EWHC 610 (Admin), Mumby J neatly summarised the common law's approach to defining death:

> Once upon a time the law, following medical science, treated death as marked by the cessation of breathing or of heartbeat. At present the law treats death as meaning brain stem death: *Re A* [1992] 3 Med LR 303, *Airedale NHS Trust v Bland* [1993] AC 789. But there may be contexts in which the law treats death as occurring at some other time. In certain circumstances the court may presume death if someone has not been heard of for at least seven years: *Chard v Chard* [1956] P 259. Section 184 of the *Law of Property Act 1925* creates for certain purposes a statutory presumption as to when death occurs when two or more persons have died in circumstances rendering it uncertain which of them survived the other or others. No doubt there are other examples of the point. (at [57])

Even though Mumby J was discussing English law, it is likely that the current Australian common law definition of death is brain stem death. In *Re A* [1992] 3 Med LR 303, a case concerning a young boy who had suffered a head injury, the trial judge found that, even though the child's autonomous functions were being carried on by artificial means, the child had died when his brain stem had ceased to function. Similar comments on 'death' being brain stem death can be found in *R v Malcherek & Steel* [1981] 2 All ER 422 and *Bland's case* [1993] AC 789 at 878 (Lord Browne-Wilkinson).

However, as the first part of the chapter illustrates, all Australian jurisdictions (except Western Australia) have put in place legislation that defines death as:

- irreversible cessation of all brain function; or
- irreversible cessation of blood circulation.

See *Human Tissue Act 1983* (NSW), s 33; *Death (Definition) Act 1983* (SA), s 2; *Human Tissue Act 1985* (Tas), s 27A; *Human Tissue Act 1982* (Vic), s 41; *Transplantation and Anatomy Act 1978* (ACT), s 45; *Human Tissue Transplant Act 1979* (NT), s 23. This definition has effect for all laws within each jurisdiction, except in Queensland (*Transplantation and Anatomy Act 1979* (Qld), s 45) where the definition is only relevant in the context of organ donation. This definition overrides the common law definition of brain stem death.

This definition was included in the legislation as a result of recommendations in the Australian Law Reform Commission (ALRC) report in 1977 (ALRC 1977) entitled *Human Tissue Transplants* (see Chapter 25). The view of the ALRC was that, as the application of common law approaches to defining death was uncertain, it was important to clarify the circumstances where death could be established in order to use an organ for the purposes of transplantation.

The ALRC did not specifically refer to the method for determining that there had been an irreversible cessation of all brain function. Instead, the ALRC report commented:

> First, detailed criteria should not be included. Secondly, a Statement of the Royal Australian Medical Colleges (if the Colleges decide that such a step is a proper and desirable one) prescribing approved criteria for professional guidance in relation to 'brain death' could serve a valuable purpose by providing specific guidelines for areas left untouched by the generality of the statutory provision. Flexibility to allow adoption of criteria to accord with the best current professional procedures is preferable to verbose legislation. The brevity of the recommended statutory provision, and the deliberate omission of detailed criteria, may be taken as a reflection and confirmation of the Australian community's general confidence in the medical profession. The creation and prescription of techniques of diagnosis should be the responsibility of the medical profession. Thirdly, although appearing in this context of transplantation, the recommended statutory definition of death is intended to have general application. It should not be limited in its legal effect to any particular kind of patient, not to patients maintained by support machinery (although, in practice it will no doubt principally, if not exclusively affect only such patients), not to transplantation. The inclusion in the statutory provision of references both to 'brain death' and to traditional criteria serves a useful

purpose. Despite the greater accuracy of determining death by reference to cessation of brain function, it is clear that in most cases, death will be certified or determined according to the traditional respiratory-circulatory-cardiac standards. There will not be a great number of cases in which the need and facilities for, and opportunity of, employing the necessary 'brain death' criteria will be present. (ALRC 1977: para 137)

Even though it is clear that the ALRC was prepared to let the medical profession determine the criteria for establishing 'brain death', there does still appear to have been an expectation that 'brain death' included the 'death' of the brain stem. The ALRC, when discussing the general acceptance of a 'brain death' criteria, said '[t]he condition described in the last sentence has been called by many "brain death". This refers to the irreversible cessation of all brain function *including brain stem function'* (ALRC 1977: para 119, emphasis added). It could be argued that the ALRC intended that in its recommended definition of death the cessation of all brain stem function was also to be included.

A discussion paper (Transplantation Ethics Working Party 1997) issued by the National Health and Medical Research Council has examined this issue. The Working Group suggested that:

> While a legislative refinement of the concept of 'all function of the brain' might be desirable, it is the argument of this paper that an understanding of the concept of death implicit in both the current definition and in current practice should be sufficient to allay fears that the current criteria are inadequate. What is most desirable in the short term is the careful use and dissemination of the current clinical criteria, along with an understanding of their philosophical presuppositions. (Transplantation Ethics Working Party 1997)

With respect, the fact that current practice may be out of step with the requirements of the law is of some concern and the conclusions of the working group may not be supported by the evidence before the Working Group. The current state of the law is therefore unsatisfactory. Tibballs has stated:

> While the law defines that organ donation may proceed when all the brain is dead, the diagnosis of brain death is determined by medical bodies, and is taken to be loss of brain-stem reflexes and coma. In this respect there is a mismatch between what is stipulated as "cessation of all brain function" in law and what is defined as brain death in Australian medical clinical guidelines. (Tibballs 2008)

One solution would be to change the definition to brain stem death, as has already occurred at common law in the UK. On one view this happened in *Krommydas v Sydney West Area Health Service* [2006] NSWSC 901. The patient was in the intensive care unit at Westmead Hospital but the hospital argued that the patient had satisfied the definition of death as laid out in s 33. The judge felt that once this determination based on 'acceptable and credible evidence' (namely brain stem criteria) had been made then there was no residual discretion remaining with the court to order continued treatment. This seems to indicate that it may be possible to treat whole brain death as having occurred when a diagnosis of brain stem death is made. But this approach is shaky and effectively paints over the cracks caused by the outdated definition.

References

Ad Hoc Committee of the Harvard Medical School (1968) 'A definition of irreversible coma'. *JAMA* **205**: 337-40.

ALRC (1977) *Human tissue transplants*. Sydney, Law Reform Commission and MD Kirby.

Annas, G (1988) 'Brain death and organ donation: you can have one without the other'. *Hastings Cent Rep* **June/July**: 28-30.

Anon (2004) Coroner: Removing man's organs was homicide, CNN, 5 October 2004.

ANZICS (1998) *Recommendations on brain death and organ donation* (2nd ed). Melbourne, Australian and New Zealand Intensive Care Society.

Bernat, JL (2006) 'Are organ donors after cardiac death really dead?' *J Clin Ethics* **17**(2): 122-32.

Bernat, JL (2006) 'Chronic disorders of consciousness'. *Lancet* **367**(9517): 1181-92.

Caplan, AL, JJ McCartney et al (2006) *The case of Terri Schiavo : ethics at the end of life*. Amherst, NY, Prometheus Books.

Class, R and W Nel (2006) 'Drug induced arousal from the permanent vegetative state'. *NeuroRehabilitation* **21**(1): 23-8.

Dosemeci, L, M Cengiz et al (2004) 'Frequency of spinal reflex movements in brain-dead patients'. *Transplant Proc* **36**(1): 17-19.

Dresser, R and E Boisaubim (1985) 'Ethics, law and nutritional support'. *Arch Intern Med* **145**: 122-4.

Evans, D (2007) 'Seeking an ethical and legal way of procuring transplantable organs from the dying without further attempts to redefine human death'. *Philos Ethics Humanit Med* **2**: 11.

Faunce, TA and C Stewart (2005) 'The Messiha and Schiavo cases: third-party ethical and legal interventions in futile care disputes'. *Med J Aust* **183**(5): 261-3.

Fine, RL (2006) 'Ethical issues in artificial nutrition and hydration'. *Nutr Clin Pract* **21**(2): 118-25.

Fins, JJ (2008) 'Neuroethics and neuroimaging: moving toward transparency'. *Am J Bioeth* **8**(9): 46-52.

Fins, JJ, ND Schiff et al (2007) 'Late recovery from the minimally conscious state: ethical and policy implications'. *Neurology* **68**(4): 304-7.

Freckelton, I (1993) 'Withdrawal of Life Support: The "Persistent Vegetative State" Conundrum'. *Journal of Law and Medicine* **1**: 35.

Gillett, G (1986) 'Why let people die?' *J Med Ethics* **12**: 83.

Hess, DC and CV Borlongan (2008) 'Stem cells and neurological diseases'. *Cell Prolif* **41 Suppl 1**: 94-114.

Institute of Medical Ethics Working Party on the Ethics of Prolonging Life and Assisted Death (1991) 'Withdrawal of life-support from patients in a persistent vegetative state'. *Lancet* **337**: 96-8.

Jennet, B (2002) *The vegetative state. Medical facts, Ethical and Legal Dilemmas*. Cambridge, Cambridge University Press.

Joannides, AJ and S Chandran (2008) 'Human embryonic stem cells: an experimental and therapeutic resource for neurological disease'. *J Neurol Sci* **265**(1-2): 84-8.

Joffe, AR (2007) 'The ethics of donation and transplantation: are definitions of death being distorted for organ transplantation?' *Philos Ethics Humanit Med* **2**: 28.

Karakatsanis, KG (2008) ' "Brain death": should it be reconsidered?' *Spinal Cord* **46**(6): 396-401.

Kellehear, A (2008) 'Dying as a social relationship: a sociological review of debates on the determination of death'. *Soc Sci Med* **66**(7): 1533-44.

Kennedy, M, J Moran et al (1996) 'Drugs and brain death'. *Med J Aust*: 394-7.

Kinney, H, J Korein et al (1994) 'Neuropathological findings in the brain of Karen Ann Quinlan'. *N Engl J Med* **330**(21): 1469-75.

Korein, J (1978) 'The problem of brain death'. *Ann New York Acad Sci* **315**: 26.

Laureys, S and M Boly (2007) 'What is it like to be vegetative or minimally conscious?' *Curr Opin Neurol* **20**(6): 609-13.

Lewis, P (2007) 'Withdrawal of treatment from a patient in a permanent vegetative state: Judicial involvement and innovative treatment'. *Medical Law Review* **15**(3): 392-9.

Lizza, J (1993) 'Persons and death: what's metaphysically wrong with current statutory definitions of death?' *J Med Philos* **18**: 351-74.

Macdonald, ME, S Liben et al (2008) 'Signs of life and signs of death: brain death and other mixed messages at the end of life'. *J Child Health Care* **12**(2): 92-105.

Modo, M (2008) 'Brain repair: how stem cells are changing neurology'. *Bull Soc Sci Med Grand Duche Luxem* **2**: 217-57.

Multi-Society Task Force on PVS (1994a) 'Medical Aspects of the Persistent Vegetative State. (First of two parts)'. *N Engl J Med* **330**(21): 1499-507.

Multi-Society Task Force on PVS (1994b) 'Medical Aspects of the Persistent Vegetative State (Second of two parts)'. *N Engl J Med* **330**(22): 1572-9.

National Health and Medical Research Council (2004) *Post-Coma Unresponsiveness (Vegetative State): A Clinical Framework for Diagnosis*. Canberra, NHMRC.

National Health and Medical Research Council (2007) *Ethical Guidelines for the Care of People in Post-Coma Unresponsiveness (Vegetative State) or a Minimally Responsive State – DRAFT*. Canberra, National Health and Medical Research Council.

Owen, A, M Coleman et al (2007) 'Response to Comments on Detecting Awareness in the Vegetative State'. *Science* **316**: 1221c.

Owen, A, R Martin et al (2006) 'Detecting Awareness in the Vegetative State'. *Science* **313**(5792): 1402.

Pallis, C (1983) *ABC of Brain Stem Death*. BMJ Devonshire Press.

Pearson, I (1995) 'Brain death and organ donation'. *Anaesth Intensive Care* **23**(1): 11-13.

Powner, D, B Ackeman et al (1996) 'Medical diagnosis of death in adults: historical contributions to current controversies'. *Lancet* **348**: 1219-23.

Powner, DJ and IM Bernstein (2003) 'Extended somatic support for pregnant women after brain death'. *Crit Care Med* **31**(4): 1241-9.

Racine, E, R Amaram et al (2008) 'Media coverage of the persistent vegetative state and end-of-life decision-making'. *Neurology* **71**(13): 1027-32.

Rousseau, MC, S Confort-Gouny et al (2008) 'A MRS-MRI-fMRI exploration of the brain. Impact of long-lasting persistent vegetative state'. *Brain Inj* **22**(2): 123-34.

Royal College of Physicians of London (2003) *The vegetative state. Guidance on Diagnosis and Management*. London, Royal College of Physicians of London.

Shann, F (1995) 'A personal comment: whole brain death versus cortical death'. *Anaesth Intensive Care* **23**(1): 14-15.

Tibballs, J (2008) 'The non-compliance of clinical guidelines for organ donation with Australian statute law'. *Journal of Law and Medicine* **16**: 335.

Tomlinson, T (1990) 'Misunderstanding death on a respirator'. *Bioethics* **4**: 253-64.

Transplantation Ethics Working Party (1997) *Certifying death: The brain function criterion*. Canberra, National Health and Medical Research Council.

Truog, R (2004) Is it time to abandon brain death? *Health Care Ethics: Critical Issues For The 21st Century*. J Monagle and D Thomasma. Sudbury, Mass, Jones & Bartlett.

Truog, R (2007) 'Brain death – too flawed to endure, too ingrained to abandon'. *J Law Med Ethics* **35**(2): 273-81.

Truog, R and J Fackler (1992) 'Rethinking brain death'. *Crit Care Med* **20**: 1705-13.

Verheidje, J, M Rady et al (2007) 'Recovery of transplantable organs after cardiac or circulatory death: Transforming the paradigm for the ethics of organ donation'. *Philos Ethics Humanit Med* **2**: 8.

Washida, M, R Okamoto et al (1992) 'Beneficial effect of 3,5,3 – Triiodothyronine and vasopressin administration on hepatic energy status and systemic haemodynamics after brain death'. *Transplantation* **54**: 44-9.

Whetstine, L (2007) 'Bench-to-bedside review: When is dead really dead – on the legitimacy of using neurological criteria to determine death'. *Crit Care* **11**(2): 208.

Young, GB, SD Shemie et al (2006) 'Brief review: the role of ancillary tests in the neurological determination of death'. *Can J Anaesth* **53**(6): 620-7.

CHAPTER 25

ORGAN DONATION AND TRANSPLANTATION

Case 1

'Ten people have been arrested for alleged involvement in a human organs racket related to 150 illegal transplants, the Hindustan Times said yesterday. Police said the 10, including three doctors, a policeman and a nursing home staff member, were charged with wrongful confinement and endangering the life of a person. They were arrested in New Delhi on Saturday after a patient, Shaukat Ali, complained a kidney had been removed without his consent. ... Police said the doctors had performed about 150 kidney transplants by luring poor people from New Delhi's Walled City area, mainly inhabited by poor Muslims. The kidneys were sold to recipients for 80,000 rupees ($A3240) – about double the amount paid to the "donors." A flourishing illegal trade in human organs – mainly kidneys and eyes – has been rampant in India. A series of scandals resulted in the Human Tissue Act of 1994, which bans kidney donations to anyone except close relatives.' (Sydney Morning Herald, 11 May 1998: 7)

Case 2

JL is a 32-year-old computer programmer who has hereditary polycystic kidney disease. He has been on dialysis for the past two years. His sister is now offering to donate her kidney to him. The social worker who has been talking to the family is concerned that the sister's main motive may not be purely altruistic, as she suspects that the sister may be under great pressure from the family.

The first kidney transplant was performed in the United States in 1954; the first heart and liver transplants were performed in 1967; and the first lung transplant in 1983. Other tissues that have been successfully transplanted include pancreas, bone marrow, pancreatic islet cells, bone, skin, intestine, peripheral nerves, adrenal glands, foetal tissue and dopaminergic brain tissue.

The majority of transplants are highly successful. Survival rates following kidney transplantation are 90% in the first year after transplant and over 75% after five years. Heart and liver transplant survival rates are around 90% in the first year and 85% after five years and pancreas transplant survival rates are 94% after one year and 87% after five years (National Clinical Taskforce on Organ and Tissue Donation 2008). Indeed, the survival rates following transplant have improved so much that the greatest risks to long-term survival among transplant recipients are not recurrence of the organ dysfunction that led to transplantation in the first place, but cancer and cardiovascular disease (Buell, Gross et al 2005). Successful transplantation dramatically increases individuals' life expectancy and quality of life, allowing many to return to active participation in the community, so it is not surprising that transplantation has been enthusiastically championed among many different communities.

The success of transplantation programs has created a major demand for transplantable tissues and organs. In Australia in 2007, 612 patients received kidney transplants, 151 received liver transplants, 59 received heart transplants, 69 had double lung transplants, eight had single lung transplants and six had heart/lung transplants, and 25 people had combined pancreas and kidney transplants. And even though there were only 198 deceased organ donors in 2007, this resulted in transplants for 668 people. (These figures illustrate how efficiently Australia is at using organs from deceased donors – in 2005 3.6 transplants resulted from each deceased Australian donor, compared with 2.4 in Spain and 2.7 in the United States.) Yet the demand still outstrips the supply for transplanted organs. By July 2008 there was a waiting list of 1357 people for kidneys, 67 for hearts, 194 for livers, 149 for lungs and 35 for pancreases (Australia & New Zealand Organ Donation register: <http://www.anzdata.org.au/anzod/v1/indexanzod.html>).

Twenty to thirty per cent of potential heart and liver recipients die while waiting for a transplant and the average waiting time for a patient needing a kidney transplant is approximately four years (National Clinical Taskforce on Organ and Tissue Donation 2008; NHMRC 2007b). Other countries have similar problems. The average wait for a cadaveric organ in the US or Britain is two to three years, in Singapore it is six to eight years, and it is probably even longer than this in the rest of Asia or the Gulf States (Rothman and Rothman 2003).

The scarcity of organs has provided the impetus for an ongoing search for new strategies to increase the number of organs available for transplantation (O'Connor and Delmonico 2005). An enormous number of strategies have been investigated, including public education aimed at 'normalising' organ donation; improved processes for identifying and recruiting potential organ donors in hospital, promulgation of 'presumed consent' policies for organ donation, development of protocols for paired kidney donation and for increasing organ procurement from people after cardiac death (DCD), further redefinition of death to include more people as dead, xenotransplantation, somatic cell nuclear transfer and regenerative medicine, non-directed (altruistic) organ donation, and financial reimbursement or even payment for living donors. The scarcity of organs has also led desperate patients to use the internet to obtain an organ for their own use and engage in organ commerce and global transplant tourism (Daar 2003; Wright and Campbell 2006).

Organ donation in Australia

Organs for transplantation are currently derived from three main sources: living donors, brain-dead donors – otherwise known as heart-beating organ donors (HBOD), and donors whose hearts have, at least briefly, stopped (Donation after Cardiac Death donors or cadaveric donors).

Australia currently has an *'opt-in'* or *'express consent'* approach to organ donation, whereby individuals are encouraged to indicate their preferences for organ donation on the Australian Organ Donor Registry (AODR) or on their driver's licence and to talk with their loved ones about their preferences. Following a potential organ donor's death, their family is always consulted and their wishes respected – so that should a family object to organ donation, then organ procurement generally does not proceed, regardless of the wishes of the deceased.

The AODR is the single national register of consent or objection to organ and tissue donation (although some States, such as New South Wales, still enable adults to register their organ donation preferences on their driver's licence). The AODR is administered by Medicare and provides registered donors with an organ donor card (<www.hic.gov.au>). As of April 2008, over 1.1 million Australians had registered on the AODR. Ninety-nine per cent of these were 'consents' to donation.

The level of support for organ donation in Australia is high with approximately 90% of Australians indicating their support for organ donation (NHMRC 2007a). Despite this, in 2007 Australia had one of the lowest solid-organ donation rates in the developed world at nine donors per million population (dpmp), compared with Spain (34.3dpmp), Belgium (28dpmp), France (24.7dpmp), United States (24.6dpmp), Germany (16dpmp) and the UK (13.2dpmp). (In contrast Australia's donation rate for corneas is near the top of international lists at 47dpmp in 2006.) (National Clinical Taskforce on Organ and Tissue Donation 2008).

The exact reason for the low donor rate in Australia is unclear but may be multi-factorial and relate to a combination of medical, political, cultural and legal factors including:

- the reduction in factors causing brain death including a reduction in neurotrauma due to improved road and gun safety, and better treatment and higher survival rates following cerebrovascular accident (stroke);
- the fact that only about 1% of deaths occur in circumstances where donation of the person's organs is possible;
- 'systems failures' including failure to identify potential donors in hospital or to approach families to request donation;
- inadequate coordination of donation processes nationally;
- an aging population;
- geographic distance; and
- a cultural reluctance to 'intervene' during times when families are dealing with the (often unexpected) death of a loved one.

In July 2008 the Commonwealth Government announced a $136.4 million national organ and tissue donation reform package to improve Australia's organ donation rate. Key aspects of this initiative, which was largely based on the recommendations of the National Clinical Taskforce on Organ and Tissue Donation, included:

- funding for organ donation specialist doctors, transplant coordinators and other staff in selected public and private hospitals;
- establishment of an independent national authority to coordinate national organ donation initiatives;
- funding for beds and infrastructure associated with organ donation;
- national public awareness and education campaigns;
- counselling services for potential donor families; and
- development of protocols for new and innovative strategies to increase organ donation, including donation after cardiac death (DCD), paired kidney donation, living donor liver transplantation, clinical 'trigger' checklists and transplant-related data collection. (National Clinical Taskforce on Organ and Tissue Donation 2008)

Living donation

Living donors have been used in kidney transplantation since 1954, in partial liver transplantation since 1989 and in lung transplantation since 1990. Living donors may choose to donate regenerative tissues such as bone marrow, blood and bone; or non-regenerative tissue such as lung, liver and kidney. The majority of donors are close relatives of a family member who requires a transplant; however, unrelated donors may donate an organ on altruistic grounds.

Living donation raises unique ethical issues – primarily because the principal risk is borne by the donor whereas the principal benefit is to the recipient. This situation raises a series of very difficult questions, including how these risks and benefits are to be balanced, and at what point does the risk of harm to the donor make it inappropriate to allow the donation to take place. While one initial response is simply to argue that respect for autonomy demands that individuals assess risks for themselves, one must ask how the ethical acceptability of allowing a young person to donate an organ to their parent would change if the risk of death was (hypothetically) 1%, 5%, 10%, 50% or 90%? In other words – there is always some point where one judges the risk that an individual may take, with the assistance of the medical system, as too great.

Although death after live donation is uncommon, it can be associated with considerable psychological and physical morbidity. Donors face risks of death or disability from the surgery itself, in addition to the higher risk of exposure to injury and disease when living with one kidney or lung. Living kidney donation is quite a safe procedure, with a mortality rate of 0.02-0.03%, but between 4 and 38% of donors experience some complications of surgery (Matas, Bartlett et al 2003). Follow-up of donors suggests that while they may develop depression, anxiety and adjustment disorders following donation, they have a low probability of significant renal dysfunction and do not have a higher chance of developing hypertension than the general population (Smith, Trauer et al 2004; Najarian, Chavers et al 1992). There is less data available regarding the risks of living liver donation. Recent reviews describe a donor mortality of 0.2%, with 16% experiencing surgical morbidity, including biliary complications and infections (Middleton, Duffield et al 2006; Munson 2007).

Live donation may also have a significant psychological impact on both donor and recipient and the success or failure of the transplant may have a profound and long-term impact on the relationship. between them. At any one time, transplant recipients may experience anxiety about early death, hope for their own future, and guilt about either the death of the donor (in the case of transplantation following brain death) or the health of the donor (in the case of living donation). They may also experience tremendous changes in their sense of identity and may feel that they never return to 'normal' following transplantation (Sanner 2003; Inspector, Kutz et al 2004). Indeed, on occasion recipients may feel overwhelmed by the 'tyranny of the gift'. Donors also may become depressed, anxious, demanding, jealous or resentful – and suicide has been reported in both donors and recipients following live volunteer donation (Shiel 1995).

Since donors are taking risks for the benefit of others, their free and informed consent becomes of central importance. The problem is that there are many pressures within the context of decisions to donate organs that may impair the voluntariness of the donor's decision. Many of the unavoidable pressures arise from the fact that the recipient may die without transplantation and that the decision is a highly emotionally charged one. This may give rise to coercion or threats compelling the donor to agree to organ donation. For some observers these pressures are sufficient to make valid consent impossible – particularly where parents are considering donating organs to their children – and may be reasonable grounds for restricting live volunteer donation to related donors. For others, restriction of either related or unrelated altruistic donation represents unjustifiable paternalism.

Non-directed living donation

While donation of organs from living relatives is widely accepted (despite the very real possibilities that these relationships make living related donation unavoidably coercive) there is much greater concern with living donation by those without a genetic or emotional link (non-directed living donation). In general terms this is because of distrust of the motives of non-related donors and disquiet about the degree of risk that strangers can accept for others. (This creates a dilemma for those who support organ donation as altruism is often encouraged in the context of blood donation, research, charity, community service and, indeed, in organ donation (Matas, Garvey et al 2000; Daar 2002). Those who object to non-directed donation point to the use of the internet by companies like 'International Medical Travellers' which can unite those seeking organ transplantation with altruistic individuals wishing to donate an organ.

The main arguments advanced in favour of allowing non-directed donation are that it is consistent with the principles of liberal democracy; that it is a justifiable expression of autonomy; that competent adults should be able to make decisions about their own health care, including decisions to donate their organs to others; that it is consistent with the social value attached to altruism; and that in most liberal democracies individuals are generally allowed to take risks – as long as those risks do not endanger others. Interestingly, non-directed donation has not been advanced as a major strategy for ameliorating the shortage of donor organs – in large measure because it is assumed that such processes are 'risky', create substantial practical difficulties and are unlikely to generate many organs for transplantation. Nevertheless, non-directed donation is now possible in a number of Australian States.

Directed donation

Importantly, while governments and services increasingly allow organ donation by strangers, there is generally little support for donors directing their organs to specific groups defined by ethnicity, age, lifestyle, gender, religious tradition, nationality or socio-economic status on the grounds that such choices offend against equity (Matas, Garvey et al 2000). Indeed, most policies explicitly pro-hibit conditional donation of this support (UK Department of Health 2000). In contrast, there has recently been a re-examination of Directed Deceased Donation (DDD) where an individual is permitted to nominate who shall receive their organ(s) in much the same way that living donors donate their kidney of liver lobe to a family member. The issues surrounding DDD continue to be the focus of debate.

Children as 'donors'

The problems of consent to organ donation are considerably greater where a child or non-competent adult is to be a living donor. This has been discussed previously in Chapter 20. The NHMRC has suggested that permitting a child to be a living donor will only be ethically sound where:

- no other suitable donors are available;
- the risks and discomfort to the child are minimal;
- the donation is to a person – such as a sibling – with whom the child has an intimate relationship (the child donor may then benefit indirectly from the benefits to the recipient, for example, in having a brother or sister survive);
- the donation is a last resort in treatment and is expected to be of great benefit to the recipient;
- the proposed transplant is of proven efficacy and expected benefit, and there is a good chance that the risks and discomforts involved for the donor child will be outweighed by the benefits of transplantation;
- an independent team considers that on balance the donation is in the donor's best interests; and
- the parents consent and the child (if he or she is able to do so) agrees or assents. The child's understanding of the donation and transplantation may be incomplete, but efforts must be made to ensure that his or her understanding is as thorough as possible, consistent with his or her age; and, to the best of the parents' (or family's) judgment, all the reasonably expected benefits (to recipient and donor) clearly outweigh all the reasonably expected risks and discomforts (to the donor and recipient). (NHMRC 2007a)

Paired donation (kidney paired exchange)

In 'direct' paired kidney donation, living potential donor-recipient pairs, such as family members or partners, who are biologically incompatible (because they have incompatible ABO blood groups or are not histocompatible), are matched with other biologically incompatible donor-recipient pairs to exchange kidneys – thereby providing both recipients with biologically compatible donor organs. (This, of course, requires that surgery on all four individuals is performed at the same time.)

Paired donation is currently practised in the United States, United Kingdom and the Netherlands and limited numbers have been performed in Australia. While paired donation may increase the number of kidney transplants (although there is some dispute as to the real impact that this policy may have on organ availability) (Waterman, Schenk et al 2006), it raises serious questions regarding coercion and distributive justice and poses substantial and logistic challenges (Ross and Zenios 2004).

Heart-beating organ donation (brain-dead donation)

Issues with the diagnosis of brain death have been discussed in Chapter 24. Regardless of whether the current definitions of brain death continue to be supported, patients with brain death are likely to continue to have the opportunity to be organ donors.

Contemporaneous consent is impossible from patients who are declared brain-dead, so considerable attention has been devoted to encouraging Australians to indicate their preferences for organ donation in advance. Approximately 35-37% of the eligible adult population has indicated their opinions regarding donation on the AODR and about a quarter of donors have done so on their driver's licence. For this and other reasons permission for organ donation following a diagnosis of brain death is usually obtained by surrogate decision-making by family members instead (Excell, Russ et al 2004).

In Australia, New Zealand, the UK and the USA, organ procurement is based on a system of express donation ('opt in') by the donor or their family. Although the ethical ideal is presumed to be a 'substituted judgment' that reflects the wishes and beliefs of the donor, it seems likely that families often make decisions that reflect their own beliefs and their own sense of altruism.

There is ongoing public debate regarding the ethical appropriateness of families being able to override the express wishes of their loved ones. Those who argue that a person's wishes should always be respected base this on the belief that respect for autonomy requires respect for an individual's choices regarding the 'disposal' of their body after death. Those who support the status quo argue that one can rarely be certain that an individual's previously expressed preferences were either informed or valid, that current mechanisms for indicating 'consent' (such as nominating one's consent online with the AODR) satisfy none of the standard requirements of valid consent and that health-care professionals should be more concerned with the potential harms of donation on those left behind that with the symbolic importance of respecting a deceased individual's wishes. This debate has led to suggestions from government and from transplant advocates that legislative measures should be introduced to prevent families from 'vetoing' a person's decision to donate their organs after their death. The problem with such measures is that they ignore medical culture, ignore concern for those left behind, ignore the social context of decision-making and the inter-relational basis of autonomy, and over-emphasise one particular view of autonomy. They are also inconsistent with the emerging critique of autonomy, particularly from within feminist bioethics, that seeks to legitimise the importance of families.

Presumed consent ('opt-out')

Presumed consent systems assume that everyone is an organ donor (subject to medical assessment for suitability) unless they have previously indicated that they did not wish to be an organ donor. Presumed consent systems operate in Singapore and Brazil and in a number of European countries, including Spain, Denmark, Finland, Norway, France, Norway, Austria, Italy and Belgium. In all but Austria there remains an obligation to consult with the deceased person's family. In Austria there is no requirement to consult relatives and those who 'opt-out' are given the lowest priority if they later need an organ for transplantation (Kondro 2006; Quigley, Brazier et al 2008).

Presumed consent, which is sometimes referred to as the 'Spanish model', is commonly cited as the best model for organ donation as Spain achieves a higher rate of donors than any other country. However, in Spain there are many other factors that may contribute to this including the national coordination of donation and transplantation services, the level of infrastructure support and staffing for donation, the high levels of neurotrauma from road traffic accidents, the use of elderly people as donors and the high numbers of doctors and ICU beds (Chang, Mahanty et al 2003).

Those who support the introduction of presumed consent (opt-out) models of organ donation argue that it will increase the number of organs and tissues available for donation and transplantation, 'normalise' donation, be more consistent with strong levels of public support for donation, and remove the ability of family members to prevent an individual's wishes regarding organ donation being actualised (if a 'strong presumed consent' system was adopted) (Benoit, Spira et al 1990; Roels, Vanreterghem et al 1990; Teo 1991). The main objections to presumed consent systems are that there is no conclusive proof that they increase rates of organ donation (Greece – which has a presumed consent system – has a lower donation rate than Australia), as well as that presumed consent models are not reflective of many cultural views regarding the body and do not encourage appropriate discussion of organ donation (Veatch and Pitt 1995; Csilag 1997; National Clinical Taskforce on Organ and Tissue Donation 2008).

Alternative approaches to maximising organ donation

A number of other strategies have been employed in different parts of the world to increase the number of available donor organs. 'Required request' has been introduced to some parts of the United States. Under this system legislation makes it mandatory for health professionals to make a formal request for organ donation to the families of eligible patients. Although such a system has been claimed to be sensitive to the values of voluntarism, altruisms and autonomy, 'required request' does not appear to have resulted in a sustained increase in the number of organ donors (Norris 1990).

'Mandated choice' or 'required response', which has been strongly supported by the ethics committee of the United Network for Organ Sharing (UNOS) in the United States, requires that all adults indicate their preference for organ donation, such as when applying for a health-care card or a driver's licence (Dennis, Hanson et al 1994). The advantage of such an approach is that it provides data on every citizen's choices. But there are many disadvantages – it forces a choice upon those who do not wish to make a choice, it does nothing to ensure the validity of the 'consent' and it does not provide any clarity about the role of the family (Siminoff and Mercer 2001). Indeed, because such systems suffer from many of the problems of advance directives, such as utility, validity and reliability, they would be unlikely to contribute greatly to reducing the shortage of donor organs. Some countries, such as Singapore, have also institutionalised financial or material incentives to donate, including tax rebates, fixed grants and subsidisation of medical expenses (Teo 1991).

The optimal method for obtaining consent to organ donation remains controversial. While a system of 'presumed consent' seems attractive, it is more likely that organ procurement in Australia will continue to emphasise voluntarism and altruism; and continue to promote higher rates of donation by attempting to 'normalise' organ donation through public education.

Consent to organ donation

When members of the health-care team attempt to obtain consent for donation it is important not to coerce patients or families through the language used. We should also not assume that documented preferences for donation – whether on a driver's licence or online organ donor registry – are either informed or include consent to all procurement practices (Truog 2008). But perhaps most importantly, we should not lose sight of the context in which donation decisions occur and the social and relational nature of these decisions.

Few decisions are as difficult as the decision to donate a loved one's organs. While knowledge of their preferences for organ donation may make such decisions easier for partners or family members – nothing can take away the enormity or complexity of the decision. In the midst of grief and in the midst of trying to find meaning in death, family members must balance their own needs, fears and desire for solidarity, with their desire to respect the wishes and memory of their loved one and the obligations they may feel are expected of them (Rodgers and Cowles 1991; Titmuss 1997; Little and Sayers 2004). Health professionals must be sensitive to the enormous importance of these occasions and be aware that discussions about organ donation may create meaning but may also cause harm.

Donation after cardiac death (DCD) or non-heart beating organ donation (NHBOD)

In recent years there has been a resurgence of interest in organ donation after cardiac death (DCD) as a source of kidneys, livers, lungs and pancreases, particularly in Europe and North America (Steen, Sjoberg et al 2001; Weber, Dindo et al 2002; Keizer, de Fijter et al 2005). DCD donors now account for 7% of all deceased donors in the United States, and many countries now also supplement their organ donor pool with DCD donors. The widespread adoption of the Maastricht categories of DCD provides the possibility of standardisation of donor protocols and international collaboration in the analysis of outcomes following DCD (Koostra 1997; DuBois 2009).

The Maastricht categories are:

- *Category 1*: Dead on scene (out of hospital) – Unknown warm ischaemic time: Uncontrolled
- *Category 2*: Unsuccessful resuscitation – Known warm ischaemic time: Uncontrolled
- *Category 3*: Waiting cardiac death after planned treatment withdrawal – Known and limited warm ischaemic time: Controlled
- *Category 4*: Cardiac arrest after confirmation of brain death but before planned organ procurement – Known and potentially limited warm ischaemic time: Uncontrolled

In Australia, DCD typically follows an initial decision that continued life-sustaining treatment would be non-beneficial or contrary to the person's wishes and should be withdrawn. In 2006 there were eight donors after cardiac death in Australia and in 2007 there were 19 such donors. During 2007 the NSW Department of Health issued guidelines for DCD permitting category 3 and 4 DCD (NSW Health 2007).

While the rationale for DCD is clear, the concept and its applications have turned out to be enormously problematic and the use of such patients as organ donors has raised a series of ethical concerns regarding end-of-life care, conflicts of interest, rituals and grieving at the end of life, the goals of medicine, consent, the appropriate treatment of bodies and the definition of death (Joffe 2007).

Regardless of the events leading up to an individual's death, the moment of death, the time immediately after death and the point where families take their leave from their loved one are periods of immense meaning. While DCD protocols emphasise the importance of respect for this 'separation' they also seek a balance between provision of compassionate end-of-life care and optimising organ viability. DCD protocols invariably recognise the social and cultural meaning of death, but there is no doubt that the very fact that there is discussion about donation, donor assessments and consideration of pre-mortem therapies limits the grieving periods following the diagnosis of cardiac death and alters end-of-life care and the experience of loved ones during this period. And while many families may negotiate the rapid shifts in status of the dying person from patient to donor to lifeless body, others may find it intolerable.

Broad recognition of these potential harms has led to the adoption of different strategies for allowing family members to be present in the ICU, operating theatre or anaesthetic bay, to formal protocols for separation and to mandatory counselling for families of DCD donors. At this point much of the debate regarding DCD is based on conjecture and it will be important to audit the impact of DCD on death and dying in a range of different contexts and different cultures.

The impact of DCD on the social and cultural rituals surrounding death and dying is most evident in discussions about the pre- and post-mortem management of the DCD donor. Concern about organ viability following DCD and the best interests of the transplant recipient has stimulated interest in pre-mortem use of agents or interventions to maintain organ integrity, such as heparin, phentolamine, cold perfusion and extracorporeal membrane oxygenation (ECMO) (Bernat 2008). While moral objections can be raised against such practices on Kantian grounds (ie, that therapy given solely for the benefit of the recipient is morally unacceptable), it may be possible to defend such practices either by early redefinition of death or, alternatively, by clear separation of donor and ICU teams and consent.

Perhaps the major issue raised by the re-emergence of DCD is the challenge to the definition of death. For DCD, as with organ donation after brain death, it is generally accepted that the 'dead donor rule' must apply. (This requires that a donor has irreversible cessation of circulatory function or brain function.) 'Irreversibility' has been variously defined as 10 minutes of asystole (Maastricht protocol), 5 minutes of asystole (the Institute of Medicine), 2-5 minutes of asystole (American College of Critical Care Medicine) and 2 minutes of asystole (Pittsburgh protocol). As dying is a biological and physiological process, it is important to recognise that the definition of cardiac death according to periods of asystole (and thereby the creation of two categories – alive and dead) is a linguistic construction designed to fulfil particular functions (in this case, to enable organ donation). The choice of definition may be based on a number of biological and social phenomena, including the possibility of autoresuscitation following cardiac arrest (the 'Lazarus phenomenon'), the need to minimise the time in which organs may be compromised by lack of oxygen, community values, the perception of public trust and the priority given to organ integrity and transplantation (Keenan, Hoffmaster et al 2002; Koogler, Stark et al 2006; Kamarainen, Virkkunen et al 2007; Joffe, Anton et al 2008; Truog and Miller 2008).

Critics of DCD have pointed out that definitions of circulatory death for DCD purposes often use very short periods of time whereas, in resuscitation, longer periods of asystole may be insisted upon before death is declared. As Joffe has argued:

> This means that patients in identical physiologic states are dead (in the DCD context) or alive (in the resuscitation context); the current state of death (at 2-5 minutes) is contingent on a future event (whether there will be resuscitation) suggesting backward causation; and the commonly used meaning of irreversible as 'not capable of being reversed' is abandoned'. (Joffe 2007)

In 2008, a number of cases were described in which hearts had been transplanted from babies declared as DCD donors after 75 seconds of asystole (their heart stopping) (Boucek, Mashburn et al 2008). The transplanted hearts functioned well in the recipients – suggesting that the donor did not meet the full criteria for circulatory death in the first place, since the cessation of cardiac function was clearly reversible (in the right biological context).

We, and many other commentators, believe that organ donation in such cases may be ethically justifiable – as long as the process is based on explicit consent, the donor is irreversibly dying and the recipient may obtain great benefit. (In these cases the donors were terminally ill, newborn babies with severe neurological disorders from birth injuries, the recipients were infants who were dying as a consequence of severe cardiac disease who were also dying and consent was obtained from the parents of both donors and recipients.) But such cases do not appear to be consistent with the 'dead donor rule'. While some commentators have suggested that the answer to this is to change the definition of death again, perhaps allowing for the fact we do not intend to resuscitate a person as being evidence that they have irreversible cardiac death (Bernat 2008), we believe that it is difficult to defend the idea that the definition of death should depend on intent.

Developments in organ transplantation mean that the point at which one declares death will likely always represent a compromise between the need to have a reliable definition of death and the need to have viable organs for transplantation (Veatch 2008). In light of this we can either continue to debate the degrees of statistical certainty required to mark the point at which death can be said to occur, we can abandon cardiac transplantation following DCD (Gawande, Caplan et al 2008) or we can abandon the 'dead donor rule' altogether to permit removal of organs from the dying, without the pretence that they are dead before surgery (Evans 2007).

We agree with Truog and Miller that the 'dead donor rule' is philosophically, biologically and clinically incoherent (although we accept that it satisfies political goals and is deeply entrenched within legal, ethical and medical institutions) (Truog and Miller 2008). But this is not the mainstream view. It is likely that the coming years will see continuing debate regarding the philosophical, ethical and legal challenges raised by DCD. (For further discussion of the dead donor rule, see Chapter 24.)

Foetal tissue transplantation

Transplantation of aborted foetal pancreatic or brain tissue has been used in the treatment of neurodegenerative disorders such as Huntington's disease and Parkinson's disease for almost 20 years (Peschanski et al 2004). Its use has generated enormous controversy. For those who object to termination of pregnancy on moral grounds, foetal tissue transplantation represents little more than a medical justification for murder. For others, the morality of abortion is largely irrelevant to the consideration of foetal tissue transplantation. According to this viewpoint, what *is* relevant is the balance between judgments of the moral or symbolic value of foetal tissue and consideration of its utility.

Xenografting

> The creatures outside looked from pig to man, and from man to pig, and from
> pig to man again; but already it was impossible to say which was which.
> (George Orwell, *Animal Farm*)

It has become increasingly evident that even with 100% consent for organ
retrieval from brain-dead donors there will still be insufficient donor organs to
meet the needs of patients. The clear implication is that an alternative source of
organs is required. The use of mechanical or bioengineered organs is one option
but the technology required is enormously complex and most development
remains at a premature stage. The use of xenografts, where organs are transplanted from animals into humans, has been proposed as an alternative means
by which the organ shortage could be ameliorated and transplantation programs
expanded (Dorling, Reisbeck et al 1997).

The idea that animals may be used as a source of solid organs for
transplantation has been tested since the early part of the 20th century. Kidneys,
liver, pancreas and hearts have all been transplanted from animals into humans
(Auchincloss 1988). In 1964 the first heart-transplant patient received his organ
from a chimpanzee. Also in 1964, a woman was transplanted with a chimpanzee
kidney – which functioned without rejection for nine months (Reemtsma,
McCracken et al 1964). In 1984 the much publicised case of Baby Fae, where a
three-week-old baby girl was transplanted with a baboon's heart and lived 21
days before dying of kidney failure, brought the issue of xenotransplantation to
public notice.

The major practical difficulty with xenografting is that most transplants fail
acutely because preformed antibodies in the recipient produce an almost immediate shutdown in circulation – a process called hyperacute rejection. In recent
years advances in immunology, pharmacotherapy and genetic therapy have
raised the possibility that immunological barriers to xenotransplantation may
be overcome by intensification of immunosuppressive therapy or by 'transgenically' modifying donor animals so that their organs are 'humanised' and so
less likely to be rejected. Current research suggests that pig organs can support
physiological function in primates and their rejection can be successfully treated,
but in the short term transplantation of tissue (such as pancreatic islet cells
responsible for producing insulin) may be more feasible than transplantation of
entire organs (Baertschiger and Buhler 2007).

In 1996 the Nuffield Council on Bioethics concluded that the use of transgenic pigs as source animals for transplantation was ethically acceptable as long
as account was taken of the extent of genetic manipulation of the donor animal,
the welfare of the animal, the type of tissue used and the infective, immunological and physiological risks to the recipient (Nuffield Council on Bioethics
1996). For many, however, the imminent emergence of xenotransplantation
raises a number of troubling issues. It is often stated that transferring organs
between species is 'unnatural', that it 'interferes with nature' or that it blurs the
distinction between humans and animals. Such arguments are relatively easy to
dismiss as it is often difficult to define what is 'natural' or 'unnatural' and it is
not clear at all why 'interfering with nature', by attempting to cure or prevent

disease, is morally wrong. Similarly, objection to the use of non-human tissue or substance has little weight given the widespread and uncontroversial use of porcine insulin by diabetics, factor VIII by haemophiliacs and porcine heart valves by those with valvular heart disease.

A more significant objection to xenotransplantation is based on animal rights and speciesism. Opponents of xenografting may claim that animals have rights to life and should not be sacrificed to save human lives. Advocates of xenografting respond to such objections in three ways. First, they may accept that animals are clearly harmed by xenotransplantation but maintain that this harm is overridden by the benefits to human recipients. Secondly, they may recognise that as animals are already used for food and medical research, their use as a source of organs should be equally acceptable. Finally, they may maintain if animals are to be used as source organs the selection of donor species can proceed on 'moral' grounds by taking account of availability, life-span and species characteristics. This has been the approach taken by the British Medical Association and the Nuffield Council on Bioethics, which concluded that while primates would be the optimal source of donor organs because of their anatomical, physiological and immunological similarity to humans, their use in xenotransplantation is ethically unacceptable because they are highly intelligent and social animals, slow breeding, have not been farmed and are either scarce or endangered. As the Nuffield report makes clear:

> When considering the use of primates for xenotransplantation, the capacities they share with human beings, notably their self-awareness, led to ethical concerns about their use for xenotransplantation. While unquestionably intelligent and social animals, there is less evidence that pigs share capacities with human beings to the extent that primates do. As such, the adverse effects suffered by the pigs used to supply organs for xenotransplantation would not outweigh the potential benefits to human beings. (Nuffield Council on Bioethics 1996)

The difficulty with using characteristics such as self-awareness, intelligence or social interaction as a basis for choosing an organ source is that it would allow not only the use of pigs but also neonates, comatose adults or the severely demented elderly.

A further practical difficulty with xenotransplantation is that it carries with it a number of risks, such as rejection, immunosuppression, psychological harm and disease transmission, that are difficult to quantify and may only be identified after they begin to cause disease. This issue is made more complex by the fact that some organisms may not cause any symptoms in animals but cause disease in humans, may only cause disease after a long incubation period (eg, Creutzfeld-Jacob disease) and may have implications not only for the organ recipient but, by creating a risk of epidemics, have implications for the wider community. These facts make consent, both in research and in clinical use, absolutely essential. The onus is clearly on the health professional to minimise risks by adequate research, by screening donor animals for disease, by long-term follow-up and by ensuring that patients are competent, adequately informed and not unjustifiably coerced by the scientific merit or altruistic gain from xenotransplantation. While the pig appears to be a relatively safe source of donor organs, most governments have banned porcine xenotransplantation until regulatory standards are established (Tallacchini 2008).

Xenotransplantation clearly has enormous potential. However, there remains a series of immune, non-immune and ethical issues that will need to be addressed before it becomes a clinical reality.

Organ commerce

As long as the global supply of tissues, cells and organs for transplant does not meet needs, organ trade is likely to continue. There is considerable profit to be made from taking advantage of the desperation of wealthy patients and the extreme poverty of vendors (Noel 2007).

In Australia, as in most other nations, organ commerce is illegal. The sale of human body parts is prohibited by the World Health Assembly Guiding Principles (Resolutions WHA 44.25). Despite this, there appears to be a flourishing global organ 'trade' involving several thousand organs per year (Rothman and Rothman 2003). A number of examples of organ commerce have come to the attention of international media, including the sale of kidneys from Turkish peasants to private hospitals in London (Wright 1991), the kidnapping and killing of people in order to obtain their organs (Strauss 2004) and the sale of organs of executed Chinese prisoners to citizens from Hong Kong, Taiwan and Singapore (Rothman 1997). (Until recently, China transplanted organs from the thousands of prisoners it executes each year to fee-paying foreigners. About five Australians are thought to have bought organs from this source per year. China always insisted that these organs were only transplanted with the consent of the prisoners, but this was often doubted by outside observers. The sale of any human body part was eventually banned in 2006 (Anon 2008a).)

There is very limited data on the organ trade (Shimazono 2007) but what there is, is extremely disturbing. Naqvi et al found that kidney vendors from Pakistan were generally young, illiterate debentured labourers whose main aim in selling their kidney was to repay a fraction of intergenerational debt (Naqvi, Ali et al 2007). Unsurprisingly, as vendors received less than 4% of the purchase price for their kidney the vast majority (85%) felt that their economic situation did not improve following the loss of their kidney. Other research has demonstrated that many vendors were depressed or suicidal following the sale of their kidney, a number developed medical complications following nephrectomy, many expressed hate and anger towards the recipient and most would not recommend that others sell their kidneys (Zargooshi 2001).

Many people express abhorrence at the concept of organ commerce, particularly in countries where there are regulated transplant programs. However, in a society that champions individual rights and bodily autonomy and accepts the sale of labour, sex, blood, sperm and ova, the sale of organs might not necessarily be intrinsically unethical. Indeed, refusing to countenance payment to organ donors, particularly those who are poor and without other 'assets', while doing nothing to alleviate their poverty, and simultaneously accepting that people may die while awaiting organ availability, may itself be ethically questionable.

Objections to the sale of organs may be based on the intrinsic morality of organ commerce, the potential consequences of any move to allow it in the marketplace and the ethics of its practice. One argument suggests that autonomy does not extend to selling one's organs and that turning organs into commodities violates the intrinsic value of bodily integrity and degrades the intrinsic worth of every person. It is further claimed that the human body is not a possession to be sold and that the morality of organ donation is only established where it is done on the basis of altruism (Wilkinson and Garrard 1996).

A second objection to organ commerce focuses on the adverse consequences that may follow from it. The fear is that it may undermine the practice of altruistic organ donation, may lead to the vulnerable being killed for their organs, may encourage governments to do little to improve the situation of the poor and may increase the risks to donors and recipients by leaving organ transplantation in the hands of those concerned more with profit than with health care. As we saw in the examples above, there is some evidence that such practices occur.

A final objection to trade in organs is that truly free and informed consent to organ sale is not possible as the context in which it occurs, of desperately needy 'sellers' and chronically or terminally ill 'buyers', is unavoidably coercive. The argument is that in situations where the only asset people have in a marketplace is themselves, then poverty is a coercion of such magnitude that voluntary consent is impossible and exploitation inevitable. The basic obligation of the state in this context is not to facilitate commerce but to protect the vulnerable from being harmed by their own actions or those of others.

While a number of novel regulatory processes have been suggested, such as 'mandated philanthropy', where a wealthy recipient would be obliged to provide relief for impoverished groups, and an 'organ futures market' whereby the right to remove a person's organs upon death may be purchased from them while they are alive and well – it is probably unrealistic to believe that an organ market could be adequately regulated. What evidence there is suggests that the pattern of commercial movement in living donor organs – from South to North, poor to rich, black and brown to white, and female to male – mirrors and entrenches the inequalities that already exist in society, and that transplant tourism harms both vendors and recipients. However, given the increasing dominance of market economics and globalisation in the moral and social spheres of life, the real question becomes what should be done about transplant tourism. National legislative frameworks appear to provide one means for reducing the organ trade. For example, legislative frameworks banning commercial transplantation adopted by China and Pakistan in 2007 resulted in closure of websites advertising commercial transplantation services in these countries and expulsion of foreign candidates for transplantation (Noel 2007). But while national legislation may be effective, an examination of the history of the organ trade suggests that, as one country ceases to be a source of organs, another market becomes available. This suggests that to truly confront transplant tourism we will need to recognise that it is a global issue and that it requires a global response based on some sense of moral commitment to justice and equity.

Organ transplantation and the ethics of allocation

Transplantation raises ethical issues at the level of transplantation programs (macroallocation) and at the level of the individual patients (microallocation) (NHMRC 2007a; NHMRC 2007b).

The prioritisation of patients for transplant is extraordinarily complex and a range of ethical, medical, 'quasi-medical' and non-medical factors determine the process and outcomes of allocation. Medical factors that may be taken into consideration in attempting to maximise the outcome of the transplant include size, blood group, HLA-type, co-morbidity, urgency of need and disease status. 'Quasi-medical' factors include age, aetiology, and compliance. Non-medical factors may include lifestyle, time on waiting list and social utility criteria (Hauptman and O'Connor 1997).

The major ethical principles underlying allocation policies are justice (equity in distribution) and utility (medical benefit and efficiency). The way in which these factors are balanced is itself an ethical concern as there will often be a trade-off between justice and utility and all decisions will ultimately reflect value judgments. For example, as compliance with immunosuppression is critical to the survival of a graft, particularly in the early post-transplant period, it may seem reasonable to privilege those who are more likely to comply with medical therapy and exclude those who are generally non-compliant with medical instructions. But in doing so one may discriminate against those with cognitive impairment, developmental delay or psychiatric illness and those who come from groups who are already disempowered or marginalised in society, including indigenous Australians and those from ethnic minorities (Veatch 2000). Indeed, there is empirical data to suggest that the incorporation of 'quasi-medical' and non-medical factors into systems of organ allocation does lead to discrimination against groups such as American blacks and Aboriginal Australians, both of whom have lower rates of transplant and longer waiting times than might be thought equitable (Lowe, Kerridge et al 1995; Epstein, Ayanian et al 2000; Cass, Cunningham et al 2003).

In Australia, complex algorithms (such as the National Organ Matching Scheme and the National Kidney Matching Scheme), incorporating many of the criteria listed above, are used to determine organ allocation; following which organs may be transported interstate, or to and from New Zealand.

Arguments can be advanced both for selecting the sickest patients as organ recipients or for allocating organs to those with the highest likelihood of graft and/or patient survival. At the very least it would seem ethically required that there is equitable access to organ resources, that allocation processes are fair and transparent, and that criteria that are clearly discriminatory, such as race, gender, social status, religious affiliation and capacity to pay, are not used as grounds for the selection of organ recipients (Childress 1987).

LEGAL ASPECTS OF ORGAN TRANSPLANTATION

Background

In 1977 the Australian Law Reform Commission (ALRC) released a report entitled *Human Tissue Transplants*. The ALRC had been asked to examine the regulation of organ donation and transplantation as there had been doubts expressed about the application of the law to human tissue transplantation and the courts had not yet been asked to address the issue of removing tissue from a deceased person's body. The ALRC expressed the view that removal of an organ from a living person, even with the consent of the person, could constitute an assault (ALRC 1977). However, the conclusions reached by the ALRC were not in any way final, and it was thought that legislation was necessary to clarify the legal position. The ALRC therefore recommended that all States and Territories should pass uniform legislation that would regulate organ donation and tissue transplantation.

All Australian States and Territories have subsequently passed such legislation. The States and Territories follow a consent-based model where either the living donor consents, the deceased donor had consented, or consent is given by the senior available next-of-kin. While presumed consent approaches have been discussed by Australian governments, the National Clinical Taskforce on Organ Donation (2008) recommended against their introduction and instead focused intention on improved communication processes and consent procedures. A $151 million package was announced in July 2008, which created a new Australian Organ and Tissue Donation Authority, which has the task of improving donation rates through the implementation of a consistent and coordinated approach to organ donation: *Australian Organ and Tissue Donation and Transplantation Authority Act 2008* (Cth).

The new authority has the task of creating new standards and policies, and providing training and education, as well as funding research into transplantation.

Table 25.1 Human tissue legislation

Jurisdiction	Legislation
NSW	*Human Tissue Act 1983*
Qld	*Transplantation and Anatomy Act 1979*
SA	*Transplantation and Anatomy Act 1983*
Tas	*Human Tissue Act 1985*
Vic	*Human Tissue Act 1982*
WA	*Human Tissue and Transplant Act 1982*
ACT	*Transplantation and Anatomy Act 1978*
NT	*Human Tissue Transplant Act 1979*

The general effect of the legislation

The legislation in the States and Territories is based substantially on the draft Bill included in the ALRC report. There are, however, a number of minor variations (such as consent processes and children) between the jurisdictions.

Living donors – adults

Regenerative tissue

A competent adult may give written consent to the removal of regenerative tissue. The removal of the tissue may be for the purpose of transplantation into the body of another person or for therapeutic, medical or scientific purposes. In Queensland the consent must be signed in the presence of the designated officer (in a hospital this is the medical superintendent or nominee). In South Australia and Western Australia the consent must not be given or signed in the presence of the donor's family (or friends in WA). All jurisdictions (apart from SA and WA) require an independent medical practitioner to certify that:

(a) the adult's consent was given in the presence of the medical practitioner;

(b) the medical practitioner explained to the person, before the consent was given, the nature and effect of the removal of the tissue; and

(c) the medical practitioner is satisfied that, at the time the consent was given:
    (i)   the person was not a child,
    (ii)   the person was of sound mind, and
    (iii) the consent was freely given.

Non-regenerative tissue

Non-regenerative tissue may be donated for transplantation into the body of another person. There must be a delay of at least 24 hours after the consent to the donation has been made before the tissue may be removed. In South Australia the consent must not be given in the presence of the donor's family. In Western Australia the consent must not be given in the presence of the adult's family and friends.

Certification

A medical practitioner may certify that:

- consent was given in the presence of the medical practitioner (in Queensland, the designated officer);
- the nature and effect of the removal of the tissue had been explained;
- the adult was of sound mind and the consent was given freely.

In all jurisdictions, except South Australia and Western Australia, the time of the consent must be included in the written consent (in New South Wales the day and time must also be included). When the written consent has been gained and the certificate signed, the tissue may be removed for the approved purpose.

Living donors – incompetent adults

The Supreme Court's *parens patriae* power can be use to approve the donation of both regenerative and non-regenerative tissue from an incompetent adult. In *Northern Sydney and Central Coast Area Health Service v CT by his Tutor ET* [2005] NSWSC 551, the Supreme Court approved the donation of bone marrow by an intellectually disabled adult (CT) to his brother NT, who was suffering from non-Hodgkin's lymphoma. Nicholas J stated:

> The exercise of the jurisdiction requires the court to regard the welfare and interests of CT as the paramount consideration. Relevant matters to be taken into account in determining what is in his best interest in all the circumstances include, in my opinion, his wishes as expressed by him and his level of understanding. I am satisfied that he at least understands that by participating in the procedure he will be helping his brother to get better and this is something he wishes to do. I infer from the evidence from both himself and his mother that he would be very distressed if he was refused the opportunity to help his brother and his brother subsequently died. This is consistent with the impression he gave me as having a genuine concern and affection for NT. (at [26])

The issue went before the Supreme Court in CT because it was clear that the NSW Guardianship Tribunal had no power to consent to any treatment which did not promote and maintain CT's health and well-being (see Chapter 13). Contrastingly, consent to the donation of regenerative and non-regenerative tissues can be given by guardianship authorities in Queensland and Victoria as a form of special health care: *Guardianship and Administration Act 2000* (Qld), s 69; *Guardianship and Administration Act 1986* (Vic), ss 3, 42B-42G. Similar provisions exist in Tasmania and the ACT, but only in relation to the removal of non-regenerative tissue (which arguably means that removal of regenerative tissue could be consented to by others): *Guardianship and Administration Act 1995* (Tas), s 45; *Guardianship and Management of Property Act 1991* (ACT), s 70.

Living donors – children

Regenerative tissue

In all jurisdictions, except the Northern Territory (which is silent on the issue), parents may consent to the removal of regenerative tissue from a child, provided the tissue is for transplantation into the child's relative (in Tasmania, Western Australia and the ACT) or the child's parent or sibling (New South Wales, Queensland, Victoria): *Human Tissue Act 1983* (NSW), ss 10, 11, 11A; *Transplantation and Anatomy Act 1979* (Qld), ss 12B, 12C, 12D, 12E; *Human Tissue Act 1985* (Tas), ss 12, 13; *Human Tissue Act 1982* (Vic), s 15; *Human Tissue and Transplant Act 1982* (WA), s 13; *Transplantation and Anatomy Act 1978* (ACT), s 13. The South Australian legislation does not specify who may be a recipient of a tissue donation, but approval from a Ministerial Committee is required before tissue may be removed: *Transplantation and Anatomy Act 1983* (SA), s 13.

Before the donation takes place a medical practitioner must sign a certificate. In all jurisdictions (barring the Northern Territory) consent must be obtained from the parents *and* from the child. The medical practitioner certifies that the nature and effect of the removal of the tissue has been explained to the parent(s) and the child; the parent and the child were each of sound mind; the parent and the child each understood the nature and effect of the removal of the tissue and the intended effect of its proposed transplantation; the consent was freely given; and the child was in agreement with the proposed removal and transplantation of the tissue.

As the child's agreement is implied, then regenerative tissue may only be removed if the child has the capacity to agree to its removal, thus limiting donation to older children, and not babies or infants.

Three jurisdictions have made provision for tissue removal from younger and incompetent children. In New South Wales, if the child is incompetent, donation can only be made to the child's sibling, and two medical practitioners must certify that:

- the parent's consent was given in his or her presence;
- before consent was given, he or she explained to the parent the nature and effect of the tissue removal and the intended effect of its transplantation;
- the parent was of sound mind;
- the parent understood the nature and effect of the removal of the tissue and the intended effect of its transplantation;
- the consent was freely given;
- the child, by reason of his or her age, is not capable of understanding the nature and effect of the removal of the tissue and the intended effect of its proposed transplantation;
- the brother or sister of the child is likely to die or suffer serious and irreversible damage to his or her health unless the tissue intended to be removed from the child is used in the treatment of that brother or sister;
- any risk to the child's health (including psychological and emotional health) caused by the removal of the tissue is minimal.

In Queensland, if the child is not competent three medical practitioners (one of whom must be a specialist anaesthetist) must certify that:

- the child, by reason of his or her age, was not capable of understanding the nature and effect of the removal and the nature of the transplantation; and
- the brother, sister or parent of the child, in the medical practitioner's opinion, is likely to die without the transplant; and
- the risk to the child, in the medical practitioner's opinion, is minimal.

In Victoria, tissue may be removed where the child is too young to understand only where it is necessary to save the life of a sibling.

The State laws are therefore highly restrictive on child donation. As a consequence, applications are sometimes made to the Family Court for it to exercise its welfare powers to order donation. The Family Court's power comes from a federal Act so it can override the State laws under s 109 of the Australian

Constitution. In *Re GWW and CMW* (1997) FLC ¶92-748, the parents of a 10-year-old boy applied to the Family Court to authorise a bone marrow harvest for donation to his aunt. The boy had an understanding of the procedure but was not competent to give his own consent. The court decided that the psychological benefit to the child of donating to his aunt outweighed the minimal risks and consequences of the procedure and therefore it was in his best interests to be a donor. The court recognised that there may have been a conflict between the *Human Tissue Act 1982* (Vic) and the exercise of the court's power to authorise the collection of the bone marrow and the potential application of s 109 of the Constitution. When the case was to be decided by the court, the Attorneys-General of each State and Territory were notified but advice was received by the court that they did not wish to intervene in the matter.

The decision in *GWW* was revisited in *Re Inaya (Special Medical Procedure)* (2007) 38 Fam LR 546. Orders were sought from the Family Court to authorise the donation of bone marrow from a 13-month-old child to the child's seven-month-old cousin who suffered from infantile osteopetrosis. The child's condition was fatal and the bone marrow transplant was the only potential cure. The Victorian Act prohibited the removal of tissue from the child for its donation to anyone except a sibling. Cronin J found that donation of regenerative tissue was within parental power given that the Act already recognised the parent's right to consent to donations to siblings or the other parent. He found that bone marrow donation was not serious or irreversible, with minimal risks. Because the power to consent was found to be within ordinary parental power and supported by the *Family Law Act 1975* (Cth), the Victorian prohibition on donation outside of immediate family members was struck down as being inconsistent with the *Family Law Act*.

Re Inaya has effectively rendered the State-based legislative restrictions on parental consent to donation of regenerative tissue void. The State parliaments need to respond by either removing the restrictions or redrafting them so that they will not be inconsistent with the *Family Law Act*.

Non-regenerative tissue

South Australia, Victoria and Western Australia have banned donation of non-regenerative tissue by children: *Transplantation and Anatomy Act 1983* (SA), s 12; *Human Tissue Act 1982* (Vic), s 14; *Human Tissue and Transplant Act 1982* (WA), s 12. The legislation in New South Wales, Queensland, Tasmania and the Northern Territory is silent on the issue. In the ACT non-regenerative tissue may be removed from a child where it is needed for a family member who is in danger of dying: *Transplantation and Anatomy Act 1978* (ACT), s 14. Consent must be gained from both parents (where available), a medical practitioner must provide a prescribed certificate and there is a 24-hour waiting period. A Ministerial Committee must also approve the potential donation. The following people comprise the committee:

- a judge of the Supreme Court;
- a medical practitioner; and
- a social worker or a psychologist.

Deceased donors

Subject to certain conditions below, a designated officer may authorise removal of tissue from the body of a deceased person where the body is at a hospital and the purpose is for transplantation to a living person or other therapeutic, medical or scientific purposes.

Deceased's views known

Where the designated officer has made reasonable inquires to determine whether the deceased had expressed a wish or had consented to removal of tissue after death and (except in Victoria) it had not been withdrawn or revoked, the removal may be authorised (in writing) in accordance with the wish or consent.

Deceased's views not known

Where there has been no explicit expression of consent by the deceased and the deceased had not objected during their lifetime, and the senior available next-of-kin does not object (in New South Wales, Queensland, Tasmania and Victoria actually consents), the designated officer may authorise the removal of tissue.

In South Australia, Victoria, the ACT and the Northern Territory, if the senior available next-of-kin cannot be contacted the designated officer may authorise the removal of tissue: *Transplantation and Anatomy Act 1983* (SA), s 21(3); *Human Tissue Act 1982* (Vic), s 26(1); *Transplantation and Anatomy Act 1978* (ACT), s 27(3); *Human Tissue Transplant Act 1979* (NT), s 18(3). 'Senior available next-of-kin' means (in the following order of priority):

- in relation to a child –
    - o a parent of the child;
    - o a brother or sister who has attained the age of 18 years; or
    - o a guardian of the child
- in relation to any other deceased person –
    - o the spouse of the deceased (some jurisdictions will recognise a same-sex relationship in this category);
    - o a son or daughter who has attained the age of 18 years;
    - o a parent of the deceased person; or
    - o a brother or sister of the deceased person who has attained the age of 18 years.

Coroner's jurisdiction

Where the death of the deceased is subject to a coroner's inquiry transplantation of the deceased person's organs would normally be prohibited. Only if the coroner consents may tissue be removed for the purposes of transplantation from the deceased person.

Autopsy

The law allows for two kinds of post-mortem examination. A post-mortem may be ordered under legislation covering coroners to assist the coroner in investigating a death. Owing to the nature of the coroner's jurisdiction, the consent of the next-of-kin is not required, although there are provisions in some jurisdictions to allow the next-of-kin to object to a coronial post-mortem (eg, s 48A of the *Coroners Act 1980* (NSW) and *Krantz v Hand* [1999] NSWSC 432).

The second kind of post-mortem examination is one that is authorised under the human tissue transplantation legislation. The rules for the authorisation of a post-mortem examination are similar to the requirements for the donation of tissue noted above.

Organ retention scandals

In the past 10 years a number of organ retention scandals have emerged concerning autopsy practice in England and Wales, Scotland, Ireland, New Zealand and Australia. In the United Kingdom, evidence was raised in the Bristol Royal Infirmary Inquiry regarding paediatric deaths from heart surgery, that it was common practice for hearts to be retained after autopsy, without parental consent. The Bristol Inquiry gave an interim report on the practice (<http://www.bristol-inquiry.org.uk/>). This then lead to nationwide concern and the health authorities performed an audit of organs that had been retained. It was discovered that a large number of organs had been retained at Alder Hey Hospital and Royal Liverpool Children's Hospital. A further inquiry was ordered. *The Royal Liverpool Children's Inquiry* (2001) found that a large collection of foetuses, children's organs and body parts had been collected for decades at Alder Hey Hospital and the Liverpool Children's Hospital without the knowledge and/or consent of the children's parents (House of Commons 2001). The collection had increased in size during the 1980-90s after the appointment of Professor Van Velzen who was found to have ordered 'the unethical and illegal retention of every organ in every case for the overriding purpose of research' (Inquiry 2001). The Inquiry found that Van Velzen was guilty of numerous serious breaches of policy and law, including the 'unnecessary excessive, illegal and unethical build up of organs following post-mortem examination, ostensibly for research but with no likelihood that the bulk of the organs stored in containers would ever be used for research' (Inquiry 2001).

Litigation was commenced in two class actions concerning thousands of litigants. Parents of the children whose organs had been retained at Alder Hey Hospital eventually settled their claim but the other class action continued. A test case was decided in *AB v Leeds Teaching Hospital NHS Trust* [2004] EWHC 644 (QB), where three lead claims were used to test the plaintiffs' assertion that there was a tort for the wrongful interference with a corpse which would make damages recoverable for psychiatric injury. Alternatively, the test cases claimed a duty in negligence which was hoped to produce a similar result.

The three claims concerned organs which had been removed from dead children in accordance with the terms of the *Human Tissue Act 1961* (UK), but in circumstances where the parents had asked that they be returned after post-mortem. In all three cases major organs such as brain, hearts and lungs and spinal cord had been kept in breach of the agreement.

Gage J dismissed the claims for wrongful interference with a corpse by finding that, once the organs had been lawfully removed under the *Human Tissue Act 1961* (UK), any rights of the family concerning burial came to an end. The parents did not have possessory or property rights over the organs of their children, even for the limited purpose of burial. Gage J also went further and said that, because the hospital had laboured on the tissue in preserving it, the possessory rights of the parents had been extinguished by the superior property rights of the hospitals (see below for more discussion on labour and property rights).

On the secondary claim of negligence Gage J recognised a general duty on the part of doctors seeking consent to post-mortem examination to properly discuss such issues with the parents of the dead children. He rejected claims that the *Bolam* test alleviated the doctors from discussing such issues with parents. He found that the practice of the medical profession not to discuss such issues, whilst universally adopted, was unreasonable as most mothers of recently deceased children would want to know if organs were to be retained.

Even though Gage J found for the existence of a general duty of care, because the claims were based on negligently inflicted psychiatric injury they had to satisfy the English law of 'nervous shock'. In England such claims are only recognised if the psychiatric illness was a foreseeable result of the defendant's negligence.

On the facts, Gage J found that the illness of only one of the plaintiffs was a foreseeable result of not being told about organ retention. The other two mothers were considered to be robust, practical and sensible women who were unlikely to collapse under strain and for that reason any psychiatric illness that they suffered was not foreseeable.

Despite the failure of the *AB case* to recognise a tort of wrongful interference the UK government introduced the *Human Tissue Act 2004* and the *Human Tissue (Scotland) Act 2006* which, amongst other things, requires consent for organs to be retained after post-mortem.

Both Ireland and Scotland have considered similar claims. In *O'Connor v Lenihan* [2005] IEHC 176, the High Court of Ireland dismissed a claim by a mother and father who had discovered that two of their deceased children had had their organs retained after post-mortem without consent. Neither parent brought evidence that they had suffered any psychiatric injury and on that basis the judge dismissed the action. Feelings of hurt and distress were not recoverable. A public inquiry was demanded but the government established a non-statutory inquiry and the report was not made public (the Dunne Inquiry). A further public inquiry was held and published (the Madden Report). Aggrieved parents sought to force the government to have another inquiry, as they believed that they had been promised one by the minister and that the previous inquiries had been ineffective. The court refused to entertain these claims: *McStay v Minister for Health and Children* [2006] IEHC 238.

Contrastingly, in the Scottish case of *Stevens v Yorkhill NHS Trust* [2006] ScotCS CSOH 143, MacAulay J found that a tort existed in Scots law of wrongful interference with a corpse which could demand damages for hurt feelings. He also agreed with Gage J in *AB* that a duty of care was owed to the family members to disclose to them that organs may be removed and retained.

In New Zealand, organ retention issues were raised concerning Green Lane Hospital in Auckland, where it was alleged that organs of children had been routinely kept without consent for over 50 years. It was alleged that over 1300 children had been harvested for organs. The practice was admitted in 2002. A class action had commenced with 42 parents, but it was recently settled, for $5000 per person, an apology and a denial of liability by the Crown (Anon 2008b).

In Australia organ retention issues were at the forefront of the Walker Inquiry (the *Inquiry Into Matters Arising from the Post-Mortem and Anatomical Examination Practices of the NSW Institute of Forensic Medicine*). This inquiry was formed after allegations had surfaced that organs and bones were being taken without consent from bodies being presented to the Glebe Morgue. It was also alleged that corpses were being experimented on without consent. Brett Walker SC found that a number of bones had been taken from corpses unlawfully and that bodies had been used for research. There appeared to be a mistaken belief amongst the staff that such research and collection were permissible under the *Human Tissue Act 1983* (NSW). Nevertheless, that Act only allows for tissue to be taken either with consent, or to determine the cause of death in a coronial autopsy. The taking of tissue for research purposes, whilst done in good faith, was not permissible under the Act. Mr Walker also found that a number of bodies which had been donated to the Institute under the *Anatomy Act 1977* were also experimented on illegally. He found that the Act only permitted bodies to be dissected, and did not permit the bodies being subjected to forensic experimentation. He recommended a number of changes to the law in New South Wales to permit experimentation with the consent of the deceased and the non-objection of the family.

The New South Wales government responded with the *Human Tissue and Anatomy Legislation Amendment Act 2003*. This Act amended both the *Human Tissue Act* and the *Anatomy Act* to require either written consent from the deceased or written consent from the senior available next-of-kin to the use of a body for anatomical examination. The definition of 'anatomical examination' included the use of the body for medical, scientific and educational purposes.

Property rights in human tissue

The organ retention cases highlight a massive gulf between the expectations of the medical profession with regards to its rights to access tissue, and the expectation of the public with regards to ownership and control of tissue. This problem can arguably be attributed to the failure of the law to create a language of rights regarding the use of human tissue. Traditionally the law has considered human tissue a *res nullius* (a thing belonging to no one) with the effect that human tissue could not be subject to property rights of ownership and control.

The rule seems to reflect the Christian aversion to notions that we own our bodies, as well as the longstanding dislike of slavery, which was abolished in the British Empire in 1804.

Professor Loane Skene is a leading advocate of why property rights should not be recognised in human tissue (Skene 2002; Skene 2007). She states that the following public policy issues justify the law's failure to recognise property rights:

- *emotional* (a repugnance at people selling their bodies and body parts);
- *familial* (stored genetic material should be available to blood relatives for their own testing, not subject to veto by one person);
- *pragmatic* (the possible consequences of such a principle for hospitals and laboratories);
- *economic* (undue fettering of teaching, research and commercialisation of biological inventions); and
- *social* (maintenance of museum collections and educational institutions). (Skene 2004)

Perhaps as a reflection of these concerns, human tissue legislation in all Australian jurisdictions prohibits trade in human tissue. This means that a living person cannot provide their human tissue to another for valuable consideration. Valuable consideration includes not only money but also other things of value such as promises, jobs, gifts etc). In some jurisdictions the legislation provides that where tissue that has been donated and then subsequently subjected to some process then the processed tissue may be sold.

It would, however, be wrong to conclude that human tissue can never be property. In the Australian case of *Doodeward v Spence* (1908) 6 CLR 406 a majority of the High Court found that the preserved foetus of a two-headed child may constitute 'property' if it has been altered by a process of labour. The majority of the court found that if the corpse (or part thereof) had been altered for the purpose of medical or scientific purposes it acquired a value and became property.

There have also been a number of recent Australian cases that have had to consider the use of tissue samples from a deceased person in testing to establish paternity. The Supreme Court of New South Wales in *Pecar v National Australia Trustees Ltd (Estate of Urlich Deceased)* (unreported, 27 November 1996) decided that tissue samples are property for the purposes of the Supreme Court Rules. The court held that as the samples were fixed in paraffin they were transformed into objects capable of constituting property (even though the question of whether such property could be 'owned' by anyone was left in doubt). Similarly, in Western Australia, Master Sanderson in *Roche v Douglas* [2000] WAR 331, a case involving tissue samples taken from the deceased and preserved in paraffin wax, found that the tissue was property but found it unnecessary to decide its ownership. Finally, in *AW v CW* [2002] NSWSC 301, Barrett J decided that the *Status of Children Act 1996* (NSW) did not authorise the taking of material from a dead body to allow parentage testing.

Doodeward v Spence has been followed in England in *R v Kelly* [1999] QB 621. The appellants in this case had been found guilty of the theft of approximately 35 human body parts from the Royal College of Surgeons. The defendants asserted that body parts were not property and therefore could not be stolen. The Court of Appeal upheld the trial judge's view that the parts were property as they had been the subject of a 'process of skill' which meant that they had acquired a usefulness or value and were capable of being stolen. It was noted that 'the common law did not stand still and it might be that in the future a court would hold that body parts were property even without the acquisition of different attributes, if, for example, they were required for use in an organ transplant' (at 631).

The danger with this labour theory of property is that it is asymmetrical in the way that it recognises property rights. In the United States decision of *Moore v Regents of University of California* 793 P 2d 479 (Cal 1990), the Californian Supreme Court found that a person had no rights of property in their own tissue, but that researchers who took the property and researched upon it could own it as property. The plaintiff (Moore) had his spleen removed in 1976 as part of his treatment for leukaemia. Between 1976 and 1983 he had samples of blood and bone marrow taken as part of his treatment. Unknown to the plaintiff, the samples were used as part of the development and patent of a cell line which had potential sales of up to US$3 billion. The Supreme Court found in favour of Moore on the basis that the surgeons had breached their fiduciary obligations to him, but they did not find that he had any rights to claim for damages due to his spleen being taken and used without permission. The operation to remove it was not a battery as Moore had consented. Nor was there an action for breach of informed consent to treatment as all the risks of treatment had been spelled out. The only remaining avenue – property rights – were denied to him primarily because of the negative economic effect on medical research of recognising such rights.

Two later US cases have continued this trend. In *Greenberg v Miami Children's Hospital* 264 F Supp 2d 1064 (2003) the plaintiffs were donors who had donated their tissue to a university researcher, so as to enable him to research into the genetic causes of Canavan disease, a degenerative disorder that causes progressive damage to nerve cells in the brain. The researcher successfully discovered the genetic link and his hospital employer patented the test. The patent meant that the hospital had control over who could access the test and how much to charge them. The donors sued the hospital for breaching informed consent, fiduciary duty, unjust enrichment, fraudulent concealment of the patent application, conversion and misappropriation of trade secrets. The Florida District Court on an interlocutory application refused to recognise that the donor had any property rights in their tissue.

In *Washington University v Catalona* 437 F Supp 2d 985 (2006), it was the researcher's turn to be denied property rights, this time by his employer. The researcher had recruited several thousand participants to provide tissue to his tissue bank for the study of prostrate cancer. The researcher left the university for a competitor institution and tried to take the tissue bank with him. The bulk of the participants wished for the tissue bank to remain in the researcher's control. Washington University stated that it owned the tissue bank. The court found for the University. It also directly disputed any property rights belonging to the participants. Limbaugh J stated:

> Medical research can only advance if access to these materials to the scientific community is not thwarted by private agendas. If left unregulated and to the whims of a RP, these highly-prized biological materials would become nothing more than chattel going to the highest bidder. It would no longer be a question of the importance of the research protocol to public health, but rather who can pay the most. Selling excised tissue or DNA on E-Bay would become as commonplace as selling your old television on E-Bay. The integrity and utility of all biorepositories would be seriously threatened if RPs could move their samples from institution to institution any time they wanted. No longer could research protocols rely on aggregate collections since individual samples would come and go. Accountability would no longer exist since institutions would merely be warehouses filling purchase orders.
>
> More alarming is the great potential for prejudicial influences into medical research. Allowing an RP to choose who can have the sample, where the sample will be stored, and/or how the sample can be used is tantamount to a blood donor being able to dictate that his/her blood can only be transfused into a person of a certain ethnic background, or a donated kidney being transplanted only into a woman or man. This kind of 'selectiveness' is repugnant to any ethical code which promotes medical research to help all of mankind. (at 1002)

With respect, these arguments are fallacious for two reasons. First, it is simply wrong to say that medical research will stop if the property rights of research participants are recognised. The research participants in both *Greenberg* and *Washington University* were people who volunteered their tissue for research in the public interest for the 'help of all mankind', not to profit personally. Nevertheless, they believed that they should have some say about what happened to their tissue. In any event the language of gift used by Limbaugh J is an implicit recognition of some form of property belonging to the participants in the first place.

Equally problematic is how one-sided the decisions are in their account of private property rights. Limbaugh J completely ignored the fact that the decision to uphold the University's private property rights can be equally as detrimental to research in the public interest. The effect of the decision is that the University controls access to the samples. The University decides who can study them. The University could sell the samples or destroy them if it saw fit. Limbaugh J's *res nullius* approach says that private property is evil when it lies in the hands of participants, but unimpeachable when it lies in the hands of universities and pharmaceutical companies. This cannot be right. Purely, from a logical perspective, property notions have either to be available to all, or to none.

The second reason for disputing the *res nullius* rule is to counter the arguments that private property would entail a free-fall into a completely free market where people could sell their kidneys, pieces of their liver and their mother's corpse. This type of argument is a form of moral panic which ignores the fact that private property is tightly controlled and regulated in all Western economies. One need only look at the fact that a person is not free to build whatever they like on their land, or to set off firearms willy-nilly, or buy stockpiles of uranium, even though all these things are considered as private property. The law has always recognised interests in gifts and dispositions which reserve rights of control and access. These types of modest private property rights would be a very suitable match for the kinds of rights being claimed by the participants in *Greenberg* and *Catalona*, and they could be tightly controlled by the same regulatory mechanisms we see in the regulation of other items of property.

Of course property rights are not a panacea. As Otlowski rightfully points out:

> [E]ven if we were to go down the property road, serious questions remain as to the extent to which the property model could provide the desired outcome of giving the donor control over the commercialisation process ... even if we were to uphold the donor as the 'owner,' that does not in fact clarify the legal obligations imposed on commercial users of that biological material. (Otlowski 2007)

But while property rights do not automatically make clear all of the rights and responsibilities over human tissue, they do provide a language within which questions can be asked about competing rights of access and control. In the absence of property rights there is no way for common law to contemplate these issues. The *res nullius* rule creates an enormous silence. Human tissue is now so valuable that the silence can no longer be tolerated.

One final point that can be made is to note the frightening parallels that exist between the rule of *res nullius* in human tissue and the, now discredited, rule of *terra nullius* in Australian land law. Chapter 29 discusses the devastating effects that the rule of *terra nullius* had on the rights of indigenous Australians. In the age of the genetic revolution, where gene patents are increasingly becoming commonplace, the *res nullius* rule takes on a similarly threatening countenance. We, as humans, run the risk of losing rights over genetic makeup, in much the same way as the indigenous peoples of the world lost their property during the 18th century period of Western colonial expansion (Stewart 2007). Any legal system which deliberately ignores the justifiable concerns of people concerning their rights runs the risk of doing great injustice. Rather than refuse to listen the common law could usefully employ property concepts in ways to preserve the public's interest in what happens to the ownership and control of genetic knowledge and tissue technologies.

References

Anon (2008a) 'The gap between supply and demand'. *The Economist* (Oct 11-17): 71-3.
Anon (2008b) Green Lane baby organ case settled. *New Zealand Herald* (8 December 2008) Auckland.
Auchincloss, H (1988) 'Xenogeneic transplantation. A review'. *Transplantation* **46**: 1-20.
Benoit, B, A Spira et al (1990) 'Presumed consent law: Results of its application/outcome from epidemiologic survey'. *Transplant Proc* **22**(2): 320-2.
Bernat, JL (2008) 'The boundaries of organ donation after circulatory death'. *N Engl J Med* **359**(7): 669-71.
Boucek, MM, C Mashburn et al (2008) 'Pediatric heart transplantation after declaration of cardiocirculatory death'. *N Engl J Med* **359**(7): 709-14.

Buell, JF, TG Gross et al (2005) 'Malignancy after transplantation'. *Transplantation* **80**(2 Suppl): S254-64.

Cass, A, J Cunningham et al (2003) 'Renal transplantation for Indigenous Australians: identifying the barriers to equitable access'. *Ethn Health* **8**(2): 111-19.

Chang, GJ, HD Mahanty et al (2003) 'Expanding the donor pool: can the Spanish model work in the United States?' *Am J Transplant* **3**(10): 1259-63.

Childress J (1987) 'Some moral connections between organ procurement and organ distribution'. *J Contemp Health Law Policy* **3**: 85-110.

Csilag, C (1997) 'Brazil's law on organ donation passed'. *Lancet* **349**: 482.

Daar, AS (2002) 'Strangers, intimates, and altruism in organ donation'. *Transplantation* **74**(3): 424-6.

Daar, AS (2003) 'Paid organ donation and organ commerce: continuing the ethical discourse'. *Transplant Proc* **35**(3): 1207-9.

Dennis, J, P Hanson et al (1994) 'An evaluation of the ethics of presumed consent and a proposal based on required response'. *UNOS Update* **10**(2): 16-21.

Dorling, A, K Reisbeck et al (1997) 'Clinical xenotransplantation of solid organs'. *Lancet* **349**: 867-71.

DuBois, J (2009) 'Increasing rates of organ donation: Exploring the Institute of Medicine's boldest recommendation'. *J Clin Ethics* **20**(1): 1-10.

Epstein, A, J Ayanian et al (2000) 'Racial disparities in access to renal transplantation'. *N Engl J Med* **2000**(343): 1537-44.

Evans, D (2007) 'Seeking an ethical and legal way of procuring transplantable organs from the dying without further attempts to redefine human death'. *Philos Ethics Humanit Med* **2**: 11.

Excell, L, G Russ et al (eds) (2004) *ANZOD Registry Report 2004.* Adelaide, South Australia, Australia and New Zealand Organ Donation Registry.

Gawande, A, A Caplan et al (2008) 'Organ donation after cardiac death: A perspective roundtable'. *N Engl J Med.*

Hauptman, P and K O'Connor (1997) 'Procurement and allocation of solid organs for transplantation'. *N Engl J Med* **336**(6): 422-31.

House of Commons (2001) *The Royal Liverpool Children's Inquiry.* London, House of Commons.

Inspector, Y, I Kutz et al (2004) 'Another person's heart: magical and rational thinking in the psychological adaptation to heart transplantation'. *Isr J Psychiatry Relat Sci* **41**(3): 161-73.

Joffe, AR (2007) 'The ethics of donation and transplantation: are definitions of death being distorted for organ transplantation?' *Philos Ethics Humanit Med* **2**: 28.

Joffe, AR, NR Anton et al (2008) 'Survey of pediatricians' opinions on donation after cardiac death: are the donors dead?' *Pediatrics* **122**(5): e967-74.

Kamarainen, A, I Virkkunen et al (2007) 'Spontaneous defibrillation after cessation of resuscitation in out-of-hospital cardiac arrest: a case of Lazarus phenomenon'. *Resuscitation* **75**(3): 543-6.

Keenan, SP, B Hoffmaster et al (2002) 'Attitudes regarding organ donation from non-heart-beating donors'. *J Crit Care* **17**(1): 29-36; discussion 37-8.

Keizer, KM, JW de Fijter et al (2005) 'Non-heart-beating donor kidneys in the Netherlands: allocation and outcome of transplantation'. *Transplantation* **79**(9): 1195-9.

Kondro, W (2006) 'Fragmented organ donation programs hinder progress'. *CMAJ* **175**(9): 1043.

Koogler, T, A Stark et al (2006) 'Parents/guardians views on donation after cardiac death'. *Crit Care Med* **33**(12 Suppl): A105.

Koostra, G (1997) 'The asystolic, or Non-Heart Beating Donor'. *Transplantation* **63**: 917-21.

Little, M and EJ Sayers (2004) 'The skull beneath the skin: cancer survival and awareness of death'. *Psychooncology* **13**(3): 190-8.

Lowe, M, I Kerridge et al (1995) 'These Sorts of People Don't Do Very Well': Race and the allocation of health care resources'. *J Med Ethics* **123**(11): 878-81.

Matas, AJ, ST Bartlett et al (2003) 'Morbidity and mortality after living kidney donation, 1999-2001: survey of United States transplant centers'. *Am J Transplant* **3**(7): 830-4.

Matas, AJ, CA Garvey et al (2000) 'Nondirected donation of kidneys from living donors'. *N Engl J Med* **343**(6): 433-6.

Middleton, PF, M Duffield et al (2006) 'Living donor liver transplantation – adult donor outcomes: a systematic review'. *Liver Transpl* **12**(1): 24-30.

Munson, R (2007) Organ transplantation. *The Oxford handbook of bioethics.* R Steinbook. Oxford, Oxford University Press.

Najarian, JS, BM Chavers et al (1992) '20 years or more of follow-up of living kidney donors'. *Lancet* **340**(8823): 807-10.

Naqvi, SA, B Ali et al (2007) 'A socioeconomic survey of kidney vendors in Pakistan'. *Transpl Int* **20**(11): 934-9.

National Clinical Taskforce on Organ and Tissue Donation (2008) *National Clinical Taskforce on Organ and Tissue Donation Final Report: Think Nationally, Act Locally.* Canberra, Commonwealth of Australia.

NHMRC (2007a) *Organ and tissue donation by living donors guidelines for ethical practice for health professionals.* Canberra, National Health and Medical Research Council.

NHMRC (2007b) *Organ and Tissue Donation After Death, for Transplantation.* Canberra, Commonwealth Government.

Noel, L (2007) 'Current concerns in transplantation'. *Bull World Health Organ* **85**(12): 905.

Norris, M (1990) 'Required request: Why it has not significantly improved the donor shortage'. *Heart Lung* **19**: 685-6.

NSW Health (2007) *Organ Donation after Cardiac Death: NSW Guidelines.* Sydney, New South Wales Government.

Nuffield Council on Bioethics (1996) *Animal-to-Human Transplants: The Ethics of Xeno-transplantation.* London, Nuffield Council on Bioethics.

O'Connor, KJ and FL Delmonico (2005) 'Increasing the supply of kidneys for trans-plantation'. *Semin Dial* **18**(6): 460-2.

Otlowski, M (2007) 'Donor Perspectives on Issues Associated with Donation of Genetic Samples and Information: An Australian Viewpoint'. *J Bioethical Inquiry* **4**: 135.

Quigley, M, M Brazier et al (2008) 'The organs crisis and the Spanish model: theoretical versus pragmatic considerations'. *J Med Ethics* **34**(4): 223-4.

Reemtsma, K, B McCracken et al (1964) 'Renal heterotransplantation in man'. *Ann Surg* **160**: 384-410.

Rodgers, B and K Cowles (1991) 'The concept of grief: An analysis of classical and contemporary thought'. *Death Studies* **15**(5): 443-58.

Roels, L, Y Vanreterghem et al (1990) 'Effect of a presumed consent law on organ retrieval in Belgium'. *Transplant Proc* **22**: 2078-9.

Ross, LF and S Zenios (2004) 'Practical and ethical challenges to paired exchange pro-grams'. *Am J Transplant* **4**(10): 1553-4.

Rothman, D (1997) ' Body Shop'. *The Sciences* **Nov/Dec**: 17-21.

Rothman, D and S Rothman (2003) Organic commerce. *The Australian Financial Review* 17 Oct. **Review:** 1-7.

Sanner, MA (2003) 'Transplant recipients' conceptions of three key phenomena in transplantation: the organ donation, the organ donor, and the organ transplant'. *Clin Transplant* **17**(4): 391-400.

Shiel, A (1995) 'Ethics in organ transplantation: The major issues'. *Transplant Proc* **27**(1): 87-9.

Shimazono, Y (2007) 'The state of the international organ trade: a provisional picture based on integration of available information'. *Bull World Health Organ* **85**(12): 955-62.

Siminoff, LA and MB Mercer (2001) 'Public policy, public opinion, and consent for organ donation'. *Camb Q Healthc Ethics* **10**(4): 377-86.

Skene, L (2002) 'Arguments Against People Legally 'Owning' Their Own Bodies, Body Parts and Tissue'. *Macquarie Law Journal* **2**: 165.

Skene, L (2007) 'Legal Rights in Human Bodies, Body Parts and Tissue'. *J Bioethical Inquiry* **4**: 129.

Skene, L (2008) *Law and Medical Practice: Rights, Duties, Claims and Defences* (3rd ed). Sydney, LexisNexis Butterworths.

Smith, GC, T Trauer et al (2004) 'Prospective psychosocial monitoring of living kidney donors using the Short Form-36 health survey: results at 12 months'. *Transplantation* **78**(9): 1384-9.

Steen, S, T Sjoberg et al (2001) 'Transplantation of lungs from a non-heart-beating organ donor'. *Lancet* **357**: 825-9.

Stewart, C (2007) 'The Human Body – The Land that Time Forgot'. *J Bioethical Inquiry* **4**: 117.

Strauss, J (2004) Russian doctors accused of killing for donor organs. *The Age* 23 September. Melbourne.

Tallacchini, M (2008) 'Defining an appropriate ethical, social and regulatory framework for clinical xenotransplantation'. *Curr Opin Organ Transplant* **13**(2): 159-64.

Teo, B (1991) 'Organs for transplantation. The Singapore experience'. *Hastings Cent Rep* **Nov-Dec**: 10-13.

Titmuss, R (1997) *The Gift Relationship: from Human Blood to Social Policy* (New edition). A Oakley and J Ashton (eds). London, London School of Economics.

Truog, RD (2008) 'Consent for organ donation – balancing conflicting ethical obligations'. *N Engl J Med* **358**(12): 1209-11.

Truog, RD and FG Miller (2008) 'The dead donor rule and organ transplantation'. *N Engl J Med* **359**(7): 674-5.

UK Department of Health (2000) *An Investigation into Conditional Organ Donations. Report of the Panel.* February 2000. UK Department of Health.

Veatch, R (2000) *Transplantation Ethics.* Washington DC, Georgetown University Press.

Veatch, RM (2008) 'Donating hearts after cardiac death – reversing the irreversible'. *N Engl J Med* **359**(7): 672-3.

Veatch, RM and JB Pitt (1995) 'The myth of presumed consent: ethical problems in new organ procurement strategies'. *Transplant Proc* **27**(2): 1888-92.

Waterman, AD, EA Schenk et al (2006) 'Incompatible kidney donor candidates' willingness to participate in donor-exchange and non-directed donation'. *Am J Transplant* **6**(7): 1631-8.

Weber, M, D Dindo et al (2002) 'Kidney transplantation from donors without a heartbeat'. *N Engl J Med* **347**(4): 248-55.

Wilkinson, S and E Garrard (1996) 'Bodily integrity and the sale of human organs'. *J Med Ethics* **22**: 334-9.

Wright, J (1991) 'Ethics, commerce and kidneys'. *BMJ* **303**: 110.

Wright, L and M Campbell (2006) 'Soliciting kidneys on web sites: is it fair?' *Semin Dial* **19**(1): 5-7.

Zargooshi, J (2001) 'Quality of life of Iranian kidney "donors".' *J Urol* **166**(5): 1790-9.

CHAPTER 26

END-OF-LIFE CARE: PALLIATIVE CARE, EUTHANASIA AND ASSISTED SUICIDE

Case 1

The following is an extract from an article written by Frederique Zwart – a junior doctor in Yorkshire – that was printed in the *British Medical Journal* in July 1997.

A very special day.

My grandmother died recently. She made the decision and chose the date and the place. She came to a point when she thought life was not worth living and, as the doctors agreed, she was allowed to die quickly and painlessly. As you have gathered she died through active euthanasia and this was made possible by the fact that she was Dutch. I am Dutch and I am working on a geriatric ward in Yorkshire. I have seen many people die, but none have died as peacefully as my gran. My gran's death was my first encounter with euthanasia, and it has made a lasting impression on me. She died at home on the anniversary of my grandfather's death.

Once the decision had been made she relaxed and said her goodbyes. I asked her if she needed to rest while saying her farewells but she replied: 'Why should I rest, I'll have plenty of time for that later.' Finally she fell asleep, totally exhausted.

The doctor came, talked to her again, and explained the procedure to us. Those who wished followed him to her room. The 'second opinion doctor' had seen her a few weeks earlier, and all the paperwork, which could have been arranged in advance, had been done. … She decided at 8am, and by 2pm the procedure had taken place. A few days before she had told her general practitioner that she had no reason to carry on and wished to die.

Case 2

JA was a 73-year-old widow, who visited her doctor – Dr Harold Shipman – in June 1998, with an exacerbation of her asthma. He wrote a prescription for antibiotics, and told her that she was suffering from pleurisy and pneumonia. Later he made an unannounced home visit at which time he gave her an injection for her condition. Half an hour later her friend found her dead.

Several months after this, police began investigating the deaths in Dr Shipman's practice, and found that he had been systematically murdering his patients – particularly the elderly women – by administering lethal doses of morphine. Many of his victims were found looking as if they had peacefully gone off to sleep, but none had wished to die. This was murder, not euthanasia. (Subsequent investigations found that Dr Shipman was Britain's worst mass murderer – having killed more than 200 of his own patients.) (Whittle and Ritchie 2000)

Case 3

According to Truog:

> *Sixty to 90% of deaths in the ICU follow the withdrawal of life-sustaining treatment, where doctors and families get together, and they say "What do you think the prognosis is here?" And then we will decide, in those cases where we think it's not good enough, to take away the ventilator. And we'll start to give morphine so that, if there was a chance that the person was going to breathe, they're probably not going to breathe after they've gotten a fair amount of morphine. And that patient dies, amidst great uncertainty as to whether they might actually have been able to survive the ICU admission or not ... This is daily life in the ICU.* (Gawande, Caplan et al 2008)

At 9.30 am on 2 January 1996, Janet Mills, a 52-year-old woman from South Australia, pushed the space-bar on the specially designed computerised 'death machine' to trigger a lethal injection – and thereby became the second person to die using the Northern Territory's *Rights of the Terminally Ill Act 1995*. News of her death was subsequently revealed on the Internet through Dr Phillip Nitschke's website 'Deliverance'. (Dr Nitschke was her general practitioner and is a vocal advocate of voluntary euthanasia legislation.) Janet Mills had a form of lymphoma known as Mycoses Fungoides. She was originally diagnosed in May 1993, but at the time of her death she was only expected to live a few weeks more. In a letter written on 1 January 1996 and subsequently released to the press, Mrs Mills wrote:

> I believe that euthanasia is the greatest thing for people who are sick with no chance of getting better ... No-one wants to die if they don't have to, but I know I have had no hesitation in asking for this. No-one should have to suffer when they don't have to. (*Sydney Morning Herald*, 6 January 1996)

Health workers who care for patients with life-threatening and chronic illnesses commonly encounter patients who ask for assistance to die, but the issue of whether this request should be granted raises a major moral and legal issue. The disquiet that many health-care professionals feel about this issue is probably because many of the same principles that dictate good, compassionate medical care may also justify euthanasia. For example, where a dying patient is experiencing great pain and suffering, and wishes to die, conventional practice would dictate ceasing curative therapy and alleviating pain with a narcotic drug – thus respecting the patient's wish to stop treatment. But such reasoning might also lead to relieving the patient's suffering through the process of euthanasia, if that was their wish.

Euthanasia – what does it mean?

While the term euthanasia means literally 'good-death' or 'dying well' from the Greek *eu* – meaning good, and *thanatos* – meaning death, there is considerable confusion about the different ways that euthanasia may be described. In the following discussion we use the term 'voluntary euthanasia' to refer to the killing of a person at their request with the intention of ending that person's suffering. 'Non-voluntary euthanasia' refers to the decision to terminate the life of a person who does not have the capacity to comprehend and so cannot provide meaningful consent (as in the cases described in Case 3 above). 'Involuntary euthanasia' is the decision to terminate the life of a person against their will or consent. This category includes murder and manslaughter as in Case 2 above. 'Active euthanasia' refers to giving a patient a treatment that directly and intentionally results in their death (Case1). 'Passive euthanasia' is sometimes used to refer to the withholding or withdrawal of a life-saving or sustaining treatment, knowing, and intending, that the omission will result in premature death of the patient involved (Case 3). These terms may be put together to form expressions such as active or passive voluntary euthanasia, active or passive non-voluntary euthanasia, and active or passive involuntary euthanasia. 'Physician-assisted suicide' refers to situations where a person provides the means, or information about the means, to allow another person to end his or her own life (often this takes the form of a doctor providing a prescription for a large dose of barbiturates) (Foley 1995).

Dying well: Palliative care, 'passive euthanasia' and the 'good death'

While bioethics continually tries to keep pace with our changing world, many of the questions that confront bioethics are, in fact, very old. Few questions are more significant than those surrounding the way that we die. While dying may facilitate a search for meaning and a dialogue with those we love, in the end our death is ours alone (Kierkegaard 1946; Heidegger 1992; Komesaroff 2008)

Concepts of death play a central role in how we view health and illness and how we view the role of the health profession. Until recently, death was regarded as a natural event or a part of God's will, and medicine's role was to recognise that death was imminent and accept the limited possibilities for cure. Over the past two centuries, however, death has become something that medicine sought to conquer and, in the process, turned from something familiar, personal and social to something lonely, lacking meaning and surrounded by the trappings of modern medicine (Illich 1990; Komesaroff 2008). Medicine's remarkable capacity to treat acute illness now means that many of us experience an extended period of decline into debility and dementia and die in hospitals, with the end coming only when we, or our loved ones, or the health professionals charged with our health care, decide that 'enough is enough' (Gillam 2008). Of the roughly 150,000 Australians who die each year, the majority die in hospitals (51-56%) or nursing homes (18-21%) and very few die at home (<20%) or in hospices (2-4%). And many of those who die do not die 'well', but die alone, in pain, terrified, confused, alienated and without dignity – particularly those who are poor, marginalised or from ethnic minorities (Smith 2000).

Increasing concern with the way that medicine had transformed and dehumanised death led, in the late 1960s, to the rise of the Hospice Movement and to the emergence of palliative care as a an area of medical speciality devoted to symptom management and the care of the sick and dying. Palliative care has transformed the experience of dying for many patients through close attention to the physical, emotional, psychological, social, cultural, spiritual and existential needs of the dying patient, through the development of particular skills in symptom management, and through a commitment to team-based care (Ashby and Stoffell 1991; Randall and Downie 1996). (At the same time however, palliative care, as with all areas of medical 'specialty', has developed its own language, politics and norms regarding the 'right' way to 'do illness' and die, and it also struggles with the challenges raised by euthanasia and assisted suicide, terminal sedation and intractable pain or suffering.)

In recent years concern about the quality of care provided for patients at the end of the lives has also led to an interrogation of what it means to have a 'good death' and the meaning of dignity, hope, suffering and care (Clark and Singer 2003; Townsend and Hardy 2008). Surprisingly, we know very little about the experience of dying, and almost nothing about the experience and needs of people from non-Western cultures, patients with dementia and non-malignant conditions, and dying children. In part this is because it is so difficult to do research with dying people and with their carers, in part it is because some aspects of dying may be 'beyond language' and in part it is because medicine has been reluctant to embrace non-quantitative research methods such as narrative methods, phenomenology and ethnography (Glaser and Strauss 1965; Kleinman 1988). We do have some idea, however, as to the factors that may contribute to a 'good death' and those that may contribute to a 'bad death' (Clark and Singer 2003). It has been argued that those things that contribute to a bad death include a lack of honest communication, difficulties in accurate prognostication, lack of control (autonomy) and a lack of planning of end-life care (Edmonds and Rogers 2003). Those things that are reported as contributing to a good death include patient control (autonomy) over a series of factors relating to terminal care, including pain and symptom control, place of death and the presence of others at the time of death; access to information, expertise, hospice care and spiritual and emotional support; the sense of achieving a sense of completion or closure of one's life; and a chance to say goodbye (Steinhauser, Clipp et al 2000).

A number of strategies have been advanced to improve end-of-life care including support for palliative care and hospice services, adoption of advance directives, education of health professionals regarding the principles of 'dying well', and integrated care pathways for the care of the dying (Hardy and Vora 2004). Such pathways generally require that there is acceptance that death is approaching, that all unnecessary interventions, medications, examinations and observations are discontinued, that pain and symptom control and basic comfort care are maximised, that all relevant moral and spiritual issues are addressed, that any unfinished business is attended to, and that patients and relatives remain fully informed throughout (Middlewood, Gardner et al 2001). But while such pathways are now often provided through palliative care, they do not allow room for patient autonomy regarding the time and manner of their death – which could loosely be described as 'active euthanasia'.

The doctrine of double effect

Hospice and palliative care are sometimes characterised as a form of 'passive euthanasia' – since they are based on removal of overly intrusive interventions, and the institution of painkillers and other treatment options that may hasten death, but whose primary aim is to relieve symptoms. It is often stated that there is a morally important distinction between passive and active euthanasia. Those who hold this view believe that, whereas it may sometimes be morally accep- table to allow a patient to die, it is not morally acceptable to intervene and intentionally kill a patient.

There is no doubt that this is true in many cases. There is clearly a great moral difference between actively killing a healthy non-consenting person, and avoiding life-sustaining CPR in a patient with metastatic carcinoma whose heart has recently stopped beating. However, there are also many cases in which the difference between withdrawing life-sustaining therapy and the institution of life-threatening therapy is not clear.

For example, patients with severe life-threatening diseases sometimes collapse in the community and are intubated and ventilated by ambulance staff before they can gain very much information about the patient. If it then turns out that the patient has a severe, painful, life-threatening illness and does not wish to be resuscitated, the patient may be extubated and the ventilator stopped. It is unclear whether disconnecting the ventilator would be 'passive euthanasia' – as it merely involves discontinuing an unwanted therapy and allowing nature to take its course, or 'active euthanasia' – because an action of the therapist will result in the patient's death.

It is sometimes argued that the difference between active and passive euthanasia lies in the intention of the therapist rather than the actual act perfor- med. If the intention is to kill, this is thought to be morally abhorrent, whereas, if the intention is to relieve suffering and allow a 'natural' dying process to con- tinue, this is thought to be morally acceptable. This argument is sometimes used to justify the use of narcotic infusions to treat terminally ill patients' symptoms even where it is recognised that this may hasten their death (Folker, Holtug et al 1996; Foley 1997; Gillon 1999).

The use of intent as a means to distinguish between forms of care that are morally permissible and those that are not is central to the philosophical argu- ment that is known as the doctrine of double effect (Quill, Dresser et al 1997). 'Double effect' was originally discussed by Thomas Aquinas (1225-74), a Christian theologian and moral philosopher of the 13th century, who identified certain conditions that he believed would morally allow the causing or permitting of evil in the pursuit of good. According to Aquinas, in order to justify performing an evil act in the pursuit of good, four conditions must be satisfied. These are:

1. The action must be good in itself.
2. The agent must intend only the good effect and not the evil effect.
3. The good effect must not be achieved through the bad effect – that is, the evil effect cannot be a means to the good effect. More importantly, the good and evil effects must follow immediately from the same action.
4. There is sufficient reason to permit the bad effect – that is, there must be a favourable balance between the good and evil effects of the action.

The central distinction that the Doctrine of Double Effect relies on is the difference between the *intentional* causation of evil, and *foreseeing* evil to be a consequence from what one does. In the context of euthanasia, the doctrine of double effect would draw a distinction between acting in such a way that death was intended, and acting in a way that caused death as the foreseen but unintended effect of the pursuit of another goal (such as a patient dying as a consequence of respiratory suppression from the sedating effects or an opiate infusion used for pain relief).

A good example of the doctrine of double effect can be found in the debate over the Northern Territory euthanasia legislation and the use of 'death machines'. For the short period of time that euthanasia was legal in the Northern Territory, Dr Phillip Nitschke used a computerised system that allowed patients to give themselves a lethal dose of medication in order to die. Such a machine is prohibited by the doctrine of double effect, because by using it the patient was using death as a means of relieving pain.

After the legislation was changed, Dr Nitschke began work on a slightly different machine, which he suggested would resolve both the legal and ethical problems associated with the first machine. He proposed a 'slightly macabre device' that would work by 'linking the person's brain activity to a constant drug infusion, aimed at keeping the patient permanently unconscious. The drugs would be a mix of morphine for pain relief and Midazolam, a form of sedative. The machine would guarantee a patient would not wake up by constantly monitoring their state of consciousness, boosting the drugs if there was any sign of waking' (Zinn 1996). Such a machine would have a very similar effect as the other machine, patients would simply die a few days later. However, this machine would not breech the doctrine of double effect – although death was foreseen, the aim of the machine was pain relief. It would also be legal.

Dr Nitschke's new machine seems designed to exploit one of the major criticisms of the doctrine of double effect – that if it is known that a bad effect will result from one's action then it seems hypocritical to say that one does not intend the bad effect. Indeed, in most other areas of human behaviour people are held to be responsible for foreseeable consequences of their actions whether they are intended or not (Brody 1993). Even when it is only possible that an unintended bad effect will occur, there remains a general assumption that as moral agents we should accept some degree of responsibility for the effects of what we do. Furthermore, we should probably also accept responsibility for effects whose risks we ought to have foreseen, even if we have not foreseen them. Thus, while the doctrine of double effect is intuitively appealing because it provides some psychological protection against the consequences of our actions, in the end we cannot completely escape the moral dilemma by simply saying that, although we foresee the probability of both good and bad effects, we only intend the good effect (Quill, Dresser et al 1997).

Intention is also a concept that is often difficult to pin down. People often have multiple intents that may conflict and, because intents are intangible and difficult to assess, it is difficult to validate them externally. Empirical research also suggests that there may be considerable ambiguity about a doctor's intention and doctors may have dual intentions (to relieve pain and to hasten death) when analgesic drugs are given (Kuhse, Singer et al 1997). Kuhse and colleagues, for example, reported that 6.5% of all deaths in Australia involved opiods 'partly intended' to hasten death, while Douglas et al reported that 36% of surgeons indicated that they had administered drugs at doses greater than necessary to relieve symptoms with the intention to hasten death (Kuhse, Singer et al 1997; Douglas, Kerridge et al 2001; Douglas, Kerridge et al 2008). The presence or absence of intention does not therefore provide an unambiguous framework for analysing the morality of actions.

Another criticism of the doctrine of double effect is that, if a patient's autonomy is the central aspect of health-care decisions, then the entire doctrine may be irrelevant.

According to Quill:

> Those who give considerable weight to patient's rights to determine their own care believe that the patient's informed consent to an action that may cause death is more fundamental than whether the physician intends to hasten death. From this perspective, the crucial moral considerations in evaluating any act that could cause death are the patient's right to self determination and bodily integrity, the provision of informed consent, the absence of less harm-ful alternatives, and the severity of the patient's suffering. (Quill, Dresser et al 1997)

The value of the doctrine of double effect is that it emphasises the need for a careful moral evaluation of a proposed action. For many reasons it is important that health professionals are able to distinguish for themselves (and explain to others if requested) the difference between the intended ends of an action and the intended means to that end; and between the intended results of one's actions and the unintended but foreseen consequences of one's actions. (Cases 1, 2 and 3 quoted at the start of this chapter demonstrate the importance of intention in end-of-life care.) But arguments such as those used by Dr Nitschke emphasise the fact that there are great problems with distinctions between passive and active euthanasia; or between intended outcomes and foreseen, but not intended, outcomes. These ideas are frequently cited by those involved in caring for patients at the end of life. At their best they may be useful in managing some end-of-life decisions. At their worst, they look foolish and may be morally duplicitous.

Killing and letting die

Active euthanasia involves killing (an act of commission) while passive euthanasia involves letting die (killing by omission). Although both killing and letting die may be morally permissible in certain circumstances, many believe that our obligation to refrain from direct killing is more binding than is our obligation not to let others die. The opposing view holds that active and passive euthanasia do not differ morally, because there is no conceptual or moral difference between killing another person and letting another die.

The British philosopher James Rachels has used a utilitarian argument to attempt to show that the difference between killing and letting die is not morally relevant (the 'Equivalence Thesis') (Rachels 1975). He used the example of the imaginary characters Smith and Jones. Smith will inherit a large fortune on the death of his six-year-old cousin. Smith drowns his cousin in the bath and makes it look like an accident. In the case of Jones, he also stands to inherit a fortune on the death of his six-year-old cousin. He enters the bathroom and plans to drown his cousin in the bath. Jones sees the child slip, hit his head and fall face down in the water. Jones watches and does nothing while his cousin drowns. Smith acted to kill his cousin while Jones 'merely' let the child die. Rachels agues that both Smith and Jones are equally reprehensible from a moral point of view; Jones is no better than Smith even though he did not directly act to kill his cousin. Rachels uses this example to argue that, in the case of Smith and Jones, there is no moral difference between killing and letting die.

However, the philosopher Daniel Callahan has no doubt that the distinction between killing and allowing to die is perfectly valid (Callahan 1993). Callahan points out that Rachels – in his Smith and Jones example – cleverly chooses to use an instance where both Smith and Jones are morally culpable. Here it makes no difference, morally speaking, whether they killed or allowed to die; they were equally responsible. However, to let a patient die from a disease that cannot be cured may be thought of as merely allowing the *disease* to act as the cause of death without moral culpability. Those who support the existence of a moral difference between active and passive euthanasia point out that cases of passive euthanasia often involve individuals who will die in a short time *no matter what intervention occurs or does not occur*. Life-support treatment is the only means by which such individuals can postpone death, and even then only for a brief period. To withhold such treatment cannot be viewed either as contributing causally to death or as *permitting* death to occur as in the Smith and Jones example.

Active voluntary euthanasia

As of November 2008 euthanasia or assisted suicide is legal in Albania, Belgium, Luxembourg, the Netherlands, Switzerland, the Autonomous Community of Andalusia (Spain) and the US States of Oregon and Washington. Since euthanasia again became illegal in Australia in 1997 a number of Australians seeking euthanasia or assisted suicide have done so with the assistance of non-government organisations including Dignitas (Switzerland), Exit International (Australia), Dying in Dignity (UK) and the Final Exit Network.

In Switzerland, lethal drugs may be administered to a Swiss citizen or a to a foreigner under Article 115 of the penal code where the recipient is competent, clearly and freely states their wish to die and takes an active role in the drug administration, and where the physicians have nothing to gain from the person's death, ie their motive is unselfish. Dignitas has estimated that it has assisted almost 1000 people to die using Nembutal overdose or helium gas since it was founded in 1998. Over half of those assisted to die have come from outside Switzerland – from Germany, the United Kingdom and Australia – taking advantage of what has been termed Suicide Tourism (*Sterbetourismus*).

Support for active voluntary euthanasia has been justified using four major forms of argument. The first is that it is generally supported by the public. Australian and international studies suggest that there is strong public support for active voluntary euthanasia among the general public and a considerable degree of support within the nursing and medical professions (Kuhse and Singer 1993; Ward and Tate 1994; Kuhse, Singer et al 1997; Cohen, van Delden et al 2008; Parker, Cartwright et al 2008). However, it may be difficult to avoid introducing bias into the phrasing of questions, and it can be extremely difficult to know how to interpret the answers of respondents. The results of surveys are also often presented as providing a single answer, a numerical indicator of support for euthanasia or physician-assisted suicide, whereas this often conceals significant differences between respondents according to their gender, age, cultural background, country of origin, ethnicity and, in the case of health professionals, specialty and experience with palliative care. In addition it is clear that polls and questionnaires cannot determine what is morally right.

The second common argument used to support euthanasia arises from liberalism – the idea that individuals within a democracy should be allowed the free exercise of their choice – including the choice of when and how they wish to die (Brock 1992). However, critics of liberalism point out that although we might respect individuals' autonomous choices, including the choice for euthanasia, this does not imply that all choices are either 'wise' or 'good'. There may be more at stake in arguments about euthanasia than individual choice, because the freedom to choose does not mean that all choices will respect the dignity of persons and the central values of society.

Those who oppose liberalist views of the right to die also argue that decisions or choices made by dying patients must not be too readily accepted, but should instead be sensitively explored with the individual. The *real* wishes and needs of the dying are often elusive or poorly expressed – because of their condition, the effect of medications, their fears and beliefs, the information presented to them and the biases, needs and beliefs of those caring for them. It seems likely that where people are sick, suffering and aware of the burden they place on others they may well choose to have their life terminated. Those who oppose euthanasia worry that the availability of a quick death may introduce subtle coercion of those who are frightened, powerless or feel that their invalid state is a burden to others (Doerflinger 1989).

Liberal argument suggests that individuals' 'right to die' is based on their rights to exercise free choice. But it can be argued that if the 'right to die' is truly a matter of *individual autonomy*, then this right should not be restricted to the terminally ill. Perhaps people who are *not* dying but who have pain, or chronic disease, or are depressed or lonely, should have the same rights to life and death. Indeed, if the issue is only concerned with choice, then people who are perfectly healthy should also have the 'right to die', and might even be able to insist that health professionals assist them to die. Critics of liberalism believe that this argument represents a major fault in proposals that would legalise euthanasia for those with terminal illnesses. Advocates of euthanasia address these concerns in two ways. For some, such as the Euthanasia Society, euthanasia should not be limited only to those who are dying but should be available to anyone who feels they would rather choose death than continue to live with what they perceive as an unacceptably poor quality of life. For others, such as those who drafted the Northern Territory legislation, euthanasia should be available only to those who are terminally ill or suffering great pain.

The third type of argument used to support euthanasia is based on consistency with philosophical argument and current clinical practice (Hope, Savulescu et al 2003). According to this argument, the introduction of active voluntary euthanasia is entirely consistent with the medical, social, legal and moral character of contemporary Australia. Proponents of this argument reject the argument that there is a morally significant distinction between euthanasia and the withholding or withdrawing of life-sustaining treatment and point to:

- the fact that there is general acceptance that suicide may be rational, is not immoral, and is no longer illegal;
- the fact that withdrawing and withholding life-prolonging treatment with the express consent of the patient has become an accepted feature of medical practice;
- the fact that where patients are terminally ill, certain treatments, such as opioid analgesic infusions, may be initiated where death is a foreseen but not intended consequence of that treatment (according to the doctrine of double effect);
- the fact that surveys indicate that doctors and nurses in many countries where euthanasia is prohibited, including Australia, the United States, Denmark and England, may already be involved in active voluntary euthanasia and physician-assisted suicide, both in response to explicit requests for assistance with dying and in the absence of explicit requests. (Asch 1996; Meier, Emmons et al 1998; Magnusson 2004)

While arguments based on consistency may be insufficient, in themselves, to justify the legalisation of euthanasia, they do serve to remind us of changing attitudes to death, terminal care and suicide, and the rise of secularism in social life, law and medicine.

The final argument in support of euthanasia is based on appeals to compassion and beneficence. Advances in medical technology have increased our ability to prolong life to the point where it may become overly burdensome. So it is argued that euthanasia may sometimes present the most humane, compassionate and dignified option for treatment. This argument is often expressed in terms of a right to 'die with dignity'. Empirical research consistently provides support for this argument, with studies demonstrating that many physicians would intensify pain relief, even if this would hasten death, and a small, but significant, number of physicians would administer drugs (including terminal sedation) with the express intention of hastening death, particularly where patients requested euthanasia, had poorly controlled symptoms and had a limited life expectancy (Emanuel, Fairclough et al 2000; Emanuel 2002; Parker, Cartwright et al 2008). This view is rejected by many of those who work in palliative care and the hospice movement, on the basis that, while it may be true that many people in our society die in pain and indignity, this could be prevented by the provision of adequate palliative care. In support of this contention, opponents of euthanasia point to the high incidence of psychiatric morbidity among those who request euthanasia or assisted suicide and the low numbers of requests for assistance with dying in situations where palliative care is available (Cherny and Catane 1995). For those who object to the legalisation of euthanasia these types of studies provide evidence that we should critically examine the palliative care services available in those countries and states where euthanasia is available, and respond to requests for assistance with dying not by killing the patient but by providing quality end-of-life care.

This argument is partly political in nature, as it partly represents an expression of the needs for greater funding of those who work in palliative care. It also ignores the ethical issue of whether people should be allowed to have euthanasia. Indeed, of those patients who requested euthanasia in the Netherlands, only a small minority gave pain as their *only* reason for wanting euthanasia. It is unlikely that increased palliative care services will 'solve' the question of euthanasia, since there is no good reason why palliative care and euthanasia could not coexist. Even in present practice, the distinction between killing (euthanasia) and letting die peacefully (palliative care) is frequently unclear (Herxheimer 1996). In fact, the evidence we do have from the Netherlands and Oregon would seem to suggest that the provision of euthanasia has actually focused attention on deficiencies in the provision of palliative care and in the appropriate management of pain.

Opponents of euthanasia also warn that any move to liberalise the law relating to the care of dying patients would herald a major change in the *ethos* of medicine, undermine the trust and confidence that patients have in their doctors and diminish the public's perception that the health professions are dedicated to the health and welfare of their patients. At this point, however, we are unable to determine whether the legalisation of euthanasia would have such an impact. Certainly there is no firm evidence from the Netherlands to suggest that this may be the case. It is worth noting that those who advocate voluntary euthanasia do not generally dismiss the importance of trust, confidence and respect in health care but argue, instead, that the role of health-care professionals and the proper function of health-care institutions is defined not by doctors but by society. In other words, if we collectively decree that a doctor's role should include euthanasia when a patient is terminally ill and suffering then it is not up to the doctor alone to tell society how medicine should proceed.

Physician-assisted suicide and euthanasia

Physician-assisted suicide occurs where a physician does not actually kill the patient, but does consciously provide them with the means to kill themselves. Although a distinction is often drawn between physician-assisted suicide and active voluntary euthanasia, in general the moral issues that arise are common to both. This fact was recognised in both Dutch and Northern Territory legislation, which allowed for patients to have access to both physician-assisted suicide and active voluntary euthanasia.

Advocates of physician-assisted suicide argue that it has the advantage of reassuring terminally ill patients that they can continue living, in the knowledge that they can end their own lives if and when they choose; and that because they die by their own hands, their action is likely to represent a voluntary and informed choice. For these reasons, many physicians report that they feel more comfortable with physician-assisted suicide than with active voluntary euthanasia (Bachman, Alchser et al 1996).

Opponents of physician-assisted suicide reject the notion that it is simply an acceptable manifestation of patient autonomy, and present a series of arguments against the legalisation of physician-assisted suicide. These include that it violates moral prohibitions against intentionally causing a patient's death, and that self-administration does not guarantee competence, voluntariness or consent, as patients may still be incompetent, coerced or ill-informed.

Both proponents and advocates of physician-assisted suicide recognise that it is discriminatory in that it is limited to those who are physically able. Furthermore, physician-assisted suicide may not always be effective, and patients, families and the health service may need to face the consequences of unsuccessful suicide attempts, such as patients who are unresponsive or seriously ill, but who are not actually dying or dead. While the final actor in physician-assisted suicide is the patient, in the end physicians must retain moral responsibility for their actions.

The slippery slope from voluntary to involuntary euthanasia

A major argument against acceptance of active voluntary euthanasia arises from what is known as the slippery slope. This argument holds that acceptance of euthanasia for the terminally ill will create a dangerous precedent, leading to a step-by-step broadening of the circumstances in which euthanasia may occur, eventually encompassing the elderly, weak, demented, socially unproductive and disabled. A further variant of the 'slippery slope' argument, the 'psychological' slippery slope, contends that once we legalise the intentional killing of patients by their physicians then we will inevitably change society's perception of the sick, the elderly and the disabled. The argument is that in time we will become accustomed to the presence of euthanasia in our midst, and lose our capacity to appreciate the unknowable and inestimable value of moments in the dying patient's life and euthanasia will eventually become a complete substitute for the natural process of dying.

The proof of the existence of a slippery slope does not necessarily mean that we will slip if we stand upon it. For example, society accepts that prenatal screening and termination of pregnancy of major foetal abnormalities represent appropriate medical practice despite the fact that there is a clear risk of the gradual acceptance of other, more questionable, bases for prenatal diagnosis such as sex-selection. Evidence about the slippery slope argument comes from the experience of the legalisation of euthanasia in both Oregon and the Netherlands.

The 'Death with Dignity Act' (DWDA) was enacted in Oregon in 1997. It entitles patients to receive a prescription for a lethal dose of medication from physicians if they meet a number of criteria. These include: a person must be an Oregon resident, 18 years of age or older, must have decision-making capacity, and must be suffering from a terminal disease that will lead to death within six months. A patient must make one written and two oral requests for medication to end his or her life, witnessed by two persons in the presence of the patient who attest that the patient is 'capable, acting voluntarily, and not being coerced to sign the request'. The patient's decision must be an 'informed' one. Another physician must confirm the diagnosis, the patient's decision-making capacity and voluntariness of the patient's decision. There are requirements for counselling if the patient is thought to be suffering from a mental disorder which may impair his or her judgment, for documentation in the patient's medical record, for a waiting period, for notification of the patient's next of kin, and for reporting to State authorities. The patient has the right to rescind the request for medication to end his or her life at any time.

After the law was passed, the number of prescriptions written for the purpose of physician-assisted suicide gradually increased, from 24 in 1998 to 67 in 2003 to 85 in 2007. The number of people who actually used the prescriptions also increased from 16 in 1998 to 42 in 2003 and 49 in 2007. This corresponds to an estimated 15.6 DWDA deaths per 10,000 total deaths or about one death in every 640 due to physician-assisted suicide (Department of Human Services Oregon). Of those patients who access lethal prescriptions under the law, most are well educated and financially secure, most are already enrolled in home hospices (suggesting that assisted suicide is not a substitute for palliative care or occurs because patients cannot access adequate palliative care), most seek assistance with dying in order to maintain their autonomy and avoid dependence on others, rather than because of intractable or unrelieved pain, and very few are depressed or anxious (Ganzini, Dobscha et al 2003; Ganzini, Goy et al 2003; Ganzini, Goy et al 2008).

In the Netherlands, medical euthanasia has been broadly accepted for 20 years. It is protected by a substantial body of case law, is based on strong public support and has been formalised in Royal Dutch Medical Association (RDMA) Guidelines since 1984. In 1990, a series of three studies, collectively known as the Remmelink Report, examined all Medical Decisions at the End of Life (MDEL) in the Netherlands, including euthanasia and assisted suicide, the alleviation of pain and symptoms, decisions to withhold or withdraw treatment and decisions not to resuscitate (van der Maas, van Delden et al 1991).

The studies found that, during 1990, 1.8% of all deaths were as a consequence of euthanasia and 0.3% were as a consequence of assisted suicide. In the majority of these cases the patients had cancer and euthanasia was estimated to have shortened their life by days to weeks. To those in favour of euthanasia, the Remmelink report provided some reassurance as euthanasia was performed in less than a third of cases where it was requested, was performed mainly on those who were terminally ill and expected to die within a week, and comprised only a small proportion of total deaths. (It is noteworthy, however, that approximately one in five Dutch patients with motor neurone disease now die of euthanasia or assisted suicide (Veldink, Wokke et al 2002).)

Of more concern, however, was the finding that in 1000 cases or 0.8% of deaths, euthanasia was performed without the explicit request of the patient. Closer examination of these cases reveals that in almost all cases the patient was suffering intolerably and that in 59% of the cases the patient was incompetent at the time of the decision, having previously discussed euthanasia with their physician whilst competent. These decisions were generally made by families in consultation with doctors and nurses, and generally resulted in life being shortened only by days. Nevertheless, it is clear that these cases did not meet the strict criteria for euthanasia. The significance of these 1000 cases has been hotly debated – and for opponents of euthanasia, this is a clear demonstration that any attempt to legislate for active voluntary euthanasia will lead to the killing of those *who do not wish to die*. These results were therefore widely reported as showing evidence for the existence of a slippery slope – leading from active voluntary euthanasia to involuntary euthanasia.

In order to address some of these issues, assess changes in practice and audit notification, two further studies into medical decisions at the end of life were commissioned in 1995 (van der Maas, van der Wal et al 1996). These studies found that patients pursued euthanasia because of fears about loss of dignity, 'unworthy dying' or dependence on others, with pain a factor in half of the requests for euthanasia but the sole reason for requesting euthanasia in only 5% of cases. Perhaps more importantly, however, these studies also found that, whilst notification of euthanasia had improved from 18-41% in 1995, the majority of cases remained unreported. In addition, there had been a small increase in the incidence of euthanasia (from 1.8-2.3% of all deaths) whereas physician-assisted suicide remained rare (0.3%). By 2001, it appeared that physicians had become more reluctant about the process of euthanasia and there had been no increase in its use (Onwuteaka-Philipsen, van der Heide et al 2003).

These studies cast doubt about the existence of the 'logical' slippery slope as there does not appear to have been any increase in the prevalence of non-voluntary euthanasia over the years 1990-2001 in Holland, and any increases in Oregon nonetheless resulted in a very limited role for physician-assisted suicide generally. However, the fact that a large number of patients continue to be euthanised in the Netherlands without an explicit request, in clear contravention of the guidelines, continues to be of great concern. It seems likely, therefore, that any legalisation of euthanasia will probably be associated with a small number of cases of involuntary euthanasia.

Some actual examples of the problems that occur with the legalisation of euthanasia in the Netherlands have been documented in a paper by Hendin and colleagues:

A wife who no longer wished to care for her sick husband gave him a choice between euthanasia and admission to a home for the chronically ill. The man, afraid of being left to the mercy of strangers in an unfamiliar place, chose to be killed; the doctor, although aware of the coercion, ended the man's life. A healthy 50-year-old woman, who lost her son recently to cancer, became depressed, refused treatment for her depression, and said she would accept help only in dying. She was assisted in suicide by her psychiatrist within 4 months of her son's death. Her refusal of treatment was considered by her physician and the Dutch courts to make her suffering unrelievable. Another Dutch physician who was filmed ending the life of a patient recently diagnosed with Amyotrophic Lateral Sclerosis [ALS] says of the patient, 'I can give him the finest wheelchair there is, but in the end it is only a stopgap. He's going to die and he knows it.' That death may be years away, but a physician with this attitude may not be able to present alternatives to this patient. (Hendin, Rutenfrans et al 1997)

Of course, it is likely that such cases also occur without legalisation of euthanasia, and euthanasia laws at least allow such attitudes and behaviour to come to light.

Euthanasia and disability

In 1983, Elizabeth Bouvia, a Californian woman with cerebral palsy, requested the assistance of the local hospital in discontinuing her naso-gastric feeding to allow her to starve to death, because she believed the quality of her life had diminished to the point that it was no longer worth living. Disability advocates did not regard this as a case that centred upon personal autonomy or people's right to die as it had been reported in the courts and the media. Rather they felt it was an example of the failure of society to provide adequate funds to enable justice for the disabled, that in turn led to unbearable conditions of living for disabled people, and subsequent requests for euthanasia (DeJong and Banja 1995). As Gill put it:

Our people are still being warehoused without hope of ever having a home or family or lifestyle of their own. When you think about it, in contrast to the vast number of us demanding our rights to first-class citizenship, only a handful of disabled people have publicly sought death. Yet ... laws are being passed at record speed to ease our way to our demise. Prominent experts (argue) for our right to die ... as defenders of our freedom, dignity, humane treatment and even 'independence' ... (yet it) has taken almost 20 years of exhausting struggle to get a basic civil rights law for disabled people. (quoted in Bach and Barnett 1995)

Some of the greatest opposition to legalised euthanasia has come from disability-rights groups. The philosopher Peter Singer, an advocate of euthanasia for severely disabled newborn infants, has been singled out in Germany and Austria for particularly extreme treatment. He has been prevented from speaking on numerous occasions and when he has spoken has been heckled and jeered. When the German weekly *Die Zeit* published two articles that discussed these issues in 1989, Franz Christoph, the leader of the 'cripples movement', chained his wheel-chair to the door of the newspaper's editorial offices. When Professor Singer (who is also one of the originators of the animal rights movement) was invited to speak at the Zoological Institute in Zurich in 1991, a group of people in wheel-chairs protested at the fact that the organisers had invited 'such a notorious advocate of euthanasia'. The lecture was prevented from occurring by a section of the audience chanting 'Singer *raus*, Singer *raus*' and Singer was assaulted by one of the audience (Singer 1993).

However, not all disabled people are opposed to the legalisation of vol-untary euthanasia. As in any diverse community, a variety of views are held by disabled people. A 1994 American poll found that 66% of people with disabilities support a right to assisted suicide, compared with 70% of the general population. But, as Batavia has noted:

> [P]erhaps the most disturbing aspect of this debate is the revelation that many people with disabilities believe that their physicians would be too quick to help them die as a "solution" to their health problems ... A substantial minor-ity of people with disabilities appear to think that their doctors believe that they would be better off dead. Clearly communication between physicians and people with disabilities must be improved. (Batavia 1997)

Within the Australian context, it should be noted that some of the oppo-sition to the Northern Territory Act came from another disadvantaged group – the Northern Territory Aboriginal population. Their opposition was based on two main concerns – that the legislation had implications in tribal law including the requirement for retribution against those who had caused another's death, and that the legislation added to their existing fears of inappropriate care in hospitals. Many Aboriginal people feel alienated by the care they receive in Northern Territory hospitals, and educators who went to Aboriginal settlements to explain the new Act were faced with distrust and hostility (Collins and Bren-nan 1997).

Many disabled people believe that they have good historical reasons to fear any program that supports euthanasia – particularly when they consider the widespread euthanasia of disabled people that was carried out under the Nazis. It is not surprising that some Aboriginal people have similar fears about eutha-nasia programs carried out by white Australians.

Euthanasia in Nazi Germany

Opponents of euthanasia sometimes point to the Aktion T4 (Euthanasia) pro-gram that operated under the Nazis, and less commonly the Holocaust itself, as arguments against the involvement of the state, and the health professions, in killing. In many ways, however, this argument is historically and logically inap-propriate.

In May 1939, just before the commencement of World War II, the Nazis commenced the Aktion T4 program – killing children under three who exhibited mental or physical disability that a panel of medical experts believed gave the child a 'life unworthy of life'. Children were killed by lethal injection. Following their deaths, autopsies were generally performed, brain samples taken for 'medical research' and false death certificates, often recording death from appendicitis or pneumonia, prepared for the child's parents. After the war began the Aktion T4 program was extended to include older children adolescents and adults, became less rigorous and dropped any pretence of medical utility. The list of those killed under this program, increasingly by carbon monoxide gas, included Jews, the 'criminally insane', 'juvenile delinquents' and those diagnosed with epilepsy, schizophrenia, syphilis, Huntington's chorea, dementia, paraplegia and chronic neurological conditions. Despite efforts to maintain secrecy, opposition to the T4 program grew within Germany, prompted not by opposition from the medical and nursing profession, who largely co-operated with the program, but by the Catholic Church and, to a lesser extent, the judiciary. While this led, in August 1941, to the cancellation of the T4, institutions and psychiatrists sympathetic to the ideals of the program continued to kill people until after the end of the war. It is estimated that 70,000 died between 1939 and 1941 and up to 275,000 by 1945 (Proctor 1988; Lifton 2000).

While the Aktion T4 program raises troubling moral issues about the participation of the health professions in state-sanctioned killing and the attitudes to the elderly and the disabled, it is not relevant to contemporary debates about the ethical and legal issues surrounding euthanasia. The Aktion T4 program was based on ideas of 'racial hygiene' and eugenics, was concerned with reducing the costs to the state of caring for disabled and institutionalised people at a time of war, was not motivated by concern for the welfare of those involved, was concerned more with the states' 'right to kill' than the citizen's 'right to die' and was conducted without consent or after extreme coercion (Lifton 2000).

Conclusion

In 1991, Dr Timothy Quill provided a lethal dose of medication to one of his patients who was dying of cancer to use if she desired to end her life. After her death, he wrote about his experience in an article in the *New England Journal* (he was subsequently prosecuted for this series of events). The patient was a long-term client of Dr Quill who had talked openly about dying with him. According to Quill:

> Diane taught me about the range of help I can provide if I know people well and if I allow them to say what they really want. She taught me about life, death and honesty and about taking charge and facing tragedy squarely when it strikes. She taught me that I can take small risks for people that I really know and care about ... Although I know we have measures to help control pain and lessen suffering, to think that people do not suffer in the process of dying is an illusion ...
>
> I wonder how many families and physicians secretly help patients over the edge into death in the face of such severe suffering. I wonder how many severely ill or dying patients secretly take their lives, dying alone in despair. I wonder whether the image of Diane's final aloneness will persist in the minds

of her family or if they will remember more the intense, meaningful months they had together before she died. (Quill 1991)

The importance of Dr Quill's description is not that it suggests that euthanasia is a good or a bad thing. Rather, it illustrates the point that underlying all the debate over active voluntary euthanasia, the deliberations of the US Supreme Court, the controversy over the Northern Territory Act, are concerns about compassion, ethics and the needs of a just society. And it is important to remember that the impetus for euthanasia legislation has arisen in part because of the medical profession's failure to provide care, compassion, respect, understanding and adequate communication to those who are terminally ill.

The Northern Territory legislation was the first instance of legalised voluntary euthanasia anywhere in the world, and it was suppressed after it had been used by only four patients. We do not know as yet whether support for voluntary euthanasia is based on a dangerously naive view of rights, autonomy and society, or whether objections to legalising voluntary euthanasia are based on illusory rather than real, slippery slopes. Until these questions can be answered, we should do our best to listen as fully as we can to patients who request euthanasia. The issues they raise are of fundamental importance to the way in which we see ourselves as health-care professionals, to the way we want our society and our health-care system to be, and the way we perceive the balance between personal morality, individual choices and public policy. Dr Quill's story illustrates the point that when people are dying, even if we are unable to provide the comfort or care that they desire, we must learn from them to work towards a better way to manage death.

LEGAL ASPECTS OF EUTHANASIA AND PALLIATIVE CARE

Mercy killing

In all Australian jurisdictions it is a crime deliberately to take another person's life or to assist another person to commit suicide. The law is unequivocal on these points. There may, however, be some discretion available to a court in the sentence that will be handed down. Also, it is not unknown for juries to furnish a 'not guilty' verdict where an accused person has been charged with murder or manslaughter after a 'mercy killing'. For example, in April 1996 a Victorian man, Mr Joseph Mohr, 74, killed his chronically ill wife, Ingrid, who was 71 years of age. In 1997 a Supreme Court jury in Melbourne took two-and-a-half hours to find Mr Mohr not guilty of murder and manslaughter charges arising from the mercy killing of his wife. A report in the *Age* newspaper (Gregory and Parsons 1997) set out the facts of this case thus:

> The jury heard Mrs Mohr had severe paralysis on her right side and difficulties with speech, eating and swallowing after her stroke in 1984. She had also been in pain from arthritis. Mr Smallwood [the barrister for Mr Mohr] said Mr Mohr visited his wife daily for 18 months in the Western Private nursing home at Footscray. Mrs Mohr had repeatedly asked her husband to help her die. On her last visit to their Footscray unit, she again asked Mr Mohr to kill her, which he did, before unsuccessfully trying to kill himself.

The *Age* reported that '[t]he president of the Voluntary Euthanasia Society of Victoria, Dr Rodney Syme, said he believed the verdict was an important landmark, being the first time in Australia a jury had acquitted someone for what they clearly regarded as an act of voluntary euthanasia – not murder'.

In 2000 a Western Australian urologist, Dr Daryl Stephens, was charged with the murder of a 48-year-old woman. The woman was suffering from terminal cancer of the kidney and allegedly died after being given an intravenous injection of antracurium and midazolam. The woman's brother and sister were also charged with murder for allegedly being present while the lethal injection was being administered. This was said to be the first time in Australia that a doctor had been charged with 'mercy killing'. The jury took just 10 minutes to acquit all three of the charges against them (Associated Press 2001).

A more recent example comes from New Zealand. The Supreme Court of New Zealand upheld a conviction for attempted murder against a woman who had killed her mother, for allegedly compassionate reasons: *Martin v R* [2005] NZSC 33. The accused, Lesley Martin, had cared for her mother who had bowel cancer. After her mother's death she published a book called ... *to die like a dog* wherein she disclosed that she had administered 60 milligrams of morphine to her mother with the intention of ending her mother's life. Martin maintained that the book was true but had a degree of literary licence.

Martin was charged with attempted murder (there was not enough forensic evidence to prove cause of death). She said her account in the book was untruthful and that her admissions were unreliable. She also said that she had no intention to kill her mother. She was convicted and sentenced to 15 months' imprisonment (she actually served seven-and-a-half months).

Martin appealed her conviction all the way to the Supreme Court of New Zealand, where she was unsuccessful. The Supreme Court found that there was no appearance of a miscarriage of justice. There was no room for any suggestion that the injection was to relieve pain rather than to kill.

Assisted suicide in Australia

'Suicide' is an intentional act of self-destruction (Magnusson 1997). In the common law a person who committed suicide was a *felo de se*, a 'self murderer'. Suicide was considered a crime against God and nature, as well as being a crime of depriving the King of a subject. Attempted suicide was also a crime, although the first recorded case does not appear in the records until 1854 in *R v Doody* (1854) 6 Cox Crim Cas 463.

The traditional punishment for suicide was a forfeiture of personal property. In early times, a person who committed suicide to escape conviction for a felony forfeited his lands, whereas other suicides forfeited their goods only. That distinction appears to have disappeared by the 17th century and the punishment of forfeiture was removed by statute in 1870.

In addition to forfeiture, a custom developed whereby the body of a suicide would be hung on a gibbet or left at a crossroads with a spike driven through it and a stone left on the suicide's head. This was done to prevent the soul of the suicide from returning and animating the corpse. After this custom was outlawed in 1823, suicides were to be buried between 9 pm and 12 midnight, without any religious rites. 'Ignominious burial', as this practice was known, was abolished in 1882 (Acts of 4 Geo 4 (1823) c 52 and 45 & 46 Vic (1882) c 19).

Committing suicide or attempting to commit suicide are no longer crimes in any Australian jurisdictions. The common law rules were abrogated by statute in New South Wales (*Crimes Act 1900*, s 31A), South Australia (*Criminal Law Consolidation Act 1935*, s 13A(1)), Victoria (*Crimes Act 1958*, s 6A) and the ACT (*Crimes Act 1900*, s 16). In Queensland, Tasmania, Western Australia and the Northern Territory suicide and attempted suicide are no longer offences (they are no longer included in the *Criminal Code* of these States).

In all Australian jurisdictions it remains an offence to assist or to encourage another to commit suicide (*Crimes Act 1900* (NSW), s 31C; *Criminal Code* (Qld), s 311; *Criminal Law Consolidation Act 1935* (SA), s 13A(5), (7); *Criminal Code* (Tas), s 163; *Crimes Act 1958* (Vic), s 6B(2); *Criminal Code* (WA), s 288; *Crimes Act 1900* (ACT), s 17; *Criminal Code* (NT), s 168). The maximum penalty for committing these offences varies between the jurisdictions, varying from life in prison in the Northern Territory to five years in prison in New South Wales for 'inciting and counselling'.

Conduct performed pursuant to a suicide pact is partly excused in New South Wales (*Crimes Act 1900*, s 31B), South Australia (*Criminal Law Consolidation Act 1935*, s 13A(3)) and Victoria (*Crimes Act 1958*, s 6B(1), (1A)). These provisions prevent the survivor of a suicide pact from being charged with murder, but they will still be criminally liable. In New South Wales, 'suicide pact' is defined by the legislation in the following way:

> 31B(2) In this section, **suicide pact** means a common agreement between 2 or more persons having for its object the death of all of them, whether or not each is to take his or her own life, but nothing done by a person who enters into a suicide pact shall be treated as being done by the person in pursuance of the pact unless it is done while the person has the settled intention of dying in pursuance of the pact.

Types of assistance

What does assistance mean? Assistance can take many forms. Clearly it covers affirmative acts whereby the defendant provides a gun, poison, knife or other instrument which suicides then use to kill themselves: *Bouvia v Superior Court* 225 Cal Rptr 207 (1986) at 306. It can also consist of advice on methods or the provision of devices to help the suicide in his or her task. It might also include active physical participation in the death of the suicide, although we will see below that in such cases the prosecution may proceed on the grounds of homicide rather than assisted suicide. The most common types of assistance involve the purchase or preparation of drugs which are then consumed by the suicide: *R v Ruscoe* (unreported, NZCA, CA 445/91, 20 March 1992, per Cooke P, Hardie Boys and Gault JJ). However, in some circumstances it has been found that merely supplying drugs is not an assistance, if the accused was not absolutely sure that the drugs were to be used in an attempt to commit suicide: *R v Fretwell* (1862) 9 Cox CC 152.

One of the leading cases on the meaning of 'aiding and abetting' suicide is *Attorney-General v Able* [1984] QB 795. In this case the Attorney-General brought a civil action against the members of a voluntary euthanasia society. A declaration was sought that the conduct of the defendants in publishing a booklet which outlined how to commit suicide effectively was unlawful. The book's aim was to reduce people's fear of dying and to reduce the incidence of unsuccessful suicide. Evidence was presented which suggested that 15 cases of suicide were associated with the booklet.

The declaration was refused on the grounds that it could hinder future conduct which may not have been criminal. Woolf J (as he was then) outlined the elements of the offence of aiding and abetting suicide. His Honour found that, in order to convict a person of assisting suicide in this fashion, the prosecution would have to prove:

> (a) that the alleged offender had the necessary intent, that is, he intended the booklet to be used by someone contemplating suicide and intended that person would be assisted by the booklet's contents, or otherwise encouraged to attempt to take or to take his own life; (b) that while he still had that intention he distributed the booklet to such a person who read it; and, (c) in addition, if an offence under section 2 is to be proved, that such a person was assisted or encouraged by so reading the booklet to attempt to take or to take his own life, otherwise the alleged offender cannot be guilty of more than an attempt. (at 812)

An interesting American case is *Donaldson v Lungren* 4 Cal Rptr 2d 59 (1992), a case where a cryogenic technician sought a declaration as to the lawfulness of his conduct. He wanted to give a terminally ill man advice and encouragement about the best ways to commit suicide, for the purpose of cryogenically freezing his corpse, so that one day in the future he could be resurrected and cured. The court found that such advice was illegal and that the statutes proscribing such conduct were not unconstitutional. The State was found to have a valid interest in criminalising the assistance of suicide in this manner. Such laws would deter those who might encourage a suicide to advance their personal motives. The state also had a valid interest in preserving the sanctity of life and protecting potential suicide victims who where mentally ill.

In Australia there have been convictions for assisting a suicide. For example, in 2003, before the Victorian Supreme Court, Alexander Maxwell pleaded guilty to aiding or abetting his wife, Margaret, to commit suicide: *R v Maxwell* [2003] VSC 278. Mrs Maxwell was diagnosed with breast cancer. As her condition deteriorated she made her husband promise to assist to end her life if her health did not improve. Mrs Maxwell reached a point where she asked her husband to honour his promise. Following instructions in the book 'Final Exit: The Practicalities of Self-Deliverance and Assisted Suicide for the Dying', Mr Maxwell assisted his wife to die. After his wife had died, he contacted a funeral director who contacted the police. He laid down beside his wife on the bed and waited for the police to arrive. Mr Maxwell was sentenced to imprisonment for 18 months. The period was wholly suspended.

Assisted suicide or homicide?

If the accused takes an active role in helping the suicide kill him or herself, the prosecution can choose to charge the accused with either assisting a suicide or homicide. The motive of the accused is irrelevant in these cases, as is the consent of the suicide. For example, in the United States, convictions for murder and manslaughter have arisen where the accused tied up and held the victim while the victim attempted to hang himself (*People v Cleaves* 280 Cal Rptr 146 (1991)); where the deceased asked the accused to strangle him to make it look like murder (*People v Matlock* 336 P 2d 505 (1959); and where the accused finished off the deceased with suffocation after the suicide attempt failed (*Gentry v State* 625 NE 2d 1268 (1993)).

Even the supply of drugs can be considered to constitute homicide. For example, in the Australian case, *R v Jemielita* (1995) 81 A Crim R 409, the deceased died pursuant to a suicide pact whereby the accused gave an injection of a substance to the victim, which could only cause death when taken with another drug. The accused injected the first drug but the victim ingested the second and subsequently died. The accused's actions were still considered as the cause of death because the accused had foresight that the final step was going to be taken by the victim.

A similar approach was taken by the Supreme Court of Michigan in *People v Kervorkian* 527 NW 2d 714 (1994), where Jack Kevorkian argued that he had been wrongfully charged with the murder of two of his patients, after he had helped the patients to suicide by providing them with a suicide machine and a carbon monoxide gas breather, which they respectively used to die. Both patients required Kervorkian's aid in attaching the machines to their bodies (by inserting an intravenous needle into one patient and by placing a gas mask over the face of the other). Both patients completed the act of suicide by turning on the apparatus to which they were attached.

The Supreme Court of Michigan found that murder should, at common law, be confined to intentional acts of the defendant where the act was the direct and natural cause of the death of the victim. In contrast the court found that:

> Where a defendant merely is involved in the events leading up to the death, such as providing the means, the proper charge is assisting in a suicide. (at 738-9)

This seems to have been the approach taken in *R v Hood* [2002] VSC 123, where the accused had assisted his ex-lover to commit suicide by buying a large packet of panadeine, which was then consumed by the deceased, along with other drugs and alcohol. The accused also had attempted at one stage to suffocate the deceased when it looked like he might not die, but the accused did not persist as it made him feel ill. The evidence suggested that this had had no effect on the cause of death, which was from combined drug toxicity, namely, codeine, morphine paracetamol, diazepam and temazepam. The judge took this into account when sentencing Hood to an 18 months' suspended sentence for assisting a suicide.

A different set of facts emerged in *R v Justins* [2008] NSWSC 1194. The accused was the de facto partner of Graeme Wylie, a retired airline pilot who had been diagnosed with Alzheimer's disease. As the disease took hold Wylie abandoned his interest in electronics, stopped reading newspapers, had very limited conversation and at times appeared disoriented. He was also clinically depressed. He expressed an interest in going to Switzerland to visit the Dignitas clinic (where he could be euthanised) but his application was refused. Dignitas was concerned that he no longer had capacity to make decisions for himself. Justins, and her friend Jennings, made arrangements for Jennings to go to Mexico to procure nembutal (also known as pentobarbitone) for the purpose of killing Wylie. Justins also took Wylie to his solicitor to have his will changed so as to substantially increase her beneficial interest. At the time the will was signed Wylie was no longer able to read but nothing was said to the solicitor, and a doctor's certificate had been provided which said that Wylie was competent to make his own decisions. Justins provided the nembutal to Wylie in a glass which he drank and then quickly died. She attempted to get a death certificate but no doctor would sign one. The police were called and an autopsy took placed which revealed the presence of the nembutal. A jury found both Justins and Jennings guilty of manslaughter. Before being sentenced Jennings killed herself. In sentencing Justins to 30 months' periodic detention (with a 22-month non-parole period) Howie J stated:

> Of course there are extremely sad cases of offences committed by persons pushed beyond endurance by concern for a loved one in never-ending pain and suffering without hope of remedy. In those circumstances the court can take a very merciful view of the criminal conduct especially when it occurs without significant planning. Such a set of facts would give rise to an offence on the lower end of the spectrum for crimes of assisting a suicide or otherwise aiding a person who professed a wish to die. But this was not such a case. On the other hand it is not at the upper limit of seriousness such as where the offender operated a commercial enterprise in assisting the deaths of members of the community for gain. But in my view it was of such seriousness that even had the offender been convicted of an offence contrary to s 31C(1) of the *Crimes Act* a gaol penalty would have been the appropriate sentence.
>
> Manslaughter is of course a more serious offence than aiding suicide. It was the offender's act that resulted in his death. The offence is aggravated by the degree of planning involved. There was a late acceptance by the offender of involvement in the death that indicates some acknowledgement of responsibility, both morally and criminally. However, I doubt that she really accepts the grave criminality of what she did. Her conduct after the killing shows that the offender knew that what she had done was unlawful ... (at [46]-[47])

Human rights and assisted suicide

Because suicide is no longer illegal, it has been argued on occasion that that there is a right to commit suicide. In *Reeves v Commissioner of Police* [1999] 3 WLR 386 at 386, Lord Hobhouse said:

> Suicide is within the range of conduct lawfully open to a person: personal autonomy includes the right to choose conduct which will cause that person's death and the right to refuse to allow others to obstruct that choice ...

Serious questions can be asked about the correctness of this approach given that most jurisdictions forgive criminal assaults which are occasioned to prevent a suicide (see, eg, *Crimes Act 1900* (NSW), s 574B).

Nevertheless, people have attempted to fashion a human right to assisted suicide in Canada, the United States and the United Kingdom. All attempts have failed. The first case occurred in Canada and was the closet to being successful. In *Rodriguez v British Columbia (Attorney-General)* (1993) 82 BCLR (2d) 273, a patient with Lou Gherig's disease wished to have a physician supply her with a 'suicide machine' so she could kill herself when she longer wished to live. She sought a declaration that would invalidate the criminal provisions which made the aiding and abetting of suicide an offence, on the basis that her human rights were being breached. She claimed that, as able bodied people could kill themselves, she should also be able to do so, but her disabilities required her to have help. The laws against assisting a suicide therefore breached her rights by discriminating against her because of her disabilities.

It was found by the majority of the Canadian Supreme Court (5:4) that the there were no human rights breaches. According to the court, the criminal prohibition may have deprived the patient of her autonomy and caused her physical pain and distress, but such a deprivation was not found to have been contrary to the principles of fundamental justice, as secured by the Canadian Charter. The court could not make fundamental changes to the long-standing and almost universal policy against euthanasia.

The Supreme Court of the United States rejected similar claims based on the United States Constitution: *Washington v Glucksberg* 521 US 702 (1997) and *Vacco v Quill* 521 US 703 (1997). The court rejected any suggestion that there was ever a right to assisted suicide. Nearly every State in America had criminalised assisted suicide and the court found that the Anglo-American tradition has punished or deterred suicide for nearly 700 years. To hold that assisted suicide was a constitutional liberty interest would 'reverse centuries of legal doctrine and practice and strike down the considered policy choice of almost every state' (at 723).

In *Vacco* the claimants argued that the laws prohibiting assisted suicide were irrational because they prevented physician-assisted suicide but allowed patients to kill themselves by refusing treatment. The Supreme Court rejected the claims. The distinction between suicide and refusing treatment was said to be rational and in accordance with well-accepted doctrines of intention and causation. The death of the patient was not intended by the physician in cases where treatment is withheld (but see the discussion in Chapter 15).

The House of Lords has also rejected claims that there is a human right to assisted suicide in the United Kingdom: *Pretty v Director of Public Prosecutions and Secretary of State for the Home Department* [2001] UKHL 61. Diane Pretty suffered from motor neuron disease and was unable to commit suicide without assistance. Pretty wished for her husband to aid her suicide but requested that the Director of Public Prosecutions undertake not to prosecute him for breaching the *Suicide Act 1961* (UK). The Director refused to give such an undertaking. She then brought an application for judicial review of the decision of the Director.

Pretty argued that under the *Human Rights Act 1998* (UK) she had a right to aid in dying, the effect of which would be to protect her husband from being charged for assisting her suicide. Pretty's main arguments were that her right to assisted suicide was based on the right to life (contained in Article 2), the prohibition of torture (Article 3), the right to respect of private and family life (Article 8), freedom of thought, conscience and religion (Article 9), and the prohibition of discrimination (Article 14). The House unanimously agreed that she failed on all counts.

With respect to the right to life it was found that while the state had no obligation to keep Mrs Pretty alive against her will, the state did not have to recognise her right to commit suicide. The right to life enjoined the state from killing and also imposed on it a duty to safeguard life. It did not include a right to kill. Moreover such a recognition would conflict with the deeply imbedded principles of the common law which distinguish between killing and letting die.

The argument based on the prohibition of torture was similarly dismissed. The 'negative' prohibition against torture did not include a 'positive' right to die. Nor was there any positive action on the part of the state to inflict pain or a failure to properly treat Mrs Pretty's condition.

With respect to the right to respect for privacy and family life, Lord Bingham believed that the right was not at all relevant to the argument, but even if it was he believed that any infringement was justifiable, on the grounds that suicide should not be encouraged and that the law should not make specific exemptions for people in similar circumstances to Mrs Pretty.

Pretty's right to freedom of thought, conscience and religion were given short thrift, Lord Steyn stating that the Article did not give individuals a right to perform any acts in pursuance of whatever beliefs they might hold.

Finally, with regards to the discrimination argument, Article 14 can only be invoked if other Articles have been offended. Given the findings of the House on the other claims, the claim based on discrimination failed. Even so, the Lords considered that there was no discrimination on any account as the criminal law applied to all equally, whether the victims of an assisted suicide were able bodied or not. An appeal to the European Court of Human Rights was also unsuccessful: *Pretty v United Kingdom* [2002] ECHR 427. Mrs Pretty died at a hospice near her home on 11 May 2002.

Double effect and the law

UK cases

The earliest known case on doctrine of double effect is *R v Adams* (unreported, 8 April 1957). The doctor, Bodkin Adams, was charged with the murder after prescribing large doses of barbiturates for a patient after she had a stroke, and even beyond the point where she had lapsed into a coma. There were accusations that Dr Adams had prescribed the drugs so as to encourage the patient to affect changes in her will. The patient left the doctor an oak chest containing silver and, if her son predeceased her, her Rolls Royce and an Elizabethan cupboard.

In his summing-up to the jury, Devlin J (as he was then) stated that 'no doctor, nor any man, no more in the case of the dying than of the healthy, has the right deliberately to cut the thread of life'. However, Devlin J also found that:

> [If] the first purpose of medicine, the restoration of health, can no longer be achieved, there is still much for a doctor to do, and he is entitled to all that is proper and necessary to relieve pain and suffering, even if the measures he takes may incidentally shorten life. (Palmer 1957)

Adams was acquitted. Later cases accepted shortening of life on the basis that the doctor was motivated by a desire to lessen the patient's pain. In *R v Arthur* (1981) 12 BMLR 1, an obstetrician was acquitted of attempting to murder a new born boy with Down's Syndrome. The child had been rejected by his parents. The mother of the child had stated that she did not wish for the child to survive. The doctor ordered a course of non-treatment for the child, in which he was to be provided with pain killers which sedated and repressed appetite. Some time later the baby died. Farquharson J stated:

> Where, perhaps, somebody is suffering from the agonies of terminal cancer and the doctor is obliged to give increasing dosages of an analgesic to relieve the pain, there comes a point where the amounts of these doses are such that in themselves they will kill off the patient; but he is driven to it on medical grounds. There again, you will, undoubtedly say that that could never be murder. That would be a proper practice of medicine.

Since *Arthur* the doctrine has been accepted by UK courts several times: *Re J (A Minor) (Wardship: Medical Treatment)* [1991] Fam 33 at 46. In *Airedale NHS Trust v Bland* [1993] AC 789, Lord Goff accepted that a doctor may lawfully administer painkilling drugs despite the fact that he knows they will shorten the patient's life. In *R v Moor* (unreported, Newcastle Crown Court, 13 May 1999, Hooper J), a doctor was acquitted of the murder of his patient after injecting him with increasing doses of diamorphine to treat pain which was thought to have been caused by terminal cancer, but which was in fact caused by an undiagnosed heart condition (Arlidge 2000). Similarly, in *Pretty v Director of Public Prosecutions and Secretary of State for the Home Department* [2001] UKHL 61, the House of Lords reaffirmed that medical treatment may be administered to a terminally ill person to alleviate pain although it may hasten death, as long as the outcome was foreseen but not intended.

According to this approach the doctrine of double effect does not protect a health-care professional if that professional provides the medication with the primary intention of killing the patient. In *R v Cox* (1992) 12 BMLR 38, Dr Nigel Cox injected his patient with a lethal dose of potassium chloride which was designed to cause the death of the patient. Potassium chloride has no analgesic effects. Cox had known the patient for 13 years and he had promised her that she would not suffer. The pain-killing medication that he prescribed was ineffective and she begged him to kill her. He gave her the injection and she died within minutes.

Cox was tried and convicted of attempted murder (the charge of murder was not available as the body had been cremated before an autopsy could be performed). Ognall J, in his summing-up to the jury, repeated the findings of Devlin J and Farquharson J that:

There can be no doubt that the use of drugs to reduce pain and suffering will often be fully justified notwithstanding that it will, in fact, hasten the moment of death. What can never be lawful is the use of drugs with the primary purpose of hastening the moment of death. (at 41)

Ognall J found that there was an 'absolute prohibition on a doctor purposefully taking life as opposed to saving it'. The task for the jury was to determine what was the primary purpose of the injection. Ognall J stated that if the primary purpose of the injection was the alleviation of suffering then Cox should be found not guilty, even if the alleviation of suffering shortened the patient's life. If the primary purpose was to bring about death then the doctor should be found guilty.

North American cases

While the majority of cases appear to come from the United Kingdom, there are pronouncements from other jurisdictions which support the use of the doctrine of double effect. For example, in *Rodriguez v British Columbia (Attorney-General)* [1993] 3 SCR 519, mentioned above, both Lamer CJ (in dissent) and Sopinka J gave approval to the doctrine. In *R v Morrison* (1998) 41 WCB (2d) 462, charges were brought but dismissed against a doctor who had allegedly killed her patient by injecting him with potassium chloride, nitroglycerine and high levels of narcotics. The patient had incurable throat cancer and was in the terminal phase of the illness when a decision was made to take him off ventilatory support. The patient experienced significant distress after being taken off the ventilator and narcotics were administered to extraordinary levels of more than 500 mgs an hour. For reasons arguably due to a defective drip the narcotics were ineffective, and the doctor was alleged to have injected the patient with potassium chloride and nitroglycerine, after which the patient soon died. Controversially a judge dismissed the charge against the doctor for lack of evidence. This decision was upheld on appeal.

The United States has also accepted the doctrine of double effect as being part of the common law. In *Vacco v Quill* 521 US 703 (1997) the Supreme Court accepted that the doctor has no intention to kill when terminally sedating a patient.

It has also been accepted at the State level. In *State v Narramore* 1998 Kan App Lexis 79, a doctor was accused of attempting to murder his patient Ruth Leach and charged with the first degree murder of another patient, Chris Willt. Narramore had attempted to terminally sedate Leach, during her final days of life. Leach suffered from terminal cancer. Narramore gave Leach opioids to relieve pain but was prevented from increasing the dosage by her son, who was afraid that the dosages would kill her. On this basis he was found guilty by a jury of attempted murder.

Narramore was also found guilty of murder after he withdrew artificial respiration from Willt, who suffered from untreated diabetes. Willt had refused treatment for his condition and had presented at the hospital with signs of a severe stroke. Narramore drugged the patient to place him on a ventilator. After three hours ventilation was withdrawn with the approval of next of kin, even though the patient exhibited body movements. Narramore withdrew ventilation as he believed the patient to be 'brain dead'. A second doctor had concurred with the removal of ventilation. Nevertheless, the jury convicted Narramore.

The Court of Appeals of Kansas overturned the findings of the jury on the basis that no rational jury could have found criminal intent and guilt beyond a reasonable doubt. Expert evidence and the evidence of doctors at the scenes of the alleged crimes showed the actions of Narramore to be medially appropriate and not of a criminal nature.

Problems with double effect

The cases above suggest that the doctrine of double effect works on two levels: it distinguishes the intention of the doctor from an intention to kill, and by doing so it is also said that death is not caused by the pain-killing medication. The problem with this analysis is that both conclusions directly conflict with fundamental principles of criminal law.

Foreseeing death is intending

As stated in Chapter 15, the common law recognises that an accused can be found to have an intention to kill when they either have an actual intention to kill, or where they act knowing that death is a probable result of their actions: *R v Crabbe* (1985) 156 CLR 464. This directly conflicts with the notion that one can foresee death resulting from administration of pain medication but not intend it. Meisel has correctly stated that:

> The Courts in right to die cases have been content to substitute platitudes about intent for analysis. They have utterly failed to examine the conventional meanings of intent in criminal law. (Meisel 1997)

In other types of homicide, the courts have accepted knowing and reckless mental states as sufficient for *mens rea*. No explanation is given in any of the authorities listed above as to why this area of homicide should be treated any differently.

The motive of the accused is irrelevant to the question of intention

The second problem with the doctrine is the way that it confuses the requirement of intention with that of the accused's motive. The motive of the defendant is irrelevant once an intention to kill has been established. As was stated in Chapter 15, it does not matter that the killing is inspired by a motive of compassion.

The idea of primary intention put forward in some of these decisions is in reality a question of motive. As Lanham puts it:

> If the only way to relieve the pain is to kill and the killer knows this, the requirement of intention to kill is satisfied. (Lanham 1994)

The idea of primary and secondary intentions has no place in the criminal law. If the doctor realises that the death of the patient will be hastened with drugs, his or her motive for providing those drugs is irrelevant for determining the issue of whether there is a sufficient *mens rea*. Therefore the bottom line is that the courts' current use of double effect is a distortion of the idea of intention, which lies at the heart of criminal law.

The doctrine of double effect is not supported by principles of legal causation

Ashby has argued that:

> If an incidental effect of accepted palliative care practice measures is to hasten the (inevitable and anticipated) death of a person, then this is not deemed to constitute a cause of death in law, because such practice does not constitute a new intervening act in a pre-existing chain of causation. (Ashby 1995)

This is specious reasoning for two reasons. First, in criminal law, a cause which hastens death as one of a number of causes is still a legal cause of death. The fact that the deceased was dying from another cause is of no consequence in determining whether the accused is causally responsible for the death of the victim.

Secondly, it is by no means clear why the doctor's treatment, if it accelerates death, would not be considered an intervening act. Independent acts of third parties will break the chain of causation when they are voluntary human responses to a situation. The doctor who knowingly provides medication that will hasten death is acting voluntary and consciously. By doing so they are certainly an intervening act, or at the very least a contributing cause of death.

Solutions to the problem of double effect in law

The above criticisms suggest that it is wrong to manipulate established criminal law principles to achieve a desired outcome. The first cost of manipulating the law is that it loses its coherence and then its ability to function as a normative system. The second cost is that doctors will not understand what the law permits and consequently take a less aggressive approach to the treatment of pain, leaving patients with sub-standard care. That is not to say that palliative care is always about hastening death. Indeed good palliative care will extend life. Nevertheless, there will be times when patients do require treatment for their pain and suffering which may hasten death, and the law should support and protect such treatment.

The better and more ethical way for judges to do this is to find a way using existing criminal law principles, or to get parliament to provide a legislative solution.

Legislative solutions

Legislative solutions exist. The *Medical Treatment (Health Directions) Act 2006* (ACT), s 17, says that patients with advance directives have a 'right to receive relief from pain and suffering to the maximum extent that is reasonable in the circumstances'. The *Consent to Medical Treatment and Palliative Care Act 1995* (SA), s 17(1), says that medical practitioners who are treating terminally ill patients, incur no civil or criminal liability for administering treatments for pain or distress:

(a) with the consent of the patient or the patient's representative; and
(b) in good faith and without negligence; and
(c) in accordance with proper professional standards of palliative care,
even though an incidental effect of the treatment is to hasten the death of the patient.

In Queensland the *Criminal Code* states that a person is not criminally responsible for providing palliative care to another person if:

(a) the person provides the palliative care in good faith and with reasonable care and skill; and
(b) the provision of the palliative care is reasonable, having regard to the other person's state at the time and all the circumstances of the case; and
(c) the person is a doctor or, if the person is not a doctor, the palliative care is ordered by a doctor who confirms the order in writing. (s 282A(1))

The section applies even if an incidental effect of providing the palliative care is to hasten the other person's death. Palliative care is reasonable when it is considered reasonable in 'good medical practice'. 'Good medical practice' is defined as:

(a) the recognised medical standards, practices and procedures of the medical profession in Australia; and
(b) the recognised ethical standards of the medical profession in Australia. (s 282A(5))

Common law solutions

In the absence of a legislative solution, common law must provide a way. There are two options: a consent-based defence and a necessity defence.

The defence of consent was discussed in Chapter 14. People are permitted to consent to activities with serious risks of injury and even death, if the activity can be said to be in the public interest: *R v Brown* [1994] 1 AC 212.

There are very good public policy reasons for finding in favour of giving doctors the power to aggressively treat pain and suffering in terminal illness. The double effect clearly secures the ethical integrity of the medical profession, by allowing members to treat the painful symptoms of terminal disease. This type of treatment is in accord with the sanctity of life in that it at least lessens the stress of patients and may, in the right circumstances, extend the life of the patient. Even in cases where the patient's life is shortened palliative care provides for a better *quality of life*. If such treatment was not available, some patients may take initiatives to end their own lives. For all of these reasons, public policy would seem to approve of the doctrine of double effect. As Otlowski states:

> [I]t is possible, at least for the purposes of the Australian common law jurisdictions, that the courts would accommodate the practice of doctors administering palliative drugs which are likely incidentally to hasten the patient's death within this concept of socially justifiable risk. (Otlowski 2001)

The major limitation of the defence is that it may only be available to patients who are still competent. This is a major problem because many patients at the end stage of a terminal illness will not be competent due to the ravages of their illness.

These limitations lead the argument towards a defence of necessity. Necessity was discussed in Chapter 14 and 15.It might be argued that the doctor should be granted immunity from criminal liability if he or she provides pain relief which shortens life, on the basis that the pain relief was necessary because it was in the patient's best interests.

Professor Glanville Williams suggested this as a solution to the problem of double effect in 1958:

> [A] physician may give an amount of drug necessary to deaden pain, even though he knows that the amount will bring about speedy or indeed immediate death. His legal excuse does not rest upon the Roman Church's doctrine of 'double effect', for it would be both human and right for him in these circumstances to welcome his patient's death as a merciful release. The excuse rests upon the doctrine of necessity, there being at this juncture no way of relieving pain without ending life. (Williams 1958)

The major stumbling block to the use of necessity was *R v Dudley and Stephens* (1884) 14 QBD 273 (which was discussed in Chapter 15). That stumbling black has been removed, as necessity has been found to be available as a defence to murder: *Re A (children) (conjoined twins)* [2000] 4 All ER 961 at 1051 (Brooke LJ); *R v Latimer* (2001) 193 DLR (4th) 577 at 596.

A doctor who employed double effect reasoning may be able to satisfy the three elements of the necessity defence. First, the acceleration of death in such a case is done to avoid the evil of continued refractory symptoms, in cases where the doctor is duty bound to act to relieve pain. Secondly, the doctor has no reasonable alternative, assuming that all other palliative options have been exhausted, for the treatment of the patient's pain. Finally, the continued palliation in response to the patient's pain would ordinarily be proportionate to the risk of a lengthy and painful dying process.

Arguably, the defence would not be available to doctors who decided to accelerate death when there were other effective treatments for the pain being suffered by the patient. Nor should such a defence be available to doctors when the evidence establishes that a lethal medicine was administered which had no analgesic or sedative effect. Such an administration would not satisfy the requirement of proportionality.

Finally, a question should be asked as to whether the defence should be restricted to the medical profession. Most commentators presume that it should be. Hart and Honore have stated that:

> The correct principle must surely be that a doctor has a duty not merely to prolong life but, when that proves no longer possible, to continue to relieve a patient's suffering. It is therefore permissible for him, when the patient is doomed to die shortly, to administer pain-killing drugs with his consent, even if they slightly shorten life. It does not follow that it would be permissible, as opposed to understandable, for someone without such a duty to do the same. In general, it is important to cleave to the principle that the slightest

acceleration of death, eg by shooting a man strapped in the electric chair, is homicide. (Hart and Honore 1985)

But what of nurses, home carers and others who are involved in administering palliative care? It should not be forgotten that medical decision-making is being increasingly delegated to the allied health professionals, as well as to non-professionals, who are increasingly being called on the care for the dying. The doctrine of double effect ordinarily has been presumed to apply only to doctors because it is presumed that only doctors administer the medication to their patients. If that is the basis for the restriction it might be argued that allied health professionals might also be able to claim the benefit of the defence should it be proven that the responsibility for administering medication had been lawfully delegated to them.

Australian legislative change

Some Australian legislators have attempted to reform the law and introduce legislation that would authorise assisting a patient to die. Notably, legislation was passed in the Northern Territory (*Rights of the Terminally Ill Act 1995*) which allowed a patient (in prescribed circumstances) to request assistance from a medical practitioner to terminate his or her life. The passage of this legislation was quite controversial and in 1997 the Commonwealth government passed legislation (*Euthanasia Laws Act 1997* (Cth)), using its power under s 122 of the Constitution (the 'Territories power'), which caused the Act to be overturned. Subsequently, in a number of jurisdictions there have been Bills drafted and placed before the legislatures. At the time of writing none of these has become law.

Rights of the Terminally Ill Act 1995 (NT)

This legislation, which was passed by the Northern Territory Assembly on 25 May 1995 after a marathon 14-hour debate, was the first of its type to be passed by any legislature in the world. The long title set out the Act's various aims in the following manner: 'An Act to confirm the right of a terminally ill person to request assistance from a medically qualified person to voluntarily terminate his or her life in a humane manner; to allow for such assistance to be given in certain circumstances without legal impediment to the person rendering the assistance; to provide procedural protection against the possibility of abuse of the rights recognised by this Act and for related purposes'.

The Act allowed a terminally ill patient to request the patient's medical practitioner to assist the patient to terminate the patient's life. A terminal illness was defined as 'an illness which, in reasonable medical judgment will, in the normal course, without the application of extraordinary measures or of treatment unacceptable to the patient, result in the death of the patient'. Before requesting such assistance the patient had to be 'experiencing pain, suffering and/or distress to an extent unacceptable to the patient'.

The Act then set out a number of conditions which had to be met before the assistance could be given (not all of the requirements have been included here):

- the patient had to be 18 years or older;
- the medical practitioner had to be satisfied that the patient was suffering from a terminal illness with no hope of cure;
- two other (unrelated) medical practitioners (one with experience with the terminal illness, the other a psychiatrist) had examined the patient and confirmed the diagnosis and ensured that the patient is not suffering from 'a treatable clinical depression';
- the illness had to be causing the patient severe pain or suffering;
- the medical practitioner had informed the patient of the nature of the illness and its likely course, and the medical treatment, including palliative care, counselling and psychiatric support and extraordinary measures for keeping the patient alive, that might have been available to the patient;
- the patient had indicated to the medical practitioner that the patient had decided to end his or her life;
- the medical practitioner had to be satisfied that the patient had considered the possible implications of the patient's decision to his or her family;
- the patient needed to be of sound mind and the patient's decision to end his or her life had to have been made freely, voluntarily and after due consideration;
- after seven days the patient had signed a certificate of request;
- the medical practitioner had witnessed the patient's signature on the certificate of request or that of the person who signed on behalf of the patient, and had completed and signed the relevant declaration on the certificate;
- the certificate of request witnessed and checked by another medical practitioner;
- not less than 48 hours had elapsed since the signing of the completed certificate of request;
- at no time before assisting the patient to end his or her life had the patient given to the medical practitioner an indication that it was no longer the patient's wish to end his or her life;
- the medical practitioner himself or herself provided the assistance and/ or is and remains present while the assistance is given and until the death of the patient.

No assistance to die could be given where there were 'palliative care options reasonably available to the patient to alleviate the patient's pain and suffering to levels acceptable to the patient'. After the assisted death of the patient information concerning the death was to be forwarded to the Coroner.

Shortly after the Act came into effect there was a challenge made in the Northern Territory Supreme Court (*Wake v Northern Territory* (1996) 124 FLR 298) with respect to the validity of the Act. The court, by majority decision, upheld the validity of the Act.

In September 1996 Mr Kevin Andrews introduced a Private Member's Bill into the Commonwealth Parliament. The Bill sought to amend the grant of legislative power given to Australian Territories under the self-government Acts. The Bill was referred to the Senate Legal and Constitutional Legislation Committee which reported in March 1997. The Committee received 12,577 submissions from every State and Territory in Australia and from several overseas countries.

On Monday 24 March 1997, the Senate passed the Bill which was assented to on 27 March 1997. The operative provisions of the Act amend the *Northern Territory (Self-Government) Act 1978* (Cth) and insert the following:

> The power of the Legislative Assembly ... does not extend to the making of laws which permit or have the effect of permitting (whether subject to conditions or not) the form of intentional killing of another called euthanasia (which includes mercy killing) or the assisting of a person to terminate his or her life.

Similar amendments were made to the *Australian Capital Territory (Self-Government) Act 1988* (Cth). Euthanasia legislation has been proposed for South Australia, Western Australia and New South Wales. These Bills tend to be Private Member Bills and are not generally debated before the respective parliaments.

Senator Bob Brown issued a challenge to the *Euthanasia Laws Act* by introducing the *Rights of the Terminally Ill (Euthanasia Laws Repeal) Bill 2008* into the Australian Senate. The Bill sought to repeal the *Euthanasia Laws Act*. The Bill was sent to the Legal and Constitutional Affairs Committee, which did not form a majority view, although it was agreed that the Bill should not proceed in its current form (see <http://www.aph.gov.au/Senate/committee/legcon_ctte/terminally_ill/report/index.htm>).

Euthanasia tourism

Questions arise as to how the law should deal with situations where people wish to travel to other jurisdictions where euthanasia is permitted. This was discussed in *Local Authority v Z* [2004] EWHC 2817 (Fam). The case concerned Mr and Mrs Z. Mrs Z had cerebella ataxia, a condition which attacks the body's motor functions. The condition is terminal, incurable and irreversible. Mrs Z had unsuccessfully attempted suicide through paracetemol poisoning and later expressed her desire to go to Switzerland to be euthanised. Her family initially were opposed but later came to support her decision. The local authority came to know of Mrs Z's decision and investigated whether she was a vulnerable person in need of protection. A social worker for the authority believed that she was competent but also expressed concern that for her decision to be carried out she would need the help of her husband and this might be a criminal act. Hedley J found that that Mrs Z was competent and that the *Suicide Act 1961* (UK) did not prohibit her committing suicide. In relation to Mr Z, Hedley J said:

> The position in relation of Mr Z, however, is much less clear. Section 2 of the *Suicide Act 1961* provides:

(1) a person who aids, abets, counsels or procures the suicide of another, or an attempt by another to commit suicide, shall be liable on conviction on indictment to imprisonment for a term not exceeding fourteen years ...

(4) ... no proceedings shall be instituted for an offence under this section except by or with the consent of the Director of Public Prosecutions.

Although it is the case that all that Mr and Mrs Z propose to do is not criminal under the law of Switzerland, it seems to me inevitable that by making arrangements and escorting Mrs Z on the flight, Mr Z will have contravened Section 2(1) above. It follows that in order for Mrs Z actually to be able to carry out her decision, it will require the criminal conduct of another. That said I remind myself of sub-section (4). Although not unique, the provision is rare and is usually found where Parliament recognises that although an act may be criminal, it is not always in the public interest to prosecute in respect of it. (at [14])

Hedley J then examined the question of whether the authority was duty bound to seek an injunction to prevent Mrs Z's travel. The judge did not believe so. The authority was only duty bound to investigate Mrs Z's competence and to refer any possible criminal activity to the police. Because the police did not intervene no further action was necessary to be taken and no injunction would be ordered.

References

Arlidge, A (2000). 'The Trial of Dr David Moor'. *Crim LJ*: 31.

Asch, D (1996) 'The role of critical care nurses in euthanasia and assisted suicide'. *N Engl J Med* **334**: 1374-9.

Ashby, M (1995) 'Hard Cases, Causation and Care of the Dying'. *Journal of Law and Medicine*(3): 152.

Ashby, M and B Stoffell (1991) 'Therapeutic ratio and defined phases: proposal of ethical framework for palliative care'. *BMJ* **302**(6788): 1322-4.

Associated Press (2001) Three cleared in WA mercy killing. *Illawarra Mercury*. Wollongong.

Bach, J and V Barnett (1995) 'Ethical considerations in the management of individuals with severe neuromuscular disorders'. *Am J Phys Med Rehab* **74**(1): S34-S40.

Bachman, J, K Alchser et al (1996) 'Attitudes of Michigan physicians and the public toward legalising physician-assisted suicide and voluntary euthanasia'. *N Engl J Med* **334**: 303-9.

Batavia, A (1997) 'Disability and physician-assisted suicide'. *N Engl J Med* **336**(23): 1671-3.

Brock, DW (1992) 'Voluntary active euthanasia'. *Hastings Cent Rep* **22**(2): 10-22.

Brody, H (1993) 'Causing, intending and assisting death'. *J Clin Ethics* **4**: 112-18.

Callahan, D (1993) *The troubled dream of life : in search of peaceful death*. New York, Simon & Schuster.

Cherny, NI and R Catane (1995) 'Professional negligence in the management of cancer pain. A case for urgent reforms'. *Cancer* **76**(11): 2181-5.

Clark, J and PA Singer (2003) 'BMJ Special Supplement. What is a good death?' *BMJ* **309**: 327.

Cohen, J, J van Delden et al (2008) 'Influence of physicians' life stances on attitudes to end-of-life decisions and actual end-of-life decision-making in six countries'. *J Med Ethics* **34**(4): 247-53.

Collins, J and F Brennan (1997) 'Euthanasia and the potential adverse effects for Northern Territory aborigines'. *Lancet* **349**(9069): 1907-8.

DeJong, G and J Banja (1995) Health care and physical disability. *Encyclopedia of Bioethics*. WT Reich. New York, MacMillan.

Department of Human Services Oregon. 'Tenth Annual Report on Oregon's Death with Dignity Act'. <ww.dhs.state.or.us/publichealth/chs/pas/pas.cfm>.

Doerflinger, R (1989) 'Assisted suicide: pro-choice or anti-life'. *Hastings Cent Rep* **19**(Sp Suppl): 16-19.

Douglas, C, I Kerridge et al (2008) 'Managing Intentions: the End-of-Life Administration of Analgesics and Sedatives, and the Possibility of Slow Euthanasia'. *Bioethics*.

Douglas, CD, IH Kerridge et al (2001) 'The intention to hasten death: a survey of attitudes and practices of surgeons in Australia'. *Med J Aust* **175**(10): 511-15.

Edmonds, P and A Rogers (2003) '"If only someone had told me ..." A review of the care of patients dying in hospital'. *Clin Med* **3**: 149-52.

Emanuel, EJ (2002) 'Euthanasia and physician-assisted suicide: a review of the empirical data from the United States'. *Arch Intern Med* **162**(2): 142-52.

Emanuel, EJ, DL Fairclough et al (2000) 'Attitudes and desires related to euthanasia and physician-assisted suicide among terminally ill patients and their caregivers'. *JAMA* **284**(19): 2460-8.

Foley, K (1995) 'Pain, physician-assisted suicide, and euthanasia'. *Pain Forum* **4**: 163-78.

Foley, K (1997) 'Competent care for the dying instead of physician-assisted suicide'. *N Engl J Med* **336**: 54-8.

Folker, A, N Holtug et al (1996) 'Experiences and attitudes towards end-of-life decisions amongst Danish physicians'. *Bioethics* **10**: 233-49.

Ganzini, L, SK Dobscha et al (2003) 'Oregon physicians' perceptions of patients who request assisted suicide and their families'. *J Palliat Med* **6**(3): 381-90.

Ganzini, L, ER Goy et al (2003) 'Nurses' experiences with hospice patients who refuse food and fluids to hasten death'. *N Engl J Med* **349**(4): 359-65.

Ganzini, L, ER Goy et al (2008) 'Why Oregon patients request assisted death: family members' views'. *J Gen Intern Med* **23**(2): 154-7.

Gawande, A, A Caplan et al (2008) 'Organ donation after cardiac death: A perspective roundtable'. *N Engl J Med*.

Gillam, L (2008) 'End of life decision-making in paediatrics'. *J Paediatr Child Health* **44**(7-8): 389-91.

Gillon, R (1999) 'Foreseeing is not necessarily the same as intending'. *BMJ* **318**: 1431-2.

Glaser, BG and AL Strauss (1965) *Awareness of dying*. Chicago, Aldine Pub Co.

Gregory, P and B Parsons (1997) 'Aged mercy killer acquitted'. *The Age*, 10 May. Melbourne.

Hardy, J and R Vora (2004) 'A good death down under'. *Int Med J* **34**: 450-2.

Hart, H and A Honore (1985) *Causation in the Law* (2nd ed). Oxford, Oxford University Press.

Heidegger, M (1992) *The concept of time*. Oxford, Blackwell.

Hendin, H, C Rutenfrans et al (1997) 'Physician assisted suicide and euthanasia in the Netherlands'. *JAMA* **277**(21): 1720-2.

Herxheimer, A (1996) 'Euthanasia and palliative care: a pseudo conflict?'. *Lancet* **348**: 1187-8.

Hope, RA, J Savulescu et al (2003) *Medical ethics and law : the core curriculum*. Edinburgh, Churchill Livingstone.

Illich, I (1990) *Limits to medicine*. London, Penguin.

Kierkegaard, S (1946) *The sickness unto death*. [S.l.], Princeton University Press.

Kleinman, A (1988) *The illness narratives : suffering, healing, and the human condition*. New York, Basic Books.

Komesaroff, PA (2008) *Experiments in Love and Death: Medicine, Postmodernism, Microethics and the Body*. Melbourne, Melbourne University Press.

Kuhse, H and P Singer (1993) 'Voluntary euthanasia and the nurse: an Australian study'. *Int J Nurs Stud*. **4**: 311-22.

Kuhse, H, P Singer et al (1997) 'End-of-life decisions in Australian medical practice'. *Med J Aust* **166**(4): 191-6.

Lanham, D (1994) 'Euthanasia, Painkilling, Murder and Manslaughter ' *Journal of Law and Medicine* **1**: 146.

Lifton, RJ (2000) *The Nazi doctors : medical killing and the psychology of genocide : with a new preface by the author.* [New York], Basic Books.

Magnusson, R (1997) 'The Sanctity of Life and the Right to Die: Social and Jurisprudential Aspects of the Euthanasia Debate in Australia and the United States'. *Pacific Rim Law and Policy Journal* **6**.

Magnusson, R (2004) ' "Underground euthanasia" and the Harm Minimisation Debate'. *J Law Medicine Ethics* **32**(3): 486-95.

Meier, D, C Emmons et al (1998) 'A national survey of physician-assisted suicide and euthanasia in the United States'. *N Engl J Med* **338**: 1193-201.

Meisel, A (1997) 'Rights and Risks to Vulnerable Communities: Physician-Assisted Suicide: A Common Law Roadmap for State Courts'. *Fordham Urban Law Journal* **24**.

Middlewood, S, G Gardner et al (2001) 'Dying in hospital: medical failure or natural outcome'. *J Pain Symptom Manage* **22**: 1035-41.

Onwuteaka-Philipsen, B, A van der Heide et al (2003) 'Euthanasia and other end-of-life decisions in the Netherlands in 1990, 1995, and 2001'. *Lancet* **362**(9381): 395-9.

Otlowski, M (2001) *Voluntary Euthanasia and the Common Law.* Oxford, Oxford University Press.

Palmer, H (1957) 'Dr Adams' Trial for Murder'. *Crim LR*.

Parker, MH, CM Cartwright et al (2008) 'Impact of specialty on attitudes of Australian medical practitioners to end-of-life decisions'. *Med J Aust* **188**(8): 450-6.

Proctor, R (1988) *Racial hygiene : medicine under the Nazis.* Cambridge, Mass, Harvard University Press.

Quill, T (1991) 'Death and dignity. A case of individualised decision making'. *N Engl J Med* **324**(10): 691-4.

Quill, T, R Dresser et al (1997) 'The rule of double effect – a critique of its role in end-of-life decision-making'. *N Engl J Med* **337**(24): 1768-71.

Rachels, J (1975) 'Active and passive euthanasia'. *N Engl J Med* **292**(2): 78-80.

Randall, F and RS Downie (1996) *Palliative care ethics : a good companion.* Oxford, Oxford University Press.

Singer, P (1993) *Practical ethics.* Cambridge, Cambridge University Press.

Smith, R (2000) 'A good death. An important aim for health services and for us all'. *BMJ* **320**(7228): 129-30.

Steinhauser, K, E Clipp et al (2000) 'In search of a good death: observations of patients, families and providers'. *Ann Intern Med* **132**: 825-32.

Townsend, SC and J Hardy (2008) 'End-of-life decision-making in intensive care: the case for an international standard or a standard of care?' *Intern Med J* **38**(5): 303-4.

van der Maas, P, J van Delden et al (1991) 'Euthanasia and other medical decisions at the end of life'. *Lancet* **338**: 669-74.

van der Maas, P, G van der Wal et al (1996) 'Euthanasia, physician-assisted suicide, and other medical practices involving the end of life in the Netherlands 1990-95'. *N Engl J Med* **335**(22): 1699-705.

Veldink, JH, JH Wokke et al (2002) 'Euthanasia and physician-assisted suicide among patients with amyotrophic lateral sclerosis in the Netherlands'. *N Engl J Med* **346**(21): 1638-44.

Ward, B and P Tate (1994) 'Attitudes among NHS doctors to requests for euthanasia'. *BMJ* **308**: 1332-4.

Whittle, B and J Ritchie (2000) *Prescription for murder: The true story of Dr Harold Shipman.* London, Time Warner.

Williams, G (1958) *The Sanctity of Life and The Criminal Law.* London, Faber and Faber.

Zinn, C (1996) 'Australian doctor builds "coma machine".' *BMJ* **314**: 1501.

CHAPTER 27

PUBLIC HEALTH

Case 1 – the Nazi war on cancer

'*Early detection was a centrepiece of Nazi-era cancer propaganda. Physicians lamented the number of late stage cancers presenting in their offices – especially among women, given the growing conviction that tumours of the uterus or breast found early stood a much greater chance of being healed ... Hans Hinselmann, inventor of the colposcope (an illuminated optical device used to screen for uterine and cervical cancer), predicted in 1938 that if his device were widely used, mortality from these diseases would virtually disappear. He also cautioned that physicians who failed to use it were complicit in the annual death of 40,000 women from uterine and cervical cancer worldwide.*

In the Nazi era, the propaganda designed to encourage (especially) women to consult their physicians was kicked up several notches. Radio and newspaper announcements urged women to submit to annual or even biannual cancer exams, while men were urged to check up on their colons as often as they would check out the engine of their car. "Cancer counselling centers" were established in most German cities, both to popularise the value of early detection and to advise people with cancer of their therapeutic options ...

There were many in the German medical community who took this need for early diagnosis quite seriously. A 1939 article in the Viennese medical weekly, by the antitobacco misogynist Robert Hofstätter, argued that all German women over the age of thirty should be required to undergo a semiannual gynaecologic cancer exam. ... He also claimed that women who failed to submit to such exams would be punished by placing an extra financial burden on the insurance bureaucracy. Women who refused the exams and chose to "go it alone" were to be awarded only half the normal insurance coverage in the event that they became sick from cancer.' (Proctor 1999)

Public health is an enormous and diverse field, including infection control, epidemiology, environmental and occupational health, health promotion, health policy, health resource allocation, developing world and global health concerns, and genetic screening. The WHO definition of public health is 'the science and art of preventing disease, prolonging life and promoting health through the organised efforts of society' (Calman and Downie 2002). Public health has also been described as 'what we, as a society, do collectively to assure the conditions for people to be healthy'. As Childress has noted, this definition suggests not only the need for cooperative behaviour but also the need for relationships built on trust and shared values (Childress, Faden et al 2002).

Public health has made enormous contributions to global health – the provisions of sewerage systems, the creation of public space, the rebuilding of slums, and the reduction in infectious diseases such as diphtheria and smallpox. But it should be remembered that, historically, public health has also created a great deal of human suffering through policies of forced sterilisation, mandatory screening of ethnic populations, eugenic policies, the detention of people with infectious diseases, quarantine and social isolation of individuals and communities, and the construction of conservative notions of 'sexual health'. The practice of public health is always, and has always been, value-laden. Until recently these values have been implicit, rather than explicit, and have been assumed to be 'good' rather than being open to critical examination (Bauman, O'Hara et al 2000). In recent years, however, many of the ethical issues raised by public health have been the focus of professional and philosophical examination, including the nature and implication of human rights in health care, the pursuit of equity, the tension between local and global concerns, the tension between individuals and population health goals and values, the role of the community in policy and decision-making, and the duties, obligations and limitations of the state in providing and protecting the health of the population (Buchanan 2000).

The ethical issues raised by public health differ somewhat from those raised in clinical medicine. Public health is unavoidably political, because political contexts are inextricably linked to the social determinants that influence health. And while there is general agreement that public health has a strong moral foundation, there is debate whether this should be based on ethical principles or on the more politicised foundation of human rights.

Discussion about ethical principles in public health tends to emphasise the concept of equity, and the tensions between autonomy, beneficence and justice. Some argue that one or other of these principles should take precedence, or that new principles that incorporate several of these concepts should be developed. For example, Baum considers that over-emphasis on autonomy and individualism is undesirable (Baum 2002), whereas Calman and Downie argue that the principle of 'utility' – of maximising the total benefits for the population involved – should be taken on as a first-order principle along with autonomy, beneficence, non-maleficence and justice (Calman and Downie 2002). Lawrence Gostin argues that public health must be concerned with principles such as individual liberty, autonomy, privacy and property, and also with collective goods such as the sustained community action needed to ensure health benefits (Gostin 2001).

Frameworks of public health ethics have been developed from communitarian, utilitarian, principle-based and duty-based perspectives. For example, the framework developed by Childress and colleagues suggests that public health should produce benefits to the population as a whole while minimising harms, fairly distributing benefits and burdens, respecting individual autonomy and privacy and honouring prior commitments (Childress, Faden et al 2002).

Many different principles have been emphasised for assessing the moral appropriateness of public health interventions including:

- effectiveness;
- proportionality (any moral harm resulting from a public health intervention must be outweighed by the benefits gained);
- necessity (the intervention must produce an outcome that cannot be created by another less invasive intervention);
- least infringement (only the least amount of restriction or breach of privacy should occur);
- public justification (any policies or interventions must be justified through public debate);
- reciprocity (individuals who comply with public health interventions, particularly where their own freedoms are restricted, should be supported); and
- transparency (interventions should be accountable and evaluated for their effectiveness).

Cole has suggested that there are three main reasons why public health interventions require moral justification: because they are enforceable by the police power of the state, because they are supported by public funds and because they are often intrusive (Cole 1995).

Public health research

While public health research follows many of the same moral guides as does clinical research, it also differs in ways that have important moral consequences:

- It examines different units of study, including families, communities, social networks and institutions.
- It may 'offer' varying degrees of participation to those being studied, from situations where participants may not even be aware that they are being studied to situations in which participants are regarded as research collaborators and help determine what research is done, how it is done and how the data is analysed and the results disseminated.
- It may emphasise prevention rather than cure, focus on health and not disease and be concerned primarily with social determinants of health rather than simple interventions.
- It may assume consent, or seek consent from communities as well as from individuals.
- It may privilege epidemiological methods, quantitative methods, database studies and tissue-banking research.
- It may seek population correlations rather than individual causation.
- It may be difficult to identify, quantify and balance the burdens and benefits of research as the benefits may accrue to a population whereas the burdens may fall on individuals.
- It may risk privacy/breaches of confidentiality through the use of data-linkage studies.

Unlike consent in clinical trials, 'group' or 'collective' consent is often used in public health research, and may supplement or even supplant individual consent. With group consent, information is usually made available to representatives authorised in some way to make decisions on behalf of members of the group. Group consent is most often used with research involving stored samples, or diseases occurring within a particular ethnic group or community.

Group consent may be justified if there are genuine risks of harm to the group as well as to individuals, or if groups are seen as being particularly worthy of respect or requiring protection. Questions about group consent include: how one defines membership of the group in question (by shared culture? shared history? geographical location? or self-identification?), and who legitimately may represent a group or community. A particularly difficult question is whether group consent can ever be entirely sufficient, or whether it can only be an additional mechanism to increase support for and participation in research. Group consent may also reinforce ill-founded ideas about the 'naturalness' of certain types of groups, such as racial groups, entrench stereotyping and increase the risk of discrimination.

An additional issue affecting public health research is that because it studies the processes, institutions and services of the state it may at times be the subject of state censorship, particularly where it investigates subjects such as the perceived failing of health services, harms to the environment or health status of vulnerable groups (Yazahmeidi and Holman 2007).

Human rights

To many public health practitioners, biomedical ethics does not provide a strong basis for public health action. They argue that the only way to protect the health of vulnerable people is through enforcement of human rights (Mann 1997).

Human rights are a particular subset of rights that are distinguishable because they apply across borders, political systems, cultures and religions. Human rights have a strong basis in international law, and it is this basis that is so attractive to commentators such as Mann. If we could persuade or even force countries to uphold their obligations under human rights law, perhaps this would provide an appropriate framework for international public health! However, there are also difficulties with human rights – they can be imprecise and vague, are open to interpretation and may conflict. In practice, using international law to enforce human rights has had variable success (Robertson 2006), and some authors have concluded that it has little practical value in some of the more important debates in public health in Australia (Gray and Bailie 2006).

Rights and ethics often overlap and complement each other and both are intrinsic to consideration of public health. Ethics and human rights build on similar principles, including respect for persons, justice, dignity, autonomy and privacy. They both provide strong arguments for action and both may be restricted according to consideration of outcomes and competing values. But ethics and rights differ in important ways. Ethics governs the relationships between people and between communities through codes, theories and laws, whereas rights establish the obligations of the state and others in power to populations and individuals through international treaties, declarations and natural law. Rights are 'what governments can do to you, cannot do for you and should do for you' (Gruskin and Tarantola 2002).

There is considerable scepticism about the practical implication of human rights for health. It is important to distinguish the concept of human rights as used in international law from the much more common use of informal concepts of human rights in health debates. The language of rights is often used far more loosely than is justifiable. All sorts of entitlements may be claimed as human rights. The 'Beastie Boys' tell us that we have to 'Fight for the right to party', and commentators such as Collard suggest that human rights even include such entitlements as access to petrol bowsers (Collard, D'Atoine et al 2005) – but while these may be rights in some communities, they are surely not human rights. O'Neill points out, 'it is too easy, all too easy, to proclaim illusory rights (there is rather less temptation to proclaim illusory obligations)' (O'Neill 2002).

Claims on human rights are often made as an emotive way of attempting to persuade – rather than as a reasoned application of international law or ethics. Using the rhetoric of human rights in this way can be very useful. Claiming a right is a powerful act:- it can recruit followers, initiate government action, and call up the might of international law. However, the widespread claiming of rights that have little basis in law or reason brings up a larger question about the ethics of attempts to persuade people (see below).

Epidemiology, preventative and community medicine

The 'father' of epidemiology is often identified as the London anaesthetist Dr John Snow. In 1854, an epidemic of cholera in London was traced to contaminated water from the Broad Street pump in Soho. John Snow disabled the pump handle – resulting in a rapid decline in the incidence of new cases of cholera (Cook 1996).

It is interesting to think of John Snow's actions from the point of view of people who depended upon the Broad Street pump for their drinking water. Some of them would have been grateful, but others would probably have regretted having to walk further for their water. Some probably thought Snow to be a busybody or just wrong, and that a better approach would have been merely to warn people of the risks and to let them do as they wished.

Since Snow's time, epidemiology has evolved from largely being concerned with the spread of communicable diseases to being concerned with all aspects of human health. As the scope of epidemiology increased, ethical reservations about the right of public health practitioners to intervene in the lives of others continued to be expressed. For example, in 1923, the American satirist HL Mencken wrote:

> Hygiene [the term used at the time for public health] is the corruption of medicine by morality. It is impossible to find a hygienist who does not debase his theory of the healthful with a theory of the virtuous. The whole hygienic art, indeed, resolves itself into an ethical exhortation. This brings it, at the end, into diametrical conflict with medicine proper. The true aim of medicine is not to make men virtuous; it is to safeguard and rescue them from the consequences of their vices. (Mencken 1922)

663

Mencken feared that much of the agenda of public health actually hides a moral agenda that is at odds with individual autonomy. However, this is not necessarily a fear that the enterprise of public health shrinks from. For example, the *Oxford Textbook of Public Health* discusses health promotion (one of the branches of Public Health) as follows:

> The health promotion movement is value driven in a way in which medicine ordinarily is not. It is committed to the view that there are better and worse ways of living one's life, and that there are better and worse ways of organising society and distributing its goods and services. In other words health promotion has moral and political commitments. (Calman and Downie 2002)

Public health measures also raise ethical concerns because recipients of public health interventions rarely request them but may receive them without their consent. Indeed, in the past there has sometimes been a presumption that public health measures are always morally justifiable and that there is little need for accurate or complete information transfer. It has also been assumed at times that a range of means of influence may reasonably be brought to bear on a reluctant public including education, persuasion, regulation and coercion (O'Neill 2002b). As Leeder has noted:

> Much public health action is taken on behalf of a faceless, anonymous, collective known only by the name public, for reasons that may not be made clear to them and over which they exercise no choice. Not always is all of the truth disclosed: occasionally public health politely keeps silent and at times for what appear to be excellent reasons. At other times the silence of public health is far from golden. (Leeder 2004)

This state of affairs is clearly unsatisfactory, and we believe that the reasoning behind any decision to treat the public should be transparent and open to critique. Consent, whether of the community or the individual, cannot ever be assumed.

Public health research interventions are invariably targeted at specific populations. Examination of the history of public health reveals how vulnerable populations may benefit from such interventions or may be stigmatised or harmed by them. It is also the case that, either through the priorities that policymakers set or the way that interventions are enacted, certain populations may be specifically excluded from public health interventions or may fail to benefit from them. This is classically the case with many health promotional campaigns, such as programs to encourage healthy eating and exercise, which are often taken up by those who need them least and miss those who are most in need. Indeed, those who are already marginalised, such as the poor, socially disadvantaged, ethnic minorities, the mentally ill and disabled, may be least likely to benefit from many public health interventions.

Autonomy, regulation and persuasion

Public health ethics is both concerned with health and with the environment in which health can be maintained. Because of these dual interests, public health ethics is situated in an uneasy domain between biomedical ethics and environmental ethics.

According to O'Neill:

> Much of biomedical ethics has concentrated on the individual patient, her rights and her autonomy; demands that medical professionals respect autonomy and rights have become a constant refrain. The implicit context of nearly all this work is the medical system of a developed society with much hospital-based medicine. Topics such as the distribution of health care within these medical systems, public health and global health distribution have been pushed to the margins in much of bioethics. Perhaps these topics have been marginalized because individual autonomy is viewed as central to medical ethics.
>
> Writing on environmental ethics has more often focused on public beliefs and public harms. Here individual autonomy is quite often seen as a source of harms, and there has been a steadily increasing emphasis on the consequent need to limit individual autonomy. Standard examples of such controls include the prohibition on discharge of raw sewage or toxic chemicals, regulation of standards for vehicle emissions or building insulation and requirements for high safety standards in biotechnology. Contemporary discussions in environmental ethics seldom view the autonomous 'life-style' choices of individuals adequate for protecting the environment. They increasingly highlight the importance of stewardship of the environment and argue that this requires public regulation and enforcement, sometimes international regulation and enforcement. (O'Neill 2002)

Public health ethics at times emphasises individual autonomy, but also at times emphasises public regulation and enforcement. There are inevitable strains between these two approaches, particularly centring on the role of individual autonomy in public health interventions. One example that illustrates some of these ethical tensions in public health is the response of public health practitioners to tobacco smoking.

Tobacco and public health

The control of tobacco smoking has become one of the major interests of modern public health. It provides a useful example of some of the ethical issues surrounding the public health enterprise.

If smoking was an entirely voluntary act, taken up by competent adults of their own free will, and not affecting others, there would be little role for public health. Its main role would be to inform of risks in an unbiased fashion and to prevent the habit spreading to children where there may be questionable evidence of decision-making capacity. Other than this, the rule of autonomy suggests that we should allow people to do what they wish. Also, if smoking were entirely voluntary, there would be little role for public health action at the government/corporate level, since such action would limit an autonomous choice.

On the other hand, if smoking were an entirely involuntary act, then there would be a clear role for public health – to lobby and act at a government and corporate level to stop access to cigarettes, and thereby prevent its ill-effects. There would be no role at an individual level for such things as gory photos and warnings on cigarette packets, because these would be unlikely to influence a behaviour which was non-voluntary but would merely distress people. The only real reason for public health to engage with the public on the issue would be to justify and explain its higher level actions.

In fact, smoking is probably best seen as a behaviour that has both voluntary and involuntary aspects, and the public health response attempts to address both of these aspects (Roemer 1993; Wikler 2004). However, there is a risk that the interventions that are directed at the voluntary aspects of smoking (ie, presentation of gory photos on cigarette packets) only serve to alienate and stigmatise those for whom smoking is involuntary. Similarly, interventions aimed at limiting access and restricting the environments of smokers, may also be seen as infringing the rights of those for whom smoking is a voluntary choice.

Many of the arguments for limiting cigarettes are based on the idea that smoking is not just a risk to the individual smoker, but also to those who do not smoke. Arguments that smoking hurts others have tended to focus on two main areas – the costs to society and the effects of passive smoking. But a case can be made that public health practitioners have exaggerated the risks of smoking to others (Sullum 1998; Copas and Shi 2000).

The costs of smoking to society are often emphasised by the anti-smoking lobby. However, many studies suggest that smoking, although causing higher health-care costs in middle age, result in savings for society in the long term, because of both the taxes that smokers pay on cigarettes, and because smokers die at a younger age, thus avoiding the need for longer pensions or social security entitlements. For example, a 1990 study found that lifetime health-care costs were actually lower for smokers than non-smokers (Lippiatt 1990), and a 1997 study estimated that in a population where no one smoked, the costs of health care would be 7% higher among men and 4% higher among women (Barendregt and et al 1997). It is possible that the non-economic costs of smoking – early loss of loved ones, pain and suffering from emphysema and similar qualitative factors – outweigh these economic considerations, although how to weigh such factors will always be a matter of controversy. However, arguments that look only at the economic costs of smoking, and ignore the economic benefits of smoking, also misrepresent the true picture.

The risks of passive smoking have probably also been misrepresented. Epidemiological studies provide evidence that second-hand smoke causes disease in adults and children including respiratory symptoms, exacerbation of asthma, cardiovascular disease, lung cancer SIDS, asthma, otitis media, and acute respiratory illnesses (Hirayama 1981). However, some of these risks have been exaggerated in the public mind by the way that they are represented.

Epidemiologists usually recommend against giving 'relative risk estimates' when discussing harm, as people are easily mislead by relative risk data. The preferred method of communication is to give absolute risk data instead. In public health campaigns against unhealthy behaviours, such as campaigns against passive smoking, it is rare to see any statistics used other than relative risk estimates. The authors were unable to find absolute risk estimates for passive smoking in any of the public health websites devoted to this topic, however it is possible to work these risks out. One commonly cited relative risk estimate is that exposure to environmental tobacco smoke is associated with approximately 20% higher risk of lung cancer for non-smokers. However, since the risk to non-smokers of dying from lung cancer is only 1 in 200 (Rudd and Rabbitts 2002), this is only a one in 1000 increase in absolute risk of death from lung cancer. This absolute risk is never quoted in public health literature about passive smoking, whereas the relative risk increase of 20% is commonly used instead.

It has also been pointed out that the risks of smoke probably come from many different types of smoke, not just from tobacco. The implications for smoke-free policies for Aboriginal smoking ceremonies, camping, barbeques, log fires and the like have not been explored with anything like the enthusiasm for the risks of tobacco (Chapman 2008). Smoking may serve important social and cultural functions such as social bonding and identity formation for Middle Eastern cultures via smoking water pipes, and via sharing cigarettes for Aboriginal people.

The desire to ban or allow tobacco in various workplaces and places of recreation has probably less to do with the immediate risks to health within these environments, but more to a general desire to decrease smoking by making it more difficult. Economic, ideological and anecdotal arguments can overpower scientific evidence in either supporting or restricting smoking in bars and clubs, hospitals or workplaces. So, for example, while the risk of second-hand smoke in external spaces such as recreational areas, beaches, sporting stadia and hospital grounds must be minimal it may still be banned for the political purpose of health promotion.

We believe that there is a definite role for public health lobbying against smoking at the government and institutional level, but this should be somewhat constrained by the fact that some smoking is voluntary and we should not unnecessarily restrict voluntary actions. The public health move to make smoking in private cars with children illegal would be one example where this may have gone to far.

There is also a role for public health in attempting to dissuade individuals from smoking, although this must be tempered by the facts that the risks to others of smoking are sometimes exaggerated, and that for some people it is an involuntary act. We should therefore not expose smokers to unnecessary stigmatisation or discomfort. Public health has a role of informing the public in an unbiased fashion of the risks of smoking, and there is a definite role for public health in preventing smoking in children – as they do not necessarily have the capacity to make an informed decision.

Such a moderate role of public health in smoking is frequently exceeded by current public health campaigns. Smokers feel stigmatised and are exposed to graphic medical images (often of extremely rare complications of smoking), and governments are encouraged to introduce draconian anti-smoking laws (Bayer 1997). However, it should be remembered that, if unchecked, idealism and rhetoric may ultimately undermine trust in health-care institutions and policy-makers.

Vaccination

Many public health interventions, such as vaccination for prevention of infectious diseases in childhood, quarantine and social isolation for control of pandemic infections, and food fortification for prevention of congenital and acquired disorders arising from vitamin deficiency, are predicated on the notion that individual benefit arises only where a population or group is 'treated'. This raises a number of ethical concerns, including the right to refuse, the balance between public good and individual rights, and the moral justification for restrictions of freedom (King 1999).

Vaccination has been hailed as one of the greatest of public health interventions – saving millions of lives, preventing significant morbidity and eradicating disease (smallpox). Few public health strategies are as cost-effective, with measles vaccination programs alone demonstrating a cost-benefit ratio of nearly 43:1 (Department of Health and Aging 2003). The rationale for its use is simple – healthy individuals can generally be safely protected from potentially fatal and/or debilitating disease through administration of a vaccine and when a certain level of coverage is reached the community as a whole benefits from what is known as 'herd immunity'.

But while vaccination appears desirable, a series of questions must be asked before introduction of any vaccine including:

- what evidence is there that it works?
- who receives the benefit – the individual or the community or both?
- who should be immunised?
- what vaccines should they receive?
- when should they be immunised?
- what are the risks of vaccination?
- who bears those risks? and
- how should vaccination be supported by public policy?

Vaccination/immunisation confers a high-value benefit to the majority at a cost to a minority. There is clear evidence, for example, that measles vaccination may cause a severe or life-threatening adverse reaction in one in a million doses (Isaacs, Kilham et al 2004). But for those who bear these costs, which include infection, developmental disorders and adverse reaction to vaccination, the cost is massively disproportionate to any benefit they may have received. Given this, and given the fact that we cannot identify in advance and protect those who may be harmed by immunisation, any vaccination program must have a strong scientific and moral foundation, and must provide support to those who are harmed by it.

Public health interventions often rely on utilitarian justifications for action (the greatest good for the greatest number). Different types of vaccination have different benefits, and risks, meaning that they require different ethical analysis. For example, while we may promulgate the importance of vaccination for influenza, if people refuse vaccination then respect for their human rights and liberty means that we do not generally insist that people be vaccinated (unless they are health workers).

In recent years there has been considerable debate about whether immunisation, particularly in childhood, should be compulsory, in part because of concerns that falling vaccination rates in some countries have reduced 'herd immunity' and led to the 're-emergence' of infectious diseases, such as pertussis (Isaacs, Kilham et al 2004). Compulsory vaccination strategies, or strategies linking vaccination with school admission, while allowing for limited religious objections, are practised in some countries, including the United States and the Netherlands. In Australia some States mandate that health professionals be vaccinated against vaccine-preventable infections as a condition of employment. In contrast, childhood immunisations are not compulsory but are supported by a national immunisation policy, public education campaigns and financial incentives for both parents and health providers. As a consequence, Australia has achieved vaccination coverage levels of approximately 91-94% in children up to the age of 12 months (Lawrence, MacIntyre et al 2004; Salmon, Teret et al 2006). Thus, with persuasion, and with community support, rather than restriction of liberty through mandatory immunisation policies, Australia has been able to achieve very high rates of coverage.

In this regard it is also important to recognise that the majority of unvaccinated children are not immunised because of various practical difficulties parents face in getting their child vaccinated, or because of concerns regarding the adverse effects of vaccination, and not because of philosophical or religious objections to vaccination (although this does occur) (Dare 1998; McIntyre, Williams et al 2003).

Verweij and Dawson have proposed seven principles for immunisation:

1. It should target serious diseases that are a public health problem.
2. Each vaccine, and the program, must be effective and safe.
3. The burdens and inconvenience for participants must be as small as possible.
4. The programs burden/benefit ration should be favourable in comparison with other prevention programs.
5. Collective programs should involve a just distribution of benefits and burdens.
6. Participation should be voluntary unless compulsory vaccination is essential to prevent a concrete and serious harm.
7. Public trust in the vaccination program should be honoured and protected. (Verweij and Dawson 2004)

If one applies these principles in different situations, it is easy to see why vaccination may be mandatory in certain (restricted) situations – such as for health workers in high risk contexts; elective in others settings, such as with tetanus vaccination; and in all situations may be adopted or abandoned as evidence of harm emerges.

Some members of the public have great concerns about vaccination. While these are sometimes unrealistic, it is unfortunate that people who do not vaccinate their children may be represented by public health as neglectful, ignorant, overly anxious, irrational, anti-intellectual or unaware of the risks of diseases prevented by these strategies (Baum 2002). In 1997, the Australian Public Health Association even criticised a television program that discussed the risk of immunisation on the grounds that it concentrated on the rare tragic consequences of vaccination – precisely the information that many parents would wish to be aware of. In fact, interviews with parents who avoid vaccination suggest these decisions are often rational and made on the basis of the parents' knowledge of risk (Baum 2002). The question arises as to why public health feels it has to go this far?

Menken's idea – that public health practitioners have an underlying 'moral' interest in people's health – probably applies at least in part here. Anti-smoking and pro-vaccination lobbyists may use figures and facts in persuasive ways (this is known as rhetoric), rather than in purely informative ways. This use of rhetoric is precisely what many practitioners object to when it is used by tobacco or drug companies or anti-vaccination lobbyists. Is it then ethical to use these techniques in the interests of health, rather than in the interests of commerce?

The ethics of rhetoric

In an episode of *South Park* called 'My future self and me', two of the characters are visited by depressing, dirty men claiming to be their future selves – who ended up that way because they tried drugs when they were young. Later it turns out that this was a hoax – from a company that specialised in keeping children away from drugs. They overhear a salesman telling parents how it is okay to lie to kids if it keeps them away from drugs (<http://en.wikipedia. org/wiki/My_Future_Self_n'_Me>). Exaggerating and lying about the risks of drug taking, premarital sex and sexually transmissible diseases have all been common tactics to attempt to persuade children out of behaviours that their parents disapprove of.

Exaggeration of the costs of tobacco and the risks of passive smoking is also part of a wider picture within public health, in which misconstruing risks is sometimes seen as legitimate method to improve public health. A good example is the 'grim reaper' ads of the Australian HIV campaign that deliberately set out to make low-risk groups overestimate their chance of contracting HIV. Other examples include portraying an 'epidemic' of chronic disease, at a time when death rates from most chronic diseases are falling, and the declaration that any alcohol intake in pregnancy puts the foetus at risk. (It has been suggested that this campaign will cause an increase in abortions of normal foetuses by mothers concerned that a few drinks have damaged their babies (Stark 2007).)

Appiah illustrates this approach with an anecdote about a medical missionary in remote Africa who is unable to persuade people that they should boil their water, because they do not believe in germ theory. Then 'the mission-ary has another idea. Look, she says, let me show you something. She takes some water and boils it. See, she says, there are spirits in the water, and when you put it on the fire they flee: those bubbles you see are the spirits escaping, the spirits that make your children sick. Now boiling water makes sense' (Appiah 2006). The missionary has not told the truth, but she has prevented disease – surely she is justified in such a white lie.

Public health practitioners no doubt also feel justified in using the language of persuasion (rhetoric) rather than the language of information because what they are doing is in the public interest. But distorting the truth is morally problematic. Although Appiah's example is only a story, the Australian experience suggests Aboriginal people want to know about germ theory and are fascinated by it. Telling people the 'true story' may be preferable to trying to persuade them (<http://www.ards.com.au/health.htm>). Telling people the truth and allowing them to decide for themselves also fits better with the principle of autonomy.

Many groups are trying to persuade us about our health behaviours. Drug companies, tobacco companies, the alcohol industry and fast food manufacturers all use marketing techniques to have us buy their messages. Even governments suppress the truths that they do not want to hear while trumpeting those that fit their agendas (d'Arcy and Holman 2008). If we object to the techniques of marketing use by such organisations, we cannot really take them on ourselves while maintaining the moral high ground. We believe that it may be reasonable to use rhetoric in the few situations where the health of the community is at stake from an individual's actions – including some types of immunisation, irresponsible drinking and unsafe driving. But in most situations where individual choices do not affect others – such as smoking, and obesity – there is no reason to persuade, and information delivery is the main requirement. In general, wherever possible it is better to stick to the facts.

Evidence-based medicine

Information in public health is largely derived from studies of groups of people, and its interventions are often applied to groups of people rather than individuals. However, many of the lessons that can be learnt from groups seem as though they should be able to be applied to individuals. For example, if a study of a large number of smokers shows that about half die from diseases related to smoking, this suggests that we can say to a smoker that they have a 50% chance of dying from their smoking. (It is important to note, however, that this apparently simple statement is extremely contentious in the philosophy of both mathematics and medicine, since probabilities cannot really be applied to individuals in any rigorous way. This is the basis of a major ideological rift in probability theory between the 'classical' and 'Bayesian' schools.)

In the past decade and a half, an extremely influential movement in medicine – 'Evidence-based medicine' (EBM) has come to dominate much clinical discussion. Evidence-based medicine is the idea that data derived in formal ways from experiments involving large groups of patients should be the 'base' of decision-making about individual patients. Evidence-based principles and practices have come to have a profound influence on the setting of biomedical research priorities, the generation of public health and clinical practice guidelines and the implementation of these guidelines in practice. At present, all funders and publishers of biomedical research and all policymakers and practitioners of clinical and public health medicine are expected to understand and implement the principles of EBM. The term 'evidence-based' has also become influential in nursing, policy and education.

EBM has developed great moral authority because it promises that both individual patient care and public health interventions can be shown to be effective, safe and efficient, that these decisions and standards can be determined (and therefore judged) in a transparent manner, and that this form of decision-making is reliable, objective and value-free.

There is not anything inherently wrong with medicine that is based on evidence, on the contrary, this is what we should be striving for. However, 'evidence based medicine' is different from 'evidence' 'based' 'medicine', in that the term 'EBM' refers to particular, ideologically and philosophically specific concepts of evidence, medicine and the relationship between them, and these specific concepts do have some difficulties.

What is EBM?

EBM first arose from the work of a group of epidemiologists and biostatisticians at McMaster University in Canada. The initial formulation of EBM was very clear: it was that medicine should be based on the 'conscientious, explicit and judicious use of current best evidence', and that 'best evidence' should be identified using epidemiological and biostatistical ways of thinking. By defining its methods like this, EBM attempted to distinguish itself from traditional medicine, which relied on unsystematic observations, medical intuition, pathological principles and clinical experience (Sackett, Rosenberg et al 1996).

What constitutes the 'best research evidence' has generally been specified in EBM by the 'evidence hierarchy' – a ranking of study designs based on judgments about which types of studies are most likely to provide estimates of 'truth'. Over 60 such evidence hierarchies exist (West, King et al 2002), and the vast majority place randomised controlled trials (RCTs) and meta-analyses near the top of the hierarchy.

Gradually EBM became incorporated into medical curricula worldwide, colonising other fields of practice such as nursing, complementary medicine and public health, and spawning journals, research centres and websites (Goldenberg 2006; Kemm 2006). EBM provided power, authority and legitimacy to a new group of academics and practitioners; it provided a means of managing increasingly complex data; it promised access to knowledge about the best, and least harmful, therapies; and it carried great normative power – so that to practise any other form of medicine seemed to be abrogating one's moral responsibilities (Gupta 2003).

However, many aspects of EBM have also been challenged – including its theoretical structure, foundations and assumptions, its methods, its practice, and its translation into policy (Shahar 1997; Lau, Ionnidis et al 1998; Tonelli 1998; Denny 1999; Miles, Grey et al 2004).

The main criticisms of EBM may be summarised as follows:

- that it may displace clinical judgment and patient values and narratives from decision-making, even where it does take account of these;
- that EBM (or at least the authority it confers) may be used to justify restriction of expenditure and patient choice;
- that it gives priority to those things for which there is good data – in a world where not everything is amenable to measurement according to the methods preferred by EBM – the RCT, systematic review and meta-analysis;

- that it promises, but is unable to, apply epidemiological data to the care of individuals;
- that it is systematically biased towards individualised interventions;
- that it has been unsuccessful in disseminating and implementing evidence into practice;
- that there is no evidence that EBM has produced better patient outcomes that 'traditional medicine' (Norman 1999); and
- that it may restrict patient choice and limit the options available to clinicians and patients (thereby limiting the autonomy of each).

Advocates of EBM have often responded to these criticisms by pointing out that they arise from a misunderstanding of EBM, result from the enthusiastic but misguided application of 'crude' EBM, or are irrelevant as they simply point to the limitations inherent in all research/practice (Gallagher 1999; Brody, Miller et al 2005).

EBM has responded to its critics by changing and incorporating some of the criticisms. A major change is that EBM has been re-defined as 'the integration of best research evidence with clinical expertise and patient values' (Sackett, Straus et al 2000). Sackett and colleagues described the new model of EBM with a Venn diagram with three interlocking circles termed research evidence, clinical expertise and patient preferences. This diagram was subsequently further modified to place evidence within interpretive art and clinical experience (Haynes, Devereaux et al 2002). Likewise, development of models of 'evidence-based patient choice', which combine EBM and patient-centred care, have emerged in response to criticisms of EBM that it excluded the patient and was concerned more with the clinicians and the passive transfer of information (Hope 2002).

It has become increasingly difficult to define exactly what EBM is and what it is not. The initial ideas about hierarchies of evidence, about the promise of EBM and about its translation into practice have all become increasingly fragmented as EBM has tried to accommodate many of the challenges about the nature, biases and value of evidence. Brody, for example, in a defence of EBM, describes how 'sophisticated EBM' 'accepts the best available evidence may be studies of different methodology, may be pathobiological data or may even be clinical experience and fully accepts uncertainty' (Brody, Miller et al 2005).

While this degree of intellectual dynamism is to be commended, it creates substantial problems for the utility and (apparent) simplicity of EBM. It is also impossible not to be reminded of Popper's description of problems that may emerge from theoretical accommodation. As he notes in *Conjectures and Refutations*:

> Some genuinely testable theories, when found to be false, are still held by their admirers–for example by introducing ad hoc some auxiliary assumption, or by re-interpreting the theory ad hoc in such a way that it escapes refutation. Such a procedure is always possible, but it rescues the theory from refutation only at the price of destroying, or at least lowering, its scientific status. (Popper 1989)

But if EBM has lost some of its original (apparent) coherence, what it has retained is its rhetorical force and its moral status. Thus, while it may be increasingly hard to recognise or describe EBM, it remains even harder to speak against it.

Ethics and EBM

EBM promises to be the most effective means for identifying and implementing the safest, most effective and most efficient health-care interventions. If it is correct, then we are morally obliged to practise EBM (Gupta 2003). But even if we accept the goals of EBM, there is good reason to question the assumptions and practices of EBM and to ask whether unreflective application of EBM can actually create harm.

Some of the ethical problems that arise from EBM concern the methods used to generate research data, and the way that EBM prioritises health problems that can be investigated with certain sorts of research method. A major problem for EBM is that many outcomes of medicine are not adequately measurable or comparable (such as pain), some may not be measurable at all (such as justice or cultural integrity) and some (such as quality of life) may not even be adequately definable (Kerridge, Lowe et al 1998). This requires either that these outcomes are somehow excluded from any calculation of efficacy or benefit, that some value is somehow assigned to such outcomes, or that such outcomes are placed outside the realm of evidence but within another domain relevant to decision-making, such as patient preferences or context, which in turn still requires some means for balancing it against empirical evidence.

The other consequence of this difficulty in defining and measuring all the relevant outcomes of health care is that it is more likely that we will conduct research into those things we can test and more likely to publish the results of studies we can easily understand and incorporate into our decision-making.

For example, parents making decisions about the use of an adrenalin syringe for a child with possible peanut anaphylaxis may decide not on the basis of extensive epidemiological and immunological data regarding risk but on the basis that if they made a decision that resulted in harm, however rationally that decision were made, they might regret it in the future. Similarly, while patients considering whether to go ahead with a bone marrow transplant may choose not on the basis of a careful consideration of the risks and benefits of transplant in their situation, but on the basis that as they confront death there is, in reality, no choice.

While it would seem highly desirable to integrate different kinds of knowledge into EBM, the recognition of qualitative or non-empirical kinds of knowledge presents a major challenge for EBM (Tonelli 1998).

Some alternative formulations to EBM have been proposed to attempt to address these issues. One alternative is to base medical decision-making not around evidence, but around values. 'Values-based medicine' has been posited as an alternative to EBM on the grounds that health care is primarily a moral enterprise based on universal values, such as caring and compassion and that these values are pervasive and are the major determinants of decisions about health, clinical practice and research (Petrova, Dale et al 2006).

Another alternative is to clearly separate the different ways of knowing such that EBM is used only as a tool to evaluate outcome derived from quantitative research – and kept distinct from other types of knowing and from other influences on decision-making, such as narrative, qualitative data, sociological and anthropological research data, pathophysiological data, and patients' goals and values. Mark Tonelli has made a case for this type of process, arguing that it would more closely mimic the 'real world' of clinical care, allow for the integration of different forms of evidence, and still enable assessment of the quality of evidence, within each category of evidence (Tonelli 2006). In a landmark paper he outlined the five topics relevant to medical decision-making:

- empirical evidence – derived from clinical research;
- experiential evidence – derived from clinical experience and from expert knowledge (of others);
- pathophysiological rationale – based on underlying theories of physiology, disease and healing;
- patient values and preferences – derived from interaction with individual patients;
- system features – including resource availability, societal and professional values, legal and cultural concerns.

Tonelli argues that none of these topics takes priority over the other and any may prove determinative in a particular clinical decision.

For Tonelli the task for clinicians is to weigh up the various warrants for action by employing both practical and theoretical reasoning skills (phronesis) and by comparing their patient to paradigm cases from the literature. This approach is appealing but it remains unclear how this approach would actually work at the level of policy-making.

PUBLIC HEALTH AND THE LAW

What is public health law? Chris Reynolds, one of Australia's leading public health lawyers, has said that a general definition of public health law might be that:

- it is the specific, often long-standing, statutory responses that assist and empower public health regulators in the range of areas where they work;
- it is the body of law and legal practice that affects public health practice and the public's health more generally;
- it recognises that changing existing laws and practices that damage the public's health is as significant a task for those involved in public health law, as the supporting of laws which stand to improve public heath. (Reynolds 2004)

In this part of the chapter there is a discussion on public health laws with a focus on regulatory approaches to public health, tobacco control, alcohol regulation, food law and cancer registries. The law's effect on communicable diseases is discussed in Chapter 28, and environmental law is discussed in Chapter 32.

Regulatory approaches to public health

Public health regulation has a long history. Reynolds speaks of three periods of public health regulation:

- the *first period*, during the 19th century when the first modern pubic health laws were drafted – these laws deal primarily with environmental hazards, or nuisances, related to air, food and water quality. They allow people to make complaints about such nuisances, and for authorities to inspect and investigate such nuisances. These laws eventually made their way into the groundbreaking *Public Health Act 1875* (UK), a model on which Australian legislation is based. During this time we also see the rudimentary beginnings of occupational health and safety laws, with the introduction of factory legislation. Initially these laws, like the *Health and Morales Apprentices Act 1802* (UK), aimed to protect the children, by reducing their working hours to 12 hours per day and providing them with cleaner accommodation (Tooma 2008). By the mid-19th century the laws aimed to protect adult workers as well, by introducing such requirements as the fencing-off of machinery, forbidding the cleaning of machinery in motion, and mandatory recording of injuries (Tooma 2008);

- the *second period*, during the 20th century, which saw the standardised use of food, alcohol and tobacco laws and the introduction of singular communicable diseases law and the successful introduction of immunisation programs; and

- the *third period*, which saw the introduction of attempts to regulate life-style diseases, relating to obesity and drug use (especially tobacco controls). (Reynolds 2004)

This development of public health law shows that the control of communicable diseases is only one aspect of the protection of the health of the public. Bidmeade and Reynolds note that:

> In the 19th century, public health laws were a "top down" process, imposed by sanitary reformers on those in want of sanitary reform. Public health law was prescriptive. Thus it required parents to vaccinate their children, it contained powers to detain for long periods of time and without any recourse to appeal people suspected of being infected. Late 20th century public health laws are generally less sweeping and less draconian in their powers, and are more concerned with specifying their objects and encouraging processes for community consultation. They are more concerned with the rights of individuals and communities than were earlier Acts. (Bidmeade and Reynolds 1997)

One of the features of public health regulation is the historical tendency for regulation to be justified by pointing out some sort of moral failing on the part of the population. Early controls on leprosy, communicable diseases (particularly, sexually transmitted disease in the sex industry) and on drug use (tobacco smoking by children or alcohol consumption by the working class) all were justified on the basis of the need to correct a moral failing, rather than to address a health problem. Racism, classism and homophobia have also historically coloured pubic health law, as seen in the treatment of European Jewry during smallpox out-breaks, the blaming of African-American men for the spread of sexually transmitted disease, and the treatment of gay men during the HIV-AIDS crisis of the 1980s. There still remains a tendency for moral panics to dictate public health policy, as was seen by the debate about the best way to approach illicit drug use, and responses to the obesity epidemic.

Jane Edginton notes that another theme of public health regulation is that laws in this field involve a conflict between two competing interests – the rights and interests of the individual to privacy and freedom, and the interests of the public to be protected from the spread of disease (Edginton 1995).

Tobacco control

Tobacco use causes significant public health problems and causes a huge burden of disease and death. Given that (unlike alcohol and food consumption) there is no safe level of use for tobacco, it is curious that it was not a highly regulated product until after the 1980s (Reynolds and Woodward 1993). While sales to children were banned in the early part of the 20th century, it was not until the 1980-90s that a more concerted regulatory effort resulted in controls on:

- advertising of tobacco products;
- restriction of access to sale;
- increased penalties for sales to children;
- the banning of promotional activities to encourage use; and
- mandatory labelling and warning statements. (Reynolds 2004)

The regulation is shared between the Commonwealth and the States. The Commonwealth primarily regulates tobacco advertising through the *Tobacco Advertising Prohibition Act 1992* and labelling through the *Trade Practices Act 1974*. The States retain control over issues such as point-of-sale advertising, vending machines, sales to children and passive smoking control. The State and Territory legislation can be found in the following table:

Table 27.1 Tobacco control laws

Jurisdiction	Legislation
NSW	*Public Health (Tobacco) Act 2008*
Qld	*Tobacco Products (Licensing) Act 1988* *Tobacco and Other Smoking Products Act 1998*
SA	*Tobacco Products Regulation Act 1997*
Tas	*Public Health Act 1997*
Vic	*Tobacco Act 1987*
WA	*Tobacco Products Control Act 2006*
ACT	*Tobacco Act 1927*
NT	*Tobacco Control Act 2002*

In some jurisdictions, smoking in a vehicle with a child is prohibited: *Public Health (Tobacco) Act 2008* (NSW), s 30; *Tobacco Products Regulation Act 1997* (SA), s 48; *Public Health Act 1997* (Tas), s 67H(2).

Personal injury litigation against tobacco companies has proven to be difficult in Australia. For example, Rolah McCabe brought an action against the British and American Tobacco group of companies, arguing that she had contracted cancer due to her smoking and that the tobacco giant was responsible, given tobacco's addictive nature. McCabe won at trial as the judge struck out the defence of the tobacco company, on the basis that the company had deliberatively destroyed relevant documents: *McCabe v British American Tobacco Australia Services Ltd* [2002] VSC 73. However, the decision was overturned on appeal by the Victorian Court of Appeal and the High Court refused to grant special leave to appeal. McCabe had died in the meantime: *British American Tobacco Australia Services Ltd v Cowell (representing the Estate of McCabe (deceased))* [2002] VSCA 197. The proceedings were remitted for a new trial, this time with a person representing McCabe's estate. That trial has yet to proceed. In the interim Cowell (McCabe's daughter and personal representative) sought to release documents to the United States Department of Justice and the Australian Consumer and Competition Commission which they had discovered during the first trial. That was permitted by a judge, but then that decision was also appealed and overturned, on the grounds that the documents were privileged: *British American Tobacco Australia Services Ltd v Cowell* [2003] VSCA 43. A former solicitor of the tobacco company also leaked documents to the solicitors for the McCabe estate and the Fairfax press. A number of applications were commenced in New South Wales to prevent the use of that information and an injunction was issued, with the proceedings being transferred back to Victoria: *British American Tobacco Australia Ltd v Gordon* [2007] NSWSC 230. The Victorian Court of Appeal has decided that the documents may be used by McCabe's estate in all its claims: *Cowell v British American Tobacco Australia Services Ltd* [2007] VSCA 301.

Other cases have had more success. In *Scholem v New South Wales Health Department* (1992) 3 APLR 45 and *Sharp v Port Kembla RSL Club* [2001] NSWSC 338, employees were able to successfully claim damages for workplace exposure to smoke.

Alcohol regulation

Reynolds notes that alcohol has traditionally been one of the least regulated drugs in Australia, which is a strange fact given the drug's major effects on public order, violence and personal health (Reynolds 2004).

Initially, alcohol regulation was based on the need for a sober workforce, but the basis for the regulation was the need to regulate a moral failing on the part of drunken workers. Even as modern medicine came to characterise alcohol addiction as a disease, rather than purely as a moral failing, the object of regulatory control was still the individual. During the early 20th century, the *Inebriate Acts* were introduced to incarcerate alcoholics as a way of removing them from the influence of alcohol. Versions of the Acts has survived into the 20th century. They empower courts or medical professionals to order an inebriate into institutionalised care for periods of time (sometimes up to 12 months): *Inebriates Act 1912* (NSW); *Alcoholics and Drug-dependent Persons Act 1968* (Vic). Other Acts provide for drunken persons to detained for short periods of time, if they are a danger to themselves or others: *Public Intoxication Act 1984* (SA); *Intoxicated People (Care and Protection) Act 1994* (ACT), s 4.

The problem with this approach (from a public health perspective) is that, by treating alcohol use as either 'normal' or 'pathological', attention becomes focused on a small minority of drinkers, and the chance to regulate the whole population of drinkers goes begging (Reynolds 2004).

The availability of alcohol is now regulated at the State and Territory level by licensing laws. Initially these laws were concerned with economic regulation but in more modern times public health concerns have started to creep in. Reynolds states that objections to licences being granted may have the ability to protect public health interests particularly from an environmental perspective (Reynolds 2004).

Unlike tobacco products, there are no direct controls on advertising, sponsorship or labelling of alcoholic products. In some jurisdictions there is a requirement for the licensees to promote responsible attitudes in relation to the promotion, sale, supply and consumption of liquor: *Liquor Act 2007* (NSW), s 99; *Liquor Licensing Act 1997* (SA), s 42; *Liquor Control Reform Act 1998* (Vic), s 115A; *Liquor Act 1979* (NT), s 31(4). In Queensland, the law more explicitly targets 'happy hours', 'all you can drink' and 'toss the boss' promotions: *Liquor Act 1992* (Qld), s 148B. Apart from these areas, advertising is generally self-regulated under the *Alcohol Beverages Advertising Code* (ABAC) of the Advertising Federation of Australia. Labelling is similarly self-regulated under the *Food Standards Code*.

Taxation is another public health tool that has an effect on alcohol consumption; however, the pricing structures are complex and do not always encourage changes that were anticipated. A taxation approach was recently adopted by the Australian government in relation to ready-to-drink mixed beverages (RTDs). The Senate Community Standards Committee recommended the increase in tax for these drinks as part of a wider program to reduce drinking in the population, especially younger persons. Senator Moore said in the conclusion to the Report:

> The public health issues of problematic drinking among young people are clear and each action that reduces such drinking makes a contribution in public health terms. For all the reasons listed above the Committee agrees with the vast majority of evidence presented to the Committee, particularly by health and medical professionals, which was supportive of the measure to increase the price of spirit-based RTDs as one of a range of measures to address harmful alcohol consumption in the community and particularly among young people. The Committee notes this is a complex issue and one that will require further effort and input from governments, professional bodies, researchers, treatment and prevention services, media, industry and the community to develop the next steps. (Standing Committee on Community Affairs 2008)

Food law

Food laws have a long ancestry and still represent a significant concern given that millions of Australian are affected by food-borne illnesses every year (Reynolds 2004). The early food laws aimed to prevent price rises and control supply (particularly relating to bread and ale in the *Assize of Bread and Ale* 51 Hen III 1266). Later attention shifted to the alteration of food, particularly the selling of food and drink which was injurious to health, like unsound meat and bread with alum added for whiteness: *Adulteration of Food and Drink Act 1860* (UK); *Sale of Food and Drugs Act 1875* (UK). Australia followed in these regulatory footsteps and by the early 20th century had a complex array of food laws which aim to keep food unadulterated, license particular food providers and control ingredients.

Modern food laws are contained in the following pieces of legislation:

Table 27.2 Food legislation

Jurisdiction	Legislation
Cth	*Food Standards Australia New Zealand Act 1991*
NSW	*Food Act 2003*
Qld	*Food Act 2006*
SA	*Food Act 2001*
Tas	*Food Act 2003*
Vic	*Food Act 1984*
WA	*Health Act 1911*
ACT	*Food Act 2001*
NT	*Food Act 2004*

These laws aim to implement a uniform set of food standards created by the Food Standards Australia New Zealand, a joint Australia and New Zealand statutory authority, created under the Commonwealth Act. The *Australia New Zealand Foods Standards Code* is implemented via the State and Territories' own legislation, in a form of co-operative federalism. Chapter 3 of the Code introduces *Food Safety Standards* for all Australian jurisdictions.

Legal issues concerning obesity are discussed in Chapter 22.

Cancer registries

One of the other public heath tools is reporting of disease. Collection of data on disease occurrence and prevalence provides an important source of data for tracking both communicable and non-communicable diseases. For example, cancer registries exist in all jurisdiction and some jurisdictions also have specific registries for cervical cytology, breast cancer screening and pap smears. The table below highlights some of the registry legislation.

Table 27.3 Cancer Registries

	Legislation
NSW	*Public Health Act 1991*
Qld	*Public Heath Act 2005*
SA	*South Australian Health Commission (Cancer) Regulations 1991* *Public and Environmental Health (Cervical Cancer Screening) Regulations 1993*
Tas	*Public Health Act 1997*
Vic	*Cancer Act 1958* *Cancer (Breastscreen Victoria Registry) Regulations 2003* *Cancer (Reporting) Regulations 2002*
WA	*Health Act 1911* *Health (Notification of Cancer) Regulations 1981* *Health (Cervical Cytology Register) Regulations 1991*
ACT	*Public Health Regulation 2000*
NT	*Cancer Registration Act* *Public Health (Cervical Cytology Register) Regulations*

References

Appiah, K (2006) *Cosmopolitanism: Ethics in a world of strangers.* London, Allen Lane.

Barendregt, J and et al (1997) 'The health care costs of smoking'. *New Engl J Med* **337**(15): 1052-7.

Baum, F (2002) *The new public health.* Oxford, Oxford University Press.

Bauman, A, L O'Hara et al (2000) 'A perspective on changes in values in the profession of health promotion'. *Health Promot J Austr* **18**(1): 3-6.

Bayer, R (1997) 'Discrimination, informed consent and the HIV infected clinician'. *BMJ* **314**: 915-16.

Bidmeade, I and C Reynolds (1997) *Public Health Law in Australia: Its current state and future directions.* Canberra, Australian Government Printing Service.

Brody, H, F Miller et al (2005) 'Evidence-based medicine: watching out for its friends'. *Perspectives in Biology and Medicine* **48**(4): 570-84.

Buchanan, D (2000) *An ethic for health promotion: Rethinking the sources of human well-being.* New York, Oxford University Press.

Calman, K and R Downie (2002) Ethical principles and ethical issues in public health. *Oxford Textbook of Public Health.* R Detels, J McEwen, R Beaglehole and H Tanaka. Oxford, Oxford University Press.

Chapman, S (2008) 'Going too far? Exploring the limits of smoking regulations'. *William Mitchell Law Review* **34**(4): 1605-20.

Childress, JF, RR Faden et al (2002) 'Public health ethics: mapping the terrain'. *J Law Med Ethics* **30**(2): 170-8.

Cole, P (1995) 'The moral bases for public health interventions'. *Epidemiology* **6**(1): 78-83.

Collard, K, H D'Atoine et al (2005) ' "Mutual" obligation in Indigenous health: can shared responsibility agreements be truly mutual?' *Med J Aust* **182**(10): 502-4.

Cook, G (1996) Tropical gastroenterological problems. *Manson's Tropical Diseases.* G Cook. London, WB Saunders Ltd.

Copas, J and J Shi (2000) 'Reanalysis of epidemiological evidence on lung cancer and passive smoking'. *BMJ* **320**: 417-18.

d'Arcy, C and J Holman (2008) 'An end to suppressing public health information'. *Med J Aust* **188**(8): 435-6.

Dare, T (1998) 'Mass immunisation programs. Some philosophical issues'. *Bioethics* **12**(2): 125-49.

Denny, K (1999) 'Evidence-based medicine and medical authority'. *J Med Humanities* **20**: 247-63.

Department of Health and Aging (2003) *Applied economic returns on public investment in health. An epidemiological and economic analysis.* Canberra, Department of Health and Aging: 71-94.

Edginton, J (1995) *Law for the Nursing Profession and allied health care professionals.* Sydney, CCH Australia Ltd.

Gallagher, E (1999) 'P <0.05: Threshold for decerebrate genuflection'. *Acad Emerg Med* **6**: 1184-7.

Goldenberg, M (2006) 'On evidence and evidence-based medicine: Lessons from the philosophy of science'. *Soc Sci Med* **62**(26): 21-32.

Gostin, L (2001) 'Public health, ethics and human rights: a tribute to the late Jonathon Mann'. *J Law Med Ethics* **29**: 121-30.

Gray, N and R Bailie (2006) 'Can human rights discourse improve the health of Indigenous Australians?' *Aust NZ J Public Health* **30**(5): 448-52.

Gruskin, S and D Tarantola (2002) Health and human rights. *Oxford Textbook of public health* (4th ed). R Detels, JE McEwen, R Beaglehole and H Tanaka. Oxford, Oxford University Press: 311-35.

Gupta, M (2003) 'A critical appraisal of evidence-based medicine: some ethical consider-ations'. *Journal of Evaluation in Clinical Practice* **9**: 111-21.

Haynes, D, D Devereaux et al (2002) 'Clinical expertise in the era of evidence-based medicine and patient choice'. *Evidence based medicine* **7**: 36-8.

Hirayama, T (1981) 'Non-smoking wives of heavy smokers have a higher risk of lung cancer: a study from Japan'. *Br Med J (Clin Res Ed)* **282**(6259): 183-5.

Hope, T (2002) 'Evidence-based patient choice and psychiatry'. *Evidence based medicine* **5**(4): 100-1.

Isaacs, D, HA Kilham et al (2004) 'Should routine childhood immunizations be compul-sory?' *J Paediatr Child Health* **40**(7): 392-6.

Kemm, J (2006) 'The limitations of "evidence-based" public health'. *Journal of Evaluation in Clinical Practice* **12**: 319-24.

Kerridge, I, M Lowe et al (1998) 'Ethics and evidence based medicine'. *BMJ* **316**(7138): 1151-3.

Lau, J, J Ionnidis et al (1998) 'Summing up the evidence: one answer is not always enough'. *Lancet* **351**(9096): 123-7.

Lawrence, GL, CR MacIntyre et al (2004) 'Effectiveness of the linkage of child care and maternity payments to childhood immunisation'. *Vaccine* **22**(17-18): 2345-50.

Leeder, S (2004) 'Ethics and public health'. *Int Med Jn* **34**: 435-9.

Lippiatt, B (1990) 'Measuring medical cost and life expectancy impacts of changes in cigarette sales'. *Preventative Medicine* **19**(5): 515-32.

Mann, J (1997) 'Medicine and public health, ethics and human rights'. *Hastings Cent Rep* **27**: 6-13.

McIntyre, P, A Williams et al (2003) 'Refusal of parents to vaccinate: dereliction of duty or legitimate personal choice?' *Med J Aust* **178**(4): 150-1.

Mencken, H (1922) *Prejudices: Third series.*

Miles, A, J Grey et al (2004) 'Developments in the evidence-based health care debate – 2004'. *Journal of Evaluation in Clinical Practice* **10**: 129-42.

Norman, G (1999) 'Examining the assumptions of evidence-based medicine'. *Journal of Evaluation in Clinical Practice* **5**: 139-47.

O'Neill, O (2002) *Autonomy and trust in bioethics.* Cambridge, UK, Cambridge University Press.

Petrova, M, J Dale et al (2006) 'Values-based practice in primary care: easing the tensions between individual values, ethical principles and best evidence'. *British Journal of General Practice* **56**(530): 703-9.

Popper, K (1989) *Conjectures and Refutations: The Growth of Scientific Knowledge*. London and New York, Routledge.

Proctor, R (1999) *The Nazi war on cancer*. Princeton, Princeton University Press.

Reynolds, C (2004) *Public Health: Law and Regulation*. Sydney, Federation Press.

Reynolds, C and A Woodward (1993) 'Tobacco and Children: What can we learn from the early legislation in Australia?' *Tobacco Control* (2): 152.

Robertson, G (2006) *Crimes against humanity – the struggle for global justice*. London, Penguin.

Roemer, J (1993) 'A pragmatic theory of responsibility for the egalitarian planner'. *Philosophy and public affairs* **22**: 146-66.

Rudd, R and P Rabbitts (2002) Lung cancer: epidemiology, causation, genetics. *Oxford Textbook of Oncology*. R Souhani, I Tannock, P Hohenberger and JC Horiot. Oxford, Oxford University Press.

Sackett, D, W Rosenberg et al (1996) 'Evidence based medicine: what it is and what it isn't'. *BMJ* **312**: 71-2.

Sackett, D, S Straus et al (2000) *Evidence-based Medicine: How to Practice and Teach EBM*. Edinburgh, Churchill Livingstone.

Salmon, DA, SP Teret et al (2006) 'Compulsory vaccination and conscientious or philosophical exemptions: past, present, and future'. *Lancet* **367**(9508): 436-42.

Shahar, E (1997) 'A Popperian perspective of the terms "evidence-based medicine".' *Journal of Evaluation in Clinical Practice* **3**: 109-16.

Standing Committee on Community Affairs, AS (2008) *Ready-to-drink alcohol beverages*. Canberra, Senate Printing Unit.

Stark, J (2007) Abortion fear over no-alcohol-in-pregnancy advice. *The Age*.

Sullum, J (1998) *For your own good: The anti-smoking crusade and the tyranny of public health*. New York, The Free Press.

Tonelli, M (1998) 'The philosophical limits of evidence-based medicine'. *Academic Medicine* **73**: 2234-40.

Tonelli, M (2006) 'Integrating evidence into clinical practice: an alternative to evidence-based approaches'. *Journal of Evaluation in Clinical Practice* **12**(3): 248-56.

Tooma, M (2008) *Safety, Security, Health and Environmental Law*. Sydney, Federation Press.

Verweij, M and A Dawson (2004) 'Ethical principles for collective immunisation programmes'. *Vaccine* **22**(23-24): 3122-6.

West, S, V King et al (2002) Systems to Rate the Strength of Scientific Evidence. Evidence Report/Technology Assessment No 47. *AHRQ Publication No 02-E016. Rockville, MD:* RTI-UoNCE-bPCuCN 290-97-0011. Rockville, MD, Agency for Healthcare Research and Quality: 64-88.

Wikler, D (2004) Personal and social responsibility for health. *Public health, ethics and equity*. S Anand, F Peter and A Sen. Oxford, Oxford University Press.

Yazahmeidi, B and CD Holman (2007) 'A survey of suppression of public health information by Australian governments'. *Aust NZ J Public Health* **31**(6): 551-7.

CHAPTER 28

INFECTIOUS DISEASES

Case 1

LD is a 22-year-old physiotherapist who was accidentally scratched by an unsheathed needle that was left in the bed of a patient with AIDS. As soon as she realised what she had done, she reported the incident to a private infectious diseases specialist, and commenced on a course of anti-retroviral medication. She did not, however, report the incident on a normal 'incident report' form, nor let any of her colleagues know about it as she feared that it may become public knowledge. The hospital did not find out about the incident, so they were unable to introduce measures to prevent such episodes happening again.

Case 2

CR is a 20-year-old student-nurse who is working on placement in a haematology outpatient department. One morning he wakes with a cold. Should he go to work?

Case 3

Following the September 11 attacks on the World Trade Center, a number of letters containing anthrax spores were sent to media and political figures in the USA resulting in five deaths. The fear that this generated caused a massive increase in spending in the area of bioterrorism – some of it directed to the biological warfare defence facility at Fort Detrick in the USA, where scientists began working on the origin of the agents used. It soon became apparent that the agent had actually originated from the biological warfare defence facility at Fort Detrick. Suspicion fell upon one scientist, who was eventually exonerated. Another scientist at Fort Detrick – Bruce Ivins – then became the main suspect, but he committed suicide shortly before his arrest.

Fort Detrick was created in the middle of World War II as the centre for America's biological warfare efforts. In 1969, Richard Nixon renounced the use of biological weapons and limited research to defensive measures only. Scientists turned to developing defensive measures against biological attack – although this also seems to have involved creating new agents to develop defences against. Bruce Ivins helped create the anthrax vaccine that soldiers in the first Iraq war were vaccinated with. This was later withdrawn because of side-effects. The motives of Ivins are unknown, but it has been suggested that they may have been to emphasise the importance of vaccination against anthrax for the coming Iraq offensive.

Infectious diseases are, by definition, contagious. The ethical implications of this have only been recently taken up by bioethicists (Francis, Battin et al 2006). The key issues are that one person's actions (such as by behaving in ways that would spread an infection) may threaten the health of other individuals and society as a whole; and the measures required to control or eradicate this risk (including mandatory reporting, surveillance, contact tracing, isolation and quarantine) may require the infringement of widely accepted human rights, professional obligations and civil liberties.

Some other aspects of infectious diseases that make them ethically significant are the high morbidity and mortality associated with some infectious diseases (smallpox, for example, allegedly killed between 300-540 million people during the 20th century – more than all the wars and epidemics of that century combined), their acuity, their treatability and preventability, their high socioeconomic impact, their distribution (particularly the fact that the burden of illness is borne most heavily by the poor) and their possible use as agents of warfare (Miller, Engelberg et al 2001; Selgelid 2005; Cooper 2006; Smith, Battin et al 2006).

One aspect of infectious diseases that has not received great attention in the ethics literature is that the ethical problems associated with them vary greatly from disease to disease. This means that a good knowledge of the biology of different diseases and treatments is essential for any discussion of ethics. An example of this is with immunisation – the ethical issues associated with immunising against tetanus (a condition in which the person immunised is the sole beneficiary of the strategy) are quite different from the ethics of polio immunisation (in which the person immunised is unlikely to derive any benefit), and to rubella immunisation (in which men are immunised with the aim of decreasing the risks to women of getting the disease and causing harm to foetuses). In this chapter we examine the ethics of infectious diseases primarily by examining two recent epidemic diseases – HIV/AIDS and SARS, and a common, but sometimes overlooked, health concern – health-care associated infections (HAIs).

HIV/AIDS

The evolution of HIV prevention, treatment and care over the past quarter century is one of the great successes of medical science (International AIDS Society 2007).

AIDS was first recognised when reports of an increased incidence of infections and malignancies in homosexual men appeared in the United States in 1981. In 1983 the Human Immunodeficiency Virus (HIV) was identified as the causative agent of AIDS. It was soon found that the natural history of AIDS progresses from an acute HIV syndrome to an asymptomatic stage and eventually to the development of AIDS.

HIV is transmitted by sexual contact, transfusion with blood or blood products, maternal/foetal and neonatal pathways and via breast milk. Heterosexual sex is the most common mode of transmission worldwide, particularly in the developing world. This stands in contrast to North America, Western

Europe and Australia where over 80% of cases are among homosexual men or intravenous drug users. The pattern of HIV transmission throughout some Asian countries such as India, Thailand, Cambodia and Burma is different again, with HIV epidemics commencing among injecting drug users and/or sex workers and subsequently spreading to the general population (Bollinger, Tripathy et al 1995). Globally, intravenous drug use is responsible for about 10% of new cases, but this is becoming the leading cause of exposure in parts of Asia and Eastern Europe (Maher, Tachedjian et al 2007).

By 2004, there were estimated to be about 40 million people living with HIV infection, and more than 20 million had died of AIDS. Two-thirds of the world's infected persons were in Africa (where HIV prevalence approaches 40% of the adult population in some countries) and one-fifth were in Asia. 1.1% of all people between 15 and 49 years of age worldwide were infected with HIV. In 2003 there were a total of 12.1 million children in sub-Saharan Africa who had been orphaned by AIDS – an increase of 2.5 million from 2001 (Steinbrook 2004). Dramatic increases in the number of AIDS cases are predicted for the two most populous nations on earth, India and China.

AIDS incidence in Australia (1.5 per 100,000 population per year) is similar to that in the United Kingdom and Canada but less than that of other Western countries such as France, Spain and the United States. The incidence of HIV infection peaked in Australia around 1985. After that there was a period of decline in incidence, but this has started to rise again since 2002 (<avert.org>).

Without treatment, HIV typically takes 9 to 11 years to progress to full-blown AIDS. The discovery of effective combination treatments for HIV infection changed this prognosis, and many people with access to these medications now have much better outlooks. Given the human rights, development and security threat posed by HIV/AIDS (where security broadly includes environmental, personal, food, economic, health, communal and political security), the WHO set out to provide antiretroviral treatment to three million people in developing countries by the end of 2005. According to Steinbrook:

> Even if this ambitious plan succeeds – which is by no means assured – only about half the people who need treatment will be receiving it. Despite substantial progress, there remains a large gap between the number of people in developing countries who need treatment (4 to 8 million) and the number being treated (about 400,000, as of the end of 2003, including about 100,000 in sub-Saharan Africa). "Dismal" would be a charitable way of describing the treatment-coverage rates in many countries. Botswana, Senegal, and Uganda are three African nations that are doing better. Brazil, which has a large-scale universal program for the distribution of antiretroviral medications, is another developing nation that has made substantial progress against the epidemic. Botswana, which has one of the highest HIV infection rates in the world, has instituted routine HIV testing and is expanding access to treatment. (Steinbrook 2004)

By 2007, it was estimated that only 28% of adults and 15% of children with AIDS worldwide were receiving anti-retroviral treatment (Maher, Tachedjian et al 2007).

The SARS epidemic

The severe acute respiratory syndrome (SARS) emerged in Southern China in late 2002, spread to Hong Kong, and then travelled via international air routes to 29 other countries around the world (Heymann 2004). In the Middle Ages it took three years for the plague to spread from Asia to Europe. The SARS virus crossed from Hong Kong to Toronto in 15 hours (Singer, Benatar et al 2003). In the 1980s, it took two years to identify HIV as the cause of AIDS. In 2003, a virus associated with SARS was isolated in two weeks and its entire genome was sequenced in two weeks more (Bloom 2003).

During the short course of the SARS epidemic, 8098 people worldwide were known to be infected with SARS and there were 774 confirmed deaths (Hill 2003). Cost estimates for the entire outbreak go as high as $11 billion.

Following the original SARS epidemic, a number of other minor outbreaks appeared. Three of these incidents were attributed to breaches in laboratory biosafety, and in one case this resulted in the death of a family member outside the laboratory. There is an ongoing risk of further outbreaks from wildlife in Southern China.

Health-care associated infections (HAIs)

Unlike pandemic infections, health-care associated infections (HAIs) generally do not cause social disruption or widespread public alarm and have not been regarded as a moral problem or at least one of interest to the bioethics community. This is both remarkable and inappropriate, as HAIs are associated with considerable excess mortality, morbidity and expense, and are largely preventable (Harbarth, Sax et al 2003). It has been estimated that, in 2002, 1.7 million HAIs occurred in hospitals in the United States and caused 99,000 deaths (Klevens, Edwards et al 2007) (<http://www.cdc.gov/ncidod/dhqp/hai.html>).

In Australia, there are estimated to be about 200,000 HAIs each year, linked to between 2000 and 3500 deaths in Australian hospitals – more people than die on Australian roads. These figures are disturbing but the likelihood is that the frequency and impact of HAIs will increase as rates of colonisation and infection with multiresistant organisms (MROs) increase and new antibiotic resistant organisms emerge.

But the major reasons that HAIs are such an important ethical issue relate less to the burden of disease and more to the cause of HAIs and the measures that may be used to prevent them. There is evidence that HAIs can be prevented by a range of measures including environmental cleaning, immunisation of health-care workers, institutional antibiotic control policies, surveillance cultures and isolation of colonised or infected patients, monitoring of selected HAI indicators and, most significantly, hand washing. But it is equally clear that such measures have achieved only moderate success due largely to poor implementation by health authorities and poor compliance by health-care professionals (Pittet, Allegranzi et al 2006; Whitby, McLaws et al 2006; Aboelela, Stone et al 2007; Huskins 2007).

The failure of health professionals to consistently wash their hands before and after patient contact appears to be largely resistant to education and persists in the face of clear evidence that it causes harm to patients. Recent proposals for improving HAI rates have included attempts to change institutional and professional 'culture' through public disclosure of infection rates, tying government funding to hospital 'performance' and the introduction of 'penalties' for non-compliance, such as mandatory education, counselling and withdrawal of clinical privileges. These measures challenge the autonomy and hegemony of the (medical) profession and suggest that new approaches to patent safety and public accountability must pay close attention to factors that motivate or deter particular behaviours. Yet such measures must be based on reliable evidence, since the introduction of mandatory behaviours and punishments for those who do not concur may have wide-ranging, and sometimes negative, side-effects.

Mandatory testing, treatment and confinement

The major intervention that was developed for the SARS epidemic was a strict process of quarantine. In Singapore, authorities used thermal scanners, web cameras and electronic surveillance to enforce quarantine. In Canada, quarantine was enforced voluntarily, but with warnings that people who broke quarantine could be institutionalised against their will (Bayer and Fairchild 2007). In Taiwan alone 130,000 people were placed in quarantine (Smith, Battin et al 2006).

The response to the HIV epidemic, while originally including quarantine in some countries, ended up using very different strategies. According to Bayer and Fairchild:

> Emerging from the complex mix of ideological, moral, and political forces was a commitment to treating AIDS differently from what the history of epidemic control might have suggested. In lieu of the compulsory tradition, that often involved mandatory case reporting by name, contact investigation, and where necessary the use of isolation, an 'exceptionalist' perspective took hold. ... A simple dictum emerged: no public health policy that violated the rights of individuals could be effective in controlling the spread of HIV. There was no tension between public health and civil liberties. Indeed the protection of civil liberties was critical to the public health. (Bayer and Fairchild 2007)

Why were these reactions different? A number of factors can be identified – the difference in the biology of the two organisms, different cultures in the countries where the diseases were first recognised, and different contexts of the disease – with HIV originally rising in the context of increasing gay militancy and self-assurance.

Some authors have suggested that, in retrospect, the quarantine provisions introduced in the SARS epidemic were overly stringent. The success of strategies introduced to control the outbreak both in areas where voluntary quarantine was instituted and in those where involuntary quarantine was instituted provides some support for this idea.

However, there continue to be requirements for compulsory quarantine for some infectious diseases. An example of this occurred in 2007 when Mr Andrew

Speaker, an American public injury lawyer was diagnosed with extensively drug-resistant tuberculosis (XDR TB) in the USA. XDR TB is caused by strains of bacteria that are resistant to the most effective drugs. Less than 30% of patients with XDR TB can be cured, and more than half die within five years of diagnosis. Mr Speaker was advised that he should not travel and an order was placed to restrict him from leaving the United States, which he evaded by crossing by car to Canada and then flying to Europe for his wedding and honeymoon. Eventually he was tracked down in Europe where an attempt was made to prevent him using commercial air services again, which he evaded by flying from the Czech republic to Canada. On returning to New York he was compulsorily detained and hospitalised while a process of screening everyone who had travelled in planes with him was instituted. (<http://www.hhs.gov/asl/testify/2007/06/t20070606a.html>; <http://edition.cnn.com/2007/HEALTH/conditions/05/31/tb.flight/>)

In the early days of AIDS, precautions such as these were also sometimes used, both out of ignorance and as part of the stigmatisation of the condition. Such precautions were in fact unnecessary, reinforcing the need for careful and sensitive treatment of the issue of quarantine. This may be made more difficult by the fact that newly emerging diseases often have unknown biology when they first arise.

Confidentiality

Health-care professionals have an ethical obligation and a legal duty to keep all information about patients confidential; except where patients consent to its disclosure or where there is an ethical or legal justification for breaching confidentiality. While the moral obligation to maintain confidentiality is important in all therapeutic relationships, protecting information about HIV is particularly important because of the social stigma of AIDS and the very real risk of discrimination against people with HIV/AIDS.

The issue of confidentiality in HIV provides one example of the conflicts between the ethics of care of the individual and the ethics of public health. As well as a need to keep information about individuals secret, there is also a real need to monitor the HIV epidemic, and to use information to stop it from progressing. Particularly in the early days of the HIV epidemic, there was great uncertainty about how information about people with HIV could be gathered and used. This was eventually solved in Western countries by anonymous testing of HIV status, legislation protecting individuals from having their HIV status revealed, and coexisting legislation preventing infected individuals from knowingly spreading HIV.

One of the more difficult issues in clinical practice is the obligation that health professionals have to inform contacts of those with HIV of their risks. It is clear that the duty to maintain confidentiality is not absolute and it may at times be overridden by competing moral considerations. Considerable controversy has surrounded the question of whether health professionals should inform the sexual partner(s) of a patient who has tested HIV positive but refuses to practise safe sex or inform their partner of their HIV status. Individuals may wish to retain the confidentiality of such information for many reasons, including the fear of discrimination, guilt, denial, or fear of losing the care and support of those he or she loves, rather than simply a callous disregard for the welfare of others. But at times health professionals are in a position where they may only be able to prevent harm to others by breaching confidentiality.

Many health professionals and ethicists believe that disclosure may be ethically required where there is a risk of definite or significant risk of harm to an innocent third party. Some have suggested that obligations arising from beneficence and non-maleficence impose a duty to care for others that overrides any moral obligation to maintain confidentiality. Stated in consequentialist terms, the magnitude of harm that accrues from an uninfected person being infected with HIV far outweighs the harm done to the individual whose confidences are breached (Gillett 1988). It has also been argued that the partner of an HIV-positive patient has a right to know the patient's diagnosis and assess for themselves what degree of risk they would find acceptable. Whether they choose to stay in the relationship, leave the relationship, or stay but insist on safe sex, is irrelevant – what is important is that they are able to make an informed, autonomous decision about their own lives. When seen in this way, it is the patient's hypocrisy in demanding confidentiality from their carers, but refusing to acknowledge the needs and values of their partner or the generally accepted moral standards of veracity and consent that undermines their own claim to confidentiality and strengthens the justifiability of any breach of confidentiality. This behaviour has been termed 'moral freeloading'.

Yet there are also a number of arguments against breaching confidentiality even in such instances. Many lawyers, civil rights advocates, philosophers and patients have argued that health practitioners' main obligation is owed to the patient and that the harm done to an individual whose confidence is breached (and to future patients) is more serious than the risk of harm resulting from HIV infection of a third party (Magnusson 1994). Effective measures to control the transmission of HIV depend in large part on the trust and cooperation of those infected or at risk of infection. If patients believe that their privacy and rights of confidentiality will not be respected and that they may be subject to prejudice and discrimination, then they are unlikely to seek medical attention or participate in open and honest relationships with their carers. Whether such fears would stop people attending for health care is largely an empirical question and one that remains uncertain (Kegeles, Catania et al 1990).

The legal and moral responses to questions of confidentiality in HIV/AIDS are still evolving. In general, a broad consensus has arisen that health professionals should regard breaching a patient's confidentiality as a last resort and to make exceptions only where patients are known to be having unprotected sex without notifying their partner. What is clear is that, where it is necessary to breach confidentiality, it should be done in a way that minimises harm to the patient, and it should be done only after every effort has been made to discuss the full implications of HIV positivity with patients and their partners. With appropriate counselling and a trusting health professional-patient relationship the vast majority of people with HIV are likely to act responsibly, to practise safe sex and to inform their partners.

Transmission between patients and health workers

A number of cases of occupationally acquired HIV have occurred in health workers in Australia and elsewhere (Macdonald, Elford et al 1995). Cross-infection between patients has also been described, particularly in countries with insufficient resources or procedures to guarantee instrument sterilisation. The best documented case from an industrialised nation was the infection of four patients in a Sydney surgery – most likely due to re-use of a contaminated local anaesthetic vial (Druce, Locarnini et al 1995).

The health professions have responded to the risk of HIV transmission from patients by emphasising the importance of universal (or 'standard') pre-cautions and by instituting systems for 'post-exposure prophylaxis' with anti-retroviral drugs.

'Universal precautions' refers to the use of infection-control measures such as handwashing, gloves, protective eyewear, masks and 'needle-less' procedures for all patients, regardless of their blood-borne virus status. This is justified on the ground that all blood and body fluids should be regarded as potentially hazardous and has become the cornerstone of risk reduction for HIV in Aust-ralian hospitals.

In AIDS treatment, the paradigm of ensuring patient consent led to res-trictions on any compulsory testing for HIV in places such as hospitals and health services (although compulsory testing did occur in many prison systems). In SARS, compulsory screening (via temperature monitoring) did occur, and the use of names in case reports of both SARS and XDR TB illustrates that many of the sensitivities around HIV have not carried over to other infectious diseases.

Refusing to care for patients with infectious diseases

When the AIDS epidemic first became visible, an acrimonious debate within the health professions sprung up about whether health professionals could refuse to care for patients with HIV. The changes that have occurred in HIV treatment from the hospital in-patient setting to the outpatient setting, and the availability of effective treatment for HIV, have decreased the volubility of this debate.

At the beginning of the AIDS outbreak numerous studies showed that many health-care professionals believed that they had the right to refuse to care for HIV/AIDS patients. Reasons for this included fear of contagion and certain death, and religious objections and disapproval of patients' lifestyles (Schneider-man and RM 1992). Some bioethicists even contended that conscientious objection to treating patients with HIV on the grounds of concern for infection risk 'is not only morally permissible, but may even, in the ultimate analysis, be morally required' (Johnstone 1994).

The response of government, patient advocacy groups, health departments and ethicists was to reject refusals to provide care and to reaffirm the obligation expected of health workers to provide care where needed, regardless of race, religion, gender, life-style or HIV status (Daniels 1991; Smolkin 1997). As the HIV epidemic continued a consensus emerged (at least within the HIV and ethics literature) that there was a clear ethical duty for health workers to care for HIV patients. This was in part due to what was seen as the minimal risk of health-care workers contracting HIV in hospitals with universal precautions. This led further to the idea that health workers' obligations to care for patients depended on the risk that health workers were exposed to: at higher levels of risk they would have less obligation, but at lower levels of risk, their obligation would be higher (Reid 2007).

This consensus was turned on its head in the SARS epidemic. SARS was noticeably more dangerous than HIV. Doctors, nurses, paramedics and janitorial staff died while caring for SARS patients. Many health professionals were required to face extremely difficult decisions – should they risk death to care for SARS patients? Was there any way that they could ethically walk away from these people? What if they had children and a family?

These questions led to a larger issue – could any of us live in a society in which the health workers walked away in the face of an epidemic? It became clear that the increasing risk associated with SARS increased the obligation of health workers – not the other way around. For many health workers, this question was not answered by referring to this bigger picture – instead the answers arose from their local situation. As Reid notes:

> Writers in the HIV/AIDS debate imagined that the limits of obligation would be reached when we reached a certain level of risk. SARS took us to vastly increased levels of risk, but at the same time showed that risk is both biologically given and socially determined. The choice is not between past risk levels and current risk levels, but between accepting current risk levels and passing them on to someone else – and particularly because of the elevated risk for healthcare workers, that 'someone else' in SARS was not a hypothetical doctor, whom the HIV patient was left to find on their own, but a colleague in the hospital setting. SARS did raise the question of duty to care for each individual healthcare worker but *ipso facto* raised the question: if not me then who? (Reid 2007)

Health workers have a duty to care for patients with infectious diseases, even if it is at a risk to themselves. This duty may conflict with other duties, and we may not all have the courage to undertake this duty, but it is our duty none-theless.

Pandemics and bioterrorism

Pandemics are epidemics of infectious disease that spread around the world. Human history has been characterised by the recurrent occurrence of pandemics – including the Black Death (which killed one-third of the European population during the 14th century) and influenza (which killed between 20-100 million people in 1918). While the threat of pandemics is always present, pandemics are rare events, and planning for pandemics must be undertaken in a measured way.

In the United States and other Western countries there has been enormous interest in the moral, legal and health implications of bioterrorism since the hijacker's attacks on the World Trade Center in 2001 and the anthrax attacks that followed them (Gostin 2002; Annas 2002). Unsurprisingly, the events of 2001 directed political and public health attention to the threat posed by 'others', facilitated a willingness to sacrifice basic civil liberties as part of a comprehensive public health response to 'bio-threats' and blurred the distinctions between homeland security and security against natural events, such as Hurricane Katrina (Annas 2002). As a consequence, there has been a marked increase in spending on 'biosecurity', and an increase in the amount of infectious disease research influenced by the aims and approaches of the US military (Cooper 2006).

The United States military's history of cooperation with doctors and scientists has led to many good outcomes – including the development of anti-malarial drugs and the investigation of diseases such as yellow fever, Ebola and malaria. However, it has also had some shameful episodes such as the use of anthropology research to direct bombs in Vietnam (Gusterson 2008), the exploitation of Canadian psychiatric patients to develop torture techniques (Klein 2007), the testing of potent hallucinogens and other agents on its own civilians, and the complicity of health professionals in torture of prisoners (Miles 2006). Other armies are probably equally as bad, but their activities have not always been as well documented. In any case, while pandemics inevitably raise security concerns and may require the suspension of individual liberties or human rights in order to protect the interests of the community, the linking of public health and infectious diseases with military interests, processes and standards of justice is generally inconsistent with a plural ethics that emphasises respect for difference, human flourishing, ontological security and community.

One of the features of infectious diseases is that they are dynamic, changing over time, with contact between species and with exposure to anti-microbial agents. New mutations in the influenza virus often arise in Southern China, where pigs, poultry and humans live close together (all of which can harbour varieties of influenza). The emergence of H5N1 strains of bird flu in Southern China, and their spread around the world, has led to a worldwide response to the possibility of a bird-flu pandemic. (The Australian government, for example, reacted quickly to the threat caused by the H5N1 virus, committing over AU\$600 million to pandemic preparedness, and the Commonwealth and State governments responded to the threat of pandemic influenza by developing 'whole of government' strategies to reduce transmission of the virus (Horvath, McKinnon et al 2006).)

How we should respond to such a pandemic depends greatly on the biological behaviour of any new organism (Kotalik 2005). Following the SARS epidemic, Singer and colleagues developed a framework incorporating 10 key ethical values relevant to SARS and five major ethical issues faced by decision-makers. The values included individual liberty, protection of the public from harm, proportionality, reciprocity, transparency, privacy, protection of communities from undue stigmatisation, duty to provide care, equity and solidarity. The major ethical issues raised by SARS included the ethics of quarantine, the privacy of personal information and the public need to know, the duty of care, the 'collateral damage' resulting from measures designed to limit the pandemic (including quarantine, social isolation and triage), and the issues raised by global interdependence (Singer, Benatar et al 2003). Similarly, Torda has suggested a number of ethical principles that should form the basis of public health responses to pandemics (in this case an influenza pandemic) (Torda 2006). These include that responses to a pandemic must be based on the best available evidence, ensure transparency of decision-making, protect workers involved in providing care, embed communication and consultation in the decision-making process, and be accountable and responsible.

A previous example where some of these principles were not followed occurred in the USA response to swine flu. This influenza strain, found in pigs, was also thought to be the start of a flu pandemic, and across the USA many soldiers and health workers were compulsorily immunised against it with an inadequately tested vaccine. This caused hundreds of cases of Guillain-Barré syndrome – a severe disease that led to complete paralysis. In turn this led to the largest successful damages claim in US history (Garrett 1994).

Epidemics and pandemics are a real threat – either arising naturally or from the laboratories of scientists via bioterrorism of biowarfare (Harbarth, Sax et al 2003). In times of emergency, civilian and military responses will occur that will involve health workers, and even place them at risk. Health workers need to give some thought to this possibility, and also be prepared to ensure that an appropriate ethical framework is part of the response to these threats (Gostin 2002; Kotalik 2005).

The 'dual use dilemma'

In 2001, Australian researchers from the Australian National University, aiming to develop a technique to induce infertility in mice as a means of pest control, accidentally produced a 'super strain' of the mousepox virus which was markedly more virulent than the 'wild' strain of mousepox and was resistant to immunisation (Jackson, Ramsay et al 2001). Smallpox researchers soon realised that the same technique – now described in the public literature – could be used to modify smallpox so it could no longer be vaccinated against.

In another study, American scientists synthesised a live polio virus from commercially available strands of DNA in accordance with a map of the polio virus (RNA) genome published on the internet (Cello, Paul et al 2002). This again brought up the idea that diseases that were nearly extinguished could be brought back to life as agents of warfare.

Another recent landmark study in infectious diseases occurred when scientists used fragments of virus recovered from the preserved remains of people who had died in the 1918 influenza epidemic to reconstruct that strain of flu (Kaiser 2005). This was particularly noteworthy as the 1918 influenza epidemic, which followed World War I, killed more people than the war itself. While the epidemic died out as increasing immunity developed in the population, it is likely that, if such an epidemic occurred again today, it would result in a similarly high number of fatalities.

While each of these studies, which were published in peer-reviewed international journals, was scientifically robust and innovative, the investigators and the academic journals that published them have been extensively criticised for providing blueprints for bioweapons. This issue, the potential use of one piece of scientific research for evil or malign purposes as well as for good, has been termed the 'dual use dilemma'.

The 'dual use dilemma' is neither new nor unique to the biological sciences – similar concerns were raised by developments in nuclear science in the early part of the 20th century (developments that ultimately made possible the atomic bombing of Hiroshima and Nagasaki and the nuclear arms race that followed World War II) and have recently been raised by developments in nanotechnology. However, these dilemmas present as extraordinarily complex problems, in part because the biomedical discoveries may lead to significant progress in human health, and in part because the values at stake are of such fundamental importance (Schweber 2000). How then are we to respond to such cases?

The US National Research Council made seven recommendations for dealing with the 'dual use' dilemma. These included:

- education of scientists about the nature of the dual use dilemma in biotechnology;

- mandatory review of research that would render vaccines ineffective, confer resistance to antibiotics or antivirals, increase transmissibility of pathogens, alter the host range of pathogens, enable the evasion of diagnostic modalities, or enable the weaponisation of biological agents or toxins;

- encouraging self-governance by scientists and scientific journals of publications for their potential national security risks;

- creation of a National Science Advisory Board for Biodefense;

- review of existing legislation and regulation relevant to biodefence; collaboration between life sciences, law enforcement and national security bodies to mitigate the risks of bioterrorism; and

- harmonisation of international oversight of the biosciences in line with the USA. (National Research Council 2004)

While many of the recommendations of this report have received broad support, neither voluntary self-censorship by the scientific community (as recommended by the report) nor censorship of science and of publishing by government or regulatory bodies seems appropriate; as both approaches may be biased and ill-informed (Selgelid 2007). It remains unclear as to how real the dual use threat actually is and whether there is a better means for regulating science, protecting public interests and preserving scientific and academic freedom.

LEGAL ASPECTS OF INFECTIOUS DISEASE

Notification of disease

All jurisdictions have legislation that regulates the notification of cases of infectious disease. The obligation falls on health professionals (such as doctors, nurse practitioners, pathologists, laboratory workers) to report to the public health authority when they have reasonable grounds for suspecting that a person has contracted a notifiable disease. The notification is primarily required for the collection of epidemiological data and to monitor the incidence of the disease (a traditional public health function). The failure to notify the health authorities may result in a very heavy fine.

Table 28.1 Australian disease notification legislation and policies

Jurisdiction	Legislation
NSW	*Public Health Act 1991* (NSW)
	Policy Directive PD2006_014, Notification of Infectious Diseases under the *Public Health Act 1991*
Qld	*Public Heath Act 2005*
SA	*Public and Environmental Health Act 1987*
Tas	*Public Health Act 1997*
	HIV/AIDS Preventative Measures Act 1993
	Guidelines for Notification of Notifiable Diseases, Human Pathogenic Organisms and Contaminants 2008
Vic	*Health Act 1958*
WA	*Health Act 1911*
ACT	*Public Health Act 1997*
	Reporting of notifiable conditions code of practice 2006
NT	*Notifiable Diseases Act 1981*

Confidentiality in reporting

In most jurisdictions either the legislation or the reporting policy requires that detail of person's identity be kept off the notification form in cases of HIV/AIDS and other sexually transmitted disease. In New South Wales, identifying information cannot be provided when reporting Category 5 conditions (HIV/AIDS), unless by consent or by order of the District Court. The Director General of Health may seek a court order to disclose the identity of the patient when it is necessary in order to safeguard the health of the public. In Queensland, notifier may give anonymised information, but the Chief Executive has the power to ask for further information, including the full name of the patient and other identifying information. In South Australia, notification of HIV, AIDS, AIDS related death, Hepatitis B or C, and sexually transmitted infections, are done on a separate form which is forwarded automatically to the doctor upon a positive laboratory result. In Tasmania, notification of sexually transmitted diseases is anonymised, unless requested by the Director of Health. The situation is the same in Victoria where Group C and D conditions (primarily sexually trans-mitted diseases and HIV/AIDS respectively) must be reported with anonymity. In Western Australia, the patient's name, address and telephone number cannot be disclosed without consent in the notification of HIV or AIDS, unless the practitioner has reasonable grounds to believe that the patient may engage in behaviour that is likely to put other persons at risk of infection.

Contact tracing

Contact tracing is a method used to track down infection. In some jurisdictions contact tracing is 'essentially a voluntary activity undertaken by the doctor with his or her patient; in other states the Health Department supervises the contact tracing process, and Department employed contact tracers assist doctors when required' (Magnusson 1996). In Queensland, the ACT and the Northern Terri-tory, specific duties are laid upon patients to provide details of contacts and contact-tracing officers are permitted to communicate with the contacts: *Public Health Act 2005* (Qld), Chapter 3, Part 3; *Public Health Act 1997* (ACT), ss 106-109; *Notifiable Diseases Act 1981* (NT), s 9.

Duties to provide information to patients

Patients with communicable diseases are owed the same duties to be informed of material risks relating to their treatment as other patients. In addition, a number of statutory duties are placed on health professionals treating patients with such diseases. These generally require a medical practitioner to provide a patient with information on measures to be taken and activities to be avoided in order to minimise the danger of passing the medical condition to another person: *Public Health Act 1991* (NSW), s 12; *Public Health (General) Regulation 2002* (NSW), reg 5; *Public Health Act 1997* (Tas), s 50; *HIV/AIDS Preventative Measures Act 1993* (Tas), ss 14-15; *Health Act 1958* (Vic), Part VI.

Duties to sexual partners

The obligations to advise the patient on testing and precautions can also give rise to a duty in negligence to the patient's sexual partner. This occurred in *BT v Oei* [1999] NSWSC 1082, where a doctor, who had negligently failed to diagnose HIV infection in his patient, was found liable to the patient's sexual partner for her subsequent HIV infection. The evidence suggested that had the HIV been diagnosed the patient would have taken precautions against infecting his sexual partner. The court found that it was reasonably foreseeable that the patient, if HIV positive, would transmit the virus to a sexual partner. A duty of care was therefore imposed on the doctor.

In *Harvey v PD* [2004] NSWCA 97, a patient (PD) was seen by Dr Harvey, a general practitioner, with her future husband (FH) to be tested for HIV or any other sexually transmitted disease. The GP saw them at a joint consultation, although this fact was not recorded on their individual medical records. There was no discussion about how the results of the tests were to be disclosed.

The test results showed that FH was HIV positive but that PD was not. PD attended the general practice to collect her results but when she asked for FH's results she was told that they were confidential to FH and the results could not be disclosed to her. FH was later told the results of his test but there was no discussion of whether FH intended to tell PD that he was HIV positive. The medical director of the practice saw FH and arranged for him to attend a specialist immunology clinic. FH did not keep his appointment with the immunology clinic. The immunology clinic informed the general practice that FH did not attend his appointment but no one contacted FH or PD.

It appears that FH altered his test results to show that he was HIV negative and showed this to PD. PD married FH and later became infected with HIV. PD sued Dr Harvey and the medical director of the practice.

In the NSW Supreme Court Cripps AJ held that the doctors had breached their duty of care because of:

- the defective pre-test counselling, including not advising the couple that in the absence of consent the doctor was legally prohibited from disclosing any information concerning the HIV or AIDS status of one to the other (*Public Health Act 1991* (NSW), s 17(2)) and not raising with the couple whether the test results were to be disclosed at a further joint consultation or separately;
- the defective advice and counselling given to FH after the result of the test was known; and
- the lack of cross-referencing of the medical records when a joint consultation had been conducted.

The judge found that if the doctors had followed an appropriate course of action they would have been aware of FH's deceit and would have been able to notify the Director-General of Health under provisions of the Act without breaching confidentiality obligations.

The doctors appealed to the NSW Court of Appeal (*Harvey v PD* [2004] NSWCA 97). The court unanimously dismissed the appeal. The majority of the judges (Spigelman CJ and Santow JA) agreed that the initial consultation was flawed, as the issue of the disclosure of the results of the tests should have been explicitly addressed. The judges decided that they did not need to express a view about the other inadequacies identified by the trial judge. Spigelman CJ did express the view, however, that he was not convinced 'that the findings as to defective record keeping were correct'. He also stated that:

> The public policy underlying this strict regime is to ensure that persons are not deterred from submitting to tests by reason of an apprehension that the fact of being tested or a positive result may be disclosed. This purpose is, in my opinion, best served by minimising the potential for disagreement on the provisions which exclude liability. (at [8])

Breaching confidentiality to protect third parties

Magnusson writes:

> One of the questions medical practitioners ask most frequently concerns the limits of the legal duty of confidentiality when an HIV infected patient continues to place unsuspecting sexual partners at risk. The legality of disclosure will depend upon: (i) the scope of confidentiality legislation which differs from state to state; or, where the legislation does not apply, (ii) whether the disclosure is justified under the 'public interest' exception to the duty of confidence, which all health care workers owe in accordance with common law principles. ... The issue is complex because a variety of statutory provisions may be relevant ... It is important to bear two distinct questions in mind when examining the scope of this legislation. First, when an HIV patient objects to disclosure, yet continues to behave irresponsibly, can the doctor inform a sexual or drug-sharing partner of the patient's HIV positive status? Second, can the doctor inform the Health Department, thereby enabling the Department to activate its public health powers? (Magnusson 1996)

In New South Wales, for example, identity can be disclosed via a court order, when it is necessary in order to safeguard the health of the public: *Public Health Act 1991* (NSW), s 18. In Tasmania, the *HIV/AIDS Preventative Measures Act 1993*, s 20, allows a medical practitioner to inform any sexual contact of a patient about the HIV status of that patient, when, after being given a reasonable opportunity:

- the patient fails take all reasonable measures and precautions;
- the patient fails to inform in advance any sexual contact or person with whom needles are shared about their infection; or
- the patient knowingly or recklessly places another person at risk of becoming infected with HIV; and
- the doctor only makes contact with the sexual partners after consultation with an approved specialist medical practitioner.

Compulsory testing, treatment and detention

In all jurisdictions the health authorities have the power to forcibly test, treat and detain a person who is reasonably suspected of suffering from specified infectious diseases. Ordinarily these orders can be made by a top bureaucrat, such as a direct-general of health or chief health officer, and they are then appealable to the courts.

Senanayake and Ferson have described two cases in New South Wales where public health orders were issued to two persons with tuberculosis (Senanayake and Ferson 2004). They outline the effects on the two patients as well as the staff and note that detention does not ensure compliance, understanding or improved behaviour. The staff were also affected by the process, reporting that they felt like jailers in both cases.

Table 28.2 Compulsory testing, treatment and detention powers

	Legislation
NSW	*Public Health Act 1991*, ss 22-23
Qld	*Public Health Act 2005*, ss 113-116
SA	*Public and Environmental Health Act 1987*, s 31-33
Tas	*Public Health Act*, ss 41-42 *HIV/AIDS Preventative Measures Act 1993*, s 10
Vic	*Health Act 1958, s 121*
WA	*Health Act 1911*, ss 251, 263, 273, 293, 307
ACT	*Public Health Act 1997*, ss 113-117
NT	*Notifiable Diseases Act 1981*, s 11

Discrimination

One of the serious problems for people with HIV/AIDS and Hepatitis C is persistent discrimination faced by them and people associated with them. The *Disability Discrimination Act 1992* (Cth) makes it unlawful to discriminate against a person on the grounds of their disability or a disability of any of their associates. The legislation defines 'disability' to include the presence in the body of an organism causing, or capable of causing, disease or illness. The definition includes a disability that presently exists, may exist in the future or is imputed to a person.

There are similar provisions in the State and Territory discrimination law, with the exception of South Australia. There is some doubt that the definition of impairment in the *Equal Opportunity Act 1984* (SA) would extend to cover asymptomatic infection although this has not yet been tested in court. The New South Wales Administrative Decisions Tribunal, however, has considered the case of disability discrimination in the provision of a health service (*Taikato and Nakhle v Western Sydney Area Health Service* [1999] NSWADT 52). Ms Taikato and Mr Nakhle were a couple in a de facto relationship but were unable to conceive a child. Ms Taikato carried the Hepatitis B and Hepatitis C virus. The couple approached a fertility clinic for treatment. The clinic was concerned about the inherent quality of the eggs produced by a female who suffered from Hepatitis C. The conduct in this matter occurred in 1993, before the definition of 'disability' was extended to cover viruses such as Hepatitis C. The tribunal (by majority) concluded that if Ms Taikato did not actively suffer from the Hepatitis C virus she would not have been excluded from the complete IVF program. In the view of the tribunal the clinic did not discharge the onus of satisfying the tribunal that the clinic did not take all practicable steps to assist Ms Taikato in the use of the IVF program. Ms Taikato was awarded $15,000 for the hurt and suffering that she suffered as a result of the discrimination.

The New South Wales *Anti-Discrimination Act 1977* also prohibits vilification on the grounds of HIV/AIDS (but does not cover other diseases such as Hepatitis C).

Criminalising infection

General criminal laws

The intentional or reckless infection of another person with an infectious disease is ordinarily covered by the laws against criminal assault, the infliction of grievous bodily harm and (in cases where death results) homicide. In *Kanengele-Yondjo v R* [2006] NSWCCA 3543, the HIV-positive applicant plead guilty to maliciously inflicting grievous bodily harm on two women whom he infected with HIV after informing them that he was regularly tested and 'would never hurt them'. Kanengele-Yondjo had received counselling and education about his HIV status and was fully informed of the need to engage in safe sex with informed partners. The New South Wales Court of Appeal upheld a sentence of 12 years' imprisonment with a non-parole period of nine years.

Similarly in *R v Reid* [2006] QCA 202, a 37-year-old Queensland gay man was convicted of committing a malicious act with intent. Reid had repeatedly promised his partner that he was HIV negative. Reid had infected his partner as a way of securing their relationship. The Queensland Court of Appeal upheld the conviction and sentence of 10 and a half years' gaol, finding that the actions of Reid were callous in the extreme and that he had shown no remorse.

In *Houghton v Western Australia* [2006] WASCA 143, the accused had had unprotected sex with the victim but had argued that he had made an honest and reasonable mistake that the HIV virus could not be transmitted if he withdrew from intercourse before ejaculating. This was rejected at trial by the judge who found that the belief had not been held by the accused, and that the accused would never had been advised to use withdrawal as a safe sex practice. He was convicted of unlawfully doing grievous bodily harm. A sentence of four years and eight months was upheld on appeal.

Engaging in sexual activity without protection and without informing the sexual partner may still be an offence even when the partner does not get infected. In *R v Parenzee* [2008] SASC 245, the accused was convicted of an act which endangered life or created a risk of serious harm under s 29 of the *Criminal Law Consolidation Act 1935* (SA). Parenzee had had unprotected sex with three woman on numerous occasions, only one of whom ended up contracting the virus. Parenzee had attempted to argue that HIV did not exist but the evidence of his witnesses was said to lack probity by the trial judge and an appeal from that decision was dismissed: *R v Parenzee* [2007] SASC 316. He then appealed on the issue of whether unprotected sex created a risk of serious harm. The Court of Criminal Appeal found that it did. Even though the exact risk of having unprotected sex was not able to be quantified the Court of Appeal was satisfied that it represented a significant risk and was an act which endangered life.

It has also been found that deliberately misleading your sexual partner about the fact you are HIV positive vitiates consent, with the result that otherwise consensual sexual acts become sexual assaults: *R v Cuerrier* [1998] 2 SCR 371. McLachlin J of the Supreme Court of Canada has said:

> Consent to unprotected sexual intercourse is consent to sexual congress with a certain person and to the transmission of bodily fluids from that person.

Where the person represents that he or she is disease-free, and consent is given on that basis, deception on that matter goes to the very act of assault. The complainant does not consent to the transmission of diseased fluid into his or her body. This deception in a very real sense goes to the nature of the sexual act, changing it from an act that has certain natural consequences (whether pleasure, pain or pregnancy), to a potential sentence of disease or death. It differs fundamentally from deception as to the consideration that will be given for consent, like marriage, money or a fur coat, in that it relates to the physical act itself. It differs, moreover, in a profoundly serious way that merits the criminal sanction. (at [72])

What if the accused did not reveal his or her disease status but engaged in safe sex practices? Would this constitute an endangerment to life? In *Police v Dalley* [2005] NZAR 682, Judge Susan Thomas of the Wellington District Court found that it was not endangering human life to have safe sex when HIV positive. The accused had used a condom for penetrative sex. On that count the judge accepted the defence evidence that condoms are 80 to 85 per cent effective, The judge found that:

> The duty under s 156 [of the *Crimes Act 1961* (NZ)] is to use 'reasonable' precautions and care. The duty is not to take failsafe precautions. Reasonable-ness is an objective standard. On the basis of the evidence, I find that in the circumstances Mr Dalley did take reasonable precautions and care. (at [49])

The accused had also had oral sex without using a condom. The judge found that the risk of transmission during oral sex was so low that it was not necessary to use a condom.

Specific laws criminalising infection

In addition to the general provisions above, specific crimes have been created in all jurisdictions (see Table 28.3 opposite) which deal specifically with situations where a person either knowingly or recklessly infects another person.

On the 16 January 2009, Michael John Neal was sentenced to 18 years and nine months jail (with a non-parole period of 13 years) for nine counts of attempting to infect a person with HIV, two counts of rape, three of reckless conduct endangering a person and one of procuring sex by fraud. He also pleaded guilty to drugs charges, child pornography charges and a charge of indecent acts with a child under 16. It was alleged that Neal had been involved with organising 'conversion parties' where uninfected men would be intentionally infected without their consent. Neal had become known to the Chief Health officer of Victoria who had issued orders against Neal, requiring him to cease having un-protected sex and to stay away from venues where gay men attend for sex. The order also required him to make daily contact with the Department of Human Services. Later the Department relaxed the conditions after considering Neal's argument that his viral load was undetectable. Neal was found not guilty by the jury of two counts of deliberately infecting a person with HIV, arguably because of his belief that he could not transmit HIV due to the undetectable viral load (Collins 2008; ABC News 2009).

Table 28.3 Criminal offences relating to communicable disease

	Legislation
NSW	*Public Health Act 1991*, s 12 (offence to fail to take reasonable precautions in a public place against spreading diseases in Categories 2-5), s 13 (offence to have sexual intercourse if you have a sexually transmissible medical condition without informed consent)
Qld	*Public Health Act 2005*, s 143 (offence to recklessly spread a controlled notifiable condition, or recklessly transmit a controlled notifiable condition)
SA	*Public and Environmental Health Act 1987*, s 37 (an infected person must take all reasonable measures to prevent transmission of the disease to others)
Tas	*Public Health Act 1997*, s 51 (person with notifiable disease must take reasonable measure to prevent transmission) *HIV/AIDS Preventative Measures Act 1993*, s 20 (an offence for a person with HIV to knowingly or recklessly infect another unless there was informed consent)
Vic	*Health Act 1958*, s 120 (offence to knowingly or recklessly infect another person, with a defence of informed consent)
WA	*Health Act 1911*, s 264 (offence for person with an infectious disease to wilfully expose themselves in public without taking precautions), s 310 (an offence to knowingly infect any other person with a venereal disease)
ACT	*Public Health Regulation 2000*, reg 21 (duty to take reasonable precautions when you suspect that you have a transmissible condition)
NT	*Notifiable Diseases Act 1981*, s 7 (a person who has reasonable grounds to believe that he or she may be an infected person has to consult a medical practitioner at the first reasonable opportunity)

Should infecting others be criminalised?

While there is no doubt that the activities of people like Neal are disturbing, questions need to be asked about the use of criminal law as an effective strategy to combat infection. The risk of prosecuting infection is that the disease is further stigmatised and infected parties will have even more reason to engage in duplicitous and misleading behaviours (Weait 2007). From a public health perspective, it may be that these prosecutions actually contribute to an increase in the number of infections. The World Health Organization has said:

> In criminal law, individuals are held responsible through penal sanctions for their actions that have been deemed to be unlawful. The emphasis is on individual responsibility for his/her deeds and the establishing of the moral culpability that underlies the claim for criminal culpability. For effective and convincing HIV/AIDS programming, it must be stressed that for all people there exists and remains a responsibility toward themselves and towards others to possibly minimize the risk of further transmission. This is crucial to safer sex campaigns, sexual health promotion campaigns and initiative as regards HIV and STI testing. Therefore, participants recommended that the potentially negative impact on public health and human rights of criminalization of so-called reckless and/or negligent transmission be carefully considered and that Member States consider the decriminalization of reckless/ negligent transmission and exposure-cases (prosecutions and convictions of

people living with HIV that engaged in unsafer sex without disclosing to their HIV-negative partners but where no HIV transmission occurred). Criminal law was viewed as a blunt instrument that can neither adequately capture the complexity of the contexts in which HIV transmission occurs nor deal effectively with matters such as the relative probability of transmission. (World Health Organization 2006)

Nevertheless, it is hard to see how any criminal law system could fail to react to the deliberate infection of another person with a communicable disease. WHO has stated that, unlike negligent and reckless infection, criminalisation can be justified in cases of intentional transmission.

References

ABC News (2009) 'HIV infected man jailed for 19 years' (<www.abc.net.au/>). 16 January.

Aboelela, SW, PW Stone et al (2007) 'Effectiveness of bundled behavioural interventions to control healthcare-associated infections: a systematic review of the literature'. *J Hosp Infect* **66**(2): 101-8.

Annas, GJ (2002) 'Bioterrorism, public health, and civil liberties'. *N Engl J Med* **346**(17): 1337-42.

Bayer, R and A Fairchild (2007) The genesis of public health ethics. *The bioethics reader: editors choice*. R Chadwick, H Kuhse, W Landman, U Schuklenk and PA Singer. Malden, MA, Blackwell.

Bloom, BR (2003) 'Lessons from SARS'. *Science* **300**(5620): 701.

Bollinger, R, S Tripathy et al (1995) 'The human immunodeficiency virus epidemic in India: current magnitude and future projections'. *Medicine* **74**: 97-106.

Cello, J, AV Paul et al (2002) 'Chemical synthesis of poliovirus DNA: generation of infectious virus in the absence of natural template'. *Science* **297**(5583): 1016-18.

Collins, S (2008) HIV-positive man guilty of attempting to infect partners. *The Age*. Melbourne.

Cooper, M (2006) 'Pre-empting emergence: the biological turn in the war on terror'. *Theory, culture and society* **23**(4): 113-35.

Daniels, N (1991) 'Duty to treat or right to refuse?' *Hastings Cent Rep* **21**(2): 36-46.

Francis, L, MP Battin et al (2006) How infectious diseases got left out – and what this omission might have meant for bioethics. *Ethics and infectious disease*. M Selgelid, MP Battin and C Smith. Malden, MA, Blackwell.

Garrett, L (1994) *The Coming Plague. Newly emerging diseases in a world out of balance*. New York, Penguin.

Gillett, G (1988) 'AIDS and confidentiality'. *Jn of Applied Philosophy* **4**(1): 15-20.

Gostin, LO (2002) 'Law and ethics in a public health emergency'. *Hastings Cent Rep* **32**(2): 9-11.

Gusterson, H (2008) 'Knowing your enemy'. *New Scientist*(2 Aug): 20-1.

Harbarth, S, H Sax et al (2003) 'The preventable proportion of nosocomial infections: an overview of published reports'. *J Hosp Infect* **54**(4): 258-66; quiz 321.

Heymann, DL (2004) 'The international response to the outbreak of SARS in 2003'. *Philos Trans R Soc Lond B Biol Sci* **359**(1447): 1127-9.

Hill, J (2003) 'Modeling SARS Daily Death Totals'. <http://www.geocities.com/SoHo/Nook/5440/WHO-SARS-data-fits.html>.

Horvath, JS, M McKinnon et al (2006) 'The Australian response: pandemic influenza preparedness'. *Med J Aust* **185**(10 Suppl): S35-8.

Huskins, WC (2007) 'Interventions to prevent transmission of antimicrobial-resistant bacteria in the intensive care unit'. *Curr Opin Crit Care* **13**(5): 572-7.

International AIDS Society (2007) 'The Sydney Declaration: good research drives good policy and planning. A call to scale up research'. August 2007, <http://www. iasociety.org/Default.aspx?pageId=63>.

Jackson, RJ, AJ Ramsay et al (2001) 'Expression of mouse interleukin-4 by a recombinant ectromelia virus suppresses cytolytic lymphocyte responses and overcomes genetic resistance to mousepox'. *J Virol* **75**(3): 1205-10.

Johnstone, M (1994) *Bioethics: A Nursing Perspective*. Sydney, Harcourt Brace.

Kaiser, J (2005) 'Resurrected influenza virus yields secrets of deadly 1918 pandemic'. *Science* **310**: 28-9.

Kegeles, S, J Catania et al (1990) 'Many people who seek anonymous HIV antibody testing would avoid it under other circumstances'. *AIDS* **4**(6): 585-8.

Klein, N (2007) *The shock doctrine*. London, Allen Lane.

Klevens, RM, JR Edwards et al (2007) 'Estimating health care-associated infections and deaths in US hospitals, 2002'. *Public Health Rep* **122**(2): 160-6.

Kotalik, J (2005) 'Preparing for an influenza pandemic: ethical issues'. *Bioethics* **19**(4): 422-31.

Magnusson, R (1994) 'Privacy, confidentiality and HIV/AIDS health care'. *Aust J Public Health* **18**: 51-8.

Magnusson, R (1996) 'Australian HIV/AIDS legislation: a review for doctors'. *Aust NZ J Med* **26**: 396-406.

Maher, L, G Tachedjian et al (2007) '4th International AIDS Society Conference on HIV pathogenesis, treatment and prevention'. *Med J Aust* **187**(11/12): 610-12.

Miles, SH (2006) *Oath betrayed: torture, medical complicity, and the war on terror*. New York, Random House.

Miller, J, S Engelberg et al (2001) *Germs: The Ultimate Weapon*. London, Simon and Schuster.

National Research Council (2004) *Biotechnology Research in an Age of Terrorism*. Washington DC, National Academic Press.

Pittet, D, B Allegranzi et al (2006) 'Evidence-based model for hand transmission during patient care and the role of improved practices'. *Lancet Infect Dis* **6**(10): 641-52.

Reid, L (2007) Diminishing returns? Risk and duty to care in the SARS epidemic. *Ethics and Infectious Disease*. MJ Selgelid, MP Battin and C Smith. Malden, MA, Blackwell.

Schweber, S (2000) *In the Shadow of the Bomb: Bethe, Oppenheimer, and the Moral Responsibility of the Scientist*. Princeton, Princeton University Press.

Selgelid, MJ (2005) 'Ethics and infectious disease'. *Bioethics* **19**(3): 272-89.

Selgelid, MJ (2007) 'A tale of two studies: Ethics, bioterrorism and the censorship of science'. *Hastings Cent Rep* **37**(3): 35-43.

Senanayake, S and M Ferson (2004) 'Detention for tuberculosis: public health and the law'. *Med J Aust* **180**: 573-6.

Singer, PA, SR Benatar et al (2003) 'Ethics and SARS: lessons from Toronto'. *BMJ* **327**(7427): 1342-4.

Smith, C, M Battin et al (2006) Are there characteristics of infectious diseases that raise special ethical issues? *Ethics and infectious disease*. MJ Selgelid, M Battin and C Smith. Malden, MA, Blackwell.

Smolkin, D (1997) 'HIV infection, risk taking, and the duty to treat'. *J Med Philos* **22**: 55-74.

Steinbrook, R (2004) 'The AIDS Epidemic in 2004'. *N Engl J Med* **351**(2): 115-17.

Torda, A (2006) 'Ethical issues in pandemic planning'. *Med J Aust* **185**(10): S73-S76.

Weait, M (2007) *Intimacy and Responsibility: The Criminalisation of HIV Transmission*. London, Routledge-Cavendish.

Whitby, M, ML McLaws et al (2006) 'Why healthcare workers don't wash their hands: a behavioral explanation'. *Infect Control Hosp Epidemiol* **27**(5): 484-92.

World Health Organization (2006) *WHO technical consultation in collaboration with the European AIDS Treatment Group and AIDS Action Europe on the criminalization of HIV and other sexually transmitted infections*. Copenhagen, WHO Publications.

CHAPTER 29

ABORIGINAL AND TORRES STRAIT ISLANDER HEALTH

Case study: Renal disease in the Northern Territory

Aboriginal people in Australia's Northern Territory experience extremely high rates of end-stage kidney disease. Nationally, the average annual incidence of renal failure among Aboriginal people between 1988 and 1993 was 440 per million people – 17.4 times that for non-Aboriginals. In the top end of the Northern Territory the figure was 635 per million, in Northern Queensland it was 678 per million, and in the Tiwi Islands off Darwin it was 2500 per million (Hoy, Mathews et al 1995; Hoy 1996).

People with end-stage renal failure (ESRF) require either renal transplant or renal dialysis in order to survive. Renal transplants involve the use of organs from either living related donors or from those that are brain-dead. In the past, the use of living related donors for Aboriginal patients was common, but since there are very high rates of renal disease in relatives of patients with renal disease, a number of kidney donors eventually required dialysis themselves. Communication problems with the donors also resulted in difficulties with the consent process, resulting in donors sometimes feeling themselves overly pressured or under-prepared for their decision. An example of some of these issues can be found in a statement recorded by one renal donor that he hoped would be relayed to other prospective donors in his community:

I want to say this in language:

Well all you mob [I'm telling you], [think] very carefully – don't just rush in [and give up] a kidney. You should realise its dangerous – really dangerous for you. It's no small thing, not something to be casual about. I know – I've had the operation myself. I spent six months in Queen Elizabeth Hospital – six months! I nearly died. I'm getting around okay now but I'm telling you mob, 'Don't even think about giving up a kidney to someone else!' Think very carefully; talk it over with the doctors at Congress first ...' Cause I know all about this business. I been through it – that's what I'm telling you mob on this tape now, be careful what you mob do. Please ask your doctors because it can be very dangerous. 'Cause you don't know what you going through, you don't know what your family gonna end up with ...' (Devitt and McMasters 1998b)

A second source of kidney donations is from organs donated by brain-dead patients. The Northern Territory and South Australia both donate more than the average number of organs per head of population, but organ donations from Aboriginal patients are rare. The causes of this are uncertain, but it is likely to be in part due to communication issues between staff and the relatives of brain-dead Aboriginal patients. Factors such as poverty and marginalisation are also associated with low donation rates in other parts of the world. Cultural issues regarding the treatment of dead bodies may be another factor.

Many Aboriginal patients have to wait for long periods on dialysis until they can obtain kidney transplants. The majority of Aboriginal patients do not receive a kidney transplant and instead use dialysis facilities. There are now some dialysis centres in Aboriginal communities, but many people still need to uproot from their communities and move to major towns.

Many Aboriginal people who require dialysis experience complications or even die because they have extended lapses of their dialysis treatment. According to Gorham:

> There may also be a significant number of people who die as a result of extended community visits that interrupt their courses of treatment. Strictly speaking this is not withdrawal. Rather it illustrates a conflict that is ever-present for people with ESRF who come from remote Indigenous communities. It may be difficult for them to reconcile leaving home for treatment that may be literally life-saving with their obligations to family, community and land. (Gorham 2001)

Despite such problems Aboriginal people value dialysis and renal transplants, and their communities demand that Aboriginal people should have the same access to them as other Australians. According to one patient in the study by Devitt and McMasters:

> I saw that the machines are good and I feel better. And I think that they are good for kidney disease ... Yes. They made me feel better, that's why I think that the machine is good ... I wasn't frightened ... Before I was feeling no good but now I'm all right, I feel better ... not like before ... Yes we always go to the machine. That machine saved a lot of people. I was finished [unconscious] but I am alive again. (Devitt and McMasters 1998a)

The health of Aboriginal people in Australia is much worse than the health of the rest of the Australian population. To many Australians, the injustices that are responsible for this difference and that arise from it are the major ethical issues confronting Australian health care.

There is very limited literature about ethics and Aboriginal health, other than that concerning Aboriginal health research. In previous editions of this book we have struggled to develop a framework for examining these issues. In this edition we will largely use the framework provided by the Nobel prize-winning economist Amartya Sen's 'capabilities framework'. This is in keeping with an increased interest in the application of Sen's work to the issues of Indigenous Australia (Pearson 2007).

Sen focused his work on concepts of justice in the development of poor nations. As we have seen in the rest of the book, justice can be approached in many different ways. Justice is intimately bound up with the idea of equality, but Sen's question is 'Equality of what?' (Sen 1979). His answer is that we should be looking for equality of freedom, that all people should be able to have the freedom to live their lives in the way that they wish. The aims of development should be for people to expand the freedoms they have reason to value so their lives will be 'richer and more unfettered' and people will be able to become 'fuller social persons, exercising our own volitions [capacities for deliberate choice] and interacting with – and influencing – the world in which we live' (Sen 1999). We believe that this analysis is also generally applicable to the ethical issues raised by Aboriginal health.

We are sensitive to Brough's caution that '[f]or Aboriginal and Torres Strait Islander communities, already too familiar with ethnocentric research, the concern about constructing "another" non-Aboriginal representation of Aboriginal problems is very real' (quoted in Baum 2007). Yet we believe that Sen's work provides a unique insight into the problems of disadvantaged people, and a new insight into some issues of Indigenous health.

Australian Aboriginal people are probably one of the most researched and written-about groups on earth. Yet much early research had the specific social and political aim of denigrating Aboriginal Australians as a race. For example, in the 19th and early 20th centuries there was a huge body of written research into the skull shapes and sizes of Aboriginal people aiming to prove that they were inferior to Europeans. A similar body of literature existed with regard to blood groups (Thomas 2004).

Not all research about Aboriginal people was done with ill intent; much research also arose from academic interest and curiosity. Unfortunately, this was equally unlikely to generate findings that were useful to Aboriginal people. According to Brady:

> As an Aboriginal person having experienced the education system at universities, I've come across a number of experts, particularly in regard to Aboriginal people. Most of these experts have come to their area of expertise, not necessarily from a will or desire to own Indigenous people, but within the European notion of an investigation, posing questions, having them resolved, finding new knowledge. It's only in recent times that we have been able to change this approach. It has come about through Aboriginal people posing those questions, also by those who are engaging in these endeavours to change the way in which they acquire and express knowledge. There has also been a desire to work in coalition or collaboration with those of us who were formerly only the subjects or objects of investigation. (Brady 1999)

This historical background led the 1981 Working Party of Aboriginal Historians for the Bicentennial History to argue that Aboriginal history should only be written by Aboriginal people, utilising Aboriginal methods of inquiry, criteria of validity, and forms of communication (Humphrey 2001). However, this view has not been generally accepted by either Aboriginal or by non-Aboriginal researchers (perhaps unsurprisingly in the latter case).

This leaves open the ethical question as to whether it is possible for non-Aboriginal people to write about Aboriginal health and ethics, as we intend to do in this book. We believe that there is a place for the 'outsider' writing about such issues. The reader must be aware however, that, no matter how hard we try to see things from other perspectives, our writings represent non-Aboriginal perspectives.

The health of Aboriginal Australians

Aboriginal people have occupied Australia for at least 60,000 years. Today there are two main groups of Indigenous Australians: Aboriginal people from the Australian mainland and Tasmania, and Torres Strait Islanders.

In the 2006 Census 455,031 people identified themselves as Aboriginal. Together they made up 2.3% of the Australian population (Australian Bureau of Statistics 2007). Aboriginal life expectancies are slowly increasing, but the gap between Aboriginal and non-Aboriginal mortality in Australia has largely been unchanged (Pink, Allbon et al 2008). For the period 1996-2001, the estimated life expectancy at birth for Aboriginal and Torres Strait Islander people was estimated to be 59 years for males and 65 years for females. In contrast, the average life expectancy at birth for all Australians for the period 1998-2000 was 77 years for males and 82 years for females (Australian Institute of Health and Welfare 2008).

Circulatory system disease (including heart disease and stroke) was the leading cause of death for Indigenous men and women in 2002-03, with standardised mortality rates of 3.2 (for men) and 2.8 (for women) times that of the total Australian population (Australian Bureau of Statistics 2003). Indigenous Australians also have significant disadvantage in other key social outcomes including lower levels of employment, lower income, lower rates of home ownership and lower educational outcomes at secondary and tertiary levels, in particular.

A number of interrelated factors can be identified that contribute to the high rates of mortality experienced by Aboriginal people. The main factors identified by Aboriginal people themselves are: destruction of Aboriginal culture, limited education about health and nutrition, high levels of unemployment and low-status jobs, and alienation from their land (Trigger, Anderson et al 1983). Increasingly, the effects of grief and childhood violence are also seen as important health determinants. Other factors include: inadequate housing, difficulty accessing medical services, inadequate electricity and sewerage systems, a sedentary lifestyle, high rates of alcohol abuse and smoking, geographical isolation, and dependence on social welfare.

If health programs are to be tailored towards Aboriginal people, it is necessary to identify Aboriginal people and be aware of their different needs. This can be a double-edged sword – for by identifying Aboriginal people as different it becomes possible to discriminate. As Patricia King has observed:

> [I]f the racial difference is ignored and all groups are considered similarly, unintended harm may result from the failure to recognise racially correlated factors. Conversely, if difference among groups or person are recognised and attempts are made to respond to past injustices and special burdens, the effort is likely to support existing negative stereotypes that contributed to the emphasis on racial differences in the first place (King 1992)

In order to look at the question in more detail, it is first necessary to consider the related definitions of 'race' and 'ethnicity'.

Race and ethnicity

Racial classifications attempt to distinguish groups of humans biologically, on the basis of skin colour and other physical characteristics. Racial ideas have often been expressed in terms of 'blood'. For example, Neville Bonner (the first Aboriginal member of the Commonwealth Parliament) commented in his maiden speech to the Senate in 1979:

> All persons who desire to be classified as Indigenous, regardless of hue of skin, and who have flowing in their veins any portion, however small, of Aboriginal or Torres Strait Islander blood are Indigenous people. It does not necessarily follow that the degree of emotional scars matches the darkness of personal pigmentation or that the lightness of one's skin necessarily indicates a lessening of knowledge of, and belief in, Aboriginal or Torres Strait Islander culture and tradition. (Burger 1979)

It is ironic that the idea that 'a single drop of black blood' defines a person as black originally derives from American laws that were aimed at increasing the numbers of potential slaves by including the illegitimate children of white slave owners. This law was upheld as recently as 1986, when a Louisiana woman whose great-great-great-great-grandmother (the mistress of a French planter) was black was found by the Supreme Court to be black on the basis of this law (Wright 1994).

In the Australian census, it is possible to classify one's self as 'Aboriginal', 'Torres Strait Islander', or both. It is not possible to classify one's self as both Aboriginal and European or Asian, although most Aboriginal people in Australia have at least some non-Aboriginal ancestors. In the USA, a move to allow 'multiracial' classifications has largely been ignored on the grounds that it would decrease the power of civil rights laws and civil rights organisations (Wright 1994). Similar concerns exist within Australia. Despite this, some people with Aboriginal ancestry are now also acknowledging multiracial heritage (see, for example, the biographical note by Paradies in Carson, Dunbar et al (2007)).

Recently, the concept of racially determined blood has been updated to the idea that race can be identified by genetic markers. Some Aboriginal people themselves have suggested the use of DNA techniques to decide whether people are Aboriginal or not (Sydney Morning Herald 2002). However, although genetic markers may provide guidance about 'descent', they do not completely resolve issues of race.

To illustrate this we can consider the use of some of the genes commonly used for such purposes – those found in mitochondrial DNA and the Y chromosome. Mitochondrial DNA is derived from one's mother, and in turn from one's mother's mother etc. Examining mitochondrial DNA shows connections to one of four grandparents, one of eight grandparents and so on. Y chromosome tracing connects a man to his father, and it connects him to only one of his four grandparents: his paternal grandfather. Continue back in this manner for a number of generations and the man is still connected to only one ancestor in that generation. The test does not connect him to any of the other ancestors in that generation to which he is also related in equal measure (Elliott and Brodwin 2002). Researchers have attempted to get around these issues by using banks of multiple DNA markers, but can still not entirely resolve this problem.

'Ethnicity' is a concept that is closely related to that of race. In older dictionaries, ethnicity is defined as 'pertaining to race'. More recently, ethnicity has come to refer to the shared characteristics of groups of people that include ancestral and geographical origins, cultural traditions and language. Unlike race, ethnicity is a fluid concept and depends upon context. According to Bhopal, '[f]or practical and theoretical reasons, the current preference is for self-assessment of ethnicity. People change their self-assessment over time, as is their prerogative' (Bhopal 1997).

In summary, the idea of race refers to how other people see us, whereas the idea of ethnicity refers mostly to how we see ourselves. Because race depends on the views of others, it has often been an excuse for disempowering and discriminating against groups. Ethnicity, on the other hand, has the potential to empower people through pride in who they are and identification with others.

Aboriginality

There is considerable debate about the definition of Indigenous people (Coates 2004). Some definitions emphasise the political subordination of Indigenous peoples by colonising powers while others focus on the sociocultural characteristics of Indigenous societies, for example, small-scale, decentralised, ongoing ties to the land that made them vulnerable to political domination, exploitation and dispossession (Anderson, Crengle et al 2006).

It has been argued by some authors that self-identification as Aboriginal is all that is required for Aboriginality. More recent works tend to shy away from this position, as it has become apparent that there may be a number of reasons why people identify as Aboriginal, and that some people who now identify as Aboriginal may not be seen as such by others.

In recent years, a number of benefits have become available to Aboriginal people to attempt to make up for the discrimination that they experience. In determining eligibility for these benefits, the Commonwealth Government has defined Aboriginality in a way that has elements of both race and ethnicity.

The Commonwealth definition of an Aboriginal person is a person who:

- is a descendant of an Indigenous inhabitant of Australia;
- identifies as an Aboriginal; and
- is recognised as Aboriginal by members of the community in which she or he lives. (Council for Aboriginal Reconciliation 1994)

The first part of the Commonwealth definition represents an attempt to include a biological criterion in the definition of Aboriginality. An Aboriginal person must be descended from another Aboriginal person, who can only be defined as such by being descended from another Aboriginal person etc. The final point, one presumes, is the time before European settlement of Australia. So, although it is not clearly stated, the definition requires that for a person to be considered Aboriginal, at least one of their ancestors should have lived in Australia before White colonisation.

Aboriginal people are sometimes required to prove this ancestry. This may be difficult or impossible, since records of Aboriginal ancestry are often incomplete. Family lines were often deliberately obscured by processes such as adoption of Aboriginal children and forcing Aboriginal people to take on non-Aboriginal identities. In many ways the estrangement of Aboriginal identity through the process of European colonisation of Australia could be seen as analogous to the estrangement of Aboriginal land as was detailed in the *Mabo* case (see below).

The second part of the Commonwealth criteria for the definition of Aboriginality is that a person must identify him or herself as Aboriginal. A corollary of this is that, according to the definition, a person may become Aboriginal part way through their life, or lose their Aboriginality, as they identify or stop identifying as Aboriginal.

The third part of the Commonwealth definition of Aboriginality requires an Aboriginal person to be recognised as such by the community. The Commonwealth does not define which community is to do this. Probably the most satisfactory answer to this would be that they should be identified by an Aboriginal community, but this also introduces some circularity. There are a number of communities in Australia who identify themselves as Aboriginal, but where this is disputed by other Aboriginal groups.

In general, although the Commonwealth definition of Aboriginality has a number of problems, it also captures some key issues. The picture of Aboriginality that arises from this definition is that Aboriginality is best seen as existing within a web of relationships. These include relationships back into ancestral times, and reciprocal relationships with other members of Aboriginal communities.

A final form of relationship that is important in defining Aboriginality, but is not mentioned in the Commonwealth definition, is the relationship with the land. Aboriginal people's relation to land may be different to many non-Aboriginal Australians. According to Rose: 'People talk about country in the same way that they would talk about a person: they speak to country, sing to country, visit country, worry about country, feel sorry for country, and long for country' (Rose, Central Land Council (Australia) et al 1995). Interactions between people and land may also contribute to Indigenous health and well-being (Burgess, Johnston et al 2005). According to Burgess and Morrison, maintenance of health and well-being is sustained through relationships of mutual care of kin, non-human affiliations and observance of ethical conduct described by the law or dreaming that is encoded within country' (Burgess and Morrison 2007).

Aboriginality and resistance

Authors such as Keeffe, Cowlishaw (Cowlishaw 1988) and Day (Day 2001) see Aboriginality in a different way – identifying at least two main strands of thought bound up in this concept. Keeffe labels these as 'Aboriginality as persistence' and 'Aboriginality as resistance' (Keeffe 1988).

Elements of the 'Aboriginality as persistence' view include a belief in the persistence of an inherently unique Aboriginal identity in the face of colonisation; the continuity of cultural practices that originate in traditional Aboriginal culture; and the common sharing of these by all Aboriginal people in Australia (Day 2001). In health, the 'Aboriginality as persistence' paradigm leads to phenomena such as the widespread use of Indigenous art in health promotion materials, reference to the beliefs and healthy lifestyles of the ancestors, and explaining modern diseases by harking back to idyllic views of a past society.

By contrast the 'Aboriginality as resistance' paradigm has described Aboriginal identity and culture in terms of resistance and opposition to non-Aboriginal culture. An example of this can be seen in Etherington's study of Kunwinjku people:

> At every step of increased contact Kunwinjku people have been forced to concede some self-esteem. From their viewpoint, contact with the non-Aboriginal world rendered them instantly incompetent in new and apparently permanent domains of life. It rendered them suddenly aware of themselves as poor, against the bounty of the outside world. The Balanda [Europeans] world of work defined them instantly as unemployable in all but the most marginal jobs. It rendered them ignorant and dependent should they seek to cross from their own world – despite the very powerful incentives to do so. They very quickly lost control over their own affairs both as a community in formation, and as individuals whose lives were redefined around relationships with powerful Balanda.
>
> ... The intensity and the degree of invasiveness of the Balanda world has increased steadily over time, for example through the compulsory nature of school attendance, the presence of state police in the community enforcing a range of laws whose origins and mechanisms are unknowable to most Kunwinjku, the regulation of funds through banking and the medicalisation of aspects of life like childbirth and circumcision. The compulsive nature of this invading world is resisted by the strong Kunwinjku principle of personal independence, articulated constantly by Kunwinjku in their dealings with others, whether Aboriginal or Balanda – 'Don't force me!' This is a constantly operational and generally shared attitude in Kunwinjku society. (Etherington 2006)

According to Cowlishaw, an Aboriginal 'oppositional culture' subverts and challenges dominant systems of meaning through everyday acts of resistance (Cowlishaw 1988). Authors such as Gibson and Sansom (Sansom 1980) have suggested that Aboriginal resistance may be expressed through drinking behaviour, and Day suggests that Aboriginal people living 'as a group in the town, barefooted, speaking their own languages and using open fires for cooking' is also a type of resistance. Other areas of resistance that have been commonly cited include breaches of law and order (Sackett 1988), negative attitudes towards working and employment (Cowlishaw 1988) and poor attendance at schools (Keeffe 1992). According to the NHMRC:

> There are a number of phenomena in the health care setting that might be interpreted as evidence of Aboriginal resistance. Aboriginal and Torres Strait Islander Peoples vigorously oppose the assimilation, integration or subjugation of their values and will defend them against perceived or actual encroachment. Researchers must be aware of the history and the continuing

potential for research to encroach on these values. (National Health and Medical Research Council 2003)

Aboriginal resistance in health care may include resistance to involvement in research activities, poor compliance with medication, poor uptake of preventative health measures, and high levels of 'absconding' from hospital and other care. Many commentators go out of their way to suggest that these factors are not evidence of Aboriginal resistance but are due to factors such as poor education and competing priorities. However it would be surprising if the task of resisting the encroachments on Aboriginal culture had no effect on such matters.

Sen's capability framework

Amartya Sen won the Nobel Prize in Economics for his work on famines and development. Sen's work concentrates on people who are disadvantaged – a condition common to many Indigenous people around the world. In Australia there is a tendency to see the problems of Australian Aboriginal people as exceptional – unlike anything elsewhere in the world. Yet a position of Aboriginal exceptionalism is in many ways like a position of cultural relativism – it stops us from gaining experience from similar situations elsewhere. By contrast, we believe that many of the problems in Aboriginal health have been addressed elsewhere, and believe that both positive and negative lessons can be learnt from this (Kunitz 1994; Kunitz and Brady 1995).

Sen's work on development is based on two key terms: 'functionings' and 'capabilities'. Sen defines 'functionings' as the things that a person does or experiences, such as being adequately nourished, being free from disease or taking part in the life of the community. Sen's idea is that we should be free to perform such functionings as we wish.

'Capability' refers to feasible alternative combinations of functionings. Capabilities are what people are able to do or able to be. People may not choose particular capabilities, but having different capabilities available is part of the definition of living a 'good life'. Sen uses the examples of two people: one a Westerner going on a fast for health reasons, the other a poor person who cannot afford to eat. Both have the same amount of nutrition, but one has the capability to choose many other alternatives, whereas the other does not (Sen 1999; Anand, Hunter et al 2005).

Sen believes that societies should strive to achieve equity in capabilities. If someone is poor, sick or disadvantaged, their capabilities are extremely limited. This leads Sen to suggest that catering to the poor, sick or disadvantaged is particularly important.

One example of the way that functionings and capabilities have been used in Aboriginal health arises from housing surveys. Much of the work on housing in Indigenous communities is based on nine 'healthy living practices' that emerged from work done in Central Australia in the mid-1980s (Bailie 2007) These nine practices are washing people, washing clothing and bedding, removing waste, improving nutrition, reducing crowding, reducing negative contact between people and animals, insects and vermin, reducing dust, controlling temperature and reducing trauma. Some of these activities (such has washing bedding) would be known as 'functionings' in Sen's terminology whereas some (such as improving nutrition) would be called 'capabilities'.

Studies of Aboriginal housing show that many of these functionings are not possible in Aboriginal houses. For example, in the NT only 54% of Aboriginal houses had capacity for washing people, 38% for appropriately storing and pre-paring food, and 62% for removing waste water (Bailie 2007). Sen's framework suggests that we should not only ensure that Aboriginal people have a full range of functionings available, but they should also have a similar range of choices to non-Aboriginal people. This means that they should have equal capabilities to live in the ways they value as the rest of us do, whether this be in a remote community or a city, a rented home or a home of their own, a tent or house.

In the health sphere, information on the use of health-care services from the 2004-05 National Aboriginal and Torres Strait Islander Health Survey (NATSIHS) showed that one in seven Indigenous Australians (15%) reported that they needed to go to a doctor in the previous 12 months, but had not gone; 8% needed to go to another type of health professional (eg, nurse, Aboriginal health worker), but had not gone; 7% needed to go to a hospital, but had not gone; and 21% needed to go to a dentist, but had not gone. From Sen's perspective this situation would be unproblematic as long as it represented a genuine choice. However, if this was because of lack of access or opportunity (as it is likely to be in part), this limitation on capabilities would clearly be unjust.

In many cases, Aboriginal people do have some capabilities (to use Sen's term) available to them – there is some housing, some nutritious food, and some employment available. But these capabilities are often built on inadequate functionings and there is rarely any freedom or choice about what is offered, so there is not equity of capabilities. Sen's ideas imply that Aboriginal people should have the same range of capabilities as the rest of Australia (although they might make different choices about how to define and live a good life). We believe that this lack of choice is one of the key, but frequently overlooked, aspects of the ethics of Indigenous health care. Lack of choice is part of the reason for Aboriginal resistance. In the following sections we show how it influences many other aspects of health care for Aboriginal people.

Cultural competence, cultural safety and trust

One approach to improving the communication and trust between different cultures is known as 'cultural competence'. It is based on health professionals and institutions developing a set of attitudes, skills, behaviours and policies that enable them to work effectively in cross-cultural situations. (For an example of the use of this concept in an Aboriginal context, see the 'Sharing the true stories' project: <http://www.sharingtruestories.com/>.)

A more client-centred approach to cultural issues is what is known as 'cultural safety'. 'Cultural safety' was originally a term that was unique to New Zealand nursing education. It arose from the poor health-care experiences of Maori people in New Zealand, and considerations about the applications of the

Treaty of Waitangi to improving this experience. 'Cultural safety' emphasises both knowledge of cultural difference and commitment to the transfer of power in the health-care arena from nurses to those receiving care. According to Wepa, '[o]nce this transfer of power has occurred the recipients of care are empowered to define what is culturally safe practice. In other words, the "lived experience" of patients determines whether or not a nurse is safe to attend to their cultural needs' (Wepa 2001).

The New Zealand Nursing Council definition of 'Cultural Safety' is:

> The effective nursing or midwifery practice of a person or family from another culture, and is determined by that person or family. Culture includes, but is not restricted to, age or generation; gender; sexual orientation; occupation and socioeconomic status; ethnic origin or migrant experience; religious or spiritual belief; and disability. The nurse or midwife delivering the nursing or midwifery service will have undertaken a process of reflection on his or her own cultural identity and will recognise the impact that his or her personal culture has on his or her professional practice. Unsafe cultural practice comprises any action which diminishes, demeans or disempowers the cultural identity and wellbeing of an individual. (Nursing Council of New Zealand 2002)

There are a number of difficulties with transplanting the New Zealand cultural safety model to Australia. One is that it is essentially a bi-cultural model, whereas Aboriginal Australians are a multicultural group. Yet the emphasis that cultural safety places on evening up power relationships and upon self-awareness of one's own culture is essential for ethical practice in Aboriginal health (Kowal and Paradies 2003).

Part of the aim of the cultural competence movement is to improve the health-care environment so it is both trustworthy and trusted by Indigenous people. Many philosophers have noted that trust exposes our weaknesses. Tom Bailey says:

> [W]hen we trust others, we are confidently relying on them to take care of something which we care about, but which they could harm or steal if they wished. When we trust, then, we make ourselves vulnerable. But we do so in the confidence that the trusted will not exploit this vulnerability, and generally in the confidence that the trusted will actively take care of what we make vulnerable. (Bailey 2002)

The historical experience of Aboriginal people in Australia would appear to give little ground for trust in non-Aboriginal institutions such as the health-care system. According to Henry and colleagues:

> We believe that Aboriginal people have lost their trust in the institutions of government, including healthcare services. Lack of respect by white Australians for Aboriginal values, the discounting of these values by those who have sought, patronisingly and paternalistically, to 'do good' to Aboriginal people (according to a 'good' defined by white fellas), leads to further erosion of trust. The lack of trust by Aboriginal people in white people and white institutions is obvious. (Henry, Houston et al 2004)

Studies of the experiences of Aboriginal people in hospitals also demonstrate this lack of trust. For example, a patient interviewed in a study of attitudes towards hospitalisation among Aboriginal people in North-East Arnhem Land reported:

> When I was in hospital in Darwin I was very sick. They changed the nurses during the night. I saw them, and they didn't write down or sign their names. That made me worried that they might do something to me. I didn't sleep that night ... I was too scared. (Amery 1999)

An Aboriginal community in the Northern Territory may receive a visit from a doctor once a week. The doctor may vary from week to week depending on current staffing. Sometimes they will be male, sometimes female. But because there is no choice and little continuity, there is little opportunity for patients to enter freely into trusting relationships. The trust described by Bailey above – where a person chooses to make themselves vulnerable by entering a trusting relationship – is not possible in these circumstances of limited health-care capabilities. Under these circumstances it is important to ask whether any real trust is possible.

According to Gilson, 'in relationships that result from lack of choice or occur in a context of inequality, such as that between health-care provider and patient, a form of involuntary trust may appear to exist. However, as trust cannot be coerced into existence, the involuntary trust seen in these relationships is more correctly seen as a form of dependency' (Gilson 2003). For many Indigenous people, the only trust available is the involuntary form of trust described by Gilson. But without real trust, there cannot be any cultural safety, as safety depends on it.

Compliance and non-compliance

'Poor compliance' is a term used when a doctor or other health professional 'orders' a course of treatment that the patient does not follow. There is an ongoing debate about the degree to which compliance is a valid construct, with most commentators believing that it is a term that should not be used (Humphery, Weeramanthri et al 2001). It has been suggested that the term 'compliance' would be better replaced with terms such as 'concordance' or 'adherence' to reflect a more collaborative approach to patient decision-making (Chatterjee 2006). Although we believe that there are great problems with the idea of compliance, we also believe that there is little to be gained by changing terms and we continue to use the term 'compliance' and 'non-compliance' in the section below.

Non-compliance is often thought of as being more of a problem in Aboriginal than non-Aboriginal populations. The research that has been done supports the idea that Aboriginal people are less compliant with medication advice (Burns 1992; Kruske, Ruben et al 1999; Humphery, Weeramanthri et al 2001). Commentators about Aboriginal compliance have warned practitioners against falling 'into the trap of "blaming" Indigenous patients for not "fitting in" with their own medical model', and have explained poor compliance in terms of educational, communication and systemic faults in health-care delivery (Bryce 2002). Sen's capability model suggests that some of this effect also might be due to the limited options offered to Aboriginal people. Perhaps non-compliance under these circumstances is better conceptualised as resistance to the limited range of options offered!

The Royal Commission into Aboriginal Deaths in Custody stated (RCADC, at para 31.3.48):

> It is essential, therefore, that health professionals working with Aboriginal clients and patients in mainstream services understand that the behaviour which they so often label as lack of compliance with expert advice is explained by both the inadequacies of the mainstream services themselves as well as the knowledge, attitudes and previous experiences of the patients. A high level of 'lack of compliance' by Aboriginal people should be a warning sign to health care service delivery personnel and administrators that problems may exist in their own styles of operating. (Johnston 1991)

From the perspective of capabilities, it is important to note that non-compliance is really only possible when a patient is only given a single option of treatment. If the doctor says 'You should take this drug', then the patient has two options – to agree or disagree. If they disagree they may often be labelled as non-compliant, but this type of labelling is not possible if more than two choices are offered. For example, if a diabetic is offered the choice of insulin, a further trial of diet and exercise, or an approach based on harm minimisation, it is difficult to say exactly what non-compliance would consist of. Even if a patient is offered the choice of taking a medication or going without, with the risks and benefits of each explained, there will be no appropriate construct of non-compliance available – if the patient chooses to do without treatment, this is not 'non-compliance' but an autonomous choice.

In a study that asked Aboriginal mothers to describe their causes for non-compliance with an antibiotic regime of otitis media, predominant causes cited by mothers were 'laziness' and 'forgetfulness'. The author suggested:

> A system that is somewhat foreign, culturally inappropriate, dominating and possibly demeaning, may significantly affect its use and the understanding of the system's process ... In other words so called 'laziness' may be constructed differently as a form of resistance to this long and inappropriate process. (Melder 2000)

A study into the attitudes of Northern Territory health practitioners' towards compliance issues noted:

> There is, in fact, an element of what could be called 'evasiveness' about a number of ... responses. This is an evasiveness born of an admirable desire to moderate or challenge the discourse of non-compliance ... Furthermore, by constituting non-compliance as unintentional, an important element of treatment refusal is eclipsed; the possibly political nature of certain acts of non-compliance or the manner in which certain instances of treatment refusal can be better read as resistance. Resistance is, we would suggest, an important factor in better grasping the complexity of treatment refusal in a Northern Territory context – although we would warn also against simply reducing non-compliance to this political factor. (Humphery, Weeramanthri et al 2001)

We believe that part of the problem with non-compliance is that it arises out of the lack of choices offered to Aboriginal people (although other factors such as misunderstanding should not be overlooked). Aboriginal people, like other people, require a range of choices for shared decision-making. But people also need to be enabled to make choices, which involves a commitment to education, development of skills in transcultural communication (including learning local languages (Bryce 2002)), cultural awareness and sensitivity, and a clear knowledge of, and ability to communicate, realistic options for treatment (Cass, Lowell et al 2002).

Consent

The process of gaining consent assumes special importance in the health care of Aboriginal and Torres Strait Islander people (Cheng, Blum et al 2004). Legal requirements for consent are the same for Aboriginal and Torres Strait Islander people as for non-Aboriginal people. Requirements for a valid consent include that the patient be fully informed, that he or she be mentally competent and that he or she be under no duress. Each of these points requires further thought when dealing with Aboriginal people.

For a person to be fully informed, he or she needs to participate in two-way communication about the range of options available and the consequences of each of these options. This often requires the use of interpreters or the use of Aboriginal Liaison Officers skilled in Aboriginal English and knowledgeable about local customs. Even if this is done appropriately, there may still come a point where the difference in culture between the patient and the health professional may lead to disagreement. Aboriginal understandings of disease may be genuinely different from Western understandings. A disease that a Western-educated doctor understands as being due to cancer may be thought by the Aboriginal client to be due to sorcery or spiritual causes. And yet such a client may nonetheless present to a Western health system, either on the off-chance that Western medicine may contribute to their cure or because a family member or health professional feels that Western medicine may be able to help (Folds 2001). Under these circumstances it is important that genuine consent be obtained.

The issue of duress is another important factor in obtaining consent in Aboriginal people. The hospital setting, with its distinctive hierarchical culture, emphasis upon rapid decision-making and sterile technological environment, may be thought to embody a degree of duress in itself. Aboriginal people may be able to resist duress better when they are accompanied by their families, when they are approached in a non-threatening environment, when they are given plenty of time to discuss things and make a decision (perhaps days or weeks), and when they are approached by an appropriate person (such as a person of the same sex).

The role of time in decision-making is one area where there are marked differences between people working within the hospital environment and Aboriginal patients. In Aboriginal societies, lengthy periods of silence are the norm, and are expected during conversation, particularly during information-sharing or information-seeking (Queensland State Government). Aboriginal peoples may also not openly explain themselves but may communicate quietly, gradually, indirectly, physically or obliquely, so that much is left to the recipient to observe, observe again, question respectfully and then derive an answer. Within Aboriginal communities enormous store is placed on talking, and the pace and style of talking is markedly different from non-Aboriginal patterns of communication. Important information may be communicated in a circular fashion or in the form of stories full of cultural nuance or metaphors of experience that may be given, not only by the individual, but also by others in attendance.

It is important, therefore, for health-care professionals to avoid the expectation of direct responses to explicit questions and to be open to listen, and to listen well, for understanding the message in discursive accounts of illness takes patience, sensitivity and training. And while this may be difficult, it is critically important as the 'stories' of Aboriginal people are the cornerstones of interaction and they need to feel able to tell them. Recognising the differences between Aboriginal and non-Aboriginal narratives and means of communicating also has practical importance as Aboriginal people are frequently able to make better decisions when they are given plenty of time to discuss things and make a decision.

Competence may also be difficult to assess in Aboriginal people. There are few validated tools for assessing cognitive abilities in Aboriginal languages (LoGiudice, Smith et al 2006). Cultural norms such as belief in sorcery may be mistaken for psychosis, or actual psychosis may be dismissed as an appropriate cultural belief. In all assessments of competence, the assessment of the normality of behaviour through use of family members and appropriate cultural and language interpreters is important.

It should be noted that there is no strict legal requirement for consent to be given in writing, even though many organisations require a consent form to be signed. Written forms can be threatening to some Aboriginal people, who fear that they are signing up for more than they are aware of. There are also some Indigenous people who cannot read or write and for whom verbal consent procedures are more appropriate.

The shape of Australian law and ethics reflects the primacy given to liberalism, autonomy and rationalism in Western societies (Maher 1999; Brough 2001). However, many Aboriginal people operate in a very different cultural milieu where it is family or community, rather than solely the individual, that is owed information and respect as the 'autonomous' decision-making 'unit'.

Aboriginal people frequently respond to the crisis of an individual's illness as a group or community, and the large numbers of people visiting and supporting an Aboriginal patient may be both puzzling and intimidating to non-Aboriginal Australians. The presence of family or community may be viewed as having a therapeutic function as well as expressing community values in what may be an unfamiliar environment. A person's spouse and family members need to mourn and care for an ill Aboriginal person as in any other community, but an Aboriginal person's spouse may not be the appropriate person to make health-care decisions (although they are usually able to say who is the appropriate person) (Nangala, Nangala et al 2008). In making a decision the patient may consider the interests of the family and community, may defer to the wisdom of an elder or may elect to use a family member as a proxy decision-maker in the consent process. This need not suggest that autonomy is, or should be, devalued – rather that 'autonomy' may be manifested in alternative frameworks.

Health-care providers must be able to recognise the different models of decision-making that may be used by Aboriginal people. Equally important is an understanding of the different notions of 'family' and their roles in decision-making. Having an understanding of the services available and appropriately utilising such services (eg, interpreters and Aboriginal Liaison Officers) may assist the Aboriginal patient and their family as well as the health-care professional in the decision-making process. This communicates respect not only for the patient, but also for elders and others with high status, and for the culture itself.

Research involving Aboriginal and Torres Strait Islander Peoples

In Australia, research involving Aboriginal and Torres Strait Islander (ATSI) communities is regulated by the NHMRC and processed through the established system of Human Research Ethics Committees (HRECs). Guidance published by the NHMRC identifies six values relevant to the conduct of research involving Aboriginal and Torres Strait islander peoples. These are:

- Reciprocity (mutual obligations and the equitable distribution of resources)
- Respect (where respect and trust provide means for promoting dignity and recognition)
- Equality (which includes the right to be different and to have equal access to social, health and biomedical resources)
- Responsibility (which requires that researchers should avoid harm to individuals or collectives through the conduct of research, publication, patenting and so forth)
- Survival and protection (acting in ways that respect and maintain the culture and values of Aboriginal and Torres Strait islander communities) and
- Spirit and integrity (respecting Aboriginal and Torres Strait Islander communities in respect of the 5 values listed above). (National Health and Medical Research Council (Australia) 2003)

The NHMRC also identified a series of issues that are key to the conduct of research in ATSI communities. These issues mark important differences with the types of ethical issues raised by research in 'white' Australian communities. First, research involving Indigenous Australians cannot be separated from the past and must recognise both the reality of the adverse impact of colonisation and dispossession, and the need for integrity of the Indigenous cultural and communal narrative. Second, while research is frequently reductionist and seeks to examine questions in isolation, this is rarely possible in the context of ATSI health, as health and illness result from a complex interplay of social determinants and political context. Third, research must recognise the importance of identity as it establishes validity and meaning, reinforces community and cultural integrity and creates the moral basis for equality as being about both sameness (as other Australians) and difference (to other Australians). This creates something of a paradox as while recognition of difference is critical to identity, it also creates the possibility of stigmatisation and discrimination. And, finally, while research involving Indigenous people must respect them as individuals, they are not disconnected individuals but live in a community and in the context of research consideration of this community is core to questions of research trial design, recruitment, consent, identification of harms, benefit-sharing and dissemination and translation of data (National Health and Medical Research Council (Australia) 2003). For all of these reasons careful planning and broad consultation is critical to ensuring that research is feasible, consistent with Indigenous cultural values and beneficial (Wand and Eades 2008).

Aboriginal medical services

Despite the fact that Aboriginal people have considerably higher rates of hospitalisation for most diseases and conditions, Aboriginal people continue to experience difficulties in accessing and utilising mainstream health services, and frequently present to health-care services later and sicker than non-Aboriginal Australians. While a number of biological, social, economic and cultural factors contribute to these health inequalities, the absence of culturally appropriate health services has been identified as a key determinant of the health status of Aboriginal peoples (Johnston 1991).

In a 2004-05 survey, 16% of Aboriginal people reported that they were treated badly by their health providers because they were Indigenous (Australian Bureau of Statistics 2006). As the Chair of the National Aboriginal Community Controlled Health Organisation has noted, 'it is a well-established fact that if health-care services are not delivered appropriately, our people won't use them' (Hunter 2001).

The notion that Aboriginal people should control, manage and deliver health-care services first arose in the 1960s as a component of an Aboriginal political reform agenda focused on a range of Indigenous rights including land rights, Aboriginal sovereignty, community cooperatives and health services (Attwood 2004). The first Aboriginal Medical Service (AMS) was set up in Redfern in 1971 staffed by Aboriginal people and non-Aboriginal volunteers. By 1989, there were 64 AMSs across Australia. AMSs were set up due to frustration with, and 'functional unavailability' of, other medical services provided for Aboriginal people (Hunter 1993). By 1999-2000 there were around 120 such services funded by the Commonwealth across Australia (Anderson and Wakerman 2005).

The availability of AMSs gives Aboriginal people increased choice and health capabilities, and has shown some health benefits for Aboriginal people (such as improved immunisation rates). In 2004-05, 60% of Indigenous Australians reported that they went to a doctor if they had a problem with their health, but 30% reported that they first went to an Aboriginal medical service (Australian Bureau of Statistics 2006). Not all Aboriginal people use AMSs, but the presence of choice of service for Aboriginal people is an important value in itself.

Health-care funding

Recent reviews looking at the overall costs of health care for Aboriginal people in Australia have concluded that Aboriginal health care has been largely underfunded for the degree of morbidity experienced. The Australian Institute of Health and Welfare note that:

> In 2004–05, estimated expenditure on health goods and services for Indigenous Australians was $2,304 million or 2.8% of total health expenditure. More than two-thirds (67%) of the 2004–05 expenditure was on publicly provided health services such as public hospitals (46%) and community health services (22%). On a per person basis, average expenditure on health goods and services for Aboriginal and Torres Strait Islander people was $4,718—some 17% higher than the expenditure for non-Indigenous people ($4,019). Considering the high level of morbidity among Indigenous Australians, and mortality rates that are more than twice those for other Australians, these figures suggest that expenditures for Aboriginal and Torres Strait Islander people were not sufficient to match needs. (Pink, Allbon et al 2008)

This issue has been examined further in a paper looking at the costs of primary health care in a small Aboriginal community. (Note that primary health care only makes up a small proportion of the total health expenditure, which includes other factors such as hospitalisation.) This paper describes a number of possible ways in which 'fairness' of budgetary allocation could be assessed (McDermott and Beaver 1996).

The authors first looked at what would happen if Aboriginal health was funded to exactly the same extent as health care for other Australians, by considering the overall spending on primary health care in Australia and dividing it by the population. Using this approach, an appropriate level of primary health-care spending would be about $700 per Aboriginal person.

However, Aboriginal people tend to be sicker than the average Australian population and live more remotely. If we adjust for these factors, we would find that an appropriate amount to spend on primary health care for Aboriginal people would be about $1400 per head.

Another way of looking at this problem would be by noting that Aboriginal people have 3.8 times the mortality of other Australians. If we paid in proportion to this mortality, we should allocate $2660 per capita for Aboriginal primary health care.

One could also adjust for cultural factors. Successful health programs in Aboriginal communities require the election and convening of health councils, properly conducted community councils, Aboriginal health workers and administrators and appropriate health promotion activities – in total $2917 per capita. Finally, if we wish to be truly culturally appropriate we might also fund healing ceremonies and visits to traditional healers – leaving a total of $3022 per capita.

At the time of this paper, primary health care for Aboriginal communities was funded at about the level suggested by the first formula – about $700 per capita. It is clear that Australia could provide a vastly increased sum on Aboriginal health – in the interests of justice – without invoking positive discrimination.

Interventions and capabilities

The poor health of Indigenous Australians results to a substantial degree from the ongoing impact of colonial histories, dispossession and marginalisation and the effects of prejudice and racism (Eades 2000). For these reasons it is vital to establish key issues and concerns as seen from an Aboriginal perspective. Language difficulties, poor communication, a lack of cultural sensitivity and an inadequate understanding of the health needs and social conditions of Aboriginal people are major barriers to appropriate health care. The perception of many Aboriginal people is that they receive inappropriate treatment in an environment that is not only insensitive to them as people, but also to their culture, values and needs.

These points are summarised in the statement of the Royal Commission into Aboriginal Deaths in Custody: '[T]he elimination of disadvantage requires an end of domination and an empowerment of Aboriginal people; that control of their lives, of their communities must be returned to Aboriginal hands' (Johnston 1991).

Treasury Secretary Ken Henry has identified seven platforms for a framework of Indigenous capability development. These provide a good example of some of the functionings and capabilities required to advance the prospects of Aboriginal people in Australia. His platforms include:

- basic protective security from violence for parents and children;
- early childhood development interventions to provide a critical foundation base for young children from pre-birth to school;
- a home environment conducive to regular patterns of sleep and study, free from overcrowding and distraction;
- ready access to a suitable primary health service infrastructure.
- In an environment where real jobs are not the norm, incentives in the welfare system cannot be allowed to work against the promotion of investment in human capital.
- There must be a realistic prospect of an educated Indigenous person securing a real job – in some places it is difficult to avoid confronting the need for mobility.
- Governance systems have to support the political freedom and social opportunities of local Indigenous people to be engaged in policy development. (Pearson 2007)

It is important to note that, while this list of capabilities maybe useful, it has been developed from a non-Aboriginal perspective. Sen (in contrast to some of his followers such as Nussbaum) has refused to specify his own list of capabilities, arguing that it is up to individuals themselves to decide what is important for them. This is in keeping with what has become probably the most widespread view about Aboriginal health – that Aboriginal people must decide health priorities themselves.

'Little children are sacred' – The Northern Territory Emergency Response

On 21 June 2007 the government announced the Northern Territory Emergency Response following details of child sexual abuse in remote Aboriginal communities in 2006 and publication of the *Ampe akelyernemane meke mekarle: 'little children are sacred'* report (Wild and Anderson 2007). The initiative, which was the largest public health response ever conducted in Australia, had three broad objectives: stabilisation to protect children and secure their communities, normalisation of services and infrastructure and, in the longer term, sustainability in order to bring Aboriginal Australians into lines with the choices other Australian enjoy (Glasson 2007).

From the outset the intervention was styled as strong, decisive action and framed as an emergency. (John Howard, then Prime Minister, described the situation of children in remote Aboriginal communities as 'Australia's Hurricane Katrina'.) This rhetoric, coming as it did after many years of inadequate funding, provided the moral justification for action that would otherwise have been subject to extensive critique. and created considerable disquiet among those living and working in Aboriginal communities (Tait 2007). Importantly, the rhetoric used by the government and social commentators was also in marked contrast to the language and text of the 'Little children are sacred' report, which supported few of the draconian measures adopted in the intervention. In fact, the *Ampe akelyernemane meke mekarle: 'little children are sacred'* report was very clear about the necessary approach to addressing the issues it raised: '

> [W]hat is required is a determined, coordinated effort to break the cycle and provide the necessary strength, power and appropriate support services to local communities, so they can lead themselves out of the malaise: in a word, empowerment! (Wild and Anderson 2007)

While few denied the need for some type of action to address the problems in Aboriginal communities, the scale, timing and manner of the intervention raised real concerns. While some parts of the intervention, including access to paediatric ENT services and an improved primary health-care system, were desirable and generally welcomed by Aboriginal communities and by the Aboriginal Medical Service Alliance Northern Territory (AMSANT) (Boffa, Bell et al 2007), other parts of the intervention, such as compulsory forensic (sexual) examinations of children (which were later abandoned), generated widespread fear and resentment, and others, including welfare changes, compulsory land acquisition by the federal government, the abolition of entry permits for Indigenous communities and the prohibition of alcohol, were poorly defined, or justified and were arguably racially discriminatory.

While the results of reviews of the intervention are ongoing, it seems clear that the intervention was poorly conceived; lacked many of the elements of good indigenous policy – respect, engagement, consultation, participation and accountability; failed to consider the long-term socio-political consequences of the intervention, including the further stigmatisation of Aboriginal men and Aboriginal communities; and did little to address the impact of cultural and social disempowerment on health (Altman and Hinckson 2007; Brown and Brown 2007, Toohey 2008). Nevertheless, the injection of funds provided by the intervention and the increased focus of government on Aboriginal communities have provided some grounds for optimism in addressing Aboriginal disadvantage. It remains unclear whether the intervention will create safe, sustainable and nurturing communities or perpetuate dysfunction, marginalisation, cultural trauma and abuse.

The Apology

On 13 February 2008, the new Labour Prime Minister, Kevin Rudd, offered an apology to the Stolen Generation and, through them, to all indigenous people.

> To the stolen generations, I say the following: as Prime Minister of Australia, I am sorry. On behalf of the government of Australia, I am sorry. On behalf of the parliament of Australia, I am sorry. I offer you this apology without qualification. (Rudd 2008)

After many years of debate regarding the necessity for, and meaning of, an apology, the day was charged with emotion and symbolic meaning, for both black and white Australians (Jackson-Pulver and Fitzpatrick 2008). For many Aboriginal people the apology provided a restored sense of decency, a sense that their suffering was acknowledged and belief that reconciliation and lasting change may be possible (Jackson-Pulver and Fitzpatrick 2008). It is important to note that the Apology was the first of five steps recommended in *Bringing Them Home: The Report of the National Inquiry into the Separation of Aboriginal and Torres Strait Islander Children from their Families* – the others being: guarantees against repetition, restitution, rehabilitation and compensation – and that it took 10 years for the apology to happen. The Commonwealth has made no commitment to reparation or compensation.

THE LAW AND ABORIGINES AND TORRES STRAIT ISLANDERS

The Indigenous people of Australia have not been well served by the law or the legal justice system. From the time of European settlement Indigenous people have not been treated equally with other inhabitants of the country. This is despite the fact that the Colonial Office in England insisted, throughout the 1830s, that Aboriginal people be treated as British subjects and receive greater protection from the white legal system.

Much of Australian law has been built upon a shaky legal fiction – that Australia was subject to the doctrine of *terra nullius* at the time of 'settlement'. International law recognised three effective ways of acquiring sovereignty over another country – conquest, cession, and occupation of territory that was *terra nullius*. According to Blackstone, English law would become the law of a country outside England either by the exercise of the Sovereign's legislative power over a conquered or ceded country, or upon first settlement by English colonists of a 'desert uninhabited' country. In the case of a conquered country, the general rule was that the laws of the country continued after the conquest until those laws were altered by the conqueror. The doctrine of *terra nullius* provides that where a land is unoccupied, settlers bring their domestic law with them as part of their 'baggage'. The opposing doctrine is that where a land is settled after conquest, the common law recognised an obligation to recognise the existing system of law, although it could be modified as appropriate.

The doctrine of *terra nullius* was first said by the courts to apply to the occupation of Australia by the Privy Council in the decision of *Cooper v Stuart* (1889) 14 App Cas 286. Blackburn J, in the case of *Milirrpum v Nabalco Pty Ltd* (1971) 17 FLR 141, felt constrained to follow the precedent set by the Privy Council. It was not until 1992 that the High Court in *Mabo v Queensland (No 2)* (1992) 175 CLR 1 (*Mabo*) rejected the application of the doctrine of *terra nullius* to Australia. Deane and Gaudron JJ observed that:

> The acts and events by which that dispossession in legal theory was carried into practical effect constitute the darkest aspect of the history of this nation. The nation as a whole must remain diminished unless and until there is an acknowledgment of, and retreat from, those past injustices. In these circumstances, the Court is under a clear duty to re-examine the two propositions. For the reasons which we have explained, that re-examination compels their rejection. The lands of this continent were not terra nullius or 'practically unoccupied' in 1788. (at 109)

In the *Mabo* decision the High Court by a 6:1 majority recognised the existence of native title for a group of Murray Islanders. In response to the decision in *Mabo* the *Native Title Act 1993* (Cth) was enacted to set the boundaries within which native title could be claimed. There were further developments in the decision in *Wik Peoples v Queensland* (1996) 187 CLR 1 where it was affirmed by the High Court that pastoral leases might not have, necessarily, extinguished native title to land. The Commonwealth Parliament responded to this judgment with a '10 point plan' and in 1998 amended the *Native Title Act 1993*. On 13 October 2004 Cooper J of the Federal Court approved the native title claim by the Wik Peoples covering about 12,500 square kilometres on the western side of the Cape York Peninsula.

Until 1967, Aboriginal and Torres Strait Islander people were effectively excluded from the Australian Constitution under s 51(xxvi) that placed responsibility for Aboriginal and Torres Strait Islander people in the hands of the States. In 1967 a referendum (with the largest majority in any Australian constitutional referendum) amended the Constitution to remove the exclusion of Aboriginal peoples from the power of Federal Parliament to make laws with respect to 'the people of any race for whom it is deemed necessary to make special laws'. The referendum also deleted s 127 of the Constitution which had stated that that in taking a census 'Aboriginal natives were not to be counted'.

Customary laws

Legislation may recognise the significance of customary law. For example, the *Family Provision Act 1980* in the Northern Territory provides in s 7(1A) that 'an Aboriginal who has entered into a relationship with another Aboriginal that is recognised as a traditional marriage by the community or group to which either Aboriginal belongs is married to the other Aboriginal, and all relationships shall be determined accordingly'. While the High Court in *Mabo* recognised the existence of native title, the court did not have to consider the extent of its application, nor did it consider the wider issue of residual rights of Indigenous people. In a decision handed down by the High Court (Mason CJ, sitting alone) on 16 December 1994, the court considered the general application of customary law. The case was *Walker v New South Wales* (1994) 182 CLR 45 which concerned an application to dismiss, or alternatively stop, criminal proceedings against an Aboriginal person in the New South Wales District Court on the ground that because the defendant was an Aboriginal person they should be tried in accordance with Aboriginal customary law.

The Chief Justice said:

> Even if it be assumed that the customary criminal law of Aboriginal people survived British settlement, it was extinguished by the passage of criminal statutes of general application. In *Mabo (No 2)*, the Court held that there was no inconsistency between native title being held by people of Aboriginal descent and the underlying radical title being vested in the Crown. There is no analogy with the criminal law. English criminal law did not, and Australian criminal law does not, accommodate an alternative body of law operating alongside it. There is nothing in *Mabo (No 2)* to provide any support at all for the proposition that criminal laws of general application do not apply to Aboriginal people. (at 50)

This does not mean, however, that customary law is no longer of any relevance. The Northern Territory Supreme Court has recognised Aboriginal customary law as relevant to the sentencing process. These include *R v Miyatatawuy* (1996) 6 NTLR 44 and *Munungurr v R* (1994) 4 NTLR 63. Such cases are principally concerned with the extent to which the courts, in fixing an appropriate sentence, can have regard to the application of customary law. During the late 1990s formalisation of this practice has occurred in remote and urban areas with the advent of Indigenous sentencing, Community Justice Groups and Circle Courts (Marchetti and Daly 2004). The aim has been to make court processes more culturally appropriate and to engender greater trust between Indigenous communities and judicial officers.

Aboriginal deaths in custody

The Royal Commission into Aboriginal Deaths in Custody investigated the deaths of 99 Aboriginal and Torres Strait Islander people who died in custody between 1 January 1980 and 31 May 1989. A five-volume report was produced in 1991 (Johnston 1991). Chapter 31 of the Report in titled *Towards Better Health*. The Royal Commission noted (at para 31.1.2):

> The link between the health of Aboriginal people in the community and these deaths in custody should be obvious: Aboriginal people in general have a very poor level of health. Their quality of life is substantially reduced by illnesses that only uncommonly affect the general Australian public. Since so many Aboriginal people experience serious sickness and injury as part of their everyday lives, it should be no surprise to find that they bring this impaired health status with them into the custodial situation. The quality of their management in these circumstances is a central theme of this report.

The Royal Commission made 23 recommendations relating to the health of Aboriginal people. The recommendations included further and better education of non-Aboriginal health professionals about Aboriginal people, their cultural differences, socio-economic circumstances and history within Australian society (recommendation 247); access to skilled interpreters (recommendation 249); the improved physical design and operation of health-care facilities (recommendation 253); and the use of Aboriginal hospital liaison officers (recommendation 261).

One of the problems noted by the Royal Commission was the stereotyped attitude of some health-care providers to Aboriginal people. As an example the Report said:

> 31.3.38 … The case of Mark Quayle is perhaps best known, owing to media publicity, as one where responsibility for the death fell on nursing and medical personnel as well as on police officers. Commissioner Wootten, in his report on the case, referred to the 'shocking and callous disregard' for Quayle's welfare on the part of the staff, and pointed out that this unacceptable behaviour reflected 'the dehumanising stereotype of Aboriginals so common in Australia'.

All Australian governments have endorsed the 1990 National Aboriginal Health Strategy and have affirmed their endorsement by approving Recommendation 271 of the Royal Commission into Aboriginal Deaths in Custody which regarded implementation of the Strategy as 'crucial'.

Despite many of the recommendations made by the Royal Commission there are still a disproportionate number of deaths of Aboriginal and Torres Strait Islander people, due to the over-representation of this group in custodial facilities and the failure of government (both State and federal) to implement the recommendations (Sripathy and Ogle 1997).

Stolen Generation report

The National Inquiry into the Separation of Aboriginal and Torres Strait Islander Children from Their Families was established in 1995. It was conducted by the Human Rights and Equal Opportunity Commission (HREOC). There was increasing concern among key Indigenous agencies and communities that the general public's ignorance of the history of forcible removal was hindering the recognition of the needs of its victims and their families, and the provision of services.

The Inquiry took evidence in public and private sittings from Indigenous people, government and church representatives, former mission staff, foster and adoptive parents, doctors and health professionals, academics, police and others. People also made written submissions. HREOC President, Sir Ronald Wilson, and the Aboriginal and Torres Strait Islander Social Justice Commissioner, Mick Dodson, conducted most hearings.

The Inquiry submitted its 700-page report to the Federal Attorney-General in April 1997. The Inquiry found that Indigenous families and communities have endured gross violations of their human rights. These violations continue to affect Indigenous people's daily lives. They were an act of genocide, aimed at wiping out Indigenous families, communities and cultures, vital to the precious and inalienable heritage of Australia. The Inquiry's recommendations are directed to healing and reconciliation for the benefit of all Australians (National Inquiry into the separation of Aboriginal and Torres Strait Islander Children from their Families 1997).

Chapter 18 of the 'Bringing them Home' report deals with mental health services. The Royal Commission into Aboriginal Deaths in Custody had already pointed out that:

> In view of the extent of mental health problems found by the Commission among the people whose deaths it has investigated, special attention needs to be directed at the component of the health care system aimed at addressing mental health problems.... [T]he prevalence of major mental disorders among Aboriginal people is probably similar to that among non-Aboriginal people, but that, for many Aboriginal people, mental distress is a common and crippling problem which largely goes unnoticed, undiagnosed and untreated. (Royal Commission into Aboriginal Deaths in Custody 1991: para [31.2.40])

The Inquiry noted:

> Indigenous mental health is finally on the national agenda. As participants in the National Mental Health Strategy, States and Territories acknowledge the importance of the issue. Some of the effects of removal including loss and grief, reduced parenting skills, child and youth behavioural problems and youth suicide are increasingly recognised. The circumstances in which a large proportion of Indigenous people live also contribute to experiences of loss and grief and to mental health and related problems. They include poverty and high rates of unemployment, marginalisation and racism. (National Inquiry into the separation of Aboriginal and Torres Strait Islander Children from their Families 1997: Chapter 18)

The Inquiry made a number of recommendations, recognising that 'a substantial injection of funding is needed to address the emotional and well-being needs of Indigenous people affected by forcible removal'. The Recommendations included:

> **Recommendation 32:** That the Commonwealth Government work with the national Aboriginal and Torres Strait Islander Health Council in consultation with the National Aboriginal Community Controlled Health Organisation

(NACCHO) to devise a program of research and consultations to identify the range and extent of emotional and well-being effects of the forcible removal policies.

Recommendation 33a: That all services and programs provided for survivors of forcible removal emphasise local Indigenous healing and well-being perspectives.

Recommendation 33b: That government funding for Indigenous preventive and primary mental health (well-being) services be directed exclusively to Indigenous community-based services including Aboriginal and Islander health services, child care agencies and substance abuse services.

Recommendation 33c: That all government-run mental health services work towards delivering specialist services in partnership with Indigenous community-based services and employ Indigenous mental health workers and community members respected for their healing skills.

Recommendation 34a: That government health services, in consultation with Indigenous health services and family tracing and reunion services, develop in-service training for all employees in the history and effects of forcible removal.

Recommendation 34b: That all health and related training institutions, in consultation with Indigenous health services and family tracing and reunion services, develop under-graduate training for all students in the history and effects of forcible removal.

Recommendation 35: That all State and Territory Governments institute Indigenous mental health worker training through Indigenous-run programs to ensure cultural and social appropriateness.

A number of members of the stolen generation have sought to sue for the damage done to them by their removal from their families. In New South Wales Joy Williams first filed a notice of motion seeking an extension of time under the *Limitation Act 1969* (NSW) to bring a claim for negligence, breach of fiduciary duty and wrongful imprisonment against the State of New South Wales. The application was rejected by Studdert J in 1993 but this decision was reversed by a majority in the Court of Appeal the following year (*Williams v Minister, Aboriginal Land Rights Act 1983* (1994) 35 NSWLR 497). In 1999 Ms Williams lost her claim before the New South Wales Supreme Court and a subsequent appeal was also unsuccessful (*Williams v Minister, Aboriginal Land Rights Act and New South Wales* (2000) Aust Torts Reports ¶81-578).

In the Northern Territory, Lorna Cubillo and Peter Gunner sued for wrongful imprisonment, breach of statutory duty, negligence and breach of fiduciary duty arising out of their removal from their families and their detention in mission run institutions. They were unsuccessful before the Federal Court (2000) and the Full Court of the Federal Court (2001). In 2002 the High Court refused special leave to appeal from this decision.

There has at least been one successful claim. In *Trevorrow v South Australia (No 5)* [2007] SASC 285, an Aboriginal plaintiff successfully brought an action against the State of South Australia for misfeasance of public office, false imprisonment, breach of duty of care and breach of fiduciary and statutory duties. It was found that the removal of the plaintiff from his family as a child had occurred without authority and had occurred illegally. By doing so the State had breached its duty of care to the plaintiff. It had falsely imprisoned the plaintiff and misused it public powers. The State, as the guardian of the plaintiff, also owed a fiduciary duty to inform the plaintiff of the circumstances of his removal and to ensure he received independent legal advice. Damages were awarded, including exemplary damages.

The law and Indigenous health

It is important to understand the ways in which the legal system has supported injustices against Indigenous people as these injustices are often at the root of the health disadvantage suffered by Indigenous people. There are also functional factors imposed by the law that has an indirect impact upon the provision of health services. The application of laws that may be advantageous amongst the wider population could have a negative impact upon some groups. For example, all jurisdictions have legislation that regulates the supply and use of certain medications. These medications may be dangerous to the health of people and, indeed, are defined by some legislation as poisons (Staunton and Chiarella 2003). The legislation is designed to protect the public by regulating a system that aims to provide for the timely, safe and efficacious use of medicines. The prescription and supply of medications is one of the few areas of health care that is specifically regulated by statute.

Richard Murray, however, has pointed out that in the Aboriginal health setting 'prescribers commonly confront the dilemma of quite reasonable and well-established medication practices by Aboriginal health workers and registered nurses that fall outside various laws and regulations' (Murray 2003). This particularly may be the case in rural and remote communities. This is because the infrastructure anticipated by the legislation may not exist in practice and that in the choice between delivering needed services and the strict interpretation and application of the statutory requirements, the delivery of needed services takes precedence. This situation may reflect a breakdown in health policy rather than inappropriate practices. Murray suggests that:

> Without a statutory framework, health services may leave treatment decisions to the discretion of remote health staff as they feel unable to expressly condone an illegal practice. This leaves individual health workers exposed and unsupported. To ensure timely, safe and efficacious use of medicines in Aboriginal communities, the way forward must include statutory reform. (Murray 2003)

These types of tensions may appear in many other areas of the law that confront health-care professionals, including consent and the assessment of the capacity of patients. The courts, when examining the application of common law principles, are always interested in the context of the particular case. Thus, the standard of care owed by a health professional will be different in a remote community compared with a modern metropolitan hospital. These concerns do not, however, relieve health professionals from considering the common law and statutory requirements; the choice is how the balance is made and justified.

Legal aspects of the Northern Territory intervention

There are legal aspects of the Northern Territory intervention (discussed above) which are profoundly disturbing. One of the primary reasons for this disturbance is that both the *Northern Territory National Emergency Response Act 2007* (Cth), ss 132-133, and the *Social Security and Other Legislation Amendment (Welfare Payment Reform) Act 2007* (Cth), ss 4-5, explicitly suspend the operation of the *Racial Discrimination Act 1975* (Cth).

The reasons given for the suspension of human rights legislation was to enable the compulsory acquisition of land by the Commonwealth under five-year leases and the imposition of compulsory income management schemes through the welfare system. Land was compulsorily acquired by the Commonwealth without consent and without compensation. Sixty-four acquisitions of leasehold have been granted to the Commonwealth, giving the Commonwealth exclusive possession and quiet enjoyment of the leasehold area.

The Northern Territory Emergency Response Review Board (NTERRB) reported in October 2008 on the effectiveness of the intervention and made a number of recommendations on how it could be improved. The NTERRB stated:

> There is intense hurt and anger at being isolated on the basis of race and subjected to collective measures that would never be applied to other Australians. The Intervention was received with a sense of betrayal and disbelief. Resistance to its imposition undercut the potential effectiveness of its substantive measures. (NTERRB 2008: 8)

One of the overarching recommendations was that government actions affecting Aboriginal communities respect Australia's human rights obligations and conform with the *Racial Discrimination Act* (NTERRB 2008: 12, 46-7). These recommendations do not look like they will be adopted by the Rudd Government.

A constitutional challenge to the legislation was launched in the High Court in October 2008 by Reggie Wurridjal and other the community elders from Maningrida: *Wurridjal v Commonwealth* [2009] HCA 2. It was argued that the intervention was illegal because it allowed the Commonwealth to acquire property without payment being made on just terms (as required under s 51(xxxi) of the Australian Constitution). A majority (6:1) found against the claim. All judges agreed that the requirement to pay just terms did apply to the Territory, but the majority itself was split. French CJ, Gummow, Hayne, Heydon and Kiefel JJ found that the acquisition of land was on just terms because the intervention legislation allowed for a 'reasonable amount of compensation' to be paid by the Commonwealth. Crennan J believed that the legislation did not effect an acquisition of property that would have required just terms compensation. Kirby J, in dissent, believed that the issue required consideration of the native title in question and of the nature of the Commonwealth's acquisition, which could only be determined after a trial. As such, the way the case was fought by the Commonwealth (on *demurrer*) was, for Kirby J, inappropriate as there had not been a trial yet on the facts.

Regardless of the outcome in *Wurridjal*, one needs to seriously question the effectiveness of a regulatory control mechanism that is apparently motivated by the desire to protect the human rights of children, but which takes as its starting point an express desire to racially discriminate against indigenous rights. It is clearly hypocritical for the Commonwealth to push for the imposition of human rights on the one hand, while with the other exempting itself from compliance with them. No one doubts that action is needed to improve the health of indigenous Australians in the Territory, but improvements should be built on respect for the rights of Aboriginal Australians, not in opposition to them.

References

Altman, J and M Hinckson (2007) *Coercive reconciliation.* Melbourne, Arena Publications.

Amery, H (1999) *Attitudes to hospitalisation amongst the Yolngu people of North East Arnhem Land – A comparative study.*, Territory Health Services.

Anand, P, G Hunter et al (2005) 'Capabilities and Wellbeing: Evidence based on the Sen-Nussbaum approach to welfare'. *Social Indicators Research* **79**: 9-55.

Anderson, I, S Crengle et al (2006) 'Indigenous health in Australia, New Zealand and the Pacific'. *Lancet* **367**: 1775-85.

Anderson, I and J Wakerman (2005) Aboriginal and Torres Strait islander primary health care and general practice. *General Practice in Australia.* DoHa Aging. Canberra, Commonwealth of Australia: 303-36.

Attwood, B (2004) *Rights for Aborigines.* Sydney, Allen and Unwin.

Australian Bureau of Statistics. (2003) '4713.0 Population Characteristics, Aboriginal and Torres Strait Islander Australians', <http://www.abs.gov.au>.

Australian Bureau of Statistics (2006) *National Aboriginal and Torres Strait Islander Health Survey 2004–05.* Canberra, ABS.

Australian Bureau of Statistics (2007) '2006 Census QuickStats : Australia', <http://www.censusdata.abs.gov.au>.

Australian Institute of Health and Welfare (2008) *Australia's Health 2008.* Canberra, AIHW.

Bailey, T (2002) 'On Trust and Philosophy', <http://www.open2.net/trust/on_trust/on_trust1.htm>.

Bailie, R (2007) Housing. *Social determinants of Indigenous health.* B Carson, T Dunbar, R Chenhall and R Bailie. Sydney, Allen and Unwin.

Baum, F (2007) Social capital. *Social Determinants of Indigenous health.* B Carson, T Dunbar, R Chenhall and R Bailie. Sydney, Allen and Unwin.

Bhopal, R (1997) 'Is research into ethnicity and health racist, unsound, or important science?' *BMJ* **1314**: 1751.

Boffa, J, A Bell et al (2007) ' The Aboriginal Medical Services Alliance Northern Territory: engaging with the intervention to improve primary health care'. *Med J Aust* **187**(11-12): 617-18.

Brady, W (1999) 'Observing the Other'. *Eureka Street* **9**(1): 28-30.

Brough, M (2001) 'Healthy imaginations: a social history of the epidemiology of Aboriginal and Torres Strait Islander health'. *Medical Anthropology* **20**(1): 65-90.

Brown, A and N Brown (2007) 'The Northern Territory intervention: voices from the centre of the fringe'. *Med J Aust* **187**(11-12): 621-3.

Bryce, S (2002) 'Improving adherence to chronic disease treatment – lessons from East Arnhem Land'. *Aust Family Physician* **13**(7).

Burger, A (1979) *Neville Bonner.* Melbourne, MacMillan.

Burgess, CP, FH Johnston et al (2005) 'Healthy country: healthy people? Exploring the health benefits of indigenous natural resource management'. *Aust NZJ Public Health* **29**(2): 117-22.

Burgess, P and J Morrison (2007) Country. *Social determinants of Indigenous health.* B Carson, T Dunbar, R Chenhall and R Bailie. Sydney, Allen and Unwin.

Burns, C (1992) 'A Pilot Study on Compliance in Aboriginal Paediatric Patients receiving Oral Antibiotic Medication'. *Australian Journal of Hospital Pharmacy* **22**(3): 217-21.

Cass, A, A Lowell et al (2002) 'Sharing the true stories: improving communication between Aboriginal patients and healthcare workers'. *Med J Aust* **176**(10): 466-70.

Chatterjee, JS (2006) 'From compliance to concordance in diabetes'. *J Med Ethics* **32**(9): 507-10.

Cheng, W, P Blum et al (2004) 'Barriers to effective perioperative communication in indigenous Australians: and audit of progress since 1996'. *Anaesth Intensive Care* **32**(4): 542-7.

Coates, C (2004) *A global history of Indigenous peoples struggles and survival*. New York, Palgrave Macmillan.

Council for Aboriginal Reconciliation (1994) *The Little Red, Yellow & Black and Green and Blue and White Book – A Short Guide to Indigenous Australians*. Canberra, Australian Institute of Aboriginal and Torres Strait Islander Studies.

Cowlishaw, G (1988) *Black white or brindle: race in rural Australia*. Sydney, Cambridge University Press.

Day, W (2001) Aboriginal fringe dwellers in Darwin: cultural persistence or culture of resistance? *Department of Anthropology*. Perth, University of Western Australia.

Devitt, J and A McMasters (1998a) *Living on Medicine: A cultural study of end-stage renal disease among Aboriginal people*. Alice Springs, IAD Press.

Devitt, J and A McMasters (1998b) *On the machine: Aboriginal stories about kidney troubles*. Alice Springs, IAD Press.

Eades, S (2000) 'Reconciliation, social equity and Indigenous health: A call for symbolic change'. *Med J Aust* **172**: 468-9.

Elliott, C and P Brodwin (2002) 'Identity and Genetic Ancestry Testing'. *BMJ* **325**: 1469-70.

Etherington, S (2006) *Learning to be Kunwinjku: Kunwinjku People Discuss Their Pedagogy*. Darwin, Charles Darwin University. PhD.

Folds, R (2001) *Crossed purposes: the Pintupi and Australia's indigenous policy*. Sydney, UNSW Press.

Gilson, L (2003) 'Trust and the development of health care as a social institution'. *Social Science and Medicine* **56**: 1453-68.

Glasson, W (2007) 'The Northern Territory Emergency response: a chance to heal Australia's worst sore'. *Med J Aust* **187**(11-12): 614-16.

Gorham, G (2001) *Prevention & Treatment Options for Renal Disease in the Northern Territory (with particular reference to the Barkly Region)*. Darwin, Cooperative Research Centre for Aboriginal and Tropical Health.

Henry, B, S Houston et al (2004) 'Institutional racism in Australian healthcare: a plea for decency'. *Med J Aust* **180**(10): 517-20.

Hoy, W (1996) 'Renal disease in Australian Aboriginals'. *Med J Aust* **165**(3): 127.

Hoy, W, J Mathews et al (1995) 'Treatment of Australian Aborigines with end-stage renal disease in the top end of the Northern Territory'. *Nephrology*: 307-13.

Humphery, K, T Weeramanthri et al (2001) *Forgetting compliance : Aboriginal health and medical culture*. [Casuarina, NT], Northern Territory University Press in association with the Cooperative Research Centre for Aboriginal and Tropical Health.

Humphrey, K (2001) Indigenous Health and Western Research. *VicHealth Koori Health Research and Community Development Unit. Discussion Paper No 2*.

Hunter, EM (1993) *Aboriginal health and history : power and prejudice in remote Australia*. Cambridge; New York, Cambridge University Press.

Jackson-Pulver, L and S Fitzpatrick (2008) 'Beyond Sorry – the first steps in laying claim to a future that embraces all Australians'. *Med J Aust* **188**(10): 556-8.

Johnston, E (1991) *Royal Commission into Aboriginal Deaths in Custody. National Report*. Canberra, AGPS.

Keeffe, K (1988) 'Aboriginality: resistance and persistence'. *Australian Aboriginal Studies* **1**(67-81).

Keeffe, K (1992) *From the centre to the city: Aboriginal education, culture and power*. Canberra, Aboriginal Studies Press.

King, P (1992) 'The dangers of difference'. *Hastings Cent Rep* **22**: 35-8.

Kowal, E and Y Paradies (2003) *Race and Culture in Health Research: A Facilitated Discussion*. Darwin, Cooperative Research Centre for Aboriginal and Tropical Health.

Kruske, S, A Ruben et al (1999) 'An Iron treatment trial in an Aboriginal community: Improving nonadherence'. *J Paediatr Child Health* **35**: 153-8.

Kunitz, SJ (1994) *Disease and Social Diversity: The European Impact on the Health of Non-Europeans*. Oxford, Oxford University Press.

Kunitz, SJ and M Brady (1995) 'Health care policy for aboriginal Australians: the relevance of the American Indian experience'. *Aust J Public Health* **19**(6): 549-58.

LoGiudice, D, K Smith et al (2006) 'Kimberley Indigenous Cognitive Assessment tool (KICA): development of a cognitive assessment tool for older indigenous Australians'. *Int Psychogeriatr* **18**(2): 269-80.

Maher, P (1999) 'A review of "traditional" aboriginal health beliefs'. *Aust Jn Rural Hlth* **7**(4): 229-36.

Marchetti, E and K Daly (2004) *Indigenous courts and justice practices in Australia. Trends and issues in crime and criminal justice*. Canberra, Australian Institute of Criminology.

McDermott, R and C Beaver (1996) 'Models for horizontal equity in resource allocation in Aboriginal health'. *Aust NZ J Publ Health* **20**(1): 13-15.

Melder, A (2000) A search for meaning? *School of Public Health*. Sydney, University of Sydney.

Murray, R (2003) 'Prescribing issues for Aboriginal people'. *Australian Prescriber* **26**: 106-9.

Nangala, T, G Nangala et al (2008) 'Who makes decisions for the unconscious Aboriginal patient?' *Aboriginal and Islander Health Worker Journal*. **32**(1): 6-8.

National Health and Medical Research Council (2003) *Values and Ethics: Guidelines for Ethical Conduct in Aboriginal and Torres Strait Islander Health Research*. Canberra, National Health and Medical Research Council. Canberra, NHMRC.

National Health and Medical Research Council (Australia) (2003) *Values and ethics : guidelines for ethical conduct in Aboriginal and Torres Strait Islander health research*. Canberra, NHMRC.

National Inquiry into the separation of Aboriginal and Torres Strait Islander Children from their Families (1997) *Bringing them home: Report of the National Inquiry into the Separation of Aboriginal and Torres Strait Islander Children from their Families*. Sydney, Human Rights and Equal Opportunities Commission.

Northern Territory. Board of Inquiry into the Protection of Aboriginal Children from Sexual Abuse, R Wild et al (2007) *Report of the Northern Territory Board of Inquiry into the Protection of Aboriginal Children from Sexual Abuse*. [Darwin, Govt Printer].

Northern Territory Emergency Response Review Board (2008) *Report of the NTER Board*. Canberra, Commonwealth of Australia.

Nursing Council of New Zealand (2002) 'Guidelines for Cultural Safety, the Treaty of Waitangi, and Maori Health in Nursing and Midwifery Education and Practice'.

Pearson, N (2007) Choice is not enough. *The Australian*.

Pearson, N (2007) Sense of obligation a route out of handout hell. *The Australian*. Melbourne. **Dec 22-23**: 22.

Pink, B, P Allbon et al (2008) *The Health and welfare of Australia's Aboriginal and Torres Strait Islander peoples, 2008*. Canberra, Australian Bureau of Statistics and Australian Institute of Health and Welfare.

Queensland State Government. 'Aboriginal English in the courts', <www.justice.qld. gov.au/courts/pdfs/handbook.pdf>.

Rose, B, Central Land Council (Australia) et al (1995) *Land management issues : attitudes and perceptions amongst Aboriginal people of central Australia*. Alice Springs, Central Land Council.

Rudd, K (2008) 'Apology to Australia's Indigenous peoples'. House of Representatives 2008, *Debates*, No 1, 13 February 2008: 167-73, <http://www.aph.gov.au/Hansard/reps/dailys/dr130208.pdf>.

Sackett, L (1988) 'Resisting arrests: drinking, development and discipline in a desert context'. *Social Analysis* **24**: 66-84.

Sansom, B (1980) *The Camp at Wallaby Cross*. Canberra, Australian Institute of Aboriginal Studies.

Sen, A (1979) Equality of what?. *The Tanner Lecture on Human Values*. Stanford University.

Sen, AK (1999) *Development as freedom*. New York; Oxford, Oxford University Press.

Sripathy, V and L Ogle (1997) *The Law Handbook: Your practical guide to the law in New South Wales*. Sydney, Redfern Legal Centre Publishing.

Staunton, P and M Chiarella (2003) *Nursing and the Law*. Sydney, Churchill Livingstone.

Sydney Morning Herald (2002) Blood lines called into question. *Sydney Morning Herald*.

Tait, P (2007) 'Protecting little children's health – or not?' *Med J Aust* **187**(11-12): 619-20.

Thomas, D (2004) *Reading Doctors' Writing: Race, politics and power in Indigenous health research 1870-1969*. Canberra, Aboriginal Studies Press.

Toohey, P (2008) 'Last drinks: the impact of the Northern territory intervention'. *Quarterly essay*(30): 1-97.

Trigger, DS, C Anderson et al (1983) 'Mortality rates in 14 Queensland Aboriginal reserve communities. Association with 10 socioenvironmental variables'. *Med J Aust* **1**(8): 361-5.

Wepa, D (2001) An exploration of the experiences of cultural safety educators, Massey University.

Wild, R and P Anderson (2007) Ampe akelyernemane meke mekarle: 'little children are sacred'. *Report of the Northern Territory Board of Inquiry into the Protection of Aboriginal Children from Sexual Abuse*. Darwin, Northern Territory Government: 13.

Wright, L (1994) 'One drop of blood'. *The New Yorker*: 46-5.

CHAPTER 30

RESOURCE ALLOCATION AND INTERNATIONAL HEALTH

Case 1

JN is a 36-year-old United Nations peacekeeper who was airlifted from East Timor to an Australian hospital with severe pneumonia. He was originally from West Africa, but has been in East Timor for six months. As part of his workup he was found to have HIV. He was unwilling to disclose contacts in East Timor, and, although it is known that he is married with children in Africa, the details of these were not known to the treating team. The question arose of what responsibility did the Australian doctors have for tracing his contacts.

Case 2

BG is a 32-year-old Indonesian fisherman who was caught illegally fishing off Australia's Northern Coast. He was brought to Darwin where he was found to have active Tuberculosis. He was treated for a short period of time in Darwin before being transported back to Indonesia with a small amount of medications. This is the second time this has happened to BG and he has told staff he is unable to afford medications in Indonesia, and must rejoin a boat as soon as he gets back in order to support his wife and children. He wishes to get back to Indonesia as soon as possible as he is concerned that his wife and children will be unable to survive without his salary.

In Australia, a person who does not take his TB medications can be forced to do so, even imprisoned if necessary. The treating team wonder what their responsibility is to this man, and to the broader community. One of their concerns is that if he is treated inadequately he will be at high risk of multi-drug resistant TB – which he may bring back to Australia at a later date. (For a discussion of Indonesian fishermen with TB, see Gray, Hansen-Knarhoi et al (2008).)

Case 3: Health care in Singapore

Since independence in 1965, the government of Singapore has emphasised the values of hard work, and economic self-sufficiency. Singaporeans have never had unemployment benefits, old-age pensions or significant supporting-mother benefits. "As Rajaratnam, a former senior minister, puts it: 'We want to teach the people that the

Government is not a rich uncle. You get what you pay for. We are moving in the direction of making people pay for everything ... We want to disabuse people of the notion that in a good society the rich must pay for the poor. We want to reduce welfare to the minimum, restricted only to those who are handicapped or old. To the others we offer equal opportunities and it is up to them what they make of it."(Barraclough and Morrow 1995)

Singapore has a high level of employment, and all employees must contribute between 6% and 8% of their incomes into the 'Medisave' scheme. Payments to the Medisave scheme are compulsory for employees, and are highly encouraged for those who are self-employed. The money that is placed in this scheme is able to be used to cover part of the costs of hospital for the contributor and their family. It is not an insurance scheme in which shared funds can be used by those who are unrelated. Singaporeans are also encouraged to pay into an insurance scheme known as Medishield that covers catastrophic illness such as intensive care, dialysis and cancer therapy. This fund will not cover the whole costs of hospitalisation – but will require co-payments by those who wish to draw benefits. Neither Medishield nor Medisave can be used to cover the costs of illnesses that are 'self-inflicted' such as AIDS, drug addiction, attempted suicide or alcoholism.

An obvious intention of the Medisave and Medishield schemes is cost-containment through the use of a price-signal. At every stage of treatment the patient, or the patient's family, is required to provide varying degrees of co-payment ... Rightly or wrongly, Singapore's policy makers clearly believe that consumers who have to fund a large part of their hospital treatment from their own savings are likely to be more frugal in their use of hospital services ... The extension of Medisave to the contributor's parents and grandparents reinforces the Confucian values of familial duty promoted through public policy in a Singapore whose leaders fear that rapid economic growth and exposure of its citizens to western culture pose threats to what they regard as traditional Asian values. (Barraclough and Morrow 1995)

Much of bioethics is concerned with the specific relationships between health professionals and patients. However, bioethics is also concerned with wider issues about the health of communities and the way society allocates its resources to maintain health standards. The ethical issues involved in resource allocation can be considered at a number of levels – international, national, regional, hospital or at the level of the professional/patient relationship. Gruen and colleagues have noted in relation to the medical profession that:

Leaders and observers of the medical profession have recently urged greater engagement of physicians in the public arena. Three compelling reasons have been given. First, community socioeconomic characteristics affect many health problems and access to health care; second, physician's expertise is essential for properly addressing major quality, access, public health and policy concerns; and third, clear and visible leadership in the interests of the public's health is regarded by many as the best way for the medical profession to regain and retain the public trust that has diminished in recent decades. (Gruen, Pearson et al 2004)

Gruen and colleagues propose a model whereby physicians have a professional obligation to take responsibility for patient care, access to care, and direct socioeconomic influences on health, and have aspirations to influence, but no direct responsibility for, the broad socioeconomic influences and broader global influences of health. Many health practitioners (medical or otherwise) would probably find this conclusion, and the reasons for limiting involvement in the public domain to be overly conservative, and would believe that the role of the health professions extends even to the global influences on health.

Resource allocation/priority setting

No health system can afford to provide every service to every citizen. The cost of health care is constantly increasing because the population is increasing and getting older, and because technological change is driving increased expectations of the services that the health-care system can offer. Decisions about the allocation of resources are therefore a feature of every health service (Pearson 2000).

Priority setting occurs at the bedside, in hospitals or regional institutions and at system-wide levels. Decisions at each of these levels are inter-related.

Priority setting involves taking account of a complex series of factors including clinical factors, patient values and system goals. Importantly, there is no real consensus regarding how these factors are weighed, and individuals and communities may differ as to how these decisions are made. The goal is therefore to establish a process which is fair and just, in which values that may guide these decisions are explicit and in which different perspectives may be heard and different needs considered.

Moral frameworks for priority setting

The 'accountability for reasonableness' framework is one example of a model for priority setting that is based on the ethical concept of fairness (Daniels 2000). This model suggests that priority setting should take account of: relevance (priority-setting decisions must rest on reasons that 'fair-minded' people agree are relevant), publicity (reasons for priority-setting decisions must be publicly accessible), revision (all decisions must be open to challenge) and enforcement (those responsible for priority setting are responsible for ensuring that other conditions of fairness are met).

At the micro level (the bedside) health professionals are often in a position where they must act, or feel under pressure to act, as gatekeepers for the health system. This is a problematic position because rationing decisions are best made according to policies rather than on a case-by-case basis and health professionals are generally not trained or willing to play such a role. In practice, rationing decisions made at the bedside often end up very unclear and vary between situations, cases and clinicians. Some may be based on patient need, others on potential for benefit, others on the capacity to pay, and many decisions are based only on the professional's clinical wisdom or their ability to advocate for the patient (Walton, Martin et al 2007).

Global poverty and public health

Worldwide, 18 million people die prematurely each year from treatable medical conditions such as infections, perinatal conditions, maternal conditions, and malnutrition. This represents 50,000 avoidable deaths per day, or one-third of all human deaths (WHO 2004). Nearly all of this avoidable mortality and morbidity occurs in poor countries, and among their poorer inhabitants in particular. The social determinants of this burden of illness are now well recognised – 800 million worldwide are undernourished, 1000 million lack access to safe water, 2400 million lack access to basic sanitation, more than 880 million lack access to basic health services, 1000 million lack adequate shelter and 2000 million have no access to electricity (UNDP 1998; UNDP 1999; UNDP 2003).

Public health practitioners increasingly demand that we pay attention to the manner in which national and international economies and political structures directly contribute to the extent of global poverty and to the deprivation of basic human rights (Pogge 2002; Farmer 2003).

In general terms it has been suggested that there are two basic ways to respond to the problem of global poverty – one is through increasing the disposable income that all people have to be able to purchase those things that contribute to good health; food, sanitation, safe drinking water, housing and so on; and the other is through ensuring increased access to public goods, such as medical therapies (Pogge 2002). Both of these 'solutions' suggest that public health interventions must be broadly political if they are to have any real impact on health.

Philosophy and global health

The philosopher Peter Singer has written extensively about issues of global equity. Singer (reasonably) assumes that suffering is bad and, because hunger is a form of suffering, hunger is bad. Singer proposes that resources should be distributed with impartiality, universalisability and equality in a way that minimises suffering. And 'if it is in our power to prevent something bad from happening, without thereby sacrificing anything of comparable moral importance, we ought, morally, to do it'. Further, he argues, from Aquinas, that 'whatever a man has in abundance is owed, of natural right, to the poor for their sustenance' and that failure to act, if one can act, is equivalent to killing (Singer 1972; Singer 2002). Singer believes that one should continue to give up to the 'Point of Marginal Utility' – the point at which contributing anything more may cause more harm to the donor than further contribution would prevent the recipient from suffering.

Singer's position is that giving is not a matter of generosity (as it is commonly perceived) but necessity and that not giving is not a matter of egocentricity or selfishness, but is morally wrong. He also argues that our obligations to help others should not take into account proximity or distance between the person or persons requiring help and the donor, and he makes no distinction between whether the person is the only one who can act or whether they are one of millions who can act. Singer's concern is the moral obligations on the donor.

Singer's paper – which demands that individuals and nations contribute aid to relieve world hunger – has evoked furious responses from philosophers and politicians (Kuper 2005).

One philosopher who has disagreed with Singer is the African-American philosopher Kwame Anthony Appiah. Appiah suggests that the logical conclusion of Singer's position would be that 'a well-off person, like you and me, must contribute to vitally effective groups, like OXFAM and UNICEF, most of the money she now has, and most of what comes her way for the foreseeable future' (Appiah 2006).

Appiah himself thinks that this goes too far, and suggests an alternative formulation: 'If you are the person in the best position to prevent something really awful, and it won't cost you much to do so, do it' (Appiah 2006). Appiah links this idea to the interesting question of 'doing one's share':

> [O]ur obligation is not to carry the whole burden alone. Each of us should do our fair share; but we cannot be required to do more … even if we could determine how each of us, depending on our resources, should contribute as his or her fair share, we can be pretty confident that some people would not give their fair share. This means there would be some unmet entitlements. What is the obligation of those who have already met their basic obligation? Is it enough simply to say, 'I know there are unmet entitlements, but I have done my part?' … For if so many people in the world are not doing their share – and they clearly are not – it seems to me I cannot be required to derail my life to take up the slack. (Appiah 2006)

So what is our fair share? Many activists in the area of international aid have suggested that rich countries should donate 0.7% of GDP to poor countries. A convincing case has been made by Clemens and Moss, that this figure is a purely arbitrary one. However, some European countries have signed up to this figure, and some already exceed it (Clemens and Moss 2005). In 2005, Australia donated 0.28% of its GDP in foreign aid – well below this recommended amount (Zwi, Grove et al 2005).

Another philosophical approach to the problem of global poverty is that taken by Onora O'Neill (O'Neill 1986; O'Neill 2007). O'Neill's approach to world hunger and famine is based on Kantian moral philosophy which, she says, states that we are obligated to treat people as ends in themselves and are therefore duty-bound to help others to act autonomously. O'Neill is clear that it is the individual's autonomy that is most central and that as people suffering from hunger have their autonomy and rationality compromised they are vulnerable to acts of coercion and deception. We have an obligation to help them become autonomous and regain independence through relief of hunger and poverty. She rejects the idea that provision of aid (calories or medicine) is sufficient and argues that what is ultimately needed is empowering people so that they can feed and support themselves. In other words she strives to build independence, foster and sustain indigenous capacities for local action and ensure justice. Importantly, she does not tell us where goods come from – only what we should do with them once we have them. Her theory, therefore, has limited application in times of crisis, but is a valuable guide as to the goals of support.

In his analysis of famine, the economist Amartya Sen has shown that hunger and famine result not so much from a shortage of food, but from injustices in access to, and distribution of, food (Sen 1987). And while aid may have an important role in crisis situations, it infrequently addresses the root political and economic causes of the crises and may have limited positive influence on the long-term growth and economic sustainability of developing countries. It may also aggravate injustices and inequity, and sustain the power imbalances and political, social and economic systems that create poverty in the first place (Kuper 2005). If Singer's ideas were to be interpreted as the provision of aid to poor countries, then they may be misplaced (Kamm 2000; Igneski 2001).

However, we must agree with both Singer and O'Neill at least that significantly more needs to be done to relieve world poverty and world hunger.

Using resources equitably

A key issue in the ethics of resource distribution is whether resources are shared 'equitably', or fairly. One concept of fairness is that money should be spent in such a way so that everyone would be equally healthy. This idea is reflected in the goal adopted by the World Health Organization of 'Health for all by the year 2000'. In retrospect it is hard to see how this goal could ever have been proposed. After all, there are many people with illnesses that simply cannot be treated; these individuals were not healthy in the year 2000, indeed they may never be healthy! (It is also worth noting that equity is not the only goal that we should pursue. It would be possible to make everybody equally healthy, by making everybody severely ill! This might be fair, but it would not be desirable.)

Another approach to equity would be to suggest that people should all have equal use of services. However, some people need more services than others, so this principle would need to be modified to say that people with equal needs should have equal use of services (Mooney 1994). Health-care systems that operate in this way generally provide some sort of subsidy to those with low incomes, so that income does not substitute for need as the basis for health-care distribution. This model does have a number of difficult technical areas such as how does one assess need, and how the health-care needs of people of different levels of need are to be assessed.

Authors including Mooney suggest a third approach to equity – equality of access for equal need. By this he means that the opportunity costs for different individuals in seeking health should be the same. So, for example, services for a paraplegic on an invalid pension should involve the same personal costs and inconvenience as for the managing director of BHP. Access can in this way be measured as an economic variable. The UK government has recently implemented a policy that resources should be distributed in such a way as to 'contribute to the reduction of avoidable health inequalities' (Hauck, Shaw et al 2002). While this would seem an ethically robust definition of equity, such an approach may not be compatible with an objective of equity of access, nor with the objective of maximising health gain.

A fourth approach, suggested by Amartya Sen, is based on equality of 'capabilities'. This idea, discussed further in Chapter 29, suggests that people would have an equal range of available life choices, including choices about health (Sen 1979).

Other ideas of equity are also sometimes included in health-care systems. In the example quoted at the start of the chapter – that of Singapore – it can be seen to be based on an equality of access to economic gains (such as jobs and business-making opportunities), that are then supposed to translate into money, and hence into an equality of access to goods such as health care. The Medisave and Medishield systems are there to ensure that some individual economic gains are set aside for health care and to provide a safety net for those who fall through the system. The emphasis on self-reliance is also reflected in the decision that these funds cannot be used for 'self-inflicted' illnesses (including HIV!) – an idea that seems out of step with many Western views of equity (Barraclough and Morrow 1995).

It is important to recognise, as economist Amartya Sen has pointed out, that definitions of health equity cannot be concerned only with the distribution of health care or the distribution of health (Sen 1992). For it is now well established that a range of factors, including genetic propensities and environmental condit-ions, work conditions, food habits and social inequalities, can have far-reaching effects on health and survival. Thus, health equity is ultimately concerned both with issues of fairness and justice within wider social arrangements, particularly the distribution of wealth and power, and with the role that health, in turn, plays in human life and freedom. The relationship between health equity and social justice is most apparent in countries like Australia when there are gross dis-parities in wealth and health between indigenous and non-indigenous citizens.

The costs of health care

Economists do not generally define the costs of goods or services in terms of money. Rather, costs are defined in terms of what must be forgone in order to obtain that item. If we wish to obtain something – such as a car, we must forgo something else – such as an overseas holiday. In this sense, the cost of the car is the overseas holiday that must be given away.

For example, in the early 1990s, it was reported that the costs of surgery and care for a child with hypoplastic left ventricle were up to US$660,000 (Boren 1994). From an economist's point of view, the real cost of the operation was the next best use that could have been made with that money. When we decide to fund an expensive operation like this, the funds are directed away from another area such as nursing homes, intensive care, or even roads or defence.

The responsibility of government to fund such surgery is clearly dependent on the resources of the country in which we live. We might argue that an Australian child may have a right to a heart transplant, as the real cost of this might only be the inability to perform a liver transplant upon someone else, or to provide some dialysis beds, or to forego part of the cost of a new jet. Yet, in a third-world country this would not be a viable argument. The cost of a heart transplant there might involve denying the right to basic health care to more than 10,000 other citizens! Therefore, if governments have an obligation to provide health care, it is evident that this can only be expressed in terms of offering citizens an equitable share of the health-care resources that they have available. This is much less evident when we use the language of rights – because we are forced to conclude that any right to health care consists more as a right to an equitable share of the health dollar than as an overall right to any particular procedure or treatment.

In a fanciful article in a 1994 edition of the *New England Journal of Medicine*, Frederick Abrams imagined a doctor waking up with two heads – one which put patient advocacy before community interests, and the other which put community interests before patient advocacy.

> 'OK, this is what we'll do,' [said the first head]. 'I will handle all the patient treatment and do everything the patient and I decide to do in pursuit of the therapeutic goal that we have chosen together. If care is going to be limited, it will be strictly on the basis of what works ...'
>
> 'You, [the second head], get to deal with the interplay between medicine and society,' he continued. 'You go to meetings and give policy people your opinion about what is cost effective. But that's not the thing to do when you're dealing with an individual patient who expects you to do everything to meet his or her goals. You can advise legislatures, health maintenance organisations and insurance companies about what you think ought to be limited for the best use of resources ...'
>
> 'So,' said one head, 'we'll use one head to advocate for the patient and the other head when we're suggesting community restrictions due to limited resources.'
>
> 'And we'll never try to use two heads at once.' (Abrams 1994)

Abrams argues that health professionals should not consider costs of treatment when they are dealing with individual patients, but may only consider them when dealing with issues at community or population levels. This approach to the problem of resource allocation is often advocated by clinicians who do not believe that it is appropriate for them to think about resources costs when dealing with the individual patient. However, from an economic perspective, this is precisely the opposite of what would be desirable; for if decisions are to be made free of the constraints of costs this is likely to cause a greatly expanding blow-out of the health budget. Furthermore, to an economist, the idea of attempting to avoid issues of cost and opportunity cost verges on the ridiculous.

> If another CT scanner is bought, the costs and use represent forgone opportunities to provide benefits, from more geriatric beds, more health visiting or ... other forms of non-health care spending. Dr Paul always robs Dr, Mr or Master Peter. As we shall see later, it is the attempt – inevitably forlorn – to ignore, bypass or overcome this basic law of economics which leads to frustration and inefficiency in the health care sector. (Mooney 1992)

In the Australian health-care system, health professionals act as agents for their patients. 'Agent' relationships occur where consumers realise that they do not have the knowledge or expertise to buy goods or services themselves, and request a more trained person to either suggest items or purchase them on their behalf. Health professionals operate for patients in this way in procuring items as diverse as housing, food, operations, drugs, pathology tests and even care-givers and companions.

The economist Gavin Mooney points out that, by making health-care professionals accountable for cost decisions as well as for clinical decisions, we expect them to enter another sort of agent relationship – acting as the agent for society to manage issues of cost and opportunity cost. Mooney points out that this agency relationship is more problematic than the other one. First, there is less of an information gap between the patient and the professional, as few professionals are any better informed on these matters than the general public. Secondly, the opportunity cost of a decision is often only evident a long way removed from the site of the original decision. For example, if a health service opens a new facility such as an MRI machine, they will have to cut services elsewhere. But the practitioners involved in planning for and using the MRI machine may have absolutely no contact with the second area where the costs become evident. Thirdly, there is often a clash of interests between the roles of professionals as patients' agents and as society's agents.

This is a difficult issue. Health professionals cannot avoid being involved in making resource decisions, yet they are poorly qualified for this role, and it may entail significant conflict of interests.

Community involvement in priority setting

Resource allocation decisions at all levels above the bedside are generally made by health bureaucrats, with health professionals often supplying expert knowledge where appropriate. Community participation in health policy and priority-setting is a recent alternative to this model (Frankish, Kwan et al 2002). Those who advocate community participation argue that health policy requires dialogue and engagement with the public, and recognition that the public has particular kinds of knowledge and expertise. Local communities have knowledge of local needs and resources and often have direct experience of health services. Advocates of community involvement also claim that the community has an important role to play both in identifying the values that should underpin resource allocation decisions, and that community participation has an important role in legitimating health policy decisions, and fostering trust and confidence in the health-care system (Frankish, Kwan et al 2002; McBride and Korczak 2007).

A number of models for public participation in health-care decision-making have been described including 'citizens' juries', community advisory boards, lay health authorities, community forums, long-term standing committees and 'whole community engagement' (in small, homogeneous and remote communities).

The role of citizens' juries has generally been to advise on policy and planning issues where value judgements are required. They are formed from a random and stratified sample of the community so that they are broadly representative. Over four days they are then briefed by experts in the field, provided with opportunities to interrogate the information provided, given time to discuss the issues in depth and then expected to draft recommendations or advice (Lenaghan 1999). Citizens' juries have become an established method for community involvement in health care in the UK and are widely regarded as a valuable resource for policy makers and economists (Lenaghan 1999).

An experiment with citizens' juries in Western Australia in 2001 found support for the following values in health care:

- greater priority setting in health;
- equity, based on equal access for equal need;
- positive discrimination for disadvantaged people;
- more spending on prevention and public health, rather than treatment of disease;
- more spending on rural and remote health;
- more focus on community-based health services. (Mooney and Blackwell 2004)

This suggests that citizens' juries may be able to think through complex issues and may be able to identify core values in health and construct broad policy agendas reflective of concerns for social justice and care for vulnerable populations. This is also consistent with research from the UK and Canada that has demonstrated that, given sufficient time, community members can understand complex information and become expert in resource allocation (Lenaghan 1999; Maxwell, Rosell et al 2003).

A number of criticisms of citizens' juries have been advanced including that it is difficult to get a representative sample for community members to participate in such exercises. Participants are often self-selecting and tend to be white, middle class, educated and motivated – which may not represent the background population.

Dialogue sessions using randomly selected citizens have been another widely used method of obtaining community involvement in Canada. At a national level such sessions defined the broad values and goals of the Canadian health-care system – universal coverage and a commitment to principles of equity, efficiency and accountability (Maxwell, Rosell et al 2003).

Another approach to community involvement in setting health priorities occurred in the US State of Oregon, where citizens were able to vote upon which procedures would receive State funding (Glass 1988; Bodenheimer 1997).

Those who advocate community participation argue that health policy requires dialogue and engagement, and demands that we develop new mechanisms for inclusion of the public. Critics of all forms of community participation claim that governments and policy-makers use participation purely as a means for co-opting citizens into a larger agenda, such as cost-cutting or introducing unpopular interventions, or simply legitimating predetermined health policy. Others are concerned that an emphasis on participation and/or consensus may serve to derail important policies or social agendas and risk recourse to populism.

The Australian health-care system

By world standards, Australia provides effective and efficient delivery of health care. Every two years, the Australian Institute of Health and Welfare puts out a report on the state of Australia's health. At the time of writing, the most current statement was the 2006 report (Australian Institute of Health and Welfare 2006) which contains data for the period leading up to 2006. This report forms the basis for much of the data within this section.

In 2003-04, Australia spent 9.7% of its gross domestic product ($78.6 billion) on health – with over two-thirds of this funded by government. Hospital services accounted for about one-third of recurrent health expenditure, whereas government expenditure on public health (disease prevention and health promotion) accounted for only 1.7% of recurrent health expenditure. One in 17 of all employed people are in the health occupations – nearly 570,000 Australians (Australian Institute of Health and Welfare 2006).

Around 85% of Australians visit a doctor at least once a year, at an average of five GP visits per Australian. However, the distribution of services is very skewed – with 4% of people having more than 50 medical services in a year but many people not going at all (Australian Institute of Health and Welfare 2006).

On any one day in Australia about 19,000 Australians are admitted to hospital and there are about 125,000 other hospital services, such as emergency department consultations. In a year there is about one hospital stay for every three Australians, however this distribution is also skewed, with some such as those on dialysis having many admissions, whereas others are rarely admitted. About 60% of hospital stays occur in the public system where the average cost of an episode of care in 2003-04 was about $3300. Almost 1 in 20 hospital separations are associated with an adverse event. Same-day admissions to hospitals now make up over half of all admissions (Australian Institute of Health and Welfare 2006).

Almost 70% of total health expenditure in Australia is funded by government, with the Australian government contributing two-thirds of this and State, Territory and local governments the other third. The Australian government's major contributions include the two national subsidy schemes: Medicare and the Pharmaceutical Benefits Scheme. These schemes subsidise payments for services provided by doctors and optometrists, and for a high proportion of prescription medications bought from pharmacies. The Australian and State and Territory governments also jointly fund public hospital services. There are also special health-care arrangements for members of the defence forces, and for war veterans and their dependants (Australian Institute of Health and Welfare 2006).

Funding of Australian health services is split between numerous parties. Government health services are funded by the Australian government, the State and Territory governments, or both. The Australian government is the major source of funds for high-level residential care (74.8%), medical services (76.8%) and health research (66.6%). State and Territory governments are the major source of funding for community health services (91.9%). Funding for public hospitals is shared between the Australian government (45.2%) and the States and Territories (47.5%), as is funding for public health activities (52.4% and 47.6% respectively). Private hospitals are largely funded by non-government sources (59.9%) (Australian Institute of Health and Welfare 2006).

Before 1975, 10-15% of Australians lacked medical insurance. In 1975, the Australian government introduced a system of mandatory health insurance. This scheme underwent several changes until the current scheme – Medicare –

was introduced in 1984. Medicare is partially funded by an annual federal income tax that is known as the Medicare levy. This pays for a small part of the total costs of medical and hospital services – with the remainder coming from other sources of revenue (Peabody, Bickel et al 1996).

A significant number of Australians continue to have private health insurance in addition to what they receive from Medicare. At the end of June 2005, 42.8% of the Australian population were covered by private hospital cover. This number has fluctuated greatly over the years in response to different incentive packages offered by governments including such measures as a tax levy of 1% of taxable income for high income earners, and the introduction of a non-means-tested 30% rebate on private health insurance premiums in 1999 (Australian Institute of Health and Welfare 2006).

Private health insurance provides for about 10.3% of total national health-care funding. For insured people it provides added benefits such as choice of doctor, choice of hospital and choice of timing of procedure, and can assist with services not covered by Medicare, such as dental, optical, physiotherapy and podiatry services. Private health insurance is highly regulated by the Commonwealth government. A system known as 'community rating' means that health funds are not allowed to change their rates for people who are sicker or the elderly.

One of the problems with systems of medical care that are largely publicly funded, and that operate at little direct cost to the customer, is that people may seek more treatment than they would if they had to pay for it. There is some evidence that this occurs in Australia. In 1992-93, Australians had an average of 9.76 doctor contacts per capita – compared with an OECD average of 6. By 2002-03, Australians were visiting doctors an average of 11.1 times per year (Australian Government Department of Health and Ageing 2004).

Governments have attempted to limit the expenditure on health care in this system in several ways. First, the number of available hospital beds has been decreased as a reaction to the perceived oversupply, resulting in an increase in waiting lists. Secondly, governments have not increased scheduled fees in line with other salaries, resulting in a fall in the income of doctors who bulk-bill. Thirdly, the government limits the adoption of expensive new technology through its control of Medicare reimbursement. Finally, the government restricts the availability of subsidised medication and can negotiate reductions in prices of some medications.

Despite such measures, the costs of health care in Australia continue to rise and there are major concerns that the quality and availability of health care have deteriorated over the past 5-10 years. As we have seen in other countries, the government is now attempting to introduce new elements as an alternative to the traditional fee-for-service. A good example of this is the 'casemix' systems that are used for allocation of funds to the hospital system. Unfortunately, there is little evidence that government policy has improved the health care of the majority of Australians or the indigenous population, and there is also little evidence that measures such as the 30% private health insurance rebate have strengthened either the public hospital system or Medicare.

In August 2003, 250 consumers, doctors, nurses, allied health and other health professionals, health managers, economists and politicians met at the Australian Health Care Summit to discuss ways in which Australia's health system could be improved. The group later issued a communiqué, *The Old Parliament House Blueprint for Health Reform,* which contained a series of recommendations regarding urgent priorities, proposals for reform and suggestions for restructuring the bureaucracy of health care. Importantly, there was general agreement on the underlying problems facing the health system and on future priorities. The problems identified included: lack of community involvement in health-care planning; waste and systemic inefficiencies; overemphasis on hospitals at the expense of primary care; failure of the Commonwealth and States to cooperate in the funding and delivery of health services; government, public and professional failure to acknowledge the need for rationing and the existence of opportunity costs; bureaucratic preoccupation with crises and micro-management; and the absence of a collective political will for meaningful reform of the health sector (Menadue 2003). In 2008, these issues are equally salient.

Conclusion

Efforts worldwide to address the complexities of resource allocation suggest that it presents intractable problems. These efforts provide some common insights. First, it is clear that there is no universal model for resolving the ethical problems of resource allocation. Secondly, resource allocation requires consideration of multiple, often conflicting, ideals such as effectiveness, equity and efficiency. Finally, while no experiment in allocation can claim absolute success, those that have achieved social and political credibility have transparency and community involvement in common (Klein, Day et al 1996).

In a limited health budget, the introduction of a new service will always involve an opportunity cost. One clear ethical principle in health-care budgeting is that, if a new service is introduced, it should be at least as good as the service it replaces. One should not introduce a new service if it is less beneficial to the public than the service it replaces. Unfortunately, in the present situation where the opportunity costs of services are often not clearly identified, such comparisons cannot be made easily. As part of a more open approach to health-care budgeting, the adverse consequences of the introduction of new services should be made more explicit.

Finally, there can be a great deal more community involvement in resource allocation decisions than is currently the case. At present, community interest in these issues is usually only stimulated by sensational stories of people being refused services, or by lobbying by individual disease interest groups. Explicit and informed community involvement would be far superior to the present system of covert decision-making by health professionals and health administrators.

LEGAL ASPECTS OF INTERNATIONAL AND GLOBAL HEALTH AND RESOURCE ALLOCATION

International law and human rights in health care

International law consists of the implied and express agreements which are binding on nation-states in the international community. Nations ordinarily become bound by international law when they sign up to agreements concerning norms of conduct (such as declarations, covenants and treaties) but there is also a body of customary international laws which, arguably, apply to all nations regardless of their consent (eg, the laws of war, laws against genocide and crimes against humanity). In Australia, international law contained in treaties does not become part of the domestic law of Australia until it is enacted in legislation, even though Australia may be a signatory to such treaties.

The Universal Declaration of Human Rights

International law is an important source of human rights and since World War II the United Nations has created a number of human rights instruments that have direct and indirect effects on health care. The originating document is the *Universal Declaration of Human Rights 1948*, which was a resolution of the General Assembly. The Declaration expressed a commitment to a number of fundamental rights. Article 25.1 states:

> Everyone has the right to a standard of living adequate for the health and well-being of himself and of his family, including food, clothing, housing and medical care and necessary social services, and the right to security in the event of unemployment, sickness, disability, widowhood, old age or other lack of livelihood in circumstances beyond his control.

The International Covenant of Civil and Political Rights and the International Covenant on Economic, Social and Cultural Rights

While having great moral authority, the Declaration as a resolution does not have binding authority on states under international law (O'Neill, Rice and Douglas 2004). Further treaties were needed. Of these the most important are the *International Covenant of Civil and Political Rights* (ICCPR) and the *International Covenant on Economic, Social and Cultural Rights* (ICESCR), Australia ratified the ICESCR in 1976 and the ICCPR in 1980. The ICCPR recognises a number of basic political and civil rights such as the right to life (Article 6), freedom from torture (Article 7), rights to liberty and security of the person (Article 9), and the right to be treated with dignity and respect (Article 10). These arguably all have some impact on health care. Interestingly, a number of the rights can be limited by public health concerns such as the right to freedom of movement (Article 12), freedom of expression (Article 19), right to peaceful assembly (Article 21) and freedom of association (Article 22).

The ICCPR also has two optional protocols, the first of which allows people who have exhausted their domestic remedies to seek the intervention of the

United Nations Human Rights Committee. Member states must submit periodic reports to the Committee which then forwards comments back to the states and on to ECOSOC (the Economic and Social Council of the United Nations). The Second Optional Protocol creates an international obligation not to execute anyone within a country's jurisdiction. Australia is a signatory to both protocols. At times the Human Rights Committee has been quite critical of Australian reports, commenting on such issues as the abolition of the Aboriginal and Torres Strait Islander Commission (ATSIC) and legislation for mandatory imprisonment in Northern Territory and Western Australia.

While the ICCPR is concerned with negative rights (freedoms from interference), the ICESCR recognises positive rights which impose obligations on member states to provide economic and social services. Rights recognised include the right to work (Article 6), the right to enjoy favourable work conditions (Article 7), the right to an adequate standard of living (Article 11) and the right to education (Article 13).

Importantly for health law, Article 12 recognises a right to the enjoyment of the highest attainable standard of physical and mental health. In pursuance of this right, member states are bound to take steps towards:

    (a) The provision for the reduction of the stillbirth-rate and of infant mortality and for the healthy development of the child;

    (b) The improvement of all aspects of environmental and industrial hygiene;

    (c) The prevention, treatment and control of epidemic, endemic, occupational and other diseases;

    (d) The creation of conditions which would assure to all medical service and medical attention in the event of sickness.

The ICESCR contains some of the more controversial statements of rights expressed in the two treaties. The treaty does not require states to give immediate effect to the rights it recognises but suggests that each state 'undertakes to take steps ... to the maximum of its available resources, with a view to achieving progressively the full realisation of the rights recognised ...' (Article 2). This has led some to argue that economic, social and cultural rights contained in the treaty are not real human rights, since they do not arise out of the human condition, but are instead dependent on economic factors within individual countries for their realisation.

The Convention on the Rights of the Child

The *Convention on the Rights of the Child* came into force in 1990 and Australia became a signatory in 1991. Many of the rights expressed in this convention were already contained in other conventions, but new rights included the right for a child to be cared for by his or her parents, and to be free of sexual abuse and exploitation. Article 24 recognises the 'right of the child to the enjoyment of the highest attainable standard of health and to facilities for the treatment of illness and rehabilitation of health'. Additionally, under Article 24, states agree to take measures to:

(a) To diminish infant and child mortality;
(b) To ensure the provision of necessary medical assistance and health care to all children with emphasis on the development of primary health care;
(c) To combat disease and malnutrition, including within the framework of primary health care, through, inter alia, the application of readily available technology and through the provision of adequate nutritious foods and clean drinking-water, taking into consideration the dangers and risks of environmental pollution;
(d) To ensure appropriate pre-natal and post-natal health care for mothers;
(e) To ensure that all segments of society, in particular parents and children, are informed, have access to education and are supported in the use of basic knowledge of child health and nutrition, the advantages of breastfeeding, hygiene and environmental sanitation and the prevention of accidents;
(f) To develop preventive health care, guidance for parents and family planning education and services.

Traditional practices which are prejudicial to children's health should be abolished and states agree to promote international cooperation to fully realise Article 24.

Article 23 requires states to recognise that mentally or physically disabled children should enjoy a full and decent life, in conditions which ensure dignity, promote self-reliance and facilitate the children's active participation in the community. Article 25 requires children in placements to have their care, protection and medical treatment periodically reviewed.

The International Convention to Eliminate All Forms of Racial Discrimination

The *International Convention to Eliminate All Forms of Racial Discrimination* entered into force in January 1969 and was ratified by Australia in September 1975. The treaty is supervised by the Committee on the Elimination of Racial Discrimination (CERD). It considers reports by governments on racial discrimination in their countries and follows up urgent cases of racial discrimination brought to its notice. At times this committee has also been critical of the Australian government.

Under Article 5 of the convention, states undertake to guarantee everyone a number of rights, including the right to public health, medical care, social security and social services.

The Universal Declaration on the Human Genome and Human Rights and the International Declaration on Human Genetic Data

The *Universal Declaration on the Human Genome and Human Rights* is a non-binding declaration. It was drafted by the International Bioethics Committee of the United Nations Education Scientific and Cultural Organization (UNESCO) in the mid-1990s and was adopted by the General Conference of UNESCO in 1997. The United Nations later endorsed the Declaration in 1998. The Declaration aims to ensure the respect of human dignity and the protection of human rights in the collection, processing, use and storage of human genetic data, human proteomic data and biological samples. In particular Article 5 mandates informed consent for research, Article 6 forbids genetic discrimination and Article 7 protects confidentiality. Article 12 states that benefits from advances in biology, genetics and medicine, concerning the human genome, shall be made available to all.

UNESCO later followed up the Universal Declaration with a further *International Declaration on Human Genetic Data*, which was endorsed in 2004 by the General Conference of UNESCO. The aim of this Declaration was to place further stipulations on the collection, use and storage of genetic materials in line with human rights principles.

The Universal Declaration on Bioethics and Human Rights

The *Universal Declaration on Bioethics and Human Rights* is another UNESCO non-binding declaration which was adopted by the UNESCO general conference in 2005. The aim of the declaration is to create a universal framework of principles and procedures to help states in the formulation of their legislation and policies. The Declaration requires respect for human dignity and human rights (Article 3); maximisation of benefit and minimisation of harm to patients, research participants and other affected individuals (Article 4); autonomy and individual responsibility (Article 5); informed consent to medical intervention and scientific research (Article 6); and special protection for persons without the capacity to consent (Article 7). Other rights recognised include a respect for human vulnerability and personal integrity (Article 8); privacy and confidentiality (Article 9); equality, justice and equity (Article 10); non-discrimination and non-stigmatisation (Article 11). In relation to the right to health care, Article 14 states that the promotion of health and social development is a central purpose of government and that the attainment of the highest possible standard of health is a fundamental right of every human being.

International health law or global health law?

As the discussion of these international human rights instruments shows, health is at the forefront of human rights and international law. Critics of these instruments say that, while they work as grand aspirational statements, they have little effect on the reality of political and social rights of people living in both the developed and developing world. International laws are only binding to the extent that states wish them to be. In that sense these international health rights have no real legitimacy as legal rights given their low levels of enforceability (Ruger 2008).

Professor Lawrence Gostin believes that the focus on international heath law as it affects individual states has not been as effective as it should be. He has argued that there are four 'grand challenges' to overcome if international law is to be more effective in pursuing better health (Gostin and Taylor 2008):

- state-centricity in the international legal system;
- skewed-priority setting;

- flawed implementation and compliance; and
- fragmentation, duplication and lack of coordination.

Professor Gostin has argued for a move away from traditional international law towards global health law. A 'global health law' approach looks to 'facilitate health-promoting behaviour among the key actors that significantly influence the public's health, including international organizations, governments, businesses, foundations, the media, and civil society'. While international law and public international organisations are important, according to Gostin and Taylor:

> [T]o be an effective global health governance strategy, global health law must evolve beyond its traditional confines of formal sources and subjects of international law. It must foster more effective collective global health action among governments, businesses, civil society and other actors. Accordingly, our definition of global health law is prescriptive as well as descriptive: it sets out the sort of international legal framework needed, but still unavailable, to empower the world community to advance global health in accordance with the value of social justice. (Gostin and Taylor 2008)

The move away from traditional international law approaches has been partially caused by globalisation. The experience of globalisation has thrown up serious challenges to traditional international law and to the global health law movement. Magnusson has written:

> The pervasive theme here is globalisation itself: a process reflected in the disappearance of boundaries, the increasing integration of the global economy, and flowing from that, the intensification of transnational interactions and influences across physical, political, social and cultural borders. The point is often made that globalization has diminished the capacity of countries to deal effectively with major health threats occurring within their borders, creating new imperatives for international cooperation, and thrusting new responsibilities onto global actors, civil society and the private sector. Globalization creates, in other words, new process challenges to an effective response to national health problems. Coordinated strategies involving partnerships between international agencies, the private sector and non-governmental organizations (NGOs) are required because few policy actors – global or not – are capable of single-handedly driving policies across multiple sectors at country level in order to lay the groundwork for population-wide health improvements. (Magnusson 2007)

Globalisation has rendered state boundaries more permeable with the result that national approaches are less likely to be effective (Bennett 2008). To that extent global health law must steer away from a state-based focus and look towards international organisations and multinational corporations as targeted areas for regulation. Moreover, the regulatory focus itself shifts to consider not only traditional regulatory mechanisms but also informal mechanisms to 'promote health-producing behaviours and discourage harmful behaviours' (Gostin and Taylor 2008). Gostin and Taylor have said:

> Governance goes well beyond setting and enforcing hard legal norms for states to obey. Instead, governance involves creating incentives for a wide array of actors; setting priorities for the most cost-effective interventions;

coordinating increasingly fragmented activities; mobilizing international aid and technical assistance; and stimulating research for new vaccines, pharmaceuticals and technologies. Scholars emphasize global health governance, rather than the prohibitory or regulatory products of 'government' because it allows easy movement across public/private boundaries of the state, markets, civil society and private life. Rather than a model of top-down social control, governance theory harnesses the creativity and channels the actions, ideas and resources of multiple actors that affect health.

Examples of global health law

Advocates of the global health law approach use two main examples of global health law. The first is *International Health Regulations* (IHR) which are a unified code of conduct for infectious disease control, binding on members of the World Health Organization (WHO) (Isasi and Nguyen 2005; Ruger 2008). They were adopted in 1951, revised in 1969 and revised again in 2005. The IHR provide a framework for a global response to pandemic threats. They also incorporate human rights principles into their framework. Gostin and Taylor are, however, critical of the way the IHR failed to provide any mechanism to assist poor countries in establishing or maintaining their national systems (Gostin and Taylor 2008).

Another example of global health law which is often cited is the WHO *Framework Convention on Tobacco Control* which requires countries to regulate tobacco sales, advertising, packaging and labelling (see Chapter 22). It also requires members to provide for education, training, communication, public awareness, and smoking cessation efforts (Ruger 2008; Magnusson 2007). Again, Gostin has been critical of the convention in the way that it failed to require independent monitoring systems, effective dispute resolution procedures, or a mechanism for providing resources to poor states to implement their treaty obligations (Gostin and Taylor 2008).

Professor Gostin has suggested a *Framework Convention on Global Health* (FCGH) as a model of innovative global health governance (Gostin 2008; Gostin 2009). He proposes that an FCGH would look, first, to building capacity so that all countries have enduring and effective health systems, and, secondly, setting priorities so that international assistance is directed to meeting 'basic survival needs'. These needs are sanitation and sewage, pest control, clean air and water, diet and nutrition, tobacco reduction, essential medicines and vaccines, and well-functioning health systems. The FCGH could set goals for spending (such as a minimum percent of GDP). It could also be used to address issues like the migration of health-care workers, the development of strong surveillance laboratories, and the creation of incentives for affordable medicines and vaccines.

Legal aspects of rationing health-care resources

Justice Michael Kirby, in his Inaugural Lecture to the Australian Institute of Health Law and Ethics, said that 'it is possible for us to recognise, in recent years, a growing understanding that the allocation of healthcare resources has an ethical dimension which sometimes presents itself in a legal case and which is ultimately the source of competing political strategies, advanced for popular endorsement'. There has been surprisingly little litigation in Australia that argues that an adverse result has come about because of rationing decisions.

This may be due to the fact that many decisions that have a resource allocation component are not presented in that way. There may also be a general willingness within Australian society to accept the inevitability of some health-care rationing, but this seems likely to change as the impact of rationing is felt by a larger number of people.

In 1990, the National Health and Medical Research Council (NHMRC) issued a Discussion Paper on ethics and resource allocation. In this discussion paper the Council said:

> In the allocation of any public resource our concern should be primarily with justice. This involves giving to each person his or her due. In allocating healthcare resources our concern is largely with the distributive justice – to distribute among members of the community those benefits and burdens due to them. The basis of distributive justice is the notion of fairness. The most appropriate criterion for a fair distribution of resources would appear to be those of equity and need. More specifically, a just allocation should offer equal treatment to those whose needs are similar. In other words, each person is entitled to enjoy an appropriate share of the sum total of resources available according to their need. However, the need which justifies one person's entitlement must be a need which can be fulfilled in a way compatible with fulfilling the similar needs of others. (National Health and Medical Research Council 1990)

Justice is particularly important when governments or institutions are making decisions about the allocation of resources. As Justice Kirby points out, 'the triage in every modern hospital represents the daily application, in the most basic way, of the allocation of scarce healthcare resources'. The triage process is not controversial in law, as long as triage represents the allocation of services assessed by need, and those with the greatest need get first access to the available resources. However, when criteria other than clinical need are used to assess access to resources, then the situation becomes less clear.

Government responsibilities to provide health care in Australia

Medicare principles and commitments

There are no broad common law or constitutional rights to access health care in Australia. Neither the *Human Rights Act 2004* (ACT) nor the *Charter of Human Rights and Responsibilities Act 2006* (Vic) recognises a right to health care.

The *Health Insurance Act 1973* (Cth), s 26, creates some recognition of the rights of patients to treatment. The Commonwealth government provides health funding to the States and Territories but on the basis that those jurisdictions adhere to certain principles and commitments of 'Medicare' (the nationalised public health insurance scheme).

A number of the Medicare principles relate to rights to health care. Principle 1 of the Medicare principles provides that 'eligible persons must be given the choice to receive public hospital services free of charge as public patients'. Principle 2 provides: 'Access to public hospital services is to be on the basis of clinical need'. Principle 3 states: 'To the maximum practicable extent, a State will ensure the provision of public hospital services equitably to all eligible persons, regardless of their geographical location'.

Additionally the Commonwealth, States and Territories are bound to Medicare commitments, namely:

> *Commitment 1*: The Commonwealth and a State must make available information on the public hospital services eligible persons can expect to receive as public patients
>
> *Commitment 2*: The Commonwealth and the States are committed to making improvements in the efficiency, effectiveness and quality of hospital service delivery.

These principles and commitments have been enshrined by most jurisdictions into legislation: *Health Services Act 1997* (NSW), s 68; *Medicare Principles and Commitments Adoption Act 1994* (Qld), s 3 (note: later repealed by the *Statute Law (Miscellaneous Provisions) Act 1999* (Qld)); *Health Act 1997* (Tas), s 5; *Health Services Act 1997* (Vic), ss 9, 10, 17AA; *Hospitals and Health Services Act 1997* (WA), s 34; *Health Act 1993* (ACT), ss 6, 7; *Medical Services Act 1982* (NT), s 6(3), Sch 2. For example, s 5 of the *Health Act 1997* (Tas) states:

> The Minister is to ensure that in providing public hospital services on behalf of the State to eligible persons –
> (a) the Medicare principles are given effect to; and
> (b) the Medicare commitments are undertaken –
> in the manner required by the Commonwealth Act.

While they appear to enshrine rights to health services, in New South Wales, Queensland, Victoria, Western Australia and the Australian Capital Territory, these Acts expressly state that the Medicare principles and commitments do not create enforceable rights that give rise to a cause of action. Therefore, if the responsible Minister fails to give effect to the principles a private citizen cannot seek redress from the courts. In the Northern Territory the Minister's obligation is to follow the Medicare principles and commitments 'when possible' (s 6(3)). The Tasmanian legislation is not qualified, nor does it expressly deny a private right of action (s 5). It would therefore be safe to conclude that (with the possible exception of Tasmania) the Medicare principles and commitments are purely aspirational rights that fail to grant rights to individuals to demand treatment.

In addition to the statutory enactment of Medicare principles, the State and Territory governments have agreed with the Commonwealth government, under what is known as the Australian Healthcare Agreements, to create *Public Patients' Hospital Charters*, which recognise the right to treatment. For example, the Queensland *Public Patients Charter* states:

> 1. You have the right to use free hospital services as a public patient. It does not matter where you live in Australia as long as you have a current Medicare card ...

2. You have the right to be treated with respect, dignity and consideration regardless of your age, gender, sexual preference, religion and culture ...

5. You have the right to treatment based on our assessment of how sick you are.

The Charters are not based in legislation, and as such it appears that they are intended to be aspirational rights rather than legal ones.

Who should make rationing decisions: governments or courts?

Who should make decisions about the allocation of scarce resources when the impact of those decisions may result in some people having to forego life-sustaining treatments? This is the area of the so-called 'tragic choice' where decision-makers must choose to let some suffer and die for the greater good (Ham 1999; Stewart 2000). There is a very strong argument that decisions concerning resource allocation should be made at a governmental level, either through the various Departments of Health or area health service levels (the name will vary depending on jurisdiction). The reason for this is that governmental decisions are, at least theoretically, open to scrutiny and are accountable to the public.

It is often said that the he courts may not review government decisions on 'pure policy', as they are 'non-justiciable'. But some aspects of decision-making may be reviewable by courts under the principles of administrative law. Administrative law allows the courts to question decisions when those decisions have been made beyond power (*ultra vires*) or in ways that breach principles of procedural fairness (sometimes called *natural justice*). Decisions can also be reviewed when the courts find that they were so irrational that no reasonable body would have come to those conclusions. This is referred to as *Wednesbury* unreasonableness: *Associated Provincial Picture House Ltd v Wednesbury Corporation* [1948] 1 KB 223 (Stewart 1999; Stewart 2000).

Earlier cases all indicated that if the decision has been made solely on resource allocation grounds there was no role for administrative review. One of the first cases in this area was *R v Central Birmingham Health Authority; R v Secretary of State for Social Services; ex p Walker* ('Walker') (1987) 3 BMLR 32. Mrs Walker applied to the court for the judicial review of a decision by the central Birmingham Health Authority not to treat her baby son for a heart operation. Due to staffing problems with a shortage of specially trained nurses a bed could not be made available until all emergency cases had been dealt with. The doctors offered to do the surgery but only when the child had reached 'emergency' status. Even then they could not guarantee that the child would receive post-operative care.

The mother sought a court order that the operation take place at once. She failed both at first instance and on appeal on the grounds that the decision not to treat was based on resource allocation priorities. The first instance judge deprecated 'any suggestion that patients should be encouraged to think that the court has a role in a case of this kind'. In the Court of Appeal, Donaldson MR stated that:

It is not for this court, or indeed any court, to substitute its judgment for the judgment of those who are responsible for the allocation of resources.

Soon after the decision in *Walker's case* further judicial review from a decision of the Central Birmingham Health Authority was sought in *R v Central Birmingham Health Authority; ex p Collier* (*'Collier'*) (unreported, Court of Appeal, 6 January 1988). The father of an infant sought the court's intervention in a series of decisions not to give an 'urgent operation' for a heart by-pass. Significantly no evidence was led as to why the operation was repeatedly cancelled. Neill LJ found that there was no evidence whatsoever that the health authority acted un-reasonably or in breach of any public duty. On the issue of whether the urgency and life-threatening nature of the decision made any difference to the question of justiciability, Stephen Brown LJ said that the court was not a position to judge allocation issues.

Perhaps the most cited case of resource allocation is *R v Cambridge Health Authority; ex p B* [1995] 1 WLR 898. This case concerned the decision of a health authority not to provide funds for the treatment of a 10-year-old girl who had non-Hodgkin's leukaemia and who had come out of remission. The doctors in charge of her treatment decided that they would only provide palliative care as the chances of a successful second course of chemotherapy and bone-marrow transplant were slim. There was some evidence raised that further treatment should be provided. It was suggested that treatment might be successful if it consisted of chemotherapy (costing £15,000) and a further bone marrow trans-plant (costing £60,000). However, B's father could not afford the cost of the treatment and he requested that the local health authority fund the treatment. The authority refused on the grounds that it was not in B's best interests and that it would not be an appropriate use of the resources of the authority to fund treatment of an 'experimental' nature.

At first instance the decision was quashed on four grounds. The first ground was that the authority's decision failed to take into account the wishes of the patient, as expressed through her family, in particular, her father. On this ground, the authority's decision was said to be manifestly *Wednesbury* unreas-onable. The second ground was that the treatment was unfairly described as being 'experimental'. Thirdly, the authority had failed to provide evidence of its financial difficulty. The trial judge stated that the authority had to provide evidence of why there were not sufficient resources to fund the treatment. Finally the trial judge found that the authority had misdirected itself deciding the request for funds as a request for a total of £75,000. Instead what was being requested was £15,000 for the initial stages of the treatment. If that failed then there would be no reason for the treatment to continue.

The Court of Appeal overturned the trial judge's decision on the grounds of non-justiciability. Again it was found that it was not the court's role to question allocation decisions. The trial judge's finding that the authority should justify its resource decisions was viewed as 'totally unrealistic' as 'no major authority could run its financial affairs in a way that would permit such a demonstration'.

Plaintiffs have had some success but only in cases where the authority making the decision has failed to comply with statutory duties, or failed to follow its own policy when making the decision. Additionally, if an authority decides not to fund treatment because of social rather than clinical factors, its policy may be struck down as irrational or because it involved irrelevant considerations. For example, a decision by a health authority not to provide treatment for trans-sexualism was found to be illegal because it had not properly considered transsexualism as an illness nor considered it in that light when it formulated its policy. The policy was also unlawful because it fettered the discretion of the health authority: *North West Lancashire Health Authority v A, D & G* [1999] Lloyd's Law Rep Med 399.

Policies will also be struck down when they are a mere sham or an effort to disguise a decision not to fund treatment. For example, in *R v Derbyshire HA; ex p Fisher* [1997] 8 Med LR 327, a local authority had limited the use of beta interferon to treatments that were part of a randomised trial of the drug. No such trial was in existence and there was little if any chance that one would be implemented. Regardless of this fact the authority insisted on withholding funds for the use of the drug unless treatment was part of a trial. The policy was found to be irrational and unreasonable. It was also in contravention of a departmental directive to provide funding for such treatments.

More recent decisions concerning policies have shown a tendency for the judges to exercise a rigorous review of decisions which impact on the human rights of the patients or which may leave them untreated with terminal conditions. A number of cases have arisen in the United Kingdom concerning drug treatments where policies indicated that new drugs would not be funded unless there were 'exceptional circumstances' justifying funding. In *R (Rogers) v Swindon NHS Primary Trust* [2006] EWCA Civ 392, the Court of Appeal said that if a policy made it impossible to satisfy 'exceptional circumstances' it would effectively be a blanket refusal and therefore irrational. In *Rogers* the policy was found to be irrational because it failed to distinguish between cases of exceptional circumstances and the decision-makers could not justify why some patients were being given treatment while others were not. In *R (Ross) v West Sussex Primary Care Trust* [2008] EWHC B15 (Admin) the claimant had a decision not to fund a new drug for multiple myeloma quashed. The judge overturned the decision on unreasonableness grounds, finding the meaning of 'exceptional' applied by the Trust meant that any case which was like another would be automatically excluded. The judge found this to be contradictory and outside of the ordinary meaning of the word 'exceptional'. The court ordered that the policy be reviewed and that the decision be made again under a revised policy.

Similar facts occurred in *R (Murphy) v Salford Primary Care Trust* [2008] EWHC 1908 (Admin), where the applicant had run out of treatments for her kidney cancer. She wished to have a new drug treatment (Sunitinib), but the local authority refused to fund it. A review panel confirmed the decision not to fund. The patient argued that the decision-making panel had misapplied its own policy and had come to a decision that was irrational. It was also argued that the panel had fallen into error as it had considered the material factors individually, but had failed to consider all the factors as a whole when making its decision.

The judge agreed with the last proposition and felt not enough weight had been given to the patient's circumstances 'in the round'. The matter was sent back to the trust for reconsideration.

Judges have also used the rigorous review technique to strike down decisions which they think cannot be held up to logical scrutiny. In *R (Otley) v Barking & Dagenham NHS Primary Care Trust* [2007] EWHC 1927 (Admin), Mitting J struck down a decision not to fund a new tumour-shrinking drug, Avastin, on a woman with advanced colorectal cancer and tumours in her liver, who had reacted badly to chemotherapy. Five cycles of the drug had been funded to shrink the tumours. They had shrunk in response but were not yet at the stage were they could be resected. Further funding was requested for another four cycles but the Trust refused. Unlike earlier cases, the policy was not attacked but rather its application by the decision-makers was said to be flawed:

> This is not a case as in *R (Rogers) v Swindon National Health Service Primary Care Trust* [2006] EWCA Civ 392, in which the policy of the Trust and its Difficult Decisions Panel is open to criticism. On the contrary, the policy is entirely rational and sensible. Nor is it a case, on close analysis, in which the availability of scarce resources is a decisive feature. The policy properly provides that the allocation of resources is an element in every decision of this kind. But the course proposed by Dr Raouf, for which he sought funding, was at least in its initial stages a course which required the allocation of only relatively small resources. His proposal was for four or five cycles of treatment, including Avastin, at the end of which imaging would be done and progress reviewed. The bleak conclusion for Ms Otley is that, if at the end of those four or five cycles no improvement is revealed, then her slim chance of long term survival will be lost. But the course proposed by Dr Raouf did not on any reasonable view require this Trust to put at risk the interests of other patients or, in the words of its own policy on difficult decisions, require it "to consider the impact of funding on the health of the whole population". Accordingly, the decision of the Panel falls to be analysed on the basis that although the allocation of resources is a factor, it is not capable of being a decisive factor in the decision which it had to make. (at [27])

All of these cases recognise the potential for review but illustrate how difficult it will be to review a resource allocation decision, which is not obviously tainted by some illegality or irrationality. One conclusion that we can make is that tragic decisions that have been properly made are unreviewable. On its face such a conclusion seems correct and proper. Tragic choices are inevitable. People will die. If the decision has been made fairly and according to law there should be no criticism and no judicial second-guessing.

Ultimately, as the law presently stands, a line has clearly been drawn around decisions purely based on resource allocation factors. The formulation of irrationality/unreasonableness is confusing and does not seem to guarantee transparency or necessarily allow for review when the decision is resource based. This is unfortunate. As Ham has pointed out:

> Given that there will often be controversy over tragic choices in health care, it is incumbent on those responsible for decision making to show that they have followed due processes and have been both rigorous and fair in arriving at their decisions. (Ham 1999)

Accountability in this area is therefore essential. Daniels and Sabin have proposed four necessary conditions to ensure such accountability:

1. *the publicity condition*- which requires that choices about new treatments need to be publicly available;

2. *the relevance condition* – that rationing of health resources is based on evidence, reasons and principles that are relevant to deciding how to meet needs of a diverse number of patients;

3. *the appeals condition* – that there is an effective and accessible mechanism for challenging decisions; and

4. *the enforcement condition* – that there are checks and balances in place to ensure that the first three conditions are met. (Daniels and Sabin 1998)

Administrative law has a role to play in all four of these conditions but the unreasonableness/irrationality tool is not necessarily as clear or predictable as it should be.

References

Abrams, F (1994) 'Doctor with two heads – the patient versus the costs'. *N Engl J Med* **328**(13): 975-7.

Appiah, K (2006) *Cosmopolitanismthics in a world of strangers*. London, Allen Lane.

Australian Government Department of Health and Ageing (2004) 'Australia: Selected Health Care Delivery and Financing Statistics – May 2004'. <http://www7.health.gov.au/haf/ozhealth/tablesupp.pdf>.

Australian Institute of Health and Welfare (2006) *Australia's health 2006*. Canberra, AIHW.

Barraclough, S and M Morrow (1995) 'Saving for hospital care costs in Singapore'. *Aust Health Rev* **18**(2): 11-18.

Bennett, B (2008) Globalising rights? Constructing Health Rights in a Shrinking World. *Brave New World of Health*. B Bennett, T Carney and I Karpin. Sydney, Federation Press: 8-20.

Boren, S (1994) 'I had a tough day today Hilary'. *N Engl J Med* **330**(7): 500-2.

Clemens, M and T Moss (2005) *Ghost of 0.7% Origins and relevance of the international aid target*. Center for Global Development.

Daniels, N and J Sabin (1998) 'The ethics of accountability in managed care reform'. *Health Ethics*. **17**: 50.

Daniels, N (2000) 'Accountability for Reasonableness'. *BMJ* **321**(7272): 1300-1.

Farmer, P (2003) *Pathologies of Power: Health, Human Rights and the New War on the Poor*. Berkeley, University of California Press.

Frankish, CJ, B Kwan et al (2002) 'Challenges of citizen participation in regional health authorities'. *Soc Sci Med* **54**(10): 1471-80.

Gostin, LO (2008) 'Global Health Law Governance'. *Emory International Law Review* **22**: 35.

Gostin, LO (2009) 'Meeting Basic Survival Needs of the World's Least Healthy People: Toward a Framework Convention on Global Health'. *Georgetown LJ* **96**: 331.

Gostin, LO and AL Taylor (2008) 'Global Health Law: A Definition and Grand Challenges'. *Public Health Ethics*. 1(1): 53.

Gray, N, M Hansen-Knarhoi et al (2008) 'Tuberculosis in illegal foreign fishermen: whose public health are we protecting?' *Med J Aust* **188**(3): 144-7.

Gruen, RL, SD Pearson et al (2004) 'Physician-Citizens – Public Roles and Professional Obligations'. *JAMA* **291**(1): 94-8.

Ham, C (1999) 'Tragic choices in health: lessons from the Child B case'. *BMJ* **319**:1258

Hauck, K, R Shaw et al (2002) 'Reducing avoidable inequalities in health: a new criterion for setting health care capitation payments'. *Health Econ* **11**: 667-77.

Igneski, V (2001) 'Distance, determinacy and the duty to aid: a reply to Kamm'. *Law and philosophy* **20**(6): 605-16.

RM Isasi and T Nguyen. (2005) 'The Global Governance of Infectious Diseases: The World Health Organization and the International Health Regulations'. *Alberta L Rev* **43**: 497

Kamm, F (2000) 'Does distance matter morally to the duty to rescue?' *Law and philosophy* **19**: 655-81.

Klein, R, P Day et al (1996) *Managing scarcity*. Buckingham, Open University Press.

Kuper, A (2005) Global poverty relief: More than charity. *Global responsibility: who must deliver on human rights?* A Kuper. New York, Routledge: 155-81.

Lenaghan, J (1999) 'Involving the public in rationing decisions. The experience of citizens juries'. *Health Policy* **49**(1-2): 45-61.

Magnusson, RS (2007) 'Non-communicable diseases and global health governance: enhancing global processes to improve health development'. *Globalization and Health* **3**:2.

Maxwell, J, S Rosell et al (2003) 'Giving citizens a voice in healthcare policy in Canada'. *BMJ* **326**(7397): 1031-3.

McBride, T and V Korczak (2007) 'Community consultation and engagement in health care reform'. *Aust Health Rev* **31 Suppl 1**: S13-5.

Menadue, J (2003) 'Healthcare reform: possible ways forward'. *Med J Aust* **179**: 367-9.

Mooney, G (1992) *Economics, Medicine and Health Care*. Hampshire, Harvester Wheatsheaf.

Mooney, G (1994) *Key issues in health economics*. Hampshire, Harvester Wheatsheaf.

Mooney, GH and SH Blackwell (2004) 'Whose health service is it anyway? Community values in healthcare'. *Med J Aust* **180**(2): 76-8.

National Health and Medical Research Council (1990) *Discussion Paper on Ethics and Resource Allocation*. Canberra, Australian Government Publishing Service.

O'Neill, O (1986) *Faces of hunger: An essay on poverty, justice and development*. London, Allen and Unwin.

O'Neill, O (2007) Kantian formula of the end in itself and world hunger. *Pojman LP ed. Ethical theory: classical and contemporary readings*. L Pojman. Belmont, CA, Wadsworth: 284-94.

Peabody, J, S Bickel et al (1996) 'The Australian health care system: Are the incentives down under right side up?' *JAMA* **276**(24): 1944-50.

Pearson, SD (2000) 'Caring and cost: the challenge for physician advocacy'. *Ann Intern Med* **133**(2): 148-53.

Pogge, T (2002) *World Poverty and Human Rights: Cosmopolitan Responsibilities and Reforms*. Cambridge, Polity Press.

Ruger, JP (2008) 'Normative Foundations of Global Health Law'. *Georgetown LJ* **96**: 423

Sen, A (1979) Equality of what? *The Tanner Lecture on Human Values*. Stanford University.

Sen, A (1992) *Inequality Reexamined*. Cambridge, MA, Harvard University Press.

Sen, AK (1987) *Food and freedom*. Washington, DC, Washington State University.

Singer, P (1972) 'Famine, affluence and morality'. *Philosophy and public affairs* **1**(3).

Singer, P (2002) Famine, affluence and morality. *Ethics: history, theory and contemporary issues* (2nd ed). S Cahn and P Markie. New York, Oxford University Press: 805-12.

Stewart, C (1999) 'Health Care and Judicial Review: A further role for the courts?' *Journal of Law and Medicine*. **7**: 212.

Stewart, C (2000) 'Tragic choices and the role of administrative law'. *BMJ* **321**: 105-7.

UNDP (1998) *Human Development Report 1998*. New York, Oxford University Press.

UNDP (1999) *Human Development Report 1999*. New York, Oxford University Press.

UNDP (2003) *Human Development Report 2003*. New York, Oxford University Press.

Walton, NA, DK Martin et al (2007) 'Priority setting and cardiac surgery: a qualitative case study'. *Health Policy* **80**(3): 444-58.

WHO (2004). The World Health Report 2004. Geneva, WHO Publications.

Zwi, A, N Grove et al (2005) 'Keeping track to keep Australia's overseas aid on track'. *Med J Aust* **183**(3): 119-20.

CHAPTER 31

BIOMEDICAL RESEARCH

Case study 1

The CLASS trial was designed to study the effects of Celecoxib – a new anti-inflammatory drug that was thought to have lower gastrointestinal side effects than older drugs (Silverstein, Faich et al 2000). This trial was reported as a three-arm trial comparing the effects of Celecoxib with two older non-steroidal anti-inflammatory drugs (NSAIDs) over a time period of six months. It showed a decrease in gastrointestinal complications for people treated with Celecoxib. These results led to a marked rise in Celecoxib prescribing around the world.

One year after the CLASS publication, it was revealed that the original intention of the trial had been very different, with a planned follow-up of 12-15 months, not six months (Juni, Rutjes et al 2002). The trial had shown no difference in gastro-intestinal adverse effects over the longer period, but when results had been restricted to six months a difference had emerged. To the original readers of the CLASS trial, none of this was evident and critical appraisal of the original article could only conclude that Celecoxib was beneficial.

Restricting the data in this way was widely thought to have been inappropriate, but it resulted in an effective marketing campaign for Celecoxib. Many people continue to be on this drug because many doctors continue to believe that it has fewer side effects.

Case study 2

Deliberate academic fraud is more common than is often appreciated. In one study almost 5% of medical authors reported fabrication or misrepresentation of results within the previous 10 years, and 17% of authors personally knew about a case of fraud in the previous 10 years. (Gardner, Lidz et al 2005)

For example, in 1990 Werner Bezwoda, a scientist at the University of Witwaters-rand, began reporting results of trials of high-dose chemotherapy with bone marrow transplantation in high-risk breast cancer patients. His published results showed markedly improved outcomes with this technique and therefore exerted a substantial influence on clinical practice worldwide. In 2000, a site visit to his laboratory was arranged to try and see how he had obtained such good results, before commencing a larger trial of this therapy worldwide. Unfortunately, the site visit revealed that the original results could only have been obtained by fraud. (Weiss, Rifkin et al 2000)

Case study 3

In June 2001, Ellen Roche, a healthy research volunteer, died at the Johns Hopkins Bayview Medical Center, following participation in a study funded by the National Institutes of Health and conducted by senior scientists at the Johns Hopkins Asthma & Allergy Center. This study was using inhaled hexamethonium to examine airway narrowing and the mechanisms underlying the development of asthma. Ellen, who was paid for participation in this study, had previously volunteered for a number of experiments at the Johns Hopkins Asthma Research Center where she worked.

Following her death, all federally funded research at Johns Hopkins was briefly halted and internal and external reviews of Roche's death found a series of failures in institutional review processes, safety monitoring, solicitation of research 'volunteers' and consent processes, and noted a culture that regarded ethics review as a bureaucratic barrier to research. (Steinbrook 2002)

The history of research ethics

Experimentation has always been a feature of medicine and medical science. Human experiments, often involving small numbers of vulnerable subjects including children, the poor, prisoners and the condemned, have long been used to investigate human anatomy, physiology and disease (Pappworth 1967). Organised, large scale human research is a more recent phenomenon, emerging in the post-industrial 19th century along with advances in statistics, epidemiology, genetics, microbiology, pathology, microscopy and public health (Ackernecht 1982). An examination of the history of human experimentation reveals an enthusiasm for knowledge and understanding with little regard for the welfare of the research subject (Katz 1972).

Many histories of research ethics begin with descriptions of the Nuremberg Code – the set of principles for medical research outlined by the Nuremberg Doctors Trial following investigation of experiments conducted by Nazi physicians, nurses and scientists in concentration camps during World War II (Weindling 2001). In fact there is a history of concerns regarding the ethics of medical research going back at least to the 1830s. The physician William Beaumont first introduced a contract with his patients and the physiologist Claude Bernard cited the ethical necessity of obtaining informed consent, while physician researchers such as Armauer Hansen and Walter Reed were criticised for their failure to obtain the consent of their research subjects and for the coercive nature of the practices. Somewhat ironically, concerns about the risks of research and the necessity for the consent of research participants led to the drafting of government directives and guidelines on research conduct by the Prussian Minister for Religious, Education and Medical Affairs (in 1900) and by the Reich Minister of the Interior in Berlin (in 1931), well before the abuses that occurred during World War II (Lock 1995; Vollman and Winau 1996).

Nevertheless, the ethics of human experimentation first gained wide recognition following the Nuremberg 'Doctors Trial' in 1947 – in which 20 doctors and three non-medical personnel were accused of war crimes and crimes against humanity for their experiments on Jews, Gypsies, Slavs, the mentally ill, political prisoners and captured members of the Allied armed forces. The accused offered a number of defences: that they were following orders; that the experiments were necessary to support the German war effort; that it was necessary to sacrifice a few individuals in order to benefit many; and that medical research (including research conducted in the United States) had historically been conducted without proper regard for the consent of research participants or for the need to minimise the harms of research. But, in the end, 16 of the defendants were found guilty and seven (including Karl Brandt, Hitler's personal physician) were hanged (Annas and Grodin 1990). The American judges in the Doctor's Trial enumerated 10 basic principles that must be observed in conducting medical experiments on human beings 'in order to satisfy moral, ethical and legal concepts'. These principles, which explicitly recognised the difference between patients and research subjects, and focused on the inalienable human rights of research subjects, rather than the responsibility of doctors to protect their research subjects, became known subsequently as the Nuremberg Code (Shuster 1997).

The Nuremberg Code has had a profound influence on the parameters of research and has been largely responsible for the requirement for informed consent in research. The basic principles outlined in the Nuremberg Code formed the basis of the Declaration of Helsinki, which was first published by the World Medical Association (WMA) in 1964 after more than a decade of drafting, and subsequently ratified in Australia in 1965..

At times it has been suggested that Nazi medicine was an aberration in the history of medicine; and in the years following Nuremberg there was a belief, encouraged in part by some professional bodies, that the Code was directed at the atrocities of Nazi physicians rather than at all researchers (Hornblum 1997). However, the Nazis were not alone in conducting barbarous and inhumane experiments during World War II.

From 1932 to 1945 Japanese doctors, scientists, pathologists and researchers under the direction of General Shiro Ishi conducted a range of experiments on the civilian population and on prisoners of war through a network of research camps in Asia stretching from Mongolia to Singapore. Up to 250,000 people are estimated to have been killed in field experiments involving intentional exposure to anthrax, cholera, yersinia and other pathogens, with smaller numbers of people being killed in barbarous 'camp' experiments involving 'testing' of surgical instruments, exposure to lethal radiation, live vivisection, intentional trauma and poisoning (Nie 2006).

While a 'Japanese Doctors Trial' was conducted in Moscow in 1949, the Japanese atrocities have had little impact on medical research or the development of codes of research ethics. There have never been any prosecutions (despite the fact that this research was against the Nuremberg Code and all subsequent relevant UN Conventions), there has never been a formal apology or offer of compensation and, until recently, this history has not been widely acknowledged in the West. There are a number of reasons why this may be the case. First, details of Japanese experiments were kept secret for many years as the result of an agreement made by the American Government to give those involved immunity from prosecution in exchange for providing all data relating to biological weaponry to the American Occupation Forces Command. Second, most of the information about Japanese experiments only came to light following freedom of information actions in the United States in the 1980s. And, third, the research was believed to have yielded 'valuable' data – which may have had military value during the Cold War

Any suggestion that inhuman or unethical research was a feature of Nazi (or Japanese) totalitarianism, and not a feature of medicine and medical research more generally, is undermined by instances of unethical research in the 'civilised' liberal democracies, like the United States and Australia. In the years since World War II, patients have been injected with cancer cells, irradiated, poisoned with LSD, infected with hepatitis and left to die from untreated syphilis or carcinoma – without their consent or even the knowledge that they were involved in an experiment (Beecher 1966). People who were already powerless or disenfranchised – women, ethnic minorities, children and prisoners – were frequently the subjects of such experiments. Studies such as the Tuskegee Study into the 'natural' history of syphilis in black Americans, the Willowbrook study into the effects of hepatitis in a group of institutionalised children, the National Women's Hospital (Auckland) study of cervical cancer and the vaccine trials conducted in Melbourne orphanages from the 1940s to the 1970s have become infamous.

There are a number of reasons why codes such as the Nuremberg Code and the Declaration of Helsinki have not prevented unethical research from occurring, including the overpowering aura of science, the entrenched power of medical professionals, self-interest and a pervasive utilitarian belief in the benefits of research (Jones and Tuskegee Institute 1993; Rothman and Michels 1994; Ettershank and Ranson 1997). Modern practices for the review of ethics, such as those laid out in Australia's National Statement on Ethical Conduct in Human Research are also unlikely to prevent all unethical research, but it is hoped that they will limit and mitigate is effects.

Research ethics

It is important to recognise that the primary aim of research is to produce knowledge, not to benefit the research subjects themselves (British Medical Association 2004). Because of this there is potential for great harm to occur to research subjects. Much of the framework that has been built around ethics in research is aimed at preventing such harms. The main way that this is done is through appropriate ethics review of all research.

Most health research in Australia is conducted under the oversight of the National Health and Medical Research Council (NHMRC), using the guidelines developed by the Australian Health Ethics Committee (AHEC) – a principal committee of the NHMRC. AHEC has produced a number of guidelines governing research in Australia – the major one being the National Statement on Ethical Conduct in Human Research (NHMRC 2007). Responsibility for the valuation and approval of health research was devolved to Human Research Ethics Committees (HRECs) in the mid-1970s (Loblay 2008). These committees refer to both the four general principles elucidated by the NHMRC: respect, research merit and integrity, justice and beneficence (similar to the four principles espoused by Beauchamp and Childress) and the guidelines produced by the NHMRC to carefully assess all research (NHMRC 2007).

In general terms research must satisfy the following standards:

- it should address an important (and answerable) question and build upon knowledge rather than simply repeating it;
- it should be rigorous, using validated research methods appropriate to the research question;
- it should be committed to the welfare of the research participant;
- it should seek to minimise the harms/risks to the participant;
- recruitment should be just and vulnerable populations should not be inappropriately excluded;
- participation should be on the basis of (informed) consent;
- participants must not be coerced and should be able freely and voluntarily to choose to participate in a study or leave it without fear of punishment/sanction;
- confidentiality and privacy should be maintained;
- special protections should be considered where appropriate for vulnerable populations;
- data should be appropriately analysed and the results disseminated to research participants and to the target population;
- researchers should take steps to avoid conflict of interest; and
- the study should undergo independent scrutiny.

Two of the main principles used by HRECs in reviewing proposals for research are the principle of autonomy and the principle of non-maleficence. The principle of autonomy, as applied to research, states that no research can be done without the research subject's informed consent. The principle of non-maleficence suggests that research should not harm research subjects. The use of the two principles together results in extremely stringent safeguards – HRECs frequently disallow studies that have little chance of causing harm if there is not informed consent; and disallow studies in which subjects are fully informed and wish to participate, if there is even a moderate risk.

Protecting research subjects in this way has had some negative consequences. The requirements for strict informed consent have restricted research greatly in populations such as children, the demented elderly and unconscious intensive-care patients. The requirement for protection has restricted research in some groups such as terminally ill cancer patients who may be willing to take on greater risks than ethics committees are willing to allow. Despite this, the authors (and many other commentators) believe that the benefits of the current system of ethical review clearly outweigh its ill effects (McNeill, Berglund et al 1990).

Given the terrible history of the abuse of vulnerable populations in medical research it is hardly surprising that considerable attention has been directed to the identification and protection of vulnerable populations in research. There are many reasons why human research participants may be vulnerable (incapable of giving consent or protecting their own interests). Cognitive limitations, medical illness, power imbalances or deferential relationships, social disvalue, restricted liberty or rights, poverty, limited education, or inadequate protections may all leave individuals or populations open to being harmed by research. The existence of inequity or vulnerability does not, however, demand exclusion from research (which may cause further disadvantage and entrench stereotypes) but, rather, recognition of vulnerability in all its forms and careful consideration of the need for specific measures to protect research participants may maximise the possible benefits that may accrue to both the research participant and the target population.

Recently there has been concern that research is being done less in academic centres with careful supervision, and more in private, for-profit research centres where there is little oversight. There was great controversy in January 2008 when an article in the *New Yorker* described the lives of professional guinea pigs who spend their lives living in research centres being experimented upon for money (Elliott 2008). There are also concerns that research institutions are increasingly switching their attention to vulnerable populations in the developing world for research subjects.

Ethics committees

Ethics committees take on a complex moral position as they seek to facilitate the capacity of autonomous individuals and populations to participate in research (a libertarian position), protect research participants from harm (a paternalistic position) and maximise the benefits of research (a consequentialist position) (Hope, Savulescu et al 2003). Achieving a balance between these approaches is not always easy, and at times HRECs may make decisions that appear to be excessively paternalistic (restricting the choice of individuals to assess the risks and benefits of research for themselves) or prevent the performance of research that seeks to answer important clinical and/or scientific questions.

Under current guidelines, HRECs must include men and women of different age groups, and include at least one member from each of the following categories:

- laywoman not associated with the institution;
- layman not associated with the institution;
- minister of religion (of any faith);
- lawyer;
- medical graduate with research experience.

The demands placed on HRECs are considerable. HRECs must consider study design, funding, conflict of interest, monitoring, risks and benefits, consent, confidentiality and the use of results of every research proposal that comes before them. And yet for the most part the Australian system of ethical review of human experimentation has worked remarkably well – particularly given persistent under-funding and a dependence on the altruistic commitment of HREC members (who are volunteers).

Questions remain, however, regarding the structure, function and membership of HRECs. Some research suggests that HRECs may be dominated by representatives from medicine, science and the law (McNeill, Berglund et al 1994) and do not reflect the needs, interests or concerns of patients and consumers (Goodare and Smith 1995). The efficiency of HRECs has also come to attention with evidence of long delays in the review process, particularly with regard to multi-centre trials (Gizzler, Davies et al 1990; Loblay and Chalmers 1999) and the suggestion that such delays may deter the introduction of beneficial therapy – such as the use of thrombolytics and aspirin in acute myocardial infarction (Collins, Doll et al 1992).

In recent years such concerns have led to increased emphasis on the education of researchers in research ethics, streamlining of processes for ethical review of multi-centre studies and research in specialty areas, such as cancer, and the separation of ethical review from 'research governance' (defined as an organisational framework through which institutions maintain standards of quality, safety, privacy, risk management and financial management of research in addition to ensuring its ethical acceptability) (Lock 1990; Cookson 1992; Walsh, McNeil et al 2005; Frew and Martlew 2007).

While most criticisms of HRECs, and indeed of the entire process of research ethics review, have come from researchers and research sponsors, others are concerned that emphasis on the instrumental functions of HRECs has obscured critical analysis of the genuine ethical difficulties that characterise research. Alex Capron, among others, has argued that the elaborate rules and processes enmeshing research ethics review have had the effect of normalising human experimentation and prevented critical engagement with researchers about moral dilemmas that are central to research, particularly the acceptance of unforeseen risks of harm so that others may benefit (Capron 2006).

Research projects

When submitting a research proposal to an ethics committee, one of the researcher's major tasks is to review the literature on the subject to be researched. This is because, as a general principle, research should be of some potential benefit and should not unnecessarily repeat work that has been done before. Research must also be scientifically valid: there must be a clear scientific hypothesis to be tested and a research methodology that is capable of testing the hypothesis. There are scientific reasons behind this, but there are also ethical ones – researchers should not waste people's time and energy, or expose them to risk, if there is no valid conclusion that can be reached from their experiment. According to the National Statement:

> Unless proposed research has merit, and the researchers who are to carry out the research have integrity, the involvement of human participants in the research cannot be ethically justifiable. (NHMRC 2007)

This point is often a problem for students who must complete a research project for an assessment, but do not have the background for major creative advances. It may also be a problem for qualitative researchers who, by virtue of their choice of research method, may not have a specific hypothesis or research question, and so may have some difficulty convincing an ethics committee comprised of quantitative-oriented scientists of the value of their work. In general, however, if there is little harm that will arise from a project, and the subjects give informed consent, ethics committees usually do not reject a study on these grounds alone.

Ethics committees must review all the documentation that is given to research subjects, and often pay great attention to the wording of patient information, on the grounds that some of it is difficult to understand or may be ambiguous.

Types of research

Clinical research using humans can be divided into two main types – observational studies and experimental studies. In observational studies, the experimental subjects are merely observed and compared, they are not changed in any way. There are many types of observational studies, ranging from the simple case report – in which an interesting case is described – to more sophisticated designs such as case/control studies. In experimental studies, on the other hand, the investigators cause some change to occur within the experimental subjects, and may compare this to the results of other interventions or placebos.

The major ethical difficulties with observational studies are issues of privacy and confidentiality. For example, a 1993 case report in the *British Journal of Psychiatry* described a case of bulimia nervosa in a 26-year-old pre-registration doctor. The story was taken up by a local newspaper, and the person who was the subject of the case study was easily identified by her friends from the details reported. She reported herself to be 'very shocked, very angry, very upset' and reported the authors of the study to the British General Medical Council for serious professional misconduct (Court 1995). The authors were found not guilty but, as a result of this case, most major medical journals released guidelines for case reports that included showing the manuscript to patients and gaining their written informed consent before manuscripts are published (International Committee of Medical Journal Editors 1995).

Some authors point to a difference between the concepts of confidentiality and privacy. Capron uses an analogy based on a burglar breaking into a house. He asks: if a burglar does not know one's identity, does not steal anything and does not even move anything – but merely spends several hours looking at one's belongings – whether one has been wronged by the burglar's actions. He argues that although confidentiality has been preserved one has nonetheless been wronged by an infringement of privacy (Capron 1991).

This situation is analogous in some ways to the techniques of epidemiological research that may examine details of one's hospital records, census details or records owned by other health agencies but attempt to maintain confidentiality about subjects' names. It has been argued that such information should not be available to researchers without the subject's express permission – but this idea has been opposed vigorously by medical researchers who believe that this restriction would severely limit epidemiological research.

Qualitative research

Whereas research ethics has historically concerned itself with experimental studies, recent attention has shifted to the ethical issues raised by different types of research methods and different research contexts, including public health research, molecular epidemiology, tissue repository research and qualitative research.

Qualitative research generates a rich and detailed account of human experience through a range of methods of data collection, including interviews and focus groups, with the aim of providing a new, original, critical or accurate (lived) insight into that particular experience. This type of research is particularly valuable in areas that are value-laden, complex, socially or culturally delineated or poorly understood. Qualitative research is also of value when used in combination with quantitative methods and in the exploration of an area of (research) interest before it is clear exactly what the research question is or should be.

While many of the ethical issues raised by qualitative research are no different from those raised by quantitative research – there are some issues specific to qualitative research or that arise more often in the conduct of qualitative research. One of the main questions to be asked of any research project is whether the method (including data collection, participant selection and exclusion, data analysis and dissemination) is appropriate and rigorous. Unfortunately, whereas there is general agreement regarding method and quality assessment in quantitative research, qualitative research is characterised by intense disagreement about theory, method and rules of quality. And as qualitative research often allows for the focus of a study to 'emerge' from the data and actively engages with the research participant it may be difficult accurately to predict (and describe to members of an ethics committee) exactly what ethical issues will be raised by the study. It may also be difficult accurately to predict the risks and benefits of participation in a qualitative study.

While research ethics (perhaps rightly) has focused on the risks to research participants, and tends to focus on the emotional or psychological risks of talking about personal issues or experiences, there is a considerable body of literature to suggest that participants in qualitative research frequently find the experience empathic, cathartic or meaningful in some way. (This may be no different in quantitative studies.) This, in turn, suggests that the consent process in qualitative research, and indeed in all research projects, should inform potential participants of the benefits, as well as the risks, of participation (Carter, Jordens et al 2008).

The final issue of particular moral relevance to qualitative research relates to the way in which listening to a participant's story creates a relationship between the researcher and participant and may alter the participant's understanding of themselves and their experience. While such relationships may be beneficial, they also pose risks to both parties and must be anticipated and managed by the researcher. Likewise, while revisiting or retelling an experience may benefit the participant, it may also disrupt a person's narrative, identity, relationships and coping mechanisms. None of these issues provides an argument against qualitative research but all must be carefully considered in relation to each study and study population.

Experimental studies

Experimental studies of medications may be divided into different phases, each of which raises different philosophical and ethical concerns. Phase 1 studies are the earliest type of experimental study and are done primarily to demonstrate safety. These studies frequently recruit healthy volunteers and include first-in-man studies, drug interaction studies, bioavailability or pharmacokinetic studies, food interaction studies and studies of disease models. Phase 2 studies use a range of different designs in order to collect information, usually from patients, on efficacy and safety. Phase 3 studies are generally comparative studies performed with the aim of establishing the risk or benefit of an intervention (often described statistically as significance, odds ratio or risk). They use a range of methodological strategies to increase rigour, including concurrent controls, randomisation, blinding, strict selection and exclusion criteria, defined endpoints/ outcomes and placebo controls. Phase 4 studies (sometimes called 'post-marketing research' are designed to collect additional information on efficacy, safety or cost-effectiveness and, because they are often designed to support the claims of the product or sponsor, are sometimes difficult to distinguish from expanded access or compassionate access programs, which are not research but are strategies to increase usage and familiarity with a product.

We have discussed the issue of consent in detail elsewhere in this book and will not discuss it again here except for one aspect: that people who enrol in trials must be clearly aware that the trial is not for their benefit, but for the benefit of the community at large. When a researcher undertakes an experimental trial of a new form of therapy, it is generally because he or she believes or hopes that the new therapy will be better in some way than what was done in the past. If the researcher knows that the new therapy is better, then he or she cannot ethically perform the trial, as this would deny a better form of therapy to the comparison group. In fact, new forms of therapy can only be trialled if the community at large is in a state of 'equipoise ' – meaning that there is genuine uncertainty about the value of the different alternatives that are used in a trial (Cheng, Lowe et al 2003). It is only if the community is genuinely unsure whether a treatment is better or worse than an existing treatment for a disease that it may be ethically sound to compare the two in a clinical trial (Hellman 1995).

There are several corollaries that arise from the concept of equipoise. The first is that, although patients sometimes attempt to enter trials in the hope that a new approach to treatment may be of benefit to them, this should be strongly discouraged, because the trial should really only go ahead if there is genuine doubt as to the value of the new therapy. The aim of the trial is not to offer half of the patients a better treatment, but to assess the benefits to the community of an uncertain treatment.

A second corollary is that, if it becomes apparent during the trial that one form of therapy is better than the other (this may occur either through the accumulated results of the trial or through other published results), then patients must be immediately given the option to withdraw from the trial or the trial must be stopped. In most large trials, an overseeing body will monitor the ongoing results of trials and cease the trial if any results become apparent during its course.

Placebos and other ethical problems

An important point about experimental trials is that new treatments should, where possible, be compared both against the best available treatment, and against placebo. In 1994, a paper by Rothman and Michels argued strongly that use of placebos in trials where a better treatment was thought to be available was unethical (Rothman and Michels 1994). This point was taken up by many (including the authors of this book) and used to argue against placebos in trials.

Since that time, trials – particularly in the field of depression – have demonstrated the value of placebos again. Because of the argument that placebos were unethical, a multitude of trials of new antidepressants dispensed with placebos, and only compared them with older agents. Most new agents showed equivalence to the older agents but with fewer side effects, and were licensed on this basis. It was only when these new agents were trialled against placebos, that it became apparent that in many cases neither the new anti-depressants nor the traditional ones had any apparent effects in the modern populations. A review of this topic suggested that about one-third to one-half of modern antidepressant trials are unable to distinguish drugs that had proven to be effective in historical trials from placebos (Temple and Ellenberg 2000).

Placebos are used in trials largely to obscure the fact that some subjects are taking a medication and some are not. However, placebos have their own action – known as the placebo effect. Recent research in patients with irritable bowel syndrome has attempted to clearly establish the basis of the placebo effect – hypothesising that it may be possible to progressively combine the factors contributing to the placebo effect as a form of 'graded dose escalation' (Kaptchuk, Kelley et al 2008). This study, a three-arm randomised controlled trial, found that enhancing the patient-practitioner relationship was the most significant contributor to the placebo effect. Findings such as this have led both to a –re-examination of the therapeutic relationship and a re-emphasis on the role of placebos in trials (Spiegel and Harrington 2008).

There are many other ethical problems that occur with medical research. These include: the historical exclusion of women, children, the elderly and minority groups from trials (McCarthy 1994; Murthy, Krumholz et al 2004;

Ballantyne and Rogers 2008); the medical care of patients during the trial (Lewis, Rachelevski et al 1994) and after the trial has finished; study design for medical conditions in which consent is impossible to obtain (Miller 1993); what to do with the results of studies that have been conducted unethically (Angel 1990); the degree of patient involvement in the design and implementation of clinical trials (Institute of Medical Ethics Working Party on the Ethical Implications of AIDS 1992); and problems that arise when communicating results between researchers (Hogue 1991) and with the public. Interested readers may find more information about these issues in the references cited in the NHMRC *Human Research Ethics Handbook* (National Health and Medical Research Council 2002) and in overviews such as that by Levine and Lebacqz (Levine and Lebacqz 1979).

Research in developing countries

A particular problem regarding the ethics of human experimentation has been that of research in developing countries (Editorial 1998). The issues surrounding HIV studies conducted in Africa and Asia in the 1990s illustrate the complexity of the issues involved.

In 1994 evidence emerged that zidovudine (AZT) prophylaxis was effective in reducing the risk of mother-to-child-transmission of HIV from 25% to 8%. But because this therapy was expensive (US$800) there was considerable interest in testing a shorter course for use in the developing world. Following this the World Health Organization (WHO), the Joint United Nations Programme on HIV and Aids (UNAIDS), the US National Institutes of Health (NIH), and the US Centers for Disease Control and Prevention (CDC) designed and funded placebo-controlled studies of short-course AZT costing only US$80. These trials were conducted in Cote d'Ivoire, Uganda, Tanzania, South Africa, Malawi, Thailand, Ethiopia, Burkina Fasso, Zimbabwe, Kenya and the Dominican Republic.

In April 1997, the US watchdog Public Citizen complained about US government sponsorship of these trials, arguing that they were unethical because a placebo control was used rather than a zidovudine control (zidovudine is proven to prevent one-third or more of perinatal transmission of HIV). These concerns were subsequently reiterated in major journals (Angel 1997; Lurie and Wolfe 1997).

The central concern shared by these authors was that according to codes of research ethics every patient – including those in the control group – should be assured of the best proven therapeutic method and that the interests of science and society should never take precedence over the well-being of the subject. If these standards are not universal, they argued, it would mean that there were two standards of research ethics: one for the rich and one for the poor, and that medical researchers would be able to conduct or fund research in the developing world that would be ruled unethical in their own country.

The response from Africa's research community and the US National Institute of Health pointed to major differences in mortality and morbidity, health care and economic status, between affluent and developing countries as the basis for difference in research methodology. It was argued that the fundamental need was for research endpoints that were of benefit to the inhabitants of that country where the study is conducted rather than those of donor nations (Varmus and Satcher 1997; Gambia Government/Medical Research Council Joint Ethical Committee 1998). The major defence offered by the sponsors of these trials was that to insist on provision of 'best proven therapeutic method' (such as AZT) as an essential element of ethical research in sub-Saharan Africa, where 8 million people die each year (68% from communicable maternal and perinatal causes), 23% of children die before the age of 15, 15 million people have been infected by the HIV virus and antiretroviral therapy is generally not available to over 90% of those infected, would seem to represent ethical imperialism and a disregard of the judgments of locally constituted research ethics committees (Murray and Lopez 1994).

From the researchers' and sponsors' perspective the use of a placebo control was justifiable because no one was deprived of care as the 'standard care' in these countries was nothing, because this study design would provide better data on absolute effectiveness (rather than relative effectiveness) and because placebo-controlled studies would enable research to be done faster and research benefits translated into the local community. In the words of the Gambian Government Medical Research Council Joint Ethical Committee (1998): 'Stopping trials, in Africa, that are trying to help improve the health of poor people so that those in affluent countries can have peace of mind seems a tortured form of ethical logic'. At the same time, the community in which a therapy is trialled should benefit from participation in the trial either through access to the therapy beyond the completion of the trial, or by gaining a 'fair benefit'.

The principles of a 'fair benefit' framework for evaluating the ethical justifiability of research conducted in the developing world suggest that trials in developing countries should offer:

- Benefits to participants during the research, including health improvement and access to collateral health services beyond those essential to the conduct of the research.
- Benefits to the population during the research, including the provision of additional health services, public health measures and economic/occupational benefits.
- Benefits to the population after the research, including availability of any proven interventions, capacity development, public health measures, long-term collaboration and sharing of financial rewards or intellectual property rights.

Collaborative partnership
- The population is able to make a free and informed decision to participate in the research.
- The population is supportive of the research.

Transparency

- An independent body creates a publicly accessible repository of all formal and informal benefits agreements.
- The research incorporates wide community consultation. (Anon 2004)

The problem with these and other efforts to address issues of exploitation and justice in research is that it is difficult to see how research conducted in the developing world is likely to be either just or coherent in a world characterised by injustice, where developed nations contribute little towards the alleviation of global poverty, where power resides in multinational corporations rather than nation states and where pharmaceutical and biotechnology companies have structural motivations, such as patent laws and trade agreements, to contribute as little as possible to their developing nation hosts (Arras 2004).

Authors such as Farmer (Farmer 1999; Farmer 2003) have argued that the developing world should not have to accept second-rate medicine – a stance that has been influential in initiatives such as the WHO programs to deliver anti-retrovirals to people with AIDS in developing countries. The success of this program means that the arguments about HIV trials in developing countries have largely been outdated. However, HIV is only one disease, and the same arguments that applied to the early HIV trials also apply to other conditions. There is an urgent need for trials of effective and cheap agents for conditions that are common in the developing world such as leukaemia and other cancers, in which Western treatments are inaccessible, and the only alternatives are ineffective.

Debates over 'standards of care', placebo controls and the obligations owed to trial participants both during and following clinical trials have been the subject of intense activity for over a decade. Efforts to reach a compromise position during the revision of the Declaration of Helsinki were ultimately unsuccessful and there is no longer any international consensus with regards to the conduct of clinical trials in the developing world. The WHO has adopted a more lenient position on the use of placebos and on the treatments owed to research participants, and discrepancies also exist between the Declaration of Helsinki and the US National Bioethics Advisory Commission and the Nuffield Council on Bioethics, among others. While this may not be a bad thing as it recognises the need for flexibility and realism and avoids ethical imperialism, it also raises questions about the care of vulnerable populations and the need to consider global health concerns, human rights and the moral failures of governments worldwide to address inequity (Selgelid 2005).

These issues are likely to become more pressing in the coming years as an increasing number of clinical trials are conducted in low-income and developing countries. Many drug trials (estimated at up to 30-40% of the total world clinical trials) are now conducted in China, India, Russia and Latin America and it is estimated that by 2020 30%of the world's clinical trials will be conducted in India.

The reasons for this are clear – these areas have large populations and disease populations (the vast majority of whom are both trial and treatment naïve), they have inadequate hospital and scientific infrastructure, the regulatory restrictions on research are limited and weak, the costs associated with research are 30-65% lower than in the United States or Europe, research studies recruit much faster than in the developed world and there is considerable enthusiasm for establishing links between medicine and industry. While the shift in research activity from the West is obviously appealing to industry and research-funding bodies, there is good reason to be concerned about the conduct of clinical trials in this setting as many of these countries are characterised by weak health systems without universal access to health care and with a dominant private sector, by limited regulation/governance of the medical profession and of private medicine in particular, by marked disparities in wealth and entrenched discrimination, by limited ethics and regulatory infrastructure, and by extensive ties between researchers, academic institutions and private enterprise. Emerging evidence regarding the extensive use of placebo-controlled studies without methodological justification, recruitment of vulnerable populations without elaboration of safety requirements, inadequate post-trial care, frequent undisclosed conflicts of interests, inadequate ethics review and trials conducted in violation of the trial protocols and ethical standards should be of concern to all those concerned with global equity, with research ethics and with the validity and generalisability of data generated from clinical research (Nuffield Council on Bioethics 2005; European Parliament 2007).

Research integrity and scientific misconduct

One definition of research is 'the attempt to derive generalisable new knowledge by addressing clearly defined questions using systematic and rigorous methods'. What this definition does not cover is the human dimension of research – researchers are human, research subjects are human, publishers are human and so are readers. As humans they share strengths and weaknesses, many of which are reflected within the scientific endeavour.

Scientists are under great pressures to produce important results. Much depends on this – their jobs, reputations, incomes and the livelihood of their staff, research students and families. Pressures from universities, commercial enterprises, funding organisations and colleagues all add to their stressors, as does the requirement to meet funding deadlines and participate in other activities including administrative tasks and research oversight. It is not surprising that scientists sometimes slip into unethical behaviour, even sometimes going as far as coercing colleagues, students and research subjects, or faking results. The falls from grace of Dr William McBride, the Australian researcher who first documented the link between thalidomide use in pregnancy and birth defects, and of Professor Hwang Woo Suk, the Korean stem-cell researcher, following exposure of data fabrication and research misconduct, illustrate the complex forces that compromise research integrity and the profound impact that research misconduct has on all involved in it (Wohn 2006).

Examples of research misconduct include putting patients in danger unnecessarily, engaging in fraud or deceit, forging consent forms, publishing a single piece of research multiple times, committing plagiarism, failing to inform or warn research participants or risks or harms, failing to obtain consent, refusing to accept HREC oversight, failing to report the results of research, accepting gift authorship or failing to declare an interest. The NHMRC's Australian Code for the Responsible Conduct of Research addresses many of these issues (National Health and Medical Research Council, Australian Research Council et al 2007). Yet there is no international consensus as to what constitutes research misconduct, with differences in understanding of research misconduct reflecting different emphasis on fraud and/or plagiarism and different perspectives on whether less serious matters (such as multiple publication) or more serious matters (such as harm to research subjects) are being included.

The exact prevalence of scientific misconduct is unknown, as is its impact on science, medicine and public trust. But while it seems likely to be uncommon, it is noteworthy that investigations of adverse outcomes of research, such as those into the deaths of research volunteers such as Ellen Roche or Jesse Gelsinger, reveal evidence of behaviour that verges on research misconduct, including the failure to adhere to research protocols, to identify and respond to adverse effects, or comply with institutional review processes. However, even in the absence of definitive data on research misconduct there is still reason to be concerned about its occurrence as false or unsupported claims arising from flawed research may lead to the development of inappropriate or harmful therapies or products, to the conduct of unnecessary research and ultimately to the erosion or loss of faith in science, medicine and the research endeavour.

Academic authorship

Few aspects of research cause as much distress and uncertainty as questions regarding authorship. Ghost authorship, multiple publication, plagiarism and selective interpretation of data according to the interests of authors are issues that many academics and researchers face in the course of their professional work. Disagreements over c authorship, in particular, are often a potent source of conflict in research. Concerns about authorship, and particularly about the naming as authors on research papers academics who had not made substantive contributions to that research, have led to the formulation of many guidelines on authorship. According to the Australian Code,

> To be named as an author, a researcher must have made a substantial scholarly contribution to the work and be able to take responsibility for at least that part of the work they contributed. Attribution of authorship depends to some extent on the discipline, but in all cases, authorship must be based on substantial contributions in a combination of:
> * conception and design of the project
> * analysis and interpretation of research data
> * drafting significant parts of the work or critically revising it so as to contribute to the interpretation. (International Committee of Medical Journal Editors 2007; National Health and Medical Research Council, Australian Research Council et al 2007)

A number of important principles follow from this. The first is that one should never accept authorship for work one is not responsible for. An interesting side effect of the Bezwoda affair (see case study above) is that some of the co-authors of the Bezwoda papers appeared to be unaware that the fraud had taken place.

It is also obviously unacceptable to publish others' works as one's own. Despite this, cases where papers are re-published under another's name, sometimes after being translated into another language, regularly arise.

Finally all authors must agree, preferentially in writing, to be included. Authorship carries responsibility, and this includes being responsible for what has been written under his or her name. So, for example, the authors of the CLASS paper are responsible for the data manipulation that occurred in this paper, and Bezwoda's co-authors are responsible for the fabricated data presented in his work.

Clinical audit

While research seeks to generate new knowledge, clinical audit seeks to ascertain whether clinical practice conforms to predetermined standards of good clinical practice, and to examine the reasons for variation. Clinical audit is a part of continuous quality improvement rather than standard medical research. The distinction between audit and research may, however, be difficult, as both can require access to medical records, both can use surveys, both can refer to control groups, both require statistical analysis, both may generate results that have relevance to patient populations and both may be published (National Health and Medical Research Council 2003). And while consent requirements may be waived in the case of audit, this is not automatically the case (Bailey 2008; Miller and Emanuel 2008). For these reasons most HRECs also have mechanisms to perform a limited review of audit, such that audit may be performed efficiently and in a timely fashion but with adequate safeguards for maintaining patient autonomy and confidentiality. There is no absolute requirement that review of audit occur through HRECs, and in some cases audit activities are evaluated through other committees such as quality committees or clinical ethics committees.

Conclusion

Research poses a particular problem for medical ethics, because the aim of research – to benefit society – may often conflict with the well-being of the animal or human subjects that are experimented upon. Humans who act as experimental subjects do so out of altruism and some make genuine sacrifices for the sake of the generation of knowledge. This act of giving should not be underestimated, and should be acknowledged specifically in dealings with research subjects. As Goodare and Smith state:

> Clinical trials cannot be done without patients, and the whole purpose of conducting trials is to benefit patients. These two indisputable statements should mean that patients should be at the front of researchers' mind when they design, conduct and report medical research. But they rarely are. Too often patients are forgotten in the complex business of conducting research.

We argue that patients should help to decide which research is conducted, help to plan the research and interpret the data, and hear the results before anyone else. (Goodare and Smith 1995)

RESEARCH AND THE LAW

The civil and criminal law applies to health research in the same way that it is applied to clinical care. A person who was to suffer harm as a result of participation in research would have recourse to the courts in order to gain compensation for damages. There is, however, very little case law involving participants in research. There is also very little in the way of legislation. Ian Kennedy and Andrew Grubb have commented that in the United Kingdom while research on animals has been regulated by law there has never been any statute regulating research on human beings (Kennedy and Grubb 1994). The situation in Australia is somewhat similar!

Researchers in Australia are expected (but not required by legislation) to comply with guidelines issued by the National Health and Medical Research Council (NHMRC). The NHMRC was originally established by a series of orders in council since 1936. In 1992 the *National Health and Medical Research Council Act 1992* (Cth) was passed which gave statutory recognition to the Council. One of the aims of the Act is 'to foster medical research and training and public health research and training throughout Australia'. To achieve this aim s 7(1) of the legislation provides:

The functions of the Council are:
(a) to inquire into, issue guidelines on, and advise the community on, matters relating to:
   (i) the improvement of health; and
   (ii) the prevention, diagnosis and treatment of disease; and
   (iii) the provision of health care; and
   (iv) public health research and medical research; and
   (v) ethical issues relating to health; and
(b) to advise, and make recommendations to, the Commonwealth, the States and Territories on the matters referred to in paragraph (a); and
(c) to make recommendations to the Commonwealth on expenditure:
   (i) on public health research and training; and
   (ii) on medical research and training; including recommendations on the application of the Reserve; and
(d) any functions incidental to any of the foregoing.

Section 35 of the Act requires the creation of the Australian Health Ethics Committee (AHEC). The functions of the AHEC are 'to advise the [NHMRC] on ethical issues relating to health and to develop and give the [NHMRC] guidelines for the conduct of medical research involving humans'. In 2003 the NHMRC was responsible for making available to researchers, both in continuing and new grants, over $300 million. In order to receive these funds researchers must agree to comply with guidelines issued by the AHEC. Thus, the major means of ensuring that researchers comply with ethical guidelines is by the threat to withdraw funds. There are no other general penalties for researchers who breach ethical guidelines, unless a subject of research who suffers damage brings a civil action.

The guidelines issued by the NHMRC are only 'mandatory', then, to the extent that researchers depend on funds from the NHMRC or from other sources that require, as a condition of granting the funding, that NHMRC guidelines be followed. Many private institutions such as CSL Limited (formerly the Commonwealth Serum Laboratory) voluntarily comply with the guidelines (Dow 1997). It is not, and is unlikely to be, known how many private organisations do not comply with the NHMRC guidelines. A former chairman of the AHEC, Professor Don Chalmers, is reported as saying that 'no drug company aiming to get a product registered in Australia would dare test it on humans outside of institutions attached to an ethics committee because the Federal Government's Therapeutic Goods Administration would never approve the results for release of the drug' (Dow 1997). Loane Skene has pointed out that a breach of the NHMRC guidelines may also have the effect of attracting adverse publicity that could damage the reputation and career prospects of the researcher and prevent publication of research results (Skene 2004).

The Privacy Act 1988 (Cth) and research

The *Privacy Act 1988* is Commonwealth legislation that aims to protect the privacy of personal information held by Commonwealth agencies or by the private sector. The Act has particular concerns with protecting sensitive information such as health information. As well as the personal concern to protect sensitive information there may be other claims that argue that access to this sensitive information is required in order to benefit society as a whole. This is frequently the case with health research. Health research is important to help the community make decisions that impact on the health of individuals and the community. Ideally this should be done in such a way as to minimise the intrusion on a person's privacy while still providing relevant information to researchers. There is a need therefore to balance the public interest in respect for privacy against the public interest in carrying out relevant research.

Sections 95 and 95A of the Act provide a process to resolve the conflict that may arise between the public interest in privacy and the public interest in research. The NHMRC (with the approval of the Federal Privacy Commissioner) has provided guidelines for the protection of privacy in medical research. The guidelines prescribe procedures that Human Research Ethics Committees and researchers must adhere to in order for the disclosures of personal information from Commonwealth agencies to be lawful.

New South Wales, Victoria and the ACT all provides similar exceptions for medical research without consent: *Health Records and Information Privacy Act 2002* (NSW), HPP 10(f); *Health Records Act 2001* (Vic), HPP 2(g); *Health Records (Privacy and Access) Act 1997* (ACT), PP 10.3. Both NSW and Victoria also have statutory guidelines for controlling the disclosure for research which are much the same as the NHMRC guidelines with respect to the *Privacy Act*.

Clinical trials

A clinical trial is a study involving humans to find out whether an intervention which it is believed may improve a person's health actually does so (National Health and Medical Research Council 2001). There are two schemes under which clinical trials involving therapeutic goods may be conducted, the Clinical Trial Exemption (CTX) Scheme and the Clinical Trial Notification (CTN) Scheme. The schemes apply when it is proposed using a drug product not entered in the Australian Register of Therapeutic Goods (ARTG), including any new formulation of an existing drug product or any new route of administration or any use of a marketed drug product beyond the conditions of its marketing approval. These schemes place some responsibilities upon Human Research Ethics Committees (HRECs). All CTX and CTN schemes must have an Australian sponsor. The sponsor is the person, body, organisation or institution that takes overall responsibility (including medico-legal responsibility) for the conduct of the trial.

Clinical Trial Exemption (CTX) Scheme

The CTX scheme is an approval process. The Therapeutic Goods Administration (TGA) is a unit of the Australian Government Department of Health and Ageing. The TGA has the responsibility for assessing and monitoring activities to ensure that the Australian community has access, within a reasonable time, to therapeutic advances. In a CTX trial the TGA evaluates data to assess safety issues and decides whether the proposed usage guidelines for the product are acceptable. A HREC then considers the proposed trial protocol after reviewing the summary information provided by the sponsor and additional comments from the TGA.

Clinical Trial Notification (CTN) Scheme

The CTN scheme is a notification scheme. In a CTN trial the data on the drug product is reviewed by the HREC (often specialist reviewers will examine issues such as toxicology). The TGA does not review the data relating to the trial before permitting it to proceed. The sponsor notifies the TGA that a clinical trial is being conducted after the HREC has given approval.

Negligence, experimental treatments and research

Paul McNeill, in his book *The Ethics and Politics of Human Experimentation* (1993), notes that there are very few reported cases on human experimentation (after 1945) and that most of the reported cases rely on legal principles established in the cases that concern medical treatment. McNeill says:

> There have been very few court cases involving non-therapeutic human experimentation. Most cases have arisen from experimental treatment that promised at least the possibility of some benefit to the subject. In the few

cases of 'non-therapeutic' medical experimentation, courts have consistently held that there can be no exceptions to the obligation to disclose all relevant information. (McNeill 1993)

This is consistent with the High Court judgment in *Rogers v Whitaker* (1992) 175 CLR 479. It would be expected that a reasonable person, when considering whether to participate in a research project, would want far more information than if only therapeutic treatment was involved.

Two of the significant cases of 'non-therapeutic' treatment are from Canada. In the first of these, *Halushka v University of Saskatchewan* (1965) 53 DLR 436, the patient had been wrongly reassured that the experimental drug was safe and had been used many times before, when this was not true. Halushka went into a complete cardiac arrest following administration of the drug. The court found that for consent for research to be valid there had to be a 'full and frank' disclosure of the facts; that had not occurred in this case. Halushka was awarded $22,500 in damages.

In the case of *Weiss v Solomon* [1989] RJQ 731 the heirs of a research subject (Weiss), who had died in the course of participating in a non-therapeutic trial, successfully sued the principal investigator and the hospital. The court held that both the researcher and the hospital, through its research ethics committee, were liable because they did not adequately warn Weiss of the risks associated with the treatment.

In the United States it has been noted that, following a 1995 report by President Clinton's Advisory Committee on Human Radiation Experiments that documented widespread abuses in the 1940s, and the 1999 death of Jessie Gelsinger, an 18-year-old who participated in gene transfer studies at the University of Pennsylvania, there have been a 'flurry of claims' (Morreim 2004). This has led to concerns being expressed that such litigation could lead to a 'more legalistic, mechanistic approach to ethical review that does not further the interests of human subjects or scientific progress' (Mello, Studdert et al 2003).

Jessie Gelsinger died in September 1999 while participating in a gene therapy trial at the Institute of Human Gene Therapy at the University of Pennsylvania. The trial was designed to treat a rare metabolic disease, ornithine transcarbamylase deficiency. Four months later he died from multi-system organ failure resulting from a liver infection. In the subsequent Food and Drug Administration investigation four issues were identified:

- he was inadequately informed of the risks involved;
- he was admitted into the study when his liver function was outside the parameters of the inclusion criteria;
- serious adverse effects in other participants had been reported, but not acted upon; and
- the investigator held a 30% interest in the sponsoring company while the university held a 5% equity, thus presenting a conflict of interest that was not disclosed.

Jessie Gelsinger's father sued the university. The case settled for an undisclosed sum. One interesting aspect of this case is that the original suit included a claim against a bioethicist, Arthur Caplan, the Director of the University of Pennsylvania's Center For Bioethics. The claim against Caplan was dropped.

Problems with informed consent were also raised in the Western Australian case of *Hassan v Minister for Health (No 2)* [2008] WASCA 149. This case concerned a pregnant woman whose unborn child had died. She had opted to have the foetus removed before labour. The clinical method chosen was to artificially induce labour and then perform a uterine evacuation to remove the foetus. As part of this treatment, the patient was invited to participate in a clinical trial of prostaglandin, in the form of the drug Misoprostal. This drug induces labour and the trial was designed to test for suitable dosages of the drug in second trimester terminations. The trial had been approved by the hospital clinical authorities. The patient experienced complications with bleeding and as the placenta was being removed the patient had a massive a massive haemorrhage which put her life in serious danger. A total hysterectomy was performed to stop the bleeding but the patient was left sterile.

The plaintiff alleged a number of breaches of duty, including a failure to warn the patient of the material risk of hysterectomy. The trial judge found that the doctor had failed to discharge her duty of care by failing to advise the patient adequately of the risks associated with the uterine evacuation and in failing to advise her of an alternative available procedure of dilatation and evacuation (D&E). Even so, the trial judge did not find that these breaches had caused or contributed materially to the hysterectomy. The hysterectomy was found to have been an unavoidable complication with the pregnancy, given the patient's obstetric history.

On appeal, the WA Court of Appeal agreed with the trial judge. The court found that, even had the patient been made aware of some risk of having to have a hysterectomy in the trial, it was clear from all the circumstances that she would still have submitted to being in the trial and having the uterine evacuation as proposed by the doctor. According to the court there was no feasible alternative course available, and it could not be said that the breach of the duty to inform had caused the damage of the hysterectomy.

When treatment is being provided as part of a research study it is incumbent on health professionals to keep abreast of any changes to the treatment protocol. *South Eastern Sydney Area Health Service v King* [2006] NSWCA 2 concerned a 13-year-old patient who had become quadriplegic as a result of a radical and experimental treatment involving radiotherapy, systemic chemotherapy and intrathecal chemotherapy. The area health service was found to be negligent as the treating doctor was unaware that the protocol for the treatment had been amended. There was also a finding of negligence in that the treating doctor had not put in place a system to ensure that recent developments were communicated to him. Hunt AJA stated the duty as being:

> I do not accept that the performance of this duty could only have been achieved by Professor O'Gorman-Hughes by undertaking *for himself* the obligation to conduct a literature search and make inquiries of the IRS Group. Practising in a leading hospital as a member of a team permits a task such as this to be delegated, so that the same searches do not have to be made by many (if not all) of the members of that team. But this duty did require

Professor O'Gorman-Hughes to ensure that, in the particular circumstances of this case (as outlined in the previous paragraph), he was placed in as good a position by a system based on collaborative teamwork as he would have been had he performed the duty himself. He had to do more in this case than merely rely in a purely reactive manner to whatever information Dr White may randomly have received from his overseas contacts. If he could not do it himself, he had to take reasonable care to ensure that someone else actively searched for material which was relevant to the task he was to undertake. (at [60])

Research involving incompetent adults and children

Some jurisdictions class medical research as a form of special treatment which requires a special form of consent or authorisation (see Chapter 13) for the laws on consent for incompetent patients).

In the *Guardianship Act 1987* (NSW) the definition of 'special treatment' includes any new treatment that has not yet gained the support of a substantial number of medical practitioners or dentists specialising in the area of practice concerned. Section 45 authorises the Guardianship Tribunal to give consent to new and unsupported treatments if it is satisfied that:

(a) the treatment is the only or most appropriate way of treating the patient and is manifestly in the best interests of the patient, and

(b) the National Health and Medical Research Council guidelines have been or will be complied with.

In Queensland the *Guardianship and Administration Act 2000* defines 'special health care' to include participation by an adult in special medical research or experimental health care. The Guardianship and Administration Tribunal may approve special medical research or experimental health care if:

(a) the special medical research or experimental health care is approved by an ethics committee;

(b) the risk and inconvenience to the adult and the adult's quality of life is small;

(c) the special medical research or experimental health care may result in significant benefit to the adult; and

(d) the potential benefit can not be achieved in another way. (s 72(1))

The tribunal may also consent to an adult's participation in special medical research or experimental health care if the tribunal is satisfied that –

(a) the special medical research or experimental health care is approved by an ethics committee;

(b) the risk and inconvenience to the adult and the adult's quality of life is small;

(c) the special medical research or experimental health care may result in significant benefit to the adult or other persons with the condition;

(d) the special medical research or experimental health care can not reasonably be carried out without a person who has or has had the condition taking part;

(e)   the special medical research or experimental health care will not unduly interfere with the adult's privacy. (s 72(2)

The Victorian *Guardianship and Administration Act 1986* used to require special approval for medical research, but after 15 July 2006 a person responsible is empowered to consent to a medical research procedure.

Research and experimental treatment involving children may also be reviewed by the courts. In Australia, it is arguable that the doctrine of non-therapeutic treatment as set out in *Marion's case* (*Secretary, Department of Health and Community Services v JWB And SMB* (1992) 175 CLR 218) could be applied to research projects and experimental treatments where there may be no demonstrable benefit from being exposed to the treatment. This issue was discussed in the case of *Re Baby A* [2008] FamCA 417. Baby A had been born with a rare and fatal metabolic disorder that had no known treatment. Her parents and treatment team wished for her to be treated with an experimental drug known as Drug X. The drug had not been tested on humans but had given promising results in mice. The judge doubted whether approval was necessary as a special treatment. The treatment was clearly the only option for the child even though no one could say what its effects would be with certainty. Nevertheless, Dessau J proceeded on the basis that the treatment did require approval as the judge wished for there to be no doubt that the parents had the power to consent to the treatment. The treatment was approved and a declaration was made that the parents were empowered to consent to it.

Similar issues were raised in the UK case of *Simms v Simms* [2002] EWHC 2734 (Fam). This case concerned both an 18-year-old and a 16-year-old sufferer of vCJD. The parents of the patients sought a declaration that it would be in the patients' best interests for them to be treated with Pentosan Polysulphate, a drug that was licensed for treatment of interstitial cystitis, thrombophlebitis or thrombosis, but not for vCJD. Dame Butler-Sloss P (as she was then) began by examining whether the treatment was supported under the *Bolam* test in medical negligence. Her Ladyship found that it was, as there was 'a responsible body of relevant professional opinion which supports this innovative treatment' (at [51]). On the best interests test Dame Butler-Sloss P stated:

> I am satisfied from all the evidence that both JS and JA have a life that is worth preserving and that any treatment that might be beneficial would be of value to them. It has to be recognised that the treatment proposed for these two patients would not lead to recovery. Nonetheless, on the totality of the medical evidence I find that there are possible benefits both to JS and JA from this pioneering treatment. The chance of improvement is slight but not non-existent. The families ought to regard that possibility as unlikely but not impossible, since no-one knows the outcome. There is, from the medical evidence, a possibility of arresting the disease temporarily, and the possibility of prolonging the life of these two patients to some extent, although whether that be in weeks, months or years is impossible to tell. ... I consider that even the prospect of a slightly longer life is a benefit worth having for each of these two patients. There is sufficient possibility of unquantifiable benefit for me to find that it would be in their best interests to have the operations and the treatment subject to an assessment of the risks. There is no alternative treatment available. (at [61])

Research fraud

Dr William McBride was an Australian specialist obstetrician and gynaecologist and was the first to publish on the teratogenicity of thalidomide. It was claimed that in 1982 Dr McBride published in a scientific journal spurious results relating to laboratory experiments on pregnant rabbits dosed with scopolamine. In January 1989 it was announced by the Medical Complaints Unit of the New South Wales Department of Health that an inquiry would be held. The allegations against Dr McBride included 44 concerning his medical practice and 24 relating to his medical research. A Medical Tribunal hearing commenced on 6 November 1989 and lasted a total of 198 days. Dr McBride was cross-examined for 41 days. Of the medical practice allegations only one minor complaint was found proved but 24 of the medical research allegations were found proved. On 29 July 1993 his name was removed from the Medical Register. An appeal to the New South Wales Court of Appeal was disallowed in July 1994 and the High Court refused leave to appeal in February 1995.

The case of Dr McBride illustrates the serious nature of scientific fraud and the effect that it can have upon a career.

References

Ackernecht, E (1982) *A Short History of Medicine*. Baltimore, Johns Hopkins Press.

Angel, M (1990) 'The Nazi hypothermia experiments and unethical research today'. *N Engl J Med* **322**(20): 1463-4.

Angel, M (1997) 'The ethics of clinical research in the third world'. *N Engl J Med* **337**: 847-9.

Annas, GJ and MA Grodin (1990) 'The Nazi doctors and the Nuremberg Code: relevance for modern medical research'. *Med War* **6**(2): 120-3.

Anon (2004) 'Moral standards for research in developing countries: from "reasonable availability" to "fair benefits"'. *Hastings Cent Rep* **34**(3): 17-27.

Arras, JD (2004) 'Fair benefits in international medical research'. *Hastings Cent Rep* **34**(3): 3.

Bailey, M (2008) 'Harming through protection?' *N Engl J Med* **358**(8): 768-9.

Ballantyne, AJ and WA Rogers (2008) 'Fair inclusion of men and women in Australian clinical research: views from ethics committee chairs'. *Med J Aust* **188**(11): 653-6.

Beecher, HK (1966) 'Ethics and clinical research'. *N Engl J Med* **274**(24): 1354-60.

British Medical Association (2004) *Medical Ethics Today* (2nd ed). London, BMJ Books.

Capron, A (1991) 'Protection of research subjects: Do special rules apply in epidemiology?' *J Clin Epidemiol* **44**(Supp 1): 81S-89S.

Capron, A (2006) Experimentation with human beings: Light or only shadows symposium. *A World Less Silent: Celebrating Jay Katz's contributions to Law, Medicine and Ethics. Yale Journal of Health Policy, Law and Ethics*. **6**:431-64.

Carter, SM, CF Jordens et al (2008) 'You have to make something of all that rubbish, do you? An empirical investigation of the social process of qualitative research'. *Qual Health Res* **18**(9): 1264-76.

Cheng, AC, M Lowe et al (2003) 'Ethical problems of evaluating a new treatment for melioidosis'. *BMJ* **327**(7426): 1280-2.

Collins, R, R Doll et al (1992) Ethics of clinical trials. *Introducing new treatments for cancer: practical ethics and legal problems*. C Williams. Bristol, John Wiley and Sons Ltd: 49-65.

Cookson, J (1992) 'Auditing a research ethics committee'. *JR Coll Physicians London* **26**: 181-3.

Court, C (1995) 'GMC finds doctor not guilty in consent case'. *BMJ* **311**: 1245-6.

Dow, S (1997) Science's playground. *The Age*.

Editorial (1998) 'Pragmatism in codes of research ethics'. *Lancet* **351**: 225.

Elliott, C (2008) 'Guinea-pigging'. *New Yorker* **Jan 7**: 36-41.

Ettershank, K and D Ranson (1997) 'Vaccine trials on orphans cause outrage in Australia'. *Lancet* **349**: 1817.

European Parliament (2007) Final Report of the Expert Meeting: 'Clinical Trials and Protection of Trial Subjects in Low-Income and Developing Countries'. Brussels, European Parliament.

Farmer, P (1999) *Infections and inequalities : the modern plagues*. Berkeley, University of California Press.

Farmer, P (2003) *Pathologies of Power: Health, Human Rights and the New War on the Poor*. Berkeley, University of California Press.

Frew, D and A Martlew (2007) 'Research governance: new hope for ethics committees?' *Monash Bioeth Rev* **26**(1-2): 17-23.

Gambia Government/Medical Research Council Joint Ethical Committee (1998). 'Ethical issues facing medical research in developing countries'. *Lancet* **351**: 286-7.

Gardner, W, C Lidz et al (2005) 'Authors' reports about research integrity problems in clinical trials'. *Contemp Clin Trials* **26**: 244-51.

Gizzler, M, J Davies et al (1990) 'Ethics committees and health services research'. *J Pub Health Med* **12**: 190-6.

Goodare, H and R Smith (1995) 'The rights of patients in research'. *BMJ* **310**: 1277-8.

Hellman, S (1995) 'The patient and the public good'. *Nature Medicine* **1**(5): 400-2.

Hogue, C (1991) 'Ethical issues in sharing epidemiological data'. *J Clin Epidemiol* **44**(Supp 1): 103S-107S.

Hope, RA, J Savulescu et al (2003) *Medical ethics and law: the core curriculum*. Edinburgh, Churchill Livingstone.

Hornblum, A (1997) 'They were cheap and available: prisoners as research subjects in twentieth century America'. *BMJ* **315**: 1437-41.

Institute of Medical Ethics Working Party on the Ethical Implications of AIDS (1992) 'AIDS, ethics and clinical trials'. *BMJ* **305**: 699-701.

International Committee of Medical Journal Editors (1995) 'Protection of patient's rights to privacy'. *BMJ* **311**: 1272.

International Committee of Medical Journal Editors (2007) 'Uniform requirements for manuscripts submitted to biomedical journals: Writing and editing for biomedical publication', <http://www.icmje.org/icmje.pdf>.

Jones, JH and Tuskegee Institute (1993) *Bad blood: the Tuskegee syphilis experiment*. New York, Maxwell McMillan International.

Juni, P, A Rutjes et al (2002) 'Are selective COX 2 inhibitors superior to traditional non steroidal anti-inflammatory drugs?' *BMJ* **324**: 1287-8.

Kaptchuk, TJ, JM Kelley et al (2008) 'Components of placebo effect: randomised controlled trial in patients with irritable bowel syndrome'. *BMJ* **336**(7651): 999-1003.

Katz, J (1972) *Experimentation with Human Beings: the Authority of the Investigator, Subject, Professions, and the State in the Human Experimentation Process*. New York, Russel Sage Foundation.

Levine, R and K Lebacqz (1979) 'Ethical considerations in clinical trials'. *Clin Pharmacol Ther* **25**(5): 728-41.

Lewis, M, G Rachelevski et al (1994) 'The termination of a randomised clinical trial for poor Hispanic children'. *Arch Pediatr Adolesc Med* **148**(4): 364-7.

Loblay, RH (2008) 'Human research ethics – a work in progress'. *Med J Aust* **188**(11): 628-9.

Loblay, RH and DR Chalmers (1999) 'Ethics committees: is reform in order?' *Med J Aust* **170**(1): 9-10.

Lock, S (1990) 'Monitoring research ethics committees'. *BMJ* **300**: 61-2.

Lock, S (1995) 'Research ethics – a brief historical review to 1965'. *J Intern Med* **238**(6): 513-20.

Lurie, P and S Wolfe (1997) 'Unethical trials of interventions to reduce perinatal transmission of the human immunodeficiency virus in developing countries'. *N Engl J Med* **337**: 883-5.

McCarthy, C (1994) 'Historical background of clinical trials involving women and minorities'. *Acad Med* **69**(9): 695-8.

McNeill, P, C Berglund et al (1990) 'Reviewing the reviewers: a survey of institutional ethics committees in Australia'. *Med J Aust* **152**: 289-96.

McNeill, P, C Berglund et al (1994) 'How much influence do various members have within research ethics committees?' *Camb Q Healthcare Ethics* **3**(522-32).

Miller, B (1993) 'The ethics of cardiac arrest research'. *Ann Emerg Med* **22**(1): 118-24.

Miller, F and EJ Emanuel (2008) 'Quality-improvement research and informed consent'. *N Engl J Med* **358**(8): 765-7.

Murray, C and A Lopez (1994) 'Global and regional causes-of-death patterns in 1990'. *Bull World Health Org* **72**: 447-80.

Murthy, VH, HM Krumholz et al (2004) 'Participation in cancer clinical trials: race-, sex-, and age-based disparities'. *JAMA* **291**(22): 2720-6.

National Health and Medical Research Council (2002) *Human research ethics handbook : commentary on the National statement on ethical conduct in research involving humans.* Canberra, National Health and Medical Research Council.

National Health and Medical Research Council, Australian Research Council et al (2007) *The Australian Code for the Responsible Conduct of Research.* Canberra, Australian Government.

NHMRC (2007) *National Statement on Ethical Conduct in Human Research.* Canberra, Australian Government.

Nie, JB (2006) 'The United States cover-up of Japanese wartime medical atrocities: complicity committed in the national interest and two proposals for contemporary action'. *Am J Bioeth* **6**(3): W21-33.

Nuffield Council on Bioethics (2005) *The ethics of research related to healthcare in developing countries.* London, Nuffield Council on Bioethics.

Pappworth, M (1967) *Human guinea pigs: experimentation on man.* Boston, Beacon Press.

Rothman, K and K Michels (1994) 'The continuing unethical use of placebo controls'. *N Engl J Med* **331**(6): 394-8.

Selgelid, MJ (2005) 'Module Four: Standards of Care and Clinical Trials'. *Developing World Bioethics* **5**(1): 55-72.

Shuster, E (1997) 'Fifty years later: the significance of the Nuremberg Code'. *N Engl J Med* **337**(20): 1436-40.

Silverstein, F, G Faich et al (2000) 'Gastrointestinal toxicity with celecoxib vs nonsteroidal anti-inflammatory drugs for osteoarthritis and rheumatoid arthritis: the CLASS study: a randomized controlled trial. Celecoxib Long-term Arthritis Safety Study'. *JAMA* **284**: 1247-55.

Spiegel, D and A Harrington (2008) 'What is the placebo worth?' *BMJ* **336**(7651): 967-8.

Steinbrook, R (2002) 'Protecting research subjects – the crisis at Johns Hopkins'. *N Engl J Med* **346**(9): 716-20.

Temple, R and S Ellenberg (2000) 'Placebo-controlled trials and active-control trials in the evaluation of new treatments. Part 1: Ethical and scientific issues'. *Ann Intern Med* **133**: 455-63.

Varmus, H and D Satcher (1997) 'Ethical complexities of conducting research in developing countries'. *N Engl J Med* **337**: 1003-5.

Vollman, J and R Winau (1996) 'Informed consent in human experimentation before the Nuremberg Code'. *BMJ* **313**: 1445-7.

Walsh, MK, JJ McNeil et al (2005) 'Improving the governance of health research'. *Med J Aust* **182**(9): 468-71.

Weindling, P (2001) 'The origins of informed consent: the International Scientific Commission on Medical War Crimes, and the Nuremburg code'. *Bull Hist Med* **75**(1): 37-71.

Weiss, R, R Rifkin et al (2000) 'High-dose chemotherapy for high-risk primary breast cancer: an on-site review of the Bezwoda study'. *Lancet* **355**: 999-1003.

Wohn, Y (2006) 'Research misconduct. Seoul National University dismisses Hwang'. *Science* **311**(5768): 1695.

CHAPTER 32

HEALTH CARE, ANIMALS AND THE ENVIRONMENT

Case study 1. Frogs

Since the early 1990s, frog populations around the world have suffered dramatic declines. This was first attributed to factors such as climate change, environmental degradation and pesticides. However the leading cause of frog population declines in many areas is now known to be the presence of a pathogen called the chytrid fungus.

Chytrid disease is a global epidemic, occurring in Australia, New Zealand, Europe, North America, Central America, South America and Africa. Worldwide, the oldest evidence of this disease comes from specimens collected in 1938 of an African frog – Xenopus laevis. This frog harbours the Chytrid fungus and can spread it to other species, but does not itself develop disease from it. Looking back through museum specimens, it can be seen that the disease first spread to Canada in the early 70s and to Australian frog specimens from 1978. But how did it spread from Africa to other species around the world?

In 1934, it was found that this particular species of frog develops clearly identifiable swelling of its ovaries if it is injected with urine of pregnant women. This formed the basis for the first pregnancy test. Exporting these frogs became an industry, with about 5000 frogs exported to overseas laboratories per year from the 1930s until the 1970s. Of course some of these frogs escaped, and feral populations have been found in Ascension Island, the United Kingdom, the United States, and Chile. It is thought that the fungus from the African frogs then spread to the native frog population. (Weldon, du Preez et al 2004)

The net result is that up to a third of the world's frog species are now at risk due to use of these frogs in pregnancy tests.

Case study 2. Fish

The American Heart Association recommends that all people should eat fish at least twice per week – a total of about 340gm per week or 17kg per year. There are currently about 6.5 billion people in the world, and this is expected to rise to 9 billion by 2050. If all of these people ate the recommended dose of fish this would come to between 110 and 153 million tonnes per year.

World wide, we currently eat about 100 million tonnes of seafood per year and, to sustain this catch, a third of the world fish stocks are over-fished (Montaigner 2007). *Increasing this catch in line with the American Heart guidelines is clearly not sustainable.*

Case study 3. Woodchucks and Chimpanzees

A study was undertaken to examine the effectiveness of a new drug for treating chronic hepatitis B called Fialuridine. Fifteen patients were randomly assigned to receive different dosages of the drug that had previously been shown to be safe when tested on animals. All patients gave informed consent to participate in the study.

Thirteen weeks into the trial, one of the patients presented to a local Emergency Department with sudden onset of hepatic failure and shock. The trial was stopped and the other patients were immediately reviewed. Seven patients were found to have liver failure; and two of these patients died immediately. The remaining five patients required urgent liver transplants, and three of these patients died post-operatively. (McKenzie, Fried et al 1995)

When these results were reported, some commentators suggested that the drug had not been tested on animals sufficiently before it was trialled on humans. One commentator noted that much of the testing had been performed on woodchucks. He went on to suggest that:

> *'Chimpanzees, whose genome is more than 98% identical to that of humans, provide a potentially much more informative model, in both safety and efficacy. Chimpanzees with chronic HBV, HCV and HIV infection are available in many research facilities. Although HBV-infected animals are in relatively short supply, this is not the case for HCV- or HIV-infected animals. These animals should be used in preliminary studies of the safety and efficacy of experimental treatments. Chimpanzee studies are often more expensive than human trials; however the potential avoidance of tragedies such as those described by McKenzie et al, is of incalculable value and deserves consideration ...'* (Prince 1996)

Bioethics emerged in the 1960s and 1970s as a new way of thinking and speaking about the ecological, moral and social universe and was not so much a simple extension of medical ethics but a break from it. The term 'bioethics', which was coined by the American biochemist, Van Rensselaer Potter in 1970, referred to a multidisciplinary field of inquiry that sought to integrate biology, ecology, medicine and human values (Potter 1971). While bioethics may have originally been conceived as having a concern with ecology, the field is often regarded as having two distinct domains – biomedical ethics and environmental ethics (O'Neill 2002). (Although this formulation of bioethics as a culture/nature dualism is rejected by some (Twine 2005).) Medical ethics is largely concerned with humans (ie, it is 'anthropocentric') in keeping with Abrahamic religions (Christianity, Judaism and Islam), and western moral philosophy, both of which presume natural hierarchies of existence, sometimes referred to as the 'Great

Chain of Being' – with God at the pinnacle and the natural world at the bottom (Lovejoy 1936). For example, the Bible (*Genesis* 1:27-8) says:

> God created man in his own image, in the image of God created he him; male and female created he them. And God blessed them, and God said unto them, be fruitful, and multiply, and replenish the earth, and subdue it: and have dominion over fish of the sea, and over fowl of the air, and over every living thing that moveth upon the earth.

However, it is now obvious to most people that humans should do more than simply exploit the other parts of the biological and physical world. Even the current Pope Benedict has protested against the use of animals in factory farms because 'degrading living creatures to a commodity' seemed to him to 'contradict the relationship of mutuality that comes across in the Bible' (Ratzinger 2002).

In contrast to biomedical ethics, environmental ethics is largely concerned with the planet and universe, ecosystems, the treatment of life forms such as plants and animals, of groups and systems of life-forms (such as ecosystems and populations) and with more abstract aspects of the environment such as species, climate change or pollution (Nash 1990; O'Neill 2002). Environmental ethics would suggest that there are two major philosophical reasons why we should respect the non-human world – one is that the environment has *instrumental* worth, the other that it has *intrinsic* worth (Brennan and Lo 2002).

The idea that the environment has predominantly instrumental worth starts from an anthropocentric perspective and argues that it is important to maintain the environment because otherwise it would be bad for humanity. For example, we should not let frog species die out because there may be some important drugs in their skins that would be useful to humanity. Or we should be concerned about the greenhouse gases emitted by hospitals because in the long term it will be bad for humanity if we don't. This approach maintains a human-centred view of the environment and presumes the world in terms of power – the power of human animals to label, define, classify, control and discipline (Komesaroff 2008).

Arguments that concentrate on the intrinsic worth of the environment suggest that we should not see things only in terms of humanity, and that the natural world has a value in itself (Verhoog 1992). These arguments do not necessarily apply to the whole environment – for example philosophers like Peter Singer argue that we should take special care of some living creatures because some are capable of feeling pleasure and pain. Singer's argument is based on the idea that avoidance of suffering – of whatever species – has intrinsic value. He says:

> The prevailing Western ethic presumes that human interests must always prevail over the comparable interests of other species. Since the rise of the modern animal movement in the 1970s, however, this ethic has been on the defensive. The argument is that, despite obvious differences between human and non-human animals, we share a capacity to suffer, and this means that they, like us, have interests. (Singer and Mason 2006)

Other values that may form the basis for an environmental ethic – for example, biodiversity (Wilson 1992), beauty, the integrity and value of the entire world, or the dignity of living creatures – may also be seen as worthy ends in themselves.

These are themes that we come back to again in the following sections where we look at a number of areas where biomedical ethics and environmental ethics converge.

Medicine and overpopulation

In a 1974 article in the Scientific American, Coale summarised the history of the human population as follows:

> The present rate of the world population increase – 20 per 1000 – is almost certainly without precedent and it is hundreds of times greater than the rate that has been the norm in most of man's history. Without doubt this period of growth will be a transitory episode in the history of the population. If the present rate were to be maintained, the population would double approximately every 35 years, it would be multiplied by 1000 every 350 years and by a million every 700 years. The consequence of sustained growth at this pace are clearly impossible: in less than 700 years there would be one person for every square foot on the surface of the earth ...
>
> Arithmetic makes a return to a growth rate near zero inevitable before many generations have passed. What is uncertain is not that the future rate of growth will be about zero but how large the future population will be and what combination of fertility and mortality will sustain it. The possibilities range from more than eight children per woman and a life that lasts an average of 15 years to slightly more than two children per woman and a life span that surpasses 75 years. (Coale 1974)

In the 30-plus years since this was written the world's average population growth has fallen from 1.79% to 1.16% per year but the world population has continued to grow from about 4 billion to 6.6 billion. Coale's two visions of the world – one where the world is crowded but with low life expectancies; and the other where it is spacious and with high life expectancies, have come to exist side by side. Japan and South Africa represent two examples of the different sorts of societies envisaged by Coale – Japan has a fertility rate of 1.2 children per woman and a life expectancy of 82 years; South Africa has a fertility rate of 2.2 children per women but a life expectancy of only 42 years (US Census Bureau 2007).

One country that has attempted to limit population growth through more stringent measures is China. China has a population of 1.3 billion people, a fertility rate of 1.8 children per woman and a life expectancy of 73 years. From the perspective of environmental ethics, China's policies have been successful. However, from the perspective of biomedical ethics, they have been extremely concerning. According to Hesketh and Zhu:

> The ugliest aspects of the policy have received great attention: female infanticide, forced abortions, and selective abortion of female fetuses. There is no doubt that all of these have occurred, but they have now disappeared completely in many places. (Hesketh and Zhu 1997)

Many commentators have argued that China's 'one child policy' is unethical, since it conflicts with humans' 'reproductive rights'. But this brings up a basic problem involving the conflict between biomedical and environmental ethics. In the case of China, should an individual's 'reproductive rights' trump our concerns about overpopulation, or should it work the other way? When can we use coercive measures that limit people's rights in order to maintain the environment? Indeed, to what extent can we exploit or sacrifice the environment for the benefit or health of humans?

China's one-child policy does not arise out of concerns for the intrinsic value of the environment. China's leaders could see that the rising impact of population growth would affect economic prosperity and the health of its people. In fact this provides one clear answer to these questions – the maintenance of the environment should take priority when further damage to it is likely to affect humanity more than it benefits humanity. But arguments of the intrinsic worth of the environment suggest that we should stop damaging the natural world well before his point.

The environmental footprint of health care

Health care is notoriously wasteful and produces enormous amounts of wastes and pollutants. For example, Susan Germain, a Canadian GP and environmental researcher, has looked at the environmental impact of Lions Gate Hospital, a mid-size Canadian hospital. In the space of a year, the hospital used over 1.7 million pairs of gloves, over 17 tonnes of plastic bags for intravenous solutions and 7 tonnes of packaging for these bags. It used 426,000 diapers, almost all for adults which, together with incontinence pads, accounted for 58 tonnes of waste (Germain 2007).

And there are other more dangerous wastes from hospitals. Disposal and incineration of the by-products of health care are a leading source of dioxin and mercury pollution – both of which have been linked to birth defects, organ toxicity and malignancy (Birnbaum 1995; Myers, Davidson et al 2003). There is approximately 1 gram of mercury in a typical thermometer. It is claimed that this is enough mercury to contaminate a lake with a surface area of about 20 acres, to the degree that the fish from it would be unsafe to eat. This has led to a move to have 'mercury-free' hospitals by replacing all mercury-based instruments such as thermometers and sphygmomanometers with electronic ones (Going Green 2002). So far this has appeared to have little impact in Australia.

Some of the waste in hospitals arises out of the high standards of hygiene required to prevent cross infections. We use universal precautions against infection for everybody –not just those whom we know to have infectious diseases. But this has an inevitable effect on the environment (such as 1.7 million rubber gloves per year). Some of this waste might be preventable if we took different approaches to patient care.

Other waste is entirely preventable. We do not need to use mercury, to photocopy on only one side of a piece of paper, or to keep lights and computers on 24 hours a day in most areas.

Health care has other effects on the environment in addition to that caused by its waste. It may even affect rare and endangered species. This is not only true of Western health care – traditional Chinese medical practices have led to the near extinction of the rhino, bear, shark and tiger!

One example is the development of the drug Paclitaxel (Taxol). In the early 1960s, the National Cancer Institute organised a collection of plants from the US for evaluation as potential sources of anti-cancer drugs. One of these plants – the Pacific Yew – was found to contain effective anti-cancer agents, leading to the development of the drug Paclitaxel. The bark of a single Pacific Yew tree yielded enough chemical to make one dose of Taxol. At their peak, Pacific yew bark collections required several hundred thousand pounds of bark per year. By this time the Pacific Yew was said to be rare in the wild and there was concern that it might be made extinct as a consequence of its use in drug production. Eventually, a way was discovered to make Taxol out of the common Yew instead of the Pacific Yew (<http://en.wikipedia.org/wiki/Taxol>).

Increasing concern with the environmental harms associated with providing health care led to the creation of a political coalition called Health Care Without Harm (HCWH) in 1996 (Heilig, Kushner et al 2001). This movement, which has since been endorsed by more than 470 medical, nursing, public health and environmental organisations, labour unions and health providers in over 50 countries, was created with the broad intention of transforming the health-care sector worldwide, without compromising patient safety or care, so that it is ecologically sustainable and no longer a source of harm to public health and the environment (<http://www.noharm.org>). The stated goals of HCWH are to:

- create markets and policies for safer products, materials and chemicals in health care;
- promote safer substitutes, including products that avoid mercury, polyvinyl chloride (PVC) plastic and brominated flame retardants;
- eliminate incineration of medical waste, minimise the amount and toxicity of all waste generated and promote safer waste treatment practices;
- transform the design, construction and operations of health care facilities to minimise environmental impacts and foster healthy, healing environments;
- encourage food-purchasing systems that support sustainable food production and distribution, and provide healthy food onsite at health-care facilities;
- secure a safe and healthy workplace for all health-care workers;
- ensure patients, workers and communities have full access to information about chemicals used in health care and can participate in decisions about exposures to chemicals; and
- promote human rights and environmental justice for communities impacted by the health-care sector, while assuring that problems are not displaced from one community or country to another.

While HCWH has established a major presence in North America and Western Europe, with limited local exceptions, environmental activism is not yet a feature of health care in Australia or New Zealand.

The stories of the Pacific Yew tree, the tiger and the pollution of the natural environment by medical waste incineration illustrate the value of rare plants and animals and the pressures the environment may come under when it is exploited. In the context of health care these stories raise the same difficult questions as population control – to what extent is it possible to weigh the benefits of medical care to humans against the damage that it causes to the environment, and should humans always take priority?

Dangerous technologies

Mercury is not the only dangerous substance found in hospitals. Many technologies that are used in health care pose some risk to the wider environment.

Perhaps the best example is that of nuclear energy. One of the leading justifications for having nuclear reactors in Australia is for their use in the production of medical isotopes. For example, the Australian Nuclear Science and Technology Organisation website introduces the organisation with the following words:

> The Australian Nuclear Science and Technology Organisation (ANSTO) is the centre of Australia's nuclear science capabilities and expertise. ANSTO's vision is to be recognised as an international centre of excellence in nuclear science and technology for the benefit of Australia. ANSTO produces radiopharmaceuticals to help in the diagnosis and treatment of a range of serious illnesses. (<www.ansto.gov.au>)

Nuclear medicine in turn produces nuclear waste, some of which is stored onsite at many Australian hospitals. There are attendant risks to all of this – both to the community and the environment at large.

Many of the techniques of nuclear medicine can be substituted with other approaches – CT angiograms instead of VQ scans, surgical thyroidectomy instead of radioactive iodine, exercise stress tests instead of thallium studies. While in many cases the replacements will not be as good, morally one must ask whether the benefits of nuclear technologies in medicine are outweighed by the environmental risks.

The use of non-human animals

Celiac disease is a common gastrointestinal illness. It can cause a range of disabling symptoms, but may be difficult to diagnose and treat. In the past, it required small bowel biopsy for a definitive diagnosis, since antibody tests were not very sensitive or specific. The development of the anti-endomysial antibody test revolutionised this problem, and now screening for celiac disease is easy and commonly undertaken.

Many people who use this test would not be aware that it is based on the presence of antibodies to a molecule found in a monkey's oesophagus – leading to a worldwide trade in these body parts. Some substitutes have been found, including umbilical cord tissue, but monkey oesophagus continues to be a common substrate for this test.

The habitat for many sorts of monkeys is decreasing in the world, and many species are under threat. The question arises as to whether we should use monkeys (or other animals) for medical purposes – be that diagnostic tests, experimentation or even transplantation.

Some of the answers to this question depend on anthropocentric arguments. For example, it can be argued that it is important to conduct experiments using animals because we value human life and this avoids exposing patients to unnecessary risk. Prince, for example, quoted in the case study above, says that the loss of five lives from fialuridine was a tragedy of 'incalculable' magnitude, and justified testing in chimpanzees (Prince 1996).

The use of animals in research dates back to Aristotle (384-322BCE) and Galen (129-199 AD). However, it was only in the 17th and 18th centuries that medical research began to make extensive and systematic use of animals in research. In the past two centuries the scope of animal experimentation has vastly increased, particularly in cellular biology, physiology, molecular biology and immunology. Animals are currently used in three main types of scientific research: the testing of product safety; research into the causes, diagnosis and treatment of disease; and 'pure' research into aspects of developmental biology, biochemistry, physiology, anatomy, pathology and genetics relevant to human disease.

The vast majority of animals used in research are invertebrates, such as fruit flies, nematode worms and shrimp, although the use of these species are generally not regulated by law and generally not included in statistics of animal experimentation.

The Nuffield Council on Bioethics has estimated that between 50-100 million vertebrate animals are used in research each year. It is estimated that less than 1 million of these animals are used in research in Australia each year. Approximately 90% of these animals are rats, mice and other rodents, with smaller numbers of domesticated animals, such as sheep, cows, and pigs; smaller numbers of cats and dogs and less than 0.5% monkeys, including marmosets, spider monkeys and macaques. Few great apes – chimpanzees, orang-utans and gorillas – are used in medical research and their use is prohibited in many countries, including the United Kingdom. The source of these animals varies between countries and species. Most are purpose-bred, but smaller numbers are taken from the wild or from animal shelters. Most animals are euthanased at the completion of the research project.

Many of those who support animal experimentation believe that the use of animals has been vital to the evolution of modern medicine. Indeed, the Declaration of Helsinki states that any research involving human participants should be based on adequately performed laboratory and animal experimentation. This requirement, in turn, is based on two questionable assumptions: a moral one (that human lives are more valuable than the lives of non-human animals), and a scientific or epistemic one (that the use of model organisms/ animal models for the study of health and disease are valid because animals have evolved from common ancestors and so have evolved comparable structures and functions, and because they enable researchers to focus on particular pathological processes or physiological outcomes without the confounding effects of environmental factors or other pathologies, co-morbidities or treat-ments). Supporters of animal experimentation point to the development of drugs such as sulfanilamide, heparin, penicillin and insulin and other medical developments, such as polio vaccination and organ transplantation, as advances that could not have been made without the use of animals (Botting and Morri-son 1997).

These arguments are not accepted by opponents of animal experimen-tation, who point out that the generalisation of the results of non-human animal studies to humans is as likely to be misleading as it is to be helpful. They suggest that much of the animal research conducted is physiologically invalid, is unable to account for the complexity of human behaviour, accounts insuf-ficiently for environmental interactions, and is irrelevant or unnecessary given alternative strategies, such as human epidemiology, plant models systems, human tissue cultures, in vitro serological assays, computer simulation (systems biology), chimeras (human animal hybrids), stem-cell cultures following somatic cell nuclear transfer and 'orphan' animal disease models (LaFollette and Shanks 1993; LaFollette and Shanks 1996; Barnard and Kaufman 1997; Moore 2001). They point to examples such as thalidomide (shown not to be teratogenic in two lines of animal testing in multiple species), fialuridine, penicillin (which is highly toxic in guinea-pigs), arsenic (which is not lethal in sheep but highly lethal in humans), morphine (which sedates humans but stimulates cats), benzene (which causes leukaemia in humans but not in any other animal), aspirin (which causes birth defects in rats and mice, poisons cats and has no effect in horses) and animal experiments that discounted the links between smoking and lung cancer (LaFollette and Shanks 1993; Barnard and Kaufman 1997). They also point to the results of systematic reviews of animal experiments that raise questions about the methodological quality and relevance of animal studies and the capacity of animal models to adequately mimic human disease (Roberts, Kwan et al 2002; Pound, Ebrahim et al 2004; Perel, Roberts et al 2007).

Proponents of animal research generally respond by asserting that there is currently no feasible replacement for many important animals, such as the transgenic 'oncomouse', and no better non-living system available for the study of complex interactions between normal and abnormal cells, tissues and organs (Moore 2001).They also suggest that the types of disanalogies described above provide evidence of the need for more appropriate animal experimentation rather than the need for abolishing it all together.

An alternative approach to the question of the use of animals in medicine comes from arguments based on animal rights or the 'intrinsic' value of animals, rather than on their value to mankind. There are two basic types of these arguments (often used together), those based on the similarity of animals to humans, and those based on the intrinsic worth or dignity of animals – even in the absence of similarities to humans.

Western views regarding the moral status of non-human animals and the differences between animals and humans have been strongly influenced by Christian thought and by moral and political philosophy. Aristotle, Augustine and Thomas Aquinas all believed that animals had no moral status because they lacked reason, while Rene Descartes (1596-1650) believed that human beings were distinguished from animals by the possession of reason, speech, the capacity for moral reasoning and an immortal soul (Armstrong and Botzler 2003).

Unfortunately, attempts to provide clear and consistent distinctions between non-human animals and humans, using properties such as intelligence, language, social interaction, learning, independence, rationality, agency, capacity to suffer, capacity to plan for the future, moral agency and an eternal soul, are difficult to sustain because many species have these capacities, some species exercise these functions better than human beings, and humans who lack these functions because of age (premature neonates) or illness (brain-injured patients, demented elderly people and those with persistent lack of consciousness) do not have their human rights withdrawn and are not regarded as having the same moral status as non-human animals. This suggests that if we continue to insist that there is a moral difference between animals and humans, then logically the only way this claim can be sustained is by appealing to a putative moral hierarchy of species, ie, humans have more moral worth than non-human animals. This argument is known as 'speciesism' (LaFollette and Shanks 1996).

LaFollette and Shanks have critiqued arguments in support of the use of animals in research which rely on distinctions between human and non-human animals through a principle they called 'causal/functional asymmetry' (LaFollette and Shanks 1996). They argue that in order to justify harming certain animals in experiments, we must first show that there are morally relevant differences between humans and the experimental animals. But if such differences between humans and non-human animals exist, then these are likely to reflect anatomical, physiological or functional differences between humans and animals as well. This conflicts with the other requirement that we have of experimental animals – that they must be physiologically similar to human beings so that experiments are testing analogous physiological systems.

An illustration of this argument can be found in the case study that introduced this chapter. The investigators tested fialuridine predominantly on woodchucks – a species that was genetically very different from humans and therefore less ethically problematic. But the physiology of the woodchuck differed from humans in a crucial way, and did not suggest the severe problems that would later be experienced. Commentators suggested that chimpanzees should have been used instead since chimpanzees have 98% of their genes in common with human beings. But this would bring up more ethical issues, as since chimpanzees are very similar to humans it would seem more difficult to justify experiments that would be forbidden using humans.

Arguments of the second type also commonly arise, such as with recent attempts to solve the problems of organ transplantation involving placing human genetic material into the genomes of pigs and using the pigs' organs for human transplantation. Several commentators have suggested that this may be unethical – as the dignity of the animals is not consistent with their use as 'organ factories' (Regan 1984; Singer 1975). Arguments about the intrinsic value of animals may emphasise their ability to suffer pain, their consciousness or even their 'dignity' or may simply be based on the idea that we should not interfere with natural things more than we need to (that we should 'walk lightly on the earth').

Even if one accepts that animals have rights or intrinsic worth or that animal research can only be explained by appeal to speciesism, the use of animals in research can still be justified on consequentialist grounds, ie if the net utility or value from using animals in research is greater than the harm caused to those animals, then it may be morally justifiable. But even here a range of factors may determine whether animal experimentation is ethically justifiable, including the type of species, the type of harm, the number of animals harmed, and the type and extent of benefit. Consider, for example, how many gorillas or guinea-pigs could be sacrificed in the pursuit of a cure for a disease that affects very few children – 1, 100, 100,000 or the entire species? And what if the point of the research was not to prolong life but to improve quality of life, or even to develop a 'better' cosmetic – how would this impact on any decision about vivisection?

There is no question that animals suffer physical, psychological or social distress and there is little reason to maintain that this suffering is less significant than human suffering simply because it is expressed differently (Rollin 1989). If animals are to be used for our purposes, it is preferable that this should be done as humanely as possible. Even those who are in favour of animal experimentation believe that strict guidelines should be laid down to regulate it and that researchers should be asked to justify their research, explain why alternative strategies are unsuitable, justify their species choice, justify the number of animals being used, justify and explain the harms that arise and include mechanisms for harm reduction. For example, McCloskey suggests that:

> Experiments must be constructed so as to minimise suffering and not use scientifically unnecessary over-testing overkill methods. More important, animals that may experience pain should be used only when the relevant information sought can be obtained only through them or human beings and not by experiments on non-sentient animals. Further, it is essential when well-thought-out ethical codes of conduct of animal experiments are laid down, it be ensured that experimentation conform with the required standards. Experimenters, whether they be experimenters on humans or animals, notoriously fail to conform with the ethical standards laid down for experimentation in the absence of effective controls and supervision. (McCloskey 1987)

Research involving animals is now the subject of international and national regulations that give expression to a 'minimal harm' ethic that permits experimentation within defined limits (Armstrong and Botzler 2003). All centres which experiment with animals must now justify their experimentation in front of an ethics committee and must comply with regulations that govern this experimentation (National Health and Medical Research Council 2004; Weatherall and Munn 2007).

While questions remains regarding the true contribution of animal research to biomedicine, the relative merits of different strategies for their use, and the extent of compliance with research regulations and norms, there appears to be broad acceptance within the research community that there must be external review of biomedical research involving non-human animals by Animal Ethics Committees, that animal experimentation must involve the minimum number of animals and cause the least possible suffering, and that animal research should be guided by the 'three Rs' – reduction and replacement of animals and refinement of procedures (Smith 2001; National Health and Medical Research Council 2004). *Replacement* of animals in research refers to the need to find alternative (and better) strategies for medical discovery. *Reduction* refers to the need to ensure that each project uses no more than the minimum number of animals necessary to ensure scientific and statistical validity, to avoid using animals in research unless essential for the purpose or design of the project and to avoid excessive breeding of animals for scientific research so that the need to kill healthy animals is minimised. *Refinement* requires that researchers maximise the animals' welfare and reduce suffering; avoid taking animals from natural habitats unless animals bred in captivity are not available or are not suitable for specific scientific purposes; use animals for the shortest duration possible; select the appropriate animals for research, taking into account their biological characteristics including behaviour, genetic attributes and nutritional, microbiological and general health status; and employ the best available educational or scientific techniques in their research and teaching (National Health and Medical Research Council 2004).

ANIMALS, THE ENVIRONMENT AND THE LAW

The legal status of animals

In the Anglo-Australian common law tradition, animals do not have legal personality, so they are governed by property law. This is most probably a reflection of the same Western approach to the moral status of animals that was discussed above. In common law, wild animals are classed as *ferae naturae*, meaning belonging to no one, but become property when they are captured or killed by humans. Pets are considered to be property and are treated as such by the criminal law, tort law and family law. Animals cannot themselves own property, but the laws of equity do recognise trusts which are established for the benefit of pets: *Pettingall v Pettingall* (1842) 11 LJ Ch 176; *Re Dean* (1889) 41 Ch D 552.

Each State and Territory has legislation intended to prevent cruelty to animals but these laws do not grant legal personality to them. In one sense these laws merely regulate the ownership of property, rather than create any rights that can be enjoyed by animals. Because of this it is very difficult (if not impossible) to speak of animal 'rights' in the common law. An animal cannot have rights because it has no ability to be a legal actor, it has no legal personality.

The fact that animals have not enjoyed legal status as juristic persons does not mean that the law could not change to accommodate them. The history of the common law is replete with many examples of human beings who were denied full legal personality by the common law but who were later granted it: married

Table 32.1 Animal cruelty legislation

Jurisdiction	Legislation
NSW	*Prevention of Cruelty to Animals Act 1979* (NSW)
Qld	*Animals Care and Protection Act 2001* (Qld)
SA	*Animal Welfare Act 1985* (SA)
Tas	*Animal Welfare Act 1993* (Tas)
Vic	*Prevention of Cruelty to Animals Act 1986* (Vic)
WA	*Animal Welfare Act 2002* (WA)
ACT	*Animal Welfare Act 1992* (ACT)
NT	*Animal Welfare Act 1999* (NT)

women, slaves, Jewish people, and convicted felons with commuted death sentences all were either denied legal personality altogether or where given a weaker and debased form of it. There are also pieces of property which have been given legal personality, such as the modern corporation. Other examples include Hindu idols and temples which are recognised as having their own legal personality in Indian and English common law and may sue or be sued: *Pramatha Nath Mullick v Pradyumna Kumar Mullick* (1925) LR 52 In App 245; *Bumper Developments Corporation v Commr of Police* [1991] 4 All ER 638. These examples show that it would not be technically difficult to bestow legal personality on animals.

The Great Ape Project is a group of scholars and activists who are trying to get governments to bestow legal personality on great apes. The project was inspired by a book edited by Paola Cavalieri and Peter Singer which argued that chimpanzees, bonobos, gorillas, and orangutans should be given some of the same rights and protections as humans, given their genetic similarity, their ability to reason and their self-consciousness (Cavalieri and Singer 1993). The Project has sought to have the United Nations endorse a declaration on great apes which would give apes a right to life, rights to individual liberty and rights against torture. The Spanish parliament recently decided to recognise the legal personality of apes in accordance with the project's recommendations (Catan 2008).

Animal research

Australian prevention of cruelty to animals statutes control all uses of animals including animal experimentation, except New South Wales where animal experimentation is controlled by a separate Act (*Animal Research Act 1985*). 'Animal' is defined in most Acts as a live member of a vertebrate species including any amphibian, reptile, bird and mammal but not a human or fish. Queensland and Victorian legislation includes fish and crustaceans. Animal experimentation is well controlled by both statute and regulation.

The *Australian Code of Practice for the Care and Use of Animals for Scientific Purposes* (7th ed), published by the National Health and Medical Research Council (NHMRC), has been recognised by most regulations under the relevant legislation (National Health and Medical Research Council 2004). The Code of Practice was prepared by a joint working party of the NHMRC, Commonwealth Scientific and Industrial Research Organisation (CSIRO), Agricultural Resource Management Council of Australia and New Zealand, Australia Research Council, Australian Vice-Chancellors' Committee and representatives of State and Territory governments and the RSPCA.

Since 1985 no research institute using animals can operate without registration and it is a condition of registration that the institute has an Animal Ethics Committee (AEC). The composition of an AEC is controlled by law and all experiments have to be approved by the Committee first. Two of the four essential members of the Committee are an active member of an animal welfare society and an independent member of the community. Some of the issues of current concern to AECs include the use of animals obtained from pounds for experimentation, the importation of exotic live virus for use as a biological pest control agent and genetic manipulation and patenting of animals.

Environmental law

The development of environmental law

Environmental law is the body of laws dealing with the control of development, the regulation of pollution (both from industrial and non-industrial sources) and the protection of plant and animal species. Environmental law began in the early common law of nuisance (a tort concerned with improper land use which interferes with the rights of neighbours) and later came to be concerned with development in the common law of restrictive covenants (where neighbours came together in contract to control the types of developments that could occur in a neighbourhood). However, the vast majority of environmental law is based in legislation, and has been from very early days. For example, in 1273 King Edward I (Edward Longshanks) prohibited the burning of coal because the smog was considered to be bad for health (Bates 2006). In 1388, Richard II prohibited the throwing of dung and filth into rivers near towns, again for health reasons (Tooma 2008). Sewers were controlled by legislation by 1531 and by the time of the Industrial Revolution in the 19th century a raft of legislation was passed culminating in the *Public Health Act 1875* (UK). Continuing problems with water pollution led to the *Rivers (Prevention of Pollution) Act 1875* (UK). In 1952, over 2000 Londoners perished due to poor air quality leading to the *Clean Air Act 1956* (UK).

The Australian colonies inherited the English law and consequently their approaches to environmental issues were based in common law. In *Oliver v Hughes* (15 June 1837, Kinchela J) the plaintiff was a haberdasher who complained that his neighbour (a grocer by trade) had taken up candle making and was rendering large amounts of putrid fat, which caused a terrible smell and made the plaintiff feel sick. The plaintiff argued that the smell gave him liver disease(!), loss of appetite and headache. A verdict was entered for the plaintiff on the grounds of nuisance. Similarly, in *Shannon v Turner* (1831) Dowlings' Select Cases 684, a publican was found to have committed a nuisance when he built a toilet on the boundary of his property, which oozed waste through a wall and into the neighbouring property.

Modern Australian environmental law is overwhelmingly based in legislation (Bates 2006). Each State and Territory has a raft of environmental statutes and the Commonwealth government also has a number of environmental laws which create significant overlap.

Environmental planning and assessment

Environmental planning and assessment has three main components: strategic planning, and development control through environmental assessment (Bates 2006). Strategic planning is achieved through State and local council planning policies, which concern development of sensitive areas such as coastlines, vegetative conservation and the management of water. Building standards for materials are also effected as are requirements for the control of waste and recycling.

Development (which concerns not only the building of structures but also changes in land use, demolition and subdivision) must be approved by local, State or Commonwealth authorities and must comply with any relevant strategic planning. Applications are normally made public and interested persons can lodge objections, which must then be considered by the decision-maker. Applications can be approved, denied or approved with conditions. Larger or sensitive development may be subject to the requirement of getting an environmental impact assessment, which ordinarily involves a statement about what the predicted outcomes will be and what will be done to management these outcomes.

Pollution law

As stated above pollution laws have a long lineage, but the majority of pollution controls up until the time of the industrial revolution were based in the private law of nuisance. Arguably, this would be because most industries were home-based and pollution would have been caused by small-scale industries within neighbourhoods. With the advent of the industrial revolution, the health effects of industry became more severe. Large-scale production and the use of steam driven-machinery were incredibly dangerous.

The pollution caused by some industry caused horrible diseases. Tooma gives the example of 'phossy jaw' which was a disease suffered by workers in the match–making industry (Tooma 2008). The disease was caused by excessive exposure to phosphorous and led to the worker's jaw bone and surrounding flesh dying with the ultimate result that the lower jaw would have to be removed entirely. Many victims committed suicide.

A number of regulatory attempts were made to make working conditions safer during the 19th century although they were at times resisted greatly by industry. In the United Kingdom the *Factories and Workshops Act 1878* combined different legislative regimes into one set of laws.

Workplace pollution is controlled in Australia at the State and Territory level under occupational health and safety laws. For example, in *Inspector Lewis v Northern Sydney and Central Area Health Service* [2006] NSWIRComm 61, health workers were made ill by fumes from an X-ray development machine. The machine had been supplied with a higher concentration mix of chemicals. When the supplier came to fix the problem he cleaned the system but then replenished it with the same chemical mix. Workers continued to be made ill. The NSW Industrial Relations Commission fined the area health service and the machine company $100,000.

Outside of the workplace, each jurisdiction also has laws criminalising pollution and damage to the environment.

Table 32.2 Pollution legislation

Jurisdiction	Legislation
NSW	*Protection of the Environment Operations Act 1997*
Qld	*Environmental Protection Act 1994*
SA	*Environmental Protection Act 1993*
Tas	*Environmental Management and Pollution Control Act 1994*
Vic	*Environmental Protection Act 1970*
WA	*Environmental Protection Act 1986*
ACT	*Environmental Protection Act 1997*
NT	*Waste Management and Pollution Control Act 1998*

Protection of biodiversity

Australia's loss of biodiversity is one of the worst on record. The 1996 Commonwealth State of the Environment Report found that loss of biodiversity was Australia's biggest environmental problem (Bates 2006). Australia has a number of international obligations to protect biodiversity including the *Convention on Biological Diversity*, the *Convention on Conservation of Nature in the South Pacific*, the *Convention on Migratory Species of Birds*, the *Convention on International Trade in Endangered Species of Wild Fauna and Flora* and the *Rio Declaration on Environment and Development*.

The primary Commonwealth piece of legislation is the *Environment Protection and Biodiversity Conservation Act 1999*, which aims to implement controls in furtherance of Australia's international obligations. The Act allows the Minister to create bio-regional plans to manage biodiversity. The Act also requires the Minister to prepare inventories of threatened species and ecological communities. It gives the Minister power to list World Heritage areas or to create 'biosphere reserves' for sustainable development studies, and Commonwealth reserves (which can be to protect particular ecosystems, areas of wilderness, national parks, national monuments or particular land or seascapes).

The States and Territories also have the power to create national parks and marine reserves.

Habitats can also be protected even when they are not in reserves. There are a number of State-based laws on habitat destruction, such as laws on the clearing of native vegetation, and controls on forestry.

References

Armstrong, S and R Botzler (2003) *The Animal Ethics Reader*. London, Routledge.

Barnard, N and S Kaufman (1997) 'Animal research is wasteful and misleading'. *Scientific American* **Feb**: 64-6.

Bates, B (2006) *Environmental Law in Australia*. Sydney, LexisNexis Butterworths.

Birnbaum, LS (1995) 'Developmental effects of dioxins'. *Environ Health Perspect* **103 Suppl** 7: 89-94.

Botting, J and A Morrison (1997) 'Animal research is vital to Medicine'. *Scientific American* **Feb**: 67-9.

Brennan, A and Y Lo (2002) 'Environmental Ethics'. *The Stanford Encyclopedia of Philosophy*. <http://plato.stanford.edu/>.

Catan, T (2008) Apes get legal rights in Spain, to surprise of bullfight critics. *The Times*. London.

Cavalieri, P and P Singer (1993) *The Great Ape Project: Equality Beyond Humanity*. London, Fourth Estate.

Coale, A (1974) 'The history of the human population'. *Scientific American* **Sept**: 15-25.

Germain, S (2007) 'Determination of the ecological footprint of a hospital'. <http://www.c2p2online.com/documents/Lionsgate.pdf>.

Going Green (2002) 'The mercury problem' *Going Green: A resource kit for pollution prevention in health care*. <http://www.noharm.org/library/docs/Going_Green_The_Mercury_Problem_-_Fast_Facts.pdf>.

Heilig, S, T Kushner et al (2001) 'Health care without harm: an ethical imperative. A consensus statement from Biomedical Ethicists in Support of Environmentally Sound Healthcare Practices'. *West J Med* **175**(4): 222-3.

Hesketh, T and W Zhu (1997) 'Health in China: The one child family policy: the good, the bad, and the ugly'. *BMJ* **314**(7095): 1685-7.

Komesaroff, PA (2008) *Experiments in Love and Death: Medicine, Postmodernism, Microethics and the Body*. Melbourne, Melbourne University Press.

LaFollette, H and N Shanks (1993) 'Animal models in biomedical research: some epistemological worries'. *Public Aff Q* **7**(2): 113-30.

LaFollette, H and N Shanks (1996) 'The origin of speciesism'. *Philosophy* **71**(275): 41-61.

LaFollette, H and N Shanks (1996) *Dilemmas of animal experimentation*. New York, Routledge.

Lovejoy, A (1936) *The great chain of being*. Cambridge, Mass, Harvard University Press.

McCloskey, H (1987) 'The moral case for experimentation on animals'. *The Monist* **70**(1): 65.

McKenzie, R, M Fried et al (1995) 'Hepatic failure and lactic acidosis due to Fialuridine (FIAU), an investigational nucleoside analogue for chronic hepatitis B'. *N Engl J Med* **333**: 1099-105.

Montaigner, F (2007) 'Still Waters: The global fish crisis'. *National Geographic* (April): 33-51.

Moore, A (2001) 'Of mice and Mendel. The predicted rise in the use of knock-out and transgenic mice should cause us to reflect on our justification for the use of animals in research'. *EMBO Rep* **2**(7): 554-8.

Myers, GJ, PW Davidson et al (2003) 'Prenatal methylmercury exposure from ocean fish consumption in the Seychelles child development study'. *Lancet* **361**(9370): 1686-92.

Nash, R (1990) *The rights of nature: a history of environmental ethics*. Sydney, The Wilderness Society.

National Health and Medical Research Council (2004) *Australian code of practice for the care and use of animals for scientific purposes*. Canberra, National Health and Medical Research Council.

O'Neill, O (2002) *Autonomy and trust in bioethics*. Cambridge, UK, Cambridge University Press.

Perel, P, I Roberts et al (2007) 'Comparison of treatment effects between animal experiments and clinical trials: systematic review'. *BMJ* **334**(7586): 197.

Potter, V (1971) *Bioethics: Bridge to the future*. Edgeworth Cliffs, NJ, Prentice Hall.

Pound, P, S Ebrahim et al (2004) 'Where is the evidence that animal research benefits humans?' *BMJ* **328**(7438): 514-17.

Prince, A (1996) 'Letter'. *N Engl J Med* **334**(17): 1136.

Ratzinger, J (2002). *God and the world: Believing and living in our time: A conversation with Peter Seewald*. San Francisco, St Ignatius Press.

Roberts, I, I Kwan et al (2002) 'Does animal experimentation inform human healthcare? Observations from a systematic review of international animal experiments on fluid resuscitation'. *BMJ* **324**(7335): 474-6.

Rollin, B (1989) *The unheeded cry*. Oxford, Oxford University Press.

Singer, P and J Mason (2006) *The ethics of what we eat*. Melbourne, Text Publishing.

Smith, R (2001) 'Animal research: the need for a middle ground'. *BMJ* **322**(7281): 248-9.

Tooma, M (2008) *Safety, Security, Health and Environmental Law*. Federation Press, Sydney.

Twine, R (2005) 'Constructing critical bioethics by deconstructing culture/nature dualism'. *Med Health Care Philos* **8**(3): 285-95.

US Census Bureau (2007) 'US Census Bureau International Data Base'. <http://www.census.gov/ipc/www/idb/country/egportal.html>.

Verhoog, H (1992) 'The concept of intrinsic value and transgenic animals'. *J Agric Ethics* **5**(2): 147-60.

Weatherall, D and H Munn (2007) 'Animal research: the debate continues'. *J Intern Med* **262**(6): 591-2.

Weldon, C, L du Preez et al (2004) 'Origin of the Amphibian Chytrid Fungus'. *Emerging Infectious Diseases* **10**(12): 2100-5.

Wilson, E (1992) *The diversity of life*. Cambridge, Mass, Harvard University Press.

CHAPTER 33

COMPLEMENTARY AND ALTERNATIVE MEDICINE (CAM)

Case 1

A 42-year-old woman presented with trouble sleeping. She appeared to be depressed, and she discussed with her GP whether she should start an antidepressant. In the end she decided against it, as she did not wish to take medications. She then visited a naturopath who treated her with massage and prescribed St John's Wort tablets. She was happy to take these as she felt that they were 'natural' and she found that the massage seemed to help her tension. When she saw her GP next time, he was quite sceptical of the benefits of this treatment, but after searching the internet he found that St John's Wort was as effective in mild depression as many antidepressants. He also found out that it has potential interactions with a large number of conventional drugs – something that he had not previously been aware of.

Case 2

AG is a 32-year-old woman who presented to the emergency department with gastroenteritis. While giving her history, she revealed that her only previous illness was when her naturopath had diagnosed her as having 'sub-clinical cancer'. This diagnosis was arrived at by a combination of iridology and a technique of placing different substances under her tongue and testing her muscle strength in response to these substances. The naturopath prescribed a course of fasting, vitamins and herbal remedies and found that the 'cancer' had been cured after one year. She has continued to see the naturopath since then but has not had any further problems.

Introduction

Community surveys from Australia, North America and Europe indicate that 35-50% of the population use complementary or alternative medicine (CAM) (MacLennan, Myers et al 2006). In Australia, expenditure on CAMs (excluding CAM practitioner visits) has been estimated to be almost twice the annual national prescription expenditure (approximately $2.3 billion annually); in the United States, it is equivalent to the amount spent out-of-pocket for all physician services (Eisenberg, Davis et al 1998; Ernst 2000; MacLennan, Wilson et al 2002).

Over the past decade the demand for, and expenditure on, CAM has approximately doubled in both the United States and the United Kingdom.

The reasons for the extraordinary growth in popularity of CAM are poorly understood but appear to be due both to general societal changes and to developments within medicine and the health sector. Exploration of the issues surrounding CAM has been made more difficult because of the enormous heterogeneity of CAM and because of the lack of a uniform definition of CAM.

The definition used by the National Centre for Complementary and Alternative Medicine in the United States is:

> [H]ealthcare practices that are not an integral part of conventional medicine. As diverse and abundant as the peoples of the world, these practices may be grouped within five major domains: alternative medical systems; mind-body interventions; biologically-based treatments; manipulative and body-based methods; and energy therapies. (Coulter and Willis 2004)

This definition is, however, problematic for a number of reasons. First, this definition describes CAM by what it is not, that is, it is not conventional/ allopathic medicine. Second, it fails to account for the enormous diversity of practices included under the rubric of CAM, which range from specific physical therapies, such as reflexology and chiropractics, to whole medical systems, such as Ayurvedic medicine and traditional Chinese medicine. Third, it fails to provide a means for resolving the social and political implications of the terms commonly used to describe CAM. For example, *alternative* suggests a medical system in opposition to conventional medicine, *complementary* suggests a secondary role for CAM after conventional medicine, and *integrative* medicine implies that CAM will undergo a process of evaluation whereas only those believed to have value, or evidence, will be subsumed with conventional medicine. No one of these terms is sufficient and none is without problems (Sanderson, Koczwara et al 2006). For this reason, in this chapter we use the abbreviation CAM (Lewith and Bensoussan 2004).

Popularity and use of CAM

It has been suggested that while 'folk' or 'home' remedies have always been a feature of health care, CAMs have recently become more popular, within Western countries in particular, because of dissatisfaction with Western scientific conceptions of health and disease and because of dissatisfaction with the care provided by modern health-care systems. Thus, CAMs are popular because of their association and continuity with spirituality, ancient traditions, nature and indigenous cultures; because they provide an alternative to the authority, reductionism and dualism of conventional medicine; because they enable the patient to retain some control or agency over their own health and life choices; because they tend to emphasise holism, care, relationships and attention to the patient's narrative; and because they may be perceived to have more to offer than conventional medicine in certain situations, such as in chronic and terminal illness, including increased energy, prolonged survival, enhanced quality of life, improved immune function, and a higher chance of cure (thus filling so called 'effectiveness gaps' in conventional medicine) (Kelner and Wellman 1997; Correa-Velez, Clavarino et al 2005; Thompson and Feder 2005; Joske, Rao et al 2006).

An alternative explanation is that the popularity of CAM is a reflection of broader, more fundamental, social changes, including societal trends to individualism (Joske, Rao et al 2006); loss of faith in medicine's ability to solve the problems of living; the growth of the consumer movement; the impact of globalisation; the erosion of medical dominance; the emergence of the 'green' movement; the increase in migration and transmission of established medicine from other countries (eg, Ayurvedic medicine) and the politicisation of health, whereby the control of health is returned to the individual and the control of the health system is returned to the community (Coulter and Willis 2004).

While these explanations provide a means for understanding the growth in popularity of CAM as a social phenomenon, they have little bearing on why an individual may decide to use CAM. It is well known that CAMs are particularly popular with certain groups of patients, such as those with chronic, refractory or terminal illnesses. It is estimated that up to 80% of people with cancer in Australia use some form of CAM alongside or (less commonly) instead of their conventional treatment (Ernst and Cassileth 1998; Senate Community Affairs Committee 2005; Joske, Rao et al 2006). The reason that such people use CAM has little to do with major dissatisfaction with 'conventional' medicine and much more to do with maintaining their sense of optimism in the face of risk, uncertainty and loss of identity; maintaining their agency or 'healthcare autonomy'; and providing them with health-care alternatives that are more congruent with their values and beliefs (Astin 1998; Bensoussan 1999).

CAM and conventional medicine

In the past, CAM has existed as a parallel and disparate set of health practices, largely ignored by conventional medical practitioners on the grounds that it had no compelling evidence-base and that what research was available had substantial methodological flaws or systematic biases and did not meet conventional standards of evidence (Tang, Zhan et al 1999; Linde, Jonas et al 2001).

A series of developments have focused attention on the interface between complementary and conventional (allopathic) medicine and the role(s) and responsibilities of medical practitioners. These include: the Pan Pharmaceuticals recall, a recent criminal case related to the death of a infant being treated by a naturopath (Williams 2004), increased concern regarding medical liability arising from failure to refer to complementary therapists (Brophy 2003), and moves to regulate complementary therapists (NSW Health 2002). These developments present challenges for conventional biomedical health-care systems and for those who practise within them. They also raise questions about the nature of evidence, about the creation of consensus in clinical practice, and about the meaning and function of complementary medicine (Thorne, Best et al 2002).

Complementary medicine and consent in conventional medical practice

The ethical obligations related to the provision of alternative health care are no different from those related to conventional medicine. Patients still require information, have a right to be involved in decision-making and must be sufficiently informed about any proposed therapy. The obligations to patients do not change with the form of therapy that is being offered to them. Thus, health professionals are ethically and legally obliged to provide patients with sufficient information such that their health-care decisions are adequately informed and that any consent they give to treatment is valid. This information includes information regarding the risks and benefits of the proposed treatment and of any alternative treatments that are material to the patient.

A strong case can be made that doctors should be aware of the benefits, risks and potential drug interactions of CAMs and should be able to advise patients of these options (Weir 2003). This is because of the frequency with which people consume both prescription pharmaceuticals and CAMs, the importance attached to their use by different members of the public, the blurring of distinctions between complementary and conventional medicine, and the increasing research into the efficacy of CAM.

This does not mean that CAM should only be discussed where patients directly ask questions about it, as there may be other times when discussions of CAM may become more significant for patients. For example, where the burden of illness is substantial; where there is no proven conventional therapy available; where the therapy that is available is invasive and/or is associated with minimal benefit or major toxicity; where complementary therapy may be of benefit and has few risks; and where the patient has an expressed an interest in, or preference for, alternative therapies. The US Institute of Medicine has suggested that when a health professional is determining what information or advice they should provide a patient regarding CAM they should consider whether evidence supports both safety and efficacy; supports safety but is inconclusive about efficacy; supports efficacy but is inconclusive about safety; or indicates either serious risk or inefficiency. Thus, where there is evidence of efficacy and safety CAM should be recommended, where there is clear evidence of harm CAM should be avoided and discouraged, and where data supports either efficacy or safety but is otherwise inconclusive, the patient should be adequately informed regarding CAM use in their particular situation and continue to be supported, treated and monitored should they choose to use that CAM (Cohen and Eisenberg 2002; Institute of Medicine (US) 2005).

If health professionals are to provide information to patients about CAMs then they should possess sufficient knowledge about CAM in order to meet the patient's information needs. While neither the law, nor the profession, nor the general public, expect medical practitioners to be experts on CAM, both the law and the profession expect that doctors should have *some* knowledge of CAMs so that they can properly inform their patients about therapeutic alternatives. The issue then becomes *what should* health professionals know about CAM and *where* should they find this information? These questions are particularly difficult to answer as the degree of knowledge required may vary according to practit-ioners' specialty and the degree to which they incorporate CAM within their own practice.

Research and evidence in CAM

An examination of the history of medicine reveals how Western medicine attained and maintained power, legitimacy and epistemic authority through development of theory, professionalisation, control of the health marketplace, clinical success and, perhaps most significantly, through its association with science, law and political power. Contemporary medicine continues to retain authority, accountability and public trust through peer review, clinical audit, public scrutiny via professional registration, codes of ethics and disciplinary authorities, the application of the processes and standards of science to all aspects of medicine and, more recently, the development of evidence-based medicine and clinical practice guidelines (Breen 2003). In contrast, while CAMs have enjoyed enormous public support, they do not have the same degree of authority or power. While there are a number of reasons for this, perhaps the most frequent relevant criticism of CAM is that it is not supported by rigorous evidence and that the research that has been done has serious methodological flaws and biases (Linde, Jonas et al 2001). While there are elements of truth in such sentiments, it is also the case that many health professionals are unin-formed about the evidence that does exist (Hyodo, Eguchi et al 2003). Taken together, this presents a major problem for those inquiring about the value of CAM.

There are a number of reasons why there is such limited data regarding CAM (Ernst, Cohen et al 2004; Shekelle, Morton et al 2005). CAM receives only a limited amount of research funding as many CAM modalities lack patent protection, and therefore commercial appeal, and clinical trials of CAM may be expensive as treatments are often therapist led, and effect sizes are often small and only appear after long periods of treatment. It is frequently difficult, but not impossible, to perform methodologically rigorous trials of CAM. Blinding patients may be impossible; it may not be possible to construct placebo controls, particularly for physical therapies; and many treatments may be complex and individualised, making trial design extremely difficult. In addition, some advocates of CAM may reject clinical trials altogether on the ground that it constitutes an inappropriate test of natural forces, life energy, spiritual energies or ultramolecular phenomena. Research may also be hampered by obscure outcomes, or by expression of therapeutic claims in metaphorical terms that can-not be evaluated or refuted, such as 'attaining wellness', 'cleansing the liver' or 'aiding the maintenance of the peripheral circulation'. Finally, recruitment of patients into clinical trials may be difficult as many research participants will feel a strong sense of attachment to CAM and will be reluctant to be randomised to a control therapy (Ernst 2003).

Despite the barriers to research into CAM, in recent years increasing attention has been devoted to applying the methodological rigour of evidence-based medicine to CAM. Whereas in the past, most CAMs had not been rigorously assessed for efficacy and there was very limited data regarding potential interactions between CAMs and conventional therapies, this situation is changing, as more attention is given to research (Vicekers 1998; Cumming 2000).

The outcomes of such research are important and noteworthy. While, on the whole, there is very limited evidence for most CAMs, how one interprets the data depends on the question being asked (efficacy or risks/burdens), the outcomes measures used, and the study design (Singh and Ernst 2008). A number of treatments have been shown to have no clinical benefit, including antioxidants for the prevention of gastrointestinal cancer (Bjelakovic et al 2004), spinal manipulation for dysmenorrhoea (Proctor, Hing et al 2004), feverfew for migraine (Pittler and Ernst 2004) and therapeutic touch for acute wounds. A number of therapies have been demonstrated to be beneficial such as cranberry juice for urinary tract infections, phytomedicines for sickle cell anaemia and horse chestnut seed for chronic venous insufficiency. Some therapies have also been demonstrated to have considerable harms, including coffee enemas, ozone therapy and chiropractic manipulation in certain patients (Ernst 2001).

However, simply asserting that evidence regarding CAM exists and that health professionals should know about this research fails to account for the limitations of this data set, the difficulties conventional practitioners have in accessing information regarding CAM, the lack of education regarding CAM in Australia's universities, and the general absence of discourse regarding CAM in the health professions.

Increasing the evidence base for CAM is unlikely to resolve questions relating to the incorporation of CAM into the medical practitioner's lexicon of therapy. Literature from the US suggests that most medical practitioners have limited knowledge of CAM therapies and that their knowledge may be primarily determined by their beliefs regarding the legitimacy of the therapies (Berman, Bausell et al 2002). There is also evidence that many conventional medical practitioners are unaware of the evidence that does already exist for CAM, both in medicine in general, and in their own areas of expertise (Hyodo, Eguchi et al 2003). While it is crucial to establish the evidence for CAMs, overemphasis on evidence, regulation or integration fails to appreciate the substantial differences between allopathic and complementary medicine, including differences in the meaning and context of health and illness, in methodology, language and culture, and in the relationship to science (Dalen 1998; Zollman and Vickers 1999; Tonelli and Callahan 2001).

Integration of CAM and conventional medicine

An examination of the history and philosophy of Western medicine reveals that while conventional and complementary medicine share various historical features, such as reference to vitalism, holism and humoral balance, there exists an enormous gulf between contemporary allopathic and complementary medicine. The absence of a language that is shared by conventional and complementary medicine is not surprising since, due to the heterogeneity of CAM, there is also no common language between complementary therapies (Bensoussan 2000).

This gulf between complementary and allopathic medicine has prompted some to suggest that what is required is integration of these forms of therapy. Indeed the World Health Organization's first global strategy on traditional and alternative medicine, released in May 2002, advocates integration (Holliday 2003).

But, as both Parker (Parker 2003) and Kaptchuk and Miller make clear, 'the philosophical, epistemological and practical differences between mainstream medicine and CAM systems defy coherent integration' (Kaptchuk and Miller 2005). For this reason the most prevalent model of integration has been the integration of CAMs that satisfy conventional standards of scientific evidence into conventional medicine (Parker 2003). But while government, the AMA and most professional bodies appear to support the integration of *evidence-based* CAM, there are significant implications of such an approach for both conventional and, particularly, complementary medicine. As others have made clear, integration may actually mean subjugation, disintegration or marginalisation, may fail to account for difference and may fundamentally alter CAM practice, emphasising standardisation, efficiency and generality at the expense of communication and individualised care (Eisenberg, Cohen et al 2002; Mizrachi, Shuval et al 2005). For these reasons, not only is it unclear whether integration of conventional and unconventional medicines is possible, but, more importantly, it is unclear if it is even desirable. If part of the attraction of CAM is its uniqueness, or its concordance with non-biomedical conceptions of health and disease, then what may happen as a result of integration is the loss of this alternative or, more likely, the expansion of conventional medicine as it absorbs evidence-based CAMs and the reshaping, shrinking and marginalisation of those CAMs that remain.

Philosophical criticisms of CAM

While criticism of CAM purely in terms of its evidence-base is sometimes misguided, there are a also a number of concepts that underpin many CAMs that are philosophically troubling. These include the use of metaphor in CAM, the normative association with nature, the appropriation and distortion of traditional culture and the emphasis on stress and internal constructions of disease causality (Coward 1989).

Metaphor is often used in medicine to explain health and illness. (A metaphor is a figure of speech in which a term is transferred to something that it does not literally apply to.) For example, a common metaphor that is used in conventional medicine is that of a war. Bacteria 'invade' the human body, we choose 'aggressive' therapies, new therapies are 'magic bullets', oncologists 'target' cancer with chemotherapy and radiotherapy, and patients, researchers and clinicians 'fight the war against cancer'.

While metaphorical views of illness are common, it is uncertain whether they add a great deal to our understandings of illness. The influential author Susan Sontag, after being diagnosed with cancer, came to the conclusion that illness is *not* a metaphor and the most truthful way of regarding illness is the one most purified of metaphoric thinking (Sontag 1979). While this is a matter of opinion, it is certainly true that major advances in the understanding of disease and in the treatment of illness have only come about through healthy and informed scepticism and through concrete, as opposed to metaphorical, views of disease causation.

CAM uses an enormous range of metaphor, using terms such as 'nature', 'energies', or 'consciousness', in ways that incorporate complex and often contradictory meanings and ideologies.

For example, most CAMs claim a close relationship with nature. 'Nature' is a commercially attractive term that is used to sell a wide range of products ranging from detergents to dishwashers to health products and services. It is not always clear how such products are related to nature, or how the processes of refining and purification used for vitamins and herbal supplements differ from those used for drugs such as morphine, digoxin, aspirin or vincristine. The view of nature that is expressed in philosophies of CAM is often highly idealised, with nature being seen as gentle, calming and restorative – an entity based on wholeness and cooperation. This often seems like the view of nature that one gets from watching it on television rather than first-hand experience. There is little room in this view for famine, disasters or crocodiles and other carnivores. In one shampoo advertisement, a naked woman walks through the rainforest as a voice says: 'The best way to be is to be close to nature'. But where are all the mosquitoes and leeches?

CAM places 'natural' therapies in opposition to 'scientific' or 'chemical' methods of treatment, yet many CAM therapies and therapists appear to have a strange ambivalence towards science, borrowing freely from scientific terminology and frequently claiming 'scientific' justification for their products or services. Terms that are based on science, and have defined meanings within science, such as 'virus' or 'immune' or 'anti-oxidant', are frequently appropriated and used metaphorically rather than in their original scientific context.

CAM also places considerable emphasis on the value of traditional cures, and cures used by tribal people. A good example of this sort of thinking comes from the book *Mutant message down under*, in which an American chiropodist describes her experiences among a 'lost' tribe of Australian Aborigines. She says:

> I too was grateful that night for being allowed into the mysterious virgin minds of these so-called uncivilised humans. I wanted to learn more about their healing techniques but I didn't want the responsibility of adding challenges to their lives ... The Real People tribe believes that we are not random victims of ill-health, that the physical body is the only means our higher level of eternal consciousness has to communicate with our personality consciousness. Slowing down the body allows us to look around and analyse the really important wounds we need to mend: wounded relationships, gaping holes in our belief system, walled up tumours of fear, eroding faith in our Creator, hardened emotions of unforgiveness and so on. (Morgan 1994)

This book has been described as 'distasteful, insulting and outrageous' by one Aboriginal reviewer (Behrendt 1994).

Arguments such as these appear to rely on several assumptions – that there are cultures in the world that are more 'primitive' than our own, that their health beliefs are more likely to be uncontaminated by cultural issues, and that such beliefs are therefore more likely to reflect 'natural' methods of healing. These ideas are closely aligned to 19th century views of the 'noble savage' and are profoundly ethnocentric, making huge assumptions about other cultures based on a limited understanding of them from the standpoint of the 'advanced' state of Western culture.

Many types of CAM appear to appropriate indigenous cultures for their own ends. The need for accurate representation of cultural beliefs and for cultural sensitivity towards traditional values and narratives is largely absent, or is dominated by commercial imperatives. Good examples of this can be found in current menus for 'Aboriginal' spa treatments, which offer such experiences as the:

Wuri Julma (Oo-ri Jul-ma) – Corroboree Dance Massage

Embrace the mystery of ancient Aboriginal therapies. An elder of a tribe – a wise man and a healer, whispered secrets of a rhythmic massage. Time has passed, we now bless you with the Wuri. A relaxing massage infused with these sacred principals, to realign energy flow. A dynamic dance of life. ... 60 minutes $105.00.

(http://www.daintree-ecolodge.com.au/Daintree_Lodge_Spa_Treatments. htm)

Before the modern era, Western medicine stressed the importance of internal humoral balance and the 'personal' basis of disease. Indeed, it is only since the advent of scientific medicine and anatomico-pathological approaches to disease causation that diseases such as tuberculosis, peptic ulceration, heart disease and cancer have ceased to be regarded as arising from flaws in personality or personal failings and have been found to be due to external factors. These ideas persist. For example, the author Katherine Mansfield, when she was dying of tuberculosis, 'had come to the conviction that her bodily health depended upon her spiritual condition. Her mind was henceforth preoccupied with discovering some way to "cure her soul"; and she eventually resolved ... to abandon her treatment and to live as though her grave physical illness were incidental' (Sontag 1979).

Such ideas continue to have currency in CAM, where disease is often thought to result from loss of internal balance or accumulation of internal stressors, and considerable emphasis is placed on individuals' capacity to heal themselves. Stress, more than any other emotion or experience, dominates CAMs conceptions of disease causation. According to Coward:

[T]here is a curious, but widespread, agreement amongst commentators that stress is much worse now then previously. Modern life, it is agreed, is infinitely worse than anything which mankind has previously had to face. Somehow it is implied that the stresses of continuous factory work, poverty, and the death of several children were less severe than contemporary stresses ... This is hardly an objective assessment of stress but rather a strong and prevalent fantasy of ourselves as victims and not beneficiaries of the twentieth century. (Coward 1989)

The concept of stress is frequently emphasised in discussions of disease causation because it provides the link between the mind and the body, and between thoughts, feelings and disease. In fact, much of the research about stress appears contradictory, and many of its apparent effects disappear when trials are conducted prospectively and rigorously. For example, psychological stress does not appear to precipitate relapse of breast cancer (Barraclough, Pinder et al 1992), flare up of herpes simplex (Rand, Hoon et al 1990), preterm labour (Peacock, Bland et al 1995), or progression of HIV (Perry, Fishman et al 1992).

Such concepts can be criticised on several levels. First, there is conflicting evidence as to whether stressful events do precipitate major disease. Secondly, it seems unlikely that a single mechanism could explain so much different pathology: for example, if stress causes a general depression of the immune system (which in itself is contentious), we would expect it to be ideal for treatment of auto-immune diseases where the immune system is overactive. Thirdly, the changing patterns of disease can be explained in other, more understandable, ways rather than being seen as due to changing patterns of stress. For example, the increasing rate of lung cancer in women is probably due to increasing cigarette usage (perhaps from tobacco companies targeting this group).

Table 33.1: Communicating about CAM

A health professional should:

- honestly answer patient's direct questions about CAM;
- elicit information about the patient's use of CAM;
- establish the patient's understanding of the conventional and complementary therapies, both those available to them, and those that they may already be taking;
- establish why the patient uses CAMs, taking the time to discover the patient's values and goals with respect to complementary and conventional therapies;
- reflect upon whether information about CAMs would be *material* for *that* patient at *that* time, taking into account the patient's burden of illness, their expressed preferences and the risks and benefits of both conventional and complementary therapy;
- take steps to become adequately informed about reasonably available CAM medicines and therapies that have been shown to be safe and effective, ineffective or harmful;
- become familiar with qualified and competent CAM practitioners (medical and non-medical) to whom referrals can be made when necessary;
- continue a relationship with the patient, continuing to monitor the patient conventionally and staying open to further discussions regarding CAM.

Much of this information can be obtained at first contact with the patient, while taking the patient's medical history, although the issues can be discussed at many points during the therapeutic relationship.

Conceiving of health and illness in this way also tends to ignore many of the public or political aspects of disease and, as such, offers a truly conservative approach to health problems. According to such concepts, political action to change the regulation of cigarettes would be useless, as the real problem with lung cancer lies within the psyche. A cholera epidemic could be treated by meditation rather than attention to the water supply, and cancer could be treated by counselling, rather than a sustained search for mechanisms of causation and for novel therapeutic agents.

Conclusion

CAM is likely to remain popular with the Australian public and, while it may become more or less integrated with conventional medicine, CAM will not disappear. Major questions regarding the evidence for CAM, the regulation of CAM practitioners, and the legal obligations of conventional practitioners regarding CAM remain; but health professionals and students no longer have any choice but to enter into a dialogue with their patients regarding CAM use and must develop some sensitivity and knowledge regarding CAM (Table 33.1 opposite) (Ezzo, Berman et al 1998; Wetzel, Kaptchuk et al 2003). In so doing, the health professions will be better able to provide care that accords with the patient's values and needs and better satisfy the ethical dimensions of health-care decision-making.

LEGAL ISSUES IN COMPLEMENTARY AND ALTERNATIVE MEDICINE

To date, there has been very little case law on the practice of complementary and alternative medicine (CAM). As the use of CAMs is quite widespread this is surprising, although we would suggest that this situation will not remain. We are seeing, however, consideration being given to the regulation of CAM with increasing concerns about the harms that may arise from unregulated practice.

Regulation of complementary medicines

The Therapeutic Goods Administration (TGA) is a unit of the Australian Government Department of Health and Ageing. The TGA carries out a range of assessment and monitoring activities to ensure that therapeutic goods available in Australia are of an acceptable standard. Within the TGA is the Office for Complementary Medicine. The TGA operates under the authority of the *Therapeutic Goods Act 1989* (Cth) which came into effect on 15 February 1991. The aim of the legislation is to provide a national framework for the regulation of therapeutic goods in Australian and to ensure their quality, safety and efficacy.

Essentially, any product for which a therapeutic claim is made must be entered in the *Australian Register of Therapeutic Goods* (ARTG) before the product can be supplied in Australia. The Act sets out the requirements for inclusion in the ARTG, including labelling, advertising, product appearance and appeal guidelines. Some areas such as the scheduling of substances and their safe storage are covered by State or Territory legislation (eg, the *Poisons and Therapeutic Goods Act 1966* in New South Wales). Therapeutic goods are broadly defined as those things that are:

- represented as having a therapeutic purpose; or
- likely to be taken as having a therapeutic purpose; or
- declared by the TGA as having a therapeutic purpose.

A therapeutic purpose is defined as a use in connection with preventing, diagnosing, curing or alleviating a disease, ailment, defect or injury, or in connection with influencing or modifying a physiological purpose in humans or animals, or for testing the susceptibility of a person to a disease or ailment. Goods that are classified as *registered* goods (eg, prescription medicines) must have demonstrated quality, safety and efficacy. Goods classed as *listed* goods (eg, vitamins and sunscreens) must have demonstrated quality and safety. Complementary medicines can be either listed or registered on the ARTG, depending on their ingredients and the claims made for them.

The listed category is for those goods made with low risk ingredients that may be used for minor, self-limiting conditions. Sponsors must hold appropriate evidence to support claims they have made about their products. A 'sponsor' is someone who imports, manufactures or exports therapeutic goods. The majority of listed medicines are self-selected by consumers and used for self-treatment. Most complementary medicines (eg, herbal, vitamin and mineral products) are listed products. All listed medicines must display an 'AUST L' number on the label of the product.

The registered, non-prescription, category is for those products that have a higher risk or are for more serious claims than allowed for in the listed category. Goods that are registered undergo a scientific evaluation for quality, safety and efficacy. The Complementary Medicines Evaluation Committee (CMEC) provides advice on the safety, quality and, where appropriate, the efficacy relating to claims made for the product to be included on the ARTG. All registered medicines must display an 'AUST R' number on the label as proof of registration.

The *Therapeutic Goods Act* includes the Standard for the Uniform Scheduling of Drugs and Poisons (SUSDP) which contains the decisions from the National Drugs and Poisons Schedule Committee, regarding the classification of drugs and poisons into schedules for inclusion into relevant legislation of the States and Territories. Also included are model provisions regarding containers and labels, product list recommended for exemptions to provisions and recommendations regarding other controls for drugs and poisons. This also includes herbs that are considered to have toxic effects. The inclusion of substances in the SUSDP results in some restriction on prescribing, such as Schedules 1-4 substances which may only be prescribed by medical practitioners, dentists or veterinarians. Dispensing of these substances is also restricted. Some Chinese herbalists have expressed concern that the substances they use are being made unavailable through scheduling that denies them access.

There are frequently concerns about whether a particular substance should be regarded as a medicine or a food for the purposes of registration. Products that may fit within the definition of either a food or a medicine are referred to a joint TGA/Food Standards Australia New Zealand Committee which recommends whether the product should be regulated as a therapeutic good or food.

Regulation of CAM practitioners

During the past 20 years there has been a significant increase in the number of CAM practitioners, training courses and professional associations. Qualifications for practitioners vary widely and many argue that, as with many health professions, there is a public interest in the regulation of CAM practitioners. Some complementary professions like chiropractic and osteopathy have been registered professions for years and soon will be regulated by standard regulation under the *National Registration and Accreditation Scheme for the Health Professions* which will commence on 1 July 2010.

Other regulatory approaches have been more sporadic. For example, Chinese traditional medicine is only regulated in Victoria. The *Chinese Medicine Registration Act 2000* came into operation on 1 January 2002 and has now been subsumed under the *Health Professions Registration Act 2005*. The Act was modelled on the various Australian medical practice Acts. The Act establishes a statutory, incorporated Chinese Medicine Registration Board, which registers Chinese herbal medicine practitioners, acupuncturists and dispensers of Chinese herbs, and conducts investigations into complaints about registrants' professional conduct or fitness to practise. Health practitioners who are already registered with another health board that has endorsed their registration to practise Chinese medicine are exempt from registering with the Chinese Medicine Registration Board.

At the time of writing no other Australian jurisdictions have adopted this approach for either Chinese medicine or any other CAM. In 2002 the New South Wales Chief Health Officer released a discussion paper – *Regulation of Complementary Health Practitioners* – which invited submissions concerning the need to regulate CAM practitioners, and offering models for implementing regulation (NSW Department of Health 2002). Malcolm Parker has argued that the process of registration and regulation of CAMs will require minimum defined standards of competence that will have to be based on scientific evidence. This, it is suggested, will create a tension with the CAM practices which have traditionally relied on peer review. He argues that 'as scientific evidence accumulates these modalities are likely to lose their identities as "alternative" and become assimilated into Western medicine' (Parker 2003).

Although there have been no other moves to register CAM practitioners there is still some oversight through the various Health Care Complaints bodies within the States and Territories. The 2002-03 Annual Report of the New South Wales Health Care Complaints Commission notes that:

> Few complaints were about alternative health care providers. The complaints this year included:

- A traditional Chinese medicine practitioner holding out to be a medical practitioner
- Three unregistered persons offering "chiropractic" work
- Dissatisfaction with treatment using the EQ4 Listen system for eczema
- The amount of money charged for natural therapies and lack of receipts
- A traditional Chinese medicine practitioner providing false medical certificates
- Poor infection control by a traditional Chinese medicine practitioner in treating haemorrhoids. (Health Care Complaints Commission 2003)

Problems with the scope of practice

One of the most difficult areas of CAM from a regulatory perspective is defining the scope of practice (Weir 2007). All Australian jurisdictions make it illegal for anyone to practise medicine without being registered as a medical practitioner.

Jurisdiction	Legislation
NSW	*Medical Practice Act 1992*, s 99
Qld	*Medical Practitioners Registration Act 2001*, s 161
SA	*Medical Practice Act 2004*, s 43
Tas	*Medical Practitioners Registration Act 1996*, s 63
Vic	*Health Professions Registration Act 2005*, s 80
WA	*Medical Act 1894*, s 19
ACT	*Health Professionals Act 2004*, s 72
NT	*Health Practitioners Act 2004*, s 101

An example of such criminal passing off occurred in *Dix, Registrar of NSW Medical Board v Lin* [2007] NSWSC 846, where a Chinese medicine practitioner plead guilty to passing himself off as a registered medical practitioner and pre-scribing misepristone (otherwise known as RU-486). Lin had told an undercover investigator that he could perform an abortion and supply RU-486. The accused also took blood pressure and asked for a urine sample. He also supplied a num-ber of tablets labelled as 'miseprestone'. The judge sentenced Lin to a suspended sentence of 13 months, primarily due to the guilty plea and his general lack of understanding about the laws concerning passing himself off as a doctor.

In other situations, fair trading laws can be applied to any representation by a CAM practitioner that is misleading or deceptive. For example, in *Commissioner for Fair Trading, Department of Commerce v Perrett* [2007] NSWSC 1130, an alternative health practitioner (Perrett) was found to have engaged in mis-leading and deceptive conduct in his practice at the 'Rutherford Health Clinic'. Perrett used the practice to provide treatments for cancer, multiple schlerosis and Huntington's disease (an incurable genetic condition). The goods included tablets, capsules, white powder, ampoules of red liquid for injecting, bags of yellow fluid for intravenous drips, bottles of 'serum', green tea capsules, black ointments, and other substances of unknown or uncertain composition. He also used a 'radiation pulsation machine'.

A number of complaints were set out by the Commissioner. For example, Perrett was found to have told patients that he worked for NASA, had trained but not competed his medical training, and had been cured of cancer and had himself cured others. He had injected a multiple sclerosis patient with a yellow substance made from a Chinese plant and when the patient complained of adverse reactions Perrett told the patient that it was a 'latent virus' coming out. He attempted to cure a breast cancer patient with a black ointment that burnt her. His explanation was that it would 'root up the cancer cells'. He also suggested using a radiation machine that was said to have the ability to 'send out magnetic fields and is a healing device. The pulsator kills bacteria. I can stop your body from producing the cancer cells. You do not need to have invasive surgery to remove the lumps and tumours'.

He also tried to treat a patient with thyroid cancer with substances such as seaweed extracts and tea. He tried to convince the patient to avoid radiotherapy because it could damage her brain. He also supplied treatments to patients with Huntington's disease.

The court found that the representations were misleading and deceptive in breach of the *Fair Trading Act 1987* (NSW). The judge ordered that Perrett cease making such claims but refused to make a further order preventing Perrett from continuing to trade. Curiously, this was because the defendant had failed to appear at trial either in person or through a lawyer, and the judge felt it inappropriate to make such orders without the benefit of hearing Perrett's side of the story. Moreover, such an order would effectively destroy his business and there was nothing to suggest that the business was illegal. Indeed some health funds provided rebates for his services.

Similar issues arose in *Commissioner for Fair Trading, Department of Commerce v Hunter* [2008] NSWSC 277. Here the misleading and deceptive conduct related to advertising by a professed naturopath which advertised 'live blood analysis' as a cure for, amongst other things, allegories, acne, eczema, psoriasis, obesity, constipation, candida, chronic fatigue syndrome, 'menopausal syndrome' and ADHD. Live blood analysis consisted of projecting a microscopic image of the patient's blood onto a screen in front of the patient. The advertisement also stated that Hunter was a 'PH.D. M.A. DOCTOR OF NATURAL MEDICINE' and that he was a member of the Australian Charter of Natural Health Practitioners. The Commissioner sought an order preventing the advertising from continuing and also an order to prevent the defendant from continuing to practise.

The judge found that the advertising was misleading and deceptive. The legal test was said to be whether it would lead the ordinary readers of the advertising to be misled and deceived on the basis that live blood analysis was found to convey no therapeutic benefits. Similarly the use of the term 'doctor of natural medicine' was said to be misleading as most people would assume it meant 'medical doctor' or 'medically qualified'. However, the court declined to find that the term 'PH.D' was misleading because the judge was not convinced that the ordinary reader would have associated the letters with being a doctorate of philosophy. The claim that Hunter was a member of the Australian Charter of Natural Health Practitioners was found to be false.

The judge also issued a permanent injunction preventing the defendant from working in the area. The judge found that the defendant had little insight into his actions or comprehension as to why it was wrong to publish the misleading advertisements. Moreover the defendant's bias, inaccuracy and his tendency to overstate his competence, qualifications and affiliations led the judge to find that there was a substantial risk that he would continue to mislead the public unless he was permanently restrained.

Standards of care and CAMs

The CAM practitioner

Many of the legal problems faced by CAM practitioners are similar to those of other health professionals. Problems will arise from failures to examine properly, diagnose, refer, treat, keep proper records, observe confidentiality, obtain consent and communicate properly. The standard of care expected of health professionals was stated by the High Court of Australia in *Rogers v Whitaker* (1992) 175 CLR 479 at 483 as 'that of the ordinary skilled person exercising and professing to have that special skill'. The question then arises, what is the standard of care expected of a CAM practitioner? This issue was examined in an English case *Shakoor (administratrix of the estate of Shakoor (deceased) v Situ (t/a Eternal Health Co)* [2000] 4 All ER 181. A fit 32-year-old man sought treatment from a Chinese medicine practitioner for multiple benign lipomas (for which Western medicine offered only surgery). He took nine doses on alternative days of a traditional Chinese remedy made from 12 herbs. He developed liver failure and died. There was a coronial inquest which found that one of the herbs used in the remedy was Bai Xian Pi or dictamnus dasycarpus which might be hepatotoxic (although there was conflicting evidence on this point).

In a civil trial for negligence it was submitted that the defendant should be judged against the standard of a general medical practitioner specialising in the treatment of skin complaints. It was argued that medical journals, including *The Lancet*, had reported risks to the liver from similar herbs. The defendant argued that he should be judged against the standards of the reasonable practitioner of traditional Chinese medicine. The Chinese medical textbooks and periodicals said that the remedy had been established over centuries to be safe and did not pose any adverse effects. The judge said that when the court adjudicates on the standard of care in cases such as this it must 'have regard to the fact that the practitioner is practising his art alongside orthodox medicine and the implications of this fact' (at 188). However, the defendant could not be judged by the standard of care expected of a general medical practitioner, as he did not hold himself out to be such a person. Nevertheless, practitioners must recognise that they are holding themselves out 'as competent to practise within a system of law and medicine which will review the standard of care he has given' (at 189).

The practitioner must also recognise the possibility that anyone having an adverse reaction to an alternative remedy may be treated in an orthodox hospital and so 'must take steps to satisfy himself that there has not been any adverse report in such journals on the remedy which ought to affect the use he makes of it' (at 189). The court held that the Chinese medicine practitioner had not been in breach of his duty of care when treating the deceased. The court also found that he had not breached his duty of care by not warning the deceased of any risks, as the risks were too low to have warranted disclosure.

This case suggests that CAM practitioners need to be aware of dangerous or toxic reactions to their treatments that may be reported within orthodox medicine (this could be done by subscribing to an association which searches the literature and circulates relevant information). Ian Freckelton has commented that this case suggests that:

> The duty of care of the alternative practitioner is largely defined by what is to be expected of a competent practitioner of her or his art. However, it is influenced by what is known outside the paradigm of that art but not wholly determined by it, because otherwise the patient's decision to leave the orthodox paradigm would be rendered otiose. (Freckelton 2003)

Issues concerning evidence of standards of care were raised in *Forder v Hutchinson* [2005] VSCA 281. In that case an osteopath, who was also a naturopath, was sued by a patient for a negligent neck manipulation. The patient had a condition which made the risk of neck manipulation greater but the osteopath had not ordered any X-rays before commencing treatment which would have uncovered the condition. A chiropractic professor (who lectured osteopathic students on how to do manipulations) and a neck surgeon had both given evidence that an X-ray should have been taken and examined before the neck manipulation. The trial judge rejected this evidence as not being relevant to the standard of care for osteopaths and dismissed the claim. The Court of Appeal overturned this decision and submitted the case for re-trial. Maxwell P stated:

> I consider that the judge erred in his analysis of the question of whether there was sufficient evidence to enable him to ascertain the standard of care required of an osteopath in the circumstances of the respondent. It will be remembered that his Honour took the view that Professor Terrett was not qualified to give evidence as an expert on that question ...
>
> In my view, that reasoning was erroneous. One may take judicial notice that chiropractic is a system of health care of which the principal method of treatment is spinal manipulation and that osteopathy is a holistic approach to health care which embraces a range of treatments, including chiropractic treatment. Self-evidently, when the respondent manipulated the appellant's neck he was using chiropractic treatment as an osteopath ... Plainly, therefore, Professor Terrett was qualified to express opinions which were directly relevant to the standard of care to be expected of an osteopath performing a spinal manipulation of the sort in question.
>
> I consider that the judge was also in error in failing to refer to or consider [the neck surgeon] Mr Kingsley Mills' unchallenged opinion that forceful manipulation rarely achieves any positive effect; that there are many recorded examples of adverse consequences, some involving major neurological loss; and that no manipulation, violent or otherwise, of the cervical spine should be undertaken without first referring to recent X-rays. Of course Mr Kingsley Mills was a leading surgeon, and the respondent was only an osteopath, and

it is not necessarily to be expected that the standards asked of an osteopath will be the same as those of a surgeon. But the standard of care to be expected of a professional is not wholly circumscribed by the standards of his profession. The question is in the end one of reasonable care and, even in the sphere of diagnosis and treatment, the *Bolam* principle has not always been applied. Therefore, taken in conjunction with Professor Terrett's evidence, it appears to me that Mr Kingsley Mills' observations were relevant to the question of whether the respondent breached the standard of care properly to be expected of him. (at [43]-[45])

Health professionals and CAM

One of the difficult issues that may arise is the situation where a health professional incorporates CAM within their own practice. What standard of care will they be judged against – that of a CAM practitioner or that of a member of their own profession? We would suggest that the standard of care would be that of a member of his or her own profession, particularly where there is a professional emphasis on evidence-based practice. Caulfield and Feasby have commented on this issue:

> [T]here are important policy implications that would flow from the adoption of an inconsistent approach to the standard of care. For example, it would send a mixed message to practitioners. Though the evidence-based approach to clinical decision making is not without problems, there are sound justifications for encouraging physicians to use the best available evidence. But when does a prudent practitioner need to be aware and guided by scientific evidence – only when conventional therapies are involved? From the perspective of a patient who has been injured by possible negligence, such a double standard seem illogical and potentially unjust. Patients should be able to rely on physicians to employ the same stringent standard regardless of the nature of the treatment. (Caulfield and Feasby 2001)

Elizabeth Brophy has examined the question of whether a doctor has a duty to provide patients with information about complementary and alternative medicine. With respect to the fear that doctors may have about being sued for disclosing or not disclosing information about complementary and alternative medicines she advises (drawing upon the principles enunciated by the High Court of Australia in *Wyong Shire Council v Shirt* (1980) 146 CLR 40) that:

> Circumstances where litigation is most likely to occur are in a context where there is a CAM treatment reasonably available for the patient's condition that has been shown to be safe and efficacious and where the conventional treatment is invasive and or where there are significant risks attached to the procedure and/or where, if the risks eventuated, the magnitude of the harm would be great. (Brophy 2003)

In her conclusion to the article, Brophy's advice to doctors (specifically referring to the AMA's Position Statement on Complementary Medicine) is to:

- elicit information from patients about use of CAM treatments;
- answer patients' direct questions about CAM;

- take steps to become informed about reasonably available CAM medicines and therapies that have been shown to be safe and effective; and
- become familiar with qualified and competent CAM practitioners (medical and non-medical) to whom referrals can be made when necessary.

While the question of what information to provide to the patient remains patient centred (what information would the *reasonable patient* attach significance to or what information has *this patient* indicated they may wish to know), the doctor is also expected to demonstrate sufficient knowledge to enable them to meet the patient's information needs. Given that a significant number of respected practitioners (as illustrated by the AMA Position Statement on Complementary Medicine) would accept that it is reasonable to inform themselves about various aspects of different CAMs in order to properly inform their patients about alternatives (including demonstrated efficacy or risks associated with them), some knowledge of CAMs would seem to be a minimal requirement.

If patients were not infrequently to request information about CAMs a question could also be raised whether it is appropriate for doctors to inform themselves of complementary and alternative therapists within their own region in order to suggest appropriate practitioners. This does raise some problems in jurisdictions where there is no registration of CAM practitioners or where a particular type of CAM has not received bureaucratic/statutory recognition.

Criminal law and the CAM practitioner

There have been a small number of cases where CAM practitioners have found themselves in trouble with the criminal law. One notable case is that of a naturopath, Reginald Fenn. Nine days after a baby was born, the baby was diagnosed to have a critical aortic stenosis, a structural defect of the heart. The only known remedy for this condition is surgery. The father of the baby had been a patient of Mr Fenn's for approximately 15 years. He took the baby to be examined by Mr Fenn. Mr Fenn prescribed jojoba drops and used an electronic 'Mora Machine' and declared the baby 'cured'. He told the parents to 'not let surgeons touch [the baby] because he was too young and would not cope' and the parents cancelled a hospital appointment for the baby to be evaluated (Williams 2004). The appointment was rescheduled after the doctors intervened but the baby died before an operation could be carried out.

Mr Fenn pleaded not guilty when he was charged with manslaughter of the 18-day-old baby. The charges were that he was grossly negligent by treating the baby when the problem was beyond his area of expertise. A jury found Mr Fenn guilty. He was sentenced to five years' jail, although the sentence was suspended because he was too ill to serve his time in prison. In handing down the sentence the judge is reported as saying:

> Those who practise alternative medicines in this state must appreciate they must not attempt to treat conditions which can only be properly treated by surgical intervention and by experienced physicians. I find it alarming that a

person who has no qualifications … be allowed to practice medicine in the way he did. They [naturopaths] should appreciate that if tragedy follows [their treatment of a patient] then the full weight of the law will fall upon them. (Williams 2004)

References

Astin, J (1998) 'Why patients use alternative medicine: results of a national study'. *JAMA* **279**(19): 1548-53.

Barraclough, J, P Pinder et al (1992) 'Life events and breast cancer prognosis'. *BMJ* **304**(6834): 1078-81.

Behrendt, L (1994) Dark places in a country built on lies. *Sydney Morning Herald, 15 Oct.* Sydney: 11.

Bensoussan, A (1999) 'Complementary medicine – where lies its appeal?' *Med J Aust* **170**: 247-8.

Bensoussan, A (2000) 'Complementary medicine: searching for the evidence'. *Aust Fam Physician* **29**: 1129-33.

Berman, B, R Bausell et al (2002) 'Use and referral patterns for 22 complementary and alternative medical therapies by members of the American College of Rheumatology: results of a national survey'. *Ann Intern Med* **162**(7): 766-70.

Bjelakovic, G, D Nikolova et al (2004) 'Antioxidant supplements for prevention of gastrointestinal cancers: a systematic review and meta-analysis'. *Lancet* **364**: 1219-28.

Breen, KJ (2003) 'Ethical issues in the use of complementary medicines'. *Climacteric* **6**(4): 268-72.

Brophy, E (2003) 'Does a doctor have a duty to provide information and advice about complementary and alternative medicine?' *Journal of Law and Medicine* **10**: 271.

Caulfield, T and C Feasby (2001) 'Potions, promises and paradoxes: complementary medicine and alternative medicine and malpractice law in Canada'. *Health Law J* **9**: 183-203.

Cohen, M H and D M Eisenberg (2002) 'Potential physician malpractice liability associated with complementary and integrative medical therapies'. *Ann Intern Med* **136**(8): 596-603.

Correa-Velez, I, A Clavarino et al (2005) 'Surviving, relieving, repairing, and boosting up: reasons for using complementary/alternative medicine among patients with advanced cancer: a thematic analysis'. *J Palliat Med* **8**(5): 953-61.

Coulter, I and E Willis (2004) 'The rise and rise of complementary and alternative medicine: a sociological perspective'. *Med J Aust* **180**: 587-9.

Coward, R (1989) *The whole truth: The myth of alternative health.* London, Faber and Faber.

Cumming, F (2000) 'Complementary medicine regulation in Australia'. *Current Therapeutics* **41**: 57-61.

Dalen, E (1998) 'Conventional and unconventional medicine: Can they be integrated?' *Arch Int Med* **158**: 2179-81.

Eisenberg, D, M Cohen et al (2002) 'Credentialing complementary and alternative medical providers'. *Ann Intern Med* **137**(12): 965-73.

Eisenberg, D, R Davis et al (1998) 'Trends in alternative medicine use in the United States, 1990-1997'. *JAMA* **280**(18): 1569-75.

Ernst, E (2000) 'Prevalence of use of complementary/alternative medicine: a systematic review'. *Bulletin World Health Org* **78**: 252-7.

Ernst, E (2001) 'A primer of complementary and alternative medicine commonly used by cancer patients'. *Med J Aust* **174**: 88-92.

Ernst, E (2003) 'Obstacles to research in complementary and alternative medicine'. *Med J Aust* **179**: 279-80.

Ernst, E and BR Cassileth (1998) 'The prevalence of complementary/alternative medicine in cancer: a systematic review'. *Cancer* **83**(4): 777-82.

Ernst, E, MH Cohen et al (2004) 'Ethical problems arising in evidence based complementary and alternative medicine'. *J Med Ethics* **30**(2): 156-9.

Ezzo, J, B Berman et al (1998) 'Complementary medicine and the Cochrane Collaboration'. *JAMA* **280**: 1628-30.

Holliday, I (2003) 'Traditional medicines in modern societies: an exploration of integrationist options through East Asian experience'. *J Med Philos* **28**(3): 373-89.

Hyodo, I, K Eguchi et al (2003) 'Perceptions and attitudes of clinical oncologists on complementary and alternative medicine'. *Cancer* **97**: 2861-8.

Institute of Medicine (US) Committee on the Use of Complementary and Alternative Medicine by the American Public. (2005) *Complementary and alternative medicine in the United States.* Washington, DC, National Academies Press.

Joske, DJ, A Rao et al (2006) 'Critical review of complementary therapies in haematooncology'. *Intern Med J* **36**(9): 579-86.

Kaptchuk, TJ and FG Miller (2005) 'Viewpoint: what is the best and most ethical model for the relationship between mainstream and alternative medicine: opposition, integration, or pluralism?' *Acad Med* **80**(3): 286-90.

Kelner, M and B Wellman (1997) 'Health care and consumer choice: medical and alternative therapies'. *Soc Sci Med* **45**(2): 203-12.

Lewith, G and A Bensoussan (2004) 'Complementary and alternative medicine – with a difference'. *Med J Aust* **180**: 585-6.

Linde, K, W Jonas et al (2001) 'The methodological quality of randomised trials of homeopathy, herbal medicine and acupuncture'. *Int J Epidemiol* **30**: 526-31.

MacLennan, A, D Wilson et al (2002) 'The escalating costs and prevalence of alternative medicine'. *Prev Med* **35**: 166.

MacLennan, AH, SP Myers et al (2006) 'The continuing use of complementary and alternative medicine in South Australia: costs and beliefs in 2004'. *Med J Aust* **184**(1): 27-31.

Mizrachi, N, JT Shuval et al (2005) 'Boundary at work: alternative medicine in biomedical settings'. *Sociol Health Illn* **27**(1): 20-43.

Morgan, M (1994) *Mutant message down under.* Harper Collins.

NSW Health (2002) *Regulation of complementary health practitioners.* Discussion paper. Sydney, NSW Health.

Parker, M (2003) 'The regulation of complementary health: sacrificing integrity?' *Med J Aust* **179**(6): 316-18.

Peacock, J, J Bland et al (1995) 'Preterm delivery: effects of socioeconomic factors, psychological stress, smoking, alcohol and caffeine'. *BMJ* **311**(7004): 531-5.

Perry, S, B Fishman et al (1992) 'Relationships over 1 year between lymphocyte subsets and psychosocial variables among adults with infection by human immunodeficiency virus'. *Arch Gen Psychiatry* **49**(5): 396-401.

Pittler, M and E Ernst (2004) 'Feverfew for preventing migraine'. *Cochrane Database Syst Rev* **1**(CD002286).

Proctor, M, W Hing et al (2004) 'Spinal manipulation for primary and secondary dysmenorrhoea'. *Cochrane Database Syst Rev* **3**(CD002119).

Rand, K, E Hoon et al (1990) 'Daily stress and recurrence of genital herpes simplex'. *Arch Int Med* **150**(9): 1889-93.

Sanderson, CR, B Koczwara et al (2006) 'The "therapeutic footprint" of medical, complementary and alternative therapies and a doctor's duty of care'. *Med J Aust* **185**(7): 373-6.

Senate Community Affairs Committee (2005) *The cancer journey: Informing choice.* Parliament of Australia. Canberra, Parliament of Australia.

Shekelle, PG, SC Morton et al (2005) 'Challenges in systematic reviews of complementary and alternative medicine topics'. *Ann Intern Med* **142**(12 Pt 2): 1042-7.

Singh, S and E Ernst (2008) *Trick or Treat? Alternative Medicine on Trial.* Ealing, Bantam Press.

Sontag, S (1979) *Illness as metaphor.* London, Allen Lane.

Tang, J, S Zhan et al (1999) 'Review of randomised controlled trials of traditional Chinese medicine'. *BMJ* **319**: 160-1.

Thompson, T and G Feder (2005) 'Complementary therapies and the NHS'. *BMJ* **331**(7521): 856-7.

Thorne, S, A Best et al (2002) 'Ethical dimensions in the borderland between conventional and complementary/alternative medicine'. *J Altern Complement Med* **8**(6): 907-15.

Tonelli, MR and TC Callahan (2001) 'Why alternative medicine cannot be evidence-based'. *Acad Med* **76**(12): 1213-20.

Vicekers, A (1998) 'Bibliometric analysis of randomised controlled trials in complementary medicine'. *Complementary Ther Med* **6**: 185-9.

Weir, M (2003) 'Obligation to advise of options for treatment – medical doctors and complementary and alternative medicine practitioners'. *J Law Med* **10**(3): 296-307.

Weir, M (2007) *Complementary medicine: ethics and law.* Brisbane, Prometheus Publications.

Wetzel, M, T Kaptchuk et al (2003) 'Complementary and alternative medical therapies: implications for medical education'. *Ann Intern Med* **138**(3): 191-6.

Williams, N (2004) Naturopaths warned over bad medicine. *The Daily Telegraph, 14 Feb*: 17.

Zollman, C and A Vickers (1999) 'ABC of complementary medicine: What is complementary medicine?' *BMJ* **319**: 93-6.

CHAPTER 34

THE PHARMACEUTICAL INDUSTRY

Case study

A pharmaceutical company offered to provide a weekly free lunch for the inter-disciplinary meeting at a large Department of Neurology. They wished in return to have a representative present to say a few words at the end of the session, and have a table with pens, literature and some knick-knacks with the company logo on them. They were also happy to provide occasional guest speakers, and to sponsor some members of the department when they went to talk to regional hospitals. Within the department there was great debate about whether this should be accepted. Eventually it was decided to reject the offer because of fears that it would introduce conflicts of interest into the department, and it was decided that all attendees at the meeting would bring their own packed lunches instead.

The money that is put into health care is enormous, and huge profits are possible for companies that are involved in health care. There are clear incentives for manufacturers to target employees of health institutions as a way of marketing their products. Many health professionals may be approached – pharmaceutical manufacturers may have relationships with pharmacists and doctors; manu-facturers of surgical equipment may have relationships with operating theatre staff, physiotherapists and occupational therapists; diagnostic equipment manu-facturers may have relationships with radiographers, physiotherapists, speech therapists; dressing manufacturers may have relationships with nurses and so on.

The best studied relationships are those between pharmaceutical manu-facturers and doctors, and these are explored further below. However, much of what is discussed is equally applicable to other manufacturers and other health professionals.

Relationships involving medical practitioners and the pharmaceutical industry raise serious concerns and controversy within both the medical profession and the broader community (Mainous, Hueston et al 1995; Gibbons, Landry et al 1998). Within the profession itself views differ sharply, from the conviction that the risks associated with such relationships are minimal, to a concern that all contact between doctors and industry involves compromise and should therefore be avoided as far as possible (Waud 1992). The relationship between the pharmaceutical industry and the medical profession includes clearly desirable aspects (eg, the cooperative efforts of industry, government and prescribers in trying to achieve quality use of medicines) and less clearly ethically justifiable ones (eg, acceptance of lavish gifts and money for entertainment expenses by doctors).

Ethical issues arising from the interaction between the pharmaceutical industry and the health professions

Health professionals and the pharmaceutical industry share a number of common interests. For example, both are concerned with encouraging effective and responsible use of existing drugs in treatment and care, monitoring of their use, and innovative research. However, the parties have different emphases and focus on different stakeholders. Health workers are interested primarily in patient care and scientific advance, while industry is interested primarily in commercial outcomes. The primary stakeholder in patient care is the patient, whereas the principal stakeholder in industry is the shareholder. The similarities and differences between participants and their interests create both a need for discourse and the potential for conflict.

The relationship between industry and physicians and between industry and academic medicine is likely to contain both risks and benefits. Industry sponsorship may support important clinical research into new therapies, may increase continuing medical education (CME) and provide valuable resources for patients and carers.

The contribution made by industry to medical knowledge and practice has been considerable. It has been estimated that it takes about $403 million to develop a new drug (DiMasi, Hansen et al 2003), and up to 80% of clinical research in the United States is now sponsored by industry (Bodenheimer 2000). But interaction between health professionals and the pharmaceutical industry may also create conflicts of interest, distort education and research, increase the costs of care and increase the amount of inappropriate prescribing (Angell 2004; Avorn 2004; Brennan, Rothman et al 2006).

In spite of the clear common interests and benefits of cooperation, four main concerns of an ethical nature have been expressed by both the medical profession and the community:

- the possibility that associations between doctors and drug companies may serve commercial objectives of industry and acquisitive interests of clinicians rather than legitimate health, educational or research goals, thereby compromising the primary ethical obligation of doctors to patients, dividing the loyalties of doctors and undermining the basic trust on which clinical relationships depend;

- the risk that drug promotion will inappropriately influence doctors' decisions;

- the danger that industry involvement in research will lead to distortions in scientific evidence and prevent independent assessment of data; and

- the risk that exposure of inappropriate relationships between health professionals and industry may erode public confidence in health professionals and health institutions, and threaten the expectation of patients that they receive interventions because they are necessary and that health-care decisions are based on sound clinical judgment unconstrained by commercial influences.

These concerns have prompted all stakeholders, including government and regulatory authorities, industry bodies, consumer groups, and professional and academic bodies, to develop policies and guidelines for regulating this relationship. No stakeholder has advocated that health professionals eliminate contact with industry, but each has provided guidelines regarding the management of conflicts of interest, the adoptions of organisational transparency and the maintenance of professional norms (World Health Organization 1988; International Federation of Pharmaceutical Manufacturers and Associations 2003; RACP 2005). There has been disagreement about whether voluntary codes are sufficient, or whether mandatory rules are needed (Langman 1988), but the self-regulatory model has so far largely prevailed in Australia.

Divided loyalties and conflicts of interest

An 'interest' is a commitment, goal or value that arises out of a particular social relationship or practice. The possibility that dealings with drug companies might lead to 'conflict of interest' has been an abiding concern. One definition of a conflict of interest is a set of conditions in which professional judgment concerning a primary interest, such as a patient's welfare or the validity of research, tends to be unduly influenced by a secondary interest, such as financial gain (Thompson 1993).

It is common for relationships to be associated with several interests, all of which may influence decisions and none of which is morally wrong, in and of itself. Interests of health professionals may include:

- patient welfare;
- community welfare;
- pecuniary interests (eg, consultancy fees, share holdings, paid employment);
- non-pecuniary interests (eg, relationships, quality of life);
- advancement of career;
- success in obtaining research grants;
- participation in student teaching;
- maintenance of professional standards;
- hospitality;
- public recognition and prestige;
- participation in research.

When a health professional is engaged in a relationship with a pharmaceutical company, a 'duality' of interests is said to exist. It cannot be assumed that such a duality will constitute a 'conflict' in each case as this will depend on the particular circumstances.

Dualities of interest are common; conflicts relatively rare. Further, whereas the distinction between the two is sometimes clear cut, at other times it may be subtle and depend on the nature of the relationship in question and the values of the community within which it occurs. Dualities of interest constitute 'conflicts' only when they are associated with competing obligations that are likely to lead directly to a compromise of primary responsibilities. To establish whether a conflict of interest exists it is necessary for the factual details to be declared and for the community to have the opportunity to scrutinise the issues publicly.

Extent of the interaction between the pharmaceutical industry and the medical profession

Recent empirical research has shown clearly that the interaction between the pharmaceutical industry, the medical profession and medical organisations is extensive, diverse, complex and interdependent. This interaction also begins early so patterns of behaviour, reciprocity and a culture of expectation are likely to be established well before physicians are given licence to prescribe (Rogers, Mansfield et al 2004). A recent Australian study found that 96% of Australian physicians accepted gifts from industry, 84% attended sponsored symposia or product launches, 52% accepted travel sponsorship for themselves and 30% for their partner, 40% had been involved in industry-sponsored research in the past year, 23% had been an active member of an advisory group in the past 12 months, 20% had received some payment from industry for teaching or research, 6% acted as a paid consultant to industry and 7% had shares in pharmaceutical companies (Henry, Doran et al 2005; Henry, Kerridge et al 2005; Kerridge, Maguire et al 2005). Similarly, a recent US survey of 3167 physicians found that 94% had some type of relationship with the pharmaceutical industry – most involving receiving food in the workplace (83%) or accepting drug samples (78%). Thirty-five per cent received payment for continuing medical education (CME) or for attendance at professional meetings and 28% received payments for consulting, giving lectures or enrolling patients in clinical trials (Campbell, Gruen et al 2007).

Drug promotion

Promotion and marketing (including advertising, gift giving and support for medically related activities such as travel to meetings) make up a very large part of the activities of drug companies; consuming a quarter to a third of their entire budgets (two to three times that spent on research and development). In the United States alone it has been estimated that in 2003 drug companies spent more than US$30,000 per practising physician on marketing (US$14 billion per annum) and employed almost 90,000 drug representatives ('detailers') (Angell 2004).

Advertising

The pharmaceutical industry uses a diverse range of strategies to increase sales, including advertising to physicians; sponsorship of medical research; sponsorship of consumer organisations; provision of 'information aids', diaries and disease management resources to patients; personal contact with health professionals by 'detailers'; provision of education material, audio-visual teaching material and software to physicians; support for continuing medical education; recruitment of health professionals to advisory boards; 'indirect' direct-to-consumer advertising; and identification and cultivation of opinion leaders likely to become 'product champions' capable of influencing many other physicians through education, research and collegiality (Moynihan 2008).

Doctors generally perceive the way they practise to be determined by knowledge and evidence, but it appears that they often fail to recognise commercial influences on therapeutic decisions and underestimate the subtle and pervasive effects of pharmaceutical promotion (Avorn 2004). It is disquieting that some practitioners rely on pharmaceutical company representatives for much of their drug information. Although physicians often deny it, there is considerable evidence that advertising affects clinical decision-making behaviour. Contact with drug company representatives leads to prescribing of their drugs (Peay and Peay 1998); physicians exposed to advertising are more likely to accept commercial rather than well established scientific views (Lexchin 1993); and drug company advertising is associated with an inability of some physicians to identify wrong claims and a propensity to engage in non-rational prescribing behaviour (Haayer 1982).

While many health professionals deny that interaction with industry has any impact on the rigour or logic of their decision-making, recent neurobiological and psychological evidence suggests that influence and reciprocity may have a significant, but largely unconscious, effect on decision-making and may lead people to behave more unethically than they otherwise would (AAMC 2007).

Direct-to-consumer-advertising (DTCA)

Expenditure on pharmaceuticals in Australia has grown more rapidly in recent years than the overall government health budget. There are numerous factors driving this.

In the USA, where prescription drugs are the fastest growing component of the health-care budget, attention has focused on the role of direct-to-consumer advertising (DTCA) (Findlay 2001). DTCA is the promotion of any health product or service directly to the general public by private enterprise and government agencies, via media sources including (but not limited to) print, internet and broadcast services.

DTCA emerged in the USA in 1997, and since that time annual expenditure on DTCA of prescription pharmaceuticals has grown exponentially, rising from US$375 million in 1995 to US$4.2 billion in 2005 (US General Accounting Office 2007). This spending represents about a third of the total spending on drug promotion in the USA. At the same time there has been a corresponding increase in sales of prescription drugs, with sales increasing by US$20.8 billion between 1999 and 2000. The same trends are evident in New Zealand – the only other country in the OECD that allows DTCA (Toop, Richards et al 2003).

In Australia, over-the-counter (OTC) pharmaceuticals and complementary or alternative therapies are regulated under the auspices of the Therapeutic Goods Advertising Code. DTCA of prescription drugs remains prohibited. This legislation is supplemented by the Code of Conduct of Medicines Australia, which regulates drug company sponsorship of medical conferences, the payment of travel and accommodation expenses of doctors attending such conferences and the provision of other forms of hospitality. The Code currently prohibits DTCA. In other words, current policy restricts the actions that industry can take to promote consumption of its products and, more broadly, restricts their communication with consumers.

The pharmaceutical industry has responded to the legislative prohibition of DTCA by arguing that this represents an inappropriate degree of government intervention in the marketplace. It has continued to push for reconsideration of the restrictions on DTCA and to challenge the legislative boundaries. This has occurred through disease awareness campaigns, internet advertising and email campaigns that 'indirectly' promote their products, through support for professional and patient organisations and through direct sponsorship of journalists. Increasingly, the distinction between advertising, promotion and education is blurred by 'advertisements' that foster awareness of particular diseases and therapies, and do not mention the name of a drug, but include a company name or logo, provide a free call number and a website, and direct patients to seek medical advice regarding treatment for their ailment. Advertising has been packaged as 'information' in a range of media to alert Australian patients to the potential availability of a number of treatments including medications for arthritis, impotence, genital herpes and obesity. It is clear from such evidence of direct and 'indirect' advertising of drugs to consumers in Australia that efforts to 'contain' DTCA within national boundaries by legislation are made largely redundant as Australian consumers increasingly encounter DTCA of prescription drugs in the pages of American magazines and websites (Lexchin 2006).

Advocates of DTCA claim that it informs and empowers patients, improves information exchange between doctors and patients, increases awareness of illness, leads to detection of undiagnosed conditions, fosters compliance, increases trust and ultimately improves health. In contrast, opponents of DTCA contend that it reinforces the link between symptoms and disease and between disease and drugs, exaggerates the benefits of pharmacotherapy, exploits the (health) fears of consumers, erodes trust and impairs the doctor-patient relationship, diverts attention away from more important health concerns, increases demand for prescription drugs, increases inappropriate prescribing, increases health-care costs and ultimately has no social benefit. Studies of DTCA – the vast majority of which have been conducted in the United States – provide some (limited) data relevant to these claims and counter-claims. For the most part, health professionals do not support DTCA while patients and consumers have either neutral or positive attitudes to DTCA (due largely to the value they place on information about therapies). DTCA also appears to have both positive and negative effects, increasing consumer awareness, visits to physicians, requests for information, requests for prescriptions, the number of new diagnoses, the number of new ons, compliance with courses of treatment and (possibly) inappropriate prescribing. DTCA also does appear to have increased the total expenditure on drugs, and so some extent has promoted brand shifting. It is not possible to say whether DTCA has contributed to increases or reduction in net health or illness .

While some commentators suggest that DTCA can be effectively managed by legislative prohibition, this appears simplistic as it fails to take account of the complexity and changing factors, including widespread use of the media to 'sell' and potentially distort health messages; the impact of the consumer movement; changes in the doctor-patient relationship; and the revolution in information technology. For all of these reasons DTCA is increasingly recognised as a force that is likely to shape pharmaceutical usage in Australia.

Gift giving

Gift giving is another widespread drug-promotion strategy. A study from the University of Toronto showed that, over a period of one year, psychiatry residents and interns attended up to 35 meetings and 70 drug lunches and received up to 75 promotional items and US$800 in gifts (although there was considerable variation) (Hodges 1995). In another study, more than 80% of medical students had received at least a book and in some cases much more (Sandberg, Carlos et al 1997).

Although many physicians deny that gifts influence their behaviour (Chren, Landefeld et al 1989; McInney, Schiedermayer et al 1990), here, too, there is clear evidence to the contrary (Wazana 2000). For example, a survey of 120 physicians in Cleveland, Ohio, showed that those who met with pharmaceutical representatives were 13.2 times more likely to request inclusion of the company's products in their hospital formulary; those who accepted money to speak at symposia were 21.4 times more likely to do so; and those who accepted money to perform research were 9.2 times more likely to do so. The authors concluded that there is a 'strong, consistent, specific and independent' association between physicians' requests that a drug be added to the hospital formulary and interactions with drug companies (Chren and Landefeld 1994).

Support for travel

There is also evidence that drug company support for travel expenses changes the prescribing behaviour of practitioners (Orlowski and Wateska 1992). Among the many studies that have demonstrated such an effect, it has been shown that a physician who accepts money to travel to a symposium is 4.5–10 times more likely to prescribe a company-sponsored drug after such sponsorship than before (even though he or she may believe in advance that prescribing behaviour will not be affected), and is 7.9 times more likely to submit a formulary request for that drug than a physician who does not (Orlowski and Wateska 1992; Chren and Landefeld 1994).

Meeting sponsorship and continuing medical education activities

Sponsorship of meetings is an important and difficult issue. There are clearly common interests between professional societies, which are usually responsible for organising conferences, and the pharmaceutical industry. The former stand to gain substantial funding from the pharmaceutical industry for their meetings and other activities, while, for the latter, meetings offer opportunities to showcase their wares. Sponsorship of conferences has been shown to lead to bias in favour of the sponsoring companies' drugs (Bowman 1986), with increases in prescriptions for sponsors' drugs in the six months after an event (Lichstein, Turner et al 1992). Similarly, pharmaceutical support for continuing medical education (CME) activities leads to increased prescribing of sponsoring companies' products. This occurs even when the course content is controlled by the society or institution and the drugs are referred to by their generic names only (Bowman 1986).

Research

While there is little question that interaction with industry may inappropriately influence prescribing, it is the impact of the pharmaceutical industry on medical research that has the greatest potential to influence practice and the delivery of health care. The majority of clinical trials in the United States (>80%) and an increasing number in Australia (>20%) are now sponsored by the pharmaceutical industry and governments worldwide are reducing the relative contributions they make to clinical research, facilitating commercial matched funding of research and encouraging research bodies and researchers to identify commercial applications of their research (Green 2008). While industry sponsorship of research may enable the investigation of new therapies and has unquestionably led to reductions in the mortality and morbidity associated with many conditions, industry sponsorship may also direct the research that is done and the results of that research, with the potential to create significant conflicts of interest. Financial conflicts of interests may occur where researchers have shares in the company whose product they are testing, are being paid to recruit subjects for research, participate as speakers, consultants or advisors for industry or work for institutions that have close academic and financial links with industry (Lemmens and Miller 2003; Brennan, Rothman et al 2006). Academic, personal and social conflicts of interest may also arise but are much more difficult to describe and measure.

The adverse impacts of pharmaceutical industry sponsorship of medical research have been extensively documented and arise from the involvement of industry in every step of the research process.

First, the research agenda may be distorted by the interests of industry such that there is less research conducted on those unable to purchase medicines (particularly those living in the developing world); less research conducted on diseases that affect only a few people ('orphan diseases'); less research on non-pharmaceutical therapies or on health prevention/promotion; less research on drugs that are no longer patent protected; more research conducted on diseases affecting the affluent 'worried well'; and more research conducted with the aim of increasing the diagnosis or treatment of existing diseases or creating entirely new categories of disease (Lexchin 2006) (Moynihan, Heath et al 2002).

Second, pharmaceutical industry sponsors or contract research organisers (CROs) hired by them may control or significantly influence study design, subject recruitment, data collection and analysis, preparation of manuscripts, and publication and dissemination of results to the extent that the validity, integrity and adequacy of the 'evidence' produced by medical research is called into question. In this regard it is noteworthy that systematic reviews have demonstrated that industry-sponsored research is more likely to produce results favourable to the (sponsored) new therapy than research funded from other sources (Bhandari, Busse et al 2004). It is also noteworthy that one in five researchers in Australia actively involved in industry-sponsored research have observed basic flaws in methodology or evidence of research misconduct and 12% acknowledged that they had participated in research where the first draft of the resultant manuscript was drafted by the sponsor or 'ghost written' (Henry, Kerridge et al 2005). There are many ways in which research findings can be directed towards producing a desired result (Bero 1996), ranging from careful design of a trial and selection of drug doses to selective reporting of favourable outcomes (Bodenheimer 2000). Studies can use a non-inferiority rather than a superiority study design (meaning that a new drug simply has to be no worse than an existing therapy); drugs can be inappropriately trialled against a placebo, against a drug known to be inferior or against too low or too high a dose of a competitor drug; trials can be too small to show a significant difference; multiple endpoints can be measured and then only those that produce favourable results reported; results from single centres in multi-centre trials can be reported; subgroup analysis can be performed and only the positive results reported; results can be published early before mature results (which may or may not be known) reveal significant adverse effects or therapeutic equivalence; and negative results can be delayed or actively suppressed (Bekelman, Li et al 2003). The prominence of a publication can also be enhanced by paying authors to participate, or publishing non-peer-reviewed material as a supplement in a respected journal (Bero, Galbraith et al 1992). Delays in the publication of unfavourable results are common, and it is speculated that the results of many clinical trials are never published at all (Chan and Altman 2005; Chalmers 2006).

Third, industry sponsorship may create dualities of interest and diminish the virtues of science and medicine – increasing secrecy and diminishing sharing of data, eroding the integrity and independence of researchers, creating multiple ties between researchers and industry sponsors, and inappropriately influencing the way that researchers treat research participants.

Fourth, industry sponsorship of research may ultimately erode public trust in research, medicine and health professionals.

Managing dualities of interest

The problem with dualities of interest is not that they exist – they are inevitable – but the extent to which they may distort primary interests or lead to morally questionable actions. The central principle that should be adopted is that arrangements between physicians and pharmaceutical companies should be open and transparent. Dualities ought to be clarified and clearly declared in the relevant context – to patients, research participants, hospital committees, and so on. Whether they constitute conflicts should generally not be left to the individuals concerned to decide, but to a process of informed public debate within the setting in which the duality arises. This debate will need to consider whether the duality of interest constitutes a conflict of interest, how legitimate the interests are, whether the duality or conflict of interest is avoidable and who is being served or harmed by those interests. Where conflicts appear likely, special procedures should be devised to avoid unacceptable outcomes. Institutions, professional bodies and academic journals instrumentalise these principles in various ways, including through policies obliging disclosure of financial interests, research review committees, independent data monitoring committees, conflict-of-interest committees, research governance structures and mechanisms for public disclosure. While such mechanisms go some way to addressing concerns regarding conflicts of interest, there is also a broad recognition that disclosure is necessary but not sufficient and that other approaches may be required, including prohibition of shareholding by researchers or participant recruitment fees, mandatory registration of clinical trials, reporting of undeclared conflicts of interest to professional registration boards or misconduct committees, penalties for researchers and/or authors found to be in breach of codes of conduct and, ultimately, restrictions on industry sponsorship of research and an increase in public funding of research (Brown 2000; De Angelis, Drazen et al 2005). In Australia, a recent decision by the Australian Competition and Consumer Commission (ACCC) requires pharmaceutical companies to report all occasions where they have provided 'support' to health professionals. The first of these reports, a Deloitte survey sponsored by the industry body Medicines Australia, listed 14,633 'educational events' over six months in 2007 where doctors were given food and drink by drug companies (SMH 2008). While this may seem substantial, the report was later criticised as a 'sham' by critics of industry on the grounds that it failed to verify the accuracy and completeness of information supplied by industry and because it did not include visits that drug company representatives made to doctors.

Management of the interactions between the pharmaceutical industry and the health professions

Ideally, drug promotion should be restricted to the dissemination of well-founded data about specific products. This would ensure reduction of costs of pharmaceuticals to the consumer as well as reassuring the community about the independence of physicians, restricting excessive claims about the effectiveness of drugs and ensuring unbiased assessment of evidence.

Benefits received from pharmaceutical companies should leave physicians' and scientists' independence of judgment unimpaired. Various levels of advice have been advanced to medical practitioners about accepting gifts. These range from blanket rejection, to a gradient of moral acceptability based on cost, to the principles that gifts should not be excessive and should not influence decision-making, to the test of whether the recipient would be willing to have the arrangements publicly known. Each approach that attempts to define a gradient of acceptability is problematic and tends to be arbitrary in its decision-making. For these reasons the simplest, and perhaps most defensible, approach is for health professionals to err on the side of rejection of gifts, even those of trivial value.

Support for travel to meetings (including conferences organised by professional societies and CME courses) should be restricted to those making formal contributions. Spouses and partners should not receive support under any circumstances. Entertainment expenses should not be lavish, although it is recognised that ideas about what constitutes 'lavishness' vary according to one's point of view. Access of drug company representatives to students and health services should be limited. These changes will not happen easily, and it is likely that fundamental changes in practice will require a cultural shift towards a lesser expectation of entertainment, grand dinners, receptions and free food in association with conferences and symposia.

Full disclosure of commercial sponsorship of meetings should be made. Sponsorship should always be provided through independently organised scientific committees; speakers should indicate dualities of interest at the time of presentation; and sources of commercial funding should not influence scientific, educational or public policy decisions of the professional body.

Regulation of the relationships between industry and the medical profession

Although opinions differ about whether voluntary guidelines or mandatory rules are the best way to monitor potential conflicts of interest, no professional bodies or institutions have proposed a ban on interactions between doctors and the pharmaceutical industry. Indeed, it is accepted that such a policy would not serve the interests of any party. It is likely that the most desirable approach is to develop an amicable relationship that allows healthy criticism and is based on clear, but non-coercive, guidelines. This is the view adopted by the Royal Australasian College of Physicians (2005).

Conclusions

In the medical and ethics literature there is a tendency to portray the interaction between the pharmaceutical industry and the medical profession in pejorative terms, with the pharmaceutical industry often characterised as 'villains' and the medical profession as innocent or, at the very least, naive 'victims'. This is a gross oversimplification. A more accurate characterisation of the relationship sees both the medical profession and pharmaceutical companies as powerful stakeholders in the practice of medicine. Each has a *stake* in medicine and in the outcome of any medical and commercial interaction.

Medical organisations are primarily concerned with maintenance of professional standards, continuing medical education, training and accreditation, political lobbying and participation in the health sector. Their concerns are with the profession and, indirectly, with patients. Pharmaceutical companies, on the other hand, are commercial enterprises, aiming to make a profit and serve the interests of their shareholders. Nevertheless, they are in the business of treating disease and so have a commercial interest in doing this well. Thus, while medical organisations and pharmaceutical companies differ in their emphases, there is sufficient commonality in their interests to ensure that cooperative inter-action between them is inevitable. Each is concerned with medical research and development, each seeks to shape medical education and pharmaceutical prescribing, and each has a stake in the definition, diagnosis and management of disease (Illich 1990).

The current pattern of relationships between doctors and the pharma-ceutical industry is the outcome of a long-established culture in which gratuities, gifts and the like are both expected and provided. As a result, change will require a substantial shift in attitudes and values and thus is likely to be slow. The major concern that arises in the interaction between the medical profession and the pharmaceutical industry is the existence of *dualities* of interest and the potential for *conflicts* of interest. Conflicts of interest in medicine are of concern primarily because of their potential to affect the process of education, the prac-tice of prescribing, and the quality, conduct, outcome and dissemination of research, subverting them to serve commercial rather than scientific or com-munity ends. More fundamentally, the medical profession also seeks to avoid real or perceived conflict of interest because of its potential to diminish the public's perception of, and trust in, the profession itself, in medical research and in the entire health endeavour.

In reviewing the relationships between medical practitioners and the phar-maceutical industry, it is clear that benefits received from pharmaceutical companies must leave the independent judgment of physicians unimpaired and that arrangements between physicians and pharmaceutical companies ought to be open and transparent. The overriding principle should be a firm belief that the values of science and clinical medicine must prevail over commercial imperatives. If these simple guidelines are followed, it is likely that much progress will be made towards allaying the concerns of both the community and the medical profession.

LEGAL ISSUES IN THE RELATIONSHIP BETWEEN HEALTH PROFESSIONALS AND THE PHARMACEUTICAL INDUSTRY

Legislating the relationship between health professions and the pharmaceutical industry

The primary legislative interface between the pharmaceutical industry and the health professions is the *Therapeutic Goods Act 1989* (Cth). The Act primarily deals with the approval of therapeutic goods for use on and in humans. Approv-ed therapeutic goods and devices are listed on registers and must be registered before they can be sold in Australia. The register is controlled by the Therapeutic

Goods Administration. While advertising of prescription medicines directly to members of the public is prohibited (s 42AA), advertising of registered goods to health professionals is allowed if it complies with the Therapeutic Goods Advertising Code: ss 42DM, 42DO. The Code is managed by the Therapeutic Goods Advertising Code Council and is authorised and gazetted by the Health Minister.

Apart from these regulations, there is no further legislative control on the advertisement and promotion of therapeutic goods to health-care professionals, whether it be through traditional advertising or through sponsorship of educational events, hospitality or gifts. The primary regulatory mechanism is therefore self-regulation through Medicines Australia's Code of Conduct, discussed above.

Medicine Australia's Code of Conduct and the Australian Competition Tribunal

Self-regulation may still need some form of approval by regulators. This occurred in 2006-07 when Medicines Australia sought approval for a new edition of its Code of Conduct from the ACCC. Approval by the ACCC is necessary under the *Trade Practices Act 1974* (Cth) because the Act requires corporations to seek the ACCC's approval for arrangements which might substantially reduce competition in Australia. The ACCC can approve uncompetitive conduct if there is an overwhelming public interest. Medicines Australia's regulation of the pharmaceutical industry does lessen competition, so its Code of Practice requires approval.

The ACCC refused to approve the Code without it being amended to include conditions requiring pharmaceutical companies (who were members of medicines Australia) to make public disclosure of all their sponsorship of educational meetings and symposia. Medicines Australia was required to publish details of the sponsorship on its website. Furthermore, a monitoring committee needed to scrutinise the details and check for inaccuracies.

Medicines Australia would not agree with these conditions. They felt the reporting requirements were too onerous and that the public would be drawn to misleading and sensational accounts of doctors being given gifts and hospitality. It appealed to the Australian Competition Tribunal: *Re Medicines Australia Inc* [2007] ACompT 4. The Tribunal upheld an amended version of the ACCC's conditions. Part of the reasons given were as follows:

> 360. The Tribunal considers that this is a case in which it is appropriate, if the authorisations are to be granted, to impose conditions to provide an incentive to compliance with the Code provisions relating to the conferring of benefits on doctors. That incentive is best secured by a combination of internal review and evaluation of such benefits and their accessibility to public scrutiny. In our opinion the existing enforcement mechanism [in the earlier version of the Code], so far as it relates to these provisions, is weak. It is also open to lenient interpretation. There is little in the way of any real deterrent to contravention or incentive to compliance. There seems to be little incentive or enthusiasm for companies to complain about one another in this area.

361. The practice of pharmaceutical companies conferring benefits upon healthcare professionals carries with it a risk that prescribing decisions may be affected or influenced by considerations not relevant to patient welfare. It also carries with it a risk of reduced public confidence in the industry and the profession. So far as such practices may affect prescribing decisions there is a species of market failure because such influences are unrelated to product quality or patient welfare. ...

363. The costs associated with the imposition of a condition such as that proposed by the ACCC have not been quantified. We are satisfied that there would be some administrative cost involved in the companies preparing records of the kind proposed by the ACCC. We are, however, prepared to take notice that such records could be produced, at least in part, as an incident of ordinary budgeting, accounting and internal corporate reporting practices. We do not consider that such burdens are unreasonable having regard to the benefit likely to be derived from the condition.

364. A further difficulty raised on behalf of Medicines Australia is that the publication of occasions of hospitality provided to healthcare professionals with costs and venues included may lead to sensationalised or misleading reporting of entirely legitimate events. The capacity to withstand public and professional scrutiny is one of the criteria adopted within the Code itself. There is a risk that public scrutiny may be misinformed. However, provided that benefits conferred on healthcare professionals remain within the kinds of limits that properly mark them as incidental to the educational purpose of the relevant event, Medicines Australia and its members should be quite capable of making their public case in support of them. ...

366. In our opinion there is a real risk that absent any requirement for regular reporting and public disclosure of the kind proposed in the ACCC condition some companies will test the boundaries and offer inappropriate benefits to healthcare professionals. Making public the nature, frequency and scale of benefits conferred will impose its own compliance constraint that companies conferring the benefit will have to be in a position to explain and justify it in public as well as to the Code Committee should a complaint be made.

Conflicts of interest, dualities of interest and the health professional

As discussed in Chapter 4, the relationship between a doctor and his or her patient is principally governed by the law of contract and tort (*Breen v Williams* (1996) 186 CLR 71), although there may be elements of the relationship that create some fiduciary obligations (eg, the obligation of confidence). By analogy these areas of law would govern the obligations between other health professionals and their patients. If a conflict of interest were to influence the practice of a registered health professional it could be that this could also amount to unsatisfactory professional conduct and lead to disciplinary proceedings against the practitioner. We will examine the ways in which each of these areas of law may deal with a conflict of interest.

Importantly the law does not recognise the concept of a 'duality of interests'. The legal doctrines of conflict of interest treat both a real conflict between interest and duty as being the same as a perceived conflict of interest and duty. The question of whether the competing obligations lead directly to a compromise of primary responsibilities is irrelevant in law. The possibility of harm to a patient is not a necessary element for a finding in law that a health professional has a conflict of interest. The law is rightly suspicious of claims made by professionals (whether they be health professionals or otherwise) that they can be trusted to deal with real or perceived conflicts without informing their clients/patients and getting their permission to continue acting as the patient's health provider.

Contract

In the absence of any special dealing between them, the contract struck between a doctor and patient obliges the doctor to advise and treat the patient with reasonable skill and care. As discussed in Chapter 4, most of the terms of the contract between the parties will not have been explicitly stated but are implied by the law. Generally, a term in the contract is implied only if it is necessary to give efficacy to the contract and will not be implied lightly (*Breen v Williams*, per Brennan CJ at 102).

In the South Australian case of *Kite v Malycha* (1998) 71 SASR 321, a Mrs Kite sued her surgeon when, following a fine needle aspiration of a lump, the histology report (which included the statement 'highly suspicious of an underlying carcinoma') was lost in his office; the surgeon never received the report and so Mrs Kite was not informed about her condition. Mrs Kite did not return to the surgery until nine months later and was subsequently diagnosed with breast carcinoma. The central issue in the case was whether she had been robbed of the chance of successfully curing the cancer or life expectancy that she otherwise might have expected to enjoy if she had been diagnosed when the report was made. Mrs Kite was successful in this action. However, she had also brought a second action against the doctor. This action was that the doctor had put himself in a position of conflict of interest in failing to advise Mrs Kite that he had given notice to his professional indemnity insurer of a possible claim against him. The claim was also made that the doctor continued to treat Mrs Kite, even after he knew that there may be the possibility of a legal claim being made against him.

The claim made by Mrs Kite was that the implied terms of contract between herself and the doctor included terms that he would (inter alia):

- keep confidential information obtained or arising from the relationship of doctor and patient;
- not act in a manner that would be in conflict with his duty to her or her interests;
- make proper disclosure to her of matters relating to her condition and treatment which came to his attention in the course of her treatment;
- enable her to obtain access to information affecting her rights in the event of a conflict of interest or duty arising.

Based on the evidence before the court it was held that there had been no breach of contract by the doctor. The court said:

> Ordinarily it would be sufficient for a medical practitioner in those circumstances simply to say to the patient that it might be suggested that he or she had been at fault in some way in failing earlier to make the diagnosis, and in those circumstances the patient might prefer to engage someone else. Whether or not the medical practitioner happens to be insured and has notified the insurer, are not matters which, in my opinion, there is any obligation to disclose. (at 358)

The clearer cases may be those where it could be argued that, because of a conflict of interest, there has been some deficiency in advising and treating the patient with reasonable skill and care. This type of case could be where insufficient information was provided to the patient to allow them to make an informed opinion about the treatment to be undertaken. Most of these cases are argued in negligence rather than in contract, although an action may be available in both areas of law.

Negligence

The High Court of Australia decision in *Rogers v Whitaker* (1992) 175 CLR 479 sets out the requirements for the information to be provided to patients when they are asked to consent to medical treatment. The Court held that patients need to be informed about 'material risks' (see Chapter 14). While the High Court in *Rogers v Whitaker* was concerned particularly about 'risks', the principle has wider application and could be read as a requirement to provide patients with 'material information'. This proposition is supported by the High Court's approval of the Full Court of the Supreme Court of South Australia's decision in *F v R* (1983) 33 SASR 189. In a later High Court judgment, *Rosenberg v Percival* (2001) 205 CLR 434 at 480, Kirby J examined some of the reasons why the reasoning in *Rogers v Whitaker* should still be followed:

(1) Fundamentally, the rule is a recognition of individual autonomy that is to be viewed in the wider context of an emerging appreciation of basic human rights and human dignity. There is no reason to diminish the law's insistence, to the greatest extent possible, upon prior, informed agreement to invasive treatment, save for that which is required in an emergency or otherwise out of necessity;

(2) Whilst it may be desirable to instil a relationship between the healthcare professional and the patient, reality demands a recognition that sometimes (as in the present case) defects of communication demand the imposition of minimum legal obligations so that even those providers who are in a hurry, or who may have comparatively less skill or inclination for communication, are obliged to pause and provide warnings of the kind that Rogers mandates;

(3) Such obligations have the added benefit of redressing, to some small degree, *the risks of conflicts of interest and duty which a provider may sometimes face in favouring one healthcare procedure over another;*

(4) Also, to some extent, the legal obligation to provide warnings may some-times help to redress the inherent inequality in power between the professional provider and a vulnerable patient; and

(5) Even those who are dubious about obligations, such as those stated in decisions such as *Rogers*, commonly recognise the value of the sym-bolism which such legal holdings afford. (emphasis added)

Thus, it could be argued that a reasonable person in the patient's position may want to know if a doctor was receiving, for example:

- a financial advantage for prescribing a particular form of treatment, or referring the patient to a nominated pathology laboratory or medical imaging service; or
- whether the doctor had a financial interest in a private hospital the patient was to be admitted to; or
- whether the doctor was receiving a financial benefit from enrolling the patient in a trial.

Of course, before a patient could be successful they would have to show that damage had occurred and that damage was causally related to the fact they were not informed of the conflict of interest.

Equity – fiduciary obligations

The word 'fiduciary' has its roots in the Latin word *fiducia*, which means 'confidence'. A fiduciary relationship is thus a relationship of trust and confidence. The person who owes the duty in the relationship is referred to as the fiduciary. If a fiduciary abuses his or her position to obtain an advantage or benefit at the expense of the other party, the other party will be able to seek relief from a court of equity (Radan, Stewart and Lynch 2005).

It has been said that the essence of fiduciary obligations is that of 'undivid-ed loyalty': *Beach Petroleum NL v Kennedy* (1999) 48 NSWLR 46-7. The fiduciary must not act in any other way than in the interests of the person to whom the duty to so act is owed. It is from this concept that we get the concept of conflict of interest.

Fiduciary obligations arise in either of two ways. First, a relationship may fall into a class of recognised fiduciary relationship, where the courts automatically apply fiduciary duties. These relationships include relationships of trustee and beneficiary, director and company, legal practitioner and client, agent and principal, and relationships between business partners.

Outside of these traditional relationships, it is possible to argue that the relationship between two parties was fiduciary, based on the facts. Unfor-tunately, there is no unifying test for whether a fiduciary duty or obligation exists. Factors which the courts look to include a relationship of trust and confidence; whether one party has undertaken to act in the interests of the other; and whether the relationship is marked by unequal bargaining power, vulner-ability and disadvantage (Dal Pont and Chalmers 2007).

Once a relationship has been described as a fiduciary relationship, the fiduciary is subject to high level duties. By and large the duties are negative (duties to refrain from acting) rather than positive. The main positive duty is to inform the beneficiary of the relationship of any current or future conflict of interest. This gives rise to two main rules:

(a) the 'no conflict rule' – a fiduciary cannot have a personal interest or inconsistent engagement with a third party where there is a real and sensible possibility of conflict; and

(b) the 'no profit rule' – a fiduciary cannot obtain an advantage from the property, powers, confidential information or opportunities afforded to the fiduciary by the principal. (Dempsey and Greinke 2004)

The High Court had the opportunity to examine the doctor/ patient relationship and determine whether it is fiduciary in nature in *Breen v Williams* (1996) 186 CLR 71. Julie Breen wished to participate in a class action in the United States to obtain compensation for the negligent manufacture of silicone breast implants. She sought access to the medical records from one of her doctors who was involved in repairing the damage from the original implants. The doctor would only release the records if he received an undertaking from Ms Breen that no legal action would be taken by her against him at any time. Amongst a number of reasons advanced before the courts was the argument that the doctor owed her a fiduciary duty to disclose to her the contents of the records. Ms Breen was unsuccessful in these arguments and was not given a right to have her medical records.

The High Court clearly rejected the proposition that there was any fiduciary duty to act positively in the interests of the patient so as to require the doctor to produce the records (Dempsey and Greinke 2004). As to whether the doctor/patient relationship could be said to be a fiduciary one the court was split. The majority of the court said that the relationship was not fiduciary although the court decided that doctors may have some fiduciary *duties* to their patient (Skene 2004). Dawson and Toohey JJ said:

[F]iduciary duties may be superimposed upon contractual obligations and it is conceivable that a doctor may place himself in a position with potential for a conflict of interest – if, for example, the doctor has a financial interest in a hospital or a pathology laboratory – so as to give rise to fiduciary obligations. (at 93-4)

Since *Breen* rejected the concept of a general fiduciary relationship existing between doctors and patients, questions have arisen as to whether a specific fiduciary duty may be owed in particular situations. Interestingly, Dal Pont and Chalmers state:

Perhaps it is regarding unauthorised profit that doctor-patient fiduciary duties are most likely to develop. For example, a doctor who prescribes medication without disclosing the receipt of a financial benefit from the provider of medication arguably breaches her or his fiduciary duty to patients. The fiduciary duty is attracted because there is no other legal avenue available to patients to redress conduct of this kind, and the gain made by the doctor introduces the required economic aspect. (Dal Pont and Chalmers 2007)

Another example may be cases of research where the medical researcher is being paid for successful patient recruitment.

In equity, a conflict of interest may be actionable even when the conflict did not result in harm to the person who was owed the duty. Nor will it matter that the conflict was generated by good intentions. The High Court explained this in *Maguire v Makaronis* (1997) 188 CLR 449 at 465:

> Equity intervenes ... not so much to recoup a loss suffered by the plaintiff as to hold the fiduciary to, and vindicate, the high duty owed to the plaintiff ... [T]hose in a fiduciary position who enter into transactions with those to whom they owe fiduciary duties labour under a heavy duty to show the righteousness of the transactions.

This principle is illustrated by *Phipps v Boardman* [1967] 2 AC 46. A solicitor, working for a trustee, discovered a good investment opportunity for the trust. He also wished to invest his own personal funds in the investment in addition to those of the trust. He sought permission from the trustees and all gave their permission barring one who was mentally ill. One of the beneficiaries later objected to the solicitor profiting from his use of information he received as a fiduciary. The solicitor was found to have breached his fiduciary duty even though all the parties profited from the investment.

It is because equity can see a conflict as existing even in situations where the position of the beneficiary of the fiduciary relationship is *improved*, that the concept of 'dualities of interest' is highly likely to be rejected by the courts. Legally, situations of duality clearly fall into the area of conflicts, and it matters not that the intention of the health professional may be good and that the patient will be better off.

Rather than seeking protection for conflict through notions of 'dualities of interest' the better approach is to actively look for potential conflicts and then seek to get the patient's fully informed consent to approve the conflict. The fully informed consent of the person to whom the fiduciary obligations are owed provides a complete defence to any claim for breach of fiduciary duty. The disclosure must be of all material facts and information that could affect the decision to give the consent. Consent has to be sought from all the persons who are owed the fiduciary duty (the solicitor in *Phipps v Boardman* was found liable for the breach because he did not get the consent of all the trustees, or alternatively the beneficiaries of the trust). In the health context this would normally involve simply getting the consent of the patient. This could be done by having the doctor disclose any financial interests in providing certain treatments or prescribing drugs or, in cases of medical research, by having the researchers clearly state that they receive a financial benefit for each patient they recruit into a study.

Professional regulation

A health professional who allowed a conflict of interest to affect the treatment of his or her patients may also be subject to discipline from an appropriate registration authority or subject to investigation by a health-care complaints body. An example of this can be seen in the Queensland Health Practitioner Tribunal decision in *Medical Board of Queensland v Raddatz* (unreported, No D 2392 of 2000). Dr Raddatz was introduced to Mannatech products in 1998. Mannatech products are not conventional medicines; in the judgment of the tribunal they are 'simply complementary, alternative, unconventional'. Dr Raddatz was an enthusiastic supporter of these products and promoted them for use by his patients. A complaint was received that he had substituted a Mannatech product for insulin in the treatment of a diabetic patient. After the complaint was received and investigated he was counselled about his use of the products. Such were the concerns of the Medical Board that he was examined by a psychiatrist who recommended that Dr Raddatz be 'directed to desist from unethical behaviour in the promoting and selling of substances which are not scientifically validated and which he endorses'. Dr Raddatz continued to deny any fault and 'stated his intention to continue to recommend Mannatech products to his patients and that his wife [would] continue to sell them'. The judgment reveals that Dr Raddatz began an association with the Mannatech Group through the use of a family trust. The tribunal found that this was a conflict of interest:

> This was, of course, an obvious conflict of interest situation. It is desirable to state what this means in the view of the Tribunal. In such a situation, there is a strong risk that the registrant will consciously or unconsciously recommend a product in which he has a financial interest direct or indirect in favour of a better product in which he has no interest ... Interests of this kind open the way for potential adverse preferences and should be frowned upon as unethical.

The tribunal decided that Dr Raddatz's registration should be cancelled for two years from 8 September 2000. The tribunal imposed a condition that he could only re-apply for registration after the two years if he had 'truly resolved ... to return to the views of his erstwhile peers and to abide by all current ethical standards, policies and practices provided by the Board'.

Other professions will also discipline their members for conflicts of interest. In *HCCC v Garry* [2008] NSWNMT 20 a nurse was found guilty of unsatisfactory professional conduct when he promoted the taking of goji berries as a treatment for mental illness, and promoted a business opportunity involving the selling of goji to one of the patients. The NSW Nurses and Midwives Tribunal stated:

> The Tribunal recognises your experience as a nurse and particularly in the area of mental health nursing. However, it expresses severe disapproval of your conduct in relation to the following:
> (i) failure to recognise the potential for conflict of interests in relation to your introduction of a colleague with a mental illness to network selling of alternative health products;
> (ii) failure to recognise that your actions had the potential to undermine patients' confidence in the treating team and health care service and to cause conflicting loyalties and anxiety amongst clients of the service ...

Another example is that of the *Physiotherapy Board of SA v Heywood-Smith* [2008] SASC 253. In this case a physiotherapist was found guilty of unprofessional conduct for asking a supplier of equipment to pay him a secret commission on purchases of health equipment made by his patients. The supplier made a complaint to the Board. The physiotherapist was also investigated for the receipt of secret commissions paid by another supplier for purchases of equipment made by his patients. The Board found that he was not guilty of unprofessional conduct for this behaviour, possibly because such a payment was considered an existing practice and had not been solicited by the physiotherapist. The decision of the Board was appealed all the way to the Supreme Court of South Australia. The Court upheld the finding of unprofessional conduct by the Board and said:

> The essence of the professional standard of which Mr Heywood-Smith fell short was the standard of a professional avoiding an actual or potential conflict of interest. This is the relevant characterisation of the consequence of undisclosed or secret commissions. There is a conflict of interest in relation to the patient in circumstances where a product may be the subject of recommendation by the physiotherapist and the physiotherapist may be influenced by the incentive of an additional commission payment.
>
> Secret commissions; that is the taking of commission by a physiotherapist for the sale of products which are recommended to patients, without disclosing the financial benefit received by the physiotherapist, amounts, in our view, to unprofessional conduct. (at [48]-[49])

Interestingly, the Supreme Court also believed that the physiotherapist was guilty of unprofessional conduct under the second count, for taking secret commissions, even though it was considered a standard practice. The court said at [51]:

> It is our view that the circumstances giving rise to the second count do in fact disclose unprofessional conduct on the part of Mr Heywood-Smith. In the course of his engagement as a physiotherapist, he advised patients and clients to purchase equipment from a supplier without disclosing to those patients or clients that he was to be paid a commission. In our view, such conduct was unprofessional and fell well below the standard of professional conduct expected of a physiotherapist.

References

AAMC (2007) *The scientific basis of influence and reciprocity: A symposium*. Washington, Association of American Medical Colleges (AAMC).

Angell, M (2004) *The truth about the drug companies : how they deceive us and what to do about it*. New York, Random House.

Avorn, J (2004) *Powerful medicines: the benefits, risks and costs of prescription drugs*. New York, Random House.

Bekelman, JE, Y Li et al (2003) 'Scope and impact of financial conflicts of interest in biomedical research: a systematic review'. *JAMA* **289**(4): 454-65.

Bero, L (1996) 'Influences on the quality of published drug studies'. *Int J Techol Assess Health Care* **12**: 209-37.

Bero, L, A Galbraith et al (1992) 'The publication of sponsored symposiums in medical journals'. *N Engl J Med* **327**: 1135-40.

Bhandari, M, JW Busse et al (2004) 'Association between industry funding and statistically significant pro-industry findings in medical and surgical randomized trials'. *CMAJ* **170**(4): 477-80.

Bodenheimer, T (2000) 'Uneasy alliance: clinical investigators and the pharmaceutical industry'. *N Engl J Med* **342**: 1539-44.

Bowman, M (1986) 'The impact of drug company funding on the content of continuing medical education'. *Mobius* **6**: 66-9.

Brennan, TA, DJ Rothman et al (2006) 'Health industry practices that create conflicts of interest: a policy proposal for academic medical centers'. *JAMA* **295**(4): 429-33.

Brown, JR (2000) 'ESSAYS ON SCIENCE AND SOCIETY: Privatizing the University – the New Tragedy of the Commons'. *Science* **290**(5497): 1701-2.

Campbell, EG, RL Gruen et al (2007) 'A national survey of physician-industry relationships'. *N Engl J Med* **356**(17): 1742-50.

Chalmers, I (2006) 'From optimism to disillusion about commitment to transparency in the medico-industrial complex'. *JR Soc Med* **99**(7): 337-41.

Chan, AW and DG Altman (2005) 'Identifying outcome reporting bias in randomised trials on PubMed: review of publications and survey of authors'. *BMJ* **330**(7494): 753.

Chren, M and C Landefeld (1994) 'Physicians' behaviour and their interactions with drug companies'. *JAMA* **271**: 684-9.

Chren, M, C Landefeld et al (1989) 'Doctors, drug companies and gifts'. *JAMA* **262**: 3448-51.

Dal Pont, GE and Chalmers, DRC (2007) *Equity and Trusts in Australia*. Sydney. Thomson Lawbook Co.

De Angelis, CD, JM Drazen et al (2005) 'Is this clinical trial fully registered? A statement from the International Committee of Medical Journal Editors'. *Lancet* **365**(9474): 1827-9.

Dempsey, G and A Greinke (2004) 'Proscriptive fiduciary duties in Australia'. *Australian Bar Review* **25**(1): 1-13.

DiMasi, J, R Hansen et al (2003) 'The price of innovation: new estimates of drug development costs'. *Journal of Health Economics* **22**: 151-85.

Findlay, S (2001) 'Direct-to-Consumer Promotion of Prescription Drugs. Economic Implications for Patients, Payers and Providers'. *Pharmacoeconomics* **19**: 109-19.

Gibbons, R, F Landry et al (1998) 'A comparison of physicians' and patients' attitudes towards pharmaceutical industry gifts'. *J Gen Int Med* **13**: 151-4.

Green, S (2008) 'Ethics and the pharmaceutical industry'. *Australas Psychiatry* **16**(3): 158-65.

Haayer, F (1982) 'Rational prescribing and sources of information'. *Soc Sci Med* **16**: 2017-23.

Henry, D, E Doran et al (2005) 'Ties that bind: multiple relationships between clinical researchers and the pharmaceutical industry'. *Arch Intern Med* **165**(21): 2493-6.

Henry, DA, IH Kerridge et al (2005) 'Medical specialists and pharmaceutical industry-sponsored research: a survey of the Australian experience'. *Med J Aust* **182**(11): 557-60.

Hodges, B (1995) 'Interactions with the pharmaceutical industry: experiences and attitudes of psychiatry residents, interns and clerks'. *CMAJ* **153**: 553-9.

Illich, I (1990) *Limits to medicine* London, Penguin.

International Federation of Pharmaceutical Manufacturers and Associations (2003) *Code of Practice of Pharmaceutical Marketing Practice*. Geneva, International Federation of Pharmaceutical Manufacturers and Associations.

Kerridge, I, J Maguire et al (2005) 'Cooperative partnerships or conflict-of-interest? A national survey of interaction between the pharmaceutical industry and medical organizations'. *Intern Med J* **35**(4): 206-10.

Langman, M (1988) 'The code for promoting drugs can do little to limit over-enthusiastic advocacy'. *BMJ* **297**: 499-500.

Lemmens, T and PB Miller (2003) 'The human subjects trade: ethical and legal issues surrounding recruitment incentives'. *J Law Med Ethics* **31**(3): 398-418.

Lexchin, J (1993) 'Interactions between physicians and pharmaceutical industry'. *CMAJ* **149**: 1401-7.

Lexchin, J (2006) 'Bigger and better: how Pfizer redefined erectile dysfunction'. *PLoS Med* **3**(4): e132.

Lichstein, P, R Turner et al (1992) 'Impact of pharmaceutical company representatives on internal medicine residency programs. A survey of residency program directors'. *Arch Intern Med* **152**: 1009-13.

Mainous, A, W Hueston et al (1995) 'Patient perceptions of physician acceptance of gifts from the pharmaceutical industry'. *Arch Fam Med* **4**: 335-9.

McInney, W, D Schiedermayer et al (1990) 'Attitudes of internal medicine faculty and residents towards professional interaction with pharmaceutical sales representatives'. *JAMA* **264**: 1693-7.

Moynihan, R (2008) 'Key opinion leaders: independent experts or drug representatives in disguise?' *BMJ* **336**(7658): 1402-3.

Moynihan, R, I Heath et al (2002) 'Selling sickness: the pharmaceutical industry and disease mongering'. *BMJ* **324**(7342): 886-91.

Orlowski, J and L Wateska (1992) 'The effects of pharmaceutical firm enticement on physician prescribing patterns'. *Chest* **102**: 270-3.

Peay, M and E Peay (1998) 'The role of commercial sources in the adoption of a new drug'. *Soc Sci Med* **26**: 1183-9.

RACP (2005) *Ethical Guidelines in the Relationship between Physicians and the Pharmaceutical Industry*. Sydney, Royal Australasian College of Physicians.

Radan, P, C Stewart and A Lynch (2005) *Equity and Trusts*. Sydney, LexisNexis Butterworths.

Rogers, WA, PR Mansfield et al (2004) 'The ethics of pharmaceutical industry relationships with medical students'. *Med J Aust* **180**(8): 411-14.

Sandberg, W, R Carlos et al (1997) 'The effect of educational gifts from pharmaceutical firms on medical students' recall of company names or products'. *Acad Med* **72**: 916-18.

Skene, L (2004) *Law and Medical Practice: Rights, Duties, Claims and Defences*. Sydney, LexisNexis Butterworths.

SMH (2008) Doctors, perks report dismissed as a sham. *Sydney Morning Herald*. Sydney.

Thompson, D (1993) 'Understanding financial conflicts of interest'. *N Engl J Med* **329**: 573-6.

Toop, L, D Richards et al (2003) *Direct to consumer advertising of prescription drugs in New Zealand: for health or for profit?* Report to the Minister of Health supporting the case for a ban on DTCA, New Zealand Departments of General Practice. Christchurch, Dunedin, Wellington and Auckland Schools of Medicine.

US General Accounting Office (2007) Prescription Drugs: Improvements Needed in FDA's Oversight of Direct-to-Consumer Advertising. GAOR Testimony.

Waud, D (1992) 'Pharmaceutical promotion – a free bribe?' *N Engl J Med* **227**: 351-3.

Wazana, A (2000) 'Physicians and the pharmaceutical industry. Is a gift ever just a gift?' *JAMA* **283**: 373-80.

World Health Organization (1988) *Ethical criteria for medicinal drug promotion, 1988*. Geneva, World Health Organization.

TABLE OF CASES

TABLE OF STATUTES

Australian Capital Territory

Northern Territory

New Zealand

INDEX

Restoring Humane Values to Medicine

A Miles Little Reader

Edited by Ian Kerridge, Chris Jordens, Emma-Jane Sayers

Emeritus Professor Miles Little has had an illustrious career as a surgeon, academic, author, ethicist and philosopher. More than this he is a great humanitarian if this Reader sample of his work is indicative. ...

Professor Little's papers challenge current practices and orthodoxies. The ethics of surgery, euthanasia, research funding, treating cancer survivors – all are dissected. Little sees a profound dichotomy at the heart of modern medicine: a reductionist, as opposed to a holistic approach to illness and care in our society – a search for objectivity, which is part of the problem not the solution. ...

Added attractions in this Reader are commentaries by an assortment of authors, including Little's peers, sociologists, ethicists, even a poet. The range of writers is not surprising when Little's own sources are appreciated. He moves with ease through the ideas of a who's who of philosophers, ancient and modern, linguistic scholars, scientists, theoretical sociologists, and the co-called post-modernists of our time. His commentators sometimes agree, sometimes disagree with him. ...

Importantly, Little does not just expose the weaknesses of the system. He aims to reconcile rather than entrench division. The crux of this Reader is that modern medicine is greedy, fallible, dishonest and driven by vested interest, but his writing is a plea for change, with constructive proposals to effect it. ...

You will not be the same after reading this book. The insights are at once of the 21st century and timeless. Justice Michael Kirby's foreword notes a personal family experience with Professor Miles Little. To his Honour, Little's work evidences the love of human beings at the heart of human dignity and universal human rights, which is the root of ethics, especially perhaps bioethics. Little's clarion call is for the restoration of exactly those humane values to medicine by rebalancing science and ethical values. Let us hope that what Little fears and calls 'moral indeterminacy' does not instead prevail.

Angela Mende, *NSW Law Society Journal*

2003 • ISBN 978 187686 108 7 • PB • 310 pp • $39.95

Understanding Ethics

Noel Preston AM

Preston provides a superb introduction to moral reasoning in a world where old certainties have vanished. His comprehensive coverage of contemporary modes of ethical reasoning, written in an elegant, accessible style, makes a marvellous text.

Professor Sandra Berns

The Planet and the Environment
- Global warming and energy policy
- Population and poverty
- Global citizenship and the Earth Charter
- Animal rights

Bioethics
- Stem cell research and cloning
- Euthanasia
- Biotechnology and developing countries

Professional Life and Workplaces
- The media and journalism
- Teachers, schools and values education
- Business ethics

Politics and Policy-making
- Social justice in Australian society
- Public sector ethics
- Conflicts of interest and codes of conduct

Life, Love and Sexuality
- Honesty and truthtelling
- Same sex marriage
- Spirituality

War, Terrorism and Violence
- Capital punishment
- War including 'just war' theory
- Terrorism and torture

Dr Noel Preston AM has combined an academic career with an activist's life. He has been a prominent grass roots campaigner and social justice commentator in Queensland from the Bjelke-Petersen years. Previously an Associate Professor at QUT and director of UnitingCare Queensland Centre for Social Justice, he is currently an adjunct Professor at Griffith University.

2007 • ISBN 978 1 86287 662 0 • PB • 256 pp • rrp $39.95

www.federationpress.com.au

In the Shadow of the Law

3rd edn

Edited by Phillip Swain & Simon Rice

Social and welfare workers need to know not just what the law is, but to understand how law and legal systems can be utilised, and how they can work in cooperation with lawyers rather than in competition.

In The Shadow of the Law examines a wide range of practice settings and user populations where social work practice and law interact. This edition is a comprehensive revision and includes new chapters on domestic violence, courts tribunals and evidence, working with interpreters, social work and sexuality, housing, adoption and post adoption practice, family law, and social work and Indigenous Australians.

Reviews of previous editions

This book is an important text for both teaching and practising social work ... highlight(s) the legal and ethical dilemmas that social workers face and their responsibility to respond professionally and competently to legal challenges to their decision-making.

Children Australia

This edition incorporates all that one would wish for in a book widely used by teachers of law to social workers. It covers the areas of law which are most likely to be encountered by social workers as well as discussion of the special needs of particular groups, that is, those who would make up the largest part of many social workers' client base.

Alternative Law Journal

Thought provoking, worthy of applause, clearly written.

Australian Social Work

Any one working in the human services would find this book profitable reading.

Journal of Family Studies

2009 • ISBN 978 1 86287 718 4 • PB • 528 pp • rrp $74.95

Also available from The Federation Press

Brave New World of Health

Edited by Belinda Bennett, Terry Carney and Isabel Karpin

The meaning of "health" was once thought fixed with self-evident foundational terms and concepts. This book argues for instability. It shows established dialogues being replaced by a "brave new world" which characterises policy debate about health (and illness or disability).

The book draws on international experts to explore both macro-level forces of change, such as globalisation, and more localised impacts through detailed case studies: pharmaceuticals, preimplantation genetic diagnosis, body modification, abortion, anorexia and post-traumatic stress disorder.

It is an important contribution to our understanding of the ways in which concepts of health, disability and illness are shaped and understood by courts, institutions, regulatory authorities, international bodies, the public and individuals.

Contributors: Lee Ann Basser, Belinda Bennett, Charles Boak, Terry Carney, Raymond De Vries, Thomas Faunce, Ian Freckelton, David Healy, Miriam Ingvarson, Susannah Jefferys, Kelly Johnston, Isabel Karpin, Trudo Lemmens, Roxanne Mykitiuk, Jeff Nisker, Margaret Otlowski, Patricia Peppin, Wendy Rogers, Kristin Savelle, David Tait, Estair Van Wagner.

2008 • ISBN 978 186287 672 9 • HB • 304 pp • rrp $69.90

www.federationpress.com.au

Social Work with Indigenous Communities

Linda Briskman

Good social work practice is marked by a recognition of the strengths of communities and an understanding of how to acknowledge and facilitate these. This book shows social workers how they can develop their knowledge and skills in this area and how they can excel in their work with Indigenous communities.

Linda Briskman covers the issues that Indigenous communities face, with specific chapters devoted to the areas of children, youth, family violence, health, and criminal justice. Case studies are supported by literature and research to provide practitioners and students with a good understanding of the circumstances they will be presented with when working with Indigenous communities.

> *The publication gives a good span of information and Indigenous perspectives, and draws the reader back to the question of how to take the information into their own practice. ... This book gives very good overview of its area and is a very welcome addition to the field.*
>
> Australian Social Work

> *This book would be essential reading for all practising social workers (and social work students) who have an interest in Indigenous issues.*
>
> Family Matters

> *[The book's] open, uncluttered style of presentation and organisation makes it accessible to entry-level social-work students, practitioners and academics alike. Its unflinching advocacy of critical/structural social-work ... keeps a sense of integrity with the community and structural aspects of social-work practice... it is [a] valuable resource ... which provides a glimpse into the myriad of complex issues encountered in practice with Indigenous communities.*
>
> Australian Aboriginal Studies

2007 • ISBN 978 1 86287 643 9 • PB • 288 pp • rrp $39.95